MUSEUM OF BROADCAST COMMUNICATIONS

Encyclopedia of

TELEVISION

SECOND EDITION

Encyclopedia of
TELEVISION
SECOND EDITION

Volume 2
D–L

Horace Newcomb
EDITOR

FITZROY DEARBORN
New York • London

Published in 2004 by
Fitzroy Dearborn
An imprint of the Taylor & Francis Group
270 Madison Avenue
New York, New York 10016

First published by
Fitzroy Dearborn Publishers
70 East Walton Street
Chicago, Illinois 60611
U.S.A.

Library of Congress Cataloging-in-Publication Data:

Encyclopedia of television / Museum of Broadcast Communications ; Horace
Newcomb, editor.—2nd ed.
    p. cm.
  Includes bibliographical references and index.
  ISBN 1-57958-394-6 (set : alk. paper) -- ISBN 1-57958-411-X (v. 1 :
alk. paper) -- ISBN 1-57958-412-8 (v. 2 : alk. paper) -- ISBN
1-57958-413-6 (v. 3 : alk. paper) -- ISBN 1-57958-456-X (v. 4 : alk.
paper)
  1. Television broadcasting--Encyclopedias. I. Title: Encyclopedia of
television. II. Newcomb, Horace. III. Museum of Broadcast
Communications.
  PN1992.18.E53 2005
  384.55'03--dc22

                2004003947

Contents

Advisory Board

Alphabetical List of Entries

Volume 1

Volume 2

Alphabetical List of Entries

Alphabetical List of Entries

Volume 3

Volume 4

Alphabetical List of Entries

D

Da Vinci's Inquest

Canadian Coroner/Detective Series

Created by Chris Haddock and coproduced in Vancouver by the Canadian Broadcasting Corporation (CBC) and Haddock Entertainment, *Da Vinci's Inquest* has completed five broadcast seasons. This popular series also airs in over two dozen European, Latin American, and Middle Eastern countries. Coroner Dominic Da Vinci (Nicholas Campbell) is pivotal to the generic mix of investigative drama and social issue themes.

Campbell's extensive acting skills and personal "bad boy" appeal lend Da Vinci the energy and competence the role requires. In his signature raincoat, he fits the show's local setting, Vancouver, which is depicted as rainy and drab yet alive with a street culture of transient and marginal figures. His investigations are marked by his candid and incisive observations and procedures as investigative coroner with a mission. A plain talker and recovered alcoholic, he has experienced loss (his father's death, divorce, and an inability to overcome alcoholism). Obsessive in his concern with injustices and lapses in the Social Service system, Da Vinci has an amiable rapport with his ex-wife (Gwynyth Walsh), chief pathologist in the coroner's office, and is a worthy dad to his teenage daughter.

Typically, Da Vinci is on the move, carrying the minimal tools of his trade to crime scenes: a brief case or shoulder tote containing camera and rubber gloves, a cell phone, and often a file tucked under one arm. He thinks out loud as he reviews and debates the circum-stances of the death in question with cops and colleagues on the scene. He is interested in the truth of the matter but also forgoes protocol to follow his instincts; as a colleague reminds him of his iconoclastic snooping, "Isn't this a little beyond the coroner's mandate?" In an episode featuring a seemingly open-and-shut case of teen suicide, he rightly suspects the family doctor of malpractice that resulted in the youth's death. By badgering the doctor on his rounds and earning the mother's trust, Da Vinci figures out that similar medical negligence was the cause of the youth's father's death a month earlier.

Da Vinci is a sociable loner with collegial links to all the show's continuing characters. Unlike Da Vinci, the continuing characters have a professional or personal counterpart. Mick (Ian Tracey), the younger detective, and Leo (Donnelly Rhodes), who is nearing retirement, work as an investigative team. Leo is an "old-school" thinker, with a homophobic streak, and is burdened by his wife's decline from Alzheimer's disease. The two women pathologists, DaVinci's ex-wife and a younger woman (Suleka Mathew) of East Indian heritage, are independent women and compatible professionals. The younger woman has had a fitful intimate relationship with Mick. Mick's brother Danny is rehabilitating himself from shady drifter to undercover operative "Bobby." On the right side of the law, Danny regains his brother's respect while he strives to revive the affection of the smart, if sometimes unethical, de-

Da Vinci's Inquest.
Photo courtesy of CBC Television

tective Angie (Venus Terzo). In a recent episode, Danny confronts Angie for her deceitful ploy with a woman implicated in murder. Angie leads the woman to believe that a witness protection program might be forthcoming in exchange for testimony against the husband.

Da Vinci's Inquest thrives on exceptional writing and nuanced performances and camera work. The well-crafted narratives and ensemble characters are located in Vancouver's street life with its ethnic and racial mix of Asians, East Indians, blacks, aboriginals, and recent immigrants. In a CBC interview, Campbell lauded the show's intelligent camera work: "It feels so real to the audience and yet has this loving touch to it...because of David Frazee's [director of photography] eye." The concluding scene of an episode near the end of the 2001–02 season, for example, is a tour de force of camera work that meshes characters and local setting. Within several city blocks, the camera captures a series of ambling conversations. Da Vinci emerges from an alleyway, and a teen contact catches up with him. The teen retreats, then a detective emerges from a tackle shop, extolling the art of "catch and release" fly-fishing. At the next alleyway, detectives Mick and Leo bump into the two men, and the foursome continues to stroll and discuss fishing and an unresolved immigration case. Through five minutes of continuous camera work, without editing, an aesthetic integrity more common to observational documentary than television is constructed.

Vancouver is as individuated a cityscape in *Da Vinci's Inquest* as Baltimore was in *Homicide: Life on the Street.* Familiar streets, skyline, docks, and dull weather shape the show's urban textures, with realist narrative glimpses of Vancouver's immigrant heritage, bag ladies, marginal citizens, and junkies.

Episodes are richly structured with dovetailing plots. Social issues and philosophical debates are injected into running conversations. One episode has DaVinci debating, with a young female police officer, the negative effects of installing surveillance cameras to control local street crime. He recalls Galileo's suspicion of new technology ("Every technological advancement is greeted by a howl of horror") and argues for human vigilance over technical surveillance. Episodes rarely offer pat conclusions, even when cases are solved. In an episode featuring a jailed teenager whose baby dies, DaVinci concludes that he doesn't "believe anybody"—not the girl, the prison guards, or the medical team. Nor does he perceive a cover-up conspiracy; rather, systemic failure and lacking communication by all parties are the culprits.

As realist drama, *Da Vinci's Inquest* has addressed the disappearance and unsolved murders of numerous Vancouver prostitutes. It has alluded to the maltreatment of "very young aboriginal women" who, some twenty years ago, were given tubal ligations by a now elderly doctor. As DaVinci's ex-wife reports to him, the doctor's "selective amnesia" makes it impossible to investigate this injustice. Such stories are known to observers of Canadian social history. *Da Vinci's Inquest* keeps them visible within television drama.

JOAN NICKS

Cast

Dominic Da Vinci	Nicholas Campbell
Chick Savoy	Alex Diakun
Rose Williams	Kim Hawthorne
Dr. Sunny Ramen	Suleka Mathew
Bob Kelly	Gerard Plunkett
Sgt. Sheila Kurtz	Sarah-Jane Redmond
Detective Leo Shannon	Donnelly Rhodes
Helen	Sarah Strange
Detective Angela Kosmo	Venus Terzo
Detective Mick Leary	Ian Tracey

Executive Producer and Writer
Chris Haddock / Haddock Entertainment, Inc.

Programming History
CBC   Sunday 9:00

Dad's Army

British Situation Comedy

The British Broadcasting Corporation (BBC) comedy series *Dad's Army* was the creation of one of the most successful British television comedy writing and production teams, Jimmy Perry and David Croft. They created 81 half-hour episodes between 1968 and 1977, with audiences of 18.5 million in the early 1970s. The program has developed a TV nostalgia popularity among its original audience, as repeat transmissions (in 1989 for instance) and sales of home videocassettes testify. One of the key factors in the program's success lay in its historical setting during the early years of World War II.

Dad's Army features the comic ineptitude of a Home Guard platoon in Walmington-on-Sea, an imaginary seaside resort on the south coast of England. The Land Defence Volunteers were formed in 1940 as a reserve volunteer force made up of men who did not meet the standards of age and fitness required for regular military service. These units were soon officially renamed the Home Guard, but they also attracted the somewhat derisory nickname of "Dad's Army."

Perry and Croft's scripts, based on vivid memories from the period, won them professional recognition with a screenwriting BAFTA Award in 1971, and their subsequent work has secured them a central place within popular British television comedy. They went on to produce *It Ain't 'Alf 'Ot Mum!* (1976–81), set in a British Army entertainment corps posted in Burma during World War II, and *Hi-de-Hi* (1980–94), set in Maplins Holiday Camp in 1959. In their own way, these programs have tapped into, and contributed to, television's myths about wartime Britain and the immediate postwar period of the 1950s. All three series feature ensemble casts of misfit characters brought together under a quasi-authoritarian order (a volunteer army, concert corps, or holiday camp staff) and whose weekly crises demand that the group pulls together against adversity.

The longevity and endearing appeal of *Dad's Army* in particular is explained in part by the way in which the series successfully constructs myths of British social unity and community spirit that were so sought after in the years following the revolutionary moment of the late 1960s. The revival of the series in the late 1980s pointed up the starker, more divided nature of

contemporary British life, riven by class, racial, and national identity tensions. *Dad's Army* depicts with humor—but obvious underlying affection—the "bulldog" spirit of Britain popularly taken to characterize public morale during the Blitz and its immediate aftermath (1940–41). Britain alone against the threat of Hitler's Nazi army occupying Europe is the subject of the program's signature tune lyrics, "Who do you think you are kidding, Mr. Hitler, if you think old England's done," written by Perry and sung by wartime entertainer Bud Flanagan in a clever recreation of a 1940s sound. The opening credit sequence depicts a map of Europe with advancing Nazi swastikas attempting to cross the English Channel. In its production style, *Dad's Army* exemplified the BBC's reputation for period detail, and many episodes featured exterior sequences shot on rural locations in southeast England. This film footage was mixed with videotape-recorded interior scenes, and a live studio audience provided laughter for the final broadcast version.

The humor of *Dad's Army* derives from a combination of ridiculous task or crisis situations, visual jokes, and a gentle mockery of English class differentiation. Perry and Croft's skill was to script dialogue for a talented ensemble of character actors constituting the Walmington-on-Sea platoon, led by the pompous Captain Mainwearing (Arthur Lowe), the manager of the local bank. The other main characters include his chief clerk, Sergeant Wilson (John Le Mesurier); Frank Pike (Ian Lavender), the junior bank clerk; and Lance Corporal Jones (Clive Dunn), the local butcher. The platoon's rank and file are made up of privates Frazer, the Scots undertaker (John Laurie); Godfrey (Arnold Ridley), a retired gentleman who lives with his two maiden sisters in a cottage; and Walker (James Beck), a "spiv" who deals in contraband goods. Mainwearing's main rival authority in Walmington is the chief air-raid warden, Mr. Hodges (Bill Pertwee), a local greengrocer. They frequently battle over use of the church hall and office of the long-suffering camp vicar (Frank Williams) and his toadying verger (Edward Sinclair).

Perry and Croft's world in *Dad's Army* is largely male, but women do feature, albeit in their absence or marginality. Underlying the appearance of the middle-class proprieties of marriage are dysfunctional relationships. Mainwearing's agoraphobic wife (Elizabeth) never appeared in the series (except once as a lump in the top bunk of their Anson air-raid shelter). They obviously share a loveless marriage with her firmly in control over domestic arrangements. Similarly, Mrs. Pike (Janet Davies) is a young widow who entertains the debonair Sergeant Wilson, and although Frank refers to him as "Uncle Arthur," there is some suspicion that the lad is their illegitimate son. The amorous, larger-than-life Mrs. Fox (Pamela Cundell) gives her matronly attentions freely to the platoon's men, and she eventually marries the elderly but eligible Corporal Jones.

Dad's Army is particularly significant in its comic treatment of English class tensions. Through narrative and character, Croft and Perry revisit a time when the war was being fought partly in the belief that the old social class divisions would give way to a more egalitarian postwar meritocracy. The chief manifestations of such tensions occur in exchanges between Captain Mainwearing and Sergeant Wilson. In a clever reversal of expectations, Croft made the captain a grammar school–educated, bespectacled, and stout man whose social status has been achieved through hard work and merit. His superiority of rank, work status, and self-important manner are nevertheless constantly frustrated by Wilson's upper-class pedigree, public school education, and nonchalant charm. Mainwearing's middle-class snobbery, brilliantly captured by Arthur Lowe, is also reflected in his attitudes toward the lower classes. A member of the managerial class, he looks down at uncouth tradesmen: "He's a greengrocer with dirty finger nails," he says of his archrival Hodges. Although *Dad's Army* is comic because it mocks such pretension, it is essentially a nostalgic look back to a social order that never existed in this form. The program celebrates values such as "amateurism," "making do," and muddling through, values that in this presentation remain comic but appear quaint to later generations of television viewers.

LANCE PETTITT

See also **British Programming**

Cast

Capt. Mainwearing	Arthur Lowe
Sgt. Wilson	John Le Mesurier
Lance Cpl. Jones	Clive Dunn
Private Frazer	John Laurie
Private Walker	James Beck
Private Godfrey	Arnold Ridley
Private Pike	Ian Lavender
Chief Warden Hodges	Bill Pertwee
Vicar	Frank Williams
Verger	Edward Sinclair
Mrs. Pike	Janet Davies
Private Sponge	Colin Bean
Private Cheeseman	Talfryn Thomas
Colonel	Robert Raglan
Mr. Blewitt	Harold Bennett
Mrs. Fox	Pamela Cundell

Producer

David Croft

Programming History

81 half-hour episodes; 1 1-hour episode; 1 insert
BBC

July 1968–September 1968	6 episodes
March 1969–April 1969	6 episodes
September 1969–October 1969	7 episodes
October 1969–December 1969	7 episodes
September 1970–December 1970	13 episodes
December 1970	Christmas special
December 1971	Christmas special
October 1972–December 1972	13 episodes
October 1973–December 1973	7 episodes
November 1974–December 1974	6 episodes
September 1975–October 1975	6 episodes
December 1975	Christmas special
December 1976	Christmas special
October 1977–November 1977	6 episodes

Further Reading

Ableman, Paul, *The Defence of a Front Line English Village,* edited by Arthur Wilson, London: BBC Books, 1989

Cook, Jim, editor, *Television Sitcom,* London: British Film Institute, 1982

Perry, J., and David Croft, *Dad's Army* (five scripts), London: Hamish Hamilton, 1975

Pertwee, Bill, *Dad's Army: The Making of a TV Legend,* London: David and Charles, 1989

Dallas

U.S. Serial Melodrama

Dallas, the first of a genre to be named "prime-time soap" by television critics, established the features of serial plots involving feuding families and moral excess that would characterize all other programs of the type. Created by David Jacobs, *Dallas*'s first five-episode pilot season aired in April 1978 on the Columbia Broadcasting System (CBS), getting poor reviews, but later high ratings put it in the top ten by the end of its limited run. The central premise was a *Romeo and Juliet* conflict, set in contemporary Texas. Pamela Barnes and Bobby Ewing were the young lovers whose two families perpetuated the feud of their elders, Jock Ewing and Digger Barnes, over the rightful ownership of oil fields claimed by the Ewings.

In the pilot episodes and the 12 full seasons that would follow, the Ewing family remained the focus of *Dallas.* Indeed, the Ewing brothers, their wives, their offspring, and all the assorted relatives passing through would continue to live under one roof on Southfork, the family ranch. Bobby's older brother J.R., played with sly wit by Larry Hagman, would become a new kind of villain for television because of his centrality to the program and the depth both actor and writers gave to the character. Abusive to his alcoholic wife Sue Ellen and ruthless and underhanded with his nemesis Cliff Barnes and any other challenger to Ewing Oil, J.R. was nevertheless a loyal son to Miss Ellie and Jock and a devoted father to his son and heir, John Ross. Hagman's J.R. soon became the man viewers loved to hate.

For prime time in the late 1970s, *Dallas* was sensational, featuring numerous acts of adultery by both J.R. and Sue Ellen; the revelation of Jock's illegitimate son, Ray Krebs, who worked as a hired hand on Southfork; and the raunchy exploits of young Lucy, daughter of Gary, the third, largely absent Ewing brother. It was the complicated stuff of daytime melodrama, done with big-budget glamour—high-fashion wardrobes, richly furnished home and office interiors, and exteriors shot on location in the Dallas area.

During the 1978–79 season, writer-producer Leonard Katzman turned the prime-time drama into the first prime-time serial since *Peyton Place,* as Sue Ellen Ewing found she was pregnant, her child's paternity uncertain. The generic formula was complete when that same season concluded with a cliff-hanger: Sue Ellen was critically injured in a car accident, and both her fate and the fate of her baby remained unresolved until September. Cliff-hanger episodes became highly promoted Friday night rituals after the following season, which ended with a freeze-frame of villain-protagonist J.R. lying shot on the floor of his office, his prognosis and his assailant unknown. "Who Shot J.R.?" reverberated throughout popular culture that summer, culminating in an episode the following season that broke ratings records, as 76 percent of all U.S. televisions in use tuned to *Dallas.* Even after 1985, when the program's ratings sagged, cliff-hanger episodes in the spring and their resolutions in the fall would boost the aging serial back into the top ten.

In the midst of an ever-expanding cast of Ewings and Barnes, scheming mistresses, high-rolling oilmen, and white-collar henchmen, the primary characters and relationships changed and evolved over the course of the serial. Bobby and Pam's marriage succumbed to J.R.'s plots to pull them apart, and both pursued other romances. After J.R. and Sue Ellen's marriage produced an heir, Sue Ellen stopped drinking and went on the offensive against J.R. Both Pam and Sue Ellen acquired careers. Ray Krebs rose from hired hand to independent rancher, always apart from the Ewing clan but indispensable to it.

Like its daytime counterparts, *Dallas* adapted to the comings and goings of several of its star actors. When Jim Davis, who played Jock Ewing, died in 1981, his character was written out of the show, with Jock's plane disappearing somewhere over South America. The character was never recast, though several plotlines alluded to his possible reappearance, and his portrait continued to preside over key scenes in the offices of Ewing Oil. Barbara Bel Geddes, the beloved Miss Ellie, asked to be relieved from her contract for health reasons in 1984, and Donna Reed stepped into the role for one season, only to be removed when Bel Geddes was persuaded to return. During the 1985–86 season, Bobby Ewing was dead, at the request of actor Patrick Duffy, but the character returned when Duffy wanted back on the show. Bobby was resurrected when his

Dallas, Patrick Duffy, Jim Davis, Larry Hagman (Season 1),
1978–91.
Courtesy of the Everett Collection

death and all the rest of the previous season were redefined as Pam's dream. Linda Gray left the show in 1989, and her character, Sue Ellen, exited as an independent movie mogul whose final act of vengeance was to produce a painfully accurate film about J.R. The serial concluded in May 1991, with J.R. alone and forced to relinquish Ewing Oil to Cliff Barnes. In the final episode, J.R. holds a drunken dialogue with the Devil (played by Joel Grey), ending with a gunshot. J.R.'s apparent suicide would prove otherwise in *Dallas: J.R. Returns,* the first of two TV movies for CBS aired after the serial's conclusion, in 1996 and 1998.

In the early 1980s, other serials joined the internationally successful *Dallas* on the prime-time schedule, each in some way defining itself in relation to the original. Among them, *Knots Landing* began as a spin-off of *Dallas,* featuring Gary Ewing and his wife, Valene, transplanted to a California suburb. The American Broadcasting Company's (ABC's) *Dynasty* both copied the *Dallas* formula and stretched it to outrageous proportions. On the other hand, hour-long dramas, most notably *Hill Street Blues,* began grafting *Dallas*'s successful serial strategy onto other genres.

Among the 1980s generation of prime-time soaps, only *Knots Landing* outlasted *Dallas.* In the 1990s, *Beverly Hills 90210* (FOX), *Melrose Place* (FOX), and *Dawson's Creek* (WB) pitched the genre to a younger generation of viewers. The short-lived *Models, Inc.* (FOX) and *Titans* (National Broadcasting Company [NBC]) featured *Dallas* alumni Linda Gray and Victoria Principal, respectively. Most recently, the multigenerational, business-and-family serial formula has been merged with the gangster genre in HBO's *The Sopranos. Dallas* continues in syndication internationally and has a fan-based presence on the Internet.

SUE BROWER

See also **Hagman, Larry; Melodrama; Spelling, Aaron**

Cast

John Ross (J.R.) Ewing, Jr.	Larry Hagman
Eleanor Southworth (Miss Ellie) Ewing (1978–84, 1985–90)	Barbara Bel Geddes
Eleanor Southworth (Miss Ellie) Ewing (1984–85)	Donna Reed
John Ross (Jock) Ewing (1978–81)	Jim Davis
Bobby Ewing (1978–85, 1986–91)	Patrick Duffy
Pamela Barnes Ewing (1978–87)	Victoria Principal
Lucy Ewing Cooper (1978–85, 1988–90)	Charlene Tilton
Sue Ellen Ewing (1978–89)	Linda Gray
Ray Krebbs (1978–88)	Steve Kanaly
Cliff Barnes	Ken Kercheval
Julie Grey (April 1978)	Tina Louise
Willard "Digger" Barnes (1978)	David Wayne
Willard "Digger" Barnes (1979–80)	Keenan Wynn
Gary Ewing (1978–79)	David Ackroyd
Gary Ewing (1979–81)	Ted Shackelford
Valene Ewing (1978–81)	Joan Van Ark
Liz Craig (1978–82)	Barbara Babcock
Willie Joe Garr (1978–79)	John Ashton
Jeb Amos (1978–79)	Sandy Ward
Kristin Shepard (1979–81)	Mary Crosby
Mrs. Patricia Shepard (1979, 1985)	Martha Scott
Dusty Farlow (1979–82, 1985)	Jared Martin
Alan Beam (1979–80)	Randolph Powell
Dr. Ellby (1979–81)	Jeff Cooper
Donna Culver Krebbs (1979–87)	Susan Howard

Character	Actor
Dave Culver (1979–82, 1986–87)	Tom Fuccello
Harve Smithfield	George O. Petrie
Vaughn Leland (1979–84)	Dennis Patrick
Connie (1979–81)	Jeanna Michaels
Louella (1979–81)	Megan Gallagher
Jordan Lee (1979–90)	Don Starr
Mitch Cooper (1979–82)	Leigh McCloskey
John Ross Ewing III (1980–83)	Tyler Banks
John Ross Ewing III (1983–91)	Omri Katz
Punk Anderson (1980–87)	Morgan Woodward
Mavis Anderson (1982–88)	Alice Hirson
Brady York (1980–81)	Ted Gehring
Alex Ward (1980–81)	Joel Fabiani
Les Crowley (1980–81)	Michael Bell
Marilee Stone (1980–87)	Fern Fitzgerald
Afton Cooper (1981–84, 1989)	Audrey Landers
Arliss Cooper (1981)	Anne Francis
Clint Ogden (1981)	Monte Markham
Leslie Stewart (1981)	Susan Flannery
Rebecca Wentworth (1981–83)	Priscilla Pointer
Craig Stewart (1981)	Craig Stevens
Jeremy Wendell (1981, 1984–88)	William Smithers
Clayton Farlow (1981–91)	Howard Keel
Jeff Farraday (1981–82)	Art Hindle
Katherine Wentworth (1981–84)	Morgan Brittany
Charles Eccles (1982)	Ron Tomme
Bonnie Robertson (1982)	Lindsay Bloom
Blair Sullivan (1982)	Ray Wise
Holly Harwood (1982–84)	Lois Chiles
Mickey Trotter (1982–83)	Timothy Patrick Murphy
Walt Driscoll (1982–83)	Ben Piazza
Jarrett McLeish (1982–83)	J. Patrick McNamara
Thornton McLeish (1982–83)	
Eugene Bullock (1982–83)	Kenneth Kimmins
Mark Graison (1983–84, 1985–86)	E.J. Andre
Aunt Lil Trotter (1983–84)	John Beck
Roy Ralston (1983)	Kate Reid
Serena Wald (1983–85, 1990)	John Reilly
Peter Richards (1983–84)	Stephanie Blackmore
Paul Morgan (1983–84, 1988)	Christopher Atkins
Jenna Wade (1983–88)	Glenn Corbett
Charlie Wade (1983–88)	Priscilla Presley
	Shalane McCall

Character	Actor
Edgar Randolph (1983–84)	Martin E. Brooks
Armando Sidoni (1983–84)	Alberto Morin
Sly Lovegren (1983–91)	Deborah Rennard
Betty (1984–85)	Kathleen York
Eddie Cronin (1984–85)	Fredric Lehne
Pete Adams (1984–85)	Burke Byrnes
Dave Stratton (1984)	Christopher Stone
Jessica Montfort (1984, 1990)	Alexis Smith
Mandy Winger (1984–87)	Deborah Shelton
Jamie Ewing Barnes (1984–86)	Jenilee Harrison
Christopher Ewing (1984–91)	Joshua Harris
Scotty Demarest (1985–86)	Stephen Elliott
Jack Ewing (1985–87)	Dack Rambo
Angelico Nero (1985–86)	Barbara Carrera
Dr. Jerry Kenderson (1985–86)	Barry Jenner
Nicholas (1985–86)	George Chakiris
Grace (1985–86)	Marete Van Kamp
Matt Cantrell (1986)	Marc Singer

Producers

David Jacobs, Philip Capice, Leonard Katzman

Programming History

330 episodes
CBS

April 1978	Sunday 10:00–11:00
September 1978– October 1978	Saturday 10:00–11:00
October 1978– January 1979	Sunday 10:00–11:00
January 1979– November 1981	Friday 10:00–11:00
December 1981–May 1985	Friday 9:00–10:00
September 1985–May 1986	Friday 9:00–10:00
September 1986–May 1988	Friday 9:00–10:00
October 1988–March 1990	Friday 9:00–10:00
March 1990–May 1990	Friday 10:00–11:00
November 1990– December 1990	Friday 10:00–11:00
January 1991–May 1991	Friday 9:00–10:00

Further Reading

Adams, John, "Setting As Chorus: An Iconology of *Dallas*," *Critical Survey* (1994)

Ang, Ien, *Watching Dallas: Soap Opera and the Melodramatic Imagination,* London and New York: Routledge, 1989

Bonderoff, Jason, *The Official Dallas Trivia Quiz Book,* New York: New American Library, 1985

Cassidy, Marsha F., "The Duke of Dallas: Interview with

Leonard Katzman," *Journal of Popular Film and Television* (Spring 1988)

Coward, Rosalind, "Come Back Miss Ellie: On Character and Narrative in Soap Operas," *Critical Quarterly* (Spring–Summer 1986)

Hirschfeld, Burt, *The Ewings of Dallas: A Novel,* New York: Bantam Books, 1980

Kalter, Suzy, *The Complete Book of Dallas: Behind the Scenes of the World's Favorite TV Program,* New York: Abrams, 1986

Liebes, Tamar, and Elihu Katz, *The Export of Meaning: Cross-Cultural Readings of Dallas,* New York: Oxford University Press, 1990

Mander, Mary S., "*Dallas:* The Mythology of Crime and the Moral Occult," *Journal of Popular Culture* (Fall 1983)

Masello, Robert, *The Dallas Family Album: Unforgettable Moments from the #1 TV Series,* New York: Bantam, 1980

Perlberg, Diane J., and Joelle Delbourgo, editors, *Quotations of J.R. Ewing,* New York: Bantam, 1980

Silj, Alessandro, and Manuel Alvarado, editors, *East of Dallas: The European Challenge to American Television,* London: British Film Institute, 1988

White, Mimi, "Women, Memory, and Serial Melodrama," *Screen* (Winter 1994)

Daly, Tyne (1947–)

U.S. Actor

Tyne Daly, best known as half of the female cop team that formed *Cagney and Lacey,* won recognition for her role as the New York City detective who was also a wife and mother. With a background in the theater, Daly brought a cultivated artistry to the working-class role of Mary Beth Lacey. As written, the character was multifaceted—a tough cop, a loving wife, a committed mother, a loyal friend. As played by Daly, Mary Beth was even more complex—innocent, compassionate, and at times funny but clear-eyed and confrontational in her dealings with both the "perps" and her best friend and partner, Christine Cagney (Sharon Gless). As Mary Beth, Daly created a female character for television who was smart though not college educated, sexy without being glamorous. Mary Beth's marriage with Harvey Lacey (John Karlen) offered what Daly called "a love story" that marked a true departure from TV marriages—a lusty, devoted partnership.

It is Mary Beth's partnership with Christine, however, that has drawn the attention of most feminist critics for its twist on the countless pairs of male partners and buddies that have populated television. The professional and personal sides of Mary Beth and Christine's relationship often blurred; feelings inevitably got involved. Though seemingly the "softer" of the two, Mary Beth's more rational approach to her job served as ballast in the twosome's investigations.

In addition to the ongoing themes of marriage and women's relationships, Daly was given the opportunity to explore a number of other women's issues. In 1985, Mary Beth discovered a lump in her breast that proved to be cancerous. As a method actor, Daly "lived" with the illness during Mary Beth's diagnosis and treatment, which involved a lumpectomy and radiation rather than the disfiguring mastectomy. She told one reporter, "I realized that as long as there are women being led astray by the medical establishment, women getting hacked into pieces, it's important that I tell the story, and it's important that I face the music." The following season, Daly's pregnancy was written into the series. The episode in which Mary Beth gave birth to Alice aired on the same day that Daly gave birth to her daughter.

As the series came to a close, Daly commented, "I played the hell out of [Lacey]. I knew everything there was to know about her." Between 1982 and 1988, Daly's craft was recognized with four Emmys for best actress in a dramatic series.

Besides her work in *Cagney and Lacey,* Daly is best known for her performance as Mama Rose in Broadway's revival of *Gypsy,* for which she received the Tony Award as best actress in a musical. Daly also continues to work in television movies and series, choosing roles of social significance. She played the mother of a child with Down syndrome in *Kids Like These* (1987), a homeless woman in *Face of a Stranger* (1991), and a prostitute, beaten and left for dead, who resolves to bring her attacker to justice in *Tricks* (1997). She has also done more comic turns on *Wings* (which stars her brother Tim Daly) and on

Judging Amy, Tyne Daly as Maxine Gray.
Courtesy of the Everett Collection

Sharon Gless's series *The Trials of Rosie O'Neill,* in which she played an "old friend" who had more in common in looks and manner with the brash Mama Rose than with shy, frumpy Mary Beth.

Daly and Gless have also reprised their roles in several *Cagney and Lacey* made-for-television-movies, two-hour presentations in which the characters, their friendship, and their professional relationship move further into midlife complexity. Beginning in 1999, Daly returned to series work for the Columbia Broadcasting System's (CBS's) *Judging Amy,* in which she plays the title character's strong-willed mother, social worker Maxine Gray.

SUE BROWER

See also **Cagney and Lacey**

Tyne Daly. Born in Madison, Wisconsin, 1947. Attended Brandeis University, Waltham, Massachusetts; American Music and Dramatic Academy. Married: Georg Stanford Brown (divorced); three daughters. Performed at American Shakespeare Festival; made television debut in *The Virginian;* appeared in film *The Enforcer,* 1976; starred in television series *Cagney and*

Lacey, 1982–88; appeared on Broadway in revivals of *Gypsy,* 1990 and 1991. Recipient: Emmy Awards, 1982, 1983, 1984, 1988, 1994; Tony Award, 1990.

Television Series

1982–88	*Cagney and Lacey*
1994–95	*Christy*
1999–	*Judging Amy*

Made-for-Television Movies

1971	*In Search of America*
1971	*A Howling in the Woods*
1971	*Heat of Anger*
1973	*The Man Who Could Talk to Kids*
1974	*Larry*
1975	*The Entertainer*
1977	*Intimate Strangers*
1979	*Better Late Than Never*
1980	*The Women's Room*
1981	*A Matter of Life and Death*
1983	*Your Place or Mine*
1987	*Kids Like These*
1989	*Stuck with Each Other*
1990	*The Last to Go*
1991	*Face of a Stranger*
1992	*Columbo: A Bird in the Hand*
1994	*Cagney and Lacey: The Return*
1994	*The Forget-Me-Not Murders*
1995	*Cagney and Lacey: Together Again*
1995	*Cagney and Lacey: The View through the Glass Ceiling*
1995	*Bye, Bye Birdie*
1996	*Cagney and Lacey: True Convictions*
1997	*Tricks*
1997	*Student Affair*
1998	*Vig*
1999	*Three Secrets*
1998	*Execution of Justice*
1999	*Absence of the Good*
2001	*The Wedding Dress*

Films

John and Mary, 1969; *Angel Unchained,* 1970; *Play It As It Lays,* 1972; *The Adulteress,* 1973; *The Enforcer,* 1976; *Telefon,* 1977; *Speedtrap,* 1978; *Zoot Suit,* 1982; *The Aviator,* 1985; *Movers and Shakers,* 1985; *The Lay of the Land,* 1998; *Autumn Heart,* 1999; *The Simian Line,* 1999; *A Piece of Eden,* 2000.

Stage

Gypsy; The Seagull; Call Me Madam; Come Back Little Sheba; Ashes; Black Angel; Gethsemane

Springs; Three Sisters; Vanities; Skirmishes; The Rimers of Eldritch; Birthday Party; Old Times; The Butter and Egg Man; That Summer That Fall; Mystery School.

Further Reading

D'Acci, Julie, *Defining Women: Television and the Case of Cagney and Lacey,* Chapel Hill: University of North Carolina Press, 1994

Gordon, Mary, "Sharon Gless and Tyne Daly," *Ms.* (January 1987)

Danger Bay

Canadian Family Adventure Series

A half-hour dramatic series coproduced by the Canadian Broadcasting Corporation (CBC) and the Disney Channel, *Danger Bay* was a family adventure series set in Canada's scenic west coast. It starred Donnelly Rhodes as Dr. Grant Roberts, a veterinarian and marine specialist at the Vancouver Aquarium who was also busy raising his children, Jonah and Nicole, played by Chris Crabb and Ocean Hellman.

The aquarium and nearby coastal waters off Vancouver provided the exotic backdrop for many of the show's adventures, which often focused on the children but always involved the whole family. Plots usually presented some kind of peril or violence to the animals at the aquarium or surrounding area, and each week the strong and daring "Doc" Roberts would foil the greedy and selfish schemes of poachers, hunters, or developers who posed a threat to the animals and environment.

Danger Bay was fairly formulaic, filled with elements that were conventional to family series. It presented a strong father figure in Donnelly Rhodes and a motherly figure in Joyce, Dr. Robert's girlfriend (played by Deborah Wakeham), and young viewers could identify with Jonah and Nicole. Moral and psychological tensions were also muted, reflecting the Disney producers' reluctance to deal with controversial issues such as sex, drugs, or alcohol, as did the other contemporary Canadian teenage drama series, *Degrassi Junior High.* Instead, dramatic tension in *Danger Bay* usually involved a morality lesson related to subjects such as lying or cheating and were always resolved with the help of patient fatherly advice. The series did, however, try to reflect a more sensitive attitude toward the environment, women (Joyce was a bush pilot), and visible minorities, but such issues very rarely drew any direct attention in the plots.

Danger Bay reflected the basic characteristics of wholesomeness and adventure. Its formulaic nature and rather innocent perspective led some Canadian critics to see it as an example of the "Disneyfication" of Canadian television drama, and it was sharply criticized for its timidity. Defenders of the series have argued that the show provided fast-paced action and fun for a young viewing audience. Nevertheless, as Canadian television drama historian Mary Jane Miller points out, it remains "a blend of action and fathering with lots of running, chasing, fixing, rescuing." *Danger Bay* ended its run on Canadian television after six seasons in the spring of 1990, at the same time that another Canadian television drama series, *Beachcombers,* ended after 19 seasons on the CBC.

MANON LAMONTAGNE

Cast

Dr. Grant Roberts	Donnelly Rhodes
Jonah Roberts	Chris Crabb
Nicole Roberts	Ocean Hellman
Joyce	Deborah Wakeham

Producers

Philip Saltzman, Mary Eilts

Programming History

123 episodes
CBC

November 1984–February 1985	Monday 8:30–9:00
November 1985–March 1986	Monday 8:00–8:30
November 1986–March 1987	Wednesday 7:30–8:00
November 1987–March 1990	Monday 7:30–8:00

Further Reading

Miller, Mary Jane, *Turn Up the Contrast: CBC Television Drama since 1952,* Vancouver: University of British Columbia Press, 1987

Skene, Wayne, *Fade to Black: A Requiem for the CBC,* Toronto: Douglas and MacIntyre, 1993

Dann, Michael (1921–)

U.S. Network Executive

Michael Dann was one of the most successful programming executives in U.S. network television during the 1950s and 1960s. He was known as a "master scheduler" and spent his most successful years at the Columbia Broadcasting System (CBS) working in tandem with CBS President James Aubrey. He began his television career shortly after World War II as a comedy writer and in 1948 joined the National Broadcasting Company (NBC), where he stayed for the next ten years. Initially hired to work in publicity, he soon moved to the programming department and eventually served as head of NBC Entertainment under David Sarnoff. In 1958, he moved to CBS as vice president of programs in New York. In 1963, he was promoted to head of programming and in 1966 was appointed senior vice president of programs. During most of his tenure, CBS consistently ranked as the number one network in prime-time audience ratings.

Dann held the head programming position at CBS longer than anyone else (from 1963 to 1970), serving under five different CBS presidents. His success was attributable, in part, to an uncanny ability to gauge CBS owner William Paley's probable reaction to most program ideas. Dann was often referred to as "the weathervane" for changing his opinions to match those of his bosses. Despite this reputation, Dann was not one to avoid controversy. Arthur Godfrey, a long-time audience favorite at CBS, had two prime-time programs ranked in the top ten; during the 1950s, he did not get along with Dann and left CBS as a result. (The fact that Godfrey disappeared from public view suggests that Dann was probably correct in his assessment that Godfrey was "over the hill.")

Dann was also able to restore and establish good and long-lasting relationships with talent producers and advertisers—an area in which CBS had suffered. He felt that viewers preferred escapist television to realist television and thought that the half-hour situation comedy was the staple of any prime-time schedule. He also believed the network should renew any program with ratings high enough to produce a profit.

Another development during Dann's regime was a significant increase in the number of specials aired. While the staple of prime-time programming was, and remains, the weekly series, Dann believed that liberal use of special programming at strategic times would only enhance the network's ratings. One could argue that he was the innovator of what has come to be called "event television."

In 1966, he recognized that television (and CBS in particular) faced a major crisis—the networks were running out of first-run theatrical movies. As a result, CBS bought the old Republic Pictures lot, turned it into the CBS Studio Center, and went into feature film production. The American Broadcasting Company (ABC) and NBC soon followed suit.

Among the many successful programs introduced under Dann's leadership were *The Mary Tyler Moore Show, The Carol Burnett Show, Mission: Impossible, Mannix, Hawaii Five-0,* and *60 Minutes.* These program development and programming skills were put to the test in one particular instance. For years CBS had trouble competing in the very important 9:00–10:00 slot on Sunday evenings despite a very strong lead-in program (*The Ed Sullivan Show*). NBC had *Bonanza,* the highly successful series, in that time period, and CBS had failed with its previous counterprogramming attempts (*The Judy Garland Show, The Garry Moore Show, Perry Mason*). Dann chose a new series for this slot, a series he believed would attract a younger audience, *The Smothers Brothers Comedy Hour.* The move proved quite successful. The Smothers Brothers' show became a hit, though not without its share of controversy. The most notable conflict arose over a 1967 episode involving folk singer Pete Seeger, who was scheduled to sing his antiwar song "Waist Deep in the Big Muddy." Dann wanted Seeger to delete one stanza of the song. When Seeger and the Smothers refused, Dann had the song deleted from the telecast. In February 1968, Seeger was again scheduled to appear. This time the song aired in its entirety.

Dann's conservative attitudes toward social and cultural standards appeared again when CBS decided to air *The Mary Tyler Moore Show.* Dann had the producers make one change—Mary could not be a divorced woman. He felt that premise too controversial and forced James L. Brooks and Allan Burns to rewrite the character as a woman who had recently broken off a long-term engagement.

Michael Dann.
Photo courtesy of Broadcasting & Cable

Dann's power at CBS began to wane in the late 1960s, as did the ratings of some of the shows he had developed and scheduled. His new boss, Robert Wood, wanted innovation, not sameness. Dann was forced out when he opposed cancellation of hit "rural" series: *The Red Skelton Show, The Jackie Gleason Show, The Beverly Hillbillies, Green Acres,* and *Hee Haw.* These shows were replaced by series such as *All in the Family,* which were deemed more socially relevant and, perhaps more important, more appealing to a younger age-group whose greater spending power attracted advertisers. The public explanation for Dann's departure was the ever-available and undefined "health reasons." His successor was his protégé, Fred Silverman, who would go on to head the programming departments of all three networks.

MITCHELL E. SHAPIRO

See also **Columbia Broadcasting System; Paly, William S.;** *Smothers Brothers Comedy Hour, The*

Michael Dann. Born in Detroit, Michigan, September 11, 1921. Educated at the University of Michigan, B.A. in economics 1941. Married: 1) Joanne Himmell, 1949 (divorced, 1973); children: Jonathan, Patricia, and Priscilla; 2) Louise Cohen, 1973. Comedy writer, 1946–47; public relations staff, New Haven Rail Road, 1947–48; trade editor, NBC press department, 1948–49, coordinator of program package sales, 1949–50, supervisor, special telecasts, 1950–52, manager, television program department, 1952–54, director, program sales, 1954–56, vice president, television program sales, 1956–58; vice president, network programming, CBS, 1958–63; vice president, programs, CBS, 1963–66, senior vice president, 1966–70; vice president and assistant to president, Children's Television Workshop, 1970s; consultant, Warner Cable, planning programming for QUBE, 1974; developed concepts for Disney's Epcot Center; senior program adviser, ABC Video Enterprises, 1980; visiting lecturer in American studies and guest fellow, Yale University, 1973–78.

Publication

"Foreword," *The Gatekeeper: My Thirty Years as Network Censor,* by Alfred R. Schneider, 2001

Further Reading

Barnouw, Erik, *A History of Broadcasting in the United States,* volume III, *The Image Empire, from 1953,* New York: Oxford University Press, 1970

Marc, David, and Robert J. Thompson, *Prime Time, Prime Movers: From I Love Lucy to L.A. Law—America's Greatest TV Shows and the People Who Created Them,* Boston: Little Brown, 1992

Metz, Robert, *CBS: Reflections in a Bloodshot Eye,* Chicago: Playboy Press, 1975

Paley, William S., *As It Happened: A Memoir,* Garden City, New York: Doubleday, 1979

Shapiro, Mitchell E., *Television Network Prime-Time Programming, 1948–1988,* Jefferson, North Carolina: McFarland, 1989

Slater, Robert, *This...Is CBS: A Chronicle of 60 Years,* Englewood Cliffs, New Jersey: Prentice Hall, 1988

Danny Kaye Show, The

U.S. Comedy/Variety Program

The Danny Kaye Show, which premiered on September 25, 1963, was designed as a showcase for the multi-talented entertainer who, before appearing on television, was already a veteran of the vaudeville circuit, the Broadway stage, film, radio, and nightclubs. The variety series was not Kaye's first foray into television: a 1957 *See It Now* program, entitled *The Secret Life of Danny Kaye,* documented Kaye entertaining children around the world on behalf of UNICEF, an organization for which he worked for many years. In 1960, Kaye signed a $1.5 million contract for three annual special programs (*An Hour with Danny Kaye,* October 30, 1960; *The Danny Kaye Special,* November 6, 1961, and November 11, 1962) that would set the pattern for his later series. Although these specials were not critically successful, audience ratings (and two Emmy nominations for his second special with Lucille Ball) were sufficient for the Columbia Broadcasting System (CBS) to offer the entertainer his own weekly series. That same season, veteran performers Jerry Lewis and Judy Garland also premiered variety series but faded quickly.

Unlike comedians such as Red Skelton or Bob Hope, whose series highlighted their monologues, Kaye's variety hour was similar in scope to Sid Caesar's *Your Show of Shows* and *Caesar's Hour.* Kaye's series was a mixture of sketches and special musical material that showcased his inimitable talents. The series attracted prominent guests who helped Kaye demonstrate his own versatility. He sang scat with Louis Armstrong and calypso with Harry Belafonte, danced with Gene Kelly, and performed in sketches with such stars as actor José Ferrer and comedian Dick Van Dyke.

Kaye's strength was his ability to work with a live studio audience. Most episodes included a "quiet" segment highlighting Kaye's ability to work one on one with his audience and provide a sense of intimacy. In this portion, Kaye would sit on a chair at the edge of the stage; then he might tell a story that would showcase his talent for dialects or tongue-twisting dialogue. On other occasions, he would engage in conversation with a child (Laurie Ichino or, later, Victoria Meyerink) or tell tales to a group of children.

The series was produced by Perry Lafferty, who had previously produced variety series for Arthur Godfrey and Andy Williams. Writers for the series included Larry Gelbart (who later created *M*A*S*H*) and Mel Tolkin, both of whom had also written for *Caesar's Hour.* Although Kaye's supporting cast did not appear on a weekly basis, they included Harvey Korman, Gwen Verdon, Joyce Van Patten, the Earl Brown Singers, the Clinger Sisters, and the Tony Charmoli Dancers.

In its first season, *The Danny Kaye Show* garnered three Emmy Awards, including one for the show and one for its star. That same season, the series also received a George Foster Peabody Award as one of the best entertainment programs for the year. During the series' four-year run, it accumulated a total of ten Emmy nominations.

Despite Kaye's enormous talents and popularity, the series failed to gain a wide audience and never achieved

The Danny Kaye Show, Clint Eastwood, Buddy Ebsen, Danny Kaye, Fess Parker, 1963–67.
Courtesy of the Everett Collection

critical success. Considering Kaye's popularity among younger viewers, his late time slot (10:00–11:00 P.M.) may have been a major reason for his show's mediocre ratings. A lack of direction in the show's format and average material often resulted in childlike antics that some critics felt were inappropriate. In addition, competition from other network programs, such as the National Broadcasting Company's (NBC's) *Wednesday Night at the Movies* and *I, Spy,* contributed to the variety show's low ratings.

However, Kaye remained popular with his audience and legions of fans. In fact, the variety series was imported to the United Kingdom in 1964 for the premiere of the British Broadcasting Corporation (BBC 2) channel and ran there for three seasons.

After his show's cancellation in 1967, Kaye returned to television in a number of special programs, mostly aimed at younger viewers, including Rankin-Bass's *The Enchanted World of Danny Kaye* (CBS, February 20,1972), Hallmark Hall of Fame's *Peter Pan* (NBC, December 12, 1976), and *Pinocchio* (CBS, March 27, 1976). In 1976, he hosted the Emmy Award–winning *Danny Kaye's Look at the Metropolitan Opera* (CBS).

His last television appearances were in the Emmy-nominated *Live from Lincoln Center: An Evening with Danny Kaye and the New York Philharmonic* (Public Broadcasting Service [PBS], 1981) and the CBS docudrama *Skokie* (CBS, November 7, 1981). For both these performances, Kaye was presented with another Peabody Award "for virtuoso performances and versatility as a superb clown and as a sensitive dramatic actor." Kaye died in Los Angeles on March 3, 1987.

SUSAN R. GIBBERMAN

See also **Kaye, Danny**

Regular Performers
Danny Kaye
Harvey Korman (1964–67)
Joyce Van Patten (1964–67)
Laurie Ichino (1964–65)
Victoria Meyerink (1964–67)

Music
The Johnny Mann Singers (1963–64)
The Earl Brown Singers (1964–67)
Paul Weston and His Orchestra

Dancers
The Tony Charmoli Dancers

Producers
Perry Lafferty, Robert Tamplin

Programming History
96 episodes
CBS
September 1963–June
  1967   Wednesday 10:00–11:00

Further Reading
Freedland, Michael, *The Secret Life of Danny Kaye,* New York: St. Martin's Press, 1985

Gottfried, Martin, *Nobody's Fool: The Lives of Danny Kaye,* New York: Simon and Schuster, 1994

Gould, Jack, "Danny Kaye Brightens Home Sets," *New York Times* (September 26, 1963)

Singer, Kurt Deutsch, *The Danny Kaye Story,* New York: Thomas Nelson, 1958

"Soliloquy," *Newsweek* (6 November 1961)

"The Wednesday Question: Want to Watch Danny Kaye?," *Newsweek* (December 23, 1963)

Dark Shadows

U.S. Gothic Soap Opera

This enormously popular half-hour gothic soap opera aired on the American Broadcasting Company (ABC) from 1966 until 1971 and showcased a panoply of supernatural characters including vampires, werewolves, warlocks, and witches. During its initial run, the series spawned two feature-length motion pictures, *House of* *Dark Shadows* (1970) and *Night of Dark Shadows* (1971), as well as 32 tie-in novels and assorted comic books, records, Viewmasters, games, models, and trading cards. Fans of the show included both adults and children (it aired in a late-afternoon time slot, which allowed young people the opportunity to see it after school), and many of these fans began to organize clubs and produce fanzines not long after the show was canceled. These groups were directly instrumental in getting *Dark Shadows* rerun in syndication on local stations (often public broadcasting stations) throughout the 1970s and 1980s and in persuading series creator Dan Curtis to remake the show as a prime-time weekly drama on the National Broadcasting Company (NBC) in 1991. Although the new show did not catch on with the public, the entire run of *Dark Shadows,* both the original series and the remake, are available on videotape. Fans continue to hold yearly conventions, write their own *Dark Shadows* fanzines, collect memorabilia, and lobby the entertainment industry.

Set in Collinsport, Maine, the original series focused on the tangled lives and histories of the Collins family. Matriarch Elizabeth Collins Stoddard (well-known classical Hollywood movie star Joan Bennett) presided over the ancestral estate, Collinwood, along with her brother Roger Collins (Louis Edmonds). The show was in danger of being canceled after its first few months on the air until the character of Barnabas Collins, a 172-year-old vampire, was introduced. As played by Jonathan Frid, Barnabas was less a monster and more a tortured gothic hero, and he quickly became the show's most popular character. Governess Victoria Winters (Alexandra Moltke), waitress Maggie Evans (Kathryn Leigh Scott), and Elizabeth's daughter Carolyn (Nancy Barrett) became the first few women to fall sway to the vampire's charms. Dr. Julia Hoffman (Grayson Hall) attempted to cure him of his affliction, although she too subsequently fell in love with him. Barnabas was protected during the day by his manservant Willie Loomis (John Karlen), although Roger's son David (David Henesy) almost discovered his secret.

One of the series' most innovative developments was its use of time travel and parallel universes as narrative tropes that constantly reshuffled storylines and characters, enabling many of the show's most popular actors to play different types of characters within different settings. The first of these shifts occurred when governess Victoria Winters traveled back in time (via a séance) to the year 1795 so that the series could explore the origins of Barnabas's vampirism. The witch Angelique (Lara Parker) was introduced during these episodes, as was the witch-hunting Reverend Trask (Jerry Lacy). After the 1795 sequence, Angelique returned to present-day Collinwood as Roger's new wife Cassandra; she continued to practice witchcraft under the direction of warlock Nicholas Blair (Humbert Allen Astredo). Other classic gothic narratives were soon pressed into service, and the 1968 episodes also featured a werewolf, a Frankenstein-type creation, and a pair of ghosts à la *The Turn of the Screw.*

Dark Shadows.
Photo courtesy of Dan Curtis Productions, Inc.

Those ghosts proved to be the catalyst to another time shift, this time to 1897, wherein dashing playboy Quentin Collins (David Selby) was introduced. His dark good looks and brooding sensuality made him a hit with the fans, and his popularity soon began to rival that of Barnabas. The 1897 sequence marked the height of the show's popularity, and the writers created intricately interwoven stories about vampires, witches, gypsies, zombies, madwomen, and a magical Count Petofi (Thayer David). Quentin was turned into a werewolf, only to have the curse controlled by a portrait, as in *The Picture of Dorian Gray.* When the show returned to the present time once again, it began working a storyline liberally cribbed from H.P. Lovecraft's "Cthulu" mythos. Through various time shifts and parallel universes, the show continued to rework gothic classics (including *Dr. Jekyll and Mr. Hyde, The Turn of the Screw, Rebecca, Wuthering Heights,* and *The Lottery*) until its demise in 1971. Ingénues came and went, including pre–*Charlie's Angels* Kate Jackson as Daphne Harridge and Donna McKechnie (*A Chorus Line*) as Amanda Harris.

The popularity of *Dark Shadows* must be set against the countercultural movements of the late 1960s: interest in alternative religions, altered states of consciousness, and paranormal phenomena such as witchcraft. *Dark Shadows* regularly explored those areas through its sympathetic supernatural creatures, while most of the true villains of the piece turned out to be stern patriarchs and hypocritical preachers. (The show did come under attack from some fundamentalist Christian groups who dubbed the series "Satan's favorite TV show.") Monstrous characters as heroic or likable figures were appearing elsewhere on TV at this time in shows such as *Bewitched, The Addams Family,* and *The Munsters.* Many fans of those shows (and *Dark Shadows*) apparently looked to these figures as playful countercultural icons, existing in a twilight world somewhere outside the patriarchal hegemony. Furthermore, since the show was shot live on tape and mistakes were rarely edited out, the series had a bargain-basement charm that appealed both to spectators who took its storylines seriously and to those who appreciated the spooky goings-on as camp. The range of acting styles also facilitated a camp appreciation, as did the frequently outlandish situations, costumes, and makeup. Despite these technical shortcomings, the gothic romance of the show appears to be one of its most enduring charms. Fan publications most regularly try to recapture the tragic romantic flavor of the show rather than its campiness, although some fans faulted the latter-day NBC remake for taking itself too seriously. Whatever their idiosyncratic reasons, *Dark Shadows* fans remain devoted to the property, and its characters remain popular icons in U.S. culture.

HARRY M. BENSHOFF

See also **Soap Opera**

Cast

Joe Haskell/Nathan Forbes	Joel Crothers
Victoria Winters	Alexandra Moltke
David Collins	David Hennessy
Elizabeth Collins	Joan Bennett
Barnabas Collins	Jonathan Frid
Roger Collins	Louis Edmonds
Dr. Julia Hoffman	Grayson Hall
Maggie Evans	Kathryn Leigh Scott
Carolyn	Nancy Barrett
Quentin Collins	David Selby
Daphne Harridge	Kate Jackson
Angelique	Lara Parker
Nicholas Blair	Humbert Allen Astredo
Reverend Trask	Jerry Lacy
Count Petofi	Thayer David
Willie Loomis	John Karlen

Producers
Dan Curtis, Robert Costello

Programming History
ABC

June 1966–April 1971	Non–prime time

Cast (prime-time series)

Barnabas Collins	Ben Cross
Victoria Winters/Josette	Joanna Going
Elizabeth Collins Stoddard/Naomi	Jean Simmons
Roger Collins/Reverend Trask	Roy Thinnes
David Collins/Daniel (age 8)	Joseph Gordon-Levitt
Dr. Julia Hoffman/Natalie	Barbara Steele
Prof. Woodward/Joshua	Stefan Gierasch
Angelique	Lysette Anthony
Willie Loomis/Ben	Jim Fyfe
Mrs. Johnson/Abigail	Julianna McCarthy
Sheriff Patterson	Michael Cavanaugh
Joe Haskell/Peter	Michael T. Weiss
Sarah Collins	Veronica Lauren
Carolyn Stoddard	Barbara Blackburn

Producer
Dan Curtis

Programming History
NBC

January 1991	Sunday 9:00–10:00
January 1991	Monday 9:00–10:00
January 1991	Friday 10:00–11:00
January 1991– March 1991	Friday 9:00–10:00
March 1991	Friday 10:00–11:00

Further Reading

Benshoff, Harry M., "Secrets, Closets, and Corridors through Time: Negotiating Sexuality and Gender in *Dark Shadows* Fan Culture," in *Theorizing Fandom: Fans, Subcultures, and Identity,* edited by A. Alexander and C. Harris, Cresskill, New Jersey: Hampton Press, 1996

Pierson, Jim, *Dark Shadows Resurrected,* Los Angeles and London: Pomegranate, 1992

Scott, Kathryn Leigh, *My Scrapbook Memories of Dark Shadows,* Los Angeles and London: Pomegranate, 1986

Scott, Kathryn Leigh, editor, *The Dark Shadows Companion,* Los Angeles and London: Pomegranate, 1990

Dateline NBC

U.S. Newsmagazine Show

After 15 failed attempts by NBC News to develop and sustain a newsmagazine series, success began on March 31, 1992, with *Dateline NBC,* co-anchored by Jane Pauley and Stone Phillips. The series' growth and contraction was erratic. A second edition, *Dateline NBC Wednesday,* started in June 1994 when the news division co-opted *Now,* a magazine series co-anchored by Tom Brokov and Katie Couric, making them "contributing anchors" on *Dateline NBC.* A third edition began in fall 1994, a fourth edition during the 1997–98 season, and a fifth edition in the summer of 1999. After maintaining five editions a week from mid-1999 through most of 2000, the series immediately shifted to three editions, with intermittent *Dateline NBC* special reports, until NBC canceled the flagship Tuesday night edition in the fall of 2003, signaling the series' inadequacy in the present landscape of network programming.

Dateline NBC grew slowly as the news division tested new editions in different time slots during the spring and summer before making a seasonal commitment. Even after establishing a time slot, new editions were temporarily shifted on the schedule or were preempted for short periods, causing producers to fear losing viewers. But NBC strategically capitalized on the demographic flow of preceding programs, locating and building a specific audience base on different nights before an edition took a permanent or constant position on the schedule.

A significant staff change occurred in 1993 at NBC News that influenced the series' leadership and direction. General Motors discovered that *Dateline NBC* placed and ignited incendiary devices under General Motors' light trucks during test crashes to vividly illustrate design dangers of side-saddle gas tanks. Michael Gartner, president of the news division, was forced to resign in March. He was replaced by Andrew Lack, once executive producer of the flashy CBS News series *West 57th* and Neil Shapiro became the series' executive producer, a position Steve Friedman, executive producer of *Nightly News,* held with the title "executive in charge of *Dateline NBC.*"

Referred to as a factory, franchise, or, according to NBC publicity releases, a "multinight franchise," *Dateline NBC* was the first newsmagazine "clone," propagating and radically changing the programming strategies of the network newsmagazine. *Dateline NBC* established brand power by "stripping" editions, an entertainment division strategy that placed a program in the same time slot every week night. When adding new editions, NBC News conceptualized, formatted, and promoted *Dateline NBC* as one series with several editions, not distinct or separate hourly programs. After reaching three editions a week, more programming options helped build audience anticipation from one edition to the next. Stories could air over multiple editions in several parts, an edition could contain five or six stories, or one hour could be dedicated to a special topic. *Dateline NBC* could offer celebrities or figures in an investigation an interview over two editions. Reinforcing the series as interconnected hourly editions, most editions promoted future stories and regularly updated past stories.

When Executive Producer Shapiro literally "put the news back into newsmagazines," the series shattered conventions. At three nights a week, *Dateline NBC* started covering breaking news, securing viewers rarely visiting network evening news programs. Breaking news segments had an urgent, sensational tone, building suspense from edition to edition as stories unfolded over weeks or months. From 1995 through 1999, *Dateline NBC*'s rapid growth period, these stories included the killings at Columbine High School, the aftermath of Swissair Flight 111, the destruction and rebuilding process after hurricanes and tornadoes, new evidence or rumors concerning the death of Jon Benet Ramsey, the Unabomber, Princess Diana's death, the explosion of TWA Flight 800, the Oklahoma City bombing, and the flight and death of Andrew Cunanan. *Dateline NBC* became a phenomenal success by the end of 1999, with at least one edition consistently ranking in the top ten. Breaking news stories are still part of the series' formula, but critics attribute their early success to recontextualizing these news stories into a more compelling form for magazine programs, the astounding and thrilling nature of the stories, and uniqueness of breaking news in a magazine format.

Dateline NBC rreconceptualized the news division's image, projecting a unified community of journalists on broadcast and cable television. Anchors and correspondents appeared regularly on MSNBC and CNBC with condensed stories from the series, especially when Jane Pauley hosted *Time and Again* on MSNBC from 1996 to 2001. Katie Couric reports stories and briefly announces others on *Today*. Tom Brokaw hosts several *Dateline NBC* specials each year, increasing visibility for *Nightly News*. Producers added correspondents to *Dateline NBC* from NBC-affiliated stations, generating audience appeal in different markets.

Shapiro aggressively differentiated *Dateline NBC* from competitors by introducing "signature" segments, produced by the unit or with media organizations such as *People* magazine, Court TV, and *Good Housekeeping*. "Signature" segments, such as "Dateline Feedback," Dateline Poll," and "Dateline Timeline," facilitated viewer participation, while other segments, such as "Picture of the Week," "State of the Art," "Dateline Survivor," "Dateline/Court TV," "Dateline People," and "Dateline/Consumer Reports," focused on specific subject matter. The longest-lasting and most popular signature segment, "Dateline Timeline," still quizzes viewers on the year that a group of historical events occurred. By combining signature segments, coverage of breaking news, regular updates of past stories, two- or three-part investigative and consumer report segments, and interviews, *Dateline NBC* retained viewers with the suspense that bridged three or four editions and audience anticipation of the unpredictable content of the next edition. NBC News attributed this formula to the series' success.

David Corvo, vice president of NBC News since 1995, became executive producer in 2001, developing documentaries with the Disney Channel, History Channel, Court TV, and Discovery Health. Segments from documentaries sometimes appeared on *Dateline NBC,* but these alliances placed the series' "brand" and image throughout the media terrain.

Populism remains central to most *Dateline NBC* stories. A six-part series on firehouses in the United States in 2002 shunned investigating the institution but chronicled the emotional journeys of individual firefighters. Producers dedicated over a year preparing stories on important issues, such as cancer drug trials and adoption of severely abused children, but the program's news qualities receded as correspondents intimately probed the emotions and psychology of participants. This was not always the primary perspective, with the series producing award-winning reports after yearlong investigations on important social conditions in the United States, such as migrant workers. But on a regular basis, segments shifted story perspective to facilitate the audience's emotional attachment to the stories' characters.

Dateline NBC became infamous for its steady stream of stories on private suffering, pain, and grief of family members. The news division defended these as investigations of "personal hardships," and reviewers denounced them as exploitive and torturous to watch. Although different circumstances tore families apart every week, these families triumphed in small ways against impossible odds.

Dateline NBC coveted consumer advocate stories, alerting the public to the horrific dangers of products and the unimaginable behavior of professionals in everyday life. That your child might be wearing recycled braces sent fear through American families. "Tired" or "old" consumer alert stories, such as credit card fraud and bacteria-infected or outdated meat reaching supermarket shelves, were invigorated with extensive use of hidden cameras, sometimes over several editions. By 1999, segment titles began with the words "Dateline Hidden Camera Investigation." Many investigations were compelling and newsworthy and provided the impetus for change, including examinations of collusion between the real estate industry and housing inspectors to the detriment of buyers and sellers and factory-enslaved children overseas producing silk for the United States. But when reverting to hidden cameras to depict aggressively impolite airline employees or to gaze at babysitters abusing children, *Dateline NBC* signaled a willingness to secure ratings from shocking and voyeuristic stories.

In 1999, the series began interactive stories where viewers voted on a website, maintained by MSNBC for *Dateline NBC,* on such circumstances as whether to convict or acquit a woman in the death of her boyfriend or whether to charge a doctor with manslaughter for falling asleep in the operating room, causing a child's death. Viewer tallies of "guilty" or "not guilty" crawled across the bottom of the television screen every 15 seconds. Interactive stories became more complex and potentially troubling with "Interactive Dateline Mystery: Shadow on the Stairs" (January 2002) after the 1989 murder of Janice Johnson was reopened with her husband, Clayton, as the primary suspect. With different evidence and witness testimonies available, at every commercial break viewers requested over the Internet evidence they needed after the break to continue evaluating the case, in essence controlling the content and direction of a serious news investigation. The series still offers these highly interactive and involving story structures.

Dateline NBC's visual style targets younger viewers while reaching out to the voyeuristically inclined. Events are reconstructed with shaky handheld cameras, sometimes slightly out of focus, from the point of view of a murderer or an imminent victim. Other stylistic techniques include rapid editing, dramatic music, exaggerated sound effects, shifting from black-and-white to color footage, and arresting and disconcerting camera angles. Shapiro defended *Dateline NBC*'s less-than-orthodox practices and subject selection, claiming that the series represented audience desires and fascination with headline news. Because newsmagazines competed with prime-time entertainment programs, Shapiro believed that formulating valuable public information into entertaining dramatic packages did not demean the importance or integrity of news.

Skepticism that *Dateline NBC* could preserve news as a valuable public commodity was raised in February 2003, when Corvo, on a directive from NBC's entertainment division, expanded a profile of Michael Jackson to two hours, hoping to ride the rating success of a competitor's exposé. Corvo characterized this decision as "all part of the game." A year earlier, Corvo accepted a commission from NBC's entertainment division for several fascinating and involving two-hour *Dateline NBC* specials.

When Jane Pauley retired as co-anchor in May 2003, the series' underlying goals became more transparent when the press noted the long-standing resentment by NBC News at Pauley's decision not to partake in the unpleasant and uncivilized battles with other networks for the big money-making star interview.

Dateline NBC radically shook up and rreconfigured network newsmagazines. They were responsible for the Columbia Broadcasting System (CBS) introducing *60 Minutes II* and for the American Broadcasting Company (ABC) adding new editions of *20/20*. *Dateline NBC*'s influence was so strong that *60 Minutes II* started even after Don Hewitt, executive producer of *60 Minutes,* said that a clone would never start while he was at CBS and led to Hewitt's announcement that to "shore up ratings," *60 Minutes* would introduce breaking news stories, ultimately unsuccessfully, in the spring of 1996. During certain times from 1997 through 2000, up to 11 hours of newsmagazine programs aired weekly. As *Dateline NBC* became an economic success and an invaluable asset to the brand image of NBC News, it created an intense competitive marketplace that critics feared would inevitably spawn moments of unethical and unprofessional broadcast journalism. Needing more prime-time newsmagazine segments, the networks loosened journalistic standards, placing false dramatic story configurations on news and information to compete with entertainment programs. Ironically, Corvo attributed the reduction of *Dateline NBC* to two weekly editions and weaker but still economically strong ratings to viewers demanding reality programs.

RICHARD C. BARTONE

See also **Brokaw, Tom; Couric, Katie; National Broadcasting Company; News, Network; Pauley, Jane**

Anchors
Stone Philips (1993–)
Jane Pauley (1993–2003)

Contributing Anchors
Tom Brokaw (1994–)
Katie Couric (1994–)
Bryant Gumbel (1994–97)
Maria Shriver (1994–2002)

Correspondents/Reporters
Michelle Gillen (1992–93)
Arthur Kent (1992–93)
Brian Ross (1992–94)
Deborah Roberts (1992–95)
Faith Daniels (1993–95)
John Larson (1994–)
Dennis Murphy (1994–)
Lisa Rudolph (1994–)
Mike Boettcher (1995–96)
Jon Scott (1995–96)
Elizabeth Vargas (1995–96)
Bob McKeown (1995–2002)
Les Cannon (1995–)
Victoria Corderi (1995–)
Keith Morrison (1995–)
Chris Hansen (1995–)
Lea Thompson (1995–)
Ed Gordon (1996–2000)
Dawn Fratangelo (1996–)
John Hockenberry (1996–)
Sarah James (1996–)
Josh Mankiewicz (1996–)
Ann Curry (1997–)
Rob Stafford (1997–)
Mike Taibbi (1997–)
Bob Costas (1997–2000)
Steve Daniels (1998–99)
Dr. Bob Arnott (1998–)
Hoda Kotb (1998–)
Margaret Larson (1998–)
David Gregory (1999–)
Edie Magnus (1999–)
Robert Bazelle (2002–)

Producers
Steve Friedman (1993); Neil Shapiro (1993–2001); David Corvo (2001–).

Programming History

Fall 1992	Tuesday 10:00–11:00
Fall 1993	Tuesday 10:00–11:00
	Wednesday 9:00–10:00; began in January 1994)
Fall 1994	Tuesday 10:00–11:00
	Wednesday 9:00–10:00
	Friday 9:00–10:00
Fall 1995	Tuesday 10:00–11:00
	Wednesday 9:00–10:00
	Friday 9:00–10:00
Fall 1996	Tuesday 10:00–11:00
	Friday 9:00–10:00
	Spring 1996 adds 7:00–8:00 edition
Fall 1997	Monday 10:00–11:00
	Tuesday 10:00–11:00
	Friday 9:00 –10:00
Fall 1998	Sunday 7:00–8:00
	Monday 10:00–11:00
	Tuesday 10:00–11:00
	Wednesday 8:00–9:00
	Friday 8:00–9:00
Fall 1999	Sunday 7:00–8:00
	Monday 10:00–11:00
	Tuesday 10:00–11:00
	Wednesday 8:00–9:00
	Friday 9:00–10:00
Fall 2000	Sunday 7:00–8:00
	Tuesday 10:00–11:00
	Friday 9:00–10:00
Fall 2001	Sunday 7:00–8:00
	Tuesday 10:00–11:00
	Friday 9:00–10:00
Fall 2002	Sunday 7:00–8:00
	Tuesday 10:00–11:00
	Friday 9:00–10:00
Fall 2003	Sunday 7:00–8:00
	Friday 9:00–10:00

Further Reading

Adalian, Josef, "'Dateline' Timeline Reaches 10th Year," *Variety* (April 29, 2002)

Carter, Bill, "The Man Reshaping Prime Time," *New York Times* (June 8, 1998)

Consoli, John, "All the News That Fits," *Media Week* (June 1, 1998)

Dugard, M., editor, *Dateline Survivors: Tales of Extraordinary Heroism by Everyday People*, New York: McGraw-Hill, 1999

Gay, Verne, "Send in the Clones," *Media Week* (September 22, 1997)

Greppi, Michele, "Decade Old 'Dateline' Counts Its Blessings," *Electronic Media* (April 22, 2002)

Greppi, Michele, "Keeping NBC News in Top Form," *Electronic Media* (January 7, 2002)

Justin, Neal, "Glossy and Sometimes Paper-Thin, Newsmagazines Shows are Proliferating on Prime-Time TV," *Star Tribune* (December 23, 1997)

Smillie, Dirk, "Newsmagazines Woo Viewers as Must-See TV Dramas," *Christian Science Monitor* (February 20, 1998)

Turner, Richard, and Mark Hosenball, "The Datelining of TV," *Newsweek* (May 4, 1998)

Willens, Michele, "Sweet Sixteen?: After Misfiring with 15 Other Newsmagazines, NBC Believes It Has an Attractive Formula for Its 'Dateline' Show," *Los Angeles Times* (March 22, 1992)

Davies, Andrew (1936–)

British Writer

Andrew Davies is an incredibly prolific award-winning writer and adapter. He began his career in 1960 writing radio plays, moving into television, stage plays, children's books, novels, and films. He combined writing with his work as a teacher, then university lecturer, until the age of 50. Both professions inform some of his writing, such as his highly autobiographical *Bavarian Night* (British Broadcasting Corporation [BBC] *Play for Today),* which deals with a parent-teacher association evening, and the hugely successful series *A Very Peculiar Practice,* about general practitioners on a university campus.

Davies has long been recognized as writing good roles for women. He created the character Steph Smith as a vehicle for his "early feminist plays" for radio. Steph was a factory worker aspiring to the life of the sales representative. Davies's first play for television, *Who's Going to Take Me On?* (on *Wednesday Play*) also featured Steph.

The mainstay of his television work has been for the BBC. Initially, he felt himself in danger of being regarded solely as a writer of BBC naturalistic material and turned to nonnaturalistic writing, such as *Fearless Frank Harris,* in the early 1970s. His other original television work includes *A Very Polish Practice,* a one-off sequel to his series, and the pilot for the London Weekend Television series *Anna Lee.*

Davies is also well known for a great many adaptations and dramatizations that have won him a string of awards. Following dramatizations of R.F. Delderfield's *To Serve Them All My Days* and *Diana,* he has adapted a host of very high-profile dramas for the BBC. After the success of dramatizations of Michael Dobbs's *House of Cards* and its sequel, *To Play the King* (for which he was accused of a left-wing bias), he was commissioned for the much-heralded, expensive and extensive version of George Eliot's *Middlemarch,* the BBC's most costly drama serial to that date. *Middlemarch* was praised in the trade press as a fast-moving, faithful adaptation of the original.

Having suggested that adapting Jane Austen would be a thankless task since so many viewers know her books word for word, Davies dramatized *Pride and Prejudice.* This BBC serial was another great popular and critical success despite the fact that it was preceded by strong reactions from tabloid newspapers over the possibility that it might feature nudity.

Davies enjoys adapting other authors' work, grateful for the existing plot in which to exercise his own humor and explore his preoccupations. There are also those originals he admires to the extent that he wishes solely to do them justice. In this category, he cites *Anglo-Saxon Attitudes* and *The Old Devils.* He was involved in a very public struggle to get screen time for *Anglo-Saxon Attitudes,* attacking ITV's "flexipool" (or "indecision pool") in the process. It was then commissioned on the back of discussions regarding "quality."

As well as writing numerous children's books, Davies is also an award-winning writer of children's television. He wrote two original series of *Marmalade Atkins* for Thames TV and dramatized *Alfonso Bonzo* as a six-part serial from his own children's novel. He has also written feature film screenplays, including *Circle of Friends* and *Bridget Jones's Diary.*

GUY JOWETT

Andrew (Wynford) Davies. Born in Rhiwbina, Cardiff, Wales, September 20, 1936. Attended Whitchurch Grammar School, Cardiff; University College, London, B.A. in English 1957. Married: Diana Huntley, 1960; children: one son and one daughter. Began career as teacher at St. Clement Danes Grammar School, London, 1958–61, and Woodberry Down Comprehensive School, London, 1961–63; lecturer, Coventry College of Education, 1963–71, and University of Warwick, Coventry, 1971–87. Wrote first play for radio, 1964; television and film writer; author of several stage plays and fiction aimed at both young and adult audiences. Recipient: *Guardian* Children's Fic-

tion Award, 1979; *Boston Globe-Horn* Book Award, 1980; Broadcast Press Guild Awards, 1980, 1990; Pye Colour TV Award, 1981; Royal Television Society Award, 1987; British Academy of Film and Television Arts Awards, 1989, 1993; Writers Guild Awards, 1991, 1992; Primetime Emmy Award, 1991.

Television Series and Miniseries (selection)

1980	*To Serve Them All My Days*
1986–88	*A Very Peculiar Practice*
1989	*Mother Love*
1990	*House of Cards*
1993	*To Play the King*
1994	*Middlemarch*
1995	*Game On* (with Bernadette Davis)
1995	*Pride and Prejudice*
1995	*The Final Cut*
1996	*Wilderness*
1998	*Vanity Fair*
1999	*Wives and Daughters*
2001	*The Way We Live Now*
2002	*Dr. Zhivago*
2002	*Daniel Deronda*
2004	*He Knew He Was Right*

Television Plays and Movies (selection)

1967	*Who's Going to Take Me On?*
1970	*Is That Your Bod, Boy?*
1973	*No Good unless It Hurts*
1974	*The Water Maiden*
1975	*Grace*
1975	*The Imp of the Perverse*
1976	*The Signalman*
1976	*A Martyr to the System*
1977	*Eleanor Marx*
1977	*Happy in War*
1977	*Velvet Glove*
1978	*Fearless Frank*
1978	*Renoir My Father*
1981	*Bavarian Night*
1983	*Heartattack Hotel*
1984	*Diana*
1985	*Pythons on the Mountain*
1987	*Inappropriate Behaviour*
1988	*Lucky Sunil*
1988	*Baby, I Love You*
1991	*Filipina Dreamers*
1992	*The Old Devils*
1992	*Anglo-Saxon Attitudes*
1992	*A Very Polish Practice*
1993	*Anna Lee*
1993	*Harnessing Peacocks*
1994	*A Few Short Journeys of the Heart*

1996	*The Fortunes and Misfortunes of Moll Flanders*
1998	*Getting Hurt*
1998	*A Rather English Marriage*
2001	*Take a Girl Like You*
2002	*Othello*
2002	*Tipping the Velvet*
2003	*Boudica*

Films

The Hospitalization of Samuel Pellett, 1964; *Getting the Smell of It*, 1967; *A Day in Bed*, 1967; *Curse on Them, Astonish Me!*, 1970; *Steph and the Man of Some Distinction*, 1971; *The Innocent Eye*, 1971; *The Shortsighted Bear*, 1972; *Steph and the Simple Life*, 1972; *Steph and the Zero Structure Lifestyle*, 1976; *Accentuate the Positive*, 1980; *Campus Blues*, 1984; *Circle of Friends*, 1995; *The Tailor of Panama*, 2001; *Bridget Jones's Diary*, 2001; *Bridget Jones: The Edge of Reason*, 2004.

Stage

Can Anyone Smell the Gas?, 1972; *The Shortsighted Bear*, 1972; *Filthy Fryer and the Woman of Mature Years*, 1974; *Linda Polan: Can You Smell the Gas?, What Are Little Girls Made of?*, 1975; *Rohan and Julia*, 1975; *Randy Robinson's Unsuitable Relationship*, 1976; *Teacher's Gone Mad*, 1977; *Going Bust*, 1977; *Fearless Frank*, 1978; *Brainstorming with the Boys*, 1978; *Battery*, 1979; *Diary of a Desperate Woman*, 1979; *Rose*, 1980; *Prin*, 1990.

Publications (selection)

The Fantastic Feats of Doctor Boox, 1972
Conrad's War, 1978
Marmalade and Rufus, 1979
Poonam's Pets, with Diana Davies, 1990; 1990
B. Monkey, 1992

Further Reading

"Pride and Prurience (Andrew Davies' Racy Adaptation of Jane Austen's Pride and Prejudice)," *The Economist* (London) (November 3, 1990)
Rafferty, Frances, "Always One Page Ahead," *Times Educational Supplement* (London) (November 8, 1991)

Day After, The

U.S. Made-for-Television Movie

The Day After, a dramatization of the effects of a hypothetical nuclear attack on the United States, was one of the biggest media events of the 1980s. Shown on the American Broadcasting Company (ABC) on Sunday, November 20, 1983, *The Day After* was watched by approximately half the U.S. adult population, the largest audience for a made-for-TV movie to that time. The movie was broadcast after weeks of advance publicity, fueled by White House nervousness about the program's antinuclear "bias." ABC had distributed half a million "viewer's guides," and discussion groups were organized around the country. A studio discussion, in which the U.S. secretary of state took part, was conducted following the program. The advance publicity was unprecedented in scale, centered on the slogan, "*The Day After*—Beyond Imagining. The starkly realistic drama of nuclear confrontation and its devastating effect on a group of average American citizens."

The show was the brainchild of Brandon Stoddard, then president of the ABC Motion Picture Division, who had been impressed by the theatrical film *The China Syndrome*. Directed by Nicholas Meyer, a feature film director, *The Day After* went on to be either broadcast or released as a theatrical feature in more than 40 countries. In Britain, for example, an edited version was shown on the ITV commercial network three weeks after the U.S. broadcast, with the U.K. airing accompanied by a Campaign for Nuclear Disarmament recruitment drive. In a country that had yet to transmit Peter Watkins's film on the topic of nuclear war, *The War Game*, most British critics dismissed *The Day After* as a travesty, a typically tasteless American treatment of this major theme.

Wherever it was shown, *The Day After* raised questions about genre and about politically committed TV and its ideological effects. Was it a drama-documentary,

The Day After.
Photo courtesy of ABC Photo Archives

a combination of fact and fiction (how do you depict a catastrophe that has not yet happened?), or was it a disaster movie? Some argued that the program stretched the limits of the medium, in the tradition of *Roots* and *Holocaust,* manipulating a variety of prestige-TV and -film propaganda devices to raise itself above the ratings war in order to attempt to address a universal audience about a 20th-century nightmare.

ABC defined the production in terms of realism (for example, rosters of scientific advisers helped design the special effects used during the depictions of missiles and the blast), and the network defined it in terms of art, as a surrealist vision of the destruction of Western civilization as it affected a midwestern town (Lawrence, Kansas) and a family (graphically represented in the movie poster). Network executives were particularly aware of the issue of taste and the impact of horror on sensitive viewers (they knew that Watkins's film had been deemed "too horrifying for the medium of television"); however, it was assumed that the majority of the audience was already inured to depictions of suffering. The delicate issue of identification with victims and survivors was handled by setting the catastrophe in a real town and using a large cast of relatively unknown actors (although John Lithgow, Jo-Beth Williams, Steve Guttenberg, and Amy Madigan would eventually become established, well-known actors) and a horde of extras, while at the center of the story stood the venerable Jason Robards as a doctor. *Time* magazine opined that "much of the power came from the quasi-documentary idea that nuclear destruction had been visited upon the real town of Lawrence, Kansas, rather than upon some back lot of Warner Brothers." Scriptwriter Edward Hume decided to downplay the more inflammatory, political aspects of the scenario: "It's not about politics or politicians or military decision-makers. It is simply about you and me—doctors, farmers, teachers, students, brothers, and kid sisters engaged in the usual love and labor of life in the month of September." (This populist dimension was reinforced when the mayor of Lawrence sent a telegram to Soviet leader Yuri Andropov.)

There is an American pastoralism at work in the depiction of prairie life. Director Nicholas Meyer (*Star Trek II*) was aware of the danger of lapsing into formulas and wrote in a "production diary" for *TV Guide,*

> The more *The Day After* resembles a film, the less effective it is likely to be. No TV stars. What we don't want is another Hollywood disaster movie with viewers waiting to see Shelley Winters succumb to radiation poisoning. To my surprise, ABC agrees. Their sole proviso: one star to help sell the film as a feature overseas. Fair enough.

Production proceeded without the cooperation of the U.S. Defense Department, which had wanted the script to make it clear that the Soviet Union started the war.

Despite sequences of *cinéma vérité* and occasional trappings of realism, the plot develops in soap opera fashion, with two families about to be united by marriage. The movie evolves, however, to present an image of a community of survivors that extends beyond the family, centered on what is left of the local university and based on the model of a medieval monastery.

Although November was a "sweeps" month, ABC decided to air no commercials after the point in the story in which the bomb fell. Even so, *The Day After*'s critics categorized the film as just another made-for-TV movie treating a sensational theme. Complained a *New York Times* editorial, "A hundred million Americans were summoned to be empathetically incinerated, and left on the true day after without a single idea to chew upon." Other critics found the movie too tame in its depiction of the effects of nuclear attack (abroad, this was sometimes attributed to American naïveté about war), a reproach anticipated in the final caption, "The catastrophic events you have witnessed are, in all likelihood, less severe than the destruction that would actually occur in the event of a full nuclear strike against the United States." Some critics did appreciate *The Day After*'s aesthetic ambitions. Since the program aired, no network has successfully attempted to match this hybrid between entertainment and information, between a popular genre like disaster and an address to the enlightened citizen.

SUSAN EMMANUEL

Cast

Dr. Russell Oakes	Jason Robards
Nancy Bauer	JoBeth Williams
Stephen Klein	Steve Guttenberg

Jim Dahlberg	John Cullum	Tom Cooper	Arliss Howard
Joe Huxley	John Lithgow	Dr. Wallenberg	Rosanna Huffman
Eve Dahlberg	Bibi Beach	Cleo Mackey	Barbara Iley
Denise Dahlberg	Lori Lethin	TV Host	Madison Mason
Alison Ransom	Amy Madigan	Cody	Bob Meister
Bruce Gallatin	Jeff East	Mack	Vahan Moosekian
Helen Oakes	Georgann Johnson	Dr. Landowska	George Petrie
Airman McCoy	William Allen Young	2nd Barber	Glenn Robards
Dr. Sam Hachiya	Calvin Jung	1st Barber	Tom Spratley
Dr. Austin	Lin McCarthy	Vinnie Conrad	Stan Wilson
Reverend Walker	Dennis Lipscomb		
Dennis Hendry	Clayton Day		
Danny Dahlberg	Doug Scott		
Jolene Dahlberg	Ellen Anthony		
Marilyn Oakes	Kyle Aletter		
Cynthia	Alston Ahearn		
Professor	William Allyn		
Ellen Hendry	Antonie Becker		
Nurse	Pamela Brown		
Julian French	Jonathan Estrin		
Aldo	Stephen Furst		

Producers

Robert Papazian, Stephanie Austin

Programming History

ABC
November 20, 1983   8:00–10:35

Further Reading

Boyd-Bowman, Susan, "*The Day After:* Representations of the Nuclear Holocaust," *Screen* (July–October 1984)

Day, Robin (1923–2000)

British Broadcast Journalist

Sir Robin Day was admired as one of the most formidable of political interviewers and commentators in British television and radio. An aspiring politician himself in the 1950s, he subsequently acquired a reputation for challenging questions and acerbic resistance to propagandist responses that made him the model for virtually all political interviewers who came after him.

As a student at Oxford, Day became president of the Oxford Union debating society and subsequently trained for the bar before realizing that a career in the media was ideally suited to his talents. With athlete Chris Chataway, he was one of the first two newscasters for the fledgling Independent Television News (ITN) and created a considerable impact with his forceful personality and style of delivery, which was in marked contrast to the stuffier and more formal style of the British Broadcasting Corporation (BBC) presenters. He also developed his skills as a political interviewer for the small screen; in 1957, for instance, while working for ITN's *Roving Report* at a time when Britain and Egypt were still technically at war over the Suez crisis, he scored a notable coup when he managed to secure an interview with Egypt's President Nasser.

After his own bid for Parliament (as a candidate for the Liberals) failed in 1959, Day moved to the BBC as a reporter and presenter of *Panorama*, which under his leadership (carrying on from that of Richard Dimbleby) consolidated its reputation as the corporation's most influential political program. Respected and indeed feared by politicians of all parties, Day became a national institution, instantly familiar with his breath-

Robin Day.
Photo courtesy of Robin Day

sucking speech, large black-rimmed spectacles, and flamboyant spotted bow ties—and a favorite subject of impersonators.

Interviewees were rarely allowed to wriggle off the hook by the relentless Day, who showed scant respect for rank and title, and on several occasions guests were bludgeoned into making disclosures that would doubtless have otherwise remained unrevealed (some viewers were appalled at Day's brusque persistence and called him rude and insensitive).

After 13 years with *Panorama,* Day hosted his own *Newsday* program and also presented radio's *The World at One* for several years. In 1979, he was the first chair of the popular *Question Time* program, based on radio's *Any Questions?,* in which prominent members of parliamentary and public life were invited to field questions on topical issues from a studio audience. Under Day's eagle eye, the program quickly established itself as the best of its kind and attracted a huge audience under both him and successive presenters. Following his departure from the program, after some ten years in the chair and by now a veteran of some 30 years of television experience and knighted in

acknowledgment of his achievements, he confined himself largely to occasional work for the satellite and regional television stations.

Some politicians found Day's dogged—even belligerent—style of questioning too much to take, and on several occasions notable figures lost their temper. Defense Secretary John Nott was a particularly celebrated victim of the master interviewer's attacks, snatching off his microphone and storming out of a television interview with Day at the time of the Falklands crisis after taking offense at Day's questions.

DAVID PICKERING

Robin Day. Born in London, October 23, 1923. Attended Bembridge School; St. Edmund Hall, Oxford, B.A. with honors in jurisprudence 1951; Middle Temple, M.A.; Blackstone Entrance Scholar, 1951; Harmsworth Law School, 1952–53. Served in Royal Artillery, 1943–47. Married: Katherine Ainslie, 1965 (divorced, 1986); children: Alexander and Daniel. Called to the bar, 1952; worked for British Information Services, Washington, 1953–54; freelance broadcaster, 1954; radio talks producer, BBC, 1955; newscaster and parliamentary correspondent, ITN, 1955–59; columnist, *News Chronicle,* 1959; worked on various ITV programs, 1955–59; ran unsuccessfully for Parliament as a Liberal, 1959; hosted numerous BBC radio and television current affairs programs, including *Panorama, Newsday,* and *Question Time,* from 1959; retired as regular presenter, 1989, but subsequently worked on satellite and regional television. LL.D.: University of Exeter, 1986; Keele University, 1988; University of Essex, 1988. Honorary Fellow, St. Edmund Hall, Oxford, 1989; Honorary Bencher, 1990. Member: Trustee, Oxford Literary and Debating Union; Phillmore Committee on Law of Contempt, 1971–74; chair, Hansard Society, 1981–83. Knighted, 1981. Recipient: Guild of TV Producers' Merit Award, Personality of the Year, 1957; Richard Dimbleby Award for factual television, 1974; Broadcast Press Guild Award, 1980; Royal Television Society Judges' Award, 1985. Died in London, August 5, 2000.

Television Series

1955–59	Independent Television News
1955–59	*Tell the People*
1955–59	*Under Fire*
1957	*Roving Report*
1959–72	*Panorama* (presenter, 1967–72)
1976	*Newsday*
1979–89	*Question Time*
1992	*The Parliamentary Programme*
1992	*The Elder Statesmen*

Radio

It's Your Line, 1970–76; *Election Call,* 1974, 1979, 1983, 1987; *The World at One,* 1979–87.

Publications (selected)

The Case for Televising Parliament, 1963
Day by Day (autobiography), 1975

The Grand Inquisitor (autobiography), 1989
... But with Respect (interviews), 1993

Further Reading

Cox, Geoffrey, *Pioneering Television News: A First Hand Report on a Revolution in Journalism,* London: John Libby, 1995
Milne, Alisdair, *DG: Memoirs of a British Broadcaster,* London: Hodder and Stoughton, 1988

Death on the Rock

British Investigative Documentary

"Death on the Rock" is the title of a program in the current affairs series *This Week,* made by Thames Television and broadcast on the ITV network on April 28, 1988. The program investigated the incident, on Sunday, March 6, 1988, when three members of the Irish Republican Army (IRA), sent to Gibraltar on an active service mission, were shot and killed by members of British special forces. The incident, and subsequently the program about it, became controversial as a result of uncertainty and conflicting evidence about the manner in which the killing was carried out and the degree to which it was an "execution" with no attempted arrest. The program interviewed witnesses who claimed to have heard no prior warning given by the Special Air Service (SAS) troops and to have seen the shooting carried out "in cold blood." Furthermore, when defenders of the special forces' actions contended the IRA team might, if allowed time, have had the capacity to trigger by remote control a car bomb in the main street, that assertion was also criticized by an army bomb disposal expert, among others.

Claiming that its transmission prior to the official inquest was an impediment to justice, the British foreign secretary, Sir Geoffrey Howe, attempted to stop the program from being broadcast by writing to the chairman of the Independent Broadcasting Authority, Lord Thomson of Monifieth. Lord Thomson refused to prevent transmission, noting that "the issues as we see them relate to free speech and free inquiry which underpin individual liberty in a democracy." Following transmission, there was widespread criticism in sections of the press of the program's investigative stance

(such as "Storm at SAS Telly Trial," *Sun;* "Fury over SAS 'Trial by TV,'" *Daily Mail;* "TV Slur on the SAS," *Daily Star*). Subsequently, a number of papers, notably the *Sunday Times* and the *Sun,* attempted to show not only that the program's procedures of inquiry were faulty but also that the character of some of its witnesses was dubious (in one case, a woman subjected to this latter charge successfully pursued a libel action against the newspapers that made it).

The debate that developed around the program intensified when one of its witnesses subsequently repudiated his testimony, and so an independent inquiry was conducted at the behest of Thames Television. This inquiry was undertaken by Lord Windlesham, a former government minister with experience as a managing director in television, and Richard Rampton, a barrister specializing in defamation and media law. The inquiry's findings, which were published as a book in 1989, largely cleared the program of any impropriety, although it noted a number of errors.

Any assessment of the "Death on the Rock" affair has to note a number of constituent factors. The hugely emotive and politically controversial issue of British military presence in Northern Ireland provides the backdrop. For much of the British public, the various bombing attacks of the IRA (many of them involving civilian casualties) seemed to give the incident in Gibraltar the character of a wartime event whose legitimacy was unquestionable. At a more focused level, the Windlesham/Rampton report analyzed, in unusual detail, the narrative structure of current affairs exposition—its movement between interview and presenter

"Death on the Rock."
Courtesy of ©FremantleMedia Enterprises

commentary, its use of location material, and its movements of evaluation. It also probed further back into the way in which the program was put together through the contacting of various witnesses and the investigations of researchers. This analysis was set in the context of long-standing tension between the Conservative government and broadcasters, particularly investigative journalists, on the matter of "national interest" and on the "limits" that should be imposed (preferably self-imposed) on work that brought into question the activities of the state.

There is obviously little space here to look at the program's form in any detail, but a number of features in its opening suggest something of its character. The program starts with a pretitle sequence featuring two of its principal witnesses, Carmen Proetta and Stephen Bullock, in "sound bites" from the longer interviews. These go as follows:

Witness 1: "There was no exchange of words on either side, no warning, nothing said; no screams, nothing; just the shots."

Witness 2: "I should say they were from a distance of about four feet and that the firing was continuous; in other words, probably as fast as it's possible to fire."

After the titles, the program is "launched" by the studio-based presenter (Jonathan Dimbleby):

The killing by the SAS of three IRA terrorists in Gibraltar provoked intense debate not only in Britain but throughout the world—and especially in the Republic of Ireland and the United States. There are perhaps those who wonder what the fuss is about, who ask, "Does it really matter when or how they were killed?"; who say "They were terrorists, there's a war on; and we got to them before they got us." However, in the eyes of the law and of the state, it is not so simple. . . . The question which goes to the heart of the issue, is this: did the SAS men have the law on their side when they shot dead [photo stills] Danny McCann, Sean Savage, and Mairead Farrell, who were unarmed at the time? [photo of bodies and ambulance] Were the soldiers acting in self-defence or were they operating what has become known as a "shoot to kill policy"—simply eliminating a group of known terrorists outside the due process of law, without arrest, trial or verdict?

Dimbleby concludes his introduction by promising the viewer something of "critical importance for those who wish to find out what really happened."

This use of a "shock" opener, followed by the framing of the report in terms that anticipate one kind of popular response but set against this expectation the need for questions to be asked, gives the program a strong but measured start. Its conclusion is similarly balanced, anticipating at least some of the next morning's complaints, by attempting to connect its own inquiries to the due process of the law:

That report by Julian Manyon was made, as you may have detected, without the cooperation of the British government, which says that it will make no comment until the inquest. As our film contained much new evidence hitherto unavailable to the coroner, we are sending the transcripts to his court in Gibraltar, where it's been made clear to us that all such evidence is welcomed.

Given the political debate it caused, there is little doubt that "Death on the Rock" is established as a marker in the long history of government–broadcaster relationships in Britain.

JOHN CORNER

Programming History
ITV
April 28, 1988

Further Reading

"A Child of Its Time," *The Economist* (4 February 1989)
Windlesham, P., and R. Rampton, *The Windlesham/Rampton Report on "Death on the Rock,"* London: Faber, 1989

Defenders, The

U.S. Legal Drama

The Defenders was American television's seminal legal drama and perhaps the most socially conscious series the medium has ever seen. The series boasted a direct lineage to the age of live television drama but also possessed a concern for topical issues and a penchant for social comment that were singularly resonant with New Frontier liberalism. With its contemporary premise and its serious tone, *The Defenders* established the model for a spate of social issue programs that followed in the early 1960s, marking a trend toward dramatic shows centered on nonviolent, professional "heroes" (doctors, lawyers, teachers, and politicians).

The series had its origins in a 1957 *Studio One* production titled "The Defender," written by Reginald Rose, one of the most prominent writers from the age of live anthology dramas. Having collaborated with Rose on the original two-part "Defender" teleplay and other productions, veteran anthology producer Herbert Brodkin teamed again with the writer to oversee the series. Brodkin and Rose were able to attract a large number of anthology alumni as writers for the series, including Ernest Kinoy, David Shaw, Adrian Spies, and Alvin Boretz. Although Rose authored only 11 of *The Defenders'* 130 episodes, Brodkin, the cast, and the writing staff always acknowledged that Rose, as senior story editor, put his own indelible stamp on the show. *The Defenders'* creators went against the overwhelming tide of Hollywood-based programs, following the tradition of the live anthologies—and the more recent police drama *Naked City*—by mounting their show in New York. Although *The Defenders* was primarily a studio-bound operation, with minimal location shooting, its success proved to be a key contributor to a small renaissance in New York–based production in the early 1960s.

The series concerned the cases of a father-and-son team of defense attorneys, Lawrence Preston (E.G. Marshall), the sharp veteran litigator, and his green and idealistic son Kenneth (Robert Reed). (Ralph Bellamy and William Shatner had originated the roles, then named Walter and Kenneth Pearson, in the *Studio One* production.) During the series' four years on the air, Ken Preston became more seasoned in the courtroom, but, for the most part, character development

took second place to explorations of the legal process and contemporary social issues.

As Rose pointed out a 1964 article, "The law is the *subject* of our programs: not crime, not mystery, not the courtroom for its own sake. We were never interested in producing a 'who-done-it' which simply happened to be resolved each week in a flashy courtroom battle of wits." Rose undoubtedly had in mind the Columbia Broadcasting System's (CBS's) other celebrated series about a defense attorney, *Perry Mason* (1957–66), when he wrote these words. Although both were nominally "courtroom dramas" or "lawyer shows," *Perry Mason* was first and foremost a classical detective story whose climax played out in the courtroom, while *The Defenders* focused on the machinery of the law, the vagaries of the legal process, and system's capacity for justice. Although the Prestons took on their share of murder cases, their aim in such instances was to mount a sound defense or plead for mercy, not unmask the real killer on the witness stand.

Certainly, *The Defenders* exploited the inherent drama of the courtroom, but it did so by mining the complexity of the law, its moral and ethical implications, and its human dimensions. Rose and his writers found much compelling drama in probing the psychology of juries, the motives of clients, the biases of opposing counsel, the flaws of the system itself, and the fallibility of their own lawyer-heroes. The series frequently took a topical perspective on the U.S. justice system, honing in on timely or controversial legal questions: capital punishment, "no-knock" search laws, custody rights of adoptive parents, the insanity defense, and the "poisoned fruit doctrine" (admissibility of illegally obtained evidence) as well as immigration quotas and Cold War visa restrictions. *The Defenders* avoided simple stances on such cases, instead illuminating ambiguities and opposing perspectives and stressing the uncertain and fleeting nature of justice before the law.

Rose declared in *The Viewer* magazine, "We're *committed* to controversy," and, indeed, the series often went beyond a strict focus on "the law" to probe the profound social issues that are often weighed in the courtroom. *The Defenders'* most controversial case was "The Benefactor" (1962), in which the

The Defenders, Robert Reed, E.G. Marshall, Lee Grant, 1961–65.
Courtesy of the Everett Collection

Prestons defend an abortion provider—and in the process mount an unequivocal argument in favor of legalized abortion (a decade before the Supreme Court's *Roe v. Wade* decision). Although the series regularly nettled some sponsors and affiliates, this particular installment marked a major crisis, with the series' three regular sponsors pulling their support from the episode. Another advertiser stepped in at the 11th hour and sponsored the show, and the network reported that audience response to the program was 90 percent positive. As one CBS executive recalled to author Robert Metz, "Everybody survived, and that was the beginning of *The Defenders* dealing with issues that really mattered." While not all of the Prestons' cases were so politically charged, the show took on current social concerns with some frequency. One of the series' most acclaimed stories, "Blacklist," offered a quietly powerful indictment of Hollywood blacklisting; in other episodes, the Prestons defended a schoolteacher fired for being an atheist, an author accused of pornography, a conscientious objector,

civil rights demonstrators, a physician charged in a mercy killing, and neo-Nazis.

The Defenders tended to take an explicitly liberal stance on the issues it addressed, but it offered no easy answers, no happy endings. Unlike *Perry Mason,* courtroom victories were far from certain on *The Defenders*—as were morality and justice. "The law is man-made, and therefore imperfect," Larry tells his son near the end of "Blacklist." "We don't always have the answer. There *are* injustices in the world. And they're not always solved at the last minute by some brilliant point of law at a dramatic moment." With all their wisdom and virtue, the Prestons were fallible, constrained by the realities of the legal system, the skill of their opponents, the whims of juries, and the decisions of the bench. Yet if *The Defenders*' view of the law was resigned, it was also resilient, manifesting a dogged optimism, acknowledging the flaws of the system, but affirming its merits—that is, its ability to change and its potential for compassion. The Prestons wearily admitted that the system was not perfect, but they returned each week to embrace it because of its potential for justice—and because it is the only system "we" have (a point that has become almost a cliché on such subsequent legal dramas as *L.A. Law* and *Law and Order*). It was this slender thread of optimism that enabled the defenders to continue their pursuit of justice one case at a time.

As a serious courtroom drama, *The Defenders* series meshed well in the early 1960s with network aims for prestige in the wake of the quiz show scandals and charges of creeping mediocrity in TV fare. The dramatic arena of the courtroom and the legal system allowed for suspense without violence and the avoidance of formula plots characteristic of traditional crime and adventure drama. With consistently strong ratings and a spate of awards unmatched by any other series of its day, *The Defenders* proved that controversy and topicality were not necessarily uncommercial. The series was in the works well before Federal Communications Commission Chairman Newton Minow's 1961 "vast wasteland" speech, but there is little doubt that the new Minow-inspired regulatory atmosphere augured well for the rise of such programming. The show's success supported the development of a number of social issue and political dramas in the following years, notably *Slattery's People* and *East Side, West Side,* and gave further impetus to a shift in network programming from action-adventure to character drama. But most significant of all, it grappled with larger ethical and political questions, pulling social problems and political debate to center stage, presenting a consistent, ongoing, and sometimes critical examination of contemporary issues and social morality. In the episode titled "The Star-Spangled Ghetto" (written by Rose), a judge takes the elder Preston to task for invoking the social roots of his clients' acts as part of his defense: "The courtroom is not the place to explore the questions of society." Lawrence Preston responds, "It is for me." So was the television courtroom for Reginald Rose and the writers of *The Defenders.*

In 1997 and 1998, *The Defenders* was revived as a series of three made-for-cable movies on Showtime: *The Defenders: Payback* (1997), *The Defenders: Choice of Evils* (1998), and *The Defenders: Taking the First* (1998). The first two films found E.G. Marshall back in court as an even more seasoned Lawrence Preston, now joined by younger son Don (Beau Bridges) and Kenneth's daughter M.J. (Martha Plimpton). In the third movie, made after Marshall's death, Bridges and Plimpton reprised their roles.

MARK ALVEY

See also **Bellamy, Ralph; Kinoy, Ernest; Rose, Reginald;** *Studio One*

Cast

Lawrence Preston	E.G. Marshall
Kenneth Preston	Robert Reed
Helen Donaldson (1961–62)	Polly Rowles
Joan Miller (1961–62)	Joan Hackett

Producers

Herbert Brodkin, Robert Maxwell, Kenneth Utt

Programming History

132 episodes
CBS

September 1961–	
September 1963	Saturday 8:30–9:30
September 1963–	
November 1963	Saturday 9:00–10:00
November 1963–	
September 1964	Saturday 8:30–9:30
September 1964–	
September 1965	Thursday 10:00–11:00

Further Reading

"The Best of Both Worlds," *Television* (June 1962)

Bodger, Lowell A., "Shooting *The Defenders*," *American Cinematographer* (July 1963)

Crean, Robert, "On the (Left) Side of the Angels," *Today* (January 1964)

Efron, Edith, "The Eternal Conflict between Good and Evil," *TV Guide* (July 1962); reprinted in *TV Guide: The First 25 Years,* edited by Jay S. Harris, New York: Simon and Schuster, 1978

Gelman, Morris J., "New York, New York," *Television* (December 1962)

Metz, Robert, *CBS: Reflections in a Bloodshot Eye,* Chicago: Playboy Press, 1975

"$108,411 for an Hour's Work," *Television* (September 1961)

Oulahan, Richard, and William Lambert, "The Tyrant's Fall That Rocked the TV World," *Life* (September 10, 1965)

Rose, Reginald, "Law, Drama, and Criticism," *Television Quarterly* (Fall 1964)

Rosenberg, Howard, "This Time, *The Defenders* Will Hold Court on Showtime," *Los Angeles Times* (September 1, 1997)

"The Show That Dared to Be Controversial," *The Viewer* (May 1964)

Smith, Sally Bedell, *In All His Glory,* New York: Simon and Schuster, 1990

Steinberg, Cobbett, *TV Facts,* New York: Facts on File, 1980

Stempel, Tom, *Storytellers to the Nation,* New York: Continuum, 1992

"Three Sponsors Withdraw from Program Dealing with Abortion; CBS to Show Drama As Scheduled," *New York Times* (April 9, 1962)

Watson, Mary Ann, *The Expanding Vista: American Television in the Kennedy Years,* New York: Oxford University Press, 1990

Degrassi (The Kids of Degrassi Street; Degrassi Junior High; Degrassi High; Degrassi Talks; Degrassi: The Next Generation)

Canadian Drama Series

During the 1980s, three *Degrassi* drama series appeared on the Canadian Broadcasting Corporation (CBC), Canada's public television network. The programs, all in a half-hour format, began with *The Kids of Degrassi Street,* followed by *Degrassi Junior High,* then *Degrassi High.* Central *Degrassi* actors reappeared in the CBC's 1991–92 season as roving interviewers and hosts of *Degrassi Talks,* a youth magazine program. This program featured such pertinent topics as sex, work, and abuse, all examined from the perspectives of Canada's youth. This point of view was in keeping with the precredit program statement, "Real kids talking to real kids from the heart." The federal government's Health and Welfare Canada was an advocacy sponsor of *Degrassi Talks,* suggesting official recognition and support of a distinct youth culture and an agenda of intentional socialization, using CBC television and the well-known *Degrassi* cast as teaching agents.

A two-hour television movie special, *School's Out!* (1992), completed the original coming-of-age cycle of three dramatic series and the magazine show. Programmed into a CBC Sunday evening slot, in early fall *School's Out!* was scheduled to coincide with the beginning of the school year. In the movie, various *Degrassi* characters are confronted with the transitions that follow high school graduation: the anticipation of attending university, the dissolution of a high school romance, a tragic highway accident, rootlessness, work prospects, and, ultimately, a fall reunion at the wedding of a long-standing couple.

An outgrowth of the original *Degrassi* project was *Liberty Street,* which featured only one former cast member, Pat Mastroianni, who played a different character than before but with a similar cocky persona. *Liberty Street* continued the *Degrassi* coming-of-age chronology, focusing on "20-something" characters struggling for independence in a downtown Toronto warehouse-apartment building that required chronic upkeep and so afforded dramatic situations demanding personal negotiations. Launched on the CBC as a series in the 1994–95 season, the *Liberty Street* characters were introduced in an earlier television movie

special, *X-Rated,* a title that recalls writer Douglas Coupland's term for disenfranchised youth, popularized by his book *Generation X: Tales for an Accelerated Culture* (1991). Linda Schuyler is credited as the creator and executive producer of *Liberty Street* in association with the CBC.

The first three *Degrassi* series had been created and produced by collaborators Schuyler and Kit Hood and their Playing with Time (PWT) Repertory Company in association with CBC drama departments and the support of Telefilm Canada. Eventually, the series drew support from associate producing entities, such as WGBH-Boston, the U.S. Corporation for Public Broadcasting, and the Public Broadcasting Service (PBS).

The three series achieved international success and sales and were programmed at various times on cable systems, including HBO, Showtime, and the Disney Channel as well as PBS. However, these international opportunities sometimes involved divergent national broadcasting and censorship standards, which revealed cultural differences between Canada and the United States. A two-part *Degrassi High* episode concerning abortion, for example, was truncated by PBS for U.S. audiences. This was not the case, however, with the CBC, which ran the complete version. PBS edited out a fetal icon from the episode's open-ended narrative designed to engage television audiences in the moral and physical complexities facing teens who seek abortion. PBS's editing decision raised public discussion in the arts and entertainment sections of major Canadian newspapers. In the short term, Canadian media coverage of PBS's action shored up the CBC's open attitude toward audiences. The corporation was willing to trust teens and their parents to make their own judgments on options presented in the complete version of the episode.

Yan Moore, head writer of the *Degrassi* series, tailored the scripts with the vital participation of the repertory cast, young people drawn from schools in the Toronto area. The situations, topics, and dialogue were vetted in regular workshops involving the young actors. In the interest of constructing valid actions and responses for the characters, consultation ensured that

Degrassi Junior High (top, l to r): Duncan Waugh, Stacie Mistysyn, Siluck Saysanasy, Pat Mastroianni, Amanda Stepto; (bottom, l to r): Christopher Charlesworth, Neil Hope, Anais Granofsky (Season 2), 1986–91.
Courtesy of the Everett Collection

the *Degrassi* series would remain youth centered and that the durable, realistic manner of the dramas would avoid the plasticity common to television's generic sitcom families. Even as the actors grew within their roles over the first three series and as new characters were added, a naturalistic acting style prevailed. If the acting at times appears untutored, it remains closer to the look and speech of everyday youths than the per-

formances of precocious kids and teens common to Hollywood film and television sitcoms.

From *The Kids of Degrassi Street* through *Degrassi High,* various schools served as narrative settings, although the dramatic situations mostly pivoted on action outside the classroom: in the corridors, around lockers and yards, to and from school, at dances and other activities, and in and around latchkey homes, with parents usually absent or at the edges of the situations to be managed by the youths themselves. These unofficial spaces outside the jurisdiction of authority figures maintained the youth-culture themes.

The backdrop for *Degrassi Talks* was a school bearing a "Degrassi High School" sign. From that location, specific *Degrassi* actors introduced the week's topic. This sense of a familiar locale hearkened back to *The Kids of Degrassi Street,* filmed on Toronto's Degrassi Street in an inner-city neighborhood. In *Degrassi Talks,* the physical references to the school and to the actors who portrayed *Degrassi* characters carried forward the history of the earlier series. The actors appeared to have graduated into role models of youth, with interspersed dramatic clips from past series serving as proof of their apprenticeship.

The evolutionary *Degrassi* series established high standards for representing youth on television, and these programs influenced the development of other mature-youth series for public and private Canadian television, such as CBC-West's *Northwood* and CanWest-Global's *Madison.* By integrating sensitive issues into the characters' narrative worlds and by foregrounding and backgrounding various continuing characters (as opposed to the convention of "principle" and "secondary" figures), the *Degrassi* series developed depth, unlike topic-of-the-week formulas. Abortion, single parenthood, sex, death, racism, AIDS, feminism, gay issues: these became conditions the characters had to work through, largely on their own individual or shared terms, within the serialized narrative structures.

A generation of Canadian kids could be said to have grown up with the *Degrassi* series. The narrative themes held out implicit lessons for the targeted youth audiences and for parental viewers. This teaching/learning ideology befitted the educational basis of the entire project as well as the cultural mandate of the CBC. With ethical lessons coded into the narratives, the characters were motivated to make mistakes, not merely choices, appropriate to them.

What made the *Degrassi* project more than a mere projection of ethical lessons in episodic-series form was the media consciousness that invited young viewers to ponder the dramatic futures of characters even when presented in genre-based television. The frequent use of freeze-frames at the ends of episodes suspended closure on dramatic topics and themes in keeping with open-ended serialization. Over time, the maturity of the writing and the character development in the *Degrassi* series brought a rich dovetailing of plots and subplots, often threaded with nondramatic cultural asides (youth gags, humor, and media allusions) that drew attention to the aesthetics of television construction and the need for informed viewership.

A useful example is "Black and White" (1988), an episode of *Degrassi Junior High* about the topic of interracial dating between a white female and a black male. Subtly, the female teen's parents reveal their primary fear of miscegenation. The two teens come to make their own choices in a climate of parental overreaction (for their daughter's "own good") and arrive at a solution for their prom-night date. In subsequent episodes, the couple faces an ethical dilemma of their own making. The young man avoids revealing to his white girlfriend that he is attracted to another young woman and has in fact been dating this black teen during the summer holiday. Jealousy follows deceit. The emotive complexity pushed viewers to recall the series' narrative past in order to contextualize the dilemma among the teens. The story thus becomes distinct from and more complex than the original plot about parental objections to interracial dating.

Degrassi: The Next Generation is an attempt to revive some of the social and ethical themes of the earlier *Degrassi* series for early 21st-century adolescent viewers shaped by new media. A series of 13 half-hour episodes was launched in October 2001 on CTV, with a one-hour special that brought original *Degrassi* characters (predominantly Joey, Caitlin, Snake, Lucy, and Spike) to the newly named Degrassi Community School for their 10-year high school reunion. The new generation is exemplified by the character Emma, 12-year-old daughter of a caring and conservative Spike who, in her adult reinvention, embodies middle-class values, unlike her working-class struggle as a *Degrassi* teen raising a baby, attending school, and working for sexist bosses.

Middle-class values shape *The Next Generation*'s narratives and characters. The episode "Secrets and Lies," for example, features a "yuppified" family with "tweens" (youths between 10 and 14 years of age) named Ash, Page, and Liberty and a dad named J.T., who admits he is gay and has a partner with whom he is in love. The transparent moral lesson concerns a father's dishonesty with his daughter and himself, but the lifestyle rhetoric and fail-safe romanticism are soap opera familiar. The camera style, which independent filmmaker Bruce McDonald established for the series' other directors, displays a polish common to prime-time TV drama but not McDonald's independent rebel filmmaking.

Executive producer/co-creator Schuyler and head writer Moore developed *The Next Generation* with Canadian private network CTV in partnership with television producer Epitome Pictures and new media producer Snap Media. This mix of production players is telling, and the CTV website emphasized the series' uniqueness as a convergent TV/Internet project. The series' narratives portray the Degrassi Community School as a wired environment for its computer-literate adolescent users. Emma and her friends spend time around the computer in her bedroom, which facilitates new moral lessons about parental control of computer access. A pedophile, posing on the Internet as romantic tween soul mate, lures Emma to a hotel room, where he attempts to molest her, with a video camera set up to record the assault. It is the wiser adults (Spike and Snake) from the original *Degrassi* series who rescue an unharmed but shaken and chastened Emma.

Convergence through CTV's interactive website allows young viewers to share their points of view and perhaps their experiences as they relate to the problem solving embedded in episodes. The website is also a tool for measuring a tween fan base built from wired activity. One key issue for television is whether convergence, in practice and in the case of this series, does create a virtual "community" of adolescent viewers or whether it largely appeases or "masters" this audience to sustain production.

JOAN NICKS

See also **Children and Television**

The Kids of Degrassi Street

Cast

Tina Sheldon	Lisa Barry
Squeeze	Shawn Biso
Connie Jacobs	Danah-Jean Brown
Benjamin Martin	Christopher Charlesworth
Casey Rothfels	Sarah Charlesworth
Noel Canard	Peter Duckworth-Pilkington II
Chuck Riley	Nick Goddard
Karen Gillis	Anais Granofsky
Sophie Brendakis	Stacey Halberstadt
Cookie	Dawn Harrison
Robin "Griff" Griffiths	Neil Hope
Pete Riley	John Ianniou
Duke Griffiths	Dave James
Irene	Nancy Lam
Rachel Hewitt	Arlene Lott
Norman	Jason Lynn
Fred Lucas	Allan Melusi
Lisa Canard	Stacie Mistysyn
Ida Lucas	Zoe Newman
Martin Schlegel	Jamie Summerfield
Billy Martin	Tyson Talbot
Leon Schlegel	Shane Toland
Dodie	Heather Wall

Producers

Kit Hood, Linda Schuyler

Programming History

CBC
26 episodes
1979–86

Degrassi Junior High/Degrassi High

Cast

Bryant "BLT" Lester Thomas	Dayo Ade
Claude Tanner	David Armin-Parcels
Melanie Brodie	Sara Ballingal
Clutch	Steve Bedernjak
Mr. Lawrence	John Bertram
Paul	Michael Blake
Tessa Campinelli	Kirsten Bourne
Archie "Snake" Simpson	Stefan Brogren
Trish	Danah-Jean Brown
Dwayne	Darrin Brown
Trudi Owens	Tammy Campbell
Simon Dexter	Michael Carry
Blaine	Tory Cassis
Nick	George Chaker
Luke	Andy Chambers
Scott "Scooter" Webster	Christopher Charlesworth
Susie Rivera	Sarah Charlesworth
Lorraine "LD" Delacourt	Amanda Cook
Alexa	Irene Courakos
Bartholomew Bond	Trevor Cummings
Mr. Walfish	Adam David
Erica Farrell	Angela Deiseach
Heather Farrell	Maureen Deiseach
Jyoti	Sabrina Dias
Scott	Byrd Dickens
Rick Munro	Craig Driscoll
Diana Economopolous	Chrissa Erodolou
Cindy	Marsha Ferguson
Karen Avery	Michelle Goodeve
Lucy Fernandez	Anais Granofsky
Kathleen Mead	Rebecca Haines
Allison	Sara Holmes
Derek "Wheels" Wheeler	Neil Hope
Joanne Rutherford	Krista Houston
Wai Lee	Ken Hung
Amy	Jacy Hunter
Bronco Davis	Dean Ifill
Alex Yankou	John Ioanniou
Mark	Andy Jekabson
Tabi	Michelle Johnson-Murray
Mahmoud	Samer Kamal
Rainbow	Anna Keenan
Liz O'Rourke	Cathy Keenan
Vula	Niki Kemeny
Vivan Wong	Colleen Lam
Maya	Kyra Levy
Doris Bell	Deborah Lobban
Casey	Andrew Lockie
Nancy Kramer	Arlene Lott
Joey Jeremiah	Pat Mastroianni
Michelle Asseth	Maureen McKay

Caitlin Ryan
Mr. Garcia
Louella Hawkins
Shane McKay
Yick Yu
Vicky Friedland
Christine "Spike"
  Nelson
Stephanie Kaye
Jason Cox
Patrick
Dorothy
Arthur Kobalowsky
Nora-Jean Rivera
Tim O'Connor
Max
Joy
Mr. Raditch

Stacie Mistysyn
Roger Montgomery
Susin Nielsen
Bill Parrot
Siluck Saysansay
Karryn Sheridan

Amanda Stepto
Nicole Stoffman
Tyson Talbot
Vincent Walsh
Annabel Waugh
Duncan Waugh
Lea-Helen Weir
Keith White
Joshua Whitehead
Lisa Williams
Daniel Woods

Producers
Kit Hood, Linda Schuyler

Programming History
CBC

Degrassi Junior High

January 1987–March 1987	Sunday 5:00–5:30 (13 episodes)
January 1988–March 1988	Monday 8:30–9:00 (13 episodes)
November 1988–March 1989	Monday 8:30–9:00 (16 episodes)

Degrassi High

November 1989–March 1990	Monday 8:30–9:00 (15 episodes)
November 1990–March 1991	Monday 8:30–9:00 (13 episodes)

Degrassi Talks

Hosts
Rebecca Haines
Neil Hope
Pat Mastrioanni
Stacie Mistysyn
Siluck Saysansay
Amanda Stepto

Producers
Kit Hood, Linda Schuyler

Programming History
CBC
6 episodes 1991–92

Degrassi: The Next Generation

Cast

Liberty Van Zandt
Dylan Michalchuk
Archibald "Snake"
  Simpson
Sean Hope Cameron
Paige Michalchuk
James Tiberius
  "J.T." Yorke
Ms. Hatzilakos
Craig Manning
Ellie Nash
Tobias "Toby" Isaacs
Jimmy Brooks
Mr. Armstrong
Gavin "Spinner" Mason
Kendra Mason
Hazel Aden
Miss Kwan
Joseph "Joey" Jeremiah
Emma Nelson
Ashley Kerwin
Caitlin Ryan
Chris Sharpe
Marco del Rossi
Terri MacGregor
Manuella "Manny"
  Santos
Angela Jeremiah
Christine "Spike"
  Nelson (Simpson)
Principal Raditch
Nadia Jamir

Sarah Barrable-Tishauer
John Bregar

Stefan Brogren
Daniel Clark
Lauren Collins

Ryan Cooley
Melissa DiMarco
Jake Epstein
Stacey Farber
Jake Goldsbie
Aubrey Graham
Michael Kinney
Shane Kippel
Katie Lai
Andrea Lewis
Linlyn Lue
Pat Mastroianni
Miriam McDonald
Melissa McIntyre
Stacie Mistysyn
Daniel Morrison
Adamo Ruggiero
Christina Schmidt

Cassie Steele
Alex Steele

Amanda Stepto
Dan Woods
Mony Yassir

Producer
Linda Schuyler

Programming History
CTV
October 2001–

Further Reading

Devins, Susan, "New Kids on the Block," *Cinema Canada* (April 1986)

Magder, Ted, "Making Canada in the 1990s: Film, Culture, and Industry," in *Beyond Quebec: Taking Stock of Canada,* edited by Kenneth McRoberts, Montreal: McGill-Queen's University Press, 1995

Miller, Mary Jane, "Will English Language Television Remain Distinctive? Probably," in *Beyond Quebec: Taking Stock of Canada,* edited by Kenneth McRoberts, Montreal: McGill-Queen's University Press, 1995

Demographics

The term "demographics" is a colloquialism that derives from demography, "the study of the characteristics of human populations." Professional demographers, such as those who work at the U.S. Census Bureau, are concerned primarily with population size and density, birth and death rates, and in- and out-migration. However, the practice of describing human groups according to distributions of sex, age, ethnicity, educational level, income, or other such characteristics has become a commonplace in many domains. These categories are called "demographics."

In the television industry, demographics are used in various ways, most of which can be characterized as either descriptive or analytic. First, demographics can be used to describe an audience. Such descriptive uses may be applied to an actual audience (for example, 54 percent female, 62 percent white, average age of 44 years), or demographics may be used to describe a desired audience, as in "younger" or "higher income."

Second, demographics can be used to sort data about people for purposes of analysis. For example, data may be available from a study designed to assess people's evaluations of an evening newscast anchor. Researchers may be interested in the average evaluation across the entire audience, in the evaluations of specific subgroups of people, or in the differences between the evaluations of specific subgroups. For either of the latter two purposes, one would divide the data according to the demographic categories of interest and calculate averages within those categories. It would then be possible to report the evaluations of women as distinct from those for men, those for higher- and lower-education groups, and so on.

Advertisers' interest in demographics arises from market research or advertising strategies that emphasize certain types of people as the target audience for their advertising. Therefore, commercial broadcasters, who earn their living by providing communication services to advertisers, are interested in demographics because the advertisers are. Because advertisers are more interested in some demographic categories than others, the commercial broadcasters have a financial interest in designing programming that appeals to people in those more desired demographic categories.

These interests result in programming artifacts, such as the low incidence of programs focused on African Americans or other racialized groups, on "neutral" constructions of matters such as religious belief, or on certain patterns of programming schedules, such as "sports on weekends when men are viewing." The increased number of distribution channels that has emerged with greater capacity for cable programming, especially when multiplied by digital capabilities, has led to some more "targeted" programming and to some increased programming options for specific groups. Thus, more programming for children is now available than in earlier periods, and some networks, such as The WB or UPN, developed specific audiences with programs focused on African Americans. The increase in programming devoted to wrestling or NASCAR automobile racing, the success of the Lifetime cable network's focus on women's topics, and Music Television's (MTV's) attention to "youth" markets can all also be linked to programmers' reliance on demographic analysis.

Independent of the specific advertising connection, demographic categories may also be used whenever generalizations are more important than precision. National television programmers must think in terms of audiences of several million people at a time, so their work is characterized by reliance on such generalizations as women like romance, men like action, and young people will not watch unless we titillate them. For other media, such as radio, magazines, cable television, and the Internet, audiences are smaller, and more information may be available about them. Yet the convenience as well as the established habit of thinking in terms of demographic generalizations continues to hold sway.

Uses of demographics to define and generalize about people is an instance of social category thinking. The rationale is that the available social categories, such as age, gender, ethnicity, and educational level, are associated with typical structures of opportunity and experience that in turn produce typical patterns of disposition, attitudes, interests, behaviors, and so on. The application of social category thinking often extends beyond that sensible rationale to include any instance where differences in a variable of interest can be associated with conveniently measured demographic differences. Age, for example, is easy to measure, amenable to being categorized, and associated with a great variety of differences in tastes and activities. No one, of course, supposes that aging causes people to watch more television, but older adults do watch more than younger adults. The convenience of that knowledge outweighs the need for precision in the television industry.

ERIC ROTHENBUHLER

See also **Audience Research; Market; Programming**

Further Reading

Becker, Lee B., "Racial Differences in Evaluation of the Mass Media," *Journalism Quarterly* (Spring 1992)

Horovitz, Bruce, "A Case for Different Strokes: Black's TV Choices Differ from General Public, Ad Study Shows," *Los Angeles Times* (April 7, 1992)

Lehmkuhl, D.C., "Seeing beyond Demographics," *Marketing and Media Decisions* (July 1983)

Mann, Judy, "Television Makes a Discovery (Orient Programs toward Women)," *Washington Post* (November 17, 1989)

Maxwell, Robert, "Videophiles and Other Americans," *American Demographics* (July 1992)

Merriam, John E., "Clues in the Media," *American Demographics* (February 1991)

Moshavi, Sharon D., "Study Shows Network's Demographic Strengths," *Broadcasting* (November 30, 1992)

Roth, Morry, "See Zip Codes a New Key to Demographics," *Variety* (May 28, 1990)

"TV and Cable Programming (U.S. Demographics)," *Television Digest* (June 21, 1993)

Dench, Judi (1934–)

British Actor

One of the leading classical actors of her generation, Judi Dench is unique in having sustained a television career that, in both breadth and depth, more than matches her work for the stage. The three roles for which she received, in the same year, a clutch of best actress awards—a cancer ward sister in the single drama *Going Gently,* Ranyevskya in *The Cherry Orchard,* and the gauche but capable Laura in the situation comedy *A Fine Romance*—epitomize the versatility of this distinctive and popular performer and the range of work with which she has been associated across a career spanning more than four decades and dozens of parts. She was made a Dame Commander of the British Empire in 1988 and, in 2001, was awarded the prestigious Fellowship of the British Academy of Film and Television Arts.

Educated at a Quaker school, the spiritual discipline of which she has suggested deeply influenced her life and work, she trained at the Central School from 1954 to 1957. Her first television appearance, a small part in a live broadcast of the thriller *Family on Trial,* came within two years of her graduation and was followed soon after by the title roles in a six-part serialization of Arnold Bennett's *Hilda Lessways* and a production by Stuart Burge of *Major Barbara.* She also played the part of a young tearaway in an early episode of *Z Cars* by John Hopkins, a character that became the basis of the disaffected daughter Terry, created for her by Hopkins in his groundbreaking family quartet *Talking to a Stranger* and for which she received the British Guild of Directors Award for Best Actress.

Dench has given notable performances in television presentations of Shakespeare. She played Katherine of France in the cycle of histories *An Age of Kings* in 1960 and at the end of the 1970s was in two screenings of Royal Shakespeare Company productions, as Adriana in *The Comedy of Errors* and opposite Ian McKellan in Trevor Nunn's landmark chamber production of *Macbeth.* In 1984 she appeared in John Barton's series of practical workshops for Channel 4, *Playing Shakespeare.* Her classical work for television also includes a substantial number of period dramas and serialized novels, but it is in her commitment to a range of largely antiheroic parts in contemporary television drama that she has most consistently won both popular and critical acclaim and where she has most effectively demonstrated her capacity for conveying what one critic called "transcendent ordinariness." In 1979 she played the real-life role of Hazel Wiles, the world-weary adoptive mother of a thalidomide child, in the British Broadcasting Corporation (BBC) play *On Giant's Shoulders,* and in 1981 she brought depth and complexity to the comparatively small role of Sister Scarli in *Going Gently.* In David Hare's *Saigon: Year of the Cat,* she played the reserved figure of Barbara Dean, an expatriate bank official caught up in a brief, passionate affair during the final days of the U.S. presence in Vietnam—a performance described by Hare in his introduction to the published script as "silkenly sexy and intelligent, as only she can be."

Judi Dench.
Photo courtesy of Judi Dench

Indeed, one of Dench's most instantly recognizable features is a vocal timbre so husky that an early commercial for which she had provided the voice-over had to be withdrawn because it was too suggestive. Other writers and directors have remarked not only on her vocal technique but on the subtlety and insight of her approach to character. Her physical appearance—stocky and soft but strongly featured (she was told at a film audition early in her career that she had everything wrong with her face)—might lend itself to comedy, but she has never fallen into the trap of comfortable typecasting. Her performance as Bridget, the ill-treated divorcée returning to play havoc with her husband's marriage to a younger woman in the four-part serial *Behaving Badly,* trod a fine line between dowdy despair and spirited heroism. In two long-running situation comedies, *A Fine Romance* (in which she played opposite her husband Michael Williams) and *As Time Goes By,* she brought to her characters the same quizzical intelligence that epitomizes her more serious work.

These two popular hits sealed Dench's reputation as one of the few classical actors able to move with ease between the differing disciplines of stage and television acting and, as was proved by the unexpected West End success of the somber stage play *Pack of Lies* in

1983 (in which she and Williams also played opposite each other), confirmed the often neglected synergy that exists between the two performance media. In 1991 she played the lead in the BBC's production of Rodney Ackland's rediscovered play *Absolute Hell,* later reprising the role on stage to great acclaim; and her performance in the National Theatre's 1996 production of *A Little Night Music* demonstrated a remarkable balance between the theatrical projection required by the musical form and the finely timed minutiae of emotional insight that had become the hallmark of her work for television. In 2000, after an absence from television (apart from several voice-overs) during which she took on a succession of major film and stage roles, Dench brought these two qualities together in Alan Plater's one-off drama *The Last of the Blond Bombshells.* Starring alongside Leslie Caron, Olympia Dukakis, and Cleo Laine, she played a former saxophonist in a World War II–era all-girl dance band attempting to reunite the old band members.

JEREMY RIDGMAN

Judi Dench. Born Judith Olivia Dench in York, England, December 9, 1934. Attended the Mount School, York; Central School of Speech Training and Dramatic Art, London. Married: Michael Williams, 1971 (died 2001); child: Tara. Stage debut, Old Vic Theatre, London, 1957; Broadway debut, 1958; actor, Old Vic Company, 1957–60; joined Royal Shakespeare Company, 1961; first television appearances, 1965; actor, dramas and situation comedies, from the early 1980s; debut as stage director, Renaissance Theatre Company, 1988. Officer of the Order of the British Empire, 1970; Dame Commander of the Order of the British Empire, 1988. Member: Royal Shakespeare Company (associate), from 1969; board of the Royal National Theatre, 1988–91. D. Litt.: University of Warwick, Coventry, 1978; University of York, 1983; University of Birmingham, 1989, University of Loughborough, 1991; Open University, Milton Keynes, 1992. Recipient: Paladino d'Argentino Award, Venice Festival, 1961; *Variety* London Critics Award, 1966; Guild of Directors Award, 1966; *Plays and Players* Award, 1980; Society of West End Theatre Awards, 1980, 1983, 1987; *Evening Standard* Drama Awards, 1980, 1983, 1987; British Academy of Film and Television Arts (BAFTA) Awards, 1965, 1981, 1985, 1987, 1988, 1997; 1998; *TV Times* Funniest Female on Television, 1981–82; American Cable Award, 1988; Academy Award for Best Supporting Actress, 1998; National Society of Film Critics for Best Supporting Actress, 1998; Tony Award for Best Actress in a Play, 1999; Golden Globe for Best Actress in a Mini-Series or Motion Picture Made for Television, 2000; Fellowship of the British Academy of Film and Television Arts, 2001.

Television Series

1981–84	*A Fine Romance*
1992–	*As Time Goes By*

Television Plays

1959	*Family on Trial*
1959	*Hilda Lessways*
1960	*An Age of Kings*
1960	*Pink String and Sealing Wax*
1962	*Major Barbara*
1963	*The Funambulists*
1963	*Made for Each Other (Z Cars)*
1964	*Parade's End*
1966	*Talking to a Stranger*
1966	*Days to Come*
1968	*On Approval*
1978	*The Comedy of Errors*
1978	*Langrishe Go Down*
1979	*Macbeth*
1979	*On Giant's Shoulders*
1979	*A Village Wooing*
1980	*Love in a Cold Climate*
1981	*Going Gently*
1981	*The Cherry Orchard*
1983	*Saigon: Year of the Cat*
1984	*Playing Shakespeare*
1985	*Mr. and Mrs. Edgehill*
1985	*The Browning Version*
1986	*Ghosts*
1989	*Behaving Badly*
1990	*Can You Hear Me Thinking?*
1990	*The Torch*
1991	*Absolute Hell*
2000	*The Last of the Blond Bombshells*

Films

The Third Secret, 1964; *A Study in Terror,* 1966; *He Who Rides a Tiger,* 1966; *Four in the Morning,* 1966; *A Midsummer Night's Dream,* 1968; *The Angelic Conversation* (voice only), 1973; *Luther,* 1973; *The Third Secret,* 1978; *Nela* (voice only), 1980; *Dead Cert,* 1985; *Wetherby,* 1985; *A Room with a View,* 1985; *84 Charing Cross Road,* 1987; *A Handful of Dust,* 1987; *Henry V,* 1990; *Jack and Sarah,* 1994; *Hamlet,* 1995; *Goldeneye,* 1995; *Mrs. Brown,* 1997; *Tomorrow Never Dies,* 1997; *Shakespeare in Love,* 1998; *The World Is Not Enough,* 1999; *Tea with Mussolini,* 1999; *Into the Arms of Strangers: Stories of the Kindertransport* (narrator), 2000; *Chocolat,* 2001; *Iris,* 2001; *The Shipping News,* 2001; *The Importance of Being Earnest,* 2002; *Die Another Day,* 2002; *The Chronicles of Riddick,* 2004; *Ladies in Lavender,* 2004.

Stage (actor; selected)

Hamlet, 1957; *Measure for Measure,* 1957; *A Midsummer Night's Dream,* 1957; *Twelfth Night,* 1958; *Henry V,* 1958; *The Double-Dealer,* 1959; *The Merry Wives of Windsor,* 1959; *As You Like It,* 1959; *The Importance of Being Earnest,* 1959; *Richard II,* 1960; *Romeo and Juliet,* 1960; *She Stoops to Conquer,* 1960; *A Midsummer Night's Dream,* 1960; *The Cherry Orchard,* 1961; *Measure for Measure,* 1962; *A Midsummer Night's Dream,* 1962; *A Penny for a Song,* 1962; *Macbeth,* 1963; *Twelfth Night,* 1963; *A Shot in the Dark,* 1963; *The Three Sisters,* 1964; *The Twelfth Hour,* 1964; *The Alchemist,* 1965; *Romeo and Jeannette,* 1965; *The Firescreen,* 1965; *Private Lives,* 1965; *The Country Wife,* 1966; *The Astrakhan Coat,* 1966; *St. Joan,* 1966; *The Promise,* 1966; *A Little Night Music,* 1966; *The Rules of the Game,* 1966; *Cabaret,* 1968; *A Winter's Tale,* 1969; *Women Beware Women,* 1969; *London Assurance,* 1970; *Major Barbara,* 1970; *The Merchant of Venice,* 1971; *The Duchess of Malfi,* 1971; *Toad of Toad Hall,* 1971; *Content to Whisper,* 1973; *The Wolf,* 1973; *The Good Companions,* 1974; *The Gay Lord Quex,* 1975; *Too True to Be Good,* 1975; *Much Ado about Nothing,* 1976; *The Comedy of Errors,* 1976; *King Lear,* 1976; *Pillars of the Community,* 1977; *The Way of the World,* 1978; *Cymbeline,* 1979; *Juno and the Paycock,* 1980; *Village Wooing,* 1981; *A Kind of Alaska,* 1982; *The Importance of Being Earnest,* 1982; *Pack of Lies,* 1983; *Mother Courage,* 1984; *Waste,* 1985; *Mr. and Mrs. Nobody,* 1987; *Antony and Cleopatra,* 1987; *Entertaining Strangers,* 1987; *Hamlet,* 1989; *The Cherry Orchard,* 1989; *The Sea,* 1991; *The Plough and the Stars,* 1991; *Coriolanus,* 1992; *The Gift of the Gorgon,* 1992; *The Seagull,* 1994; *Absolute Hell,* 1995; *A Little Night Music,* 1996; *Amy's View,* 1997; *The Royal Family,* 2001.

Stage (director)

Much Ado about Nothing, 1988; *Look Back in Anger,* 1989; *The Boys from Syracuse,* 1991; *Romeo and Juliet,* 1993.

Further Reading

Eyre, Richard, *Utopia and Other Places,* London: Bloomsbury, 1993; revised edition, London: Vintage, 1994

Jacobs, Gerald, *Judi Dench: A Great Deal of Laughter,* London: Weidenfeld and Nicholson, 1985

Miller, John. *Judi Dench: With a Crack in Her Voice,* New York: Welcome Rain, 2000

Denmark

Since the late 1980s, Danish television has experienced a revolutionary transition from a system of public service broadcasting monopoly to a multichannel system with satellite delivery, national private stations, public service stations, and local stations. This transition caused fundamental changes. The public service tradition historically was rooted in the public sphere, where politicians, citizens' interests groups, and artists took an active role in determining the structure and content of television. In the new television system, these aspects of television are influenced by far more market-oriented concerns.

The first Danish television experiments started in the late 1940s in the radio monopoly Statsradiofonien, later renamed Danmarks Radio and later again *DR,* and for a trial period from 1951 until 1954, there were three hours of transmission weekly. In 1954, television was inaugurated officially in Denmark. The main reason for this delay was a tight economic situation in the postwar period. The minister of finance in the liberal-conservative government was against spending money on television until the electronics industry had convinced him that domestic broadcasting would support the export of television sets. Thus Danish television was conceived as part of industrial and financial policy. In 1953, a new Social Democratic government removed the remaining opposition against television by referring to the "threat" of cultural influence from German television, and since then television policy has indisputably been considered a matter of cultural policy.

Television developed slowly in Denmark because of the economic situation and very high prices of television sets. In 1953, the number of licensed viewers was 800; in 1956, 16,000; and in 1959, 250,000. In the beginning, Statsradiofonien used every opportunity to broadcast popular programs as a tool to attract new viewers in order to increase the revenue derived from license fees on sets. The transmission time per week was extended from 10 hours in 1954 to 25 hours in 1961. From the mid-1960s, television was well established with about one million set owners, and gradually the programming policy was changed to one of more classical public service programming.

Throughout these developments, television has been seen as a powerful medium, and the political parties have wanted to control television as they had controlled radio. Therefore, the existing radio monopoly was ex-

tended for the provision of television. The main ideology was, and to a certain extent still is, that television should be used as a public service in the interest of the citizens in a democratic society. The Social Democratic Party, the labor movement, and strong popular movements have all seen radio and television as a great opportunity for enlightenment, as media that could pass on art and culture to all people in an egalitarian society. In the 1960s and 1970s, television was an integrated part of the development of the Danish welfare state model. Even though the idea of public service television has changed over time because of cultural, political, and management transformations, Danish television has been ruled by some basic public service principles.

Public service television has to be available nationwide to all at an equal, low price (the cost of the license fee and an antenna). Public service television is also obliged to provide a many-sided and manifold programming policy. An overall ambition has been to enlighten the audience culturally and to serve the public with sufficient information so that citizens can participate in the democratic process. Programming must be critical and put all authorities and institutions under scrutiny, and the programming must cater to various interests and needs of small as well as large population groups.

The public service station is obliged to broadcast a substantial amount of nationally produced programs, to participate actively in the creative arts, and to promote artistic and cultural innovation. These principles are important in a relatively small country like Denmark with 5.2 million inhabitants because national programs are much more expensive than imported fare.

Public service has to be independent of all vested interests as well as of specific political interests. Historically, this goal has led to problems. The main issue has been the conflict between the Parliament's legitimate right to create certain general obligations in the public interest and the attempts of the government and the different parties to cultivate specific interests. The demand of independence from all vested interests resulted in the prohibition against any advertising in Danish television until 1988, when the second Danish terrestrial channel, the publicly owned TV 2, started out as a partly commercial and partly license fee–financed station.

Apart from the more classical public service programs, informative, educational, art, and high culture, Danish television from the very beginning broadcast entertainment such as quiz shows, variety shows, sports, and foreign popular drama. The two types of programming have been broadcast side by side, but in the public debate popular entertainment has generally been depreciated.

Programming in the monopoly era consisted mainly of single programs from among various genres. Only the news was scheduled at the same time every day. People checked the schedule and turned on the set whenever they found something of interest and as a natural choice turned off the set afterward. Concepts such as scheduling, program flow, and formats played no significant role. The concept of the program was the decisive factor in terms of its content, form, and duration, and only a small part of the schedule was serialized. The popularity of a program was secondary to the program idea, and even successful series were scheduled for only 6 or 12 shows—or as long as the producers enjoyed producing them.

Even though public service television in many ways succeeded in Denmark in the monopoly era and even though there has in general been political consensus for maintaining public service television in Denmark, the programming policy has been discussed fiercely within a political and a cultural framework. The formal responsibility for the programming policy in Danmarks Radio was placed in a Radio Council, where the members were appointed by the political parties in accordance with their representation in the Parliament. This organizational construction resulted in a politicized television environment both externally and internally. Danmarks Radio had a privileged position and therefore was under constant monitoring, especially in terms of news coverage and journalistic programs. Politicians from both the right and the left complained over what they perceived as a biased programming policy, and there were continuous debates over whether a given single program should be impartial or whether it was the total output that should be balanced. This question was never solved, and after some fierce battles in the Radio Council in the late 1970s and the beginning of the 1980s, it seemed that the producers gave up progressive ideas and began to practice forms of self-censorship in order to avoid further trouble.

Further, Danmarks Radio developed a paternalistic attitude toward the audience that caused a cultural conflict. Under shelter of the public service obligations to educate, enlighten, and give the public access to a unified culture, the station presented the middle- and high-brow stance of the cultural elite in Copenhagen, and the station showed contempt for the popular culture and the popular products from the entertainment industry. Another contributory cause of this form of paternalism was that the general public was not the primary audience for the TV stations. It was instead the politicians, who decided the size of the license fee, and the critics and public opinion makers, who gave the only public feedback. The general public was rarely heard, and there were no regular ratings. This attitude and a bureaucratic organization caused some difficulties for Danmarks Radio in adjusting to the new competitive television situation in which the audience is addressed as consumers in a market instead of as citizens in a democratic society.

The transition from a monopoly to a multichannel system began in 1982, when satellite television was introduced in Europe. The "threat" from the sky caused the Danish politicians to strengthen the national terrestrial output as a protection against the influence from foreign TV stations.

When TV 2 was conceived in 1987, the right-wing politicians wanted a private alternative to the monopoly, which in their view was biased in favor of the Social Democratic Party. After a fierce political fight, the right-wing government succeeded in breaking the monopoly but had to compromise on the financial aspect, and TV 2 was launched in 1988 as a nonprofit public service station financed partly by commercials and partly by license fees. The rules for advertising on TV 2 were strict, and even though they have been modified several times, commercials still may appear only between programs.

TV 2 was immediately an innovative force in Danish television with a commercially inspired programming strategy and a more forthcoming attitude toward the audience. As a result, the channel has been a popular success. The most significant rating successes have been persistent scheduling of standardized commercial formats, national and local news, and a variety of Danish entertainment and factual programs. TV 2 had a Danish version of the game show *Wheel of Fortune* airing almost daily since its launch in 1988 until 2001. Furthermore, TV 2 has a great variety of programs and extensive regional programming, so the service has in broad outline fulfilled its public service obligations even though the station lacks sufficient national drama and other expensive program types.

The Danish television model with two competing public nonprofit public service stations has been successful in containing the influence from foreign television stations. The transnational satellite stations have established only a marginal position, even though the cable and satellite penetration increased from 58 percent in 1992 to 70 percent in 2003. In the early and mid-1990s, Danmarks Radio and TV 2 were able to establish a kind of duopoly situation with a combined audience share in 1992 of 75 percent. Danish television viewers want to watch national programs because of the languages and the cultural heritage. Still, subtitled foreign programs (American and British) are a significant and popular part of the program supply on the national channels.

The main challenge to the public service stations has instead come from private satellite channels aimed at the Danish market and from a network of local stations. The most successful provider has been the Swedish-owned TV3 (Modern Times Group [MTG], a daughter company of Kinnevik). The channel was launched in 1987 from England under British jurisdiction and is therefore allowed to broadcast commercials within single programs. In the beginning, TV3 consisted mainly of American series, some high-profile sports events, and less than 10 percent Danish programs. MTG has over the years launched several channels, and in 2003 the service offers two channels, TV3 and TV31, providing mainly entertainment and sport programs, one all-sports channel (Viasat Sport), and two pay channels with movies. Gradually, TV3 and TV31 have increased the national output of cheaply produced but very popular entertainment shows based mostly on international formats. The biggest successes have been a Danish version of the game show *Robinson,* soccer's Champion League, and Danish soccer. The other significant player is the American-owned Scandinavian Broadcasting System (SBS), which controls a terrestrial network of local stations, TVDanmark 2, with 80 percent national coverage. The local stations provide local programming for one to two hours daily, and the rest is networked entertainment. In 2000, SBS launched a satellite channel from England, TVDanmark 1, with entertainment and sports programs.

DR and TV 2 have responded to the challenge from the commercial channels by launching supplementary satellite channels. DR2 was launched in 1996 using a varied programming strategy with many programs targeting small population groups. A main goal was to relieve the main channel of some of the public service obligations so that the main channel could be more streamlined. Initially, DR2 was criticized for breaking one of the basic public service principles because the station was not available terrestrially. In 2000, TV 2 launched Zulu, targeting the commercially attractive age-group of 15 to 30 years with mainly entertainment programs.

In 2002, the two public service stations continuously were the most popular with a combined audience share of 70 percent—DR1 had 28%, DR2 4 percent TV 2 35 percent, and Zulu 3 percent. The MTG and SBS channels were taking the lion's share of the remaining viewing time (11 and 7 percent, respectively). The plethora of transnational satellite channels and stations from neighboring countries have established only a marginal position with around 12 percent of the viewing time.

Throughout the revolutionary changes in the Danish television situation, the so-called Danish model, with two nonprofit public service stations, has been very successful in finding a significant new cultural role in the marketplace for modernized public service programming. To the satisfaction of the Danish viewing public, it has been possible to maintain a significant part of the Danish television system within the framework of cultural policy. The public service stations will face new political, technological, and economic challenges in the coming years. The current right-wing government has decided to privatize TV 2 in 2004 as part of a general liberalization of the media market. A privatized TV 2 will, to a large extent, still be prescribed to fulfill the existing public service obligations. The government wants the private TV 2 to continue the current programming policy, even though the financial conditions will be changed dramatically. In 2002, TV 2 had U.S.$87 million in license fees and $160 million in advertisement revenues out of a total television advertisement market of $262 million, so a new private owner of TV 2 will face tremendous financial challenges in an ever-increasing competitive television market on the brink of digitalization.

POUL ERIK NIELSEN

DePoe, Norman (1917–1980)

Canadian Broadcast Journalist

Norman DePoe was a pioneering figure in Canadian television news reporting, one of the heroic figures of frontline journalism. He was among the first of the Canadian Broadcasting Corporation's (CBC-TV's) high-profile television correspondents and helped establish the traditions of television journalism in

Norman DePoe.
Photo courtesy of National Archives of Canada/CBC Collection

Canada. In the 1960s, he was a national institution, his gruff voice heard in almost every major news report on CBC-TV, when the public broadcaster dominated Canadian television news.

DePoe began his broadcasting career with CBC Radio in 1948, moved to the fledgling television service in 1956, joined the CBC-TV parliamentary bureau in 1959. He was named chief Ottawa correspondent in 1960. He became the first television reporter admitted to the parliamentary press gallery and helped provide legitimacy to the handful of broadcasters (five in 1959) whose attempts to gain admission to the gallery had been strenuously resisted by many newspaper writers. As media historian Allan Levine has put it in *Scrum Wars: The Prime Ministers and the Media* (1993), "DePoe was the first television journalist who could compete on an intellectual level with the other stars of the gallery." He was well read and a skillful writer. Years after he had left the air in 1975, DePoe's hard-edged reporting style continued to set the standard for broadcast journalists. Politicians were quicker than print reporters to identify DePoe as a key player in the gallery and to foresee the dominance of television news in politics.

DePoe's physical features were assets on the screens of the 1960s but in a way that would make him ill suited to the glamorized television newsroom that came later. Raspy voiced and rumpled, wrinkled and weary, DePoe cut an oddly romantic figure in the Humphrey Bogart mold. He possessed a prodigious memory and a healthy disregard for those in power, whether they were in political offices, government bureaucracies, or the management suites of the CBC. DePoe was famously contemptuous of producers and was not above criticizing them on air. For him, political reporting was a solitary exercise and at times a splendid joust with those he covered. His contributions to national newscasts were much-envied models of economical incisiveness.

Even during his spell as the principal reporter on national affairs, DePoe was assigned to cover significant political stories in the United States and elsewhere in the world. An unabashed patriot, his comments about U.S. politics could be biting. The visibility afforded by foreign assignments only added to his reputation as an authoritative commentator on politics for the English-language television audience in Canada. For many Canadians in the late 1950s and 1960s, especially rural audiences served by few other national media, he was perhaps the most credible authority on political affairs in Ottawa and elsewhere. It is estimated that he gave some 5,000 television news reports, including coverage of 31 elections, several leadership conventions, and other major political events.

Although DePoe was widely revered, there was another side to his career. He led a romanticized life in journalism, full of the kind of carousing bellicosity often stereotyped in American cinematic treatments of news work. According to a successor in the Ottawa post, he was visibly inebriated during a live stand-up on at least one occasion, and the memoirs of contemporaries are replete with candid anecdotes or unmistakable hints about his rough-edged lifestyle. With respect to gossip about his drinking, he once remarked that "90 percent of the stories are just not true." He fell out of favor with assignment editors in the early 1970s, and in 1975 he returned to radio news, finally retiring in 1976.

At the time of his death in 1980, DePoe was remembered by Knowlton Nash, another of the CBC's well-known correspondents and one-time head of CBC News, as "the most memorable reporter of our lifetime...the most enjoyable, most charismatic, most effective electronic reporter Canada has ever seen, with a colorful, irrepressible style." DePoe was regarded with wary respect by political leaders for his standard of integrity, his toughness, and his incisive reporting.

FREDERICK J. FLETCHER AND ROBERT EVERETT

Norman DePoe. Born in Portland, Oregon, May 4, 1917. Educated at the University of British Columbia, 1934–38; University of Toronto, 1946–49. Married: 1) Madeline Myra, 1942, seven children; 2) Mary Elizabeth, 1974. Served as captain, the Royal Canadian Signal Corps, 1938–46. Reporter in CBC's overseas unit, war and postwar reports, 1939–52; joined CBC's News Department, 1948; news editor, *Graphic,* 1956; CBC television parliamentary correspondent, 1952–69; host, *The Public Eye,* 1965–69; interviewer, *Weekend,* 1969–72; host, *Newsmagazine* (later *CBC Newsmagazine*), 1973–75; retired from CBC, 1976. Died in 1980.

Television Series

1965–69	*The Public Eye*
1969–72	*Weekend*
1973–75	*Newsmagazine*

Further Reading

Levine, Allan, *Scrum Wars: The Prime Ministers and the Media,* Toronto: Dundurn, 1993

Lynch, Charles, *A Funny Way to Run a Country: Further Memoirs of a Political Voyeur,* Edmonton, Alberta: Hurtig, 1986

Taras, David, *The Newsmakers: The Media's Influence on Canadian Politics,* Toronto: Nelson, 1990

Troyer, Warner, *The Sound and the Fury: An Anecdotal History of Canadian Broadcasting,* Rexdale, Ontario: Wiley, 1980

Deregulation

When applied in the United States, the concept of "deregulation" describes most American electronic media policy of the past three decades. Largely a bipartisan effort, this fundamental shift in the approach of the Federal Communications Commission (FCC) to radio and television regulation began in the mid-1970s as a search for relatively minor "regulatory underbrush" that could be cleared away for more efficient and cost-effective administration of the important rules that would remain. Congress largely went along with this trend and initiated a few deregulatory moves of its own. The arrival of the Reagan administration and FCC Chairman Mark Fowler in 1981 marked a further shift to a fundamental and ideologically driven reappraisal of regulations long held central to national broadcasting policy. Ensuing years saw removal of many long-standing rules, resulting in an overall reduction in FCC oversight of station and network operations. Congress grew increasingly wary of the pace of deregulation, however, and began to slow the FCC's deregulatory pace by the late 1980s.

Specific deregulatory moves, some undertaken by the FCC and some by Congress, include (a) extending television station licenses from three to five years in 1981 and to eight in 1996; (b) expanding the number of television stations any single entity could own from the long-traditional 7 to 12 in 1985, 18 in the early 1990s, and a larger but not clearly determined number after 1996; (c) loosening restrictions on the number of stations one owner can control in a single market; (d) abolishing guidelines for minimal amounts of non–entertainment programming in 1985; (e) elimination of the Fairness Doctrine in 1987; (f) dropping in 1985 FCC guidelines on how much advertising could be carried; (g) leaving technical matters largely in the hands of station licensees rather than the FCC; and (h) considerable post-1980 deregulation of cable television, affecting its ownership, rates charged, programs carried, and public interest requirements.

Proponents of deregulation do not perceive station licensees as "public trustees" of the public airwaves, required to provide a wide variety of services to many different listening groups. Instead, broadcasting has been increasingly seen as just another business operating in a commercial marketplace, an industry that did not need its management decisions questioned by government overseers. Opponents argue that deregulation violates key parts of the Communications Act of 1934—especially the requirement that broadcasters operate in the public interest—and allows broadcasters to seek profits with little public service programming required in return. These opponents further contend that certain postderegulation changes in the television industry (the growing number of stations on the air, the increasing number of television networks, and the considerable expansion of cable and other competing services) all provide evidence to support their contentions about deregulation's harmful effects—presumably, the television industry would not have expanded so dramatically if profit-seeking businesses thought they would incur significant costs by serving the public. Backers of deregulation argue, however, that this growing plethora of competing service options will do more for the public interest than any government policy ever could.

The Telecommunications Act of 1996, although concerned only in small part with electronic media issues, greatly accelerated the pace of deregulation. Furthermore, the George W. Bush administration (beginning in 2001) appeared ready to do away with many of the few remaining television restrictions.

American deregulation has been widely emulated in other countries in spirit if not in detail. Developed and developing countries have introduced local stations to supplement national services; have begun to allow (if not encourage) competing media, such as cable, satellite services, and videocassettes; and have sometimes loosened regulations on traditional radio and television. Advertising support along the lines of the American model has become more widely accepted in other nations, especially as television's operating costs rise. However, the American example of relying on competition more than regulation also threatens many countries' traditional public service broadcasting, which must meet increasing competition for viewers by offering more commercially appealing programs, usually entertainment, rather than culture-based programming.

Since the late 1990s, the dramatic expansion of the Internet has increased the pressure on traditional broadcasters as more consumers turn to web-based information and entertainment resources, often instead of television. The availability of the Internet's many suppliers and services also gives new force to arguments for the deregulation of older services; such a move, deregulation proponents contend, will allow television to better compete with new media forms.

CHRISTOPHER H. STERLING

See also **Federal Communications Commission; License; United States: Cable**

Further Reading

Broadcast Deregulation, New York: Station Representatives Association, 1979

Congressional Research Service, *Should the Federal Government Significantly Strengthen the Regulation of Mass Media Communication in the United States?,* 96th Congress, 1st Session, House Document 96–167, Washington, D.C.: Congressional Research Service, 1979

Fowler, Mark S., and Daniel L. Brenner, "A Marketplace Approach to Broadcast Regulation," *Texas Law Review* (February 1982)

Horwitz, Robert Britt, *The Irony of Regulatory Reform: The Deregulation of American Telecommunications,* New York: Oxford University Press, 1989

Johnson, Leland L., *Toward Competition in Cable Television,* Cambridge, Massachusetts: MIT Press, 1994

Krattenmaker, Thomas G., and Lucas A. Powe, Jr., *Regulating Broadcast Programming,* Cambridge, Massachusetts: MIT Press, 1995

Le Duc, Don R., *Beyond Broadcasting: Patterns in Policy and Law,* White Plains, New York: Longman, 1987

Powe, Lucas A., Jr., *American Broadcasting and the First Amendment,* Berkeley: University of California Press, 1987

Tunstall, Jeremy, *Communications Deregulation: The Unleashing of America's Communications Industry,* Oxford: Basil Blackwell, 1986

Weiss, Leonard W., and Michael W. Klass, editors, *Regulatory Reform: What Actually Happened,* Boston: Little, Brown, 1986

Desmond's

British Situation Comedy

Produced by Charlie Hanson and Humphrey Barclay, *Desmond's* was first broadcast on Channel 4 in 1989 and finally came to an end in December 1995, a short time before its leading star, Norman Beaton, died. The half-hour weekly program has often been referred to as an "ethnic sitcom" in the sense that it featured a black family and their predominantly black friends. However, the series managed to reach a mainstream audience and thus appeal to viewers of all ages and cultures in Britain. It has also been popular in the Caribbean and in the United States, where it has been broadcast on the cable network Black Entertainment Television.

Desmond's was also distinguished by its West Indian writer, Trix Worrell, previously an actor and graduate from the National Film and Television School in Britain. Although Worrell went on to direct *Desmond's,* the series was initially coproduced and directed by Charlie Hanson. Hanson had previously been an originator and producer for *No Problem!,* Channel 4's first "black comedy" (1982–85). Many have argued that the

Desmond's comic formula was more successful than previous "ethnic sitcoms." Although the series has often been compared to *The Cosby Show,* it can be seen as the first light entertainment program to embrace fully the black community within a British context.

The series was based in Desmond's, a barbershop in Peckham. A core group of characters used the shop as a social meeting place. Norman Beaton played Desmond, a West Indian traditionalist, and Carmen Munroe played his loving and supportive wife, Shirley. Together they ran the southeast London barbershop, where their children and friends would often congregate. The couple's children were Gloria (Kim Walker), Sean (Justin Pickett), and Michael (Geff Francis). The dynamics and relationships among these various characters formed the basis of the comedy.

The setting of the program was unique—a black sitcom based in the workplace. The series' antecedents, such as *No Problem!* and *The Fosters,* tended to focus on black family relationships within the family home. The cast of *Desmond's* were not passive characters in a stagnant setting but socially mobile people in multiracial Britain. In this context, the comedy introduced new types of protagonists, such as Desmond, the black entrepreneur, and his two sons, one an aspiring bank employee and the other a bright student. The characters in *Desmond's* were quite distinct types, neither caricatures nor stereotypes. Worrell was very keen to emphasize differences within the African-Caribbean diaspora, and so the audience was witness to racism and prejudice between, for example, the African eternal student Matthew (Gyearbuor Asante) and the West Indian characters. The series depicted a myriad of types, spanning across generations, lifestyles, and politics, thus dispelling any notion of there being an essential black British subject. Indeed, generational and other differences among characters often triggered the hilarity.

Desmond's had its own unique method of team writing. To some extent, it became a training ground for young, multicultural, creative talent. Many aspiring writers, producers, directors, and production staff members gained experience on the program by learning how to create a long-running fresh situation comedy. Although the series lasted for five years on British television, those involved in the production often mentioned the pressures of producing what was generally perceived as a black comedy. Both Worrell and Hanson have spoken of the expectations placed on them, simply because there were so few other black comedies on television. In the 1992 television documentary *Black and White in Colour,* Hanson commented that "Black situation comedy comes under the microscope far more than any other situation comedy on television." At the same time, the program marked a progression in that most black British sitcoms have tended to focus on dysfunctional families and social problems. Carmen Munroe sees *Desmond's* as a landmark program; in *Black and White in Colour,* she notes that "we have successfully created a space for ourselves, where we can just be a real, honest, loving family, with problems like lots of people, and we can present that with some degree of truth and still not lose the comedy."

SARITA MALIK

Cast

Desmond	Norman Beaton
Shirley	Carmen Munroe
Gloria	Kim Walker
Sean	Justin Pickett
Michael	Geff Francis
Matthew	Gyearbuor Asante

Producers
Charlie Hanson, Humphrey Barclay

Programming History
Channel 4
1989–95

Detective Programs

Detective programs have been a permanent presence on American television; like their more numerous siblings, police shows, their development enacts in miniature many aspects of the larger history of the medium as a whole. They began as live programs, recycling prose fiction, movies, and radio shows, the earliest of them such as *Man against Crime* (1949–56, Columbia Broadcasting System [CBS], National Broadcasting Company [NBC], Dumont) and *Martin Kane, Private Eye* (1949–54, NBC) conceived and produced in New

York City by advertising agencies. Erik Barnouw's history of American broadcasting discloses that the tobacco sponsors of *Man against Crime* prohibited fires and coughing from all scripts to avoid negative associations with their product and also describes the technical and narrative crudity of these early programs. The length of radio episodes could be gauged accurately by counting the words in the script, but the duration of live action on TV was unpredictable, varying treacherously from rehearsal to actual broadcast. To solve this problem, Barnouw writes, every episode of *Man against Crime* ended with a search that the hero (played by Ralph Bellamy) could prolong or shorten, depending on the time available.

Even the earliest detective shows can be subdivided into recognizable subgenres. *Man against Crime* and *Martin Kane* are simple versions of the hard-boiled private eye, a figure invented in the 1920s in stories and novels by Dashiell Hammett and Raymond Chandler and reincarnated in the movies of Humphrey Bogart and other tough-guy actors. Other 1950s series recycle detectives in the cerebral, puzzle-solving tradition of Agatha Christie and Arthur Conan Doyle, author of the Sherlock Holmes stories. The character Holmes makes his first appearance on American television in 1954 in a syndicated filmed series that lasts only a single season. Ellery Queen, an American Sherlock Holmes, is born in a cycle of popular novels beginning in 1929, transfers to radio a decade later in a long-running weekly program, and migrates to television in 1950 in a live series, *The Adventures of Ellery Queen* (1950–51, Dumont; 1951–52, American Broadcasting Company [ABC]). This is the first of four series devoted to Ellery Queen, a mystery writer and amateur detective who is the direct inspiration for Angela Lansbury's long-running character in *Murder, She Wrote* (1984–96, CBS). The classic whodunit pleasures of *Ellery Queen*—as well as its relative indifference to social or psychological realism—are crystallized in its structure: Queen's adventures in all media usually conclude with a summary of the story's clues and a challenge to the reader or viewer to solve the mystery before Ellery himself supplies the answer in the epilogue.

A third subgenre of the detective story also makes an early appearance in the new medium. A hybrid of screwball comedy and mystery, this format usually centers on the adventures of a married or romantically entangled couple, amateurs in detection who are often distracted in the face of villainy and mortal danger by their own erotically charged quarrels. Examples include *Boston Blackie* (1951–53, syndicated), *Mr. and Mrs. North* (1952–53, CBS; 1954, NBC), and, a bit later, *The Thin Man* (1957–59, NBC). Each of these escapist half comedies placed more emphasis on interpersonal badinage than on the realities of urban crime,

although the social whirl of the modern city was often a background in all three series.

Like most television detectives of the 1950s, these protagonists had originated in older media. A durable embodiment of disreputable and elegant self-reliance, Blackie first appears in American magazine stories at the turn of the century, a jewel thief who moves easily in high society and has served time in prison but now prevents crime instead of committing it. Surreptitious and resilient, he turns up in silent films and reappears in sound movies and on radio in the 1940s. Still quick with a wisecrack, he is more respectable in his TV incarnation than his prototypes in the older media, according to several commentators, and, aided by a girlfriend named Mary and a dog named Whitey, is said to have been remodeled in the image of the movie version of Nick Charles, hero of *The Thin Man,* who is also in partnership with a woman and a dog.

Mr. and Mrs. North has a similar mixed-media ancestry, originating in prose fiction in 1940 by a writing couple, Richard and Frances Lockridge, then in the very next year is thrice reborn—in a Broadway play, in a Hollywood movie starring Gracie Allen as Mrs. North, and, most durably, in a weekly radio series that runs on CBS and later NBC until 1956, outlasting the TV series to which it gave rise. Gracie Allen's presence in this catalog is a decisive clue to the stereotype of the lovably addled female on which *Mr. and Mrs. North* relies.

No such stereotype mars *The Thin Man,* but despite an energetic performance by Phyllis Kirk as Nora, the TV version is a mere derivative echo of its famous predecessors, Hammett's 1934 novel and especially the series of five MGM movies starring William Powell and Myrna Loy as Nick and Nora Charles (1934, 1936, 1939, 1941, 1944). The Kirk character hints at what comes across with charming serious authority in Myrna Loy's definitive Nora: unlike her imitators and competitors, this woman is no mere sidekick but rather her detective husband's true moral and intellectual equal: a rare female in this masculine genre.

Following the success of *I Love Lucy* (1951–61, CBS) and *Dragnet* (1952–59; revived, 1967–70, NBC; and yet again 2003– , ABC), both filmed in Hollywood, production shifts to film and to the West Coast, and the economic structure of the new medium is stabilized: production companies sell programs to the networks, which peddle commercial slots to advertisers who have no direct creative control over programming. The standard format for crime shows changes from 30 minutes to an hour in the late 1950s and early 1960s, and crime series begin to exhibit a richer audiovisual texture, learning to exploit such defining features of television as its reduced visual field and the mandatory commercial interruptions.

Such an embrace of some of television's distinctive features surely helps explain the success of the Raymond Burr *Perry Mason* (1957–66, CBS), one of the first TV series to achieve greater complexity—and popularity—than the books and radio episodes from which it derives. An American version of the whodunit, the program is a kind of primer on the uses and gratifications of genre formulas. Both a courtroom melodrama and a detective story, its appeal to viewers and its power as drama are grounded in TV-specific features. Its highly segmented narrative structure, for example, exploits the commercial interruptions, organizing the plot in predictable units that offer viewers the simultaneous pleasures of recognizable variations (different performers, settings, motives, and so on) within a familiar, orderly pattern. Every episode begins with a minidrama, establishing a roster of plausible suspects for the murder in which it culminates. Every episode dramatizes the arrest and imprisonment of Perry's client, known to be innocent by the very fact that Perry has taken on the defense. The second half hour of every episode is always a courtroom trial in which Perry's deductive genius and brilliance in cross-examination combine to force a confession from the real murderer. Every episode contains an explanatory epilogue, often at table in a restaurant or other convivial space signifying the restoration of normality and order, in which Perry discloses the chain of reasoning that led him to the truth. This intensification of the structural constraints inherent in the format of the weekly series strengthens what must be called the mythic or ritual content of *Perry Mason:* an endlessly renewing drama of murder, justice perverted, and justice redeemed.

The very title sequence of *Perry Mason* signals something of the way TV drama by the late 1950s had begun to develop an appropriately minimized audiovisual vocabulary: a confident, swooping camera glides through a courtroom to a close-up of the hero, its graceful dipping motion a visual tracing of the rhythms of Fred Steiner's dramatic theme music.

Similar audiovisual effects are intermittently present in two notable series created by Blake Edwards, *Richard Diamond, Private Detective* (1957–60, CBS, NBC) and *Peter Gunn* (1958–61, NBC, ABC), both of which center on wiseacre heroes whose sexual bravado is more important to their appeal than their brains or their marksmanship. Richard Diamond's place in TV history is secured by two of its cast members: the protagonist was played by a young David Janssen, smooth faced, not furtive, and just learning to mumble, in rehearsal for his memorable work in *The Fugitive* (1963–67, ABC) and *Harry O* (1974–76, ABC), and the role of Diamond's throaty secretary belonged briefly in 1959 to Mary Tyler Moore, who received no billing in the credits and, in keeping with the macho ob-

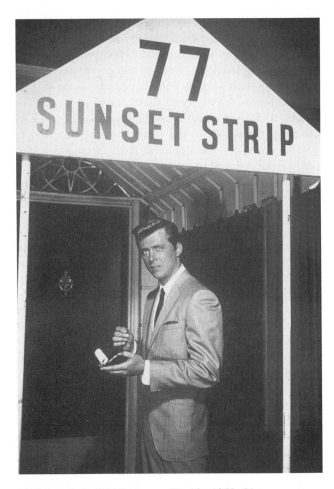

77 Sunset Strip, Edd Byrnes as Kookie, 1958–64.
©*Mark Marmor/Courtesy of the Everett Collection*

jectification of women common in detective mythology, was shown on camera only from the waist down.

Especially in its music, *Peter Gunn* was a more compelling program than *Richard Diamond,* though its plots were reductive and often as violent as those of *The Untouchables* (1959–64, ABC), notorious even in its own day for its surfeit of murder. Henry Mancini's original jazz variations (later collected in two best-selling albums) provided an elegant, haunting accompaniment to the show's moody, film-noirish editing and camera work. Gunn himself, portrayed in a minimalist physical style by Craig Stevens, often repaired to a nightclub called "Mother's," where his girlfriend Edie Hunt (Lola Albright) sang jazz (and wore extreme décolletage) for a living.

Peter Gunn had a genuine individuality, but its half-hour episodes, photographed in black and white, must have seemed obsolete by the end of the decade. Hour-long series, shot in glossy, high-key color in exotic locales and filled with physical action became the standard during the 1960s. In a sense, this trend was part of the industry project of finding ways to adapt action-adventure material to the exigencies of the small screen. Car chases and acrobatic action were not impossible on television, though such things could never be as riveting here as in the movies. But artful editing and clever camera placement—emphasizing action in depth that moved toward or away from the camera and avoided trajectories that ran across the screen into its confining borders—could create plausibly exciting effects. Glossy production values, then, often as an end in themselves, set the tone for most TV detectives of the 1960s.

One of the founding programs in this gloss-and-glamour mode was *77 Sunset Strip* (1958–64, ABC), produced by Warner Brothers and created by Roy Huggins from his own 1946 novel. The theme music and lyrics for the show aimed for a tone of jivey, youthful "cool" and included the sound of snapping fingers. The show appealed strongly to younger viewers, primarily through the character of a jive-talking parking lot attendant called "Kookie" (Edd Byrnes), who was perpetually combing his luxuriant wavy hair and trying to persuade the detective heroes, played by Efrem Zimbalist, Jr., and Roger Smith, to let him work on their investigations. The series title named the agency's upscale Hollywood address, but many episodes required travel to exotic foreign locales where the camera could ogle wealth and pulchritude. Roger Smith wrote and directed the most memorable episode of the series, "The Silent Caper" (first telecast June 3, 1960), in which the hero learns about a mob kidnapping from newspaper headlines in the opening sequence and proceeds to rescue the distressed damsel in a series of heroic improvisations, the entire adventure unfolding without a single line of dialogue.

In this period of what might be called technical exploration, the private-eye genre, like other forms of action-adventure, remains essentially plot driven, and despite the fact that the protagonist returns each week for new adventures, every episode remains self-contained, void of any memory of prior episodes. Often subtle visually but superficial in content, some of these programs even differentiated their heroes by strangely external and implausible attributes. *Cannon* (1971–76, CBS), played by William Conrad, was balding and fat, but his excessive weight and his fittingly cumbersome Lincoln Continental did not noticeably inhibit his scriptwriters, who provided fisticuffs and races by foot and by vehicle sufficient to challenge an Olympic athlete or Grand Prix driver. Even more implausibly, James Franciscus's *Longstreet* (1971–72, ABC) was blind and brought his seeing-eye dog and a special electronic cane to all investigations.

Barnaby Jones (1973–80, CBS) starred an aged Buddy Ebsen at the end of a long career that had apparently culminated in the role of Jed Clampett, patriarch of *The Beverly Hillbillies* (1962–71, CBS). The

Honey West, Anne Francis, 1965–66.
Courtesy of the Everett Collection

later detective series turned its protagonist's geriatric aura to some use by emphasizing his country slyness and old-fashioned integrity, but there was unintended irony, a reminder of Ebsen's visible decrepitude, in this remark by his policeman friend Lieutenant Biddle (John Carter) in an episode first broadcast in 1976: "Barnaby, if I ever get to heaven I expect I'll find you there first, checking out the pearly gates for me."

Mannix (1967–75, CBS) was perhaps the representative private-eye series of the era. Played by the rugged and athletic Mike Connors, Mannix was not physically challenged, but one might be tempted to doubt his brainpower, for he was quick to the punch and seemed to conduct most of his investigations by assault and battery. This thoughtless tough-guy element was so pronounced that, as Brooks and Marsh report, it incited the radio comedians Bob and Ray to create a continuing parody of the program, titled Blimmix, "in which the hero always held a polite conversation with some suspect, calmly agreeing that mayhem was the only answer, and then was invariably beaten to a pulp."

Finally, in its third or "mature" stage, roughly corresponding to the mid-1970s and beyond, the private-eye series combines the visual subtlety achieved over more than 25 years of such programming with a new complexity in content. The best detective shows develop a

Mike Hammer: Private Eye, Stacy Keach, 1984–87.
Courtesy of the Everett Collection

Columbo (1971–77, NBC; continuing as an occasional TV movie), was technically a *policier* but in spirit one of American television's wittiest variations on the mystery-puzzle format: the detective as triumphant (and dogged) rationalist as well as working-class avenger, writer-producers Richard Levinson and William Link's most memorable creation. *Tenafly* (1973–74, NBC) was a short-lived but thoughtful series centered on a black private eye, played by James McEachin, whose gentleness and husbandly decency undermine many media stereotypes.

Magnum, PI (1980–88, CBS) starred Tom Selleck as an engaging and self-deprecating Vietnam veteran living in the guest cottage on a picturesque estate in an even more picturesque Hawaii; Magnum's character deepened as the series continued, and some episodes explored the show's relation to its detective-story ancestry with modesty and wit. *Moonlighting* (1985–89, ABC) was a frequently brilliant though also abrasive postmodern variation on the *Thin Man* formula, with Bruce Willis and Cybill Shepherd trading insults and cracking wise through the run of the series.

But *Harry O* and *Rockford* are the most compelling private detectives in television history. Both series are the work of writers, directors, and producers with long experience in the crime genre and a specific history of collaboration with their stars. Janssen's creative ensemble included Howard Rodman, creator of the show and writer of the two pilot films that led to the series; producer-director Jerry Thorpe; directors Paul Wendkos, Richard Lang, and Jerry London; and writers Michael Sloan, Robert C. Dennis, Stephen Kandel, and Robert Dozier. Garner's collaborators included his former agent-turned-executive producer Meta Rosenberg and such TV veterans as Roy Huggins, Stephen J. Cannell, Juanita Bartlett, Chas. Floyd Johnson, and David Chase, some of whom had worked with him in movies and in his earliest jobs in television. (Chase joined the show as a producer in 1976 and wrote or co-wrote 18 episodes, several of which deal with New Jersey mobsters who are clear ancestors of the characters in *The Sopranos,* the landmark Home Box Office [HBO] series Chase created in 1999.)

Antiheroic in tone, both series draw creatively on their stars' previous work and also reflect something of the legacy of the antiwar movement and the broad social turmoil of the late 1960s and early 1970s. In a way, both Harry and Rockford are adult dropouts, living unpretentiously along the beaches of southern California. (Rockford's minimal domicile is actually a mobile home.) But both protagonists are a generation older than the youthful protestors of that era, and they project a wariness and skepticism that seem to originate not in naïveté or adolescent discontent but in part

memory, the hero's prior adventures bear on his current ones, and characters from earlier episodes or seasons reappear, adding complexity to themes and relationships. In the richest such programs, character, not violent action, drives the story, and the subject matter itself engages reality more seriously and topically than the muscle-flexing violence of earlier shows had generally allowed.

Harry O (1974–76, ABC) and *The Rockford Files* (1974–80, NBC) are the primary examples of these principles of accretion and refinement. Equivalent instances among police shows are *Police Story* (1973–77, NBC), *Hill Street Blues* (1981–87, NBC), *NYPD Blue* (1993– , ABC), *Law and Order* (1990– , NBC) and *Homicide* (1993–1999, NBC). But a significant minority of other detective series beginning in the 1970s and after also achieve new levels of excellence and imaginative energy, combining memorable acting with elegant cinematography and, often, superior writing to become, at the least, provocative entertainment.

Kojak, Telly Savalas, 1973–78.
Courtesy of the Everett Collection

in the muddles, disillusionments, even the physical humiliations of middle age.

Janssen's Orwell especially is a figure of pain and diminished expectations, divorced and solitary, living on a disability pension from the San Diego Police Department. Fitting himself with rueful slowness into his broken-down toy of a sports car, middle aged and sagging like its owner, or stiffly climbing the wooden steps of his rickety beach house, he seems a subversively modest hero, the fugitive grown older and wiser.

Less melancholy and wincing than Harry O, Rockford is unpretentious and decent, equally postheroic, probably the only TV detective to spend more time nursing his own injuries than inflicting hurt on others. Both Rockford and Orwell are great wheedlers, more likely to coddle or flatter information out of their sources than to threaten them. "Why should I answer you?" asks an officious bureaucrat in one episode of *Harry O.* Janssen's response is characteristic, a half-audible mumble, delayed for a moment as he settles on the edge of the bureaucrat's desk: "Because my feet hurt?"

Rockford is the richer, more various and more playful text, partly because it had the advantage of lasting six years, while *Harry O* was canceled abruptly after its second season despite reasonably strong ratings, possibly a casualty of the crescendo of complaints against media violence that developed in the mid-1970s.

Like the police series that appear in the same "late" period of the network era, Rockford is something of a hybrid, combining elements of comedy and the daytime continuing serial with the private-eye format. Though Rockford's adventures are self-contained, usually concluding within the confines of a single episode, his father "Rocky" (Noah Beery) and a wide circle of friends and professional colleagues are recurring characters, and the momentum of their lives as well as their unstable, shifting intimacy with Rockford himself deepen and complicate the program. The recurring women in *Rockford*—Jim's tough, competent lawyer Beth Davenport (Gretchen Corbett); the blind psychologist Megan Dougherty (Kathryn Harrold), a client who becomes Jim's lover; and Rita Capkovic (Rita Moreno), a resilient, loquacious prostitute who enlists Rockford's help in changing her life—exhibit qualities of intelligence, moral courage, and independence rare in women characters in our popular culture and virtually nonexistent among the dolls and molls of detective stories.

"I hope these nuances are not escaping you, Orwell," says Lieutenant Trench (Anthony Zerbe), Harry's police contact, in a typically abrasive encounter during his second season. Harry shakes his head. For viewers of *Harry O* and *The Rockford Files,* his answer ramifies: "I'm very good at nuances."

Private-eye series were scarce in the television of the affluent 1980s and 1990s, the years of Reagan and Clinton and the Internet stock market bubble, though police shows continued to thrive. As the broadcast era yielded to the dubious plenitude of cable and satellite television, the prime-time schedule came to be dominated by "reality programming," and the old genres, at least for a time, fell into disrepute. Moreover, the medium's preference for law-and-order heroes working for the police or government agencies was much intensified after the terrorist attacks of 9/11. Loner protagonists sympathetic to underdogs and suspicious of authority disappeared even from the reruns.

The only notable private detective of the early years of new millennium, *Monk* (USA 2002–) rejects even the modest subversions of *Harry O* or *Rockford.* Wonderfully acted by Tony Shaloub (who won an Emmy Award in 2003 for best actor in a comedy series for his portrayal of Monk), Monk is a former cop on medical leave, suffering from obsessive-compulsive disorder. A variation of the *Columbo* formula, though less carefully scripted than its classic ancestor, *Monk* is a private-eye show in name only, for its protagonist works as a special consultant for the San Francisco Police Department on cases that are cerebral puzzles or locked-door mysteries. The detective's character is compelling in this escapist series, and the plots are routine and derivative. Afraid of heights, germs, physical contact, and compulsively driven to straighten, repair, and disinfect the world's disorder, Monk cannot function without his nurse-protector Sharona (Bitty Schram), a female Watson for this phobic, American Sherlock Holmes.

Valuable as a corrective to the still-widespread notion that TV programs and especially crime shows are interchangeable and entirely ephemeral, the essentially internal history proposed here must be complicated and supplemented by other perspectives. Cultural studies or anthropological approaches would understand the TV detective show as part of a larger project in which the conventions of genre function in part as enabling devices, their reassuring familiarity licensing an exploration of topics that might otherwise be too disturbing or threatening to acknowledge or discuss openly. On this view, all television programs, and particularly the prime-time genres, collectively sustain an open-ended, ongoing conversation about the nature of American culture, about our values and the norms of social life. Cop and private-eye shows are fables of justice, heroism, and deviancy, symbolically or imaginatively "policing" the unstable boundaries that define public or consensus ideas about crime, urban life, gender norms, and the health or sickness of our institutions. The progression, that is, from *Dragnet* to *Hill Street Blues* and thence to the *Law and Order* spin-offs and surveillance fables generated by the terror of September 11, discloses aspects of a social history of our society. But this is not a simple affirmation of such stories or of some comforting progress myth. For our genre texts carry and rehearse and diffuse the lies, the prejudices, and the self-delusions of our society as well as its ideals. *Harry 0* and *Rockford* share the

prime-time schedule with *Mannix* and *Charlie's Angels* (1976–81, ABC). Inevitably ambivalent, in conflict with themselves, genre stories reflect and embody cultural divisions.

A chief virtue, then, of television's most fundamental of all programs, the series, is precisely that it is continuing and, theoretically, endless. In this, the TV series embodies a useful truth: that culture itself is a process—not any fixed thing at all but a shifting, ongoing contention among traditional and emerging voices, forces, and ideologies.

DAVID THORBURN

See also **Columbo; Hill Street Blues; Homicide: Life on the Street; Law and Order; Magnum, PI; Moonlighting; Murder, She Wrote; NYPD Blue; Perry Mason; Police Story; Rockford Files, The**

Further Reading

Barnouw, Barnouw, *The Image Empire,* New York: Oxford University Press, 1970

Brooks, Tim, and Earle Marsh, *The Complete Directory to Prime Time Network TV Shows,* New York: Ballantine Books, 1985

Gianakos, Larry James, *Television Drama Series Programming: A Comprehensive Chronicle, 1959–1975,* Metuchen, New Jersey: Scarecrow Press, 1978

Kerr, Paul, "Watching the Detectives," *Primetime Magazine* (London), Vol. 1, No. 1 (July 1981)

McNeil, Alex, *Total Television,* New York: Penguin Books, 1984

Meyers, Richard, *TV Detectives,* San Diego, California: A.S. Barnes, 1981

Norden, Martin F., *"The Detective Show"* in *TV Genres: A Handbook and Reference Guide,* edited by Brian G. Rose, Westport, Connecticut: Greenwood Press, 1985

Tibballs, Geoff, *The Boxtree Encyclopedia of TV Detectives,* London: Boxtree Ltd, 1992

Thorburn, David, "Is TV Acting a Distinctive Art Form?" *New York Times* (August 14, 1977)

The author acknowledges the valuable research assistance provided by Micky Dupree and Lilly Kam.

Development

The term "development" refers to the process in U.S. television program production (usually involving prime-time dramatic series) whereby a network pays an outside program supplier or the program producer to develop a potential series. This often involves an elaborate step deal, beginning with a verbal pitch of

the series concept by the supplier. If the network is interested, it provides funds with which to develop story and script and eventually the actual production of a pilot or the originating episode of the series. The network may or may not choose to air the pilot; if the pilot is run and performs satisfactorily, the network may decide to "pick up" the series for its regular schedule. The networks develop far more programs than they can possibly air, and thus program development clearly favors the networks despite the mutual dependency between buyers and suppliers. Indeed, program development well indicates the networks' long-standing control over television programming, which they maintain today, even in the age of cable.

This was not the case in the early years of U.S. network television, when the industry relied primarily on the "radio model" of program development. As in network radio, television programs were conceived and produced by advertising agencies on behalf of sponsors. The agencies also decided which network would air the program and in many cases the actual time slot on the network schedule. The radio model proved untenable in the burgeoning TV industry, however, for three principal reasons. First, the increasing cost and complexity of TV series production made it difficult for sponsors to underwrite shows and for ad agencies to produce them. Second, the heavy emphasis on ratings and on scheduling meant that the ad agency's and sponsor's notion of an appropriate program and time slot might not (and often did not) jibe with the network's strategy for attracting and maintaining the largest possible audience during the crucial evening hours. And third, it was becoming ever more obvious that syndication (off-network reruns) would generate huge revenues for the companies that owned the programs and controlled their off-network afterlife. Thus, the networks gradually took control of programming and scheduling in the late 1950s, which had significant impact on TV program development.

Network control of programming was severely undercut in the early 1970s, however, which had a tremendous impact on the process—and the standardization—of program development. In the 1972–73 season, the networks' collective control of the television industry was challenged, primarily on antitrust grounds, by the Justice Department, the Federal Trade Commission, and the Federal Communications Commission (FCC). The most significant of these challenges in terms of programming (and development) were the FCC's so-called fin-syn (financial interest and syndication) regulations, which restricted the networks' right to finance and syndicate programs. As a direct result, program development quickly evolved from a haphazard, informal process to a standardized and heavily regulated set of procedures. With most prime-time dramatic series production now being farmed out, development became the primary focus of the industry—particularly the growing ranks of mid-management "development executives" at both the networks and the program suppliers.

Program development under fin-syn regulations was a rule-bound, pitch-to-pilot ritual. The pitch had to be verbal since anything in writing required a contractual agreement. If the network-buyer was sufficiently interested in the pitch, the supplier was contracted to develop the concept into a story treatment (synopsis), then into one or more scripts, and then into an actual series pilot. Depending on the supplier's track record and clout with the network, there might be guarantees with regard to airing the pilot or even picking up the series—a so-called play-or-pay deal. But for the most part, series development was a high-cost, high-risk venture, with the supplier sharing the risk because the costs for producing a pilot often exceeded what the network paid. In most cases, this investment was simply lost since even successful TV producers could expect only about 10 percent of the series they developed to actually be picked up by a network.

Suppliers were more willing than ever to take the risks since fin-syn assured them the ownership and syndication rights to their series. The potential syndication payoff also increased dramatically in the late 1970s because of cable, which created a surge in the number of independent television stations and thus a wider market for off-network reruns. The emergence of cable networks and superstations in the 1980s further complicated program development by increasing the number of program buyers and also by enhancing the off-network currency of even moderately successful series. Moreover, cable brought back the first-run syndicated dramatic series (most notably via *Star Trek: The Next Generation* in 1986), which had been phased out in the 1960s. These factors, along with the network penchant for "quick-yank" cancellation of weak series after only a few episodes, rendered development an even more crucial and pervasive aspect of the industry in the cable era. By the early 1990s, according to *Broadcasting* magazine, "70% to 80% of a network's costs [were] tagged to program development."

Program development persisted in the mid-1990s, although a number of trends in the television and cable industries, and in the "entertainment industry" at large, may very well increasingly affect the process in the new millennium. One trend has been the move by several studios (FOX, Warner Brothers, and Paramount) to create their own broadcast or cable networks, thereby serving not only as program suppliers but as buyers and distributors as well. A related trend involves the recent wave of mergers and acquisitions as media conglomerates move into every phase of production, distribution, and exhibition. Yet another related trend involves the deregulation of the television industry, most notably the 1995 scaling back of the FCC's fin-syn regulations.

Now that the networks again can finance and syndicate their own programs, merging with suppliers is not only logical but inevitable.

Nevertheless, program development persists for a number of reasons. First, development has been part of the industry's entrenched bureaucracy since the 1970s, and it will not be easily or readily dismantled. Second, although the networks clearly favor their in-house suppliers, the highly competitive nature of television programming necessarily will encourage the networks to look outside for fresh ideas or, even more likely, for top talent—especially proven writer-producers and established stars who wish to maintain a degree of independence. Finally, and perhaps most important, the networks have grown accustomed to developing far more programs than they actually can purchase or schedule. This enables them to keep their options open, to test-market potential series, and to share the risks of development. Program suppliers continue to accommodate the networks because the long-term syndication payoff is still much higher for a series that has aired on a major broadcast network. Thus, program development remains a buyer's market and a routine industry practice even in the era of cable, deregulation, and media mergers, with the networks enjoying considerable industry power.

THOMAS SCHATZ

See also **Financial Interest and Syndication Rules; Media Conglomerates; Mergers and Acquisitions**

Further Reading

Anderson, Christopher, *Hollywood TV: The Studio System in the Fifties,* Austin: University of Texas Press, 1994

Barnouw, Erik, *Tube of Plenty: The Evolution of American Television,* New York: Oxford University Press, 1975

Cantor, Muriel G, *Prime-Time Television: Content and Control,* Beverly Hills, California: Sage, 1980

Flint, Joe, "Networks Win, Hollywood Winces as Fin-Syn Barriers Fall," *Broadcasting* (November 22, 1993)

Freeman, Mike, "How Drama Boldly Goes First-Run," *Broadcasting* (February 17, 1992)

Gitlin, Todd, *Inside Prime Time,* New York: Pantheon, 1983

McClellan, Steve, "The TV Networks in Play," *Broadcasting* (November 11, 1991)

Reel, A. Frank, *The Networks: How They Stole the Show,* New York: Scribner's, 1979

Robins, J. Max, "TV Biz Sweats It Out in Development Hell," *Variety* (April 22–28, 1996)

Robins, J. Max, and Brian Lowry, "Pilot Poker Is Now for High Rollers Only," *Variety* (April 4–10, 1994)

Development Communication

Communication for development involves the strategic application of communication processes and technologies to advance socially beneficial goals. These interventions are implemented by development agencies and social movement organizations in their efforts to engage social change. Although development projects typically transfer resources from wealthy nations to those with fewer financial means, these strategies are appropriately used in any community involved in social change.

Building on a broad understanding of television as a dominant social and cultural force in our societies, development planners attempt to use this tool in their strategic interventions. Early development communication scholars encouraged the introduction of television systems as a symbol of modernity. As many countries began to gain their political sovereignty following World War II, national politicians used development assistance to build media systems, seen as a way to disseminate national development agendas. Television and other media systems were assumed to help foster empathy among individuals as a precurser to democratic participation and economic entrepreneurship. The underlying model of media effects advocated in this approach assumed that television would help diffuse information to a receptive audience.

One of the earliest examples of television used in development communication comes from the National Aeronautics and Space Administration (NASA)-India Satellite Instructional Television Experiment (SITE). Indian and U.S. space agencies coordinated satellite television service to more than 2,000 villages in the mid-1970s. Television programming on these channels was designed to address a number of development concerns, such as family planning, agriculture, education, national integration, and health.

Television continues to be frequently used in social marketing and entertainment education strategies, two dominant models of development communication practice. In the first approach, public service commercials are created to disseminate information to targeted audiences. The marketing orientation is differentiated from advertising in its emphasis on audience behavior change rather than exposure to the mediated message. Advertisements produced by nonprofit organizations, promoting topics such as family planning, nutrition, and vaccinations, fit this social marketing model.

Entertainment education programs differ from social marketing campaigns in that they incorporate socially beneficial messages into longer narratives rather than rely on short segments between other programs. Entertainment education projects attempt to appeal to audiences interested in fictional programs while offering strategic messages designed to change knowledge, attitudes, or behaviors. Indian television, for example, devoted a serial, *Hum Log*, to addressing family issues, such as limiting fertility and promoting gender equity.

Many of these development interventions are designed to diffuse information to targeted audiences. The hierarchical nature of this dominant diffusion model has been critiqued on both ethical and efficacy grounds. These critiques inspired the growth of a participatory approach to development communication based on the principle that communities should share in the definition and resolution of social problems rather than be mere receptacles of information determined by external development agencies.

How participation actually becomes interpreted in development projects can vary greatly. Development institutions interested in creating efficient and effective projects understand participation as formative research or needs assessments. Social marketing projects, for example, involve extensive interviews and conversations with intended beneficiaries in project planning stages. A television advertisement would be created only after beneficiaries had been consulted in their understanding of the problem and possible solutions and in their reactions to types of messages, sources, visuals, and other aspects of the campaign. These types of interventions utilize participation as a means toward an end, defined by the institution itself.

Other development institutions concerned with the ethical aspects of participation are more likely to conceive of participation as an end in itself regardless of project outcomes. Community members are encouraged to define their own social problems and to engage actively in their resolution. Some projects, for example, teach video production skills so that local participants can create their own mediated texts, building on what came to be known as the "Fogo Process" after Canadian development strategies implemented it in the mid-1980s.

Another form of development communication engages media as a site for resistance against dominant power structures and ideologies. Social movement or-

ganizations may actively use television channels to mobilize supporters, gain public support, counter dominant ideas, and offer alternative frames. Media advocacy strategies target television news, along with other channels, to draw attention to particular issues. In an early example, a media advocacy campaign contrasted actual with toy guns, with little discernible difference between them, producing compelling visuals that were then used in television news stories.

Across many different approaches to development communication, television is a popular medium. This channel may be a particularly effective means of reaching audiences for whom televisions are affordable. In areas where access to television is limited, however, any benefits accrued through televised campaigns remain with the elite. Current enthusiasm regarding interactive and computer-integrated television formats must again be subject to this concern with access. Given that fewer than one-quarter of the world's population have access to computer technologies, television's interactive potential remains a privileged resource.

Traditional evaluations of development communication projects assess a hierarchy of effects, charting exposure to the disseminated message, knowledge gained, attitudes formed, and behavior changed. With adequate political and economic support, along with appropriate theoretical understanding of the issues and communities engaged, development communication projects have the potential to contribute to social change. The first step requires that the targeted audiences have access to the information. This does not necessarily require that televisions be individually owned but that people have some place to watch them, even in a community setting. Some campaigns specifically target knowledge, such as teaching modes of HIV transmission, whereas others focus on attitudes, such as reinforcing more equitable gender roles. Others build on knowledge and attitudes to encourage behavior change, such as the cessation of smoking, boiling water, or using condoms. Although changing behavior occurs considerably less frequently in response to communication campaigns than contributing to knowledge or reinforcing attitudes, this level of success is possible particularly when communities identify with the concern addressed and have the appropriate means suggested for the problem's resolution. Evaluations on the effects of these communication campaigns demonstrate that limited success can occur if social and cultural circumstances warrant the campaign and if political and economic resources adequately support it.

In addition to considering the possible manifest and latent consequences of interventions, communication for development needs to be understood within political and economic processes and structures. As a discourse, development communicates the agenda of a powerful few, with the ability to define problems and create knowledge toward their resolution. Development intervention allocates resources and articulates ideologies across cultural and political boundaries within a global sphere. It is important to question how television works to facilitate or constrain development communication.

KARIN WILKINS

Further Reading

Mody, B., *Designing Messages for Development Communication: An Audience Participation-Based Approach,* New Delhi: Sage, 1992

Singhal, A., and E.M. Rogers, *Entertainment-Education: A Communication Strategy for Social Change,* Mahwah, New Jersey: Lawrence Erlbaum Associates, 1999

Wallack, Lawrence, Lori Dorfman, David Jernigan, and Makani Themba, *Media Advocacy and Public Health: Power for Prevention,* Newbury Park, California: Sage, 1993

Wilkins, K., editor, *Redeveloping Communication for Social Change: Theory, Practice & Power.* Boulder, Colorado: Rowman & Littlefield, 2001

Diana. *See* **Princess Diana: Death and Funeral Coverage**

Dick Van Dyke Show, The

U.S. Situation/Domestic Comedy

Even more than *I Love Lucy* or *The Honeymooners, The Dick Van Dyke Show,* which ran from 1961 to 1966 on the Columbia Broadcasting System (CBS), ushered in the golden age of the situation comedy, poised as it was on the threshold between the comedy-variety star vehicles of the 1950s (frequently still grounded in vaudeville) and the neorealist sociocomedies of the early 1970s (whose mainstay Mary Tyler Moore carried *The Dick Van Dyke Show*'s pedigree). It was among the first network series to bring itself electively to closure in the manner of *M*A*S*H, The Mary Tyler Moore Show,* and *Cheers* and has proven one of the most resilient in syndication. As social document, it managed to operate largely contemporaneously with the New Frontier and the thousand days of the Kennedy presidency.

The show was largely the autobiographical exegesis of Carl Reiner, whose previous tenure in workaday television had been with the legendary stable of writers surrounding *Your Show of Shows* and the Sid Caesar sketch vehicles of the mid-1950s. This same group went on to literally redefine American humor: on the Broadway stage (Neil Simon), on the high and low roads of screen comedy (Woody Allen and Mel Brooks, respectively), and in television, both early and late (Larry Gelbart, *M*A*S*H*). But first and foremost was *The Dick Van Dyke Show,* based loosely on Reiner's 1958 novel *Enter Laughing* (he directed a tepid screen version in 1967), in which his Alan Brady is a thinly veiled Caesar—a comic monster, sporadically seen but ubiquitously felt.

Brady's writing staff comprises the college-educated Rob Petrie (the eponymous Dick Van Dyke), assigned to interject new blood into his team of more experienced subordinates, Buddy Sorrell (Morey Amsterdam) and Sally Rogers (Rose Marie), loosely patterned after *Show of Shows* writers Mel Brooks and Selma Diamond. This sense of autobiography even stretched to the Petries' New Rochelle address (Reiner's own, save for a single digit) as well as his immediate family (his son Rob Reiner in turn became the archetypal early 1970s postadolescent as Michael Stivic on *All in the Family,* raising certain intriguing Freudian possibilities in the evolution of the sitcom genre). Rounding out the domestic American Century optimism is Rob's wife, Laura (Mary Tyler Moore).

As author David Marc has noted, for all intents and purposes, the movies destroyed vaudeville once and for all and, as a form of penance, made it into a kind of "biblical era of modern mass culture." This impulse was inherited wholesale by television of the 1950s (a quick survey of *I Love Lucy* reruns should suffice to illustrate this point), and it was in turn carried forward rather elegiacally in the many blackouts built into this show within a show. Van Dyke, a gifted physical performer, never missed an opportunity to reprise his mewling Stan Laurel or engage in a bit of Catskills shtick (invariably veiled in nostalgia). Entire episodes were given over to aging radio scribes or vaudeville fixtures who had been brushed aside by the space-age wonder of broadcast TV. Even sidekicks Buddy and Sally, real-life vaudeville veterans, often seemed little more than human repositories of the history of formalist comedy ("Baby Rose" Marie was a child singer on radio; Amsterdam, a cello prodigy whose act recalled Henny Youngman or Jack Benny, cohosted the *Tonight Show* forerunner *Broadway Open House* in 1950 and—in a bit of New Frontier prescience—wrote the paean to U.S. imperialism "Rum and Coca-Cola" for the Andrews Sisters).

Yet perhaps to counterbalance these misted reveries, *The Dick Van Dyke Show* just as often displayed an aggressive, Kennedy-era sophistication and leisure-class awareness. Initially competing for the central role were Van Dyke and that other Brubeck hipster grounded squarely in midwestern guilelessness, Johnny Carson (and if truth be known, another prominent casualty of after-hours blackout drinking). Meanwhile, all the hallmarks of the Kennedy zeitgeist are somewhere in attendance: Laura as the Jackie surrogate, attired in capri pants and designer tops; the Mafia, via the imposing Big Max Calvada (executive producer Sheldon Leonard); Marilyn Monroe, represented by the occasional *Alan Brady* guest starlet or lupine voluptuary; and intelligence operatives who commandeer the Petries' suburban home on stakeout. Camelot references abound, with a Robert Frost–like poet, a Hugh Hefner surrogate, Reiner as a Jackson Pollack–modeled abstract painter, or Laura's praise for baby guru Dr. Spock.

Sophisticated film homages appear throughout: *Vertigo*'s "Portrait of Carlotta" becomes "the Empress Carlotta brooch," and *Citizen Kane*'s "Rosebud" turns up as son Ritchie's middle name. (According to confidante Peter Bogdanovich, Orson Welles reportedly took a break every afternoon to watch the show in reruns.) Civil rights are often squarely front and center as well, with Leonard claiming that one racially

The Dick Van Dyke Show, Mary Tyler Moore, Dick Van Dyke, 1961–66.
Courtesy of the Everett Collection

themed episode, "The Hospital," specifically allowed him to cast *I Spy* with Bill Cosby, in turn the medium's first superstar of color. Even Van Dyke's own little brother, Jerry Van Dyke, is afforded a brief nepotistic berth from which to triumph—in his case, over painful shyness, social ineptitude, and a somewhat pesky somnambulism rather than innate ruthlessness and the reputation as White House hatchet man. And for purists, there is even a working conspiracy of sorts—the name "Calvada" is scattered portentously throughout (Big Max "Calvada," "Drink Calvada" scrawled on a billboard, and the name of their production company); the term is, in fact, a modified acronym for the show's partners: *CA*-rl Reiner, Sheldon *L*-eonard, Dick *VA*-n Dyke, and *DA*-nny Thomas.

Serving as more than vague inspiration, the Kennedys directly participated in the show's genesis. In 1960, Reiner wrote a pilot titled *Head of the Family,* virtually identical to the *Dick Van Dyke Show* in every way, save for casting himself in the lead role. The package made its way to Rat Pack stalwart Peter Lawford, a burgeoning producer and brother-in-law of the future president. Family patriarch Joseph P. Kennedy, seeking to oversee family business during the campaign, read the pilot personally and volunteered production money. Although the pilot was unsuccessful, its recasting led directly to the later series.

In 1966, *The Dick Van Dyke Show* ended with a final episode surveying Rob's "novel"—a collection of favorite moments from the five-year run—which Alan Brady dutifully agrees to adapt as a TV series, thus re-upping the autobiographical subtext one more level and providing Reiner the last laugh. The termination of the show was perhaps in light of CBS's decision to enforce a full-color lineup the following season. As such, the series' cool, streamlined black and white mirrors perfectly the news images of the day and functions as one of the few de facto time capsules on a finite and much-celebrated age.

PAUL CULLUM

See also **Comedy, Domestic Settings; Moore, Mary Tyler; Van Dyke, Dick**

Cast

Rob Petrie	Dick Van Dyke
Laura Petrie	Mary Tyler Moore
Sally Rogers	Rose Marie
Maurice "Buddy" Sorrell	Morey Amsterdam
Ritchie Petrie	Larry Mathews
Melvin Cooley	Richard Deacon
Jerry Helper	Jerry Paris
Millie Helper	Ann Morgan Guilbert
Alan Brady	Carl Reiner
Stacey Petrie	Jerry Van Dyke

Producers

Carl Reiner, Sheldon Leonard, Ronald Jacobs

Programming History

158 episodes

CBS

October 1961–December 1961	Tuesday 8:00–8:30
January 1962–September 1964	Wednesday 9:30–10:00
September 1964–September 1965	Wednesday 9:00–9:30
September 1965–September 1966	Wednesday 9:30–10:00

Further Reading

Butsch, Richard, "Class and Gender in Four Decades of Television Situation Comedy: *Plus ca change....*" *Critical Studies in Mass Communication* (December 1992)

Hamamoto, Darrell Y., *Nervous Laughter: Television Situation Comedy and Liberal Democratic Ideology,* New York: Praeger, 1989

Haralovich, Mary Beth, "Sitcoms and Suburbs: Positioning the 1950s Homemaker," *Quarterly Review of Film and Television* (May 1989)

Javna, John, *The Best of TV Sitcoms: Burns and Allen to the Cosby Show, The Munsters to Mary Tyler Moore,* New York: Harmony, 1988

Jones, Gerard, *Honey, I'm Home!: Sitcoms, Selling the American Dream,* New York: Grove Weidenfeld, 1992

Leibman, Nina C., *Living Room Lectures: The Fifties Family in Film and Television,* Austin: University of Texas Press, 1995

Lipsitz, George, "The Meaning of Memory: Family, Class, and Ethnicity in Early Network Television," *Camera Obscura* (January 1988)

Marc, David, *Demographic Vistas: Television in American Culture,* Philadelphia: University of Pennsylvania Press, 1984; 2nd edition, 1996

Marc, David, *Comic Visions: Television Comedy and American Culture,* Boston: Unwin Hyman, 1989; 2nd edition, Malden, Massachusetts: Blackwell Publishers, 1997

Rowe, Kathleen, *The Unruly Woman: Gender and the Genres of Laughter,* Austin: University of Texas Press, 1995

Spigel, Lynn, *Make Room for TV: Television and the Family Ideal in Postwar America,* Chicago: University of Chicago Press, 1992

Weissman, Ginny, and Coyne Sanders, *The Dick Van Dyke Show: Anatomy of a Classic,* New York: St. Martin's Press, 1983

Different World, A

U.S. Situation Comedy

A Different World, a spin-off of the top-rated *The Cosby Show,* enjoyed a successful run on the National Broadcasting Company (NBC) from 1987 to 1993. The half-hour, ensemble situation comedy was the first to immerse an American audience in student life at a histor-ically black college. Over the course of its run, the show was also credited with tackling social and political issues rarely explored in television fiction and opening doors to the television industry for unprecedented numbers of young black actors, writers, producers, and directors.

A Different World, Darryl Bell, Lou Myers, Cree Summers, Glynn Turman, Sinbad, Charnele Brown, Jasmine Guy, Kadeem Hardison, Dawnn Lewis (Season 3), 1987–93. *Courtesy of the Everett Collection*

Set at Hillman College, a fictitious, historically black college in the South, the series began by focusing on the college experiences of sophomore Denise Huxtable (Lisa Bonet)—one of the four daughters featured on *The Cosby Show.* Denise's attempts to adjust to life away from her family's upper-middle-class nest and her relationships with her roommates typically fueled the plot of each episode. One of those roommates, Jaleesa Vinson (Dawnn Lewis), was a young divorcée who considered Denise to be something of a spoiled snob. Another roommate, Maggie Lauten (Marisa Tomei), was one of the few white students on the mostly black campus; for her, as it was for much of the show's audience, Hillman was indeed "a different world." Other recurring characters were added throughout the course of the first season: Whitley Gilbert (Jasmine Guy) was a rich southern belle, Dwayne Wayne (Kadeem Hardison) was a fast-talking but studious New Yorker, Ron Johnson (Darryl Bell)

was Dwayne's scheming sidekick, and Warren Oates (Sinbad) was the dorm director and gym teacher. Bonet and her character, Denise, left the show after the first season because of Bonet's real-life pregnancy.

Despite dismal initial reviews, *A Different World* capitalized from its Thursday at 8:30 P.M. time slot on NBC—between *The Cosby Show* and the ever-popular sitcom *Cheers*—and finished second in the ratings its first season. The show and its creative staff were revamped for the second season, leading to third- and fourth-place finishes for the 1988–89 and 1989–90 seasons, respectively. Among black viewers, the show consistently ranked first or second throughout most of its run.

As *The Hollywood Reporter* noted, the series was transformed "from a bland *Cosby* spin-off into a lively, socially responsible, ensemble situation comedy" only after Debbie Allen took over as producer-director following the first season. Allen, a prominent black dancer, choreographer, and actress—and a graduate of historically black Howard University—drew from her college experiences in an effort to reflect accurately in the show the social and political life on black campuses. Moreover, Allen instituted a yearly spring trip to Atlanta, Georgia, where series writers visited two of the nation's leading black colleges, Morehouse and Spelman. During these visits, ideas for several of the episodes emerged from meetings with students and faculty. Perhaps symbolizing the show's transformation between the first and second seasons, "the queen of soul," Aretha Franklin, was chosen in season two to replace Phoebe Snow as vocalist for the title theme.

During Allen's tenure, casting changes also transformed the look and feel of the series. Several new characters were added, while certain characters from the first season were featured more prominently in order to add some spice. A cafeteria cook, Mr. Gaines (Lou Meyers), was added to give the series a flavor of southern culture. A hardworking, premedical student, Kim Reese (Charnele Brown), was also introduced as a foil for Whitley; she worked for Mr. Gaines in the cafeteria and eventually found herself caught in an on-again, off-again romantic relationship with Ron, one of the original characters. Similarly, Dwayne became entangled in a love-hate relationship with Whitley. Their eventual marriage became a major event in the storyline. Other new characters included Col. Taylor (Glynn Turman), the campus ROTC commander; Freddie Brooks (Cree Summer), an environmental activist with metaphysical leanings; Terrence Taylor (Cory Tyler), the son of Col. Taylor; and Lena James (Jada Pinkett), a feisty freshman from a Baltimore, Maryland, housing project. Each new season brought an incoming class of freshmen and new featured characters. In short, following the departure of Bonet's character after the first season, the series became a true ensemble situation comedy.

A Different World is also notable for its attempts to explore a range of social and political issues rarely addressed on television—let alone in situation comedies. Featured characters regularly confronted such controversial topics as unplanned pregnancy, date rape, racial discrimination, AIDS, and the 1992 Los Angeles uprisings. Many observers also commended the series for extolling the virtues of higher education for African-American youth at a time when many black communities were in crisis.

In the final analysis, *A Different World* might best be remembered for its cultural vibrancy, its commitment to showcasing black history, music, dance, fashion, and attitude. This quality, no doubt, was due in large measure to the closeness of the series' creative staff to the material: the series featured a black woman as producer-director (Allen), another as head writer (Susan Fales), and several other people of color (male and female) in key creative positions. Few series in the history of television can claim a comparable level of black representation in key decision-making positions.

DARNELL M. HUNT

See also **Cosby Show, The**

Cast

Denise Huxtable (1987–88)	Lisa Bonet
Whitley Gilbert	Jasmine Guy
Jaleesa Vinson	Dawnn Lewis
Dwayne Wayne	Kadeem Hardison
Ron Johnson	Darryl Bell
Maggie Lauten (1987–88)	Marisa Tomei
Millie (1987–88)	Marie-Alise Recasner
Stevie Rallen (1987–88)	Loretta Devine
J.T. Rallen (1987–88)	Amir Williams
Gloria (1987–88)	Bee-be Smith
Allison (1987–88)	Kim Wayane
Walter Oakes (1987–91)	Sinbad
Lettie Bostic (1988–89)	Mary Alice
Col. Clayton Taylor (1988–93)	Glynn Turman
Terrence Johann Taylor (1990–92)	Cory Tyler
Winifred "Freddie" Brooks (1988–93)	Cree Summer
Kim Reese (1988–93)	Charnele Brown
Vernon Gaines (1988–93)	Lou Myers
Ernest (1988–90)	Reuben Grundy
Julian (1990–91)	Dominio Hoffman
Lena James (1991–93)	Jada Pinkett
Charmaine Brown (1992–93)	Karen Malina White
Gina Devereaux (1991–92)	Ajai Sanders
Byron Douglas III (1992)	Joe Morton
Shazza Zulu (1992)	Gary Dourdon
Clint (1992–93)	Michael Ralph

Producers

Marcy Carsey, Tom Werner, Anne Beatts, Thad Mumford, Debbie Allen, George Crosby, Lissa Levin

Programming History

144 episodes
NBC

September 1987–June 1992	Thursday 8:30–9:00
July 1991–August 1991	Monday 8:30–9:00
July 1992–November 1992	Thursday 8:00–8:30
November 1992–January 1993	Thursday 8:30–9:00
May 1993–June 1993	Thursday 8:00–8:30
July 1993	Friday 8:00–8:30

Further Reading

Beller, Miles, "A Different World," *The Hollywood Reporter* (September 21, 1989)

Dates, Janette, and William Barlow, editors, *Split Image: African Americans in the Mass Media,* Washington, D.C.: Howard University Press, 1990

"A Different World," *Variety* (October 7, 1987)

Gray, Herman, *Watching Race: Television and the Struggle for "Blackness,"* Minneapolis: University of Minnesota Press, 1995

Haithman, Diane, "Different Touch to *Different World,*" *Los Angeles Times* (October 6, 1988)

Honeycutt, Kirk, "Breaking through the Walls: Tonight *A Different World* Broadcasts Its 100th Episode on NBC," *The Hollywood Reporter* (October 17, 1991)

Letofsky, Irv, "A Different World," *The Hollywood Reporter* (September 24, 1992)

MacDonald, J. Fred, *Blacks and White TV: Afro-Americans in Television since 1948,* Chicago: Nelson-Hall, 1992

McNeil, Alex, *Total Television: A Comprehensive Guide to Programming from 1948 to 1980,* Harmondsworth, England, and New York: Penguin Books, 1980; 4th edition as *Total Television: A Comprehensive Guide to Programming from 1948 to the Present,* New York: Penguin Books, 1996

Vittes, Laurence, "A Different World," *The Hollywood Reporter* (September 20, 1990)

Digital Television

Increasingly, digital technology has been applied to television in the process of producing and transmitting television programming. Television was developed as an "analog" medium, but the replacement of analog technology with digital technology throughout the television production and transmission process promises to increase the capabilities of the medium.

The term "digital" refers to a type of electronic signal in which the information is stored in a sequence of binary numbers ("on" or "off," representing one and zero, respectively) rather than in a continuously varying signal (known as an analog signal). Almost all naturally occurring communication media, including sound and light waves, are analog signals. Because these signals are composed of waves, they are extremely susceptible to interference, as the waves of external, extraneous signals can interact with a specific signal, altering the shape of the wave. Digital signals are much less susceptible to interference because a slightly altered sequence of "on" and "off" can still be read as the original sequence of ones and zeroes.

The primary attributes of a digital signal are the sampling frequency and the bit rate. In order to convert an analog signal to digital, the signal must be "sampled" by measuring the height of the analog signal at discrete points in time. The "sampling frequency" is a measure of how many samples are taken to represent the analog wave. A higher sampling frequency indicates more samples, providing a more faithful reproduction of the analog signal. But doubling the sample rate means doubling the amount of data needed to represent the original analog signal. Bit rate refers to the number of different "bits" (zero/one values) used to represent each sample. A higher bit rate results in a greater number of values for the signal and hence a higher resolution. (Each additional bit doubles the number of values for each signal, so that an eight-bit signal has twice the resolution of a seven-bit signal.) Most digital audio signals use eight or 16 bits of information for each sample.

Digital signals have a number of advantages over analog signals. The primary advantage is that they allow for perfect copies (and perfect copies of copies and so on). Digital signals may also be manipulated by computers, allowing for elaborate modifications of both video and audio signals. The primary drawbacks of digital versus analog signals are that it takes a great deal more space to store digital than it does analog signals and that extra equipment is needed to covert analog video and audio signals to digital and later convert the digital signals back to analog.

Digital technology was first applied to television to create special video effects that were impossible using analog technology. The analog images were digitized, and mathematical algorithms processed the resulting data, allowing a picture to be blown up, shrunk, twisted, and so on. The next innovation was the creation of digital video recorders, which stored television signals as a sequence of binary numbers. Digital video recording is extremely complicated because the sequence of numbers used to represent a single picture required much more storage space than the corresponding analog signal. However, copies of digital signals are exactly the same as the original, enabling higher-quality pictures during the editing process, especially when many signals have to be "layered" together to create a single picture or sequence.

The television production process is gradually moving from a system that interconnects a variety of digital sources with analog equipment to the use of an all-digital environment. Along the way, analog and digital tape formats have been replaced by new digital recording devices similar to computer disk drives, allowing random access to any portion of a recording.

Digital technology has also been applied to the process of transmitting television signals. The bandwidth required for high-definition television required development of a means of transmitting up to five times the video information of a traditional television signal in the same bandwidth. The solution was the application of digital compression technology. Digital compression is the process by which digital signals are simplified by removing redundancy. (For example, each of the 30 individual pictures used to create one second of video is quite similar to the previous picture. Instead of transmitting the entire picture again, some compression algorithms transmit only the parts of the picture that change from one picture to the next.) There are two general types of digital compression: "lossless" compression, in which the decompressed signal is exactly the same as the uncompressed signal, and "lossy" compression, in which the decompressed signal contains less information (or less detail) than the original, uncompressed signal.

The flexibility of digital signals has led many engineers to develop uses for digital broadcasting other than high-definition television. The use of digital compression will allow the transmission of at least four, and perhaps eight or more, standard-definition channels of programming in the same bandwidth required for a single analog channel. Furthermore, the fact that digital signals are less susceptible to interference will eventually allow more television stations on the air in a market. (Interference problems with analog signals requires wide spacing of television stations transmitting on the same or adjacent channels, resulting in the use of only a few channels in most cities to protect stations in nearby cities.)

The flexibility of digital signal transmission has led to the development of 18 varieties of digital television transmission in the United States, ranging from standard-definition images that are comparable to traditional, analog television to high-definition images that provide clarity comparable to 35-millimeter film. In choosing among the 18 formats, U.S. broadcasters must consider tradeoffs between the number of different signals they can transmit simultaneously and the quality of each individual signal. The more signals transmitted, the less information—and lower quality—is available for each channel.

From the viewer's perspective, the primary drawback of digital broadcasting is that it will require viewers to either buy new receivers or obtain adapters to convert digital signals to analog form for viewing on a traditional television receiver. Many cable television subscribers have digital converter boxes that perform such a conversion for digital signals transmitted through a cable television system. Ultimately, the use of television by consumers may be revolutionized as they begin buying digital receivers and digital video recorders and enjoy the quality and flexibility provided by digital technology.

AUGUST GRANT

Further Reading

Alten, S., *Audio in Media* (4th ed.), Belmont, California: Wadsworth, 1994

Seel, P.B., and M. Dupagne, "Digital Television," in *Communication Technology Update* (8th ed.), edited by A.E. Grant and J.H. Meadows, Boston, Massachusetts: Focal Press, 2002

Digital Video Recorder

The brief history to date of the digital video recorder in the United States provides a vivid illustration of the ways in which the prospect of technological innovation can call into question the fundamental business models and cultural assumptions undergirding commercial television. This new digital device combines the time-shifting capabilities of the VCR with the ability to pause or replay the incoming television signal as well as to search for and record programs through an interactive electronic program guide connected by modem to the digital video recorder's provider. Introduced in the United States in 1998 via direct sales from small start-up manufacturers TiVo and Replay TV, the digital video recorder moved to the mass market the following year in the forms of stand-alone set-top boxes sold through consumer electronics retailers and of embedded devices within decoder boxes supplied by satellite broadcasters EchoStar and DirecTV. Contrary to wildly optimistic sales estimates from some early observers, the number of digital video recorders sold through the middle of 2002 was modest (an estimated 1–2 million units), especially compared to the phenomenal commercial success of the DVD player and the growing sales of digital television sets during the same period. However, the digital video recorder's slow penetration into American living rooms has not discouraged extravagant and often apocalyptic predictions of the device's eventual effect on the commercial television industry and on the wider economic assumptions of mass marketing. The slower-than-expected diffusion of the digital video recorder has already provoked new alliances and rivalries within the U.S. television industry and between it and consumer electronics and personal computer industries. For many executives and media pundits, the digital video recorder promised (or threatened) to radically alter the economic value of the traditional 30-second TV commercial, the nature of TV viewing, the expectations of personal privacy, and even the place of the live television broadcast as token and tool of national identity. Given its contested status, it is not surprising that the digital video recorder has been greeted by threatened and actual lawsuits from Hollywood studios and commercial networks and by attempts to draft federal legislation to restrict its use.

To many observers, the relatively slow consumer acceptance of the digital video recorders reflected the difficulty of marketing a genuinely new domestic appliance, one distinguished by several distinct and unprecedented features. The digital video recorder, despite its name, is not a simple functional replacement for the VCR, which was found in 90 percent of U.S. homes by 2002. Despite the VCR's long-standing capacity to time-shift broadcast programs, most households use the device nearly exclusively for the playback of prerecorded tapes (only 4 percent of total TV viewing time in the United States is devoted to the playback of recorded television programs). Thus, while U.S. sales of DVD players exceeded those of VCRs for the first time in 2001, suggesting that the VCR's role as a playback platform for prerecorded material was in eclipse, the technological shift of the VCR's time-shifting function to the digital video recorder is less certain. Much of the debate about the economic and cultural implications of the digital video recorder concerns the extent to which consumers will take up the novel features of the new digital device, including the ability to pause and perform "instant replays" of an incoming TV signal, instantaneously scan through commercials of recorded programs, and seek out and record programming via an interactive electronic program guide that can learn and anticipate viewing habits (and sell such information to advertisers). While the commercial-scanning capabilities of the traditional VCR are already familiar, recently enhanced by the widely licensed Commercial Advance technology, which automatically speeds through recorded commercials on playback, when Replay TV's manufacturer announced that its 2002 model would be equipped with the same licensed feature, it was sued by a group of TV networks and production studios even before the new digital video recorders hit the market. Although the number of digital video recorder–equipped homes is still quite small, survey data suggest that most consumers routinely use the devices to evade commercials, and a large percentage report watching much less "live" TV generally. Likewise, the diffusion of the digital video recorder is widely expected to undermine the economic value of a network brand identity and challenge conventional notions of program flow, schedule, and day part as viewers select programs without regard to the channel or hour they are offered. More broadly, some observers have worried that the decline of "live" reception at the hands of the digital video recorder would weaken network broadcasting's traditional function as agent of

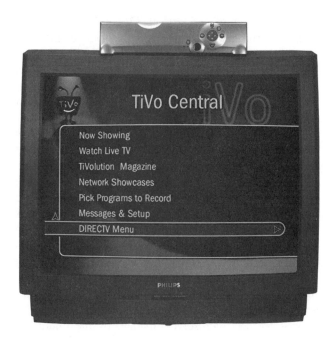

© 2001 Tivo Inc.

national identity and community. Many observers have argued that the ease with which viewers armed with digital video recorders might avoid viewing traditional TV commercials would lead to a proliferation of more invasive advertising techniques, including product placement, banner ads, and advertiser-supplied programming, though more sanguine observers argue that TV viewers will remain interested in viewing commercials that are more carefully designed to appeal to them. They point to TiVo's announcement that the segment of the 2002 Super Bowl broadcast that TiVo users most frequently selected for instant replay was not the last-minute winning field goal or any on-field action but instead a halftime Pepsi commercial featuring performer Britney Spears. In any event, the patterns of use among today's early adopters of the digital video recorder may be of little predictive power as the technology becomes more widely diffused.

Meanwhile, the business models and hardware platforms on which the digital video recorder will eventually be based remain unsettled. TiVo, the U.S. market leader, draws on distinct revenue paths of monthly subscriptions, manufacturing and licensing royalties, and advertising revenues generated from its electronic program guide and dedicated advertising programming. The experience of the U.S. computer software giant Microsoft suggests the uncertain market for the digital video recorder; Microsoft integrated digital video recorder capability into its existing WebTV service in the 2001 launch of its Ultimate TV service, only to retreat from the market in the face of consumer indifference at the beginning of 2002. Replay TV, like TiVo, a late 1990s Silicon Alley start-up, burned through its original capital before being acquired by Sonic Blue in 2001, and its products have not yet been successful in mass-market terms. Internationally, the only other significant market for the digital video recorder to date has been the United Kingdom, where the devices are found in less than 1 percent of homes both in the form of TiVo stand-alone models and as part of enhanced set-top boxes from Rupert Murdoch's Sky satellite service. One fundamental unsettled issue in the digital video recorder market in the United States and abroad is whether the technology will reach consumers as single-purpose devices or be integrated into the set-top boxes provided by satellite broadcasters and cable operators or instead be integrated into DVD players, video game consoles, personal computers, new "home entertainment servers," or simply TV sets themselves. In fact, by the middle of 2002, the largest single supplier of digital video recorders in the United States was the satellite broadcaster EchoStar, which was expected to place 1 million recorders in the homes of its 6 million satellite TV subscribers. At this point in the product cycle, the crucial market for digital video recorder manufacturers may be less the electronics retailer and individual consumer than the handful of major cable operators who are currently rolling out enhanced digital cable backbones and household devices for millions of U.S. homes. In sum, while the ultimate consumer appeal of the unique features of the digital video recorder seems ensured (as does the digital video recorder's potential to supply broadcasters and advertisers a more targeted audience), the specific mix of industry players, revenue models, and hardware platforms associated with the device are still unresolved. Furthermore, the validity of the often-extravagant predictions of the economic and social impact of the technology will take some time to be fully tested. Even if those effects turn out to be slower and more diffused than the most alarmist observers have predicted, they promise to revise the way in which commercial television is funded and consumed in the United States in significant ways.

WILLIAM BODDY

See also **Advertising; Digital Television; Interactive Television; Satellite; Videocassette; WebTV**

Further Reading

"Big Brother Is You, Watching," *The Economist* (April 13, 2002)

Brown, Roger, and Jeff Baumgartner, "Probing the Minds of Cable's Braintrust: Five of the Industry's Best and Brightest Discuss Their Agendas for Advanced Services Such as iTV, VOD, HDTV, VoIP and Home Networking," *Communications Engineering and Design* (May 1, 2002)

Fyffe, Steven, "Home Ownership; Who Controls the Household Entertainment Hub?," *CommVerge* (May 1, 2002)

Kovsky, Steve, *High-Tech Toys for Your TV: Secrets of TiVo, Xbox, ReplayTV, UltimateTV and More,* New York: Que, 2002

Lewis, Michael, *Next: The Future Just Happened,* New York, W.W. Norton, 2001

Diller, Barry (1942–)

U.S. Media Executive

For more than four decades, Barry Diller has played a prominent role in redefining the television industry. Widely regarded as both an innovative programmer and an expert deal maker, Diller's influence on the media industries has been widely felt. Among his impressive list of accomplishments, he has helped developed new television formats, launched the careers of several leading executives including Michael Eisner and Jeffrey Katzenberg, and created a viable fourth network, FOX, which went on to challenge the dominance of the American Broadcasting Company (ABC), the Columbia Broadcasting System (CBS), and the National Broadcasting Company (NBC).

Diller began his career in 1961, when he dropped out of the University of California, Los Angeles (UCLA), and began work in the mail room of the William Morris agency. He moved up the ranks quickly, becoming an assistant and then junior agent for the talent firm. In 1966, he began his first job in the television industry as an assistant to Leonard Goldberg at ABC. At the age of

26, he became head of programming, responsible for negotiating with the major studios for broadcast rights to feature films.

In 1969, Diller inaugurated ABC's *Movie of the Week,* a regular series of 90-minute films made exclusively for television. Made-for-television movies (MFTs) had aired sporadically since the mid-1960s; however, it was with Diller's influence that they became a regular fixture on ABC's schedule. Under his supervision, MFTs focused increasingly on social issues, such as homosexuality (*That Certain Summer,* 1972), the Vietnam War (*The Ballad of Andy Crocker,* 1969), and drugs (*Go Ask Alice,* 1973). In addition to providing a huge ratings boost to ABC, MFTs could be produced quickly and cheaply. A typical program was made for approximately $350,000—and often fared better in the Nielsen ratings than a theatrically released film.

Diller remained at ABC through the early 1970s, moving up to become vice president of entertainment. In addition to his supervision of MFTs, Diller also became involved in the development of the network's miniseries. Prior to his departure from ABC in 1974, he approved the production of the ambitious courtroom drama *QB VII.* Shortly thereafter, Diller moved on to become chair of Paramount Pictures, where he supervised the studio's film and television divisions.

During his ten years at the Gulf 1 Western subsidiary Paramount Pictures, Diller managed a studio operating at its peak. Diller and his top-rate executive staff—which included Jeffrey Katzenberg, Don Simpson, and Michael Eisner—generated an impressive list of critical and commercial successes, including *Saturday Night Fever* (1977), *Grease* (1978), *Star Trek* (1979), *Raiders of the Lost Ark* (1981), *Reds* (1981), *Terms of Endearment* (1983), and *Beverly Hills Cop* (1984). The company had an equally remarkable string of television hits; its programs included *Laverne and Shirley* (1976–83), *Taxi* (1978–83), *Family Ties* (1982–89), and *Cheers* (1982–93).

Following the death of Gulf 1 Western's head, Charles Bluhdorn, and the ascension of Martin S. Davis, Diller left Paramount to become chair of 20th Century-Fox. On arriving at FOX, Diller found the studio to be a financial mess. Matters were worsened by the unwillingness of the company's owner, Marvin Davis (no relation to Martin), to put the necessary funds back into the studio. Diller subsequently turned to Australian newspaper mogul Rupert Murdoch for financial support; Murdoch ultimately assumed full ownership of the studio in 1985.

With Murdoch's backing, Diller not only put the studio back on solid financial ground but also spearheaded the company's launch of a fourth broadcast network. Whereas Gulf 1 Western had previously

Barry Diller.
Photo courtesy of USA Interactive

blocked Diller's efforts to create a fourth network, Murdoch enthusiastically provided him with the means to buy major market television stations, recruit experienced executives, and compensate top creative figures. Though the new network's early years were bumpy, by the time Diller left the company in February 1992, the FOX network had become competitive with the "Big Three." With younger-skewing hit programs such as *In Living Color, Married... with Children,* and *The Simpsons,* FOX had successfully branded itself as the "alternative" network.

Despite the fact that he was the only executive at the time to oversee both a movie studio and a television network, ultimately Diller wanted more. Shortly after his 50th birthday, he left FOX to become an entrepreneur who owned his "own store." Diller spent the next several months traveling across the United States, visiting with numerous executives from computer, cable, and high-tech firms. His travels ended with his arrival at home shopping channel QVC, where he invested $25 million and became chair of the company. Though publicly professing his newfound faith in the future of "transactional" television, his own business transactions were repeatedly aborted during his time at QVC. First, antitrust concerns halted his effort to merge QVC and the Home Shopping Network (HSN), and then Viacom outbid him for Paramount. Diller's reign at QVC ended in the summer of 1994 after he was unable to complete a sale of his new company to CBS because of objections by key QVC investors.

His next venture into home shopping would prove to be much more enduring. In August 1995, Diller started the lengthy process of building his next media company by becoming a 20 percent equity partner—and head—of HSN. In this new position, he also controlled Silver King Communications, a group of UHF and low-power television stations.

Although the initial holdings of HSN were relatively limited, Diller quickly began acquiring an interest in a variety of media companies, including Savoy Pictures Entertainment, the Internet Shopping Network, and Ticketmaster. A series of relatively minor purchases culminated with a major deal with Seagram's chief executive office, Edgar Bronfman, in the fall of 1997. Through a series of complicated exchanges of assets and cash, Diller's company acquired Seagram's television holdings, including the Universal television production arm and the USA and Sci-Fi cable channels. Seagram retained a 45 percent interest in the newly formed operation, which was called USA Networks. In discussing his rationale for making the deal, Bronfman explained that it was "the only way I could be in business with Barry Diller."

At the helm of USA Networks, Diller continued to explore the relationships that could be forged between broadcasting and cable, production and distribution, and new media and old. He repeatedly spoke of the need for a fresh business model for media in which revenue would be generated from a combination of advertisements, subscriptions, and direct sales. Recognizing the increasing fragmentation of the marketplace, he sought to develop brands that could be promoted across a number of different media holdings. In television, his vision was realized with the Universal-produced *Law & Order: Special Victims Unit.* Original episodes of the program aired on NBC and then were re-aired less than two weeks later on the USA cable channel.

Diller's involvement with USA proved profitable. In 2000, Vivendi acquired Universal from Seagram, thereby assuming the 45 percent stake in USA Networks. Then, in December 2001, Diller sold back the Universal assets to Vivendi for $10.3 billion, thereby getting back more than double the amount he had originally paid. Despite Diller's earlier declarations that he would never work for anyone again, he continued to remain on Vivendi's payroll, serving as chief executive of the newly formed Vivendi Universal Entertainment. At the same time, he also remained in control of his own company, which was rechristened USA Interac-

tive and focused almost exclusively on accumulating Internet assets.

The relationship between Diller and Vivendi-Universal became more complex as Vivendi faced mounting financial difficulties. Management shake-ups at Vivendi led Diller to assume the title of interim chief executive officer during late 2002. He retained this position until March 2003, when he resigned to focus on USA Interactive (which was then renamed InterActiveCorp). His involvement with Universal continued indirectly, as InterActive held a 5.4 percent stake in its assets and Diller personally held a 1.5 percent interest.

As of early 2003, Diller had departed from television industry, only to emerge as a vocal critic of its trade practices. He issued a general call for re-regulation as a means of combating what he perceived to be excessive media concentration. In addition, Diller argued for the return of the financial interest and syndication rules—the very rules that he had been integral in helping eliminate during his time at FOX in the late 1980s and early 1990s.

With television behind him, Diller attended to building InterActive, which continued to expand its role in information and services, e-commerce, and travel-oriented online properties. By developing such holdings as Expedia, Hotels.com, Match.com, CitySearch, and Lending Tree, InterActive ranked first growth among Fortune 500 companies—surpassing Amazon.com, eBay, and Yahoo! in revenue and standing as one of the few online companies to consistently turn a profit.

ALISA PERREN

See also **American Broadcasting Company; Eisner, Michael; FOX Broadcasting Company; Financial Interest and Syndication Rules; Home Shopping; Movies On Television; Murdoch, Rupert K.; Vivendi Universal**

Barry Diller. Born in San Francisco, California, February 2, 1942. Married: Diane von Furstenberg. Mail room, William Morris agency, 1961; assistant to agent, William Morris agency, 1964; assistant to vice president in charge of programming, ABC, 1966; executive assistant to vice president in programming and director of feature films, ABC, 1968; vice president, feature films and program development, ABC, 1969; created TV movies of the week and miniseries as vice president, feature films, Circle Entertainment, division of ABC, 1971; vice president, prime-time entertainment, ABC, 1973; board chair and president, Paramount Pictures, 1974; president, Gulf 1 Western Entertainment and Communications Group (while retaining Paramount titles), 1983; resigned from Paramount and joined 20th Century-Fox as board chair and chief executive officer, 1984; chair and chief executive officer, Fox, Inc., 1985;

named to board, News Corp. Ltd, June 1987; resigned from 20th Century-Fox, February 1992; chairman and chief executive officer, QVC Network, 1992; resigned from QVC, December 1994; chairman of board, Home Shopping Network, August 1995; chairman and chief executive officer of HSN, Inc. (formed by merger of Silver King Communications, Home Shopping Network, and Savoy Pictures Entertainment), December 1996; chairman and chief executive officer, USA Networks, February 1998; chairman and chief executive officer, Vivendi Universal Entertainment (while retaining title of chair and chief executive officer of reformulated USA Networks, renamed USA Interactive and operating as a stand-alone entity), December 2001; Interim co–chief executive officer, Vivendi Universal (while retaining previous titles), November 2002; resigned from Vivendi Universal positions, March 2003; chairman and chief executive officer, InterActiveCorp (renamed from USA Interactive), 2003. Board of directors: the Washington Post Company; the Coca-Cola Company; Conservation International; Channel 13/WNET. Trustee: New York University. Executive board: Medical Sciences at UCLA. Board of Councilors, School of Cinema-Television, University of Southern California.

Further Reading

Block, Alex Ben, *Outfoxed: Marvin Davis, Barry Diller, Rupert Murdoch, Joan Rivers and the Inside Story of America's Fourth Television Network,* New York: St. Martin's, 1990

Boliek, Brooks, "Diller Warns Broadcasters about Perils of Deregulation," *Hollywood Reporter,* (April 8, 2003)

Grover, Ronald, and Tom Lowry, "The New Barry Diller," *BusinessWeek* (September 10, 2001)

Mair, George, *The Barry Diller Story,* New York: Wiley, 1997

Mermigas, Diane, "Small Pieces All Add Up for Diller," *Electronic Media* (February 1, 1999)

Mullaney, Timothy J., and Ronald Grover, "The Web Mogul," *BusinessWeek* (October 13, 2003)

Rose, Frank, "Barry Diller Has No Vision for the Future of the Internet," *Wired* (April 2003)

Thompson, Anne, "The Man Who Would Be King," *Premiere* (May 2003)

Dimbleby, Richard (1913–1965)

British Broadcast Journalist

Richard Dimbleby was the personification of British television current affairs broadcasting in the 1950s and early 1960s, and he set the standard for succeeding generations of presenters on the network, by whom he was recognized as the virtual founder of broadcast journalism. After working on the editorial staff of several newspapers, he joined the British Broadcasting Corporation (BBC) as a radio news observer in 1936. When war broke out three years later, he became the BBC's first war correspondent, and, as such, within the constraints of often stifling official censorship, he brought the reality of warfare into homes throughout the length and breadth of Great Britain. Notably graphic broadcasts included dispatches from the battlefield of Al-Alamein and from the beaches of Normandy during the D-Day landings and a report sent back from a Royal Air Force bomber on a raid over Germany (in all, he flew as an observer on some 20 missions). He was also the first radio reporter to reach the concentration camp at Belsen, from which he sent a moving account of what he saw, and he was the first to enter Berlin.

After the war, Dimbleby worked as a freelance broadcaster and made the switch to television, in time becoming the BBC's best-known commentator on current affairs and state events. Among the important state occasions he covered were the coronation of Elizabeth II in 1953 and the funerals of John F. Kennedy and Sir Winston Churchill. The coronation broadcast was a particular personal triumph, establishing Dimbleby as the first-choice commentator on all state events and, incidentally, promoting television sales by some 50 percent. Other milestones in his career included his participation in 1951 in the first Eurovision television relay and, in 1961, his appearance in the first live television broadcast from the Soviet Union.

In 1955, Dimbleby was selected as anchor for the much-respected current affairs program *Panorama,* and it is with this show that his name is usually associated. Quizzing politicians of all colors with equal severity on behalf of the nation, he was praised by many as a defender of the public interest and became almost synonymous with the BBC itself as a bastion of fairness and perspicuity in political debate. Under Dimbleby's direction, *Panorama* established itself as the current affairs program par excellence, the weekly showing almost a political event itself, raising issues that Parliament hastened to address in order to show that it was responsive to the electorate thus represented.

Viewers hung on the presenter's every word and besieged him with letters, begging him to use his evident influence to intervene personally in political issues of all kinds, from proposals for new roads to the Cuban missile crisis. One rare remark that did not go down so well was an infamous aside, "Jesus wept," which was unfortunately picked up by the microphone and prompted a stream of letters criticizing him for blasphemy.

Dimbleby did, however, also tackle lighter fare and was much loved as chair of the radio program *Twenty Questions* and as presenter of the homely *Down Your Way* series, in which he sought out prominent members of a given locality and passed the time of day with them. His standing with the British listening and viewing public was officially honored in 1945, when he was made an Officer of the British Empire, and again in 1959, when he was promoted to Companion of the British Empire.

Dimbleby's premature death from cancer at the age of 52, shortly after broadcasting to 350 million people on the state funeral of Winston Churchill, was regretted by millions of viewers, and subsequently the annual Richard Dimbleby lectures were established in his memory. These were not his only legacy, however, for two of his sons, David and Jonathan, pursued similar careers in current affairs broadcasting and in their turn became two of the most familiar faces on British screens, earning reputations as fair but tough-minded interrogators of the political leaders of their generation. David Dimbleby emulated his father by, in 1974, becoming anchorman of *Panorama*, while Richard Dimbleby has occupied a similar role on such current affairs programs as *This Week* and *First Tuesday*.

DAVID PICKERING

See also **Panorama**

Richard Dimbleby. Born in Richmond-upon-Thames, London, England, May 25, 1913. Attended Mill Hill School, London. Married: Dilys, 1937; children: Jonathan, David, Nicholas, and Sally. Began career with the family newspaper, *The Richmond and Twickenham Times,* 1931; subsequently worked for the *Bournemouth Echo* and as news editor for *Advertisers Weekly,* 1935–36; joined BBC Topical Talks department as one of the first radio news reporters, 1936; accompanied British Expeditionary Force to France as first BBC war correspondent, 1939; reported from front line in Middle East, East Africa, the Western Desert, and Greece, 1939–42; flew about 20 missions with Royal Air Force Bomber Command and was first reporter to enter Belsen concentration camp, 1945; after war, became foremost commentator on state occasions, including coronation of Elizabeth II, 1953, and funeral of Winston Churchill, 1965; managing director, Dimbleby newspaper business, from 1954; presenter of BBC's *Panorama,* 1955–63. Officer of the Order of the British Empire, 1945; Commander of the Order of the British Empire, 1959. Died in London, December 22, 1965.

Television Series

1955–63   *Panorama*

Radio

Twenty Questions; Down Your Way; Off the Record.

Further Reading

Dimbleby, Jonathan, *Richard Dimbleby: A Biography,* London: Hodder and Stoughton, 1975

Miall, Leonard, *Inside the BBC: British Broadcasting Characters,* London: Weidenfeld and Nicholson, 1994

Milne, Alasdair, *DG: Memoirs of a British Broadcaster,* London: Hodder and Stoughton, 1988

Trethowan, Ian, *Split Screen,* London: H. Hamilton, 1984

Dinah Shore Show, The (Various)

U.S. Music-Variety Show

A popular radio and television performer for more than 40 years, Dinah Shore was known for the warmth of her personality and for her sincere, unaffected stage presence. Television favored her natural, relaxed style,

and like Perry Como, to whom she was often compared, Shore was one of the medium's first popular singing stars. Even though by her own admission Dinah Shore did not have a great voice, she put it to good advantage by enunciating lyrics clearly and singing the melody without distracting ornamentation. The result was the very definition of "easy listening."

By the time Shore first appeared on television, she was already well known as a big-band singer and radio performer. In 1952, she was chosen most popular female vocalist by a Gallup poll. She was also appearing in the best nightclubs, making motion pictures, and selling approximately 2 million phonograph records per year. Shore's subsequent two decades of television work merely enhanced her already remarkable career.

Dinah Shore first appeared on television in 1951, when she began a twice a week program over the National Broadcasting Company (NBC). This 15-minute show was broadcast on Tuesday and Thursday evenings at 7:30. Jack Gould, the *New York Times* radio and television critic, enthused about the program, "Last week on her initial appearance, she was the picture of naturalness and conducted her show with a disarming combination of authority and humility."

The 15-minute program was produced by Alan Handley, who made a special effort to make the musical production numbers interesting. The imaginative backdrops he provided for Shore's songs were inspired by travel posters, *New Yorker* cartoons, history, literary classics, and Hollywood. Handley often checked department store window displays and went to the theater to get ideas for these numbers. On one occasion, he used a Georgia O'Keefe painting of a bleached cattle skull as a backdrop for a song called "Cow Cow Boogie." On another occasion, he made a living Alexander Calder–inspired mobile out of his vocal quintet "The Notables" by suspending them from the ceiling of the studio.

In 1956, Shore began a one-hour program on NBC, *The Dinah Shore Chevy Show.* The program was extremely popular, and its theme song, "See the USA in Your Chevrolet," always ending with Shore's famous farewell kiss to the television audience, remains a television icon. The high production values of her 15-minute program continued on the 60-minute show. The lineup usually contained two or three guests drawn from the worlds of music, sports, and movies. Shore was able to make almost any performer feel comfortable and could bring together such unlikely pairings as Frank Sinatra and baseball star Dizzy Dean.

The Dinah Shore Chevy Show was produced in Burbank, California, by Bob Banner, who also directed each episode. The choreographer was Tony Charmoli, who occasionally danced on camera. Often the production numbers took advantage of special visual effects. For "76 Trombones," Banner used prisms mounted in front of the television cameras to turn 12 musicians into several dozen. The number was so popular that it was repeated on two subsequent occasions. For "Flim

The Dinah Shore Show, Dinah Shore, 1951–56.
Courtesy of the Everett Collection

Flam Floo," Banner used the chromakey so that objects appeared and disappeared, and actors floated through the air without the aid of wires. In his review of the opening show of 1959, Gould called the program "a spirited and tuneful affair." Shore, he wrote, "sang with the warmth and infectious style that are so distinctly her own," and he judged that she "continues to be the best-dressed woman in television."

Shore's musical variety program went off the air in May 1963. After that time, she appeared in a number of specials and later did a series of interview shows in the 1970s, including *Dinah!, Dinah and Friends, Dinah and Her New Best Friends,* and *Dinah's Place.* Throughout her career, Shore remained one of the great women of the entertainment world.

HENRY B. ALDRIDGE

See also **Shore, Dinah**

The Dinah Shore Show

Regular Performers
Dinah Shore
The Notables, quintet (1951–55)
The Skylarks, quintet (1955–57)

Dinah Shore Show, The (Various)

Music
Ticker Freeman, Piano
The Vic Schoen Orchestra (1951–54)
The Harry Zimmerman Orchestra (1954–57)

Producer
Alan Handley

Programming History
NBC
November 1951–July 1957   Tuesday and
                                                     Thursday 7:30–7:45

The Dinah Shore Chevy Show

Regular Performers
Dinah Shore
The Skylarks, quintet (1956–57)
The Even Dozen (1961–62)

Dancers
The Tony Charmoli Dancers (1957–62)
The Nick Castle Dancers (1962–63)

Music
The Harry Zimmerman Orchestra (1957–61,
   1962–63)
Frank DeVol and His Orchestra (1961–62)

Producer
Bob Banner

Programming History
NBC
October 1956–June 1957   Friday 10:00–11:00
October 1957–June 1961   Sunday 9:00–10:00
October 1961–June 1962   Friday 9:30–10:30
December 1962–
   May 1963   Sunday 10:00–11:00

Further Reading
"Dinah Shore's TV Art," *Look* (December 15, 1953)
Eells, G., "Dinah Shore," *Look* (December 6, 1960)

Dingo, Ernie (1956–)

Australian Actor

Ernie Dingo is an aboriginal Australian actor who has had an extensive career in film and television. Best known to international audiences through his film roles as Charlie in *Crocodile Dundee II* and as the Australian detective who chases William Hurt around the globe in Wim Wenders's *Until the End of the World,* Dingo has also become a familiar and popular figure on Australian television.

Dingo's television career is particularly significant for the way it has broken new ground in the medium's presentation of cultural difference. Initially taking roles scripted specifically for an aboriginal actor by white writers and directors, he has worked consistently to broaden expectations of what aboriginality can include and to introduce and popularize an understanding of aboriginal perspectives on Australian life.

Ernie Dingo grew up around the small Western Australian town of Mullewa, where the local aboriginal people still speak the traditional Wudjadi language. He first moved into acting in Perth when a basketball team to which he belonged formed a dance and cultural performance group, Middar. From there, he moved into stage roles in plays by Western Australian aboriginal playwright Jack Davis before gaining a role in the television miniseries *Cowra Breakout* (1985) by Kennedy Miller for the Channel 10 network. Dingo's background in traditional and contemporary aboriginal culture have been important to his work in television because, as he points out, working as an aboriginal actor frequently involves working also (usually informally) as a consultant, cultural mediator, co-writer, and translator.

Dingo's first major screen roles were in film in *Tudawali* (1985), *Fringe Dwellers* (1986), and *State of Shock* (1989), all of which had white script writers and directors but dealt sympathetically with problems of racism and disadvantage encountered by aboriginal people. All three were small-release productions designed substantially for television adaptation and/or distribution. In 1988, he was awarded the Special Jury Prize at the Banff Television Festival for his powerful performance as one of Australia's first aboriginal screen actors, Robert Tudawali, in *Tudawali*.

One of Dingo's main skills as an actor is an ability to engage audiences with an open, easy screen presence and use of humor while also capturing serious moods dramatically and convincingly. It is perhaps this versatility, above all, that has made him highly effective as a cross-cultural communicator. Dingo's ability with lighter roles was first demonstrated by his performances in children's drama series, including *Clowning Around* (1992) and *A Waltz through the Hills* (1990), for which he received an Australian Film Institute award for best actor in a telefeature for his performance as an aboriginal bushman, Frank Watson.

However, his first emergence as a popular figure of mainstream commercial television occurred with his inclusion in the comedy-variety program *Fast Forward*. He is particularly remembered for his comic impersonation of prominent financial commentator Robert Gottliebsen, in which he imitated Gottliebsen's manner and appearance but translated his analysis of movements in share prices and exchange rates into colloquial aboriginal English.

From *Fast Forward*, Dingo has moved on to roles in other popular programs, such as *The Great Outdoors* and *Heartbreak High*. The latter two roles, as well as his role in *Fast Forward*, are significant because they are not clearly marked as specifically aboriginal. In *The Great Outdoors*, Dingo appears alternately with other well-known Australian television personalities as a compere, or master of ceremonies, in light feature stories about leisure, travel, and the environment. In *Heartbreak High*, he appeared as Vic, a media studies teacher at multicultural Hartley High. Both roles have done much to normalize the appearance of aboriginal people on Australian television and have provided an important counter to the often-fraught treatment of aboriginal issues in news and current affairs.

Dingo has also continued with serious dramatic roles with a major role as an aboriginal police liaison officer, Vincent Burraga, in the Australian Broadcasting Corporation's highly acclaimed drama series *Heartland*. The series was in many ways groundbreaking, not only in its inclusion of aboriginal people in script writing and production and frequent adoption of aboriginal perspectives but also for its naturalistic treatment of a cross-cultural romance between Vincent and white urbanite Elizabeth Ashton (Cate Blanchett). The series' ability to negotiate issues of cultural and political sensitivity was significantly dependent on Dingo's skills and magnetic screen presence.

Ernie Dingo has been acclaimed by some as one of Australia's finest contemporary actors. In addition, he has established a place as a major figure in extending mainstream awareness and understanding of aboriginal Australia.

MARK GIBSON

See also **Heartbreak High**

Ernie Dingo. Born July 31, 1956. Married to Sally Dingo; two children: Willard and Jurra. Began career as part of the Middar Aboriginal Dance Theatre, 1978; had various stage roles; in television, from 1985; appearances in episodes of *The Flying Doctors, Relative Merits, Rafferty's Rules, The Dirtwater Dynasty,* and *GP;* in film, from 1985; currently host of travel magazine television series, *The Great Outdoors.* Recipient: Banff Television Festival special prize; Australian Film Institute Award, 1990; National Aboriginal and Islander Day of Observance (NAIDOC) Aboriginal of the Year, 1994. Order of Australia, 1990.

Television Series

1987	*Relative Merits*
1990	*Dolphin Cove*
1989–93	*Fast Forward*
1992	*Clowning Around*
1993	*The Great Outdoors*
1994	*Heartland*
1994–95	*Heartbreak High*

Television Miniseries

1985	*Cowra Breakout*
1990	*A Waltz through the Hills*

Made-for-Television Movies

1986	*The Blue Lightning*

Films

Tudawali, 1985; *The Fringe Dwellers,* 1986; *Crocodile Dundee II,* 1988; *Cappuccino,* 1988; *State of Shock,* 1989; *Until the End of the World,* 1991; *Blackfellas,* 1993; *Mr. Electric,* 1993; *Deadheart,* 1996; *The Echo of Thunder,* 1998.

Dingo, Ernie

Further Reading

Coolwell, Wayne, *My Kind of People,* St. Lucia: University of Queensland Press, 1993

Lewis, Berwyn, "Comedian with a Sting," *Australia Now* (1993)

McKee, Alan, "Ernie Dingo: Reconciliation (A Love Story Forged against the Odds?)," *Australian Studies,* Vol. 14, Nos. 1–2 (1999)

van Nunen, Linda, "The Games Ernie Plays," *Australian Magazine* (January 1991)

Direct Broadcast Satellite

Satellite Delivery Technology

Direct Broadcast Satellite (DBS) is one of two direct-to-home (DTH) satellite-delivered program services meant for home reception. DTH programming is, in most respects, the same as that available to cable television subscribers. However, DTH subscribers access their programs not from terrestrial cable systems but rather directly from telecommunications satellites stationed in geosynchronous orbit approximately 22,000 miles above the Earth. Like cable systems, DTH program suppliers package a variety of program service channels and market them to prospective DTH subscribers for a monthly fee.

The second DTH service, and the older of the two, was originally referred to as TVRO (for "television receive only"), but now it is more commonly known as "C-band" service. C-band households (of which there were approximately 1 million in 2001) receive programming via a satellite dish that measures between six and eight feet in diameter; this programming is transmitted from a satellite transponder at low power (10–17 watts) in the 3.7- to 4.2-GHz frequency range, a range that occupies a portion of the frequency spectrum known as the C-band. C-band customers receive some unscrambled programming but may also subscribe to a package of scrambled (called "encrypted") program services for a monthly fee. Some 250 program channels provided by about 20 satellites were available to C-band customers in 2001.

DBS is the newer DTH service and by far the most popular, comprising a U.S. customer base (in 2001) of nearly 16 million households. Two DBS providers—DirecTV, owned by Hughes Electronics, and the DISH Network, owned by EchoStar Communications—provide similar program packages to their customers, all available via a receiving dish that measures about 18 inches in diameter. DBS programming is delivered by satellite transponders operating in the 12.2- to 12.7-GHz portion of the frequency spectrum (called the Ku band) and transmitted at a power range that may exceed 100 watts. The higher power allows a more directed satellite-to-receiver signal and, thus, requires a much smaller receiver dish than is required for C-band reception.

The origins of DBS date to 1975, when Home Box Office (HBO) first utilized a satellite to deliver its program service to local cable television systems. Numerous individuals, especially those living in rural areas beyond the reach of cable television, erected TVRO dishes on their property and accessed whatever programming they wanted as it flowed from satellites. Program suppliers soon objected to free receipt of their product by TVRO owners. As a result, HBO and similar services began scrambling their signals in 1985. TVRO owners thereafter were required to pay a subscription fee to receive such programming.

The first effort to create a true DBS service in the United States occurred in 1980, when the Satellite Television Corporation (STC) proposed such a service to the Federal Communications Commission (FCC). The FCC approved STC's proposal and invited other companies to propose DBS services. Of the 13 companies that responded to the FCC, proposals from eight of them (including such electronics industry giants as Western Union and Radio Corporation of America [RCA]) eventually were approved. By the early 1990s, however, the high start-up cost of establishing a DBS service (estimated at more than $1 billion) had forced many of the original DBS applicants either to delay or to abandon their projects altogether. DBS companies were uncertain that program suppliers that heretofore had provided programming exclusively to cable systems would extend their services to DBS. That matter was settled when the Cable Television Consumer Protection and Competition Act of 1992 prohibited cable

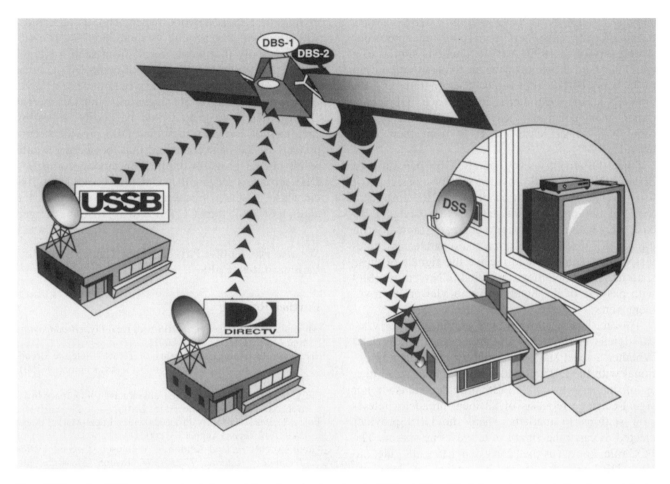

How DBS works: DBS programming is beamed from broadcast centers to DBS satellites. Digital programming is then beamed down from satellites to the 18-inch satellite dish attached to the side of a home. A set-top receiver picks up the programming signals. *Illustration courtesy of DIRECTV*

program suppliers from refusing to sell their services to DBS operators.

FCC permission to launch DBS services included satellite transponder (or transmitter) assignment and DBS orbital slot assignment. Satellites providing a DBS service are allowed to occupy eight orbital slots positioned at 61.5, 101, 110, 119, 148, 157, 166, and 175 degrees west longitude.

A consortium of cable television system owners launched the first-generation DBS service, called Primestar, in July 1991. Ten years later and after the appearance and subsequent merger of several upstart DBS companies, only DirecTV, serving some 10 million customers, and DISH Network, serving some 6 million customers, were operating. However, the customer base of these two DBS services combined now accounted for a nearly 16 percent share of the national multichannel video program distribution (MVPD) market. Cable TV systems controlled about 80 percent of that market, but cable has been losing market share

over the years to its more aggressive DBS competitor. DBS subscribership, in fact, grew at nearly three times cable's growth rate between June 1999 and June 2000. DBS growth has been most pronounced in rural areas where cable has not yet penetrated and among disenchanted former cable customers or customers new to the MVPD marketplace. Significant numbers of C-band customers also have been moving to DBS in recent years.

The cost for DBS service will vary somewhat, but the cost of equipment purchase and installation (in 2001 figures) is about $300, and the monthly subscription fee is approximately $55 for a 130-channel program package. Both DirecTV and DISH Network subscription fees and program packages are comparable. DBS customers also have access through broadband capabilities to high-definition television (HDTV) as well as high-speed connection to the World Wide Web. DBS does offer pay-per-view (PPV) programming, but it is not yet capable of providing video-on-demand (VOD). As a VOD substitute, DBS services began offering customers a personal video recorder (PVR) service in 1999. A PVR functions similar to a computer hard drive, allowing customers to record up to 35 hours of DBS-delivered PPV programming for viewing at the customer's convenience. DBS customers must either purchase their PVR at a cost of roughly $400 or lease the PVR from their DBS provider.

Since the industry's beginnings, DBS had suffered in the inability of DBS providers to carry the signals of local broadcast television stations to DBS customers living in markets where the stations were located. DBS customers had to either use "rabbit ears" (antennae on top of the TV set) or subscribe to a separate cable television service in order to receive the signals of these stations. The problem was rectified in November 1999 with passage of the Satellite Home Viewer Improvement Act.

This act finally allowed DBS providers to carry local signals in a process known as "local-into-local." Whether a local station's signal was carried was optional with the DBS provider, but the FCC ruled that, as of January 1, 2002, DBS providers must honor signal-carriage requests of all local broadcast television stations in markets where the DBS provider elected to carry the signal of at least one station. The FCC rule, known as the "carry one, carry all" rule, did allow DBS providers to decline carriage of a local station's signal if the quality of that signal was deemed unacceptable. The FCC also allowed some local stations, generally those associated with the four major broadcast television networks (the National Broadcasting Company [NBC], the Columbia Broadcasting System [CBS], the American Broadcasting Company [ABC], and FOX), to request payment for carriage by DBS providers. By early 2001, either DirecTV or DISH Network or both were providing local-into-local service in at least 40 major television markets.

The DBS industry's corporate structure stood on the brink of major change as 2001 neared an end. Earlier in the year, DISH Network owner EchoStar tendered a $30 billion offer to acquire its rival DirecTV. The virtual monopoly that would result from such a merger raised significant concentration-of-control issues that the U.S. Department of Justice would have to resolve. Opponents of the DISH Network/DirecTV merger claimed that consumers would be poorly served by such lack of competition among DBS providers. Proponents of the deal countered that the merger would result in less program duplication among competing DBS providers serving the same market and more efficient use of scarce frequency spectrum space. In the autumn of 2002, the FCC failed to approve the merger.

RONALD GARAY

See also **Pay Cable; Pay-per-View Cable; Satellite; United States: Cable**

Further Reading

Albiniak, Paige, "Ergen: Let DBS Bird Deal Fly," *Broadcasting and Cable* (December 10, 2001)

"Delivery Technologies, Glossary of Terms," Satellite Broadcasting and Communications Association, 2001, http://www.sbca.com

"FCC Sees DBS Gaining while Cable Rates Still Outpace Inflation, *Satellite Week* (January 15, 2001)

Foley, Theresa, "DirecTV Proceeds with a Local-Market Plan," *New York Times* (August 13, 2000)

Grant, August E., and Kenton T. Wilkinson, *Communication Technology Update: 1993–1994,* Boston, Massachusetts: Focal, 1994

Higgins, John M., "EchoStar-DirecTV Players Square Off," *Broadcasting and Cable* (November 12, 2001)

Higgins, John M., and Gerard Flynn, "Cable Slows, DBS Sprints," *Broadcasting and Cable* (June 4, 2001)

Hudson, H.E., *Communication Satellites: Their Development and Impact.* New York: Free Press, 1990

Hudson, Kris, "Satellite, Cable Chase 'On Demand' Program Technology in Infancy," *Denver Post* (June 17, 2001)

Mirabito, Michael M.A., *The New Communications Technology* (2nd ed.), Boston, Massachusetts: Focal Press, 1994

Rees, D.W.E., *Satellite Communications: The First Quarter Century of Service,* New York: Wiley, 1990

Terry, Ken, "Why DBS Is Pushing PVRs," *Cablevision* (October 22, 2001)

Director, Television

The television director, who sits atop the chain of command of the crew during the actual filming or taping of the show, is responsible for the visualization of the TV program, selecting the different camera angles and compositions that will used. Beyond this most general definition, however, the nature of the director's job and the relative importance of the director's creative contribution to the finished product vary greatly among different forms and genres of television.

One basic distinction in TV production exists between single-camera (film-style) and multicamera work. In single-camera production, each shot is staged individually, allowing precise camera positioning and lighting. Repeated "takes" are shot until the director is satisfied with the results. The action is filmed or taped out of sequence, based on a logic of setups for camera and lighting. Actors must break their performance into noncontinuous bits that still appear coherent when assembled later in the editing room. In this type of production, then, performance is adjusted to fit the visual scheme. Virtually all prime-time television dramas, programs generally one hour or longer, are produced in this manner. Common genres include action-adventure, crime, medical, courtroom, melodrama, and "prime-time soap opera." The television drama is the format in which the TV director has the most control and the most creative input and operates most like a feature film director. Yet even here, the director's role is more limited than a film director's. The series nature of television necessitates an exceptionally demanding production schedule and a rigid organization of labor, giving the director certain responsibilities, removing or restricting others.

In the production of films for theatrical exhibition, directors frequently devise and initiate their own projects. Many film directors, such as Oliver Stone and Quentin Tarrantino, write their own screenplays. Even in cases where the director is hired after a producer has initiated a project and a script has already been commissioned, the director has great leeway to interpret the material in his or her own way. In addition to controlling visual style, the director may also develop the themes, work with actors on characterizations, and even participate in the rewriting of the script.

Television directors, however, work on a per-episode basis. Because of the highly compressed production schedule, any series will employ several different directors during a season. When the director arrives on the scene, the characterizations, themes, and basic style of the show have already been established by previous episodes. In fact, such creative decisions were often made by the show's producer in the development of the series, and they remain the province of the producer during the run of the show. The director, then, takes an existing, basic aesthetic setup and works out the details for the episode at hand. When film directors such as Steven Speilberg, Michael Mann, and David Lynch work in television, they generally act as producers because from that position the more important creative choices are made.

Nevertheless, the direction of TV drama episodes still offers excellent opportunities for creative expression. A number of TV drama directors, including Spielberg, have gone on to become film directors. This was even more the case in the 1950s and 1960s, when television served as a training ground for some of the most prominent directors to work in the U.S. film industry. Arthur Penn, Sidney Lumet, Sam Peckinpah, Delbert Mann, Robert Altman, and other directors moved from television to the big screen. This path became less common by the late 1980s, and by the turn of the millennium, Hollywood was more likely to recruit new directors of feature films from the world of music video production than from series television. In the 1990s, the connection between film and TV directing occasionally flowed in the other direction, as established film directors could be found directing an episode of series television now and then. This was especially true where the director was also the program's producer, as with Lynch and *Twin Peaks* or Barry Levinson and *Homicide*. In the spring of 1995, Tarrantino elected to direct the concluding episode of the first year of the National Broadcasting Company (NBC) series *E.R.* because he found the show compelling.

In contrast to single-camera style, multicamera television production requires that the visual scheme be adjusted around the performance. The on-camera talent deliver their performances in real time, and the visualization is created by switching among a series of cameras trained on the unfolding event (and, in many cases, among several channels of electronically stored graphics). All "live" programs, including news and sports broadcasts, are produced this way. So, too, are talk, discussion, and game shows, which are shot "live-to-tape," then later broadcast with minimal editing. Directing in these genres offers less opportunity for creativity. The multicamera style in itself introduces great technical limitations, but these are often less restricting than the constraints defined by the forms themselves—how much visual flair is desirable in a shot of ABC News anchorman Peter Jennings reading a report of the latest Mideast conflict? Usually, then, the visual elements in presentational "event" programs, such as news, talk, or sports, generally follow a rigid, preset pattern. This is a necessity given that the production needs to be created almost instantaneously, with little or no time to prepare for the specifics of the particular episode. (Indeed, much of the visual excitement in "live" events such as sports derives from technical features such as instant replay.)

Directing this type of production is more a craft than an art. Although it requires great skill, the demands are mostly technical. Directors of multicamera television productions generally sit in a control room, viewing a bank of monitors on which the images from each camera and graphics source are displayed. They do not operate any studio controls, as they must keep their eyes glued to the monitors. They should not even look away to check notes or a script; instead, they must simply know how the program should unfold and be able to keep their mind ahead of the developing action. The director of an American football game must be ready for the cut to the downfield camera before the quarterback throws the pass, for example, whereas the talk show director should anticipate an outburst of audience response. This intensity must be maintained for long periods, with commercials serving as brief breaks from the action. In some ways, multicamera direction is a verbal art form. The director literally "talks" the show into existence, calling out cues for edits, camera movements, effects, and audio transitions while different specialized crew persons, listening via headset, execute these commands.

During the 1950s, television drama specials and anthology series were shot in this multicamera style and often broadcast live. Directing in this context was especially challenging, requiring the dramatic skill of a stage director, the visual skills of a film director, and the technical skills of a live-TV director. These programs were often intimate psychological dramas. They called for relatively exacting visuals, which necessitated complicated camera-and-actor blocking schemes. For example, a primary camera and the lead actor had to be precisely positioned in order to get the required close-up without obstructing a second camera's view of the lead actress for the next shot. All these movements, of both cameras and actors, had to be executed perfectly in real time. It is easy to understand why, once the major film studios opened their facilities for TV productions, prime-time narrative shows quickly turned to film-style production. The producers were then able to establish considerably more control over the production process.

Daytime drama (soap opera in the United States) is a different story. Because multicamera production can be completed much more quickly and is therefore much less expensive than film-style production, soaps are still shot live-to-tape using multiple cameras. With little time for preproduction or rehearsal, the director must establish a visual sequence that can be executed essentially in real time. Yet that visual design must also serve the dramatic needs of the show. This task is made somewhat easier by the formulaic nature of the genre, but the combination of technical and aesthetic challenges makes directing the soap opera one of television's more difficult and underappreciated tasks. This technique has been adopted for the production of prime-time serials throughout Europe, for the *téléroman* in Quebec, and for *telenovelas* throughout Latin America.

The one other contemporary TV genre that employs the multicamera technique is the situation comedy. Until the 1960s and early 1970s, most sitcoms were shot in single-camera film style, with the laugh track dubbed in later. Beginning with *All in the Family,* however, comedy producers adopted multicamera production techniques. This enabled actors to perform complete scenes before a live audience, generating natural laughter. In some cases, it also allowed the producer to schedule two performances of the same script, which enabled the selection of the "biggest" laughs for use in the soundtrack.

Sitcom production is actually a hybrid form, more likely to be shot with film cameras than video cameras. When this is the case, instead of cutting between cameras in real time with a switcher, all the cameras record the entire scene from different angles, and edits are made in postproduction, as in film-style work. Generally, the shows are performed not from beginning to end in real time but rather scene by scene, with breaks and retakes as needed. (The live audiences are apparently willing to laugh at the same joke more than once.) Still, this type of production is more a version of filmed theater than pure moving-picture work, and a sitcom director operates more like a stage director. Sitcom visualization is usually very simple—lots of long shots to catch the physical nature of the comedy are intercut with a few close-up reaction shots. More extensive use of close-ups would be out of place since the actors usually employ broad gestures and strong vocal projection to communicate the performance to the back row of the live audience. The overall effect of this form is the creation of a "proscenium style," as in the theater. The camera serves as the surrogate audience and establishes a "fourth wall" that is rarely crossed.

In this production style, the director concentrates on working with the actors on timing and execution, and successful sitcom directors are known primarily for their ability to communicate with the stars of their shows. In many cases, these directors work with a single show for its entire run, directing almost all the episodes. Jay Sandrich, for example, is noted for his work on *The Mary Tyler Moore Show* and *The Cosby Show,* and James Burrows is equally acclaimed for his direction of *Cheers.*

In many countries other than the United States, the television director is afforded a role of greater prominence, much more akin to that of the film director. In most cases, this situation holds because television productions have been limited to one or two episodes or to the miniseries. This role may change, however, as more and more television systems come to rely on regular schedules built around series production, with its attendant demand for tight production schedules and minimal preproduction opportunities. It is this industrial organization, itself the result of particular economic imperatives, that has defined the present role of the American television director, a role in which participation in the creative process is often secondary to that of the producer.

DAVID J. TETZLAFF

See also **Allen, Debbie; Almond, Paul; Cartier, Rudolph; Mann, Delbert; Producer in Television; Schaffner, Franklin**

Further Reading

Aldridge, Henry B., and Lucy A. Liggett, *Audio/Video Production: Theory and Practice,* Englewood Cliffs, New Jersey: Prentice Hall, 1990

Armer, Alan A., *Directing Television and Film,* Belmont, California: Wadsworth, 1990

Directors Guild of America, *Constitution and Bylaws,* Los Angeles, California: Directors Guild of America, 1991

Green, Kathleen, "The Other Side of the Camera: Behind-the-Scenes Jobs in Television and Motion Pictures," *Occupational Outlook Quarterly* (Spring 1995)

Hickman, Harold R., *Television Directing,* New York: McGraw-Hill, 1991

Lewis, Colby, *The TV Director/Interpreter,* New York: Hastings House, 1968

Kindem, Gorham, *The Live Television Generation of Hollywood Film Directors: Interviews with Seven Directors,* Jefferson, North Carolina: McFarland, 1994

Randolph, Laura B., "Debbie Allen on Power, Pain, Passion, and Prime Time," *Ebony* (March 1991)

Ravage, John W., *Television: The Director's Viewpoint,* Boulder, Colorado: Westview, 1978

Richards, Ron, *A Director's Method for Film and Television,* Boston, Massachusetts: Focal, 1992

Rose, Brian G., *Directing for Television: Conversations with American TV Directors,* Lanham, Maryland: Scarecrow Press, 1999

Schihl, Robert J., *Single Camera Video: From Concept to Edited Master,* Boston, Massachusetts: Focal, 1989

Schihl, Robert J., *Talk Show and Entertainment Processes and Procedures,* Boston, Massachusetts: Focal, 1992

Shanks, Bob, *The Cool Fire,* New York: Vintage, 1977

Taylor, Don, *Days of Vision: Working with David Mercer; Television Drama Then and Now,* London: Methuen, 1990

Thomson, David, "Walkers in the World: Alan Clarke," *Film Comment* (May–June 1993)

Wicking, Christopher, and Tise Vahimagi, *The American Vein: Directors and Directions in Television,* New York: Dutton, 1979

DirecTV. *See* **Covergence**

Disasters and Television

Natural and human-made disasters are ideal subjects and settings for television, which continually seeks the dramatic, the emotionally charged, and even the catastrophic in order to capture audience attention. In the process, the medium sometimes serves a vital function, informing and instructing viewers in matters pertaining to safety and recovery.

This article focuses primarily on natural catastrophes, such as earthquakes, floods, hurricanes, blizzards, and drought, and technological accidents of a dramatic scale, such as fatal plane crashes, nuclear reactor failures, oil or chemical spills, and similar emergencies. While they are less emphasized here, human conflicts such as riots and political coups cannot be strictly segregated from the notion of "disaster." The chaos and drama inherent in these forms of violence

are certainly as intriguing to television as "acts of god," and television often frames them in ways that parallel the medium's interpretations of natural disasters. Furthermore, coverage of violent conflicts at times becomes inextricably linked to the coverage of "natural" catastrophes. For instance, reporting on the Rwandan civil wars involved coverage of the massive problems of disease and famine to which those wars contributed. Likewise, in the time since the terrorist attacks on New York City and Washington, D.C., on September 11, 2001, much media attention has been cast on the suffering caused by the ongoing drought in Afghanistan and its implications for political stability in that nation and around the world.

During the actual moments of a disaster, television plays multiple roles. It is purveyor of information, storyteller, and sometimes agent of change. It can impart news of impending disaster, convey the effects of events that have taken place or are unfolding, and assign meaning. The use of particular camera angles, editing techniques, and added special effects render televised disaster footage ever more visually stunning, dramatic, and sensational. All this is possible by virtue of the medium's technology, its aesthetic, and its cultural authority.

Actual disasters have been the topic of numerous TV genres and forms, including made-for-TV movies, programming on specialized cable channels (such as the Weather Channel), public service announcements for relief organizations such as the Red Cross, and entertainment-oriented musical relief efforts such as the Live Aid concert/telethon or the Band Aid music video. Yet while the range of television genres employed in framing disasters has broadened, by far most attention to disasters is still found in the news.

It has been argued that people are psychologically drawn to disaster news because it feeds an innate voyeuristic tendency. Whether or not that is the case, natural and technological disasters are "newsworthy" because they are out-of-the-ordinary events, because they wreak havoc, and, particularly important in television, because they are the stuff of interesting, dramatic video footage. The way a disaster is reported on television depends on the characteristics of the disaster itself, but it also depends on characteristics of television news practice and television technology.

Television news is often a useful means of relaying information about stages of disasters as they develop. Natural disasters, such as hurricanes and tornadoes, can be reasonably predicted because of available sophisticated meteorological technology. In such instances, television may serve as a warning mechanism for residents of an area about to be hit by severe weather. In contrast, some natural events, such as earthquakes, are difficult to predict, and it can be virtually impossible to predict specific technological disasters, such as plane crashes or oil spills. However, even without the benefit of warning, television is capable of transmitting news of a disaster as it unfolds. In the aftermaths of the 1989 Loma Prieta earthquake in California, the 1994 Los Angeles earthquake, the 1994 crash of the Delta Airlines shuttle outside Chicago, and the 1996 crash of TWA flight 800, television news provided immediate, up-to-the-minute reports about the extent of damage and the cleanup and investigative efforts under way. In some cases, such as the September 11, 2001, collapse of the World Trade Center towers in New York City, television news captured the disaster as it was taking place, transmitting live the image and sounds of that catastrophe. The challenge for television news in such cases is to provide information continuously while trying to make sense of sudden chaos While earthquakes and plane crashes are relatively confined in both space and time, other disasters are more widespread and unfold over a much more slowly. In 1993, the great flood in the midwestern United States developed throughout the summer and traveled south with the overflowing rivers. The drought and famine in Somalia and Ethiopia were also widespread and were covered by television over a period of months, even years. The challenge for television news in such ongoing disasters is to search continually for fresh angles from which to report and new and interesting video to shoot. For example, during the 1993 flood, on one night, network television news might devote a news segment to the disaster's effects on farmers; on another night, another segment would cover the effects on small businesses; and then a story on local and national relief efforts would be reported on yet another evening. All the while, the news would regularly update the audience on the progress of rising floodwaters.

The role of television news in disasters is also spatially varied. In local settings or in the immediate area within which disaster has struck or is striking, television news is one of the primary means of disseminating information that may be vital to the physical and emotional health and safety of community residents. Television provides information about the risks communities are under, where residents can go for relief, and who they should contact for specific needs. At times, television becomes a conduit for personal messages. When severe weather conditions or the need for immediate access make television the only viable means of communication, individuals may use the medium to let others know they are safe or where they can be found.

In other situations, a disaster may have a profound impact on an area far from its epicenter. In such cases, television is often the fastest way to convey personal information to affected viewers. Shortly after the December 1988 crash of Pan Am flight 103 in Lockerbie, Scotland, local television newscasters in Syracuse, New York, quickly obtained passenger lists to read over the evening news because many of the passengers were students at Syracuse University and most of their friends and relatives were unsuccessful in confirming passenger information with Pan Am. One of the greatest challenges to the local newsroom during periods of disaster is to coordinate efforts with local safety and law enforcement officials so that accurate and necessary information is conveyed to the public in an efficient manner. Local television news staffs also find that they must abandon typical daily routines in favor

The aftermath of the *Exxon Valdez* disaster.
Courtesy of AP/Wide World Photos

of quick action and greater flexibility in fulfilling tasks.

National television news plays a different role in reporting disaster. A national newscast crosses local boundaries and shares disaster stories with a nationwide audience, evoking empathy, community, solidarity, and, sometimes, national action. Hurricane Andrew, which struck the southeastern United States in 1993; the 1993 and 1997 Midwest floods; the January 1994 Los Angeles earthquake; and a number of raging forest fires in the northwestern United States during the late 1990s and early 2000s all developed as "national" disasters by virtue of the network television coverage they received. Network news reported daily on the damaging effects of these disasters. Network news anchors traveled to and reported from the disaster sites, helping to convey, even create, a sense of national significance. The effect of this type of coverage can be a national outpouring of sympathy and grassroots relief efforts. Daily footage of damage and homelessness brought on by a storm, flood, fire, or earthquake can prompt residents from distant parts of the nation (or the world) to coordinate food and clothing drives to help the recently victimized communities.

National disaster coverage can also lead to political action. TV coverage of the *Exxon Valdez* oil spill in Alaska's Prince William Sound in March 1989, particularly the pictures of damage to wildlife and the ecosystem, brought attention to a technological disaster and stoked the outrage of environmental groups such as Greenpeace. The action of environmentalists in their cleanup efforts and their battles with Exxon became significant angles in the development of that disaster news story.

However, television also has the power to divert audiences from these more complex questions of politics and responsibility. On January 17, 1994, for example, immediately after the Los Angeles earthquake, all the U.S. networks sent news teams to Los Angeles. Each shot scene after scene of the most devastating effects of this seismic tragedy: broken water mains, exploding gas lines, dismantled freeway systems, and the horrified, panicked, and awestruck faces of the earthquake victims. Larger issues, however, went unexplored. Working under the time constraints of broadcast news and emphasizing the pictorial chaos of disaster, television typically cannot or does not develop other aspects of a disaster, such as related governmental or policy problems, or the event's historic implications.

Yet another type of political consequence may emerge from news reports of distant international disasters, especially when they involve U.S. coverage of disasters in developing nations. Critics have charged the U.S. press with geographic bias in covering disasters from developing nations. Their argument, supported by detailed content analysis of news stories broadcast in the United States, points out that much of the reporting from these nations focuses on disasters and political upheaval. This practice is seen as creating distorted images of these nations as chaos ridden and prone to disaster, representations that support and perpetuate unequal power relations between dominant and developing nations.

Critics also argue that U.S. broadcasters often decide which disasters should receive airtime according to the perceived connections between a given disaster and the interests of the United States. Those disasters in which Americans or American interests are harmed tend to receive prominent coverage by the U.S. press (including on television), while other disasters may be given minor coverage or be overlooked altogether. All these charges speak to television's ability to construct and assign meaning to the events it covers, including disasters.

In this context, then, television news does not merely convey information about disasters. It has the power to *define* disaster. Television's penchant for striking visual content encourages news gatherers to use the camera lens and various camera angles and shot lengths to frame numerous images of drama and chaos and then to edit footage together in such a way as to represent and redefine the drama and chaos. As a result, television coverage of natural disasters is often framed in such a way as to convey hopelessness, presenting them as battles between powerless humans and powerful nature, whereas coverage of technological disasters is typically framed to convey humanity's profound powerlessness over technologies of all sorts.

This power to create and assign meaning demonstrates television's central role in contemporary societies. Consider, for example, the 1986 Chernobyl nuclear reactor disaster in the Soviet Union. One line of analysis suggests that the accident would never have been international news had it not been for television and emphasizes the contrast between the international coverage and that seen on domestic Soviet television, where, by carefully choosing which images would be included on the news, the Soviet government failed to warn its citizens adequately about the effects of the disaster. However, U.S. news groups covering the disaster were themselves duped by outside agents, as when news producers accepted videotape of what they believed was actual footage from Chernobyl—footage that turned out to be scenes shot somewhere in Italy. Such incidents speak both to the power of television and to the power of those who can control it to serve their own interests.

Besides framing disasters a certain way, assigning them a certain meaning, television producers also have some power to decide which disasters will be of significant interest to those outside the immediate area affected. For example, earthquakes that affect a large number of people, whether within a nation's borders or abroad, tend to receive far more coverage than earthquakes that register the same measurement on the Richter scale but do not wreak the same social havoc.

The importance of disasters as defined by television has even reached beyond news coverage, moving increasingly into entertainment television. Real-life disasters have become fodder for entertainment, and since the mid-1980s the line between fact and fiction, news and entertainment, has been increasingly blurred on TV. For example, the 1985 Live Aid rock concert/telethon, an international relief effort for famine victims in Ethiopia, was produced by Bob Geldof and transmitted internationally via satellite television. In this case, television first defined an international disaster through news coverage, then offered its own televised "solution" to the disaster by airing the Live Aid concert for relief.

Real-life disasters also can be the subject of made-for-TV movies. Sometimes called "virtual disasters,"

TV movies based on actual disasters became more common from the early 1990s onward. *Triumph over Disaster: The Hurricane Andrew Story* is an example of television's efforts not only to capitalize on disaster for ratings points but also to define the order of reality.

As the example of Live Aid suggests, television coverage of disasters can be used to raise money. The Red Cross has employed images of disaster in televised public service announcements, editing together news footage of recent hurricanes, floods, and earthquakes into 30-second spots that urge viewers to contribute money so that the charity can fund relief for disaster victims. Not all efforts to make money from disaster footage are philanthropic; some cable channels, such as the Weather Channel, air specials on significant and dramatic natural disasters and then sell videos of these programs to consumers.

The power of television as a tool for information, for making money, and for defining reality can be witnessed throughout the coverage of natural and technological disasters. As television becomes more competitive, the drama guaranteed by disaster images practically ensures an audience across increasingly blurred genres.

KATHERINE FRY

Further Reading

Benthall, Jeremy, *Disasters, Relief, and the Media,* London: I.B. Tauris, 1993

Boltanski, Luc, *Distant Suffering: Morality, Media, and Politics,* translated by Graham Burchell, Cambridge and New York: Cambridge University Press, 1999

Deppa, Joan, *The Media and Disasters: Pan Am 103,* New York: New York University Press, 1993

Fensch, Thomas, *Associated Press Coverage of a Major Disaster: The Crash of Delta Flight 1141,* Hillsdale, New Jersey: Lawrence Erlbaum Associates, 1990

Lasorsa, Dominic L., and Stephen D. Reese, "News Source Use in the Crash of 1987: A Study of Four National Media," *Journalism Quarterly* (1990)

Lippert, Barbara, "Get Real: NBC's Week of Virtual Disasters Showed How TV Reality Is Collapsing into Itself," *Media Week* (1993)

Mellencamp, Patricia, "TV Time and Catastrophe; or, Beyond the Pleasure Principle of Television," in *Logics of Television,* edited by Mellencamp, Bloomington: Indiana University Press, and London: British Film Institute, 1990

Moeller, Susan D., *Compassion Fatigue: How the Media Sell Disease, Famine, War, and Death,* New York: Routledge, 1999

Newhagen, John E., and Marion Lewenstein, "Cultivation and Exposure to Television Following the 1989 Loma Prieta Earthquake," *Mass Comm Review* (1992)

Rubin, David M., "How the News Media Reported on Three Mile Island and Chernobyl," *Journal of Communication* (1987)

Singer, Eleanor, and Phyllis M. Endreny, *Reporting on Risk: How the Mass Media Portray Accidents, Disease, Disasters, and Other Hazards,* New York: Russell Sage Foundation, 1993

Singer, Eleanor, Phyllis Endreny, and Marc B. Glassman, "Media Coverage of Disasters: Effect of Geographic Location," *Journalism Quarterly* (1991)

Smith, Conrad, *Media and Apocalypse: News Coverage of the Yellowstone Forest Fires, Exxon Valdez Oil Spill, and Loma Prieta Earthquake,* Westport, Connecticut: Greenwood, 1992

Vincent, Richard C., Bryan K. Crow, and Dennis K. Davis, "When Technology Fails: The Drama of Airline Crashes in Network Television News," *Journalism Monographs* (November 1989)

Wei, Ran, "Earthquake Prediction: Did the News Media Make a Difference?," *Mass Comm Review* (1993)

Discovery Channel

U.S. Cable Network

Higher-education consultant John S. Hendricks founded Discovery Channel (DC) in 1982 to provide documentary programming on cable television that "enlightens as it entertains" (*PR Newswire,* 1985). Two decades later, Discovery Communications, Inc. (DCI), comprises five analog cable networks and five digitally tiered channels reaching 650 million subscribers in 155 countries through 33 languages. To promote the networks and extend the brand, DCI operates 170 Discovery Channel retail stores, online services, theme-park attractions, and publishing, video, outdoor apparel, and multimedia product lines.

In the three years before DC's June 17, 1985, launching to 2 million households through 100 local cable systems, Hendricks attracted $4.5 million in venture capital and an agreement with Group W Satellite Communications to distribute the channel. A ready supply of inexpensive international documentary programming and a deregulatory cable TV environment in the United States facilitated DC's launching. While few documentaries could be found on U.S. television in the 1980s, documentary programming prospered in the United Kingdom, Canada, Australia, and New Zealand, where a fuller commitment to state-subsidized educational television existed. At this time, 60 percent of DC's programs were imported from these countries for $250 to $400 per film hour.

This informational programming proved valuable to U.S. cable operators who were looking to add additional channels to justify substantial subscriber rate increases after the Cable Communications Policy Act of 1984 lifted rate restrictions. This encouraged four major multisystem cable operators (Tele-Communications Inc., Cox Cable Communications Inc., United Cable Television Corp., and Newhouse Broadcasting Corp.) to take a 10 percent stake each in DC. As Cox Cable president remarked, "The Discovery Channel becomes a very useful marketing and community relations tool as we in the cable industry approach deregulation" (*PR Newswire,* 1986). With vertical ties to the largest cable operators, a national advertising revenue-sharing plan with all cable affiliates, and an advertiser-desired "upscale" target audience, DC grew quickly to 9 million U.S. subscribers in the first year, 50 million by 1990, and 82 million by 2001, the second most widely distributed cable network behind Turner Broadcasting System (TBS).

In its first four years, DC organized its wholly acquired programming into topical blocks (the natural world, science and space, geography, exploration, and history), with periodic, high-profile themed weeks, including *Science and Technology Week,* and the ongoing summer franchise *Shark Week.* In 1990, expanded distribution brought revenues that DC used to produce or coproduce original programs for half its schedule. By 1995, a $110 million programming budget produced 400 hours of original programs filling 60 percent of the schedule, with 30 percent acquired from overseas and 10 percent from U.S. producers. Refinements to DC's 18-hour-per-day schedule include a morning hour of commercial-free educational programming called Assignment Discovery (1989) and home improvement/decorating series in the late morning and afternoon with hosts Lynette Jennings (1991) and Christopher Lowell (1996). Undifferentiated prime-time nature, science, and historical programming was gradually shaped into branded nightly series, including the nature-themed *Wild Discovery* (1995), the science anthology *Sci-Trek* (1995), and the behind-the-scenes-oriented *On the Inside* (1999). Special-event series include the extreme adventure race *Eco-Challenge* (1996) and *Expedition Adventure*

Courtesy of Discovery Networks

(1997), which partially funds and films expeditions, including the shipwrecked *Titanic* (1998), the recovery of the Mercury space capsule *Liberty Bell 7* (1999), and a French archaeological exhumation of a woolly mammoth (2000). DC's most substantial coproduction partner is BBC Worldwide, the commercial branch of the U.K. public broadcasting network. In 1998, a five-year deal worth $565 million included network partnerships in the United States (Animal Planet and BBC America) and Latin America (People 1 Arts and Animal Planet Latin America) and coproduced computer graphic designed specials, including *Walking with Dinosaurs,* and nature spectaculars, such as *Blue Planet: Sea of Life.*

Low-cost programming and broad distribution brought surplus revenues and carriage leverage that DCI used to launch and/or acquire additional nonfiction cable networks. In 1991, DCI purchased the Learning Channel from the Financial News Network, excised its for-credit telecourses and daytime infomercials, and focused programming on "the world of ideas," a somewhat distinct focus from the "experiential, physical world" of DC programs. In 1996, DCI launched Animal Planet, a network dedicated to wildlife documentaries and domestic pets. The analog network expanded quickly as DCI moved the wildly successful nature franchise *Crocodile Hunter* from DC to Animal Planet and paid cable/satellite distributors a substantial fee for carriage. DCI also acquired Travel Channel in 1997, launched Discovery Health in 1999, and acquired the Health Network from FOX Cable Networks Group in 2002. In anticipation of digital compression technologies, in 1995 DC planned to create dozens of digital "clubs," such as "Astronomy Club" or "Science Club," that would function as separate pay-per-view services offering on-demand programs rather than additional multiplexed niche channels. The initiative, an offshoot of a more ambitious project to create a broader video-on-demand system called "Your Choice TV," gave way to the creation

of four digitally tiered channels in 1996 (Discovery Home and Leisure, Discovery Civilization, Discovery Science, and Discovery Kids) and a fifth in 1998 (Discovery Wings).

The growth of cable/satellite infrastructures internationally facilitated DCI's rapid expansion into the following regions: in 1989, DC Europe (Benelux, Scandinavia); in 1994, DC Asia (Brunei, Papua New Guinea, the Philippines, South Korea, Taiwan, Thailand, and Singapore), DC Latin America (Central America, South America, and the Caribbean), and the Middle East; in 1995, Canada, India, and Australia/New Zealand; in 1996, Africa, Italy, and Germany; and in 1997, Japan and Turkey. Discovery Networks International (DNI), DCI's subsidiary for international expansion, typically partners with local and regional cable/satellite carriers to share risk, resources, and local expertise and to satisfy foreign ownership restrictions. Often the regional channels are initially offered free to cable/satellite carriers to secure distribution, then small per-subscriber fees are charged. Because little advertising is sold on most of these channels as yet, most of the revenues come from subscriber fees, and as of 2001, only DC Europe has turned a profit. DNI's professed commitment to "localizing" each channel typically begins with locally produced promotional campaigns, then a gradual splitting of feeds for language/dialect diversification. For example, the Miami-based DC Latin America began in 1994 as a single Spanish-subtitled channel and then in 1996 added the Portuguese-language DC Brazil. By 1999, DNI had created separate Spanish-language feeds for the southern cone of Latin America, Spain, and the U.S. Hispanic market. The bulk of DC's programming remains panregional, and special-event programs are designed for global promotion and reach, such as "Watch with the World" events, which are shown in all regions simultaneously in prime time, including *Cleopatra's Palace: In Search of a Legend* (1999), *Raising the Mammoth* (2000), and *Inside the Space Station* (2000).

In 1985, *Science* magazine described the newly arrived DC as "something like a Sorbonne of the tube—a loosely structured, informal university where you can take in whatever classes or lectures interest you" (Meyer, p. 90). In the new millennium, DCI rather resembles a globally integrated media conglomerate where branded content designed for international markets drives programming decisions. As DCI President Judith McHale boasted with reference to *Raising the Mammoth,* "Our wide reach lets us extend this global media event across our worldwide network of branded channels, in concert with our many other content and retail platforms" (*PR Newswire,* 2000). DCI sold prehistoric-themed merchandise through its retail stores,

Discovery.com offered online sweepstakes, the Travel Channel promoted "Discovery-branded" trips to archaeological digs, and all companion networks produced "complementary" programs to promote the event.

JOHN MCMURRIA

Further Reading

Chris, Cynthia, "All Documentary, All the Time?: Discovery Communications Inc. and Trends in Cable Television," *Television & New Media,* Vol. 3, No. 1 (2002)

Herman, Edward S., and Robert W. McChesney, *The Global Media: The New Missionaries of Corporate Capitalism,* London: Cassell, 1997

Izod, John, and R.W. Kilborn, *An Introduction to Television Documentary: Confronting Reality,* Manchester: Manchester University Press, and New York: St. Martin's Press, 1997

Meyer, Alfred, "The Discovery Channel," *Science,* Vol. 6 (1985)

Parson, Patrick R., and Robert M. Frieden, *The Cable and Satellite Television Industry,* Boston, Massachusetts: Allyn and Bacon, 1998

Waterman, David, and Andrew A. Weiss, *Vertical Integration in Cable Television,* Cambridge, Massachusetts: MIT Press, 1997

Discovery Channel (Canada)

Canadian Cable Network

Canada's Discovery Channel was granted a license in June 1994 and made its debut on New Year's Eve later that year as a national, English-language specialty channel. Like its American namesake, Discovery Canada offers a mix of content dedicated to science, technology, nature, the environment, and adventure. The Canadian offshoot was among the first international Discovery franchises in what has become a globe-spanning media brand.

The license was originally held by a partnership called "Adventure Unlimited" uniting Labatt breweries and a number of smaller Canadian investors with Discovery Networks International (DNI), the American parent corporation of Discovery, which exercised its option to purchase 20 percent of the enterprise. Majority ownership ultimately passed to a media consortium called NetStar. Then, in early 1999, Canada's largest private broadcaster, CTV, purchased 80 percent of NetStar. A year later, CTV itself was taken over by Bell Globemedia, the media subsidiary of giant BCE Inc., amid a wave of takeovers in Canada that brought Discovery under the umbrella of the country's largest media conglomerate.

The advent of the digital era in Canada in the 1990s and the subsequent proliferation of services licensed by the Canadian Radio-television and Telecommunications Commission presented DNI and its sundry partners with opportunities to expand and diversify the Discovery line. As a result, DNI also holds shares in Discovery Civilization and Animal Planet (also in conjunction with Bell Globemedia), Discovery Health (in partnership with Alliance Atlantis), and Discovery Kids (with Corus Entertainment). Many of these newer channels are available only in digital mode, and their potential and actual audiences are relatively small. Discovery Canada is the undisputed ratings champion within the Canadian branch of the extended family.

The founding president of the Discovery Channel was Trina McQueen. Lured away from the Canadian Broadcasting Corporation (CBC) after helping to launch the all-news channel Newsworld, McQueen is a leading television executive and a pioneering woman broadcaster in Canada. Her surprise departure from CBC represented something of a coup for Discovery. Reflecting on the early years of Discovery Canada, McQueen took pride in helping to establish popular domestic programming. She believed that Discovery's winning formula was based on being "cool" and therefore attractive to cable subscribers (and, not insignificantly, to advertisers.) She boasted that the service had been able to maintain credibility with the scientific community even as it cultivated and entertained a diverse audience.

Many other conventional and specialty channels provide at least some space for content similar in kind to the programs offered by Discovery. Writing in *Marketing,* Muriel Draaisma noted that McQueen has emphasized that Discovery is not an "educational or instructional" service. She prefers to describe Discovery's mandate in terms such as "curiosity," "drama," and "exploration." Discovery Canada is also differentiated by theme weeks in which different aspects of a particular topic are in scope on successive weekday evenings.

Discovery has been among the industry leaders since its inception and is well positioned in terms of both average hours of viewing by adults and reach (its rating are the highest among the batch of seven services that debuted in 1994). The channel takes pains to report that viewer surveys point to impressive levels of viewer satisfaction.

A typical weekly rotation for Discovery includes a good deal of content originating with the American channel and other foreign producers, especially in the peak hours of prime time. However, the original condition of license (successfully renewed in 2001) obliges Discovery to invest 45 percent of its annual revenues in domestic content. The result has been the production of a number of acclaimed series that have appeared in syndication on other services at home and abroad. Discovery must also present at least 60 percent domestic content overall (50 percent in the prime evening hours). Short documentary films, a staple for which Canadians are often said to have a particular fondness, occupy much of the schedule.

The flagship show on Discovery is @*discovery.ca.* Airing nightly in the prime 7:00 P.M. slot, it is billed by the channel as the "world's first and only daily science and nature news magazine." It is one of the service's most popular programs. According to a profile in the *Ryerson Journalism Review* by Rebecca Davey, in 1997 approximately 1.5 million viewers tuned into @*discovery.ca* at least once during the week, and, surprisingly, one-third of the audience is composed of women over the age of 18. In a reverse of the customary south-to-north flow of content, the Canadian show was picked up by Discovery Science in the United States.

The series is produced and presented by well-known science popularizer Jay Ingram, an award-winning radio host, television personality, print journalist, and former university educator. He joined Discovery prior to the ser-

vice's launch and helped design the show. His presence infuses the evening showcase with eclectic and witty perspectives on topical science stories. On any given night, the segments range across live remote interviews with astronauts in space or scientists in their labs, quizzes for both viewers and professionals, scientific demonstrations, and minidocumentaries. The pace is fast, and the banter between Ingram and his on-air partners is bright. One of the features is an interactive segment called "You Asked For It," in which viewers can make special feature requests or pose questions of experts.

Discovery's programming is complemented by an ambitious website. The site was a first for Canadian television. Launched simultaneously with the channel in 1994 with the prosaic address of www.discovery.ca, the site was rechristened EXN (Explorer Network) in 1996. Users are able to access a wide variety of information on the site, including archived video and text material along with entries in "Jay's Journal," a sampling of Ingram's typically engaging investigations of scientific curiosities.

ROBERT EVERETT

See also **McQueen, Trina**

Further Reading

An, Lisa, "Lights! Camera! Action!: Do Dramatic Elements in Documentaries Deceive the Audience or Do They Enhance Storytelling? Do Viewers Really Care?" *Ryerson Review of Journalism* (Spring 1999)

Davey, Rebecca, "Bringing the Test Tube to the Boob Tube, the Discovery Channel's Flagship Show Makes Science Sizzle," *Ryerson Review of Journalism* (Summer 1997)

Draaisma, Muriel, "Selling the Fun Side of Science," *Marketing* (March 22, 1999)

Woolery, Alexander, "Blazing a Trail in Canadian Broadcasting," *Carleton University Magazine* (Winter 2002)

Disney, Walt (1901–1966)

U.S. Animator, Producer, Media Executive

Walt Disney was a visionary filmmaker who brought his film library, his love of technology, and his business sense to American television in the mid-1950s. His groundbreaking television program, *Disneyland,* helped establish fledgling network ABC, pointed the way to-

ward that network's increasing reliance on Hollywood-originated filmed programming, and provided much-needed financing for Disney's pioneering theme park.

From the late 1920s on, Disney was a public figure, Hollywood's best-known independent studio head. He first achieved success with animated short subjects starring the character with whom he is best associated, Mickey Mouse. In 1937, his studio produced the first full-length animated motion picture, *Snow White and the Seven Dwarfs.* In the late 1940s, beginning with *Song of the South* (1946), the Disney studio also branched out into live-action films, but it was associated, then as now, primarily with animation.

Unlike many other studios, Disney's did not prosper during World War II, when it devoted much of its energies to producing films for the U.S. government. Indeed, the Disney studio had never made a great deal of money because of the time- and labor-intensive nature of animation work. After the war, Walt Disney hoped to expand his enterprises. The key to this expansion, according to Christopher Anderson in *Hollywood TV* (1994), was diversification. Disney was ready to set his sights beyond the film industry.

Disney flirted with the new medium in the early 1950s, producing a one-hour special for the National Broadcasting Company (NBC) in 1950 and another in 1951. He discussed a possible series with both NBC and the Columbia Broadcasting System (CBS), but only the American Broadcasting Company (ABC), the third-place network, was willing to give him what he wanted in exchange—funding for the amusement park he dreamed of opening in Anaheim, California. ABC executives were desperate to obtain programming that would enable them to compete with their more established rivals and were particularly interested in courting the growing family market in those baby-boom years.

Walt Disney and his brother Roy convinced the network to put up $500,000 toward the construction costs for the park, to be called (like the television program) Disneyland, and to guarantee its bank loans. In exchange, ABC would obtain 35 percent of the park and would receive profits from Disneyland concessions for ten years. Even more important to the network, Disney would deliver them a weekly, hour-long television program that would take advantage of his family-oriented film library.

The program *Disneyland* debuted on October 27, 1954, and quickly became ABC's first series to hit the top ten in ratings. A number of early episodes showed old Disney films or promoted new ones. (A documentary chronicling the filming of the upcoming *20,000 Leagues Under the Sea* added to the audience for that film and also earned Disney his first Emmy Award, for best documentary.)

The program's success was clinched in December 1954 with the introduction of the first of three episodes focusing on Davy Crockett. The day after the December 15 telecast of "Davy Crockett, Indian Fighter," Crockett mania swept through the country.

Walt Disney, c. 1950s.
Courtesy of the Everett Collection

The "Davy Crockett" episodes established another new Disney tradition. Not only would Disney move his feature films to television, but he would also reverse the process. Although ABC broadcast only in black and white, the Disney studio shot the "Davy Crockett" episodes in Technicolor. After telecasting each of the three hours twice during the winter and spring months of 1954 and 1955, the studio edited them into a film, which it released to theaters nationally and internationally in the summer of 1955. The film's high attendance increased the visibility of the *Disneyland* television program—and of all Disney's enterprises, including his new park.

When the park opened in July 1955, ABC aired a live special honoring the new tourist mecca of the United States and its founder. Within a year, millions of viewers whose amusement appetites had been whetted by Disney's television program poured into Disneyland. In its first year, it grossed $10 million. Walt Disney and his company had shaped two new entertainment forms—and had made more money than ever before.

Disney himself served as the affable host of his program. In light of its success, his studio quickly gener-

Courtesy of the Everett Collection

ated other youth-oriented television shows for ABC. *The Mickey Mouse Club,* a daily daytime program featuring a likable group of youngsters known as the Mouseketeers, premiered a year after *Disneyland* and lasted for four seasons. *Zorro,* an adventure series about a masked, swashbuckling Spaniard in 19th-century California, ran from 1957 to 1959.

Disney continued to be best known, however, for the weekly program he hosted. In 1959, this show changed its name to *Walt Disney Presents.* In 1961, it moved to NBC and changed its name to *Walt Disney's Wonderful World of Color.* NBC's parent company, Radio Corporation of America (RCA), offered the Disney studios an appealing sponsorship deal, hoping that Disney's colorful telefilms would help market color-television receivers.

Disney was still the host of this version of the program at the time of his death in December 1966. His avuncular on-screen personality had endeared him to viewers of all ages. And his re-creation of American recreation through the dual marketing of the two Disneylands had forged new patterns in American cultural history, inextricably linking television to the film and amusement industries.

TINKY "DAKOTA" WEISBLAT

Walt (Walter) Elias Disney. Born in Chicago, Illinois, December 5, 1901. Attended McKinley High School, Chicago; Kansas City Art Institute, 1915. Married Lillian Bounds, 1925; children: Diane and Sharon. Served in France with Red Cross Ambulance Corps, 1918. Became commercial art apprentice to Ub Iwerks, 1919; joined Kansas City Film Advertising Company, producing, directing, and animating commercials for local businesses, 1920; incorporated Laugh-o-Gram Films, 1922; went bankrupt, 1923; moved to Hollywood and worked on several animated series, including *Alice in Cartoonland,* 1923; ended *Alice* series and began *Oswald the Lucky Rabbit* series, 1927; formed Walt Disney Productions, 1927; created *Steamboat Willie* (first cartoon to use synchronized sound and third to feature his creation Mickey Mouse), 1928; began distributing through Columbia, 1930; *Flowers and Trees* released through United Artists, first cartoon to use Technicolor and first to win Academy Award, 1932; began work on *Snow White and the Seven Dwarfs,* his first feature-length cartoon, 1934; Disney staff on strike, 1941; Disney developed several TV programs, 1951–60; formed Buena Vista Distribution Company for release of Disney and occasionally other films, 1954; hosted *Disneyland* TV series; opened Disneyland, Anaheim, California, 1955; premiered numerous television shows, including *The Mickey Mouse Club* and *Walt Disney's Wonderful World of Color;* Walt Disney World opened, Orlando, Florida, 1971. Recipient: Special Academy Award, 1932, 1941; Irving G. Thalberg Award, 1941; Best Director (for his work as a whole), Cannes Film Festival, 1953; two Emmy Awards. Died in Los Angeles, California, December 15, 1966.

Television Series

1954–58	*Disneyland*
1955–59	*The Mickey Mouse Club*
1958–61	*Walt Disney Presents*
1961–66	*Walt Disney's Wonderful World of Color*

Films (director, animator, and producer)

Newman Laugh-o-Grams series, 1920; *Cinderella; The Four Musicians of Bremen; Goldie Locks and the Three Bears; Jack and the Beanstalk; Little Red Riding Hood; Puss in Boots,* 1922; *Alice's Wonderland; Tommy Tucker's Tooth; Martha,* 1923; *Alice* series (12 episodes), 1924; *Alice* series (18 episodes), 1925; *Alice* series (9 episodes), 1926; *Alice* series (17 episodes), 1927; *Oswald the Lucky Rabbit* series (11 episodes), 1927; *Oswald the Lucky Rabbit* series (15 episodes), 1928.

Films (as head of Walt Disney Productions; coproduced with Ub Iwerks)

Steamboat Willie, 1928; *Mickey Mouse* series (12 episodes), 1929; *Mickey Mouse* series (3 episodes), 1930; *Silly Symphonies* series, 1929; *Night,* 1930; *The Golden Touch,* 1935.

Films (as head of Walt Disney Productions)

Flowers and Trees, 1932; *Three Little Pigs,* 1933; *The Tortoise and the Hare,* 1934; *Snow White and the Seven Dwarfs,* 1937; *Ferdinand the Bull,* 1938; *Fantasia,* 1940; *Pinnochio,* 1940; *The Reluctant Dragon,* 1941; *Dumbo,* 1941; *Bambi,* 1942; *Victory Through Air Power,* 1943; *The Three Caballeros,* 1944; *Make Mine Music,* 1946; *Song of the South,* 1946; *Fun and Fancy Free,* 1947; *Melody Time,* 1948; *So Dear to My Heart,* 1948; *Ichabod and Mr. Toad,* 1949; *Cinderella,* 1950; *Alice in Wonderland,* 1951; *The Story of Robin Hood and His Merrie Men,* 1952; *Peter Pan,* 1953; *The Sword and the Rose,* 1953; *Rob Roy, the Highland Rogue,* 1953; *Toot, Whistle, Plunk and Broom,* 1953; *20,000 Leagues Under the Sea,* 1954; *The Littlest Outlaw,* 1954; *Lady and the Tramp,* 1955; *Davy Crockett and the River Pirates,* 1955; *The Great Locomotive Chase,* 1956; *Westward Ho the Wagons!,* 1956; *Johnny Tremain,* 1957; *Old Yeller,* 1957; *The Light in the Forest,* 1958; *Sleeping Beauty,* 1958; *Tonka,* 1958; *The Shaggy Dog,* 1959; *Darby O'Gil and the Little People,* 1959; *Third Man on the Mountain,* 1959; *Toby Tyler, or Ten Weeks with a Circus,* 1959; *Kidnapped,* 1960; *Pollyanna,* 196; *Ten Who Dared,* 1960; *Swiss Family Robinson,* 1960; *One Hundred and One Dalmatians,* 1960; *The Absent-Minded Professor,* 1960; *Moon Pilot,* 1961; *In Search of the Castaways,* 1961; *Nikki, Wild Dog of the North,* 1961; *The Parent Trap,* 1961; *Grayfriar's Bobby,* 1961; *Babes in Toyland,* 1961; *Son of Flubber,* 1962; *The Miracle of the White Stallions,* 1962; *Big Red,* 1962; *Bon Voyage,* 1962; *Almost Angels,* 1962; *The Legend of Lobo,* 1962; *Savage Sam,* 1963; *Summer Magic,* 1963; *The Incredible Journey,* 1963; *The Sword in the Stone,* 1963; *The Misadventures of Merlin Jones,* 1963; *The Three Lives of Thomasina,* 1963; *A Tiger Walks,* 1964; *The Moon-Spinners,* 1964; *Mary Poppins,* 1964; *Emil and the Detectives,* 1964; *Those Calloways,* 1964; *The Monkey's Uncle,* 1964; *That Darn Cat,* 1965; *The Ugly Dachshund,* 1966; *Lt. Robin Crusoe, U.S.N.,* 1966; *The Fighting Prince of Donegal,* 1966; *Follow Me, Boys!,* 1966; *Monkeys, Go Home!,* 1966; *The Adventures of Bullwhip Griffin,* 1966; *The Gnome-Mobile,* 1966; *The Jungle Book,* 1967.

Further Reading

Anderson, Christopher, *Hollywood TV: The Studio System in the Fifties,* Austin: University of Texas Press, 1994

Bailey, Adrian, *Walt Disney's World of Fantasy,* New York: Everest House, 1982

Eliot, Marc, *Walt Disney: Hollywood's Dark Prince: A Biography,* Secaucus, New Jersey: Carol, 1993

Field, Robert Durant, *The Art of Walt Disney,* London: Collins, 1942

Finch, Christopher, *The Art of Walt Disney: From Mickey Mouse to the Magic Kingdoms,* New York: H.N. Abrams, 1975

Finch, Christopher, *Walt Disney's America,* New York: Abbeville, 1978

Heller, Scott, "Dissecting Disney," *Chronicle of Higher Education* (February 16, 1994)

Jackson, Kathy Merlock, *Walt Disney: A Bio-Bibliography,* Westport, Connecticut: Greenwood, 1993

Kurland, Gerald, *Walt Disney, The Master of Animation,* Charlotteville, New York: SamHar, 1971

Maltin, Leonard, *The Disney Films,* New York: Crown, 1984

Schickel, Richard, *The Disney Version: The Life, Times, Art, and Commerce of Walt Disney,* New York: Simon and Schuster, 1968

Shows, Charles, *Walt: Backstage Adventures with Walt Disney,* La Jolla, California: Windsong, 1980

Smoodin, Eric, editor, *Disney Discourse: Producing the Magic Kingdom,* New York: Routledge, 1994

Thomas, Bob, *Walt Disney: An American Original,* New York: Simon and Schuster, 1976

Thomas, Bob, "Mickey and His Walter Ego," *Life* (November 1988)

Distant Signal

Cable Television Transmission Technology

The term "distant signal" refers to a television station transmission made available to one or more local cable systems by means other than off-air reception. Traditionally, distant signals have been imported via terrestrial microwave relays; today, however, communications satellites are also used for distant signal importation.

The earliest cable systems of the late 1940s and early 1950s, then known as CATV (Community Antenna Television), were little more than very tall community antennas connected by wire to homes within a given community. Under these conditions, retransmission of distant signals was limited to communities no more than approximately 100 miles from the nearest television stations. Consequently, many communities, particularly small communities in sparsely populated states of the western United States, were unable to benefit from community antennas.

By the mid-1950s, however, a number of these western towns had CATV systems served by microwave relays. The relays made it possible to retransmit broadcast signals over many hundreds of miles. The first such system, launched in 1953, brought a Denver, Colorado, signal to Casper, Wyoming. Within the next decade, microwave relays—many of which had been connected to form networks—covered a large portion of the West.

Eventually, microwave technology began to be used as more than simply a substitute for community antenna service. By the late 1950s, some cable operators were using microwave-carried signals to supplement signals received off the air. As improved technology brought about increased CATV channel capacity, operators began to seek extra programming options in order to make their service more attractive to potential subscribers. In the early 1960s, independent stations from large cities such as New York and Chicago became popular CATV channel options because of the quantity of movies and local sports in their schedules.

Also, in the mid- to late 1950s, some operators began using microwave relays to bypass local or nearby signals entirely in order to provide their subscribers with more popular stations from distant cities. In most cases, the program quality of a local station serving only several thousand people could not be expected to equal that of a station serving millions, and with the technical capability to carry distant stations, CATV operators had little incentive to use the lower-quality local programming. An outcry arose from the small-market broadcasters, who felt that CATV would draw viewers away. As local viewership decreased, they argued, so would advertising revenues. Hearings on this issue were held throughout the late 1950s by both Congress and the Federal Communications Commission (FCC), but no decisive regulatory action was taken to limit this type of CATV competition with broadcasters until a landmark 1963 Supreme Court decision.

In this case, *Carter Mountain Transmission Corp. v. FCC,* a small Wyoming broadcast station challenged the FCC's licensing of a microwave company that intended to deliver distant signals to a CATV system in a community where the station's signal could be re-

ceived off air. The FCC ultimately denied the microwave license because the microwave outfit not only refused to guarantee the local station protection against program duplication on imported stations but also refused to require the CATV to carry the local station's signal. The commission reasoned that, because microwave threatened to destroy a local broadcaster, it also threatened the loss of television service to a substantial rural population without access to CATV as well as to any other CATV nonsubscribers. To grant the microwave company a license unconditionally would have been in direct conflict with the commission's policies favoring localism in broadcasting.

The *Carter Mountain* decision set in motion a series of FCC decisions on the status of CATV, culminating in its 1965 First Report and Order and the 1966 Second Report and Order. These two rulings recognized that CATV had become more than simply a retransmission medium for areas not served by broadcast television. It was beginning to enter broadcast markets, sometimes replacing local signals with distant signals. Even when local stations were offered in addition to distant stations in these markets, subscribers often would watch the distant rather than local stations. Thus, the two rulings focused on setting guidelines for the carriage of local signals by CATV systems and on restricting the duplication of the local stations' programming by channels that carried imported distant stations. In addition, the 1966 rules temporarily limited the growth of CATV in the nation's top 100 broadcast television markets, a provision strengthened by a 1968 FCC ruling that completely froze growth in the top 100 markets, pending further study of cable developments.

The 1972 Cable Television Report and Order, the next major FCC ruling regarding cable, also focused in large part on the importation of distant signals into broadcast markets. This extensive ruling contained one provision that affected the importation of distant independent stations and another that protected local stations' exclusive rights to syndicated programming. The latter, known as "syndicated exclusivity" or "syndex," became increasingly difficult to enforce as the number of cable program services grew, especially after satellites were introduced to the cable industry in the mid-1970s. Still, pressure from broadcasters continued to focus regulators' attention on the issue, and in 1990 an updated version of the syndex rules was enacted. Since then, cable operators have been obligated to black out any syndicated programming on distant signals that duplicates syndicated programs offered by local stations.

Distant signal importation has been important to the growth of the cable industry in that it has allowed cable operators some degree of selection in the types of broadcast signals they retransmit to their subscribers.

The most popular distant signals used by modern cable systems are satellite-carried superstations, such as WGN in Chicago, WOR in New York, and Ted Turner's WTBS in Atlanta, Georgia.

MEGAN MULLEN

See also **Microwave; Must Carry Rules; Superstation; Translators; United States: Cable**

Further Reading

Gay, Verne, "Syndex Simplified," *Newsday* (December 31, 1989)

LeDuc, Don R., *Cable Television and the FCC: A Crisis in Media Control,* Philadelphia, Pennsylvania: Temple University Press, 1973

Seiden, Martin H., *Cable Television U.S.A.: An Analysis of Government Policy,* New York: Praeger, 1972

Dixon of Dock Green

British Police Series

Beginning in 1955 and finally ending in 1976, *Dixon of Dock Green* was the longest-running police series on British television. Although its homeliness would later become a benchmark to measure the "realism" of later police series, such as *Z Cars* and *The Bill,* it was an enormously popular series. *Dixon* should be seen as belonging to a time when police were generally held in higher esteem by the public than they have been subsequently. The series was principally set in a suburban police station in the East End of London and concerned uniformed police engaged with routine tasks and low-level crime. The ordinary, everyday nature of the people and the setting was further emphasized in early episodes of the series with the old, British music-hall song "Maybe It's Because I'm a Londoner"—with its sentimental evocations of a cozy community—being used as the series theme song.

Unlike later police series, *Dixon* focused less on crime and policing and more on the family-like nature of life in the station with Dixon, a warm, paternal, and frequently moralizing presence, as the central focus. Crime was little more than petty larceny. However, as the 1960s and the early 1970s brought ever more realistic police series from both sides of the Atlantic to the British public, *Dixon of Dock Green* would seem increasingly unreal, a rosy view of the police that seemed out of touch with the times. Yet the writer of the series maintained to the end of the program's time on air that the stories in the episodes were based on fact and that *Dixon* was an accurate reflection of what goes on in an ordinary police station.

Police Constable (PC) George Dixon was played by veteran actor Jack Warner. The figures of both Dixon and Warner were already well known to the British public when the series was launched. Warner had first played the figure of Dixon in 1949 in the Ealing film *The Blue Lamp.* A warm, avuncular policeman, his death at the end of the film at the hands of a young thug (played by Dirk Bogarde) was memorably shocking and tragic. British playwright Ted Willis, who, with Jan Read, had written the screenplay for *The Blue Lamp,* subsequently revived the figure of Dixon for a stage play and then wrote a series of six television plays about the policeman. Thus, the British Broadcasting Corporation (BBC) took little chance in spinning off the figure and the situation into a television series.

If Dixon was well known to the public, the actor Jack Warner was even better known. Born in London in 1900, Warner had been a comedian in radio and in his early film career. Starting in the early 1940s, he had broadened his range to include dramatic roles, becoming a warmly human character actor in the process. However, in addition to playing in films with dramatic themes, such as *The Blue Lamp,* Warner continued to play in comedies, such as the enormously successful Huggett family films made between 1948 and 1953.

In *Dixon of Dock Green,* Dixon was a "bobby" on the beat—an ordinary, lowest-ranking policeman on foot patrol. With the inevitable heart of gold, Dixon was a widower raising an only daughter Mary (Billie Whitelaw in the early episodes, later replaced by Jeannette Hutchinson). Other regular characters included Sergeant Flint (Arthur Rigby), PC Andy Crawford (Peter Byrne), and Sergeant Grace Millard (Moira Mannon). From 1964, Dixon was a sergeant.

The series was the creation of writer Ted Willis, who not only wrote the series over its 20 years on British television but also had a controlling hand in the production. Long-time producer of the series was Douglas

Moodie, whose other television credits include *The Inch Man* and *The Airbase. Dixon* was produced at the BBC's London television studios at Lime Green. The show began on the BBC in 1955 and ran until 1976. Altogether, some 439 episodes were made, at first running 30 minutes and later 45 minutes. The early episodes were in black and white, while the later ones were in color.

The BBC scheduled *Dixon* in the prime family time slot of 6:30 P.M. on Saturday night. At the time it started on air in 1955, the drama schedule of the BBC was mostly restricted to television plays, so that *Dixon of Dock Green* had little trouble in building and maintaining a large and very loyal audience. In 1961, for example, the series was voted the second-most-popular program on British television, with an estimated audience of 13.85 million. Even in 1965, after three years of the gritty and grimy procedural police work of *Z Cars,* the audience for *Dixon* still stood at 11.5 million. However, as the 1960s wore on, ratings for *Dixon* began to fall, and this factor, together with health questions about Warner, led the BBC to finally end the series in 1976.

ALBERT MORAN

Cast

George Dixon	Jack Warner
Andy Crawford	Peter Byrne
Mary Crawford	Billie Whitelaw/Jeanette Hutchinson
Sgt. Flint	Arthur Rigby
Insp. Cherry	Stanley Beard/Robert Crawdon
PC Lauderdale	Geoffrey Adams
Duffy Clayton	Harold Scott
Johnny Wills	Nicholas Donnelly
Tubb Barrell	Neil Wilson
Grace Milard	Moira Mannion
Jamie MacPherson	David Webster
Chris Freeman	Anne Ridler
Bob Penney	Anthony Parker
Alex Jones	Jan Miller
PC Jones	John Hughes
Kay Shaw/Lauderdale	Jacelyne Rhodes
Michael Bonnet	Paul Elliott
Jean Bell	Patricia Forde
Bob Cooper	Duncan Lamont
PC Swain	Robert Arnold
Liz Harris	Zeph Gladstone
Shirley Palmer	Anne Carroll
Betty Williams	Jean Dallas
PC Burton	Peter Thornton
DS Harvey	Geoffrey Kean
PC Roberts	Geoffrey Kenion
Insp. Carter	Peter Jeffrey
Ann Foster	Pamela Bucher
Brian Turner	Andrew Bradford
DC Pearson	Joe Dunlop
PC Newton	Michael Osborne
DC Webb	Derek Anders
Sgt. Brewer	Gregory de Polney
Alan Burton	Richard Heffer
Len Clayton	Ben Howard

Producers

Douglas Moodie, G.B. Lupino, Ronald Marsh, Philip Barker, Eric Fawcett, Robin Nash, Joe Waters

Programming History

154 30-minute episodes; 285 45-minute episodes
BBC

July 1955–August 1955	6 episodes
June 1956–September 1956	13 episodes
January 1957–March 1957	13 episodes
September 1957–March 1958	28 episodes
September 1958–March 1959	27 episodes
September 1959–April 1960	30 episodes
October 1960–April 1961	30 episodes
September 1961–March 1962	27 episodes
September 1962–March 1963	27 episodes
October 1963–March 1964	26 episodes
September 1964–March 1965	26 episodes
October 1965–April 1966	31 episodes
October 1966–December 1966	13 episodes
September 1967–February 1968	20 episodes
September 1968–December 1968	16 episodes
September 1969–December 1969	16 episodes
November 1970–March 1971	17 episodes
November 1971–February 1972	12 episodes
September 1972–December 1972	14 episodes
December 1973–April 1974	16 episodes
February 1975–May 1975	13 episodes
March 1976–May 1976	8 episodes

Further Reading

Cotes, Peter, "Obituary: Lord Willis," *The Independent* (December 24, 1992)

Scott, Richard, "Villainy by the Book," *Times* (London) (November 12, 1994)

West, Richard, "Sunday Comment: Bring Back the Friendly Bobby," *Sunday Telegraph* (June 13, 1993)

Doctor Who

British Science Fiction Program

Doctor Who, the world's longest continuously running television science fiction series, was made by the British Broadcasting Corporation (BBC) between 1963 and 1989 (with repeats being shown in many countries thereafter and a made-for-television movie broadcast on both the BBC and the U.S. network FOX in 1996). *Doctor Who's* first episode screened in Britain on November 23, 1963, the day after the assassination of President John F. Kennedy. Consequently, this first episode of a low-budget series was swamped by "real life" television and became a BBC institution quietly and by stealth in the interstices of more epic television events. Similarly, in the first episode, the central character is a mysterious ("Doctor Who?") and stealthy figure in the contemporary world of 1963, not even being seen for the first 11 and a half minutes and then appearing as an ominous and shadowy person who irresponsibly "kidnaps" his granddaughter's schoolteacher in his time machine (the Tardis). This mystery was the hallmark of the series for its first three years (when William Hartnell played the lead), as was the antihero quality of the Doctor (in the first story he has to be restrained from killing a wounded and unarmed primitive).

The Doctor was deliberately constructed as a character against stereotype: a "cranky old man" yet also as vulnerable as a child, an antihero playing against the more obvious "physical" hero of the schoolteacher Ian (played by the well-known lead actor in commercial television's *Ivanhoe* series). Its famous, haunting signature tune was composed at the new BBC Radiophonic Workshop, adding a futuristic dimension to a series that would never be high on production values. The program always attracted ambitious young directors, with (the later enormously successful) Verity Lambert as its first. The decision to continue with the series in 1966 when Hartnell had to leave the part and to "regenerate" the Doctor on screen allowed a succession of quirkily different personas to inhabit the Doctor. When it was decided in 1966 to reveal where the Doctor came from (the Time Lord world of Gallifrey), the mysteriousness of the Doctor could be carried on in a different way—via the strangely varied characterization. Following Hartnell, the Doctor was played by the Chaplinesque "space hobo" Patrick Troughton; the

dignified "establishment" figure of Jon Pertwee; the parodic visual mix of Bob Dylan and Oscar Wilde, Tom Baker; the vulnerable but "attractive to young women" Peter Davison; the aggressive and sometimes violent Colin Baker; the gentle, whimsical Sylvester McCoy; and, in the 1996 movie, the romantic and emotional Paul McGann.

These shifts in personas were matched by shifts in generic style, as each era's producers looked for new formulas to attract new audiences. The mid-1970s, for example, under producer Philip Hinchcliffe, achieved a high point in audience ratings and was marked by a dramatic gothic-horror style. This led to a "TV violence" dispute with Mary Whitehouse's National Viewers and Listeners Association. The subsequent producer, Graham Williams, shifted the series to a more comic signature. This comedy became refined as generic parody in 1979 under script editor Douglas Adams (author of *Hitchhiker's Guide to the Galaxy*). *Doctor Who's* 17th season, for which Adams edited scripts and wrote certain episodes ("The Pirate Planet" and "The City of Death"), became notorious with the fans, who hated what they saw as the self-parody of *Doctor Who* as "*Fawlty Towers* in space" (John Cleese appeared briefly in a brilliantly funny parody of art critics in "The City of Death").

Throughout *Doctor Who's* changes, however, the fans have remained critically loyal to the series. Fiercely aggressive to some producers and to some of the show's signature players, the fans' intelligent campaigns helped keep the program on the air in some of the more than 100 countries where it has screened; and in the United States, huge conventions of fans brought *Doctor Who* a new visibility in the 1980s. However, the official fans have never amounted to more than a fraction of the audience. *Doctor Who* achieved the status of an institution as well as a cult.

Doctor Who's reputation attracted high-level, innovative writers; its formula to educate and entertain encouraged a range of storylines from space opera through parody to environmental and cultural comment. Its mix of current technology with relatively low budgets attracted ambitious young producers and led to what one producer called a "cheap but cheerful" British show that fascinated audiences of every age-

Doctor Who, Jon Pertwee, 1963–89.
Courtesy of the Everett Collection

group worldwide. Above all, its early, ambiguous construction opened the show to innovative, often bizarre, but always dedicated acting. With so many different characterizations and acting styles, the program, like the Doctor, was continuously "regenerating" and so stayed young.

JOHN TULLOCH

See also **Lambert, Verity; Nation, Terry; Newman, Sidney; Pertwee, John; Science Fiction Programs; Troughton, Patrick**

Cast

The Doctor (first)	William Hartnell
The Doctor (second)	Patrick Troughton
The Doctor (third)	Jon Pertwee
The Doctor (fourth)	Tom Baker
The Doctor (fifth)	Peter Davison
The Doctor (sixth)	Colin Baker
The Doctor (seventh)	Sylvester McCoy
The Doctor (eighth)	Paul McGann

Susan Foreman	Carole Ann Ford
Barbara Wright	Jacqueline Hill
Ian Chesterton	William Russell
Vicki	Maureen O'Brien
Steven Taylor	Peter Purves
Katarina	Adrienne Hill
Sara Kingdom	Jean Marsh
Dodo Chaplet	Jackie Lane
Polly Lopez	Anneke Wills
Ben Jackson	Michael Craze
Jamie McCrimmon	Frazer Hines
Victoria Waterfield	Deborah Watling
Zoe Heriot	Wendy Padbury
Liz Shaw	Caroline John
Jo Grant	Katy Manning
Sarah-Jane Smith	Elizabeth Sladen
Harry Sullivan	Ian Marter
Leela	Louise Jameson
Brigadier Lethbridge-Stewart	Nicholas Courtney
K9	John Leeson
Romana (first)	Mary Tamm
Romana (second)	Lalla Ward
Adric	Matthew Waterhouse
Nyssa	Sarah Sutton
Tegan Jovanka	Janet Fielding
Turlough	Mark Strickson
Perpugilliam Brown	Nicola Bryant
Melanie Bush	Bonnie Langford
Ace	Sophie Aldred
Master (1971–73)	Roger Delgado
Master (1981–89)	Anthony Ainley
Master (1996)	Eric Roberts
Doctor Grace Holloway	Daphne Ashbrook

Producers

Alex Beaton, Peter Bryant, Philip Hinchcliffe, Matthew Jacobs, Verity Lambert, Barry Letts, Innes Lloyd, John Nathan-Turner, Mervyn Pinfield, Derrick Sherwin, Peter Ware, John Wiles, Graham Williams II, Jo Wright, Philip Segal, Peter Wagg, Jo Wright

Programming History

BBC
679 approximately 25-minute episodes
15 approximately 50-minute episodes
1 90-minute special anniversary episode
1 90-minute made-for-television movie

November 1963–September 1964	42 episodes
October 1964–July 1965	39 episodes

September 1965–July 1966	45 episodes
September 1966–July 1967	43 episodes
September 1967–June 1968	40 episodes
August 1968–June 1969	44 episodes
January 1970–June 1970	25 episodes
January 1971–June 1971	25 episodes
January 1972–June 1972	26 episodes
December 1972–June 1973	26 episodes
December 1973–June 1974	26 episodes
December 1974–May 1975	20 episodes
August 1975–March 1976	26 episodes
September 1976–April 1977	26 episodes
September 1977–March 1978	26 episodes
September 1978–February 1979	26 episodes
September 1979–January 1980	20 episodes
August 1980–March 1981	28 episodes
January 1982–March 1982	26 episodes
January 1983–March 1983	22 episodes
November 25, 1983	90-minute anniversary special
January 1984–March 1984	22 25-minute episodes, 2 50-minute episodes
January 1985–March 1985	13 50-minute episodes
September 1986–December 1986	14 episodes
September 1987–December 1987	14 episodes
October 1988–January 1989	14 episodes
September 1989–December 1989	14 episodes
May 27, 1996	90-minute made-for-television movie (first aired in U.S. on FOX, on May 14, 1996)

Further Reading

Bentham, Jeremy, *Doctor Who: The Early Years,* London: Allen, 1986

Dicks, Terrance, and Malcolme Hulke, *The Making of Doctor Who,* London: Allen, 1980

Haining, Peter, *Twenty Years of Doctor Who,* London: Allen, 1983

Haining, Peter, *Doctor Who: 25 Glorious Years,* London: Allen, 1988

Rickard, Graham, *A Day with a TV Producer,* Hove, England: Wayland, 1980

Road, Alan, *Doctor Who: The Making of a Television Series,* London: Andre Deutsch, 1982

Tulloch, John, and Manuel Alvarado, *Doctor Who: The Unfolding Text,* London: Macmillan, 1983

Tulloch, John, and Henry Jenkins, *Science Fiction Audiences: Watching Doctor Who and Star Trek,* London: Routledge, 1995

Docudrama

The docudrama is a fact-based representation of real events. It may represent contemporary social issues—the "facts-torn-from-today's-headlines" approach—or it may deal with older historical events. U.S. television examples include *Brian's Song* (1971), the biography of Brian Piccolo who played football for the Chicago Bears and died young from cancer; *Roots* (1977), the history of a slave and his family; *Roe v. Wade* (1989), the history of the Supreme Court decision legalizing abortion; *Everybody's Baby: The Rescue of Jessica McClure* (1989), the rescue of an 18-month-old baby from a well; and three versions of the Amy Fisher and Joey Buttafuoco affair (1993). The sources of the form derive from 19th- and 20th-century journalism, movies, and radio.

In most cases, a docudrama is produced in the manner of realist theater or film. Thus, events are portrayed by actors in front of an invisible "fourth wall," shooting techniques obey the conventions of mainstream film or television (that is, establishing shots with shot/reverse shots for dialogue, lighting constructed in a verisimilar manner, nonanachronistic mise-en-scène), no voice-over narrator comments on the actions once the events begin, and little or no documentary footage is interspersed. Unlike mainstream drama, however, the docudrama does make claims to provide a fairly accurate interpretation of real historical events. In other words, it is a nonfictional drama.

Thus, the docudrama is a mode of representation that, as its name reflects, combines categories usually perceived as separate: documentary and drama. This transgression, however, is not an actual one. Texts that claim to represent the real may be created out of vari-

Eleanor and Franklin: The White House Years, Edward Herrmann, Jane Alexander, 1977.
©*ABC/Everett Collection*

ous sorts of documents, such as photographs, interviews, tape recordings of sounds, printed words, drawings, and narrators who attempt to explain what happened. Nonfictional texts may also use actors to reenact history. In all cases, the real is being represented and is thus never equal to the reality it represents. Some people point out that having any filmic recording of an event is a "text" with the same status as these other types of documents: film footage is necessarily taken from a particular angle and thus is an incomplete representation of an event.

The docudrama should be distinguished from fictional dramas that make use of reality as historical context but do not claim that the primary plotline is representing events that have actually occurred. An example of such a fictional use of history would be an episode in *Murphy Brown* in which Brown insists on questioning President Bush at a press conference and is then thrown out. The use of the real person Bush as backdrop to a fictional plot creates a "reality effect" for the fictional program but would not qualify the episode to be a docudrama.

Docudramas do not have to conform to the previously mentioned aesthetic conventions. An early U.S. example of a series devoted to reenacting past events is *You Are There. You Are There* derived from the radio program *CBS Is There,* which ran from 1947 through 1950. On television it appeared from February 1953 through October 1957. *You Are There* violated the traditional taboo of avoiding anachronisms by having contemporary television reporters interview historical figures about the events in which they were supposed to have been participating, for example, during the conquest of Mexico.

The *You Are There* form for a docudrama, however, is very unusual. Most docudramas employ standard dramatic formulas from mainstream film and television and apply them wholesale to representing history. These conventions include a goal-oriented protagonist with clear motivations, a small number of central characters (two to three) with more stereotyping for secondary characters, causes that are generally ascribed to personal sources rather than structural ones (psychological traumas rather than institutional dynamics), a dramatic structure geared to the length of the program (a two-hour movie might have the normal "seven-act" structure of the made-for-television movie), and an intensification of emotional ploys.

The desire for emotional engagement by the viewers (a feature valuable for maintaining the audience through commercials) produces an inflection of the docudrama into several traditional genres. In particular, docudramas may appeal to effects of suspense, terror, or tears of happiness or sadness. These effects are generated by generic formulas, such as those used in the detective, thriller, or horror genre. Although the outcome was known in advance, *Everybody's Baby* operates in the thriller mode: how will Baby Jessica be saved? Judicial dramas such as *Roe vs. Wade* or murder dramas such as *Murder in Mississippi* (the death of three civil rights workers) use suspense as a central affective device. Examples of terror are docudramas of murders or attempted murders by family members or loved ones or of larger disasters, such as the Chernobyl meltdown or plane crashes.

One of the most favored effects, however, is tears, produced through melodramatic structures. Some critics point out that docudramas tend to treat the "issue of the week" and that such a concern for topical issues also produces an interest in social problems that might have melodramatic resolutions. Docudramas have treated incest, missing children, wife or child abuse, teenage suicide, alcoholism and drug addiction, adultery, AIDs-related deaths, eating disorders, and other "diseases of the week." The highly successful *Brian's Song,* which won five Emmys and a Peabody, is an excellent example of this subtype of docudrama. Its open sentimentality and use of male-buddy conventions, along with the treatment of an interracial friendship, uses the event of an early death by cancer to promote images of universal brotherhood. *The Burning Bed* (1984) and *The Karen Carpenter Story* (1989) wage war against pressures producing, respectively, domestic violence and anorexia nervosa.

Such implicitly or explicitly socially conscious programs, however, raise the problem of interpretation. Indeed, docudramas, like other methods of representing reality, are subject to controversy regarding their offer of historical information through storytelling. Although historians now recognize how common it is to explain history through dramatic narratives, they are still concerned about what effects particular types of dramatic narratives may have on viewers. Debates about docudramas (or related forms, such as "reality TV") include several reservations.

One reservation is related to "dramatic license." In order to create a drama that adheres to the conventions of mainstream storytelling (particularly a sensible chain of events, a clear motivation for character behavior, and a moral resolution), writers may claim they need to exercise what they call dramatic license—the creation of materials not established as historical fact or even the violation of known facts. Such distortions include created dialogues among characters, expressions of internal thoughts, meetings of people that never happened, events reduced to two or three days that actually occurred over weeks, and so forth. Critics point out that it is the conventions of mainstream drama that compel such violations of history, while writers of docudramas counter that they never truly distort the historical record. Critics reply that the dramatic mode chosen already distorts history, which cannot always be conveniently pushed into a linear chain of events or explained by individual human agency.

Another reservation connected to the first is the concern that spectators may be unable to distinguish between known facts and speculation. This argument proposes not that viewers are not sufficiently critical but that the docudrama may not adequately mark out distinctions between established facts and hypotheses and that, even if the docudrama does mark the differences, studies of human memory suggest that viewers may be unable to perceive the distinctions while viewing the program or remember the distinctions later.

A third reservation focuses on the tendency toward simplification. Critics point out that docudramas tend toward hagiography or demonization in order to compress the historical material into a brief drama. Additionally, complex social problems may be personalized so that complicated problems are "domesticated."

Adding phone numbers to call to find help for a social problem may be well intentioned but may also suggest that sufficient solutions to the social problem are already in place.

Outside the United States, many of these problems have been addressed in different but related ways, and while the term "docudrama" is often used in a generic fashion, it may be applied to a range of forms. In the United Kingdom, for example, *Cathy Come Home* (1966) stands as one of the earliest and strongest explorations of the problem of homelessness. Created by writer Jeremy Sandford, producer Tony Garnett, and director Ken Loach, this program refuses the more conventional structures of dramatic narrative, inserting a strong "documentary" style of photography into the presentation and using "Cathy's" own voice as narrator-analyst for the harsh social situation in which she finds herself. Another voice, however, presents factual information in the form of statistics and other information related to the central topic of the piece. *Cathy Come Home* has been described as a "documentary-drama," a term that seeks to emphasize the serious and factual qualities of the show against the more conventional docudrama.

In Australia, versions of docudrama have often been used to explore social and national history. Productions such as *Anzacs, Gallipoli,* and *Cowra Outbreak* have focused on Australian participation in both world wars and, in some views, are crucial texts in the construction of national identity.

In Canada, critics have applied the docudrama designation to a broader range of production styles, including works such as *The Valour and the Horror,* which combined documentary exploration with dramatized sequences. This program led to an ongoing controversy over the nature of the "real" and the "true." Because the presentation challenged received notions of Canadian involvement in World War II (notions themselves constructed from various experiences, memories, and records), the conflict took on an especially public nature. So, too, did arguments surrounding *The Boys of St. Vincent,* which dealt with child molestation in a church-run orphanage. The dramatization in this case was more complete but clearly paralleled a case that was still in court at the time of production and airing.

What all these examples suggest is, on the one hand, that docudrama is a particularly useful form for television, whether for advertising profit, the exploration of social issues, the construction of identity and history, or some combination of these ends. On the other hand, the varied examples point to an ongoing aspect of television's status as a medium that both constructs narratives specifically defined as "fiction" and purports to somehow record or report "reality." *You Are There* mixed "news," history, and fiction, categories often (and uncritically) considered distinct and separate. The mixture, the blurred boundaries among the conventions linked to these forms of expression and communication, and the public discussions caused by those blurrings and mixings remain central to any full understanding of the practices and the roles of television in contemporary society.

All these concerns came to the fore in late 2003 in the United States, when the Columbia Broadcasting System (CBS) declined to air *The Reagans,* a docudrama based on the lives and careers of President Ronald Reagan and his wife, Nancy. Although the network had commissioned the work and, presumably, had been aware of its content and approach throughout the production process, Leslie Moonves, chief executive officer of CBS, made the decision not to air the program on the prime-time schedule after strong objections were raised in various quarters. Some of the response came from political groups aligned with the Republican Party. Some came from conservative critics who charged that the docudrama was a left-wing attack on a beloved president. Another line of critique cited the casting of Mr. James Brolin, husband of Ms. Barbra Streisand, as Ronald Reagan. This criticism pointed to Ms. Streisand's strong support of the Democratic Party. Moonves's personal explanation claimed that he found the work "unbalanced" and that his decision was a "moral call." Although the program was not aired on CBS, it was made available on

Showtime, a premium cable network also owned by Viacom, parent company of CBS. In addition to the docudrama itself, in its complete and original form, Showtime presented a panel discussion in which historians and media critics discussed the project. The network also conducted a poll of viewers. Those who responded split almost evenly between those who felt that the controversy was "very warranted" (34 percent) and those who felt that it was "not at all warranted" (37 percent). Previously in the same year, CBS aired *Hitler: The Rise of Evil.* While this docudrama also raised questions (and eyebrows) regarding the use of actual events in television dramatic productions, it proved modestly successful and was also sold widely to other television organizations throughout the world.

JANET STAIGER AND HORACE NEWCOMB

See also **Cathy Come Home; Power Without Glory; Six Wives of Henry VIII; Valour and the Horror, The**

Further Reading

Caughie, John, "Progressive Television and Documentary Drama," in *Popular Film and Television,* edited by Tony Bennett et al., London: British Film Institute, 1981

Goodwin, Andrew, et al., *Drama-Documentary,* London: British Film Institute, 1983

O'Connor, John E., *American History/American Television: Interpreting the Video Past,* New York: Ungar, 1983

Rapping, Elaine, *The Movie of the Week: Private Stories, Public Events,* Minneapolis: University of Minnesota Press, 1992

Documentary

A documentary is defined as a nonfiction report that devotes its full-time slot to one thesis or subject, usually under the guidance of a single producer. Part of the fascination with documentaries lies in their unique blend of writing, visual images, soundtracks, and the individual styles of their producers. In addition to their particular contribution to the television medium, documentaries are notable because they have intertwined with wrenching moments in history. These characteristics have inspired some to describe documentaries as among the finest moments on television and as a voice of reason, while others have criticized them as inflammatory.

TV documentaries, as explained by A. William Bluem in the classic *Documentary in American Television,* evolved from the late 1920s and 1930s works of photojournalists and film documentarians, such as Roy Stryker, John Grierson, and Pare Lorentz. Bluem writes, "They wished that viewers might share the adventure and despair of other men's lives, and commiserate with the downtrodden and underprivileged." The rise of radio in World War II advanced the documentary idea, especially through the distinguished works of writer Norman Corwin of the Columbia Broadcasting System (CBS) and the reporting of Edward R. Murrow. In 1946, Murrow created the CBS documentary unit, which linked documentary journalism with the idea that broadcasters owed the public a news service in exchange for lucrative station licenses.

Technology has also been a force in the documentary's evolution. The editing of audiotape on the 1949 CBS record *I Can Hear It Now* facilitated the origin of the radio documentary. On National Broadcasting Company (NBC) radio, the *Living* series (1949–51) used taped interviews and helped move the form away from dramatizations and toward actualities.

The genesis of the American TV documentary tradition is attributed to the CBS series *See It Now,* started in 1951 by the legendary team of Murrow and Fred Friendly. *See It Now* set the model for future documentary series. Producers shot their own film rather than cannibalize other material, worked without a prepared script and allowed a story to emerge, avoided using actors, and produced unrehearsed interviews. This independence contributed to the credibility of *See It Now*'s voice, as did Murrow and Friendly's courage in confronting controversy.

The most notable of the *See It Now* programs include several reports on McCarthyism, an episode that illustrates the uneasy association that exists between controversial documentaries, politics, and industry economics. The Aluminum Company of America (Alcoa) sought to sponsor *See It Now,* which featured the esteemed Murrow, to improve its image following antimonopoly decisions by the courts.

As McCarthyism increasingly damaged innocent reputations, Murrow and Friendly used their series to expose the groundless attacks. "A Report on Senator Joseph R. McCarthy" in 1954 employed the senator's own words to discredit his false claims. Such programs made CBS and Alcoa uneasy. Alcoa refused to publicize or pay for some of the productions. Changing market conditions forced the company to withdraw sponsorship at the end of the 1955 season, and the program lost its weekly time period.

In June 1955, CBS began airing *The $64,000 Question,* which greatly increased revenues for its time slot as well as for adjacent periods. In a climate that included political pressure on the network and its sponsor, coupled with economic pressures that favored revenues over prestige, support for *See It Now* waned, and the program was scaled back to occasional broadcasts that lasted until the summer of 1958.

Other notable series of the 1950s include television's first major project in the compilation tradition, *Victory at Sea* (1952–53). Produced by Henry Solomon, this popular NBC series detailed World War II sea battles culled from 60 million feet of combat film footage. It was a paean to freedom and the overthrow of tyranny. Another popular series ran on CBS

Frontline: "The Secret File on J. Edgar Hoover."
Photo courtesy of Photo Assist

from 1957 to 1966. *The Twentieth Century* was a history class for millions of American TV viewers, produced throughout its entire run by Burton (Bud) Benjamin.

The absence of the American Broadcasting Company (ABC) as a major presence in the documentary field in the 1950s is a telling indicator of television history. ABC was the weak, third network, lacking the resources, affiliate strength, and audience of its rivals. Since CBS and NBC dominated the airwaves, each could counterprogram the other's entertainment hits with documentaries. The more the industry tended toward monopoly, the better the climate for documentaries.

Documentaries soared in quality and quantity during the early 1960s, a result of multiple factors. In *The Expanding Vista: American Television in the Kennedy Years,* Mary Ann Watson articulates how the confluence of technology with social dynamics energized the television documentary movement. Following the quiz show scandals, pressure on the industry to restore network reputations spurred the output of high-quality nonfiction programming.

Against the Odds: "The Artists of the Harlem Renaissance, William Henry Johnson."
Courtesy of the Everett Collection/CSU Archives

The May 1961 "Vast Wasteland" speech by Federal Communications Commission (FCC) chairman Newton Minow and the "raised eyebrow" of government further motivated the networks to accelerate their documentary efforts as a way of protecting broadcast-station licenses and stalling FCC hints that the networks themselves should be licensed. President John F. Kennedy was also an advocate of documentaries, which he felt were important in revealing the inner workings of democracy.

The availability of lightweight 16-millimeter film equipment enabled producers to get closer to stories and record eyewitness observations through a technique known as *cinéma vérité,* or direct cinema. A significant development was the wireless synchronizing system, which facilitated untethered, synchronized sound-film recordings, pioneered by the Drew Associates.

Primary (1960) was a breakthrough documentary. Produced by Robert Drew and shot by Richard Leacock, the film featured the contest between Senators John Kennedy and Hubert Humphrey in the 1960 Wisconsin primary. For the first time, viewers of Time-Life's four television stations followed candidates through crowds and into hotel rooms, where they awaited polling results. Through the mobile-camera technique, *Primary* achieved an intimacy technique never before seen and established the basic electronic news-gathering shooting style. In *Crisis: Behind a*

Presidential Commitment, Drew Associates producer Gregory Shuker took cameras into the Oval Office to observe presidential meetings over the crisis precipitated by Alabama Governor George Wallace, who authorized the use of physical force to block the entry of two African-American students to the University of Alabama. The program aired in October 1963 on ABC and triggered a storm of protest over the admission of cameras into the White House.

The peak for TV documentary production was the 1961–62 season, when the three networks aired more than 250 hours of programming. Each network carried a prestige documentary series. *CBS Reports,* produced by Friendly, premiered in 1959 and became a weekly documentary series in the 1961–62 season. *NBC White Paper,* produced by Irving Gitlin, first aired in November 1960 and immediately thrust itself into hotly contested issues, such as the U-2 spy mission and the Nashville, Tennessee, lunch-counter sit-ins. The *White Paper* approach featured meticulous research and analysis.

At ABC, the job of developing a documentary unit fell to John Secondari. Since sponsor Bell and Howell produced film cameras and projectors, the artistic quality of the filmed presentation was important and engendered an attention to aesthetics that carried over in later years on ABC News documentaries. Like others of the period, the *Bell and Howell Close-Up!* series, which also aired productions by Drew Associates, dealt with race relations ("Cast the First Stone" and "Walk in My Shows") and Cold War themes ("90 Miles to Communism" and "Behind the Wall").

Minow's emphasis on the public service obligations of broadcast licensees also spurred network affiliates to increase documentary broadcasts. Clearances for *CBS Reports* jumped from 115 to 140 stations. The production of local documentaries surged, creating a favorable environment for independent producers. David Wolper, whose Wolper Productions enjoyed a growth spurt in 1961, said, "Maybe we should thank Newton Minow for a fine publicity job on our behalf." Wolper's unique contributions to syndicated TV documentaries include "The Race for Space" (1958) and the series *Biography,* the *National Geographic Society Special,* and *The Undersea World of Jacques Cousteau.*

The favorable climate for TV documentaries in the Kennedy era also nurtured an international collaboration that began in late 1960. *Intertel* came into being when five groups of broadcasters in the four major English-speaking nations formed the International Television Federation. The participants were Associated Rediffusion, Ltd, of Great Britain, the Australian Broadcasting Commission, the Canadian Broadcasting Corporation, and, in the United States, the National

American Masters—John Cage: "I have nothing to say and I am saying it."
Courtesy of the Everett Collection

Educational Television (NET) and Radio Center and the Westinghouse Broadcasting Company. In the United States, *Intertel* was piloted by NET's John F. White and Robert Hudson and by Westinghouse Group W executives Donald McGannon and Richard M. Pack. *Intertel* sought to foster compassion for the human problems of member nations—to teach countries how to live together as neighbors in a world community, which Bluem characterized as "the greatest service which the television documentary can extend."

In a speech reported in *Television Quarterly,* historian Erik Barnouw characterized the documentary as a "necessary kind of subversion" that "focuses on unwelcome facts, which may be the very facts and ideas that the culture needs for its survival." Throughout the turbulent 1960s, documentaries regularly presented "unwelcome facts." ABC offered a weekly series beginning in 1964 called *ABC Scope.* As the Vietnam War escalated, the series became "Vietnam Report" from 1966 to 1968. NBC aired *Vietnam Weekly Re-*

The Louvre: *A Golden Prison.*
Photo courtesy of Monterey Home Video and Lucy Jarvis

view. CBS launched an ambitious seven-part documentary in 1968 called *Of Black America.*

The year 1968 also marked a change in the influence of network news and a drop in TV documentary production. Affiliate stations bristled over network reports on urban violence, the Vietnam War, and antiwar protests. The Nixon administration launched an assault on the media and encouraged station owners to complain about news coverage in exchange for deregulation. TV coverage of the Democratic National Convention triggered protests against network news.

During this social, political, and economic revolution, network management experimented with less controversial programs. Each network introduced a newsmagazine to complement evening news and documentaries. Ray Carroll reports that the newsmagazine became a substitute for documentaries in the late 1960s and throughout the 1970s and that the number of long-form reports dropped. *60 Minutes* on CBS premiered in 1968, and, after a slow start for several years, it achieved unparalleled success. NBC followed in 1969 with *First Tuesday.*

ABC's answer was *The Reasoner Report,* launched in 1973, the same year the network resurrected the *CloseUp!* documentary series. In the 1970s, ABC's entertainment programs began to attract large audiences. To establish itself as a full-fledged network, ABC strengthened its news division and added the prestige documentary series *ABC CloseUp!,* produced by Av Westin, William Peters, Richard Richter, and Pam Hill. Under Hill's guidance, the *CloseUp!* unit excelled in documentary craft, featuring artfully rendered film, poetic language, and thoughtful music tracks.

The three-way competition for prime-time audiences reduced airtime for documentaries. However, ABC's reentry into the documentary field forced competitors to extend their documentary commitment, a rivalry that carried into the Reagan years. Pressure continued to mount against documentaries, however, in the 1970s. In the most celebrated case, the 1971 CBS documentary *The Selling of the Pentagon* resulted in a congressional investigation into charges of unethical journalism.

Network documentaries virtually disappeared during the Reagan years; in 1984, there were 11. Under Mark Fowler, the FCC eliminated requirements for public service programming. Competition from cable, independents, and videocassettes eroded network audiences. The Reagan administration advocated a society based on individualism; economics became paramount, while support for social programs declined.

Documentaries also suffered from controversies over the CBS programs *The Uncounted Enemy: A Vietnam Deception* and *People Like Us,* from an increase in libel suits, and from deregulation, which offered financial incentives to broadcasters in lieu of public service programming. In this environment, the network documentary, which was rooted in the Franklin Delano Roosevelt era and frequently endorsed collective social programs, became an anachronism. The documentary's decline in the Reagan years is one indicator of the ebbing of the New Deal influence on American culture.

After the three network sales in the mid-1980s, the new owners required news divisions to earn a profit. The most successful experiments were the 1987 NBC Connie Chung lifestyle documentaries, *Scared Sexless* and *Life in the Fat Lane.* These programs demonstrated that a combination of celebrity anchor, popular subjects, and updated visual treatments could appeal to larger audiences. In time, as entertainment costs rose and ratings fell, these "infotainment" programs evolved into a stream of popular newsmagazines, which became cost-effective replacements for entertainment shows.

As the documentary presence continued to recede at the commercial networks, the best place for American viewers to find documentaries on free, over-the-air television was on the Public Broadcasting Service (PBS) as a new generation of producers committed themselves to prolonging long-form programs. As of 2002, *NOVA,* the science documentary series, was still on the air after more than 25 years. In 1983, PBS launched *Frontline,* an investigative series produced by David Fanning. *Frontline* is regarded as the flagship public affairs series for PBS and "the last best hope for broadcast documentaries." *The American Experience* first appeared in 1988, led by Judy Crichton and others, who created lush portrayals of memorable events and people in American history. *P.O.V.* gave opportunities to independent producers whose works did not fit into series' themes.

Several notable PBS documentary series examined specific periods in American history. The 13-hour *Vietnam: A Television History* aired in 1983. In 1987, the network broadcast *Eyes on the Prize.* Produced by Henry Hampton, this moving series chronicles the story of the modern civil rights movement from the beginnings of the Montgomery, Alabama, bus boycott to the passage of the Civil Rights Act of 1964. The success of the first *Eyes on the Prize* series failed to translate into easier fund-raising for the second series, which was more controversial.

Whereas commercial broadcast documentaries were ephemeral, many of those appearing on PBS became available to viewers and scholars through postbroadcast products. One of the dominant figures using this technique in the 1990s was Ken Burns. Burns carved a niche as a filmmaker able to tackle large sweeps of history in multipart documentaries such as *The Civil War, Baseball,* and *Jazz.* These programs also enjoyed commercial success through the sale of companion books, videotapes, and compact discs. Burns offered serious, in-depth research; careful use of expert consultants; and exquisite use of photography, sound, narration, fluid camera, and other techniques to make the past vivid. Programming of this style also benefited from enough historical distance to skirt controversy of the type raised by the *Vietnam* series or Hampton's second series of *Eyes on the Prize.* His brother Ric Burns employed similar techniques in such PBS series as *New York: A Documentary Film.* Consequently, both Burns brothers were able to attract large corporate sponsors to support their work on public television. In the fall of 2002, many of Ken Burns's documentaries were presented in a retrospective series devoted to his works. For this special presentation, the films were remastered and offered in superb visual quality not always available in the original airings. Michael Apted has also maintained a presence on PBS with projects such as *7 Up,* in which he followed a group of individuals to document the progressions in their lives at seven-year intervals. Another Apted series, *Married in America,* aired in 2002.

A leading documentary producer on cable television is Bill Kurtis. Kurtis, a former Chicago newsman and national correspondent for CBS News, founded Kurtis productions and began producing investigative, long-form series for the A&E cable television network, as well as PBS, in 1991. Home Box Office, the Discovery Channel, the Learning Channel, the History Channel, and the Cable News Network (CNN) give cable viewers a wide selection of documentary programs and independent films, including extended series. CNN produced the 24-part *Cold War* in 1998, and the History Channel telecast series such as *A History of Britain,* with six parts in 2000 and another five installments in 2001. A recent development in documentary programming is the access to information beyond the telecast on specially designed sites of the World Wide Web.

During five decades of documentary television, some patterns have emerged. Documentary series have been used to give in-depth attention to major cultural issues but also as a publicity device to raise the visibility of a network. Broadcast and cable networks have used documentary programming to raise their credibility. Certain individuals have become prominent within the industry because of their association with, or innovations in, documentaries. On public television, the popularity of documentary series has become a marketing tool for attracting contributions from viewers and corporate sponsors.

Within this environment are two recurring tensions. One relates to economics. In early times, documentaries were more expensive to produce than regular news programs, but the expense was outweighed by prestige and evidence of public service. In later years, documentaries continued to be more expensive than news but became less expensive than entertainment programs. This characteristic led to the development of a niche for news in prime time on commercial broadcast television as well as inexpensive programming for filling hours of cable network schedules. When a network cannot afford entertainment programming, cannot be without a visible public service commitment, or cannot lose its viewer base (as on PBS), it relies on documentary programming.

The other tension relates to controversy, politics, and timing. When controversial documentaries butted heads with declining powers, they were acclaimed. *See It Now* succeeded in its indictments of Wisconsin Senator Joseph McCarthy in part because McCarthy's career was waning. CBS prevailed in the controversy over *The Selling of the Pentagon* in part because, by the 1970s, the Vietnam War had reduced the clout of the military in public affairs. In the 1980s, a shift in the political climate hindered government support for public television and for aggressive commercial network documentaries. Political conservatives objected to what was perceived as a liberal bias in this kind of programming. In the commercial arena, the threat or act of litigation, often supported by conservative interest groups, put pressure on executives responsible for documentary programming, which resulted in a lowering of the networks' documentary voices. In the public television arena, attacks by conservative politicians on controversial documentaries created a disincentive to embrace the form.

The one sweeping change in documentary programming since its inception on American television is that it was once provided without regarded for its profitability. However, that is no longer the norm. Documentaries produced today are, by and large, expected to attract money directly.

Tom Mascaro

See also **Black and White in Color; Burns, Ken;** *Civilisation;* **Death on the Rock; Drew, Robert;** *Eyes on the Prize; Eyewitness to History; Fifth Estate;* **NBC Reports; NBC White Papers; Secondari, John;** *Selling of the Pentagon; Sylvania Waters; This Hour Has Seven Days; Tour of the White House with Mrs. John F. Kennedy; Uncounted Enemy, The; Valour and the Horror; Vietnam: A Television History; World in Action*

Further Reading

Barnouw, Erik, *Documentary,* New York: Oxford University Press, 1993

Benjamin, Burton, *Fair Play: CBS, General Westmoreland, and How a Television Documentary Went Wrong,* New York: Harper and Row, 1988

Bluem, A. William, *Documentary in American Television,* New York: Hastings House, 1965

Brown, Les, "The FCC Proudly Presents the Vast Wasteland," *Channels of Communications* (March/April 1983)

Carroll, Raymond Lee, "Factual Television in America: An Analysis of Network Television Documentary Programs, 1948–1975," Ph.D. diss., University of Wisconsin, 1978

Curtin, Michael, "Packaging Reality: The Influence of Fictional Forms on the Early Development of Television Documentary," *Journalism Monographs* (February 1993)

Curtin, Michael, *Redeeming the Wasteland: Television Documentary and Cold War Politics,* New Brunswick, New Jersey: Rutgers University Press, 1995

Diamond, Edwin, and Alan Mahony, "Once It Was *Harvest of Shame*—Now We Get *Scared Sexless,*" *TV Guide* (August 27, 1988)

Einstein, Daniel, *Special Edition: A Guide to Network Television Documentary Series and Special News Reports, 1955–1979,* Metuchen, New Jersey: Scarecrow Press, 1987

Hammond, Charles Montgomery, Jr., *The Image Decade,* New York: Hastings House, 1981

Jacobs, Lewis, *The Documentary Tradition: From Nanook to Woodstock,* New York: Hopkins and Blake, 1971; 2nd edition, New York: Norton, 1979

Kilborn, Richard, and John Izod, *An Introduction to Television Documentary: Confronting Reality,* Manchester, England: Manchester University Press, 1997

Leab, Daniel, J., "See It Now: A Legend Reassessed," in *American History/American Television: Interpreting the Video Past,* edited by John O'Connor, New York: Frederick Ungar Publishing, 1983

Levin, Roy, *Documentary Explorations,* Garden City, New York: Anchor Press, 1971

Mascaro, Tom, "Lowering the Voice of Reason: The Decline of Network Television Documentaries in the Reagan Years," Ph.D. diss., Wayne State University, 1994

NBC News, *The Invention of the Television Documentary: NBC News, 1950–1975,* New York: NBC, 1975

Nichols, Bill, *Representing Reality: Issues and Concepts in Documentary,* Bloomington: Indiana University Press, 1991

Rosteck, Thomas, *"See It Now" Confronts McCarthyism: Television Documentary and the Politics of Representation,* Tuscaloosa: University of Alabama Press, 1994

Swisher, Kara, "*Discovery*'s Long, Hard Road," *Washington Post* (June 17, 1991)

Unger, Arthur, "*Frontline*'s David Fanning: Upholding the Documentary Tradition" (interview), *Television Quarterly* (Summer 1991)

Waldman, Diane, and Janet Walker, editors, *Feminism and Documentary,* Minneapolis: University of Minnesota Press, 1999

Watson, Mary Ann, "The Golden Age of the American Television Documentary," *Television Quarterly* (1988)

Watson, Mary Ann, *The Expanding Vista: American Television in the Kennedy Years,* New York: Oxford University Press, 1990

Docusoap

"Docusoap" is the partly descriptive and partly pejorative name given to a broad subgenre of popular factual entertainment that first appeared mostly in Britain and Europe (but not exclusively there) during the 1990s. Docusoaps can be seen as one strand of "reality television," another loose category that indicates a whole range of popular factual formats to appear on television since the 1980s. Among these formats, the first developments appeared in the form of factual shows focusing on the work of police and emergency services, with FOX's *America's Most Wanted* (1988) and *Rescue 911* (Columbia Broadcasting System [CBS] 1989–) providing classic early examples on U.S. television. Among the later developments are the highly formatted game-documentaries in the line of *Big Brother* (Endemol 1999–) and the British *Pop Idol* (ITV 2002–) and its American counterpart, *American Idol* (FOX 2002–). Somewhere in the middle, although nearly all the varieties of reality television continue to be active in European television, comes the docusoap.

Docusoaps are generally a "quiet" form of reality television, using show-length narratives in series format to follow a selected group of people through the events and interactions of mundane, mostly occupational life. The "casting" of such shows can be compared with that of soap operas and sitcoms, but docusoaps have generally also drawn extensively on the tradition of observational filmmaking on location, within whose terms an unfolding plane of action and speech is accorded firm roots in nontelevisual reality. High-profile family-based series such as *An American Family* (Public Broadcasting Service [PBS] 1973) and *The Family* (British Broadcasting Corporation [BBC] 1974) provide an important part of the lineage here. However, it is work rather than family life that goes on in most docusoap: hotel staff keep their establishments running, airport desk clerks process passengers, vets attend sick animals, and parking wardens give offending motorists fines (to cite a few British examples).

This raises important questions about the degree of directorial intervention at all stages of the production, but it makes the programs distinct from series such as *The Real World* (Music Television [MTV] 1992–) and *Big Brother,* where the artificial terms of the protelevisual situation is an open condition of the programs' making and imposes constraints (as well as providing possibilities) for all that follows.

The appeal of docusoap to the audience's sense of ordinary life, a life portrayed without any clear propositional intent (for instance, there is no framing of what is observed in terms of larger problems and issues), connects strongly with the British and European tradition of soap opera fictions that focus on working-class families and situations rather than following the U.S. emphasis on the wealthy and privileged. However, whereas soaps in most countries has stayed centrally and sometimes exclusively with the themes of family relationships within the small community, docusoaps have successfully exploited the interest and entertainment potential of people at work or people being trained. Thus, an interest in private lives and in the world of feelings is connected to an interest in routine working settings, relationships, and encounters. This is doubly innovative, although there are clearly precedents for the televising of the mundane.

In tracing the history of the docusoap in Britain, the success of the BBC's series *Vet's School* (1996) and *Driving School* (1997) are important. The first series had drawn on the unexpectedly high ratings for the BBC series *Animal Hospital* in 1994, connecting the sick-animal theme outwards to issues of professional training and allowing stronger narrative and character development to figure, shadowing fiction at points in its construction. *Driving School* became a national phenomenon through its portrayal of one particular trainee in her bid to gain a license. These early series suggested the further possibilities of using an observational style to follow people in everyday situations outside the domestic frame. The requirement was a small "cast" to give character continuity and growing audience familiarity and a relatively stable workplace setting to give continuity of action, space, and time across the edited episodes. Sheer fascination with the kinds of activity observed carried the viewing experience. Stylistically, the format could incorporate both voiced-over commentary (essential to provide background information and useful in strengthening the comic development) and interview sequences (mostly informal, perhaps spoken while the subject was undertaking an occupational task). It could work with lengthy sections in real-time duration and yet also crosscut across different locations and time collapses as the material suggested.

Shows developed in the docusoap format within Britain and elsewhere in Europe varied considerably in the recipe by which they combined their more obvious "soap" factors with the exploration of the spaces and routines of work. Some, such as the BBC's *Hotel* (1997), looking at the working lives of a small group of people in a Liverpool hotel, seem to carry substantial documentary value, whatever shaping interventions are brought to bear in order to ensure that the audience is entertained. And it is easy to see the appeal of both the BBC's *Airport* (1997) and ITV's *Airline* (1998) in the context of general public fascination with the procedures and processes associated with air travel and the various problems and tensions that can arise.

To some of those working in documentary departments, the docusoaps seemed to threaten the integrity of their craft. They were seen to do this by a very relaxed approach to "staging" at every level, a preoccupation with what could be seen as the trivial, and a level of audience success that threatened to take the funding and scheduling opportunities away from more serious projects. All these charges have a measure of truth, particularly the final one. However, other pro-

ducers and directors saw the success of docusoaps as opening up the possibilities for more imaginative documentary ventures in a serious vein and as reconnecting the broad documentary approach with a popular audience. The issue was the subject of intensive debate within the television industry during the period 1995–2000, after which point the mutated varieties of docusoap seemed to be more or less fully absorbed within national television systems. As the novelty effect waned, commissioning and prime-time scheduling dropped back.

British newspapers carried a run of stories in the late 1990s about the "scandal" of docusoaps, particularly their sometimes dubious practices of preshoot preparation and action management, which often aligned them very closely with fictional productions. However, the audience seemed to regard them with a mixture of quiet disdain and casual affection rather than seeing them as a threat to the integrity of the medium itself. While they did not undercut the core practices of documentary output (as some critics feared and some hoped), they did significantly modify the terms of popular factual representation in ways that will continue to be active in television culture.

JOHN CORNER

See also **Big Brother; Real World, The; Reality Programming**

Further Reading

Bruzzi, Stella, *New Documentary: A Critical Introduction,* London: Routledge, 2000
Dovey, Jon, *Freakshow,* London: Pluto 2000
Holmes, Su, and Jermyn, Deborah, editors, *Understanding Reality TV,* London: Routledge, 2004
Kilborn, Richard, *Staging the Real,* Manchester: Manchester University Press, 2003

Dolan, Charles F. (1926–)

U.S. Media Executive

Charles F. Dolan is one of the least known but most powerful moguls in the modern cable television industry in the United States. In early 1995, his corporate creation, Cablevision Systems Corporation, ranked as the fifth-largest operator in the United States, serving some 2.6 million subscribers in 19 states, about 1.5

million of them in the New York metropolitan area. "Chuck" Dolan's Cablevision Systems also owns and controls a number of noted cable television networks, headed by the popular and influential American Movie Classics (AMC). In 1995, the *New York Times* estimated Dolan's net worth at $175 million.

Headquartered in Long Island, New York, Dolan organized Cablevision Systems in 1973. He had started in the cable TV business a decade earlier with Sterling Television, an equipment supplier, which acquired the cable franchise for the island of Manhattan in the 1960s. Then, in 1970, he founded Home Box Office (HBO). When Time Life Inc. purchased HBO and Sterling Manhattan Cable, Dolan used the substantial proceeds from the deal to buy some Long Island systems that he turned into Cablevision Systems.

Dolan correctly figured that the action for cable would move to the suburbs and turned the locus of Cablevision Systems to the millions of potential customers living in areas surrounding New York City, particularly in Long Island's close-in Nassau and Suffolk counties. In time, Dolan also acquired franchises controlling 190,000 customers in Fairfield, Connecticut; 250,000 more in northern New Jersey; and 60,000 in Westchester County, New York. He also purchased or built cable TV systems across the United States, in Arkansas, Illinois, Maine, Michigan, Missouri, and Ohio.

In 1988, Dolan added the National Broadcasting Company (NBC) as a minority partner. General Electric had recently purchased NBC and prior to that had helped Dolan finance the expansion of Cablevision Systems. After that, Dolan, with help from NBC, moved into cable network programming in a major way. He crafted AMC into the top classic movie channel on cable. Building through grassroots marketing, AMC quietly became one of the fastest-growing cable networks of the early 1990s. Soon the *New York Times* was lavishing praise on AMC:

> It's more than nostalgia. It's a chance to see black-and-white films which may have slipped through the cracks. It's wall-to-wall movies with no commercials, no aggressive graphics, no pushy sound, no sensory MTV overload, no time frame. There's a sedate pace, a pseudo-PBS quality about AMC. It's the *Masterpiece Theater* of movies.

Dolan has also done well with sports programming, but on a regional basis. Dolan's regional sports channels broadcast all forms of sports to millions of subscribers to his and other cable systems in the New York City area. The New York Yankees and New York Mets baseball games are particularly successful. By 1994, Dolan had done so well that he partnered with billion-dollar conglomerate ITT to purchase Madison Square Garden for $1 billion. Suddenly, Cablevision Systems was the major player in sports marketing in the New York City area, owning the Knicks basketball team, the Rangers hockey team, the Madison Square Garden cable TV network, and the most famous venue for indoor sports in the United States. However, Dolan's

Charles F. Dolan.
Courtesy of Cablevision Systems Corporation

other great experiments, 24-hour local news on cable TV and the Bravo arts channel, were not as profitable.

Local around-the-clock news began in 1986 as News 12 Long Island. This niche service came about because New York City's over-the-air TV stations seemed unable to serve Long Island. Viewers appreciated not only News 12's basic half-hour news wheel but also its multipart reports that ran for a half hour or more. Under current economic constraints, New York City television stations could never telecast such programs.

With prize-winning series on breast cancer, drug abuse, and Alzheimer's disease, News 12 Long Island established a brand image. During election campaigns, the channel regularly staged candidate debates, and local politicians loved having their faces presented there. But little money came in to pay for these features, and only after a decade did it seem that News 12 would finally make money.

The same difficult economic calculus affected the arts-oriented Bravo channel. It was popular with well-off consumers, but too few of these tuned in on a regular basis. In the mid-1990s, Bravo seemed doomed, but when it partnered with NBC, its fortunes improved, doing well through the opening of the 21st century.

Dolan's accomplishments have been considerable. Though not well known to the general public, he helped establish cable television as an economic, social, and cultural force in the United States during the final quarter of the 20th century. He represents the TV entrepreneur in the true sense of the word, comparable to more publicized figures who started NBC and the Columbia Broadcasting System (CBS), David Sarnoff and William S. Paley.

Dolan continues to look to the future, seeking significant positions for his menu of cable programming networks and franchises on the "electronic superhighway." Like other cable entrepreneurs of the late 20th century, he pledged to make available 500 channels, movies on demand, and interactive video entertainment and information. However, not all such promises have been fulfilled. By 2001, Dolan had turned most of the day-to-day operations to his son James, and for its core profits, the company still depended on its 2.9 million cable TV subscribers in the suburbs of New York City. As the 21st century began, Cablevision System's high-speed Internet plans were proceeding very slowly. Having acquired The Wiz electronics stores and the Clearview Cinema chain in the late 1990s, the company, like many other new media corporations, seems unsure where to find the next television breakthrough.

DOUGLAS GOMERY

Charles F. Dolan. Born in Cleveland, Ohio, October 16, 1926. Attended John Carroll University. Married: Helen; children: MariAnne, Theresa, Deborah, James, Patrick, Thomas. Served briefly in the U.S. Air Force at the end of World War II. Worked at a radio station during high school, writing radio scripts and commercials; operated sports newsreel business; joined Sterling Television, 1954; built first urban cable television system, in New York City, 1961; president, Sterling Manhattan Cable, 1961–72; creator, Home Box Office pay movie service, 1970; sold interests in Manhattan cable service and HBO to Time Life, Inc., 1973; created and served as chair and chief executive, Cablevision Systems, one of the country's largest cable installations, since 1973; developed first local all-news channel for cable; created Rainbow Program Enterprises, operator of regional and national cable networks, including American Movie Classics, Bravo, and SportsChannel; elected chair of the National Academy of Television Arts and Sciences, 1996.

Further Reading

Burgi, Michael, "Cablevision's Bold Visionary," *MediaWeek* (July 4, 1994)

"Chuck Dolan of Cablevision on Making the Most of Cable's Head Start in the Wired Nation" (interview), *Broadcasting* (October 31, 1988)

Lieberman, David, "A Cable Mogul's Daring Dance on the High Wire," *BusinessWeek* (June 5, 1989)

Donahue, Phil (1935–)

U.S. Talk Show Host

In recent years, the talk show has become the most profitable, prolific, and contested format on daytime television. The sensationalist nature of many of these shows has spawned much public debate over the potential for invasion of personal privacy and the exploitation of sensitive social issues. In this environment, Phil Donahue, who is widely credited with inventing the talk show platform, appears quite tame. But in the late 1960s, when *The Phil Donahue Show* first aired on WLW-D in Dayton, Ohio, Donahue was considered a radical and scintillating addition to the daytime scene.

Working at the college station KYW as a production assistant, Donahue had his first opportunity to test his on-air abilities when the regular booth announcer failed to show up. Donahue claims it was then that he became "hooked" on hearing the transmission of his own voice. The position he took after graduation, news director for a Michigan radio station, allowed him to try his hand at broadcast reporting and eventually led to work as a stringer for the *CBS Evening News* and an anchor position at WHIO-TV in Dayton in the late 1950s. There he first entered the talk show arena with his radio show *Conversation Piece,* on which he interviewed civil rights activists (including Martin Luther King, Jr., and Malcolm X) and war dissenters.

After Donahue left WHIO and worked a subsequent three-month stint as a salesman, the general manager of WLW-D convinced him to host a call-in TV talk show. The show would combine the talk-radio format with television interview show. However, *The Phil Donahue Show* would start with two major disadvantages: a small budget and geographic isolation from the entertainment industries, preventing it from garnering star guests. In order to attract an audience, Donahue and his producers had to innovate—they focused on issues rather than fame.

The first guest on *The Phil Donahue Show* was Madalyn Murray O'Hair, an atheist who contended that religion "breeds dependence" and who was ready to mount a campaign to ban prayer in public schools. During that same week in November 1967, the show featured footage of a woman giving birth, a phone-in vote on the morality of an anatomically correct male doll, and a funeral director extolling the workings of his craft. The bold nature of these topics was tempered by Donahue's appealing personality. He was one of the first male television personalities to exude characteristics of "the sensitive man" (traits and behaviors further popularized in the 1970s by actors such as Alan Alda), acquired through his interest in both humanism and feminism.

Donahue's affinity with the women's movement, his sincere style, and his focus on controversial topics attracted a large and predominantly female audience. In 1992, he told a *Los Angeles Times* reporter that his show

> got lucky because we discovered early on that the usual idea of women's programming was a narrow, sexist view. We found that women were interested in a lot more than covered dishes and needlepoint. The determining factor [was], "Will the woman in the fifth row be moved to stand up and say something?" And there's a lot that will get her to stand up.

Donahue attempted to "move" his audience in a number of ways, but the most controversial approach involved educating women on matters of reproduction. Shows on abortion, birthing techniques, and a discussion with Masters and Johnson were all banned by certain local affiliates. According to Donahue's autobiography, WGN in Chicago refused to air a show on reverse vasectomy and tubal ligation because it was "too educational for women...and too bloody." Nevertheless, Donahue's proven success with such a lucrative target audience led to the accumulation of other major Midwest markets as well as the show's eventual move to Chicago in 1974 and then to New York in 1985 (the show's name was shortened to just *Donahue* when production moved to Chicago). By then, the range of topics had broadened considerably, even to include live "space bridge" programs. Cohosted with Soviet newscaster Vladimir Pozner, these events linked U.S. and Soviet citizens for live exchanges on issues common to both groups.

Phil Donahue.
Courtesy of the Everett Collection

By the 1980s, however, the increasing popularity of *Donahue* had led to a proliferation of local and nationally syndicated talk shows. As competition increased, the genre became racier, with less emphasis on issues and more on personal scandal. Donahue retained his niche in the market by dividing the show's focus, dabbling in both the political and the personal. He was able to provide interviews with political candidates, explorations of the AIDS epidemic, and revelations of the savings-and-loan crisis, alongside shows on safe-sex orgies, cross-dressing, and aging strippers.

In 1992, with 19 Emmy Awards under his belt, Donahue was celebrated by his fellow talk show hosts on his 25th anniversary special as a mentor and kindly patriarch of the genre. Fellow talk show host Maury Povich was quoted in *Broadcasting and Cable* as saying at the event, "He's the granddaddy of us all and he birthed us all." Phil Donahue broadcast out of New York, where he lives with his wife, actress Marlo Thomas, until 1996. Early in that year, he announced that television season would be his last. Ratings for *Donahue* were declining, and a number of major stations, including his New York affiliate, had chosen to drop the show from their schedules. In the spring of 1996, Donahue taped his final show, an event covered on major network newscasts, complete with warm sentiment, spraying champagne, and expected yet undoubted sincerity.

After the ending of this hugely successful run for a syndicated program, Donahue retired from television work, dedicating himself to political causes and public service while remaining in the public eye as a spokesman for organizations such as the American Civil Liberties Union and a supporter of third-party presidential hopeful Ralph Nader. Then, in April 2002, Donahue surprised many by agreeing to return to the television arena, signing a contract with the struggling cable news network MSNBC to host a prime-time current events program scheduled opposite the FOX News Channel's *The O'Reilly Factor* and the Cable News Network's (CNN's) new show, *Connie Chung Tonight.* The latest program to be called *Donahue* debuted in July 2002. After six months of faring poorly in the ratings, however, the show was canceled on February 25, 2003.

SUSAN MURRAY

See also **Talk Show**

Phil (Phillip) John Donahue. Born in Cleveland, Ohio, December 21, 1935. Educated at the University of Notre Dame, B.B.A. 1957. Married: 1) Marge Cooney, 1958 (divorced, 1975); children: Michael, Kevin, Daniel, Jim, Maryrose; 2) actress Marlo Thomas, 1980. Began career as announcer, KYW-TV and AM, Cleveland, 1957; bank check sorter, Albuquerque, New Mexico; news director, WABJ radio, Adrian, Michigan; morning newscaster, WHIO-TV, where interviews with Jimmy Hoffa and Billy Sol Estes were picked up nationally; hosted *Conversation Piece,* phone-in talk show, 1963–67; debuted *The Phil Donahue Show,* Dayton, Ohio, 1967, syndicated two years later; relocated to Chicago, 1974–85; host, *Donahue,* 1974–96; relocated to New York City, 1985; host of cable program, also called *Donahue,* July 2002–February 2003. Recipient: 20 Emmy Awards; Best Talk Show Host, 1988; Margaret Sanger Award, Planned Parenthood, 1987; Peabody Award, 1980.

Television Series

1969–74	*The Phil Donahue Show* (syndicated; from Dayton, Ohio)
1974–85	*Donahue* (syndicated; from Chicago)
1985–96	*Donahue* (syndicated; from New York)
2002–03	*Donahue* (MSNBC)

Publications

Donahue: My Own Story, 1980
The Human Animal, 1985

Further Reading

Carbaugh, Donald A., *Talking American: Cultural Discourses on Donahue,* Norwood, New Jersey: Ablex Publishing, 1988
Haley, Kathy, "From Dayton to the World: A History of the Donahue Show," *Broadcasting* (November 2, 1992)
Haley, Kathy, "Talking with Phil" (interview), *Broadcasting* (November 2, 1992)
Heaton, Jeanne Albronda, and Nona Leigh Wilson, *Tuning in Trouble: Talk TV's Destructive Impact on Mental Health,* San Francisco, California: Jossey-Bass, 1995
Kurtz, Howard, "Father of the Slide," *The New Republic* (February 12, 1996)
McConnell, Frank, "What Hath Phil Wrought?," *Commonweal* (March 22, 1996)
Mifflin, Laurie, "The Price of Being Earnest," *New York Times* (January 21, 1996)
Priest, Patricia Joyner, *Public Intimacies: Talk Show Participants and Tell All TV,* Cresskill, New Jersey: Hampton, 1996
Unger, Arthur, "I Cannot Be the BBC in an MTV World!" (interview), *Television Quarterly* (Spring 1991)

Dowdle, James Charles (1934–)

First President and Chief Executive Officer of the Tribune Broadcasting Company

James Charles Dowdle is credited with the significant growth and diversification of the Tribune Company's broadcast efforts in programming and station acquisitions. On his promotion to executive vice president of Tribune Media Operations, Dowdle was responsible for the Tribune Company's newspaper publishing, broadcasting, and entertainment businesses, including the Chicago Cubs baseball franchise.

In 1962, Dowdle joined KWTV in Oklahoma City as national sales manager. Two years later, he joined Hubbard Broadcasting's KSTP in Minneapolis as national sales manager and, in 1973, was promoted to vice president and general manager of Hubbard's independent WTOG in Tampa, Florida. He remained in Tampa until 1981, when he rejoined the Tribune Company as president and chief executive officer of the newly formed Tribune Broadcasting Company. In that capacity, Dowdle was responsible for the company's owned-and-operated television and radio stations and its subsidiary Tribune Entertainment Company, which was founded in 1982. Within four years, he was elected to the Tribune board of directors.

Visionary in his approach to media and dedicated to the concept of growth, from the outset Dowdle worked at moving Tribune to new and ever more profitable levels. The Chicago Cubs were purchased by Tribune in the summer of 1981. Approximately two years later, in combination with Viacom Enterprises, he formed TV-NET, a prime-time program service aimed at monthly distribution of major theatrical films not seen on network television. But, most important, under Dowdle's direction, by early 1985 Tribune had increased its ownership of independent stations from three to five with top-ranked independents in Chicago, Denver, and New Orleans and second-ranked independents in New York and Atlanta. Then, on May 16, 1985, the Tribune announced plans to buy Los Angeles–based KTLA-TV for a reported $510 million (reputedly the highest price ever paid for a single television station). KTLA was targeted at revenues of approximately $100 million in 1985 and would expand Tribune's reach to 19.6 percent of all U.S. television households.

The KTLA acquisition, reported *BusinessWeek* on June 13, 1985, was "crucial to Dowdle's ambitious plan to use the combined viewership of his stations as a captive customer base for his own programming." To that end, he pursued various joint ventures in program production in various formats, signed the controversial Geraldo Rivera in 1987 for a daily daytime talk show that culminated in a successful 11-year run, and in April 1990 signed a 10-year contract with Ted Turner's Cable News Network (CNN). Under terms of the arrangement, Tribune stations would become CNN affiliates, and the two companies would coproduce documentaries, miniseries, and news specials.

In 1991, Dowdle was directing the operations of six television stations, four radio stations, and a variety of subsidiaries that produced and distributed programming for both media. Earlier in the year, the Tribune had also launched ChicagoLand Television (CLTV) under the banner of Tribune Regional Programming, Inc., a service dedicated to Chicago-area news, sports, and information utilizing the resources of the *Chicago Tribune,* WGN radio, WGN television, and the Chicago Cubs. Within two years, Tribune Regional Programming combined with Tele-Communications, Inc. (TCI), to provide CLTV to TCI's 300,000 cable customers in the Chicago metropolitan area 24 hours a day.

For his efforts, Dowdle was named a corporate vice president of the parent Tribune Company in July 1991. Then, in 1994, at the age of 60, he was appointed executive vice president of Tribune Media Operations. Overseeing publishing, broadcasting, and entertainment, Dowdle was responsible for approximately 90 percent of the more than $2 billion in company revenues. In this position, he worked to direct expansion and media crossover strategies, improve operational efficiencies, and increase new services for the advertiser who wanted to use print and broadcast simultaneously. He also continued to direct the 24-hour local CLTV news service.

On November 2, 1993, *PR Newswire* carried Dowdle's announcement that the Tribune Broadcasting Company would join with Warner Brothers to create The WB, a new prime-time television network slated to begin operations in the fall of 1994. Tribune television stations in New York, Los Angeles, Philadelphia, Atlanta, Denver, and New Orleans were initially slotted as affiliates, and the network, emphasizing programming for 18- to 49-year-olds in prime-time evening slots, would instantly cover 85 percent of American households. Then, in 1996, Tribune added six new television stations to its stable for a total of 16 when it agreed to buy Renaissance Communications Corporation for $1.13 billion. Including a station that it managed in Washington, D.C., Tribune was now broadcasting in nine of the country's top 11 markets.

Dowdle stepped down from his position as executive vice president of the Tribune Company effective December 31, 1999, and was succeeded by Tribune Broadcasting's president, Dennis FitzSimons.

JOEL STERNBERG

See also **Cable News Network (CNN); Rivera, Geraldo; Turner, Ted; WB Television Network**

James C. Dowdle. Born in Chicago, Illinois, March 12, 1934. Education: B.S., University of Notre Dame, accounting, 1956. Married: Sally. Served as officer in U.S. Marines. Worked for *Chicago Tribune,* automotive advertising sales, Chicago, 1956; after military service returned to Edward Petry Company, sales staff, Chicago; Katz Company, sales staff, Chicago; KWTV, national sales manager, Oklahoma City, Oklahoma, 1962–64; KSTP, national sales manager, Minneapolis, Minnesota, 1964–73; WTOG, vice president and general manager, Tampa, Florida, 1973–81; Tribune Broadcasting, president/chief executive officer, Chicago, 1981–97; Tribune Company Board of Directors, Chicago, 1985–2000; Tribune Company, corporate vice president, Chicago, 1991–99; Tribune Media Operations, executive vice president, Chicago, 1994–99. Retired, December 31, 1999. Has served as director on boards of Chicago's Loyola University, Loyola University Health System, the Advertising Council, the Television Operators Caucus, Television Bureau of Advertising, Television Information Office, the Chicago Museum of Broadcast Communications, and Maximum Service Television Inc. Trustee on Chicago's Museum of Science and Industry and served as director for such charitable and civic-minded causes as Junior Achievement of Chicago, the Robert R. McCormick Tribune Foundation, the Chicago Center for Peace Studies, and Catholic Charities Big Shoulders campaign. Inducted into the Broadcasting and Cable Hall of Fame (1992); named Person of the Year by

Chicago's Broadcasting Advertisers Club (1994); received the National Academy of Television Arts and Sciences Trustees Award (1995), the United States Marine Corps Semper Fidelis Award (1995), the Hazelden Chicago Distinguished Leadership Award (1997), and the National Association of Broadcasters Distinguished Service Award (1998).

Further Reading

Caray, Harry, and Verdi, Bob, *Holy Cow!*, New York: Villard Books, 1989

Davidson, Jean, "Tribune Co. Reorganization Boosts Focus on New Media," *Chicago Tribune* (July 28, 1994)

Ellis, James E., "Sorry Mr. Murdoch, the Fourth Network May Not Be Yours," *BusinessWeek* (June 13, 1985)

"FitzSimons to Lead Tribune," *Broadcasting & Cable,* Vol. 129 (November 15, 1999)

Freeman, Mike, "Tribune on Late Night: 'We Shall Return,'" *Broadcasting,* Vol. 122 (July 27, 1992)

"From Doorstep to TV Set: The Evolving Strengths of the Tribune Co.," *Broadcasting,* Vol. 109 (December 30, 1985)

Heuton, Cheryl, "James Dowdle Tribune Broadcasting Co.," *Channels,* Vol. 10 (August 13, 1990)

Holtzman, Jerome, "Two Who Helped Harry Caray Become Harry Caray," *Chicago Tribune* (February 21, 1998)

"New Divisions at Tribune," *New York Times* (July 28, 1994)

Storch, Charles, and Greenberg, Herb, "Tribune Co. to Buy L.A. TV Station $510 Million Price Is Highest Ever," *Chicago Tribune* (May 17, 1985)

Strupp, Joe, "Tribune Co. No. 2 Spot Shifts from Dowdle to FitzSimons," *Editor & Publisher,* Vol. 132 (November 13, 1999)

Tribune Company 2000 Annual Report, Chicago: Tribune Company, 2001

"Tribune Restructuring Boosts Dowdle, Bosau," *Broadcasting & Cable,* Vol. 124 (August 1, 1994)

Warren, James, "FitzSimons to Oversee Tribune TV Stations," *Chicago Tribune* (January 3, 1992)

Ziemba, Stanly, "Tribune Co. Reaches an Agreement to Add 6 TV Stations for $1.1 Billion," *Chicago Tribune* (July 2, 1996)

Downs, Hugh (1921–)

U.S. Television Host

A venerable and extremely affable television host, Hugh Downs is known for his intelligence, patience, and decency. The *Guinness Book of World Records* reports that Downs, among the most familiar figures in the history of the medium, has clocked more hours on television (10,347 through May 1994) than any other person in U.S. TV history.

Downs began his broadcasting career as a radio announcer at the age of 18 in Lima, Ohio, moving later to NBC Chicago as a staff announcer. In 1957, he became well known to U.S. audiences as Jack Paar's sidekick on *The Tonight Show,* and he remained in that spot through 1962. In 1958, he began hosting the original version of *Concentration,* helping to establish his niche of doing more serious and thought-provoking television even within the game show format.

He served as the National Broadcasting Company's (NBC's) utility host for many of the network's 1950s and early 1960s news, information, and entertainment programs. He added *The Today Show* to his list of network assignments, replacing John Chancellor, who had served for just 15 months as Dave Garroway's replacement on the original *Today Show.*

Downs was the primary host of the *Today Show* for nine years.

Downs's reassuring, professional manner in the roles of announcer, sidekick, host, and anchor has been unrivaled in U.S. television. He has said that he tries to be the link between what goes on behind and in front of the camera and the audience at home, hoping that he serves as an "honest pipeline to the audience." He believes that television works best when a familiar presence is there to help guide viewers in and out of features and stories, however abbreviated that function may be. From 1978 to 1999, he demonstrated that commitment as the anchor or co-anchor of the American Broadcasting Company's (ABC's) *20/20,* a job he came out of retirement to take after a nearly disastrous premier almost kept the show off the air.

His great affability and smooth manner have made it possible for Downs to get along well with whomever he has been paired. For example, he repeatedly took the edge off some of the sharper moments with Jack Paar, who was well known for his outbursts, tantrums, and eccentricities. Downs proved his diplomacy once again in 1984, when Barbara Walters took the position

Hugh Downs.
©*ABC/Courtesy of the Everett Collection*

across from him on *20/20,* just after a major brouhaha had developed because she had been asked to leave her position as the first female network news co-anchor, paired unsuccessfully with Harry Reasoner. The chemistry between Walters and Downs was right, and the two worked together successfully from 1984 until Downs left *20/20.*

Intimates refer to Downs as one of the last "renaissance men." He is a proficient sailor and aviator—even though he is color blind. He has composed, published, and had orchestral pieces performed; has hosted *Live from Lincoln Center* for the Public Broadcasting Service (PBS) since 1990; and is exceptionally knowledgeable about science and health. One of his special interests is the U.S. space program. Another focuses on issues surrounding aging, and he has earned a postgraduate certificate in geriatric medicine while hosting *Over Easy* for PBS, the first successful television program in the United States about aging. Always modest, Downs shuns the "renaissance" label, preferring instead to call himself "a champion dilettante."

Downs is the author of numerous books, including *Perspectives,* a collection of his 10-minute radio commentaries for ABC Radio; an autobiography; a collec-

tion of his science articles (on astronomy and the environment); an account of a sailing voyage across the Pacific; and several books on the subjects of aging, health, and psychological maturity. Downs's public service commitments are also notable. He is chairman emeritus of the board of the United States Committee for UNICEF, chair of the Board of Governors of the National Space Society, an elected member of the National Academy of Science, and a past member of NASA's Advisory Council. He received an award from the American Psychiatric Association for his work on the ABC News special *Depression: Beyond the Darkness,* and he received an Emmy for his work on *The Poisoning of America,* about damage to the environment. He was named broadcaster of the year by the International Radio and Television Society in 1990. In 1995, he was honored with a special salute ceremony by the Museum of Broadcast Communications in Chicago.

In 1999, Downs began a very active retirement, leaving ABC and *20/20* after 21 years and after 62 years in broadcasting. The same year, Arizona State University named the Hugh Downs School of Human Communication for Downs. He occasionally lectures there. Downs has also branched out to the Internet, creating and "appearing" on the web-based network iNEXTTV's Executive Branch TV channel in the programs *My Take with Hugh Downs* and *Conversations with Hugh Downs: Values in America.* Downs also recently composed a musical piece for cellist Yo-Yo Ma and had it performed by Ma, accompanied by a 98-piece orchestra.

ROBERT KUBEY

See also **Talk Show,** *20/20*

Hugh (Malcolm) Downs. Born in Akron, Ohio, February 14, 1921. Attended Bluffton College, Ohio, 1938–39; Wayne State College, 1940–41; Columbia University, 1955–56. Married: Ruth Shaheen, 1944; children: Hugh Raymond and Deirdre Lynn. Began career as staff announcer and program director, WLOK, Lima, Ohio, 1939–40; staff announcer, WWJ, Detroit, Michigan, 1940–42; staff announcer, NBC-Radio, Chicago, Illinois, 1943–54; in television, from 1949; chairman, board of directors, Raylin Productions, Inc., from 1960; special consultant to United Nations on refugee problems, 1961–64; science consultant to Westinghouse Laboratories and the Ford Foundation. Member: Actors' Equity Association; Screen Actors Guild, American Federation of Television and Radio Artists; National Space Institute; chair, U.S. Committee for UNICEF; Center for the Study of Democratic Institutions. Recipient: Emmy Award.

Television Series

1949	*Kukla, Fran, and Ollie* (announcer)
1950	*Hawkins Falls*
1951–55	*American Inventory*
1951	*Your Luncheon Date* (announcer)
1954–57	*The Home Show* (announcer)
1956–57	*Sid Caesar's Hour* (announcer)
1957–62	*The Jack Paar Show* (announcer)
1958–68	*Concentration* (emcee)
1962	*The Tonight Show* (announcer)
1962–72	*The Today Show* (host)
1972	*Not for Women Only* (host)
1974	*Variety* (host; pilot only)
1977–83	*Over Easy*
1978–99	*20/20* (anchor)
1985	*Growing Old in America* (host)

Made-for-Television Movie

1976	*Woman of the Year*

Television Specials

1975	*Broken Treaty at Battle Mountain: A Discussion* (moderator)
1986	*Liberty Weekend Preview* (reporter)
1986	*NBC's 60th Anniversary Celebration* (reporter)
1987	*Today at 35* (reporter)

Films

Nothing by Chance (documentary; executive producer and narrator), 1974; *Oh God! Book II,* 1980.

Radio

WLOK, Lima, Ohio, 1939–40; WWJ, Detroit, Michigan, 1940–42; NBC Radio, Chicago, Illinois, 1943–54.

Publications

A Shoal of Stars, 1967
Rings around Tomorrow, 1970
Potential: The Way to Emotional Maturity, 1973
Thirty Dirty Lies about Old Age, 1979
The Best Years Book: How to Plan for Fulfillment, Security, and Happiness in the Retirement Years, 1981
On Camera: My Ten Thousand Hours on Television, 1986
Fifty to Forever, 1994
Perspectives, 1995

Further Reading

"Hugh Downs," *Ad Astra* (July–August 1991)
"Hugh Downs: TV's Marathon Man," *Broadcasting* (February 5, 1990)

Dr. Kildare

U.S. Medical Drama

Dr. Kildare, the award-winning series that aired on the National Broadcasting Company (NBC) from September 28, 1961, through August 30, 1966, was one of television's most popular and influential medical dramas. The show was loosely based on a series of MGM films, also titled *Dr. Kildare,* written by Max Brand and starring Lew Ayres in the title role. However, the television series departed from its film predecessor in several significant ways.

Norman Felton, the show's producer, capitalized on the familiarity of the Dr. Kildare name but created a new formula for medical series, one that stressed the compassion of doctors and followed a young intern's passage into the practice of medicine. *Dr. Kildare* maintained the older doctor–younger doctor dynamic of the film version but sought to add a more realistic dimension to the depiction of medicine and the intern's life.

Each Thursday night, NBC viewers could tune in to watch Dr. Kildare at Blair General Hospital, where he worked as a gifted and caring intern, training under the expert tutelage of Dr. Leonard Gillespie. Together they offered healing and comfort to patients who arrived at the hospital in moments of stress and crisis. Throughout the course of the show's five-year run, Dr. Kildare and Dr. Gillespie dealt intimately and personally with

Richard Chamberlain as Dr. Kildare, 1961–66.
Courtesy of the Everett Collection

issues ranging from alcoholism and malpractice to suicide and mental illness. These stories informed the audience about the ailment of the week as they entertained millions of viewers. Episodes included a nonstop stream of guest stars, from William Shatner and Peter Falk to Robert Redford, all of whom contributed to the popularity and freshness of the show.

Beyond the appeal of its compelling stories, many viewers tuned to *Dr. Kildare* to watch the handsome young actor Richard Chamberlain in the title role. From the pilot episode, viewers showed intense interest in Chamberlain, whose good looks made him especially popular with female viewers. Chamberlain was also portrayed in the press in a way that conflated his own attributes with those of the fictional Dr. Kildare. He was said to be "good," "high-minded," and "trustworthy," and it was noted that he looked up to Raymond Massey, the actor who played Dr. Gillespie, in much the same way that the young intern admired his

mentor. For many viewers, Chamberlain's face became the face of medicine, and magazine and newspaper stories often focused on the phenomenon of fans writing to Chamberlain for medical advice or stopping him in Central Park to ogle him.

Chamberlain and *Dr. Kildare* shared the medical stage with Vince Edwards of *Ben Casey,* the American Broadcasting Company's (ABC's) medical drama that ran from 1961 to 1966 on Monday nights. The two shows were different in emphasis and style, however, with Edward's Dr. Casey a less "user-friendly" hero for the small screen, a difficult and hotheaded doctor who at times allowed his temper to get the better of him. Edwards and Chamberlain were frequently compared in the press, with descriptions of their personalities mirroring those of the characters they played on television.

Producer Felton's conception of *Dr. Kildare* stressed the human elements over medical accuracy. Guided by the American Medical Association (AMA), whose imprimatur appeared at the end of every program, the series did use on- and off-set technical advisers to maintain "cutting-edge" procedures. But producers were willing to gloss over some details when a storyline demanded more drama. And other "opposing forces" were also at work. Media executives, advertisers, and the AMA all had an effect on the end product, and innovative medical techniques were tempered with compassion, personality, and even humor.

Not all the compromises garnered praise, however. During the period of *Dr. Kildare's* run, the practice of medicine was itself changing. Hospital strategies no longer focused on a one-on-one approach but more frequently relied on teams of doctors, specialists, nurses, and administrators working in concert. Costs were escalating, and the Kennedy administration was proposing Medicare to help senior citizens pay for health care. The AMA was opposed to Medicare, and several critics in the *New York Times* and the *Wall Street Journal* charged that the AMA's association with *Dr. Kildare* prohibited the show from exploring any aspect of what was often referred to as "socialized medicine." Indeed, the AMA and the advisory board for the show did want to maintain *Dr. Kildare* as a promotion for mainstream medicine. For the most part, the show's agenda received little criticism, and the AMA's gamble paid off.

JOSEPH TUROW AND RACHEL GANS

See also **Ben Casey**

Dragnet

U.S. Police Drama

From the distinctive four-note opening of its theme music to the raft of catchphrases it produced, no other television cop show has left such an indelible mark on American culture as *Dragnet*. It was the first successful television crime drama to be shot on film and one of the few prime-time series to have returned to production after its initial run. In *Dragnet,* Jack Webb, who produced, directed, and starred in the program, created the benchmark by which subsequent police shows would be judged.

The origins of *Dragnet* can be traced to a semidocumentary film noir, *He Walked by Night* (1948), in which Webb had a small role. Webb created a radio series for the National Broadcasting Company (NBC) that had many similarities with the film. Not only did both employ the same Los Angeles Police Department (LAPD) technical adviser, but they also made use of actual police cases, narration that provided information about the workings of the police department, and a generally low-key, documentary style. In the radio drama, Webb starred as Sgt. Joe Friday, and Barton Yarborogh played his partner. The success of the radio show led to a *Dragnet* television pilot that aired as an episode of *Chesterfield Sound Off Time* in 1951 and resulted in a permanent slot for the series on NBC Television's Thursday night schedule in early 1952. Yarborogh died suddenly after the pilot aired and was eventually replaced by Ben Alexander, who played Officer Frank Smith from 1953 to the end of the series in 1959.

Dragnet was an instant hit on television, maintaining a top-ten position in the ratings through 1956. The series was applauded for its realism—actually a collection of highly stylized conventions that made the show an easy target for parodists and further increased its cultural cachet. Episodes began with a prologue promising that "the story you are about to see is true; the names have been changed to protect the innocent," then faded in on a pan across the Los Angeles sprawl. Webb's mellifluous voice intoned, "This is the city. Los Angeles, California," and usually offered statistics about the city, its population, and its institutions. Among the show's other "realistic" elements were constant references to dates, the time, and weather conditions. Producing the series on film permitted the use of stock shots of LAPD operations and location shooting in Los Angeles. This was a sharp contrast to

the stage-bound "live" detective shows of the period. *Dragnet* emphasized authentic police jargon, the technical aspects of law enforcement, and the drudgery of such work. Rather than engaging in fistfights and gunplay, Friday and his partner spent much screen time making phone calls, questioning witnesses, or following up on dead-end leads. Scenes of the detectives simply waiting and engaging in mundane small talk were common. To save on costly rehearsal time, Webb had actors read their lines off a TelePrompTer. The result was a clipped, terse style that conveyed a documentary feel and became a trademark of subsequent series produced by Webb, including *Adam-12* and *Emergency.* *Dragnet* always concluded with an epilogue detailing the criminal's fate, accompanied by a shot of the character shifting about uncomfortably before the camera.

Dragnet's stories, many written by James Moser, ran the gamut from traffic accidents to homicide. Other stories played on critical middle-class anxieties of the postwar period, including juvenile delinquency, teenage drug use, and the distribution of "dirty" pictures in schools. Moral complexity was eschewed for a crime-doesn't-pay message sketched in stark, black-and-white tones. Friday put up with little from lawbreakers, negligent parents, or young troublemakers. Program segments often concluded with the sergeant directing a tight-lipped homily to miscreants coupled with a musical "stinger" and an appreciative nod from his partner.

By 1954, *Dragnet* was watched by over half of U.S. television households. This success prompted Warner Brothers to finance and distribute a theatrical version of *Dragnet* (1954), signaling the rise of cross promotion between film and television. Further evidence of the show's popularity was found in the number of TV series that imitated its style, notably *The Lineup, M Squad,* and Moser's *Medic,* based on cases from the files of the Los Angeles County Medical Association. Conversely, other series such as *77 Sunset Strip* and *Hawaiian Eye,* featuring younger, hipper detectives, were developed to provide an antidote to *Dragnet*'s dour approach to crime fighting. As *Dragnet* neared completion of its initial run in 1959, Friday was promoted to lieutenant, and Smith passed his sergeant's exam. Seven years later the show was revived by NBC as *Dragnet 1967.* Until it was canceled in 1970, *Dragnet* was always followed by the year to distinguish the

Dragnet, Jack Webb, Harry Morgan, 1967–70.
Courtesy of the Everett Collection

new series from its 1950s counterpart. In the new series, Friday was once again a sergeant, now paired with Officer Bill Gannon (Harry Morgan). Though the style and format of the show remained the same, the intervening years and the rise of the counterculture had changed Friday from a crusading cop to a dyspeptic civil servant, alternately disgusted by the behavior of the younger generation and peeved at his partner's prattle about mundane topics. The program's conservatism was all the more apparent in the late 1960s, as Friday's terse warnings of the 1950s gave way to shrill lectures invoking god and country for the benefit of hippies, drug users, and protestors.

Webb's death in 1982 did not prevent another revival of *Dragnet* from appearing in syndication during the 1989–90 season. Two younger characters filled in for Friday and his partner, but the formula remained the same. This little-seen effort failed quickly in part because series such as *Hill Street Blues* and *COPS* had significantly altered the conventions of realistic police dramas. Those programs, and such others as *NYPD Blue,* must be considered the true generic successors to the original *Dragnet.* As the archetypal television police drama, *Dragnet* has remained a staple in reruns and continues to be an object of both parody and reverent homage.

ERIC SCHAEFER

See also **Police Programs; Webb, Jack**

Cast

Sgt. Joe Friday	Jack Webb
Sgt. Ben Romero (1951)	Barton Yarborough
Sgt. Ed Jacobs (1952)	Barney Phillips
Officer Frank Smith (1952)	Herb Ellis
Officer Frank Smith (1953–59)	Ben Alexander
Officer Bill Gannon (1967–70)	Harry Morgan

Producer/Creator

Jack Webb

Programming History

1952–59	263 episodes
1967–70	100 episodes

NBC

January 1952–December 1955	Thursday 9:00–9:30
January 1956–September 1958	Thursday 8:30–9:00
September 1958–June 1959	Tuesday 7:30–8:00
July 1959–September 1959	Sunday 8:30–9:00
January 1967–September 1970	Thursday 9:30–10:00

Further Reading

Anderson, Christopher, *Hollywood TV: The Studio System in the Fifties,* Austin: University of Texas Press, 1994

"Detective Story," *Newsweek* (January 14, 1952)

Hubler, Richard G., "Jack Webb: The Man Who Makes *Dragnet,*" *Coronet* (September 1953)

"Jack, Be Nimble!" *Time* (March 15, 1954)

Luciano, Patrick, and Gary Coville, "Behind Badge 714: The Story of Jack Webb and *Dragnet* (Part One)." *Filmfax* (August–September 1993)

Luciano, Patrick, and Gary Coville, "Behind Badge 714: The Story of Jack Webb and *Dragnet* (Part Two)," *Filmfax* (October–November 1993)

Tregaskis, Richard, "The Cops' Favorite Make-Believe Cop," *Saturday Evening Post* (September 26, 1953)

Dramedy

"Dramedy" is best understood as a television program genre that fuses elements of comedy and drama. According to R. Altman, new genres emerge in one of two ways: "either a relatively stable set of semantic givens is developed through syntactic experimentation into a coherent and durable syntax, or an already existing syntax adopts a new set of semantic elements." "Semantic elements" are the generic "building blocks"

The Days and Nights of Molly Dodd, Maureen Anderman, William Converse-Roberts, James Greene, Blair Brown, David Strathairn, Allyn Ann McLerie, 1987–91.
Courtesy of the Everett Collection

out of which of program genres are constructed—those recurring elements such as stock characters, common traits, and technical features such as locations and typical shots. "Syntax," or "syntactic features," describes the ways in which these elements are related and combined. The recurring combination of semantic and syntactic elements creates a conventional type or category of program called a genre.

As a commercial enterprise, television piques audience members' interest and attracts viewers, at least in part by offering innovations on familiar genre forms. Thus, while dramedy may have taken the final step from invention to genre evolution in the 1980s, several series during the 1970s occasionally experimented with individual "dramedic" episodes, including *M*A*S*H* (1972–83), *Barney Miller* (1975–82), and *Taxi* (1978–83). After *Moonlighting* (1985–89) had garnered both popular success and critical acclaim, a number of television producers turned to dramedy's unique duality as a means of attracting audiences. Other television series that some critics have called

dramedies include *The Days and Nights of Molly Dodd* (1987–91), *Hooperman* (1987–89), *The Wonder Years* (1988–93), *Northern Exposure* (1990–95), *Brooklyn Bridge* (1991–93), *Sports Night* (1998–2000), *and Ally McBeal* (1997–2002).

Arguably one of the clearest examples of the dramedy genre emerged in 1985 and 1986, when the Directors Guild of America nominated the hour-long television series *Moonlighting* for both best drama and best comedy, an unprecedented event in the organization's previous 50 years. *Moonlighting* combined the semantic elements or conventions of television drama (serious subject matter, complex and rounded central characters, multiple interior and exterior settings, use of textured lighting, and single-camera shooting on film) with the conventional syntactic features of television comedies (four-act narrative structure, repetition, witty repartee, verbal and musical self-reflexivity, and hyperbole).

Not all dramedies, however, are an hour long. For example, the half-hour series *Frank's Place* (1987–88) and *Sports Night* dealt with serious issues; had rounded and complex central characters, textured lighting, and multiple interior settings; and featured single-camera shooting on film with no studio audience or canned laugh track. However, given the economic organization of the American television schedule, in which "half-hour" is usually equated with "comedy" and "hour-long" with "drama," creators of dramedies have frequently had some difficulty persuading television networks to air their half-hour genre hybrids without laugh tracks. In the case of *Sports Night,* for example, producer Aaron Sorkin and director Thomas Schlamme spent much of the series' first season trying to persuade the American Broadcasting Company (ABC) that the laugh track the network demanded was destroying the series.

Television, like most popular culture forms, is strongly generic; audiences come to television program viewing experiences with definite expectations about genre conventions; indeed, according to Robert Warshow, audiences welcome originality "only in the degree that intensifies the expected experience without fundamentally altering it." So, too, do the networks. *Frank's Place* lasted only one season, while *Sports Night* lasted only two. In the case of the latter program, however, as *New Yorker* critic Ted Friend noted, producer Aaron Sorkin and director Thomas Schlamme managed during those two years "to take the half hour visually, where Steven Bochco had taken the hour with *Hill Street Blues.*"

Ally McBeal, an hour-long dramedy on the FOX network, featured one of the most innovative settings on television—prime time's first unisex bathroom—as well as the series' self-reflexive visual special effects (such as Ally fantasizing herself and her high school/college/law school lover sharing a steamy kiss in a giant coffee cup and Ally's breasts growing to the point where her bra bursts as she looks in the mirror and acknowledges to herself that she does wish her bustline were a little bigger).

Critics have praised television dramedies' sophistication and innovation, calling these innovative series "quality television" for "quality audiences," and have suggested that the appearance of such creative hybrids whose self-reflexivity and intertextual references require a substantial degree of both popular and classic cultural literacy from viewers for full appreciation of their allusions and nuances signifies a change in the relationships among television, audiences, and society and indicates that television has "come of age" as an artistic medium.

LEAH R. VANDE BERG

See also Ally McBeal; Moonlighting

Further Reading

Alley, Robert S., "Television Drama," in *Television: The Critical View,* edited by Horace Newcomb, New York: Oxford University Press, 1976; 2nd edition, 1979

Altman, R., "A Semantic/Syntactic Approach to Film Genre," in *Film Genre Reader,* edited by B.K. Grant, Austin: University of Texas Press, 1986

Brown, C., and R. Marin, "Sitcom or Tragedy: High Drama and Low Ratings at *Sports Night,*" *Newsweek* (November 9, 1998)

Cawelti, J.G., *Adventure, Mystery and Romance: Formula Stories As Art and Popular Culture,* Chicago: University of Chicago Press, 1976

deLauretis, T., "A Semiotic Approach to Television As Ideological Apparatus," in *Television: The Critical View,* edited by Horace Newcomb, New York: Oxford University Press, 1976; 2nd edition, 1979

Eaton, M., "Television Situation Comedy," in *Popular Television and Film,* edited by T. Bennett, S. Boyd-Bowman, C. Mercer, and J. Wollacott, London: British Film Institute, 1981

Franklin, N., "The Sporting News," *The New Yorker* (January 11, 1999)

Friend, T., "Laugh Riot: What Happens When a Newcomer Tries to Bend the Rules of the Most Venerable and Conservative of Cultural Forms—The American Sitcom?," *The New Yorker* (September 28, 1998)

Horowitz, J., "Sweet Lunacy: The Madcap behind *Moonlighting,*" *New York Times Magazine* (March 30, 1986)

Mintz, L.E., "Situation Comedy," in *TV Genres: A Handbook and Reference Guide,* edited by B. Rose, Westport, Connecticut: Greenwood Press, 1985

Newcomb, Horace, *TV: The Most Popular Art,* Garden City, New York: Anchor/Doubleday, 1974

Newcomb, Horace, "Toward Television History: The Growth of Styles," *Journal of the University Film Association* (1978)

Vande Berg, Leah R., "Dramedy: *Moonlighting* As an Emergent Generic Hybrid," *Communication Studies* (1989)

Warshow, Robert, *The Immediate Experience: Movies, Comics, Theatre, and Other Aspects of Popular Culture,* Garden City, New York: Doubleday, 1962

Williams, J.P., "When You Care Enough to Watch the Very Best: The Mystique of Moonlighting," *Journal of Popular Film and Television* (1988)

Drew, Robert (1924–)

U.S. Documentary Film Producer

Robert Drew is a documentary producer who, during the late 1950s and 1960s, pioneered a new documentary form for application in the network news departments. This form, which Drew dubbed "candid drama," also known as "*cinéma vérité*" or "direct cinema," did not, ultimately, reshape news programming, but it did provide the medium with a radically different way of covering historical and cultural events.

"Candid drama," according to Drew, is a documentary filmmaking technique that reveals the "logic of drama" inherent in almost all human situations. In sharp contrast to typical television documentaries, which are simply "lectures with picture illustration" (and for that reason usually are "dull"), the candid drama documentary eschews extensive voice-over narration, formal interviews, on-air correspondents, or other kinds of staged and framed television formulae. Instead, through the slowly acquired photography and long, single takes—called real-time photography—of vérité technique, the details and flavor of a scene become the important elements: the fatigue experienced by candidates on a campaign trail (*Primary*) or the fervid concentration of a race car driver (*On the Pole*) captures our attention as much as the factual information about a campaign or the Indianapolis 500. According to Drew, the purpose of candid documentary is to engage the viewer's "senses as well as his mind." Over a career that spans more than 30 years, Drew has produced over 100 films and videotapes, most of which employ the theory and methods of vérité technique; and unlike other practitioners of the form, he has also tried to procure a regular slot for vérité on prime-time network programming.

Drew was first introduced to the power of documentary photography just after World War II while demonstrating a new fighter plane for a *Life* magazine reporter and photography team (Drew had served as a fighter pilot during the war). Struck by the power of the resulting article, Drew, at the age of 22, became a staff reporter for *Life.* In 1955, he accepted a Nieman Fellowship at Harvard to formally pursue the problem of an alternative news theory in the medium of film. It was a time of rigorous talk, study, and analysis, according to Drew, and on his return to *Life,* he began making films as well as reporting. Some of these early experiments premiered on *The Ed Sullivan Show* and *The Jack Paar Show.* In 1960, Drew moved to Time's broadcast division, where, with the backing of Wes Tullen, vice president in charge of television operations, he obtained the funds for his first project and the means necessary to develop lightweight portable equipment. The engineering of the first small sync sound and picture camera unit, which he undertook with filmmaker Richard Leacock, has undoubtedly had an enormous impact on numerous documentarians working both for the major networks and independently. Sensitive and ephemeral moments could now be more easily captured than with the cumbersome camera, large camera crew, and lighting system that had been used in news coverage to date.

Also at this time, Drew formed his company, Drew Associates, which enabled him to hire freelance cameramen and filmmakers, some of whom, such as D.A. Pennebaker, Richard Leacock, and Albert Maysles, have since gone on to establish celebrated careers of their own. By March 1960, Drew was ready to select their first subject and settled on the Democratic presidential primary in Wisconsin, which pitted the young John Kennedy against Hubert Humphrey. For the last week of the campaign, three two-man crews tracked both Kennedy and Humphrey as they made their rounds of the hustings, photo sessions, and the rare, private moments in between.

Primary, as this first film was named, still stands today as one of Drew Associate's best-known and celebrated works. It won the Flaherty Award for best documentary and the Blue Ribbon at the American Film Festival while in Europe, according to Drew, "it was received as a kind of documentary second-coming." (The rough immediacy of the handheld camera is

Robert Drew.
Photo courtesy of Drew Associates, Inc.

said to have influenced Goddard's *Breathless.*) Kennedy, on viewing *Primary,* liked it so much that he consented to Drew's request to make further candid films in his role as president. "What if I had been able to observe F.D.R. in the 24 hours before he declared war on Japan?" he said. And indeed, Drew Associates gained permission to film the president during a period of crisis. Called *Crisis: Behind a Presidential Commitment* (1963), this documentary chronicles the showdown between Alabama Governor George Wallace and the federal government over the integration of the University of Alabama. As in *Primary,* domestic and personal details of the two main protagonists (Wallace and then–Attorney General Robert F. Kennedy) are intercut with the film's history-making moments— Wallace's initial refusal to back down and the government's decision to employ state troops. To Drew's great chagrin, however, the films were not broadcast over the networks. While regional outlets were found on occasion, the regular scheduling of these films and the many others he produced proved an elusive goal.

However, a joint sponsorship between Time, Inc., and the American Broadcasting Company (ABC) allowed Drew Associates to produce a series of films in 1960 for television, including a portrait of Indianapolis race driver Eddie Sachs, *On the Pole,* and *Yanki No!,* about Latin American reaction to American foreign policy in the region. These two films prompted a Time, Inc.–ABC liaison to offer Drew a contract for a regular supply of candid documentary. In rapid-fire succession, the company made about a half dozen more. They form a diverse list, including a profile of Nehru (which grew to a 20-year documentary relationship with the Nehru "dynasty," with subsequent films on Indira Gandhi and her son, Rajiv). Yet the first season's series was to be the last produced under the arrangement; again, the regular scheduling of the films, which Drew had made the bedrock of his candid drama theory, did not materialize.

The reasons proffered for the ambivalence of the television industry include the political infighting that arose between Time and ABC and the growing difficulty of attracting a single sponsor for the projects; but perhaps the most compelling reason was the networks' unshakable preference for correspondent-hosted or narrated reporting. The predictable (and containable) effects of a regular news anchor has prevailed, with exceptions, over more poetic candid documentary. (Moments of vérité reporting have nonetheless been produced in a few instances by the networks, Drew maintains, most notably the network coverage of American troops in Vietnam.) Once the first season of programming was complete, the three-way contractual relationship between Drew Associates, Time, and ABC formally ended. The production company since then has managed to survive and produce prolifically on an independent contractual basis with a variety of sponsors, including ABC, the Public Broadcasting Service (PBS), the British Broadcasting Corporation (BBC), corporations, and government agencies, as well with its own Drew Associates funds as an independent producer.

The resulting oeuvre consists of a wide variety of historical and high-profile moments, intermingled with scenes of the ordinary in modern life. *Jane* (1962) shows us a young Jane Fonda at her Broadway debut. *A Man Who Dances* (1968), produced as part of series on the arts for Bell Telephone, about ballet dancer Edward Villella, won Drew an Emmy. Many have dealt with subjects the networks have hesitated to tackle in house; responding to a request by Xerox Corporation for a film "that the networks won't touch," Drew made *Storm Signal* (1966), a documentary on drug addiction; a three-part series on gangs, produced for PBS's *Frontline* (1983–84) delves into the world of gangs and an inner-city high school. A full ten years later, Drew Associates completed *L.A. Champions,* also for PBS, about the basketball teams that play the streets of South Central Los Angeles, which, like Drew's first films, unobtrusively follows its main characters and without a word of narration tells a stirring story.

SUSAN HAMOVITCH

See also **Documentary**

Robert Lincoln Drew. Born in Toledo, Ohio, February 15, 1924. Served in U.S. Army Air Force, 1942.

Reporter for *Life,* 1946, Detroit bureau chief, 1949, assistant picture editor, New York, 1950, Chicago correspondent, 1951; documentary filmmaker for film and television. Recipient: Nieman Fellowship from Harvard University, 1954; American Film Festival, Blue Ribbon Award, 1961 and 1978; Venice Film Festival, First Prize, 1964, 1965, and 1966; Council on International Non-Theatrical Events, Cine Golden Eagle, 1964, 1965, 1966, 1967, 1968, 1969 (twice), 1970, 1975, 1976, 1977 (twice), 1978, 1980, 1982, 1985, 1986, and 1991; International Cinema Exhibition, Bilboa, First Prize, 1967 and 1968; International Documentary Film Festival, First Prize, 1967; Emmy Award, 1969; Chicago Film Festival, Silver Hugo, 1978; Peabody Award, 1982; American Bar Association, Silver Gavel Award, 1983; International Film and TV Festival of New York, Gold Award, 1983; Education Writers Association, First Prize, 1985; DuPont-Columbia Award, Best Documentary, 1985–86.

Documentary Films (selection)

Key Picture (Magazine X), 1954; *American Football,* 1957; *The B-52,* 1957; *Weightless (Zero Gravity),* 1958; *Balloon Ascension,* 1958; *Bullfight,* 1959; *Yanki No!,* 1960; *Primary,* 1960; *On the Pole,* 1960; *X-Pilot,* 1961; *The Children Were Watching,* 1961; *Adventures on the New Frontier,* 1961; *Kenya (Part I: Land of the White Ghost; Part II: Land of the Black Ghost),* 1961; *Eddie,* 1961; *David,* 1961; *Petey and Johnny,* 1961; *Mooney vs. Fowle,* 1961; *Blackie,* 1962; *Susan Starr,* 1962; *Nehru,* 1962; *The Road to Button Bay,* 1962; *The Aga Khan,* 1962; *The Chair,* 1962; *Jane (The Jane Fonda Story),* 1962; *Crisis: Behind a Presidential Commitment,* 1963; *Faces of November,* 1964; *Mission to Malaya,* 1964; *Letters from Vietnam,* 1965; *In the Contest of the Queen,* 1965; *Assault on Le-Mans,* 1965; *The Big Guy,* 1965; *The Time of Our Lives,* 1965; *Men Encounter Mars,* 1965; *Storm Signal,* 1966; *Another Way,* 1966; *A Man's Dream: Festival of Two Worlds,* 1966; *International Jazz Festival,* 1966; *The New Met: Countdown to Curtain,* 1966; *On the Road with Duke Ellington,* 1967; *The Virtuoso Teacher,* 1967; *Carnival of the Menuhins,* 1967; *Edward Villella: A Man Who Dances,* 1968; *Jazz: The Intimate Art,* 1968; *Nelson Rockefeller,* 1968; *Another World, Another Me,* 1968; *Confrontation in Color,* 1968; *The Space Duet of Spider and Gumdrop,* 1969; *Songs of America,* 1969; *The Martian Investigators,* 1970; *The Sun Ship Game,* 1971; *Beyond the Limits,* 1972; *Late Start,* 1973; *Deal with Disaster,* 1973; *Saving the Birds,* 1973; *Helping the Blind,* 1973; *Junior Achievement,* 1973; *Teaching Reading,*

1973; *Children's Hospital,* 1973; *School Bus,* 1973; *State Legislature,* 1973; *Pittsburg, Kansas,* 1973; *Mississippi,* 1973; *Typewriter,* 1973; *Oceanography,* 1973; *Who's Out There? (Orson Wells and Carl Sagan),* 1974; *Life in Outer Space,* 1973; *The Mind of Man,* 1973; *Saving Energy, It Begins at Home,* 1974; *Junk Cars,* 1974; *A Feat of Talent,* 1975; *The Tall Ships Are Coming,* 1975; *Christmas Birds,* 1975; *Ohio River,* 1975; *Conserving Energy,* 1975; *Apollo Soyez,* 1975; *Children Learn to Write by Dictating,* 1975; *World Food Crisis,* 1975; *Things Are Changing Around This School,* 1976; *Los Nietos, Urban League Training Center,* 1976; *Lodi Lady,* 1976; *Mr. Vernon Distar,* 1976; *Congressman Ruppe,* 1976; *What's in a Name?,* 1976; *Men of the Tall Ships,* 1976; *Six Americans on America: Chatham Massachusetts; Morristown, New Jersey; Savannah, Georgia; San Antonio, Texas; Freelandville, Indiana; San Francisco, California,* 1976; *Parade of the Tall Ships,* 1976; *Kathy's Dance,* 1977; *A Unique Fit—LTV Merger,* 1978; *Talent for America,* 1978; *Grasshopper Plague,* 1979; *Maine Winter,* 1979; *One Room Schoolhouse,* 1979; *Undersea at Seabrook,* 1979; *Images of Einstein,* 1979; *The Zapper,* 1979; *The Snowblower,* 1979; *Freeway Phobia,* 1980; *1980*

Census, 1980; *Durham Diets,* 1980; *Endorphins,* 1980; *Professor Rassias,* 1980; *Alcohol Car, 1980;* *Apex City,* 1980; *LTV '80,* 1980; *Spot Car,* 1980; *Blitz the Cities,* 1981; *Herself, Indira Gandhi,* 1982; *Fire Season* (also director), 1982; *784 Days That Changed America* (also writer), 1982; *Build the Fusion Power Machine,* 1984–85; *Being with John F. Kennedy,* 1984; *Frontline: Shootout on Imperial Highway,* 1984; *Warnings from Gangland* (also director), 1984–85; *Marshall High Fights Back* (also codirector), 1984–85; *The Transformation of Rajiv Gandhi,* 1985–86; *For Auction: An American Hero,* 1985–86; *OK Heart,* 1985–86; *Frontline: Your Flight Is Cancelled,* 1987; *Messages from the Birds* (also photographer), 1987–88; *River of Hawks,* 1987–88; *Kennedy versus Wallace,* 1988–89; *London to Peking: The Great Motoring Challenge* (also photographer, writer), 1989–90; *Life and Death of a Dynasty* (also photographer), 1990–91; *L.A. Champions,* 1993.

Further Reading

O'Connell, P.J., *Robert Drew and the Development of Cinema Verité in America,* Carbondale: Southern Illinois University Press, 1992

Dubbing

Dubbing has two meanings in the process of television production. It is used to describe the replacement of one soundtrack (music, sound effects, dialogue, natural sound, and so on) by another. The technique is used in the production of both audio and audiovisual media. It is a postproduction activity that allows considerable flexibility in "editing" the audio component of the visual. Dubbing includes activities such as the addition of music and sound effects to the original dialogue, the omission or replacement of unwanted or poorly recorded audio, or the re-recording of the entire dialogue, narration, and music. Much like literary editing, dubbing allows considerable freedom to re-create the product. Synonymous terms include postsynchronizing, looping, revoicing, re-recording, and electronic line replacement.

Dubbing is also one of the two major forms of "language transfer," the translation of audiovisual works. Dubbing, in this sense, is the replacement of the dialogue and narration of the foreign or source language (SL) into the language of the viewing audience, the target language (TL).

Inherited from cinema, dubbing is extensively used for translating other-language television programs. Some countries and cultures prefer dubbing to subtitling and voice-over. In Europe, for example, the "dubbing countries" include Austria, France, Germany, Italy, Spain, and Switzerland.

Dubbing, unlike subtitling, which involves a translation of speech into writing, is the oral translation of oral language. However, unlike "interpretation," in which the SL speaker and the TL interpreter are separate persons talking in their own distinct voices, dubbing requires the substitution of the voice of each character on the screen by the voice of one actor. It is, thus, a form of voice-over or revoicing. Dubbing is, however, distinguished from voice-over by the former's strict adherence to lip synchronization. In order to seem "natural" or authentic, the performed translation in a dubbed program must match, as closely as possible, the lip movements of the speaker on the screen. Moreover, there should be a strict though easy-to-achieve equivalence of extralinguistic features of voice, especially gender and age. The matching of other markers of speech, such as personality, class, and ethnicity, is most difficult because these features are not universally available or comparable. Another requirement of successful dubbing is the compatibility of the dubber's voice with the facial and body expressions visible on the screen.

Lip synchronization is usually seen as the strongest constraint on accurate translation. The script editor modifies the "raw translation" of each utterance in order to match it with the lip movements of the person seen on the screen. Given the enormous differences between even closely related languages such as English and German, it is difficult to find TL words that match the SL lip movements; this is especially the case when speakers are shown in close-up. It has been argued, however, that a word-by-word or sentence-by-sentence translation is not needed, especially in entertainment genres such as soap operas. Lip synchronization can be better performed with a more pragmatic "plot-oriented translation." If translation aims at conveying the general tone of each scene rather than locating meaning in each sentence, there will be more freedom to find appropriate words for lip synchronization. Moreover, it is important to seek the equivalence of not only word and sentence meanings but also genres, text quality, character, and cultural context. This approach is consistent with the claims of pragmatics, a new field of study that examines language use in social interaction. In either case, it would be more realistic to view dubbing, like other forms of language transfer, as an activity involving a re-creation of the original text.

As the transnationalization of television and film increases the demand for language transfer, the controversy about the aesthetics, politics, and economics of dubbing and subtitling continues in exporting and importing markets and in multilingual countries where language transfer is a feature of indigenous audio-visual culture. The polarized views on dubbing/subtitling highlight the centrality and complexity of language in a medium that privileges its visuality. Audience sensitivity to language can even be seen in the considerable volume of intralanguage dubbing. The miniseries *Les filles de Caleb,* for example, produced in the French language of Quebec, was dubbed into the French standard for audiences in France. Latin American producers and exporters of *telenovelas* have generally adopted a Mexican form of Spanish as their standard, following the lead of the earliest successful programs. Thus, dialect also acts as a barrier in the transnationalization of television within the same language community and highlights the complex issues surrounding this apparently simple industrial process.

AMIR HASSANPOUR

Further Reading

Gambier, Yves, *Language Transfer and Audiovisual Communication: A Bibliography,* Manchester, England: St. Jerome Publishing, 1997

Gambier, Yves, and Henrik Gottlieb, editors, *(Multi)Media Translation: Concepts, Practices, and Research,* Amsterdam: John Benjamins Publishing Company, 2001

Kilborn, Richard, "'Speak My Language': Current Attitudes to Television Subtitling and Dubbing," *Media, Culture, Society* (1993)

Luyken, Georg-Michael, *Overcoming Language Barriers in Television: Dubbing and Subtitling for the European Audience,* Manchester, England: European Institute for the Media, 1991

Yvane, J., "The Treatment of Language in the Production of Dubbed Versions," *EBU Review* (1987)

DuMont, Allen B. (1901–1965)

U.S. Inventor and Media Executive

In 1931, Allen B. DuMont founded Allen B. DuMont Laboratories, Inc., in his garage with $1,000—half of it borrowed. The company achieved its initial success as the primary U.S. manufacturer of cathode-ray tubes,

which had become critical to the electronics industry. DuMont entered into television broadcasting—first experimentally, then as a commercial venture—in 1938. In fact, the only way to receive NBC-RCA's historic

Allen B. DuMont.
Photo courtesy of the Museum of Broadcast Communications (MBC)

public broadcast of television outside the company's 1939 World's Fair pavilion was on sets made by Du-Mont Labs.

DuMont first became involved in broadcasting by building a radio transmitter and a transmitter and receiver out of an oatmeal box while suffering from polio. In 1924, he received an electrical engineering degree from Rensselaer Polytechnic Institute. After graduation, he joined the Westinghouse Lamp Company as an engineer at a time when 500 tubes a day were being produced. Later, DuMont became supervisor and initiated technical improvements that increased production to 5,000 tubes per hour. In 1928, he worked closely with Dr. Lee DeForest on expanding radio but left later to explore television.

DuMont achieved a number of firsts in commercial television practice, but with little success. He tried to expand his network too rapidly in terms of both the number of affiliates and the number of hours of programming available to affiliates each week. Even as DuMont was developing into the first commercial television network, the other networks, most notably the Columbia Broadcasting System (CBS) and the National Broadcasting Company (NBC), were preparing

for the time when rapid network expansion was most feasible—experimenting with various program formats and talent borrowed from their radio networks as well as encouraging their most prestigious and financially successful radio affiliates to apply for television licenses.

Prime-time programming was a major problem for DuMont. The network would not or could not pay for expensive shows that would deliver large audiences, thereby attracting powerful sponsors. When a quality show drew a large audience in spite of its budget, it was snatched by CBS or NBC. DuMont televised the occasional successful show, including *Cavalcade of Stars* (before Jackie Gleason left), *Captain Video,* and Bishop Fulton J. Sheen's *Life Is Worth Living.* However, the network never seemed to generate enough popular programming to keep it afloat—possibly because it lacked the backing of a radio network.

The NBC, CBS, and American Broadcasting Company (ABC) radio networks provided financial support for their television ventures while the fledgling industry was growing—creating what the Federal Communications Commission (FCC) deemed "an ironic situation in which one communications medium financed the development of its competitor." DuMont's only outside financial assistance came from Paramount Studios between 1938 and 1941. The company created and sold class-B common stock exclusively to Paramount for $1 per share and a promise to provide film-quality programming that was never delivered. The sale was performed to offset heavy investments in research, development, and equipment manufacture, but as a result, Allen DuMont relinquished half interest in his company, and Paramount gained a strong measure of "negative" control—with its board members able to veto motions and withhold payment of funds.

Although it ceased financially assisting DuMont in 1941, Paramount maintained a presence on DuMont's board of directors. The FCC ruled in 1948 that Du-Mont and Paramount must combine the number of stations they owned under ownership rules, hurting DuMont's ability to secure exclusive network owned-and-operated programming outlets. One question that remains unanswered is the amount of control Paramount actually did have over the DuMont organization. In 1949, the number of Paramount-controlled DuMont board-of-directors positions was reduced from four to three, but the FCC decision on Paramount control was not reversed.

The FCC "freeze" from 1948 to 1952 hurt the Du-Mont Network because DuMont could add few additional affiliates during a period when the company was financially capable of expansion due to profits from

TV set sales. DuMont did claim a large number of affiliates compared to the other networks, but many of these appear to have taken only a few shows per week from DuMont and relied primarily on an affiliation with CBS and NBC. Analysts have suggested that DuMont's lack of primary affiliates was a key factor in the network's demise.

One important factor contributing to the demise of the DuMont Network was Allen B. DuMont himself. Many people thought of him as a "bypassed pioneer" with no head for business. Major stockholders began to question publicly the soundness of his decisions, especially his desire to keep the TV network afloat despite major losses. In 1955, concerned holders of large blocks of DuMont stock began to wrest control from the company founder.

When the fiscally weakened DuMont corporation spun off its television broadcasting facilities in 1955, *Business Week* claimed that DuMont had been forced into television programming in order to provide a market for his TV receivers. No evidence has been found to support this claim, however. In markets where licenses for television stations were being granted during the postwar period, there were sufficient license applicants to provide audiences with programming to stimulate set sales. One reason DuMont television sales lagged behind those of other manufacturers was that his sets were of higher quality and consequently much more expensive. In fact, in 1951, DuMont cut back television set production by 60 percent—although profits from this division had been subsidizing the TV network—because other manufacturers were undercutting DuMont's prices.

After the DuMont Television Network and its owned-and-operated stations were spun off into a new corporation, there remained only two major divisions of Allen B. DuMont Laboratories, Inc. In 1958, Emerson Electric Company purchased the DuMont consumer products manufacturing division. DuMont was no longer employed by his own company when the last division—oscillograph and cathode-ray tube manufacturing—was sold to Fairchild in 1960. DuMont was hired by Fairchild as group general manager of the A.B. DuMont Division of Fairchild Camera and Instrument Corporation until his death in 1965.

DuMont may have remained in television broadcasting despite fiscal losses in order to uphold the title once given him, "the father of commercial television." His company pioneered many important elements necessary to the growth and evolution of the industry. DuMont engineers perfected the use of cathode-ray tubes as TV screens, developed the kinescope process as well as the "magic eye" cathode-ray radio-tuning indicator, and the first electronic viewfinder. DuMont was an intelligent and energetic engineer who took risks

and profited financially from them—becoming history's first television millionaire. But when the big radio networks entered the field of television, DuMont was unable to compete with these financially powerful, considerably experienced broadcasters.

PHILIP J. AUTER

See also **Army-McCarthy Hearings; United States: Networks**

Allen B(alcom) Dumont. Born in Brooklyn, New York, January 29, 1901. Educated at Rensselaer Polytechnic Institute, Troy, New York, B.S. in electrical engineering 1924. Married: Ethel; children: Allen B., Jr., and Yvonne. Began career with the Westinghouse Lamp Company; conducted TV experiments in his garage, 1920s; developed an inexpensive cathode-ray tube that would last for thousands of hours (unlike the popular German import tube, which lasted only 25 to 30 hours), DeForest Radio Company, 1930; left to found his laboratory, 1931; incorporated DuMont Labs, 1935; sold a half interest to Paramount Pictures Corporation to raise capital for broadcasting stations, 1938; DuMont Labs was first company to market home television receiver, 1939; granted experimental TV licenses in Passaic, New Jersey, and New York, 1942; DuMont Television Network separated from DuMont Labs, sold to the Metropolitan Broadcasting Company; Emerson Radio and Phonograph Corporation purchased DuMont's television, phonograph, and stereo producing division, 1958; remaining DuMont interests merged with the Fairchild Camera and Instrument Corporation, 1960; named group general manager of DuMont divisions of Fairchild, 1960; named senior technical consultant, 1961. Honorary doctorates: Rensselaer and Brooklyn Polytechnic Institutes. Recipient: American Television Society, 1943; Marconi Memorial Medal for Achievement, 1945; several trophies for accuracy in navigation and calculations in power-boat racing. Died in Montclair, New Jersey, November 16, 1965.

Further Reading

Auter, Philip. J., and Douglas A. Boyd, "DuMont: The Original Fourth Television Network," *Journal of Popular Culture* (Winter 1995)

Barnouw, Erik, *Tube of Plenty: The Evolution of American Television,* New York: Oxford University Press, 1975; 2nd revised edition, 1990

Bergreen, Laurence, *Look Now, Pay Later: The Rise and Fall of Network Broadcasting,* New York: Doubleday, 1980

Bochin, Hal W., "The Rise and Fall of the DuMont Network," in *A Sourcebook on the History of Radio and Television,* edited by Lawrence Lichty and Malachi Topping, New York: Hastings House, 1975

Brooks, Tim, and Earle Marsh, *The Complete Directory to Prime Time Network TV Shows: 1946–Present,* New York: Ballantine, 1976; 3rd edition, 1985

DuMont, Allen B.

"The Five-Year Color War," *Television-Radio Age* (September 28, 1987)

Hess, Gary. N., *An Historical Study of the Du Mont Television Network,* New York: Arno Press, 1979

"Pioneer of TV DuMont Dies," *Washington Post* (November 16, 1965)

Sterling, Christopher H., and John M. Kittross, *Stay Tuned: A Concise History of American Broadcasting,* Belmont, California: Wadsworth, 1978; 3rd edition, Mahwah, New Jersey: Lawrence Erlbaum Associates, 2002

U.S. Federal Communications Commission, *Seventh Annual Report,* Washington, D.C.: U.S. Government Printing Office, 1941

White, Timothy R., "Hollywood's Attempt to Appropriate Television: The Case of Paramount Pictures," Ph.D. diss., University of Wisconsin, 1990

Dyer, Gwynne (1943–)

Canadian Journalist, Producer

Gwynne Dyer is a Canadian journalist, syndicated columnist, and military analyst. He is best known for his documentary television series *War,* which echoed the peace movement's growing concern over the threat of nuclear war in the early 1980s. Nominated for an Oscar in 1985, *War* was based on his own military experience and extensive study.

After serving in the naval reserves of Canada, the United States, and Britain, Dyer completed his doctoral studies in military history at King's College, University of London, in 1973. He lectured on military studies for the next four years before producing a seven-part radio series, *Seven Faces of Communism,* for the Canadian Broadcasting Corporation (CBC) and the American Broadcasting Company (ABC) in 1978. This quickly led to other radio series, including *War,* in six parts, in 1981. Based on this series, he was invited by the National Film Board of Canada, the country's public film producer, to enlarge the project into a seven-part film series in 1983. On release to critical acclaim, the series was broadcast in 45 countries.

War was a reflection of Dyer's own growing concern about the proliferation of new technology, its impact on the changing nature of warfare, and the growing threat of nuclear annihilation. Filmed in ten countries and with the participation of six national armies, it examined the nature, evolution, and consequences of warfare. It featured interviews with top-level North Atlantic Treaty Organization (NATO) and Warsaw Pact military leaders and strategist, many of whom spoke to the Western media for the first time. The series argued that in an era of total war, professional armies were no longer able to fulfill their traditional roles. The growth of nationalism, conscript armies, and nuclear technology had brought the world perilously close to Armageddon. *War* offered the unique perspective of the soldier, from the rigorous training of young U.S. Marine recruits at the Parris Island Training Depot in South Carolina to the field exercises conducted by NATO and Warsaw Pact countries in Europe. It presented military officers from both sides talking frankly about how nuclear technology had changed their profession and followed them as they vividly described how any superpower conflict would inevitably lead to an all-out nuclear war. Dyer argued that the danger posed by the explosive mix of ideology and nuclear technology could be mitigated only by a total elimination of nuclear arsenals.

This award-winning series was soon followed by another production for the National Film Board of Canada in 1986, *The Defence of Canada,* an examination of Canada's military role on the international scene. Following arguments similar to those postulated in *War,* Dyer called for Canada to set an example by rethinking its position in NATO and the North American Air Defense Command (NORAD). He maintained his ties in the Soviet Union and from 1988 to 1990 produced a six-part radio series, *The Gorbachev Revolution,* which followed the thunderous changes occurring in Eastern Europe. He served as a military commentator in Canada during the Gulf War, and in 1994 his series *The Human Race* was broadcast nationally on the CBC. It was a personal inquiry into the roots, nature, and future of human politics and the threat posed by tribalism, nationalism, and technology to the world's environment. The next year, his television documentary on the war in Bosnia, *Protection Force,* aired.

Dyer continues to write a syndicated column on international affairs, which is published in 150 newspapers in 30 nations. He also lectures frequently on military history and global instability in the current world.

MANON LAMONTAGNE

Gwynne Dyer. Born in St. John's, Newfoundland, Canada, April 17, 1943. Educated at Memorial University of Newfoundland, B.A. in history, 1963; Rice University, Houston, Texas, M.A. in military history 1966; King's College, University of London, Ph.D. in military and Middle Eastern history 1973. Served as reserve naval officer, Royal Canadian Naval Reserve, 1956–64, 1966–68; U.S. Naval Reserve, 1964–66; British Royal Navy Reserve, 1968–73. Lecturer in military history, Canadian Forces College in Toronto; senior lecturer in war studies, Royal Military Academy, Sandhurst, England, 1973–77; producer of various radio and television special series, since 1978; syndicated columnist, international affairs, since 1973. Recipient: International Film Festival Awards; International Film Festival Awards, 1984; Best Writing Gemini for *The Space Between,* 1986.

Television Documentaries

1983   *War* (co-writer and host)
1986   *The Defence of Canada*

1994   *The Human Race* (host)
1995   *Protection Force*

Films

The Space Between (co-writer/host), 1986; *Harder Than It Looks,* 1987; *Escaping from History* (writer), 1994; *The Gods of Our Fathers* (writer), 1994; *The Tribal Mind* (writer), 1994; *The Bomb under the World* (writer), 1994.

Radio

Seven Faces of Communism, 1978; *Goodbye War* (writer and narrator), 1979; *War,* 1981; *The G orbachev Revolution,* 1988–90; *Millennium,* 1996.

Further Reading

Dodds, Carolyn, "Too Close for Comfort," *Saturday Night* (August 1988)
"Dyer's Contrived Truth Doesn't Tackle the Real Consequences," *Vancouver Sun* (September 3, 1994)
"Recording a Global Culture," *Maclean's* (March 25, 1996)

Dyke, Greg (1947–)

British Media Executive

As director general of the British Broadcasting Corporation (BBC), Greg Dyke heads one of Britain's best-known institutions and largest employers and is custodian of the nation's most important cultural body. In April 2000, Dyke was named to succeed Sir John Birt at the BBC, which at that time had an annual income of $4.5 billion and a staff of 23,000. Clearly, the BBC governors chose Dyke because he had previously proven himself to be a genius in supplying popular, widely watched television for independent companies. Dyke had been one of the most powerful leaders among the British independent television companies, having headed TV-AM, Television South, and London Weekend Television (LWT). His 1995 departure from network television to become head of the television interests of the Pearson Group and member of the board of the satellite-delivered television group British Sky Broadcasting (BSkyB) signaled a shift of his considerable influence from mainstream television to the new multichannel systems. In 2000, his friend Sir Christopher Bland, who had been promoted from chairman of LWT to chairman of the BBC's board of governors, called Dyke back to the mainstream in order to boost BBC ratings. Bland has said of Dyke, "Television is a mass medium and Greg understands that. You have to have a mass audience if you are going to succeed."

Dyke's success in the industry has proved that it is no longer necessary for top British television people to come from "Oxbridge" (Oxford and Cambridge Universities) and start their careers with the BBC. Unlike most BBC executives, Dyke had a varied career after leaving grammar school at age 16: he worked for various local papers and gained a politics degree at York University as a mature student.

Dyke's television career began when he joined *The London Program* in the 1970s, and he rapidly rose to become producer of *Weekend World* and deputy editor of *The London Program.* In 1981, he was given command of his own creation, *The Six O'clock Show,* an energetic magazine program. Dyke proved to his production teams that he was an inspirational manager and able administrator.

Dyke's greatest success in the early chapters of his television career came when he, almost single-handedly, saved TV-AM. The 1981 franchised breakfast company was heading for bankruptcy when Dyke was called in to bring back its audience. Dyke took the ailing breakfast show "down-market," signaling this move with the introduction of bingo numbers, horoscopes, and a clueless puppet called Roland Rat. Viewership rose from 200,000 to 1.8 million in 12 months, and the eventual gain was 20-fold. Better ratings were regarded as more important than cultural qualities.

Dyke eventually resigned from TV-AM because of a conflict over budget cuts, and he was quickly hired by Television South as director of programs; from that appointment, he returned to LWT as director of programs and then chief executive. Perhaps his most significant promotion was to replace his good friend and former colleague Birt on the ITV Program Controllers' group. When Dyke rose to become chair of that vital group, he effectively orchestrated the ITV companies' scheduling against the BBC.

By 1993, Dyke was chief executive of London Weekend Television Holdings, chair of the ITV Association, and chair of ITV Sport. Under his command, LWT flourished as never before, with excellent programs such as *Blind Date* and *Beadle's About*. But successful companies always risk the danger of being taken over unless they are protected by government regulation, as was the case for ITV companies. When the Conservatives abolished these restrictions in 1993, LWT was at risk. Granada swallowed LWT for $900 million in 1994, and Dyke resigned rather than work under Granada control. With $1.75 million in stock options, Dyke made a $12 million profit from the Granada bid.

Dyke is perhaps the outstanding ITV "baby boomer": generous, perennially optimistic, and very widely experienced. His friends say that he is motivated and streetwise and understands popular TV. His critics suggest that he is a lightweight, with a tendency to speak out quickly, an impression that is fostered by his blue-collar London accent and approachable personality. Certainly his impact on ITV was considerable. His move to Pearson and BSkyB illustrated clearly that the traditional ratings war between ITV and the BBC is no longer the only competition in the British television market. As head of the largest terrestrial broadcaster in the United Kingdom, the BBC, he must protect its share of the market from both ITV and cable and satellite programming.

Dyke's first two years with the BBC yielded mixed results; among the low points, he lost the Match of the Day Premiership Football highlights to commercial interests in 2001. Dyke has been faced with correcting the overly bureaucratic approach to management promoted by the previous director general, his ex-LWT colleague Birt. Dyke's plans for "One BBC" included reducing the amount of money spent on running the BBC from 24 to 15 percent of its total income, freeing up an additional $300 million for programming. He described this scheme as "more leadership, less management...our aim is to create one BBC, where people enjoy their job and are inspired and united behind the common purpose of making great programs and delivering outstanding services." The key change under this plan has been the creation of three programming divisions: Drama, Entertainment, and Children; Factual and Learning; and Sport. Each programming division reports directly to the director general and has a seat on the new executive committee.

ANDREW QUICKE

See also **British Production Companies; British Sky Broadcasting**

Greg(ory) Dyke. Born May 20, 1947. Attended Hayes Grammar School; University of York, B.A. in politics. Two sons and two daughters. Had varied career, 1965–83, before being appointed editor in chief, TV-AM, 1983–84; director of programs, TVS, 1984–87; director of programs, 1987–91, deputy managing director, 1989–90, managing director and subsequently group chief executive, 1990–94, London Weekend Television; director, Channel 4 Television, 1988–91; chair, ITV Council, 1991–94; director, BSkyB, 1995–2000; chair, Pearson Television, 1995–2000; director general of the BBC since 2000.

Dynasty

U.S. Serial Melodrama

Premiering as a three-hour movie on January 12, 1981, the prime-time soap opera *Dynasty* aired on the American Broadcasting Company (ABC) until 1989. *Dynasty* quickly worked its way into the top-five rated programs, finishing fifth for the 1982–83 season and third for the 1983–84 season. It was the number one ranked program for the 1984–85 season but rapidly began losing viewers. By its final season (1988–89), *Dynasty* finished tied for 57th place and was unceremoniously dumped from ABC's roster leaving numerous dangling plotlines. These plotlines were tied up in a two-part, four-hour movie, *Dynasty: The Reunion,* which aired on ABC on October 20 and 22, 1991, some two years after the series' cancellation.

The soap opera focused primarily on the lives and loves of Blake Carrington (John Forsythe), a wealthy Denver, Colorado, oil tycoon; his wife Krystle (Linda Evans); ex-wife Alexis (Joan Collins); daughter Fallon (Pamela Sue Martin, Emma Samms); sons Steven (Al Corley and Jack Coleman); and Adam (Gordon Thomson), as well as numerous extended family members and associates, including Fallon's husband/ex-husband Jeff Colby (John James) and Krystle's niece and Steven's wife/ex-wife Sammy Jo (Heather Locklear).

The program relied on both camp and excess for its appeal. Its characters and plotlines were sometimes absurd and broadly drawn, but it was the trappings of wealth, glamour, and fashion that drew viewers in some 70 countries to the program. With a weekly budget of $1.2 million ($10,000 of which went for clothing alone, including at least ten Nolan Miller creations per episode), *Dynasty* placed more emphasis on style than on plot.

The plotlines of this prime-time soap opera often resembled those of its daytime counterparts: kidnapped babies, amnesia, pregnancy, infidelity, and treachery. In fact, *Dynasty* made extensive use of one soap opera staple: the return to life of characters presumed dead. Both Fallon and Steven Carrington were killed off, only to return in later seasons played by different actors.

Just as often, however, *Dynasty*'s plots leaned toward the campy and absurd. One of the most talked about and ridiculed plots was the 1985 season-ending cliffhanger, which saw the Carringtons gathered for a wedding in the country of Moldavia. Terrorists stormed the ceremony in a hail of machine-gun fire, but when the smoke cleared (at the start of the next season, of course), all the primary characters were alive and basically unscathed.

While often criticized for its weak and at times absurd plots, *Dynasty* did provide juicy roles for women, notably Joan Collins's characterization of Alexis. Her character—scheming, conniving, and ruthless—was often referred to as a "superbitch" and was the quintessential "character you love to hate." Alexis was set in opposi-

Dynasty, Linda Evans, Pamela Bellwood, Heather Locklear, Pamela Sue Martin, Joan Collins, and John Forsythe, 1981–89.
Courtesy of the Everett Collection

tion to Krystle, who was more of a "good girl"—sweet, loyal, and loving. One of the best-known scenes in *Dynasty*'s history was the 1983 "cat fight" between Alexis and Krystle, in which they literally fought it out in a lily pond. Alexis met her match in the character of wealthy singer and nightclub owner Dominique Devereaux (Diahann Carroll), the first prominently featured African-American character on a prime-time soap opera.

During its nearly nine-year run, *Dynasty* spawned the short-lived spin-off *Dynasty II: The Colbys* (1985–87) and gave rise to numerous licensed luxury products, including perfume, clothing, and bedding. Never before had television product licensing been so targeted to upscale adults.

When *Dynasty* left the air in 1989, it also marked the demise of the prime-time soap opera, which had been a staple of television programming through the 1980s. Produced in part by Aaron Spelling, whose programs (such as *Charlie's Angels; The Love Boat; Beverly Hills, 90210;* and *Melrose Place*) have emphasized beauty, wealth, and glamour, *Dynasty* had proved the perfect metaphor for 1980s greed and excess. In declaring *Dynasty* the best prime-time soap of the decade, *TV Guide* asserted that the program's "campy opulence gave it a superb, ironic quality—in other words, it was great trash."

SHARON R. MAZZARELLA

*See also **Dallas;** **Forsythe, John;** **Melodrama***

Cast

Blake Carrington	John Forsythe
Krystle Jennings Carrington	Linda Evans
Alexis Carrington Colby	Joan Collins
Fallon Carrington Colby (1981–84)	Pamela Sue Martin
Fallon Carrington Colby (1985, 1987–89)	Emma Samms
Steven Carrington (1981–82)	Al Corley
Steven Carrington (1983–88)	Jack Coleman
Adam Carrington/Michael Torrance (1982–1989)	Gordon Thomson
Cecil Colby (1981–82)	Lloyd Bochner
Jeff Colby (1981–85, 1987–89)	John James
Claudia Blaisdel (1981–86)	Pamela Bellwood
Matthew Blaisdel (1981)	Bo Hopkins
Lindsay Blaisdel (1981)	Katy Kurtzman
Walter Lankershim (1981)	Dale Robertson
Jeannette	Virginia Hawkins
Joseph Anders (1981–83)	Lee Bergere
Kirby (1982–84)	Kathleen Beller
Andrew Laird (1981–84)	Peter Mark Richman
Sammy Jo Dean	Heather Locklear
Michael Culhane (1981, 1986–87)	Wayne Northrop
Dr. Nick Toscanni (1981–82)	James Farentino
Mark Jennings (1982–84)	Geoffrey Scott
Congressman Neal McEane (1982–84, 1987)	Paul Burke
Chris Deegan (1983)	Grant Goodeve
Tracy Kendall (1983–84)	Deborah Adair
Farnsworth "Dex" Dexter (1983–89)	Michael Nader
Peter de Vilbis (1983–84)	Helmut Berger
Amanda Carrington (1984–86)	Catherine Oxenberg
Amanda Carrington (1986–87)	Karen Cellini
Dominique Deveraux (1984–87)	Diahann Carroll
Gerard (1984–89)	William Beckley
Gordon Wales (1984–88)	James Sutorius
Luke Fuller (1984–85)	William Campbell
Nicole Simpson (1984–85)	Susan Scannell
Charles (1984–85)	George DiCenzo
Daniel Reece (1984–85)	Rock Hudson
Lady Ashley Mitchell (1985)	Ali MacGraw
Danny Carrington (1985–88)	Jameson Sampley
Joel Abrigore (1985–86)	George Hamilton
Garrett Boydston (1985–86)	Ken Howard

Producers

Richard and Ethel Shapiro, Aaron Spelling, E. Duke Vincent, Philip Parslow, Elaine Rich, Ed Ledding

Programming History

ABC

January 1981–April 1981	Monday 9:00–10:00
July 1981–September 1983	Wednesday 10:00–11:00
September 1983–May 1984	Wednesday 9:00–10:00
August 1984–May 1986	Wednesday 9:00–10:00
September 1986–May 1987	Wednesday 9:00–10:00
September 1987–March 1988	Wednesday 10:00–11:00
November 1988–May 1989	Wednesday 10:00–11:00

Further Reading

"The Best Prime-Time Soaps," *TV Guide* (April 17, 1993)
Dynasty: The Authorized Biography of the Carringtons, Garden City, New York: Doubleday, 1984

Feuer, Jane, "Reading *Dynasty:* Television and Reception Theory," *South Atlantic Quarterly* (Spring 1989)

Geraghty, Christine, *Women and Soap Opera: A Study of Prime Time Soaps,* Cambridge: Polity, 1991

Gripsrud, Jostein, "The *Dynasty*-Event in Norway: The Role of Print Media," *Edda: Nordisk Tidsskrift for Litteraturforskning/Scandinavian Journal of Literary Research* (1989)

Gripsrud, Jostein, "Toward a Flexible Methodology in Studying Media Meaning: *Dynasty* in Norway," *Critical Studies in Mass Communication* (1990)

Gripsrud, Jostein, *The Dynasty Years: Hollywood Television and Critical Media Studies,* London and New York: Routledge, 1995

Schroder, Kim Christian, "The Playful Audience: The Continuity of the Popular Cultural Tradition in America," *The Dolphin: Publications of the English Department, University of Aarhus* (1989)

White, Mimi, "Women, Memory, and Serial Melodrama," *Screen* (Winter 1994)

E

E! Entertainment Network

U.S. Cable Network

E! Networks launched E! Entertainment Television in 1990 as the only 24-hour network with programming dedicated to the world of entertainment. Now majority owned by Comcast Communications Corporation and available in more than 80 million Nielsen homes, E! has become a mainstay for adult audiences who want the latest news on celebrities, Hollywood, and the scandals that intermittently afflict the rich and famous. As the largest producer and distributor of entertainment and lifestyle-related programming, E! offers a scheduling mix of entertainment news, celebrity interviews, docudramas, reality programming, behind-the-scenes specials, comedy, movie previews, and extensive coverage of the entertainment industry's award shows.

E! emerged in 1990 when Time Warner and Home Box Office (HBO), acting as the managing partner for five major cable operators, sought to transform the floundering cable network Movietime into one providing 24-hour coverage of the entertainment industry. Movietime was subsequently revamped and relaunched under a new name and logo, E! Entertainment Television, which premiered that year as the only 24-hour network with original, short-form programming dedicated to the world of entertainment. Long-form programming production began at E! in 1991 with *Talk Soup,* a daily, half-hour parody of America's daytime talk show phenomenon. Hosted by Greg Kinnear, *Talk Soup* became the network's first major hit.

Capitalizing on the nation's increasing hunger for round-the-clock access to celebrities, E!'s first Oscar guide show premiered in 1991, setting the stage for E!'s signature program *Live From the Red Carpet.* In 1994, comedian Joan Rivers became the host of E!'s live Oscar telecast, transforming the coverage into a ratings bonanza and establishing a decade-long network franchise.

Several months after Rivers's debut with *Live From the Red Carpet,* E! launched *Howard Stern,* a nightly, half-hour show featuring a compilation of raunchy sketches from the shock jock's morning radio program. *Howard Stern* quickly became one of the network's top-rated series, albeit a perennially controversial one.

E! benefited from more controversial programming the following year when it ran full, gavel-to-gavel coverage of the O.J. Simpson murder trial. The network's trial coverage posted huge ratings gains and cemented the network's reputation for bold, irreverent, and revealing programming.

Seeking to further brand itself as the leading source on television for the inside scoop on celebrity lifestyles, in 1996 E! launched the docudrama, *The E! True Hollywood Story,* as a one- and two-hour exposé into the real-life dramas of the rich and famous. *True*

Courtesy of E! Entertainment Television

Hollywood Story, with celebrity profiles including Demi Moore, Martha Stewart, Diana Ross, Eminem, Anna Kournikova, and Michael Jackson, became a nightly prime-time program in 1999. That same year, *Rolling Stone* named the Emmy-nominated program as one of the decade's most influential shows.

Other significant recent E! programming ventures include *Revealed* and *It's Good to Be. Revealed* debuted with host Jules Asner in 2001 as a one-hour series that sheds light on the lives of A-List celebrities, including Julia Roberts, Jennifer Lopez, George Clooney, and Halle Berry. *It's Good to Be* debuted on the network soon thereafter and turns the spotlight on celebrities' financial assets and extravagant spending habits.

As it has since its inception, E! continues to target the prized 18-to-49 adult demographic and remains one of the most recognizable brands in cable television for this age-group, ranking in the top 15 out of more than 100 established cable networks in brand awareness. The network has increasingly struggled, however, to maintain a healthy share of this audience in the face of mounting competition from rival cable channels such as Music Television (MTV) and Video Hits 1 (VH1) and new and highly successful reality programming ventures from the broadcast networks.

In order to maintain and expand its share of style-conscious, entertainment-oriented young adults, E! developed its own reality-programming roster with entries such as *The Anna Nicole Smith Show,* which debuted in the summer of 2002 to favorable ratings and critical infamy. *The Anna Nicole Smith Show* ran for two seasons as a weekly, half-hour reality sitcom featuring the life of outlandish model/playmate/pop culture sensation Anna Nicole Smith and her unique circle of family and friends. More recent E! forays into reality programming have included *Celebrities Uncensored* and *Wild On.*

Leveraging its strength in the fashion sector of entertainment and by repurposing shows such as *Fashion Emergency,* a groundbreaking makeover program, E! launched the Style Network in 1998 as the only 24-hour network devoted to lifestyle programming. The Style Network features original series covering a broad range of categories within the lifestyle genre, including appearance, home, food and entertainment, and leisure. Style Network currently covers more than 30 million Nielsen homes.

E! Networks controls production for both E! Entertainment Television and the Style Network from its Los Angeles–based headquarters. Advertising and affiliate sales offices for the network are based in New York with additional affiliate sales offices in Connecticut. Both networks maintain websites, and E! Online—which provides entertainment news, original features, gossip, reviews, games, live-event coverage, and E!-branded merchandise—averages more than 100 million page views per month.

The Comcast Communications/Walt Disney Company partnership assumed 80 percent control of E! Entertainment Network in 1997, with 50 percent of that block solely owned by Comcast. Comcast, the largest cable operator in the United States, remains the network's largest shareholder with Disney and Liberty Media holding significant stakes as well.

CHRISTOPHER SMITH

Further Reading

Romano, Allison, "At E! Youth Will Be Served," *Broadcasting & Cable* (July 22, 2002)

Romano, Allison, "E!'s Great Big Blonde Surprise," *Broadcasting & Cable* (August 12, 2002)

Early Frost, An

U.S. Television Movie

An Early Frost, broadcast on November 11, 1985, on the National Broadcasting Company (NBC), was the first American made-for-television movie and the second prime-time dramatic program to acknowledge the presence and spread of AIDS in the 1980s. Because the movie was about the potentially controversial topic of homosexuality and the impact of AIDS on the beleaguered community of gay men, much care went into the preproduction process. First, for more than a year, there was much interaction between writers Dan Lipman and Ron Cowen and NBC's Broadcast Standards and Practices department about the script. Such thorough development is highly unusual for most made-for-television movies. This interaction attempted to ensure a delicate balance in the presentation of sensitive subject matter. In addition, NBC gathered a cast of actors—Aidan Quinn, Gena Rowlands, Ben Gazzara, and Sylvia Sidney—who were most often associated with theatrically released films. The network also secured the service of Emmy Award–winning director Jon Erman for the project. These choices, they hoped, would enhance the production's aura of quality and deflect any criticism about exploitation of the tragic pandemic.

Scriptwriters Lipman and Cowen consciously framed the narrative about AIDS in the generic conventions of the family melodrama. Strategically, this approach provided a familiar, less threatening environment in which to present information and issues surrounding gay men and the disease. At one level, the narrative of *An Early Frost* exposes the tenuous links that hold the middle-class Pierson family together. On the surface, life appears to be idyllic. Nick Pierson is the successful owner of a lumberyard. He and his wife Kate have reared two seemingly well-adjusted children in a suburban neighborhood. Son Michael is a rising young lawyer in Chicago. Daughter Susan has replicated her parents' lifestyle, married with one child and expecting a second.

Under the surface, however, several familial fissures exist. Nick's upwardly mobile class aspirations are stalled. Kate's creative talent as a concert pianist has been sublimated into the demands of being a wife and mother. Susan acquiesces to her own husband's demands rather than follow her own desires. Unknown to the family, Michael, a closeted gay man, lives with his

lover Peter. The fragile veneer of familial stability bursts apart when Michael learns he has AIDS, exposing all the resentments that various family members have repressed.

The script also includes a parallel narrative thread exploring the conflicts in the gay relationship between Michael and Peter. Their relationship suffers from Michael's workaholic attitude toward his job. Conflict also grows out of Peter's openness about his homosexuality and Michael's inability to be open about his sexuality. The tension between the two is further exacerbated when Michael discovers that Peter has been unfaithful because of these conflicts.

When broadcast, *An Early Frost* drew a 33 share of the viewing audience, winning its time slot for the

An Early Frost, Ben Gazzara, Gena Rowlands, Aidan Quinn, 1985.
Courtesy of the Everett Collection

evening's ratings and thus suggesting that the American public was ready to engage in a cultural discussion of the disease. Even so, the ratings success did not translate into economic profits for NBC. According to Perry Lafferty, the NBC vice president who commissioned the project, the network lost $500,000 in advertising revenues because clients were afraid to have their commercials shown during the broadcast. Apparently, advertisers believed that the subject matter was too controversial because of its homosexual theme and too depressing because of the terminal nature of AIDS as a disease.

These concerns inhibited further production of other made-for-television scripts about AIDS until 1988. Ironically, the production quality of *An Early Frost* became a hallmark by which members of the broadcasting industry measured any subsequent development of movie scripts about AIDS. Arthur Allan Seidelman, director of an NBC afternoon school-break special about AIDS titled *An Enemy among Us,* has stated, "There was some concern after *An Early Frost* was done that 'How many more things can you do about AIDS?'" Any new scripts had to live up to and move beyond the standard set by Cowen and Lipman's original made-for-television movie. Although providing the initial mainstream cultural space to examine AIDS, *An Early Frost* also hindered, in some ways, increased discussion of the disease in prime-time American broadcast programming precisely because it achieved its narrative and informational goals so well.

RODNEY A. BUXTON

See also **Sexual Orientation and Television**

Cast

Nick Pierson	Ben Gazzara
Michael Pierson	Aidan Quinn
Katherine Pierson	Gena Rowlands
Beatrice McKenna	Sylvia Sidney
Susan Maracek	Sydney Walsh
Bob Maracek	Bill Paxton
Victor DiMato	John Glover
Peter Hilton	D.W. Moffett
Dr. Redding	Terry O'Quinn
Christine	Cheryl Anderson

Producer

Perry Lafferty

Programming History

NBC
November 11, 1985

Further Reading

Buxton, Rodney, "Broadcast Formats, Fictional Narratives and Controversy: Network Television's Depiction of AIDS, 1983–1991," Ph.D. diss., University of Texas at Austin, 1992

Farber, S., "A Decade into the AIDS Epidemic the TV Networks Are Still Nervous," *New York Times* (May 2, 1991)

Russo, Vito, *The Celluloid Closet: Homosexuality in the Movies, Revised,* New York: Harper and Row, 1987

Watney, Simon, *Policing Desire: Pornography, AIDS, and the Media,* Minneapolis: University of Minnesota Press, 1987

East Side/West Side

U.S. Drama

East Side/West Side, an hour-long dramatic series, first appeared on the Columbia Broadcasting System (CBS) in September 1963. Though it lasted only a single season, it is a significant program in television history because of the controversial subject matter it tackled each week and the casting of black actor Cicely Tyson in a recurring lead role as secretary Jane Foster.

During the Kennedy years, with an increased regulatory zeal emanating from the Federal Communications Commission, the networks attempted to deemphasize the violence of action-adventure series. One result was an increase in character dramas. There was a trend toward programs based on liberal social themes in which the protagonists were professionals in service to society. As one producer of that era explained, "The guns of gangsters, policemen, and western lawmen were replaced by the stethoscope, the law book, and the psychiatrist's couch." This new breed of episodic TV hero struggled with occupational ethics and felt a disillusionment with values of the past.

East Side/West Side.
Photo courtesy of CBS Worldwide, Inc.

Unlike action-adventure series in which heroes often settled their problems with a weapon, the troubles in New Frontier character dramas were not always resolved. Writers grappled with issues such as poverty, prejudice, drug addiction, abortion, and capital punishment, which do not lend themselves to tidy resolutions. Although the loose ends of a plot might be tied together by story's end, the world was not necessarily depicted as a better place at the conclusion of an episode.

East Side/West Side, produced by David Susskind and Daniel Melnick, was among the best of the genre and won instant acclaim. The program, about a New York social worker, appealed to sophisticates because, according to Lawrence Laurent of the *Washington Post,* it violated "every sacred tenet for television success." Typical TV heroes all had a similar look, said Laurent, "short straight noses, direct from a plastic surgeon, gleaming smiles courtesy of a dental laboratory." But, observed Laurent, Neil Brock (played by George C. Scott) was "hooknosed and disheveled."

An exemplary episode of *East Side/West Side* titled "Who Do You Kill?" aired on November 4, 1963. The story portrays how a black couple in their early 20s living in a Harlem tenement face the death of their infant daughter, who is bitten by a rat while in her crib. Diana Sands played the mother who works in a neighborhood bar to support the family. Her husband, played by James Earl Jones, is frustrated by unemployment and grows more bitter each day.

The week after the broadcast, Senator Jacob Javits, a liberal, pro–civil rights Republican, moved that two newspaper articles be entered into the *Congressional Record:* "A CBS Show Stars Two Negroes: Atlanta Blacks It Out," from the *New York Herald Tribune,* and, from the *New York Times,* "TV: A Drama of Protest." Javits praised CBS for displaying courage in airing "Who Do You Kill?" and told his Senate colleagues he was distressed that not all southern viewers had the opportunity to see the drama. The program, Javits said, "dealt honestly and sensitively with the vital problems of job discrimination, housing conditions, and the terrible cancerous cleavage that can exist between the Negro and the white community." "Who Do You Kill?" he said, was "shocking in its revelations of what life can be like without hope."

The stark realism of the series was discomforting. Most viewers did not know what to make of a hero who was often dazed by moral complexities. For CBS, the series was a bust; one-third of the advertising time remained unsold, and the program was not renewed. A few years later, David Susskind reflected on the ratings problem of *East Side/West Side:* "A gloomy atmosphere for commercial messages, an integrated cast, and a smaller Southern station lineup, all of these things coming together spelled doom for the show. I'm sorry television wasn't mature enough to absorb it and like it and live with it."

MARY ANN WATSON

Cast

Neil Brock	George C. Scott
Frieda Hechlinger	Elizabeth Wilson
Jane Foster	Cicely Tyson

Producers

David Susskind, Don Kranze, Arnold Perl, Larry Arrick

Programming History

26 episodes
CBS
September 1963–September
1964 Monday 10:00–11:00

Further Reading

Watson, Mary Ann, *The Expanding Vista: American Television in the Kennedy Years,* New York: Oxford University Press, 1990

EastEnders

British Soap Opera

EastEnders is one of Britain's most successful television soap operas. First shown on the British Broadcasting Corporation (BBC 1) in 1985, it enjoys regular half-hour prime-time viewing slots, originally twice, later three times a week, and since August 2001 four times weekly, and it is repeated in an omnibus edition on the weekend. Within eight months of its launch, it reached the number one spot in the ratings and has almost consistently remained among the top ten programs ever since (average viewing figures per episode are around 16 million, ranging, since 1997, from 12 million to up to 24 million for episodes where strong storylines climax). A brief dip in audience numbers in the summer of 1993 prompted a rescheduling masterstroke by the then BBC 1 controller, Michael Grade, in order to avoid the clash with ITV's more established soap, *Emmerdale Farm.* The brainchild of producer Julia Smith and script editor Tony Holland, *EastEnders* is significant in terms of both the survival of the BBC and the history of British popular television drama.

In an increasingly competitive struggle with independent television to present quality programs and appeal to mass audiences, the BBC claimed to have found in *EastEnders* the answer to both a shrinking audience and criticisms of declining standards. The program is set in Walford, a fictitious borough of London's East End, and it focuses on a number of predominantly working-class, often interrelated, families living in Albert Square. The East End of London was regarded as the ideal location for an alluring and long-running series since its historical significance in Britain renders it instantly recognizable; the location was also thought to be illustrative of modern urban Britain because it possesses a mix of individuals who are, according to Smith and Holland, "multi-racial, larger-than-life characters." Much of the action takes place in and around the local pub, the Queen Vic, traditionally run by the Watts—originally villainous Den and his neurotic wife Angie and later by their estranged adoptive daughter, Sharon, who after a few years' absence took it over again from strong-minded Peggy Mitchell.

The main characters were connected originally with the closely knit Fowler/Beale clan, specifically, Pauline and Arthur Fowler and their eldest children,

Mark, an HIV-positive market trader, and Michelle, a strong-willed, single mother, together with café owner Kathy Beale, her son Ian, and the long-suffering Pat Butcher. The Butcher/Mitchell clan has been expanding through the years, providing the show with some of its strongest characters and storylines: for example, overprotective mum Peggy divorced naughty husband Frank Butcher, who renewed his love for ex-wife Pat and almost ruined her marriage with his business partner Roy Evans, and bully son Phil Mitchell cheated on his brother Grant with Grant's wife Sharon, became an alcoholic, sold stolen cars for a living, and eventually got shot by pregnant ex-girlfriend Lisa. Additional figures and families come and go, illustrating the view that character turnover is essential if a contemporary quality is to be retained. At any one time, around eight families, all living or working in Albert Square, will feature centrally in one or another narrative.

EastEnders exhibits certain formal characteristics common to other successful British soap operas (most notably, its major competitor, Granada's *Coronation Street*), such as the working-class community setting and the prevalence of strong female characters (Pauline, Peggy, Rosa, Bianca, Mo, Melanie, Kat, Janine, and Sonia). In addition, a culturally diverse cast strives to preserve the flavor of the East End, while a gender balance is allegedly maintained through the introduction of various "macho" male personalities (Grant, Phil, Beppe, Dan, and Nick). The expansion of minority representation signals a move away from the traditional soap opera format, providing more opportunities for audience identification with the characters and hence a wider appeal. Similarly, the program has come to include more teenagers and successful young adults in a bid to capture the younger television audience. The program's attraction, however, is also a product of a narrative structure unique to the genre. The soap opera has been described as an "open text," a term relating primarily to the simultaneous development and indeterminate nature of the storylines and the variety of issue positions presented through the different characters. Such a structure invites viewer involvement in the personal relationships and family lives of the characters without fear of repercussions through recognition of "realistic" situations or personal dilem-

EastEnders.
Courtesy of the Everett Collection

mas rather than through identification with a central character. *EastEnders* is typical of the soap opera in this respect, maintaining at any one time two or more major and several minor intertwining narratives, with cliff-hangers at the ends of episodes and (temporary) resolutions within the body of some episodes.

To fulfill its public service remit, the program aims to both entertain and educate. The mystery surrounding the father of Michelle's baby and the emotional weight of the AIDS-related death of Mark's girlfriend Jill, the controversy around Dot Cotton's mercy killing of sick friend Ethel, and the moral dilemma of schoolgirl Sonia saying good-bye to baby Chloe all illustrate how a dramatic representation of social issues in contemporary Britain successfully combines these elements. Throughout *EastEnders*' long history, issues such as drug addiction, abortion, AIDS, breast cancer, homosexuality, death, euthanasia, racial and domestic violence, murder, theft, stabbings, adoption, divorce, infidelity, betrayal, and teenage pregnancy have graced the program's social and moral agenda. *EastEnders* strives to be realistic and relevant rather than

issue led, with the educational element professed as an incidental outcome of the program's commitment to realism. Such endeavors have been attacked, with criticisms of minority-group tokenism, depressing issue mongering, and, paradoxically, lapses into Cockney stereotyping. However, over the past few years, the number of "overly diagrammatic characters" such as "Colin the gay" (so described by Andy Medhurst in *The Observer*) appears to have decreased, with new characters being introduced for their dramatic contribution rather than their sociological significance.

As with other British soaps, *EastEnders* differs from American soaps by its relentless emphasis on the mundane and nitty-gritty details of working-class life (no middle-class soap has yet succeeded for long in Britain) among ordinary-looking (rather than attractive) and relatively unsuccessful people. This potentially depressing mix is lightened by a dose of British humor and wit, by the dramatic intensity of the emotions and issues portrayed, and by the nostalgic gloss given to the portrayal of solidarity and warmth in a supposedly authentic community. In terms of the image of "ordinary life" conveyed by the program, *EastEnders* is again typical of the soap opera for its ambivalences: showing strong women who are nonetheless tied to the home, a community that tries to pull together but a relatively disaffected youth, and a romantic faith in love and marriage and yet a series of adulterous affairs and divorces. For its audience, *EastEnders* is highly pleasurable for its apparent realism, its honesty in addressing contentious issues, and its cozy familiarity.

A regular feature of the weekly schedules, *EastEnders* has become a fundamental and prominent part of British television culture. Public and media interest extends beyond plot and character developments to the extracurricular activities of cast members. While maintaining the essential soap opera characteristics, *EastEnders* distinguishes itself from the other major British soaps, appearing coarser, faster paced, and more dramatic than *Coronation Street* yet less controversial and more humorous than *Brookside*. In the words of Medhurst of *The Observer*, "*EastEnders* remains the BBC's most important piece of fiction, a vital sign of its commitment to deliver quality and popularity in the same unmissable package." Although *EastEnders* is in many ways typical of the genre, the obvious quality, cultural prominence, and audience success of the program has established the soap opera as a valued centerpiece of early prime-time broadcasting in Britain.

DANIELLE ARON AND SONIA LIVINGSTONE

See also **British Programming;** *Brookside; Coronation Street;* **Soap Opera**

Cast

Ian Beale	Adam Woodyatt
Laura Beale (Dunn)	Hannah Waterman
Lucy Beale Casey	Anne Rothery
Peter Beale	Joseph Shade
Steven Beale	Edward Savage
Jim Branning	John Bardon
Bianca Butcher (Jackson)	Patsy Palmer
Frank Butcher	Mike Reid
Janine Butcher	Charlie Brooks
Ricky Butcher	Sid Owen
Dot Cotton	June Brown
Nick Cotton	John Altman
Zoe Cotton	Tara Ellis
Beppe di Marco	Michael Greco
Joe di Marco	Jake Kyprianou
Sandra di Marco	Clare Wilkie
Barry Evans	Shaun Williamson
Natalie Evans (Price)	Lucy Speed
Pat Evans (Harris, Beale, Wicks, Butcher)	Pam St Clement
Roy Evans	Tony Caunter
Mark Fowler	Todd Carty
Martin Fowler	James Alexandrou
Pauline Fowler (Beale)	Wendy Richard
Mo Harris	Laila Morse
Garry Hobbs	Ricky Groves
Robbie Jackson	Dean Gaffney
Sonia Jackson	Natalie Cassidy
Asif Malik	Ashvin Luximon
Kim McFarlane	Krystle Williams
Mick McFarlane	Sylvester Williams
Billy Mitchell	Perry Fenwick
Jamie Mitchell	Jack Ryder
Peggy Mitchell (Butcher)	Barbara Windsor
Phil Mitchell	Steve McFadden
Trevor Morgan	Alex Ferns
Melanie Owen (Healy)	Tamzin Outhwaite
Steve Owen	Martin Kemp
Terry Raymond	Gavin Richards
Lisa Shaw	Lucy Benjamin
Charlie Slater	Derek Martin
Harry Slater	Michael Elphick
Kat Slater	Jessie Wallace
Lynne Slater	Elaine Lordan
Maureen "Little Mo" Slater	Kacey Ainsworth
Zoe Slater	Michelle Ryan
Dan Sullivan	Craig Fairbrass
Anthony Trueman	Nicholas R. Bailey
Patrick Trueman	Rudolph Walker
Paul Trueman	Gary Beadle
Sharon Watts (Mitchell)	Letitia Dean

Producers

Julia Smith, Mike Gibbon, Corinne Hollingworth, Richard Bramall, Michael Ferguson, Pat Sandys, Helen Greaves, Leonard Lewis, Matthew Robinson, Nigel Taylor, Lorraine Newman, Nicky Cotton, John Yorke

Programming History

BBC
February 1985–

Further Reading

Buckingham, David Dennis, *Public Secrets: EastEnders and Its Audience,* London: British Film Institute, 1987

Frentz, Suzanne, editor, *Staying Tuned: Contemporary Soap Opera Criticism,* Bowling Green, Ohio: Bowling Green State University Popular Press, 1992

Geraghty, Christine, *Women in Soap Operas: A Study of Prime Time Soaps,* Oxford: Polity Press, 1990

Liebes, Tamar, and Livingstone, Sonia M., "The Structure of Family and Romantic Ties in the Soap Opera: An Ethnographic Approach to the Cultural Framing of Primordiality," *Communication Research,* Vol. 21, No. 6 (1994)

Liebes, Tamar, and Livingstone, Sonia M., "European Soap Operas: The Diversification of a Genre, *European Journal of Communication,* Vol. 13, No. 2 (1998)

Livingstone, Sonia M., "Why People Watch Soap Opera: An Analysis of the Explanations of British Viewers," *European Journal of Communication,* Vol. 3 (1988)

Livingstone, Sonia M., *Making Sense of Television: The Psychology of Audience Interpretation,* Oxford: Pergamon, 1990; 2nd edition, London: Routledge, 1998

Livingstone, Sonia M., and Liebes, Tamar, "Where Have All the Mothers Gone? Soap Opera's Replaying of the Oedipal Story," *Critical Studies in Mass Communication,* Vol. 12 (1995)

Ebersol, Dick (1947–)

U.S. Media Executive

In his various executive positions, Duncan Dickie Ebersol has contributed several innovations to the National Broadcasting Company (NBC). He shepherded *Saturday Night Live* onto the air, then returned as producer to "rescue" the show in the early 1980s. As president of NBC Sports, he pursued several inventive and sometimes risky programming packages, such as the Olympics "Triple Cast" and the Baseball Network. Throughout his career, he has been recognized as one of television's more creative programmers.

Ebersol became hooked on television sports when he saw the debut of *ABC's Wide World of Sports* in 1963. Later, when that show was shooting in his area, he got errand jobs with the crew. By the winter of 1968, he was working as a research assistant for the American Broadcasting Company's (ABC's) coverage of the winter Olympics in Grenoble, France, and while finishing his studies at Yale, he worked full-time as a segment producer. In 1971, following graduation, he became an executive assistant and producer with Roone Arledge, vice president of ABC Sports and creator of *Wide World of Sports.*

NBC tried to hire Ebersol in 1974 by offering to name him president of their sports division, but at the age of 27, he decided he was not ready to compete against Arledge. Instead, he moved to NBC with a new title: director of weekend late-night programming. At that time, the programming slots following the Saturday and Sunday late news were a dead zone for all three networks. Affiliates made more money with old movies than with network offerings—in NBC's case, reruns of *The Tonight Show.* The network charged Ebersol with finding something, anything, to replace the Carson reruns.

Ebersol conceived of a comedy-variety revue aimed at young adults, an audience generally thought to be away from home—and television—on weekends. He assumed that enough of them would stay home to watch a show featuring "underground" comedians such as George Carlin and Richard Pryor, especially when supported with a repertory cast picked from new improv-based, television-savvy comedy groups, such as Second City, the National Lampoon stage shows, or the Groundlings. Ebersol also discovered Lorne Michaels, a former writer for *Rowan and Martin's Laugh-In,* who had produced specials for Lily Tomlin and Flip Wilson and had been lobbying for just the kind of program Ebersol was thinking of.

As Michaels assembled the cast and writers, Ebersol ran interference for *Saturday Night Live* before nervous network management and affiliates. The pair spurned NBC's suggestions for safe hosts such as Bob Hope and Joe Namath and secured Pryor, Carlin, and Tomlin for that role. As *Saturday Night Live* took off, NBC promoted Ebersol to vice president of late-night programs, with an office in Burbank and responsibility over every late show that did not belong to Johnny Carson. Ebersol had become, at 28, the youngest vice president in NBC history.

By 1977, he had become head of NBC's comedy and variety programming. Unfortunately, this was a fallow time for comedy, especially for NBC. Ebersol has said that his only success in this period was hiring Brandon Tartikoff away from ABC to be his associate. After a confrontation with new programming director Fred Silverman, Ebersol quit his position at NBC, and Tartikoff replaced him. He went into independent production, taking over *The Midnight Special* and various sports programming. Shortly afterward, however, NBC asked him to rescue *Saturday Night Live.*

Lorne Michaels had left *Saturday Night Live* after the 1979–80 season, and the original cast and writing

Dick Ebersol, 1987.
Photo courtesy of National Broadcasting Company, Inc.

staff left as well. Replacement producer Jean Doumanian's tenure proved a disaster: the show's daring, edgy satire went over the edge with sketches such as "The Leather Weather Lady." NBC executives had seen enough with Doumanian's 12th show, when cast member Charles Rocket absent-mindedly said "fuck" on the air. Doumanian was fired, and Ebersol agreed to produce the show if NBC would end *Midnight Special.*

Ebersol took *Saturday Night Live* off the air for a month of "retooling." Following this hiatus, only one show was broadcast before a writers' strike in early 1981 halted production until fall. Meanwhile, he fired all the cast except rising stars Joe Piscopo and Eddie Murphy and hired Christine Ebersole (no relation), Mary Gross, and Tim Kazurinsky. He also brought back the head writer from the first season, the brilliant but intimidating Michael O'Donoghue (who was fired by the following January).

Critics considered Ebersol's *Saturday Night Live* an improvement over the previous season, but the ratings were still lower than in the Doumanian era. The show's guest hosts devolved from hip comedians to NBC series players or stars of current movies.

In 1983, No Sleep Productions, Ebersol's production house, had brought *Friday Night Videos* to NBC, where Michael Jackson's groundbreaking "Thriller" video debuted. The next year, Ebersol took over *Fri-day Night Videos* full time and shared the reins on *Saturday Night Live* with Bob Tischler. For the 1984–85 season, the two shored up *Saturday Night Live*'s ratings with experienced comics such as Billy Crystal, Harry Shearer, Christopher Guest, and Martin Short. Afterward, Ebersol quit to spend more time at home, and Brandon Tartikoff, now his boss, hired Lorne Michaels as producer.

Ebersol continued to produce *Friday Night Videos* for NBC, while his wife, the actress Susan St. James, starred in the Columbia Broadcasting System's (CBS's) *Kate and Allie* with Jane Curtin. In 1985, he produced *The Saturday Night Main Event,* a series of World Wrestling Federation matches, to rotate in *Saturday Night Live*'s off weeks. In 1988, he produced the very late-night *Later with Bob Costas.*

Ebersol returned to NBC in April 1989 as president of NBC Sports. That July, he was also named senior vice president of NBC News, a position that paralleled the situation of his mentor, Roone Arledge, at ABC. As the executive for the *Today Show,* Ebersol presided over Jane Pauley's removal from the anchor desk in favor of Deborah Norville. He took the heat for the resulting bad publicity and was relieved of his *Today Show* duties.

Ebersol has enjoyed much greater success in sports programming. He helped NBC snare several Super Bowl contracts, then brought the National Basketball Association back to network television at the height of its popularity. NBC's coverage of the 1992 Olympic Games in Barcelona received excellent ratings, but the network lost money, largely from its "Triple Cast" coverage offered on three pay-per-view cable channels. Corporate parent General Electric expressed its commitment to the Olympics, though, when they announced that Ebersol would be executive producer of the 1996 Atlanta games.

Ebersol aided in the formation of the Baseball Network, an unusual joint venture between NBC, ABC, and Major League Baseball. The league produced its own coverage of Friday or Saturday night games; ABC or NBC alternated scheduling *Baseball Night in America,* and affiliates chose games of local interest to carry. The Baseball Network opened after the 1994 All-Star Game but was cut short by that year's players' strike. In 1995, as the delayed baseball season opened without a labor agreement and no guarantee against another strike, both networks pulled out of the venture.

In 1998, Ebersol was named chairman of NBC Sports and NBC Olympics. The following year, he gained the rights to NASCAR coverage for NBC, with a six-year contract starting in 2001. With the World Wrestling Federation, NBC under Ebersol ccofounded the XFL, a professional football league that was both a critical and a popular failure and that folded after only one season. In 2002, Ebersol's division suffered another blow when the 12-year relationship between NBC and the National Basketball Association came to end; in 2003, professional basketball games began to be aired on ABC and Entertainment and Sports Network (ESPN).

MARK R. McDERMOTT

See also **Arledge, Roone; *Saturday Night Live;* Sports and Television**

Dick Ebersol. Born in Torrington, Connecticut, 1947. Graduated from Yale University, New Haven, Connecticut, 1971. Married: Susan St. James, 1982; three children. Began broadcasting career as researcher, ABC Sports, 1967; segment producer, ABC Sports, 1969; executive assistant to Roone Arledge, ABC Sports, 1974; director, late-night weekend programming, NBC-TV, 1974; vice president, late-night weekend programming, NBC-TV, 1975; vice president, comedy, variety, and event programming, NBC-TV, 1977; independent producer, 1979; executive producer, *Saturday Night Live,* 1981; president, NBC Sports, since 1989; senior vice president, NBC News, since 1989; chairman of NBC Sports since 1998.

Television Series (executive producer)
1981–85   *Saturday Night Live*
1983   *Friday Night Videos*
1985   *The Saturday Night Main Event*
1988   *Later with Bob Costas*

Further Reading

Clark, Kenneth R., "Reincarnated: In Susan Saint James' New Life, She's Betty Aster, Radio Star," *Chicago Tribune* (June 1, 1993)
Graham, Stedman, Joe Jeff Goldblatt, Lisa Delpy Neirotti, and Dick Ebersol, *The Ultimate Guide to Sports Marketing,* New York: McGraw-Hill Trade, 2001
Hill, Doug, and Jeff Weingard, *Saturday Night: A Backstage History of Saturday Night Live,* New York: Beech Tree, 1986
Holtzman, Jerome, "On Baseball," *Chicago Tribune* (June 13, 1993)
"Live from New York—It's Dick Ebersol." *Broadcasting* (December 4, 1989)
Mandese, Joe, "'There's a Lot Left for Me in Sports,'" *Advertising Age* (September 6, 1993)
Niedetz, Steve, "On TV/Radio Sports," *Chicago Tribune* (January 23, 1995)
Shales, Tom, and James Andrew Miller, *Live from New York: An Uncensored History of Saturday Night Live,* New York: Little, Brown, 2002
Shapiro, Mitchell E. *Television Network Prime-Time Programming, 1948–1988,* Jefferson, North Carolina: McFarland, 1989

Ebert and Roeper at the Movies. *See* Siskel and Ebert

Ed Sullivan Show, The

U.S. Variety Show

The Ed Sullivan Show was the definitive and longest-running variety series in television history (1948–71). Hosted by the eponymous awkward and fumbling former newspaperman, the show became a Sunday night institution on the Columbia Broadcasting System (CBS). For 23 years, Sullivan's show fulfilled the democratic mandate of the variety genre: to entertain all the audience at least some of the time.

In the late 1940s, television executives strove to translate the principles of the vaudeville stage to the new medium, the amalgamation referred to as "vaudeo." As sports reporter, gossip columnist, and master of ceremonies of various war relief efforts, Ed Sullivan had been a fixture on the Broadway scene since the early 1930s. He had even hosted a short-lived radio series that introduced Jack Benny to a national audience

Ed Sullivan Show, Ed Sullivan, Louis Armstrong, 1948–71;
1961 episode.
Courtesy of the Everett Collection

in 1932. Although Sullivan had no performing ability (comedian Alan King quipped, "Ed does nothing, but he does it better that anyone else on television"), he understood showmanship and had a keen eye for emerging talent. CBS producer Worthington Miner hired him to host the network's inaugural variety effort *The Toast of the Town,* and, on June 20, 1948, Sullivan presented his premiere "really big shew," in the lingo of his many impersonators who quickly parodied his wooden stage presence and multitudinous malapropisms.

The initial telecast served as a basis for Sullivan's inimitable construction of a variety show. He balanced the headliner, Broadway's Richard Rodgers and Oscar Hammerstein (who, like most headliners to follow, were unassailable legends), with up-and-coming stars—on the opening program, Dean Martin and Jerry Lewis, fresh from the nightclubs in their television debut. He also liked to juxtapose the extreme ends of the entertainment spectrum: the classical—here pianist Eugene List and ballerina Kathryn Lee—with the novel—a group of singing New York City fireman and six of the original June Taylor Dancers, called the Toastettes.

From the beginning, Sullivan served as executive editor of the show, deciding in rehearsal, in consultation with producer Marlo Lewis, how many minutes each act would have during the live telecast. In 1955, the title was changed to *The Ed Sullivan Show.*

Sullivan had a keen understanding of what various demographic segments of his audience desired to see. As an impresario for the highbrow, he debuted ballerina Margot Fonteyn in 1958 and later teamed her with Rudolf Nureyev in 1965, saluted Van Cliburn after his upset victory in the Tchaikovsky competition in Moscow, and welcomed many neighbors from the nearby Metropolitan Opera, including Roberta Peters, who appeared 41 times, and the rarely seen Maria Callas, who performed a fully staged scene from *Tosca.* As the cultural eyes and ears for middle America, he introduced into the collective living room such movie and Broadway legends as Pearl Bailey, who appeared 23 times; Richard Burton and Julie Andrews, in a scene from the 1961 *Camelot;* Sammy Davis, Jr., with the *Golden Boy* cast; former CBS stage manager Yul Brynner in *The King and I;* Henry Fonda reading Abraham Lincoln's Gettysburg Address; and the rising star Barbra Streisand singing "Color Him Gone" in her 1962 debut. Occasionally, he devoted an entire telecast to one theme or biography: "The Cole Porter Story," "The Walt Disney Story," "The MGM Story, and "A Night at Sophie Tucker's House."

What distinguished Sullivan from other variety hosts was his ability to capitalize on teenage obsession. His introduction of rock and roll not only brought the adolescent subculture into the variety fold but also legitimized the music for the adult sensibility. Elvis Presley had appeared with Milton Berle and Tommy Dorsey, but Sullivan's deal with Presley's manager, Colonel Tom Parker, created national headlines. The sexual energy of Presley's first appearance on September 9, 1956, jolted the staid, Eisenhower conformism of Sullivan's audience. By his third and final appearance, Elvis was shot only from the waist up, but Sullivan learned how to capture a new audience for his show, the baby-boom generation.

In 1964, Sullivan signed the Beatles for three landmark appearances. Their first slot on February 9, 1964, was at the height of Beatlemania, the beginning of a revolution in music, fashion, and attitude. Sullivan received the biggest ratings of his career, and, with a 60 share, that episode was one of the most watched programs in the history of television. Sullivan responded by welcoming icons of the 1960s counterculture into his arena, most notably the Rolling Stones, the Doors, Janis Joplin, and Marvin Gaye. One performer who never appeared was Bob Dylan, who walked off when

CBS censors balked at his song "Talkin' John Birch Society Blues."

Although called "the great stone face" on screen, Sullivan was a man of intense passion off camera. He feuded with Walter Winchell, Jack Paar, and Frank Sinatra over his booking practices. He wrangled with conservative sponsors over his fondness for African-American culture and openly embraced black performers throughout his career, including Bill "Bojangles" Robinson, Ethel Waters, Louis Armstrong, and Diana Ross. He also capitulated to the blacklisting pressures of *Red Channels* and denounced performers for pro-communist sympathies.

Sullivan saw comedy as the glue that held his demographically diverse show together and allowed a nation to release social tension by laughing at itself. He was most comfortable around Borscht Belt comics, as seen by the funnymen he most often enlisted: Alan King (37 times), Myron Cohen (47 times), and Jack Carter (49 times). When Sullivan's son-in-law Bob Precht took over as producer in 1960, there was a movement to modernize the show and introduce a new generation of comedians to the American audience, led by Mort Sahl, Woody Allen, Richard Pryor, and George Carlin. The comic act that appeared most on the Sullivan show was the Canadian team of Johnny Wayne and Frank Shuster (58 times); the parodic sketches of Wayne and Shuster assured Sullivan a sizable audience north of the border.

Sullivan was always on the lookout for novelty acts, especially for children. His interplay with the Italian mouse Topo Gigio revealed a sentimental side to Sullivan's character. He also was the first to introduce celebrities from the audience and often invited them on stage for special performances. Forever the sports columnist, he was particularly enthralled by athletic heroes and always had time on the show to discuss baseball with Mickey Mantle or Willie Mays and learn golf from Sam Snead or Ben Hogan.

The Ed Sullivan Show reflected an era of network television when a mass audience and, even, a national consensus seemed possible. Sullivan became talent scout and cultural commissar for the entire country, introducing more than 10,000 performers throughout his career. His show implicitly recognized that the United States should have an electronic exposure to all forms of entertainment, from juggling to opera. The Vietnam War, which fractured the country politically, also helped splinter the democratic assumptions of the variety show. By 1971, *The Ed Sullivan Show* was no longer a generational or demographic mediator, and it was canceled as the war raged on. Later in the decade, the audience did not require Sullivan's big tent of variety entertainment any longer; cable and the new technology promised immediate access to any programming desired. The Sullivan library was purchased by producer Andrew Solt in the 1980s and has served as the source of network specials and programming for cable services. In 2001, *The Ed Sullivan Show* began airing on public television, fulfilling, according to one executive, the educational mandates of the Public Broadcasting Service (PBS).

RON SIMON

See also **Sullivan, Ed; Variety Programs**

Host
Ed Sullivan

Music
Ray Bloch and His Orchestra

Dancers
The June Taylor Dancers

Producers
Ed Sullivan, Marlo Lewis, Bob Precht

Programming History
CBS

June 1948	Sunday 9:00–10:00
July 1948–August 1948	Sunday 9:30–10:30
August 1948–March 1949	Sunday 9:00–10:00
March 1949–June 1971	Sunday 8:00–9:00

Further Reading

Bowles, Jerry, *A Thousand Sundays: The Story of the Ed Sullivan Show,* New York: Putnam, 1980

Harris, Michael David, *Always on Sundays—Ed Sullivan: An Inside View,* New York: Meredith, 1980

Henderson, Amy, *On the Air: Pioneers of American Broadcasting,* Washington, D.C.: Smithsonian Institution Press, 1988

Leonard, John, *A Really Big Show,* New York: Viking Studio Books, 1992

Educational Television

Broadcasting in the United States evolved as a commercial entity. Within this system, efforts to use the medium for educational purposes always struggled to survive, nearly overwhelmed by the flood of entertainment programming designed to attract audiences to the commercials that educated them in another way—to become active consumers. Despite its clear potential and the aspirations of pioneer broadcasters, educational television has never realized its fullest potential as an instructional medium. Educational television (ETV) in the United States refers primarily to programs that emphasize formal, classroom instruction and enrichment programming. In 1967, ETV was officially renamed "public television" and was to reflect new mandates of quality and diversity as specified by the Public Broadcasting Act. Public television incorporated "formal" (classroom) and "informal" (cultural, children's, and lifelong learning) instructional programming into a collective alternative to commercial television. Despite commercial dominance, however, educational initiatives in American television continue to change with the introduction of new telecommunications technology. Cable and new media challenge and enhance the traditional definition of ETV in the United States.

Interest in ETV was expressed early. Educators envisioned television's potential as an instructional tool and sought recognition by Congress. The short-lived Hatfield-Wagner amendment proposed to reserve one-fourth of the broadcast spectrum for educational stations. But the Communications Act of 1934 became law without this specification, although the Federal Communications Commission (FCC) promised to conduct further inquiry into ETV.

The immediate postwar years created a deluge of requests for broadcast licenses. So overwhelmed, the FCC initiated a "television freeze" in 1948 (forbidding the issuance of new licenses) in order to reorganize the current system and to study the ultra-high-frequency (UHF) band. The period of the "TV freeze" was an ideal opportunity to resurrect the debate over allotment of spectrum space for educational channels.

The FCC's commissioner, Freida Hennock, led the crusade. She understood that this would be the only opportunity to reserve spectrum space for ETV. When educators would be financially and technically prepared for television experiments, spectrum space might be unavailable. Hennock raised the consciousness of educators and citizens alike and convinced some of them to form the first ad hoc Joint Committee for Educational Television (JCET). Financial assistance from the Ford Foundation provided legal expertise and enabled the JCET to successfully persuade the FCC to reserve channel space for noncommercial ETV stations. In 1953, the FCC allotted 242 channels for education. KUHT in Houston, Texas, was the first noncommercial television licensee.

Although this was a major victory, the development of ETV was a slow process. The majority of educators did not have the financial or technical capabilities to operate a television station. Commercial broadcasters recognized their dilemma as a lucrative opportunity.

Commercial broadcasters lobbied against the reservation of channels for education. Although they claimed they were not opposed to ETV as a programming alternative, they were opposed to the "waste" of unused spectrum space by licensees who were financially unable to fill broadcasting time. Persuaded in part by the argument for economic efficiency, the FCC permitted the sale of numerous ETV stations to commercial broadcasters. Many universities, unable to realize their goals as educational broadcasters, profited instead from the sale of their unused frequencies to commercial counterparts.

From its inception, then, ETV was continually plagued with financial problems. As a noncommercial enterprise, ETV needed to rely on outside sources for funding. Federal funding created the potential for programming biases, and private foundations, such as the Ford Foundation, would not be able to sustain the growing weight of ETV forever. In 1962, the Educational Television Facilities Act provided temporary relief. Thirty-two million federal dollars was granted for the creation of ETV stations only. Programming resources were still essential, however.

The establishment of the Carnegie Commission in 1965 was critical to the survival of ETV. For two years, the commission researched and analyzed the future relationship between education and television. Some of their proposals included increasing the number of ETV stations, imposing an excise tax on all television sets sold, the interconnection of stations for more efficient program exchange, and the creation of a "Corporation for Public Television." These mandates prompted Congress to enact the 1967 Public Broadcasting Act as an amendment to the Communications Act of 1934.

The evolution of ETV into "public television" forever changed the institution. The ETV curriculum of formal instruction was too narrow to entice sweeping federal recognition. As a result, ETV was endowed with a new name and a new image. The mandate of public television was diversity in programming and audience. Public television promised to educate the nation through formal instruction and enrichment programming emphasizing culture, arts, science, and public affairs. In addition, it would provide programming for "underserved" audiences (those ignored by commercial broadcasters), such as minorities and children. Ultimately, public television promised to be the democratization of the medium. Sadly, however, these public service imperatives could never flourish as originally intended in a historically commercial system.

Educational television provides programming that emphasizes formal instruction for children and adults. Literacy, mathematics, science, geography, foreign language, and high school equivalency are a few examples of ETV's offerings. The most successful ETV initiatives in the United States are public television's children's programs. Staples such as *Barney, Sesame Street, 3-2-1 Contact, Mister Rogers' Neighborhood,* and *Reading Rainbow* teach children academic fundamentals as well as social skills.

Higher-education initiatives in television, "distance learning," boasts an impressive but modest history. Distance learning programs, while significantly more intensive abroad, have been integral to realizing the American ETV "vision." Nontraditional instruction via telecourse is an alternative learning experience for adults who cannot or do not choose to attend a university.

Closed-circuit TV (CCTV) was used as early as the 1950s by universities to transmit classroom lectures to other locations on campus. The Pennsylvania State University CCTV project is an early example. In 1952, the Pennsylvania State CCTV system (sponsored by the Ford Foundation) was created to offer introductory college courses via television in order to eliminate overcrowded classrooms and faculty shortages. Although moderately successful in achieving these goals, overall the CCTV system proved unpopular with students because of the absence of student–teacher contact and the lackluster "look" of the programs, especially in comparison with the familiar alternative of commercial television. This experiment made clear a continuing reality; the appeal of an instructional program is often dependent on its production quality.

The Chicago Television College was a more suc-

cessful endeavor. Teacher training was another initiative undertaken by the Ford Foundation in the early days of ETV, and in 1956 the Chicago Television College was created as a cost-effective way to accomplish this task. Approximately 400 students earned their associate of arts degrees from the college. The majority of graduates were inmates from particular correctional facilities and home-bound physically challenged individuals.

The Public Broadcasting Service (PBS) is a significant participant in distance learning. Its Adult Learning Service (ALS) distributes telecourses to universities nationwide that are broadcast by participating PBS stations. In conjunction with ALS is the Adult Learning Satellite Service (ALSS), which provides a more efficient delivery system of telecourses. Similarly, the Instructional Television Fixed Service (ITFS) transmits college courses to high school students via satellite and microwave relay. Workbooks and examinations often supplement the video "lessons." The ITFS also transmits its signals to social service centers, correctional facilities, and community colleges.

Formal instruction efforts by commercial broadcasters are historically scarce. A notable example, however, was the CBS/New York University collaboration titled *Sunrise Semester.* For nearly three decades, a New York University lecture would air at 6:00 A.M. for the edification of early risers.

Adult learners are only not the only beneficiaries of ETV's instructional programs. Preschool, elementary, and secondary school students are all target audiences of ETV services. The National Instructional Television Satellite Schedule (NISS) is a primary distributor of such programming. *3-2-1 Contact* (science), *Futures* (math), and *American Past* (history) are just a few examples of NISS offerings. Enrichment programs such as these are used to enhance, not replace, traditional classroom instruction.

Sesame Street is the ETV staple of preschool children internationally. Heralded for its ability to successfully combine education and entertainment, *Sesame Street* is an anomaly. No other broadcast or cable program has seriously rivaled its formula for success. (It is even used in Japan to teach high school students English.)

Educational television is not unique to the home and classroom. More specialized uses have proliferated. For example, CCTV is frequently used by medical institutions as a more effective means to demonstrate surgical procedures to doctors and medical students, and workplace programming is often used by corporations for training purposes or to teach safety procedures. Distance learning, classroom instruction, and workplace programming represent part of the ETV mosaic, which is generally defined by programming that emphasizes formal and informal learning.

But ETV also includes "enrichment" programming emphasizing culture, the arts, and public affairs as an alternative to commercial choices. Popular entertainment programs such as *Masterpiece Theater,* public affairs and news programs such as *Frontline* and *The MacNeil/Lehrer News Hour,* and nature programs such as *Nova* all attempt to meet the requirements of ETV as defined by broadcast law in the United States.

The expansion of the telecommunications environment has also yielded additional outlets for ETV. The surge of cable television has been the most significant challenge to ETV as it is defined and provided by public television. Public television has always justified its very existence in the United States in terms of its role as the sole provider of educational programming. However, the emergence of cable services such as Bravo, A&E, the Learning Channel, Discovery, and Nickelodeon have challenged public television's position. These outlets provide viewers with the same quality programming as public television. Often, cable networks compete with public stations for the rights to the same programs, from the same program suppliers.

Advocates of public television will often justify its existence with two words: *Sesame Street.* Noncommercial programming, availability in all households, and quality children's programming such as *Sesame Street* are the examples used by public broadcasters to warrant their claims to federal and viewer support. Cable television's contribution cannot be completely ignored, however.

Indeed, the vision of ETV is perhaps best exemplified by cable's public, educational, and government (PEG) access channels. While not mandatory, most cable companies are willing to provide these channels as part of their franchise agreements. They point to the existence of PEG channels as examples of their philanthropy. PEG channels demonstrate a grassroots approach to television. Public access encourages individual program efforts that often contribute to the enlightenment of the immediate community. Paper Tiger Television is one example of such video "activism."

Education provided on access channels offers much of the same formal instruction as public television. The Cable in the Classroom organization distributes programs created by various cable networks (e.g., A&E, the Cable News Network [CNN], and The Learning Channel [TLC]) for classroom use. The programs are commercial free. Like public television, educational access offers formal instruction and distance learning. One of its most recognized services is the Mind Extension University, which offers credit for college courses taken at home.

Government access channels supply viewers with the discussion of local and national policy debates. City council and school board meetings are presented here. For a national/international perspective, most cable systems offer C-SPAN and C-SPAN II in their basic service. PEG channels foster localism and serve the public interest. They are valid interpretations of broader concept of ETV.

Globally, ETV plays a more significant role than in the United States. Most international broadcasting systems developed as noncommercial public service organizations. Public service broadcasters or state broadcasters are supported almost exclusively by license fees—annual payments made by owners of television receivers. Because the community directly supports the broadcaster, there is a greater commitment by the broadcaster to meet their multitudinous programming needs. As a result, these systems more effectively exemplify the mandates of the American public television system: quality and diversity.

Sweeping deregulation, increased privatization, and the introduction of cable television have posed new problems for the public service monoliths, however. The introduction and proliferation of commercially supported television casts doubt on the need for license fees. Public service broadcasters must find new ways to compete, to sustain their reputations as cultural assets. Educational television and its relationship to higher education is most developed and more successful as a learning device in what has been called the "open university" system. The lack of higher-education opportunities in many countries has contributed to the validation of distance learning. Open universities are provided by public (service) broadcasters on every continent. The British Open University is the most notable example, existing as an archetype for similar programs worldwide. Created in 1969, the Open University confers college degrees to students enrolled in telecourses. Programs are supplemented by outside exams and work/textbooks. Degrees from the Open University are as valued as traditional college diplomas.

The University of Mid-America (UMA) was a failed attempt by public broadcasters in the United States to emulate the British system. In existence from 1974 to 1982, UMA attempted to provide traditional higher education through nontraditional methods. Funding problems, coupled with a society unreceptive to the open university culture, hastened UMA's demise.

Educational television is similar throughout the industrialized world. The combination of formal classroom instruction and enrichment programming defines the genre. Educational television in the developing world also includes programming that directly affects the quality of life of its viewers. For example, in areas where television penetration is very low, audiences may gather at community centers to view programs on hygiene, literacy, child care, and farming methods. In this respect, ETV provides the group with practical information to improve living standards. Such programming best exemplifies the global aims of ETV.

The Internet is impacting ETV. Subtle nuances continue to emerge as a result of new technologies and the combination of old ones. Satellite technology has already provided a more effective delivery system for programming. Interactivity has revitalized instructional television in particular. Teleconferencing, for example, links classrooms globally. These services not only provide access to traditional learning but also enhance the cultural literacy of students worldwide.

PBS has recognized the primacy of the Internet in education with its popular children's program *Cyberchase*. The show features a "good guy," Motherboard, and the evil Hacker. Child viewers help Motherboard via mathematics and logic games.

The relationship between education and television in the changing telecommunications environment continues to evolve. As television becomes more "individualized," providing, for example, "menus" of lessons, applications, and experiments, ETV may become the programming of choice. The synergisms between the significant players (broadcasters and cablecasters, telephone, hardware and software companies, educators, and government) will ultimately determine new outlets for ETV across the globe, but audiences—students and users—will reap the ultimate benefits.

SHARON ZECHOWSKI

See also Blue Peter; **Children and Television; National Education Television; Public Service Broadcasting;** *Sesame Street;* **Sesame Workshop**

Further Reading

Adler, Richard, and Walter S. Baer, *Aspen Notebook: Cable and Continuing Education,* New York: Praeger, 1973
Barnouw, Erik, *A History of Broadcasting in the United States. Vol. II—1933–1953, The Golden Web,* New York: Oxford University Press, 1968
Carnegie Commission on Educational Television, *Public Television, a Program for Action: The Report and Recommendations of the Carnegie Commission on Educational Television,* New York: Harper and Row, 1967
Fuller, Linda K., *Community Television in the United States: A Sourcebook on Public, Educational and Governmental Access,* Westport, Connecticut: Greenwood, 1994
Gibson, George H., *Public Broadcasting: The Role of the Federal Government 1912–1976,* New York: Praeger, 1977
Granger, Daniel. "Open Universities: Closing the Distances to Learning," *Change* (July/August 1990)
Hawkridge, David, and John Robinson, *Organizing Educational Broadcasting,* Paris: UNESCO Press, 1982
Head, Sydney W., and Christopher H. Sterling, *Broadcasting in America: A Survey of Electronic Media,* 6th edition, Boston, Massachusetts: Houghton Mifflin, 1990
Howell, W.J., *World Broadcasting in the Age of Satellite: Comparative Systems, Policies and Issues in Mass Telecommunication,* Norwood, New Jersey: Ablex, 1986
Hoynes, William, *Public Television for Sale: Media, the Market, and the Public Sphere,* Boulder, Colorado: Westview, 1994
Kahn, Frank J., editor, *Documents of American Broadcasting,* Englewood Cliffs, New Jersey: Prentice Hall, 1968; 3rd edition, 1978

Egypt

Egypt began its television system, considered one of the most extensive and effective among all undeveloped countries of Asia and Africa, in 1960. Because of a well-financed radio service and film industry already in existence, Egypt, unlike other Arab countries, was able to start television production without importing engineering staff from abroad. Even with this beginning, however, the development of television in Egypt has been complicated by many social and cultural factors.

In the late 1950s, following the 1952 revolution, President Gamal Abdel Nasser realized television's potential for helping to build Egypt into a new nation. Although the decision to start television service had been made earlier, the joint British–French–Israeli Suez invasion delayed work until late 1959. Egypt then signed a contract with Radio Corporation of America (RCA) to provide the country with a television network and the capacity to manufacture sets. After the RCA contract was signed, Egypt began construction of a radio and television center, completed in 1960, and the first television pictures appeared on July 21, 1960, using the 625-line European standard.

From the start, Egypt did everything on a grand scale. Thus, while most nations began their systems modestly with one channel, Egypt began with three. Initially, the government totally subsidized the entire system, through a direct grant made every year. In 1969, however, an annual license fee of $15 per set was introduced, and after 1979, revenue from advertising and from the sales of programs to other countries also helped in financing. At the present time, a surcharge that goes to the broadcasting authority is added to all electricity bills and provides additional funding for the system.

Egyptian television began its multichannel operation under the control of the Ministry of Culture and National Guidance, an organization that figured prominently in the Nasser regime from the start and that used radio and television broadcasting to disseminate propaganda in support of the ruling regime. Television's role in the culture was heightened following the June 1967 war with Israel, which resulted in an Egyptian defeat that was militarily, economically, and psychologically devastating to that nation. Immediately after the war, there was a decrease in the amount of foreign programming shown. The third channel, over which much programming had been telecast, was eliminated, and the British and U.S. programs that constituted the bulk of imported programs were deemed unacceptable because of the break in diplomatic relations with those countries. Almost all forms of programming on television placed less emphasis on Egypt's military capability, tending instead toward the nationalistic, the educational, and the religious. Moving closer to the country's new military supplier, the former Soviet Union, television began showing films about Soviet and Eastern European life. These programs were either provided free of charge or inexpensive to purchase or lease.

The general technical quality of Egyptian television declined between 1967 and 1974, a period when there was less money for new equipment. Generally, however, the change in government after Nasser's death and Anwar al-Sadat's ascendancy to the presidency in 1970 did not appear to have much effect on television programming or the structure of the federation. On August 13, 1970, radio, television, and broadcast engineering were established as separate departments under the Ministry of Information. The new decree formally established the Egyptian Radio and Television Union (ERTU) and created four distinct sectors—radio, television, engineering, and finance—each of which had a chairman who reported directly to the minister.

Following the October 1973 war, the various Egyptian media took very different approaches to the national situation. Television programming, which took longer to produce and air than radio information, was somewhat more upbeat. As good news came in, television reflected confidence in an Egyptian recovery. After the Egyptian–Israeli engagement, Egyptian television shows dealt more often with the United Nations, European countries, the United States, and Israel. Agreements regarding military disengagements received a high priority for broadcast on the air. More than any other Egyptian mass medium, television was set to reflect the changing international political orientation of the country. Sadat's government gradually changed Egypt during the 1970s from a socialist orientation to one that was more hospitable to free enterprise and decidedly pro-West. After 1974, the door was formally opened to the West. Consequently, the number of Western programs on Egyptian television schedules increased.

The television organization decided during this time to continue the development of color technology. Although some believed that color television was a luxury that Egypt could not afford, the favorable attitude toward it among broadcasting officials prevailed. The French government had been successful in persuading Egypt to adopt the French color system (SECAM) and had installed its equipment in one of the Egyptian studios before the 1973 war. After the war, the decision was made to convert both production and transmission facilities to color, an action that improved the technical quality of Egyptian television by discarding the monochrome equipment that had been installed by RCA long before 1970. Older switchers and cameras, which were becoming difficult to repair or to purchase, were replaced. The new equipment was necessary for the production of programs to be sold to other countries that were also converting to color, and after 1974 television revenues derived from advertising and from program sales to other Arab countries increased significantly. The Egyptian broadcasting authority changed from the SECAM system to PAL, however, in both studio and transmission in 1992.

Because of Egypt's peace treaty with Israel, a number of Arab countries sought to isolate Egypt, remove it from the Arab League, and boycott its exports. Many of these countries broke diplomatic relations with Egypt or reduced the size of their diplomatic missions in Cairo. Nations that supported the boycott no longer purchased Egyptian television programs, stating that they did not need to buy directly from Egypt because so much quality material was available from Egyptian artists living outside Egypt's borders. One response held that "the boycott organizers are interested in drawing the distinction between the Egyptian people and the Egyptian government." Indeed, many Egyptian producers moved to Europe to produce programs for sale to the Arab countries. However, Egyptian television program sales to the Arab world did not decrease as a result; they actually increased.

During this period, the Egyptian government was very seriously considering plans for a new satellite system. Technical staff personnel had already been sent to be trained in the United States. This undertaking, called the Space Center Project, was designed mainly for the distribution of television signals that would link the country through ground stations that would receive and rebroadcast programming to the villages. The proposal became active when the Egyptian president signed a document for the beginning, in 1995, of Nile Satellite (Nilesat), a satellite operation that not only covers the Egyptian state but also services the larger Arab community.

In addition to the two centralized television networks, a new strategy to decentralize the television broadcasting system was introduced in 1985 during President Hosni Mubarak's era. The policy was implemented by starting a third television channel that covers only the capital city. This was followed in 1988 by Channel 4, which covers the Suez Zone. Yet another channel was added in 1990 to cover Alexandria, and in 1994 Channel 6 was created to cover the Middle Delta. Most recently, in late 1994, Channel 7 was introduced in southern Egypt. In 1990, Egypt became the first Arab state to start an international television channel when the Egyptian Space Channel was introduced to the Arab world and later to Europe and the United States. Egypt was also the first to start a foreign national network, Nile TV, to serve expatriates in Egypt as well as to promote tourism in English and French languages.

In part as a result of these available channels, a television set has become a priority for any young Egyptian couple getting married. Most prefer buying a television set to purchasing other important things for the house. A color TV set is considered a normal part of the household in middle-class families, and the number of such sets has increased greatly since 1970. The price of television sets purchased in Egypt, however, reflects high import taxes, sometimes reaching 200 percent. This expense has led most Egyptians to buy their sets from abroad. Most Egyptian people working outside the country, especially in Saudi Arabia and the other Gulf states, return to Egypt with television sets because of the lower prices in the Gulf countries. Others acquire secondhand sets from individuals or from dealers who sometimes help finance such transactions. Egyptian shops do carry a variety of television receivers. These include foreign brands as well as sets assembled in Egypt, but the imported sets have a reputation of being more reliable. The government is attempting to reduce prices of locally made sets. In 1995, the number of television sets in Egypt was estimated at 6.2 million.

Programming

From the beginning, Egyptian television has had strong ties with Arab culture. Historical, religious, geographical, political, and linguistic bonds linked Egypt to the Arab countries. Egyptian television was influenced Arab literature, religion, philosophy, and music. The producers of the first programs—influenced to some extent by the example of contemporary programs from the Eastern European countries and the Soviet Union, which were heavily cultural in content—quite naturally regarded Egyptian television programs as a proper vehicle for Arab literature and the arts. Egyptian television thus performs the function of reinforcing and enhancing Arab culture, which is defined as a heritage in creative endeavor and thought. Its programs also raise the cultural level of the ordinary viewer by presenting refined items covering scientific, literary, and artistic fields as well as a great deal of Arab music and drama on traditional themes.

Television is an ideal medium for disseminating Egyptian culture because that culture is family oriented and tends to center much of its education and entertainment around the home. Nevertheless, the content and style of television broadcasting available to these viewers has changed over time. The government still owns and operates the medium and sometimes uses it to convey political messages, but programming is now characterized by somewhat less politically motivated programming than was typical in the 1960s and 1970s. Contemporary Egyptian television contains more entertainment and popular culture, and the Ministry of Information is trying to stress these aspects and reduce the amount of political content.

Entertainment programs such as Egyptian soap operas and Egyptian music and songs are very popular. Foreign programs are also popular, especially those from Europe and the United States, which provide Egypt with many series, such as *The Bold and the Beautiful, Knots Landing, Love Boat,* and *Knight Rider.* The famous American series, *Dallas,* however, was banned from Egyptian television because officials thought it conveyed immoral messages to the public, especially to youth and children.

News is an important aspect of programming in Egypt because of the country's regional position and the fluctuating nature of political alignments in the Arabic-speaking area. As previously suggested, the 1960s, especially the events surrounding the 1967 war, was an era of crisis. Egyptian television penetrated the region. It was important for the government to maintain a strong news front in order to present its particular point of view. Newscasts in Egypt included a segment of official "commentary" when there was some special concern to be articulated. From these news broadcasts, as well as other programs, the policies of President Nasser were clear to the viewer, as were the identities of those who were considered the enemies of those policies.

Compared to the beginning of the 1960s, there was a significant increase in the emphasis on education at the beginning of the 1970s. It had taken almost the entire previous decade for the Ministry of Education to be convinced of the value of educational programs. Moreover, the educational programs were run first under the initiative of the broadcasters, who resisted turning any time over to the ministry. However, enlightenment programs remain important in the schedule of Egyptian television and have increased measurably through the years.

Religion, of course, carries great weight in Egypt, an Islamic center. Readings from the Koran have always been broadcast on a regular basis by Egyptian television, and religious commentaries or advice on proper moral and ethical behavior are featured. Coverage of the rituals of the Muslim Holy Day is presented as part of the attempt to maintain Islamic traditions and values. During the Muslim holy month of Ramadan, Egyptian television is exceptionally active in religious programming, exhorting the faithful and explicating the pertinence of Islamic history. In the period from 1980 to 1985, a close observer could notice an increase in religious programs.

Children's programming, which formerly was completely of foreign origin, has changed to suit the Egyptian culture. Almost all Egyptian programs for youth and women and programs dealing with art and literature have been given increased time on the television schedule.

The Current Broadcasting Industry

Egyptian information media have always been closely tied to politics. Television in Egypt is typically a monopoly under direct government supervision, operation, and ownership. There are several reasons for this. First, the minimum cost of establishing a radio or television system is far greater than the minimum cost of establishing a newspaper, for example, and thus far beyond the capability of nearly all private persons in a developing country. Second, this high cost encourages the pooling of resources, or a monopoly. In addition, because the broadcast media reach beyond borders and literacy barriers, the government has a much greater interest in controlling them or at least keeping them out of hostile hands. Anyone with a printing press has the technical capability of reaching the literate elite, and while this is seen by the government as a potential

threat, it is not nearly as great a political liability as a monopoly radio station broadcasting to millions. Radio and television, which have the potential of instantaneously reaching every single person in the country and many outside it, are regarded by the Egyptian government as too important to be left to private interests. Third, radio and television are newer media, and the trend is toward greater authoritarian control over all media.

In October 1990, cable television made an entry to Egypt when the government approved the establishment of Cable News Egypt (CNE) in a cooperative arrangement with the Cable News Network (CNN) to extend for 25 years. The main purpose of CNE was to retransmit Cable News Network International (CNNI) in Egypt. At the end of 1994, CNE underwent a major change. Cable News Egypt, the name of the original company, was changed to be Cable Network Egypt. The renamed company then made an agreement with a South African–based company, MultiChoice Africa, to market CNE in Egypt. Within the framework of this agreement, MultiChoice began selling a new decoder and introduced new services such as CNN; Music Television (MTV); the Showtime channel; MNet, a movie channel that carries mostly American movies and was rated first among the other networks in terms of popularity from CNE subscribers; KTV, a children's channel carrying mostly American children's television programs as well as movies; and Super Sports.

Around the turn of the 21st century, Egypt launched its first generation of Nilesat digital satellites, the state-of-the-art *Nilesat-101* (operational June 1998) and *Nilesat-102* (operational September 2000). Although the cost of the Nilesat project is almost $158 million, the country is looking forward to gaining maximum benefits from it in many different areas. Each satellite carries 12 transponders, each with a capability of transmitting a minimum of eight television channels. Transmitting across North Africa and the Arabian peninsula, the Nilesat satellites beam down more than 160 digital television channels and 40 radio channels. The ERTU is making use of many of Nilesat's channels, which gives Egypt the chance to produce and broadcast its own specialized channels for the first time. As of 2001, ERTU broadcast from the satellites the Nile TV specialized package, which includes Nile Drama (made-for-television movies, soap operas, and drama), Nile News, Nile Sports, Nile Culture, and Nile Children as well as educational channels. In addition to these channels, the Nile TV ShowTime package offers CNN, the Movie Channel, Discovery, and Nickelodeon, among other networks. Arab Radio and Television (ART), a Saudi network, also has a package, called 1st NET, on Nilesat. Through this combination of packages, Nilesat is intended to serve both Arabic- and English-language audiences.

It is expected that as a national satellite, Nilesat will save Egypt a great deal of money, the estimated $3.5 million that has been spent annually to transmit the Egyptian Satellite Channel. The project is being supervised by a joint stock company, the Egyptian Company for Satellites; as of 2001, around 40 percent of the shares of this company belonged to ERTU, with the rest being held by Egyptian banks and foreign investors.

Founded in 1992 and still expanding a decade later, the Egyptian Media Production City (EMPC) is a product of the government efforts to attract international investors and media companies to its " Media Free Zone," in which the state offers tax and customs exemptions to private media entities that produce in the zone but still regulates editorial content through ERTU. Located in Sixth of October City, southwest of Cairo, EMPC has three production complexes: two built by EMPC and comprising 11 studios with indoor-filming, production, and postproduction facilities and one called the Mubarak International Media Complex, which contains 18 individual television studios. In addition, 11 outdoor shooting locations are located within the Media City.

A continuing challenge for Egyptian television concerns its staffing levels. State-run Egyptian television employs almost 14,000 people. Obviously, this large number of television workers is far above that required to produce programs and fill broadcasting time, and there are more workers than necessary for efficient operation of the two centralized television channel services. The figure is especially excessive for a country with limited financial resources.

Along with advertising revenue and license fees (added monthly to the electricity bill), Egypt depends on sales of Egyptian programs to other countries as the main resource to finance television. Since the peace treaty with Israel, many Arab countries have boycotted Egypt's exports, including media products; however, Egyptian television is still the most influential in the region.

Despite recent technological advances and changes in strategy, the financing of radio and television broadcasting will continue for some time to be a serious problem for the Egyptian government. Although the state recognizes the importance of electronic media industry to the internal and external political success of Egypt, funds to disseminate that industry's services have become increasingly scarce, especially as the educational and health needs of the country have grown more significant. It is obvious, then, that Egypt must continue to struggle and compromise to find funds needed to continue national broadcasting services.

HUSSEIN Y. AMIN

Further Reading

Amin, Hussein Y., "An Egypt Based Model for the Use of Television in National Development," doctoral diss., Ohio State University, 1986

Amin, Hussein Y., and Douglas Boyd, "The Impact of Home Video Cassette Recorders on Egyptian Film and Television Consumption Patterns," *European Journal of Communication* (1993)

Boyd, Douglas A., *Broadcasting in the Arab World,* Ames: Iowa State University Press, 1993

Head, Sydney, *Broadcasting in Africa,* Philadelphia, Pennsylvania: Temple University Press, 1975

Rugh, William A., *The Arab Press,* New York: Syracuse University Press, 1987

Eisner, Michael (1942–)

U.S. Media Executive

Michael Eisner joined the Disney Company in 1984 and helped recraft it throughout the 1980s and 1990s. In the process, he helped make Disney into a television powerhouse, climaxing those efforts with a takeover of Capital Cities-ABC (American Broadcasting Company) on the last day of July 1995. Through the final sixth of the 20th century, the Disney Company, with its ever increasing profits, was held up as a quintessential American business success story. It produced popular culture fare embraced around the world. Yet when Michael Eisner assumed leadership of the company, Disney was in trouble. It was Eisner and his staff who turned the ailing theme-park company into a media powerhouse.

Eisner brought a rich base of executive experience to Disney. He had begun his career at the ABC televi-

Michael Eisner, 1977.
Courtesy of the Everett Collection/CSU Archives

sion network and then moved to Paramount under former ABC boss Barry Diller. The two men made Paramount the top Hollywood studio during the late 1970s and early 1980s. By 1978, just two years after Diller and Eisner arrived, Paramount had moved to the head of the major studio race. Led by *Grease, Saturday Night Fever,* and *Heaven Can Wait,* Paramount took in one-quarter of the Hollywood box office in that year.

When Eisner moved to Disney, he immediately sought to revitalize the company. He hired Hollywood's new "Irving Thalberg," Jeffrey Katzenberg, then barely 30 years old, to make movies under two new "brand names": Touchstone Pictures and Hollywood Pictures. (Eisner and Katzenberg worked well together until 1994, when Katzenberg moved to Dream Works, with new partners Steven Spielberg and David Geffen.)

The new Disney turned out hit feature films, including *Down and Out in Beverly Hills* and *Ruthless People.* In 1987, when *Three Men and a Baby* pushed beyond $100 million in box office gross, it became the

first Disney film ever to pass that vaunted mark. *Three Men and a Baby* represented a quintessential example of the new Disney, drawing its stars, Ted Danson and Tom Selleck, from the world of television.

From the base of solid feature-film profits, Eisner then began to remake Disney into a TV power. The studio quickly placed hits such as *Golden Girls* on prime-time schedules. By the early 1990s, Disney's *Home Improvement* and *Ellen* consistently ranked in TV's prime-time top ten. Disney also expanded into the TV syndication business. The company created a very successful syndicated program by hiring film critics Gene Siskel and Roger Ebert to review movies, including those produced by Disney.

Not all Disney moves into television have prospered. In 1986, Eisner revived Disney's family-oriented Sunday night TV show in a prized 7:00 P.M. time slot on ABC, with himself as host. However, he proved not to be "Uncle Walt," and he was forced to cancel *The Disney Sunday Movie,* for which he also served as executive producer, in 1988. The National Broadcasting Company (NBC) then picked up a modified version of the program, now called *The Magical World of Disney;* with Eisner as executive producer and host, this Sunday evening program aired for two years, 1988 to 1990, before succumbing to the fate of its ABC predecessor. Like many before and after him, it seemed that Eisner could not compete successfully with the Columbia Broadcasting System's (CBS's) *60 Minutes.* Seven years later, however, Eisner returned to executive produce and host yet another edition of this show, *The Wonderful World of Disney,* for ABC on Sunday nights. This program may not beat *60 Minutes* in the ratings, but it has fared well with a mixture of original made-for-television movies, such as the musical *Annie* and the drama *Ruby Bridges,* and broadcasts of Disney features, such as *Babe* and *The Princess Diaries.*

Some of Disney's TV syndication efforts also failed to mint gold. *Today's Business* was an early-morning show that, although it aired initially in half the television markets in the United States, lasted but a few painful months in 1985. The Walt Disney Company pulled out, suffering a $5 million loss.

Eisner had more success with cable TV as he expanded efforts to make the Disney Channel a pay–cable TV power. Using a seemingly infinite set of cross-promotional exploitation opportunities, the Disney Channel began to make money by 1990. By that year, the channel could claim 5 million subscribers (out of a population of some 60 million cable households).

Eisner may have had the most early success in home video. He accomplished this in spades by packaging and proffering the "classics" of Disney animation in the expanding home-video market. These video revenues provided an immediate boost to the corporate bottom line. In 1986 alone, home-video revenues added more than $100 million of pure profit. In October 1987, when *Lady and the Tramp* was released on video, the Disney company had more than 2 million orders in hand before it ever shipped a copy. By the late 1980s, *Bambi* and *Cinderella* were added to the list of the all-time best-sellers on video. Eisner placed *Bambi* and even *Fantasia* into "video sell through" so every family could buy and own a copy. *Aladdin* and *The Lion King* created even more profit and made the Disney operation Hollywood's leader in home-video sales.

With all this, Eisner made the Disney balance sheets glow. From mid-1985 through late 1990, the company broke profit records for more than 20 straight quarters. Based on the good times of the 1980s, operating margins and cash flow tripled. It was no wonder that, in order to underscore their thriving new corporate colossus, Eisner and company president Frank Wells changed the company name from Walt Disney Productions to the Walt Disney Company.

By 1991, the Walt Disney Company had become a true corporate power. Specifically, as 1991 began, it ranked in the top 200 of all U.S. corporations in terms of sales and assets, an outstanding 43rd in terms of profits. In terms of its stock value, Disney had grown into a $16 billion company, with mind-boggling sales of $6 billion per annum and profits approaching $1 billion per year. This was a media corporate giant, of a rank comparable to that of Time Warner or Paramount, no marginal enterprise anymore.

It came as no surprise in July 1995 that Disney announced its most important move in television, the takeover of a broadcast television network. What was surprising, however, is that the network chosen by Disney was ABC, then the leading network, and its parent company, Capital Cities. Additional surprise came from the quiet, unsuspected nature of the deal making. As the story is reported, Eisner and Capital Cities President Thomas Murphy began their negotiations only days before the final deal was struck—and managed to keep it from reporters. For an announced $19 billion, Disney had suddenly become one of the world's major media conglomerates. A few weeks later, the surprise continued when Michael Ovitz, head of the Creative Artists Agency—who was at that time often referred to as the most powerful man in Hollywood—became president of the new company.

For all his successes, Eisner has been well rewarded. In 1990 surveys of the best-paid corporate executives in the United States, he ranked in the top ten. From 1986 to 1990, he had been paid nearly $100 million for his efforts. In 2000, Eisner received a stock options bonus worth nearly $38 million despite the fact that during the previous three years company profits fell by half. The Disney Company hit a publicity apex in May 1989, when it was revealed that Michael Eisner was the highest-paid executive in the United States for 1988, at more than $40 million. Michael Eisner must be credited with creating in the Disney Company one of the true media powerhouses of the late 20th century. However, the dawn of the 21st century proved unkind to Eisner. During the summer of 2001, Disney's blockbuster *Pearl Harbor* did not do as well as expected at the box office. Around the same time, conservatives attacked Eisner for his liberal policies regarding homosexuals. Then the September 11, 2001, terrorist attacks on the World Trade Center and the Pentagon devastated the theme-park business.

DOUGLAS GOMERY

See also **American Broadcasting Company;** *Walt Disney* **Programs**

Michael Eisner. Born in Mt. Kisco, New York, March 7, 1942. Educated at Lawrenceville School, Lawrenceville, New Jersey, and Denison University, Granville, Ohio, B.A., 1964. Married: Jane Breckenridge; three sons: Michael (Breck), Eric, and Anders. Began career in programming department of CBS; assistant to national programming director, ABC, 1966–68, manager, specials and talent, director of program development, East Coast, 1968–71, vice president, daytime programming, 1971–75, vice president, program planning and development, 1975–76, senior vice president, prime-time production and development, 1976; president and chief operating officer, Paramount Pictures Corp., 1976–84; chairman and chief executive officer, Walt Disney Company, since 1984.

Television Series

1986–88	*The Disney Sunday Movie*
1988–90	*The Magical World of Disney*
1997–	*The Wonderful World of Disney*

Publication

Work in Progress, with Tony Schwartz, 1998

Further Reading

Auletta, Ken, "The Human Factor," *The New Yorker* (September 26, 1994)

Auletta, Ken, "Awesome: Michael Eisner's Comeback," *The New Yorker* (August 14, 1995)

Boroughs, Don L., "Disney's All Smiles," *U.S. News and World Report* (August 14, 1995)

Flower, Joe, *Prince of the Magic Kingdom: Michael Eisner and the Re-Making of Disney,* New York: John Wiley, 1991

Grover, Ron, *The Disney Touch: How a Daring Management Team Revived an Entertainment Empire,* Homewood, Illinois: Business One Irwin, 1991

Huey, John, "Eisner Explains Everything," *Fortune* (April 17, 1995)

Jacobs, Rita D., "Modern Medici: Michael Eisner" (interview), *Graphis* (September–October 1992)

Masters, Kim, *The Keys to the Kingdom: How Michael Eisner Lost His Grip,* New York: Morrow, 2000; revised edition as *The Rise of Michael Eisner and the Fall of Everybody Else,* New York: HarperBusiness, 2001

"Meet the Boss," *Harper's Magazine* (October 1995)

Schatz, Thomas, "Boss Men," *Film Comment* (January–February 1990)

Elderly and Television, The

The elderly, defined here as individuals 65 years old and above, represent a significant portion (12.4 percent) of the total U.S. population. According to the United States Census of 2000, this population segment had increased by 12 percent from the previous decade, numbering more than 35 million and growing. As of 2000, the Center for Disease Control estimated that the average life expectancy for males was 74.1 years, 79.5 years for females. With advancements in the surgical and pharmaceutical fields, life expectancy will increase, creating greater numbers of individuals beyond the population's median age. Thus, the elderly category will expand, generating a larger television viewing audience of older Americans.

The Elderly Audience

Seniors now average more hours of television watching per week than any other age category. Many use television as a critical source of information, enabling them to actively participate in public issues on a local, state, or federal level. Local and national network news reports as well as dedicated news channels, such as C-SPAN, the Cable News Network (CNN), and MSNBC, help older individuals stay abreast of pending legislation that may impact their quality of life. Most recently, for example, topics such as social security and health care have received wide coverage. By staying informed through the television medium, which sometimes allows for immediate interactivity via the call-in format, older citizens have the ability to remain or become active.

In addition to boosting political interest, television provides cultural stimulus through the broadcasting of concerts, theater performances, bibliographies, and cultural documentaries. The elderly audience generally favors these types of programming, found in the United States on channels such as the Public Broad-

casting Service (PBS), A&E, The Learning Channel (TLC), the Discovery Channel, the History Channel, and even the Food Network. These offerings enable elderly individuals, who may be confined to their homes for health or economic reasons, to virtually explore the world and its peoples.

Television's audio component can also provide a type of companionship in the home for older women and men who find themselves alone. Not only is the noise from television a comfort, but viewers often feel a connection with television personalities. Historically, favorite characters and personalities of this age-group include mystery sleuths such as Perry Mason, Columbo, and Jessica Fletcher (*Murder, She Wrote*); performers such as Lawrence Welk, Lucille Ball, and Carol Burnett; and game show hosts Pat Sajak and Vanna White (*Wheel of Fortune*), Alec Trebek (*Jeopardy*), and Bob Barker (*The Price Is Right*). Further, aging viewers tend to prefer characters, storylines, and formats that reflect and reinforce their existing ideologies rather than exploring more radical options. For instance, the character Jessica Fletcher is well liked because she is successful, conventionally moral, and intelligent and is an older character. Additionally, older adults tend to prefer stories that are resolved within a single episode (with the exception of traditional soap operas), as opposed to plotlines that run throughout the series.

Representation of Elderly Characters

Often, older characters are depicted as feisty grouches, such as Grannie (*Beverly Hillbillies*), Archie Bunker (*All in the Family*), Frank Costanza (*Seinfeld*), or Frank Barone (*Everybody Loves Raymond*). Otherwise, they are portrayed as scatterbrained, as exemplified by Edith Bunker (*All in the Family*) and Rose Nylund (*Golden Girls*). Seniors are repeatedly shown to be feeble, as seen in the popular "Help! I've Fallen and I Can't Get Up!" commercial of the 1980s. Further, there is little racial or ethnic diversity among older characters. The vast majority is Caucasian. There are exceptions, such as Fred Sanford (*Sanford and Son*), but even this character fell victim to some stereotypes of black Americans. Still, as channel and programming options increase, a greater diversity of representation across all age categories, races, and socioeconomic groups may emerge.

Perhaps many of these issues are exemplified in one program that focused completely on elderly characters, *The Golden Girls.* This situation comedy ran from 1985 to 1992 and featured four females in their senior years, each exhibiting a distinct background and persona. The women were shown to have active lifestyles, including dating (many jokes centered around sex), and to face serious concerns (characters dealt with housing issues and health emergencies). This very popular show, filled with humor and touching moments, represents one of the few series that afforded a great deal of attention to the often disregarded elderly community.

It is likely that the elderly community is largely ignored in series television because the group is also frequently overlooked as a demographically defined target market. Nevertheless, elderly individuals are consumers as well as viewers. Average annual expenditures for Americans between the ages of 65 and 74 years were more than $32,000 in 2001, according to the U.S. Department of Labor Bureau of Labor Statistics. Yet advertisers, other than those selling products made specifically for aging adults such as denture cream or pharmaceuticals, tend to focus on the 18-to-34 demographic. The U.S. network capitalizing most extensively on elderly viewership is the Columbia Broadcasting System (CBS). With programs that are popular among older audiences, such as *Touched by an Angel* and *60 Minutes,* CBS has become known as the only major network catering to senior viewers.

Home shopping, however, is also a potential site at which television addresses the elderly and provides a different approach to financial interaction. The Home Shopping Network (HSN) and QVC are popular among elderly buyers because these stations allow them to make purchases without leaving their homes, and the phone-in format, as opposed to Internet shopping, is easier for some elderly consumers. Further, the hosts of these shows, who often use direct address of the camera to attract the viewer, can serve as companions in the homes of isolated audience members.

Television use cannot, of course, be studied solely on the basis of age categories. Education and economic status, individual tastes, and cultural background all certainly influence viewing choices and behaviors. While researchers have found that the elderly as a demographic group generally favor certain genres, formats, and characters, elderly viewers are a diverse group who ultimately live with the medium according to their own distinct, individual needs.

STACY ROSENBERG

See also **Columbia Broadcasting System (CBS); Columbo; Golden Girls; Murder, She Wrote; Perry Mason; 60 Minutes; Touched by an Angel**

Further Reading

Bell, J., "In Search of a Discourse on Aging: The Elderly on Television," *The Gerontologist,* Vol. 32 (1992)

Davis, Richard H., *Television and the Aging Audience,* Los Angeles: University of Southern California Press, 1980

Davis, Richard H., and Westbrook, G., "Television in the Lives of the Elderly: Attitudes and Opinions," *Journal of Broadcasting and Electronic Media,* Vol. 29, No. 2 (1985)

Mundorf, N., and Brownell, W., "Media Preferences of Older and Younger Adults," *The Gerontologist,* Vol. 30 (1990)

Riggs, Karen E., *Mature Audiences: Television in the Lives of Elders,* New Brunswick, New Jersey: Rutgers University Press, 1998

Ellen

U.S. Situation Comedy

Ellen, which premiered as *These Friends of Mine* in March 1994, was a situation comedy in the *Seinfeld* mold: built around successful stand-up comic Ellen DeGeneres, it focused on a 30-something woman and her group of friends. Although its premise was unremarkable, *Ellen* entered television history in the spring

Ellen DeGeneres.
Photo courtesy of ABC Photo Archives

of 1997 when its title character came out as a lesbian, making the show the first to feature a gay lead character, a move that received heightened publicity because of Ellen DeGeneres's virtually simultaneous coming out in mass media.

In the first season, Ellen Morgan was a bookstore manager in Los Angeles who endured the vicissitudes of life and love with her roommate, Adam Greene (Arye Gross), a slob and aspiring photographer, and her friends Holly (Holly Fulger) and Anita (Maggie Wheeler). By the 1994 fall season, the show's name had changed, Ellen owned the bookstore (Buy the Book), and she had a new supporting cast. Although her roommate Adam remained for one more year, her new friends included Joe Farrell (David Anthony Higgins), a co-worker who ran the coffee bar at the bookstore, and her glamorous and self-centered childhood friend Paige Clark (Joely Fisher), a film executive. In the 1995–96 season, Buy the Book had been destroyed in an earthquake; after rebuilding it, Ellen sold out to a chain, although she remained as manager. By the end of the season, another new character, Ellen's annoyingly naive friend Audrey Penney (Clea Lewis), had been added, and Adam had been replaced by a new roommate, Spence Kovak (Jeremy Piven), Ellen's cousin and a former doctor who had moved to Los Angeles to start a new life. Ellen's parents, Lois and Harold Morgan (Alice Hirson and Steven Gilborn), as well as her gay friend Peter (Patrick Bristow) also made occasional appearances.

The sitcom's tone was a combination of the "single woman on her own" premise originally popularized by *The Mary Tyler Moore Show* and a kind of physical comedy reminiscent of *I Love Lucy,* featuring DeGeneres's talent for physical antics and sight gags. Indeed, one review of the show's first season referred to DeGeneres as a combination of Mary Richards and Lucy Ricardo. Much of the humor revolved around Ellen's active but unsuccessful dating life. Although it performed respectably, the show was never an unqualified ratings success. By the end of its first season, there was speculation that the sitcom's seemingly unrelenting focus on Ellen Morgan's lack of success at romance was the problem and that Ellen lacked chemistry with men because she was gay, an interpretation bolstered by her somewhat androgynous style and by the way the comedy milked her clear discomfort and ineptitude at dating for laughs. Joyce Millman, television critic for the *San Francisco Examiner,* wrote, "As a single gal sitcom, *Ellen* doesn't make any sense at all, until you view it through the looking glass where the unspoken subtext becomes the main point. Then

Ellen is transformed into one of TV's savviest, funniest, slyest shows. Ellen Morgan is a closet lesbian."

Speculation about DeGeneres's own sexuality also was a factor in rumors about the sitcom. DeGeneres was notoriously private, refusing to speak about her personal life in public, but allusions to her sexuality in the press were more frequent by 1996. In the summer of that year, DeGeneres began to discuss the implications of coming out with her publicist. A story in a September 1996 issue of *TV Guide* noted that the producers of *Ellen* were considering a storyline about Ellen Morgan's coming out in the 1996–97 season, and the show itself began to feature comic allusions to the possibility in its fall episodes.

Fearing the reaction of conservative groups and advertisers, the American Broadcasting Company (ABC) and Touchstone Television (which produced *Ellen* and was a subsidiary of Disney, ABC's parent company) proceeded carefully, admitting that a coming-out episode was planned but might not necessarily be aired. Once the decision was made, ABC scheduled the episode during the 1997 spring sweeps and moved the show to a later hour in the schedule, presumably to avoid targeting an audience with young children. In April 1997, DeGeneres was featured on the cover of *Time* magazine with a photo caption that read, "Yep, She's Gay," discussed her coming out and the sitcom in appearances on both *20/20* and *Oprah* shortly before the episode was broadcast, and both she and her parents appeared in an episode of ABC's *Prime-Time Live* immediately after the coming-out episode (referred to as "The Puppy Episode," a jokey allusion to the idea that the "real" news of the episode was that Ellen was getting a puppy).

The coming-out episode that aired on April 30, 1997, focused on Ellen Morgan's own realization that she might be gay. It drew the largest audience of the week, a phenomenon traceable to its enormous publicity and its roster of guest stars, such as lesbian icons k.d. lang and Melissa Etheridge as well as Oprah Winfrey (who played Ellen's therapist) and Laura Dern (who played Ellen's love interest). Two more episodes in the spring season dealt with coming-out issues; one focused on Ellen coming out to her parents, and the other centered on Ellen coming out to her boss at the bookstore. In the fall of 1997, *Ellen* won two Emmys for "The Puppy Episode," one for editing and another for writing. It also received a Peabody Award for the episode.

Despite the initial favorable reaction to the coming-out storyline, the 1997–98 season of *Ellen* was troubled. The high ratings for the coming-out episode were not sustained, and, as Ellen Morgan began to explore her new identity through a romantic relationship with a woman, complaints that the show was "too gay" began to surface. ABC placed parental advisories before the episodes and gave them a TV-14 rating, prompting protests from both DeGeneres and gay rights organizations. By the spring of 1998, ABC had cancelled the sitcom. There were accusations from DeGeneres that the network had not been supportive of the show, claims from ABC executives that the sitcom had turned into her personal soapbox, and arguments from television critics and commentators that it had simply ceased to be funny. Regardless, there was widespread agreement that *Ellen* had changed the face of television by introducing a gay lead character, a view that gained strength from the large number of programs with gay themes that followed in its wake and that faced little controversy.

BONNIE J. DOW

Cast

Ellen Morgan (1994–98)	Ellen DeGeneres
Adam Greene (1994–96)	Arye Gross
Holly (1994)	Holly Fulger
Anita (1994)	Maggie Wheeler
Joe Farrell	David Anthony Higgins
Paige Clark	Joely Fisher
Audrey Penney (1995–98)	Clea Lewis
Spence Kovak (1995–98)	Jeremy Piven
Peter	Patrick Bristow
Lois Morgan	Alice Hirson
Harold Morgan	Steven Gilborn

Producers

Ellen Degeneres (producer), David Flebotte, Alex Herschlag, Mark Wilding (coproducers), Mark Driscoll, Eileen Heisler, DeAnn Heline, Vic Kaplan, Dava Savel (executive producers), Lawrence Broch, Matt Goldman (co–executive producers)

Programming History

108 episodes
ABC

March 1994–May 1994	Wednesday 9:30–10:00
August 1994–September 1994	Tuesday 9:30–10:00
September 1994–March 1995	Wednesday 9:30–10:00
March 1995–April 1995	Wednesday 8:30–9:00
April 1995–May 1995	Tuesday 9:30–10:00
May 1995–September 1995	Wednesday 8:30–9:00
September 1995–November 1996	Wednesday 8:00–8:30
December 1996–February 1997	Wednesday 9:30–10:00
March 1997–April 1997	Tuesday 8:30–9:00
April 1997–March 1998	Wednesday 9:30–10:00
May 1998–July 1998	Wednesday 9:30–10:00

Further Reading

Cagle, Jess, "As Gay As It Gets?" *Entertainment Weekly* (May 8, 1998)

Dow, Bonnie J., "*Ellen,* Television, and the Politics of Gay and Lesbian Visibility," *Critical Studies in Media Communication,* Vol. 18 (2001)

Gross, Larry, *Up from Invisibility: Lesbians, Gay Men, and the Media in America,* New York: Columbia University Press, 2001

Handy, Bruce, "He Called Me Ellen DeGenerate?" *Time* (April 14, 1997)

Handy, Bruce, "Roll Over, Ward Cleaver," *Time* (April 14, 1997)

Hubert, Susan J., "What's Wrong with This Picture? The Politics of *Ellen*'s Coming Out Party," *Journal of Popular Culture,* Vol. 33 (1999)

Jacobs, A.J., "Will the Real Ellen Please Stand Up?" *Entertainment Weekly* (March 24, 1995)

Millman, Joyce, "The Sitcom That Dare Not Speak Its Name," *San Francisco Examiner* (March 19, 1995)

Svetkey, Benjamin, "Is Your TV Set Gay?" *Entertainment Weekly* (October 6, 2000)

Walters, Suzanna Danuta, *All the Rage: The Story of Gay Visibility in America,* Chicago: University of Chicago Press, 2001

Ellerbee, Linda (1944–)

U.S. Broadcast Journalist

Linda Ellerbee, respected and outspoken broadcast journalist, has functioned as a network news correspondent, anchor, writer, and producer. She is currently president of her own production company, Lucky Duck Productions. Gaining fame in the 1970s and 1980s for her stints as an NBC News Washington

Linda Ellerbee.
Photo courtesy of Gittings/Skipworth, Inc.

correspondent, *Weekend* co-anchor, reporter, and co-anchor of *NBC News Overnight,* Ellerbee came to represent a distinctive type of reporter: literate, funny, irreverent, and never condescending. Her personal style attracted a diverse and dedicated following of viewers for her stories, which covered everything from politics to pop culture. "And so it goes" is her trademark broadcast tagline as well as the title of her 1986 best-seller *"And So it Goes": Adventures in Television,* an amusing and candid look at the realities of the profession.

Ellerbee's 12-year career as a correspondent and anchor at NBC News climaxed with her appointment as co-anchor of an overnight news broadcast, *NBC News Overnight.* Although the program failed with audiences, Ellerbee and the concept were critical successes. The duPont Columbia Awards cited *Overnight* as "possibly the best written and most intelligent news program ever." She left the network news business in 1986, after serving a stint as anchor for ABC News' short-lived *Our World.*

Ellerbee's television production company, Lucky Duck Productions, has a reputation as a supplier of outstanding children's programming. Ellerbee writes and hosts the weekly *Nick News* and the quarterly *Nick News Special Editions* (the Nickelodeon news-

magazine for children and young people), both produced by Lucky Duck Productions. These shows have given Lucky Duck a reputation for introducing quality news journalism on a broad range of subjects to its audience. These series have been honored with the Peabody, duPont Columbia Awards, the recognition of the National Education Association, and the Parents Choice Awards. The Peabody citation given in 1991 notes the award was given for presenting news in a thoughtful and noncondescending manner for both children and adults. Other Lucky Duck productions for such clients as Nickelodeon, Music Television (MTV), Home Box Office (HBO), FOX, and Time-Life include several projects for young adults and documentary or news shows for all viewers.

In 1996, Ellerbee was again involved in expanding and experimenting with media forms. She began writing and hosting a monthly online public affairs interview program, *On the Record,* produced by Microsoft and Lucky Duck Productions, which combined print, television, and computer technology. She continues to write, following up her 1991 best-seller *Move On* with an eight-part series for middle-school children titled *Get Real.* A breast cancer survivor, Ellerbee also travels the country giving inspirational speeches about her life and her challenges. In 1999, she was awarded a Peabody for her accomplishments on *Nick News.*

ALISON ALEXANDER

See also **Children and Television; Nickelodeon**

Linda Ellerbee (Linda Jane Smith). Born in Bryan, Texas, August 15, 1944. Educated at Vanderbilt University, Nashville, Tennessee, 1962–64. Married: 1) Mac Smith, 1964 (divorced, 1966); 2) Van Veselka, 1968 (divorced, 1971); children: Vanessa and Joshua; 3) Tom Ellerbee, 1973 (divorced, 1974). Disc jockey, WSOM, Chicago, 1964–65; program director, KSJO, San Francisco, 1967–68; reporter, KJNO, Juneau, Alaska, 1969–72; news writer, Associated Press, Dallas, Texas, 1972; television reporter, KHOU, Houston, Texas, 1972–73; general assignment reporter, WCBS-TV, New York City, 1973–76; reporter, Washington bureau of NBC News, 1976–78; co-anchor, network newsmagazine *Weekend,* 1978–79; correspondent, *NBC Nightly News,* 1979–82; co-anchor, *NBC News Overnight,* 198–84; co-anchor, *Summer Sunday,* 1984; reporter, *Today,* 1984–86; reporter, *Good Morning, America,* 1986; anchor, ABC news show *Our World,* 1986–87; commentator, Cable News Network (CNN), 1989; president, Lucky Duck Productions, since 1987; producer, writer, and host, *Nick News,* since 1991; writer and founder, host, *On the Record,* online production with Microsoft, from 1996. Recipient: Peabody Awards, 1991, 1998.

Television Series

1978–79	*Weekend*
1979–82	*NBC Nightly News*
1982–84	*NBC News Overnight*
1984	*Summer Sunday*
1984–86	*Today*
1986–87	*Our World*
1991–	*Nick News*

Television Specials (selected)

1997	*Addicted*
1998	*The Other Epidemic: What Every Woman Needs to Know About Breast Cancer*
2001	*Turning Ten: A Nick News Celebration*
2002	*Faces of Hope: The Children of Afghanistan*

Film

Baby Boom, 1987.

Radio

The Lives of Children, 1995.

Publications

"And So It Goes": Adventures in Television, 1986
Move On: Adventures in the Real World, 1991
Girl Reporter Blows Lid Off Town!, 2000
Girl Reporter Sinks School!, 2000
Girl Reporter Stuck in Jam!, 2000
Girl Reporter Snags Crush!, 2000
Ghoul Reporter Digs Up Zombies!, 2000
Girl Reporter Rocks Polls!, 2000
Girl Reporter Gets The Skinny!, 2001
Girl Reporter Bytes Back!, 2001

Further Reading

Lamb, Chris, "From TV Commentator to KFS Columnist," *Editor and Publisher* (October 27, 1990)
"Linda Ellerbee: Telling Her Own Stories," *Broadcasting & Cable* (September 11, 1995)
Orenstein, Peggy, "Women on the Verge of a Nervy Breakdown," *Mother Jones* (June 1989)

Emerson, Faye (1917–1983)

U.S. Television Personality

Faye Emerson was one of the most visible individuals in the early days of U.S. television. A "television personality" (meaning talk show host and more), her omnipresence during the infant days of TV made her one of the most famous faces in the United States and earned her the unofficial titles of "Television's First Lady" and "Mrs. Television."

Before television settled into stricter genre forms, when prime time was dominated by more presentational types of programming, "personalities" prospered. Variety shows abounded, as did low-cost, low-key talk shows that took advantage of TV's intimate nature. While the hosts of some of these shows were men—Ed Sullivan, Garry Moore, and Arthur Godfrey are among the better-known "personalities"—the majority were female: Ilka Chase, Wendy Barrie, Arlene Francis, and others.

Emerson had been a marginally successful film and stage actress before she embarked on her second career in television. After noticing her in a local theater production, a talent scout offered Emerson a contract with Warner Brothers, and she starred or costarred in various "A" and "B" movies. Her career took an upswing in 1944, when she married for a second time, to Elliot Roosevelt, son of President Franklin Delano Roosevelt. The studio's publicity machine used this union to bring her greater fame and expanded Emerson's nonacting opportunities. As a "first daughter-in-law," she took part in presidential ceremonies and, with her husband, staged a successful trip to the Soviet Union in the late 1940s. She also acted on Broadway and on radio.

Emerson made her first television appearance of note in 1949 as a panelist, with her husband, on a game show. Her quick wit and breadth of knowledge—which upstaged her husband to such a degree that she apologized on his behalf on air—made her something of a sensation. Later that year, actress Diana Barrymore was forced by illness to drop out of her soon-to-premiere local New York talk show. The producers phoned Emerson to take over, and she accepted.

Faye Emerson.
Courtesy of the Everett Collection

The Faye Emerson Show premiered in October 1949 and went national over the Columbia Broadcasting System (CBS) the following March. It quickly gained a following, snagging an average 22 rating. One month after that program's national debut, Emerson began a second talk show, this time on the National Broadcasting Company (NBC). This made her one of the first people to have two shows simultaneously on two networks.

The late-night talk show of its day, Emerson frequently welcomed celebrity guests (actors, authors, and other personalities). Sometimes the show was more free form. Sometimes it was simply Faye talking about her life and goings-on about town.

In retrospect, Emerson seemed a natural for early television, a medium that had to bridge the gap between the art of live drama and the appeal of wrestling. Emerson's combination of Hollywood good looks and social connections—along with her old-fashioned common sense, her pleasant personality, and her friendly conversations about peoples, places, and parties—made audiences want to welcome her into their homes. Adding to her appeal were her much-talked-about designer gowns featuring plunging necklines. It was believed such décolletage helped her attain much of her male viewership. (One wit would later say that Faye Emerson put the "V" in "TV.") The topic was such hot copy for a time that it inspired fashion/photo spreads in *Life* and other magazines. Finally, to move past it, Emerson brought it to a vote on her show. She asked viewers what she should wear. Ballots ran 95 percent in favor of Emerson's style staying as it was.

However, Emerson was more than just window dressing. During the height of her fame, she was a frequent substitute host for Edward R. Murrow on *Person to Person* and for Garry Moore on his show. She took part in so many game shows that a magazine once labeled her "TV's peripatetic panelist."

Emerson's omnipresence as a television performer should not be underemphasized. Before cable and satellites, the average household was lucky to receive a handful of channels. As she hosted various shows on various networks for much of the 1950s meant, even the most infrequent of audiences had to be aware of Emerson as one of TV's first citizens. A viewing of her work today reveals a pleasant, largely unflappable but somewhat stiff talent. Still, she radiates glamour and remarkable camera presence.

In 1950, after divorcing Roosevelt, Emerson announced on her evening program her plans to marry musician Lyle C. "Skitch" Henderson. (It is believed that she was the first person ever to make such an announcement on television.) In 1953, the two teamed for the show *Faye and Skitch*. Earlier, in 1951, Emerson began hosting one of the medium's most expensive programs, *Faye Emerson's Wonderful Town*, in which she traveled the United States and profiled different cities.

As the 1950s came to a close, TV "personalities" found themselves with fewer opportunities. Some, like Arlene Francis, brilliantly reinvented themselves; others found themselves relegated to guest appearances before moving into retirement. Emerson was in this latter group. She continued to make TV appearances until 1963, when, rich and weary of show business, she sailed off for a year in Europe. Finding it to her liking, she seldom returned to the United States and died abroad in 1993.

Several factors explain why Emerson, "Mrs. Television," did not endure on the small screen but her masculine counterpart, "Mr. Television" (Milton Berle), did. Perhaps most important, those individuals such as Emerson who fit the role of TV personality never had a single marketable trait: neither comic nor singer, they were more like the good host at a private, intimate party. By the late 1950s, as talk shows left prime time, the party was over. TV production moved out of New York and left Emerson's kind of glamour behind. In contrast, a variety-show performer such as Berle could adapt more easily as television evolved as an entertainment media. Still, it is worth remembering that, at its beginnings, television needed a friendly, unifying factor, a symbol to initiate audiences into its technology—and for millions of viewers that envoy was Faye Emerson.

CARY O'DELL

Faye Emerson. Born in Elizabeth, Louisiana, July 8, 1917. Married: 1) William Wallace Crawford, Jr., 1938 (divorced, 1942); one child: William Wallace III; 2) Elliot Roosevelt, 1944 (divorced, 1950); 3) Lyle C. "Skitch" Henderson, 1950 (divorced, 1958). In films from 1930s; in television from 1949 as host, guest performer, panelist. Died in Deyva, Spain, March 9, 1983.

Television Series

1949–52	*With Faye*
1950	*The Faye Emerson Show*
1951–52	*Faye Emerson's Wonderful Town*
1953–54	*Faye and Skitch*

Films

Bad Men of Missouri, 1941; *Wild Bill Hickok Rides,* 1941; *Nine Lives Are Not Enough,* 1941; *The Nurse's Secret,* 1941; *Lady Gangster,* 1942; *Murder in the Big House,* 1942; *Secret Enemies,* 1942; *Juke Girl,* 1942; *The Hard Way,* 1942; *Find the Blackmailer,* 1943; *Destination Tokyo,* 1943; *Air Force,* 1943; *The Desert Song,* 1943; *Between Two Worlds,* 1944; *The Mask of Dimitrios,* 1944; *Crime by Night,* 1944; *Very Thought of You,* 1944; *Hotel Berlin,* 1945; *Danger Signal,* 1945; *Her Kind of Man,* 1946; *Nobody Lives Forever,* 1946; *Guilty Bystander,* 1950; *A Face in the Crowd,* 1957.

Stage

With St. James Repertory Company, Carmel, California, from 1935; *The Play's the Thing,* 1948; *Back to Methuselah,* 1958; *The Vinegar Tree,* 1962.

Further Reading

O'Dell, Cary, *Women Pioneers in Television,* Jefferson, North Carolina: McFarland, 1996

Emmy. *See* Academy of Television Arts and Sciences

E.N.G.

Canadian Drama

E.N.G., a Canadian television drama series set in the news studio of a local television station, ran successfully on the private CTV network for five seasons from 1989 to 1994. After a slow start, which almost led to its cancellation at the end of the first season, the series steadily gained in popularity as audiences responded to its blend of personal and public issues. It was sold to many countries and well received when it appeared on the Lifetime cable network in the United States and on Channel 4 in the United Kingdom.

The letters in the title stand for "Electronic News Gathering" and were often seen on black-and-white images of news footage supposedly viewed through the monitors of handheld video cameras. Through its depiction of news gathering and studio production work, the series was able to respond to topical issues and comment on the role of the media in contemporary culture. The news stories were framed by the personal and professional relationships of the news makers as the objectivity demanded of news reporting collided with the subjective feelings of the reporters or with commercial or political pressures.

The series began with the arrival of Mike Fennell (Art Hindle) to take over as news director, a position to which the executive producer, Ann Hildebrand (Sara Botsford), had expected to be promoted. As these two characters endeavored to establish a professional relationship amid the various crises of the newsroom, Ann carried on a supposedly secret affair with Jake Antonelli (Mark Humphrey), an impetuous cameraman who often broke the rules and found himself in dangerous situations. In the course of the series, Mike and Ann became personally involved, and the final episodes left them trying to balance their careers and their relationship after the station's owners decided to adopt a "lifestyles" format.

The major significance of *E.N.G.* stems from its attempt to negotiate between the traditions of Canadian television and the formulas of the popular American programs that dominate CTV's schedule. In media coverage of the series, it was often compared with the Canadian Broadcasting Corporation's (CBC's) *Street Legal,* which began two years earlier and which set its personal and professional entanglements in a Toronto law office. Both series were compared to such American hits as *L.A. Law* and *Hill Street Blues,* but both presented recognizably Canadian situations and settings. Since most original Canadian television drama has been produced by the CBC, a public corporation, the success of *E.N.G.* raised hopes that the private networks would offer more support to Canadian producers.

E.N.G. did have one foot in the Canadian tradition associated with the CBC and the National Film Board, a tradition of documentary realism and social responsibility, and the series gave work to a number of veteran film and television directors. Yet the major project of the series was clearly to deliver the pleasures of "popular" television, using a formula that owed more to the melodramatic structures of the daytime soaps than to traditional Canadian suspicion of "crisis structures." When *E.N.G.* began, it used a fairly strict series format, each episode presenting a complete story with little cross-reference between episodes. The later seasons saw a movement toward a serial format as the personal lives of the characters assumed more importance.

However, the basic formula remained the same throughout. A number of loosely connected stories were interwoven, offering viewers a variety of characters and situations and inviting them to make connections among the stories and to activate memories of other episodes in the series (and to make comparisons to other similar series). In "The Souls of Our Heroes" (March 1990), for example, the main story dealt with competing accounts of the events in Tiananmen Square, while Ann received an unexpected visit from a childhood friend and her two children and a producer attempted to enliven the Crime Catchers segment of the news with fictional reenactments. "In the Blood" (January 1991) used the motif of "blood" to link its two main stories: an attempt to cap-

ture a day in the life of an AIDS victim and an investigation into an alleged miracle involving a bleeding statue of Jesus. In these episodes, and most others, the focus was on the implications of the way the news is reported for the news makers themselves, for the people on whom they are reporting, and for the community that watches the final product.

Although *E.N.G.* was clearly indebted to similar American series, its ability to blend melodrama with a serious treatment of topical issues was not shared by *WIOU,* a short-lived series with a remarkably similar premise that appeared on the Columbia Broadcasting System (CBS) in the fall of 1990.

JIM LEACH

See also **Canadian Programming in English**

Cast

Mike Fennell	Art Hindle
Ann Hildebrand	Sara Botsford
Jake Antonelli	Mark Humphrey

Producer
Robert Lantos

Programming History
CTV/Telefilm
1989–94

E.N.G.
Photo courtesy of Alliance International

English, Diane (1948–)

U.S. Writer, Producer

Diane English is in the enviable position of having several successful shows to her credit, a credit often shared with coproducer and husband, Joel Shukovsky. In addition to the programs—*Murphy Brown, Love and War,* and the earlier *Foley Square* and *My Sister Sam*—their company also manages a lucrative eight-figure multiseries contract with the Columbia Broadcasting System (CBS). The couple started their careers in public television (New York City's WNET) with English's adaptation of *The Lathe of Heaven,* and English went on to write nine TV movies before being offered the opportunity to "create-write-produce" the pilot for *Foley Square,* which, like her later shows, featured a strong female central character.

In a demanding profession, however, English's career has not been without controversy. *Murphy Brown* was attacked by Vice President Dan Quayle in the summer of 1992 when the main character on the series, a single professional woman played by Candice Bergen, decided not to terminate her unplanned pregnancy. Quayle's primary criticism was that the series mocked the importance of fathers by having a woman bear a child alone and call it "just another lifestyle choice." Quayle and English engaged in a heated and prolonged dispute through the media, which made the series, and English herself, a household word. Some industry experts called the incident the single most important element contributing to the long-term ratings success of the show. For advertisers, in the following season, *Murphy Brown* was the most expensive show in television, with 30-second commercials on the show costing an average $310,000. Syndication sales were said to exceed $100 million. Because of her unusual combination of business and creative skills, English is often mentioned as the only woman in television now capable of taking over the entertainment division at a major network.

CHERYL HARRIS

See also **Murphy Brown**

Diane English. Born in Buffalo, New York, 1948. Graduated from Buffalo State College, 1970. Married: Joel Shukovsky. High school English teacher, Buffalo, New York, 1970–71; WNET-TV, New York City, 1970s; columnist, *Vogue* magazine, New York City, 1977–80; in commercial television from 1985; creator, writer, producer, *Murphy Brown,* 1988–98. Recipient: Writers Guild Award, 1990; Genie Award, American Women in Radio and Television, 1990; Commissioners' Award, National Commission on Working Women.

Television Series

1985–86	*Foley Square*
1986–87	*My Sister Sam*
1988–98	*Murphy Brown*

Diane English and Joel Shukovsky.
Photo courtesy of Schukovsky/English Entertainment

Further Reading

Alley, Robert S., and Irby B. Brown, *Murphy Brown: Anatomy of a Sitcom,* New York: Delta Books, 1990
DeVries, Hibry, "Laughing Off the Recession," *New York Times* (January 3, 1993)

Englishman Abroad, An

This award-winning 65-minute drama from the British Broadcasting Corporation (BBC; 1983) brought together writer Alan Bennett and director John Schlesinger, who created a film around the British spy Guy Burgess, one of the so-called Cambridge spies of the 1930s to 1950s. Burgess, although not under suspicion, defected to the Soviet Union with fellow spy Donald Maclean in 1951.

The film's origins are curious, as indicated in its epigraph: "Although some incidents are imaginary…this is a true story. It happened to Coral Browne in 1958" (ellipsis in original). In that year, the Anglo-Australian actress Coral Browne was performing in a British touring production of Shakespeare's *Hamlet* that was visiting Moscow. There, by chance, she encountered Burgess, visited his apartment for lunch, and, on returning to London, undertook his requests to have clothes ordered from his tailor and shoemaker. In the television piece, Browne, 25 years on, plays herself and reenacts a version of these events. From Browne's personal history, Bennett and Schlesinger constructed a deft television drama, permeated by two overriding and overlapping themes: the issue of identity (national, ideological, and cultural) and the nature of loyalty.

It begins in the middle of a performance of *Hamlet,* with Browne on stage and an evidently unwell Burgess (played by Alan Bates) in the audience, attempting to leave his seat. In (crumpled) evening dress and bow tie, attempting to excuse himself in a poor mixture of Russian and English, he already seems out of step with the Muscovites around him. While trying to locate his old Cambridge University friend (playing Claudius) during the interval, Burgess is forced to dive into the nearest doorway—that of Browne's dressing room—to be sick. So begins the unlikely encounter, and the first scenes conclude with Burgess stealing Browne's soap, English cigarettes, and vodka: some small but telling luxuries in the Soviet Union in the 1950s.

Accepting Burgess's invitation to lunch the next day, Browne struggles to locate the address, and a visit to the British Embassy is of little assistance. In the part of the film where, one suspects, Bennett's characterization had the freest reign, Browne struggles to get help from a double act of arrogant, youthful diplomats whose mannerisms and puerility seem to perpetuate a vision of diplomatic life as a continuation of Oxbridge college life. Their behavior and repartee, as they seek to persuade Browne not to visit Burgess, smacks of the university revue or the music hall; but they also serve to put into context, albeit in a caricature fashion, a set of class and gender prejudices (for they also belittle their female secretary) that help the viewer make sense of Burgess's struggle with his background.

Once at Burgess's drab, messy apartment in a run-down block, Browne spends longer than anticipated in his eccentric company, for he is not allowed to leave home until he gets a call from, as he puts it, "my people." She declines "lunch" (a couple of tomatoes), measures him up for his clothes, and listens to music, and they discuss England, communism, gossip, and gay sex, all with Burgess's verbal sprightliness. While they are funny and light, these central scenes are also where the film's purple passages occur.

Bates's Burgess, in his disheveled eccentricity and shabby charm, seems to shy away from much that might be called earnestness. Yet in his finely judged performance and in Bennett's sharp script, the questions of loyalty and identity emerge but are never labored. This "Englishman abroad" encapsulates the paradoxes of someone who has politically and ideologically rejected his national and class background while being a social and cultural product of it. Spurred on by Burgess's sense of irony, Browne makes the mistake of wondering what there is to admire in the Soviet Union. Burgess responds calmly but forcefully: "the system—though being English, you wouldn't be interested in that." He frequently comments on the society and the social class he has left, where seemingly minor details, such as going to the right tailor or having the right school tie, establish who one is rather than one's beliefs. He rails against those who want to change England, but, as a spy (someone whose raison d'être is to subvert the nation and the system), his view of his native country is deeply conflicted:

> So little, England; little music, little art, timid, tasteful, nice. Yet one loves it. You see, I can say I love London, I can say I love England. I can't say I love my country. I don't know what that means.

It would be easy to overstress the sentimental and nostalgic layers of *An Englishman Abroad*. On one level, Bates's Burgess may seem to evade reaching conclusions about the fundamental sadness (as Browne sees it) of his condition, rather like the characters of Bennett's *Talking Heads* monologues. There is considerable evidence for such a view: he punctuates his banter with the phrase "the Comrades, though splendid in every other respect…" to introduce yet another deficiency of Soviet life; he is shadowed constantly by secret police, and his movements are restricted; his life is immeasurably poorer materially; he struggles with a half-understood language, a harsh winter, no meaningful social context, and no family (the camera passes over a photo of his mother in England); and he even wonders whether his Russian lover/partner is part of the surveillance operation.

Yet when Browne upbraids Burgess for presenting his treason as a merely a kind of Wildean social transgression, she implicitly highlights the lifelong role manipulation that has characterized Burgess's life, and viewers must be cautious about the conclusions they draw. Burgess later insists, "I do like it here—don't tell anyone I don't"; and at one level of this complex personality, that must be taken at face value. At this level, the chaos of his life masks someone who, as history documents and he himself avers, took politics and ideas so seriously as to define the course of his life by them because "at the time I thought it was the right thing to do."

Given the film's gay writer and gay director and the indiscreet homosexuality of Burgess before his defection, one might expect the theme of homosexual identity (the sexual outsider) to be aligned with that of the political outsider. However, this is not the case: homosexuality is here a secondary, even a neutral, factor in the English upper-middle-class context. In contrast to Burgess, the gay subversive, the British establishment, in the guise of the two diplomats, is effeminate *and* misogynistic.

Visually, Schlesinger harks back to the British television tradition of the documentary and to his own early working-class realist films. Although the film is shot in color, the handheld camera work, in conjunction with the extraordinarily effective mock-Moscow scenes (provided by the bleak landscapes of Dundee), provide the very opposite of a glossy period reconstruction.

The film's settings and themes are also conveyed by telling musical choices. A soundtrack of atmospheric, occasionally discordant tones with Russian elements establishes geographical context and ambience. This is interspersed by specific and telling musical references to give resonance to the "Englishman abroad" theme. Burgess intones a classic English hymn ("Oh God Our Help in Ages Past") in the theater lavatory: a striking mismatch of music and physical context. Browne is treated to Burgess's one and only record, played on a windup gramophone: Jack Buchanan's "Who Stole My Heart Away," a wistful popular evocation of prewar lost love, made more relevant by Coral Browne's real-life romantic involvement with Buchanan ("we were almost married," she comments). Burgess and his Russian partner even do a bizarre intercultural Gilbert and Sullivan rendition on balalaika and piano. And in the film's most openly emotional scene, Burgess is moved to tears by the choir at an Orthodox church.

Music also dominates the final images of *An Englishman Abroad*. A newly resplendent Burgess, fitted out in his pristine London-made suit, hat, and shoes, strides out into the Moscow snow, a dapper object of consternation to the Muscovites. This is overlaid with more Gilbert and Sullivan, from *HMS Pinafore,* as a rousing chorus sings:

> But in spite of all temptations
> To belong to other nations,
> He remains an Englishman!
> He remains an Englishman!

MARK HAWKINS-DADY

See also **Bennett, Alan**

Cast

Guy Burgess	Alan Bates
Coral Browne	Coral Browne
Toby (diplomat)	Douglas Reith
Giles (diplomat)	Peter Chelsom
Tolya (Burgess's partner)	Alexei Jawdokimov

Screenplay, Direction, Production

Director	John Schlesinger
Screenplay	Alan Bennett
Music	George Fenton
Producer	Innes Lloyd
Production Company	BBC
Director of Photography	Nat Crosby

Programming History

Single television film, 1983

Further Reading

Bennett, Alan, *Single Spies,* London: Samuel French, 1991 (contains the later stage versions of *An Englishman Abroad*)

Brandt, George W., editor, *British Television Drama in the 1980s,* Cambridge and New York: Cambridge University Press, 1993

Goode, I., "A Pattern of Inheritances: Alan Bennett, Heritage and British Film and Television," *Screen,* Vol. 44, No. 3 (2003)

Wolfe, Peter, *Understanding Alan Bennett,* Columbia: University of South Carolina Press, 1998

Entertainment Tonight

Entertainment Tonight, or *ET,* as it has dubbed itself, has proven an influential leader in the way television looks, setting a style-conscious, flashy tone that has influenced not only a proliferation of similar programming but also the overall look of television in the multichannel universe.

For more than 20 seasons, *ET* has aired in first-run syndication (in November 2000 it aired its 5,000th show), maintaining consistently high ratings and clearance in 95 percent of the American markets (already secured in several through 2009) as well as more than 70 countries worldwide. It debuted on September 14, 1981, ideally suited for local stations looking to program a half hour of their federally mandated prime-access daypart (the hour slot preceding prime time). The brainchild of Al Masini, otherwise known for creations such as *Lifestyles of the Rich and Famous, Solid Gold,* and *Star Search, ET* is an "infotainment" magazine presenting news-style coverage focused on the world of entertainment. This narrow-focus news approach was novel in 1981, as was the innovative strategy of satellite delivery it helped pioneer. Since very few local stations owned satellite dishes at the time, some reports credit *ET*'s distribution partner with promising stations free satellite dishes in exchange for licensing the series. Then, rather than receive the show physically (on tape, say, via courier), local stations could tape the satellite broadcast of the show and air it at their convenience anytime that same day. This meant that the show had the "up-to-the-minute" feel of a newscast. Such timeliness was not previously associated with nonnetwork programming, and *ET* played it up by modeling its look and presentation on the news (complete with two anchors—one of each gender—introducing stories from a desk in a studio) and emphasizing the freshness, indeed the date, of each program (with such features as "today's" celebrity birthdays).

For local stations, the show was thus fresher than off-network, syndicated reruns while being much cheaper than producing their own programming for the prime-access daypart. For national advertisers, *ET* became an alternative to networks for the airing of time-sensitive spots, including, not coincidentally, ads for music, television, and feature films—the very subject matter of *ET*'s enthusiastic reporting. Indeed, *ET* has so successfully branded itself a crucial entertainment news outlet that press agents consider it a promotional must-stop, and, as one station rep remarked, "if you're advertising a movie you have to be in there." The cheerful, uncontroversial, and promotional atmosphere thus marks the program in ad-speak as "family friendly" and therefore "basically ad friendly"—so much so that recent estimates suggest the program makes as much as $90 to $100 million per year.

Despite this appealing strategy, *ET* experienced a tumultuous first season, going through four executive producers in one year. Two of the original three anchors were also quickly replaced. Soap actor Tom Hallick left in the first month. Former Miss World Marjorie Wallace was replaced with Dixie Whatley the next month. By the start of the second season, current anchor Mary Hart had in turn replaced Whatley. This early turmoil resulted in part from what has continued to be if not the animating tension of the show then at least a sore spot: negotiating between serious journalism and gossipy promotion. The show began by attempting to present a pleasing atmosphere of celebrity-driven news while simultaneously acting as an industry "watchdog." Thus, early shows presented investigative reports on the Moral Majority's media influence or the "Washington–Hollywood connection," while the same episodes also went "behind the scenes" of soon-to-be-released Hollywood films. *ET* thus takes its news gathering seriously (the Associated Press cites the show as a source, and longtime anchor Mary Hart has been inducted into the Broadcasting and Cable Hall of Fame) but recognizes that the "puff" pieces are what makes the show attractive.

Another source of attraction stems from the innovative way in which the show packages its content. Eager to attract and hold viewers, each show begins with a tightly produced teaser of that day's stories, leading into a garish title sequence before revealing the two smiling anchors. Throughout each show, dazzling bumpers tease the viewer with upcoming stories. The celebrated graphics of the title sequence won the show an Emmy in 1985, and the overproduced look of the show (set, graphics, lighting, editing, and so on) is constantly updated. The successful *ET* formula has proven style itself to be a crucial production strategy. Along with the latest entertainment news, the viewer experiences the latest in televisual production techniques. In this way, the show's emphasis on promotion extends first and foremost to itself, exemplifying what television scholar John Thornton Caldwell has termed "televisuality," an intentional production strategy of "stylistic exhibitionism" that emerged (along with *ET*) in the early 1980s as a means of attracting attention amidst an increasingly crowded array of viewing options.

Indeed, utilizing the latest technology in its distribution and production, *ET* not only has covered the explosion of a conglomeratized media universe since its inception but is itself a living product of it. Originally produced as a collaboration between such companies as Paramount, a Hollywood studio, and Cox Broadcasting, a conglomerate with production and cable interests, the show was financially positioned from the start outside the network system. A harbinger of deregulated changes in the industry, *ET* is now wholly owned by Paramount (who had bought out its partners' interests by 1997), itself now a subsidiary of Viacom.

ET's success has not been warmly received by all. Critics cite the show for the tabloidization of the media, inspiring a host of programming such as *Access Hollywood, Extra, Hard Copy, Inside Edition, A Current Affair,* the Cable News Network's (CNN's) *Showbiz Today,* even the cable channel E! Entertainment Network. As such, *ET* is blamed for encouraging a culture of gossip and scandal where distinctions between politics, entertainment, gossip, and news are blurred and celebrity and entertainment have been "elevated" to the status of news.

Despite these concerns, the show can be credited with (or blamed for) fostering a new kind of entertainment consumer, one informed by a certain kind of economic understanding of the industry (budgets and box office), the minutiae of production concerns, the pitfalls of celebrity, and a "behind-the-scenes" understanding of the products offered by the industry. Certainly the show has catalyzed changes in the way the entertainment industry promotes its products. The innovative behind-the-scenes features, reporting of TV ratings, movie box office returns, and album sales numbers it initiated in a popular context are now all standard promotional techniques.

SHAWN SHIMPACH

See also **E! Entertainment Network; Prime-Time Access Rule; Satellite; Syndication Tabloid Television; Television Aesthetics**

Credits

Current Reporting Staff
Mary Hart: Anchor (joined show in 1982)
Bob Goen: Anchor (joined show in 1993, assumed anchor in 1996)
Jann Carl: Weekend anchor/correspondent (joined show in 1995)
Mark Steines: Weekend anchor/correspondent (joined show in 1995)
Leonard Maltin: Film historian/correspondent (joined show in 1982)

Former Anchors
Tom Hallick (1981), Marjorie Wallace (1981), Ron Hendron (1981–84), Dixie Whatley (1981–82; weekends, 1982–84), Steve Edwards (weekends, 1982–83), Alan Arthur (weekends, 1983–84), Robb Weller (1984–86; weekends 1984–89), Leeza Gibbons (weekends, 1984–95), Julie Moran (1995–2001), John Tesh (1986–96)

Former Correspondents and Commentators
Rona Barrett, Bill Harris, Pat O'Brien, Ron Powers, Scott Osborne, Jeanne Wolf, Richard Hatch, among others

Current Executive Producer
Linda Bell Blue (1995–)

Former Producers
Andy Friendly (1981), Vin Di Bona (1981–83), James Bellows (1981–83), George Merlis (1983–84), Jim Van Messel (1989–95)

Programming History
Syndicated, 1981–present
Produced by Paramount Domestic Television. First aired September 14, 1981. Continues in first-run syndication five days a week in half-hour slot. In addition, a weekend version called *Entertainment*

This Week aired from 1981 to 1999 as an hour-long recap. Since 1999, it has been called *Entertainment Tonight Weekend.*

Further Reading

Ault, Susanne, "*ET:* The Business Behind the Buzz," *Broadcasting & Cable,* Vol. 131, No. 28 (July 2, 2001)

Buck, Jerry, "Shakeup for Industry Newscast," Associated Press (October 31, 1981)

Caldwell, John Thornton, *Televisuality: Style, Crisis, and Authority in American Television,* New Brunswick, New Jersey: Rutgers University Press, 1995

Littleton, Cynthia, "*ET—Access* War Taxes Flacks," *Variety,* Vol. 372, No. 10 (19–25 October 19–25, 1998)

Martin, Ed, "Trio Holds Tight for More Than a Decade: 'ET,' 'Jeopardy!,' 'Wheel' Beat Trends to Return Every Season," *Advertising Age,* Vol. 70, No. 3 (January 18, 1999)

Skaff, Didi M., *Television and the Law: A Comparative Study of Entertainment Tonight and ABC World News Tonight,* doctoral diss., Harvard Law School, 1985

Equal Time Rule

U.S. Broadcasting Regulatory Rule

The equal time rule is the closest thing in broadcast content regulation to the "golden rule." The equal time—or, more accurately, equal opportunity—provision of the U.S. federal government's Communications Act requires radio and television stations and cable systems that originate their own programming to treat legally qualified political candidates equally when it comes to selling or giving away airtime. Simply put, a station that sells or gives one minute to candidate A must sell or give the same amount of time with the same audience potential to all other candidates for the particular office. However, a candidate who cannot afford time does not receive free time unless his or her opponent is also given free time. Thus, even with the equal time law, a well-funded campaign has a significant advantage in terms of broadcast exposure for the candidate.

The equal opportunity requirement dates back to the first major broadcasting law in the United States, the Radio Act of 1927. Legislators were concerned that without mandated equal opportunity for candidates, some broadcasters might try to manipulate elections. As one congressman put it, "American politics will be largely at the mercy of those who operate these stations." When the Radio Act was superseded by the Communications Act of 1934, the equal time provision became Section 315 of the new statute.

A major amendment to Section 315 came in 1959, following a controversial Federal Communications Commission (FCC) interpretation of the equal time provision. Lar Daly, who had run for a variety of public offices, sometimes campaigning dressed as Uncle Sam, was running for mayor of Chicago. Daly de-

manded free airtime from Chicago television stations in response to the stations' news coverage of incumbent mayor Richard Daley. Although the airtime given to Mayor Daley was not directly related to his reelection campaign, the FCC ruled that his appearance triggered the equal opportunity provision of Section 315. Broadcasters interpreted the FCC's decision as now requiring equal time for a candidate whenever another candidate appeared on the air, even if the appearance was not linked to the election campaign.

Congress reacted quickly by creating four exemptions to the equal opportunity law. Stations who gave time to candidates on regularly scheduled newscasts, news interviews shows, documentaries (assuming the candidate was not the primary focus of the documentary), or on-the-spot news events would not have to offer equal time to other candidates for that office. In creating these exemptions, Congress stressed that the public interest would be served by allowing stations the freedom to cover the activities of candidates without worrying that any story about a candidate, no matter how tangentially related to his or her candidacy, would require equal time. The exemptions to Section 315 have also served the interests of incumbent candidates since by virtue of their incumbency they often generate more news coverage then their challengers.

Since 1959, the FCC has provided a number of interpretations to Section 315's exemptions. Presidential press conferences have been labeled on-the-spot news, even if the president uses his remarks to bolster his campaign. Since the 1970s, debates have also been considered on-the-spot news events and therefore exempt from the equal time law. This has enabled stations or other parties arranging the debates to choose which candidates to include in a debate. Before this ruling by the FCC, Congress voted to suspend Section 315 during the 1960 presidential campaign in order to allow Richard Nixon and John Kennedy to engage in a series of debates without the participation of third-party candidates. The FCC has also labeled shows such as *Oprah* and *Good Morning, America* as news interview programs. However, appearances by candidates in shows that do not fit under the four exempt formats will trigger the equal opportunity provision, even if the appearance is irrelevant to the campaign. Therefore, during Ronald Reagan's political campaigns, if a station aired one of his films, it would have been required to offer equal time to Reagan's opponents.

Another provision of Section 315 prohibits a station from censoring what a candidate says when he or she appears on the air (unless it is in one of the exempt formats). Thus, a few years ago when a self-avowed segregationist was running for the governorship of Georgia, the FCC rejected citizen complaints regarding the candidate's use in his ads of derogatory language toward African Americans. More recently, the FCC has also rejected attempts to censor candidate ads depicting aborted fetuses. However, the FCC has permitted stations to channel such ads to times of day when children are less likely to be in the audience.

The equal opportunity law does not demand that a station afford a state or local candidate any airtime. However, under the public interest standard of the Communications Act, the FCC has said that stations should make time available for candidates for major state and local offices. With regard to federal candidates, broadcast stations have much less discretion. A 1971 amendment to the Communications Act requires stations to make a reasonable amount of time available to federal candidates. Once time is made available under this provision, the equal time requirements of Section 315 apply.

The 1971 amendments also addressed the rates that stations can charge candidates for airtime. Before 1971, Congress only required that the rates charged candidates be comparable to those offered to commercial advertisers. Now Section 315 commands that as the election approaches, a station must offer candidates the rate it offers its most favored advertiser. Thus, if a station gives a discount to a commercial sponsor because it buys a great deal of airtime, the station must offer the same discount to any candidate regardless of how much time he or she purchases. As with any advertiser, the rate charged to the candidate is time sensitive; therefore, candidates wishing to advertise in prime viewing or listening periods will face higher costs for airing those messages.

HOWARD KLEIMAN

See also **Deregulation; Federal Communications Commission; Political Processes and Television**

Further Reading

Carter, T. Barton, Marc A. Franklin, and Jay B Wright, *The First Amendment and the Fifth Estate: Regulation of Electronic Mass Media,* Mineola, New York: Foundation Press, 1986; 5th edition, 1999

Daus, Matthew A., "Are Politicians a Protected Class? The Constitutionality of 'Reasonable Access' Media Rights under the Communications Act," *CommLaw Conspectus,* Vol. 6 (Summer 1998)

Gillmor, Donald M., and Jerome A Barron, *Mass Communication Law: Cases and Comment,* St. Paul, Minnesota: West, 1969; 6th edition, with Todd F. Simon, Belmont, California: Wadsworth Publishing, 1998

Kleiman, Howard, "Government Licensed Public Broadcast Stations and Candidates Access to Political Campaigns," *Communication Law and Policy,* Vol. 1 (Spring 1996)

Melcher, Douglas C., "Free Air Time for Political Advertising: An Invasion of the Protected First Amendment Freedoms of Broadcasters," *George Washington Law Review* (1998)

Williams, Andrea D., "The Lowest Unit Charge Provision of the Federal Communications Act of 1934, As Amended, and Its Role in Maintaining a Democratic Electoral Process," *Federal Communications Law Journal,* Vol. 45 (1993)

Ernie Kovacs Show, The (Various)

U.S. Comedy/Variety Program

In a few brief years in the 1950s, there were actually a number of different Ernie Kovacs shows. The first, *Ernie in Kovacsland,* originated in Philadelphia, Pennsylvania, and appeared on the National Broadcasting Company (NBC) from July until August 1951. *The Ernie Kovacs Show* (first known as *Kovacs Unlimited*)

The Ernie Kovacs Show.
Photo courtesy of Edie Adams Archive

was programmed on the Columbia Broadcasting System (CBS) from December 1952 to April 1953, opposite Milton Berle on NBC. Yet another *Ernie Kovacs Show* aired on NBC from December 1955 to September 1956. The existence of these separate shows is testament to both the success and the failure of Ernie Kovacs. A brilliant and innovative entertainer, he was a failure as a popular program host; praised by critics, he was avoided by viewers.

Kovacs was one of the first entertainers to understand and utilize the television as a true "medium," capable of being conceived of and applied in a variety of ways. He recognized the potential of live electronic visual technology and manipulated its peculiar qualities to become a master of the sight gag. Characters in pictures on the walls moved, sculptures undulated, and pilots flew away without their planes. For one gag that lasted only a few seconds, he spent $12,000: when a salesman (played by Kovacs) slapped the fender of a used car, the car fell though a platform. According to Kovacs, "Eighty percent of what I do is in the category of sight gags, no pantomime. I work on the incongruity of sight against sound."

Television was a new toy to Kovacs, a fascinating array of potential special effects. He created an invisible girlfriend who gradually disappeared as she undressed. He cut a girl in half with a hula hoop. As another young lady relaxed in a bathtub, a succession of characters climbed out through the soap bubbles. Ernie taped an orange juice can to a kaleidoscope, placed the can in front of a camera lens, turned a flashlight into the lens, and created what might be the first psychedelic effect on TV. Kovacs loved the unusual, the unexpected. He tilted both the television camera and a table so that as a character seated at the table attempted to pour milk, the milk appeared to defy gravity and flow to the side.

Many of Kovacs's effects were remarkably simple. He used his face to illustrate the effects of the horizontal and vertical controls of a television set. As he adjusted the vertical, his face grew longer; as he adjusted the horizontal, it stretched side to side. To aid viewers who had black-and-white television sets, Kovacs labeled each piece of furniture on the set so viewers would know its color. As he opened a book, sound effects illustrated the plot. As he prepared to saw in half a woman inside a cabinet, two voices were heard from within.

Many of his characters were also simplistic. Percy Dovetonsils drank martinis and read poetry. The three apes of the Nairobi Trio never spoke: one played the keyboard, one directed the music, and the third hit the director with a set of drumsticks. Eugene, perhaps Kovacs's most memorable character, never spoke but managed to sustain a 30-minute program and win Kovacs an Emmy.

He did not neglect sound but used it in its proper place, as a compliment to the visuals. He captured the sound of a bullet rolling inside a tuba. He used music to accompany the movements of office furniture: filing cabinets opened and closed, typewriter keys typed, telephone dials rotated, and water bottles gurgled, all to the rhythm of music.

The influence of the Ernie Kovacs shows has been extensive. Dan Rowan, one of the hosts of *Rowan and Martin's Laugh-In,* said that many of that show's ideas came from Ernie Kovacs. On *Saturday Night Live,* another show directly influenced by the earlier comic, sight gags were so much a staple that when Chevy Chase received an Emmy for his performance on the show, he thanked Kovacs. And Kovacs's character "The Question Man," who supplied questions to answers submitted by the audience, reappeared as "Carnac" on *The Tonight Show Starring Johnny Carson.*

The Ernie Kovacs shows were products of the time when television was in its infancy and experimentation was acceptable. It is doubtful that Ernie Kovacs would find a place on television today. He was too zany, unrestrained, and undisciplined. Perhaps Jack Gould of the *New York Times* said it best: for Ernie Kovacs, "the fun was in trying."

LINDSY E. PACK

See also **Kovacs, Ernie**

Ernie in Kovacsland

Regular Performers
Ernie Kovacs
The Tony DeSimone Trio
Edith Adams

Producer
Ned Cramer

Programming History
NBC
July 1951–August 1951

The Ernie Kovacs Show (Kovacs Unlimited)

Regular Performers
Ernie Kovacs
Edie Adams
Ernie Hatrack
Trigger Lund
Andy McKay

Programming History
CBS
December 1952–April 1953

The Ernie Kovacs Show

Regular Performers
Ernie Kovacs
Edie Adams
Bill Wendell (1956)
Peter Hanley (1956)
Henry Lascoe (1956)
Al Kelly (1956)
Barbara Loden (1956)

Producers
Barry Shear, Jack Hein, Perry Cross

Programming History
NBC
December 1955–September 1956

Further Reading

Gould, Jack, "The Humor of Ernie Kovacs," *New York Times* (January 21, 1962)
"Kovacs Explains Wordless Shows," *New York Times* (December 21, 1955)
Rico, Diana, *Kovacsland: A Biography of Ernie Kovacs,* San Diego, California: Harcourt Brace, 1990
Whalley, David G., *Nothing in Moderation: A Biography of Ernie Kovacs,* New York: Drake, 1975

ESPN (Entertainment and Sports Network).

See **Sports and Television; Sportscasters**

Ethics and Television

Television ethics are derived from early professional codes of broadcasting that began in the late 1920s and are grounded in problems and issues identified in early radio. For U.S. television, these ethical systems came into their own and grew rapidly, in conjunction with the development of the new medium, during the 1960s. However, they now no longer exist as they once did.

Like radio for a previous generation, television has the ability to penetrate the private home, and its potential obtrusiveness has been the subject of concern. It is, after all, a "guest" in the home, and in that capacity it is able to serve the public interest—informing, instructing, and enlightening. It also has the power, recognized early on, to serve private interests driven by the desire for economic gain. The keen awareness of potential confrontation between service on the one hand and the desire for laissez-faire operation on the other historically led to another set of possible conflicts—between self-regulation and regulation by government. The U.S. broadcasting industry placed its faith and its interests in self-regulation.

The industry created its own Code of Broadcasting, which consisted of eight "rules." Four had to do with advertising and concern over "overcommercialization." The other rules dealt with general operations and responsible programming: no "fraudulent, deceptive,

or obscene" material. Many of these same ideas and even the language appeared again in the Television Code established in the early 1950s.

Early on, a vexing problem for the code, a potential problem in any ethical system, surfaced. It was the issue of penalties for violating the code. As in any system of self-regulated ethics, there was little room for harsh sanctions. The only penalty called for violators to be investigated and notified. Later, the penalty was strengthened by adding notification of violations to the broadcast community—the threat of ostracism among colleagues. When television came on the scene, American radio had recently experienced rapid growth in its commercialization. With that growth came continuing threats of further, more far-reaching regulation from the Federal Communications Commission and the Federal Trade Commission. In an effort to keep the government regulators at bay, the broadcasters' Code of Good Practice became more definitive. One of the main elements focused on regulation of the amount of time that should be devoted to commercials.

The evolution of the code can be seen by examining the use of commercial time in the 1930s. While there could be some advertising (of a goodwill nature) before 6:00 P.M., according to the code, "commercial announcements, as the term is generally understood,

817

should not be broadcast between 7 and 11 P.M." That restriction then evolved to allow increased broadcasting of commercial messages to 5 minutes, then 10, and then 18 by 1970. When television assumed a dominant place in broadcasting, beginning in the early 1950s, the rules affecting commercial time in that medium evolved the same way, increasing the allowed time slowly over the years.

Although the National Association of Broadcasters (NAB) created a separate set of ethical guidelines for television, distinct from radio, the existing concerns were applied to the newer medium: time limits of advertising, types of products advertised, fraud (especially in advertising), and special sensitivity to programming and advertising directed to children. Other program themes, obviously taboo in their times, such as sexual suggestiveness and explicit violence, were also addressed.

At the same time, each U.S. network installed its own staff for network Standards and Practices (S and P) to enforce the network's particular policies for advertising and programming. These were the offices and individuals often thought of as "network censors." Large corporations also created statements of policies concerning their professional ethics as related to broadcasting.

These network and company rules for self-regulation were supplementary to the NAB's continuation of its two nationally visible codes, one for radio and one for television. These codes, however, were becoming unwieldy. A dozen or so pages of the Television Code of Good Practice contained a long list of programming prohibitions: hypnotism, occultism, and astrology as well as obscene, profane, or indecent material and programs that ridiculed those with disabilities.

Still, the NAB codes remained an important public relations device for the industry. At the apex of the codes' use, NAB President Vince Wasilewski stated, "Our Codes are not peripheral activities. No activity of NAB is closer to the public."

As social mores changed and social and cultural climates became more permissive, so too did television programming. By the late 1970s and early 1980s, the code seemed hopelessly outdated, continually violated, unenforceable, and generally ignored by the broadcasters.

In 1982, when advertisers were lined up for a limited amount of available time on the television networks, it appeared that the networks gave favor for its best time slots to the largest advertisers. Displeased, one of the smaller advertisers pointed out this practice to the U.S. Justice Department, claiming unfair competitive practices, a violation of antitrust laws. The Justice Department took action against the NAB because, it said, the NAB code, which limited the amount of available commercial time, was responsible for the network practice. The court agreed and ordered the NAB to purge that part of the code. After some initial hesitancy, the NAB agreed.

For eight years, from 1982 to 1990, neither radio nor television in the United States had a code of professional ethics. During that period, research showed that although the networks and some large corporate broadcasters had their own codes (or standards and practices), there still seemed to be no universal guidance. One study, based on a national sample of broadcast managers, suggested that broadcasters preferred self-regulation rather than government regulation. It also suggested some concern that without such self-regulation, government regulation might increase.

In 1990, the NAB issued a new "Statement of Principles of Radio and Television Broadcasting," designed as a brief, general document intended to reflect the generally accepted standards of American broadcasting. The statement encouraged broadcasters to write individually their own specific policies. It also encouraged responsible and careful judgment in the selection of material for broadcast rather than forming a list of prohibitions, as was the case with the old code. Caution was advised in dealing with violence, drugs and substance abuse, and sexually oriented materials, but there was also positive encouragement for responsible artistic freedom and responsibility in children's programming. The statement made it clear that these principles are advisory rather than restrictive. Finally, the 1990 statement mentioned First Amendment rights of free speech and encouraged broadcasters to align themselves with the audiences' expectations and the public interest. In sum, the new philosophy concerning ethics in broadcasting reveals that (1) they are advisory rather than prohibitive; (2) they should be centered in individual stations or corporations rather than a national organization like the NAB; (3) since there is no provision for monitoring and enforcement on the national level, any concerns about ethics should come from individual stations and listeners/viewers; and (4) the decentralization of ethics may be indicative of a pluralistic society, where values and mores reflect distinct group perspectives rather than a national standard.

Some observers bemoan the fact that there is no nationally visible standard—no way of measuring whether the language of a daring new television program is actually on the "cutting edge" or merely "bravado bunk." Yet since the broadcast industry itself has been largely deregulated, the question remains whether this means there is now room for more self-regulation or whether self-regulation itself should also be deregulated.

VAL E. LIMBURG

See also **National Association of Broadcasters**

Further Reading

"Broadcasters Seek to Clean Up the Industry and Hope to Regulate Commercial Activities on the Air," *New York Times* (April 7, 1929)

Donaldson, Tom, "Ethical Dilemmas," *Electronic Media* (March 29, 1988)

Limburg, Val E., "The Decline of Broadcast Ethics: U.S. v. N.A.B.," *Journal of Mass Media Ethics* (1989)

Limburg, Val E., *Electronic Media Ethics,* Boston, Massachusetts: Focal Press, 1994

National Association of Broadcasters, *The Challenge of Self-Regulation,* Washington, D.C.: National Association of Broadcasters, 1966

National Association of Broadcasters, *Statement of Principles of Radio and Television Broadcasting,* Washington, D.C.: National Association of Broadcasters, 1990

"National Broadcasters Meet at Chicago and Adopt Code of Ethics," *New York Times* (March 16, 1929)

White, Llewellyn, *The American Radio,* Chicago: University of Chicago Press, 1947

Ethnicity. *See* Racism, Ethnicity, and Television

European Audiovisual Observatory

The European Audiovisual Observatory is an information service network for the audiovisual profession. It was initiated by professional media practitioners in conjunction with government authorities to meet increasing information needs in the audiovisual sector. These groups expressed a common commitment toward improved flow and access to information and toward more transparent information related to the television, cinema, video/DVD, and new media sectors of the media industries. The observatory was set up to provide reliable information services and also to improve the infrastructure of information collection and dissemination in Europe.

Established in December 1992, the observatory's membership in 2002 included 35 European states and the European Community (represented by the European Commission). With its headquarters in Strasbourg, France, the observatory was created under the auspices of Audiovisual Eureka and functions within the framework of the Council of Europe.

A unique European public service organization, the observatory provides information services to the European television, cinema, video, and new media industries. In particular, the observatory serves the information needs of the decision makers of production, broadcasting, and distribution. Public administrators, consultants, lawyers, researchers, and journalists needing information on the audiovisual sector are all target user groups of its services.

The observatory provides market, economic, legal, and practical information relevant to audiovisual production and distribution. In particular, it aims to direct those requesting information to the best information available, and it coordinates pan-European work to collect and analyze data in ways that foster insightful comparisons across national boundaries.

The observatory has several core services. These services provide rapid response to daily information needs as well as to long-term development needs for better data collection methods. The information service desk handles individual requests for information. It is designed to answer questions quickly and accurately and covers all three information areas of the observatory: market, legal, and practical information.

In addition, the observatory disseminates several publications, including an annual *Statistical Yearbook: Cinema, Television, Video, and New Media in Europe;* a monthly journal, *IRIS—Legal Observations of the European Audiovisual Observatory;* and studies such as *Public Aid Mechanisms for the Film and the Audiovisual Industry in Europe,* which offers comparative information about sources of government funding for production in various European nations. Available from the observatory's online publications department are numerous documents on such topics as industrial taxes, copyright law, television–film coproduction contracts, advertising aimed at children, digital television's development, licensing laws in specific nations, and supply and demand in European Internet usage. The observatory's website further provides copies of its press releases and many links to additional sources of information and to directories of industry contacts.

To fulfill its objective to coordinate the establishment of transparent European data, the observatory advises on questions relating to data collection and the accessibility of information sources, and it organizes expert workshops seeking improved and more comparable European data in the audiovisual sector. Furthermore, as part of its 2000–02 "action plan," the observatory has placed high priority on creating online databases providing integrated data to researchers.

The information services of the observatory are based on its network of partners and correspondents. Covering greater Europe, this cooperative network currently includes hundreds of information providers: public and private research and information organizations, universities, consultants, individual experts, ministries and administrations, and regional network organizations in the media field. By centrally coordinating this multitude of sources, the observatory gives access to the most reliable and updated information on the European audiovisual industry.

Partners are information or research organizations that have an established track record of providing reliable information in the audiovisual field on the European or the global level. Each partner has a specific responsibility or thematic area regarding information collection and provision. Partners help the observatory perform its services and play an essential role in assisting the observatory in its work toward harmonization of European audiovisual information.

Correspondent organizations are professional information organizations, and they complement and assist the observatory and its partners in collecting information from the member states. Correspondent organizations also advise on data collection and on the accuracy and relevance of the information from their specific country. In each member state, there are different correspondents for legal, market and economic, and practical information.

European professional organizations are widely represented in the observatory's advisory committee. Some of these organizations collect and maintain databases from their own areas of interest in the audiovisual sector. These organizations have also agreed to collaborate with the observatory in collecting and providing the most reliable data in their field of specialty.

ISMO SILVO AND ELIZABETH NISHIURA

Further Reading

Statistical Yearbook 2001: Cinema, Television, Video and New Media in Europe, Strasbourg, France: European Audiovisual Observatory, 2001

European Broadcasting Union

The European Broadcasting Union (EBU) is the largest professional association of national public service broadcasters in the world. It acts as a broker through which broadcasters in the European region and worldwide can exchange radio and television services and, in particular, news footage and complete programs via Eurovision for television and Euroradio for radio. It stimulates and coordinates coproductions and provides a full range of other operational, commercial, technical, legal, and strategic services.

The EBU has its administrative headquarters in Geneva, where it also maintains the Eurovision control center. It has TV news coordination bureaus in New York, Washington, and Moscow and an office in Brussels, which represents the interests of public service broadcasters before the European institutions. Its much smaller and younger counterpart, the Association of Commercial Television in Europe (ACT), caters to the interests of commercial/private broadcasting stations in Europe.

The EBU was founded on February 12, 1950, by 23 mainly Western European broadcasting stations at a conference in the Devonshire coastal resort of Torquay, England. Following the political changes in Eastern Europe, in 1993 the EBU merged with the International Radio and Television Organization (OIRT), the former umbrella organization of radio and TV services in Eastern Europe. The EBU now has 71 active full members from 52 countries in Europe, North Africa, and the Middle East and 45 associate members in 28 more countries. Members are radio and television companies, most of which are public service broadcasters or privately owned stations with public missions. Full active members are based in countries from Algeria to the Vatican, including almost all European countries. Associate members are not limited to those from European countries and the Mediterranean but include broadcasters from Australia, Canada, Japan, Mexico, Brazil, India, and Hong Kong as well as many others. Associate members from the United States include the American Broadcasting Company (ABC), the Columbia Broadcasting System (CBS), the National Broadcasting Company (NBC), and the Corporation for Public Broadcasting. At a global level, EBU works in close collaboration with sister unions on other continents: the Asia Pacific Broadcasting Union (ABU), the North American Broadcasters' Association (NABA), the Union of National Radio & Television Organizations of Africa (URTNA), the Arab States Broadcasting Union (ASBU), and the Organización de la Televisión Iberoamericana (OTI).

Based in Geneva, the EBU is a nongovernmental international association governed by Swiss law and its own statutes. It is the successor to the first international association of broadcasters, the International Broadcasting Union (1925), which was also based in Geneva. Its principal aims are to promote cooperation between members and with broadcasting organizations throughout the world and to represent its members' interests in the legal, technical, and programming fields.

The EBU is administered by a general assembly that meets annually and elects an administrative council composed of 15 active members. A president and two vice presidents are chosen by the assembly from among the representatives of the members making up the council. Council membership is for four years, with reelection permitted. Because the EBU is based in Switzerland, the Swiss member, Société Suisse de Radiodiffusion et Télévision (SSR), has a permanent seat on the council. Four permanent committees—the Radio Department, the Television Department, the Legal Department, and the Technical Department—report to the council on their working and ad hoc groups. Day-to-day operations are carried out by the Permanent Services staff, headed by the secretary-general.

One of the major activities of the EBU is the Eurovision scheme, consisting of program pooling and joint purchasing operations. Eurovision was the idea of Marcel Bezençon, once director of the SSR and president of the EBU. Eurovision was and is a television program clearinghouse that facilitates the exchange of programming between national networks throughout Europe. One of the early successes of the EBU was the relay on June 2, 1953, of the transmission of the coro-

© EBU

nation of Queen Elizabeth II to France, Belgium, the Netherlands, and Germany. The official birth of Eurovision as an international television network occurred on June 6, 1954, when the Narcissus Festival from Montreaux, Switzerland, opened a series of live transmissions, the "Television Summer Season of 1954."

Today the Eurovision permanent global network (of up to 50 digital channels on five different satellites) carries constant exchanges of news and programs. Each year, around 30,000 news items and 4,000 programs are transmitted. The EBU is often the operator of the only generally available broadcasting facilities in crisis situations, such as during the Gulf War or the conflicts in Rwanda, the Balkans, and the Middle East. The news exchange began on a trial basis in 1958 and became regularized in 1961. It has been supplemented by a multilingual channel known as Euronews, which began broadcasting in English, French, German, Italian, and Spanish on January 1, 1993, from Lyon, France. Euronews is designed to provide Europeans with world and local news coverage from a European viewpoint. The individual coverage of television channels (members and non-members) also transits via the Eurovision network. In 2001, the EBU's operational staff routed more than 120,000 transmissions.

Another major Eurovision activity is cultural and sports programming. Approximately 12,000 hours of sports and cultural programs are transmitted on an annual basis. Eurovision operates a joint purchasing scheme for international sporting events such as the Olympic Games and the World Soccer Championships. When members from two or more EBU countries are interested in a sporting event, they request coordination from the EBU, which either carries on negotiations itself or deputizes a member to do so on behalf of the EBU. Members may not carry out negotiations for national rights after joint negotiations have commenced, unless the joint negotiations fail. If the joint negotiations succeed, the rights are acquired on behalf of the interested members, who share the rights.

Television cooperation is also important in other areas ranging from educational programs, documentaries, and coproductions of animation series to competitions for young musicians, young dancers, and screenwriters as well as traditional light entertainment, such as the Eurovision Song Contest.

Radio collaboration is a multifaceted activity covering music, news, sports, youth programs, and local and regional stations. The Euroradio satellite network carries, on average, some 2,000 concerts and operas, 400 sports events. and 120 major news events each year. In 1998, the EBU launched the first interbroadcaster European music channel, specializing in classical music (Euroclassic-Notturno). The EBU's next goal is to become a major player in popular contemporary music. The new Eurosonic unit is developing partnerships with artists and record labels and acquiring broadcasting rights to major rock and pop festivals.

Cooperation in the technical sphere is another of the EBU's major activities. The EBU is at the forefront of research and development of new broadcast media and digital online services and has led or contributed to the development of many new radio and TV systems: radio data system (RDS), digital audio broadcasting (DAB), digital video broadcasting (DVB), and high-definition TV (HDTV).

JAN SERVAES

See also **Eurovision Song Contest**

Further Reading

Brack, Hans, *The Evolution of the EBU Through Its Statutes from 1950 to 1976,* Geneva, Switzerland: European Broadcasting Union, 1976

Eugster, Ernest, *Television Programming Across National Boundaries: The EBU and OIRT Experiences,* Dedham, Massachusetts: Artech, 1983

Type, Michael, "Facing the Future with Confidence: The EBU Celebrates 40 Years of Achievement," in *EBU Review: Programmes, Administration, Law,* Geneva, Switzerland, 1990.

European Commercial Broadcasting Satellite

ASTRA, the first independent European commercial satellite broadcasting system, commenced transmissions via a single satellite in early 1989. By 1995, with four satellites operative, it had already achieved penetration of more than 60 million households (more than 150 million people) in 22 European countries. This equaled 35 percent of the estimated 160 million TV households within the geographical target area and a 15 percent increase since 1993. By September 2001, coverage had increased enormously to 12 satellites, offering 53 analogue (PAL or D2Mac standard) and 595 digital television channels, plus 415 analog and digital radio channels, together reaching more than 89 million households.

The ASTRA system is owned and operated by SES ASTRA (originally Société Européen des Satellites), which began as a private company incorporated in Luxembourg and trading under a 25-year renewable franchise agreement with the Grand Duchy, which retains a 20 percent interest. Founded in March 1985 with the backing of private commercial interests all over Europe, SES ASTRA has headquarters at the Château de Betzdorf in Luxembourg. From there, it uplinks TV and radio signals to the orbiting satellite craft that constitute the system. The company's revenue is generated largely by leasing satellite transponders—effectively the equivalent of channel slots—to broadcasting organizations that pay annual rentals reputedly as high as £5 million per transponder. In 2001, there were as many as 176 separate transponders on the system, which continues to expand with the addition of further craft. Despite the challenges of economic recession, media deregulation, audience fragmentation, and the rise of the Internet, SES ASTRA has found no shortage of potential customers, with transponder availability on each new satellite subject to heavy demand from broadcasters willing to gamble high investment costs and short-term unprofitability for healthier returns later.

The ASTRA satellite system began as an analog-only enterprise but has progressively moved over to digital technology. The very first satellite, *ASTRA 1A,* was launched in December 1988 from the European Space Center in Kourou, French Guiana, aboard an *Ariane 4* rocket. It became operational in February 1989, 35,975 kilometers above the equator at its geostationary orbital position of 19.2 degrees east longitude. This was the first commercial European satellite specifically dedicated to television and radio transmission. The system was subsequently augmented by the launch of *ASTRA 1B* in March 1991, while *1C* followed in May 1993, *1D* in November 1994, and *1E* in October 1995, all co-located at the same orbital position and with an active life span of 10 to 12 years. The "footprint," or geographical universe, of this satellite constellation extends from Iceland and Norway in the north to coastal Morocco, Sardinia, and Belgrade in the south and from the Canary Islands in the west to Warsaw and Budapest in the east, with some reception possible even as far east as Helsinki.

ASTRA 1D inaugurated a significant new phase of technological development, for it was the first satellite in the system capable of operating in the Broadcast Satellite Services (BSS) frequency band reserved for digital transmissions. As such, it provided capacity for the first European digital test transmissions conducted in collaboration with key hardware manufacturers and programmers. Additional satellites carrying digital capability were progressively added to the system—*1F* in 1996, *1G* in 1997, and *1H* in 1999—with the initial series of satellites co-located at 19.2 degrees east, due for completion with the launch of *1K* in 2002. Meanwhile, SES ASTRA had begun to open up new orbital slots with a second series of powerful broadcasting satellites: *ASTRA 2A* was launched into position at 28.2 degrees east in August 1998, to be followed in September 2000 by *2B,* in December 2000 by *2D,* and in June 2001 by the delayed *2C,* bringing the system up to a total of 12 satellites. A third orbital slot at 23.5 degrees east was used for the inauguration of the third series, with the launch of *ASTRA 3A* in 2002.

The available services are accessed via one of three methods of delivery, the most visible being an individual, direct-to-home dish antenna (DTH), which can be fixed or motorized and which, for successful reception in the footprint's central belt, can be as small as 60 centimeters in diameter for analog signals or even smaller for digital ones. Alternatively, in the case of viewers in multioccupancy dwellings, reception is via communal, satellite master antenna systems (SMATV). Many other viewers, including a large proportion in Germany, the Netherlands, and Belgium, receive satellite-originated signals relayed over cable networks.

Courtesy of ASTRA

A major factor in the early success of SES ASTRA was Rupert Murdoch's 1988 decision to become ASTRA's first commercial client, taking four transponders initially on *ASTRA 1A* for his incipient Sky Television Service (subsequently renamed British Sky Broadcasting, or BSkyB), aimed principally at English-speaking audiences in the United Kingdom and western Europe. A considerable number of German broadcasting interests also migrated early to ASTRA's evolving system, which was soon enabling diverse program services in a wide variety of languages, ushering in a new era of themed private television and radio channels as alternatives to the general entertainment models commonly associated with terrestrial broadcasting. Many of these channels are transmitted in encrypted or scrambled form, available only to contracted subscribers possessing the necessary decoding device. Movies, sports, music, news, children, documentary, nostalgia, and shopping channels are the most consistently popular, while a large number of "adult" channels broadcast late at night.

Networks and program providers were quick to respond to the digital delivery options presented by SES ASTRA in the 1990s. In November 1994, the profitable French subscription channel Canal Plus concluded a long-term agreement with SES ASTRA, covering six transponders for digital transmission of the channel's program bundle to the various European-language markets. In 1998, BSkyB began its Sky Digital service via the second series of ASTRA satellites while beginning progressively to phase out analog transmissions. Hundreds of television and radio channels can be accessed via the BSkyB Electronic Programme Guide (EPG), made possible by the compression ratio available under ASTRA's digital technology. In addition to regular subscription offerings, pay-per-view and interactive program services have become commonplace, while new program propositions (including the British Broadcasting Corporation's [BBC's] new digital channels) continuously vie for audience attention.

Being first to market has helped SES ASTRA achieve a position of increasing dominance, to the extent that it has developed into a truly global media player. In 1998, the company completed its initial offering on the Luxembourg Stock Exchange. A year later, it acquired a 34 percent stake in AsiaSat and went on to purchase extensive holdings in Nordic Satellite and Embratel Satellite, thereby extending its reach to the Scandinavian and Latin American markets. In 2001, SES ASTRA combined with GE Americom to create a worldwide satellite operation and restructured itself as a wholly owned company of SES GLOBAL. The company's activities have diversified with the rapid development of broadband Internet and positioned it at the forefront of multimedia by satellite. Its ASTRA-NET platform enables content-rich data to be delivered at high speeds to personal computers in businesses and homes, allowing Internet service providers to offer conventional Internet access via existing digital satellite antennas. Another SES ASTRA project, the Broadband Interactive System, provides send-and-receive capability for data, video, and audio at speeds of up to 2 megabits. In less than two decades, a modest Luxembourg-based private company has successfully pioneered the distribution of nonterrestrial television across Europe and evolved into a public multimedia enterprise of international significance.

TONY PEARSON

See also **British Sky Broadcasting**

Further Reading

Alderman, Bruce, "Europe's TV Hopes Soar with Astra: Finally Launched DBS Bird's 16 Channels Promise a New Era for Commercial TV," *Variety* (December 14, 1988)

"Astra, Euro Broadcast Satellite, Augurs New Era on Continent," *Variety* (February 8, 1989)

Collins, Richard, *Satellite Television in Western Europe,* London: John Libbey, 1990

Fox, Barry, "Satellite Broadcasters Battle in the Sky," *New Scientist* (October 22, 1988)

Fox, Barry, "Astra Ups Its Options with Extra Satellites, *New Scientist* (December 15, 1990)

Levine, Jonathan B., "This Satellite Company Runs Rings around Rivals," *BusinessWeek* (February 11, 1991)

Margolis, Irv, "Europe's Satellite Picture: Cloudy or Bright?" *Television-Radio Age* (June 27, 1988)

Marwick, Peat, *Satellite Personal Communications and Their Consequences for European Telecommunications, Trade, and Industry: Executive Summary: Report to the European Commission,* Brussels: European Commission, 1994

Spellman, James D., "Private Satellites," *Europe* (November 1993)

Television by Satellite and Cable, Strasbourg, France: Council of Europe, 1985

Towards Europe-Wide Systems and Services: Green Paper on a Common Approach in the Field of Satellite Communications in the European Community, Brussels: Commission of the European Communities, 1990

European Union: Television Policy

The process of European integration was launched on May 9, 1950, when France officially proposed to create "the first concrete foundation of a European federation." Six countries (Belgium, Germany, France, Italy, Luxembourg, and the Netherlands) joined from the very beginning. In 2002, after four waves of accessions (1973: Denmark, Ireland, and the United Kingdom; 1981: Greece; 1986: Spain and Portugal; 1995: Austria, Finland, and Sweden), the European Union (EU) has 15 member states and is preparing for the accession of 13 eastern and southern European countries. Among the most important objectives for the founding of a European Federation were the creation of a common market and an increase in economic integration among the member states.

Television policy in the EU reflects the underlying purpose of promoting European integration and abolishing national barriers to the free movement of goods and services within the common market. By decision of the European Court of Justice in Sacchi (1974), a television signal is considered a provision of services under Articles 59 and 60 of the Treaty of Rome, and national barriers to cross-frontier broadcasting or the establishment of broadcasters from one member state in another are intended to be abolished in most circumstances.

The EU's audiovisual policy is based on regulations and financial instruments. In a matter of about ten years, this policy has gained a firm footing both internally, with the so-called Television Without Frontiers (TWF) Directive, the MEDIA Plus program, and the intervention of the European Investment Bank and externally with its position in World Trade Organization negotiations. The EU's single most important initiative in audiovisual policy is the promotion of a single EU audiovisual market, the TWF Directive of October 3, 1989. It secures access for viewers and listeners in all member states to broadcasting signals emanating from any other member state and regularizes EU broadcast advertising standards.

The European Parliament's Hahn Report on Radio and Television Broadcasting in the EC (1982) laid the groundwork for the formal TWF Directive. The Hahn Report advocated establishment of a unified European television channel and saw satellite television technology leading to a reorganization of the media in Europe and breaking down of the boundaries of national television networks.

The original TWF Directive was amended on June 30, 1997, to "increase the legal certainty and update the wording of the Directive." As of 2003, the directive is undergoing another revision in order to assess the impact of technological and market developments. The main issues in the debate on the TWF Directive revolve around the following:

- Programming quotas: broadcasters should, where practicable, reserve a majority of airtime for European programs. Additionally, 10 percent of a broadcaster's schedule should be programs made by independent producers.
- Advertising: there are detailed rules on the content of television advertising (e.g., concerning children), the duration (15 percent of daily broadcasting time, 20 percent per hour), the methods of program interruptions, the form of natural breaks, and ethical considerations (particularly for children). Advertising that promotes discrimination on grounds of race, sex, or nationality; that is offensive to religious beliefs; or that encourages behavior prejudicial to health, safety, or the protection of the environment is prohibited or restricted.

In addition, the TWF Directive lays down minimum standards that, if met by any television program, allow it to freely circulate within the EU without restriction, provided that it complies with the legislation of the country of origin. The directive contains chapters devoted to promotion of television program production and distribution, protection of minors, television sponsorship, access of the public to major (sports) events, and right of reply. A right of reply is accorded to any person or organization whose legitimate interests have been damaged by an incorrect assertion of fact in a television program. Therefore, the European Consumers' Organization (BEUC) wants clear provisions concerning an effective processing system for complaints while ensuring that the rights of consumers in their own country are not unduly infringed on by television broadcasts from other countries.

The TWF Directive also lays down two other policies that have an effect similar to the establishment of quotas on broadcasting in the EU. First, the directive requires member states to ensure "where practicable" and by "appropriate means" that broadcasters reserve for "European works" a majority of their transmission time, exclusive of news, sports events, game shows, advertising, and teletext services. This is intended to protect 50 percent or more of transmission time so defined from foreign (non-EU) competition. The second quota, designed to stimulate the production of European drama work, requires broadcasters to reserve 10 percent or more of their transmission time (as above) or, alternatively, 10 percent of their programming budget for European works created by producers who are "independent of broadcasters" (TWF Directive, art. 5). The time between a film being released and being broadcast on television shall be two years and one year for films coproduced with radio.

During the late 1980s and early 1990s, concern developed in Europe that a single market in television was an economic threat to national broadcasting markets and national media as well as a threat to cultural and linguistic diversity in Europe. The threat is seen to derive from English-language services and productions in that only the United States is considered to have film and television industries organized on a scale large enough to take advantage of the single market. However, according to the 2001 Eurofiction poll, national works account for 75 percent of TV fiction broadcast during prime time in France, 56 percent in Germany, 51 percent in Spain, and 43 percent in Italy, even though American productions still represent 50 percent for the day's transmission time as a whole on most European channels.

Therefore, concern at the European level for the protection and aid of European programming has led to audiovisual industry subsidy programs, such as the European Commission's MEDIA Action Plan for Advanced Television and MEDIA Plus programs and the Council of Europe's Eurimages fund. These are collectively intended to support and stimulate independent production and distribution networks for European works that are currently considered noncompetitive with U.S. programming imports.

The EU's television policy thus simultaneously pursues the economic objective of creating a single market in broadcasting along with the fostering of cultural pluralism and protection of existing national and subnational broadcasting markets and institutions. The TWF approach, rooted in the fundamental purpose of the EU, has so far had more impact than other protectionist policies. However, there are sharp differences between member states that could ultimately lead to less economic integration and more cultural and economic protectionism.

In addition, the European Commission is advocating a more integrated approach to audiovisual and digital technologies. To this end, it has launched a number of programs under the overall heading of the European Information Society.

JAN SERVAES

Further Reading

Aubry, Patrice, *The "Television Without Frontiers" Directive, Cornerstone of the European Broadcasting Policy,* Strasbourg: European Audiovisual Observatory, 2000

European Audiovisual Observatory, *The Yearbook Film, Television, Video and Multimedia in Europe,* 5 volumes, 8th edition, Strasbourg: European Audiovisual Observatory, 2002

European Commission, "The Fabulous Destiny of European Cinema. Challenges for an EU Audiovisual Policy," *Le Magazine. Education and Culture in Europe,* Issue 17 (2002)

Lange, Andre, "The Imbalance of Trade in Films and Television Programmes Between North America and Europe Continues to Deteriorate" (April 9, 2002), http://www.obs.coe.int/about/oea/pr/desequilibre.html

Liikanen, Erkki, "The New Communications Directives and Their Benefits for the Audiovisual Sector," in *Paper European Voice Conference "Television Without Frontiers,"* Brussels: European Commission, March 21, 2002

Nikoltchev, Susanne, "Changing Aspects of Broadcasting: New Territory and New Challenges," *Iris Plus. Legal Observations,* Issue 10 (2001).

Reding, Viviane, *European Voice Conference on "Television Without Frontiers."* Brussels: European Commission, March 21, 2002

Eurovision Song Contest

International Music Program

The Eurovision Song Contest (ESC) is a live, televised music competition that has received widespread ridicule since its debut in 1956. Certainly this has been true of the contest's reception in the United Kingdom, which informs the perspective from which this entry is written. Yet, as its longevity indicates, the program's importance within European television history is undeniable. While critics plead for the plug to be pulled on this annual celebration of pop mediocrity, the ESC continues unabated, extending its media reach (if not its musical scope) from year to year. The competition is truly massive in terms of its logistical and technical requirements, the audience figures and record sales it engenders, and the significance of the popular cultural moments it produces.

The ESC is the flagship of Eurovision light-entertainment programming. Eurovision is the television network supervised by the European Broadcasting Union (EBU) and was established in the early 1950s to serve two functions: to share the costs of programming with international interest among the broadcasting services of member nations and to promote cultural appreciation and identification throughout western Europe. At the time of the first Eurovision broadcast in 1954, there were fewer than 5 million television receivers on the whole continent (90 percent of these were in England). The network now stretches into northern Africa, the Middle East, and eastern Europe, with most transmissions conveyed via satellite to the receiving stations of member nations for terrestrial broadcast.

The overwhelming majority of Eurovision transmissions have fallen into the sports, news, and public affairs categories. In the 1950s, EBU officials, perceiving the need for the dissemination of popular cultural programming to offset the influence of the U.S. media, decided to extend Italy's San Remo Song Festival into a pan-European occasion. This became the ESC, with the first competition being held in Lugano, Switzerland, and relayed to fewer than 20 na-

Sertab Erener, representing Turkey, winner of the 2003 Eurovision Song Contest.
© EBU

tions. Since that time, the contest has developed into a spring ritual now viewed by around 600 million people in more than 30 countries, including several in Asia, the Middle East, and the Americas (some of these nations do not even send representatives to the competition).

The ESC is a long, live Saturday-evening showcase of pop music talent that typically ranges from the indescribably bad, through the insufferably indifferent, to a few catchy little numbers. Contestants are chosen by their respective nations during preliminary stages. The duly nominated acts, as cultural ambassadors for their countries, then attend the big event and perform their tunes.

Conventionally, the host nation is determined by the winner of the previous year's contest. For example, Gigliola Cinquetti's triumph of 1964, "Non ho l'età," resulted in Radiotelevisione Italiana playing host in 1965. When an Estonian duo, Tanel Padar and Dave Benton, won in 2001, there was some question as to whether Estonia's economically troubled public televi-

sion channel, ETV, had the funds to produce the program (or any other programming) in 2002. In the end, ETV secured a government loan and decided that the publicity for the nation was worth the expense.

The ESC is designed to be a grand affair, with expensive sets, full orchestra accompaniment, and a "special night out" atmosphere. Best behavior is expected from all concerned. Following the performances, panels of judges from each nation submit their point allocations to the central auditorium where the contest is taking place, and a "high-tech" scoreboard tabulates the cumulative scores. As even the most ardent of critics will attest, this is a special moment for home viewers—one where elements particular to the ESC (technological accomplishment, anticipation induced by the live event, and intercultural differences) combine for curious effect. Will your country's representatives beat the competition and incur the envy of other Europeans? Will the juries throw objectivity to the wind and vote according to national prejudice? Or will, as occurred to Norway's hapless Jahn Teigen on that unforgettable May night in 1978, a contestant endure the humiliating fate of receiving no points whatsoever?

Like its late-lamented Eurovision companion, Jeux Sans Frontières (JSF), the ESC pays homage to clean, amateur fun and the elevation of the unknown to the status of national hero. Unlike the excessively carnival-esque JSF, however, the ESC attempts to avoid the very absurdity and mockery it unwittingly generates. For its first decade, the ESC was a wholesome, formal affair: the amorous ballads it featured helped create a chasm between the competition's cultural mission and that of rock music that has never been bridged. In the late 1960s and early 1970s, youth orientation became a primary factor in determining victory. The 1968 winner, "La la la..." from Spain's Massiel, inspired a succession of entries incorporating childish lyrics that avoided identifiable linguistic origins in order to garner wide jury appeal. A similar delve into formulism was initiated by the British Sandy Shaw the following year: "Puppet on a String" evoked a generically pan-European musical heritage with its oompah brass and circus-ground melodies. In their triumphant international debut on the ESC in 1974, Abba opted to perform in English and sang about a continentally recognizable historical event in a song titled "Waterloo." The Swedish quartet's glam sensibilities and subsequent commercial success multiplied the contest's kitsch quotient tenfold and launched a string of two-girl/two-boy combos in its wake. Indicating its own concern over the increasingly imitative nature of the competition, the EBU stipulated various edicts that generated a spate of regional, folk-influenced entries in the late 1970s, all of which scored poorly with the judges. The 1980s witnessed the ascension of overchoreographed performance and more explicit attempts to excite juries and viewers with soft, sanitized sex appeal. Efforts to resuscitate the ESC as a viable musical forum have resulted in more recent efforts to modernize the look and style of the contest and to encourage a more professional approach to promotion through the participation of the corporate music industry.

In estimating the significance of the ESC, perhaps less attention should be given to its bloated festivity or the derivative nature of the contenders' music. While its cultural merits are dubious, the event has become a television landmark. Its durability and notoriety have led the EBU to support the Eurovision Competition for Young Musicians and the Eurovision Competition for Young Dancers in order to further promote Eurocentric cultural understanding through televised stage performance.

MATTHEW MURRAY

See also **European Broadcasting Union**

Further Reading

Barnes, Julian, "Pit Props," *New Statesman* (April 6, 1979)

Collins, Michael, "Eurotrash," *Punch* (May 5, 1989)

Dessau, Bruce, "Song Without End," *The Listener* (April 28, 1988)

Eugster, Ernest, *Television Programming Across National Boundaries: The EBU and OIRT Experience,* Dedham, Massachusetts: Artech House, 1983

Kressley, Konrad M., "EUROVISION: Distributing Costs and Benefits in an International Broadcasting Union," *Journal of Broadcasting* (Spring 1978)

Experimental Video

Experimental video, video art, electronic art, alternative TV, community video, guerrilla television, computer art: these are a few of the labels that have been applied to a body of work that began to emerge in the United States in the 1960s. Arguably, the most important of these labels is "experimental." The dominant goal of this video movement over the past 30 years has been change, achieved through the strategy of experimentation. The consistent target for this change has been television—commercially supported, network broadcast, mainstream television—whose success with mass audiences was the result of the repetition of proven formulas rather than aesthetic, ideological, or industrial innovation or experimentation. It is perhaps commercial television's ability to interpret the uncertain world within the context of familiar conventions that makes it an essential part of everyday life in America. And it is this body of familiar interpretations that became the challenge of experimental video artists.

In his book *Expanded Cinema* (1970), media visionary Gene Youngblood states that "commercial entertainment works against art (experimentation), exploits the alienation and boredom of the public, by perpetuating a system of conditioned response to formulas."

Youngblood's manifesto goes on to argue that any community requires experimentation in order to survive. He concludes, "The artist is always an anarchist, a revolutionary, a creator of new worlds imperceptibly gaining on reality."

One of the earliest of the video revolutionaries was Korean-born artist Nam June Paik. When he landed in the United States in 1964, Paik was already anxious to lead the experimental video revolution. One of his earliest works, *TV Magnet* (1965), challenged the viewing public to reexamine "television." Paik took a piece of furniture, the TV set, and changed its meaning by presenting it as sculpture. He demystified television by altering the magnetic polarity of the cathode-ray tube, demonstrating that the lines of light on the screen were clearly controlled by the large magnet sitting on top of the set rather than by some magical connection to the "real world." Most significant, he changed the viewers' role as passive consumers to active creators by allowing them to interact with the piece by moving the magnet, thereby participating in the creation of the light patterns on the screen.

Paik is also credited with purchasing the first Sony Portapak, the first truly portable videotape recorder, in 1965. Usually, the Sony Portapak and not the altered TV set has been identified with the beginning of experimental video. For the first time, the low cost of the Portapak and its portability gave the experimental artists access to the means of producing television. Legend has it that Paik met a cargo boat in New York harbor, grabbed a Portapak, rode through the city in a cab shooting video, and that night showed his street scenes, including the visit of Pope Paul VI, in Cafe a Go Go.

But Paik was not operating alone. In 1964, the same year Paik moved to the United States, Marshall McLuhan published *Understanding Media*. His declaration that "the medium is the message" became key passwords for Paik and a generation of experimental video makers who hoped to design and build a "Global Village" through alternative uses of telecommunications.

Many of these video artists followed the tradition of avant-garde filmmakers, seeking to define the unique properties of their medium. By the early 1970s, experimental video makers were trying to find ways to isolate the unique properties of video's electronic image. A profusion of technical devices began to appear, most notably among them a variety of color synthesizers. Paik developed one synthesizer in collaboration with Shuya Abe. Concurrently, Stephen Beck, Peter Campus, Bill and Louise Etra, Stan VanderBeek, and Walter Wright built their own versions. These synthesizers allowed artists to work directly with the materials of the TV machine. They brought into the foreground TV's glowing surface composed of tiny points called pixels. By controlling voltages and frequencies, artists could change the color and intensity of the phosphorous pixels. In the process, they pushed the viewer away from the representational properties of TV and toward its powers of abstraction, to forms and patterns akin to those of modern painting.

None of the experimenters was more systematic in their pursuit of the unique properties and language of video than Steina and Woody Vasulka. The Vasulkas founded a studio/exhibition hall/meeting place, The Kitchen, in New York City as a locus of experimentation in video, dance, and music. As a teacher at the State University of New York at Buffalo, Woody Vasulka established a video class that included the mathematics of television. Working first with the analog signal and then learning to digitize the electronic signal, Vasulka and his colleagues created a dialogue between the artist's imagination and the inner logic of the TV machine. Slowly, an electronic vocabulary and grammar began to emerge and to shape to works such as *The Commission* (1983), in which electronic imaging codes are used to render the virtuosity of violinist Niccolo Paganini into visual narrative elements.

For many other video experimenters, however, the essence of the video revolution did not lie inside the machine, in its technical or formal qualities. These "video anarchists" responded instead to the Marxist call for the appropriation of the means of production. Their interpretation of McLuhan's famous phrase was that control of the medium determined the meaning of the message and that as long as corporate American controlled the commercial TV, the message would be the same—"consume." The Sony Portapak gave these video makers a chance to produce. It did not matter that the Portapak produced low-resolution black-and-white images, that the tape was almost impossible to edit, or that the equipment was sold by a large corporation. It was cheap, it was portable enough for one person to operate, and it reproduced images instantly. It was finally a technology that gave the constitutional guarantee of "freedom of speech" a place on TV. The Federal Communications Commission (FCC) boosted the vision of a media democracy by requiring cable television companies to provide free public access channels in order to obtain franchises, and these access channels often provided the distribution and exhibition sites for experimental video makers.

Charismatic leaders such as George Stoney, who had worked in Canada's Challenge for Change program, rallied young video activists to the cause of media democracy. Throughout the 1970s, public access centers, media centers, and video collectives sprung up across the country. Their names suggest their utopian intentions: Top Value TV (TVTV), People's Video

Theater, the Alternate Media Center, Videofreex, Global Village, Video Free America, Portable Channel, Videopolis, and Paper Tiger. These groups and many others nurtured the movement. Global Village started a festival, The Kitchen hosted the First Women's Video Festival, and Paper Tiger organized a cable network of 400 sites linked via satellite. Deep Dish Television, as the network is called, still continues, airing controversial programs on such issues as censorship of the arts, the Gulf War, and AIDS.

As the United States moved into a more conservative social climate in the 1980s and 1990s, the idea of giving distribution access to the people has lost much of its influence on public policy. The FCC eliminated the public access requirements, and the Telecommunications Act of 1996 leaves the notion of public access greatly weakened.

Nevertheless, neither the movement to explore the TV machine nor the movement to create more democratic media went unnoticed by the more mainstream forms of television. In fact, the U.S. system of public television, the Public Broadcasting Service (PBS), takes as part of its mission the provision of a site for alternate voices, innovation, and the airing of controversy. These directives, it would seem, made PBS a natural forum for experimental video. Experience has proven otherwise.

In the early 1970s, WGBH producer Fred Barzyk created the New Television Workshop in Boston. Barzyk offered artists the use of non–broadcast quality half-inch video (the Portapak did not meet FCC blanking requirements) and then showed their work on *Artists' Showcase*. Other PBS venues followed, such as WNET's TV Laboratory in New York, KQED's Center for Experiments in Television in San Francisco, KTCA's *Alive from Off Center* in Minneapolis, and the syndicated series *P.O.V.* These programs flourished in the 1970s and early 1980s, yet most shut down because PBS station programmers across the country were always ambivalent about experimental media. They felt that their public trust required them to respond to ratings as did their counterparts in the commercial arena, and ratings for the experimental showcases were never large.

The commercial networks have made their own forays into the experimental movement. The Columbia Broadcasting System (CBS), for example, explored the possibility of producing a show called *Subject to Change* with Videofreex. In the end, executives decided the show was "ahead of its time." The National Broadcasting Company's (NBC's) *Today* show did hire Jon Alpert, codirector of the Downtown Community Television Center in New York City. Alpert's handheld, personal, vérité-style technique made him one of the few experimental artists who could move back and forth between the mainstream and alternate TV forums. He received both praise and criticism for doing so, as did others, such as John Sanborn, who made music videos for Music Television (MTV), and William Wegman, who presented his famous dogs on David Letterman's programs. Michael Shamberg and the Raindance Corporation, in their publication *Guerrilla Television* (1971), had admonished "anyone who thinks that broadcast-TV is capable of reform just doesn't understand the media. A standard of success that demands 30 to 50 million people can only tend toward homogenization." The question for many experimenters, then, was whether Wegmen's dogs, who had seemed so unique in half-inch black and white, had been turned into "stupid pet tricks" by David Letterman.

As this example indicates, throughout the past three decades, the dilemma for experimental video artists has been to work with the substance of mass media without being swallowed by it. For many of them, working inside the networks has proven less satisfying than "making television strange" by placing it in new contexts, such as museums, alternate spaces, and shopping malls.

Nam June Paik and his conceptual artists group Fluxus had led the way in the 1960s with their "decollage" method that started with the removal of the TV set from its familial context in the home. Probably the most famous image of the experimental movement, however, is Ant Farm's *Media Burn* (1975). In this piece, a futuristic-looking Cadillac drives headlong through a burning pyramid of TV sets. Even viewers who missed the actual performance and have seen only a photograph of *Media Burn* could not miss Ant Farm's satirical stab at the power and influence of commercial television.

During the early years of the experimental video movements, the Everson Museum of Art, the Whitney Museum, the Museum of Modern Art, the Long Beach Museum of Art, and the Walker Art Center initiated video exhibition programs. Many of these works, often known as "video installations," were multichannel. Gary Hill's *Inasmuch as It Is Always Already Taking Place* (1990) was a 16-channel installation with 16 modified monitors recessed in a wall. The multichannel capability allowed the artist to create new environments and contexts for the viewer. In their *Wraparound* (1982), Kit Fitzgerald and John Sanborn wanted to give the viewer the "everyday task of assimilating simultaneous information and eliminating the unwanted." In a measure of how far the artist intended to go to shake viewers out of their TV habit, Bill Viola placed a small TV set next to a pitcher and glass of water in what was depicted as a *Room for St. John of the Cross* (1983). Viola's ambition was to rediscover—in the context of the age of television—the experience of "love, ecstasy, passage through the dark night, and flying over city walls and mountains" that the 16th century mystic described in his poetry.

All these works have taken the artists away from the low-cost and low-tech Portapak. Instead, they have embraced the advances, especially in three-quarter-inch color video, computer editing, and mixing. Moreover, the budgets required for many of the installation works had put the artists back in contact with mainstream corporate America. El Paso Gas Company and the Polaroid Corporation, for instance, had contributed to the creation of Viola's *Room for St. John of the Cross.* No project symbolized more the ambition and frustrations of the experimental video artists learning to work with the commercial world than Dara Birnbaum's video wall constructed for the Rio Shopping Complex in Atlanta. A brilliantly conceived design related to Birnbaum's background in architecture and video, the wall, made up of 25 monitors, was a giant electronic bulletin board in the middle of the Rio mall's town square. The content of the monitors was triggered by the motion of the shoppers in the square and contained images that included news coming out of the Atlanta-based Cable News Network (CNN) as well as reflections on the natural landscape that existed before the construction of the mall. The record of the contract negotiations involved in the creation of this project gives an indication of the struggle between a real estate developer and an artist to find a common language for their project. Beginning with the concept that the "art was a work for hire," the negotiations eventually reversed the point and concluded that the artist should retain the rights to the art and license it to the developer. In the end, developer Charles Ackerman told *Business Atlanta* magazine "this center will just smack you in the face with the idea that it is different. When you look at, you will think there is no limit to the imagination. Things don't have to be the way they always are."

By the 1980s and 1990s, experimental video attracted a whole new generation of artists. Many of the best of these were women, black, Hispanic, Asian, or gay. Most brought to their work a social or political agenda. Specifically, they challenged the white male power structure that dominated myth, history, society, the economy, the arts, and television. They questioned the whole narrative framework with its white male heroes conquering dark antagonists who threatened helpless females. Starting with the camera lens—which they described as an extension of the male gaze directed at the commodified woman—they deconstructed the whole apparatus of image making and image consuming.

Speaking for these artists, the narrator in Helen DeMichiel's *Consider Anything, Only Don't Cry* (1988), lays out their strategy:

> I rob the image bank compulsively. I cut up, rearrange, collage, montage, decompose, rearrange, subvert, recontextualize, deconstruct, reconstruct, debunk, rethink, recombine, sort out, untangle, and give back the pictures, the meanings, the sounds, the music, that are taken from us in every moment of our days and nights.

In DeMichiel's portrait of a woman trying to discover both her personal and her culture identities, the intention was to produce a video quilt made up of images ranging from home movies to commercial ads. Indeed, the quilt, a favorite metaphor for the feminists' communal approach to art, produced in the viewer a perception of many pieces being stitched together rather the perception of monolithic unity derived from conventional narrative. The video quilt invited viewers into the making of the work by patching in their own associations stimulated by the personal and public images rather than asking them to uncover the message of the author.

Joan Braderman, in *Joan Does Dynasty* (1986), assumed the role of the viewer by skillfully layering a masked image of herself into scenes with *Dynasty* star Joan Collins. Once "in" the scene, Braderman carried on her own commentary about Alexis's plot to wrest power from the Carrington patriarchy. Unlike Fluxus's appropriation of the TV set, Braderman did not want to leave the familiar grounds of popular television. She wanted in, but on her own terms—with her own lines and her own images. In effect, she wanted to rearrange "television."

The challenge to the hegemony of white males spread rapidly in the 1980s and 1990s. Rea Tajiri and Janice Tanaka produced tapes to reclaim their memory and history that lay forgotten in the internment of Asian Americans during World War II. In *Itam Hakin Hopit* (1984), Victor Masayesva used cutting-edge technology to celebrate the relevance of the Hopi's worldview. Edin Velez, in his *Meta Mayan II* (1981), used slow motion to enhance the effect on the American audience of the return gaze of a Mayan Indian woman. In 1991, African-American artist Philip Mallory Jones launched his *First World Order Project,* designed to take advantage of the global "telecommunity" that had been created by technologies such as the satellite and the Internet. Jones's project focused on the knowledge and wisdom that rise out of the differences that exist in "others."

By the summer of 1989, the "differences" in "others" was too much for the establishment. Conservative political and cultural groups targeted the National Endowment for the Arts and its support of "morally reprehensible trash." The most famous examples were Robert Mapplethorpe's photos of brutal and extreme homosexual acts. The most infamous experimental film/video was *Tongues Untied* by African-American and gay artist Marlon Riggs. Campaigns were mounted against this critically acclaimed work, which was to air on the PBS series *P.O.V.* in the summer of 1991. In the end, 174 PBS stations refused to show the film. Marlon Riggs summed up the reaction of many in the experimental art field when he stated that "a society that shuts its eyes cannot grow or change or discover what's really decent in the world."

In *Expanded Cinema,* Gene Youngblood called for the "artist [to be] an anarchist, a revolutionary, a creator of new worlds imperceptibly gaining on reality." Experimental artists from Nam June Paik to Marlon Riggs responded. Scholars such as Youngblood look on the experimental movement as a protean force, constantly taking new shapes and revealing additional facets of life and humanity. Critics view it as a many-headed Hydra; each head when cut off is replaced by two others.

In 1984, Paik titled his live satellite broadcast between Paris, New York, and San Francisco *Good Morning, Mr. Orwell.* The technology of Big Brother had arrived. Of course, the playful Paik's ambition was to demonstrate to Orwell how ridiculous technology was and how easily it could be humanized. In his book *Being Digital* (1995), Nicholas Negroponte supports Paik's optimism about human beings actively appropriating technology to achieve change:

> The effect of fax machines on Tiananmen Square is an ironic example, because newly popular and decentralized tools were invoked precisely when the government was trying to reassert its elite and centralized control. The Internet provides a worldwide channel of communication that flies in the face of any censorship and thrives

especially in places like Singapore, where freedom of the press is marginal and networking ubiquitous.

This is finally the proper context in which to judge the American experimental video movement. It is the desire to be free that has driven the experiments of American video artists, and it is the possibility of liberating the full potential of all human beings that will lead them into experimental collaborations in the future.

ED HUGETZ

See also **Paik, Nam June**

Further Reading

Frohnmayer, John, *Leaving Town Alive: Confessions of an Arts Warrior,* New York: Houghton Mifflin, 1993

Hall, Doug, and Sally Jo Fifer, editors, *Illuminating Video: An Essential Guide to Video Art,* New York: Aperture Foundation, 1990

Hanhardt, John, editor, *Video Culture: A Critical Investigation,* New York: Visual Studies Workshop, 1986

Heiferman, Marvin, Lisa Phillips, and John G. Hanhardt, *Image World: Art and Media Culture,* New York: Whitney Museum of American Art, 1989

Huffman, Kathy Rae, *Video: A Retrospective,* Long Beach, California: Long Beach Museum of Art, 1984

Huffman, Kathy Rae, and Dorine Mignot, editors, *The Arts for Television,* Los Angeles, California: Museum of Contemporary Art, and Amsterdam Stedelijk Museum, Amsterdam, 1987

Judson, William D., *American Landscape Video: The Electronic Grove,* Pittsburgh, Pennsylvania: Carnegie Museum of Art, 1988

London, Barbara, *Video Spaces: Eight Installations,* New York: Museum of Modern Art, 1995

Negroponte, Nicholas, *Being Digital,* New York: Knopf, 1995

Penny, Simon, editor, *Critical Issues in Electronic Media,* Albany: State University of New York Press, 1995

Popper, Frank, *Art of the Electronic Age,* New York: Harry N. Abrams, 1993

Zippay, Lori, editor, *Electronic Arts Intermix: Video,* New York: Electronic Arts Intermix, 1991

Eyes on the Prize

U.S. Documentary Series

Eyes on the Prize, a critically acclaimed 14-part series dealing with the U.S. civil rights movement, was broadcast nationally by the Public Broadcasting Service. The first six programs, *Eyes on the Prize: America's Civil Rights Years* (1954–65), were aired in

January and February 1987. The eight-part sequel, *Eyes on the Prize II: America at the Racial Crossroads* (1965–85), was broadcast in 1990.

Produced over the course of 12 years by Blackside, Inc., one of the oldest minority-owned film and televi-

Eyes on the Prize, The 1963 March on Washington, 1987.
Courtesy of the Everett Collection

footage and contemporary interviews with participants in the struggle for and against civil rights, the series presented the movement as multifaceted. Watched by over 20 million viewers with each airing, it served as an important educational tool, reaching a generation of millions of Americans who have had no direct experience with the historic events chronicled. Though the series included such landmark events as the Montgomery, Alabama, bus boycott of 1955–56; the 1963 March on Washington; and the assassination of Dr. Martin Luther King, Jr., in 1968, it also documented the workings of the movement on a grassroots level, presenting events and individuals often overlooked.

Eyes on the Prize I, narrated by Julian Bond, was launched by the episode titled "Awakenings." It documents two events that helped focus the nation's attention on the oppression of African-American citizens: the lynching of 14-year-old Emmett Till in 1955 and the Montgomery bus boycott, motivated by the arrest of Rosa Parks, who refused to relinquish her seat on a public bus to a white person. Parts 2 through 6 covered such topics as the key court case *Brown v. the Board of Education,* the nationwide expansion of the movement, James Meredith's enrollment at the University of Mississippi, the Freedom Rides, and the passage of the Voting Rights Act.

Despite the critical and popular success of the first six episodes, executive producer Henry Hampton had a difficult time raising the $6 million needed to fund the sequel. The reticence of both corporate and public granting organizations is attributed to the subject matter of *Eyes II:* the rise of the Black Panther Party, the Nation of Islam, the black consciousness movement, the Vietnam War, busing, and affirmative action.

FRANCES K. GATEWARD

See also **Documentary; Racism, Ethnicity, and Television**

Further Reading

Barol, Bill, "A Struggle for the Prize: Documenting the Last 20 Years of Civil Rights," *Newsweek* (August 22, 1988)
"Eyes on Henry Hampton," *The New Yorker* (January 23, 1995)
Lord, Lewis J., "A Journey to Another Time and, to Many, Another World," *U.S. News and World Report* (March 9, 1987)
Lyon, Danny, "Ain't Gonna Let Nobody Turn Me Round: Use and Misuse of the Southern Civil Rights Movement," *Aperture* (Summer 1989)

sion production companies in the country, the series received over 23 awards, including two Emmys (for Outstanding Documentary and Outstanding Achievement in Writing), the duPont Columbia Award, the Edward R. Murrow Brotherhood Award for Best National Documentary, the International Documentary Association's Distinguished Documentary Award, Program of the Year and Outstanding News Information Program by the Television Critics Association, and the CINE Golden Eagle.

In addition to its positive receptions from television critics and professionals, *Eyes on the Prize* was also lauded by historians and educators. Using archival

Eyewitness to History

U.S. News Program

CBS News conceived *Eyewitness to History* to cover U.S. presidential diplomacy and the Soviet Union during the last five months of 1959. Before the series settled into its Friday 10:30 to 11:00 P.M. period in September 1960, 16 of 28 programs were brought to the public before 8:30 P.M., with only two covering stories unrelated to President Dwight Eisenhower, Premier Nikita Khrushchev, President Charles de Gaulle, and the summits in Paris. In September 1961, the series returned as *Eyewitness,* with the narrow, original focus gone but the same need to cover late-breaking national and international news. For four seasons, *Eyewitness to History* stood as the center of growth at CBS News and made a 30-minute daily news program feasible in the eyes of network executives.

In the spring of 1963, *Eyewitness* was canceled after the news division was given permission for a 30-minute nightly newscast. It was canceled not just to return time to the network schedule but also to shift executive producer Leslie Midgley and many of his producers to work on the *CBS Evening News,* assisting Don Hewitt, executive producer of the new program.

Midgley took pride in airing on Friday stories that would appear in the national newsmagazines on Monday. The series pioneered construction of a program with combinations of live telecast, videotape, and film and broke through many self-imposed limitations of news reporting. For the first time, video cameras were shipped and used overseas, covering Eisenhower. Unfortunately, the bulky nature of these cameras, difficult to move once optimally positioned, posed problems when crowds did not cooperate. In the United States, video cameras were used extensively to cover Khrushchev's visit in 1959, but the use of cameras in crowds again disrupted coverage on such historic programs as "Khrushchev on the Farm." The series also struggled with the early uses of two-inch videotape. The tape was fed to New York with specific time cues signaling when to start and stop. Unable at that time to edit two-inch tape electronically, film editors would actually cut two-inch tape, compiling the necessary sections. According to the producers, what initially made the series as historic as the events themselves was the use of a jet air-

plane to ship back tape and film of Eisenhower in Italy, India, Brazil, West Germany, England, Paris, Iran, Greece, and Japan.

As the series pushed for coverage of events with multidimensional background stories, the production crew developed appropriate strategies. Editors cut negative film and projected it directly over the air by reversing the polarity in the control room. Certain stories aired only because the unit employed a two-projector system, switching between one projector, the studio camera, the other projector, and sometimes the video projector. Realizing the historical value of the two-inch tape, Midgley asked Sig Mickelson, president of CBS News, to start a tape archive. He refused, preferring to reuse the tape—and part of the video record of significant historical, social, and cultural events was lost.

In its second season, the series quickly gained a reputation for changing the announced topic, sometimes as late as Friday morning. Midgley began to send "field producers," a term that included unit members with other official titles, to different locations, sometimes holding open the possibility of any one of five stories. The series production relied heavily on news judgments of the field producers, who included Bernie Birnbaum, Russ Bensley, John Sharnick, Av Westin, and Philip Scheffler, individuals who would go on to major roles in the television news industry. Their decisions led to crucial alterations in plans and schedules. Twice, for example, in the second season, last-minute developments growing out of tension over school integration in New Orleans, Louisiana, were given precedence over already developing stories. Similarly, on the day when the production unit was taping John F. Kennedy's announcement and introduction of cabinet appointments, two jet airliners crashed over New York City, and Midgley decided to cover the crash. The resulting journalism illustrated the production unit's expert response to such events— they were faster than units in news divisions in New York. Even late-breaking international stories received the unit's attention. They covered Yuri Gagarin orbiting the Earth, causing cancellation of two shows on the Adolf Eichmann trial in Israel, and another on the events surrounding the Bay of Pigs and the return of prisoners. When antigovernment factions seized the cruise ship *Santa Maria* off the coast of Brazil, Charles Kuralt was dispatched on another ship to intercept and film the incident, providing coverage for two weeks. If events surrounding a story halted, as they did during negotiations with the hijackers of *Santa Maria,* or if two events were simultaneously breaking, the series sometimes aired two 15-minute segments. After the second year, the Columbia Broadcasting System (CBS) television network illustrated to potential advertisers the timeliness of the program by citing listings of the stories the series was preparing to cover.

Although the title changed, *Eyewitness* remained committed to covering presidential trips and diplomacy, keeping the production unit on tight deadlines according to the president's schedule. Certain shows, such as "Spring Arrives in Paris" and "The Big Ski Boom," were prepared over a two- or three-week period and were aired on the basis of the happenstance of events unfolding and the logistics needed to cover the president. After the title change, coverage of diplomacy changed only slightly, as the flow of events became placed in something of a larger context, such as "En Route to Vienna" and "The President in Mexico." This shift was made possible by the developing expertise of the unit.

During its first year, *Eyewitness to History* highlighted correspondents Robert Pierpoint, Alexander Kendrick, Robert Trout, David Schoenbrun, Lou Cioffi, Ernest Leiser, Daniel Schorr, and especially Charles Collingwood, assigned to accompany the president. With Walter Cronkite as anchor in New York, two or three additional correspondents appeared in programs, from Washington, D.C., and from different parts of the world determined according to an event's implications. This structure remained constant throughout the series for coverage of presidential trips as well as for international incidents, such as "The Showdown in Laos" and "India at War." Midgley utilized CBS reporters around the world, even those assigned to the *CBS Evening News,* setting the stage for *Eyewitness*'s own cancellation and the unit's reassignment as a support mechanism for Walter Cronkite's 30-minute broadcast.

Network politics at this time occasioned a period of instability with regard to the anchor seat. Charles Kuralt was named anchor for the second season of *Eyewitness to History.* Midgley and others inside CBS perceived Kuralt as following in the footsteps of Edward R. Murrow. But James Aubrey, president of CBS, disliked Kuralt's on-camera appearance and convinced

Midgley to return Cronkite as anchor in January 1961. Cronkite's role as New York correspondent provided a scope of credibility absent from his other projects. When Cronkite went to the *CBS Evening News* on April 16, 1962, Charles Collingwood became anchor of *Eyewitness.*

At the series start, a critical dimension was added to the objective task of presenting news, with Howard K. Smith's commentary on programs focused on diplomacy. In covering certain issues, the distinct perspectives and arguments between producer and reporter became evident, as in the case of "Diem's War—Or Ours" and other reports on Vietnam.

Critics and the public were engaged by the urgency and depth *Eyewitness* brought to contemporary issues. Even when considering the new trend in jazz music, bossa nova, the producers presented a "critical look" at jazz. Even so, the announcement of the program "Who Killed Marilyn Monroe?" brought such an outcry from Hollywood that Midgley changed the title to "Marilyn Monroe, Why?"

For three years, *Eyewitness to History* aggressively pursued such topics as changes in the labor movement, government fiscal policy, the medical establishment, and U.S. foreign relations. It was the training and proving ground for television journalists whose careers spanned most of the second half of the century they covered. And the series signaled CBS's turn to prominence in network television journalism.

RICHARD BARTONE

See also **Documentary**

Anchors

Charles Kuralt	1960–61
Walter Cronkite	1961–62
Charles Collingwood	1962–63

Programming History
CBS

August 1959–December 1959	Irregular schedule of specials
September 1960–June 1961	Friday 10:30–11:00
September 1961–August 1963	Friday 10:30–11:00

Further Reading

Adams, Val, "Exchange Visits Get TV Sponsor," *New York Times* (August 2, 1959)

"Cronkite and Midgley: 'I Love Luce-id,'" *Variety* (January 3, 1962)

Crosby, John, "The Journey," *New York Herald Tribune* (December 23, 1959)

Delatiner, Barbara, "CBS Had a Full Roster of Marilyn Experts," *Newsday* (August 13, 1962)

Gates, Gary Paul, *Air Time: The Inside Story of CBS News,* New York: Harper and Row, 1978

Guidry, Frederick, "Video Turns to Current History: *Eyewitness*—Foot Loose Scribe," *Christian Science Monitor* (October 5, 1960)

Midgley, Leslie, *How Many Words Do You Want?,* New York: Birch Lane, 1989

"Midgley's 'Take 5, Use 1.'" *Variety* (April 5, 1961)

Ranson, Jo, "*Eyewitness to History* to Get Shorter Title in Fall," *Radio TV Daily* (May 1, 1961)

Schoenbrun, David, *On and Off the Air: An Informal History of CBS News,* New York: Dutton, 1989

"The Speed Up in Television News Coverage," *Broadcasting* (January 2, 1961)

"Stop the Cameras!" *TV Guide* (November 10, 1962)

Van Horne, Harriet, "Disasters Test TV News," *New York Telegram* (December 20, 1960)

F

Fairness Doctrine

U.S. Broadcasting Policy

The policy of the U.S. Federal Communications Commission (FCC) known as the "Fairness Doctrine" is an attempt to ensure that all coverage of controversial issues by a broadcast station be balanced and fair. In 1949 the FCC took the view that station licensees were "public trustees" and as such had an obligation to afford reasonable opportunity for discussion of contrasting points of view on controversial issues of public importance. The commission later held that stations were also obligated to seek out actively issues of importance to their community and air programming that addressed those issues. With the deregulation sweep of the Reagan administration during the 1980s, the commission dissolved the Fairness Doctrine.

This doctrine emerged when a large number of applications for radio stations were being submitted but the number of frequencies available was limited. It was intended to ensure that broadcasters did not use their stations simply as advocates with a singular perspective. Rather, they were supposed to allow all points of view. That requirement was to be enforced by FCC mandate.

From the early 1940s, the FCC had established the "Mayflower Doctrine," which prohibited editorializing by stations. However, that absolute ban softened somewhat by the end of the decade, allowing editorializing only if other points of view were aired, balancing that of the station. During these years, the FCC had established dicta and case law guiding the operation of the doctrine.

In ensuing years the FCC ensured that the doctrine was operational by laying out rules defining such matters as personal attack and political editorializing (1967). In 1971 the commission set requirements for the stations to report, with their license renewal application, efforts to seek out and address issues of concern to the community. This process became known as "Ascertainment of Community Needs" and was to be done systematically and by the station management.

The Fairness Doctrine ran parallel to Section 315 of the Communications Act of 1934, which required stations to offer "equal opportunity" to all legally qualified political candidates for any office if they had allowed any person running in that office to use the station. The attempt was to balance—to force an even-handedness. Section 315 exempted news programs, interviews, and documentaries. The doctrine, however, would include such efforts. Another major difference should be noted here: Section 315 was federal law, passed by Congress. The Fairness Doctrine was simply FCC policy.

The FCC fairness policy was given great credence by the 1969 U.S. Supreme Court case of *Red Lion Broadcasting Co., Inc. v. FCC*. In that case, a station in Pennsylvania, licensed by Red Lion Co., had aired a "Christian Crusade" program wherein an author, Fred J. Cook, was attacked. When Cook requested time to reply, in keeping with the Fairness Doctrine, the station refused. Upon appeal to the FCC, the commission declared that there had been a personal attack in the program and the station had failed to meet its obligation. The station appealed, and the case wended its way through the courts and eventually to the Supreme Court. The court ruled for the FCC, giving sanction to the Fairness Doctrine.

The doctrine, nevertheless, disturbed many journalists, who considered it a violation of First Amendment rights of free speech/free press, which should allow reporters to make their own decisions about balancing stories. Fairness, in this view, should not be forced by the FCC. In order to avoid the requirement to go out and find contrasting viewpoints on every issue raised in a story, some journalists simply avoided any coverage of some controversial issues. This "chilling effect" was just the opposite of what the FCC intended.

By the 1980s, many things had changed. The "scarcity" argument, which dictated the "public trustee" philosophy of the commission, was disappearing, and an abundant number of channels became available on cable TV. With many more voices in the marketplace of ideas, there were perhaps fewer compelling reasons to keep the Fairness Doctrine. This was also an era of deregulation, when the FCC took on a different attitude about its many rules, which were seen as an unnecessary burden by most stations. The new chairman of the FCC, Mark Fowler, appointed by President Reagan, publicly avowed to kill the Fairness Doctrine.

By 1985 the FCC issued its *Fairness Report,* asserting that the doctrine was no longer having its intended effect, might actually have a "chilling effect," and might be in violation of the First Amendment. In a 1987 case, *Meredith Corp. v. FCC,* the courts declared that the doctrine was not mandated by Congress and the FCC did not have to continue to enforce it. The FCC dissolved the doctrine in August of that year.

However, before the commission's action, in the spring of 1987, both houses of Congress voted to put the Fairness Doctrine into law—a statutory fairness doctrine that the FCC would have to enforce, like it or not. President Reagan, in keeping with his deregulatory efforts and his long-standing favor of keeping government out of the affairs of business, vetoed the legislation, however, and there were insufficient votes to override the veto. Congressional efforts to make the doctrine into law surfaced again during George H.W. Bush's administration. As before, the legislation was vetoed, this time by Bush.

The Fairness Doctrine remains just beneath the surface of concerns over broadcasting and cablecasting, and some members of Congress continue to threaten to pass it into legislation. Currently, however, there is no required balance of controversial issues as mandated by the Fairness Doctrine. The public relies instead on the judgment of broadcast journalists and its own reasoning ability to sort out one-sided or distorted coverage of an issue. Indeed, experience over the past several years since the demise of the doctrine shows that broadcasters can and do provide substantial coverage of controversial issues of public importance in their communities, including contrasting viewpoints, through news, public-affairs, public-service, interactive, and special programming.

VAL E. LIMBURG

See also **Deregulation; Federal Communications Commission; Political Processes and Television**

Further Reading

Aufderheide, Patricia, "After the Fairness Doctrine: Controversial Broadcast Programming and the Public Interest," *Journal of Communication* (Summer 1990)

Benjamin, Louise M., "Broadcast Campaign Precedents from the 1924 Presidential Election," *Journal of Broadcasting and Electronic Media* (Fall 1987)

Brennan, Timothy A., "The Fairness Doctrine as Public Policy," *Journal of Broadcasting and Electronic Media* (Fall 1989)

Cronauer, Adrian, "The Fairness Doctrine: A Solution in Search of a Problem," *Federal Communications Law Journal* (October 1994)

Donahue, Hugh Carter, "The Fairness Doctrine Is Shackling Broadcasting," *Technology Review* (November–December 1986)

Hazlett, Thomas W., "The Fairness Doctrine and the First Amendment," *Public Interest* (Summer 1989)

Krueger, Elizabeth, "Broadcasters' Understanding of Political Broadcast Regulation," *Journal of Broadcasting and Electronic Media* (Summer 1991)

Rowan, Ford, *Broadcast Fairness: Doctrine, Practice, Prospects: A Reappraisal of the Fairness Doctrine and Equal Time Rule,* New York: Longmans, 1984

Simmons, Steven J., *The Fairness Doctrine and the Media,* Berkeley: University of California Press, 1978

Streeter, Thomas, "Beyond Freedom of Speech and the Public Interest: The Relevance of Critical Legal Studies to Communications Policy," *Journal of Communication* (Spring 1990)

United States Congress, House Committee on Energy and Commerce Subcommittee on Telecommunications and Finance, *Broadcasters and the Fairness Doctrine: Hearing before the Subcommittee on Telecommunications and Finance of the Committee,* Washington, D.C.: U.S. Congressional Documents, 1989

Falk, Peter (1927–)

U.S. Actor

Most notable for his role as television's preeminent detective, Lieutenant Columbo, Peter Falk has developed a long and distinguished career in television and film. For his efforts, Falk has received numerous Emmy Awards for a detective role that has taken its place alongside other legendary literary sleuths. Since the late 1970s Falk has continued to appear in feature films as well as reprise his Columbo character on television.

One of Falk's earliest roles was in *The Untouchables,* a series that launched a number of stars, including Robert Redford. Falk became a popular dramatic actor appearing in several anthology programs, including *Bob Hope Presents the Chrysler Theater* and *The DuPont Show of the Week.* He won his first of several Emmys in 1962, for his portrayal of Dimitri Fresco in *The Dick Powell Show*'s presentation of the teleplay *The Price of Tomatoes.*

In 1965 Falk landed the title role in the CBS series *The Trials of O'Brien.* A precursor to the Columbo character, O'Brien acted diligently in his professional duties yet slovenly in his personal life. The series lasted one season before cancellation. During the 1960s, Falk also appeared in a number of feature films, including *Murder, Inc.,* which garnered him an Oscar nomination.

The Columbo character, brainchild of veteran television producers Richard Levinson and William Link, came to Falk quite by accident. According to Mark Dawidziak, author of *The Columbo Phile,* Levinson and Link had experimented with the Columbo persona when they were writing for NBC's *Chevy Mystery Theater.* In that and subsequent versions, Columbo was always portrayed by an elderly gentleman. Thus, in 1968, when Levinson and Link approached Universal television with the idea for a TV movie based on their stage play *Prescription: Murder,* the writers hoped to enlist Lee J. Cobb or Bing Crosby as Columbo. Falk, a friend of Levinson and Link, had seen the script and was interested; when Cobb and Crosby refused the part, Falk won it.

NBC was interested in turning the film into a series, but neither Falk nor Levinson and Link wanted to do weekly episodic television at the time. Three years later, when NBC promised to package *Columbo* in rotation with two other series in the *NBC Mystery Movie,*

Falk and Levinson and Link agreed. The series enjoyed a successful run from 1971 to 1977; much of that success is due to Falk's brilliant portrayal of Columbo. According to Dawidziak, "Everything clicked—the disheveled appearance, the voice, the squint caused by his false right eye. It was all used to magnificent advantage in Falk's characterization."

In 1989 Falk reprised the Columbo role, this time for the *ABC Mystery Movie;* new *Columbo* episodes have been produced since. Between 1971 and 1990, Falk won four Emmy Awards for his role as Columbo.

Peter Falk.
Courtesy of the Everett Collection

Since 1978 Falk has also appeared in both feature films and made-for-television movies focused on Columbo.

MICHAEL B. KASSEL

See also Columbo

Peter Michael Falk. Born in New York City, September 16, 1927. Educated at Hamilton College, Clinton, New York; New School for Social Research, New York, B.A. 1951; Syracuse University, M.A. in public administration 1953. Married: 1) Alyce Mayo, 1960 (divorced, 1976); two daughters; 2) Shera Danese, 1976. Served 18 months as cook in merchant marine, 1945–46. Management analyst, Connecticut State Budget Bureau, 1953–55; began acting career with Mark Twain Maskers, Hartford, Connecticut; studied acting under Eva La Gallienne, White Barn Theater, Westport, Connecticut, 1955; moved to New York to pursue theatrical career, 1955; professional stage debut in Moliere's *Don Juan,* New York, 1956; studied acting with Jack Landau and Sanford Meisner, 1957; made film debut in *Wind across the Everglades,* 1958; considered for Columbia contract but rejected because of glass eye; formed Mayo Productions company in mid-1960s; created character of Lieutenant Columbo in made-for-television movie *Prescription: Murder,* 1968; starred in television series *Columbo,* 1971–77; directed several *Columbo* episodes. Recipient: Emmy Awards, 1962, 1972, 1975, 1976, and 1990.

Television Series

1965–66	*The Trials of O'Brien*
1971–77	*Columbo* (also directed several episodes)

Made-for-Television Movies

1961	*Cry Vengeance*
1966	*Too Many Thieves*
1968	*Prescription: Murder*
1971	*Ransom for a Dead Man*
1976	*Griffin and Phoenix: A Love Story*
1989	*Columbo Goes to the Guillotine*
1990	*Columbo Goes to College*
1991	*Columbo: Grand Deception*
1991	*Caution: Murder Can Be Hazardous to Your Health*
1992	*Columbo: A Bird in the Hand*
1992	*Columbo: No Time to Die*
1993	*Columbo: It's All in the Game*
1994	*Columbo: Butterfly in Shades of Grey*
1994	*Columbo: Undercover*
1995	*Columbo: Strange Bedfellows*
1995	*The Sunshine Boys*
1997	*Columbo: A Trace of Murder*
1997	*Pronto*
1998	*Columbo: Ashes to Ashes*
2000	*A Storm in the Summer*
2000	*Columbo: Murder with Too Many Notes*
2001	*A Town without Christmas*
2003	*Columbo: Columbo Likes the Nightlife*
2003	*Finding John Christmas*
2003	*Wilder Days*

Television Miniseries

2001	*The Lost World*

Television Specials

1961	*The Million Dollar Incident*
1966	*Brigadoon*
1971	*A Hatfull of Rain*
1986	*Clue: Movies, Murder and Mystery*
1995	*Cassavetes: Anything for John*
1997	*Frank Capra's American Dream*
2000	*'70s: The Decade That Changed Television*
2001	*The 100 Greatest TV Characters*

Films

Wind across the Everglades, 1958; *Pretty Boy Floyd,* 1959; *The Bloody Broad,* 1959; *Murder, Inc.,* 1960; *The Purple Reef,* 1960; *Pocketful of Miracles,* 1961; *Pressure Point,* 1962; *The Balcony,* 1962; *It's a Mad, Mad, Mad, Mad World,* 1963; *Robin and the Seven Hoods,* 1964; *Italiana brava gente,* 1964; *The Great Race,* 1965; *Penelope,* 1966; *Luv,* 1967; *Lo sbarco di Anzio,* 1968; *Gli Intoccabili,* 1968; *Castle Keep,* 1969; *Rosolino paterno, soldato,* 1969; *Husbands,* 1970; *Step Out of Line,* 1970; *Machine Gun McCann,* 1970; *The Politics Film* (narrator), 1972; *A Woman under the Influence,* 1974; *Mikey and Nicky,* 1976; *Murder by Death,* 1976; *Opening Night,* 1977; *The Cheap Detective,* 1978; *The Brink's Job,* 1978; *The In-Laws,* 1979; *The Great Muppet Caper,* 1981; *All the Marbles,* 1981; *Sanford Meisner: The Theater's Best Kept Secret,* 1984; *Big Trouble,* 1986; *Happy New Year,* 1987; *Duenos del silencio,* 1987; *Wings of Desire,* 1987; *The Princess Bride,* 1987; *Rattornas Vinter,* 1988; *Vibes,* 1988; *Cookie,* 1989; *In the Spirit,* 1990; *Aunt Julia and the Scriptwriter,* 1990; *Tune in Tomorrow,* 1990; *My Dog Stupid,* 1991; *The Player,* 1992; *Roommates,* 1994; *Cops 'n' Robbers,* 1995; *Vig,* 1998; *Enemies of Laughter,* 2000; *Lakeboat,* 2000; *Hubert's Brain,* 2000; *Made,* 2001; *Corky Romano,* 2001; *Undisputed,* 2002; *Shark Tale,* 2004 (voice).

Stage

Don Juan, 1956; *The Changeling,* 1956; *The Iceman Cometh,* 1956; *St. Joan,* 1956; *Diary of a Scoundrel,* 1956; *Bonds of Interest,* 1956; *The Lady's Not for Burning,* 1957; *Purple Dust,* 1957; *Comic Strip,* 1958; *The Passion of Josef D,* 1964; *The Prisoner of Second Avenue,* 1971; *Light Up the Sky,* 1987; *Glengarry Glen Ross,* 1985.

Further Reading

Dawidziak, Mark, *The Columbo Phile: A Casebook,* New York: Mysterious, 1989
"Interview," *Photoplay* (January 1979)
"Peter Falk," *Conversations* by Don Shay, New York: Kaleidoscope, 1969

Fall and Rise of Reginald Perrin, The

U.K. Sitcom

Madness was the central theme of this 1970s sitcom that used flights of fantasy and dream sequences to further its serial story of an office worker becoming increasingly disillusioned with his lot. At the start of the story, Reggie is barely holding his life together, balancing the routine of the office with the routine of his home life. But already cracks are beginning to appear, and as he veers dangerously toward a nervous breakdown, we see both his professional and personal life unravel before our eyes. But the show is not just about Reggie's mental issues; it also dealt with the lunacy of office life, and the casual insanity of his fellow workers.

Reggie works in an executive position for confectionary company Sunshine Desserts. His boss is CJ, a superior type whose use of business jargon and metaphors may seem impressive on the surface but is in fact meaningless, empty corporate lingo. His often repeated claims of "I didn't get where I am today... ," followed by some ludicrous example of what he did or did not do, are equally ridiculous. CJ is a walking bundle of clichés and inconsistencies, his air of sophistication and worldliness in direct opposition to his penchant for the whoopee cushion, omnipresent on the seat of visitors to his office. Reggie's other colleagues are no better. Tony and David are would-be whiz kids, who converse solely in superficial banter (Tony: "Great!"; David: "Super!") and, despite their surface differences (Tony always confident; David forever on the verge of panic), are in fact two sides of the same coin. The firm's ancient doctor, Morrisey, is an incompetent fool. The only light on Reggie's horizon is his secretary, Joan, a loyal, efficient woman who forever seems on the verge of throwing herself on Reggie in a sudden fit of passion. When they are alone together the air fairly crackles with sexual tension. At home Reggie has his equally loyal wife, Elizabeth, and endures visits from his terminally dull son-in-law (Tom) and eccentric ex-military brother-in-law Jimmy.

Reggie's life is mind-numblingly repetitive (the same hellos to the same acquaintances on the way to the station, the same train, which is always precisely 11 minutes late, the same welcome at the office), which propels the midlife crisis that sees him gradually losing his grip on sanity and taking drastic actions to stop himself from descending into total madness. His solution is extreme but perhaps understandable in the circumstances. He fakes his own death (by leaving a suicide note and all his clothes on a beach) and re-enters the world as Martin Welbourne, a bearded, exaggerated version of himself. Unable to resist attending his own funeral, he finds himself once again falling in love with his his wife, Elizabeth, newly appealing as a widow.

But Reggie's descent into lunacy is not to be thwarted so easily. In the second series of the show, he brings himself back from the dead and attempts to change his lifestyle rather than his identity. Soon, in a bout of seeming insanity, which turns out to be a stroke of genius, he opens a shop called Grot, which is dedicated to selling useless things. To everyone's astonishment, it is hugely successful, and later—when a crisis hits Sunshine Desserts—Reggie employs his former colleagues. A third series sees Reggie, launching Perrins, a commune for middle-class, middle-aged men where a harmonious lifestyle and generous philosophy help counteract midlife crises.

The Fall and Rise of Reginald Perrin was a complex, thoughtful comedy, with each of the three series based on a different book written by David Nobbs and then adapted (by the author) for television. The themes of the midlife crisis and the nervous breakdown resonated throughout the episodes, but as the story progressed, it became clear that it was the world, not Reggie, that was insane. Nobbs cast a jaundiced eye on the vacuous lives of those working in highly regarded positions in companies that produced little of significance. The fact that the Grot shop intentionally sold useless things and was so successful was an unsubtle but nonetheless telling comment on a society obsessed with material things.

The series was brilliantly written and rib-achingly funny, benefiting from a sensational performance by Leonard Rossiter in the title role. His intense, convincing portrayal of a man on the edge, combined with his fine instinct for comedy, ensured that the series was elevated even further beyond mainstream sitcom fare.

A U.S. version, *Reggie,* appeared in 1983 (ABC) with Richard Mulligan in the title role. Although Mulligan was a good choice for Reggie and the show appeared promising, something was certainly lost in the translation. The U.S. version lacked subtlety, with Reggie's breakdown treated hastily and conveyed by wide-eyed caricature. The following year, a series on Channel 4 in the United Kingdom, *Fairly Secret Army* (also written by Nobbs), recounted the adventures of a character very similar to Perrin's brother-in-law Jimmy and played by the same actor (Geoffrey Palmer).

In 1996 the BBC presented a new Perrin series, *The Legacy of Reggie Perrin,* once again based on a Nobbs book. It took place after Reggie's death, and after the death of the actor Leonard Rossiter. Many of the original cast members returned in a story that saw Reggie's influence over his friends, relatives, and colleagues extend from beyond the grave. He left them a vast fortune in his will, on the condition that they each do something utterly ludicrous. Unfortunately, *The Legacy of Reggie Perrin* was a misguided idea, devoid of the charm of the original and a sad epitaph to a marvelous series.

DICK FIDDY

Cast

Reginald Perrin/Martin Welbourne	Leonard Rossiter
Elizabeth Perrin	Pauline Yates
CJ	John Barron
Joan Greengross/Webster	Sue Nicholls
Tony Webster	Trevor Adams
David Harris Jones	Bruce Bould
"Doc" Morrisey	John Horsley
Jimmy Anderson	Geoffrey Palmer

Producers

Gareth Gwenlan, John Howard Davies (1 episode), Robin Nash (1 episode)

Writer

David Nobbs

Programming History

The Fall and Rise of Reginald Perrin

22 episodes
BBC
September 1976–January 1979 (+ 1 Christmas Special, 1982)

Series 1: September 8–October 20, 1976, BBC 1		Wednesday 9:25–9:55
Series 2: September 21–November 2, 1977, BBC 1		Wednesday 9:25–9:55
Series 3: November 29, 1978–January 24, 1979, BBC 1		Wednesday 9:35–10:05

The Legacy of Reginald Perrin

7 episodes
BBC
September–October 1996
September 22–October 31, 1996, BBC 1 mostly Sunday at approximately 8:30

Further Reading

Lewisohn, Mark, *The Radio Times Guide to TV Comedy,* London: BBC, 1998, 2002

Famille Plouffe, La

Canadian Serial Drama

La famille Plouffe was created in 1953 in response to a lack of Francophone television programming in Canada. Unlike its counterpart in English Canada, which could pick up shows from U.S. stations, the Francophone division of the CBC, la Société Radio-Canada (SRC), was compelled to develop with very few resources its own programs. The early programs grew out of Quebec's strong tradition of radio drama, a tradition grounded in serial narratives. One such serial, *Un homme et son péché,* was heard by nearly 80 percent of the Quebec audience. It was only natural that such a formula would find its way to television. Teleromans, as these serials were called, were launched in the fall of 1953 with the debut of *La famille Plouffe,* which was broadcast live every Wednesday night. It was an instant hit, and its phenomenal success prompted Radio-Canada to develop more shows of this genre, which came to dominate the weekday prime-time schedule.

The Family Plouffe/La famille Plouffe chronicled the daily life of a Quebec working-class family in the postwar era. It was an extended family that included Théophile, the father, a former provincial cycling champion who had traded in his bicycle—and his youth—for work as a plumber; Joséphine, the naive and kindhearted mother who doted on her adult children like a worried mother hen; Napoléon, the eldest child and protector of his siblings, who mentored his younger brother Guillaume's dream of one day playing professional hockey; Ovide, the intellectual of the family, whose education and love of art and music gave him an arrogant demeanor; and Cécile, the only daughter, who, like many women in the postwar era, was faced with the choice between the traditional marriage, children, and security, on the one hand, and new aspirations of career independence, on the other.

Plots were generally cast in the form of quests—for love, career advancement, security, or a sense of personal and national identity. These themes were woven with the daily problems and choices that confronted members of the family. Some commentators have argued that the Plouffes reflected the common experience of the "typical" French Canadian family and that viewers in Quebec could easily identify with the char-acters, their aspirations, the plots, and the settings. As nostalgic as this view may be, the Plouffes were still fictional. Moral ambiguities were almost always resolved to fit the conventional values of postwar Quebec. Women were expected to be homemakers, wives, and mothers. Those women who strayed from these norms, such as Rita Toulouse, were often depicted as wily and unpredictable. Men were expected to be good providers and strong patriarchs, as symbolized by the fact that Théophile let his treasured bicycle fall into disrepair. It was only to be expected that Cécile would opt for marriage to Onésime Ménard and that Ovide would reconcile his elitist aspirations with his working-class environment.

A year after the successful premiere of the original series, CBC programmers decided to launch an English version. The version was essentially the same as its French counterpart, though modifications were made in the script to remove profane and vulgar language and any references to sex. The scripts were written by Roger Lemelin, the original and only French author, and the same cast of actors were used for the live broadcasts, which were aired later in the week.

This decision was a unique experiment. Using the magic of television, all Canadians were able to follow the same story, and although *The Family Plouffe* received good ratings in some smaller Canadian centers, the CBC's own internal surveys showed that the experiment to create a common Canadian cultural icon was a failure. In large cities where viewers had access to U.S. stations, Anglophone Canadians preferred to watch American programming. By the end of the 1958–59 season, the CBC had abandoned the practice of broadcasting language-versioned programming.

La famille Plouffe/The Family Plouffe was a unique "made-in-Canada" live drama. Nostalgic memories of its success prompted a return in 1982 to the family kitchen in a television special, *Le crime d'Ovide Plouffe,* which was also versioned and broadcast to Anglophone Canadians. After more than two decades of separate programming, another attempt was made to broadcast a series to both English and French audiences in the late 1980s. The series *Lance et compte/He Shoots, He Scores* (1987–88) was intended to appeal to

Canadians' common love of hockey, but like earlier experiments, ratings demonstrated that Francophone and Anglophone viewers wanted very different kinds of programs. The true legacy of *La famille Plouffe* was its influence in the development of the *teleroman*, which was and has remained a uniquely "made-in-Quebec" television genre.

MANON LAMONTAGNE

Cast

Théophile Plouffe	Paul Guèvremont
Joséphine Plouffe	Amanda Alarie
Napoléon Plouffe	Emile Genest
Ovide Plouffe	Jean-Louis Roux, Marcel Houben
Guillaume Plouffe	Pierre Valcour
Cécile Plouffe	Denise Pelletier
Gédéon Plouffe	Doris Lussier
Démérise Plouffe	Nana de Varennes
Onéisme Ménard	Rolland Bédard
Rita Toulouse	Lise Roy, Janin Mignolet
Blanche Toulouse	Lucie Poitras
Jeanne Labrie	Thérèse Cadorette
Stan Labrie	Jean Duceppe
Révérend Père Alexandre	Guy Provost
Martine Plouffe	Margot Campbell
Aimé Plouffe	Jean Coutu
Flora Plouffe	Ginette Letondal
Agathe Plouffe	Clémence Desrochers
Rosaire Joyeux	Camille Ducharme
Jacqueline Sévigny	Amulette Garneau
Alain Richard	Guy Godin
Hélène Giguère	Françoise Graton
Alphonse Tremblay	Ernest Guimond

Directors

Guy Beaulne; Jean Dumas; Jean-Paul Fugère (both versions)

Programming History

194 episodes
Société Radio-Canada/CBC
French version

November 1953–May 1959	Wednesdays 8:30–9:00
English version	
November 1954–May 1955	Thursdays 8:00–8:30
November 1955–May 1956	Fridays 10:00–10:30
November 1956–May 1958	Fridays 8:30–9:00
November 1958–May 1959	Fridays 9:30–10:00

Further Reading

Raboy, Marc, *Missed Opportunities: The Story of Canada's Broadcasting Policy,* Montreal: McGill-Queen's University Press, 1990

Rutherford, Paul, *When Television Was Young: Primetime Canada, 1952–1967,* Toronto: University of Toronto Press, 1990

Trofimenkoff, Susan, *The Dream of Nation,* Toronto: Gage, 1983

Family

U.S. Domestic Drama

Family, a weekly prime-time drama about a southern California suburban family, ran from 1976 to 1980 on ABC. The show's pilot, which became the first episode of a six-part miniseries that aired in March 1976, was created by novelist and screenwriter Jay Presson Allen (*Forty Carats*), directed by film director Mark Rydell (*On Golden Pond*), and produced by film director Mike Nichols (*Who's Afraid of Virginia Woolf?; The Graduate*) as well as television moguls Aaron Spelling and Leonard Goldberg (*Charlie's An-gels; Starsky and Hutch*). The success of the miniseries—it recorded an astonishing 40 shares in the ratings—led ABC to pick up *Family* as a regular series for the network's 1976–77 season. During its five seasons, *Family* received 17 Emmy Award nominations, 3 of them for Outstanding Drama Series. The show won four awards in acting categories: Outstanding Lead Actress in a Drama Series (Sada Thompson in 1977), Outstanding Supporting Actress in a Drama Series (Kristy McNichol in 1976 and 1978), and Out-

Family.
Courtesy of the Everett Collection

standing Supporting Actor in a Drama Series (Gary Frank in 1976).

Despite their impressive credentials, the creative forces behind *Family* had to fight for three years (beginning 1973) before convincing ABC to give the series a chance. As Rowland Barber has explained, during development ABC found the family portrayed in the series "at various critical times...too well-educated and too well-dressed...too true to life for Family Viewing Time...and...simply 'too good for television'" (see Barber). These attempts to dismiss the project were discarded once the miniseries proved to be a hit both with audiences and critics.

Family also benefited from a renewed interest in dramatic shows during the mid-1970s (as witnessed by the huge popularity of the miniseries *Rich Man, Poor Man*). In general, police/detective shows such as *Police Woman, Charlie's Angels, S.W.A.T., Starsky and Hutch, Switch,* and *Kojak* dominated the televisual panorama of the 1975–76 season. The appearance of nonviolent, well-crafted, and well-acted programs like

Family constituted a refreshing alternative to the predominant action-packed TV scene and were readily embraced by TV audiences.

Family follows the saga of the Lawrences, a white, middle-class family from Pasadena, California. The clan consists of the parents, Kate and Doug (played by Sada Thompson and the late James Broderick), and their three offspring: Nancy, a divorced mother of an infant, Timmy, and a lawyer (originally played in the miniseries by Elaine Heilveil; portrayed in the regular series by Meredith Baxter-Birney); Willie, a high school dropout and a talented and idealistic aspiring writer (played by Gary Frank); and free-spirited teenager Letitia, better known as "Buddy" (played by Kristy McNichol). During its 1978–79 season, a new regular character joined the series: Annie Cooper, an 11-year-old orphan girl whom the Lawrences decide to adopt (played by Quinn Cummings).

Throughout its five seasons, the series engaged a range of contemporary social issues within the parameters of its melodramatic structure. For example, the miniseries opened with a pregnant Nancy divorcing her husband, Jeff (played by John Rubinstein), after finding him in bed with one of her girlfriends. This development allowed the series to explore, through the character of Nancy, issues related to the social position of a divorced, professional woman who is also a mother. On a couple of occasions, the show dealt with issues pertaining to homosexuality. In one episode, Willie's best friend comes out of the closet, forcing Willie to reconsider his positions about both friendship and homosexuality. In a similar vein, Buddy faces issues about bigotry when a teacher she admires is to be fired because that teacher is a lesbian. On several occasions, the Lawrence matriarch, Kate, finds herself in difficult social, moral, and ethical positions related to her social situation as a middle-aged woman. In one instance, an older-than-40 Kate faces the dilemma of possibly having to have an abortion because she is expecting a child at an age when risks and complications related to pregnancy are higher than they are for younger women. In another episode, Kate confronts her insecurities and fears when she decides to take a job outside the house. At a different point in the series, she deals with having breast cancer.

Family not only reclaimed a place for hour-long (melo)dramatic series dealing with everyday topics affecting middle-class Americans during an age when action series ruled; it also prepared the ground for the prime-time soap operas centered around affluent and glamorous nuclear families—shows such as *Dallas, Dynasty, Knots Landing,* and *Falcon Crest* that exploded in popularity during the late 1970s and 1980s.

GILBERTO M. BLASINI

See also **Melodrama; Spelling, Aaron**

Cast

Kate Lawrence	Sada Thompson
Doug Lawrence	James Broderick
Nancy Lawrence Maitland (1976)	Elayne Heilveil
Nancy Lawrence Maitland (1976–80)	Meredith Baxter-Birney
Willie Lawrence	Gary Frank
Letitia "Buddy" Lawrence	Kristy McNichol
Jeff Maitland	John Rubinstein
Mrs. Hanley (1976–78)	Mary Grace Canfield
Salina Magee (1976–77)	Season Hubley
Annie Cooper (1978–80)	Quinn Cummings
Timmy Maitland (1978–80)	Michael David Schackelford

Producers

Aaron Spelling, Leonard Goldberg, Mike Nichols

Programming History

94 episodes
ABC

March 1976–February 1978	Tuesday 10:00–11:00
May 1978	Tuesday 10:00–11:00
September 1978–March 1979	Thursday 10:00–11:00
March 1979–April 1979	Friday 8:00–9:00
May 1979	Thursday 10:00–11:00
December 1979–February 1980	Monday 10:00–11:00
March 1980	Monday 9:00–10:00
June 1980	Wednesday 8:00–9:00

Further Reading

Barber, Rowland, "Three Strikes and They're On," *TV Guide* (January 21, 1978)

Family on Television

The introduction of television after World War II coincided in the United States with a steep rise in mortgage rates, birthrates, and the growth of mass-produced suburbs. In this social climate, it is no wonder that television was conceived as, first and foremost, a family medium. Over the course of the 1950s, as debates raged in Congress over issues such as juvenile delinquency and the mass media's contribution to it, the three major television networks developed prime-time fare that would appeal to a general family audience. Many of these policy debates and network strategies are echoed in the more recent public controversies concerning television and family values, especially the famous *Murphy Brown* incident in which Vice President Dan Quayle used the name of this fictional unwed mother as an example of what is wrong with the cultural values of the United States. As the case of Quayle demonstrates, the public often assumes that television fictional representations of the family have a strong impact on actual families in the United States. For this reason, people have often also assumed that these fictional households ought to mirror not simply family life in general, but their own personal values regarding

it. Throughout television history, then, the representation of the family has been a concern in Congress, among special-interest groups and lobbyists, the general audience, and, of course, the industry that has attempted to satisfy all of these parties in different ways and with different emphases.

In the early 1950s, domestic life was represented with some degree of diversity. There were families who lived in suburbs, cities, and rural areas. There were nuclear families (such as that in *The Adventures of Ozzie and Harriet*) and childless couples (such as the Stevenses of *I Married Joan* or Sapphire and Kingfish of *Amos 'n' Andy*). There was a variety of ethnic families in domestic comedies and family dramas (including the Norwegian family of *Mama* and the Jewish family of *The Goldbergs*). In addition, anthology dramas such as *Marty* sometimes presented ethnic working-class families. At a time when many Americans were moving from cities to mass-produced suburbs, these programs featured nostalgic versions of family and neighborhood bonding that played on sentimentality for the more "authentic" social relationships of the urban past. Ethnicity was typically popular so

An American Family, The Loud Family (Top row: Lance, Michelle; Middle row: Kevin, Delilah, Grant; Front row: Pat, Bill), 1971.
Courtesy of the Everett Collection

long as it was a portrayal of first-generation European immigrants; the lives of black, Hispanic, and Asian families were almost never explored. When minorities were represented, it was generally to provide humor or to play upon racist stereotypes; examples include the Cuban Ricky Ricardo, with his Latin temper, or the African-American Beulah, with her job as the happy maid/mammy in a white household.

Meanwhile, in 1950s documentaries and in fiction programming, the family often served as the patriotic reason "why we fight" communism, much as it served as a source of patriotism in the Norman Rockwell magazine covers of World War II. Action-adventure programs, such as the syndicated series *I Led Three Lives,* included numerous episodes in which communists infiltrated families and threatened to pervert American youth. Paradoxically, however, the family also provided a reason why Americans should fight the more extremist versions of anticommunism, especially that espoused by Senator Joseph McCarthy. In 1952 Edward R. Murrow's *See It Now* presented "The Case of Milo Radulovich," about an air force pilot who was suspected of communist sympathies. Murrow used interviews with Radulovich's sister and father to convince viewers that he was not a communist but instead a true American with solid family values. From the outset, the family on television served both sentimen-

tal and political/ideological functions, which were often intertwined.

By the mid-1950s, as television production moved to Hollywood film studios and was also controlled by Hollywood independent production companies such as Desilu, the representation of family life became even more standardized in the domestic comedy. By 1960, the ethnic domestic comedies and dramas disappeared, and the suburban domestic comedy rose to prominence. Programs such as *The Donna Reed Show, Leave It to Beaver,* and *Father Knows Best* presented idealized versions of white middle-class families in suburban communities that mirrored the practices of ethnic and racial exclusion seen in U.S. suburbs more generally. Even while these programs captured the American imagination, there was a penchant for social criticism registered in 1950s science fiction/horror anthologies (such as *The Twilight Zone*'s "Monsters on Maple Street," which explored the paranoid social relationships and exclusionary tactics in American suburban towns).

Within the domestic comedy form itself, the nuclear family was increasingly displaced by a counterprogramming trend that represented broken families and unconventional families. Coinciding with rising divorce rates in the 1960s, numerous shows featured families led by a single father (including comedies such as *My Three Sons* and *Family Affair* and the western *Bonanza*), while others featured single mothers (including comedies such as *Julia* and *Here's Lucy,* and the western *The Big Valley*). In all these programs, censorship codes demanded that the single parent not be divorced; instead the missing parent was always explained through a death in the family. By 1967 the classic domestic comedies featuring nuclear families were all canceled, while these broken families, as well as a new trend of "fantastic families" in programs like *Bewitched* and *The Addams Family* accounted for the mainstay of the genre.

At the level of the news, these fictional programs were met by the tragic breakup of the U.S.'s first family, as the coverage of President John F. Kennedy's funeral haunted American television screens. It could be argued that the proliferation and popularity of broken families in television entertainment genres provided a means for American society to respond to, and aesthetically resolve, the loss of the nation's father and the dream or nuclear family life that he and his family represented.

As the nation mourned, other program genres showed cause for more general sorrow. Despite the fact that domestic comedy families were well-to-do, the 1960s also included depictions of the American underclass in hard-hitting socially relevant dramas such as the short-lived *East Side/West Side,* which explored issues of child abuse and welfare in New York slums. Television also presented documentaries such as *Hunger in America* and *Harvest of Shame,* which depicted underprivileged children, while other documentaries such as *Middletown* or *Salesmen* chronicled the everyday lives of typical Americans, demonstrating the impossibility of living up to the American family ideal. This trend toward social criticism was capped off in 1973, when PBS aired *An American Family,* which chronicled the everyday life of Mr. and Mrs. William Loud and their suburban family by placing cameras in their home and surveying their day-to-day affairs. As the cameras watched, the Louds filed for divorce and their son came out as a homosexual. The discrepancies between these documentary/socially relevant depictions of American families and the more idealized images in the domestic comedy genre were now all too clear.

More generally, the 1970s were a time of significant change, as the portrayal of family life became more diverse, although never completely representative of all American lifestyles. Network documentaries continued to expose the underside of the American Dream, while other genres took on the burden of social criticism as they attempted to reach a new demographic of young urban professionals, working women, and a rising black middle class. Programs such as Norman Lear's *All in the Family, Maude,* and *The Jeffersons* flourished. *All in the Family* presented a working-class milieu and drew its comedy out of political differences among generations and between genders in the household; *Maude* was the first program to feature a divorced heroine, who, in one two-part episode, also had the first prime-time abortion. African-American families were presented in shows ranging from *The Jeffersons,* who had, as the opening theme song announced, finally got "a piece of the pie," to programs set in ghettos such as *Good Times.* Interracial families such as *Webster* depicted white parents bringing up black children (although the reverse was never the case). From the mid-1970s through the present, these new family formations have included programs featuring single moms (who were now often divorced or never married) such as *Kate and Allie, One Day at a Time,* and *Murphy Brown.* Drawing on previous working-girl/mother sitcoms like *Our Miss Brooks* or *Here's Lucy,* the MTM studio precipitated a shift from literal biological families to a new concept of the family workplace. Here, in programs such as *The Mary Tyler Moore Show,* coworkers were also codependents, so that relationships were often ambiguously collegial and familial. Despite these innovations, the 1970s and early 1980s still featured sentimental versions of family life including daytime soap operas, family dramas such as *Family* and *Eight Is Enough,* historical-family dramas such as *The Waltons* and *Little House on the Prairie,* and the popular comedy *The Brady Bunch.*

Over the course of the 1980s, the genre of prime-time soap opera served as television's answer to the Reagan-era dream of consumer prosperity. Programs such as *Dallas* and *Dynasty* presented a world of high fashion, high finance, and, for many, high camp sensibilities. Despite their idealized upper-class settings, these programs, like daytime soaps or the 1960s *Peyton Place,* dealt with marital infidelity, incest, rape, alcoholism, and a range of other issues that pictured the family as decidedly dysfunctional. Perhaps because these families were extremely wealthy, audiences could view their problems as a symptom of upper-crust decadence rather than a more general failure in American family life experienced by people of all social backgrounds. Wealth was also apparent in the enormously popular *The Cosby Show,* which featured black professionals living an ideal family life. Unlike *Dallas* or *Dynasty,* however, which were widely appreciated for their escapist fantasies and/or camp exaggeration, *Cosby* was often taken to task for not being realistic enough.

In addition to prime-time soaps and family comedies, other programs of the 1980s and 1990s showcased dysfunctional families and/or families in crisis. Made-for-TV-movies such as *The Burning Bed* detailed the horrors of spousal abuse. In addition, during this period, the television talk show took over the role of family therapist as programs such as *Geraldo, The Oprah Winfrey Show,* and *The Jerry Springer Show* feature real-life family feuds with guests who confess to incest, spousal abuse, matricide, codependencies, and a range of other family perversions. Unlike the daytime soap operas, these programs lack the sentiment of family melodrama and thus appear more akin to their contemporary cousin, the TV tabloid. These syndicated "tabloid" shows such as *COPS* or *America's Most Wanted* offer a range of family horrors as law enforcement agencies and vigilantes apprehend the outlaws of the nation. Tabloids not only demonstrate how to catch a thief and other criminals, they also engage in didactic editorializing that either explicitly or implicitly suggests that crimes such as robbery, prostitution, or drug dealing are caused by dysfunctional family lives rather than by political, sexual, racial, or class inequities.

Still, in other instances, the family remains "wholesome," especially in the age of cable when the broadcast networks often try to win a family audience by presenting themselves as more clean-cut than their cable competitors. (For example, in various seasons on different nights, ABC and NBC have both fashioned lineups of family-oriented programs aimed at mothers and children.)

Over the course of the 1980s and through the present, innovation on old formats has also been a key strategy. Programs such as the popular sitcom *Family Ties* reversed the usual generational politics of comedy by making the parents more liberal than their conservative, money-obsessed son. In the later 1980s, the new FOX network largely ingratiated itself with the public by displaying a contempt for the "white-bread" standards of old network television. Programs such as *Married…with Children* parodied the middle-class suburban sitcom, while sitcoms such as *Living Single* and the prime-time soap *Melrose Place* presented alternate youth-oriented lifestyles. ABC's *Roseanne* followed suit with its highly popular parody of family life that included such unconventional sitcom topics as teenage sex, spousal abuse, and lesbian romance. In 1994 ABC broadcast *All-American Girl,* the first sitcom to feature the generational conflicts in a Korean family.

Parody and unconventional topicality were not the only solutions to innovation. If portrayals of contemporary happy families seemed somewhat disingenuous or at best cliché by the end of the 1980s, television could still turn to nostalgia to create sentimental versions of family togetherness. For example, family dramas such as *The Wonder Years* and *Brooklyn Bridge* presented popular memories of the United States during the baby boom. Both nostalgia and parody are also the genius in the system of the cable network Nickelodeon, which is owned by Viacom, the country's largest syndicator. Its prime-time lineup, which it calls "Nick at Nite," features Viacom-owned reruns of mostly family sitcoms from television's first three decades, and Nick advertises them through parodic slogans that make fun of the happy shiny people of old TV. Other cable networks have also premised themselves on the breakdown of nuclear family ideology and living arrangements by, for example, rethinking the conventional depictions of home life on broadcast genres. For instance, MTV's Generation X and Y serialized programs under the general title *The Real World* chronicle the real-life adventures of young people from different races and sexual orientations living together in a house provided by the network. Nevertheless, cable has also been extremely aware of ways to tap into the ongoing national agenda for family values and has turned this into marketing values. Pat Robertson's Family Channel is an example of how the Christian Right has used cable to rekindle the passion for a particular kind of family life, mostly associated with the middle-class family ideals of the 1950s and early 1960s. In this regard, it is no surprise that the Family Channel showed reruns of *Father Knows Best,* but without the parodic, campy wink of Nick at Nite's evening lineup.

More generally, the rise during the 1990s of multichannel cable TV has meant that audience shares for any one show are much lower than in the past. By the new millennium, what is often called "postnetwork" television presented a host of different kinds of family shows aimed at smaller "niche" audiences' varying tastes and different lifestyles. The Christian family values of WB's drama *7th Heaven* attracted one audience, while sitcoms like NBC's *Seinfeld* or Comedy Central's *Strangers with Candy* either ironically mocked or else openly rejected the premises of nuclear family life. While some critics have deplored these contemporary "no family" sitcoms, others have championed them as a welcome relief to our culture's narrow definition of what a family is and should be.

So too, numerous shows in the 1990s began to feature gay and lesbian households, presenting lifestyles predicated on the rights of individuals to form families with same-sex partners. In 1997, when Ellen Degeneres's character came out as a lesbian on the ABC sitcom *Ellen,* she followed a longer line of network flirtations with lesbian characters (ranging from lesbian episodes of such shows as CBS's *All in the Family* to NBC's *The Golden Girls* to ABC's *Roseanne*). Yet, unlike these earlier examples, which flirted with lesbian lifestyles in a single episode/storyline of a series, *Ellen* was the first major sitcom to feature a lesbian as a continuing lead character. In this regard, Ellen represented a clear sign that lesbian love was beginning to be depicted as part of the mainstream of television entertainment (if only because advertisers felt there was money to be made in that market). Since 1998 NBC has aired the popular *Will & Grace,* which centers on the extremely close relationship between a heterosexual woman and her best friend, a gay man.

Although television has consistently privileged the family as the "normal" and most fulfilling way to live one's life, its programs have often presented multiple and contradictory messages. At the same time that a sitcom featured June Cleaver wondering what suit to buy the Beaver, a documentary or news program showed the underside of family abuse or the severe poverty in which some families were forced to live. Because television draws on an enormous stable of representational traditions and creative personnel, and because the industry has attempted to appeal to large nationwide audiences, the medium never presents one simple message. Instead it is in the relations among different programs and genres that we begin to get a view of the range of possibilities. Those possibilities have, of course, been limited by larger social ideologies such as the racism or homophobia that affects the quality and quantity of shows depicting nonwhite and nonheterosexual households. Despite these ongoing exclusions, however, it is evident that the family on television is as full of mixed messages and ambivalent emotions as it is in real life.

LYNN SPIGEL

See also Adventures of Ozzie and Harriet; Amos 'n' Andy; Bewitched; Bonanza; Brady Bunch; Cosby Show; Dallas; Dynasty; Family Ties; Father Knows Best; Goldbergs; Good Times; I Love Lucy; Jeffersons; Julia; Kate and Allie; Leave It to Beaver; Married...with Children; Mary Tyler Moore Show; Maude; My Three Sons; Peyton Place; Roseanne; Waltons; Wonder Years

Further Reading

Boddy, William, *Fifties Television: The Industry and Its Critics,* Urbana: University of Illinois Press, 1990

Friedan, Betty, "Television and the Feminine Mystique," *TV Guide* (February 1 and 8, 1964)

Hamamoto, Darrell Y., *Nervous Laughter: Television Situation Comedy and Liberal Democratic Ideology,* New York: Praeger, 1989

Haralovitch, Mary Beth, "Sitcoms and Suburbs: Positioning the 1950s Homemaker," *Quarterly Review of Film and Video* (May 1989)

Leibman, Nina C., *Living Room Lectures: The Fifties Family in Film and Television,* Austin: University of Texas Press, 1995

Lipsitz, George, "The Meaning of Memory: Family, Class, and Ethnicity in Early Network Television," *Camera Obscura* (January 1988)

Marc, David, *Demographic Vistas: Television in American Culture,* Philadelphia: University of Pennsylvania Press, 1984; 2nd edition, 1996

Marc, David, *Comic Visions: Television Comedy and American Culture,* Boston: Unwin Hyman, 1989; 2nd edition, Malden, Massachusetts: Blackwell Publishers, 1997

Meehan, Diana, *Ladies of the Evening: Women Characters of Prime-Time Television,* Metuchen, New Jersey: Scarecrow Press, 1983

Mellencamp, Patricia, "Situation Comedy, Feminism, and Freud: Discourse of Gracie and Lucy," in *Studies in Entertainment: Critical Approaches to Mass Culture,* edited by Tania Modleski, Bloomington: Indiana University Press, 1986

Spigel, Lynn, *Make Room for TV: Television and the Family Ideal in Postwar America,* Chicago: University of Chicago Press, 1992

Taylor, Ella, *Prime-Time Families: Television Culture in Postwar America,* Berkeley: University of California Press, 1989

Family Ties

U.S. Domestic Comedy

Few shows demonstrate better than *Family Ties* the resonance between the collectively held fictional imagination and what cultural critic Raymond Williams has called "the structure of feeling" of a historical moment. Airing on NBC from 1982 to 1989, this highly successful domestic comedy explored one of the intriguing cultural inversions characterizing the Reagan era: a conservative younger generation aspiring to wealth, business success, and traditional values serves as inheritor to the politically liberal, presumably activist, culturally experimental generation of adults who had experienced the 1960s. The result was a decade, paradoxical by the United States' usual post–World War II standards, in which youthful ambition and social renovation came to be equated with pronounced political conservatism. "When else could a boy with a briefcase become a national hero?"

queried *Family Ties'* creator Gary David Goldberg, during the show's final year.

The boy with the briefcase was Alex P. Keaton (Michael J. Fox), a competitive and uncompromising, baby-faced conservative whose absurdly hard-nosed platitudes seemed the antithesis of his comfortable, middle-class, white, midwestern upbringing. Yet Alex could also be endearingly (and youthfully) bumbling when tenderness or intimacy demanded departure from the social conventions so important to him. He also could be riddled with self-doubt about his ability to meet the high standards he set for himself. During the course of the show, Alex aged from a high school student running for student council president to a college student reconciled to his rejection by Princeton University.

Alex's highly programmatic views of life led to continual conflict with his parents Steven (Michael Gross)

Family Ties, Tina Yothers, Justine Bateman, Michael Gross, Meredith Baxter-Birney, Michael J. Fox, 1982–89.
Courtesy of the Everett Collection

and Elyse (Meredith Baxter-Birney). Former war protesters and Peace Corps volunteers, these adults now found fulfillment raising their children and working, respectively, as a public television station manager and as an independent architect. If young Alex could be comically cynical, his parents could be relentlessly cheerful do-gooders, whose causes occasionally seemed chimerical. Yet (especially with Elyse) their liberalism could also emerge more authoritatively, particularly when it assumed the voice, not of ideological instruction, but of parental conscience and loving tolerance. And so *Family Ties* explored not just the cultural ironies of politically conservative youth, but the equally powerful paradox of liberal conscience. Here, that conscience was kept alive within the loving nuclear family, a social form so constantly appropriated by conservatives as a manifestation of their own values.

Significantly, the show's timely focus on Alex and his contrasts with his parents was discovered rather than designed. *Family Ties'* creator Goldberg was an ex-hippie whose three earlier network shows had each been canceled within weeks, leading him to promise that *Family*

Ties would be his last attempt. He undertook the show as a basically autobiographical comedy that would explore the parents' adjustments to 1980s society and middle-aged family life. The original casting focused on Gross and Baxter-Birney as the crucial Keatons. Once the show aired, however, network surveys quickly revealed that audiences were more attracted by the accomplished physical comedy, skillful characterization, and good looks of Fox's Alex. Audience reaction and Fox's considerable, unexpected authority in front of the camera prompted Goldberg and his collaborators to shift emphasis to the young man, a change so fundamental that Goldberg told Gross and Baxter-Birney that he would understand if they decided to quit. The crucial intergenerational dynamic of the show thus emerged in a dialogue between viewers, who identified Alex as a compelling character, and writers, who were willing to reorient the show's themes of cultural succession around the youth. Goldberg's largely liberal writers usually depicted Alex's ideology ironically, through self-indicting punch lines. Many audiences, however, were laughing sympathetically, and Alex Keaton emerged as a model of the clean-cut, determined, yet human entrepreneur. *Family Ties* finished the 1983 and 1984 seasons as the second-highest-rated show on television and finished in the top 20 for six of its seven years. President Ronald Reagan declared *Family Ties* his favorite program and offered to make an appearance on the show (an offer pointedly ignored by the producers). Fox was able to launch a considerable career in feature films based on his popularity from the show.

Alex had three siblings. Justine Bateman played Mallory, the inarticulate younger sister who, unwilling to compete with the overachieving Alex, devoted herself to fashion and boyfriends, including the elder Keaton's nemesis, junkyard sculptor Nick (played by Scott Valentine). Tina Yothers played the younger daughter, Jennifer, an intelligent observer who could pronounce scathingly on either Alex's or the parents' foibles. During the 1984 season, a baby boy named Andrew joined the Keaton family; this character was played by three separate children, as, by the next season, he quickly developed into a toddler.

Both *Family Ties*' creator and its production style are products of a specific set of events in Hollywood that, in the mid-1980s, granted promising writer-producers unusual opportunity and resources to pursue their creative interests. Goldberg's first jobs in television were as a writer and writer-producer for MTM Productions, the independent production company founded by Grant Tinker and Mary Tyler Moore. The company was initially devoted to the production of "quality" comedies and known for the special respect it accorded writers. In the early 1980s the booming syndication market and continued vertical integration prompted Hollywood to consider writers who could create new programs as important long-term investments. Paramount Studios raided MTM for its most promising talents, among them Goldberg. Like many of his cohorts, Goldberg was able to negotiate for a production company of his own, partial ownership of his shows, and a commitment from Paramount to help fund his next project—all in exchange for Paramount's exclusive rights to distribute the resulting programs. Goldberg applied the methods of proscenium comedy production he had learned at MTM, developing *Family Ties* as a character-based situation comedy, sustained by imaginative dialogue, laudable acting, and carefully considered scripts that were the focus of a highly collaborative weekly production routine. (*Inside Family Ties*, a PBS special produced in 1985, shows actors, the director, and writers each taking considerable license to alter the script; Goldberg mentions that he takes it for granted that 60 percent of a typical episode will be rewritten during the week.) Each episode was shot live before a studio audience, to retain the crucial excitement and unity of a stage play.

In *Family Ties*' third season, the program played an unprecedented role in the production industry's growing independence from the declining broadcast networks. Paramount guaranteed syndicators that it would provide them with a minimum of 95 episodes of *Family Ties*, though only 70 or so had been completed at the time. Anxious to capitalize on the booming syndication market, Paramount was, in effect, agreeing to produce the show even if NBC canceled it—a decision anticipating Paramount's later, successful distribution of *Star Trek: The Next Generation* exclusively through syndication.

Michael Saenz

See also **Comedy, Domestic Settings; Family on Television**

Cast

Elyse Keaton	Meredith Baxter-Birney
Steven Keaton	Michael Gross
Alex P. Keaton	Michael J. Fox
Mallory Keaton	Justine Bateman
Jennifer Keaton	Tina Yothers
Andrew Keaton (1986–89)	Brian Bonsall
Irwin "Skippy" Handelman	Marc Price
Ellen Reed (1985–86)	Tracy Pollan
Nick Moore (1985–89)	Scott Valentine
Lauren Miller (1987–89)	Courteney Cox

Producers

Gary David Goldberg, Lloyd Garver, Michael Weinthorn

Programming History

180 episodes
NBC

September 1982–March 1983	Wednesday 9:30–10:00
March 1983–August 1983	Monday 8:30–9:00
August 1983–December 1983	Wednesday 9:30–10:00
January 1984–August 1987	Thursday 8:30–9:00
August 1987–September 1987	Sunday 8:00–9:00
September 1987–September 1989	Sunday 8:00–8:30

Family Viewing Time

Prompted by widespread public criticism, in 1974 the United States Congress exhorted the Federal Communications Commission (FCC) to take action regarding the perennial issues of alleged excesses of sex, crime, and violence in broadcast programming. Early in 1975 FCC chairman Richard E. Wiley reported to Senate and House Communications and Commerce Subcommittees recent steps taken by the FCC. They included discussions with corporate heads of television networks that resulted in four strategies for addressing the issues. The network heads adopted a self-declared "family viewing" hour in the first hour of network evening prime time (8:00–9:00 P.M., Eastern time). Actions by the National Association of Broadcasters' Television Code review board expanded that "family hour" forward one hour into local station time (7:00–8:00 P.M.). The NAB also proposed "viewer advisories" related to program content that might disturb members of the audience, especially younger people. And the FCC made further efforts to define what it construed as "indecent" under the law, in a case involving Pacifica's WBAI(FM), New York.

Arthur R. Taylor, president of CBS Inc., had championed more acceptable early-evening programming but could only do so at CBS if competing networks followed suit. FCC chairman Wiley urged reluctant executives to adopt these actions. But to avoid intercorporate collusion they felt the professional association (NAB) could best orchestrate the effort through its self-regulatory Industry Code of Practices. Enacting the code led to several results. Some early-evening shows with comedy and action deemed less suited for young viewers were displaced to later hours. West Coast producers, directors, and writers claimed the new structure infringed on their creative freedom and First Amendment rights. Later scheduling also led to lower audience ratings, partly from the stigma attached to some programs as inappropriate for viewing by families. Popular sitcom *All in the Family* suffered from the ruling; its producer Norman Lear protested against the policy and with celebrity colleagues and professional guilds mounted a lawsuit against it. Meanwhile some public-interest groups, including major religious organizations, objected to the policy for not going far enough; they claimed it sanitized only an hour or two of TV programming, leaving the rest of the 24-hour schedule open to "anything goes."

After extensive hearings U.S. district court judge Warren Ferguson ruled that, while the concept might have merit, the FCC had acted improperly in finessing the result by privately persuading the three network representatives to marshall the NAB's code provisions. Normal FCC procedure was to openly announce proposals for rulemaking, then hold public hearings to develop a record from which federal rulings might be developed. Thus the Family Viewing policy was scuttled, apparently to the satisfaction of not only the creative community that produced programs but to most network personnel who had the complicated task of applying the principle to specific shows and time slots, with direct impact on ratings and time sales for commercial spots. Syndicators of off-network reruns also were relieved because the early-evening "fringe time" programmed by local stations had been brought into the ambit of the code's provisions, limiting the kinds of shows aired then. But the reversal was frustrating to many members of Congress, to FCC chairman Wiley, and to CBS chief Arthur Taylor. Dubbed by many the "father of Family Viewing," Taylor had proclaimed the policy as the first step in 25 years to reduce the level of gratuitous TV violence and sex. John Schneider, president of the CBS/Broadcast Group, issued a statement after the court's decision: "The Court recognizes the right of an individual broadcaster to maintain programming standards, yet it denies this same right to broadcasters collectively, even though these standards are entirely voluntary. . . . To rule that broadcasters cannot, however openly and publicly, create a set of programming standards consonant with the demonstrated wishes of the American people leaves only two alternatives: no standards for the broadcasting community or standards imposed by government, which we believe would dangerously violate the spirit of the First Amendment. CBS's belief that family viewing is an exercise of broadcaster responsibility in the public interest is confirmed by its popular acceptance" reported by a major publication's two national polls.

The episode demonstrated the daunting task of guiding a complex mass entertainment medium in a pluralistic society with varied perspectives and values. Through the decades television came under increasing scrutiny for alleged permissiveness in drama and comedy programs. The theme of excessive "sex and violence" was sounded regularly in congressional sessions from Senator Estes Kefauver in the 1950s to Senator Thomas Dodd in the 1960s and Senator John Pastore in the 1970s. By 1975 House Communications Subcommittee chairman Torbert MacDonald, fearing the Family Viewing plan was no more than a public relations ploy, raised the perennial threat of licensing the source of national program service, the commercial networks. Meanwhile, the FCC sought to clarify the U.S. Code provision (Title 18, §1464) prohibiting obscene, indecent, or profane language, to extend explicitly to visual depiction of such material.

The issue joined, of course, is the broadcaster's freedom to program a station or network without censorship by governmental prior restraining action (or by ex post facto penalty that constitutes implied restraint against subsequent actions). That freedom is closely coupled with the diverse public's right to have access to a wide range of programming that viewers freely choose to watch. The other side of that coin is the audience's right to freedom *from* what some consider offensive program content broadcast over a federally licensed airwave frequency defined by Congress in 1927 and 1934 as a "natural public resource" owned by the public. The problem arises from the medium's pervasiveness (the Supreme Court's wording) that reaches into homes and beyond to portable receivers, readily available to young children often unable to be supervised around the clock by parents. FCC chairman Wiley explained to the Senate Commerce Committee in 1975: "we believe that the industry reforms strike an appropriate balance between two conflicting objectives. On the one hand, it is necessary that the industry aid concerned parents in protecting their children from objectionable material; on the other hand, it is important that the medium have an opportunity to develop artistically and to present themes which are appropriate and of interest to an adult audience." The issue recurred, as deregulation of broadcast media in the 1980s and growing permissiveness of program content on proliferating cable channels was succeeded in the 1990s by widespread calls for "family values" in media. Senator Paul Simon engineered a waiver of antitrust provisions enabling major networks and cable companies to collaborate on voluntary self-regulatory practices, to preclude threatened government enactments.

JAMES A. BROWN

See also **Censorship, Programming**

Further Reading

Cowan, Geoffrey, *See No Evil: The Backstage Battle over Sex and Violence on Television,* New York: Simon and Schuster, 1979

Rowland, Willard D., *The Politics of TV Violence: Policy Uses of Communication Research,* Beverly Hills, California: Sage, 1983

Farnsworth, Philo T. (1906–1971)

U.S. Inventor

Philo T. Farnsworth has been called the forgotten father of television. Those who knew him said he was a genius from birth. At the age of 13, he won a prize offered by the *Science and Invention* magazine for developing a thief-proof automobile ignition switch. Most remarkable from his high school experience was the diagram he drew for his chemistry teacher. This drawing established the pattern for his later experiments in electronics and was instrumental in Farnsworth winning a patent interference case pitting him against Radio Corporation of America (RCA). Farnsworth's work spanned the continent. His first laboratories were in his Hollywood home; later he and his family moved to San Francisco, Philadelphia, Fort Wayne, Indiana, and Salt Lake City, Utah. In 1926 he established his first corporation, in San Francisco, Everson Gorrell and Farnsworth Inc. The first patents for the Farnsworth television system were filed in January 1927. In 1929 the corporation became Television Laboratories Incorporated. Among the first television images created from the Farnsworth system were laboratory smoke, a single dimension line, a dollar sign printed on glass. The first woman to appear on television was Elma G. Farnsworth, Philo's wife. Her photograph was transmitted in the San Francisco Green Street laboratory on September 19, 1929.

In 1931 Farnsworth moved to Philadelphia to establish a television department for Philco. By 1933 Philco decided that television patent research was no longer a part of its corporate vision, and Farnsworth created

Farnsworth Television Inc. In August 1934 this company provided the world's first public demonstration of an all-electronic television system, which ran for ten days at the Philadelphia Franklin Institute. In 1938 Farnsworth established the Farnsworth Television and Radio Corporation. This research and manufacturing company created defense technology throughout World War II and was later purchased by the International Telephone and Telegraph Company (IT&T), which still stands in Fort Wayne, Indiana. Farnsworth's work for IT&T included both television and nuclear fusion.

In December 1938 Farnsworth moved to Salt Lake City to organize his last venture: Philo T. Farnsworth and Associates. Its purpose was to continue the work he started at IT&T on fusion, which was expected to be inexpensive alternative energy source. This work ended at this death.

Farnsworth was an independent experimenter, a charismatic scientist, an idea person who was able to initiate ideas and convince investors. However, his primary focus was always in the laboratory. He was a workaholic and often left the business, investment, and management responsibilities of his corporations to others as his experiments continued. He was so immersed in his inventions that he reportedly would forget to eat. His health proved to be a challenge throughout his life.

Farnsworth's wife worked constantly at his side and helped maintain his health. She worked in the earliest labs as a technician and a bookkeeper. Farnsworth himself said, "my wife and I started television." After he died, it was his wife who worked to ensure he was recognized for his inventions and his place in history. In many ways, Farnsworth's posthumous awards recognize the bygone era of independent inventors that he represented. He was the recipient of numerous awards from scientific and honors societies, and a 1983 U.S. postage stamp commemorates the inventor. In 1981 a historical marker was placed on the San Francisco Green Street building where the first Farnsworth television image was projected. In 1990 a statue was dedicated in Washington's Statuary Hall: the inscription reads "Philo Taylor Farnsworth: Inventor of Television."

DONALD G. GODFREY

See also **Television Technology**

Philo T(aylor) Farnsworth. Born in Beaver Creek, Utah, August 19, 1906. Educated at Rigby Idaho High School; attended Brigham Young University, 1923–25. Married Elma "Pem" Gardner, 1926, four children. Research director, Crocker Research Labs, 1926; founded Television Laboratories Incorporated, 1929; organized television department for Philco, 1931–33; vice president, founder, and director of research and engineering, Farnsworth Television and Radio Corporation, 1938; researcher in television and nuclear fusion, International Telephone and Telegraph Company, from 1949; president and director of research, Farnsworth Research Corporation, 1957; president and director, Philo T. Farnsworth and Associates, Inc., 1968. Honorary doctorates of science from the Indiana Institute of Technology, 1951; Brigham Young University, 1968. Member: American Physics Society. Named to the National Inventors Hall of Fame, 1968. Died in Salt Lake City, Utah, March 11, 1971.

Further Reading

Everson, George, *The Story of Television: The Life of Philo T. Farnsworth,* New York: Norton, 1949

Farnsworth, Elma G., *Distant Vision: Romance and Discovery on an Invisible Frontier,* Salt Lake City, Utah: Pemberly Kent, 1990

Godfrey, Donald G., and Alf Pratte, "Elma 'Pem' Gardner Farnsworth: The Pioneering of Television," *Journalism History* (Summer 1994)

Hofer, Stephen F., "Philo Farnsworth: Television's Pioneer," *Journal of Broadcasting* (Spring 1979)

Schwartz, Evan I., *The Last Lone Inventor: A Tale of Genius, Deceit, and the Birth of Television,* New York: HarperCollins, 2002

Stashower, Daniel, *The Boy Genius and the Mogul: The Untold Story of Television,* New York: Broadway Books, 2002

Father Knows Best

U.S. Domestic Comedy

Father Knows Best, a family comedy of the 1950s, is perhaps more important for what it has come to represent than for what it actually was. In essence, the series was one of a number of middle-class family sitcoms, representing stereotypical family members. Today, many critics view it, at best, as high camp fun, and, at worst, as part of what critic David Marc once labeled the "Aryan melodramas" of the 1950s and 1960s.

Father Knows Best, Lauren Chapin, Elinor Donahue, Robert Young, Jane Wyatt, Billy Gray, 1954–60.
Courtesy of the Everett Collection

The brainchild of the series' star Robert Young, who played insurance salesman Jim Anderson, and producer Eugene B. Rodney, *Father Knows Best* first debuted as a radio sitcom in 1949. In the audio version, the title of the show ended with a question mark, suggesting that father's role as family leader and arbiter was dubious. The partners' production company, Rodney-Young Enterprises, transplanted the series to television in 1954—without the question mark—where it ran until 1960, appearing at various times on each of the three U.S. networks (CBS reran it from 1960 to 1962; ABC broadcast reruns from 1962 to 1963).

Young and Rodney, friends since 1935, based the series on experiences each had with wives and children; thus, to them, the show represented "reality." Indeed, careful viewing of each of the series' 203 episodes reveals that the title was actually more figurative than literal. Despite the lack of an actual question mark, father did not always know best. Jim Anderson occasionally lost his temper, and he was not always right. Although wife Margaret Anderson, played by Jane Wyatt, was stuck in the drudgery of domestic servitude, she was nobody's fool, often besting her husband and son, Bud (played by Billy Gray). Daughter Betty Anderson (Elinor Donahue), known affectionately to her father as

Princess, could also take the male Andersons to task, as could the precocious Kathy (Lauren Chapin), the baby of the family, who was also called "Kitten."

Like *Leave It to Beaver* creators Bob Mosher and Joe Connelly, Young and Rodney were candid about their attempts to provide moral lessons throughout the series. While none of the kids experienced the sort of social problems some of the real-life actors faced (Young was an alcoholic and the adult Chapin became a heroin addict), this was more the fault of television's then-myopic need for calm than Young and Rodney's desire to sidestep the truth. The series certainly avoided the existence of the "Other America," as did most other American institutions.

Young won two Emmy Awards for his role, and Wyatt won three. A well-known film actor before his radio and television days, Young went on to later success in the long-running series *Marcus Welby, M.D.,* which may have been more appropriately called "Doctor Knows Best." After *Father Knows Best* moved into prime-time reruns in 1960, Donahue played Sheriff Andy Taylor's love interest, Miss Ellie, on *The Andy Griffith Show.* In 1977 NBC brought the Andersons back in two reunion specials, *Father Knows Best: The Father Knows Best Reunion* (May 1977) and *Father Knows Best: Home for the Holidays* (December 1977).

MICHAEL B. KASSEL

See also **Comedy, Domestic Settings; Family on Television; Young, Robert**

Cast

Jim Anderson	Robert Young
Margaret Anderson	Jane Wyatt
Betty Anderson (Princess)	Elinor Donahue
James Anderson, Jr. (Bud)	Billy Gray
Kathy Anderson (Kitten)	Lauren Chapin
Miss Thomas	Sarah Selby
Ed Davis (1955–59)	Robert Foulk
Myrtle Davis (1955–59)	Vivi Jannis
Dotty Snow (1954–57)	Yvonne Lime
Kippy Watkins (1954–59)	Paul Wallace
Claude Messner (1954–59)	Jimmy Bates
Doyle Hobbs (1957–58)	Roger Smith
Ralph Little (1957–58)	Robert Chapman
April Adams (1957–58)	Sue George
Joyce Kendall (1958–59)	Jymme (Roberta) Shore

Producers
Eugene Rodney, Robert Young

Programming History
203 episodes

CBS
October 1954–March 1955   Sunday 10:00–10:30
NBC
August 1955–September
 1958   Wednesday 8:30–9:00
CBS
September 1958–September
 1960   Monday 8:30–9:00

Further Reading

Denis, Christopher Paul, and Michael Denis, *Favorite Families of TV,* New York: Citadel, 1992

Leibman, Nina C., *Living Room Lectures: The Fifties Family in Film and Television,* Austin: University of Texas Press, 1995

Taylor, Ella, *Prime-Time Families: Television Culture in Postwar America,* Berkeley: University of California Press, 1989

Father Ted

British Sitcom

Father Ted managed the difficult feat of being a comic triumph for two cultures. As a British-produced show it was exciting and innovative, scored a massive cult success, and gave Channel 4 its only real classic sitcom. As an Irish comedy it signaled a new cultural confidence to match the economic "Celtic tiger" of the 1990s—a not entirely unaffectionate debunking of national stereotypes and sacred cows.

Graham Linehan and Arthur Mathews, who had previously penned an unsuccessful sitcom, *Paris,* wrote the series. Geoffrey Perkins, head of comedy at British Independent producer Hat Trick, commissioned *Father Ted,* its series about three hopeless priests: the elderly, hideously debauched and incoherent Father Jack Hackett, the childlike young idiot priest Father Dougal McGuire, and the central protagonist, middle-aged Father Ted Crilly. The trio live on the remote and backward Craggy Island with their overhospitable housekeeper, Mrs. Doyle, who lives for tea-making and servitude.

Like many great sitcoms, the show consists of a group of ill-matched characters thrown into a situation they cannot escape. These are not simply physical confines, however, but a prison of their own making. The priests have been banished to the island by their nemesis, Bishop Brennan, for heinous crimes: Jack for general depravity, Dougal for accidental carnage involving nuns, and Ted for financial irregularities.

Linehan has said that he and Mathews thought of the series as being in the British sitcom tradition, and there are certainly familiar elements—the enclosed situation, a circular narrative structure, and the ability to eke out laughter from every aspect of human failure and natural disaster. However, there is also a wild creative surrealism through which every episode is caught up in a whirlwind of madness, whether it is a plague of rabbits, an invasion of zombiefied housewives, or the priests winning the Eurovision Song Contest. *Father Ted* is like Monty Python blended with the Irish literary tradition of Samuel Beckett and Flann O'Brien. While apparently anything can happen, in fact everything has its own logic based on how the characters react to particular circumstances. Events and actions are merely just taken to their ultimate bizarre conclusions.

Jack, Dougal, and Mrs. Doyle quickly became cult favorites across Britain and Ireland. Playgrounds and offices rang out with catchphrases: Jack's "Drink!!!!" and "Girls!" and Mrs. Doyle's pleas of "Ah go on, go on, go on." Their extreme physical comedy is hugely pleasurable, but they are essentially one-note characters—caricatures that by their nature lack subtlety or development.

The real joy of the series is Ted himself. He alone is played straight, as the calm center amid the chaos. Ted thinks he is the only normal person present and sees himself as a man of intelligence and discernment surrounded by idiots. But in the best comic tradition, he is perhaps the biggest idiot of all. Ted is only too susceptible to earthy pleasures beyond his calling, particularly to the possibility of acquiring large amounts of cash. The "financial irregularities" that consigned him to the island are the subject of much mirth. Any allusion to this leads to Ted fiercely protesting, "That was a routine relocation of funds. That money was just resting in my account." But as Dougal says, "It was resting for a long time, Ted."

Ted's dishonesty is matched only by his capacity for lying. Much of the comic energy derives from Ted's inability to admit the slightest mistake or endure the smallest embarrassment. Instead he invents the most bizarre, contorted lies to try and escape the situation. Inevitably they just catapult the story further and further into pandemonium.

Yet Ted is not portrayed as a venal monster, nor is he a smart amoral operator like Sergeant Bilko in *The Phil Silvers Show* or Norman Fletcher in *Porridge.* Rather, he is all too much like us—he tries his best to be good but is hopelessly flawed. This reality is summed up best in the final episode, when Ted is offered a parish in Los Angeles. He asks the American priest recruiting him, "Tell me, is it really as false and artificial as they say it is?" When assured this is the case, he says wistfully, "I'd love that."

Father Ted's anarchic brand of humor was deceptively gentle, but it managed to aim some fairly sharp blows at the Catholic Church. Not only are the Craggy Island priests utterly dysfunctional, corrupt, and less than spiritual, their colleagues in the cloth are no better. The complacency, sexism, and corruption of the Church are mercilessly, if subtly, mocked (coinciding with a massive decline in its influence in Ireland).

Linehan and Mathews decided to end the show after three series, while it was still at the height of its powers. Just after the last episode was filmed, Dermot Morgan, who played Ted, died of a heart attack. But *Father Ted's* popularity remains undimmed. Videos have sold well and Channel 4 has the series on virtually continual rerun.

PHIL WICKHAM

See also **Channel 4; Ireland; Religion on Television**

Cast

Father Ted Crilly	Dermot Morgan
Father Dougal McGuire	Ardal O'Hanlon
Father Jack Hackett	Frank Kelly
Mrs. Doyle	Pauline McLynn
Bishop Brennan	Jim Norton
Father Noel Furlong	Graham Norton

Writers

Graham Linehan and Arthur Mathews

Directors

Declan Lowney (series 1 and 2 and Christmas special), Andy de Emmony (studio director, series 3), Graham Linehan (location director, series 3)

Producers

Mary Bell (executive producer), Geoffrey Perkins (series 1), Lissa Evans (series 2 and 3 and Christmas special)

Programming History

Hat Trick Productions for Channel 4
24 episodes and 1 Christmas special

April 1995–May 1995	6 episodes
March 1996–May 1996	10 episodes
Christmas special 1996	
March 1998–May 1998	8 episodes

Further Reading

Clarke, Steve, "Father Ted Brings Blessed Relief," *Daily Telegraph* (March 2, 1996)

Fennel, Nicky, "Drink! Girls! Feck!," *Film West* 25 (Summer 1996)

Linehan, Graham, and Arthur Mathews, *Father Ted: The Complete Scripts,* London: Boxtree, 1999

Sarler, Carol, "Last Rites," *Sunday Times* (March 15, 1998)

Thompson, Ben, "In the Name of the Father," *Independent on Sunday* (April 23, 1995)

Fawlty Towers

British Situation Comedy

Considered to be one of the finest and funniest examples of British situation comedy, *Fawlty Towers* became a critical and popular success throughout the world to the extent that all 12 of its episodes now stand as classics in their own right. The series succeeded in combining the fundamentals of British sitcom both with the traditions of British theatrical farce and with the kind of licensed craziness for which John Cleese had already gained an international reputation in *Monty Python's Flying Circus.* Comic writing of the highest quality, allied to painstaking attention to structure and detail, enabled *Fawlty Towers* to depict an extraordinarily zany world without departing from the crucial requirement of sitcom—the maintenance of a plausible and internally consistent setting.

As with so many sitcoms, the premise is simple, stable, and rooted in everyday life (reputedly being based on the proprietor of a genuine Torquay hotel in which Cleese and the *Monty Python* team stayed while shooting location footage). Basil Fawlty (Cleese) and his wife, Sybil (Prunella Scales), run the down-at-heel seaside hotel of the title, hampered by a lovingly drawn cast of believable characters embellished in varying degrees from comic stereotype. Yet *Fawlty Towers* stands out from the commonplace through its intensity of pace and exceptional characterization and performance, with the result that otherwise simple narratives are propelled, through the pandemonium generated by Basil and Sybil's prickly relationship, to absurd conclusions.

Cleese plays Basil as a man whose uneasy charm and resigned awkwardness scarcely contain his inner turmoil. An inveterate snob, Basil is trapped between his dread of Sybil's wrath and his contempt for the most of the hotel's guests—the "riffraff" whose petty demands seem to interfere with its smooth running. In Sybil, Prunella Scales created a character who is the equal of Basil in plausible idiosyncrasy—more practical than him but entirely unsympathetic to his feelings, a gossiping, overdressed put-down expert who can nevertheless be the soul of tact when dealing with guests.

Fawlty Towers turns on their relationship—an uneasy truce of withering looks and acidic banter born of her continual impatience at his incompetence and pomposity. For Basil, Sybil is "a rancorous coiffeured old sow," while she calls him "an aging brilliantined stick insect." With Basil capable of being pitched into wild panic or manic petulance at the slightest difficulty, the potential is always present for the most explosive disorder.

Powerless against Sybil, Basil vents his frustrations on Manuel (Andrew Sachs), the ever-hopeful Spanish waiter, whom he bullies relentlessly and with exaggerated cruelty. Manuel's few words of English and obsessive literalism ("I know nothing") draw on the comic stereotype of the "funny foreigner" but reverses it to make him the focus of audience sympathy, especially in later episodes. When the final show reveals Manuel's devotion to his pet hamster (actually a rat!), it is gratifying to find it named "Basil."

Connie Booth, co-writer of the series and Cleese's wife at the time, completed the principal characters as Polly, a beacon of relative calm in the unbalanced world of *Fawlty Towers*. As a student helping out in the hotel, her role is often to dispense sympathy, ameliorating the worst of Basil's excesses or Manuel's misunderstandings.

Fawlty Towers, John Cleese, Connie Booth, 1974–79. *Courtesy of the Everett Collection*

Such was Cleese's reputation, however, that even the smaller roles could be cast from the top drawer of British comedy actors. Among these were Bernard Cribbins, Ken Campbell, and, most notably of all, Joan Sanderson, whose performance as the irascible and deaf Mrs. Richards remains her most memorable in a long and successful career.

Beyond the tangled power relations of its principal characters, a large part of the comic appeal of *Fawlty Towers* lay in its combination of the familiar sitcom structure with escalating riffs of *Python*esque excess. The opening of each episode (with hackneyed theme tune, stock shots, and inexplicably rearranged nameboard) and the satisfying circularity of their plotting shared with the audience a "knowingness" about the norms of sitcom. Yet it was this haven of predictable composition that gave license to otherwise grotesque or outlandish displays that challenged the bounds of acceptability in domestic comedy. Basil thrashing his stalled car with a tree branch, concealing the corpse of a dead guest, or breaking into Hitlerian goose-stepping before a party of Germans were incidents outside the traditional capacity of the form, which could have been disastrous in lesser hands.

The British practice of making sitcoms in short series gave Cleese and Booth the luxury of painstaking attention to script and structure, which was reflected in the show's consistent high quality. An interval of nearly four years separated the two series of *Fawlty Towers,* and some episodes took four months and as many as ten drafts to complete. Perhaps as a result, the preoccupations of the series reflected those of the authors themselves. Basil's character is a study in the suppression of anger, a subject later explored in Cleese's popular psychology books. This, together with an acute concern with class, contributes to the peculiarly English flavor of the series and may have had its roots in his boyhood. A long-standing fascination with communication problems seems to have been the motivation for the creation of Manuel and is characteristic of much of the interaction in the show (as well as being the title of the episode involving Mrs. Richards).

Fawlty Towers has been shown repeatedly throughout the world. In the 1977–78 season alone, it was sold to 45 stations in 17 countries, becoming the BBC's best-selling program overseas for the year, although the treatment of Manuel caused great offense at the 1979 Montreux Light Entertainment Festival, where *Fawlty Towers* was a notorious flop. More recently, however, it has successfully been dubbed into Spanish, with Manuel refashioned as an Italian, and in 2001, with references to Hitler tactfully changed, the show was remade with a German cast—a project that involved Cleese as a consultant. In Britain *Fawlty Towers* has almost attained the status of a national treasure, and Basil's rages and many of his more outlandish outbursts ("He's from Barcelona"; "Whatever you do, don't mention the war"; "*My wife* will explain") have passed into common currency.

PETER GODDARD

See also **British Programming; Cleese, John; Scales, Prunella**

Cast

Basil Fawlty	John Cleese
Sybil Fawlty	Prunella Scales
Manuel	Andrew Sachs
Polly	Connie Booth
Major Gowen	Ballard Berkeley
Miss Tibbs	Gilly Flower
Miss Gatsby	Renee Roberts

Producers
John Howard Davies, Douglas Argent

Programming History
12 30-minute episodes
BBC
September 19, 1975–October 24, 1975
February 19, 1979–March 26, 1979

Further Reading

Bright, Morris, and Robert Ross, *Fawlty Towers: Fully Booked,* London: BBC, 2001

Cleese, John, and Connie Booth, *The Complete Fawlty Towers,* London: Methuen, 1988

Skynner, Robin A.C., and John Cleese, *Families and How to Survive Them,* London: Methuen, 1983

Wilmut, Roger, *From Fringe to Flying Circus,* London: Methuen, 1980

FBI, The

U.S. Police Procedural

The FBI, appearing on ABC from 1965 to 1974, was the longest-running series from the prolific offices of QM Productions, the production company guided by the powerful television producer Quinn Martin. Longtime Martin associate and former writer Philip Saltzman produced the series for QM with the endorsement and cooperation of the Federal Bureau of Investigation (FBI). As Horace Newcomb and Robert Alley report in *The Producer's Medium,* Martin professed that he did not want to do the show, primarily because he saw himself and the FBI in two different political and philosophical camps (*see* Newcomb and Alley). However, through a series of meetings with FBI director J. Edgar Hoover and other bureau representatives, and at the urging of ABC and sponsor Ford Motor Company, Martin proceeded with the show.

F.B.I., Efrem Zimbalist Jr., 1965–74.
Courtesy of the Everett Collection

The FBI marked the first time QM Productions chronicled the exploits of an actual federal law enforcement body, and each episode was subject not only to general bureau approval but also the personal approval of Hoover himself. Despite this oversight, Martin reported to Newcomb and Alley that the bureau never gave him any difficulties regarding the stories produced for the show. The FBI's only quibbles had to do with depicting the proper procedure an agent would follow in any given situation.

The FBI featured Inspector Lewis Erskine (Efrem Zimbalist, Jr.). For the first two seasons, Agent Jim Rhodes (Stephen Brooks) was Erskine's associate and boyfriend to his daughter, Barbara (Lynn Loring). Agent Tom Colby (William Reynolds) was Erskine's sidekick for the remainder of the series. All the principals answered to Agent Arthur Ward (Philip Abbot). Erskine was a man of little humor and a near-obsessive devotion to his duties. Haunted by the memory of his wife, who had been killed in a job-related shoot-out, Erskine discouraged his daughter from becoming involved with an FBI agent, hoping to spare her the same pain. However, his capacity for compassion ended there. This lack of

breadth and depth set Erskine apart from other protagonists in QM programs, but neither he nor his partners allowed themselves to become emotionally involved in their work, which focused on a range of crimes, from bank robbery to kidnapping to the occasional communist threat to overthrow the government.

Martin's attempts, with his team of writer-producers, to develop a multidimensional Lewis Erskine were met with resistance from the audience. Through letters to QM and ABC, viewers expressed their desire to see a more stoic presence in Erskine—one incapable of questioning his motives or consequences from his job. Erskine, Ward, Rhodes, and Colby were asked to view themselves simply as the infantry in an endless battle against crime. The audience, apparently in need of heroes without flaws, called for and received assurance in the form of these men from the bureau. A female agent, Chris Daniels (Shelly Novack), appeared for the final season of the show.

The series drew critical scorn but was very successful for ABC, slipping into and out of the top-20 shows for the nine years of its run, and rising to the tenth position for the 1970–71 season. Shortly after the series left the air, Martin produced two made-for-television films, *The FBI versus Alvin Karpis* (1974), and *The FBI versus the Ku Klux Klan* (1975).

In spite of the critics' negative attitude toward the series, *The FBI* was Quinn Martin's most successful show. Media scholars point to the program as most emblematic of QM's approval and advocacy of strong law enforcement. The period from the late 1960s into the early 1970s was one of significant political and social turmoil. *The FBI* and other shows like it (*Hawaii Five–O, Mission: Impossible*) proposed an answer to the call for stability and order from a video constituency confused and shaken by domestic and international events seemingly beyond its control.

Despite this social context, however, the series differed from other QM productions in its steady avoidance of contemporary issues of social controversy. *The FBI* never dealt substantively with civil rights or domestic surveillance or the moral ambiguities of campus unrest related to the Vietnam War. One departure from this pattern was sometimes found in the standard device that concluded many shows: Zimbalist would present to the audience pictures of some of the most wanted criminals in the United States and request assistance in capturing them. One of the more prominent names from this segment was James Earl Ray, assassin of Dr. Martin Luther King, Jr.

Within the dramatic narrative of *The FBI,* however, a resolute Erskine would pursue the counterfeiter or bank robber of the week bereft of any feelings or social analysis that might complicate the carrying out of his duties. For Martin, a weekly one-hour show was not the forum in which to address complex social issues. He did do so, however, in the made-for-television movies mentioned above.

The FBI occupies a unique position in the QM oeuvre. It is one of the most identifiable and recognizable of the QM productions. It is also representative of the genre of law-and-order television that may have assisted viewers in imposing some sense of order on a world that was often confusing and frightening.

JOHN COOPER

See also **Martin, Quinn; Police Programs**

Cast

Inspector Lewis Erskine	Efrem Zimbalist, Jr.
Arthur Ward	Philip Abbott
Barbara Erskine (1965–66)	Lynn Loring
Special Agent Jim Rhodes (1965–67)	Stephen Brooks
Special Agent Tom Colby (1967–73)	William Reynolds
Agent Chris Daniels (1973–74)	Shelly Novack

Producers

Quinn Martin, Philip Saltzman, Charles Larson, Anthony Spinner

Programming History

236 episodes
ABC

September 1965–September 1973	Sunday 8:00–9:00
September 1973–September 1974	Sunday 7:30–8:30

Further Reading

Martindale, David, *Television Detective Shows of the 1970s: Credits, Storylines, and Episode Guides for 109 Series,* Jefferson, North Carolina: McFarland, 1991

Meyers, Richard, *TV Detectives,* San Diego, California: Barnes, and London: Tantivy, 1981

Newcomb, Horace, and Robert S. Alley, *The Producer's Medium: Conversations with Creators of American TV,* New York: Oxford University Press, 1983

Powers, Richard Gid, *G-Men: Hoover's F.B.I. in American Popular Culture,* Carbondale: University of Southern Illinois Press, 1983

FCC. *See* Federal Communications Commission

Fecan, Ivan (1954–)

Canadian Television Programming Executive

For years, Ivan Fecan was known to the Canadian broadcasting industry as TV's controversial "wunderkind." In 1985, when he was 31 years old, the Toronto native was recruited by the U.S. television network NBC as the new vice president of programming under then-programming chief Brandon Tartikoff. NBC and CBC had the Canadian comedy series *Second City TV* in common at that time, and Fecan met with Tartikoff to discuss new program ideas. Impressed with the young man, Tartikoff, himself a young executive, offered Fecan the NBC job.

After two years at NBC, the head of English-language CBC, Denis Harvey, brought Fecan home as director of programming, where he began to institute program development, especially in comedy. He moved the award-winning young people's series, *Degrassi Junior High,* to Monday nights in prime time, where it flourished. He also hired a Canadian script doctor at CBS, Carla Singer, to work with the producer on *Street Legal,* the drama series about a group of Toronto lawyers. Although it started out with weak scripts and pedestrian directing, the series found its legs, became much more professional—some would say more "American"—and lasted eight years.

Fecan's rise to the highest levels of the industry can indeed be described as meteoric. Fecan began as a producer of the popular and respected three-hour radio magazine show, *Sunday Morning.* Moses Znaimer recognized his talent and took him away to be news director of Citytv, the hip new upstart local station. Two years later he became program director at CBC's Toronto station, CBLT. He updated that flagship station by bringing in electronic news gathering (ENG) equipment, two-way radios, and more reporters. Leaving news for the entertainment side of the business, Fecan spent 16 months as head of CBC-TV's Variety Department. He is said to have renewed variety programming there by using more independent producing talent.

Fecan's goals were to make CBC programming break even, to attain an all-Canadian schedule, and to produce high-quality shows that audiences wanted to see. There are two schools of thought on his tenure as CBC's director of programming. One is that he brought polish and quality to the national network while boosting Canadian-produced shows; the second is that he turned the public broadcaster into a veritable clone of the American networks. What is not in dispute is that he shepherded some of the finest TV movies during his leadership, including *The Boys of St. Vincent, Conspiracy of Silence, Love and Hate, Glory Enough for All, Where the Spirit Lives, Life with Billy, Princes in Exile, Dieppe,* and *Liar, Liar.* In fact, *Love and Hate* (about the true story of a Saskatchewan politician who murdered his ex-wife) was the first Canadian movie of the week to be aired on a major U.S. network (NBC). The series *Kids in the Hall, The Road to Avonlea, North of 60, Scales of Justice, 9B, Degrassi High, The Odyssey,* and *Northwood* came into existence because of Fecan. *Kids in the Hall* went on to become a hit on American television and *The Road to Avonlea* won awards all over the world and ran for seven years. In addition to *Kids in the Hall,* in the comedy arena, he launched *The Royal Canadian Air Farce, CODCO,* and *This Hour Has 22 Minutes.*

Fecan made professional use of competitive scheduling and programming tools he had learned from Tartikoff and Grant Tinker at NBC. Negotiating that delicate balance between Canadian content and American revenues that has so often been a problem, he programmed American series in prime time to help bring in much-needed money—*Kate and Allie, Hoop-*

Ivan Fecan.
Photo courtesy of Ivan Fecan

erman, The Golden Girls, and *The Wonder Years.* Some argued that *Street Legal* had become too Americanized, like *L.A. Law,* its counterpart, despite the obvious Toronto locations and the Canadian legal traditions and local issues. (The shows were developed and coincidentally went on air about the same time.) *Street Legal* also, however, began to draw more than a million viewers a week, a hit by Canadian standards, after two seasons of mediocrity.

A much more risky and dubious decision was to create *Prime Time News* at 9:00 P.M. to replace the Canadian tradition of *The National* and *The Journal* at 10:00 P.M. It turned out to be an unwise move and *The National* was soon returned.

Such shows as *Adrienne Clarkson Presents,* Harry Rasky's world-famous documentary specials, the documentary anthology *Witness,* and Patrick Watson's *The Struggle for Democracy* illustrate Fecan's commitment to Canadian production that is neither American-style nor draws large audiences. Canadian content grew from 78 percent to 91 percent under Fecan's direction, and the amount of U.S. programming dropped. Although criticized for concentrating too much on the national network instead of on regional programming, Fecan strengthened the main network in a time when local stations were about to be cut or closed altogether by severe budget restraints not in his control. It has been claimed that CBC's audience share declined over his tenure, but in boom years for cable and pay, his work probably prevented much greater declines in ratings that all networks, even the three U.S. majors, suffered.

Fecan left CBC and joined Baton Broadcasting in January 1994 as senior group vice president and became executive vice president and chief operating officer in January 1995. From 1996 to 2001, he was president and CEO of CTV, a commercial, national network overseen by Baton. During his tenure at CTV, Fecan carried out significant restructuring programs, acquisitions, and mergers, which turned CTV into a leading player in the realms of both traditional broadcasting and specialty channels.

In 2000 Ivan Fecan was named president and CEO of Bell Globemedia, while remaining CEO of CTV, Inc., which is owned by Bell Globemedia. In addition to CTV, Bell Globemedia owns several other Canadian brands, including *The Globe and Mail,* Globe Interactive, and Sympatico-Lycos.

JANICE KAYE

See also **Canadian Programming in English; Citytv; CODCO; Degrassi; Kids in the Hall; National; North of 60; Road to Avonlea; Royal Canadian Air Farce; Second City TV; Street Legal**

Ivan Fecan. Born in Toronto, Canada, 1954. Educated at York University, Toronto, B.A. in fine arts. Producer, *Sunday Morning* radio show; news director, Citytv; program director, CBC, Toronto, head of network Variety department; moved to Hollywood as vice president of creative development, NBC, 1985; director of television programming, CBC, 1987; vice president, Baton Broadcasting, 1994, chief operating officer, 1995.

Radio
Sunday Morning (producer).

Further Reading

"Baton Promotes Fecan to COO," *Financial Post Daily* (Toronto), January 18, 1995
"Hefty Bonuses for Broadcasters," *Financial Post* (Toronto), November 26–28, 1994
"Passing the Baton: Douglas Bassett Spearheads an Overhaul of Baton Broadcasting with Visionary Ivan Fecan," *Financial Post* (Toronto), April 29–May 1, 1995

Federal Communications Commission

U.S. Regulatory Commission

The U.S. Federal Communications Commission (FCC), created by an act of Congress on June 19, 1934, merged the administrative responsibilities for regulating broadcasting and wired communications under the rubric of one agency. Created during "The New Deal" with the blessings of President Franklin D. Roosevelt, the commission was given broad latitude to establish "a rapid, efficient, Nation-wide, and worldwide wire and radio communication service." On July 11, 1934, seven commissioners and 233 federal employees began the task of merging rules and procedures from the Federal Radio Commission (FRC), the Interstate Commerce Commission, and the Postmaster General into one agency. The agency was organized into three divisions: Broadcast, Telegraph, and Telephone. As of 2002, the FCC employed approximately 2,000 people and operated on a $245 million annual budget. The commission has extensive oversight responsibilities in new technologies such as wireless, satellite, and microwave communications.

The 1934 Communications Act and the Organization of the FCC

The FCC is an independent regulatory government agency. It derives its powers to regulate various segments of the communications industries through the Communications Act of 1934. Government radio stations are exempt from FCC jurisdiction. Congress appropriates money to fund the agency and its activities, although recently the FCC also has raised revenues through an auction process for the frequency spectrum. Divided into titles and sections, and amended numerous times since 1934, the Communications Act enumerates the powers and responsibilities of the agency and its commissioners.

Title I describes the administration, formation, and powers of the FCC. The 1934 Act called for a commission consisting of seven members (reduced to five in 1983) appointed by the president and approved by Senate. The president designates one member to serve as chairperson. The chair sets the agenda for the agency and appoints bureau and department heads. Commissioners serve for a period of five years. The president cannot appoint more than three members of one political party to the commission. Title I empowers the commission to create divisions or bureaus responsible for various specific work assignments.

Title II concerns common-carrier regulation. Common carriers are communication companies that provide facilities for transmission but do not originate messages, such as telephone and microwave providers. The act limits FCC regulation to interstate and international common carriers, although a joint federal-state board coordinates regulation between the FCC and state regulatory commissions.

Title III of the act deals with broadcast station requirements. Many determinations regarding broadcasting regulations were made prior to 1934 by the FRC, and most provisions of the Radio Act of 1927 were subsumed into Title III of the 1934 Communications Act. Sections 303–307 define many of the powers given to the commission with respect to broadcasting. Other sections define limitations placed upon the commission. For example, section 326 within Title III prevents the commission from exercising censorship over broadcast stations. Provisions in the U.S. code also link to the Communications Act. For example, 18 U.S.C. 1464 bars individuals from uttering obscene or indecent language over a broadcast station. Section 312 mandates access to the airwaves for federal candidates, whereas section 315, known as the Equal Time Rule, requires broadcasters to afford equal opportunity to candidates seeking political office who wish to air campaign messages. Previously, section 315 also included provisions for rebuttal of controversial viewpoints under the contested fairness doctrine. However, in October 2000 the commission relaxed the political-attack rules related to section 315.

Title V enumerates the powers of the commission to impose fines and forfeitures. Title VI describes provisions related the cable regulation. Title VII enumerates miscellaneous provisions and powers, including the power of the president to suspend licenses and transmission during times of war.

Many of the alterations to the Communications Act since its passage in 1934 have come in response to the numerous technological changes in communications

Chair Michael K. Powell.
Photo courtesy of the FCC

that have taken place during the FCC's history, including the introduction of television, satellite and microwave communications, cable television, cellular telephone, digital broadcasting, and personal communications services (PCS). As a result of these and other developments, new responsibilities have been added to the commission's charge. The Communications Satellite Act of 1962, for example, gave the FCC new authority for satellite regulation. The passage of the Cable Act of 1992 and the Telecommunications Act of 1996 required similar revisions to the 1934 law. Nonetheless, it has been the flexibility incorporated into the general provisions that has allowed the agency to survive for seven decades. In 1996 the passage of the Telecommunications Act provided a congressional mandate for the FCC to develop policies that would accelerate technological innovation and competition within various segments of the communications industry.

The FCC has broad oversight over all broadcasting regulation. The commission licenses operators for a wide variety of services and has used auctions as a means of determining who would be awarded licenses. The commission enforces various requirements for wire and wireless communication through the promulgation of rules and regulations. Major issues can come before the entire commission at monthly meetings; less important issues are "circulated" among commissioners for action. Individuals or parties of interest can challenge the legitimacy of the regulations without affecting the validity or constitutionality of the act itself. The language of the act is general enough to serve as a framework for the commission to promulgate new rules and regulations related to a wide variety of technologies and services. Although the agency has broad discretion to determine areas of interest and regulatory concern, the court, in *Quincy Cable TV, Inc. v. FCC,* reminded the FCC of its requirements to issue rules based on supportable facts and knowledge.

Under Chairman Michael Powell (2001–), the commission's bureaus were reorganized under function titles. The newly formed Media Bureau, created in 2002, combines the functions of the former Mass Media and Cable Bureaus, with the new bureau overseeing the licensing and regulation of broadcasting services and the enforcement of provisions of the Cable Act of 1992. Telephone services are split between the Wireless Telecommunications Bureau, which handles wireless and PCS services, and the Wireline Competition Bureau, which promulgates rules related to long-distance and other wireline services. The Consumer and Governmental Affairs Bureau provides linkage to consumers, states, and other governmental organizations. The Enforcement Bureau oversees the Investigations and Hearings Division and resolves complaints related to implementation of regulations promulgated by the commission. The International Bureau represents the commission in matters related to satellite and international communication. The Field Operations Bureau carries out enforcement, engineering, and public outreach programs for the commission. Ten offices within the FCC support the bureaus. The Office of Engineering and Technology provides engineering expertise and knowledge to the commission and tests equipment for compliance with FCC standards. The Office of Plans and Policy acts like the commission think tank.

The FCC and Broadcasting

Scholars differ on whether the FCC has used its powers to enforce provisions of the Communications Act wisely. Among the broad responsibilities placed with the FCC under section 303 are the power to classify stations and prescribe services; assign frequencies and power; approve equipment and mandate standards for levels of interference; make regulations for stations with network affiliations; prescribe qualifications for station owners and operators; levy fines and forfeitures; and issue cease-and-desist orders.

The most important powers granted to the commission are powers to license, short-license, withhold, fine, revoke, or renew broadcast licenses and con-

struction permits. The exercise of these powers is based on the commission's own evaluation of whether the station has served in the public interest, although a provision of the Telecommunications Act of 1996 has made it more difficult for the FCC to withhold the license of a broadcast station that fulfills its minimum obligations. Historically, therefore, much of the debate over the FCC's wisdom has focused on the determination of what constitutes fulfillment of a broadcast licensee's responsibilities under the "public interest, convenience, and necessity" standard. Definitions and applications of this standard have varied considerably depending upon the composition of the commission and the mandates given by Congress. Although the FCC can wield the life-or-death sword of license revocation as a means of enforcing its regulations, the commission has rarely used this power in its 70-year history.

Indeed, critics of the FCC argue that it has been too friendly and eager to serve the needs of large broadcast interests. Early FCC proceedings, for example, illustrate a pattern of favoring business over educational or community interests in license proceedings. And yet, the FCC has at times taken action against big broadcast interests by promulgating Duopoly, Prime-Time Access Rules (PTARs), and Syndication and Financial Interest Rules, all aimed at reducing the influence of large multiple-license owners. However, recent mergers and acquisitions allowed by the FCC, and made possible as a result of ownership changes specified in the Telecommunications Act of 1996, suggest that the Congress is interested in allowing economies of scale to work within the broadcasting and telecommunications industry.

The commission has restated the public-interest requirements numerous times over its 70-year history. The Blue Book, the 1960 Programming Policy Statement, and the Policy Statement Concerning Comparative Hearing were examples of FCC attempts to provide licensees with guidance as to what constituted adequate public service. In the early 21st century, the FCC's reliance on "marketplace forces" to create competitive programming options for viewers reflects the belief of the congressional majority that economic competition is preferable to behavioral regulation in the broadcast industry. Implementation of the Telecommunications Act of 1996 has focused on reducing unnecessary regulation for an industry that is largely regarded as mature. A biennial review process, mandated by Congress, is used to ensure that regulation is not over-burdensome.

Viewed over its 70-year history, FCC decision making is generally seen as ad hoc. As economic and technological conditions warranted changes in regulatory policy, the commission has issued decisions that have frequently reversed the direction of its policymaking. Before the present era of deregulation, the FCC had promulgated extremely complex and detailed technical and operating rules and regulations for broadcasters, but it also gave licensees great latitude to determine what constituted service in the public interest based on local needs under its Ascertainment Policy. Once a station was licensed, the operator was required to monitor the technical, operational, and programming aspects of the station. Files on all aspects of station operations had to be kept for several years. As of 2002, under the general guidance of the "market," filing and renewal requirements for broadcasters have been greatly reduced. Previously, when two or more applicants competed for the same license, or when a Petition to Deny challenge was mounted, the commission made a determination as to which of the competing applicants was best qualified using a comparative hearing process. In the past, license challenges and competing applications frequently dragged on for years, costing interested parties thousands of dollars in legal fees. In 1993 the courts ruled the comparative process was arbitrary and capricious, and in 1997, Congress mandated that the FCC utilize a competitive bidding process in awarding broadcast licenses.

Reliance on "the marketplace rationale" began under Chairman Charles D. Ferris (1977–81), when the FCC embraced a new perspective on regulation and began licensing thousands of new stations in an effort to replace behavioral regulation with the forces of competition. Chairman Mark Fowler (1981–87) endorsed the marketplace model even more willingly than his predecessor. Still, despite the flood of new stations, the Scarcity Rationale, based on limitations of the electromagnetic spectrum, remained a primary premise for government regulation over electronic media. However, new technologies have reduced the validity of the scarcity principle in recent years, although the federal government still warehouses a large portion of the electromagnetic spectrum.

Broadcast licensees do not enjoy the same First Amendment rights as other forms of mass media. Critics have charged that entry regulation—either through utilizing the concept of "natural monopoly" or severely limiting the number of potential licenses available—effectively uses the coercive power of government to restrict the number of parties who benefit from involvement in telecommunications. Recently, broadcasters have sought to limit the introduction of new broadcast services, such as low-power FM, citing spectrum crowding and increased competition from other nonbroadcast services. Steven Breyer and Richard Stewart note that, "Commissions operate in hostile environments, and their regulatory policies become conditional upon the acceptance of regulation by the regulated groups. In the long run, a commission is forced to come to terms with the regulated groups as a condition of survival." Critics say both the FRC and the FCC became victims of client politics, as these two regulatory agencies were captured by the industries they were created to regulate; however, recent analysis suggests political influence is also an important factor in decision making.

Broadcast Regulation and FCC Policy Decisions

Throughout its history, a primary goal of the FCC has been to regulate the relationship between affiliated stations and broadcast networks, because the Communications Act does not grant specific powers to regulate networks. When the commission issued Chain Broadcasting regulations, the networks challenged the commission's authority to promulgate such rules and sued in *National Broadcasting Co., Inc. et al. v. United States.* The U.S. Supreme Court upheld the constitutionality of the 1934 Act and the FCC's rules related to business alliances, noting the broad and elastic powers legislated by Congress. The FCC has used the network case as a precedent to ratify its broad discretionary powers in numerous other rulings.

On another front, at various times the commission has promulgated rules to promote diversity of ownership and opinion in markets and geographical areas. The Seven-Station Rule limited the number of stations that could be owned by a single corporate entity. Multiple-ownership and cross-ownership restrictions dealt with similar problems and monitored multiple ownership of media outlets—newspapers, radio stations, television stations—in regions and locations. Rules restricting multiple ownership of cable and broadcast television were also applied in specific situations. However, as more radio and television stations were licensed, restrictions limiting owners to few stations, a limitation originally meant to protect diversity of viewpoint in the local market, made less sense to the commission. The FCC made changes to ownership rules in 1985 and again in 1992, but Congress mandated a broad relaxation of ownership rules with the passage of the Telecommunications Act of 1996. In the early 21st century, broadcasters are not limited by the number of stations they can own, although the FCC enforces a market cap that limits the number of stations that can be owned within each market. Restrictions on ascertainment, limits on commercials, ownership, antitrafficking, and syndication and financial interest rules also have been eased as well. Recent waivers with regard to ownership and duopoly rules suggest that further deregulation is likely.

Still, it is the issue of First Amendment rights of broadcasters that has generated more public controversy in the history of the Communications Act of 1934 than any other aspect of U.S. communication law. Since the earliest days of regulation the FRC and then the FCC insisted that because of "scarcity," a licensee must operate a broadcast station in the public trust rather than promote only his or her point of view. The constitutionality of the Fairness Doctrine and Section 315 was upheld by the U.S. Supreme Court in *Red Lion Broadcasting v. FCC* (1969). Broadcasters complained that the doctrine produced a "chilling effect" on speech and cited the possibility of fighting protracted legal battles in Fairness Doctrine challenges. Generally, though, the FCC determined station "fairness" based on the overall programming record of the licensee. The court reaffirmed the notion that licensees were not obligated to sell or give time to specific opposing groups to meet Fairness Doctrine requirements as long as the licensee met its public trustee obligations. However, as commissioners embraced deregulation, they began looking for ways to eliminate the Fairness Doctrine. In the 1985 Fairness Report, the FCC concluded that scarcity was no longer a valid argument and the Fairness Doctrine inhibited broadcasters from airing more controversial material. Two cases gave the commission the power to eliminate the doctrine; in *TRAC v. FCC* (1986), the court ruled that the doctrine was not codified as part of the 1959 Amendment to the Communications Act as previously assumed. Second, the FCC applied the Fairness Doctrine to a Syracuse, New York, television station after that station ran editorials supporting the building of a nuclear power plant. Meredith Corporation challenged the doctrine and cited the 1985 FCC report calling for the doctrine's repeal. The courts remanded the case back to the commission to determine whether the doctrine was constitutional and in the public interest. In 1987 the FCC repealed the doctrine, with the exception of the personal-attack and political-editorializing rules. Then, in 2000, the courts ordered the FCC to rescind the personal attack and political editorializing rules.

Other First Amendment problems facing the commission include enforcing rules against indecent or obscene broadcasts (*FCC v. Pacifica* [1978]). After *Pacifica*, the FCC enforced a ruling preventing broadcasters from using the "seven dirty words" enumerated in comedian George Carlin's "Filthy Words" monologue on the air. However, "shock jocks" (radio disc jockeys, such as Howard Stern, who routinely test the

boundaries of language use) and increasingly suggestive musical lyrics moved the FCC to take action against several licensees in 1987. In a formal Public Notice, the FCC restated a generic definition of indecency, which was upheld by the U.S. Court of Appeals. Spurred by Congress, the commission stepped up efforts to limit the broadcast of indecent programming material, including the graphic depiction of aborted fetuses in political advertising. As of 2002, the FCC enforces a "safe harbor" restriction for broadcast material. Indecent programming is limited to times when children are not likely to be in the audience (10 P.M. until 6 A.M.).

Other perennial areas of concern for the commission include television violence, the number of commercials broadcast in given time periods, the general banality of programming, and many issues related to children's television. Several FCC chairmen and commissioners have been successful in using the "raised eyebrow" as an informal means of drawing attention to problems in industry practices. Calling television "a vast wasteland," a phrase adopted by many critics of television, FCC chairman Newton Minow (1961–63) challenged broadcasters to raise programming standards. In 1974, under Richard Wiley (1972–77), the commission issued the Children's Television Programming and Advertising Practices policy statement, thereby starting a review of industry practices. Alfred Sikes (1989–92) called for "a commitment to the public trust" when he criticized television news coverage. William Kennard (1997–2001), the FCC's first African-American chairman, encouraged minority ownership of media and equality of services in new technologies. Chairman Michael Powell has pushed for voluntary standards as a way to speed the development of digital television.

Interest in children's television was further renewed in 1990 by the passage of the Children's Television Act, which reinstated limits on the amount of commercial time broadcast during children's programming and required the FCC to consider programming for children by individual stations when those stations seek license renewal. Television stations must air at least three hours of prosocial programs for children every week. The commission, under Chairman Reed Hundt (1993), adopted a new Notice of Inquiry on compliance in this area. In 1996 Congress became increasingly interested in reducing the amount of violence on television. Industry representatives agreed to development of a ratings system that could be used in conjunction with V-Chip technology available in modern televisions.

The contemporary FCC has many critics who contend that the agency is unnecessary and the Communications Act of 1934 outdated. Calls to move communication policymaking into the executive branch, through the National Telecommunications and Information Administration (NTIA), or to reform the FCC have been heard from both industry and government leaders. Congress has grappled with FCC reform through the legislative process in its most recent sessions. Also, the FCC has refocused its regulatory priorities as a result of the passage of the Telecommunications Act of 1996 and the Balanced Budget Act of 1997. Digital radio and television authorizations, deployment of broadband telecommunications services, and media ownership are among the items that required the FCC to promulgate new rules in order to meet its mandates. Legislative initiatives have provided the FCC with a substantial agenda of items over the past decade, and the creation of new telecommunications services through spectrum auctions has provided substantive revenues for the government. However, concerns over the growth of a "digital divide" (inequity in the deployment of telecommunications services among rural and urban users), have prompted watchdog organizations to charge the FCC with inadequate oversight and probusiness rulemaking. Convergence of telephone and broadcasting technologies could make the separate service requirements under Titles II and III difficult to reform. Whether the commission will be substantially changed in the future is uncertain, but rapid changes in communications technology are placing new burdens on the commission's resources.

FRITZ J. MESSERE

See also **Allocation; Censorship; Children and Television; Deregulation; Equal Time Rule; Financial Interest and Syndication Rules; Hennock, Frieda B.; Hooks, Benjamin Lawson; License; Ownership; Political Processes and Television; Prime-Time Access Rule; Public Interest, Convenience, and Necessity; Station and Station Groups; Telcos; U.S. Policy: Communications Act of 1934; U.S. Policy: Telecommunications Act of 1996**

Further Reading

Baughman, James L., *Television's Guardians: The FCC and the Politics of Programming, 1958–1967,* Knoxville: University of Tennessee Press, 1985
Benjamin, Louise, *Freedom of the Air and the Public Interest: First Amendment in Broadcasting to 1935,* Carbondale: Southern Illinois University Press, 2001
Besen, Stanley, M., et al., *Misregulating Television: Network Dominance and the FCC,* Chicago: University of Chicago Press, 1984
Breyer, Stephen G., and Richard B. Stewart, *Administrative Law and Regulatory Policy,* Boston: Little, Brown, 1979
Bush, Darren, "The Marketplace of Ideas: Is Judge Posner

Chasing Don Quixote's Windmills?," *Arizona State Law Review* (Winter 2000)
Cole, Barry, and Mal Oettinger, *Reluctant Regulators: The FCC and the Broadcast Audience,* Reading, Massachusetts: Addison-Wesley, 1978
Cowan, Geoffrey, *See No Evil: The Backstage Battle Over Sex and Violence on Television,* New York: Simon and Schuster, 1979
Dizard, Wilson, *The Coming Information Age,* New York: Longman, 1982
Engle, Eric, "FCC Regulation of Political Broadcasting: A Critical Legal Studies Perspective," *Communications and the Law* (September 1992)
Federal Communications Law Journal, special issue on the 60th anniversary of the Communications Act of 1934 (December 1994)
Federal Radio Commission, *Annual Reports Numbers 1–7, 192–33,* New York: Arno Press, 1971
Flannery, Gerald V., *Commissioners of the FCC, 1927–1994,* Lanham, Maryland: University Press of America, 1995
Frohock, Fred M., *Public Policy: Scope and Logic,* Englewood Cliffs, New Jersey: Prentice Hall, 1979
Ginsburg, Douglas H., Michael H. Botein, and Mark D. Director, *Regulation of the Electronic Mass Media,* St. Paul, Minnesota: West Publishing, 1979; 2nd edition, 1991
Greer, Douglas F., *Industrial Organization and Public Policy,* New York: Macmillan, 1980; 3rd edition, 1992
Havick, John J., editor, *Communications Policy and the Political Process,* Westport, Connecticut: Greenwood, 1983
Head, Sydney, Christopher Sterling, and Lemuel Schofield, *Broadcasting in America,* Boston: Houghton Mifflin, 1956; 7th edition, 1994
Hilliard, Robert L., *The Federal Communications Commission: A Primer,* Boston: Focal Press, 1991
Horowitz, Robert Britt, *The Irony of Regulatory Reform,* New York: Oxford University Press, 1989
Imhoff, Clement, "Clifford J. Durr and the Loyalty Question: 1942–1950," *Journal of American Culture* (Fall 1989)
Kahn, Frank J., editor, *Documents of American Broadcasting,* Englewood Cliffs, New Jersey: Prentice Hall, 1969; 4th edition, 1984
Kittross, John M., editor, *Documents in American Telecommunications Policy,* vol. 1, New York: Arno Press, 1977
Krasnow, Erwin G., and Lawrence D. Longley, *The Politics of Broadcast Regulation,* 2nd edition, New York: St. Martin's Press, 1978
Lavey, Warren G., "Inconsistencies in Applications of Economics at the Federal Communications Commission," *Federal Communications Law Journal* (August 1993)
Lowi, Theodore, *The End of Liberalism,* New York: Norton, 1969; 2nd edition, 1979
Lung, Albert N., "Must-Carry Rules in the Transition to Digital Television: A Delicate Constitutional Balance," *Cardozo Law Review* (November 2000)
McChensney, Robert W., *Telecommunications, Mass Media, and Democracy, The Battle for the Control of U.S. Broadcasting, 1928–1935,* New York: Oxford University Press, 1993
McMillan, John, "Selling Spectrum Rights," *Journal of Economic Perspectives* (Summer 1994)
National Association of Broadcasters, *Broadcast Regulation,* Washington, D.C.: National Association of Broadcasters, 1995
Paglin, Max D., editor, *A Legislative History of the Communi-*

cations Act of 1934, New York: Oxford University Press, 1989

Ray, William B., *FCC: The Ups and Downs of Radio-TV Regulation,* Ames: Iowa State University Press, 1990

Rivera-Sanchez, Milagros, "Developing an Indecency Standard: The Federal Communications Commission and the Regulation of Offensive Speech, 1927–1964," *Journalism History* (Spring 1994)

Schwartman, Andrew J., "The FCC and the Fowler Years," *Television Quarterly* (Fall 1990)

Slotten, Hugh R., *Radio and Television Regulation: Broadcast Technology in the United States 1920–1960,* Baltimore, Maryland: Johns Hopkins, 2000

Smith, F. Leslie, Milan Meeske, and John W. Wright, *Electronic Media and Government,* White Plains, New York: Longman, 1995

Sterling, Christopher H., and John M. Kittross, *Stay Tuned: A Concise History of American Broadcasting,* Belmont, California: Wadsworth, 1978; 3rd edition, Mahwah, New Jersey: Lawrence Erlbaum Associates, 2002

U.S. Congress, Office of Technology Assessment, *Critical Connections: Communication for the Future,* Washington, D.C.: U.S. Government Printing Office, 1990

U.S. Department of Commerce, *NTIA Telecom 2000: Charting the Course for a New Century,* Washington, D.C.: U.S. Government Printing Office, 1988

U.S. Federal Communications Commission, *Information Seeker's Guide: How to Find Information at the FCC,* Washington, D.C.: Public Service Division, Office of Public Affairs, Federal Communications Commission, 1994

Veraldi, Lorna, "Gender Preferences," *Federal Communications Law Journal* (April 1993)

Federal Trade Commission

U.S. Regulatory Agency

In 1914 Congress passed the Federal Trade Commission Act (FTCA), thereby creating the Federal Trade Commission (FTC). The commission was given the mission of preventing "unfair methods of competition" (Pub. L. No. 203, 1914) and was designed to complement the antitrust laws. As such, the FTC originally was conceived as a protector of business and competition, with no direct responsibility to protect consumers.

In some of its first decisions, however, the commission found that the two interests were not mutually exclusive, since it was possible to steal business from a competitor by deceiving consumers. In fact, the FTC used this justification to protect consumers during its first 15 years of operation. But in 1931 the Supreme Court announced that the FTCA did not permit the commission to protect consumers, except where protection was a mere by-product of protecting competitors (*FTC v. Raladam,* 283 U.S. 643). Consequently, in 1938, Congress amended the FTCA to enable the commission to protect both competitors and consumers, by adding power over "unfair or deceptive acts or practices" to the FTC's authority (Pub. L. No. 447).

Today, the FTC is the primary federal agency responsible for preventing citizens from being deceived, or otherwise injured, through advertising and other marketing practices. This responsibility applies to broadcast and print media, as well as any other means of communicating information from seller to buyer. In accord with its original mission, it also protects businesses from the unfair practices of competitors and, along with the Justice Department, enforces the antitrust laws. Each of these areas of commission jurisdiction touches the broadcast industry.

The FTC and the Antitrust Division of the Justice Department have an agreement to inform each other about their investigations and expected litigation, to avoid duplication of effort. The general mission for both is to preserve the competitive process, so that it functions in the most economically efficient manner possible and best serves the interest of the public.

The phrase "unfair methods of competition" is not defined in the FTCA, because it was designed to allow the FTC to adapt to an ever-changing marketplace. Courts have determined this power to be quite extensive. Consequently, the commission's oversight of competition generally involves enforcement of the Sherman and Clayton Acts, as well as the Robinson-Patman Act.

Thus, FTC antitrust actions can arise in cases of vertical restraints, entailing agreements between companies and their suppliers that might harm competition, and in cases of horizontal restraints, where direct competitors enter into a competition-limiting agreement. Those agreements can be subject to regulation whether their primary impact is on prices or on some nonprice aspect of competition. This means that the FTC may intervene in situations intentionally designed to reduce competition, such as mergers and buyouts, or in circumstances where competition may be unintentionally affected, as where a professional association adopts a "code of ethics" agreement.

During the 1970s, the FTC was perceived as being particularly aggressive at enforcing the antitrust laws. Some critics felt it also was somewhat inconsistent in its decisions. But under the Reagan administration, in the early 1980s, the agency's regulatory philosophy changed. At President Reagan's direction, the agency experienced an infusion of "Chicago School" economists committed to deregulation and the belief that some of the commission's previous actions were actually injurious to consumer welfare. The result has been less regulation of vertical restraints and price restrictions, and a greater focus on the benefits and costs to society in regulating horizontal restraints. Any contract or other agreement between competing businesses, even through a trade association, may be subject to FTC scrutiny. However, no regulation is likely unless the agency believes the harms to competition will outweigh the benefits.

With regard to television, the FTC's role in antitrust activity has focused on the flurry round of mergers and acquisitions taking place in the 1980s and 1990s. The commission paid close attention to the purchase of Capital Cities/ABC television network by the Disney company, and to the merger of AOL and Time Warner.

In the realm of advertising regulation the FTC has authority over both "deceptive" and "unfair" advertising and other marketing practices. For television, the commission's focus is on the content and presentation of commercials.

The "unfairness" power never was used extensively and, as a response to criticism that the power was too broad and subjective, it was somewhat limited by Congress between 1980 and 1994. But in 1994 Congress amended the FTCA to define "unfairness" and thereby circumscribe the commission's authority in that area.

The newer definition of unfairness permits the commission to regulate marketing practices that (1) cause or are likely to cause substantial injury to consumers, (2) are not reasonably avoidable by consumers, and (3) are not outweighed by countervailing benefits to consumers or to competition.

By far, most regulation of advertising and marketing practices is based on the commission's "deceptive-

ness" power. As in the antitrust arena, advertising regulation experienced a shift in FTC philosophy during the Reagan presidency. The flow of Chicago School economists into the agency at that time led to a widespread perception that the FTC was engaged in less advertising regulation than it had been in earlier years. And in 1983, when the commission redefined the term "deceptive" (*Cliffdale Associates,* 103 F.T.C. 110), many observers felt the new definition greatly diminished protection for consumers.

Under that new definition, the FTC will find a practice deceptive if (1) there is a representation, omission, or practice that (2) is likely to mislead consumers acting reasonably under the circumstances, and (3) is likely to affect the consumer's choice of, or conduct regarding, a product. The first requirement is obvious, and the FTC generally assumes that the last requirement is met. The second requirement, therefore, is the essence of this definition. The issue is not whether an advertising claim is "false." The issue is whether the claim is likely to lead consumers to develop a false belief.

The previous definition required only a "capacity or tendency" to mislead, rather than a "likelihood" and allowed protection of consumers who were not "acting reasonably." These changes were what bothered critics. But after a few years criticism virtually disappeared, and this definition continues to be FTC policy.

JEF RICHARDS

See also **Advertising**

Further Reading

Ford, Gary T., and John E. Calfee, "Recent Developments in FTC Policy on Deception," *Journal of Marketing* (July 1986)

Kovacic, William E., "Public Choice and the Public Interest: Federal Trade Commission Antitrust Enforcement During the Reagan Administration," *The Antitrust Bulletin* (Fall 1988)

Rosden, George Eric, and Peter Eric Rosden, *The Law of Advertising,* New York: Matthew Bender, 1996

Shenefield, John H., and Irwin M. Stelzer, *The Antitrust Laws: A Primer,* Washington, D.C.: AEI Press, 1993

Swindle, Orson, "Combating Deceptive Advertising—The Role of Advertisers, the Media, and the FTC," Aggressive Advertising and the Law Conference, Federal Trade Commission, New York, April 28, 2003. Available at http://www.ftc.gov/speeches/swindle/030428aggressive.htm

Ward, Peter C., *Federal Trade Commission: Law Practice and Procedure,* New York: Law Journal Seminars-Press, 1988

Fifth Estate, The

Canadian Public-Affairs Program

In an attempt to mirror the huge success of the U.S. program *60 Minutes,* the Canadian Broadcasting Corporation (CBC) in 1975 inaugurated its weekly public-affairs program *The Fifth Estate.* Following the "four estates" of the clergy, nobility, the legislature, and print journalism, the "fifth estate" refers to the role of electronic broadcasting in society.

At the outset, the program's stated format and mandate was to be a weekly hour of innovative and inquisitive personal journalism. As such, the program adapted the American style of segmenting individual stories, introduced and narrated, and from time to time produced, by one of the program's hosts. Dubbed a magazine-type show, *The Fifth Estate* typically runs three such segments per show. Although based on American forms of public-affairs programs, *The Fifth Estate* maintains a distinct link with Canada's tradition of documentary filmmaking. In particular, as a CBC-produced program whose mandate is to foster Canadian national identity, *The Fifth Estate*'s subject matters are drawn from all regions of the country. The program, therefore, also serves to educate Canadians about their own nation, its distinctive geography, cultures, languages, and social problems.

The show is under the public-affairs section of CBC programming, and its stories are framed within the language of contemporary news journalism. Not unlike the evening news or beat reporter, *The Fifth Estate* sees its role as a watchdog of government and public policy. And not surprisingly the program's hosts are usually drawn from the ranks of Canada's metropolitan daily newspapers. Similarly, hosts such as Hana Gartner have used the program as a stepping-stone to prestigious anchor positions with the network's flagship newscast, *The National.*

The journalistic experience on *The Fifth Estate*'s staff has resulted in an aggressive and topical approach to public affairs in both Canada and abroad. From time to time this stance has raised the ire of individuals in question. In September 1993, for example, *The Fifth Estate* made front-page news when an entrepreneur unsuccessfully petitioned a Canadian court to place an injunction banning the broadcast of the prime-time program. At the international level, *The Fifth Estate*'s documentary segment "To Sell a War," originally broadcast in December 1992, received widespread attention and acclaim for its detailing, in no uncertain terms, the Citizen's for a Free Kuwait misinformation campaign in the months leading up to the Gulf War. In 1993 "To Sell a War" was awarded the International Emmy for Best Documentary, one of the dozens of awards won by the show and its journalists. In the same decade, other notable stories on *The Fifth Estate* included two covering the life of Ty Conn, a criminal who was first profiled on the program in 1994, when his life served as a case study in a story about the consequences of child abuse. After that story aired, *The Fifth Estate* journalist Linden MacIntyre and producer Theresa Burke maintained a friendly relationship with Conn, and soon after he escaped from a maximum security prison in 1999, he called them. While on the telephone with Burke, 32-year-old Conn fatally shot himself. The events became the subject of another story on *The Fifth Estate,* and MacIntyre and Burke co-authored a book about Conn's life and death.

GREG ELMER AND ELIZABETH NISHIURA

Interviewers/Hosts (selected)
Adrienne Clarkson (1975–82)
Eric Malling (1976–90)
Bob McKeown (1981–90)

The Fifth Estate.
Photo courtesy of CBC Television

Peter Reilly (1975–77)
Warner Troyer (1975–76)
Ian Parker (1978–81)
Hana Gartner (1982–95, 2000–)
Sheila MacVicar (1988–90)
Victor Malarek (1990–2000)
Stevie Cameron (1990–91)
Gillian Findlay (1990–91)
Lynden MacIntyre (1991–)
Bob Johnstone
Anna Maria Tremonti (1997–)

Producers
Glenn Sarty, Ron Haggart, Robin Taylor

Programming History
CBC
September 1975–   One hour weekly, fall/winter
                    season

Further Reading

Stewart, Sandy, *Here's Looking at Us: A Personal History of Television in Canada,* Toronto: CBC Enterprises, 1986

FilmFour/Film on Four

British Film Series

The series *Film on Four* was announced on the opening night of Channel 4 in November 1982 and helped to immediately draw attention to the distinctions between this and the three existing British television channels. Ostensibly, *Film on Four* occupies a curious position within British television. It was established by Jeremy Isaacs, Channel 4's first chief executive, following a European model, to encourage mainly new, independent filmmakers by offering funding for fictional, mainly feature-length films. This was intended to lead to cinema distribution in many cases, where a film might gain a reputation before transmission on Channel 4. *Film on Four* is often considered to be particularly significant within film culture for providing vital financial support and for commissioning many films that have gained high regard. Indeed, Isaacs's film investment policies made little economic sense in strictly television terms. He managed to secure around 8 percent of Channel 4's total programming funds and allocated it to fictional one-offs that would fill only 1 percent of airtime. However, it would be constrictive to overlook *Film on Four*'s integral position within television culture.

Traditionally the BBC had been the prime producer and supporter of television drama. However, in the period leading up to the early 1980s, it became increasingly difficult for the BBC to produce the single play for reasons involving changing production values, censorship, and declining resources. The first head of *Film on Four,* David Rose, whose background was in BBC regional drama, commissioned a series of films that collectively represent a renaissance of highly contemporary drama. The films Rose promoted followed a writerly formula of neorealism with socially displaced characters firmly positioned in a regional landscape. The resultant work, including Neil Jordan's *Angel* (1982) and Colin Gregg's *Remembrance* (1982), has been defined as being uncompromised by television's institutional modes of representation or by cinematic demands of impersonal spectacle.

Film on Four's only early success in the cinema was Peter Greenaway's *The Draughtsman's Contract* (1982), and, although the series had been established to encourage new ideas, in the early years the media argued that most of its products brought little that was innovative to television. Media support, credibility, and international acclaim started to be gained three years on, primarily by Rose's investment in Wim Wender's art-house classic *Paris, Texas* (1984) and his funding of the surprise success *My Beautiful Launderette* (Stephen Frears, 1984). Rose was awarded a special prize at Cannes (1987) for services to cinema and was heralded in Britain as the savior of the film industry. *Film on Four*'s successful output began to multiply with films such as *A Room with a View* (1985), *Hope and Glory* (1987), *Wish You Were Here* (1987), and *A World Apart* (1987), doing well at both the domestic and international box office. In addition to promoting new directors such as Stephen Frears and Chris Menges, *Film on Four* encouraged the work of established filmmakers including Peter Greenaway, Derek Jarman, and Agnès Varda. After touring the festival circuit and cinema distribution, the films were transmitted on television to respectable, although by no means outstanding, view-

Film on Four: Shallow Grave.
Photo courtesy of Channel Four

ing figures—audiences averaged 3 million per film in 1990.

As only a minority of *Film on Four* products succeeded in returning any money to Channel 4, a general agreement was reached at the end of the 1980s that a large portion of the budget needed to be diverted to higher-rated, long-form drama. Rose was succeeded by David Aukin, who continued to implement the recent policy of deliberate undercommissioning. With its much reduced budget, *Film on Four* could not keep up with massive inflation in production costs. Additionally, a sense of a general decrease in the quality of new projects and emerging talent surrounded the organization. Aukin showed less interest in promoting the film industry than in television itself and aimed to concentrate on films a television audience would want to watch, rather than cinema award winners.

In 1994 Channel 4 had a worldwide hit with the film *Four Weddings and a Funeral* (1994). In the wake of this success, Channel 4 increased *Film on Four*'s annual budget to £16 million. The successful streak initiated by *Four Weddings and a Funeral* continued with the critically acclaimed *Shallow Grave* (1994), *Sense and Sensibility* (1995), and *Secrets and Lies* (1996).

David Aukin stepped down in 1997. The chief executive of Channel 4, Michael Jackson, introduced Film-Four Ltd., a production studio headed by Paul Webster. With doubled investments in filmmaking, FilmFour produced another hit, *East is East* (1999), which took £10 million at the U.K. box office.

Despite these successes in the 1990s, the early 2000s have been difficult. In 2000, FilmFour signed a three-year deal with Warner Brothers. However, the first film produced under this deal, *Charlotte Gray* (2002), was a critical and box office failure. This was a blow for FilmFour, given its lack of a hit since 1999.

Under Mark Thompson, who replaced Michael Jackson as chief executive of Channel 4 (Jackson left at the end of 2001), FilmFour Ltd. was closed. The focus has been returned to airing films on television, under the name FilmFour.

NICOLA FOSTER

See also **Channel 4; Isaacs, Jeremy; Jackson, Michael**

Further Reading

Saynor, James, "Writer's Television," *Sight and Sound* (November 1992)

Financial Interest and Syndication Rules

U.S. Broadcasting Regulations

The Financial Interest and Syndication Rules (Fin-Syn), or more precisely their elimination, altered the U.S. television and film entertainment landscape as much as any event in the 1990s. The Federal Communications Commission (FCC) implemented the rules in 1970, attempting to increase programming diversity and limit the market control of the three broadcast television networks (ABC, CBS, and NBC). The rules prohibited network participation in two related arenas: the financial interest of the television programs they aired beyond first-run exhibition, and the creation of in-house syndication arms, especially in the domestic market. Consent decrees executed by the U.S. Justice Department in 1977 solidified the rules and limited the amount of prime-time programming the networks could produce themselves.

The rationales for Fin-Syn were numerous. The FCC was concerned that vertical integration (control of production, distribution, and exhibition) unfairly increased the power of the networks. By taking away the long-term monetary rights to programs created by the networks, and severely restricting their participation in syndication, the FCC eliminated incentives for the networks to produce programs, thus separating production from distribution. Those in favor of Fin-Syn hoped that the rules would benefit independent television producers by giving them more autonomy from the networks (because financial interest would be solely in the hands of the production company), and by allowing the producers to benefit from the lucrative syndication market. Proponents believed that by privileging independent producers in this way, the rules would cultivate more diverse and innovative television content. Another potential advantage of the rules was that independent television stations would benefit from the separation of the networks from syndication. If the networks owned the syndication rights to off-network programs, they might "warehouse" their programs or steer popular reruns to network-owned-and-operated stations and network affiliates in order to make those stations stronger in a particular market.

From the very beginning, however, the Fin-Syn Rules were controversial and contested. The networks contended that Fin-Syn was unfair and did not solve the problems the policy was intended to fix. One argument against Fin-Syn noted that the expense of starting a national broadcast network—the financial barriers to entry—much more significantly explained the networks' control of television than their vertical integration. Others argued that the Fin-Syn Rules undermined the role of independent producers rather than enhanced them. Small independent producers, for example, often cannot afford to engage in the "deficit financing" required by the networks. Deficit financing involves receiving a below-cost payment from the networks during the first run of a program. Large production organizations—such as the Hollywood-connected Warner Television—are much more financially able than smaller companies to cope with the necessary short-term losses in revenue, hoping to strike it rich in syndication. Critics of Fin-Syn therefore noted that Hollywood studios, rather than independents, grew stronger because of Fin-Syn, and that the smaller independents tended to produce conventional, but inexpensive, programs like talk shows and game shows rather than innovative programs.

In 1983 the FCC, swayed by these arguments against Fin-Syn and the general political climate favoring deregulation in many arenas, proposed eliminating most of the rules. However, a massive lobbying effort by Hollywood production organizations—efforts helped by a former Hollywood actor, President Ronald Reagan—kept the rules in place.

In the early 1990s other arguments were levied against Fin-Syn. When the rules were first implemented in the 1970s, before cable and the launching of the fourth network (FOX), the networks' combined share of the television audience was around 90 percent. By the early 1990s, this share had dropped to roughly 65 percent because of the new forms of competition. Fin-Syn opponents also argued that the presence of vertical integration among other media companies—including organizations with television production arms such as Time Warner—was unfair.

In 1991 the FCC relaxed the Fin-Syn Rules after an intense lobbying war pitting the major television producers (for Fin-Syn) against the major television distributors (against Fin-Syn). Appeals courts later relaxed the rules even further, in essence eliminating all traces of Fin-Syn by November 1995.

The elimination of the Fin-Syn Rules has had several long-term consequences for television. The first consequence has been the merging of production organizations with distribution organizations. One example of this is increased in-house production by the "Big Three" networks (ABC, CBS, NBC). By 1992, for example, NBC was the single largest supplier of its own prime-time programming. In addition to the distribution firms of television becoming more involved in production, production firms have gotten more involved in distribution. The creation of three new broadcast networks from 1986 to 1995 illustrates this development. FOX Broadcasting, supported by its direct relationship with a Hollywood studio, was an early innovator here. In fact, the spark that led to the Fin-Syn elimination was FOX Broadcasting's 1990 request for Fin-Syn revisions. FOX, both a major producer and a mininetwork, wanted its transition to full network status to be unimpeded by Fin-Syn. Once the rules against the merging of production and distribution were on their deathbed, Viacom (owner of Paramount) and Time Warner (owner of Warner Brothers) soon joined FOX in forming studio-based television networks (UPN and the WB, respectively). Studios also bought established networks in blockbuster deals in the mid- and late 1990s, including Disney's purchase of Cap Cities/ABC in 1995 and Viacom's purchase of CBS a few years later. With the latter deal, the Viacom entertainment corporation was now owner of two national television networks, CBS and UPN.

The future of independents—both independent producers and independent stations—may also be significantly affected by the demise of Fin-Syn. Independent producers worry that, at worst, the networks will no longer require their services and, at best, the networks will demand a share of syndication rights to programs and will privilege in-house productions with the best time slots. With the networks involved in the production of over half of their prime-time programs by 2000, many industry observers have wondered if the disappearance of Fin-Syn also means the disappearance of independent production and diverse programming sources. Groups such as the Coalition for Program Diversity, made up of both large and small independent program producers, lobbied the FCC and Congress in 2003 to reinstate mandatory percentages for non-network production, but their request was denied. Independent stations worry that the networks will warehouse their best off-network programs, now that they will own the syndication rights. As early as 1994, some television observers charged that "self-dealing" and warehousing were the motivations behind syndicating The Simpsons (which airs in first run on the FOX net-

work) to approximately 70 FOX affiliates. Such potential favoritism led to high-profile lawsuits. David Duchovny, former star of FOX's The X-Files and a point participant in that program's syndication revenues, sued FOX for favoring FOX-affiliated stations and cable outlets, arguing that the corporation was sacrificing maximum syndication revenue for affiliate loyalty and corporate promotion.

Finally, other critics note the dangers to programming diversity and advertising interference that may result from the deregulation. Now that the networks may benefit from syndication, for example, will they have an incentive to put on programs with high syndication potential, such as situation comedies? Some critics believe the networks have privileged critically panned and unimpressively rated sitcoms (such as NBC's mid-1990s programs Suddenly Susan and Veronica's Closet) because of the financial stake in production that the networks hold. Also, during the Fin-Syn era, prime-time network producers were at least superficially insulated from advertiser influence because of the separation of production from distribution. Advertisers paid the networks rather than the producers of TV content. Because the categories of production and distribution have collapsed together after Fin-Syn, advertisers may have more direct access to network production because they now write checks directly to organizations that produce as well as distribute. For example, CBS is a participant in the Survivor Entertainment Group, the production company of the reality-based program Survivor. In its early installments, that program featured significant advertiser involvement, including product placement by such sponsors as Doritos and Pontiac, with these brands of snack foods and cars featured prominently in several episodes.

Changes in the Financial Interest and Syndication Rules illustrate the significance of communication policy in affecting the daily menu of television choices available to the public. As much as alterations in technologies, techniques, and personalities, changes in the Fin-Syn Rules had an immediate, significant effect on the television industry and television audiences.

MATTHEW P. McALLISTER

See also **Deregulation; Federal Communications Commission; FOX Broadcasting Company; Programming; Reruns; Syndication**

Further Reading

Auletta, Ken, *Three Blind Mice: How the TV Networks Lost Their Way,* New York: Random House, 1991

Besen, Stanley M., et al., *Misregulating Television: Network Dominance and the FCC,* Chicago: University of Chicago Press, 1984

Carter, Bill, "Ruling Lets Networks Join Risk of Syndication," *New York Times* (November 16, 1993)

Carter, Bill, "Networks Cleared to Syndicate Programs for 7-to-8 P.M. Slot: FCC Strikes Down a 25-year-old Access Rule," *New York Times* (July 29, 1995)

Covington, William G., "The Financial Interest and Syndication Rules in Retrospect: History and Analysis," *Communications and the Law* (June 1994)

Creech, Kenneth, *Electronic Media Law and Regulation,* Boston: Focal, 1993

Ginsburg, Douglas H., *Regulation of the Electronic Mass Media: Law and Policy towards Radio, Television, and Cable Communications,* St. Paul, Minnesota: West Publications, 1979; 3rd edition, by Michael Botein, as *Regulation of the Electronic Mass Media: Law and Policy for Radio, Television, Cable, and the New Video Technologies,* St. Paul, Minnesota: West Group, 1998

Jessell, Harry A., "Comments Box Fin-Syn Compass (FCC Receives Comment on New TV Syndication Rules)," *Broadcasting* (June 25, 1990)

Jessell, Harry A., "White House Sends Loud and Clear Fin-Syn Signal," *Broadcasting* (February 18, 1991)

Kaplar, Richard T., *The Financial Interest and Syndication Rules: Prime Time for Repeal,* Washington, D.C.: The Media Institute, 1990

McClellan, Steve, "Fin-Syn," *Broadcasting and Cable* (January 24, 2000)

"Opening on Capitol Hill: 'The Fin-Syn Story,'" *Broadcasting* (June 26, 1989)

Stern, Christopher, "Faster End for Fin-Syn?," *Broadcasting and Cable* (April 10, 1995)

United States Federal Communications Commission Network Inquiry Special Staff, *New Television Networks: Entry, Jurisdiction, Ownership, and Regulation,* Washington, D.C.: U.S. Government Printing Office, 1980

Finland

In terms of television, Finland belongs to the Scandinavian and North European pattern, with a strong public-service system coexisting with commercial channels. However, the Finnish television system also offers some distinctive characteristics: an unusual combination of public and private systems; a radical view of the role of broadcasting in society; and the unique influence of television across the cold war border between Finland and Estonia.

The first regular television transmissions seen in Finland came from the Soviet Union, extended to the Estonian capital Tallinn in 1954, just 40 miles south of Finland's capital Helsinki, across the Baltic Sea. The Leningrad transmitter reached Finnish communities behind the border in the southeastern part of the country. The spillover signal encouraged Finns to buy receivers and put out antennas using the standards applied in the Soviet Union.

This happened at a time when little progress was being made regarding the establishment of national television in Finland. Beginning in the late 1940s, some experimental initiatives with the new medium had taken place in technical circles under the auspices of the state-dominated public-service broadcasting corporation YLE. But the Parliament-controlled management of YLE was reluctant to take rapid steps while its political attention and financial resources were occupied by an ambitious project to cover the wide but sparsely populated country with an FM radio network (among the first in the world). Most politicians dismissed proposals to use advertising as an additional income for the new medium, either because of concerns that this would reduce advertising revenues for the printed press, or due to the principle that public broadcasting should remain free from commercialism.

However, the prospects of an expanding Soviet television in a Western country began to galvanize politicians, especially when NATO embassies in Helsinki began to report their concern. Like the German "threat" in Denmark some years earlier, the Soviet "threat" in Finland became an argument (skilfully used by the technical lobby) to persuade hesitant decision makers to enter the television era in 1957. Another, even stronger argument for an official introduction of television in Finland was the fact that the technical and private interests, spearheaded by the radio laboratory of the Helsinki University of Technology, had already started experimental transmissions in the mid-1950s. These enthusiasts were frustrated by the slow action of YLE, and as with the introduction of radio in the 1920s, private initiatives served as catalysts to mobilize the public sector. Administratively this was not difficult to carry out, because Finland did not have a legally based state monopoly of broadcasting; even YLE operated under a license from the government.

YLE television started with a transmitter (made in the United States) in the highest tower in Helsinki, fed by an old AM radio station remodeled into a TV studio.

After nearly a year of experimental transmissions, the beginning of 1958 brought regular programs—five days a week excluding a summer break—in both of the official languages, Finnish and Swedish (the latter spoken by 6 percent of the population). Program production was divided between YLE and a subsidiary company created for dealing with advertising, made up of major advertisers, advertising agencies, film companies, and YLE itself. The motive was to ensure financing of the new medium, but the arrangement also brought along additional programs in separate time blocs designated for the commercial subsidiary called MTV (in Finnish "Mainos-TV" for "Advertising TV").

MTV soon accounted for 20–30 percent of the total programming time, and about the same share of costs. The costs of television for YLE grew rapidly, along with the building of new transmitters throughout the country. Both the studios and transmitters were operated by YLE. MTV hired time for the use of these facilities with the income acquired from the advertisers. Additional revenues for YLE were raised by a new viewing fee for households with a TV set, along with a traditional radio-listening fee.

The expansion of television in the early 1960s was quite rapid, both in terms of transmitter coverage throughout the country, and the number of homes with television sets. With its visible and popular share of the program supply, MTV became an integral part of this success story. YLE alone was allowed to send news and current affairs, while MTV specialized in entertainment. YLE and MTV both created independent productions and imported foreign programs, especially American serials such as *Highway Patrol* and *Peyton Place*. The parent YLE and the subsidiary MTV shared the same channel, MTV having its clearly marked time blocs, partly within prime time and partly in the later hours (for movies).

Accordingly, commercial television entered Finland quite smoothly, without notable opposition—neither from the print media (which did not, contrary to initial fears, lose advertising), nor from political circles (which were skillfully handled by the commercial lobbies). Its introduction was carried out as a series of pragmatic steps. Commercial television in Finland was further strengthened by the independent TV pioneers, which continued transmissions in Helsinki and extended them to the next largest cities of Tampere and Turku, effectively creating a parallel private network financed by advertising. However, this network was doomed to lose the market to the nationally expanding YLE-MTV conglomerate, and in 1965 these stations were sold to YLE. This led to the establishment of the second channel, with its studios and personnel located in Tampere, and its mission directed toward the provinces, which were soon reached by a rapidly growing transmitter network. Apart from news, which was centralized to the main channel, the second channel had a full profile of programming, including documentary and drama productions of its own. And MTV had its commercial time blocs in this public service channel as well.

The Finnish case led to a peculiar duopoly, in which a public-service corporation coexisted with a commercial company, the latter having a monopoly on television advertising. Although Finnish commercial television had some limitations (operating under YLE's license; no news and current affairs programs; no membership in EBU), it was more profoundly commercial than most European systems, because it not only had advertising (and not just in bulletins between programs but in breaks within programs); it also constituted a whole program production and purchasing organization, which made it into a real empire (MTV) within an empire (YLE). As a whole, the YLE-MTV conglomerate had grown by the 1970s to provide the Finnish public with a more abundant supply of programs than the other Nordic countries could, with their public-service monopolies operating on a single channel. Finnish television was not only more commercial, but also more American than other Scandinavian television, especially because MTV bought many series and movies from the United States.

The YLE-MTV duopoly was a symbiosis of public-service and commercial systems, at first natural, if uneasy, but later filled with strain and conflicts. YLE wanted more income, while MTV wanted more status; YLE continued to take MTV literally as its subsidiary, while MTV had growing ambitions to become a truly independent commercial company.

MTV was granted permission to launch its own news program in the mid-1980s, and in 1993 it was finally given its own operating license and a channel. Channel 3 was developed after five years of experimenting with a hybrid channel jointly owned by YLE, MTV, and Nokia (originally a manufacturer of rubber and electronic products, later specializing in mobile phones). With its own channel, it adopted a new name (distinguishing it from the international Music Television): MTV3. This fully independent commercial television company was bought by the second-largest print media group in the country, Alma Media, which is 20 percent owned by the Bonniers group in Sweden. Technically there was still space for yet a fourth channel, and it was granted to a subsidiary of Finland's largest print media group, SanomaWSOY, founded when the leading newspaper, *Helsingin Sanomat,* merged with the largest book publisher WSOY and entered the European magazine market.

The Finnish story would be incomplete without mention of the "informational broadcasting policy" as elaborated at YLE in the late 1960s. The stated objective of this policy was to promote democracy and a well-informed public through the mass media in general and television in particular. It abandoned the conventional establishment-dominated and entertainment-oriented approach and advocated an active role for broadcasting as a participant in the political and cultural life of society. Its call to cover social reality in all of its aspects was meant not only to be truthful but also to fight ignorance and prejudice.

The new policy classified media systems into three types: (1) confessional, in which information from around the world is selected for presentation on the basis of how well it fits in with a preestablished belief system; (2) commercial, in which information is selected based on how well it sells and brings profit; and (3) informational, in which information follows neither the logic of faith, nor a logic of market, but is based on the principle of turning people's worldview maximally truthful. This classification has a clear anticommercial bias, which served as ammunition in YLE's conflict with MTV.

The informational broadcasting policy was, in many respects, a reform plan resembling that prepared by Edward R. Murrow for President Kennedy. However, unlike similar U.S. plans, the Finnish initiative was actually implemented—to a degree. The new policy was developed by a brain trust of YLE's top management between 1966 and 1968, when the institution was headed by a group of cultural liberals and the political environment in the country was dominated by a left-wing majority in the Parliament, with a center-left coalition government. At that time, Finnish society underwent a dynamic change not only due to the rapid spread of television, but because of drastic shifts in economic and demographic structures while the country was shifting from an agricultural to an industrial economy.

The reform policy resonated with the new generation of television program makers (producers not only of news and current affairs programs, but also of entertainment and drama programs), and new ideas were put into practice so energetically that a liberal-democratic approach was sometimes replaced by a dogmatic-elitist form of radicalism. By the end of the 1960s, the promising reform had turned into a political backlash against YLE, which was used by conservative forces of all kinds as a scapegoat for practically all problems affecting the country. The informational broadcasting policy went out of fashion and suffered a bad reputation, although a significant portion of its ideas has survived as a key aspect of Finnish public-service television in the new millennium.

It is within the contexts of this history that the YLE-MTV duopoly was replaced by a classic dual system in the late 1990s. On the one hand, there is the public-service corporation, which is legally still a limited company. Although 98 percent is owned by the state, it no longer requires a government license due to a 1993 law passed by Parliament. YLE operates two noncommercial TV channels, in addition to a number of radio channels, all including services in the minority language of Swedish.

On the other hand, there are two commercial TV companies, fiercely competing in the advertising market. Two unique features separate the Finnish media landscape from normal dual systems: first, cross-media ownership is the rule rather than an exception; and second, the commercial companies pay an annual "public-service fee" that is used to partially finance YLE.

Despite an abundant supply of television programs, the Finnish public has watched them only in moderate numbers. Since the 1960s the daily viewing time has remained at the average level of two hours per person per household; by 2000 it had reached three hours. Radio, newspapers, magazines, books, and other media (including the Internet) occupy together twice the time devoted to television. The share of all media advertising moneys channeled into television remains significantly lower in Finland (just over 20 percent) than the European average (around 30 percent).

The audience is divided fairly evenly between the two public-service channels and the two commercial channels: YLE 1 and 2 together take typically 44 percent of the audience, while MTV3 takes 38 percent and Channel 4 takes 11 percent. Cable and satellite channels together take just 6 percent; they have never gained a major audience in Finland. The profile of YLE's programming is more versatile, with higher diversity indices than those measured in the commercial channels, but even the latter receive rather high scores when compared internationally.

The analogue full-service television is complemented with new digital thematic channels. The Finnish choice has been to build the digital terrestrial distribution infrastructure, and to give this task to YLE. After postponements, digital TV broadcasting began in 2001 and the share of households of digital receivers has since grown steadily, amounting to some 8% at the end of 2003. YLE has its own multiplex with two simulcast and three new specialized channels, whereas two multiplexes are for commercial operators. In principle, digital television is free to air, but commercial channels have developed some pay-TV services.

The unique cross-border influence between Finland and Estonia during the cold war era should be briefly mentioned. This unusual situation not only played a role in the early history of Finnish television—it became an even more significant factor in the 1970s and 1980s, when the Finnish television signal was clearly and reliably received in northern Estonia. Estonians, who speak a language closely related to Finnish, tuned in to Finnish television more frequently than Soviet-Estonian television, until the period of glasnost in the late 1980s, when emancipated Estonian television became an instrument of an exciting political struggle. Finnish television—YLE as well as MTV—had a significant political and cultural impact on Estonian society during the last decades of Soviet rule. Estonia was the first Soviet republic to break away from the USSR in the 1990s, and it is not just a joke to say that one of the strategic factors that contributed to the collapse of the Soviet Union was Finland's television.

KAARLE NORDENSTRENG

Further Reading

Aslama, Minna, Heikki Hellman, and Tuomo Sauri, "Does Market-entry Regulation Matter? Competition in Television Broadcasting and Programme Diversity of Finland, 1993–2002," *Gazette* (London), 66:2 (2004)

Endén, Rauno, editor, *Yleisradio 1926–1996: A History of Broadcasting in Finland,* Helsinki: Finnish Historical Society, 1996

Hellman, Heikki, *From Companions to Competitors: The Changing Broadcasting Markets and Television Programming in Finland,* Tampere: University of Tampere, 1999

Hujanen, Taisto, "Programming and Channel Competition in European Television," in *Television Across Europe,* edited by J. Wieten, G. Murdoch, and P. Dahlgren, London, Thousand Oaks, and New Delhi: Sage Publications, 2000

Hujanen, Taisto, *The Power of Schedule: Programme Management in the Transformation of Finnish Public Service Television,* Tampere: Tampere University Press, 2002

Nordenstreng, Kaarle, "A Policy for News Transmission," in *Sociology of Mass Communications,* edited by D. McQuail, Harmondsworth: Penguin, 1972

Nordenstreng, Kaarle, editor, *Informational Mass Communication: A Collection of Essays,* Helsinki: Tammi Publishers, 1973

Nordenstreng, Kaarle, "Hutchins Goes Global," *Communication Law and Policy* 3:3 (1998)

Nordenstreng, Kaarle, and Tapio Varis, *Television Traffic—A One-Way Street?,* Paris: Unesco Reports and Papers on Mass Communication, No. 70, 1974

Wiio, Juhani, *Managing Strategic Change in the Changing Radio and Television Market: A Finnish Example 1985–1998,* Helsinki: Finnish Broadcasting Company, 2000

Fireside Theatre

U.S. Anthology Series

Fireside Theatre was the first successful filmed series on American network television. In an era when live television dominated network schedules, the series demonstrated that filmed programming could be successful, and from the fall of 1949 to the spring of 1955, it was one of the ten most-watched programs in the United States. Following *The Milton Berle Show* on Tuesday nights on NBC, *Fireside* was an anthology drama that presented a different half-hour story each week. In 1955 the series' name was changed to *Jane Wyman Presents the Fireside Theatre,* and although it soon became a distinctly different series under the title, *Jane Wyman Theater* (1955–58), the title *Fireside Theatre* usually refers to the entire run of the series.

For the first two years of network series television (1947 to 1949), all television shows were broadcast live from New York and many were anthology dramas, presenting weekly, hour-long plays. *Kraft Television Theatre, Studio One,* and *Philco Television Playhouse*

are outstanding examples of the form that dominated network schedules through the early 1950s. Videotape would not be available until 1956, and film was initially thought to be too expensive for weekly television production. For television critics working during the early years of the medium, the hour-long anthology dramas, with their adaptations of literary classics, serious dramas, and social relevance, represented the best of television. The worst was cheap, half-hour, Hollywood telefilms that did not, in the critics' view, aspire to so-called serious drama or social relevance. *Fireside Theatre* fit this latter category.

The television series most often cited as the innovator in filmed programming is *I Love Lucy* (which was produced in Hollywood). However, when *I Love Lucy* premiered on CBS in 1951, *Fireside Theatre* had already been on the air for two years. To the show's sponsor and owner, Procter and Gamble, film offered several distinct advantages over live production. It

Fireside Theatre, Angela Lansbury, William Lundigan, Martha Vickers, George Brent, 1949–55; "The Indiscreet Mrs. Jarvis," 1955.
Courtesy of the Everett Collection

made possible the creation of error-proof commercials. It allowed for closer control of content and costs. It created opportunities for added profits from syndication when programs were sold for repeated airing. And it enabled cost-effective distribution to the West Coast, not yet hooked into the coaxial cable network that linked East Coast and Midwest stations.

Producer, director, writer, and host Frank Wisbar is often considered the reason for *Fireside Theatre*'s success. Frank Wisbar Productions was the sole production company from 1951 to 1955, and for the show's first several seasons, Wisbar produced and directed most episodes, even serving as host in the 1952–53 season. To control costs, he wrote many episodes himself and used public domain and freelance stories. Writers such as Rod Serling and Budd Schulberg saw

their stories produced, and then-little-known and second-string movie actors such as Hugh O'Brian, Rita Moreno, and Jane Wyatt appeared on the series.

When *Fireside Theatre* premiered in April 1949, it began a three-month experimental period. Some of the 15-minute episodes were live and some were filmed. Genres were mixed and included comedies, musicals, mysteries, and dramas. A half-hour format that presented two 15-minute filmed stories per episode was chosen for the 1949–50 season. These early episodes were often mysteries, reflecting Wisbar's background in horror and mystery moviemaking. (When these episodes were first shown in syndication, they were called *Strange Adventure.*) Later seasons presented half-hour dramas, and while the stories continued to vary in genre (westerns, comedies, melodramas, mysteries), family remained the central theme.

From 1953 to 1955 film actor Gene Raymond served as host, but by the end of the 1954–55 season, as ratings declined, *Fireside Theatre* was completely overhauled—it became a different series. The title and theme music changed. Most significantly, film star Jane Wyman became host and producer. Wyman chose the scripts and acted in many of the episodes and her company, Lewman Productions, produced the series. It was now Wyman's show, which would remain on NBC until 1958.

Fireside Theatre established its place in the history of television by being the first successful filmed network series in the era of live broadcasting. It was also the first successful filmed anthology series in an era of prestigious live anthology dramas. Scorned by critics, it was, for most of its seven seasons, a top-ten show on U.S. television.

MADELYN M. RITROSKY-WINSLOW

See also **Anthology Drama; Wyman, Jane**

Hosts
Frank Wisbar (1952–53)
Gene Raymond (1953–55)
Jane Wyman (1955–58)

Producers
Frank Wisbar, Jane Wyman

Programming History
268 episodes
NBC

April 1949–June 1957	Tuesday 9:00–9:30
September 1957–May 1958	Thursday 10:30–11:00

Further Reading

Lafferty, William, "'No Attempt at Artiness, Profundity, or Significance': *Fireside Theatre* and the Rise of Filmed Television Programming," *Cinema Journal* (1987)

First Peoples Television Broadcasting in Canada

First Peoples of Canada have become internationally recognized as having the most advanced and fair indigenous broadcasting system in the world, based on a legislated recognition (1991) of their collective communications and cultural rights as Peoples with a special status ("First Peoples" represents an inclusive term referring to the Inuit, known in Alaska and elsewhere as "Eskimos," the Métis, and the Amerindian populations, the latter of whom are also known as First Nations). Aboriginal-initiated Canadian television has had a relatively long history when compared with Fourth World/indigenous communities elsewhere. The stages through which this broadcasting history have evolved were initiated by First Peoples themselves as they struggled for their inclusion in the national policy and practice decisions pertaining to broadcasting services to be received by their communities, first in the North (north of 55th latitude line) and then in the rest of the country. The inclusion of aboriginal television in Canada's technical and programming infrastructure, as well as its legislation, has contributed to it being a model of media resistance against the overwhelming forces of continental integration in North America.

Until the launching of the Anik satellite in 1972, northern regional radio was limited and television service was nonexistent except for the local circulation of videos. In 1973 the North was hooked up to the South through radio and television services and for the first time, Inuit, Métis, and First Nations were able to have access to the images, voices, and messages that United States and metropolitan-based Canadians produced with southern audiences in mind. The parachuting in of southern, culturally irrelevant television programming into northern communities by the CBC Northern Service acted as a catalyst for indigenous constituency groups to organize broadcasting services in their own languages (dialects), reflecting their own cultures. Almost immediately after its initial mystique dissipated, First Peoples and their southern supporters began to lobby for culturally relevant radio and television programming and network services. They wanted participatory and language rights, as well as decision-making responsibilities about programming and southern service expansion. By the mid-1970s, First Peoples across the country had secured funding, had established Native Communications Societies (NCS) to be the responsible administrative entity for their communications activities, and had begun operating local community radio and television projects.

Beginning in 1976, in response to First Peoples clearly articulated demands, the federal government made large grants available to native organizations to be used for technical experiments with the Hermes (1976) and Anik B satellites (1978–81). In 1976 the Alberta Native Communications Society and Taqramiut Nipingat Incorporated (TNI) of Northern Quebec received this money to do interactive audio experiments with the Hermes satellite. In 1978 funding was provided to Inuit Tapirisat [Brotherhood] of Canada (ITC has recently changed its name to Inuit Tapiriit Kanatami, which means "Inuit are united") of the Northwest Territories and TNI to complete a more sophisticated interactive series of technical, community development, and educational experiments on audio/video using Anik B. By 1981, after the establishment of five northern television production studios, after two and a half years of staff training, and after six months of experimental access, it was unquestionably demonstrated that TNI and ITC were capable of:

1. organizing complex satellite-based audio/video interactive experiments involving five communities;
2. managing five production centers and satellite uplink/downlink ground stations;
3. coordinating a large staff in different locations, as well as a budget of over 1 million dollars;
4. producing hundreds of hours of high-quality television program output;
5. documenting technical data related to satellite experimentation and viable uses of the satellite for northern interactive communications; and, finally,
6. documenting the whole process as evidence of their credibility as a potential television broadcasting licensee.

In 1981, based on the positive results of its Anik B demonstration project "Inukshuk," the Inuit Broadcasting Corporation was licensed as a northern television service by the Canadian Radio-television and Telecommunications Commission (CRTC—Canada's regulatory agency) to provide Inuktitut-language services to the Northwest Territories, Northern Quebec, and Labrador. In this same period, other NCS across the North were at varying stages of radio and television development, also in preparation for the licensing process and all in support of the establishment of a legislated recognition of their media demands as a distinct constituency group within the Canadian state.

At this time, the federal government undertook a one-year consultation and planning process, the outcome of which was the Northern Broadcasting Policy (1983), and an accompanying program vehicle, the Northern Native Broadcast Access Program (NNBAP). These policy and funding decisions became the foundation for both the eventual enshrinement of aboriginal broadcasting in the 1991 Broadcasting Act and for the establishment of the Aboriginal Peoples Television Network (1999).

The Northern Broadcasting Policy set out the principle of "fair access" to production and distribution of programming by aboriginal northerners in their territories and ensured a process of consultation with First Peoples before southern-based decisions were to be made about northern telecommunications services. By 1983, 13 regional NCS had been established to be the recipients of funding from the NNBAP administered by the Department of the Secretary of State (Native Citizens Directorate). NNBAP coordinators were mandated to distribute $40.3 million over a four-year period to be used for the regional production of 20 hours of radio and 5 hours of aboriginal television per week. Funding has eroded annually, but the program is still operational.

After an initial "honeymoon" period, it became apparent that fair distribution of radio and television programming was a key problem because of the implicit assumption within the Northern Broadcasting Policy that this task would be taken care of by either CBC Northern Service or by CANCOM (Canadian Satellite Communications Inc.), a private northern program distributor. In both cases, negotiations between NCS and broadcasters had become bogged down over prime time access hours and preemption of national programming.

In 1988 the federal government responded to persistent native lobbying by the National Aboriginal Communications Society (a lobby group representing the interests of the NCS groups) for more secure distribution services by laying out $10 million toward the establishment of a dedicated Northern satellite transponder (channel). In 1991 a new Broadcasting Act was passed in which aboriginal programming was enshrined. Soon after, there followed a public hearing in Hull (October 28, 1991) where the CRTC approved the Television Northern Canada (TVNC) application for an aboriginal television license to serve northern Canada's cultural, social, political, and educational programming needs (Decision CRTC 91–826). By doing so, the commission recognized the importance of northern-based control over the distribution of aboriginal and northern programming. By 1992 TVNC was on the air and became the vehicle through which First

Peoples began to represent themselves and their concerns to the entire North. They would no longer be restricted by geography or technology to local or regional self-representation and identity building. In this sense, the licensing of TVNC constituted de facto recognition of the communication rights of the First Peoples in the North.

Owned and programmed by 13 aboriginal broadcast groups, plus government and education organizations located in the North, TVNC was a pan-Arctic satellite service that distributed 100 hours of programming to 94 Northern communities as a primary level of service. TVNC was not a programmer, but a distributor of its members' programming whose service covered an area of over 4.3 million kilometers (one-third of Canada's territory). In 1995 TVNC applied for permission from the CRTC to be placed on the list of eligible channels to be picked up by cable operators in the South. This approval was granted, making it possible for TVNC to become available in a variety of southern Canadian markets, as part of cable's discretionary packages. It was already accessible on an off-air basis to those who owned satellite dishes because its signal was not scrambled.

Obstacles to TVNC becoming a national network included financial barriers, cross-culturally sensitive issues such as programs showing the hunting and killing of animals, and the cost of acquisition of rights for broadcasting in the South, which would multiply due to the expansion of target audiences. Despite these challenges, TVNC's Pan-Northern successes convinced its board of directors and staff to aggressively pursue a nationwide network by soliciting support from the Assembly of First Nations (AFN) and other national aboriginal organizations.

In January 1998 TVNC hired Angus Reid (a public opinion consulting firm) to conduct an audience survey among a representative cross section of 1,510 adult Canadians regarding the desirability of establishing a national aboriginal broadcasting undertaking. Results indicated that 79 percent, or two out of three Canadians, supported the idea of a national aboriginal TV network, even if it would mean displacing a currently offered service (APTN Fact Sheet, 1999).

By February 1998, the CRTC called for TVNC's application for a "programming service to reflect the diversity of the needs and interest of aboriginal peoples throughout Canada" (TVNC Newsletter, March 1998, p. 1). In June 1998 the Aboriginal Peoples Television Network application was submitted. To be economically viable, it was to be a mandatory service, available to nearly 8 million households with cable, as well as those with direct-to-home and wireless service providers, including ExpressVu, Star Choice, and Look TV (APTN Fact Sheet, 1999, p. 1). The service targeted both aboriginal and nonaboriginal audiences of all ages with a wide range of programming consisting of educational and animation shows, cultural and traditional programming, music, drama, dance, (inter)national films, news and current affairs, as well as live coverage of special events and interactive programming. Initially, APTN promised 90 percent Canadian content with the remaining 10 percent consisting of indigenous programming from around the world, including the United States, Australia, New Zealand, and Central and South America (APTN Fact Sheet, 1999, p. 2). This has been modified to a more realistic Canadian content level of approximately 65 percent.

On February 22, 1999, the CRTC approved TVNC's application to become APTN and granted it mandatory carriage on basic cable throughout Canada. To provide continuity of service to the 96 communities in the North, a separate feed was to be established to ensure that special programming, including legislative coverage and special events, would be broadcast in the North on an ongoing basis at no cost (TVNC, March 1999, p. 1).

In the South, APTN provides access only for cable subscribers. It attracts niche, not mass audiences. In trying to figure out how to maintain secure funding over long periods of time, the CRTC introduced a social cost to cable operators for carriage of APTN. Subscriber costs of $ .15 per month are paid to cable operators who then transfer the money to APTN to be used for television production costs in communities that are not economically viable enough to sustain their media economies. To complement this funding strategy, APTN carries advertising and receives external funding from CTV/BCE for the establishment and maintenance of a network of regional news centers located in the Atlantic, Toronto, British Columbia, Montreal, Ottawa, and Northern regions as part of their social benefits package. When Bell Canada Enterprises acquired CTV, a private national network, the CRTC required that it pay a social cost for its acquisition in the form of subsidizing the development of APTN's news and current affairs departments. This allowed APTN to expand its regional coverage across the country and gave it a more reasonable budget with which to work. This is an emergent financial model by which states can ensure the sponsorship and sustenance of public-service programming that might be otherwise unaffordable.

APTN began broadcasting on September 1, 1999. Until programming surpluses could be created, programs were repeated three times daily. Broadcast language content is 60 percent English, 15 percent French, and 25 percent in a variety of aboriginal languages.

As the sole international broadcaster in the world that carries exclusively indigenous programming, APTN is a hybrid between what has traditionally been defined as public and private broadcasting, although it models its programming style after public-service television. It is multilinguistic, multicultural, and multiracial in content and production staff and management. It attempts to be both local and global. It does a small amount of original production, such as a daily news and current affairs show, but mainly distributes local and regionally produced programming, as well as (inter)nationally acquired aboriginal programs. The board of directors hopes to eventually expand APTN's international scope enabling it to become comparable to channels such as CNN and BBC World Service, but with an aboriginal perspective.

Despite challenges for more secure, long-term funding and improved access at no cost to any of its viewers, that is, a first-tier placement on the channel grid, First Peoples of Canada have established themselves as pioneers in the development of cross-cultural television links across the vast Canadian territory. Technical advances in local, regional, and national telecommunications services, conjoined with the social and cultural goals of First Peoples broadcasters, have demonstrated that it is possible to use media in a sensitive manner to express cultural heterogeneity, rather than homogeneity. First Peoples have refashioned Canadian television broadcasting. They have indigenized it, transforming it into an inclusive tool for the improvement of intercommunity and cross-constituency relations. They have utilized television programming as a vehicle of mediation into their own historically ruptured pasts and as a pathway into more globally integrated networks and futures. Much can be learned by international minority groups from the cross-cultural infrastructures and pathways that First Peoples of Canada have set in place.

LORNA ROTH

See also **Canadian Programming in English; Canadian Programming in French; Racism, Ethnicity and Television**

Further Reading

Aboriginal Peoples Television Network, APTN Fact Sheet, 1999, available at http://www.aptn.ca/facts.html

Alia, Valerie, *Un/Covering the North: News, Media, and Aboriginal People,* Vancouver: UBC Press, 1999

Browne, Donald R., *Electronic Media and Indigenous Peoples: A Voice of Our Own?,* Ames: Iowa State University Press, 1996

CRTC, Decision CRTC 91–826, Television Northern Canada Incorporated, Ottawa CRTC, October 28, 1991

CRTC, "Native Broadcasting Policy," Public Notice CRTC 1990–1989, September 20, 1990

CRTC, "The Northern Broadcasting Policy—a News Release," March 10, 1983. Government of Canada. June 4, 1991. Broadcasting Act.

Roth, Lorna, "The Crossing of Borders and the Building of Bridges: Steps in the Construction of the Aboriginal Peoples Television Network in Canada," Special Issue on Canadian Communications, *Gazette* (*International Journal of Communication Studies,* Vol. 62(3–4): 251–269), London, Thousand Oaks, and New Delhi: Sage Publications, 2000

Television Northern Canada, "North Link TVNC Newsletter," Ottawa, March 1998, 1999

Fisher, Terry Louise (1946–)

U.S. Writer, Producer

Terry Louise Fisher began her career not in television but as a lawyer in the Los Angeles District Attorney's Office. She later sidestepped into a specialty in entertainment law and in 1982 wrote for and produced the Emmy Award–winning series *Cagney and Lacey.* Other shows followed: *Cutter to Houston* and *The Mississippi* for CBS, the television movies *This Girl for Hire* and *Your Place or Mine?* (all 1983). But she is best known for her work as cocreator (with Steven Bochco) and supervising producer of *L.A. Law* from 1986 to 1988. *L.A. Law,* which ended its run in 1994, was considered the quintessential example of 1980s "appointment television," perfectly capturing the greed, glitz, and power-seeking of the decade, and capturing in the process of its narratives an audience intrigued by those very elements.

The power struggles among the show's law partners were echoed in Fisher's 1987 legal battle with Bochco, when a negotiation for Fisher to take over from Bochco as executive producer failed and he banned her from the set. Since then Fisher has published two novels, has produced other series and several made-for-television movies, and in the mid-1990s she co-wrote *Cagney and Lacey: The Return* (1994) and *Cagney and Lacey: Together Again* (1995). She also participated in a pilot for *Daughters of Eve,* the first international prime-time soap opera, starring Sophia Loren and financed by Procter and Gamble.

CHERYL HARRIS

See also **Cagney and Lacey; L.A. Law**

Terry Louise Fisher. Born in Chicago, Illinois, 1946. Entered law school at University of California, Los Angeles, 1968. Married and divorced. Worked as trial lawyer, Los Angeles District Attorney's Office; switched to entertainment law; worked on *Cagney and Lacey* series, 1982–85; supervising producer, *L.A. Law,* 1986–88; independent producer, made-for-television movies and television series, from 1988. Recipient: Emmy Awards, 1987 and 1988.

Television Series

1982–88	*Cagney and Lacey*
1983	*Cutter to Houston*
1983	*The Mississippi*
1986–94	*L.A. Law*
1987	*Hooperman* (co-writer)
1992	*2000 Malibu Road* (creator)
1995	*Daughters of Eve* (pilot)

Made-for-Television Movies

1983	*Your Place or Mine?*
1983	*This Girl for Hire*
1987	*Sister Margaret and the Saturday Night Ladies*
1990	*Blue Bayou*
1994	*Cagney and Lacey: The Return*
1995	*Cagney and Lacey: Together Again*

Publications

A Class Act (novel), 1976
Good Behavior (novel), 1979

Further Reading

Kort, Michele, "Terry Louise Fisher: How She Dreamed Up the Women of *L.A. Law*," *Ms.* (June 1987)

Flintstones, The

U.S. Cartoon Comedy Series

The Flintstones was the first animated situation comedy shown in prime-time television. Premiering on ABC on September 30, 1960, it gained high ratings in its first season, thus establishing animation as a viable prime-time format. Produced by Hanna-Barbera (William Hanna and Joseph Barbera), *The Flintstones* was patterned after Jackie Gleason's *The Honeymooners.* Designed as a program for the entire family, *The Flintstones* was not categorized as "children's television" until its rebroadcast by NBC in 1967. Scheduled in the 8:30 P.M. Friday time slot, its popularity with teenagers, however, presaged the late 1960s move to animation as the preeminent format for children's programming.

Fred and Wilma Flintstone and their best friends, Barney and Betty Rubble, lived in the prehistoric city of Bedrock but faced the problems of contemporary working-class life. After a day at the rock quarry, Fred and Barney arrived home in a vehicle with stone wheels and a fringe on top. Their lives revolved around their home, friends, and leisure activities: a world of drive-ins, bowling, and their "Water Buffalo" lodge. A baby dinosaur and a saber-toothed tiger replaced the family dog and cat. In 1962 and 1963, Pebbles and Bamm Bamm appeared as the daughter and adopted son of the Flintstones and Rubbles, respectively.

In addition to being the first animated series made for prime time, *The Flintstones* also broke new ground in that each episode contained only one story that lasted the full half hour. Until the 1960s, cartoons were generally only a few minutes long. Half-hour animated programs used three or four shorts (three- to four-minute cartoons) and a live "wraparound," usually presented by a friendly "host," to complete the program. In another innovation, Hanna-Barbera produced *The Flintstones* using limited animation techniques. This

The Flintstones, Wilma Flintstone, Bam Bam Rubble, Barney Rubble, Betty Rubble, Pebbles Flintstone, Fred Flintstone, 1960–66.
Courtesy of the Everett Collection

made in their likenesses, critics attacked the practice of advertising vitamins to children, and such ads were withdrawn in 1972. The *Flintstones* characters still appear in commercials for Pebbles-brand cereals, and other tie-ins include films (live-action motion pictures in 1994 and 2000), traveling road shows, toys, and other children's products.

The Flintstones played on ABC in prime time for six seasons (166 episodes) through September 1966. The series was rebroadcast on Saturday mornings by NBC from January 1967 through September 1970. Various spin-offs and specials also appeared on the CBS or NBC Saturday morning lineup throughout most of the 1970s, and they continue to reappear. *The Flintstones* is still available almost daily on cable channels such as The Cartoon Network.

ALISON ALEXANDER

See also **Cartoon; Children and Television; Hanna, William, and Joseph Barbera**

Cast (Voices)

Fred Flintstone	Alan Reed
Wilma Flintstone	Jean Vander Pyl
Barney Rubble	Mel Blanc
Betty Rubble (1960–64)	Bea Benaderet
Betty Rubble (1964–66)	Gerry Johnson
Dino the Dinosaur	Mel Blanc
Pebbles (1963–66)	Jean Vander Pyl
Bam Bam (1963–66)	Don Messick

Producers

William Hanna, Joseph Barbera

Programming History

166 episodes
ABC

September 1960–September 1963	Friday 8:30–9:00
September 1963–December 1964	Thursday 7:30–8:00
December 1964–September 1966	Friday 7:30–8:00

Further Reading

Barnouw, Erik, *Tube of Plenty: The Evolution of American Television,* New York: Oxford University Press, 1975; 2nd revised edition, 1990

Turow, Joseph, *Entertainment, Education, and the Hard Sell: Three Decades of Network Children's Television,* New York: Praeger, 1981

Woolery, George, *Children's Television: The First Thirty-Five Years, 1946–1981: Part I: Animated Cartoon Series,* Metuchen, New Jersey: Scarecrow Press, 1983

assembly-line method of creating drawings, combined with reduced and simplified body movement, made it possible to manufacture animation cells more cheaply. Because of the lowered cost and the appeal of animation to children, limited animation became the format of choice for children's television in the 1960s, a decade in which children's programming became almost entirely animated.

The Flintstones helped establish Hanna-Barbera Productions as a major Hollywood animation studio, and by the late 1960s the company was the world's largest producer of animated entertainment films. *The Flintstones* also launched a multimillion-dollar merchandising business, with hundreds of toys and novelties placed on the market. Perhaps the most enduring product developed in this ancillary line was Flintstones Vitamins, also used as a sponsor for the program. Citing the difficulties children might have in distinguishing cartoon characters from the products

Flip Wilson Show, The

U.S. Comedy Variety Program

The Flip Wilson Show was the first successful network variety series with an African-American star. In its first two seasons, its Nielsen ratings placed it as the second-most-watched show in the United States. Flip Wilson based his storytelling humor on his background in black clubs, but he adapted easily to a television audience. The show's format dispensed with much of the clutter of previous variety programs and focused on the star and his guests.

Clerow "Flip" Wilson had been working small venues for over a decade when Redd Foxx observed his act in 1965 and raved about him to Johnny Carson. As a result, Wilson made more than 25 appearances on the *Tonight Show,* and in 1968 NBC signed him to a five-year development deal.

Wilson made guest appearances on shows such as *Rowan and Martin's Laugh-In* and the first episode of *Love, American Style.* On September 22, 1969, he appeared with 20 other up-and-coming comics in a Bob Hope special, which was followed by a *Flip Wilson Show* special, a pilot for the series to come. Wilson's special introduced many distinctive elements that would be part of the series, the most striking element being the small, round stage in the middle of the audience, from which Wilson told jokes and where guests sang and performed sketches with minimal sets.

For his opening monologue on that special, Wilson told a story about a minister's wife who tried to justify her new extravagant purchase by explaining how "the Devil made me buy this dress!" The wife's voice was the one subsequently used for all his female characters, whether a girlfriend or Queen Isabella ("Christopher Columbus going to *find* Ray Charles!"). Later in the special, he put a look to the voice in a sketch opposite guest Jonathan Winters. Winters played his swinging granny character, Maudie Frickert, as an airline passenger, and when Wilson donned a contemporary stewardess's outfit—loud print miniskirt and puffy cap—Geraldine Jones was born. The audience howled as Winters apparently met his match.

Encouraged by the special, NBC decided to go forward with a regular series, and *The Flip Wilson Show* joined the fall lineup on September 17, 1970. Wilson appeared at the opening and explained that there was no big opening production number, because it would have cost $104,000. "So I thought I would show you what $104,000 looks like." Flashing a courier's case filled with bills before the camera and audience, he asked, "Now, wasn't that much better than watching a bunch of girls jumping around the stage?"

That monologue illustrated the sort of chances Wilson and his producer, Bob Henry, took. They did away with the variety show's conventional chorus lines, singers, and dancers, and allowed the star and his guests to carry the show. The creative gamble paid off as *The Flip Wilson Show* defeated all other programs airing in its time slot and won two Emmy Awards in 1971: as Best Variety Show and for Best Writing in a Variety Show.

The show was also a landmark in the networks' fitful history of integrating its prime-time lineup. Nat "King" Cole had been the first African American to host a variety show, which NBC carried on a sustaining basis in 1956. Despite appearances by guests such as Frank Sinatra, Tony Bennett, and Harry Belafonte, that program could neither attract sponsors nor obtain sufficient clearances from affiliates. Cole left the air at the end of 1957. Later, NBC was more successful with Bill Cosby in *I Spy,* and Diahann Carroll as *Julia.* The week after *The Flip Wilson Show*'s premiere, ABC debuted its first all-black situation comedy, an unsuccessful adaptation of Neil Simon's *Barefoot in the Park.*

During the run of his show, Wilson created several other characters who flirted with controversy. There was the Reverend Leroy, of the Church of What's Happenin' Now, whose sermons were tinged with a hint of larceny; Freddy the Playboy, always, but unsuccessfully, on the make; and Sonny, the White House janitor, who knew more than the president about what was going on.

However, Geraldine Jones was by far the most popular character on the series. Wilson wrote Geraldine's material himself and tried not to use her to demean black women. Though flirty and flashy, Geraldine was no "finger-popping chippie." She was based partly on Butterfly McQueen's character in *Gone with the Wind:* unrefined but outspoken and honest ("What you see is what you get, honey!"). She expected respect and was devoted to her unseen boyfriend, "Killer." It also helped that Flip had the legs for the role and did not burlesque Geraldine's build, though NBC Standards and Practices did ask him to reduce slightly the size of Geraldine's bust.

Another aspect of the show's appeal was its variety of guests. Like Ed Sullivan, Wilson tried to appeal to

The Flip Wilson Show, Flip Wilson, Hank Aaron, 1970–74.
Courtesy of the Everett Collection

as wide an audience as possible. The premiere saw James Brown, David Frost, and the *Sesame Street* Muppets. A later show offered Roger Miller, the Temptations, Redd Foxx, and Lily Tomlin, whom Freddy the Playboy tried to pick up. Roy Clark, Bobby Darin, and Denise Nicholas joined Wilson for a "Butch Cassidy and the Suntan Kid" sketch.

The Flip Wilson Show turned out to be one of the last successful variety shows. CBS's 1972 offering *The Waltons* became a surprise hit, winning the Thursday time slot in which *The Flip Wilson Show* aired. By the 1973–74 season, it was John-Boy and company who had the second-most-popular show of the season. NBC put Wilson's show to rest, airing its last episode on June 24, 1974.

MARK R. MCDERMOTT

See also **Variety Programs; Wilson, Flip**

Regular Performers
Flip Wilson
The Jack Regas Dancers
The George Wyle Orchestra

Producer
Bob Henry

Programming History
NBC

September 1970–June 1971	Thursday 7:30–8:30
September 1971–June 1974	Thursday 8:00–9:00

Further Reading

Adir, Karin, *The Great Clowns of American Television,* Jefferson, North Carolina: McFarland, 1988
Amory, Cleveland, "The Flip Wilson Show," *TV Guide* (October 10, 1970)
"Flipping It," *Newsweek* (August 12, 1968)
Franklin, Joe, *Joe Franklin's Encyclopedia of Comedians,* Secaucus, New Jersey: Citadel, 1979
"I Don't Care If You Laugh," *Time* (October 19, 1970)
O'Neil, Thomas, *The Emmys: Star Wars, Showdowns, and the Supreme Test of TV's Best,* New York: Penguin, 1992
Pierce, Ronchitta, "All Flip Over Flip," *Ebony* (April 1968)
Robinson, Louie, "The Evolution of Geraldine," *Ebony* (December 1970)

Flow

The concept of flow as it relates to television and television theory has its origins in the writings of Welsh cultural theorist Raymond Williams (1974). It was provoked by his startled introduction to the experience of watching American television. He was struck by the way that the on-screen sequence was organized to per-

suade the viewer to "go with the flow" and stay tuned. Watching television was just that:

> In all developed broadcasting systems the characteristic organization, and therefore the characteristic experience, is one of sequence or flow. This phenomenon, of planned flow, is then perhaps the defining characteristic

of broadcasting, simultaneously as technology and cultural form. (Williams, p. 86)

For one trained in the literary criticism of high modernist theater (Williams wrote *Drama from Ibsen to Brecht*), this "defining characteristic" was new, since theater, like literature, was traditionally experienced in highly bounded performances of single works.

Williams coined the term "planned flow," but he did not originate the concept. It was propounded by another British literary critic, Terence Hawkes, in a 1967 radio talk published in *The Listener* (June 8, 1967), which was Williams's own vehicle for TV criticism (Hawkes, pp. 229–41; O'Connor, 1989). Hawkes proposed that the "television experience" included "plays,...news bulletins, comedy shows, music, and other diverse activities, *in the same unit*." Reception defined television: "the basic and irreducible constituent of the medium is *not* the...individual programme...but the much larger unit...that emerges from the receiving set'"—as shaped by other shows and by the home and family context of reception (p. 234). He argued that "detailed analysis of a text" was not appropriate to television, and that "television's ephemerality in fact forms part of its nature, as an element in its grammar that relates directly to the structure of its units" (pp. 237–38).

Planned flow had occurred before television. Popular cinema had evolved a programming repertoire in which a session contained comedy cartoons, cliffhanger serials, newsreels, travelogues, B and A features—the "cultural form" that Williams ascribed to television. Radio broadcasting had been defining itself for more than half a century, and audiences were habituated to planned flow in the home. Even TV's theatrical antecedents, such as music hall, were hybrid forms with internal segmented flow, which transferred directly to television (e.g., the long-running *Sunday Night at the London Palladium* and *Royal Variety Shows*).

Thus, flow was not a new or newly noticed phenomenon when Williams leant his weight to it. His intervention was important because it marked a change in theoretical perspective. Television simply defeated high modernist textual empiricism (Hawkes, pp. 235–37), not least because some of its most important textual content was the "television that wasn't there," such as advertisements, trailers, station Ids, and other gaps between the programs that produced the flow (Hartley, ch. 11). Analysis of single shows could not lead to an understanding of television. Rather, it was necessary to relate the organization of production and distribution (i.e., the "planned" aspect of planned flow) to the family home context of viewing, the experience of consumption, and the identity or subjectivity of audiences. The flow that they were thought to experience cleared the necessary theoretical ground for a turn away from textual analysis to the subsequent flood of audience ethnographies in TV studies.

Television criticism, as an attempt to educate audiences in civic virtues or aesthetic values, was abandoned. Instead, television studies arose as an attempt to specify the relation between producers and audiences in terms of power. Audiences were not seen as having the freedom to form their own opinions and conclusions regarding what they saw on television. On the contrary, the notion of planned flow allowed the consumer experience to be thought of in the most general and abstract terms, as subject to the plans of broadcasters—namely, to be an ideological practice. Analyzing actual flows as experienced by individual viewers was rarely undertaken, because Williams had installed planned flow as a defining characteristic of television, not as a hypothesis to be tested against evidence.

Television was watched in households and nations, both highly fraught and ideological institutions where gender, class, race, and other aspects of identity were constantly in contention and pervaded by power, whether power was understood in Marxist terms (as struggle) or in Foucault's (as the administration of life). Individuals' experience of flow did not interest investigators (unless it was their own), because they already knew what it meant as an instance of abstract power relations. In this respect flow was not unlike other "fabulous powers" (Ian Connell's phrase) that people have attributed to electronic media throughout modernity. Jeffrey Sconce made the connection: "fantastic conceptions of media presence" (grounded in a "metaphysics of electricity") "have often evoked a series of interrelated metaphors of 'flow,' suggesting analogies between electricity, consciousness and information" (p. 7).

Flow became prominent via its uptake in cinema studies just as that field was going through a highly abstract theory-oriented phase. But even as they paid their respects to Williams, film theorists could not bring themselves to agree with his concept of flow. Thus John Ellis in the United Kingdom and Jane Feuer in the United States, among many others, refined and redefined the concept. Ellis determined that the "smallest signifying unit" of television was the segment, which led to "segmented flow." Feuer pointed out that there was no such thing as pure flow, only a dialectic between segmentation and flow. Previously, Hawkes had drawn attention to the fact that watching television could result in "disconcerting juxtaposition" (the opposite of flow) when shows or segments were in jarring contradiction to one another. For example, he mentioned having seen *The Black and White Minstrel Show* followed immediately by a news program marked by a main story of race riots in the United States (Hawkes, p. 238; see also Corner, chs. 5–6). John Caldwell mounted an especially spirited critique of the concept of flow in his book *Televisuality* (Caldwell, pp. 158–64, 264).

People do not remember flows; they only remember shows. But once installed as a founding concept in television theory, flow remained available for application to new media to which it was even less suited, that is, interactive and computer-based media. Ellen Seiter, for instance, suggested that in the hands of commercial and advertising "programmers" the Web resembled television; here, planned flow consisted of the attempt to "guide the user through a pre-planned sequence of screens and links." But at best the new interactive media could only claim "flow, interrupted," since the "cultural form" of interactivity meant that users could not be carried along uncontrollably (though they could follow a planned sequence if they chose to). Therefore, the concept has limited application to new media and serves mostly as a reminder of the period when ideology theory required users who were passive and uncritical, at the mercy of the persuasive blandishments of the marketing communication that wants them to stay tuned, during prime time, at any price.

JOHN HARTLEY

See also **Television Studies**

Further Reading

Caldwell, John, *Televisuality: Style, Crisis, and Authority in American Television,* New Brunswick, New Jersey: Rutgers University Press, 1995

Corner, John, *Critical Ideas in Television Studies,* Oxford: Oxford University Press, 2000

Ellis, John, *Visible Fictions: Television, Cinema, Video,* London: Routledge and Kegan Paul, 1982

Feuer, Jane, "The Concept of Live Television: Ontology as Ideology," in *Regarding Television: Critical Approaches—An Anthology,* edited by E. Ann Kaplan, Los Angeles, California: University Publications of America, Inc./AFI, 1983

Hartley, John, *Tele-ology: Studies in Television,* London and New York: Routledge, 1992

Hawkes, Terence, *Shakespeare's Talking Animals: Language and Drama in Society,* London: Edward Arnold, 1973

O'Connor, Alan, editor, *Raymond Williams on Television: Selected Writings,* New York and London: Routledge, 1989

Sconce, Jeffrey, *Haunted Media: Electronic Presence from Telegraphy to Television,* Durham, North Carolina: Duke University Press, 2000

Seiter, Ellen, *Television and New Media Audiences,* Oxford: Oxford University Press, 2000

Williams, Raymond, *Television: Technology and Cultural Form,* London: Fontana 1974; New York: Schocken, 1975

Fontana, Tom (1951–)

U.S. Writer, Producer

Since 1982 Tom Fontana has emerged as one of the most creative and influential forces in television. Fontana has been at the center of some of the most widely acclaimed and daring dramatic series in television history, including *St. Elsewhere* (1982–1988), *Homicide: Life on the Street* (1993–1999), and *Oz* (1997–2003).

Growing up in Buffalo, New York, he enrolled at the State University of New York at Buffalo, graduating in 1973 with a degree in theater. In 1975 he moved to New York City to pursue a career as a playwright, and by the early 1980s he had secured a position as the playwright-in-residence at the Williamstown Theater. Fontana continues to be active in the theater: several of his plays have been produced in New York City, San Francisco, Cincinnati, and Buffalo. He recently served as the playwright-in-residence at The Writer's Theater in New York City.

While at the Williamstown Theater, one of Fontana's plays, *The Spectre Bridegroom,* attracted the attention of television producer Bruce Paltrow, who was then producing *The White Shadow* at MTM Enterprises and was about to go into production on a new MTM show, *St. Elsewhere.* Paltrow offered Fontana a job as a writer on *St. Elsewhere,* where he stayed for the next six years. Like *Hill Street Blues,* another MTM series, *St. Elsewhere* was an ensemble drama with a large cast, set in a broken-down urban institution: in this case a hospital in a blighted section of Boston. *St. Elsewhere* and its writers became known not only for often stunningly moving stories, but also for a dark, irreverent wit and a willingness to play fast and loose with genre and character. Fontana's writing on the series earned him two Emmy Awards, a Humanitas Prize, and a Writers Guild Award.

Following the departure of *St. Elsewhere* from the television schedule in 1988, Fontana teamed up with Paltrow for two more series: *Tattingers* (1988–89) and *Home Fires* (1992). *Tattingers* was initially an hour-long comedy-drama set in a New York restaurant and filmed on location in Manhattan. The series was canceled in midseason, retooled, and brought back three months later as a half-hour sitcom called *Nick and Hillary*. The series was canceled permanently after only two weeks in the new format. *Home Fires* was a situation comedy that revolved around a middle-class suburban family who began each episode in therapy. Neither of these series caught on the way that *St. Elsewhere* did, and neither lasted into the next season.

In 1992 Fontana received word from Barry Levinson that he was going to be developing a cop show and wanted to meet with Fontana about coming on board as an executive producer. Though skeptical of the possibility of improving on what *Hill Street Blues* had already accomplished in the police genre, Fontana agreed to meet with Levinson. *Homicide: Life on the Street* was conceived as an hour-long series based on the book, *Homicide: A Year on the Killing Streets,* by David Simon, a crime reporter for the *Baltimore Sun.* Levinson told Fontana that *Homicide* would be a different kind of cop show: there would be no car chases or gun battles or other melodramatic mainstays of the genre. Thinking the whole project impossible, but looking for a challenge, Fontana signed on to the series. *Homicide* was indeed a different kind of cop show. It used shaky handheld cameras and jump cutting to add visual punch to a series that was more interested in the way the detectives thought and talked than how good they were with guns. With Fontana at the helm (developing story ideas, writing scripts, and having the final word on each episode), the series went on to become one of the most critically acclaimed dramas of the 1990s, gaining three Peabody Awards, and earning Fontana another Emmy Award for writing, along with two Writers Guild Awards.

By the time *Homicide* was nearing the end of its network run, Fontana had emerged as one of the most powerful players in television drama. He had formed his own production company, Fatima Productions and, together with Levinson, had formed The Levinson/Fontana Company; in 1997 they had production deals for new series at NBC, ABC, and HBO.

Nevertheless, Fontana's network efforts in the waning days of *Homicide* proved to be less than totally successful. Three pilots (one for each of three major networks), ABC's *Philly Heat,* CBS's *Firehouse,* and NBC's *The Prosecutors* all failed to be picked up as series. Only *The Beat,* a cop series produced for UPN during the 1999–2000 season, and based on two young uniformed officers in New York City, made it on to the schedule. *The Beat* took the stylistic ticks of *Homicide* to the level of edgy excess, careening between fairly standard compositions shot on film, and grainy video footage with an abundance of canted angles shot with a wide-angle lens. The series failed to connect with the younger UPN audience and was unceremoniously removed from the network's lineup after only a handful of episodes.

When it seemed Fontana's reign as one of television's premiere innovators was being threatened, HBO picked up his idea for a serial drama set inside a maximum-security prison. While HBO had already ventured into series programming with *The Larry Sanders Show, Oz* represented the cable network's first foray into the hour-long drama format. The series quickly earned a reputation as one of the most daring and provocative programs on television and helped launch HBO as perhaps the most important force in television at the turn of the century, setting the stage for HBO's blockbuster hit, *The Sopranos.* As the series' guiding force, Fontana wrote the entire first season (eight episodes) entirely on his own. Writing for HBO freed Fontana from the frustrating constraints imposed by network censors and allowed him to explore in grim and honest detail the kinds of stories that would likely emerge in a prison environment. *Oz* is known for its graphic violence, nudity, profanity, and its exceptional writing. While *Oz* has not received the same kind of industry accolades as its HBO brethren *The Sopranos* and *Six Feet Under,* the series and its creator helped open the door to a new era in television drama.

This commitment to innovation most adequately describes Fontana's personality as a writer and producer. Perhaps because he is the beneficiary of the tutelage he received from Bruce Paltrow, Fontana is known for his generosity in helping to develop young writers. His willingness to engage the human condition in all of its toughness, oddity, darkness, and humor has placed him among the ranks of television's most important and innovative storytellers.

JONATHAN NICHOLS-PETHICK

See also **HBO;** *Homicide: Life on the Street; Sopranos, The; St. Elsewhere*

Tom Fontana. Born in Buffalo, New York, September 12, 1951. Educated at State University of New York at Buffalo, B.A. in theater, 1973. Served as playwright in residence at the Writers Theatre in New York City, 1975–90. Playwright-in-residence at the Williamstown Theatre Festival, Williamstown, Massachusetts, 1978–80. Member of the board of directors, American Writers Theatre Foundation, 1975–90. Writer and producer of various television series since 1982. Founder of Fatima Productions; cofounder, The Levinson/Fontana Company. Recipient: Emmy Awards for Outstanding Writing for a Drama Series, 1984, 1986, 1993.

Television Series (writer and executive producer)

1982–88	*St. Elsewhere* (writer and producer)
1988–89	*Tattingers*
1989	*Nick and Hillary*
1991–92	*Home Fires*
1993–99	*Homicide: Life on the Street*
1997–	*Oz*
2000	*The Beat* (also creator)

Television Movies (writer and executive producer)

1996	*The Prosecutors*
1997	*Firehouse*
2000	*Homicide: The Movie*
2000	*Path To War* (producer)

Television Specials

1985	*The Fourth Wiseman* (writer)
1999	*Barry Levinson on the Future in the 20th Century: Yesterday's Tomorrows* (executive producer)

Stage

Johnny Appleseed: A Noh Play, 1970; *This Is On Me: Dorothy Parker*, 1971; *An Awfully Big Adventure: An Entertainment*, 1975; *One/Potato/More*, 1975; *Nonsense!*, 1977; *The Underlings,*1978; *The Overcoat, or Clothes Make the Man*, 1978; *Old Fashioned*, 1979; *The Spectre Bridegroom*, 1981; *Movin' Mountains*, 1982; *Mime*, 1982; *Imaginary Lovers*, 1982.

Further Reading

"Caron-Fontana," *On Writing 11,* Writers Guild of America, East Publications (April 2000)

Fretts, Bruce, "Nasty As He Wanna Be," *Entertainment Weekly* (July 11, 1997)

Rohrer, Trish, "Escape From New York," *New York* (July 14, 1997)

Thompson, Robert J., *Television's Second Golden Age: From Hill Street Blues to ER*, New York: Continuum Publishing Company, 1996

Troy, Patricia, "Sixty-Minute Men and Women: Writing the Hour Drama," *Written By* (September 1997)

Food Network

U.S. Cable Network

Food Network offers one of the best examples of how cable television can fulfill its promise of narrowcasting—that is, catering to specialized audience and advertiser interests. Although narrowcasting has long been articulated as a major advantage of cable, it was not until the mid-1990s that a group of networks began to demonstrate how this could be done successfully in a commercially driven television environment. Among the critical factors were solid financial backing, a favorable regulatory climate, a program category with established popularity, and a program schedule that could be linked to a large number of viewer interests and advertised products. Food Network met these criteria at the start and went on to develop even more successful programming and scheduling practices.

Food Network, known in its first incarnation as Television Food Network (TVFN), was the brainchild of Reese Schonfeld, a veteran of cable television programming who had been one of the founders of CNN in the early 1980s. Schonfeld first began to develop the Food Network concept in 1993, in partnership with the Providence Journal Company. He has been quoted widely for his idea that a cable network dedicated to food preparation and consumption is not really catering to a specialized audience, since "everybody eats." Even so, it was made clear from the beginning that the primary target was young to middle-aged women—a market niche considered to be underrepresented on cable.

The cable programming market had become fairly competitive by the time TVFN was ready to launch, with many new start-up ventures competing for the small amount of "shelf space" left over after local cable operators had filled their lineups with established favorites such as USA, MTV, CNN, and Nickelodeon. In this climate, TVFN benefited from the passage of the 1992 Cable Act and its retransmission consent provisions, which mandated that cable systems compensate local broadcast stations—financially or otherwise—for the use of their signals. Schonfeld immediately observed the success with which broadcast networks used their own major-market affiliate stations (O & O's) as leverage in drawing subscribers for their start-up cable ventures (such as FX, America's Talking/MSNBC and ESPN2), and thus formulated a plan to help build TVFN's subscriber base. He successfully approached the Chicago Tribune Company, a major television station owner, with an offer of a 20 percent ownership in TVFN in exchange for their retransmission rights—guaranteeing TVFN access to 10 million homes at its start.

Among TVFN's early programs were *Essence of Emeril* with Emeril Lagasse, *Molto Mario* with Mario Batali, *Chillin' and Grillin'* with Bobby Flay, *Too Hot Tamales* with Mary Sue Milliken and Susan Feniger, *Chef du Jour* featuring a variety of celebrity chefs, *How to Feed Your Family on a Hundred Dollars a Week* with Michelle Urvater, and *Food News & Views* with Donna Hanover and David Rosengarten. Reruns of Julia Child's classic, *The French Chef,* purchased for $500,000, helped to boost TVFN's recognition. This lineup proved solid overall, and many of the personalities from the network's early years continued to populate its schedule as of 2003.

TVFN was quietly sold to Belo Broadcasting in 1995 (Schonfeld retained a 5 percent ownership stake), with virtually no change in programming practices. Then in October 1997, the E.W. Scripps Company took over control of TVFN. Scripps had acquired 56 percent of the network from Belo in exchange for two broadcast stations in San Antonio (Scripps's ownership had increased to 68 percent by the end of 2001). Scripps was best known for its holdings in newspapers and television stations, but already was a player in cable narrowcasting, having launched the Home and Garden Television (HGTV) network in 1994.

One of Food Network's major success stories—both before and since the Scripps takeover—has been the cultivation of its star chef, Emeril Lagasse. New Orleans chef Lagasse was hired at the launch of TVFN at $300 an episode for his first show, *Essence of Emeril.* While this was a traditional-style television cooking show, with the chef host preparing recipes behind a kitchen console, Emeril's boisterous personality clearly set the program apart from its predecessors. His blue-collar dialect, jabs at elite food culture, and trademark exclamations "Bam!" and "Let's kick it up a notch!" endeared him to the widest possible cross section of the television audience. TVFN began capitalizing on this appeal with promos featuring raucous groups of home viewers, including male sports fans. A logical next step was the creation of *Emeril Live!,* a cross between traditional cooking show and late-night talk show that features a studio audience and a house. It seems clear that Emeril owes his celebrity—indeed the very concept of television chef as superstar—to Food Network. Emeril currently appears Fridays on *Good Morning America* and also starred in the short-lived 2001 NBC sitcom, *Emeril.* He also markets a product line, including his trademark Essence seasoning.

Following in Emeril's footsteps, other chefs have attained national recognition through their Food Network programs. Sara Moulton (also executive chef at *Gourmet* magazine) has a populist appeal not unlike that of Emeril; this comes across most poignantly in *Cooking Live,* a show in which Moulton often downplays her own expertise in order to accept the advice of audience members who call in. Other chefs, such as Wolfgang Puck, have used Food Network to boost existing celebrity status. And homemaking guru Martha Stewart has linked Food Network to her marketing empire via the popular program, *From Martha's Kitchen.* The presence of known—and widely cross-promoted—personalities such as these, in turn, builds Food Network's reputation.

By the end of 2001, Food Network reached 76.4 million homes, up from 59 million two years earlier and 28 million at the time of its acquisition by Scripps. While celebrity chefs play a critical role in Food Network's programming, surely the network also owes much of this success to the ways in which it has broadened its programming niche. Recent additions to the schedule include *Food Finds,* which seeks out unique prepared food products (most available by mail order) from across the United States, and *Good Eats,* part instructional cooking show and part science education. Imports have also contributed to Food Network's popular programming mix—including British shows *Two Fat Ladies* and *The Naked Chef,* and the Japanese cult favorite, *Iron Chef.*

MEGAN MULLEN

See also **Cable Networks; Narrowcasting**

Further Reading

Goldner, Diane, "Channel Surfers Get a Snack Bar," *New York Times* (January 26, 1994)

Grimes, William, "Can't Stand the Heat? Change the Channel," *New York Times* (August 23, 1998)

Schonfeld, Reese, *Me and Ted Against the World: The Unauthorized Story of the Founding of CNN,* New York: Cliff Street, 2001

Foote, Horton (1916–)

American Writer

Horton Foote is one of America's most successful and honored dramatists for television, cinema, and the theater. He is an award-winning writer from television's Golden Age of live drama, best known perhaps for the teleplays *The Trip to Bountiful* (1953) and *The Traveling Lady* (1957) and his adaptations of William Faulkner's *Old Man* (1958 and 1997) and *Tomorrow* (1960 and the 1972 version). He is also the recipient of Academy Awards for his screenplays of *To Kill a Mockingbird* in 1962 and *Tender Mercies* in 1983.

Born in Wharton, Texas (which he immortalized as the fictional town of Harrison in his plays), Foote decided in his youth to become an actor, with his father financing his early training in Dallas and Pasadena. This onstage ambition led him to New York, where he eventually discovered that he was better suited to writing. By the time his *Only the Heart* reached Broadway in 1944, it was clear that his writing was much more highly regarded than his acting.

Foote's first professionally produced play, *Texas Town* (1942), heralded the subject matter for all his later work (the themes of home and a sense of belonging, populated by realistic characters that are vulnerable to all sorts of human foibles). His early career in writing for the theater segued into writing for television, with dramas for such early anthology showcases as *Kraft Television Theatre*, *Philco TV Playhouse*, *Playhouse 90*, and *U.S. Steel Hour*. His teleplays include adaptations of his own stage plays and of works by southern authors, most notably William Faulkner.

During television's formative years in the early 1950s, Foote, in the company of such outstanding writers as Paddy Chayevsky and Rod Serling, helped usher in the Golden Age of live television drama. Horton Foote's first successful teleplay was *The Trip to Bountiful* (for *Philco TV Playhouse*), a simple and touching story about an old lady who is bullied and nagged by her overbearing daughter-in-law, and who runs away for a last glimpse of her old home in the now-deserted hamlet called Bountiful. During this time Foote also enjoyed success on Broadway, with *The Traveling Lady* with Kim Stanley, followed by *The Trip to Bountiful* with Lillian Gish.

His television work in the 1950s with producer Fred Coe (often in tandem with director Arthur Penn) illuminated and enhanced the small-screen theater strand with its emotional dramatics and its poignant tales. *A Young Lady of Property* (*Philco*) featured Kim Stanley as an adolescent girl in a Southern town whose mother is dead and whose father is about to marry again. *The Oil Well* (*Philco*), with fine performances by E.G. Marshall and Dorothy Gish, presented an atmospheric piece about a Texas farmer who believes there is oil on his property.

Gulf Playhouse: 1st Person featured the unusual (but apt) use of a subjective camera to tell its stories from the viewpoint of a central character. Two of Foote's original teleplays were produced for this fascinating *1st Person* form. *Death of an Old Man* told a sensitive story about the man of the title (who was never seen, but his thoughts were articulated by the voice of William Hansen) who had spent his life helping others and consequently has no material wealth, lying on his deathbed worrying about the welfare of his unmarried daughter. *The Tears of My Sister*, with the first-person narrative provided by Kim Stanley, presented a moving drama about a young girl forced to marry a much older, and unwanted, man so that she could provide for her mother and sister. Although it was the subjective camera around which the development of the drama was structured, these *1st Person* teleplays were considered fine additions to Foote's television body of work. As a *Variety* (August 19, 1953) reviewer noted, "Foote is building up a fictional Texan world that is approaching the stature as well as volume of William Faulkner's Mississippi work."

In 1957 Kim Stanley (a tirelessly inventive Foote interpreter) repeated her earlier Broadway role of a Texas-traveling wife whose life is being shattered by a wastrel, drunken husband reverting to type while on parole in Foote's *The Traveling Lady* for *Studio One*.

Often compared with Faulkner as a perceptive chronicler of southern Americana, Foote is also regarded as one of Faulkner's most fluent translators, his adaptations conveying a sensitive, moving, and noble expression to the work. Foote's adaptation of Faulkner's *Old Man* for *Playhouse 90*, a powerful tale of a convict rescuing a stranded, pregnant woman during a Mississippi flood, made "a memorable 90 minutes of overwhelming drama" (*Variety*, November 26,

1958); for this presentation, Foote received an Emmy nomination for Best Writing of a Single Drama. Faulkner's warmly old-fashioned love story between a deserted pregnant wife and a hired hand in *Tomorrow* was adapted by Foote for another *Playhouse 90* presentation in 1960, and again as a screenplay for the 1972 feature *Tomorrow* starring Robert Duval.

When filmed television drama superseded live, original production, Foote turned to Hollywood, where he was rewarded with an Academy Award for his eloquent adaptation of Harper Lee's *To Kill a Mockingbird*. But then, some two years later, when *Baby the Rain Must Fall* (an adaptation of his own *The Traveling Lady*) was released to lukewarm reviews, he started to grow somewhat disillusioned with the Hollywood treatment of his work (particularly with the 1966 feature version of *The Chase,* from a screenplay adaptation by Lillian Hellman).

Foote withdrew to New Hampshire, an escape from both Broadway and Hollywood. It was during the 1970s that he created *The Orphans' Home Cycle* (1974–77), nine plays chronicling the life of a Texas family from 1902 to 1928, a semiautobiographical look at his family. To date, five of these nine plays have been filmed for both cinema and television.

Over his long and varied career, Horton Foote has distinguished himself as a major American voice and has been honored by the Writers Guild of America, receiving its 1962 award for *To Kill a Mockingbird,* and by the Academy of Television Arts and Sciences, with its 1997 Emmy Award for *William Faulkner's Old Man* (Outstanding Writing for a Miniseries or a Special).

TISE VAHIMAGI

See also **Anthology Drama; Golden Age of Television Drama; *Playhouse 90***

Horton Foote. Born in Wharton, Texas, March 14, 1916. Graduate, Wharton High School; attended Pasadena Playhouse School Theatre, California; Tamara Daykarhanova School of Theatre, NYC. Married: Lillian Vallish. Actor, American Actors Theatre, NYC, 1939–42; Theatre Workshop, King-Smith School of Creative Arts, Washington DC, 1944–45; manager, Productions Inc, Washington DC, 1945–48. Pulitzer Prize in Drama, 1995; American Academy of Arts and Letters Gold Medal for Drama, 1998; PEN/Laura Pels Awards for Drama, 2000; National Medal of Arts, 2000.

Television Plays

1948	*Only the Heart* (*Kraft Television Theatre*)
1952	*The Travelers* (*Goodyear TV Playhouse*)
	The Old Beginning (*Goodyear TV Play house*)
1953	*The Trip to Bountiful* (*Philco TV Playhouse*)
	A Young Lady of Property (*Philco TV Play house*)
	The Oil Well (*Philco TV Playhouse*)
	The Rocking Chair (*The Doctor*)
	Expectant Relations (*Philco TV Playhouse*)
	Death of the Old Man (*Gulf Playhouse: 1st Person*)
	The Tears of My Sister (*Gulf Playhouse: 1st Person*)
	John Turner Davis (*Philco TV Playhouse*)
	The Midnight Caller (*Philco TV Playhouse*)
1954	*The Dancers* (*Philco TV Playhouse*)
	The Shadow of Willie Greer (*Philco TV Playhouse*)
1955	*The Roads to Home* (*U.S. Steel Hour*)
1956	*Flight* (*Playwrights '56*)
	Drugstore Sunday Noon (*Omnibus*)
1957	*A Member of the Family* (*Studio One*)
	The Traveling Lady (*Studio One*)
1958	*Old Man* (*Playhouse 90*)
1960	*Tomorrow* (*Playhouse 90*)
	The Shape of the River (*Playhouse 90*)
1961	*The Night of the Storm* (*DuPont Show of the Month*)
1964	*Gambling Heart* (*DuPont Show of the Month*)
1978	*The Displaced Person* (*American Short Story*)
1980	*Barn Burning* (*American Short Story*)
1983	*Keeping On* (*American Playhouse*)
1987	*The Orphan's Home* (*American Playhouse*)

Made-for-Television Movies

1992	*The Habitation of Dragons*
1996	*Lily Dale*
1997	*William Faulkner's Old Man* (aka *Old Man*)
	Alone (aka *Horton Foote's Alone*)

Films

Storm Fear (from novel by Clinton Seeley), 1955; *To Kill a Mockingbird* (from novel by Lee Harper), 1962; *Baby the Rain Must Fall* (from own original play *The Traveling Lady*), 1964; *Hurry Sundown* (coscreenplay with Thomas C. Ryan from novel by KB Gilden), 1967; *Tomorrow,* 1972; *Tender Mercies,* 1983; *1918, The Trip to Bountiful,* 1985; *On Valentine's Day,* 1986; *Convicts,* 1991; *Of Mice and Men* (from novel by John Steinbeck), 1992.

Stage (as writer; selected)

Texas Town, 1942; *Only the Heart,* 1944; *Celebration,* 1948; *The Chase,* 1952; *The Trip to Bountiful,*

1953; *The Traveling Lady,* 1954; *The Dancers,* 1963; *Gone With the Wind,* 1971; *The Widow Claire,* 1986; *The Young Man from Atlanta,* 1995.

Publications

The Chase, 1956
Three Screenplays: The Trip to Bountiful; Tender Mercies; To Kill a Mockingbird, 1989

Farewell: A Memoir of a Texas Childhood, 1999
Beginnings: A Memoir, 2001

Further Reading

Barr, Terry, and Gerald Wood, "A Certain Kind of Writer," *Literature/Film Quarterly,* Vol. 14 (1986)
Tanner, Louise, "An Interview with Horton Foote," *Films in Review,* Vol. 37 (1986)
Wood, Gerald, "Horton Foote: An Interview," *Post Script,* Vol. 10 (1991)

For the Record

Canadian Dramatic Anthology Series

For the Record was one of the most successful series ever produced and broadcast by the CBC. It used an anthology format, offering four to six new episodes each year linked only by the series title and a documentary-style approach to topical stories. Many episodes proved controversial, but the series was critically acclaimed for its thoughtful and intense treatment of difficult issues.

The idea for the series originated with John Hirsch, who was appointed head of television drama at the CBC in 1974. He felt that CBC drama should have the same urgency and relevance as the network's well-regarded current affairs programming and recruited Ralph Thomas as executive producer of a new series, which would become *For the Record.*

Although the producers and writers contributed a great deal to the success of the series, one of the key decisions made by Thomas was to hire directors who had contributed to the growth of Canadian cinema in the 1960s and early 1970s. These filmmakers were part of Canada's "direct cinema" movement of low-budget feature films based on documentary techniques developed at the National Film Board. In the mid-1970s Canadian film moved toward the production of supposedly more commercial imitations of Hollywood style, and, as a result, leading filmmakers, both Anglophone and Francophone, were pleased to find an outlet for their talents in a television series that stressed its difference from the U.S. network programs that dominated Canadian television screens.

The series officially got under way in 1977, but the basic approach was established in the previous season when five topical dramas were broadcast under the title *Camera '76.* These included "Kathy Karuks Is a Grizzly Bear" (written by Thomas and directed by Peter Pearson), about the exploitation of a young long-distance swimmer, and "A Thousand Moons" (directed by prolific Quebec filmmaker Gilles Carle), about an old Métis woman who lives in a city but dreams of returning home to die. Six new programs were broadcast in the following season, when the series got its permanent name: two ("Ada" and "Dreamspeaker") were contributed by another Quebec director, Claude Jutra, while documentary filmmaker Allan King directed "Maria," about a young Italian-Canadian who attempts to unionize a garment factory. The most controversial production of the 1977 season was undoubtedly "The Tar Sands," written and directed by Pearson, which provoked a libel suit because of its depiction of recent dealings between the oil industry and politicians in Alberta.

By the end of the 1977 season, the format and possibilities of the series had been firmly established, but these did not fit comfortably into existing categories of television programming. The episodes were presented as television dramas, but the location shooting made them seem more like films. After the legal problems with "The Tar Sands," the CBC disavowed the term "docudrama" that had been applied to the series and suggested instead "journalistic drama" or "contemporary, topical drama that is issue oriented."

Whatever the term, the series did allow for a range of approaches. Dramatized treatments of specific topical events (such as "The Tar Sands") were rare, although viewers could often relate the fictional stories to similar stories recently in the news. More common were episodes (such as "Maria") that dealt with an identifiable "social problem" in terms of its impact on characters seen as both individual and representative. While the "social problem" was a necessary ingredient, some episodes, notably those directed by Carle and Jutra, took on a poetic dimension with subjective fantasy sequences emerging from their social realism.

Some memorable episodes from later seasons dealt with rape ("A Matter of Choice," 1978), hockey violence ("Cementhead," 1979), separatism ("Don't Forget 'Je Me Souviens,'" 1979), television evangelism ("Blind Faith," 1982), farm bankruptcies ("Ready for Slaughter," 1983), gender discrimination ("Kate Morris, Vice President," 1984), and the beauty myth ("Slim Obsession," 1984).

The series was praised for its refusal to allow personal dramas to obscure the social implications of the issues. Whatever the outcome for the characters, the endings did not create the impression that the issues had been resolved, implying that solutions still needed to be sought in reality. Supporters of public broadcasting in Canada pointed to *For the Record* as an alternative to the formulas of commercial television, with its demand for clearly defined conflicts and happy endings, and there was a widespread agreement that the series fulfilled the CBC's mandate to provide insight into Canadian society and culture. Its cancellation in 1985 could be seen as a response to commercial and political pressures on the CBC, although the public network has continued to broadcast similar realist dramas exploring topical issues.

JIM LEACH

See also **Canadian Programming in English**

Producer
Ralph Thomas

Programming History
CBC
1976–85

Further Reading

Collins, Richard, *Culture, Communication and National Identity: The Case of Canadian Television,* Toronto: University of Toronto Press, 1990
Feldman, Seth, editor, *Take Two,* Toronto: Irwin, 1984
Gervais, Marc, "Lightyears Ahead: *For the Record,*" *Cinema Canada* (March 1977)
Henley, Gail, "On the Record: *For The Record*'s 10 Distinctive Years," *Cinema Canada* (April 1985)
Miller, Mary Jane, *Turn Up the Contrast: CBC Television Drama since 1952,* Vancouver: University of British Columbia Press, 1987
Morris, Peter, *The Film Companion,* Toronto: Irwin, 1984

Ford, Anna (1943–)

British Broadcast Journalist

Anna Ford was independent television's first female newsreader and in time became one of the most popular and experienced of female news presenters in British television. Critics ascribed her early success as a newsreader primarily to her attractive looks, but she subsequently demonstrated even to her detractors that she was more than competent as a presenter and furthermore ready to brave controversy (something she was well used to even as a student, due to her committed socialist views).

Before her recruitment as ITN's (Independent Television News) answer to the BBC's popular, though less-vivacious, newsreader Angela Rippon in the late 1970s, Ford had already amassed some experience as a television presenter through her work as a reporter for *Reports Action, Man Alive,* and other programs. Reflecting her early training in education (e.g., she taught social studies to Irish Revolutionary Army internees in Belfast's Long Kesh prison), she had also worked on broadcasts for the Open University and had then presented *Tomorrow's World* for a time before resigning because, she explained, she had no wish to become "a public figure." Ironically, this is exactly what she was shortly afterward fated to become as a high-profile newsreader for *News at Ten.*

The most controversial stage in Ford's career opened in the early 1980s, when she was one of the "Famous Five" celebrities behind the launching of the

Anna Ford.
Photo courtesy of Anna Ford

ill-starred TV-AM company, for which she presented the breakfast program *Good Morning Britain.* When the new enterprise failed to attract the required audiences, Ford (and Rippon) were unceremoniously sacked, and it was speculated that her career in television was over. Ford's response to this was to pour a glass of wine on her former employer, Member of Parliament Jonathan Aitken—an incident that hit the headlines and only confirmed Ford's reputation for belligerence.

Similarly controversial was Ford's widely reported refusal to wear flattering makeup on television to disguise the effects of aging, in protest, she said, of the "body fascism" of television bosses who insisted that female newscasters were only there to provide glamour. Critics of her stand attacked her for being aggressive and overtly feminist (they also expressed shock that she sometimes read the news while not wearing a bra), but many more admired her for her forthrightness. Those who had automatically written her off as "just a pretty face" were obliged to think again. It was a mark of her success in the argument that, some six years after the TV-AM debacle, Ford—then age 45—was readmitted to the fold as a newsreader for the BBC's prime-time *Six O'Clock News.* She has also

continued to present occasional programs on a wide range of educational and other issues.

DAVID PICKERING

Anna Ford. Born in Tewkesbury, Gloucestershire, England, October 2, 1943. Attended Minehead Grammar School and White House Grammar School, Brampton; Manchester University. Married: 1) Alan Brittles in 1970 (divorced, 1976); 2) Mark Boxer, 1981 (died, 1988); children: Claire and Kate. Taught at Open University in Belfast for two years before joining Granada Television as researcher, 1974; moved to BBC, 1976; newscaster, ITN, 1978–82; also worked as researcher and presenter of school programs; founder-member of TV-AM, 1980; freelance broadcaster and writer, 1982–86; newscaster, BBC, 1989; chancellor, University of Manchester, 2001. Trustee, Royal Botanic Gardens, Kew, 1995. Recipient: TV Times Most Popular TV Personality (Female), 1978.

Television Series

1974	*Reports Action*
1976–77	*Man Alive*
1977–78	*Tomorrow's World*
1978–80	*News at Ten*
1983	*Good Morning Britain*
1984	*Did You See...?*
1986	*Understanding Adolescents*
1987–89	*Network*
1987	*Understanding Families*
1987	*On Course*
1989–99	*Six O'Clock News*
1999–	*One O'Clock News*

Television Specials

1984	*West End Stage Awards*
1985	*Starting Infant School*
1985	*Communication*
1985	*Handicapped Children*
1985	*Children's Feelings*
1985	*Starting Secondary School*
1985	*Approaching Adolescence*
1985	*Warnings from the Future?*
1985	*Have We Lived Before?*
1986	*London Standard Film Awards*
1986	*Television on Trial*
1986	*Puberty*
1987	*Richard Burton Drama Award*
1987	*The Search for Realism*
1987	*The Struggle for Land*
1987	*The Price of Marriage*
1987	*Veiled Revolution*
1987	*ITV Schools: Thirty Years On*

1987	*Kimberley Carlile—Falling through the Net*	1992	*Family Planning Association*
1988	*Harold Pinter*	1994	*Against All Odds*
1988	*Wildscreen 88*	1994	*Evening Standard British Film Awards 1993*
1988	*Fight to Survive?*	1994	*Understanding the Under-12s*
1988	*Network in Ireland*		
1989	*British Academy Awards*		
1989	*Mary Stott*		
1992	*Edvard Munch: The Frieze of Life*		

Publication

Men: A Documentary, 1984

Format Sales, International

"Format" is the term used in television industries to describe a set of program ideas and techniques already successfully used in one market and subsequently adapted—usually under license—to produce programs elsewhere. Many past examples of such program mimicking come to mind. In radio's heyday, for example, NBC's *What's My Line?* was remade by the BBC. A decade later, the United Kingdom's *Till Death Us Do Part* was adapted for U.S. television as *All In The Family*. Typically, the business arrangements concerning these and many other program translations tended to be informal, ad hoc. and undertaken on a one-off basis. Not surprisingly, there was also a good deal of international borrowing of formats that involved neither authorization nor the payment of fees. Numerous unauthorized U.S. format adaptations turned up in The Netherlands, Australia, and many South American countries. However, the most significant case was the New Zealand remake of the U.K. game show *Opportunity Knocks*. In 1989, Hughie Green, U.K. format originator/producer, brought legal action against the New Zealand Broadcasting Corporation. Charges included infringement of format copyright. However, the charges were not upheld in New Zealand and a U.K. appeal to the Privy Council was also dismissed.

Despite this doubt about whether formats enjoyed copyright protection, the past ten years have seen an explosion in global traffic in TV program formats. One main reason for such an increase lies in the worldwide expansion of television channels thanks to deregulation, new technology and the advance of laissez-faire economic policies. Faced with an ever more desperate struggle for ratings success, TV producers and broadcasters frequently prefer to adapt an already successful program format, rather than take a chance on an original, untried format.

This increase in the volume of format adaptation has been accompanied by a determined attempt to ensure that players stick to a set of rules. Several elements are at work here. First, the fact that format trade now occurs at such industry conventions as MIPCOM rather than by overseas producers, surreptitiously recording off-air in L.A. hotel rooms, means that at least some parts of the trade are controlled. In addition, producers continue to believe that formats do carry legal protection. Paying according to rules helps maintain business reputations. Further, format licensing fees tend to be relatively modest, being partly determined by the kind of asking price that might be set for the broadcasting of an imported version of the same program. Additionally, to dissuade producers from plagiarizing a format off-air, an owner also usually makes available a series of important ancillary elements as part of the format licensing package. These can include: titles and other software; set designs, production schedules, and so on; scripts; videotapes of on-air episodes; confidential ratings and demographic information; and consultancy services. Finally, there is always the threat of legal action such as, for instance, occurred in 1999 when the U.K. producer of the reality program *Survivor* undertook a lawsuit against Endemol, producer of *Big Brother,* alleging format infringement.

One further sign of an attempted regularization of exchange in television program formats has been the organization of a trade association. In 2000, the Format Recognition and Protection Association (FRAPA) was established in London. FRAPA's functions are threefold. First, it has established a system of dispute arbitration between members to avoid legal action, which is often unpredictable, costly, and usually slow. Second, it acts as an information clearinghouse. Third, it hopes to lobby sympathetic national governments to enact format protection legislation. Not surprisingly, FRAPA has succeeded in signing up the major agencies in the international field of format trade, including Endemol, Pearson, Columbia TriStar, King World, Distraction, Mentorn International, Action Time, Hat Trick Productions, Celador, and Expand Images.

Harry de Winter, head of Dutch IDtv, believes that the international TV program format business will ultimately end up in the hands of two or three giants with smaller independent companies being the ones that actually generate the ideas. The U.K.'s FremantleMedia (formerly Pearson Television) and Endemol from The Netherlands are likely to be the central agencies in the format trade of the near future.

Pearson Television was an arm of the U.K.-based Pearson media group. Already owner of Thames Production, the company set out to acquire an extensive program format catalogue in the early 1990s. In 1995 it took over Grundy Worldwide, thereby acquiring a library in the areas of game shows and drama. The 1997 acquisition of All American Fremantle International gave it control of the Mark Goodson library of game shows including such classics as *The Price Is Right, Family Feud,* and *Card Sharks.* Successful Grundy drama formats were already on the air in Australia, The Netherlands, and Germany with new adaptations of formats such as *Sons and Daughters* and *Prisoner* appearing more recently in Sweden, Finland, Germany, and Greece. In turn, Pearson also acquired additional formats through the takeover of a string of small production companies in the United Kingdom, Germany, Italy, and South Africa. To concentrate on Spanish markets in the United States and in Latin America, it established a production company in Miami in 1999.

With an extensive format catalogue at its disposal, it was inevitable that Pearson would see strategic market advantage in joining a vertically integrated media group. From 1997, Pearson was part of the U.K. Channel 5 broadcasting consortium and in 2000 merged with the German based CTL-UF to form the RTL Group. The company changed its name to FremantleMedia in 2001. By that point, the company had over 160 programs in production in 35 different territories with particular production strengths in the United Kingdom, Germany, Sweden, the United States, and Australia.

Endemol was created in 1993 with the merger of two independent Dutch companies, Joop van den Ende Productions and John de Mol Productions. It was floated as a public company on the Amsterdam stock exchange in 1996 and the capital inflow this has created has led to an aggressive expansion. Endemol now has companies in 17 different territories in Western and Eastern Europe, the United Kingdom, Australia, South Africa, the United States, and Argentina. In 2000, it linked with the Telefonia group, the largest supplier of telecommunications and Internet services in the Spanish- and Portugese-speaking worlds. It now provides content for broadcasting companies as well as for Internet, third-generation cellular telephones, and other distribution platforms. The basis of Endemol's remarkable expansion has been its catalogue of TV formats, which now numbers over 400 titles. These include not only some of the older pre-1993 formats such as *Forgive Me* and *All You Need Is Love* but also more recently originated ones, especially *Big Brother.* Indeed, the latter format has provided the basis for a comprehensive franchising operation involving the systematic exploitation of rights in relation to new distribution platforms that may be a significant clue to future directions in the format business.

Finally, it is important to note that, despite FRAPA's efforts, many producers outside the United States and Western Europe refuse to accept any rules. This is particularly the case in the People's Republic of China, where the state does not support the notion of intellectual property. Even in other parts of the world where rules are in play, it is still often difficult to distinguish between a format infringement and general generic imitation.

ALBERT MORAN

See also All in the Family; **Reality Programming;** *Survivor; Till Death Do Us Part*

Further Reading

Moran, Albert, *Copycat TV: Globalisation, Program Formats and Cultural Identity,* Luton, United Kingdom: University of Luton Press, 1997

Forsyte Saga, The

British Serial Drama

The Forsyte Saga, one of the most celebrated of British period drama series ever made, was first shown in 1967 and subsequently in many countries around the world, to universal acclaim. Based on the novels of John Galsworthy, the series was made in black and white and comprised 26 episodes covering the history of the aristocratic Forsyte family between the years 1879 and 1926 (actually rather longer than the period covered in the novels themselves).

The project was the brainchild of producer Donald Wilson, who first conceived the idea in 1955 and spent years planning the series and getting the necessary backing for it. The series finally got the go-ahead on the strength of the distinguished cast who were signed up for it. They included Kenneth More (Jolyon Forsyte), Eric Porter (Soames Forsyte), Nyree Dawn Porter (Irene Forsyte), Fay Compton (Ann Forsyte), Michael York ("Jolly" Forsyte), and newcomer Susan Hampshire (Fleur Forsyte). The plot revolved around the feuds and machinations of the Forsyte family and their London merchants' business (paving the way for such glossy soap operas of the 1980s as *Dallas* and *Dynasty*). Each episode culminated in a "cliff-hanger" ending designed to persuade viewers to tune in once again the following week. Among the most famous scenes was one in which the hapless Irene, unloved by her cold and possessive husband, Soames, was brutally raped by him as their marriage fell apart. The scene was rendered even more convincing by bloodstains on Irene's dress (Eric Porter had inadvertently cut his hand on her brooch when tearing off her bodice).

The series enjoyed vast audiences, the first showing, on BBC 2, attracting some 6 million viewers and the second showing, now on BBC 1, attracting some 18 million. Publicans and vicars alike complained that they might just as well shut up shop on Sunday evenings as everyone stayed at home to see the next episode of the gripping saga. Similar success greeted the series in other parts of the world, including the United States, and *The Forsyte Saga* also earned the distinction of being the first BBC series to be sold to the Soviet Union. The worldwide audience was estimated as something in the region of 160 million.

The success of the series, which won a Royal Television Society Silver Medal and a BAFTA award for Best Drama, prompted the BBC to invest further resources into similar blockbusting "costume" dramas, a policy that in ensuing years was to produce such results as *The Pallisers* (which was also produced by Donald Wilson) and *Upstairs, Downstairs.* In the United States, *Forsyte*'s success promoted the development of the miniseries in competition with the open-ended perpetual drama serial. Indeed, the bosses of one U.S. television station decided its viewers could not be expected to wait for the next episode and showed the entire series in one chunk, which lasted 23 hours and 50 minutes.

In 2001 Granada Television Ltd. put a remake of *The Forsyte Saga* into production, with Rupert Graves as Young Jolyon, Gina McKee as Irene, Damian Lewis as Soames, Corin Redgrave as Old Jolyon, Wendy Craig as Aunt Juley, and Ioan Gruffud as Bosinney.

DAVID PICKERING

See also **Adaptations; Miniseries**

Cast

Jolyon Forsyte	Kenneth More
Irene Forsyte	Nyree Dawn Porter
Soames Forsyte	Eric Porter
Old Jolyon	Joseph O'Connor
Fleur	Susan Hampshire
Jon	Martin Jarvis
Montague Dartie	Terence Alexander
Michael Mont	Nicholas Pennell
Winifred	Margaret Tyzack
"Jolly"	Michael York

Producer

Donald Wilson

Programming History

26 episodes
BBC 2
January 1967–July 1967

The Forsyte Saga, Kenneth More, Eric Porter, 1967.
Courtesy of the Everett Collection

Forsythe, John (1918–)

U.S. Actor

With his tanned, handsome mien, silver hair and urbane style, John Forsythe has been a recognizable television personality associated with suavity and upper-class elegance since the 1950s. He has made his mark chiefly in debonair paternal parts in several long-running television series. The actor's distinctive voice and precise diction have also served him well, particularly in parts where the actor was never seen on-screen, as in the 1970s Aaron Spelling hit *Charlie's Angels,* in which Forsythe voiced the role of Charlie Townsend, the eponymous employer of a trio of female detectives.

Forsythe's first roles permitted him to hone and showcase his vocal talents. After studying at the University of North Carolina, he began his career as a sports announcer for the Brooklyn Dodgers at Ebbets Field and then segued into acting in radio soap operas. Subsequent appearances on Broadway led to a motion picture contract with Warner Brothers and a Hollywood debut with Cary Grant in the film *Destination Tokyo.*

After World War II Forsythe went on to starring roles in a number of Broadway productions. While still in New York, he appeared in many of the live television shows based there, such as *Studio One, Kraft Television Theatre, Robert Montgomery Presents,* and *Schlitz Playhouse of Stars.* He subsequently moved to Los Angeles and took a starring role as a playboy Hollywood attorney responsible for raising his orphaned niece in the television series *Bachelor Father,* which was broadcast from 1957 to 1962. Forsythe was nominated for an Emmy for this television role, his first as a father figure, and he would be nominated again for his portrayal of the head of the Carrington clan in the hit show *Dynasty* in the 1980s.

ABC's answer to hit CBS show *Dallas, Dynasty* featured Forsythe in the role of patriarch Blake Carrington, head of a wealthy Denver, Colorado, family, plagued by a scheming ex-wife, a bisexual son, and other tribulations. The show, which ran roughly in tandem with the Reagan era, was known for its opulent atmosphere, lavish sets and costumes, and typical preoccupation with the problems of the wealthy, ranging from murder and greed to lust and incest. The show, which hit its ratings peak in 1984–85, solidified Forsythe's "nice guy" image even in the role of a ruthless oil magnate, exploring plotlines focusing on his emotional reactions to Joan Collins's villainy, his son's sexuality, and his attempts to maintain the family. Blake Carrington even pitched his own line of cologne in advertisements featuring his love for his wife, who, in a commercial narrative extending from *Dynasty,* had the fragrance designed for him.

Forsythe won two Golden Globe Awards for Best Actor in a Dramatic Television Series for his work in *Dynasty.* Since the series ended in 1989, he has recreated his role as Blake Carrington in a reunion movie and appeared as the on-camera host for *I Witness Video.* He also starred in a 1992–93 series, a political

John Forsythe.
Courtesy of the Everett Collection

satire sitcom called *The Powers That Be* and reprised his television role of Charlie for the feature film version of *Charlie's Angels* in 2000.

DIANE M. NEGRA

See also **Charlie's Angels; Comedy, Domestic Settings;** *Dynasty*

John Forsythe (John Lincoln Freund). Born in Penn's Grove, New Jersey, January 29, 1918. Educated at the University of North Carolina and the New York Actor's Studio. Married: 1) Parker McCormick (divorced); one child: Dall; 2) Julie Warren (died, 1994); two children: Page and Brooke. Served in U.S. Army Air Corps. Public address announcer, Brooklyn Dodgers at Ebbets Field; appeared in radio soap operas; acted on stage, since early 1940s, actor in films, since 1944; actor on television, since 1947; host of Hollywood Park Feature Race, 1971–74. Member: United Nations Association; American National Theatre and Academy. Recipient: Golden Globe Awards, 1983, 1984.

Television Series

1957–62	*Bachelor Father*
1965–66	*The John Forsythe Show*
1970–82	*World of Survival*
1971	*To Rome with Love*
1976–81	*Charlie's Angels* (voice)
1981–89	*Dynasty*
1992–93	*The Powers That Be*
1993–94	*I Witness Video*
1998	*People's Century* (narrator)

Made-for-Television Movies

1964	*See How They Run*
1968	*Shadow of the Land*
1971	*Murder Once Removed*
1973	*The Letters*
1973	*Lisa: Bright and Dark*
1974	*Cry Panic*
1974	*The Healers*
1974	*Terror on the 40th Floor*
1975	*The Deadly Tower*
1976	*Amelia Earhart*
1977	*Tail Gunner Joe*
1977	*Never Con a Killer*
1978	*Cruise into Terror*
1978	*The Users*
1978	*With This Ring*
1980	*A Time for Miracles*
1981	*Sizzle*
1982	*The Mysterious Two*
1987	*On Fire*
1990	*Opposites Attract*
1991	*Dynasty: The Reunion*

Films

Destination Tokyo, 1944; *The Captive City,* 1952; *It Happens Every Thursday,* 1953; *The Glass Web,* 1952; *Escape from Fort Bravo,* 1953; *The Trouble with Harry,* 1956; *The Ambassador's Daughter,* 1956; *The Captive City,* 1962; *Kitten with a Whip,* 1964; *Madame X,* 1966; *In Cold Blood,* 1968; *Topaz,* 1969; *The Happy Ending,* 1970; *Goodbye and Amen,* 1977; *And Justice for All,* 1979; *Scrooged,* 1988; *Stan and George's New Life,* 1991; *Hotel de Love,* 1997; *Charlie's Angels,* 2000.

Stage

Dick Whittington and His Cat, 1939; *Vickie,* 1942; *Yankee Point,* 1942; *Winged Victory,* 1943; *Yellowjack,* 1945; *Woman Bites Dog,* 1946; *All My Sons,* 1947; *It Takes Two,* 1947; *Mister Roberts,* 1950; *The Teahouse of the August Moon,* 1953; *Detective Story,* 1955; *Weekend,* 1968; *The Caine Mutiny Court Martial,* 1971; *Sacrilege,* 1995.

Four Corners

Australian Current Affairs Program

Four Corners is Australia's longest-running current affairs program and is often referred to as the "flagship" of the government-funded Australian Broadcasting Corporation (ABC). *Four Corners* has gone to air continuously on the ABC since 1961 and has established itself not only as an institution of Australian television but more widely of Australian political life. The program has frequently initiated public debate on impor-

Liz Jackson, host of *Four Corners*.
Courtesy of Australian Broadcasting Corporation

tant issues as well as precipitated governmental or judicial inquiries and processes of political reform.

Four Corners was originally conceived as a program with a magazine format offering an informed commentary on the week's events. It filled a space on Australian television roughly comparable to the British Broadcasting Commission's *Panorama* (from which it often borrowed material in the 1960s) or the early current affairs programming developed by Edward R. Murrow for the Columbia Broadcasting System (CBS) in the United States. It was also notable for providing the first truly national orientation on news and current affairs in Australia, either on television or in print.

Stylistically, *Four Corners* has been an innovator in documentary strategies for Australian television and film. The program frequently presents itself as frankly personalized and argumentative. The narrator has generally appeared on-screen, a significant break with the off-screen "voice-of-God" narration that was the dominant convention in 1950s documentary. The involve-

ment of the narrators-reporters with their subject, usually on locations, gives the program an immediacy and realism, while also opening up subjective points of view. As Albert Moran argues in "Constructing a Nation: Institutional Documentary since 1945," these developments paralleled the emergence in the 1960s of direct cinema and cinema verité, as well as an increasing cultural pluralism reflected in documentary subject matter.

Since the mid-1970s the program has developed the format of a 45-minute topical documentary introduced by a studio host, occasionally varied with studio debate. The most frequently cited examples are investigative reports that have had a direct impact on political institutions, such as a 1983 program, "The Big League," which disclosed interference in court hearings of charges laid against prominent figures in the New South Wales Rugby League, or the 1988 program "The Moonlight State," which revealed corruption at high levels in the Queensland police force. However, the program has also been important for its "slice of life" portrayals of the everyday worlds of social relations, work, health, and leisure, which have increased awareness of social and cultural diversity. *Four Corners* was very early to represent Australia as a multicultural society, with a report, for example, in 1961 on the German-speaking community in South Australia.

Four Corners made an early reputation for testing the boundaries of expectations of television as a medium, as well as the limits of political acceptability. At a time when television current affairs genres were still unfamiliar, this sometimes involved little more than taking the camera outside the controlled space of the studio or the inclusion of unscripted material. A 1963 program on the Returned Servicemen's League (RSL), for example, stirred controversy for showing members of the organization in casual dress drinking at a bar, rather than exclusively in the context of formally structured studio debate. However, controversy extended also to the kinds of political questions that were raised. The story on the RSL directly challenged the organization on its claim to political neutrality. Another story from the same period drew attention to the appalling living conditions and political disenfranchisement of aboriginal people living on a reserve near Casino in rural New South Wales, an issue that had almost no public exposure at the time.

Four Corners has consistently been accused of political bias, particularly of a left-wing orientation, and critics charge it with failing to abide by the ABC's charter, which requires "balance" in the coverage of news and current affairs. The program is generally defended by its makers, ABC management, and supporters on the grounds that the importance of open public debate outweighs the damage that might be caused to interested parties and that, while the program may be argumentative, it is not unfair.

The program is also a frequent point of reference in debates over government-funded broadcasting. *Four Corners* has never achieved high ratings by the standards of the commercial networks and is often contrasted in content and style to commercial rivals such as the Nine Network's *Sixty Minutes,* which is able to claim much wider popular appeal. Despite increasing pressure on the ABC to become more commercially oriented, however, the program has continued to articulate values that are distinct from considerations of popularity—the importance of representing the positions and points of view of minorities, the necessity of forcing public institutions to accountability, and a place for television current affairs that performs an educative role. In doing so, *Four Corners* is often taken as representative of the position and identity of publicly funded broadcasting as a whole.

MARK GIBSON

Presenters
Michael Charlton (1961–63)
Gerald Lyons (1963)
Frank Bennett (1964)
John Penlington (1964)
Robert Moore (1964–67)
John Temple (1968)
Michael Willessee (1969–71)
Brian King (1971)
David Flatman (1972)
Peter Ross (1972)
Caroline Jones (1972–81)
Andrew Olle (1985–94)
Liz Jackson (1995)

Reporters
Keith Smith
Bob Sanders (1963)
Robert Moore (1964–67)
Bill Peach (1966)
Peter Reid (1967–73)
Richard Oxenburgh (1964–)
John Penlington (1963–71)
Jim Downes (1967–83)
Peter Couchman
Brian King (1969–72)
John Temple (1970–83)
David Flatman (1971–)
Richard Carleton (1972)

Stuart Littlemore (1972)
Alan Hogan (1972–78)
Peter Ross (1973–83)
Pat Burgess (1974)
Gordon Bick (1971–)
Ken Burslem (1973–76)
Jeff Watson (1974—80)
Ray Martin (1974–78)
Brian Davies (1975–)
Maryanne Smith (1975–81)
Kerry O'Brien (1975–77)
Peter Luck (1975–76)
Paul Lyneham (1976–81)
Andrew Olle (1977–78)
Bob Pride (1977–)
Jeff McMullen (1977–83)
Charles Wooley (1979–)
Bob Hill (1978–81)
Mark Colvin (1979)
Noel Norton (1980–81)
Peter Wilkinson (1980–81)
Geoff Herriot (1980)
Chris Sweeney (1980–84)
Pamela Paddon (1981)
Richard Palfreyman (1981)
Jack Pizzey (1982–83)
Mary Delahunty (1983)
Chris Masters (1983–)
Jenny Brockie (1983–86)
David de Vos (1984–84)
Allan Hogan (1984)
Tony Jones (1984–91)
Kerry O'Brien (1985–86)
Sarah Wall (1985–86)
David Marr (1985)
Clare Petre (1985–87)
John Beeston (1985)
Marian Wilkinson (1987–89)
Paul Barry (1987–89)
Peter Couchman (1987–89)
Pamela Bornhorst (1987–88)
Mark Colvin (1987–91)
Neil Mercer (1988–92)
John Millard (1989)
Deborah Snow (1989–90)
John Budd (1990)
Walter Hamilton (1990)
Jenny Brockie (1990)
David Marr (1991)
Paul Barry (1991, 1993–94)
Ross Coulthart (1991–)
Jonathan Holmes (1991, 1994)
Deb Whitmont (1992, 1998–)
Frank McGuire (1992)

Mark Westfield (1992)
Deb Richards (1993)
Marian Wilkinson (1993)
Liz Jackson (1994–)
Murray Hogarth (1994–)
Sally Neighbour (1995–)
David Hardaker (1995–98)
Murray McLaughlin (1995–98)
Andrew Fowler (1995–)
Mick O'Donnell (1995)
Margo O'Neill (1996–98)
Mark Davis (1998–99)
Geoff Parish (1998–99)
Peter George (1998–99)
Tony Jones (1998)
Quentin McDermott (1999–)
Stephen McDonnell (2000–)
Jill Colgan (2000)
Ticky Fullerton (2001)

Executive Producers
Bob Raymond (1961–63); Allan Ashbolt (1963–64); Ivan Chapman (1964); Gerald Lyons (1963); John Power (1964); Robert Moore (1965–67); Sam Lipski (1968); Allan Martin (1968–72); Tony Ferguson (1973); Peter Reid (1973–80); Brian Davies

(1980–81); Paul Lyneham (1980–81); John Penlington (1980–81); John Temple (1980–81); Jonathan Holmes (1982–85); Peter Manning (1985–88); Ian Macintosh (1989–90); Marian Wilkinson (1991–92); Ian Carroll (1992–95); Harry Bardwell (1995); Paul Williams (1995); John Budd (1995–99); Bruce Belsham (1999–)

Programming History
Australian Broadcasting Corporation
August 1961–November 1981   Saturday 8:30–9:20
March 1982–December 1984   Saturday 7:30–8:20
March 1985–June 1985   Tuesday 8:30–9:20
July 1985–   Monday 8:30–9:20

Further Reading

King, Noel, "Current Affairs TV," *Australian Journal of Screen Theory* (1983)
McKee, Alan, "*Four Corners:* Convincing Bias," in his *Australian Television: A Genealogy of Great Moments,* Melbourne: Oxford University Press, 2001
Moran, Albert, "Constructing the Nation: Institutional Documentary since 1945," in *The Australian Screen,* edited by Moran and Tom O'Regan, Melbourne: Penguin, 1989
Pullan, Robert, *Four Corners: Twenty-Five Years,* Sydney: Australian Broadcasting Corporation, 1986

FOX Broadcasting Company

U.S. Network

The FOX television network was established amid shock, controversy, legal wrangling, and uncertainty in 1985. The historic significance of this event may be judged by six interrelated factors: the daring prime mover, Rupert Murdoch; the economic environment at the time; the complacency of the major television networks; disenchanted affiliate stations; the Federal Communications Commission (FCC); and the volatile nature of television programming.

In 1984 Murdoch purchased half ownership of the Twentieth Century Fox film corporation. The following year he acquired the remaining half of the corporation. These two purchases, totaling $575 million gave him control over an extensive film library and rights to numerous television series (e.g., *L.A. Law* and *M*A*S*H).*

With this enormous programming potential in hand, he was in a good position to form a television network, the FOX Broadcasting Company. In October 1985 Murdoch bought six independent, major market stations (WNEWTV, New York; KTTV-TV, Los Angeles; WFLD-TV, Chicago; WTTG-TV, Washington, DC; KNBN-TV, Dallas; KRIV-TV, Houston). Later he acquired WFXT-TV in Boston. These stations enabled him to reach about 20 percent of all television households in the United States. For the first time since the 1960s the major networks were to experience a kind of aggressive competition that would threaten their very existence.

The founding of the FOX Broadcasting Company must be placed within a context of the general economic uncertainty and decline of network television.

Courtesy of Fox Broadcasting Company

According to Sydney Head and Christopher Sterling, 1985 was the first year that network revenues fell slightly. By 1987 total revenues of ABC, CBS, and NBC had dropped to $6.8 billion. For the first time ever, CBS recorded a net loss for the first quarter. As a result, all three networks adopted austerity measures, cutting budgets, laying off personnel, and dumping affiliates.

To the big three networks, the competition of the FOX network could hardly have occurred at a worse time. FOX itself was not spared financial hardship. In 1988 the company lost $90 million and in 1989, $20 million. To hedge against increased profit erosion the three networks began to diversify their interests in cable television and shore up their owned and operated stations.

Economic uncertainty also affected network affiliate relationships. ABC, NBC, and CBS tended to dominate the powerful and lucrative VHF stations throughout the United States, with the less profitable UHF stations being in the hands of independents. With the advent of the FOX network, a number of the VHF stations, previously affiliated with the major networks, jumped ship, providing a lucrative advantage to Murdoch. Some claim that Murdoch's exclusive National Football League contract was an added incentive to switch their allegiance. In one agreement with station group owner New World, the FOX network gained 12 new stations, which ended their affiliation with "Big Three" networks. Such "fickle behavior" on the part of affiliates sent shock waves through the established networks, which had complacently relied upon their loyalty.

Opposition to Murdoch's aggressiveness did not go unchallenged. The FCC licensing regulations specified that only American citizens could own broadcasting stations. The FCC also regulated cross-ownership of media companies to avoid antitrust abuses. In an attempt to thwart Rupert Murdoch's growing influence, the FCC, spurred on by NBC and the NAACP, investigated his citizenship and the ownership structure of the FOX network. Murdoch became an American citizen in 1985, just prior to the founding of the FOX network. He also disclosed that FOX would assume virtually all economic risk for and reward of acquired stations. His disclosures were backed by sworn declarations of key FCC staffers and the independent legal counsel of Marvin Chirelstein of Columbia Law School. Nevertheless, some reports claimed the disclosures were deceptive. Murdoch's Australia-based News Corporation owned 24 percent of the FOX voting stock (just below the legal limit of 25 percent); the remaining 76 percent belonged to Barry Diller (Twentieth Century Fox) who was an American citizen. In fact, News Corporation indirectly owned 99 percent, a reality that the FCC either ignored or failed to see. Still, in keeping with deregulation trends, and despite temporary congressional freezes, the FCC found in favor of Murdoch. This decision was a great victory for Murdoch and a major disappointment to the networks.

The new FOX network strengthened its position with several strategies. By reducing the number of prime-time hours offered each week and by providing no morning shows or soap operas, FOX has given its affiliates much more freedom to schedule their own shows and commercial announcements. Rather than compete with the major networks using counterprogram strategies, FOX has tried to offer entertaining, low-cost shows to its affiliates. Some late-night programs fringe (such as the talk shows hosted by Joan Rivers and Chevy Chase) have fared poorly, but others such as *Married…with Children, 21 Jump Street, The Tracy Ullman Show, Beverly Hills 90210,* and *The Simpsons* have been successful. The probable reason for these successes is that they target younger viewers devoted to light entertainment. In addition to this trendsetting, somewhat controversial program strategy, Murdoch has spent lavishly to obtain the rights to National Football League football, a major coup.

FOX's vertically integrated structure (a combination of Twentieth Century Fox, FOX network, and FOX stations) is also well suited to produce and distribute a large number of quality shows. The substantial collection of films in the vaults of Twentieth Century Fox remains a rich resource, still to be developed.

Early in the new millennium, the FOX network appeared to be taking advantage of the vertical integration of its corporate structure and the convergence of its constituent media partners and affiliates through the Internet. News Corporation, the parent company of the FOX network, declared a profit of $370 million as of June 30, 2003. This is a great improvement over the previous year's loss of $1.74 for the same period (the loss was attributed to the write-off of an investment in Gemstar-TV Guide International Inc., whose founder was accused of securities fraud).

In comparison with the mainline networks, FOX remains a loosely connected and frugal network that is controversial and cutting-edge. At times it appears to revel in its challenging, unorthodox, and politically incorrect stance, which may be the reason for its continued popularity. In addition to the abrasive lineup of animated cartoon shows such as *The Simpsons, King of the Hill,* and *Futurama,* FOX was the home of the paranoid drama *The X-Files.* It currently hosts offbeat sitcoms such as *Malcolm in the Middle* and *Arrested Development.*

RICHARD WORRINGHAM

See also **Murdoch, Rupert**

Further Reading

Fanning, Dierdre, "A Different Brand of Entertainment," *Forbes* (November 30, 1987)

"FOX Gives Itself Three Years to Pass Big 3 Network," *Television Digest* (June 26, 1995)

Head, Sidney, and Christopher Sterling, *Broadcasting in America,* Boston: Houghton Mifflin, 1956; 7th edition, Princeton, New Jersey: Houghton Mifflin, 1990

Larson, Eric, "Will Murdoch Be Outfoxed?" *Time* (April 17, 1995)

Merrill, John, John Lee, and Edward Friedlander, *Modem Mass Media,* New York: Harper and Row, 1990

Robins, Max, "How Foreign Is Fox?" *Variety* (December 5, 1994)

Schmuckler, Eric, "NBC Challenges Fox Ownership," *Media Week* (December 5, 1994)

Smith, F. Leslie, *Perspectives on Radio and Television,* New York: Harper and Row, 1990

Vivian, John, *The Media of Mass Communication,* Boston: Allyn and Bacon, 1993

Wharton, Dennis, "Rupert Requests Relief," *Variety* (May 15, 1995)

Zoglin, Richard, "Room for One More? The Fox Network Makes Its Move into Prime Time," *Time* (April 6, 1987)

Zoglin, Richard, "Murdoch's Biggest Score," *Time* (June 6, 1994)

Zook, Kristal Brent, *Color by Fox: The Fox Network and the Revolution in Black Television,* New York: Oxford University Press, 1999

France

In no other country in Europe have the audiovisual media been a greater stake in political struggles than in France, despite the fact that television, in particular, was very late in getting started and slow to develop in that nation. This lag may be attributed to both French anxiety about image-based culture and uncertainty about new technology. Within the public-service tradition administered by a Jacobin state, television was tightly controlled and part of electoral spoils. Its informational and educational programs achieved a high standard before deregulation in the 1980s, while popular programming languished in the shadow of American imports and the low cultural esteem in which they were held on the "audiovisual landscape." Television, unlike the cinema, was never considered part of the national culture, and so French program makers contributed little to the international circulation of programs, nor did intellectuals make much contribution to media theory.

French television's origins were not propitious. A few experiments in the 1930s culminated in the first regular programming in 1939, transmitted from the Eiffel Tower to a limited number of sets in Paris only. The postwar government revoked the Vichy law conceding broadcasting to the private sector, and the resulting state monopoly would remain unchallenged for four decades. Heavy regulation and a centralized bureaucracy explain the slow development of a network compared with the United Kingdom or Germany. Studios were built in a suburb of Paris, and for many years the "Buttes-Chaumont" label connoted a heavily dramatic style, then scorned by the young *cinéphiles* in the sway of the *Nouvelle Vague.* Television was perceived as the refuge of classical academicism and the untalented; it was not until the 1980s that the pioneer *"réalisateurs de télévision"* began to receive their critical due. There were still only 3.5 million sets by 1963, but the figure was increasing dramatically each year of the "30 Glorieuses" in the Gaullist period, often stimulated by international broadcast events (the Eurovision Song Contest, World Cup football). The evening news at 8:00 became a national ritual, *"la grande messe."*

Under the Fifth Republic, television legislation mutated every four to five years on average, as governments pondered how best to govern what its intellectuals considered a monster in the living room, undermining literate culture and opening the way to commercial influences from abroad. But the government and the opposition distrusted TV, each believing it favored the other. Under the control of Ministers for Information, then for Culture, and occasionally for Communication itself, there was no accountability, little audience research, and scarcely any cultural legitimacy. Employees of state broadcasting had the status of civil servants, which made their right to free expression precarious. During the Algerian War, President Charles DeGaulle became the first head of state to use TV to justify his policy, but the government openly interfered with the news coverage of the conflict, and many journalists quit or were dismissed. Legislation in 1959 transformed Radio-Télévision de France into a body (ORTF) with industrial and commercial objectives, but rejected both private TV and any protection against the threat of censorship.

A new breed of professionals came to the medium in the mid-1960s, when French television experienced something of a golden age under the ethos that the medium could make culture accessible to the people. The television diet leaned toward turgid studio productions of classic plays and novels (the spicy history serial *Les Rois Maudits* is remembered as refreshing in this context) and pedagogic series of "initiation" (*Lectures pour Tous, Le Camera Explore le Temps*). In the way of entertainment, there were variety shows, often associated with the popular crooner Guy Lux, and slapstick games shows like the French-originated *Jeux sans Frontières,* but little middlebrow fare, except for the *Inspecteur Maigret* mysteries. A brief period of liberalization occurred after 1964 when a second channel (A2) was created, despite the fear of where competition might lead. (The new 615-line technical system was noncompatible with the rest of Europe, but was propagated to the Soviet bloc.) A third channel (FR3) was created in 1973 with a regional structure. An ORTF strike coincided with the events of May 1968, and 200 staff were fired. Less noticed that year was the first authorization of advertising, which would lead to a slow increase in the number of advertising minutes per hour, to the collection of ratings, and in turn to the breakup of ORTF.

In 1973 President Georges Pompidou was able to proclaim that television was the "voice of France" at home and abroad. It was the only country with three public-service channels, none of which was autonomous from the government or in competition with each other for viewers. It was considered axiomatic that removing the monopolistic structure would lead to mediocrity. Neither the political left nor right was committed to freedom of communication, each for its own reasons. By 1974 there were 14 million sets receiving 7,400 program hours a year produced by 12,000 staff at ORTF. That year, the decision was finally taken to break up the ORTF; its functions were divided among seven autonomous bodies, but the government still drew the line on private broadcasting and maintained its right to appoint broadcast executives. In fact, the production wing would still get 90 percent of program commissions; there was very little independent production; and executives were still chosen for their political docility. Experimentation was left to INA, the Institut National de l'Audiovisuel, which also managed the archives and professional training. (Jean-Christophe Averty is usually singled out as the first producer to forge a specifically televisual style, one relying heavily on chroma-key effects.) Programs remained much as before, and studio programs seemed even more boring and didactic. Imports from Britain (*The Forsyte Saga*) and the United States (*Roots, Holocaust*) merely raised the alarm among cultural elites about the public taste for serial fiction and about a marked decline in domestic quality programming. Television investment had become a major factor in film production.

President Giscard d'Estaing's government also launched France into telecommunications research and development in 1979, with a DBS satellite agreement with Germany, one of the first efforts to counter United States' and Japanese hegemony in this field. The D2MAC format, an intermediate step toward high definition, would prove an expensive mistake ten years later, another unfortunate consequence of the technocratic hold over the media.

Paradoxically, in the light of the Socialists' historical opposition to private ownership of the airwaves, it was under Socialist president François Mitterrand that deregulation finally occurred. In 1981 the Moinot Commission, charged with examining the state of affairs since the breakup of ORTF in 1974, found that decentralization and competition between the three channels were illusory and not promoting creative programming; serious programs were being pushed to the edges of the schedules, in favor of a high quotient of popular imports, a trend for which *Dallas* became the inflammatory example. A 1982 law abolished the state monopoly and "freed" communications: the prime channel, TF1, was sold outright; and licenses for two more were granted, including the pay channel Canal Plus, which quickly became a major player in the audiovisual industries, spinning off its own feature film production company. Meanwhile, a belated attempt to cable the major cities got under way. Political controversy dogged the attribution of these private channels (Italian media mogul Silvio Berlusconi won one franchise) as well as the appointment of directors of the increasingly beleaguered state channels. The composition and powers of a relatively feeble regulatory agency changed with almost every government. The private TF1 quickly became the channel of reference, with almost half the general audience, while the revenues and audience share of France 2 and France 3 (as the state channels were renamed in 1994) gradually shrank.

At the international level, France had become the leading exponent of protectionist quotas for film and television, as well as of the view that the audiovisual market could be a way of creating—or defending—a common European cultural identity. France eschewed both cost-sharing initiatives with foreign partners and involvement in experiments in pan-European television, although it was increasingly worried about satellite penetration. Instead it chose the path of "Francophony," with the TV5 satellite channel in partnership with French-speaking countries, and conducted a lobbying effort within the European parliament to endorse a European channel.

Surrounded by bitterness among socialist supporters that the government had surrendered the media to private interests, Culture Minister Jack Lang exploited both a lingering anti-Americanism and a revived Europeanism in order to launch a new public-service channel with the habitual mission of exploiting new technologies and a cultural remit. *La Sept,* initially a wholly French channel lodged on the frequency of a bankrupt private channel, became ARTE when Germany became an equal partner in 1991.

The French view that cultural and political identity are necessarily linked predominated in European audiovisual policy; the debates on "world image battles" led to the European Community White Paper *Television without Frontiers,* which tackled the problem of English-language domination of the world image market by enjoining its member states to ensure, by all necessary means, that at least half the content of their television channels was of European origin. France's own quota was higher—60 percent—but the irony is that whatever its status as proponent of the European public cultural space, its domestic broadcasting policy has run in the direction of deregulation, to such an extent that the national regulatory body (Conseil Supérieur Audiovisuel) has been unable to enforce these quotas or to inhibit French investors from putting up money for English language films, ranging from *The Piano* to *Under Seige.* In fact, certain aspects of American production—like the use of multiple scriptwriters—have gradually been adopted in France. Nevertheless, the various governments under President François Mitterrand, even the conservative ones, consistently proclaimed the importance of national and high cultural goals. France continued to argue for protectionism, as in the GATT discussions in 1993, when a lobby of intellectuals helped to secure the exclusion of film and TV from the treaty.

The state of French television in the mid-1990s was a mixed but unbalanced system, with the private TF1 and Canal Plus becoming major players in the international media market. The audiences for FR2 and FR3 shrunk slightly each year, as the *redevance* (license fee) did not keep pace with rising program costs and was widely flouted by viewers turning to the growing cable sector. The Franco-German cultural channel ARTE shared a wavelength with a daytime educational channel, which seemed to perpetuate the same intellectual values that have always characterized French TV: didactic and avant-garde offerings, especially "authored" documentaries and "personal" films, made by the elites for the masses.

The following channels are currently operative in France: TF1, France 2, France 3, La 5éme, M6, Arte, Canal1, and Canal Satellite. They offer a variety of programming, including news, sports coverage, music programs, family programs, and films.

SUSAN EMMANUEL

Further Reading

Crane, Rhonda J., *The Politics of International Standards: France and the Color TV War,* Norwood, New Jersey: Ablex, 1979

Emanuel, Susan, "Culture in Space: The European Cultural Channel," *Media, Culture and Society* (April 1992)

Mattelart, Armand, and Michèle Mattelart, *Re-Thinking Media Theory,* Minneapolis: University of Minnesota Press, 1991

Miege, Bernard, "France: A Mixed System. Renovation of an Old Concept," *Media, Culture and Society* (January 1989)

Rigby, Brian, *Popular Culture in Modern France: A Study of Cultural Discourse,* London: Routledge, 1991

Scriven, Michael, and Monia Lecomte, *Television Broadcasting in Contemporary France and Britain,* Oxford and New York: Berghahn Books, 1999

Francis, Arlene (1908–2001)

U.S. Talk Show Host, Performer

Arlene Francis played a key role in television's first decades as performer, talk show host, and guest star, appearing on many shows and proving herself to be one of the medium's most durable personalities. At the height of her popularity in the mid-1950s, she was rated the third-most-recognized woman in the United States.

Francis had a diverse and successful career on television, preceded by a versatile career as "femcee," actress, and radio performer. Her film career began in 1932 with *Murders on the Rue Morgue.* In the collection of the Museum of the Television and Radio in New York, one can listen to her work as an actress on radio as early as 1936 on the Columbia Radio Workshop. During World War II she was the "femcee" of a radio show called *Blind Date,* a forerunner of *The Dating Game.* She was the first female game show host on ABC. During this time she also worked regularly as a featured actress on the Broadway stage, before coming to television in the early 1950s. She appeared in a simulcast version of *Blind Date* from 1949 to 1952, and also on such shows as *By Popular Demand* and *Prize Performance,* but it was as a regular panelist on the popular quiz show *What's My Line?* that Francis became a household name on television. Known for her elegance and good humor, Francis would trade repartee each week with such figures as columnist Dorothy Kilgallen, publisher Bennet Cerf, and poet Louis Untermeyer.

Although *What's My Line?* was her bread-and-butter show over the next 25 years, versatility continued to mark Francis's career. In September 1950, shortly after she joined the panel of that word-and-wit show, she became the first "mistress" of ceremonies for NBC's *Saturday Night Revue: Your Show of Shows,* and she appeared frequently on other television shows in the 1950s, 1960s, and 1970s.

Francis also made a major contribution to the history of television talk as host and managing editor of NBC's *Home* show. *Home* was the afternoon show teamed with *Today* and *Tonight* in NBC president Sylvester "Pat" Weaver's trilogy of daily talk on NBC in the 1950s, each show anchored by a "communicator." Network executives knew that women represented a major part of the daytime audience and were

key decision makers on consumer purchases. *Home* was NBC's attempt to capture that audience. To quote from the 1954 film *On the Waterfront,* Francis "coulda been a contender" as a titan of television talk had she continued on *Home.* She was certainly one of the foremost talk show hosts on television in the 1950s, and if her show had continued into the 1960s, her national status as a major talk show host would have been assured. But *Home,* despite great popularity among its audience, was canceled after three and a half years when Weaver was forced out of NBC by network founder David Sarnoff. Ultimately, Francis's career as a national talk show host was a casualty of forces that were moving network television away from strong women hosts, serious topics, sustaining shows, and public service, and toward immediate bottom-line profits—the same forces that drove Edward R. Murrow from the air at CBS.

As host of *Home,* Francis established patterns of daytime talk that are still with us today. This daytime talk "magazine" of the air was designed to provide intelligent conversation and up-to-date information for a largely female audience, although men were in the audience as well. Indeed, from 1954 to 1957, Francis was, along with Arthur Godfrey, Murrow, Dave Garroway, and Jack Paar, one of the founders of television talk. It was not until Phil Donahue rose to national syndication prominence two decades later that another national talk show host would make a similar appeal to women audiences. With more support from NBC management, or if Weaver had been able to continue as president, the *Home* show might have continued to build an audience and sustained itself as *Today* and *Tonight* did. As it is, the story of Francis's role on *Home* reveals the limitations placed on women talk show hosts in the male-dominated world of 1950s television.

The tensions placed on Francis's life as the managing editor and "boss" of her show were reflected in a 1957 *Mike Wallace Interview* on ABC. Wallace began his interview with Francis by saying that a lot was being said and written about "career women" in the United States. "What," he asked her, "is it that happens to so many career women that makes them so brittle? That makes them almost a kind of third sex?" Francis replied:

Arlene Francis.
Courtesy of Peter Gabel

Well, what happens to some of [the women] who have these qualities you've just spoken of, is that I suppose they feel a very competitive thing with men and they take on a masculine viewpoint and forget primarily that they are women.... Instead they become aggressive and opinionated. While men do it, it is part of the makeup of a man, and a man has always done it all his life. I do not think it is a woman's position to dominate.

Yet when NBC came to Francis toward the end of Dave Garroway's long reign to ask her to cohost *Today* with Hugh Downs, but not host her own show, she refused. Unresolved issues of power, issues that Barbara Walters was to struggle with and resolve in the 1960s and 1970s, limited Francis's options in the mid-1950s. By the end of her life, Francis was considerably more reflective about her dilemma. In her autobiography, she wrote that she had come to realize "how deeply my inability to express myself without becoming apprehensive about what 'they' might think had affected me. In short, my 'don't make waves' philosophy had inhibited my life to an incalculable extent.... I had forgotten that a few waves are necessary to keep the water from becoming stagnant."

In the later 1960s and 1970s, it was Francis's friend Walters, the person who did take the cohost position

with Downs on the *Today* show, who became the preeminent national woman host of public affairs and news talk on television.

When Arlene Francis died on May 31, 2001, the tributes and accolades from family, friends, colleagues, and fans poured in. One of the most useful and fitting memorials was a beautifully designed website (www.arlenefrancis.com) containing biographical highlights, tributes, a timeline with photographic illustrations of her remarkable and prolific career, and much other valuable information.

BERNARD M. TIMBERG

See also **Talk Shows; Weaver, Sylvester "Pat"**

Arlene Francis. Born Arline Francis Kazanjian in Boston, Massachusetts, October 20, 1908. Attended Finch Finishing School and Theatre Guild School, New York City. Married: 1) Neil Agnew, 1935 (divorced, 1945); 2) Martin Gabel, 1946; one child: Peter. Actress in film and radio from 1932; debuted on stage, 1936; took time off in World War II to sell war bonds; hosted and starred in television shows from 1949; regular panelist on *What's My Line?*, 1950–67; host and editor-in-chief, NBC-TV's daytime talk show *Home*, 1954–57. Died in San Francisco, California, May 31, 2001.

Television Series (selected)

1949–55	*Soldier Parade*
1949–53	*Blind Date*
1950	*By Popular Demand*
1950	*Prize Performance*
1950	*Saturday Night Revue (Your Show of Shows)*
1950–67	*What's My Line?*
1953–55	*Talent Patrol*
1953	*The Comeback Story*
1954–57	*Home*
1957–58	*The Arlene Francis Show*

Made-for-Television Movie

1972	*Harvey*

Films

Murders in the Rue Morgue, 1932; *Stage Door Canteen,* 1943; *All My Sons,* 1948; *One Two Three,* 1961; *The Thrill of It All,* 1963; *Fedora,* 1979.

Radio (selected)

45 Minutes From Hollywood; March of Time; The Hour of Charm; Cavalcade of America; Portia Blake; Amanda of Honeymoon Hill; Mr. District At-

torney; Betty and Bob; Central City; What's My Name?; Helpmate; Blind Date; It Happens Every Day; The Affairs of Ann Scotland; The Arlene Francis Show; Emphasis; Monitor; Luncheon at Sardi's; Fun for All.

Stage

One Good Year; The Women; Horse Eats Hat; Danton's Death; All That Glitters; Journey to

Jerusalem; Doughgirls; The Overtons; The French Touch; Once More With Feeling; Tchin-Tchin; Beekman Place; Mrs. Daily; Late Love; Dinner at Eight; Kind Sir; Lion in Winter; Pal Joey; Who Killed Santa Claus?; Gigi; Social Security.

Publication

Arlene Francis: A Memoir, with Florence Rome, 1978

Frank N. Magid Associates

Although little known by the public at large, Frank N. Magid Associates is one of the most successful and influential television and entertainment consulting companies in existence. Founded in 1957 by a young social psychologist, the company has grown to more than 350 employees and serves clients around the world. The first broadcasting client was television station WMT (now KGAN) in Cedar Rapids, Iowa. The company is still headquartered in neighboring Marion, Iowa, but has 37 worldwide locations, including full-services offices in New York, Los Angeles, and London.

Magid Associates emphasizes custom research on audience and client attitudes and behavior, and this specifically tailored work is designed to answer questions about business strategy. For local television, the company operates in considerably more than the top-100 markets in the United States. In each market, it provides consulting to one television station. It also provides various services for each of the U.S. networks and many studios and syndicators. Magid's services have been extended to clients elsewhere in the entertainment industries, such as record companies and movie producers, and the company contracts with any other businesses desiring marketing or survey research. It is increasingly employed by international clients in television and other media.

A significant part of Magid operations, indeed the work for which they are best known, is consulting with the news departments of local television stations. The company became the leading news consultant of the 1970s, amid growing controversy over its influence. Magid is often credited—or blamed—for design of the "Action News" format, and the sameness of local news broadcasts from station to station and city to city is

seen as a result of their advice and that of similar news consulting firms. This sameness is produced by the repetition of news presentation techniques. The formulas include the use of coanchors, a reliance on short news stories with time for chatting and expressing emotional reactions between items, an emphasis on graphics and live shots irrespective of their contribution to the news story, special attention to the looks and clothes of the news presenters, and the use of lighter stories and positive news in a mix with sensational crime and accident stories.

On the other hand, Magid does consistently emphasize the importance of local news. It claims that its client stations win more journalism awards than their competitors, and it promotes the generalization that stations that lead their markets in news usually also lead in overall ratings. This perspective provides a rationale for localism in a business—network TV—that often ignores local issues. Certainly, the news presentation styles that Magid Associates promote have attracted an audience and been successful for television as a business. From the financial perspective, it is important that local news broadcasts include as many or more minutes of local advertising time as any other programming activity. The news programs are a major source of direct income, making the profitability of the local news one of the most important factors in the business success of a television station.

A typical news consulting operation involves a meeting of a team of consultants, researchers, and the management of a television station to identify the concerns of the local managers. The consultants' primary research method is the telephone survey, sometimes interviewing people who have agreed ahead of time to watch the newscast in question and compare it with the newscast they regularly watch. The consultants may also mail videotapes to selected interviewees or use focus groups for trial broadcasts. The newscast in question is subjected to expert critique and compared with the competitors' newscasts, national trends, and leading newscasts in other markets. Finally, the consultants offer advice on anything from personnel hiring and firing, through story selection and news scriptwriting, to set design, graphics, promotions, lighting, camera angles, on-camera demeanor, clothes, makeup, and hairstyles.

Using similar research techniques, which emphasize data gathered from audience members asked to make evaluative comparisons, Magid Associates consult on any aspect of television station operations of concern to the client, on program evaluations, or on marketing research. The basic rationale of Magid's consulting is that television stations and other entertainment businesses will be more successful if they attract and hold a sizable audience; that the best way to do this is to give the audience what it finds attractive; and finally, that since audience members are not often articulate about what they want, researchers and expert consultants are needed to identify what the audience will find attractive.

ERIC ROTHENBUHLER

See also **Market; News, Local and Regional**

Further Reading

Goldman, Kevin, "Consultant Hired to Tinker with NBC-TV: *Today* and News under Scrutiny," *Variety* (December 21, 1983)

"Magid Firm Jumps from ABC to NBC," *Broadcasting* (January 2, 1984)

Stein, M.L., "Making Research Relevant: Panelists Debate Role of Market Information, Methods of Gathering and Analyzing Data," *Editor and Publisher* (June 30, 1990)

Frank, Reuven (1920–)

U.S. Broadcast Journalist, Producer, Executive

In a career that parallels the rise and ebb of network television journalism, Reuven Frank helped shape the character of NBC News through his work as a writer and producer, a documentary and newsmagazine pioneer, a news division president, and especially through his innovative coverage of national party conventions. In 1956 Reuven Frank teamed Chet Huntley with David Brinkley to coanchor the political conventions, a move that catapulted the two correspondents and NBC News to national fame.

Beginning with his first job at NBC in 1950, Reuven Frank realized he had an affinity for the process of film editing and an appreciation for the visual power of television, which became the signature of his career in TV news. The process of shaping film clips into coherent stories left an indelible impression on Frank. Competitor CBS News had built its strong reputation in radio, which emphasized words. *Camel News Caravan,* NBC's original 15-minute evening news program, on which Frank served as a writer, evolved from the newsreel tradition. An early partisan of television, Reuven Frank sought to exploit the medium's advantage over newspapers and radio to enable the audience to see things happen. "Pictures *are* the point of television reporting," he wrote.

This visual sense is clearly evident in the coverage of political conventions. Frank developed a method for orienting a team of four floor reporters—all but lost in a sea of convention delegates—toward live cameras. He established a communication center that simultaneously controlled news gathering, reporting, and distribution. The filter center, linked to the entire crew, advised the decision level when a report was ready for air. On cue from the decision level, the technical team would air the report. This tiered system of communication control became the industry standard.

The Huntley-Brinkley Report premiered in October 1956, with Reuven Frank as producer, and lasted until Huntley's retirement in 1970, when the report was renamed *The NBC Nightly News.* Frank was the program's executive producer in 1963 when the report was expanded from 15 to 30 minutes. In a memo to his staff, Frank outlined NBC News policies for gathering, packaging, and presenting news reports. The guiding principle for developing NBC newscasts was based on Frank's belief that "the highest power of television journalism is not in the transmission of information but in the transmission of experience."

The early years of television provided Frank with opportunities to develop his ideas and to experiment with half-hour weekly series. In 1954 he introduced *Background,* which featured "history in the making" through specially shot films, expert commentary, and the newly designed process of electronic film editing. The documentary-style series went through several iterations, including *Outlook, Chet Huntley Reporting, Time Present…Chet Huntley Reporting,* and *Frank McGee Reports.*

A fierce advocate of free speech, Reuven Frank staunchly defended television's right and obligation to deliver unsettling news. He supported rival CBS in controversies over the documentaries *Harvest of Shame* (1960) and *The Selling of the Pentagon* (1971). He championed network coverage of the civil rights movement, the Vietnam War, and the riot at the 1968 Democratic National Convention in Chicago. Frank also produced the acclaimed NBC documentary *The Tunnel,* which depicts the escape of 59 East Germans beneath the newly constructed Berlin Wall in 1962. NBC aired the program over objections by the U.S. State Department, which delayed the broadcast because it came on the heels of the Cuban missile crisis. *The Tunnel* is the only documentary ever to win an Emmy Award as Program of the Year.

The Tunnel, as well as other programs, exemplified one of Reuven Frank's lasting contributions to the content of NBC News reports, his attention to narrative structure and visual images. In the 1963 operations memo to his staff, Frank wrote,

> Every news story should, without sacrifice of probity or responsibility, display the attributes of fiction, of drama. It should have structure and conflict, problem and denouement, rising and falling action, a beginning, a middle, and an end. These are not only the essentials of drama; they are the essentials of narrative. We are in the business of narrative because we are in the business of communication.

Among Frank's other innovative series are *Weekend* and *NBC News Overnight. Weekend* was a 90-minute late-night, youth-oriented newsmagazine introduced in 1974, which alternated with rock concerts and *Saturday Night Live. Weekend* evolved from *First Tuesday* (later called *Chronolog*), NBC's answer to *60 Minutes.* Later, in response to competition from the innovative all-news-network CNN's late-night news feeds, Frank developed *Overnight,* a program hosted by Lloyd Dobyns and Linda Ellerbee and produced on a shoestring budget in a newsroom carved out of studio space. *Overnight* was a literate magazine show that af-

Reuven Frank.
Photo courtesy of Tom Mascaro

fected a wry, thoughtful, and highly visual presentation of the news.

The title of Reuven Frank's memoir, *Out of Thin Air: The Brief Wonderful Life of Network News,* reflects his sense and appreciation of fortuitous timing. Frank credits former NBC president Robert Kintner for elevating the status of NBC News:

> Those early years with Kintner emphasized news programs as never before, or since, on any network. There was money for reporters; there was money for documentaries; there was money for special programs. In his seven years as president, Kintner placed his stamp upon NBC as no one else in my four decades.

Reuven Frank left his mark on one of American television's premier news reporting services. After advancing through several roles and contributing to the development of a worldwide TV news network, Frank became president of NBC News in the tumultuous year of 1968. He held that position through the coverage of watershed events in the history of TV news, until 1973 when he returned to producing special projects for

NBC News. In 1982 Frank was asked again to head the News Division, which he did until 1984. Robert E. Mulholland, then president of NBC, said of Frank's contributions, "Reuven wrote the book on how television covers the political process in America, has trained more top broadcast journalists than anyone alive, and simply embodies the very best professional traditions of NBC News."

Frank produced documentaries for NBC News under a contract that expired in December 1986. At that time, network executives were cutting costs to maximize profits, and many loyal and experienced employees were let go, including Frank. He still comments on the television industry in radio features for *All Things Considered* on National Public Radio, *Marketplace* on Public Radio International, and as a columnist for *The New Leader,* a New York–based public-affairs magazine.

TOM MASCARO

Reuven Frank. Born in Montreal, Quebec, December 7, 1920. Educated at Harbord Collegiate Institute, Toronto; University College of the University of Toronto, 1937–40; City College of New York, B.S. in social science 1942; Graduate School of Journalism, Columbia University, M.S. 1947. Married: Bernice Kaplow, 1946; children: Peter Solomon and James Aaron. Served in the U.S. Army, 1943–46. Reporter, rewrite man, and night city editor, Newark *Evening News,* 1947–50; news writer, NBC News, 1950; news editor and chief writer, *Camel News Caravan,* 1951–54; supervised experiments in half-hour news forums such as *Background, Outlook,* and *Chet Huntley Reporting,* 1954 to early 1960s; executive vice president of NBC News, 1967–68, president, 1968–72, senior executive producer, and various other positions, 1972–82. Member: National Academy of Television Arts and Sciences; Writers Guild of America. Recipient: Sigma Delta Chi television news writing award, 1955; several Emmy Awards; Yale University Poynter Fellow, 1970.

Television Series (selected)

1954–55	*Background* (managing editor)
1956–70	*The Huntley-Brinkley Report* (producer)
1958–63	*Chet Huntley Reporting* (producer)
1956–58	*Outlook* (producer)
1960	*Time Present…Edwin Newman Reporting* (producer)
1974–79	*Weekend* (producer)
1982–83	*NBC News Overnight*

Television Specials (producer)

1953	*Meeting at the Summit*
1955	*The First Step into Space*
1956	*Antarctica: The Third World*
1958	*Kaleidoscope* ("The S-Bahn Stops at Freedom")
1958	*Kaleidoscope* ("The American Stranger")
1959	*Kaleidoscope* ("Our Man in the Mediterranean")
1959	*Kaleidoscope* ("The Big Ear")
1959	*Back to School*
1959	*Too Late for Reason*
1960	*World Wide '60* ("Freedom Is Sweet and Bitter")
1960	*World Wide '60* ("The Requiem for Mary Jo")
1960	*World Wide '60* ("Where Is Abel, Your Brother?")
1961	*Our Man in Hong Kong*
1961	*Berlin: Where the West Begins*
1961	*The Great Plane Robbery*
1962	*Our Man in Vienna*
1962	*The Land*
1962	*Clear and Present Danger*
1962	*The Tunnel*
1962	*After Two Years: A Conversation with the President*
1963	*The Trouble with Water…Is People*
1963	*A Country Called Europe*
1965	*The Big Ear*
1966	*Daughters of Orange*
1973	*If That's a Gnome, This Must Be Zurich*
1980	*If Japan Can…Why Can't We?*
1981	*America Works When America Works*
1985	*The Biggest Lump of Money in the World*
1986	*The Japan They Don't Talk About*
1987	*Nuclear Power: In France It Works*

Publications

Out of Thin Air: The Brief Wonderful Life of Network News, 1991

"Let's Put on a Convention," *Media Studies Journal* (Winter 1995)

Further Reading

Bluem, A. William, *Documentary in American Television,* New York: Hastings House, 1965

"Dialogue: Reuven Frank and Don Hewitt," *Television Quarterly* (November 1962)

Einstein, Daniel, *Special Edition: A Guide to Network Television Documentary Series and Special News Reports, 1955–1979,* Metuchen, New Jersey: Scarecrow Press, 1987

Matusow, Barbara, *The Evening Stars,* New York: Houghton Mifflin, 1983

Watson, Mary Ann, *The Expanding Vista: American Television in the Kennedy Years,* New York: Oxford University Press, 1990

Frankenheimer, John (1930–2002)

U.S. Director

John Frankenheimer is sometimes likened to a "wunderkind in the tradition of Orson Welles" because he directed numerous quality television dramas while still in his 20s. He was also one of a handful of directors who established their reputation in high-quality, high-budget television dramas and later moved on to motion pictures.

As with other television directors of the 1950s, Frankenheimer began his training in the theater, first with the Williams Theater Group at Williams College and then as a member of the stock company and director at Highfield Playhouse in Falmouth, Massachusetts. He later moved to Washington, D.C., where he acted in an American Theater Wing production. While in Washington, he both acted in and directed radio productions and began working at WTOP-TV.

After a stint with the U.S. Air Force, during which he directed two documentaries, Frankenheimer began his television career as an assistant director at CBS. He worked on weather and news shows, and moved on to *Lamp unto My Feet, The Garry Moore Show,* and Edward R. Murrow's *Person to Person.* As his career advanced, Frankenheimer directed dramatizations on *See It Now* and *You Are There* (working under director Sydney Lumet). He also directed episodes of the comedy series *Mama* (CBS, 1949–57, based on John Van Druten's play *I Remember Mama*), but it was his directorial efforts on television anthologies where Frankenheimer made his mark.

Frankenheimer began directing episodes of the suspense anthology series *Danger* in the early 1950s. Producer Martin Manulis hired Frankenheimer as a codirector on the critically acclaimed *Climax!* (CBS, 1954–58), an hour-long drama series that originally aired live. When Manulis moved on to CBS's *Playhouse 90* in 1954, he brought Frankenheimer with him. Over the next few years, Frankenheimer directed 140 live television dramas on such anthologies as *Studio One* (CBS), *Playhouse 90, The DuPont Show of the Month* (CBS), *Ford Startime* (NBC), *Sunday Showcase* (NBC), and *Kraft Television Theatre* (NBC). He directed such productions as *The Days of Wine and Roses* (October 2, 1958), *The Browning Version* (April 23, 1959; Sir John Gielgud's television debut), and *The Turn of the Screw* (October 20, 1959; Ingrid Bergman's television debut).

Frankenheimer's production of Ernest Hemingway's *For Whom the Bell Tolls* (*Playhouse 90*) was one of the first dramas to be presented in two parts (March 12 and 19, 1959) and, at $400,000, was the most expensive production at that time. Unlike most of his other productions, *For Whom the Bell Tolls* was taped for presentation because the actors were involved in other theatrical productions in New York. The production's intensive five-week rehearsal and ten-day shooting schedule had to be organized around the actors' other theatrical appearances.

Most directors of live television came from a similar theatrical background and, as such, used a static camera and blocked productions in a manner similar to a live stage play. A firm believer that a production is the sole creative statement of its director, Frankenheimer was one of the first directors of the "Golden Age" to utilize a variety of camera angles and movement, fast-paced editing, and close-ups to focus the audience's attention. However, some critics have labeled his technique as gimmicky or contrived. Frankenheimer's most famous use of the camera appears in his 1962 film *The Manchurian Candidate,* in which one shot is slightly out of focus. Ironically, the shot, which has been widely acclaimed as artistically brilliant, was, according to the director, an accident and merely the best take for actor Frank Sinatra.

Frankenheimer went on to make other memorable films, such as *The Birdman of Alcatraz* (which, in 1955, he had wanted to do as a live *Playhouse 90* production), *Seven Days in May, Grand Prix, The Fixer,* and *The Iceman Cometh.* Personal problems and a decline in the number of quality scripts offered him forced Frankenheimer to take a leave from the industry. Returning to television in the 1990s, Frankenheimer directed the original HBO production *Against the Wall* (March 26, 1994) about the 1971 Attica Prison riot. Always drawn to intimate stories and psychological portraits, in this production Frankenheimer explored the relationship between an officer taken hostage and the inmate leader of the uprising. More recently, he directed the miniseries *Andersonville* (March 3 and 4, 1996) and *George Wallace* (August 24 and 26, 1997) for TNT, and in May 2002 his final television project, *Path to War,* about the escalation of the Vietnam War during the Johnson administration, aired

John Frankenheimer.
Courtesy of the Everett Collection

on HBO in May 2002. Two months later, on July 6, Frankenheimer died of a stroke due to complications from spinal surgery.

Frankenheimer received nine Emmy nominations for his directorial work on television: *Portrait in Celluloid* (1955, *Climax!*, CBS), *Forbidden Area* (1956, *Playhouse 90*, CBS), *The Comedian* (1957, *Playhouse 90*), *A Town Has Turned to Dust* (1958, *Playhouse 90*), *The Turn of the Screw* (1959, *Ford Startime*, NBC), *Against the Wall*, *The Burning Season* (1994, HBO), *Andersonville*, and *George Wallace*.

SUSAN R. GIBBERMAN

John (Michael) Frankenheimer. Born in Malba, New York, February 19, 1930. Williams College, B.A. 1951. Married: 1) Carolyn Miller, 1954 (divorced, 1961); two daughters: Elise and Kristi; 2) Evans Evans, 1964. Served in Film Squadron, U.S. Air Force, 1951–53. Began career as actor, 1950–51; assistant director, later director, CBS-TV, New York, from 1953; director, *Playhouse 90* television series, Hollywood, 1954–59; directed first feature film, *The Young Stranger*, 1957; formed John Frankenheimer Productions, 1963. Recipient: Christopher Award, 1954; Grand Prize for Best Film Director, 1955; Critics Award, 1956–59; Brotherhood Award, 1959; Acapulco Film Festival Award, 1962. Died in Los Angeles, California, July 6, 2002.

Television Series (selected)

1948–58	*Studio One*
1950–55	*Danger*
1953–57	*You Are There*
1954–58	*Climax!*
1954–59	*Playhouse 90*

Television Miniseries

1996	*Andersonville*
1997	*George Wallace*

Made-for-Television Movies

1982	*The Rainmaker*
1994	*Against the Wall*
1994	*The Burning Season*
2002	*Path to War*

Films (selected)

The Young Stranger, 1957; *The Young Savages*, 1961; *The Manchurian Candidate* (also coproduced), 1962; *All Fall Down*, 1962; *Birdman of Alcatraz*, 1962; *Seven Days in May*, 1963; *The Train*, 1964; *Grand Prix*, 1966; *Seconds*, 1966; *The Extraordinary Seaman*; 1968; *The Fixer*, 1968; *The Gypsy Moths*, 1969; *I Walk the Line*, 1970; *The Horsemen*, 1970; *L'Impossible Objet (Impossible Object)*, 1973; *The Iceman Cometh*, 1973; *99 44/100 Dead*, 1974; *French Connection II*, 1975; *Black Sunday* (also bit role as TV controller), 1976; *Prophecy*, 1979; *The Challenge*, 1982; *The Holcroft Covenant*, 1985; *52 Pick Up*, 1986; *Across the River and into the Trees*, 1987; *Dead Bang*, 1989; *The Fourth War*, 1989; *The Island of Dr. Moreau*, 1996; *Ronin*, 1998; *Reindeer Games*, 2000; *Ambush* (short), 2001.

Publications

"Seven Ways with Seven Days in May," *Films and Filming* (June 1964)
"Criticism as Creation," *Saturday Review* (December 26, 1964)
"Filming *The Iceman Cometh*," *Action* (January/February 1974)

Further Reading

Applebaum, R., "Interview," *Films and Filming* (October–November, 1979)
Au Werter, Russell, "Interview," *Action* (May–June 1970)
"Backstage at *Playhouse 90*," *Time* (December 2, 1957)
Broeske, P., "Interview," *Films in Review* (February 1983)
Casty, Alan, "Realism and Beyond: The Films of John Frankenheimer," *Film Heritage* (Winter 1966–67)

Combs, Richard, "A Matter of Conviction," *Sight and Sound* (1979)

Cook, B., "The War between the Writers and the Directors: Part II: The Directors," *American Film* (June 1979)

Cook, B., "Directors of the Decade: John Frankenheimer," *Films and Filming* (February 1984)

"Dialogue on Film: John Frankenheimer," *American Film* (March 1989)

"A Director Trying to Reshoot His Career," *New York Times* (March 24, 1994)

Drew, B., "John Frankenheimer: His Fall and Rise," *American Film* (March 1977)

Filmer, Paul, "Three Frankenheimer Films: A Sociological Approach," *Screen* (July–August 1969)

Gross, L., and R. Avrech, "Interview," *Millimeter* (August 1971)

Higham, Charles, "Frankenheimer," *Sight and Sound* (Spring 1968)

Higham, Charles, and Joel Greenberg, *The Celluloid Muse: The Directors Speak,* London: Angus and Robertson, and Chicago: Regenery, 1969

"Interview," *Films and Filming* (February 1985)

Macklin, Tony, and Nick Pici, editors, *Voices from the Set: The Film Heritage Interviews,* Lanham, Maryland: Scarecrow Press, 2000

Madsen, Axel, "99 and 44/100 Dead," *Sight and Sound* (Winter 1973–74)

Mayersberg, Paul, "John Frankenheimer," *Movie* (December 1962)

Morgenstern, Joe, "A Hollywood Giant Who Cut His Teeth Working in TV," *Wall Street Journal* (July 10, 2002)

Pratley, Gerald, *The Cinema of John Frankenheimer: Forty Years in Film,* Bethlehem, Pennsylvania: Lehigh University Press, 1998

Scheinfeld, Michael, "The Manchurian Candidate," *Films in Review* (1988)

Thomas, John, "John Frankenheimer, the Smile on the Face of the Tiger," *Film Quarterly* (Winter 1965–66)

Weinraub, Bernard, "Back to Hollywood's Bottom Rung, and Climbing," *New York Times* (March 24, 1994)

Weinraub, Bernard, "John Frankenheimer Is Dead at 72; Resilient Director of Feature Films and TV Movies," *New York Times* (July 7, 2002)

Frank's Place

U.S. Dramedy

Frank's Place, an exceptionally innovative half-hour television program sometimes referred to as a "dramedy," aired on CBS during the 1987–88 television season. The program won extensive critical praise for its use of conventions of situation comedy to explore serious subject matter. As *Rolling Stone* writer Mark Christensen commented, "rarely has a prime-time show attempted to capture so accurately a particular American subculture—in this case that of blue-collar blacks in Louisiana."

In 1987 *Frank's Place* won the Television Critics Association's Award for Outstanding Comedy Series. One 1988 episode, "The Bridge," won Emmy Awards for Best Writing in a Comedy Series (with the award going to writer and coexecutive producer Hugh Wilson) and Outstanding Guest Performance in a Comedy Series (Beah Richards). Tim Reid, star and coexecutive producer, received a National Association for the Advancement of Colored People (NAACP) Image Award. In spite of its critical success, however, the show did not do well in the ratings and was not renewed by CBS.

Frank's Place was developed by Wilson and Reid from a suggestion by CBS executive Kim LeMasters.

Wilson, an alumnus of the heyday of MTM Productions, had previously produced *WKRP in Cincinnati,* a sitcom favorite in which Reid played supercool disc jockey Venus Flytrap. The premise for their new show centered on Frank Parrish (played by Reid), an African-American college professor from Boston who inherits a New Orleans restaurant from his estranged father. Wilson, who had directed for film as well as television, decided against using the standard situation comedy production style, that of videotaping with three cameras in front of a live audience. He opted instead for film-style production, using a single camera and no laugh track. Thus, from the beginning, *Frank's Place* looked and sounded different from other television fare. The broad physical humor and snappy one-liners that characterize most situation comedies were nowhere to be found. They were replaced with a more subtle, often poignant humor, as Frank encounters situations his formal education has not prepared him for. He is the innocent lost in a bewildering world, a rich and complex culture that appears both alien and increasingly attractive to him, and he is surrounded by a surrogate family, who wish him well but know he must ultimately learn from his mistakes.

Frank's Place, Don Yesso, Tim Reid, Tony Burton, 1987.
Courtesy of the Everett Collection

The ensemble cast included Hannah Griffin (played by Daphne Maxwell Reid), a mortician who becomes a romantic interest for Frank, and Bubba Weisberger (Robert Harper), a white Jewish lawyer from an old southern family. The restaurant staff included Miss Marie (Frances E. Williams), the matriarch of the group, Anna-May (Francesca P. Roberts), the head waitress, Big Arthur (Tony Burton), the accomplished chef who rules the kitchen, Shorty La Roux (Don Yesso), the white assistant chef, Tiger Shepin (Charles Lampkin), the fatherly bartender; and Cool Charles (William Thomas, Jr.), his helper. Reverend Deal (Lincoln Kilpatrick), a smooth-talking preacher in constant search of a church or a con-man's opportunity, was another regular.

Frank's journey into the world of southern, working-class African Americans begins when he visits Chez Louisiane, the Creole restaurant he has inherited and plans to sell. The elderly waitress Miss Marie puts a voodoo spell on him to ensure that he will continue to run the restaurant in his father's place. After Frank returns to Boston, his plumbing erupts, telephones fail him, the laundry loses all his clothes, his girlfriend leaves him, and his office burns. Convinced he has no choice, he returns to New Orleans, to the matter-of-fact welcome of the staff, the reappearance of his father's cat, and the continuing struggle to turn the restaurant into a profitable venture.

Storylines in many episodes provide comic and pointed comments on the values and attitudes of the dominant culture. In one story, college recruiters bombard young basketball star Calvin with virtually identical speeches about family and tradition and campus life. Calvin's naive expectations of becoming a professional athlete contrast with Frank's concern about academic opportunities. In another episode, the chairman of a major corporation stops in for a late-night dinner. Commenting on efforts to oust him, he eloquently condemns speculators who use junk bonds to buy companies about which they know nothing and with which they create no real value or service. The plot takes an ironic turn when this chairman realizes his partners may have made mistakes in plotting the takeover and he enthusiastically schemes to thwart them.

Class and race issues emerge in many storylines. On Frank's first night back in New Orleans, he wonders why there are so few people in the restaurant. Tiger explains with a simple observation: their clientele are working people who eat at home during the week, and white people are afraid to come into the neighborhood at night. In a later episode, Frank is flattered when he is invited to join a club of African-American professionals. Not until Anna-May pulls out a brown paper bag and contrasts it with Frank's darker skin does he understand that those who extended the invitation meant to use him to challenge the light-skin bias of the club members.

Throughout the series, tidy resolutions are missing. A group of musicians from East Africa, in the United States on a cultural tour, stop at Frank's Place. One of them, who longs to play the jazz that is forbidden at home, decides to defect. Frank refuses to help him, and he is rebuffed by jazz musicians. In the closing scene, however, as he sits listening in a club, the would-be jazz artist gets an inviting nod to join the musicians when they break. The final frame freezes on a close-up of his face as he rises, suspended forever between worlds. In another episode, a homeless man moves into a large box in the alley and annoys customers by singing and begging in front of the restaurant. Nothing persuades him to leave until one evening Frank tries unsuccessfully to get him to talk about who he is, where he is from, and the reasons for his choices.

When Frank steps outside the next morning, the man is gone. A final image, of Frank dusting off the hat left on the sidewalk, resonates with a recognition of kinship and loss. Visual sequences in many episodes suggest the loneliness of Frank's search for father, self, and his place in this community.

Various explanations have been offered for the decision to cancel *Frank's Place* after one season. In spite of a strong beginning, the show's ratings continued to drop. Viewers who expected the usual situation comedy formula were puzzled by the show's style. Frequent changes in scheduling made it difficult for viewers to find the show. CBS, struggling to improve its standing in the ratings, was not willing to give the show more time in a regular time slot to build an audience. The large ensemble and the film-style techniques made the show expensive to produce. In the end, it was undoubtedly a combination of reasons that brought the series to an end.

Frank's Place, however, deserves a continuing place in programming history. As Tim Reid told *New York Times* reporter Perry Garfinkel, it did present blacks not as stereotypes but as "a diverse group of hard-working people." Wilson attributed this accuracy to the racially mixed group of writers, directors, cast, and crew. Authenticity was heightened by the careful researching of details. Individual stories were allowed to determine the style of each episode. Some were comic, some serious, some poignant. All of them, however, were grounded in a compelling sense of place and a respect for those who inhabit Chez Louisiane and its corner of New Orleans.

LUCY A. LIGGETT

See also **Comedy, Workplace; Dramedy; Racism, Ethnicity and Television; Reid, Tim**

Cast

Frank Parish	Tim Reid
Sy "Bubba" Weisburger	Robert Harper
Hannah Griffin	Daphne Maxwell Reid
Anna-May	Francesca P. Roberts
Miss Marie	Frances E. Williams
Mrs. Bertha Griffin-Lamour	Virginia Capers
Big Arthur	Tony Burton
Tiger Shepin	Charles Lampkin
Reverend Deal	Lincoln Kilpatrick
Cool Charles	William Thomas, Jr.
Shorty La Roux	Dan Yesso

Producers

Hugh Wilson, Tim Reid, Max Tash

Programming History

CBS

September 1987–November 1987	Monday 8:00–8:30
December 1987–February 1988	Monday 8:30–9:00
February 1988–March 1988	Monday 9:30–10:00
March 1988	Tuesday 8:00–8:30
July 1988–October 1988	Saturday 8:30–9:00

Further Reading

Christensen, Mark, "Just Folks," *Rolling Stone* (March 10, 1988)

Collier, Aldore, "Hollywood's Hottest Couple," *Ebony* (January 1988)

Garfinkel, Perry, "*Frank's Place:* The Restaurant As Life's Stage," *New York Times* (February 17, 1988)

Gray, Herman, *Watching Race: Television and the Struggle for "Blackness,"* Minneapolis: University of Minnesota Press, 1995

Hill, Michael E., "*Frank's Place* Serving Rich Television with No Calories," *Washington Post TV Week* (December 16, 1987)

Newcomb, Horace, "The Sense of Place in *Frank's Place,"* in *Making Television: Authorship and the Production Process,* edited by Robert J. Thompson and Gary Burns, New York: Praeger, 1990

O'Connor, John J., "Two New Series in Previews," *New York Times* (September 15, 1987)

Reeves, Jimmie L., and Campbell, Richard, "Misplacing *Frank's Place:* Do You Know What It Means to Miss New Orleans?," *Television Quarterly* (1989)

Spotnitz, Frank, "Tim Reid," *American Film* (October 1990)

Thompson, Robert J., and Burns, Gary, "Authorship and the Production Process," *Millimeter* (March 1988)

White, Mimi, "What's the Difference? *Frank's Place* in Television," *Wide Angle* (July–October 1991)

Franz, Dennis. *See NYPD Blue*

Frasier

U.S. Situation Comedy

When *Frasier* debuted on September 16, 1993, as a *Cheers* spin-off, it faced tremendous odds against succeeding. One *Cheers* spin-off, *The Tortellis,* had already failed, as had other spin-off programs such as *After M*A*S*H.* As it turned out, *Frasier* fared more like another spinoff, *Lou Grant,* whose character of the same name had moved to a different town and career at the conclusion of *The Mary Tyler Moore Show.* Like *Cheers, Frasier* focuses tremendously on character humor.

Dr. Frasier Winslow Crane (Kelsey Grammer), erstwhile psychiatrist and graduate of Oxford and Harvard, was not an original *Cheers* character, but became a regular in the third season as Diane Chambers's (Shelley Long) psychiatrist and love interest. Chambers sought psychiatric assistance after one of many clashes with her lover, bar owner Sam Malone (Ted Danson). Chambers later left Frasier at the altar, but he continued frequenting the bar. He later married (1988), and subsequently divorced (1992), fellow psychiatrist Dr. Lilith Sternin (Bebe Neuwirth), nicknamed "Dr. Sigmund Frost" by *Cheers* regulars. Their son, Frederick, was born in November 1989. He lives in Boston with his mother and occasionally visits Frasier in Seattle. Unbeknownst to Lilith, Frasier was previously married to children's entertainer Nanny Gee.

On *Frasier,* the divorced Dr. Crane moved back to his hometown of Seattle, trading his bar stool and psychiatric practice for talk radio. As on *Cheers,* Frasier encountered a cast of characters who frequently attacked his pomposity. *Frasier* revolves around his social life, apartment, and job at KACL 780-AM. Instead of a bar, Frasier relaxes at Café Nervosa, a coffee shop where he meets his brother, coworkers, and friends.

Frasier's producers faced some dilemmas at the outset. Frasier variously told *Cheers* regulars he was an only child and his parents were research scientists and/or were dead. Yet, Dr. Hester Crane (Nancy Marchand), Frasier's mother, was featured in *Cheers* episode 52, which aired November 22, 1984, although she never again appeared on the show. In Seattle, we discover Frasier's mother was indeed dead, but he had a living father, Martin Crane (John Mahoney), and a younger brother, Dr. Niles Crane (David Hyde Pierce), also a psychiatrist. Martin, a down-to-earth retired cop, came to live with Frasier in his magnificent, trendy apartment with a panoramic view of Seattle's skyline. Martin enjoys drinking beer and watching sports at the neighborhood bar or on television, from his beloved recliner (which is held together with duct tape). He also enjoys walking Eddie (Moose), his Jack Russell terrier. Martin, whose hip was disabled when he was shot on the job, stands in direct contrast to his prissy sons, with their intellectual pretensions. Martin brought along England native Daphne Moon (Jane Leeves), his live-in, semipsychic physical therapist.

The character of snobby, competitive Niles was modeled on an idea of what Frasier would be like if he had not moved to Boston and hung out at Cheers. To prepare for his part, Pierce studied early *Cheers* episodes. As with Norm's wife on *Cheers,* Niles was married for several years to Maris, whom viewers hear about, but never see. Niles spent six years secretly in love with Daphne. After numerous twists involving other relationships, marriages, and engagements, including his quickie marriage to Dr. Melinda "Mel" Karnofsky (Jane Adams), Niles finally revealed his true feelings to Daphne at her foiled wedding to divorce lawyer Donny Douglas (Saul Rubinek). At the end of the ninth season, Niles and Daphne married.

At KACL-AM, Frasier's primary foils are his producer, Roz Doyle (Peri Gilpin), and characters that either manage the station, host their own program, or call the *Frasier Crane Show.* Roz is more than Frasier's coworker; she is a friend who has grown progressively closer to him over the years. She enjoys her relationships with men and does not shy away from talking about them. She had a baby by one of her younger lovers, which forced her to become more mature, responsible, and reliable. Early on, one of Frasier's coworkers and chief tormentors was Robert "Bulldog" Briscoe (Dan Butler), macho and aggressive host of KACL's *Gonzo Sports Show.* After the first few seasons, Bulldog lost his job and the character was phased out. Other KACL hosts include food critic Gil Chesterton, traffic reporter

Chopper Dave, green grocer Ray, and auto lady Bonnie Weems.

Callers to KACL's *Frasier Crane Show* are actually celebrities who are paid scale to call their lines into the studio from all over the world. It is fun for both the celebrities and viewers, who anxiously look for callers' names in the credits. Each *Frasier* episode begins with an animated view of Seattle's skyline featuring a small twist, such as lights, fireworks, an aircraft, or a rising moon. The show ends with a theme song, which features a different closing line each time.

Frasier is the first comedy series to win five consecutive Emmys for Outstanding Comedy Series, one more than four-time winners *The Dick Van Dyke Show, All in the Family,* and *Cheers. Frasier,* its actors, writers, and producers have won 21 Emmys overall, a Peabody Award, the Humanitas Prize, People's Choice Awards, Golden Globes, Screen Actors Guild (SAG) Awards, Television Critics Association Awards, and others. Grammer has been Emmy-nominated 12 times for his portrayal of Frasier Crane on *Cheers* and *Frasier.* David Hyde Pierce holds the record for the most SAG award nominations at 15, followed closely by Grammer's 14 nominations. Producer David Angell died in the September 11, 2001, terrorist attacks on the United States, but *Frasier* continued, as perhaps television's most intelligent situation comedy.

W.A. KELLY HUFF

See also **Cheers**

Cast

Dr. Frasier Crane	Kelsey Grammer
Dr. Niles Crane	David Hyde Pierce
Retired Police Officer Martin Crane	John Mahoney
Physical Therapist Daphne Moon	Jane Leeves
Rozalind "Roz" Doyle	Peri Gilpin
Robert "Bulldog" Briscoe	Dan Butler
Eddie	Moose the Dog
Frederick Crane (1996–)	Trevor Einhorn
Nanette Stewart	Karen Ann Genaro
Café Nervosa Waitress	Luck Hari
Bebe Glazer	Harriet Sansom Harris
Gil Chesterton (1994–)	Edward Hibbert
Noel Shempsky (1994–)	Patrick Kerr
Weird Bruce	Garett Maggart
Sherry Dempsey (1996–1997)	Marsha Mason
Station Manager Kenneth "Kenny" Daly (1997–)	Tom McGowan
Dr. Lilith Sternin-Crane (1994–)	Bebe Neuwirth
Donny Douglas (1998–)	Saul Rubinek
Station Manager Kate Costas (1995)	Mercedes Ruehl
Lorna Lenley/Lana Gardner (1999–)	Jean Smart
Simon Moon (2000–)	Anthony LaPaglia
Mrs. Gertrude Moon (2000–)	Millicent Martin
Dr. Melinda "Mel" Karnofsky (1999–2000)	Jane Adams

Producers

David Angell, Peter Casey, David Lee, Dan O'Shannon, Kelsey Grammer, Rob Hanning

Programming History

251 Episodes (2003)
NBC

September 1993–August 1994	Thursday 9:30–10:00
September 1994–May 1998	Tuesday 9:00–9:30
September 1998—May 2000	Thursday 9:00–9:30
September 2000—Present	Tuesday 9:00–9:30

Further Reading

Angell, David, Peter Casey, David Lee, and Christopher Lloyd, *The Frasier Scripts,* New York: Newmarket Press, 1999

Bailey, Bailey, and Warren Martyn, *Goodnight Seattle: The Unauthorized Guide to the World of "Frasier,"* London: Virgin Publishing, 1998

Bly, Robert W., *What's Your "Frasier" IQ: 501 Questions and Answers for Fans,* Sacramento, California: Citadel Press, 1996

Entertainment Weekly, The 100 Greatest TV Shows of All Time, New York: *Entertainment Weekly* Books, 1998

Graham, Jefferson, *Frasier,* New York: Pocket Books, 1996

Grammer, Kelsey, *So Far…,* New York: A Dutton Book, 1995

Javna, John, *The Best of TV Sitcoms,* New York: Harmony Books, 1988

McNeil, Alex, *Total Television: A Comprehensive Guide to Programming from 1948 to the Present,* 3rd edition, New York: Penguin Books, 1991

Sackett, Susan, *Prime-Time Hits: Television's Most Popular Network Programs 1950 to the Present,* New York: Billboard Books, 1993

Frederick, Pauline (1908–1990)

U.S. Broadcast Journalist

Pauline Frederick's pioneering broadcast career covered nearly 40 years and began at a time when broadcasting was virtually closed to women. During these decades, she was the primary correspondent covering the United Nations for NBC and was the first broadcast newswoman to receive the coveted Peabody Award for excellence in broadcasting.

Frederick began her career as a teenager, covering society news for the *Harrisburg Telegraph*. She turned down a full-time position there in favor of studying political science at American University in Washington, D.C. Later she received her master's degree in international law and, at the suggestion of a history professor, combined her interests in journalism and international affairs by interviewing diplomats' wives. She broke into broadcasting in 1939 when NBC's director of women's programs, Margaret Cuthbert, asked her to interview the wife of the Czechoslovakian minister shortly after Germany overran that country.

Her interviews continued until the United States joined World War II. She then worked a variety of jobs for NBC, including scriptwriting and research. After touring Africa and Asia with other journalists—over the protests of her male boss at NBC who thought the trip too difficult for a woman—she quit her job with NBC and began covering the Nuremberg trials for ABC radio, the North American Newspaper Alliance, and the Western Newspaper Alliance.

Denied a permanent job because she was female, she worked as a stringer for ABC, covering "women's stories." Her break came when she was assigned to cover a foreign ministers' conference in an emergency: her male boss had two stories to cover and only one male reporter. In a few months, the United Nations became her regular beat, and in 1948 ABC hired her permanently to cover international affairs and politics. In 1953 NBC hired her to cover the United Nations.

Over the next two decades, she covered political conventions, the Korean War, Middle Eastern conflicts, the Cuban missile crisis, the cold war, and the Vietnam War. After retiring from NBC, she worked for National Public Radio as a commentator on international affairs. Frederick received many honors, including election to the presidency of the United Nations Correspondents Association, being named to Sigma Delta Chi's Hall of Fame in 1975, and 23 honorary doctorate degrees in journalism, law, and the humanities.

Of her life, Frederick once said, "I think the kind of career I've had, something would have had to be sacrificed. Because when I have been busy at the United Nations during crises, it has meant working day and night. You can't very well take care of a home when you do something like that, or children." Through her work she advanced the position of women in broadcast news and became an important role model for newswomen everywhere.

LOUISE BENJAMIN

Pauline Frederick, 1954.
Courtesy of the Everett Collection

Pauline Frederick. Born in Gallitzin, Pennsylvania, February 13, 1908. Educated at American University in Washington, D.C., B.A. in political science, M.A. in international law. Married: Charles Robbin, 1969. Feature writer for newspapers and magazines, from late 1930s; radio interviewer, NBC, 1938–45; war correspondent, North American Newspaper Alliance, 1945–46, political reporter, ABC, 1946–53; reporter and interviewer, NBC, 1953–74; foreign affairs commentator, National Public Radio, 1974–90. Recipient: Peabody Award, 1954; Paul White Award from the Radio-Television News Directors Association, 1980; Alfred I. duPont Awards' Commentator Award. Died in Lake Forest, Illinois, May 9, 1990.

Television

1946–53	ABC News (reporter)
1953–74	NBC News (reporter)

Radio

NBC (reporter) 1938–45; National Public Radio (commentator), 1974–90.

Publication

Ten First Ladies of the World, 1967

Further Reading

Foremost Women in Communications, New York: Foremost Americans Publications Corporation, 1970

Gelfman, Judith, *Women in Television News,* New York: Columbia University Press, 1976

Hosley, David, and Gayle Yamada, *Hard News: Women in Broadcast Journalism,* New York: Greenwood, 1987

Nobile, Philip, "TV News and the Older Woman," *New York Times* (August 10, 1981)

Talese, Gay, "Perils of Pauline," *Saturday Evening Post* (January 26, 1963)

Freed, Fred (1920–1974)

U.S. Documentary Producer

Fred Freed was a leading practitioner of prime-time documentary during the genre's heyday of the 1960s. Working on the network flagship series *NBC White Paper,* he produced close to 40 major documentaries, which earned him seven Emmy and three Peabody Awards. Describing himself as an "old-fashioned liberal," Freed believed that documentary could stimulate change by providing audiences with detailed information about pressing social issues. Yet Freed was also a prominent member of a generation of documentary producers who courted mass audiences with narrative techniques that would later spread to network news reporting and television magazine programs.

Freed began his media career after a stint in the navy during World War II. Starting out as a magazine editor, he moved to radio and ultimately, in 1956, to network television. One year later, he joined CBS as a documentary producer working under Irving Gitlin, the head of creative projects in the news and public-affairs division. During the late 1950s, CBS News was well endowed with talented personnel and the competition for network airtime was extremely fierce. The CBS evening schedule almost exclusively featured entertainment fare, with the exception of irregularly scheduled broadcasts of *See It Now,* produced by Edward R. Murrow and Fred Friendly. The cancellation of this series in 1958 generated intense dissatisfaction among the news and public-affairs staff, many of them frustrated with the marginal time periods devoted to information fare. Partly in response to internal dissension, CBS management in 1959 announced the inauguration of a new prime-time documentary series, *CBS Reports.* Gitlin and his colleagues were disappointed to learn, however, that Friendly had been tapped for the slot of executive producer. Shortly thereafter, Gitlin, Freed, and producer Albert Wasserman were wooed away by NBC president Robert Kintner, who promised them a prestigious prime-time series of their own.

Beginning in 1960, *NBC White Paper* was a central component of the "peacock" network's efforts to dislodge CBS from its top billing in broadcast news. A former journalist, Kintner was a vigorous supporter of the news division, believing it essential to both good citizenship and good business. Over the next several years, NBC News grew rapidly and its documentary efforts earned widespread acclaim from critics and

Fred Freed.
Courtesy of the Everett Collection/ CSU Archives

opinion leaders. Under Gitlin's leadership, Freed and Wasserman produced numerous programs focusing on significant foreign policy issues, then a key concern of the Kennedy administration and Federal Communications Commission (FCC) chair Newton Minow. Programs on the U-2 debacle, the Berlin crisis, and political unrest in Latin America received prominent attention. Yet all three documentarians were also determined to use narrative techniques in an effort to make such issues accessible to a broad audience. At the time Freed commented, "In a world so interesting we always manage to find ways of making things dull. This business of blaming audiences for not watching our documentaries is ridiculous."

With this credo in mind, Freed produced documentaries about "The Death of Stalin" and "The Rise of Khrushchev," which featured tightly structured storylines with well-developed characters. Similarly, his analyses of the Bay of Pigs invasion and the Cuban missile crisis were built around dramatic moments in which historical figures struggled against Promethean odds. Freed's increasingly creative use of audio and vi-

sual elements is conveyed in a tightly edited opening sequence of the latter documentary in which a nuclear missile ominously emerges from its silo accompanied by the piercing sound of a military alarm claxon. Much like a feature film, the editing of the visual imagery dramatically sets the terms for the story that follows.

Freed and his documentary colleagues also experimented during the early 1960s with camera framing techniques that would later become standard conventions of television news. For example, Freed would have his camera operator zoom in for tight close-ups during particularly emotional moments of an interview. This was a significant break from the standard head-and-shoulders portrait shots then used on nightly news and Sunday talk shows. It was intended to engage viewers on both an affective and intellectual level.

Despite these dramatic techniques, network documentaries only occasionally generated ratings that were comparable with entertainment fare. By the middle of the decade, all three networks trimmed back their commitment to the genre for a variety of reasons, and producers Wasserman and Gitlin moved on to other opportunities. Yet Freed remained with *White Paper* and continued to play a leading role with the series into the 1970s. He made major documentaries about the urban crisis, gun control, and environmental issues. He also produced numerous instant specials on breaking news events as well as three superdocumentaries, which featured an entire evening of prime time devoted to a single issue. This concept, which was distinctive to NBC, originated in 1963 with a program on civil rights. It was followed in 1965 by Freed's 20-year survey of U.S. foreign policy, and in 1966 by his program on organized crime. In 1973 he produced NBC's last superdocumentary, an evening devoted to "The Energy Crisis." One year later, in the midst of a busy schedule of documentary production, Freed succumbed to a heart attack at the age of 53. His passing also marked the demise of *NBC White Paper,* for the network mounted only three more installments before the end of the decade. Although *White Paper* has very occasionally returned to prime time since then, it lacks the autonomy, prestige, and resources that were characteristic of the series during the Freed era.

MICHAEL CURTIN

See also NCB White Paper

Fred Freed. Born August 25, 1920. Began career as magazine editor and writer; in broadcasting from 1949; managing editor, NBC-TV, for the daytime program *Home,* 1955; documentary producer, CBS-TV, late 1950s; producer, NBC's *Today Show,* 1961; exclusively in documentary production later. Recipient:

three Peabody Awards; two duPont-Columbia Awards; seven Emmy Awards. Died March 1974.

Television Specials (selected)

1961   *NBC White Paper: Krushchev and Berlin*
1962   *NBC White Paper: Red China*
1962   *The Chosen Child: A Study in Adoption*
1962   *Dupont Show of the Week: Fire Rescue*
1963   *Dupont Show of the Week: Comedian Backstage*
1963   *Dupont Show of the Week: Miss America: Behind the Scenes*
1963   *NBC White Paper: The Death of Stalin: Profile on Communism*
1963   *NBC White Paper: The Rise of Krushchev: Profile on Communism*
1964   *Dupont Show of the Week: The Patient in Room 601*
1964   *NBC White Paper: Cuba: Bay of Pigs*
1964   *NBC White Paper: Cuba: The Missile Crisis*
1965   *NBC White Paper: Decision to Drop the Bomb*
1965   *American White Paper: United States Foreign Policy*
1965   *NBC White Paper: Oswald and the Law: A Study of Criminal Justice*
1966   *NBC White Paper: Countdown to Zero*
1966   *American White Paper: Organized Crime in America*
1967   *The JFK Conspiracy: The Case of Jim Garrison*

1968   *NBC White Paper: The Ordeal of the American City: Cities Have No Limits*
1968   *NBC White Paper: The Ordeal of the American City: The People Are the City*
1969   *NBC White Paper: The Ordeal of the American City: Confrontation*
1969   *Who Killed Lake Erie?*
1969   *Pueblo: A Question of Intelligence*
1970   *NBC White Paper: Pollution Is a Matter of Choice*
1971   *NBC White Paper: Vietnam Hindsight: How It Began*
1971   *NBC White Paper: Vietnam Hindsight: The Death of Diem*
1973   *NBC Reports: And Now the War Is Over…The American Military in the 1970s*
1973   *NBC Reports: Murder in America*
1973   *NBC Reports: But Is This Progress?*
1974   *NBC White Paper: The Energy Crisis: American Solutions*

Further Reading

Bluem, A. William, *Documentary in American Television,* New York: Hastings House, 1965

Curtin, Michael, *Redeeming the Wasteland: Television Documentary and Cold War Politics,* New Brunswick, New Jersey: Rutgers University Press, 1995

Einstein, Daniel, *Special Edition: A Guide to Network Television Documentary Series and Special News Reports, 1955–1979,* Metuchen, New Jersey: Scarecrow Press, 1987

Hammond, Charles Montgomery, Jr., *The Image Decade: Television Documentary, 1965–1975,* New York: Hastings House, 1981

Yellin, David, *Special: Fred Freed and the Television Documentary,* New York: Macmillan, 1973

"Freeze" of 1948

On September 30, 1948, the Federal Communications Commissions (FCC) of the United States announced a "freeze" on the granting of new television licenses (those already authorized were allowed to begin or continue operations). The commission had already granted more than 100 licenses and was inundated with hundreds of additional applications. Unable to resolve several important interference, allocation, and other technical questions because of this rush, the FCC believed that the freeze would allow it to hold hearings and study the issues, leading to something of a "master blueprint" for television in the United States. This " time-out" was originally intended to last only six months, but the outbreak of the Korean War, as well as the difficult nature of some of the issues under study, extended the freeze to four years. During this time, there were 108 VHF television stations on the air and more than 700 new applications on hold. Only 24 cities had two or more stations; many had only one. Most smaller and even some major cities (e.g., Denver, Colorado, and Austin, Texas) had none at all.

Ultimately, five major, not unrelated, issues became the focus of deliberations: (1) the designation of a standard for color television; (2) the reservation of channel space for educational, noncommercial television; (3) the reduction of channel interference; (4) the establishment of a national channel allocation map or scheme; and (5) the opening up of additional spectrum space.

With the April 14, 1952, issuance of the commission's *Sixth Report and Order,* the freeze was finally lifted. This document presented to an anxious broadcast industry and impatient viewers the resolutions to the five questions.

The decision on color came down to a choice between an existing but technologically unsophisticated CBS mechanical system, which was incompatible with existent television receivers (i.e., "color" signals could not be received on black-and-white television sets) and an all-electronic system proposed by RCA, which was compatible with black-and-white TV sets but still in development. The commission approved the CBS system, but it was never implemented because the television set manufacturing industry refused to build what it considered to be inferior receivers. The FCC rescinded its approval of the CBS system in 1950, and in 1953 it accepted the RCA system as the standard.

The reservation of channel space for noncommercial, educational television was spearheaded by FCC commissioner Frieda B. Hennock. When the channel reservation issue was raised for radio during the deliberation leading up to the Communications Act of 1934, the industry view prevailed. Broadcasting was considered too valuable a resource to entrust to educators or others who had no profit motive to spur the development of the medium. Absolutely no spectrum space was set aside for noncommercial (AM) radio. Hennock and others were unwilling to let history repeat in the age of television. Against heavy and strident industry objection (*Broadcasting* magazine said such a set-aside was "illogical, if not illegal"), advocates of noncommercial television prevailed. Two hundred and forty-two channels were authorized for educational, noncommercial television, although no means of financial support was identified. The commission acquiesced because it reasoned that if the educators succeeded, the FCC would be viewed as prescient; if the educators failed, at least the commission had given them an opportunity. Additionally, Hennock and her forces were a nuisance; the noncom-

mercial channel issue was helping keep the freeze alive and there were powerful industry and viewer forces awaiting its end.

Channel interference was easily solved through the implementation of strict rules of separation for stations broadcasting on the same channel. Stations on the same channel had to be separated by at least 190 miles (some geographic areas, the Gulf and northeast regions, for example, had somewhat different standards). A few stations had to change channels to meet the requirements.

Channel allocation took the form of city-by-city assignment of one or more channels based on the general criterion of fair geographic apportionment of channels to the various states and to the country as a whole. The "assignment table" that was produced gave some cities, such as New York and Los Angeles, many stations. Smaller locales were allocated fewer outlets.

The question of opening up additional spectrum space for more television stations was actually the question of how much of the UHF band should be utilized. Eventually, the entire 70-channel UHF band was authorized. Therefore, the television channels then available to U.S. broadcasters and their viewers were the existing VHF channels of 2 through 13 and the new UHF channels of 14 through 83.

KIMBERLY B. MASSEY

See also **Allocation; Color Television; Educational Television; Federal Communications Commission; Hennock, Frieda B.; License**

Further Reading

Barnouw, Erik, *A History of Broadcasting in the United States,* volume 2, *The Golden Web, 1933–53,* New York: Oxford University Press, 1968

Barnouw, Erik, *A History of Broadcasting in the United States,* volume 3, *The Image Empire, from 1953,* New York: Oxford University Press, 1970

Barnouw, Erik, *Tube of Plenty: The Evolution of American Television,* New York: Oxford University Press, 1975; 2nd revised edition, 1990

Bergreen, Laurence, *Look Now, Pay Later: The Rise of Network Broadcasting,* Garden City, New York: Doubleday, 1980

The First 50 Years of Broadcasting: The Running Story of the Fifty Estate, Washington, D.C.: Broadcasting Publications, 1982

Kahn, F.J., *Documents of American Broadcasting,* New York: Appleton-Century-Crofts, 1968

Sterling, Christopher H., and John M. Kittross, *Stay Tuned: A Concise History of American Broadcasting,* Belmont, California: Wadsworth, 1978; 3rd edition, Mahwah, New Jersey: Lawrence Erlbaum Associates, 2002

French, Dawn (1957–)

British Actor

Dawn French is one-half of Britain's top female comedy duo, French and Saunders, as well as a highly successful writer, comedian, and actress in her own right. She and partner Jennifer Saunders have become an outstanding double act while also pursuing successful solo careers.

French's television debut was an auspicious one, as a member of a group of "alternative" comedians known as the Comic Strip, on the opening night of Britain's fourth TV channel, Channel 4, in 1982. "Five Go Mad in Dorset," a spoof of author Enid Blyton's popular children's adventure books, clearly showed that French was a comic actress to watch. The following two years saw two series of *The Comic Strip Presents* in which French played everything from housewives to hippies.

In 1985 French approached the kind of comedy that she and Saunders would eventually make very much their own. *Girls on Top,* a sitcom about four bizarre young women sharing a flat in London, gave French, as costar and co-writer, a chance to develop further the type of character she loves to play. Amanda was an overgrown teenager, sexually inexperienced and yet aware of the sexual powers of woman. A second series followed in 1986, as did appearances with Saunders on Channel 4's cult late-night comedy show *Saturday Live,* but in 1987 French and Saunders moved as a double act to the BBC for their own co-written series, *French and Saunders.* This was broadcast on BBC 2, the nurturing ground for so much of Britain's new generation of comic talent. This first series took the form of a cheap and badly rehearsed variety show, hosted by the two women. Saunders was the rather grumpy, irritable half of the partnership, with French portraying a bouncy, enthusiastic, schoolgirlish character. This format was dropped for the second series, and instead the programs were a mixture of sketches and spoofs.

With an uncanny ability to pick up on the foibles and fears of childhood, and particularly teenage girlhood, French always played the fervent, excitable girl, generally leading the more sullen and awkward Saunders into mischief. This ability to draw on universal but commonplace memories of what now seem petty and trivial matters of girlhood (such as crushes on boys) and turn them into fresh and original comedy is one of the things that has set French and her partner above virtually all other female performers except, perhaps, Victoria Wood. Further series of *French and Saunders* have seen their transfer from BBC 2 to BBC 1. While their inventiveness has increased, there has been no diminution in their ability to latch on to the way women behave with each other. In particular they have become skilled at extraordinarily clever film spoofs, with French playing Julie Andrews in *The Sound of Music* one week and Hannibal Lecter in *Silence of the Lambs* the next.

French's first solo starring role came in 1991 with *Murder Most Horrid,* a series of six comic dramas with a common theme of violent death, in which she played a different role every week. The series was commissioned for French and enabled her to play everything from a Brazilian au pair in "The Girl from Ipanema" to a naive policewoman in "The Case of the Missing." Further series of *Murder Most Horrid* have seen the roles becoming even more ambitious.

If there had been any doubt about French's acting ability, this had been dispelled the previous year, 1993, in the BBC Screen One drama *Tender Loving Care.* In this work, French played a night nurse in the geriatric ward of a hospital. There, she helped many of her charges "on their way" with her own brand of tender loving care, believing that by killing them she is doing them a service. It was a beautifully understated and restrained performance.

After the General Synod of the Church of England voted to permit women to become priests, one *French and Saunders* sketch concerned French's receipt of a vicar's outfit after having received permission to become the first female comedy vicar, complete with buck teeth and dandruff. This soon proved prophetic, when French was cast as the Reverend Geraldine Granger, "a babe with a bob and a magnificent bosom," in Richard Curtis's *The Vicar of Dibley.* French's portrayal of a female vicar sent to a small, old-fashioned, country parish is possibly her most popular to date. The public quickly took this series to their hearts, and French shone even within an ensemble cast of experienced character actors.

French's influence can probably be felt in other areas of British comedy too. She is married to Britain's top black comedian, Lenny Henry, and is often quoted as having influenced him during the early stage of their relationship to abandon his then somewhat self-

French and Saunders, Dawn French and Jennifer Saunders.
1987–present.
Courtesy of the Everett Collection

deprecating humor, in order to explore what it is like to be a black Briton today.

French and Saunders currently have an exclusive contract with the BBC that gives them a wide scope for expanding beyond the confines of their double act. Their first project, *Dusty,* a documentary about Dusty Springfield, was not entirely successful, and the sitcom *Let Them Eat Cake,* set during the French Revolution, was not well received by either critics or public. Further solo projects, such as *Ted and Alice* and *Wild West,* have not found favor with the public either. However, the now all-too-infrequent special editions of *French and Saunders* are as fresh and funny as ever, with the movie spoofs including *Harry Potter* and *The Lord of the Rings.* French also remains a stalwart of the BBC's biannual fund-raising for the charity Comic Relief. There can be no doubt that whether it is as part of a double act or as a solo actress, Dawn French can be assured of a place at the heart of British television for a considerable number of years.

PAM ROSTRON

See also **Saunders, Jennifer**

Dawn French. Born in Holyhead, Wales, October 11, 1957. Attended St. Dunstan's Abbey, Plymouth; Central School of Speech and Drama, London. Married: Lenny Henry, 1984; child: Billie. Met Jennifer Saunders at Central School of Speech and Drama and formed alternative comedy partnership with her, appearing at the Comic Strip club, London, from 1980; participated with Saunders in the Channel 4 *Comic Strip Presents* films and then in own long-running *French and Saunders* series; has also acted in West End theater.

Television Series

1982–92	*The Comic Strip Presents* ("Five Go Mad in Dorset," "Five Go Mad on Mescalin," "Slags," "Summer School," "Private Enterprise," "Consuela," "Mr. Jolly Lives Next Door," "The Bad News Tour," "South Atlantic Raiders," "GLC," "Oxford," "Spaghetti Hoops," "Le Kiss," "The Strike")
1985	*Happy Families*
1985–86	*Girls on Top* (also co-writer)
1987–	*French and Saunders*
1991; 1994–	*Murder Most Horrid*
1993	*Tender Loving Care*
1994	*The Vicar of Dibley*

Film
The Supergrass, 1985; *Harry Potter and the Prisoner of Azkaban,* 2004

Stage (selection)
When I Was a Girl I Used to Scream and Shout; An Evening with French and Saunders; The Secret Policeman's Biggest Ball; Silly Cow.

Publication
A Feast of French and Saunders, 1992

Friendly, Fred W. (1915–1998)

U.S. Broadcast Journalist, Media Commentator

Fred W. Friendly, a pioneering CBS News producer and distinguished media scholar, enjoyed a 60-year career as remarkable for its longevity as for its accomplishments. As the technically creative and dramatically in-spired producer for CBS correspondent Edward R. Murrow, Friendly helped enliven and popularize television news documentary in the decade after World War II, when television news was still in its infancy. After

Fred W. Friendly.
Photo courtesy of Fred Friendly

resigning from CBS as its news division president in 1966, Friendly found a second career as an author and as creator of a series of moderated seminars on media and society.

Friendly got his start in broadcasting during the Great Depression with a staff position at a small radio station in Providence, Rhode Island. It was as a successful radio producer that Friendly was teamed with Murrow in the late 1940s to create a series of documentary albums entitled *I Can Hear It Now.* When Murrow made the jump to television reporting, he brought Friendly with him as his principal documentary producer. Armed with a flair for the dramatic and his experience as a technical innovator in radio, Friendly set out to do for television what he had already done for radio documentaries. The result, in 1952, was the debut of the highly acclaimed *See It Now,* a weekly series hosted by Murrow that broke new ground with its intrepid probing into subjects of serious sociopolitical significance and its stunning visual style. The successful combination of Friendly's energy and Murrow's stature hit its professional peak in 1954, with

their decision to broadcast a documentary attack on Senator Joseph McCarthy that helped change the tide of popular opinion against the anticommunist demagogue.

In his later years at CBS, Friendly was given broader responsibility to create a variety of news programs, including the landmark hourly documentary series, *CBS Reports,* and a political forum that would later be known as *Face the Nation.* As president of CBS News in the mid-1960s, Friendly struggled to keep his news division independent of profit-conscious and entertainment-oriented corporate decision making at CBS Inc., which he considered a threat to the autonomy and integrity of his news operations. In March 1966 Friendly argued vociferously to management that CBS had a journalistic obligation to carry extensive live coverage of the first Senate hearings to question U.S. involvement in Vietnam. When the network opted instead to air reruns of *I Love Lucy,* Friendly resigned from CBS in protest.

In his post-CBS years Friendly turned his interests to writing and teaching about media and law. In a span of 20 years, Friendly traced the history of people involved in landmark Supreme Court cases in books including *Minnesota Rag, The Good Guys, The Bad Guys and the First Amendment,* and *The Constitution: That Delicate Balance.* At the Ford Foundation in the mid-1970s and, later, as the Edward R. Murrow Professor of Broadcast Journalism at Columbia University, Friendly collaborated with some of the nation's leading lawyers, journalists, and politicians to create a series of roundtable debates on media and society. Now known as *The Fred Friendly Seminars,* these Public Broadcasting Service programs remained under Friendly's stewardship until shortly before his death in 1998.

MICHAEL M. EPSTEIN

See also **Army-McCarthy Hearings; Columbia Broadcasting System; Murrow, Edward R.;** *Person to Person; See It Now*

Fred W. Friendly. Born Ferdinand Friendly Wachenheimer in New York City, October 30, 1915. Educated at Cheshire Academy and Nichols Junior College. Married: Ruth W. Mark; two sons, one daughter (from previous marriage), and three stepsons. Served in U.S. Army, Information and Education Section, 1941–45. Broadcast producer, journalist for WEAN radio, Providence, Rhode Island, 1937–41; wrote, produced, and narrated radio series *Footprints in the Sands of Time,* 1938, later, at NBC, *Who Said That,* quiz based on quotations of famous people; collaborated with Edward R. Murrow in presenting oral history of 1932–45 (recorded by Columbia Records under title *I Can Hear It Now*); *I Can Hear It Now: The Sixties* with Walter Cronkite; editor and correspondent in India, Burma, and China for CBI Roundup, 1941–45; coproducer, CBS radio series

Friendly, Fred W.

Hear It Now, 1951, and CBS TV series *See It Now,* 1952–55; past executive producer, with Edward R. Murrow, CBS TV show *CBS Reports,* 1959–60; president, CBS News, New York, 1964–66; Edward R. Murrow professor emeritus broadcast journalist Columbia University Graduate School of Journalism, and director, Seminars on Media and Society, from 1966; adviser on communications, Ford Foundation, 1966–80; director, Michele Clark Program for minority journalists, Columbia University, 1968–75; member, Mayor's Task Force on CATV and Telecommunications, New York City, 1968; distinguished visiting professor, Bryn Mawr College, 1981; visiting professor, Yale University, 1984; commissioner, Charter Revision Committee for City of New York, 1986–90; Montgomery fellow, Dartmouth College, 1986. Honorary degrees: Grinnell College, University of Rhode Island; New School for Social Research; Brown University; Carnegie-Mellon University; Columbia College, Chicago; Columbia University; Duquesne University; New York Law School; University of Southern Utah; College of Wooster, Ohio; University of Utah. Member: American Association of University Professors; Association for Education in Journalism. Military awards: Decorated Legion of Merit and four battle stars; Soldier's Medal for heroism. Recipient: 35 major awards for *See It Now,* including Overseas Press Club, Page One Award, New York Newspaper Guild, and National Headliners Club Award, 1954; 40 major awards for *CBS Reports;* 10 Peabody Awards for TV production; numerous awards from journalism schools; DeWitt Carter Reddick Award, 1980. Died in New York City, March 3, 1998.

Television Series

1952–55	*See It Now*
1958–59	*Small World*
1959–60	*CBS Reports*

1980–98	*Media and Society Seminars*
1986	*Managing Our Miracles: Healthcare in America* (moderator)
1989	*Ethics in America*

Radio

Producer, reporter, correspondent: WEAN, Providence, Rhode Island, 1937–41; NBC Radio, 1932–45; CBS Radio, 1951

Publications

See It Now, edited with Edward R. Murrow, 1955
Due to Circumstances beyond Our Control, 1967
The Good Guys, The Bad Guys, and The First Amendment: Free Speech vs. Fairness in Broadcasting, 1976
Minnesota Rag: The Dramatic Story of the Landmark Supreme Court Case That Gave New Meaning to Freedom of the Press, 1981
The Constitution: That Delicate Balance, with Martha J.H. Elliott, 1984

Further Reading

"Bar Association Honors Fred Friendly (American Bar Association Lifetime Achievement Gavel Award)," *New York Times* (August 12, 1992)
Boyer, Peter J., *Who Killed CBS?: The Undoing of America's Number One News Network,* New York: Random House, 1988
Gates, Gary Paul, *Air Time: The Inside Story of CBS News,* New York: Harper and Row, 1978
Kendrick, Alexander, *Prime Time: The Life of Edward R. Murrow,* Boston: Little, Brown, 1969
Klages, Karen, "Ethics on TV," *ABA Journal* (January 1989)
Schoenbrun, David, *On and Off the Air: An Informal History of CBS News,* New York: Dutton, 1989
Sperber, A.M., *Murrow, His Life and Times,* New York: Freundlich, 1986

Friends

U.S. Situation Comedy

In 1994 NBC introduced a new situation comedy that would prove a mainstay for its popular "Must See TV" Thursday night lineup and would spark both marketing and generic crazes. Initially scheduled between the successful *Mad About You* and *Seinfeld, Friends* was intended to serve as a bridge for maintaining the young hip audiences already loyal to these two shows. Shot live on video, the show was directed by situation comedy veterans such as James Burrows (*The Mary Tyler Moore Show, Taxi*) and Michael Lembeck (*Coach,*

Ellen—he took home a 2000 Emmy for *Friends'* "The One That Could Have Been"). It would quickly establish itself as the anchor for the successful Thursday night NBC schedule that has included other successful shows such as *ER, Frasier, Scrubs,* and *Will & Grace.*

The first successful television series to address the Generation X phenomenon, *Friends* chronicles the loves and lives of six cool, quirky 20-somethings living in New York City and spending an inordinate amount of time hanging out in their local coffeehouse, Central Perk: nerdy paleontologist Ross Geller (David Schwimmer), his obsessive-compulsive chef sister Monica Geller (Courteney Cox-Arquette), wisecracking, hapless number cruncher Chandler Bing (Matthew Perry), hunky Italian-American actor Joey Tribbiani (Matt LeBlanc), spoiled ex-prom queen Rachel Green (Jennifer Aniston), and spacey massage therapist Phoebe Buffay (Lisa Kudrow, who garnered the 1998 Emmy for Outstanding Supporting Actress in a Comedy Series). In the wake of Nirvana and *Reality Bites* (1994), the *Friends* ensemble depicted and hailed this desirable demographic while simultaneously eliminating the alienation, apathy, despair, and cynicism often associated with the group. With Chandler and Joey living across the hall from Monica and Rachel, their apartments often served as a site for the group to meet and bond as the characters developed into a strong family unit, helping one another through the trials faced by young adults at the end of the 20th century (romance, careers, family, etc.).

Though the creators transformed the grunge aesthetic associated with Generation X into one of unrealistic conspicuous consumption (their spacious and well-decorated apartments would not be viable options for people sliding in and out of marginally lucrative jobs), each character was a charming combination of glamorous movie star and everyman. Episodes largely dealt with light topics such as finding Ross's lost monkey, discovering that urine is the only cure for a jellyfish sting, or deciding what to do when you realize you have free porn. Titles such as "The One With Chandler's Work Laugh," "The One With the Racecar Bed," and "The One Where Phoebe Hates PBS" illustrate the levity of each individual episode.

However, the lasting popularity of the show, which aired for ten seasons, can partially be attributed to the show's efficient combination of long-term and short-term stakes. While each episode effectively stands alone as a piece of entertainment, the show also followed the lead of earlier series such as *Cheers* and *Murphy Brown* by developing recurring plotlines. Ross's pregnant wife left him for another woman prior to the first episode, and consequently the first several seasons dealt with his neurosis regarding his wife's lesbianism (including television's first lesbian wedding), the birth of their son, Ben, and attempts to raise him in an unconventional family. In addition, anticipation mounted as the characters became more than just platonic friends. Several seasons engaged the "will they or won't they" quandary regarding Ross and Rachel's on-again, off-again romance (which continued into the show's final seasons, when Rachel and Ross, after an alcohol-induced night together, had a baby) and Monica eventually cured Chandler's recurring fear of commitment as season six climaxed in a candlelit marriage proposal. These ever-changing relationships converted the traditional amnesic plotlines of the situation comedy into ones akin to episodic drama. With seasonal cliff-hangers, *Friends* maintained its audience from one season to the next by providing escapist comedy alongside exciting soap-operatic romantic developments.

As the seasons carried on and recurring plotlines surfaced and abated, the show's creators integrated various techniques to keep the show fresh. The common inclusion of guest stars provided the network grounds for dubbing episodes "special." Elliot Gould and Christina Pickles frequently resurfaced as Ross and Monica's parents, while television's *That Girl,* Marlo Thomas, played Rachel's mother. Along with celebrities such as Tom Selleck, Susan Sarandon, and Bruce Willis (who took home a 2000 Emmy for Outstanding Guest Actor in a Comedy Series), Cox-Arquette's and Aniston's real-life husbands David Arquette and Brad Pitt made appearances, and fellow NBC contemporaries Noah Wiley and George Clooney of *ER* appeared as versions of their prime-time alter egos. Additionally, when the "reality television" craze began to threaten the show's Nielsen position, a practice of occasionally " supersizing" episodes was implemented. During February of 2001, at the height of the ratings battle with the popular show *Survivor,* NBC aired four 40-minute *Friends* episodes followed by miniepisodes of *Saturday Night Live, Friends* outtakes, and other supersized NBC sitcoms. The practice was occasionally revived in the following seasons.

Not only was America obsessively watching the show (it continuously ranked in the top ten, seldom dropping below number four), but also they were wearing it, drinking out of it, and dancing to it. Within a couple of seasons, American women fully embraced Rachel and Monica's "shag" haircuts, and the cast's wardrobes represented various factions of cool youth. In addition, the production company hawked a successful line of *Friends* merchandise (hats, T-shirts, oversized coffee mugs, etc.) in its chain of Warner Brothers mall shops. Number 35 in sales and 1 in airplay, the show's theme "I'll Be There For You" rocketed the heretofore-obscure band The Rembrandts into overexposure, as MTV and VH1 showed the cast members goofing off in the music video.

The show's popular and critical success translated into both a financial jackpot and hailstorm. Following *Seinfeld*'s and *Mad About You*'s immense salary negotiations, the young, previously little-known *Friends* actors fought Warner Brothers for escalating salaries. Initially earning around $22,000 per episode, the cast successfully held out for $75,000 in 1997, eventually earning as much as $750,000 per episode in 2002. However, while the show brought Warner Brothers headaches, it also proved to be a syndication bonanza. Expected to eventually surpass *Seinfeld*'s projected 2 billion dollars, *Friends* grossed approximately 1.5 billion in its first six-year syndication cycle. Its second run is expected to push the numbers over three billion.

This sweeping success brought about an immediate wave of *Friends* clones. In an attempt to capitalize on the Generation X craze and marketing boom, the networks scrambled to present young Americans with varying incarnations of everyone's favorite *Friends*. Shows such as *Dweebs, Partners, Can't Hurry Love*, and *Coupling* (originally a British show, which was successful, although a U.S. version failed) flooded in and out of the network schedules, while select shows such as *The Drew Carey Show* and *Caroline in the City* successfully hailed their desired youth audience and lasted past their freshman season. Regardless, *Friends* successfully takes its place as the show that best personified popular notions of Generation X and contributed to the changing face of situation comedy narrative.

KELLY KESSLER

See also **Burrows, James;** *Seinfeld; Survivor*

Cast

Monica Geller	Courteney Cox-Arquette
Ross Geller	David Schwimmer
Rachel Green	Jennifer Aniston
Joey Tribbiani	Matt LeBlanc
Chandler Bing	Matthew Perry
Phoebe Buffay	Lisa Kudrow

Producers

Kevin Bright, David Crane, Marta Kauffman

Programming History

1994–2004	242 episodes
NBC	
September 1994–	
February 1995	Thursday 8:30–9:00
February 1995–May 1995	Thursday 9:30–10:00
September 1995–May 2004	Thursday 8:00–8:30

Further Reading

"Best of Friends: The Ultimate Viewer's Guide," *Entertainment Weekly* (Fall 2001)

Cagle, Jess, "Entertainers of the Year," *Entertainment Weekly* (December 29, 1995)

Carter, Bill, "*Friends* Cast Bands Together to Demand a Salary Increase," *New York Times* (July 16, 1996)

Grego, Melissa, "What's 2 Bil Among *Friends*?," *Variety* (April 23, 2001)

Karger, Dave, and David Hochman, "Fool's Paradise," *Entertainment Weekly* (January 24, 1996)

Kolbert, Elizabeth, "A Sitcom Is Born: Only Time Will Tell," *New York Times* (May 23, 1994)

LaFranco, Robert, "Comedy Cash-In: Dig Out Those Old Joke Books from the Attic—There's Never Been a More Lucrative Time to Be Funny," *Forbes* (September 23, 1996)

Rice, Lynette, "Funny Money," *Entertainment Weekly* (May 26, 2000)

Tomashoff, Craig, "The Joy of Six," *People Weekly* (April 27, 1995)

Wild, David, "Six Lives on Videotape," *Rolling Stone* (May 18, 1995)

Wild, David, "Television the Buddy System: The Networks' New Fall Shows Ask, 'Can't We All Be *Friends*?'" *Rolling Stone* (September 7, 1995)

Front Page Challenge

Canadian Panel Quiz/Public-Affairs Program

Front Page Challenge, television's longest continuously running panel show, was one of the most familiar landmarks on the Canadian broadcasting landscape. During much of its 38-season run on the Canadian Broadcasting Corporation (CBC), from 1957 to 1995, it was among Canadian television's most popular programs, regularly drawing average audiences of 1 to 2 million in the small Canadian market; toward the end,

Front Page Challenge.
Photo courtesy of CBC Television

however, viewership dropped, numbering about 500,000 in the show's final season. A book was published in 1982 to mark the show's 25th anniversary.

Front Page Challenge was first born as a summer fill-in show; at the time, it was one of many quiz shows on the air, a genre popular because of the low production costs involved, and *Front Page Challenge* was in fact named after a U.S. quiz favorite of the time, *The $64,000 Challenge.* A half-hour program, *Front Page Challenge* featured four panelists, usually well-known journalists, who would ask yes-or-no questions in an attempt to correctly identify a mystery challenger connected to a front-page news item, as well as the news item itself. After the panelists had guessed correctly—or been stumped—they would proceed to interview the challenger.

Equal parts quiz show and current affairs panel, *Front Page Challenge*'s hybridization of televisual genres drew in not only audience members attracted by the entertainment value of the quiz show format but also viewers who were curious about who the week's mystery

challengers would be and eager to hear them interviewed by *Front Page Challenge*'s panel of crack journalists. Long before current affairs programs like *CBC Newsworld* or all-news channels such as CNN began to offer similar fare, *Front Page Challenge* provided Canadians with a humane look at the newsmakers they read about in their morning papers. Over the years, some of the show's guests included figures as diverse as Indira Gandhi, saying she would never go into politics; Eleanor Roosevelt; hockey player Gordie Howe; Tony Bennett; and Errol Flynn, along with Mary Pickford, a Canadian and one of cinema's first stars. Walter Cronkite even announced his new job as CBS anchor on the program.

As a television program noted for its attention to the newspaper, *Front Page Challenge* panelists were almost exclusively eminent Canadian newspaper workers. For most of the show's run, well-known reporter Gordon Sinclair and journalist-writer Pierre Berton joined actress Toby Robins to form the panel, with a guest panelist making a fourth, and Fred Davis hosting the show. Broadcaster Betty Kennedy replaced Robins in 1961, and upon Gordon Sinclair's death in 1984, he was replaced by author and columnist Alan Fotheringham. Another prominent reporter, Jack Webster, was added as a permanent fourth panelist in 1990.

That *Front Page Challenge* pointed not to the everyday world, but to other points within the media universe—the television program's very name evokes the newspaper—is significant as more than a sign of the times. By building a show in which competence in recalling newspaper headlines is the most important attribute, *Front Page Challenge* helped reinforce the social importance attached to what is reported in the media. The show's use of the newspaper as a frame of reference for significant events had the effect of perpetuating the idea that news happens in the real world, and that the media simply reflect these goings-on. As much research has shown, however, what we read in the newspaper is as much the result of the institutionalized conditions of newspaper reporting as it is of what goes on "out there"—the news is constructed by the media. *Front Page Challenge,* then, was an early example of the proliferation of television programs that recycle media content as news—*Entertainment Tonight* is perhaps the best-known example—and demonstrates how this type of programming tends, among other things, to contribute to the "aura" of media, in which the media world comes to stand in for the lived world.

As the product of the quiz show genre popular in the 1950s and 1960s, *Front Page Challenge* stood both within and outside of that television format, and thus provides a unique vantage point from which to look at the quiz or game show. Whereas the game show is characterized by its catapulting unknown, everyday individuals from the private sphere into the public sphere of television—providing home viewers with an easy locus of identification—*Front Page Challenge* featured only well-known public figures or newsmakers. Indeed, the only way an ordinary viewer might hope to participate in the program, other than becoming involved in a news event, was by successfully writing to *Front Page Challenge* and suggesting a front-page story to be used. Unlike other game or quiz shows, there was little competition—the panel worked together as a team—and almost no prizes to be won. Even the home viewers themselves were positioned in an unorthodox way on *Front Page Challenge:* whereas in other game shows the viewer plays along with the contestants, often shouting out the answer in her or his living room before it emerges from the television speaker, the *Front Page Challenge* viewer was actually able to see the mystery challenger, who stood behind the panelists, hidden from their eyes, but in full view of the camera.

Eliminating the elements of the quiz show genre seen as crass or vulgar helped to provide *Front Page Challenge* with an air of legitimacy and respectability that the straight quiz show did not enjoy; the show's evocation of the newspaper's seriousness, its panelists, and its location on the state broadcasting network marked it as a "quality" television program. This controlled distance from what was seen as "American mass culture" helped distance it considerably from the quiz show scandals that plagued U.S. broadcasting in the 1960s—including *The $64,000 Challenge.*

When *Front Page Challenge* was taken off the air in 1995, a move emblematic of major restructuring at the CBC, it signaled the end of an era in Canadian television broadcasting. The program's mixing of quiz show and public affairs, its lending of journalistic credence to the game show genre, and the interest with which audiences tuned in to hear and watch newsmakers of the day all exemplified television's ability to convey the humane qualities and attributes of those who were in the news.

BRAM ABRAMSON

See also **Berton, Pierre; Canadian Programming in English**

Hosts
Win Berron, Fred Davis

Panelists
Toby Robbins, Alex Barris, Gordon Sinclair, Betty Kennedy, Pierre Berton, Alan Fotheringham, Jack Webster

Moderators
Win Barron, Alex Barris, Fred Davis

Producers
Harvey Hart, James Guthro, Andrew Crossan, Don Brown, and others

Programming History
CBC
1957–95   Weekly half-hour

Further Reading

Barris, Alex, *Front Page Challenge: The 25th Anniversary,* Toronto: Canadian Broadcasting Corporation, 1981

Gould, Terry, "Front Page Challenged," *Saturday Night* (July–August 1995)

Knelman, Martin, "The Eternal Challenge," *Saturday Night* (March 1992)

Stam, Robert, "Television News and Its Spectator," in *Regarding Television,* edited by E. Ann Kaplan, Frederick, Maryland: American Film Institute, 1983

Tuchman, Gaye, *Making News: A Study in the Construction of Reality,* New York: Free Press/Macmillan, 1978

Valpy, Michael, "No More *Front Page Challenge.* No More Canada?" *The Globe and Mail* (April 15, 1995)

Frontline

U.S. Public-Affairs Program

The Public Broadcasting System's series *Frontline* has served as one of the major documentary and public-affairs program on American television since its debut in 1983. Emerging at a time when the U.S. television networks were dramatically cutting back on documentary and public-affairs television, producer David Fanning and his team have produced a series of award-winning programs on issues ranging from programs on the Gulf War, Afghanistan, and Iraq, to producer Ofra Bikel's investigation of the Little Rascals sexual abuse case to Martin Smith and Lowell Bergman's chronicle of America's drug wars.

Originating from PBS's WGBH Boston affiliate, *Frontline* has won all of the major awards for broadcast journalism, including Emmy Awards, Peabody Awards, George Polk Awards, and DuPont Columbia University Awards. The series has specialized in current affairs documentaries, producing programs on U.S. military interventions in the Reagan era and on the Panama invasion and Gulf War during the presidency of George H.W. Bush. There have also been documentaries on the presidential candidacies, and the lives of Bill Clinton and Bob Dole (*The Choice*, 1996) and on Al Gore and George W. Bush in 2000.

Frontline has also produced many provocative documentaries on the U.S. economy and political system, such as the investigations of the savings and loan scandal, *Other People's Money* and *The Great American Bailout*. Its probing investigative studies of the bank BCCI (*The Bank of Crooks and Criminals*) and the examination of the *Exxon Valdez* Alaskan tragedy, *Anatomy of an Oil Spill,* are also noteworthy.

The series creator and senior executive producer is David Fanning. In 2002 Michael Sullivan was promoted to executive producer for special projects after serving as the series senior producer. Sullivan has supervised the production of many major *Frontline* projects, including *Faith and Doubt at Ground Zero* in 2002, a probing examination of theological questions regarding the existence of God and good and evil in the wake of the events of September 11, 2001. Under Sullivan's supervision, the program continued to produce the high-quality documentaries for which it is renowned—including *Cyber War!* on hi-tech warfare, *Truth, War, & Consequences* on the chaotic aftermath of the Iraq war, and *Chasing the Sleeper Cell* on the Islamic terrorism—into the 2003–04 season.

Frontline's excellent website makes available transcripts and streaming videos of many of its programs (http://www.pbs.org/wgbh/pages/frontline/). For instance, one can access *Truth, War, & Consequences* from the website. The program is divided into sections, much like a DVD, with textual commentary surrounding the screen. The program's website also makes accessible transcripts of interviews with the characters in the documentary, textual analysis of the material and issues in the program, and links to other Internet resources. Thus *Frontline* continues its tradition as a top documentary and public-affairs television series, while providing cutting-edge educational material on the Internet.

Frontline has won numerous awards for several of its productions, including Peabody Awards, Emmy Awards, Robert F. Kennedy Journalism Awards, and Edward R. Murrows Awards. In 1995 *Frontline* received the Distinguished Achievement in Journalism Award from the Journalism Alumni Association of the University of Southern California.

DOUGLAS KELLNER

See also **Documentary; Public Television**

Senior Executive Producer
David Fanning

Executive Producer for Special Projects
Michael Sullivan

Programming History
1983–
PBS

Courtesy of the Everett Collection

Frost, David (1939–)

British Broadcast Journalist, Producer

David Frost is an outstanding television presenter, political interviewer, and producer, who is successful on both sides of the Atlantic. The awards recognizing his achievements in television include two Golden Roses from the Montreux international festival (for *Frost over England*), as well as two Emmy Awards (for *The David Frost Show*) in the United States. His long career was recognized when he was granted a knighthood in 1993.

Frost was one of the first generation of university graduates who bypassed print journalism and went straight into television. While at Cambridge he showed his satirical talent in the *Footlights Revue* and edited the university newspaper, *Granta*. In 1961 he moved to London to work for ITV during the day and perform in cabarets at night. His nightclub performance drew the attention of BBC producer Ned Sherrin, who invited him to host *That Was the Week That Was,* often called *TW3*. In the "satire boom" of the early 1960s the irreverent, topical, and politically oriented *TW3* introduced satire to television in Britain. Among others topics, the program poked fun at the Royal family, the Church, high politics, and the respectable tenets of British life. *TW3* brought the divisions of British society to the surface, and the ensuing controversy made the BBC discontinue it. From 1964 to 1965 Frost co-hosted the next, milder satirical program, *Not So Much a Programme, More a Way of Life*. At its most successful, this program bore significant resemblance to *TW3* and reached the same end.

The success of *TW3* made Frost a transatlantic commuter, after NBC bought the rights to the program and aired the American version (1964–65) with executive producer Leland Hayward. The shorter, less political, and less outspoken program never had the same impact as its British counterpart, but it nevertheless made Frost's name in the United States.

Back in Britain, the BBC's new show *The Frost Report* (1966–67) focused on one topic per program and tackled social and contemporary issues, as opposed to the political and topical focus of *TW3* and *Not So Much*. Drawing on the talents of John Cleese, Ronnie Barker, and Ronnie Corbett, the program brought humor to the topics of education, voting, and the like.

The working environment provided for the development of a new humorous trend in Britain, and five of the comedians went on to form *Monty Python's Flying Circus.*

From 1966 to 1968, *The Frost Programme* at ITV showed the beginning of Frost's transition from comedian to serious interviewer. Frost pioneered such TV techniques as directly involving the audience in the discussions and blending comedy sketches with current affairs. From this time on, Frost's mixture of politics with entertainment would draw mixed responses from critics. At this time his "ad-lib interviewing" style, as he calls it, was characterized by rather remorseless fire on well-chosen subjects and led to his label as the "tough inquisitor."

From anchorman to executive producer, Frost filled many different roles in the television business. In 1966 he founded David Paradine Ltd., and as an entrepreneur he put a consortium together to acquire the ITV franchise for London Weekend Television (LWT) in 1967. LWT's programming did not live up to its franchise undertaking in the long run and was criticized in Britain for emphasizing entertainment to the detriment of substantial programming.

On the strength of his British chat shows, Group W (the U.S. Westinghouse Corporation television stations) selected Frost to anchor an interview daily from 1969 to 1972. Frost kept his London shows and fronted *The David Frost Show* in the United States. He used more one-to-one interviews than before and managed to mix friendly conversation with confrontation. Throughout these endeavors, Frost's instinct for television, his handling of the audience, and his ability to put guests at ease and make them accessible justified the moniker "The Television Man," given him years earlier by the BBC's Donald Baverstock.

Frost's television personality status and ability to market himself well enabled him to attract prominent interviewees. He has interviewed every British prime minister since Harold Wilson, as well as leading politicians and celebrities from a number of different countries. His U.S. television specials *The Next President* (1968, 1988, 1992) featured interviews with presidential candidates in the run-up for the presidency. The most famous of the big interviews characterizing Frost's recent focus were *The Nixon Interviews* (1977). This program offered the only televised assessment Richard Nixon gave about his conduct as president, including the Watergate affair. The interviews were syndicated on a barter basis and were subsequently seen in more than 70 countries.

When interviewing leading public figures, Frost retains his persistence, but he has refined his style into an apparently soft interrogative method where the strength of a question is judged more by the range of possible responses. As a result, he has sometimes been criticized for "toadying," presenting an overly sympathetic ear to his influential guests. Unlike his entertainment-oriented shows, which were often followed by rows over questions of bias, the big interviews are usually judged as fair and balanced.

On the way to fame as a serious political interviewer, Frost had a new chance to combine politics and satire. As executive producer, he helped to launch the British program *Spitting Image* in 1984. This show, a scathing satire, picked up on already existing perceptions of politicians and highlighted them in puppet caricatures. When Margaret Thatcher was portrayed as a bald man who ate babies and lived next door to Adolf Hitler, the life-size puppets were thought to be as dangerous to politicians as *TW3* had been. As a result, before the 1987 U.K. elections, the program was not broadcast. In another transatlantic parallel, this popular program also made it into the United States. In 1986 NBC carried *Spitting Image: Down and Out in the White House,* hosted by David Frost, and in 1987 *The Ronnie and Nancy Show* appeared on U.S. television screens.

In 1982 Frost successfully bid for a commercial breakfast television franchise, TV-AM, and became director of the new venture. Despite the five famous flagship presenters, TV-AM as a whole faced the same criticism as London Weekend Television. Its leisurely approach to hard news, especially during the Gulf War, was thought to cost it the franchise in 1991.

After losing TV-AM, Frost moved to the BBC to front a weekly interview program, *Breakfast with Frost.* Despite years of success, the value of the program for the channel is currently being examined. In addition, Frost's ten-week ITV documentary *Alpha: Will It Change Their Lives?* about a popular evangelical introduction to Christianity for yuppies stirred controversy in the summer of 2001.

In the United States, Frost signed a contract with the Public Broadcasting Service in 1990 to produce *Talking with David Frost,* a monthly interview program. Frost took advantage of newly declassified documents and

David Frost.
Photo courtesy of David Paradine Television, Inc.

made a two-part documentary, *Inside the Cold War with Sir David Frost,* in 1998. On cable, he is currently presenting *One-on-One with David Frost* for Arts and Entertainment, and *Millennium Monday,* a series of historical documentaries, for the National Geographic Channel. In 2000 he signed a deal with Newsplayer. com, a website that offers subscription access to archived newsreel footage, to make his interviews available on the Web.

Frost's business ventures also include filmmaking, where he acts as executive producer. The satirical *The Rise and Rise of Michael Rimmer* (1970), featuring Peter Cook taking over the prime ministership, and the documentary *The Search for Josef Mengele* (1985) exemplify the variety of films he has produced. Most recently, in 1999, he produced *Rogue Trader,* based on the story of Nick Leeson who brought down Barings Bank. As a writer, Frost draws on his commuter observations. Along with other writings, he has published his autobiography (1993).

In Britain, Frost has often been criticized for his mannerisms and his apparent ability to use the fame bestowed by television to further his career in a number of different fields. Nevertheless, his flair for television and his ability to produce high-quality current affairs and interview programs are widely recognized. His excellent political interviews show how television is able to provide insights into political decisions and contribute to the historical record. Throughout his long career, Frost has always been ready to experiment with something new. His personal contributions to satire and political programs, as well as his business ventures, make him a prominent figure of broadcasting.

RITA ZAJACZ

See also **British Programming;** *Spitting Image;* *That Was the Week That Was*

David (Paradine) Frost. Born in Tenderden, Kent, England, April 7, 1939. Attended Gillingham Grammar School; Wellington Grammar School; Gonville and Caius College, Cambridge, M.A. Married: 1) Lynne Frederick, 1981 (divorced, 1982); 2) Carina Fitzalan-Howard, 1983; children: Miles, Wilfred, and George. Served as presenter of Rediffusion specials, 1961; established name as host of *That Was the Week That Was,* 1962–63; later gained reputation as an aggressive interviewer on *The Frost Programme* and other shows; cofounder, London Weekend Television; chair, David Paradine Group of Companies since 1966; served on British/U.S. Bicentennial Liaison Committee, 1973–76, and has hosted shows on both sides of the Atlantic; interviewed Richard Nixon for television, 1977; director, TV-AM, from 1981; helped launch TV-AM commercial breakfast television company, 1982. L.L.D., Emerson College, Boston. President, Lord's Taverners, 1985, 1986. Order of the British Empire, 1970; knighted, 1993. Recipient: Golden Rose of Montreux (twice); Royal Television Society Silver Medal, 1967; Richard Dimbleby Award, 1967; Emmy Awards, 1970, 1971; Guild of Television Producers Award, 1971; TV Personality of the Year, 1971; Religious Heritage of America Award, 1971; Albert Einstein Award, 1971.

Television Series

1961	*This Week*
1961	*Let's Twist on the Riviera*
1962–63	*That Was the Week That Was*
1963	*A Degree of Frost*
1964–65	*Not So Much a Programme, More a Way of Life*
1966–67	*The Frost Report*
1966–67	*David Frost's Night Out in London*
1966–68	*The Frost Programme*
1967	*At Last the 1948 Show* (producer)
1967–70	*No—That's Me Over Here!* (producer)
1968	*The Ronnie Barker Playhouse* (producer)
1968–70	*Frost on Friday*
1969–72	*The David Frost Show*
1971–73	*The David Frost Revue*
1973	*A Degree of Frost*
1973	*Frost's Weekly*
1974	*Frost on Thursday*
1975–76	*We British*
1976	*Forty Years of Television*
1977	*The Frost Programme*
1977–78	*A Prime Minister on Prime Ministers*
1977–78	*The Crossroads of Civilization*
1978	*Headliners with David Frost*
1979–82	*David Frost's Global Village*
1981–86	*David Frost Presents the International Guinness Book of World Records*
1981–92	*Frost on Sunday*
1982	*Good Morning Britain*
1986–88	*The Guinness Book of Records Hall of Fame*
1987–88	*The Next President with David Frost*
1987–88	*Entertainment Tonight*
1987–93	*Through the Keyhole*
1989	*The President and Mrs. Bush Talking with David Frost*
1991–98	*Talking with David Frost*
1993–	*Breakfast with Frost*

Made-for-Television Movies

| 1975 | *James A. Michener's Dynasty* |
| 1978 | *The Ordeal of Patty Hearst* |

Television Specials (selected)

1966	*David Frost at the Phonograph*
1967	*Frost over England*
1968	*Robert Kennedy, The Man*
1970	*Frost over America*
1972–77	*Frost over Australia*
1973–74	*Frost over New Zealand*
1973	*That Was the Year That Was*
1975	*The Unspeakable Crime*
1975	*Abortion: Merciful or Murder?*
1975	*The Beatles: Once Upon a Time in America*
1975	*David Frost Presents the Best*

1976	*The Sir Harold Wilson Interviews*
1977	*The Nixon Interviews*
1978	*Are We Really Going to Be Rich?*
1979	*A Gift of Song: Music for Unicef Concert*
1979	*The Bee Gees Special*
1979	*The Kissinger Interviews*
1980	*The Shah Speaks*
1980	*The American Movie Awards*
1980	*The 25th Anniversary of ITV*
1980	*The Begin Interview*
1980	*Elvis: He Touched Their Lives*
1981	*The BAFTA Awards*
1981	*Show Business*
1981	*This Is Your Life: 30th Anniversary Special*
1981	*The Royal Wedding*
1981	*Onward Christian Soldiers*
1982	*The American Movie Awards*
1982	*A Night of Knights: A Royal Gala*
1982	*Rubinstein at 95*
1982	*Pierre Elliott Trudeau*
1982	*The End of the Year Show*
1982–83	*Frost Over Canada*
1983	*David Frost Live by Satellite from London*
1983	*The End of the Year Show*
1984	*David Frost Presents Ultra Quiz*
1985	*That Was the Year That Was*
1985	*The Search for Josef Mengele*
1985–86	*Twenty Years On*
1986	*Spitting Image: Down and Out in the White House*
1987	*The Ronnie and Nancy Show*
1987	*The Spitting Image Movie Awards*
1987–88	*The Spectacular World of Guinness Records*
1988	*ABC Presents a Royal Gala*
1991	*The Nobel Debate*
1998	*Inside the Cold War with Sir David Frost*
2000	*The Debate of a Lifetime*
2000	*Ross Meets Frost*
2000	*Elizabeth Taylor: A Musical Celebration*
2001	*Alpha: Will It Change Their Lives?*

Films (producer)

The Rise and Rise of Michael Rimmer, 1970; *Charley One-Eye,* 1972; *Leadbelly,* 1974; *The Slipper and the Rose,* 1975; *The Remarkable Mrs. Sanger,* 1979; *Rogue Trader,* 1999

Radio

David Frost at the Phonograph, 1966, 1972; *Pull the Other One,* 1987– .

Stage

An Evening with David Frost, 1966.

Publications

That Was the Week That Was, 1963

How to Live Under Labour: Or at Least Have As Much a Chance As Anybody Else, 1964

To England with Love, 1967

The Presidential Debate, 1968

The Americans, 1970

Whitlam and Frost, 1970

I Gave Them a Sword: Behind the Scenes of the Nixon Interviews, 1978

I Could Have Kicked Myself, with Michael Deakin, 1982

Who Wants to Be a Millionaire?, with Michael Deakin, 1983

David Frost's Book of the World's Worst Decisions, with Michael Deakin, 1983

David Frost's Book of Millionaires, Multimillionaires, and Really Rich People, with Michael Deakin, 1984

The Mid-Atlantic Companion, with Michael Shea, 1986

The Rich Tide, with Michael Shea, 1986

David Frost: An Autobiography (Part One: From Congregations to Audiences), 1993

Billy Graham in Conversation, 1998

Further Reading

Briggs, Asa, *The History of Broadcasting in the United Kingdom, Volume V: Competition,* London: Oxford University Press, 1995

Frischauer, Willi, *Will You Welcome Now…David Frost,* London: Michael Joseph, 1971

Tinker, Jack, *The Television Barons,* London: Quartet, 1980

Frum, Barbara (1937–1992)

Canadian Broadcast Journalist

Barbara Frum was one of Canada's most respected and influential woman journalists. She began her career in journalism as a freelance writer and commentator for various CBC Radio programs. She quickly branched out into the print media, writing various columns for national newspapers such as the *Globe and Mail, The Toronto Star,* and a television column for the *Saturday Night* magazine. In 1967 she made a brief foray into television as a cohost for an information program, *The Way It Is,* but it was in radio that she first gained fame.

In the fall of 1971 she took on the cohosting duties of *As It Happens,* a new, innovative newsmagazine show on CBC Radio that followed the 6:00 P.M. news. At a time when the national broadcaster was struggling to develop programs that would keep its listeners beyond the supper-hour newscast, the show's young producer, Mark Starowicz, proposed a format based largely on newsmaker interviews that would provide an in-depth examination of the stories behind the headlines. Through the use of long-distance telephone and radio, listeners were connected to world events. In this format, Frum shone. She quickly gained the reputation as a tough, incisive, and well-informed interviewer. For ten years she interviewed numerous world leaders, national politicians, and other newsmakers, as well as those affected by the news. Frum was honored with numerous awards during her tenure, most notably the National Press Club of Canada Award for Outstanding Contribution to Canadian Journalism in 1975; Woman of the Year in the literature, arts, and education category of the Canadian Press in 1976; and the Order of Canada in 1979.

In the 1980s CBC Television decided to move its national newscast, *The National,* from its traditional 11:00 P.M. time slot to 10:00 P.M. The news division of CBC Television had long been considering such a move, hoping to capture a larger audience, since studies had shown that a large number of viewers retired to bed prior to 11:00 P.M. Realizing that it was a huge gamble, CBC executives appointed Starowicz, the producer of *As It Happens,* to translate his radio success to the newsmagazine program, *The Journal.* He, in turn, looked to Frum, who had been instrumental in the success of *As It Happens.* After months of preparation, the new current affairs program, *The Journal,* was launched on January 11, 1982. In the weeks that followed, it became the most watched and highly respected newsmagazine show in Canada.

The Journal featured many innovations and made use of the latest electronic news gathering technology. Features, such as field reports and short documentaries, public forums, and debates, as well as a series of reports on business, sports, arts and entertainment, and science news were interwoven with the interview portion of the program. The show featured two female hosts. Frum was joined by Mary Lou Finley in the hosting duties, and a higher profile was assigned to women reporters and journalists than on most other stations.

The show relied heavily on Frum's skill as an interviewer. The interview portion of *The Journal* accounted for 60 percent of the program. She remained the dominant and permanent presence on a show that saw many new cohosts. All of Canada was deeply saddened by the news of her sudden death on March 26, 1992, from complications of chronic leukemia. Tributes poured in from colleagues, coworkers, and the public at large. Months following her passing, the CBC announced that it would move its newscast and newsmagazine program, *The National* and *The Journal,* from 10:00 P.M. to 9:00 P.M. Once again, executives argued that studies showed that aging baby boomers were retiring to bed at an earlier time. This move proved to be less successful than the first endeavor, and two years later the CBC was forced to reverse itself after ratings had fallen off by half. Amid these changes and reversals, *The Journal* was transformed into the *Primetime News. As It Happens* continues its run, having celebrated more than three decades on the air.

MANON LAMONTAGNE

See also **Canadian Programming in English;** *National, The/The Journal;* **Starowicz, Mark**

Barbara Frum. Born in Niagara Falls, New York, September 8, 1937. Married: Murray, 1957; children: David, Linda, Matthew. Educated at University of Toronto, Canada, B.A. in history 1959. Began career as radio commentator and writer of reviews and magazine articles; worked briefly in television, 1961; current affairs interviewer in radio, CBC, 1971–82; co-host, *The Journal*, television news magazine, 1982–92. Recipient: four ACTRA Awards; National Press Club of Canada Award, 1975; Order of Canada, 1979. Died in Toronto, March 26, 1992.

Television Series

1967	*The Way It Is*
1981–92	*The Journal* (host-interviewer)

Radio

Weekend (interviewer-contributor), 1969–72; *As It Happens* (associate), 1971–82; *Barbara Frum* (host), 1974–75; *Quarterly Report* (cohost), 1977–82.

Further Reading

"CBC Pays Tribute to Barbara Frum," *Globe and Mail* (June 22, 1993)

"Friends Gather to Bid Colleague Goodbye," *Globe and Mail* (April 6, 1992)

Levine, Allan, *Scrum Wars: The Prime Ministers and the Media,* Toronto: Dundurn Press, 1993

Stewart, Sandy, *Here's Looking at Us: A Personal History of Television in Canada,* Toronto: CBC Enterprises, 1986

Taras, David, *The Newsmakers: The Media's Influence on Canadian Politics,* Toronto: Nelson, 1990

Barbara Frum.
Photo courtesy of National Archives of Canada/ CBC Collection

Fugitive, The

U.S. Adventure/Melodrama

Popularly known as the longest chase sequence in television history, the original series of *The Fugitive* ran through 118 episodes before a climactic two-part episode brought this highly regarded program to a close, with all the fundamental story strands concluded. The wrap-up ending was a rather rare and unusual decision on behalf of the producers as well as something of a television "first." Premiering on ABC on Tuesday September 17, 1963, *The Fugitive* went on to present some of the most fascinating human-condition dramas of that decade, all told in a tight, self-contained semidocumentary style. By its second season, the program was ranked fifth in the ratings (27.9) and later received an Emmy Award for Outstanding Dramatic Series of 1965. For its fourth and final season, the program was produced in color, having enjoyed three years of suitably film-noir-like black-and-white photography, ending on a high note that drew the highest TV audience rating (72 percent) up to that time.

Based on a six-page format, inspired by Victor Hugo's *Les Miserables,* by writer-producer (and *Maverick* and *77 Sunset Strip* creator) Roy Huggins, ABC brought in executive producer Quinn Martin to supervise the project. He in turn brought on board line producer Alan Armer (who went on to oversee 90 episodes) and hired David Janssen to play the title character. While Huggins's original outline saw the wrongly convicted character behave like an oddball, since society was treating him like one anyway, Mar-

The Fugitive, David Janssen, 1963–67.
Courtesy of the Everett Collection

tin's concept of the character was something less bizarre: a put-upon but basically decent person. At first, however, ABC executives worried that perhaps viewers would feel the only honorable thing for Kimble to do would be to turn himself in. Martin's production expertise, evidenced in the footage the executives viewed, changed their minds. In the pilot episode, "Fear in a Desert City," the audience was introduced to the story of Dr. Richard Kimble, arriving home in the fictional town of Stafford, Indiana, to witness a one-armed man running from his house, leaving behind Kimble's murdered wife. In the same episode, "blind justice" saw fit to charge Kimble himself with the murder and sentence him to death. This narrative immediately aroused viewer sympathy and interest. That the train en route to the prison where Kimble was to be executed was accidentally derailed, rendering his captor Lieutenant Philip Gerard unconscious and thus allowing Kimble to escape, propelled the hero into a "willed irresponsibility without a concomitant sense of guilt," as Roy Hug-

gins put it. In other words, the (mid-1960s) TV viewer felt perfectly at ease with this particular "outlaw" because what was happening was not his fault.

Not unlike the hero of the western, which U.S. television had embraced since the 1950s and with which it still had something of an infatuation, Kimble had the appeal of the rootless wanderer whose commitments to jobs, women, or society were temporary, yet who at the same time deserved the viewer's sympathy as something of a tragic figure. The series' and the introspective character's success rested largely with the appeal of actor David Janssen's intense portrayal (Janssen's first television hit had been as the lead in the slick *Richard Diamond, Private Detective* series of the late 1950s). The drama of the stories derived not so much from the transient occupations of the fleeing hero (such as sail mender in Hank Searls's "Never Wave Good-bye" or dog handler in Harry Kronman's "Bloodline") but from the dilemma of the Kimble character himself, something Janssen was able to convey with an almost nervous charm.

The other principal members of the cast were Canadian actor Barry Morse as the relentless, Javert-like Lieutenant Gerard, who only appeared in about one out of four stories but who seemed always ominously present; Jacqueline Scott as Kimble's sister, Donna Taft; Diane Brewster as Kimble's wife, Helen (in occasional flashbacks); and the burly Bill Raisch as the elusive one-armed man, Fred Johnson. Raisch, who had lost his right arm during World War II but nevertheless went on to become a stand-in for Burt Lancaster, may have been the prime motivation for Kimble to stay one step ahead of the law, but his character was rarely seen on-screen; during the first two years of production, Raisch worked on the program only four days.

Using the general format of an anthology show, but with continuing characters (in the manner of the contemporary Herbert Leonard series *Naked City* and *Route 66*), the producers, writers, and directors were given license to deal with characters, settings, and stories not usually associated with what was in essence a simple man-on-the-run theme. Under various nondescript aliases (but most frequently as "Jim"), Kimble traversed the United States in pursuit of the one-armed man, and along the way became involved with ordinary people who were usually at an emotional crossroads in their lives. The opportunities for some magnificent guest performances as well as interesting locations were immense (in the early years of production, the crew spent six days on each episode with about three of those days on location): Sandy Dennis in Alain Caillou and Harry Kronman's "The Other Side of the Mountain" (West Virginia), Jack Klugman in Peter Germano and Kronman's "Terror at High Point" (Salt Lake City, Utah), Eileen Heckart in Al C. Ward's "Angels Travel on Lonely Roads," parts one and two (Revenna, Nevada, and Sacramento, California), Jack Weston in Robert Pirosh's "Fatso" (Louisville, Kentucky). The series also featured a number of interesting directors, including Ida Lupino, Laslo Benedek, Walter Grauman, Robert Butler, Richard Donner, Mark Rydell, Gerd Oswald, and Joseph Sargent; Barry Morse even had an opportunity to direct an episode.

Then, on Tuesday, August 29, 1967, "the running stopped." So declared actor William Conrad in his final *Fugitive* narration after four years of keeping viewers tuned in to Kimble's circumstances and thoughts. By the fourth year of production, Janssen was physically and emotionally exhausted. When ABC, which had grossed an estimated $30 million on the series, suggested a fifth year, Janssen declined the offer and Quinn Martin, in a move quite unorthodox to series television, decided to bring Kimble's story to a conclusion. The definitive two-part episode, "The Judgment," written by George Eckstein and Michael Zagor, and directed by Don Medford, saw Kimble track the one-armed man to an amusement park in Santa Monica, California, where in a climactic fight, with Kimble about to be killed, the real murderer is shot down by Gerard. The final episode pulled a Nielsen score of 45.9. Now, with Kimble exonerated, both he and Gerard were free to pursue their own paths. Janssen, too, continued his own career. After *The Fugitive* he starred in *O'Hara, U.S. Treasury* (1971–72) and *Harry O* (1974–76).

While other series with similar themes followed (*Run for Your Life;* the comedy *Run, Buddy, Run*), it is to *The Fugitive*'s credit that it remains one of the more fondly remembered drama series of the 1960s. Harrison Ford starred as an energetic Kimble in Warner Brothers' successful 1993 feature remake, *The Fugitive,* with Tommy Lee Jones as Gerard. Jones was recalled for the unfortunate film sequel-of-sorts, *U.S. Marshals* (1998), reprising his character Chief Deputy Marshal Sam Gerard. The only actual connection of this movie to the original television series was the statement "based on characters created by Roy Huggins" in the film's credits. Two years later, in October 2000, CBS premiered a remake of *The Fugitive* series. Warner Brothers Television chose the 1993 movie as the source, rather than the 1960s drama original, and the resulting program shared little more than the motions of the original premise, lacking a comparably deep exploration of the characters. The new version lasted only one season.

TISE VAHIMAGI

See also **Jannsen, David; Martin, Quinn**

Cast (1963–67 version)

Dr. Richard Kimble	David Janssen
Lieutenant Philip Gerard	Barry Morse
Captain Carpenter (1963–64)	Paul Birch
Donna Taft	Jacqueline Scott
Fred Johnson (the one-armed man)	Bill Raisch

Narrator (1963–67 version)
William Conrad

Producers (1963–67 version)
Alan A. Armer (1963–66), Wilton Schiller (1966–67), George Eckstein (1966–67)

Cast (2000–01 version)

Dr. Richard Kimble	Tim Daly
Lieutenant Philip Gerard	Mykelti Williamson
The One-Armed Man	Stephen Lang

Producers (2000–01 version)
D. Scott Easton, David Ehrman, R.W. Goodwin, Vladimir Stefoff

Programming History

120 episodes
ABC
September 1963–August 1967   Tuesday 10:00–11:00
22 episodes
CBS
October 2000–May 2001   Friday 8:00–9:00

Further Reading

Cooper, John, *The Fugitive: A Compete Episode Guide,* Ann Arbor, Michigan: Popular Culture, 1994

Coyle, Paul Robert, "Great Shows: *The Fugitive,*" *Emmy,* vol. 4 (November/December 1982)

Dern, Marian, "Ever Want to Run Away from it All?" *TV Guide* (February 22, 1964)

Harding, H., "Rumors about the Final Episode," *TV Guide* (February 27, 1965)

Marc, David, and Robert J. Thompson, *Prime Time, Prime Movers: From I Love Lucy to L.A. Law—America's Greatest TV Shows and the People Who Created Them,* Boston: Little, Brown, 1992

Robertson, Ed, *The Fugitive Recaptured,* Los Angeles: Pomegranate, 1993

Furness, Betty (1916–1994)

U.S. Actor, Media Personality, Consumer Reporter

Betty Furness—whose first regular television appearances were in 1945 and whose last were in 1992—enjoyed one of the most diverse, remarkable careers in U.S. television, both as a commercial spokeswoman and, later, as a pioneering consumer reporter.

Born Elizabeth Mary Furness in New York City in 1916, Furness was raised in upper-class fashion by a Park Avenue family. Her first job was in 1930 when, at the age of 14, she began modeling for the Powers Agency. Her pert and pretty looks, and her educated speaking voice, soon gained the attention of Hollywood. She was signed by RKO movie studios in 1932 and moved with her mother to California. While taking her senior year of school on the studio lot, Furness starred in her first film. She would go on to act in more than 30 films, the majority of them forgettable. After seeking greater fulfillment in stage roles on the West Coast, and after the birth of her daughter and the failure of her first marriage, Furness journeyed with her daughter to New York, hoping to land theater parts. A self-described "out of work actress," Furness found herself able and willing to break into the very infant medium of television.

For a few months in the spring of 1945, Furness endured the blistering heat of the lights needed to illuminate the set, and the inconveniences of other primitive technologies, to host DuMont's *Fashions Coming and Becoming.* By 1948 she was in front of the television cameras again, as an actress for an episode of *Studio One,* an anthology program sponsored by Westinghouse appliances. In that era of live television, many commercials were also done live, frequently performed to the side of the main set. Furness was unimpressed with the actor hired to perform the commercial and offered to take a stab at it. Company executives were impressed and offered her $150 per week to pitch their products. Following her philosophy of never turning down a job, Furness signed on.

At this point in the history of television, audiences had not yet grown jaded about TV commercials and the people who appeared in them. Furness's blend of "soft sell" and common sense was soon moving the merchandise. Her delivery was always smooth and memorized (she refused cue cards), her tone pleasant and direct, and her look pretty and approachable. In lit-

tle time, the company signed her to be its sole pitchwoman, and soon her pitches were selling out stores and she was receiving, on average, 1,000 pieces of fan mail a week.

Furness's place in the popular culture canon was assured after her work for Westinghouse at the 1952 national political conventions. Westinghouse was the conventions' sole sponsor, and, as the company spokesperson, Furness was in every ad. By the end of the conventions, she had logged more airtime than any speaker from either party and made her tagline, "You can be SURE if it's Westinghouse," into a national catchphrase. From January to July 1953, Furness hosted *Meet Betty Furness,* a lively, informative daily talk show—sponsored by Westinghouse—on NBC. Later she acted as hostess on the Westinghouse-sponsored *Best of Broadway* and made regular appearances on *What's My Line?* and *I've Got a Secret.*

Furness's affiliation with Westinghouse ended (by mutual agreement) in 1960. Though financially well-off, Furness wanted to keep working. She attempted to obtain jobs at the networks as an interviewer but found the going rough. Furness was facing the challenge of putting her commercialized past behind her—an experience shared by Hugh Downs and Mike Wallace. While waiting for another break in TV, Furness worked in radio and for Democratic political causes. She also entered the last of her three marriages when she married news producer Leslie Midgely in 1967.

While preparing for that wedding, Furness received a call from President Lyndon B. Johnson. Familiar with her work on behalf of Democrats, and impressed with her work ethic, Johnson offered her the job of special assistant for consumer affairs. Furness, again following her job philosophy, took the position and with it transformed herself from actor-spokeswoman into political figure. She later recalled it as the best decision of her life.

Still in the public mind as the "Westinghouse lady," consumer groups voiced criticism of her appointment. However, Furness threw herself into learning consumer issues, testifying before Congress, and traveling the country. Within the year she had silenced her critics and won over such forces as Ralph Nader and the influential consumer affairs magazine *Consumer Re-*

Betty Furness.
Photo courtesy of Westinghouse Electric Corporation

ports. Furness held her White House position until the end of the Johnson administration in 1969. Later she headed the consumer affairs departments of both New York City and New York State. Then she reentered broadcasting for the second act of her television career. She was signed by WNBC in New York specifically to cover consumer issues, the first full-time assignment of its kind. At age 58, Furness found herself pioneering a new type of TV journalism.

Over the next 18 years, Furness took a hard line against consumer fraud and business abuse. Her reports criticized Macy's and Sears department stores, and the women's clothing chain Lane Bryant, among other businesses. She was also the first to report on the Cabbage Patch Doll craze and on defective Audi automobiles. In 1977 her local show *Buyline: Betty Furness* won the Peabody Award.

Earlier, in 1976, Furness filled in as cohost on *Today,* between the tenures of Barbara Walters and Jane Pauley. From that time on, she contributed regular consumerist pieces to the program. Furness made her last TV appearances in 1992. Since battling cancer in 1990, Furness had abbreviated her workweek to four days. NBC used that reason to oust her, and she was

given notice in March in one of the most blatant examples of ageism in media history. Both *Today* and WNBC aired tributes to her during her last week, but Furness did not keep her frustration out of the press, nor did she hide her desire to keep working. A reemergence of cancer prevented the resumption of her career, however, and she passed away in April 1994.

It is hard to place Furness's career in a historical context because it was so eccentrically one of a kind. Of the legions who pitched products from the 1950s and 1960s, hers remains the only name still very much a part of popular history. In her movement from political insider to TV commentator, she laid the groundwork for Diane Sawyer and Mary Matalin. In her work as a consumer advocate, she predated John Stossel and others who have since adopted that as their beat.

In assessing the career of Furness, one stumbles upon a feminist retelling of the Cinderella story: a smart, savvy woman who turned her back on TV make-believe and soft sell to embrace hard news and tough issues. That one individual's life encompasses such breadth and depth speaks well not only for the far-reaching talents of one woman but also for the progression of women's roles in the latter half of the 20th century and for the dynamic development of television.

CARY O'DELL

See also **Today Show**

Betty Furness. Born in New York City, January 1916. Attended Brearly School, New York City, 1925–29; Bennett School, Millbrook, New York, 1929–32. Married: 1) John Waldo Green, 1937 (divorced, 1943); daughter: Barbara Sturtevant; 2) Hugh B. Ernst, Jr., 1945 (died, 1950); 3) Leslie Midgley, 1967. Began career as teenage model, John Robert Powers Agency; movie picture actor, 1932–39; appeared in stage plays, including *Doughgirls,* 1937–60; appeared on CBS Radio, *Ask Betty Furness,* 1961–67; columnist, *McCall Magazine,* 1969–70; special consumer affairs assistant to U.S. president, 1967–69; worked for Common Cause, 1971–75; joined WNBC-TV as consumer reporter, 1974, and weekly contributor to *Today,* 1976. Honorary degrees: L.L.D., Iowa Wesleyan College, 1968, Pratt Institute, 1978, Marymount College, 1983; D.C.L., Pace University, Marymount College Manhattan, 1976. Died in New York City, April 2, 1994.

Television Series

1950–51	*Penthouse Party*
1951	*Byline*

1953	*Meet Betty Furness*
1954–55	*The Best of Broadway* (host, spokesperson)
1976–92	*Today Show*

Films (selected)

Renegades of the West, 1932; *Scarlet River,* 1933; *Headline Shooter,* 1933; *Crossfire,* 1933; *Midshipman Jack,* 1933; *Professional Sweetheart,* 1933; *Emergency Call,* 1933; *Lucky Devils,* 1933; *Beggars in Ermine,* 1934; *Life of Vergie Winters,* 1934; *A Wicked Woman,* 1934; *The Band Plays On,* 1934; *Aggie Appleby,* 1934; *Beggars in Ermine,* 1934; *Gridiron Flash,* 1935; *Calm Yourself,* 1934; *McFadden's Flats,* 1935; *Here Comes Cookie,* 1935; *Keeper of the Bees,* 1935; *Magnificent Obsession,* 1935; *Mister Cinderella,* 1936; *All-American Chump,* 1936; *Swing Time,* 1936; *The President's Mystery,* 1936; *Mama Steps Out,* 1937; *They Wanted to Marry,* 1937; *Fair Warning,* 1937; *North of Shanghai,* 1939.

Radio

Dimensions, 1962; *Ask Betty Furness,* 1961–67.

Stage (selected)

Doughgirls.

Further Reading

O'Dell, Cary, *Women Pioneers in Television,* Jefferson, North Carolina: McFarland, 1996

G

Game Shows. *See* **Quiz and Game Shows**

Garner, James (1928–)

U.S. Actor

James Garner has been called the United States' finest television actor; he has been compared more than once to Cary Grant but also has been deemed dependably folksy. Possessed of a natural gift for humor, a charm that works equally well for romantic comedy and tongue-in-cheek adventure, Garner patented the persona of the reluctant hero as his own early in his career but also exhibited an understated flair for drama that has deepened with age. Garner began his television career in the 1950s, becoming a movie star in short order, and still maintains an active presence in both media.

Transplanted to Hollywood after a knockabout adolescence and stints in the merchant marine and Korea, the strapping Oklahoman came to acting almost by chance, at the urging of an old friend-turned-talent agent. Although his first job, in a touring company of *The Caine Mutiny Court Martial,* was a nonspeaking role, it enabled the 25-year-old actor to work with—and learn from—Henry Fonda and led to a bigger part in a second national tour of the play. Spotted by Warner Brothers producers, he was hired for small parts on two episodes of the western series *Cheyenne,*

after which the studio signed him to a contract. After a turn as a con man in an installment of the anthology *Conflict* and small parts in two Warner features, Garner landed a major role as Marlon Brando's pal in *Sayonara.* On the heels of this breakthrough, Garner was signed as the lead in *Maverick,* a new western series created by Roy Huggins. As wandering gambler Bret Maverick, Garner perfected a persona that would remain with him throughout his career: the lovable con man with a soul of honor and a streak of larceny. *Maverick* put more emphasis on humor than gunplay, but while Bret and brother Bart (Jack Kelly) were a bit more pragmatic (not to say cowardly) than most TV heroes, the series was not a wholesale satire on westerns, although it did parody the genre, and TV favorites like *Bonanza,* on occasion.

Immediately upon signing as Maverick, Garner found himself cast in leading roles in Warner Brothers features. He made three routine films for the studio during breaks from the series—but he was still being paid as a television contract player. When Warner suspended the young star in 1960 during a writers' strike,

James Garner.
Courtesy of the Everett Collection

Garner walked off the series and out of his contract. The studio sued, and lost, and Garner would not return to television, apart from guest shots in comedy-variety shows, or golf tournaments, for a decade.

Garner made a comfortable transition to features, becoming a bankable box-office name in the early 1960s. He made 18 features during the decade, a mix of adventures (*The Great Escape*), westerns (*Duel at Diablo*), and romantic comedies (*The Thrill of It All*). Garner tested his dramatic muscles in downbeat psychological thrillers like *Mister Buddwing* and made a calculated turn against type as a grim, vengeful Wyatt Earp in *Hour of the Gun,* but his most successful films emphasized his innate charm and flair for irony. Save for a boost from the tongue-in-cheek western *Support Your Local Sheriff,* by the late 1960s Garner's drawing power as a movie star was in decline.

Garner returned to form, and to television, in 1971 with the turn-of-the-century western *Nichols*. The series also marked Garner's return to Warner Brothers, this time as a partner and coproducer (through his Cherokee Productions) rather than an employee. *Nichols* was an affectionate depiction of the death of

the old west, with Garner cast in the title role as the sheriff of a small Arizona town (also called Nichols), circa 1914. Nichols was an unwilling lawman, who did not carry a gun and who rode a motorcycle instead of a horse; he was amiably shady à la Maverick, but more greedy and less honorable. An innovative concept peopled with offbeat characters, *Nichols* premiered to mediocre ratings that were not aided by schedule juggling. The network, theorizing that Garner's character was too avaricious and unlikable, decreed a change: Sheriff Nichols was murdered in the last episode aired and replaced by his more stalwart twin brother Jim Nichols. Before the strategy could be tested in additional episodes, or an additional season, the program was canceled. It remains the actor's favorite among his own series.

After returning to the big screen for a few fairly undistinguished features (e.g., *They Only Kill Their Masters*), in 1974 Garner was cast in what might be called the second defining role of his television career, as laid-back private detective Jim Rockford in *The Rockford Files*. A product of writer-producers Roy Huggins and Stephen J. Cannell, *Rockford* was in some ways an updated version of *Maverick*, infusing its mysteries with a solid dose of humor, and flirting with genre parody. At the same time, however, thanks to fine writing and strong characters, the series worked superbly as a realistic private-eye yarn in the Raymond Chandler tradition. Garner left *Rockford* in 1980, in the middle of the series' sixth season, suffering from the rigors of its action-packed production. Soon after, Universal sued the actor for breaching his contract, but in 1983 Garner, ever the maverick off-screen, brought a $22.5 million suit against the studio for using creative accounting to deprive him of his *Rockford* profits; six years later Universal settled for an undisclosed, reportedly multimillion dollar, sum.

Garner had dusted off his gambler's duds in 1978 for two appearances as Bret Maverick in the pilot and first episode of a short-lived series. *Young Maverick* (same concept as the first series, now featuring a young cousin as the wandering hero). A year after exiting *Rockford*, Garner revived his original roguish alter ego once more in a new series, *Bret Maverick,* with the dapper cardsharp now older and more settled as a rancher and saloon owner in an increasingly modern west. Despite good ratings, the show was canceled after one season, ostensibly because its demographics skewed too old.

Garner took on the occasional movie role throughout the 1980s, in such hits as *Victor, Victoria* (1982) and *Murphy's Romance* (1985)—which earned him an Oscar nomination—and such misses as *Tank* (1984) and *Sunset* (1988). But feature work became almost a sideline for the actor as he entered a new phase of his career, cultivating his dramatic side in a succession of made-for-television movies and miniseries. Apart from a fairly pedestrian role in the soap-epic miniseries *Space,* Garner's performances in *The Long Summer of George Adams, The Glitter Dome, My Name Is Bill W.,* and *Decoration Day* allowed him to explore and expand his palette as a character actor. He earned some of the best notices of his career (and two Emmy nominations) for his performances in *Heartsounds,* as a physician facing his own mortality, and *Promise,* as a self-involved bachelor faced with the responsibility of caring for his schizophrenic brother. Garner also won praise as Joanne Woodward's curmudgeonly husband in *Breathing Lessons,* and for his portrayal of the taciturn Woodrow Call in *Streets of Laredo,* a miniseries sequel to Larry McMurtry's *Lonesome Dove.*

The affable charmer Garner did not completely abandon the light touch, however. In 1991 he returned to series television in the half-hour comedy *Man of the People,* as a gambler and con man appointed by corrupt politicos to fill the city council seat of his late ex-wife. Independent and honorable (in his way), Councilman Jim Doyle managed to confound his patrons and do some good for the community while lining his own pockets. (Shades of *Nichols,* low ratings prompted producers to try to make the character "warmer" after a few months, but the tinkering did not help and the show was canceled at midseason.) Two years later Garner was cast as RJR-Nabisco executive Ross Johnson in HBO's *Barbarians at the Gate,* in large part to ensure that at least one character in the cast of corporate cutthroats would have some likability. When *Maverick* was reincarnated as a theatrical film in 1993 (with Mel Gibson as Bret), Garner was there as an aging lawman who turns out to have more than a passing connection to the Maverick legend. And P.I. Jim Rockford returned, his relaxed attitude and wry antiheroics intact, in a series of made-for-television *Rockford Files* movies airing between 1994 and 1999. Between *Rockford*s there were more features, more TV movies, and then it was back to series television in 2000, as the voice of God in the animated comedy *Bob, the Devil, and God,* and in a recurring role as a hospital administrator in *Chicago Hope.* In 2002 he began costarring in a new CBS series about the U.S. Supreme Court, *First Mondays,* playing the chief justice. With more feature films and television projects in the pipeline, Garner has never been busier—or better. As he enters his fifth decade as an actor, Garner demonstrates true maturity at his craft (he would undoubtedly call it a "job").

Described as "amiable" and "lovable" in countless career profiles, Garner's warmth and likability are best suited, perhaps, to the intimacy of television's small screen and serial storytelling forms. And yet from the very beginning, his career has constituted a unique exception in the hierarchy of Hollywood stardom, as he has passed back and forth with relative ease between television and feature work. Like many of Hollywood's greatest actors, he tends to play an extension of himself—like Jimmy Stewart, Spencer Tracy, Cary Grant, and his mentor Henry Fonda. Like them, Garner is affecting not because of his ability to obliterate himself and become a character, but because of his ability to exploit his own personality in creating a part. Admittedly, it is a different sort of talent than that of a Robert De Niro or Robert Duvall. Yet, as Jean Vallely has written in *Esquire,* De Niro is probably unsuited to television stardom—he may not be the kind of star we want to see in our living room. "On the other hand," Vallely argues, "you love having Garner around. He becomes part of the fabric of the family. You really care about him." Where De Niro impresses us with his skill, Garner welcomes us with his humanity. Which is why he may indeed be the quintessential TV actor, and why he surely will be remembered by television audiences as he has said he wishes to be: "with a smile."

MARK ALVEY

*See also **Maverick; Rockford Files***

James Garner. Born James Scott Baumgarner in Norman, Oklahoma, April 7, 1928. Attended University of Oklahoma; studied acting at Herbert Bergof Studios, New York. Served with U.S. Merchant Marines in Korean War (awarded Purple Heart). Married: Lois Clark, 1956; children: Greta, Kimberly, and Scott. Began career with stage production *The Caine Mutiny Court Martial,* early 1950s; offered contract with Warner Brothers, 1956; film debut, *Toward the Unknown,* 1956; title role in *Maverick,* 1957–62; title role in *The Rockford Files,* NBC-TV, 1974–80. Recipient: Emmy Awards, 1977 and 1986.

Television Series

1957–62	*Maverick*
1971–72	*Nichols*
1974–80	*The Rockford Files*
1981–82	*Bret Maverick*
1991	*Man of the People*
1994	*Chicago Hope*
2000	*God, the Devil and Bob*
2002	*First Monday*

Television Miniseries

1985	*Space*
1993	*Barbarians at the Gate*

| 1995 | *Larry McMurtry's Streets of Laredo* |
| 1999 | *Shake, Rattle, and Roll: An American Love Story* |

Made-for-Television Movies

1974	*The Rockford Files*
1978	*The New Maverick*
1981	*Bret Maverick*
1982	*The Long Summer of George Adams*
1984	*Heartsounds*
1984	*The Glitter Dome*
1986	*Promise* (also producer)
1989	*My Name Is Bill W.* (also producer)
1990	*Decoration Day*
1994	*Rockford Files: I Still Love L.A.*
1994	*Breathing Lessons*
1995	*The Rockford Files: A Blessing in Disguise*
1996	*Rockford Files: If the Frame Fits…*
1996	*Rockford Files: Friends and Foul Play*
1996	*The Rockford Files: Godfather Knows Best*
1996	*The Rockford Files: Crime and Punishment*
1997	*Dead Silence*
1997	*The Rockford Files: Murder and Misdemeanors*
1998	*Legalese*
1999	*The Rockford Files: If It Bleeds…It Leads*
1999	*One Special Night*
2000	*The Last Debate*
2002	*Roughing It*

Films

Toward the Unknown, 1956; *The Girl He Left Behind*, 1956; *Shoot-Out at Medicine Bend*, 1957; *Sayonara*, 1957; *Darby's Rangers*, 1959; *Up Periscope*, 1959; *Cash McCall*, 1959; *Alias Jesse James*, 1959; *The Children's Hour*, 1961; *Boy's Night Out*, 1962; *The Great Escape*, 1963; *The Thrill of It All*, 1963; *The Wheeler Dealers*, 1963; *Move Over, Darling*, 1963; *The Americanization of Emily*, 1964; *36 Hours*, 1964; *The Art of Love*, 1965; *Mister Buddwing*, 1965; *A Man Could Get Killed*, 1966; *Duel at Diablo*, 1966; *Grand Prix*, 1966; *Hour of the Gun*, 1967; *How Sweet It Is*, 1968; *The Pink Jungle*, 1968; *Marlowe*, 1969; *Support Your Local Sheriff*, 1969; *A Man Called Sledge*, 1970; *Support Your Local Gunfighter*, 1971; *Skin Game*, 1971; *They Only Kill Their Masters*, 1972; *One Little Indian*, 1973; *The Castaway Cowboy*, 1974; *H.E.A.L.T.H.*, 1979; *The Fan*, 1981; *Victor, Victoria*, 1982; *Tank*, 1984; *Murphy's Romance*, 1985; *Sunset*, 1988; *The Distinguished Gentleman*, 1992; *Fire in the Sky*, 1993; *Maverick*, 1994; *My Fellow Americans*, 1996; *Twilight*, 1998; *Space Cowboys*, 2000; *Atlantis: The Lost Empire* (voice only), 2001; *Divine Secrets of the Ya-Ya Sisterhood*, 2002; *The Notebook*, 2004.

Further Reading

Anderson, Christopher, *Hollywood TV: The Studio System in the Fifties*, Austin: University of Texas Press, 1994

Beck, Marilyn, "James Garner Makes a Decision to Act His Age," *Austin American-Statesman* (March 2, 1986)

Cameron, Julia, "James Garner Regards Acting As Just a Job," *Austin American-Statesman* (February 9, 1986)

Collins, Max, and John Javna, *The Best of Crime and Detective TV*, New York: Harmony, 1988

Green, Tom, "Garner Grows into Deeper Roles," *USA Today* (December 12, 1986)

Grillo, Jean B., "A Man's Man and a Woman's Too," *New York Daily News—TV Week* (June 10, 1979)

Hall, Jane, "The Man Is Back," *People Weekly* (April 22, 1985)

Harwell, Jenny Andrews, "James Garner: A Softhearted Maverick," *The Saturday Evening Post* (November 1981)

Hawkes, Ellen, "Gentle Heart, Tough Guy," *Parade* (July 12, 1992)

"James Garner," *People Weekly/Extra* (Summer 1989)

Martindale, David, *The Rockford Phile*, Las Vegas: Pioneer, 1991

Murphy, Mary, "Meet a James Garner You'll Hardly Recognize," *TV Guide* (December 13,1986)

"Playboy Interview: James Garner," *Playboy* (March 1981)

Robertson, Ed, *Maverick: Legend of the West*, Beverly Hills, California: Pomegranate, 1994

Robertson, Ed, *"This Is Jim Rockford…": The Rockford Files*, Beverly Hills, California: Pomegranate, 1995

Strait, Raymond, *James Garner: A Biography*, New York: St. Martin's Press, 1985

Torgerson, Ellen, "James Garner Believes in Good Coffee—and a Mean Punch," *TV Guide* (June 2, 1979)

Vallely, Jean, "The James Garner Files," *Esquire* (July 1979)

Ward, Robert, "Never Play Poker with James Garner," *GQ* (March 1984)

Willens, Michelle, "James Garner: On Being a Barbarian," *TV Guide* (March 20, 1993)

Garnett, Tony (1936–)

British Producer

Tony Garnett, producer, was a central figure in the group (including writer Dennis Potter and director Ken Loach) that revolutionized British television drama in the 1960s, creating something of a golden age.

Originally an actor, Garnett was recruited by Sidney Newman in 1963 as a script editor for a new BBC drama series, *The Wednesday Play*. British television drama in the 1950s had been dominated by classic theatrical texts done in the studio, normally live, with occasional 35 mm film inserts. The coming of videotape meant only that these productions were done live-to-tape. *The Wednesday Play*, with a commitment to new talent and new techniques, changed all this. Influenced by the theater of Joan Littlewood (*Oh What a Lovely War*) and the cinema of Jean-Luc Goddard (*A bout de souffté*), Garnett sought contemporary, overtly radical scripts for the series, which he was producing by 1964.

In 1966 he produced, with Loach directing, *Cathy Come Home*. Many British viewers were complacent that their nation's welfare system was among the best in the world, and this documentary-style film of the devastating effects of homelessness on one young family had enormous impact. It was the first of many controversies. Between 1967 and 1969, Garnett mounted 11 productions ranging in subject from the plight of contemporary casualized building workers (*The Lump* by Jim Allen, directed by Ken Loach) to aristocratic corruption in Nazi-era Germany (*The Parachute* by David Mercer, directed by Anthony Page). Garnett's productions became TV "events."

In the 1970s the pace slowed but not the combative quality of the work. In 1975 *Days of Hope*, a Jim Allen miniseries, rewrote the history of the decade before the 1926 General Strike as a betrayal of the working class by its own leaders. In 1978 another Allen miniseries, *Law and Order*, caused an uproar by treating professional criminals as just another group of capitalist entrepreneurs trying to turn a profit.

The Cockney criminal slang in *Law and Order* was so authentic that the BBC program guide had to provide a glossary. The language and northern accents in *Kes*, Garnett's first feature script, produced in 1969, were also so authentic that this story of a disadvantaged boy and a kestrel (small falcon) had to be subtitled.

Uncompromising politics ("self-righteous idealism" as Garnett recalls it) and rigorous authenticity created a passionate, if completely uncommercial, oeuvre. But Garnett then discovered the critical importance, the "disciplines," of popular genres during the 1980s, a decade he spent in Hollywood. Here he learned "a movie should never be about what it's about." Thus, for example, in *Sesame Street Presents Follow That Bird* (1985) and *Earth Girls Are Easy* (1988), he produced two films about racial prejudice disguised as, respectively, a *Sesame Street* adventure and a comedy about space aliens.

In the 1990s, back in England, Garnett revisited the subjects of earlier work, but now in popular genre form. *Between the Lines* was a hit crime series that focused on police corruption and set in the internal investigation department of the force. *Cardiac Arrest* was a bitter examination of the state of Britain's socialized medical system but in the form of a black situation comedy series. Garnett, characteristically, continued to rely heavily on new talent.

Tony Garnett has been, and remains, one of the major shaping intelligences of British television drama.

BRIAN WINSTON

Tony Garnett. Born in Birmingham, West Midlands, April 3, 1936. Attended local primary and grammar schools; University of London. Began career as assistant manager and, briefly, actor; script editor for producer James McTaggart on *The Wednesday Play* series, BBC, meeting longtime collaborator Ken Loach, 1964; first collaboration as producer with Loach, on *Cathy Come Home*, 1966; cofounded, with Loach, Kestrel Films, 1969; debut as film director, 1980. Chairman, World Productions since 1990. Visiting professor of Media Arts, Royal Holloway College, University of London, 2000.

Television Series (selected)

1975	*Days of Hope*
1978	*Law and Order*
1992–94	*Between the Lines*
1994–96	*Cardiac Arrest*
1996–2001	*Ballykissangel*

1996–97	*This Life*
1998–	*The Cops*
2000	*Attachments*

Television Plays

1962	*Climate of Fear*
1962	*The Boys*
1965	*Up the Junction*
1966	*Cathy Come Home*
1966	*Little Master Mind*
1967	*The Lump*
1967	*In Two Minds*
1967	*The Voices in the Park*
1967	*Drums along the Avon*
1967	*An Officer of the Court*
1968	*The Golden Vision*
1968	*The Gorge*
1968	*The Parachute*
1969	*Some Women*
1969	*The Big Flame*
1970	*After a Lifetime*
1972	*The Gangster Show: The Resistible Rise of Arturo Ui*
1973	*Hard Labour*
1973	*Blooming Youth*
1974	*Steven*
1974	*The Enemy Within*

1975	*The Five-Minute Films*
1976	*The Price of Coal*
1978	*The Spongers*
1979	*Black Jack*
1980	*The Gamekeeper*
1991	*Born Kicking*
1997	*Hostile Waters*

Films (selected)

Kes (also writer), 1969; *The Body,* 1970; *Family Life,* 1971; *Prostitute* (also director), 1980; *Deep in the Heart/Handgun* (also director and writer), 1983; *Sesame Street Presents Follow That Bird,* 1985; *Earth Girls Are Easy,* 1989; *Fat Man and Little Boy/Shadowmakers,* 1989; *Beautiful Thing,* 1996.

Publications (selected)

"Up the Junction by Nell Dunn," *Radio Times* (1965)
"Film versus Tape in Television Drama," *Journal of the Society of Film and Television Arts,* (Spring 1966)
"Recipe for a Dust-up," *Sight and Sound* (1998)
"Contexts," in *British Television Drama: Past, Present and Future,* edited by Jonathan Bignell, Stephen Lacey, and Madeleine Macmurraugh-Kavanagh, 2000

Garroway at Large

U.S. Musical Variety Show

Garroway at Large was the definitive program series emanating from the Chicago School of Television during the late 1940s and early 1950s. An intimate, low-budget musical variety program, this critically acclaimed series allowed its host, Dave Garroway, to wander the NBC studio "at large" during the actual telecast. In the process, the show combined a number of elements later defined as being in the Chicago style: improvisation, a lack of scripts, and interpretive camerawork.

Garroway began his career in broadcasting in 1938, when he landed a $16-a-week page position at NBC New York. Enrolling in the network's announcer school, he placed an unimpressive 23rd out of a class of 24 but did manage to find work as a special events announcer at Pittsburgh's KDKA. In September 1939 he joined the announcing staff at NBC Chicago's WMAQ radio outlet.

From the opening strains of "Sentimental Journey" to his trademark expression of "peace," Garroway's "hip," esoteric broadcasting persona developed and crystallized on Chicago radio. His local *11:60 Club,* jazz music and conversation at midnight, led him into network radio with his Sunday evening *Dave Garroway Show* and his daytime *Reserved for Garroway.* From there he moved quickly into network television. *Garroway at Large* premiered on April 16, 1949, within four months of NBC television beginning operations in Chicago.

Taking advantage of Garroway's intellect, unique personality, and relaxed, intimate broadcasting style, *Garroway at Large* scripts were more conceptual than specific and placed minimal emphasis on elaborate production. Under the watchful eye of producer Ted Mills, writer Charles Andrews, and directors Bob Banner and Bill Hobin, the show worked to create illusions and gently shatter them with the reality of the television studio. In the best tradition of Chinese Opera, commedia dell'arte, or the Pirandellian manipulation of reality, Garroway would wander in and out of scenes or from behind sets, stopping to hold quiet conversations with occasional guest celebrities, the home viewing audience, technicians, and cast members (vocalists Connie Russell, Bette Chapel, and Jack Haskell; comic actor Cliff Norton; and orchestra leader Joseph Gallicchio). Using raised eyebrows, slight gestures, and knowing shrugs, he communicated eloquently and brought a cool, glib, offbeat humor to prime-time television.

Garroway at Large broadcast its last show from Chicago on June 24, 1951. On January 14, 1952, NBC's *Today* show premiered in New York with Garroway as host. *Garroway at Large* was revived, but working under the production pressures of New York, the show lost much of the charm of the Chicago version and left the air after one season.

Through the 1950s, Garroway's workload increased to between 75 and 100 hours per week. In addition to his efforts on *Today*, he hosted NBC's *Wide, Wide World* (1955–58) and NBC radio's *Monitor* series. An exhausted Garroway left the *Today* show in 1961, and, while he continued to appear on television in various shows and formats, he never again achieved comparable success or popularity. Dave Garroway died on July 21, 1982, at the age of 69.

JOEL STERNBERG

See also **Chicago School of Television**

Regulars
Dave Garroway
Jack Haskell
Cliff Norton
Bette Chapel (1949–51)
Carolyn Gilbert (1949)
Connie Russell (1949–51)
Jill Corey (1953–54)
Shirley Harmer (1953–54)
Songsmiths Quartet (1949)
The Daydreamers (1950)
The Cheerleaders (1953–54)

Dancers
Russell and Aura (1950–51)
Ken Spaulding and Diane Sinclair (1953–54)

Orchestra
Joseph Gallicchio (1949–51)
Skitch Henderson (1953–54)

Producer
Ted Mills

Programming History
NBC
April 1949–July 1949   Saturday 10:00–10:30
July 1949–June 1951   Sunday 10:00–10:30
October 1953–June 1954   Friday 8:00–8:30

Further Reading

Adams, Val, "The Easy-Going Mr. Garroway," *New York Times* (February 12, 1950)
"Banner Exits Garroway Show for Waring Slot," *Variety* (December 14, 1949)
Crosby, John, *Out of the Blue,* New York: Simon and Schuster, 1952
"Dave and the Chickens," *Newsweek* (January 25, 1954)
Deeb, Gary, "Dave Garroway Ends Own Life," *Chicago Sun-Times* (July 22, 1982)
"Ex-TV Host Garroway Kills Himself," *Chicago Tribune* (July 22, 1982)
"Garroway Pacted to 5-Yr. NBC Deal," *Variety* (November 2, 1949)
"Garroway Signs," *Broadcasting* (November 7, 1949)
Gould, Jack, "Television in Review," *New York Times* (October 5, 1953)
Hamburger, Philip, "Television: The Garroway Idea," *The New Yorker* (January 28, 1950)
Metz, Robert, *The Today Show,* Chicago: Playboy Press, 1977
Morris, Joe Alex, "I Lead a Goofy Life," *The Saturday Evening Post* (February 11, 1956)
"Prop Man at Large," *Life* (October 10, 1949)
Railton, Arthur R., "They Fool You Every Night," *Popular Mechanics* (October 1951)
Remenih, Anton, "Television News and Views," *Chicago Tribune* (October 6, 1953)
Rothe, Anna, and Lohr, Evelyn, "Garroway, Dave," in *Current Biography 1952: Who's News and Why,* New York: Wilson, 1952
Stasheff, Edward, and Rudy Bretz, *The Television Program: Its Direction and Production,* New York: Hill and Wang, 1962
Weaver, Sylvester, "Dave Garroway...a Fond Farewell," *Television Quarterly* (Summer 1982)

Gartner, Hana (1948–)

Canadian Broadcast Journalist

Hana Gartner is cohost of the Canadian Broadcasting Corporation's (CBC) major evening newscast, *Prime Time News.* Her long broadcasting career has made her one of the most visible journalists in Canada.

In 1970 Gartner worked for Montreal radio station CJAD as both an interviewer and a features reporter. She subsequently joined Standard Broadcast News, a syndicated radio news service, as parliamentary correspondent in Ottawa, the federal capital. In 1974 Gartner made her first switch to television. She returned to Montreal as cohost of *The City at Six,* CBC Montreal's local daily news hour. The following year, she relocated to Toronto for a position as host of *In Good Company* on CBC Toronto television. In 1976, however, Gartner returned briefly to radio to host the CBC's signature network radio program, *This Country in the Morning.*

The movement between radio and television, and among various cities, is typical of CBC journalists. Not only does it contribute to their training. but also it allows the CBC to use its various radio and television stations as "farm teams" for network programming. This system has also helped launch many Canadian journalists on successful international careers.

In 1977 Gartner made her second and decisive switch to television when she joined CBC Toronto's local news hour, *24 Hours,* as cohost and interviewer. She also became host of a CBC television network daytime interview program, *Take 30.*

In 1982 Gartner was selected to cohost CBC television's flagship public-affairs news and investigation program, *The Fifth Estate,* which is best known for breaking new stories and for presenting complex issues in compelling narrative style. In this capacity, she has reported from around the world on a huge range of topics. In 1978 she was given her own summer series, *This Half Hour.*

Gartner's interview style combines toughness, honesty, and sympathy. She is capable of uncomfortable directness, and even irony, in her questioning of subjects; however, she does not stray into gratuity or nastiness. She is capable of revealing a personal attitude or orientation toward an issue without betraying journalistic objectivity. On the contrary, these qualities win the sympathy of viewers who identify with her. As is characteristic of Canadian news and information programming generally, the overall tone of Gartner's work is sober, with a focus on issues and their intricacies rather than personality or glamour.

In 1985 Gartner won the Gordon Sinclair Award for excellence in broadcast journalism. In 1994 she was given a CBC series of special interviews, *Contact with Hana Gartner.* In 1995 she became cohost of *Prime Time News,* the most visible journalistic position in Canada.

Paul Attallah

See also **Canadian Programming in English;** *Fifth Estate; National, The/The Journal*

Hana Gartner. Born in Prague, Czechoslovakia, 1948. Educated at Loyola College (now Concordia

Hana Gartner.
Photo courtesy of National Archives of Canada/ CBC Collection

University), Montreal, Quebec, B.A. in communications 1970. Married: Bruce Griffin, 1987; two children. Began career as radio show host, CJAD, Montreal, 1970; began television career at CBC, Montreal, 1974; host, interviewer, reporter, various television and radio programs. Recipient: Gordon Sinclair Award, 1985; three Geminis.

Television Series

1977–82	*Take 30* (host)
1978	*This Half Hour*
1982–95, 2000–	*The Fifth Estate* (host)
1995–	*Prime Time News* (cohost)
1995–	*The National Magazine*

Television Special

1994	*Contact with Hana Gartner* (host)

Radio

CJAD Montreal (interviewer), 1970; *This Country in the Morning,* 1976.

Further Reading

"Gartner to Join Mansbridge: The Current Host of *The Fifth Estate* Will Replace Wallin on Prime Time News," *Globe and Mail* (June 3, 1995)

"The *National*'s New Face: Hana Gartner Brings Gutsy Style to CBC TV," *Maclean's* (September 18, 1995)

"Star Power Gets in the Way (for Hana Gartner)," *Globe and Mail* (June 22, 1993)

Gelbart, Larry (1923–)

U.S. Writer, Producer

As producer of *M*A*S*H,* Larry Gelbart provided numerous contributions to one of television's most innovative and socially aware sitcoms. Beyond this accomplishment, he has been a dynamic force in broadcasting for more than 40 years. Gelbart has written for radio, television, film, and the stage. After leaving television in the early 1980s, Gelbart went on to produce feature films, including *Oh, God!* (1977) and *Tootsie* (1982). In the 1990s he returned to television to write a trio of notable made-for-cable movies for HBO: *Mastergate* (1992), an adaptation of his stage play parodying a congressional hearing about events reminiscent of the Iran-Contra scandal; *Barbarians at the Gate* (1993), which is based on the true story of F. Ross Johnson's attempt to purchase the Nabisco corporation and serves as a commentary on 1980s corporate culture; and *Weapons of Mass Distraction* (1997), a satire about media executives' greed as they battle to own a professional football team. Gelbart also served as executive producer for the latter project.

During the 1940s Gelbart began working as a writer for Fanny Brice's radio show, and as a gag writer for Danny Thomas. After a brief stint in the U.S. Army, where he wrote for Armed Forces Radio, Gelbart joined the writing staff of *Duffy's Tavern,* a popular radio program. He also wrote for Bob Hope, whom he followed to television.

In the early 1950s Gelbart became part of the extraordinarily talented crew of writers on Sid Caesar's *Your Show of Shows.* This group, which included Carl Reiner, Howard Morris, Mel Brooks, and Woody Allen, helped define the medium in its earlier days. Shortly after becoming head writer for *The Pat Boone Show,* Gelbart became disgusted by broadcasting's communist witch hunts and moved to England. While in London, he continued to work in British film and television.

In the early 1970s Gene Reynolds, who was developing a television version of the film *M*A*S*H,* enticed Gelbart to write the pilot script. Gelbart was leery about returning to American television, but he became interested when he learned that CBS was willing to allow the series to depict the horrors of war realistically. When CBS picked up the series in 1972, Gelbart became its creative consultant. One year later, Gelbart joined Reynolds as coproducer.

Gelbart provided numerous innovations to an idea that had already been covered in a best-selling novel and a box office hit. Recalling a Lenny Bruce bit on draft dodgers, Gelbart created Corporal Klinger, a character who dressed in women's clothing in hopes of getting a "Section Eight" discharge. Written as a one-time character, Gelbart's Klinger, played by Jamie Farr, became central to the long-running series. When

Larry Gelbart.
Courtesy of the Everett Collection

actor McLean Stevenson decided to leave the series, Gelbart was involved in the decision to "kill off" Stevenson's character, Colonel Henry Blake. This was the first time a series regular had met such a fate. Furthermore, Gelbart is credited with "The Interview" episode, an innovative script in which journalist Clete Roberts, playing himself, interviews the doctors of the *M*A*S*H* unit. Produced with a cold opening (no teaser, lead-in, or commercial), filmed in black and white, and shot in documentary style, this episode paved the way for the numerous innovations carried out by later *M*A*S*H* producers. After four seasons with *M*A*S*H,* Gelbart became worried he would grow repetitive and left the series.

In 1973 Gelbart and Reynolds created *Roll Out,* a disappointing series about an army trucking company set in World War II. Gelbart's last outing with series television, the highly touted *United States,* also failed to score with the public. One of television's first stabs at dramatic sitcoms (dramedy), it fizzled out two months after its March 1980 debut.

MICHAEL B. KASSEL

*See also M*A*S*H*

Larry Gelbart. Born in Chicago, Illinois, February 25, 1923. Served U.S. Army, 1945–46. Married: Pat Marshall, 1956; children: Cathy, Paul, Becky, Adam, and Gary. Began career as radio writer, *Danny Thomas (Maxwell House Coffee Time),* 1945; television writer for Bob Hope, 1948–52; best known for *M*A*S*H* series, 1972–76; artist-in-residence, Northwestern University, Evanston, Illinois, 1984–85. Honorary degree: LittD, Union College, 1986. Member: Motion Picture Association of Arts and Sciences; Writers Guild of America; Writers Guild of Great Britain; ASCAP. Recipient: Sylvania Award, 1958; Emmy Awards, 1958 and 1973; Tony Awards, 1963, 1990 (twice); Peabody Awards, 1964 and 1975; Montreaux Television Festival Golden Rose Award, 1971; Humanitas Award, 1976; Edgar Allen Poe Awards, 1977 and 1990; Writers Guild of America Awards, 1977, 1978, and 1982; Christopher Award, 1978; Laurel Award, 1981; Los Angeles Film Critics Award, 1982; New York Film Critics Award, 1982; Pacific Broadcasting Pioneer Award, 1987; Lee Strasberg Award, 1990; Outer Critics Circle Awards, 1990 (twice); New York Drama Critics Circle Award, 1990; Beverly Hills Theater Group Award, 1991.

Television Series (writer or writer-producer)

1952	*The Red Buttons Show*
1953	*"Honestly, Celeste!" (The Celeste Holm Show)*
1954–62	*The Patrice Munsel Show*
1954	*The Pat Boone Show*
1955–57	*Caesar's Hour (Your Show of Shows)*
1958–59	*The Art Carney's Specials*
1963	*The Danny Kaye Show* (consultant)
1971	*The Marty Feldman Comedy Machine*
1972–83	*M*A*S*H* (also directed several episodes)
1973–74	*Roll Out*
1975	*Karen*
1980	*United States*
1983–84	*After M*A*S*H*

Made-for-Television Movies

1992	*Mastergate*
1993	*Barbarians at the Gate*
1997	*Weapons of Mass Distraction* (also executive producer)
2003	*And Starring Pancho Villa as Himself*

Television Specials

1985, 1986	*Academy Award Show*

Films

The Notorious Landlady, 1962; *The Thrill of It All,* with Carl Reiner, 1963; *The Wrong Box,* with Burt Shevelove, 1966; *Not with My Wife, You Don't,* with Norman Panama and Peter Barnes, 1966; *A Funny Thing Happened on the Way to the Forum,* 1966; *A Fine Pair,* 1969; *Oh, God!,* 1977; *Movie, Movie,* 1977; *Rough Cut* (as Francis Burns), 1978; *Neighbors,* 1981; *Tootsie,* 1982; *Blame It on Rio,* 1984; *Bedazzled,* 2000; *C-Scam,* 2000.

Radio

Danny Thomas (Maxwell House Coffee Time), 1945; *The Jack Paar Show,* 1945; *Duffy's Tavern,* 1945–57; *The Eddie Cantor Show,* 1947; *Command Performance (Armed Forces Radio Service),* 1947; *The Jack Carson Show,* 1948; *The Joan Davis Show,* 1948; *The Bob Hope Show,* 1948.

Recordings

Peter and the Wolf, 1971; *Gulliver,* 1989.

Stage

My L.A., 1948; *The Conquering Hero,* 1960; *A Funny Thing Happened on the Way to the Forum,* 1962; *Jump,* 1971; *Sly Fox,* 1976; *Mastergate,* 1989; *City of Angels,* 1989; *Power Failure,* 1991.

Further Reading

Dennison, Linda T., "In the Beginning . . . ." (interview), *Writer's Digest* (April 1995)

Frutkin, Alan James, "When at First You Do Succeed, Try, Try Again," *New York Times* (May 5, 2002)

Kalter, Suzy, *The Complete Book of M*A*S*H,* New York: H.N. Abrams, 1984

Reiss, David S, *M*A*S*H: The Exclusive, Inside Story of TV's Most Popular Show,* Indianapolis, Indiana: Bobbs-Merrill, 1983

Rothstein, Mervyn, "Is There Life After M*A*S*H?" *New York Times Magazine* (October 8, 1989)

Geller, Henry (1924–)

U.S. Telecommunications Legal Expert

Henry Geller is a telecommunications attorney and law professor with a distinguished career in U.S. communications policymaking and regulation. He worked at the Federal Communications Commission (FCC) at several intervals from 1949 until 1973, serving as general counsel for six years (1964–70) and then becoming assistant to FCC chair Dean Burch. He later served as administrator of the National Telecommunications and Information Administration (NTIA) for three years (1978–81) during the Carter presidency. Geller's contributions to national telecommunications policymaking led to the National Civil Service Award in 1970.

Geller has since served as a telecommunications adviser for a number of nongovernmental organizations, including Duke University's Washington Center for Public Policy Research, the Rand Corporation, and the Markle Foundation. His advice on policy matters was solicited because of his experience as a Washington telecommunications insider, and because of his iconoclastic views on communications spectrum issues.

Geller has long espoused that the electromagnetic spectrum allocated for telecommunications purposes is a finite national resource, and that fees should be collected from all users of that spectrum. In 1979, while at the NTIA, Geller first broached the idea of auctioning spectrum for then-new technologies such as cellular telephony and wireless cable (MMDS). Free users of this resource such as radio and television broadcasters were adamantly opposed to such proposals, claiming that they (the broadcasters) were serving the public interest by providing news and other informative programming.

Geller felt that broadcasters, especially at the local level, had neglected their public-interest programming obligations, and that the FCC should eliminate all "public fiduciary" regulation in favor of a fee-for-spectrum arrangement. The benefits of such a system, as Geller described it, would involve an end to the lackluster provision of public-affairs and children's programming, and would allow the public, rather than the buyers and sellers of existing broadcast licenses, to

Henry Geller.
Photo courtesy of Henry Geller/ Ankers Photographers, Inc

benefit from spectrum auctions. He proposed that funds raised from spectrum auctions be dedicated to the development of public broadcasting services—much like the traditional British model of public support for national programming.

The irony of Geller's position on spectrum auctions is that the FCC now conducts such auctions for emerging communications technologies such as Personal Communications Services (PCS). However, the revenues collected are allocated for federal deficit reduction instead of supporting public broadcasting. Henry Geller is a well-informed critic of the status quo in telecommunications policymaking, and the recent adoption of the spectrum auctions in the United States reaffirms a position that he has long advocated for the benefit of the public, rather than private, interest.

PETER B. SEEL

See also **National Telecommunication and Information Administration**

Henry Geller. Born in Springfield, Massachusetts, February 14, 1924. Educated at University of Michigan, B.S., 1943; Northwestern Law School, J.D. Law

clerk for Illinois Supreme Court Justice Walter V. Schaffer, 1950; attorney, Federal Communications Commission (FCC), 1949–50, 1952–55, and 1961–73; general counsel, FCC, 1964–70; special assistant to the chair, 1970; helped write cable television rules and definitive explication of the Fairness Doctrine, 1972; worked on projects concerning communications law, Rand Corporation, 1973–74; Communications Fellow, Aspen Institute Program on Communications and Society, 1975; consultant, House Communications Subcommittee, 1976; assistant secretary, Communications and Information and Administrator of the National Telecommunications and Information Administration (NTIA), U.S. Department of Commerce, functioned as chief adviser to President Jimmy Carter on telecommunications policy, 1978–81; founder and director of the Washington Center for Public Policy Research, 1981–89; professor (of practice), Duke University, 1981–89; communications fellow, John and Mary R. Markle Foundation, from 1990; senior fellow, Annenberg Washington Program, 1991–96. Recipient, National Civil Service Award, 1970.

Publications (selected)

The Fairness Doctrine in Broadcasting, 1973
Newspaper-Television Station Cross Ownership: Options for Federal Action, with Walter S. Baer and Joseph A. Grundfest, 1974
A Modest Proposal to Reform the Federal Communications Commission, 1974
The Mandatory Origination Requirement for Cable Systems, 1974
Charging for Spectrum Use, with D. Lambert, 1989
"Looking Not Far into the Future," *Society* (July–August 1989)
"Baby Bells As Information Servers," *New York Times* (November 27, 1991)
Fibre Optics: An Option for a New Policy, 1991
1995–2005: Regulatory Reform for Principal Electronic Media, 1994
"Fairness and the Public Trustee Concept: Time to Move On," *Federal Communications Law Journal* (October 1994)

Further Reading

Jessell, Harry A., "The Government Can't Do Quality . . . At All" (interview), *Broadcasting and Cable* (August 15, 1994)
"Regulation, Deregulation, and the Future of Communication Policy: At New York Seminar, Media Watchers Assess the Regulatory Climate," *Broadcasting* (November 21, 1988)
"Turmoil over Takeovers: The Subject of Takeovers—Long Simmering on Washington Burners—Came to a Boil Last Week," *Broadcasting* (July 15, 1985)

Gender and Television

In a two-part article written for *TV Guide* in 1964, Betty Friedan, author of *The Feminine Mystique,* claimed that television represented the American woman as a "stupid, unattractive, insecure little household drudge who spends her martyred, mindless, boring days dreaming of love—and plotting nasty revenge against her husband." Almost 30 years later, Pulitzer Prize–winning journalist Susan Faludi suggested that the practices and programming of network television in the 1980s were an attempt to get back to those earlier stereotypes of women, thereby countering the effects of the women's movement that Friedan's messages had inspired in the late 1960s and 1970s.

Although the analyses of Friedan and Faludi are undeniable on many levels, it is important to remember that television provides less-than-realistic stereotypes of men as well (although these stereotypes embody qualities—courage, stoicism, rationality—that society values), and the images of femininity justifiably disturbing to Friedan and Faludi are not necessarily read by female viewers in the ways intended by program producers and advertisers. Recent scholarship has studied not only female fan groups that rework television texts in their own writings but has also suggested that narratives and images are polyvalent and dependent on contextual situations for meaning. For example, television scholar Andrea Press studied women's responses to *I Love Lucy,* finding that middle-class women drew strength from Lucy Ricardo's subversion of her husband's dominance and Lucille Ball's performing talents, while working-class women tended to find Ball as Lucy Ricardo funny, but thought the character was silly, unrealistic, and manipulative.

While scholarship such as Press's, motivated by an agenda of understanding cultural products and practices, attempts to understand how audiences negotiate the meanings of gender and class in their encounters with television, commercial broadcasting also has a history of research into audience composition and desires. Of course its agenda is mainly focused on understanding the audience as consumers, since the economic basis of commercial broadcasting is selling products to consumers. As early as the late 1920s, market research suggested to advertisers the importance of the middle-class female consumer in terms of her primary role in making decisions regarding family purchases. Early radio programs included some targeted to the female listener. Advertisers found success with how-to and self-help programs that could highlight the use of a food, cosmetic, or cleaning product in their generous doses of advice patter. By the early 1930s, household product advertisers successfully underwrote serialized dramas ("soap operas") in the daytime hours, and their assumptions that women were the primary listeners during those hours meant that narratives often revolved around central female characters and that segmentation of story and commercial must conform to the working woman's activities as she listened.

Several of the popular radio soap operas made the transition to television, with many new ones created for the medium that would eventually eclipse radio in audience numbers. As with their radio predecessors, these shows were programmed for the daytime hours and featured commercials aimed at the housewife, that "drudge" Friedan described as the stereotype of the postwar American culture. Daytime hours on television also included game and talk/advice shows, whose rhetorical strategies assumed women's capacity as caretaker of the family's economic and emotional resources. The makeup of daytime programming on the broadcast networks has stayed remarkably the same over the years, although soap opera plots seem to take into account the presence of male viewers (not only making male characters more important, but mixing action genre ingredients into the narratives). Perhaps even more significant as programming strategy, game shows have given way on the schedule to talk shows.

This latter trend began with the tremendous success of *Donahue,* which started in 1967 as a local Dayton, Ohio, call-in talk show aimed at women. Host Phil Donahue was interested in serving the needs of the woman at home who was intelligent and politically sophisticated, but unrecognized by other media. Appearing at a time of considerable political and gender unrest and change, by 1980 *Donahue* was carried on 218 stations around the country, delivering the "right numbers" to advertisers—women aged 18 to 49. Oprah Winfrey also started locally (in Chicago) and two years later, in 1986, *The Oprah Winfrey Show* went national, not only beating *Donahue* in the ratings, but also becoming the third-highest-rated show in syndication. Winfrey is now one of the wealthiest working women in the country and has her own production company to produce theatrical and television films, of-

The Ann Sothern Show, Ann Sothern, 1958–61.
Courtesy of the Everett Collection

I Dream of Jeannie, Barbara Eden, 1965–70.
Courtesy of the Everett Collection

ten about African-American women. Like Donahue, Winfrey aims her show at intelligent women at home, but she attempts more intimacy with her viewers by relating her guests' problems to her own difficulties with weight, drugs, and sexual abuse. The success of Donahue and Winfrey led to a glut of talk shows on daytime television, and the fierce competition among them has resulted in an exploration (some would say exploitation) of once-unspoken or repressed experiences of gender and sexuality (transvestitism, homosexuality, prostitution, incest, adultery, abortion, etc.).

Ironically, prime-time television, once considered more "serious" than daytime programming, has continued to cause controversy in the 1980s and 1990s when dealing with issues (abortion, homosexuality) now regularly discussed on daytime talk shows. Prime-time television has been considered by the networks and media critics and historians as more serious because of the presumably "adult" dramas, mostly with male characters as central figures, scheduled during the late, 9:00–11:00 P.M. time slots. Of course, the unspoken assumption here is that these shows are serious because they appeal to male viewers, who are stereotyped as more interested in violence, the law, and the sometimes socially relevant aspects of nighttime drama.

Many prime-time dramas of the 1950s, 1960s, and early 1970s drew on the "masculine" emphasis of genres successful in other, prior media forms—novels, films, and radio. The western, the detective/police thriller, science fiction, and the medical drama featured controlling male characters, having adventures, braving danger, solving problems through reason and/or violence. Many critics have pointed to the goal-oriented nature of these generic forms, as opposed to the more open-ended, process orientation of the serialized melodrama assumed to appeal to the female viewer. Yet the prime-time dramas addressing the male audience have never precluded the development of characters and community. Some of the primary pleasures of westerns, such as *Gunsmoke* and *Wagon Train,* derived from their emphasis on community and the "feminine" values of civilization over the male hero alone in the wilderness. Yet, *Wagon Train* and two other long-running westerns, *Rawhide* and *Bonanza,* had no regular female characters. Likewise, medical dramas of the period, such as *Dr. Kildare, Ben Casey,* and *Marcus Welby,* had rational male doctors diagnosing hysterical female patients and, as in the western *Bonanza* or the sci-fi show *Star Trek,* whenever a serious relationship developed between a female character and one of the

Charlie's Angels, Jaclyn Smith, Kate Jackson, Farrah Fawcett, 1976–81.
© Columbia Pictures/Courtesy of the Everett Collection

Cagney and Lacey, Tyne Daly, Meg Foster, 1982–88.
Courtesy of the Everett Collection

shows' heroes, she would usually die before the episode concluded.

The detective and cop thriller tended to fit most securely within the action-oriented, goal-driven narrative form assumed to be compatible with stereotypes of masculine characteristics. From the police procedural *Dragnet* to the buddy cop thrillers *Starsky and Hutch* and *Streets of San Francisco,* women were usually criminals or distractions. In many ways, these were men's worlds.

This trend was borne out in the statistics gathered by media researchers: in 1952, 68 percent of characters in prime-time dramas were male; in 1973, 74 percent of characters in these shows were male. These kinds of numbers, as well as the qualities of the portrayals of women, spurred the National Organization for Women (NOW) to action in 1970. NOW formed a task force to study and change the derogatory stereotypes of women on television, and in 1972 they challenged the licenses of two network-owned stations on the basis of their sexist programming and advertising practices. Although they were unsuccessful in this latter strategy, NOW and other women's groups provided much

needed pressure when CBS tried to cancel *Cagney and Lacey,* a "buddy" cop show and the first prime-time drama to star two women. Conceived in 1974 by Barbara Corday and Barbara Avedon, two women inspired by critic Molly Haskell's study of women's portrayal in film, *Cagney and Lacey* was originally turned down by all three networks, only getting on the air after eight years. Producer Barney Rosenzweig worked closely with organized women's groups and female fans to support the show during threats of cancellation, after CBS fired the first actress to portray Christine Cagney because she was not considered "feminine enough," and during periods when the show aired controversial episodes on such topics as abortion clinic bombings.

Despite the controversy over *Cagney and Lacey,* by the time it got on the air, there were already other changes in prime-time dramas that reflected the impact of the women's movement and the networks' increasing desire to capture the female market in prime time. *Hill Street Blues, St. Elsewhere,* even the detective thriller *Magnum, P.I.,* with its Vietnam vet hero, had begun to emphasize characters' emotional developments over action, with the former two programs adopting the serialized form once more common in the daytime soap operas (*NYPD Blue* and *Homicide* inherited these changes in the 1990s). Made-for-television movies, scheduled almost every night of the week during the 1970s and 1980s often featured female characters in central roles, causing many critics to suggest that they filled the void of women's pictures now vanished from the theatrical feature film world. In the mid- to late 1980s, shows such as *China Beach* (about nurses in Vietnam), *Heartbeat* (women doctors at a women's health clinic), and *L.A. Law* (with both male and female law partners) suggested new trends in prime-time drama. Yet, in 1987, 66 percent of characters in prime time were still male.

The situation comedy, which filled the early prime-time hours from the early fifties to the present, has tended to be more hospitable to female characters, at least in terms of numbers. Because most comedy shows focused on the family, women were mainly seen as wives, mothers, and daughters. Within that context, the programs might center on the value of the mother's nurturance and work, as in *Mama* or *The Goldbergs* (which star Gertrude Berg produced), or marginalize her in decision making about the family's resources and children, as in *Leave It to Beaver* (the mother in *The Brady Bunch* of the late 1960s–1970s is heir to June Cleaver in that regard). Zany wives, who continually acted against their husband's wishes, were featured in *I Love Lucy, I Married Joan,* and *My Favorite Husband;* while *Private Secretary* and *Our Miss Brooks* represented single working women as only slightly less irrational. It would be wrong to suggest that these shows ignored gender tensions—some of the programs were fraught with them. In *Father Knows Best,* for example, although father Jim Anderson is the moral center of the show, his intelligent wife, Margaret, and ambitious daughter Betty are confronted in more than one episode with some of the agonies of the polarized choices (wife and mother or career) women faced in the 1950s. Likewise, Donna Stone of *The Donna Reed Show* questions the connotations of the media's use of "housewife" in one episode, and Lucy Ricardo of *I Love Lucy* is probably the most ambitious and dissatisfied woman in all of television history.

In the 1960s restlessness with domesticity appears in shows where the female characters have to literally use magic to leave their roles, as in *Bewitched* and *I Dream of Jeannie,* or in the girlish pretensions of would-be actress Ann Marie in *That Girl.* Although critics now point to her idealized feminine looks and her sometimes subservient response to boss Mr. Grant, Mary Richards of *The Mary Tyler Moore Show* was a refreshing relief from the frustrated women in sitcoms of the 1950s and 1960s. Coming on the air the same year NOW organized its task force, this show still

stands out in not compromising Mary's single status, in its development of her career as a news producer, in its portrayal of a character basically happy as a non-married, working woman. Her smart and sarcastic friend Rhoda was so popular with viewers that she starred in a spin-off show. While producer Norman Lear's *All in the Family* more successfully satirized male stereotypes than female, other Lear productions like *Maude* and *One Day at a Time* worked against earlier portrayals of wives and mothers. These women were married more than once, raised children, stood up for their rights and beliefs. Maude even had an abortion in one of the most controversial programs in television history.

Although sitcoms of the 1980s and 1990s, such as *Kate and Allie, Designing Women, Golden Girls, Roseanne, Murphy Brown,* and *Grace Under Fire* continued the trend of the 1970s in representing working women, female friendships, and nontraditional family formations, television producers during this period persisted in creating family sitcoms that banished mothers. Although in reality a statistically small number of households involve single fathers, *Full House, My Two Dads, Empty Nest, Blossom, The Nanny,* and *I Married Dora* featured men as both mothers and fathers (who sometimes have a great housekeeper/nanny). The mother was present in *The Cosby Show,* but some critics suggested she was too present, claiming the program hardly captured the reality of a working attorney who was also a mother of five. The show's depiction of Claire Huxtable as free from the tensions of career versus motherhood caused some critics to label her character "postfeminist." At the opposite end of the spectrum, *Murphy Brown* and *Roseanne* have come under fire for depicting motherhood in too "nontraditional" ways.

While current broadcast network programming arguably presents a greater variety of representations of women than in previous decades due to changes in gender roles in society since the women's movement, this is as much because the "new woman" is recognized as a consuming audience member as it is because networks feel a responsibility to break down cultural stereotypes. Such marketplace-driven political correctness even motivated the creation of Lifetime, a cable network for women, in 1984. At first relying mostly on acquired programming, which included many prime-time reruns from the broadcast networks, in the late 1980s the channel began producing original TV movies and programs appealing to women on the basis of central female characters and behind-the-camera female personnel, such as director-actress Diane Keaton directing a TV movie. When NBC canceled *The Days and Nights of Molly Dodd,* a "dramedy" about a wistful, divorced, working woman, Lifetime acquired the reruns and produced 30 original episodes of its own. While this decision did not generate the ratings hoped for, it was a great public relations move and raised awareness of the channel. Morning hours concentrate on advice shows for young mothers, and the rest of daytime hours are filled with reruns of shows with proven appeal to women, such as *Cagney and Lacey, The Tracy Ullman Show,* and *L.A. Law.* Although the channel refuses to identify itself as feminist—it only admits to avoiding programming that "victimizes" women—its existence does suggest that women are far from ignored by television.

Currently, the greatest gaps in television programming's representation of women probably reside in sports and news. Broadcast networks rarely cover women's sports (newer sports cable channels do a little better if only because they have 24 hours of coverage to fill), and when they do, media scholars have noted that the sportscasters often refer to female athletes by their first names and use condescending or paternal adjectives in describing them. Female TV news journalists have had their own problems in getting airtime and are usually submitted to sexist biases about feminine appearance. Women in television news divisions, both behind and in front of the camera, organized groups in the 1970s and 1980s to pressure executives to give women in these areas more power and representation. There were well-publicized sex discrimination and sexual harassment suits at this time, but change has come slowly. But CNN, a cable channel needing to fill 24 hours, has put more women on the air (including an all-women news show, *CNN and Co.*), and the profitability of increasing the number of "newsmagazines" on the air prompted the broadcast networks to include more female anchors in the early 1990s. Yet women are used as experts on news shows only about 15 percent of the time, an issue of representation as important as their presence as news anchors. Many media critics look to an increase in the use of women as experts as a possible catalyst for change in all areas of television programming. When women are seen as authority figures in our culture, their representation in fiction as well as nonfiction media forms will perhaps change for the better.

MARY DESJARDINS

See also **Bewitched; Cagney and Lacey; Donahue, Phil;** *I Love Lucy;* **Lifetime;** *Mary Tyler Moore Show; Murphy Brown; Roseanne; That Girl;* **Winfrey, Oprah**

Further Reading

Allen, Robert, *Speaking of Soap Operas,* Chapel Hill, North Carolina: University of North Carolina Press, 1985

Alexander, Sue, "Gender Bias in British Television Coverage of Major Athletic Championships," *Women's Studies International Forum* (November–December 1994)

Atkin, David, "The Evolution of Television Series Addressing Single Women, 1966–1990," *Journal of Broadcasting and Electronic Media* (Fall 1991)

Bacon-Smith, Camille, *Enterprising Women: Television Fandom and the Creation of Popular Myth,* Philadelphia, Pennsylvania: University of Pennsylvania Press, 1992

Baeher, Helen, and Gillian Dyer, editors, *Boxed In: Women and Television,* New York: Pandora, 1987

Brown, Mary Ellen, editor, *Soap Opera and Women's Talk: The Pleasure of Resistance,* Thousand Oaks, California: Sage, 1994

Brown, Mary Ellen, editor, *Television and Women's Culture: The Politics of the Popular,* Sydney: Currency Press, 1990

Butsch, Richard, "Class and Gender in Four Decades of Television Situation Comedy: Plus ca Change... ," *Critical Studies in Mass Communication* (December 1992)

D'Acci, Julie, *Defining Women: Television and the Case of Cagney and Lacey,* Chapel Hill: University of North Carolina Press, 1994

Dates, Jannette, "Range and Shade: TV's Women of Color," *Television Quarterly* (Spring 1994)

Davis, Donald M., "Portrayals of Women in Prime-time Network Television: Some Demographic Characteristics," *Sex Roles: A Journal of Research* (September 1990)

Deming, Robert, "The Return of the Unrepressed: Male Desire, Gender, and Genre," *Quarterly Review of Film and Video* (July 1992)

Dow, Bonnie J., "Femininity and Feminism in 'Murphy Brown',," *Southern Communication Journal* (Winter 1992)

Faludi, Susan, *Backlash: The Undeclared War Against American Women,* New York: Crown, 1991

Friedan, Betty, "Television and the Feminine Mystique" and "The Monster in the Kitchen." *TV Guide* (February 1964). Reprinted in *TV Guide: The First 25 Years,* Harris, Jay S., editor, New York: Simon and Schuster, 1978

Geraghty, Christine, *Women and Soap Opera: A Study of Prime Time Soaps,* Cambridge: Polity Press, 1991

Gray, Ann, *Video Playtime: The Gendering of a Leisure Technology,* London and New York: Routledge, 1992

Gray, Frances, *Women and Laughter,* Basingstoke: Macmillan, 1994

Heide, Margaret J., *Television Culture and Women's Lives: Thirtysomething and the Contradictions of Gender,* Philadelphia: University of Pennsylvania Press, 1995

Hill, George H., with Lorraine Raglin and Chas. Floyd Johnson, *Black Women in Television: An Illustrated History and Bibliography,* New York: Garland, 1990

Kaler, Anne K., "Golden Girls: Feminine Archetypal Patterns of the Complete Woman," *Journal of Popular Culture* (Winter 1990).

Lewis, Lisa A., *Gender Politics and MTV: Voicing the Difference,* Philadelphia: Temple University Press, 1990

Meehan, Diana M., *Ladies of the Evening: Women Characters of Prime-time Television,* Metuchen, New Jersey: Scarecrow Press, 1983

Messner, Michael A., "Separating the Men from the Girls: The Gendered Language of Televised Sports," *Gender and Society* (March 1993)

Nelson, E.D., "'Reality Talk' or 'Telling Tales'?: The Social Construction of Sexual and Gender Deviance on a Television Talk Show," *Journal of Contemporary Ethnography* (April 1994)

Nochimson, Martha, *No End to Her: Soap Opera and the Female Subject,* Berkeley: University of California Press, 1992

Press, Andrea L., *Women Watching Television: Gender, Class, and Generation in the American Television Experience,* Philadelphia: University of Pennsylvania Press, 1991

Rakow, Lana F., "Women as Sign in Television News," *Journal of Communication* (Winter 1991)

Rowe, Kathleen, *The Unruly Woman: Gender and the Genres of Laughter,* Austin: University of Texas Press, 1995

Sanders, Marlene, and Marcia Rock, *Waiting for Prime Time: The Women of Television News,* Urbana: University of Illinois Press, 1988

Schlesinger, Philip, with others, *Women Viewing Violence,* London: British Film Institute, 1992

Spigel, Lynn, and Denise Mann, editors, *Private Screenings: Television and the Female Consumer,* Minneapolis: University of Minnesota Press, 1992

Steenland, Sally, "Women and Television in the Eighties," *Television Quarterly* (Summer 1990)

Vande Berg, Leah R., "Prime-time Television's Portrayal of Women and the World of Work: A Demographic Profile," *Journal of Broadcasting and Electronic Media* (Spring 1992)

Veraldi, Lorna, "Gender Preferences," *Federal Communications Law Journal* (April 1993).

Ziegler, Dhyana, "Women and Minorities on Network Television News: An Examination of Correspondents and Newsmakers," *Journal of Broadcasting and Electronic Media* (Spring 1990)

General Electric Theater

U.S. Anthology

General Electric Theater featured a mix of romance, comedy, adventure, tragedy, fantasy, and variety music. Occupying the Sunday evening spot on CBS following the *Toast of the Town/Ed Sullivan Show* from February 1, 1953, to May 27, 1962, *General Electric Theater* presented top Hollywood and Broadway stars in dramatic roles calculated to deliver company-voice advertising to the largest possible audience.

Despite a long technical and practical experience with television production, previous attempts by General Electric (GE) to establish a Sunday evening company program had fared poorly. In the fall of 1948, General Electric entered commercial television for the first time with the *Dennis James Carnival,* a variety show dropped after one performance. A quiz program entitled *Riddle Me This* substituted for 12 weeks and was also dropped. In April 1949 GE returned to Sunday evenings with the musical-variety *Fred Waring Show.* Produced by the Young and Rubicam advertising agency under the sponsorship of GE's Appliance, Electronics, and Lamp Divisions, the program occasionally included company-voice messages. In November 1951 GE transferred television production to the Batten, Barton, Durstine and Osborn (BBDO) advertising agency, under whose direction the *General Electric Theater* debuted February 1, 1953, as an "all-company project" sponsored by GE's Department of Public Relations Services.

The first two seasons of *General Electric Theater* established the half-hour anthology format of adaptations of popular plays, short stories, novels, magazine fiction, and motion pictures. "The Eye of the Beholder," for example, a Hitchcock-like telefilm thriller starring Richard Conte and Martha Vickers, dramatized an artist's relationship with his model from differing, sometimes disturbing, psychological perspectives.

The addition of Ronald Reagan as program host at the start of the third season, beginning September 26, 1954, reflected GE's decision to pursue a campaign of continuous, consistent company-voice advertising. Reagan's role as program host and occasional guest star brought needed continuity to disparate anthology offerings. The casting of Don Herbert of TV's *Watch Mr. Wizard* fame in the role of "General Electric Progress Reporter" established a clear-cut company identity for commercials. "Outstanding entertainment" became the watchword of GE's public and employee relations specialists. Reagan, in the employ of BBDO, helped market the concept within the company itself. In November 1954 the first of many promotional tours orchestrated by BBDO and the GE Department of Public Relations Services sent Reagan to 12 cities with GE plants to promote the program idea, further his identity as spokesman, and become familiar with company people and products. By the time *General Electric Theater* concluded its eight-year run in 1962, Reagan claimed to have visited GE's 135 research and manufacturing facilities, meeting some 250,000 individuals. In later years, Reagan's biographers would look back upon the tour and the platform it provided as an opportunity for the future president of the United States to sharpen his already considerable skill as a communicator.

By December 1954, after only four months on the air with Reagan as program host, the new *General Electric Theater* achieved Nielsen top-ten status among all programs and was television's most popular weekly dramatic program. The format accommodated live telecasts originating from both coasts, as well as the increasing use of telefilms by Revue Productions, the motion picture production company of the Music Corporation of America (MCA). During Reagan's tenure as president of the Screen Actors Guild (SAG) in 1952, and again in 1954, SAG granted unprecedented talent waivers to MCA-Revue. These waivers allowed MCA-Revue to dominate the fledgling telefilm industry, as the studio could now simultaneously represent artists *and* employ them in telefilms it produced. MCA's stars appeared on Revue's *General Electric Theater,* and ratings soared. Many made television debuts in dramatic roles. Joseph Cotten starred in "The High Green Wall," an adaptation of Evelyn Waugh's *A Handful of Dust;* Jack Benny starred in "The Face Is Familiar," a comedy about a man whose face no one could remember; Alan Ladd starred in "Committed," a mystery about "an author who advertises for trouble and finds it." Joan Crawford made her only 1954 television appearance in "The Road to Edinburgh," a story of "terror on a lonely road." "The Long Way Around" featured Ronald Reagan and Nancy Davis Reagan, who solved "a unique marital problem to reunite a family." In a direct dramatic tie-in with a company-voice theme, Burgess Meredith portrayed "Edison the Man," a telecast coinciding with GE's commemoration of "Light's Diamond Jubilee."

General Electric Theater saturated its audience with Reagan's genial progress talk in introductions, segues, and closing comments, and with Herbert's commercials. From the viewpoint of its sponsors, the program's entertainment component seemed less important than audience "recall scores," "impact studies," and the "penetration" of company messages that culminated with the motto, "Progress is our most important product." Commercials from the 1954 fall season, for example, included "Kitchen of the Future," "Lamp Progress," "Jet Engine Advancement," "Turbosupercharger Progress," "Sonar Development," "Atomic Safety Devices," and so on. "Kitchen of the Future" achieved the highest impact score (90 percent audience recall) recorded to date by the polling firm of Gallup-

General Electric Theater "Tell Me Where It Hurts."
Photo courtesy of Wisconsin Center for Film and Theater Research

Robinson, whose specialists reported the *General Electric Theater* as "the leading institutional campaign on television for selling ideas to the public." Following a 1956 Herbert "progress report" on the subject of steam turbine generators and their contributions to "progress toward a fuller and more satisfying life," Reagan reiterated, "In the meantime, remember: from electricity comes progress; progress in our daily living; progress in our daily work; progress in the defense of our nation; and at General Electric, progress is..."

By 1957 *General Electric Theater* had hit its stride with a top-rated program package that was equal to the company's early technical proficiency in television. While GE's product divisions developed individual sponsorships to reach appliance, lamp, and electronics consumers via *The Jane Froman Show, The Ray Milland Show, I Married Joan, Ozzie and Harriet,* and *Today,* the *General Electric Theater* aspired to the overarching sale of "Total Electric" living. One telecast featuring Jimmy Stewart, for example, celebrated the first anniversary of the electric utilities' "Live Better Electrically" campaign and "National Electric Week." The closing commercial featured Nancy and

Ronald Reagan in the kitchen of a Total Electric home. "When you live better electrically," Reagan told viewers, "you lead a richer, fuller, more satisfying life. And it's something all of us in this modern age can have." In his 1965 autobiography, *Where's the Rest of Me?,* Reagan recalled that GE installed so many appliances in his home in Pacific Palisades, California, that the electrical panel needed to serve them soon outgrew the usual pantry cupboard and had to be relocated in a 3,000-pound steel cabinet outside the house. *General Electric Theater* was no less loaded with the corporate stewardship of personal and social improvement, expressed over and over by Reagan: "Progress in products goes hand in hand with providing progress in the human values that enrich the lives of us all."

In 1962 *General Electric Theater* left the air in a welter of controversy surrounding the U.S. Justice Department's antitrust investigation of MCA and the SAG talent waivers granted to MCA-Revue. The hint of scandal lessened Reagan's value as company spokesman and program host. As SAG president in 1952, Reagan had, after all, signed one of the waivers, and he later benefited from the arrangement as a *General Electric Theater* program producer himself. The suggestion of impropriety fueled Reagan's increasingly antigovernment demeanor on tour, and his insistence upon producing and starring in episodes combating communist subversion in the final season of *General Electric Theater.*

WILLIAM L. BIRD, JR.

See also **Anthology Drama; Reagan, Ronald**

Host
Ronald Reagan (1954–62)

Producers
Harry Tugend, William Morwood, Joseph Bantman, Stanley Rubin, William Frye, Mort Abrahams, Bob Mosher, Joe Connelly, Gilbert A. Ralston, Joseph Sistrom, Arthur Ripley

Programming History
200 episodes
CBS
February 1953–September 1962   Sunday 9:00–9:30

Further Reading

Cannon, Lou, *Reagan,* New York: Putnam's, 1982
Matthews, Christopher J., "Your Host, Ronald Reagan: From G.E. Theater to the Desk in the Oval Office," *New Republic* (March 26, 1984)
Owens, Patrick, "The President from G.E," *The Nation* (January 31, 1981)
Reagan, Ronald, with Richard C. Hubla, *Where's the Rest of Me?,* New York: Duell, Sloan, and Pearce, 1965
Wills, Gary, *Reagan's America: Innocents at Home,* Garden City, New York: Doubleday, 1987

Genre

Genre is one of the most useful concepts for understanding television from a wide variety of perspectives. Drawn from literary and film studies to distinguish between major types of narratives, television genres have become important categorizing tools for television critics, creators, executives, and audiences. Genre studies have intersected with major trends in critical television studies, drawing upon ritual theories, ideological analysis, and cultural studies. Even at the level of everyday viewers or *TV Guide,* the useful categorization of programming into genres like science fiction or soap operas is a central component of how television is understood and experienced around the world.

The origin of genre studies dates back to the ancient Greeks, as Aristotle's theory of literature distinguished between major categories like epic, tragedy, and comedy. As literary studies developed in the modern era, scholars looked at genre fiction as a facet of popular culture, considering categories like romances and mystery as key popular genres. Film scholars adopted this approach, examining the underlying structure and cultural meanings of important film genres like westerns and musicals. As television developed into the prevalent storytelling medium it is today, genre categories like sitcoms and game shows became part of a broader generic vocabulary.

Genres may be categorized by a broad range of criteria; probably the most central approach focuses on narrative structure. Thus the detective genre is predicated on a puzzling criminal disruption of the status quo, which the detective hero investigates and eventually solves. Likewise, romances and thrillers are dependent on their own familiar narrative structures. Another important way genres have been defined focuses on setting and iconography. Westerns, for example, might have a variety of plots (some even resembling detective stories or romances), but they are all set in a common era and locale, featuring horses, guns, and frontier décor. Medical shows, legal dramas, science fiction, workplace comedies, and espionage programs are all distinguished by their common set of locations, characters, and iconography. Other genres may be categorized by their intended audience reaction: the goal of comedy is laughter, while horror wishes to provoke a frightened reaction.

Television challenges these differing modes of categorization. Unlike film and literature, the television schedule regularly features both narrative and nonnarrative programs, and both fictional and nonscripted shows. A key aspect of genre categorization that transects both scripted and nonscripted programming is a reliance on particular *conventions*. Some of these conventions are tied to plot (such as the overheard misunderstandings typical of many sitcoms) while others are rooted in the setup of a given genre (game shows featuring prizes and contests of luck and skill). Thus a talk show might be identified by a number of conventions such as the empathetic (or controversial) host, an active studio audience, guest experts, and sensationalist issues. But there is little uniformity in what types of conventions are relevant across genres, as the importance of conventions like setting or intended emotional affect in one genre may have no relevance in another.

On the one hand, these different criteria for categorization are easily understood. Once viewers see enough of any genre, they can identify the common ground without even noticing inconsistencies between genre categories, as they soon learn to identify typical traits as part of a general set of expectations. But problems can arise with these various modes of categorization. For example, how might genre critics examine a program like *The X-Files?* The narrative follows detective story structures, but the setting draws upon science-fiction traditions, while the audience reaction often invites horror (and even occasionally comedy). Does the show belong to all of these genres? Or is it a program that makes genre categories irrelevant? In some ways both are true. Like many programs, *X-Files* mixes genres to a point that it cannot be viewed as a pure case of any one genre, but it still draws upon

Adam 12, Kent McCord, Martin Milner, 1968–75.
Courtesy of the Everett Collection

genre traditions to play with the form and formulas that are commonplace across television. To understand some of the show's more creative moments, it is important for viewers to be familiar with the conventions of horror, detective shows, and science fiction that *X-Files* tweaks in original ways.

This points to one of the functions of genre within television: it allows producers and programmers to more efficiently create and schedule television shows. Given the sheer number of hours that any network or channel must program, shortcuts are essential. Genres provide a shorthand set of assumptions and conventions that producers can draw upon to make a new program familiar to audiences and easier to produce. Some critics see this facet of television in a negative light, pointing to the formulaic nature of television programming and devaluing its creativity and originality. For example, Todd Gitlin has argued that television programming is inherently "synthetic," featuring originality primarily in the "recombination" of formulas and conventions. It is undoubtedly true that genres often serve as baseline formulas for producers, creating a core set of assumptions and patterns that can be drawn upon to make the production of so many hours of original programming more efficient and streamlined. Producers face the tension between originality and sameness, needing to rely upon formulas to make programs accessible and recognizable to fickle audiences, while still making shows original enough to distinguish themselves from the pack.

However, many of the finest works of popular culture have been rooted in genre traditions, from Sher-

Little House on the Prairie, Matthew Laborteaux, Melissa Gilbert, Michael Landon, Karen Grassle, (behind Grassle) Dean Butler, Lindsay Greenbush, Melissa Sue Anderson, Linwood Boomer, 1974–83.
Courtesy of the Everett Collection

lock Holmes detective stories to John Ford's cinematic westerns. This is true for television as well, as classic sitcoms like *The Dick Van Dyke Show,* detective dramas like *The Rockford Files,* and science fiction like the multiple *Star Trek* series all accepted the conventions of their genres and sought to explore the creative possibilities within generic boundaries. Even programs that seem to rebel against strict genre categorization, like *The X-Files,* use the conventions of their multiple genres to elicit and often contradict audience expectations. Thus a celebrated "art" program like *Twin Peaks* does not dismiss genres in exchange for a purer, original creative vision, but rather plays with the assumptions and conventions of soap operas, detective dramas, and supernatural horror to highlight the limits of formulas, while still embracing some of their conventional pleasures. It is hard to imagine television programming that operates outside of the system of genre, not because all television is too formulaic and unoriginal, but because genre categories are immensely useful to both the industry and audience.

The question of what meanings genre categories have for audiences and their broader cultural contexts has been the focus of much genre analysis from a variety of theoretical positions. One school of thought follows the pejorative vision of genres, pointing to the ways in which particular genres embody cultural ideologies and dominant norms. Following this ideological approach, genres serve as factory-produced formulas that standardize culture and limit the possibilities of both artistic expression and viewer stimulation. This position stems from the Frankfurt School theories primarily of Theodor Adorno, who asserted (before the era of television) that mass culture is inherently formulaic, repetitive, and lacking in social uplift and intellectual engagement. An ideological analysis of a genre like sitcoms would point to its inherent conservatism, as trite problems are treated as major crises and then unrealistically solved over the course of a half-hour narrative, often by promoting dominant ideals like consumerism and traditional familial structures. Ideological analyses of genres have looked at narrative structures as a central means of perpetuating dominant ideals through repetition and conventions, while some have considered nonnarrative genres like game shows as formulaic celebrations of capitalism and consumer culture.

Ideological approaches to genre assume a one-way flow of meaning from producers to programming and into collective audience consciousness. Other approaches pose the question of what uses genres serve for audiences themselves. An important development in television criticism focused on the ritual facet of genres, working through the particular cultural anxieties of a society through the repetitive narratives of a given genre. Horace Newcomb pioneered this ritual approach, examining a number of genres to explore their cultural function for American television viewers. He argues that, while sitcoms may feature exaggerated narrative closure that could reinforce dominant ideologies, this may not be their central appeal to audiences. Rather, the particular disruptions to the status quo offered by sitcoms serve as an arena or "cultural forum" to debate various positions concerning anxieties over assumed gender roles, generation gaps, and the balance between domestic and office life. Newcomb contends that the narrative closure may not be the dominant appeal for audiences. Instead, the ritualistic working through of cultural issues allow genres to function as sites of social engagement rather than escape.

This audience-centered approach has been developed further under the theoretical rubric of "cultural studies." Under this paradigm (as explored by John Fiske), television programs are viewed as open to multiple interpretations; while they often present a dominant ideological message, most viewers do not accept those meanings in full, as they make little sense to their own lives and contexts. Instead, the majority of viewers negotiate with the meanings encoded in programming, accepting some as relevant and rejecting others out of hand. A sitcom viewer might accept the consumerist messages in her favorite programs, but disregard the family values presented if they seem out of touch with her own contexts. Research on actual audience practices have often supported these theories, as people rarely see the messages of television genres as completely compelling and accurate depictions of their worlds; instead, most viewers pick and choose the facets of programs and genres that they find most pleasurable and relevant to them, while rejecting other messages as unrealistic or unpleasant. Cultural studies acknowledges that both ideological and ritual readings can be accurate for some contexts, but that to truly understand the possible meanings offered by a genre, we must look at the wide-ranging practices of diverse audiences.

The cultural studies perspective highlights one of the pitfalls of genre analysis: it is easy to overstate the uniformity of any genre category. As genres are a shorthand highlighting the similarities between shows—and thus glossing over differences—genre programs can often be misread as more consistent and uniform than they actually are. Looking at a genre historically is one key corrective to this position. The evolution of the American police drama demonstrates the wide range of differences possible within this seemingly uniform category. Programs from the 1950s, such as *Dragnet* and *Highway Patrol,* highlighted a fully functional criminal justice system, effectively upholding law and order with little personality or conflict. By the 1970s, the conventions of the maverick cop, bucking the unyielding system to more effectively dole out justice in unconventional terms, found its way onto programs like *Baretta* and *Starsky and Hutch.* The genre mixing of *Hill St. Blues* incorporated melodramatic serial storytelling into its gritty vision of urban crime, both humanizing the individual officers and the system itself, which teetered on the edge of breakdown for many seasons. The 1990s returned to more procedural concerns, with *Law and Order* and *Homicide: Life on the Street* focusing on the casework of humanized police, while questioning simplistic divisions between criminal and legal behaviors. All of these programs clearly belong to the police drama genre, yet they offer widely divergent meanings, conventions, and assumptions as to what the police drama says about its cultural context. Genre analysis has to look at the historical evolution of genres, rather than thinking of genre categories as transhistorical unchanging definitions.

One way of thinking about genres that alters the terms of the debate somewhat is to consider how genres operate as categories themselves, rather than as shorthand for their collected programs. Thus instead of examining the evolving meanings of police shows, we might examine how the television industry, critics, and audiences have made sense of the category of "police drama" throughout different contexts—whether police dramas are assumed to be critical or supportive of social norms, tied to real-life cases or functioning as escapist fantasies. Obviously these cultural assumptions filter into programs, as producers shape their work to convey their own take on the genre, and successful programs then reshape the assumptions linked to genre categories. But genre categories can be shaped outside of the process of production as well. Jason Mittell considers how the cartoon genre has shifted throughout its history on television via practices like scheduling on Saturday mornings in the 1960s and channel branding through the creation of Cartoon Network in the 1990s. As a set of assumed meanings and values, the cartoon genre changed from a mass-audience component of theatrical film bills in the 1940s, to a lowbrow, highly commercialized kids-only genre in the 1960s, to a hip, nostalgic facet of Americana in the 1990s, even when the actual cartoons themselves were consistent, as with Bugs Bunny shorts created in the 1940s. The study of television genres should look beyond just programs categorized by genre labels to consider how the categories themselves are constituted, challenged, and changed by audiences, industries, and critics.

One case study that synthesizes many of these approaches to television genre is Robert C. Allen's seminal analysis of the soap opera. At the formal level, Allen considers how the serialized narrative structure of the soap opera is its core definitional attribute, arguing that this structure elicits a particular form of generic pleasure for its audiences: witnessing the effects of narrative events on a community of relationships across the fictional world. To understand this generic pleasure, he suggests critics must take a viewer-centered perspective, seeing as soap opera fans regularly watch "their stories" for decades and thus experience the genre from a position quite different from detached critics. Yet Allen acknowledges that the genre is not solely a product of the programs themselves, noting how the genre term "soap opera" is itself a pejorative label, given by critics in the 1930s who dismissed the genre's dual facets of melodrama and commercialism. He explores how the institutional basis of the genre differs from viewers' experiences, and how these categorical definitions change over time, especially with the growing serialization of prime-time television, making soap operas a component of more mainstream and less stigmatized programming. Allen's example points to the importance of analyzing genres both from within the programs they categorize and in broader circulation among viewers, programmers, and critics, all as tied to historical contexts.

There is no doubt that genre remains an important facet of television programming and practices to this day. Even as many programs incorporate mixed genres to appeal to broad audiences and explore innovation through recombination, the importance of genre conventions and assumptions remains central. The rise of narrowcasting has foregrounded genres as a branding mechanism to label channels unified by their dedication to specific genres, from news to music videos, sports to science fiction. New technological developments, like digital program guides incorporated into cable, satellite, and digital video recorders, allow for genres to be used as a searching and sorting mechanism to find desirable programming, suggesting the continued importance of genres as an organizing principle for both the television industry and audience. Understanding the ways in which genre categories and programming continue to be used by producers, critics, industries, and audiences is crucial to the development of television into the 21st century.

JASON MITTELL

See also **Detective Programs; Narrowcasting; Police Programs; Soap Opera;** *X-Files, The;* **Western**

Further Reading

Allen, Robert C., *Speaking of Soap Operas,* Chapel Hill: University of North Carolina Press, 1985

Creeber, Glen, *The Television Genre Book,* London: British Film Institute, 2001

Feuer, Jane, "Genre Study and Television," in *Channels of Discourse, Reassembled,* edited by Robert C. Allen, Chapel Hill: University of North Carolina Press, 1992

Fiske, John, *Television Culture,* New York: Routledge, 1987

Gitlin, Todd, *Inside Prime Time,* New York: Pantheon Books, 1985

Mittell, Jason, *Genre and Television: From Cartoons to Cop Shows in American Culture,* New York: Routledge, 2004

Newcomb, Horace, *TV: The Most Popular Art,* Garden City, New York: Anchor Press, 1974

Rose, Brian G., editor, *TV Genres: A Handbook and Reference Guide,* Westport, Connecticut: Greenwood Press, 1985

Geography and Television

The importance of a geographical understanding of television lies in recognizing that television always has been produced for, has circulated across, and has been engaged through particular sites and different scales. In the 19th century, decades before the invention of the cathode-ray tube, "tele-vision" was an ideal and objective accompanying the development of telegraphy and telephony—technologies for distributing (through networks) sounds and images over distance. Collectively, tele-technologies and tele-communication became instruments of modernization, conducting commercial transactions and transporting people, goods, and information over increasingly great distances. In this respect, the idea of television emerged as a response to spatial questions and to modern ways of imagining and representing geography and mobility.

Is there such a thing as a geography of television? Since the 19th century the "televisual" never has been a discrete object but the assemblage and reassemblage of technologies within and across different social spaces and environments. Although one may choose to talk about the distinctive properties of television (e.g., as an industry, a technology, a narrative or cultural form, an audience), it is just as necessary to recognize that any definition draws strategically on examples of practices from particular locations where televisuality has been assembled, instituted, and made to matter in particular ways. Similarly, any such definition risks ignoring how these distinctive properties have always been site-specific, complexly conjoined, along with other practices, to particular environments and on different scales. Considering the televisual in this way makes untenable the notion that television has a single history and emphasizes instead that TV has been developed and deployed unevenly around the world, and that TV is as much a product of as a contributing factor to the redefinition of social space and territoriality. If, therefore, television can be said to have a geography, it is a geography produced, deployed, and made to matter in different and changing ways in and across different places and social spaces.

There are several interrelated ways to consider the televisual as a product of and as productive of social space. One concerns the commercial and institutional sites and networks of television production and broadcasting. Given that broadcast television emerged through the established national and local centers of radio broadcasting, its early geography of production followed radio's. Over the 1950s in the United States, for instance, national television production moved from New York (the center of national radio production) to Los Angeles (the center of film production), while various U.S. cities (more rapidly than anywhere in the world) developed and broadcast programming for their local populations. By the early 1950s most cities in the United States had at least one television station that was formed out of one of the city's radio stations and that was affiliated with a national broadcasting network whose central location was one of that nation's most prominent commercial and cultural centers. The capability, since the early 1950s, of remote broadcasting, and, by the mid-1960s, of remote recording by video, however, has meant that television, like radio, has not always had a fixed, centralized site of production. Over the late 1980s and early 1990s, the video "camcorder" (in conjunction with videocassette recorders for households) transformed the domestic sphere into a site of production for the television monitor; refashioned the television set as a technology of self, family, and domestic life; provided a portable accoutrement for personal travel; and occasionally became a resource for commercial television networks (e.g., clips on *America's Funniest Home Videos,* tornado-chaser videos for weather channels, and the infamous video of Rodney King's beating at the hands of the Los Angeles police).

Besides having been organized through commercial and institutional sites, the televisual has organized physical places and concrete environments, and their relation to one another. Some of this has occurred through televisual representations (visual and narrative constructions) of places and landscapes. There is, for instance, a difference between watching a sports event in a stadium and watching it on a television screen, even though the former activity has been coordinated with the latter in the age of television. The regularization of TV images and narratives also has shaped widely held assumptions about particular landscapes and places (the household, suburb, the city, the nation) and their relation to one another. For example, since the late 1980s, the ivy-covered outfield fence and brick walls of Wrigley Field, the "home" of the Chicago Cubs, and the oldest professional baseball stadium in the United States, have become through televised broadcasts (distributed nationally via WGN) one of the most widely recognized images of Chicago. Television has been instrumental in reshaping and renegotiating conventionalized representations of places. Television coverage of the collapse of the World Trade Center and of the "reclamation" of the site, for instance, has been instrumental in refashioning the identity of New York since the terrorist attacks of September 11, 2001.

While television has been one of many technologies involved in an ongoing process of constructing the identity of places and of remapping the relation among places, television also has aspired to and/or claimed the role of cultural atlas, a compendium of places (old and recent) that have mattered for those cultures that television has organized. Televisual representations of place, as a technology of touring, most recently have been organized in the United States through channels devoted exclusively to travel and tourism (e.g., the Travel Channel), although travel and tourism-oriented programs have become integral to other channels devoted to lifestyles (e.g., MTV, E!, the Disney Channel, the Food Channel), to weather (e.g., the Weather Channel), and to the popularization of scientific exploration (e.g., the Discovery Channel, Animal Planet, MSNBC's "National Geographic Explorer").

The televisual also has contributed to the organization and physical construction of places and concrete environments, and their relation to one another. There are very specific features of television's material infrastructure and circulation: the location of studios and transmitter towers; the use of microwave relay or satellite stations; cable strung from poles or buried underground; the uneven reliance upon antennae, cable, or satellite dishes for reception in the same neighborhood and in different parts of the world; and the local, regional, national, and global scales of broadcasting systems. Television sets, as an accoutrement of households and other interior spaces, have contributed to the design and organization of domestic and leisure spaces. The portability of television, not only within interior spaces but also outdoors (away from electrical outlets) or in automobiles and planes, has accompanied a broad renegotiation of mobility and of the relation between private and public activity spaces. In one respect, then, television viewing has been about one's relation from an inside to an outside, to somewhere else—that is, a tour from one's home, residential district, city, nation, or hemisphere. In another respect, however, the increased portability of the video camera and the television monitor has involved television's integration into technologies of travel and transport. Television viewers have formed cognitive maps of environments they inhabit in part through their engagements with particular televisual mappings of social space from particular places and through their capacity for moving about with portable forms of screen media such as television. Furthermore, through the circulation and consumption of representations of places, and through networks of distribution, the televisual has been instrumental in shaping concrete, material relations among places: for example, as a technology of mass suburbanization and "mobile privatization" during the 1950s and 1960s; as a burgeoning national network that realigned regions (as when the three major U.S. television networks broadcast civil rights demonstrations occurring in the South during the early 1960s while southern stations instigated local blackouts of those national broadcasts); and as a basis during the 1980s for the emergence of certain cities, such as Atlanta, Georgia, as new centers within a national and global cultural and tourism-oriented economy.

The spread and containment of the televisual have been fraught with political conflicts and inspired legislation over a variety of sites, borders, and kinds of territory. Campaigns to regulate the consumption of pornography, for example, have found television's place in the domestic sphere to be particularly alarming. In this case, regulating television involves politics and technologies for regulating the relation of the domestic sphere to an outside. In the case of the nation-state, the implementation of national coding of broadcast signals (e.g., NTSC, PAL, or SECAM) has served as an invisible border against the international flow of television broadcasting, or (as in the case of Latin America) as a means of facilitating the transnational circulation of Spanish-language television. In Western Europe, for instance, where there was a significant diversity of broadcast frequency codes, these televisual borders began to erode with the increased reliance upon satellite broadcasting, which occurred concurrently with efforts to organize a European Union. Still, language and other cultural differences have deterred a European televisual formation, and the difficulties faced in legislating and regulating the cultures of a "European television" have been a recurring impediment to actualizing the European Union or of treating television as merely another commodity in a European common market. The uses of television among Australian aboriginal communities have not only raised issues of autonomy, territoriality, and governance within and among these communities but have been the subject of the Australian government's efforts to implement policy regarding "national" broadcast space. And along with the impact of transnational televisual flows on the collapse of the Soviet Union, the televisualization of the dismantling of the Berlin Wall in 1989 attested to the capability of television to conjoin a global audience in an event that signaled a profound transformation in geopolitical borders. Moreover, that event also served as an occasion for national commentators and audiences to reformulate national cultural maps of the world. As these instances affirm, the location of television is organized through emerging and residual social and cultural formations, of which the televisual is one. However, the location of television is also organized through policies and commercial interests bent on preserving, or dismantling, residual formations or on nurturing or containing emerging ones—or on co-opting both.

The history of the televisual, then, is a history of how various sites and environments—domestic, urban, rural, regional, national, or global space—have shaped and been shaped through the place of television in a broad array of everyday activities. Emphasizing the sites and (overlapping or conflicting) territories of the televisual makes it impossible to conceive of a uniform and universal history of television. For instance, the televisual only became central to the formation of social relations and to everyday life after World War II, a period characterized by a broad restructuring of cities and of the relation between domestic space and the outside world. As Raymond Williams has noted, the expansion of cities and the proliferation of suburbs hastened at this time. The developments were sustained by technologies such as telephony, a greater reliance upon automobile travel, and broadcasting, all of which were supposed to facilitate flows to and from these new settlements. Williams's observations describe a general set of conditions, however, that were more common in North America, Britain, and Australia during the 1950s and 1960s than in other parts of the world. That is, the observations explain why television became more quickly and deeply embedded in the everyday life of some places, amid certain historical convergences, rather than others.

To say that the televisual lacks a discrete, continuous history is not to ignore that there have in fact been certain historically parallel, converging, and interdependent developments. For instance, the televisual developed through certain spatial logics and arrangements that had underpinned geopolitics since the 1920s. Television technology, along with the development of telephony and radio technology, all continued to be crucial in the social organization and conceptualization of national territory and sovereignty after World War II, such that the "national" could be defined as a networked space with a single center of cultural production (as London was to Britain, Hollywood to the United States, or Rome to Italy). Although the geographic connection between Hollywood film and television production after World War II deepened the global paths for distributing U.S. television programs, the global distribution of U.S. television was relatively meager before the 1980s because of the nationalized structures of broadcasting around the world. The rapid and widespread reliance upon cable and satellite technologies after the mid-1970s contributed to the erosion of a geography of broadcasting that had remained relatively intact since the 1920s. Throughout the 1980s, national broadcasting systems' competition, often with expanding local, regional, or "private" foreign companies, began to reconfigure that model of the nation. During the 1980s, some cities became equally or more aligned to flows outside their national boundaries than had previously been the case. And while in the early 21st century the increased reliance upon Internet sources of news and upon extranational television news sources have challenged the prerogative of national broadcasting systems as arbiters of "national representations," national television broadcasting (most notably the efforts in Western national television broadcasting after September 11, 2001, to brand al-Jazeera television as an unreliable source of news, while simultaneously relying on its images and news accounts to help cover the "war on terrorism") continues to occupy a position of authority grounded in the historical experience of viewers as well as broadcasters.

Since the late 1940s the development of the televisual has occurred through a changing set of relations between the home and other sites and spaces, through making certain environments available and open to certain populations (TV as a technology of settlement and "home"), through practices of social segregation (TV as a technology for maintaining distance and the "proper" place of populations, social classes, and identities), and through the maintenance of a broad social arrangement (a distribution/agreement) as televisual community. In part, this has been a process of linking the home to a circuit and assemblage of sites, vectors, and spaces (TV as a technology that matters in shaping a broad social arrangement). It has also been a process of aligning new domestic spaces, in new settlements, with already built (but, in the wake of resettlement, changing) places and spheres of community. The role of television in colonizing and expanding the domestic sphere and of mediating new and old places (and other flows between them) has not just involved the material networking of homes. It has also been contingent upon television audiences' investment in and mobility between the home and other sites. Such an investment has only partially to do with "watching television," but everything to do with television's role in mediating the places of everyday life. It has occurred in part through television narratives about settlement and domesticity. These narratives have mythologized certain architectural ideals of domestic space and domestic space's relation to other spheres.

The set design of ranch homes in TV westerns in the United States during the early 1960s, in series such as *Bonanza, High Chaparral, The Virginian,* or *The Big Valley,* contributed, for instance, to concrete and imaginary relations of suburban homes to suburban settlement. These sets drew upon the western genre's mythology of settlement for an era of planned development, appropriating the postwar ideals of other domestic narratives and domestic design magazines to valorize a "ranch" style (on a grander scale than most early postwar "ranch homes") for 1950s and early 1960s suburban "settlers." Television comedies produced in the United States from the late 1950s to the early 1960s rarely involved characters who abandoned or ventured too far outside the suburbs. Contemporaneous crime series, such as *Peter Gunn,* were set in an inner city where vice and eccentricity were made to seem beyond the realm of everyday life in the suburbs but, through television, having a vital connection to the domestic, suburban domain. At other times, U.S. television narratives (indeed whole series) have been about displacement and resettlement—a televisual discourse about television's changing relation to a changing material and symbolic environment (e.g., the Goldbergs' move to suburbia during the early 1950s on *The Goldbergs;* the Clampetts' move from a "simple," rural America to the suburban dream-world of Beverly Hills, California, in the early 1960s on the sitcom *The Beverly Hillbillies;* or the Jeffersons' move "up" and out from Queens, New York, to Manhattan in the mid-1970s on the sitcom *The Jeffersons*).

That television has played a mediating role amid the flows of people reshaping cities has also been evident in the postcable/postsatellite era when television became an invaluable instrument in the "revitalization" projects of certain cities. Particularly in the United States, where cable/satellite broadcasting first became widely established, Chicago and Atlanta transformed local network affiliates (Chicago's WGN and Atlanta's WTBS) into "superstations," capable of broadcasting across the United States via satellite and the rapidly expanding cable companies. Through sports broadcasting in particular, these superstations maintained a circuit of fans and thus of potential tourists to cities that were concurrently attempting to "rehabilitate" their old commercial centers as new tourist sites/sights through "restoration" projects. Wrigley Field became a nationally circulating image of a presuburban Chicago, and Turner Broadcasting's ownership of and regular recycling of *Gone With the Wind* functioned similarly for the contemporaneous "restoration" of the area surrounding Atlanta's Peachtree Street as a retail/tourist center. In both instances, the televisual worked to spatially redefine and to reimagine the relation of current development to an urban past. Since the 1970s the modifications to these cities have developed alongside the construction of Disney World in Orlando, Florida, and the initiation of the Disney Channel that promoted the theme park, and alongside the Nashville Network's promotion of the city of Nashville, Tennessee, as country-music mecca and museum. Through television, these cities emerged as "new" centers of national popular culture (after New York and Los Angeles), while their reproduction of an urban past already partially constituted as televisual and cinematic past. These urban "revitalization" projects precipitated and were fueled by a reterritorialization of national and global economic flows, by the movement of people (as "settlers" or "tourists") to these cities, and by broadcasts from them.

The flow of television broadcasting via cable, fiber optics, and satellites has affected the geographic features of the televisual and its environment in a variety of ways. It has brought traditional broadcast television into close relations with the paths and flows of telecommunications and telematics, although these convergences have been fraught with commercial and political conflicts over territory. It has occurred amid a redistribution of people and economic/cultural capital. Not every home and not every nation and few rural areas are equally connected to these potentially global flows. To the extent that new modes of transmission and new industry alliances have made the televisual a global formation, this formation is at best tenuously sustained through various conjunctions and divisions among the domestic, the urban, the rural, the regional, and the national. Furthermore, recognizing only the global flow of television risks ignoring how the movement of people from one part of the world to another often involves their "assimilation" into a new environment, shaped politically, economically, and culturally, at least in part, through televisual mediation of their new sense of place and/or their relation to their former homeland. This has occurred through Spanish-language television broadcasting across the Western Hemisphere; through television produced by and for Iranian exiles in Los Angeles; through television broadcast via satellite by the Italian RAI foreign service to Italian-American audiences in New York; through video rentals and pirating for video playback where there are no broadcasts for immigrant audiences; or through audiences whose sense of place is bound up with their consumption of television that arrives from abroad (e.g., Europeans watching *Dallas* or Australian aborigines watching *Diff'rent Strokes*).

The televisual has always been appended to particular sites and located within particular environments, mediating various spheres of sociality. However, the current interdependence of television with telecommunication and telematics suggests that what has been known so far as "the televisual" was composed of spatial formations and forms of spatial modeling whose effectivity belonged to a vanishing set of environmental conditions. In certain respects, the first wave of televisual technologies emerged within established infrastructures, networks, and environmental conditions. Through these conditions the televisual flourished as a means of spatially organizing social relations. However, the flow of images and the formation of discourses through the current technological convergence have already been predicated upon changing concentrations and dispersals of economic and cultural capital, and cultural capital, after all, is the basis for accessing these flows, as opposed to merely inhabiting an environment conditioned by them. Despite the enthusiastic proclamations about the democratizing potential of new technological convergences, then, access to global media flows is still unequally distributed at the level of home and region. The televisual thus remains as a residual formation, still an organizing feature of homes, cities, and nations, even as their relations are once again being redefined spatially through technologies appended to television. In another sense, however, the emergence of Internet technologies involves a deepening of concerns about managing distance that has made televisuality an ideal and objective since the 19th century.

JAMES HAY

See also **Coproductions, International; Satellite; Superstation**

Further Reading

Castells, Manuel, *Rise of the Network Society,* Cambridge, Massachusetts, 1996; 2nd edition, Oxford and Malden, Massachusetts: Blackwell, 2000

Innis, Harold Adams, *Empire and Communications,* Oxford: Clarendon, 1950

Mattelart, Armand, *The Invention of Communication,* translated by Susan Emanuel, Minneapolis: University of Minnesota Press, 1996

McCarthy, Anna, *Ambient Television: Visual Culture and Public Space,* Durham, North Carolina: Duke University Press, 2001

Michaels, Eric, *Bad Aboriginal Art: Tradition, Media, and Technological Horizons,* Minneapolis: University of Minnesota Press, 1994

Morley, David, *Home Territories: Media, Mobility, and Identity,* London and New York: Routledge, 2000

Naficy, Hamid, *The Making of Exile Cultures: Iranian Television in Los Angeles,* Minneapolis: University of Minnesota Press, 1993

Spigel, Lynn, *Make Room for TV: Television and the Family Ideal in Postwar America,* Chicago: University of Chicago Press, 1992

Wark, McKenzie, *Virtual Geography: Living with Global Media Events,* Bloomington: Indiana University Press, 1994

Williams, Raymond, *Television: Technology and Cultural Form,* London: Fontana, 1974; New York: Schocken, 1975

George Burns and Gracie Allen Show, The

U.S. Domestic Comedy

The George Burns and Gracie Allen Show, which premiered on October 12, 1950, was one of the first comedy series to make the successful transition from radio to television. Similar in format to the radio program in which George Burns and Gracie Allen played themselves, the CBS domestic comedy was set in their home and was the first television series to depict the home life of a working show-business couple.

The half-hour series was broadcast live for the first two seasons. The first six episodes were broadcast from New York, but the show soon moved to Hollywood, making it only the third CBS series to emanate from the West Coast (after *The Ed Wynn Show* and *The Alan Young Show*). On Burns's insistence, the show was broadcast on alternate weeks in order to provide sufficient time for rehearsals and alleviate some of the pressures of live broadcasts. During its biweekly period, the series alternated with the anthology series *Starlight Theater* and, later, with *Star of the Family.* After two seasons of live performances, the series switched to a weekly filmed broadcast. Although not filmed before a studio audience, the final filmed product was previewed to an audience and their reactions recorded. At a time when many series relied on mechanically reproduced ("canned") laughter, Burns

claimed that his series only "'sweetened' the laughter when a joke went flat and there was no way of eliminating it from the film." Even then, "we never added more than a gentle chuckle."

Like other television pioneers such as Desi Arnaz and Jack Webb, Burns must be credited for his contributions behind the scenes. *Burns and Allen* incorporated a number of television "firsts," although Burns noted that "television was so new that if an actor burped, everyone agreed it was an innovative concept and nothing like it had ever been done on television before." Burns was the first television performer to use the theatrical convention of "breaking the fourth wall" between the audience and the performer. He frequently stepped out of a scene and out of character to address the audience, then rejoined the story. This convention was later imitated by others, but not used effectively until *It's Garry Shandling's Show* in the 1980s.

The staff writers for the series were those who had written for the *Burns and Allen* radio program or worked with the team in vaudeville, including Paul Henning (who later created *The Beverly Hillbillies*), Sid Dorfman (who later wrote for *M*A*S*H* and produced *Good Times* for Norman Lear), Harvey Helm, and William Burns (George's younger brother). To

George Burns and Gracie Allen Show, George Burns, Gracie
Allen, 1950–58.
Courtesy of the Everett Collection

keep dialogue and situations consistent with the characters' personalities and ages, the *Burns and Allen*
writers adhered to policies and practices established
during their radio show. The stories stayed away from
topical humor, fantastic characters, and absurd situations, focusing instead on more universal aspects of
daily life. Plots were simple (e.g., Gracie attempting to
learn Spanish) and, like the couple's vaudeville routines, the comedy emanated from Allen's uniquely
skewed interpretation of the world and the resulting
confusion. Burns played the quintessential straight
man to the giddy, scatterbrained Allen.

Each episode began with Burns standing, trademark
cigar in hand, before the proscenium surrounding the
living room set. He presented a brief monologue and
offered the audience a few comments regarding the situation they were about to see.

Allen's success, and her enormous popularity, emanated from her ability to underplay her character. Her
convincing sincerity makes illogical premises, such as
sewing buttons on her husband's shirttails so no one
would notice if he lost one, seem logical.

Episodes ended with a Burns and Allen dialogue
reminiscent of their vaudeville routines. At the conclusion of every episode, Burns would turn to Allen and
say, "Say goodnight, Gracie," to which Allen would
obligingly turn to their audience and fondly bid them,
"Goodnight."

The supporting cast continued in roles established in
the original *Burns and Allen* radio program. Bea Benaderet and Hal March played the Burns' neighbors,
Blanche and Harry Morton. Bill Goodwin, as himself,
played the show's announcer and friend of the family,
and Rolfe Sedan played mailman Mr. Beasley, with
whom Gracie gossiped. During the run of the series, the
role of Harry Morton was subsequently played by John
Brown, Fred Clark, and Larry Keating. In the second
season, announcer Goodwin left to host his own variety
series for NBC (*The Bill Goodwin Show*) and was replaced by Harry Von Zell. A musical entr'acte entertainment was provided by the Singing Skylarks. The
Burns' son Ronnie later joined the cast as himself.

Although *Burns and Allen* was never among the top-
rated series, it maintained consistently high ratings
throughout its eight seasons. The show garnered a total
of 12 Emmy nominations: four for Best Comedy Series, six for Allen as Best Actress and Comedienne,
and two for Bea Benaderet as Best Supporting Actress.

On September 22, 1958, the series ended, following
Allen's decision to retire from show business. Burns
continued working in a revamped version of the show,
The George Burns Show (NBC, October 21, 1958, to
April 14, 1959), in which he again played himself, now
in the role of a theatrical producer. Bea Benaderet and
Larry Keating reprised their roles as Blanche and Harry
Morton, but now portrayed Burns's secretary and ac-
countant, and Harry Von Zell repeated his role as
Burns's announcer. The series lasted only one season.

After Allen's death (August 24, 1964), Burns returned to series television as producer and star of
Wendy and Me (ABC, September 14, 1964, to September 6, 1965), in which he played an apartment building
owner who narrated and commented on the action.
Burns's McCadden Productions continued to produce
other situation comedies, such as *Mr. Ed, The Bob
Cummings Show, The People's Choice,* and *The Marie
Wilson Show.* At age 89, Burns hosted the short-lived
half-hour comedy anthology series *George Burns
Comedy Week* (CBS, September 18, 1985, to December 25, 1985). He died on March 9, 1996, at age 100.

SUSAN R. GIBBERMAN

See also **Allen, Gracie; Burns, George**

Cast

George Burns	Himself
Gracie Allen	Herself
Blanche Morton	Bea Benaderet

Harry Morton (1950–51)	Hal March
Harry Morton (1951)	John Brown
Harry Morton (1951–53)	Fred Clark
Harry Morton (1953–58)	Larry Keating
Bill Goodwin (1950–51)	Himself
Harry Von Zell (1951–58)	Himself
Mr. Beasley, Mailman	Rolfe Sedan
Ronnie Burns (1955–58)	Himself
Bonnie Sue McAfee (1957–58)	Judi Meredith

Producers

Fred DeCordova, Al Simon, Ralph Levy, Rod Amateau

Programming History

239 episodes
CBS

October 1950–March 1953	Thursday 8:00–8:30
March 1953–September 1958	Monday 8:00–8:30

Further Reading

Blythe, Cheryl, and Susan Sackett, *Say Goodnight Gracie: The Story of George Burns and Gracie Allen,* Rocklin, California: Prima Publishing and Communications, 1989

Burns, George, "George Burns and Gracie Allen," in *Lovers: Great Romances of Our Time through the Eyes of Legendary Writers,* edited by John Miller and Aaron Kenedi, Boston: Little Brown, 1999

Burns, George, *Gracie: A Love Story,* New York: Putnam, 1988

Burns, George, and Cynthia Hobart Lindsay, *I Love Her, That's Why!: An Autobiography,* New York: Simon and Schuster, 1955

"Burns and Allen Bow on Television: Radio Comedians Successful in Transition to Video; Gracie As Zany As Ever," *New York Times* (October 13, 1950)

Clements, Cynthia, and Sandra Weber, *George Burns and Gracie Allen: A Bio-bibliography,* Westport, Connecticut: Greenwood Press, 1996

"George Burns and Gracie Allen," *Current Biography* (1951)

"Gracie Ends Act with George," *Life* (September 22, 1958)

Janik, Vicki K., "George Burns and Gracie Allen: The Jewish Vaudeville Tradition," in *Fools and Jesters in Literature, Art, and History: A Bio-bibliographical Sourcebook,* Westport, Connecticut: Greenwood Press, 1998

Morris, J.K., "Gracie Allen's Own Story: Inside Me," *Woman's Home Companion* (March 1953)

Staples, Shirley Louise, "From 'Barney's Courtship' to Burns and Allen: Male-Female Comedy Teams in American Vaudeville, 1865–1932," Ph.D. dissertation, Tufts University, 1981

Weisblat, Tinky, "Will the Real George and Gracie and Ozzie and Harriet and Desi and Lucy Please Stand Up? The Functions of Popular Biography in 1950s Television," Ph.D. dissertation, University of Texas at Austin, 1991

Germany

Origins

Television in Germany began as an integrated part of an existing public broadcasting system. Although it took seven years in the 1950s to establish fully TV as a mass medium, its history started before World War II. The first tests with wireless transmission of television pictures without sound were regularly offered by the German Reichpost in 1929. As a result of these tests, the first made-for-television movie, *Morgenstund hat Gold im Mund* (*The Early Bird Catches the Worm*), was produced in 1930. It was not until 1934, however, that programs combining pictures and sounds were produced.

The National Socialist Party enforced further technical developments in order to create a new instrument for propaganda. The first regular television network, "Paul Nipkow," began operation on March 22, 1935, under control of Reichssendeleiter Eugen Hadamovsky. To fulfill the propaganda function, reception was made available only in public television rooms. These venues, which operated quite similarly to movie theaters and presented programs three nights a week, were set up in Berlin. The first highlight, shown in 28 television rooms, was live coverage of the 1936 Olympic Games in Berlin. Private reception of television was made technically possible by the *Deutsche Fernseh-Einheitsempfaenger,* but the system could not be introduced to the market because of the beginning of World War II. Television programming adapted to the situation, and by 1941 a series of variety shows, *Wir senden Frohsin—Wir spenden Freude* (*We Broadcast Joy—We Spend Happiness*), were broadcast for injured soldiers in Berlin. Following the presentation of programs in Hamburg, television was also broadcast in occupied Paris from 1942 until 1944. The same programs produced for the injured soldiers were aimed in French at the inhabitants of Paris.

West German Television

The development of television in Germany following World War II began when the Western Allies founded new networks in their occupied areas, patterned on the network systems of their home countries. A common aim of the Western Allies was to prevent the future abuse of broadcasting by the German government. Thus, the different regional networks were placed under control of the state governments of the Federal Republic of Germany (FRG; West Germany): NWDR (northern and west Germany, which were split, during the 1950s, into NDR and WDR); Radio Bremen (Bremen); BR (Bavaria); HR (Hessia); SR, SDR, and SWF for southwest Germany.

In 1948 the British Allies allowed the NWDR to broadcast television programs for the northern part of Germany. A general television programming test phase, organized by Werner Pleister, started on September 25, 1950. Pleister and members of a television committee traveled to the United States and several European countries to become more familiar with television standards. In 1950 the NWDR presented a two-hour program between 8:00 and 10:00 P.M., which included news, variety shows, movies, and television plays. In 1951 additional programs for children (*Television's Children's Hour with Ilse Obrig*) and women (*Television's Tea Hour with Eva Baier Post*) were broadcast in the afternoon. Further gaps in the daily schedule were filled during the 1950s, and, in addition to the NWDR, other federal networks also started to develop television programs.

In the time of the test phase, between 1950 and 1952, it seemed necessary to promote the new medium by pointing out the technical differences that distinguished television from its "big brothers," radio and film. By presenting live reports with both visual and sound components, television was described as the fifth wall in the living room, or as the "Miracle Mirror." Television was celebrated as the "window to the world," which transferred directly into German homes. Two major events assisted in efforts to change television into a mass medium—the live coverage of the coronation ceremony of Queen Elizabeth II on June 2, 1953, and the final game of the soccer World Cup in Switzerland on July 4, 1954. Many Germans who did not yet own a television set watched these events in pubs.

In 1954 a regular television schedule began through the cooperation of all federal networks, which had formed an association named Arbeitsgemeinschaft der oeffentlich-rechtlichen Rundfunkanstalten der Bundesrepublik Deutschland (ARD). ARD was financed by license fees paid by the audience and, after 1956, with a few minutes of commercials presented in the early evening. During the 1950s the basic television genres in the central areas of entertainment, information, and education were established, and television plays developed as television's own specific art form. Because of the lack of a recording technique, these plays, as well as other types of shows, were presented live. In 1954 the first family series, *Unsere Nachbarn heute Abend: Familie Schoelermann* (*Our Neighbors Tonight: The Schoelermann Family*), appeared. The lifestyle depicted on the program served as an ideal for the audience, which resulted in many letters expressing gratitude for helpful advice. Documentaries, under the heading *Zeichen der Zeit* (*Sign of the Time*), also gave direct insights into several parts of German society.

Improvements in the technical quality of television sets, reduced prices, and better programs resulted in a steady increase in license holders, and their number reached 1 million on October 1, 1957. This success and new, still unused frequencies motivated Konrad Adenauer, chancellor of the West German government, to increase his influence by founding a second channel, "Free Television," financed by the industry and with the central goal of presenting government opinions. The federal governments protested against these activities, and they were finally stopped by a court ruling in 1961. The ARD also presented a second schedule of programs from January 1, 1961, until January 4, 1963. In addition, the federal governments allowed the several ARD networks to found regional third channels, which, from 1964, presented educational and cultural programs in addition to local information.

The ZDF (Second German Television) was founded by the FRG in 1963 as the long-promised second national network. In contrast to the ARD, whose networks distributed several radio programs as well, the ZDF was centrally organized solely for the production of television programs. According to a decision by the federal governments, programming had to be planned in cooperation with the ARD, with the aim of presenting contrasting elements on the two channels. Still, the well-established ARD perceived the ZDF as a competitor and reacted to it by offering viewers enhanced news coverage and several international reports. New political magazine programs such as *Panorama* created controversial public discussions as a result of their investigative journalism. The ZDF did not yet have enough journalists to cover these areas with the same standard. Instead, it increased its efforts in presenting entertainment in order to gain a larger audience. The arrival of color TV in 1967 increased the presentation of popular programs for both ARD and ZDF, whose schedules by then included many U.S. series, such as *Bonanza*. With the increasing influence of popular television shows, the star system also became far more significant. Still, as in the 1950s, the highlight of the era came in the form of live coverage—especially the images of the first man on the moon on July 21, 1969.

Serials dominated prime-time television broadcasts in the 1970s. In the early years of the decade, the liberalization movements initiated by students started to influence television. In 1971 Wibke Bruhns became the first female news anchor. *Wuensch Dir was* (*Desire Something,* 1969–72) was the first game show intended to improve social behavior of the contestants. The first German sitcom series, *Ein Herz und eine Seele* (*One Heart and One Soul,* 1973), criticized the conservative attitude and the chauvinistic behavior of its protagonist, Ekel Alfred. Television plays tried to present realistic daily life routines in the tradition of Egon Monk's *Wilhelmsburger Freitag* (*Friday in Wilhelmsburg,* 1964). Even television series such as Rainer Werner Fassbinder's *Acht Stunden sind kein Tag* (*Eight Hours Don't Form a Day,* 1972) followed realistic dramaturgy in order to present the necessity of political engagement. This aim also influenced informational programs, which were mainly presented in magazine format, and, in addition to political magazines, there were also magazines for seniors, car owners, and others. Politics was approached from another direction when the election campaign in 1976 was used to develop new formats for the presentation of political items, and television debates between the main candidates were established.

In the late 1960s the government founded a commission to analyze possible influences of new media technologies, but the commission did not present its report until 1976. It made clear that cable technology made new, commercially financed television channels possible. Although a 1981 legal decision guaranteed the audience further educational and information programs supplied from public television, this period saw major changes resulting from the rise of commercial broadcasting that was made possible by these new technologies.

With the foundation in 1984 of privately organized pilot projects in Ludwigshafen, Berlin, and Dortmund, the media landscape in West Germany, long dominated by public television, changed rapidly. Ratings, instead of quality, now formed the basic criteria for assessing the success of programming. ARD and ZDF, the state-supported competitors to the commercial systems, altered their schedules in attempts to secure their financial situation. The general public-service goal of integrating social minorities through the development

and broadcasting of special programming was now supplanted by the dominance of economic measurements. Public television systems did produce their own series with specific regional orientations. This programming—for example, *Landarzt* (*Country Doctor*), broadcast in a coastal region of northern Germany—was quite successful.

East German Television

From the postwar division of Germany into two nations until the collapse of the Berlin Wall, television broadcasting in the German Democratic Republic (GDR; East Germany) remained under government control and served as a propaganda instrument for socialistic ideals. Regular programming officially started on March 3, 1956, as an alternative to West German television, but it reached only few regions across the border. By contrast, ARD broadcasts could be seen in most parts of the GDR.

As in West Germany, there had been a test phase in the GDR, begun on June 3, 1952, under the control of Hermann Zille. TV officials traveled to Moscow to gain insight into socialist models for television practices. For political reasons, Zille was fired in 1953 and replaced by Heinz Adameck in June 1954, who remained as head of the system until 1989. The first East German television play was an adaptation of E.T.A. Hoffmann's *Des Vetters Eckfenster* (*The Cousin's Corner Window,* January 22, 1953).

The purpose of television was to form the morality of socialist people. Television shows and old DEFA movies were presented as entertainment in order to keep the audience from watching West German channels. In the 1960s TV novels were popular, presenting historical plots in miniseries format. The news *Aktuelle Kamera* (*Current Camera*) was directly controlled by members of the government. *Der Schwarze Kanal* (*The Black Channel*), with anchorman Karl Eduard von Schnitzler, reacted directly to West German news coverage with propaganda material.

In response to the West German television landscape, a second program schedule, presented in color, was founded in 1969 to complement the original schedule. In its early period, this channel presented color versions of programs the audience already knew from the first schedule. Additionally, the leaders of Soviet troops in the GDR demanded a series of Russian movies, *Fuer die Freunde der Russischen Sprache* (*For Friends of the Russian Language*), which were presented in the original language. In the late 1970s the second schedule began several educational and cultural programs.

During the 1980s, East German television tried to react against commercial tendencies in West Germany. More movies and popular series were placed in the schedules to keep citizens from watching West German channels. By the 1989–90 season, following political changes in East Germany and the unification of East and West Germany, the central issue for television was the matter of news coverage. Journalists of the ARD claimed to have encouraged the political changes with their information policy. In essence, East German television was adapted to the West German broadcasting system, with various services integrated in the ARD.

Television Since Reunification

From the mid-1980s on, the steadily increasing number of channels in Germany created a growing demand for programs. It was quite expensive to produce programming, but the prices for licenses exploded as well. Many Hollywood movies and U.S. series, such as *Dallas, Dynasty,* and *The A-Team,* were broadcast. The commercial networks RTL and SAT.1 established the form of the daytime series with productions like *The Springfield Story.* Game show and talk show formats were both successful and inexpensive to produce. RTL tried to gain public attention by breaking existing taboos—*Tutti Frutti* (1990) was the first striptease show presented on German TV. Soft news dominated the information sector. Instead of seriously discussing a topic, RTL talk shows were based on the principle of "confrontainment."

At the beginning of the 1990s, RTL and SAT.1 improved their financial situation. Simultaneously, ARD and ZDF, as public networks, experienced a financial crisis because of the decreasing number of commercials they carried. With their new prominence, RTL and SAT.1 started several campaigns to improve their image. They promised a higher percentage of self-produced made-for-television movies and series, more information, and less sex in future programming. They brought in stars in order to deepen the identification between the viewers and their networks. ARD and ZDF increasingly adapted the successful formats of their competitors, which had themselves already taken up popular public-television formats such as folklore programs.

From 1992 to 1994 "reality TV" shows were a successful format on every channel. The blurred lines between reality and fiction in these programs created controversial public discussions and led to their slow disappearance during the later 1990s. Several forms of emotionalized shows like *Ich bekenne* (*I Confess*) or *Verzeih mir* (*Pardon Me*) presented weeping guests comforted by weeping hosts. Flirtation and love shows such as *Traumhochzeit* (*Dream Wedding*) offered exciting possibilities for finding a partner or even for marriage in front of studio cameras.

During the 1990s, several specialty channels were created. In addition to news (N-TV), sports (DSF), and music channels (Viva I and Viva II), local channels (HH1, Puls TV) were founded. Even more new channels are expected in the future as digital television technologies make more networks possible.

In the 1990s and early 2000s, Leo Kirch, head of KirchMedia, one of the two main media conglomerates dominating the German network television market (along with Bertelsmann), tried to strengthen his company's financial resources by establishing several forms of pay-TV, beginning with the program bouquet of DF1, which was later combined with Premiere World. Kirch also invested a large amount of money to buy world rights for the live coverage of sporting events, particularly soccer matches (including the World Cup) and Formula One automobile races. However, despite such appealing offerings, German viewers still generally refused to pay for television programs, and KirchMedia became mired in debt, with Leo Kirch resigning from the company in April 2002 after it filed for insolvency.

Around the same time that Kirch was expanding and then collapsing, U.S. cable entrepreneur John C. Malone also tried to enter Germany's pay-TV market, striking a $4.7 billion deal in 2001 to acquire from the German telecommunications company Deutsche Telekom its interest in cable television services reaching the majority of German households with cable. However, Malone's efforts were thwarted in 2002 by German regulators, who cited concerns that the deal would ultimately lead to higher prices for cable subscriptions and thus harm the interests of consumers. Other foreign investors, such as Rupert Murdoch, continue to seek inroads into the German television market.

In 2000 the reality show *Big Brother* was the biggest television event in Germany. On this program and via its Internet site, viewers could observe ten people living together in a household where every room was observed by cameras. The high ratings of *Big Brother* encouraged the production of many more reality shows until this trend was stemmed by the success of quiz shows in 2001.

It remains to be seen whether the new, combined German system of television will continue a familiar path of creating new channels to serve viewer interests, or become something quite different. Throughout the world, television as medium of "mass" communication has begun to fragment into several forms of individual communication. New possibilities for interactive television try to change viewers into active users. Still, it is likely that many of those now sitting before the television set will cling to this medium as a favorite source for information, stories, and human insights.

JOAN KRISTIN BLEICHER

Further Reading

Boyle, Maryellen, "Building a Communicative Democracy: The Birth and Death of Citizen Politics in East Germany," *Media, Culture, and Society* (April 1994)

Charlton, Michael, and Ben Bachmair, editors, *Media Communication in Everyday Life: Interpretative Studies on Children's and Young People's Media Actions,* Munich and New York: K.G. Saur, 1990

Murray, Bruce A., and Christopher J. Walken, editors, *Framing the Past: The Historiography of German Cinema and Television,* Carbondale: Southern Illinois University Press, 1992

Willett, Ralph, *The Americanization of Germany, 1945–1949,* London and New York: Routledge, 1989

Gerussi, Bruno (1928–1995)

Canadian Actor

After an extensive career in stage, radio, television, and film, Bruno Gerussi became one of Canada's most highly recognizable actors and television personalities. Despite the diversity of his career, the Canadian-born Gerussi is best known for his role as Nick Adonidas on Canada's longest-running television series, *The Beachcombers* (1972–90).

Gerussi began his acting career on the stage, where he performed both supporting and leading roles in Canadian Players and Stratford Festival productions such as *Twelfth Night, Romeo and Juliet, Julius Caesar,* and *The Crucible.* The exposure and experience provided in the theater allowed Gerussi to make a smooth transition into the expanding arena of Canadian television production of the late 1950s and early 1960s. During this time the Canadian Broadcasting Corporation (CBC) developed a number of televised dramas, including *The Crucible* (1959), *Riel* (1961), and *Galileo* (1963), in which Gerussi assumed important dramatic roles.

After a two-year stint (1967–68) with his own nationally broadcast midmorning CBC radio show, *Gerussi, Words and Music,* Gerussi won the lead role on the popular CBC family-adventure series *The Beachcombers* created by Marc and Susan Strange (produced by Philip Keatley and Derek Gardner). Gerussi portrayed Nick Adonidas, the Greek-born owner of Nick's Salvage Company and father figure for a set of characters who inhabited the fishing village of Molly's Reach. Although largely consistent with the family-adventure genre, *Beachcombers* (*The* was dropped from the title in 1988) stretched the limitations of the form sufficiently to allow the various characters to evolve and the series to stay fresh during its extensive run. Over the course of the series, for example, the romantic, free spirit nature of Gerussi's character became increasingly responsible and fatherly toward his substitute family.

A total of 324 half-hour *Beachcomber* episodes were produced over a 19-year period. At its peak in 1982, the series attracted an audience of 1.94 million (25 percent of the available audience) during the "CBC Sunday night family hour" (7:30 P.M. time slot). *Beachcombers* was one of the few Canadian productions of its time to be widely exported, broadcast in a single season in as many as 34 countries, including Greece, Australia, Italy, and Britain. The location of the production, Gibson's Landing, a small fishing village on the coast of British Columbia, generated upwards of 100,000 tourists a year as a result of the show's popularity.

Despite the international appeal of *Beachcombers,* the program was often interpreted by Canadians as the quintessential Canadian program. This was true both in terms of its economic development—a relatively low-budget product of the publicly subsidized CBC, as well as culturally, in the sense that it presented a relatively innocent, unglamorous group of characters and storylines, which distinguished the series from much of the U.S. prime-time programming distributed on Canadian airwaves. Ironically, CBC management attempted to revamp the series in its last years by increasing the level of action and violence in the storylines, decreasing the contrast with its competition. This move was publicly criticized by longtime cast members, particularly Gerussi, who saw this as an "Americanization" of Canadian programming. By the 1988–89 season, *Beachcombers*' audience fell to

Bruno Gerussi.
Photo courtesy of Bruno Gerussi

990,000, and the program was canceled the following year.

From the 1970s, Gerussi accumulated dozens of television credits as a guest character on various Canadian and U.S.-Canada coproductions, including *E.N.G., McQueen, Seeing Things, Hangin' In, Wojeck, Wiseguy,* and CBC's *Side Effects.* Gerussi was often cast in roles that took advantage of his "larger than life" persona. For example, Gerussi acted as the host of the Canada Day telecast, and the opening of the Canada's National Arts Centre. Gerussi also hosted his own CBC afternoon cooking program for four years entitled *Celebrity Cooks.* This weekday production, often shot in one take, drew on the host's personality and ability to interact with the celebrities who acted as guest chefs. Through his association with the *Beachcombers* series, and his decision to locate his career permanently in Canada rather than in the larger U.S. market, Gerussi developed a particularly strong link to Canada and its television industry.

KEITH C. HAMPSON

See also ***Beachcombers;* Canadian Programming in English**

Bruno Gerussi. Born in Medicine Hat, Alberta, 1928. Educated at the Banff School of Fine Arts. Joined the Stratford Festival and the Canadian Players as a stage actor, mid-1950s; star of morning CBC radio show *Gerussi, Words and Music,* 1967–68; star of CBC television adventure series *The Beachcombers,* 1972–90; host of afternoon show *Celebrity Cooks,* 1975–79. Died in Vancouver, British Columbia, November 21, 1995.

Television Series (selected)

1972–90	*The Beachcombers*
1975–79	*Celebrity Cooks*

Television Special

1995	*Artisans de notre histoire* (actor)

Films

Alexander Galt: The Stubborn Idealist, 1962; *The Stage to Three,* 1964; *Do Not Fold, Staple, Spindle, or Mutilate,* 1967.

Radio

Gerussi, Words and Music, 1967–68.

Stage (selected)

Twelfth Night; Romeo and Juliet; Julius Ceasar; The Crucible.

Further Reading

"Beachcomber Gerussi Rakes CBC Officials for Cancelling Show," *Montreal Gazette* (June 26, 1990)
"Gerussi Award Planned Bruno Award," *Globe and Mail* (January 19, 1996)
"Gerussi Busy Despite Demise of *Beachcombers,*" *Winnipeg Free Press* (September 19, 1991)
"Gerussi Moves On, But Still Pines for *The Beachcombers,*" *Vancouver Sun* (September 20, 1991)
"Stormy Weather on the Sunshine Coast: Bruno Gerussi Has His Doubts about Head Office," *Globe and Mail* (August 1, 1989)

Get Smart

U.S. Spy Parody

The premise of this cult-classic television comedy series is that an evil organization, KAOS, is attempting to take over the world. The forces of good, symbolized by the organization CONTROL, constantly battle KAOS to preserve order in the world. Maxwell Smart (Don Adams) is CONTROL Secret Agent 86. Yet Smart is anything but smart. A stupid, self-centered man, he is the antithesis—and parody—of everything conventionally represented by secret service agents in popular culture.

Smart's immediate superior is the Chief (Ed Platt), the head of the Washington Bureau of CONTROL. In his fight against KAOS, Smart is assisted by his sidekick, Agent 99, played by former model Barbara Feldon. Unfailingly faithful to Maxwell Smart and always willing to let him take credit for her proficiency, 99's admiration of Smart goes well beyond professional respect. It is obvious to anyone, except of course Maxwell Smart, that Agent 99 is in love with him, and, indeed, in a later show they marry.

The success of *Get Smart* has been linked to three primary factors. The first was the spy craze that was all the rage in early 1960s popular culture. Second was the talent of persons involved in the production of the series both in front of and behind the camera. And third was the more tenuous sense of a new mood in the American public, a willingness to accept television humor that went beyond sight gags and family situation comedies. In the aftermath of 1950s McCarthyism, the civil rights movement, and increasing criticism of U.S. policy in Vietnam, these newer forms of television humor included satiric jabs at an increasingly questioned status quo.

In the mid-1960s, spies were hot: *The Man from U.N.C.L.E.* aired on NBC in 1964. *I Spy* appeared in 1965. *The Avengers,* a British production, came to U.S. television in March 1966. *Burke's Law* premiered in 1963 but in the 1965 season changed its name to *Amos Burke—Secret Agent.* In the same year *The Wild, Wild West* appeared on the small screen. *Honey West,* a *Burke* spin-off, featured Anne Francis as a female private detective who depends on technological marvels—tear-gas earrings and garters that convert into gas masks—to solve crimes. CBS imported *Secret Agent* from Britain, and ABC aired *The FBI.*

In this context, Mel Brooks (whose film credits include *The Producers, Blazing Saddles, Spaceballs*), Buck Henry (*The Graduate, Saturday Night Live*), Jay Sandrich (director of *Soap, The Mary Tyler Moore Show,* and *The Cosby Show*), and Carl Reiner (*Mary Tyler Moore*) were brought together by Dan Melnick and David Susskind. Melnick and Susskind owned Talent Associates, the company that had produced the highly acclaimed television series *East Side/West Side* (1963–64). Brooks and Henry developed the idea for *Get Smart.*

Get Smart, K-9 (Fang), Don Adams, 1965–70.
Courtesy of the Everett Collection

Don Adams had played a house detective on *The Danny Thomas Show* before signing on as Agent 86. His ability to deliver memorable lines was uncanny. On several occasions, for example, after being asked if he understands that his current assignment means he will be in constant danger, be unable to trust anyone, and face torture or even death, Smart, assuming a cavalier stance, responds with, "And loving it." Another catchy phrase, "Sorry about that, Chief," was usually uttered when Smart accidentally caused his boss some problem.

Finally, the mood of the American public seems to have contributed to the success of a program like *Get Smart*. In 1965 protests against the war in Vietnam, riots by African Americans in many urban centers, organized efforts by Mexican and Mexican-American migrant workers to strike for higher wages, and an increase in new political activism on the part of women eventually led to a questioning of fundamental assumptions about the role of the U.S. government in domestic and world affairs. A television series such as *Get Smart* was able to make pointed—some might say subversive—statements about many political issues in a nonthreatening, humorous way. In her book on the series, Donna McCrohan identifies one example of *Get Smart*'s political dialogue as "probably the strongest anti-bomb statement made by situation comedy up to that time" (see McCrohan). The exchange she cites takes place between Smart and Agent 99 in the episode titled "Appointment in Sahara." Behind the two characters is an image of a mushroom cloud:

99:     Oh, Max, what a terrible weapon of destruction.
Smart: Yes. You know, China, Russia, and France should outlaw all nuclear weapons. We should insist upon it.
99:     What if they don't, Max?
Smart: Then we may have to blast them. That's the only way to keep peace in the world.

Get Smart is credited with paving the way for other comedy programs and broadening the parameters for the presentation of comedy on television. While it was on the air from 1965 to 1970, a total of 138 half-hour episodes of the series were produced.

In the 1994–95 television season, an attempt was made to revive the series with some of the original actors. This time Don Adams was cast as the Chief, Barbara Feldon was a congresswoman, and Secret Agent Smart was their son. The series lasted only a few episodes; its jokes, and perhaps its cast, unable to attract a large audience.

RAUL D. TOVARES

See also **Spy Programs**

Cast

Maxwell Smart, Agent 86	Don Adams
Agent 99	Barbara Feldon
Thaddeus, The Chief (1965–70)	Edward Platt
Agent 13 (1965–70)	Dave Ketchum
Carlson (1966–67)	Stacy Keach
Conrad Siegfried (1966–69)	Bernie Kopell
Starker (1966–69)	King Moody
Hymie, the Robot (1966–69)	Dick Gautier
Agent 44 (1965–70)	Victor French
Larrabee (1967–70)	Robert Karvelas
99's Mother (1968–69)	Jane Dulo

Producers
Leonard B. Stern, Jess Oppenheimer, Jay Sandrich, Burt Nodella, Arnie Rosen, James Komak

Programming History
138 episodes
NBC

September 1965–September 1968	Saturday 8:30–9:00
September 1968–September 1969	Saturday 8:00–8:30
CBS	
September 1969–February 1970	Friday 7:30–8:00
April 1970–September 1970	Friday 7:30–8:00

Further Reading

Green, Joey, *The Get Smart Handbook,* New York: Collier, 1993
McCrohan, Donna, *The Life and Times of Maxwell Smart,* New York: St. Martin's Press, 1988

Gleason, Jackie (1916–1987)

U.S. Comedian, Actor

Jackie Gleason must be counted alongside Milton Berle, Sid Caesar, and Red Skelton among the small group of creative comedy-variety stars who dominated, and to some degree invented, early television. Perhaps more than any of the others, Gleason explored the limits of broad physical gesture and loud verbal bombast in the contextual frame of the small screen. His highly stylized and adroitly choreographed blustering, prancing, smirking, and double-taking led Gilbert Seldes to describe Gleason as "a heavy man with the traditional belief of heavy men in their own lightness and grace." Gleason's work in the 1950s constitutes a vital contribution to the invention of television comedy.

Born in a poor section of Brooklyn, New York, and abandoned by an alcoholic father, he dropped out of school at an early age and supported himself as a pool hustler, professional boxer, and carnival barker before establishing himself as "Jumpin' Jack" Gleason, a nightclub comic and vaudeville emcee known for his spirited exchanges with hecklers. Following a brief, unsuccessful stint in Hollywood as a Warner Brothers contract player, Gleason's career reached an apparent plateau. He worked as a stand-up comic and a master of ceremonies in venues ranging from middle-level nightspots to seamy dives in the New York area.

In 1949, at age 33, he landed the title role in a TV adaptation of *The Life of Riley,* a popular radio series about a culturally displaced Brooklyn factory worker who follows his job to a new life in a southern California suburb. The plodding, moralistic narrative structure of the sitcom, however, obscured Gleason's verbal rancor and physical comedy. The series was not renewed; however, it was successfully revived several years later when its radio star, William Bendix, was freed from a movie contract that had enjoined him from appearing on television.

Gleason was once again called on as a substitute when Jerry Lester, the host of DuMont's *Cavalcade of Stars,* suddenly quit the show in 1950. This time it turned out to be the break of his career. The live-from-New York, comedy-variety format played directly to Gleason's strengths, allowing him to wisecrack as emcee, engage in off-the-cuff chats with guests, and move in and out of short sketch material that emphasized physical humor rather than narrative resolution. The show became DuMont's biggest success.

It was on *Cavalcade* that Gleason originated most of the sketch characters he would play for the rest of his career: the absurdly ostentatious millionaire Reginald Van Gleason, III; the Poor Soul, a pathetic street character played in pantomime; the hapless, bumbling Bachelor; and, his greatest creation, Ralph Kramden, a bus driver tortured by a life that will not support his ego. All were to some degree autobiographical fantasies, personal visions of despair and grandeur culled from his poverty-stricken Brooklyn childhood, meditations on who the comedian could, would, or might have been. It was on the DuMont show that Gleason created his persona of The Great One; he also began his lifelong association with Art Carney, a *Cavalcade* regular.

Impressed by Gleason's performance on the screen and in the ratings, William Paley personally wooed the star away, offering him five times his DuMont salary and the far greater market coverage of CBS. *The Jackie Gleason Show* debuted in 1952, quickly propelling the comedian into national stardom. By 1954 Gleason was second only to Lucille Ball in the ratings. Taking advantage of this success, he secured rights that allowed him to dominate thoroughly every aspect of production, from casting to set design to script approval.

Glitz was Gleason's watchword. The June Taylor Dancers opened each show with a high-stepping chorus-line dance number that always included at least one overhead kaleidoscope shot of the Busby Berkley variety. A troupe of personally auditioned beauties, known as the Glea Girls, escorted the star around the stage and brought him "coffee" (he always sipped it as if were something stronger) and lit his cigarettes on camera. Unable to read music, Gleason composed his own musical theme, "Melancholy Serenade," which he hummed out for a professional songwriter. (Gleason also produced several gold albums of romantic music this way in an LP series titled *For Lovers Only.*) The show ended each week with an unprecedented but justifiable personal credit: "Entire production supervised by Jackie Gleason."

Riding high, the comedian paid little attention to the relationship between his sudden rise in fortune and the medium that had facilitated it. The Gleason style was

Jackie Gleason.
Courtesy of the Everett Collection

utterly suited to 1950s comedy-variety: the vaudeville trappings, including a live audience; the emphasis on slapstick, constant close-ups, blackout segues, splintered segments, and so on. But ever the *arriviste,* the star remained extremely defensive about his talents and status, yearning to prove himself in "higher" forms, especially the movies.

Attempting to make time for new ventures, he came up with a radical format for retaining his CBS Saturday night hour in the 1955–56 season. Gleason repackaged the most popular feature of his show, "The Honeymooners," into a 30-minute sitcom, while the second half of the hour was contracted to the Dorsey Brothers for a big-band musical program. The best of the old Ralph Kramden sketch material was reworked into the 39 *Honeymooners* episodes that have run in continuous syndication ever since.

For pure economy of style and setting, *The Honey-*

mooners has never quite been equaled. Often using only a single set, rarely employing more than the four regular characters, each episode is completely dependent upon the bravura performances of the show's stars: Gleason, as Ralph Kramden, the incorrigible egoist who, when not being teased about his weight, is repeatedly humiliated by his failed get-rich-quick schemes; Art Carney, as Ed Norton, a best friend and sidekick whose physical and mental slowness play foil to Gleason's mania in a kind of TV variation on Laurel and Hardy; and Audrey Meadows as Alice, the stoic, sensible wife who is forced to function as parent as much as spouse. Signature lines and gestures, such as Ralph's threats to send Alice "to the moon," or Ralph's throwing Norton out of his apartment, are ritually repeated to extraordinary comic effect.

Unfortunately that season marked the end of Gleason's most creative period. He would continue to hold down a prime-time slot (with some gaps) until 1970, but he never created any new noteworthy characters or elaborated further on the style he had developed. Casting about for a fresh format in which he could demonstrate versatility, he hosted a game show (*You're in the Picture,* 1961), conducted a one-on-one talk show (*The Jackie Gleason Show,* 1961) and returned to comedy-variety, promising (but not delivering) an innovative social satire approach (*Jackie Gleason and His American Scene Magazine,* 1962–66). The results were all critically disappointing, though the last of the three did prove that he could still deliver a top-20 audience with a comedy-variety format.

In 1964 all pretense was dropped, and the Saturday night hour with relaunched as *The Jackie Gleason Show,* a reprise of the familiar comedy-variety form of a dozen years earlier. Gleason spent much of the rest of his TV career doing increasingly tiresome replays of *The Honeymooners* and his other 1950s creations. Perhaps the only notable feature of the final series is that it was the only show in prime time not made in Los Angeles or New York—Gleason had moved his home and his show to Miami Beach, Florida.

Jackie Gleason's career illustrates much about the lot of television comedians. A small-timer with an erratic career, Gleason found a medium perfectly suited to his talents. He refused, however, to respect either the medium or the genre that had made him. Rather than pursue further depth as a TV sketch artist, he tried to prove that his talents transcended medium and genre. Others who would make this mistake include Dan Aykroyd, Katherine O'Hara, Chevy Chase, and Joe Piscopo. Gleason finally did achieve some popular success in the movies playing a southern sheriff in the three *Smokey and the Bandit* films made between 1977 and 1983.

DAVID MARC

See also **Honeymooners, The**

Jackie Gleason (Herbert John Gleason). Born in Brooklyn, New York, February 26, 1916. Married: 1) Genevieve Halford, 1936 (divorced, 1971); children: Geraldine and Linda; 2) Beverly McKittrick, 1971 (divorced, 1974); 3) Marilyn Taylor Horwich, 1975. Began career by winning stand-up comedy contest at age 15, 1931; master of ceremonies, Halsey Theater, Brooklyn, 1931; worked and toured in variety of entertainment jobs, including carnival barker, master of ceremonies, bouncer, amateur boxer, and disc jockey, 1935–38; signed to Warner Brothers, 1940; prominent television career beginning with *Cavalcade of Stars,* 1950; "The Honeymooners" debuted as segment on *Cavalcade of Stars,* 1951; wrote and recorded six albums of mood music, *Music for Lovers Only.* Recipient: "Best Comedian of the Year," *TV Guide,* 1952; Television Hall of Fame, 1985; Antoinette Perry (Tony) Award for "Best Actor," 1960. Died in Fort Lauderdale, Florida, June 24, 1987.

Television Series

1949–50	*The Life of Riley*
1950–52	*Cavalcade of Stars*
1952–55	*The Jackie Gleason Show*
1953	*The Laugh Maker*
1955–56	*The Honeymooners*
1957–59	*The Jackie Gleason Show*
1959	*Time of Your Life*
1961	*You're in the Picture*
1961	*The Jackie Gleason Show*
1961	*The Million Dollar Incident*
1962–66	*Jackie Gleason and His American Scene Magazine*
1964–70	*The Jackie Gleason Show*

Made-for-Television Movie

1985	*Izzy and Moe*

Films

Navy Blue, 1941; *Springtime in the Rockies,* 1942; *The Desert Hawk,* 1950; *The Hustler,* 1961; *Gigot* (wrote, starred in, and composed music), 1962; *Requiem for a Heavyweight,* 1962; *Soldier in the Rain,* 1963; *The Time of Your Life,* 1963; *Papa's Delicate Condition,* 1966; *Skidoo,* 1968; *How to Commit a Marriage,* 1969; *Don't Drink the Water,* 1969; *How Do I Love Thee?,* 1970; *Mr. Billion,* 1977; *Smokey and the Bandit,* 1977; *Smokey and the Bandit II,* 1980; *The Toy,* 1982; *Sting II,* 1983; *Smokey and the Bandit III,* 1983; *Fools Die,* 1985; *Nothing in Common,* 1986.

Stage

Hellzapoppin', 1938; *Keep Off the Grass,* 1940; *Follow the Girls,* 1944; *Artists and Models,* 1943; *Along Fifth Avenue,* 1949; *Take Me Along,* 1959–60; *Sly Fox,* 1978.

Further Reading

Bacon, James, *How Sweet It Is: The Jackie Gleason Story,* New York: St. Martin's Press, 1985
Bishop, Jim, *The Golden Ham: A Candid Biography of Jackie Gleason,* New York: Simon and Schuster, 1956
Henry, William A., *The Great One: The Life and Legend of Jackie Gleason,* New York: Doubleday, 1992
McCrohan, Donna, *Honeymooner's Companion,* New York: Workman, 1978
Weatherby, William J., *Jackie Gleason: An Intimate Portrait of the Great One,* New York: Pharos, 1992

Gless, Sharon (1943–)

U.S. Actor

Sharon Gless, who worked primarily in supporting roles for a number of series and TV movies in the late 1970s and early 1980s, rose to stardom as Christine Cagney in the female cop show *Cagney and Lacey* (1982–88).

Two of her more prominent roles before *Cagney and Lacey* anticipated aspects of the Cagney character. In a short-lived NBC sitcom, *Turnabout* (1979), Gless played Penny Alston, whose mind and spirit are exchanged with those of her husband. Gless's character thus explored gender differences through the split between a feminine exterior and masculine motivations. Three years later, Gless was tapped to take over the costarring role in *House Calls* when Lynn Redgrave was forced out of the series.

Sharon Gless.
Photo courtesy of Sharon Gless

It was the experience of trying to take over in the wake of a popular actor's departure that made Gless hesitate when she was offered the role of Christine Cagney. In the TV movie, Cagney had been played by Loretta Swit, and in the first season of the series, the character had been portrayed by Meg Foster. A CBS executive touched off a protest from fans, however, when he made a statement suggesting Foster was not feminine enough for the role, making the team of Chris Cagney and Mary Beth Lacey (played by Tyne Daly) look like "a pair of dykes." Renewal of the series was contingent on replacing Foster with someone "softer." Though initially seen by fans as a sellout to the network, Gless soon gained acceptance from the devoted audience of *Cagney and Lacey*. Ironically, she developed a substantial following among lesbian viewers, according to critic Julie D'Acci.

Not only did Cagney contrast with her married, working-class partner, but, as played by Gless, Christine Cagney embodied a number of contradictions in class and gender. Her soft blonde beauty played against the tough shell she maintained both on the job and in many of her personal encounters. Her working-class Irish cop identity, inherited from her father, clashed with the sleek, upper-crust veneer she had ac-

quired from her mother. Her career success contrasted with a string of unhappy romances in her personal life.

Although Gless has said she considers herself primarily a comedian, *Cagney and Lacey* provided the opportunity for her to grow as a dramatic actor. In the first three years of the series, Gless was nominated for an Emmy, but Daly received the award for Best Actress in a Dramatic Series. The following two years, however, the Emmy went to Gless, and in the final year of the series, the Emmy went back to Daly. Gless took pride in her contribution to the substance and quality of the series: "We're pioneering," she said in a story for *McCall's*. "We're showing women who can do a so-called man's job without ever forgetting that they are women."

Since the end of *Cagney and Lacey* in 1988, Gless has married Barney Rosenzweig, who created another series for her, *The Trials of Rosie O'Neill* (1990–91). In the role of the title character, Gless again portrayed a single, upscale character connected with the law—this time a newly divorced, well-healed lawyer, working in the cramped, underfunded offices of Los Angeles public defenders. Gless won a Golden Globe Award for her work in the series before it was canceled. In the 1990s she joined Tyne Daly in four *Cagney and Lacey* reunion movies and has appeared in a number of other TV and theatrical movies. In 2001 Gless returned to series work, in a departure from her upscale roles, as Debbie Novotny, Michael's waitress mother, in *Queer As Folk* for Showtime.

SUE BROWER

See also **Cagney and Lacey**

Sharon Gless. Born in Los Angeles, California, May 31, 1943. Attended Gonzaga University. Married Barney Rosenzweig, 1991. Actress in television from 1973. Recipient: Emmy Award, 1986 and 1987; Golden Globe Award, 1985 and 1990; Coalition for Clean Air Crystal Airwaves Media Award, 1987; Viewers for Quality TV Best Actress Award, 1988; Milestone Award, 1988; SI Award, 1991; Gideon Media Award, 1992; Distinguished Artist Award, 1992.

Television Series

1973–74	*Faraday and Company*
1974–75	*Marcus Welby, M.D.*
1975–78	*Switch*
1979	*Turnabout*
1981–82	*House Calls*
1982–88	*Cagney and Lacey*
1990–91	*The Trials of Rosie O'Neill*
2001–	*Queer As Folk*

Television Miniseries

1978	*The Immigrants*
1978	*Centennial*
1979	*The Last Convertible*

Made-for-Television Movies

1970	*Night Slaves*
1972	*All My Darling Daughters*
1973	*My Darling Daughters' Anniversary*
1976	*Richie Brockelman: The Missing 24 Hours*
1978	*The Islander*
1978	*Crash*
1979	*Kids Who Knew Too Much*
1980	*Moviola: The Scarlett O'Hara Wars*
1980	*Revenge of the Stepford Wives*
1980	*Hardhat and Legs*
1981	*The Miracle of Kathy Miller*
1983	*Hobson's Choice*
1984	*The Sky's No Limit*
1985	*Letting Go*
1989	*The Outside Woman*
1991	*Tales of the Unexpected*
1992	*Honor Thy Mother*
1994	*Separated by Murder*
1994	*Cagney and Lacey: The Return*
1995	*Cagney and Lacey: Together Again*
1995	*Cagney and Lacey: The View through the Glass Ceiling*
1996	*Cagney and Lacey: True Convictions*
1998	*The Girl Next Door*

Films

Airport 1975, 1974; *The Star Chamber*, 1983; *Ayn Rand: A Sense of Life* (narrator), 1997; *Smoke and Mirrors: A History of Denial* (narrator), 1999; *Bring Him Home*, 2000.

Stage

Watch On the Rhine, 1989; *Misery*, 1992–93; *Chapter Two*, 1995.

Further Reading

D'Acci, Julie, *Defining Women: Television and the Case of Cagney and Lacey,* Chapel Hill: University of North Carolina Press, 1994

Gordon, Mary, "Sharon Gless and Tyne Daly," *Ms.* (January 1987)

Globalization

Television is perhaps the most global of all mass media, at times extending its services to vast audiences around the world regardless of age, gender, literacy, nationality, or income. By comparison, newspapers usually serve local or in some cases national subscribers. Magazines, although national or in some cases international in reach, tend to cater to niche groups of readers. Radio transcends the literacy barrier, which is especially important in poor countries, yet increasing access television in these societies tends to displace the primacy of radio, and consequently to fragment the audience. As for the Internet—a medium that provides rapid communication around the world, regardless of political or regulatory constraints—its explosive growth over the past decade has been restricted to elite, well-educated users. Only movies come close to television as a global competitor, yet even blockbuster movies are more commonly viewed on a TV screen (via broadcast, cable, videotape or DVD) than in a theater.

Television is a pervasive presence in wealthy societies around the world, and even in relatively poor countries, such as India and People's Republic of China, TV viewing is now a common experience among the majority of the population. Television is also the popular medium of choice during historically significant moments, such as the fall of the Berlin Wall or the September 11, 2001, attack on the World Trade Center. At such times, huge audiences turn to television news services both for information and for cultural engagement, seeking somehow to participate in momentous events with global significance. Furthermore, television is the purveyor elaborately staged media events, including political campaigns, beauty pageants, the Olympics, and the Academy Awards. Some critics even include major military campaigns among such staged events, arguing that the Gulf War and the U.S. invasion of Afghanistan were elaborately choreographed in order to cater to global television audiences. For the first time in human history, vast numbers of people participate in such public events on a global basis. What is more, television facilitates the global circulation of performers, narratives, and program formats, thereby creating a loosely shared repertoire of popular cultural forms. Television heightens one's sense of connection to ideas and events from near and far, fostering tentative inklings of global connectedness, and perhaps even global community.

No matter how inchoate these feelings may be, and despite the fact that this sense of community is fraught with cultural differences and political tensions, television nevertheless makes possible widespread awareness of the global context in which human events and cultural forms unfold. Yet it would be folly to contend that the technology of television is the driving force in globalization. It is instead one element in a complex process of social change that stretches back at least 500 years. Television at once is a barometer of change and a contributor to change. Furthermore, television has its own distinctive histories and institutional logics. Consequently, we might explore the significance of global television by examining it from three perspectives: institutional, historical, and intellectual.

Institutionally, one can discern significant changes in the medium over the course of its history. Originally television, like radio before it, emerged as a quintessentially national medium. In almost every country, the state played an active role in its deployment, hoping that television would serve purposes of national integration, social development, public enlightenment, and popular entertainment. Using their power to grant broadcasting licenses and therefore limit the number of national network broadcasters, governments carefully controlled access to the airwaves either by creating public-service broadcast systems that served the interests of the state or by licensing domestic commercial broadcasters who pledged to serve the national interest. In fact, with the exception of the Western Hemisphere, most nations around the world opted for public-service television during early years of the medium. In countries like France, the government organized powerful, centralized television networks that focused on the promotion of national culture, while in poorer countries like India and China, television was mobilized to address pressing concerns related to economic and social development. Whether a commercial or public service, audiences in most countries had few channels to choose from during this classical era of national network television and broadcasters consequently placed their first priority on serving a mass audience.

During the 1980s, however, television institutions began to change dramatically. For example, economic reversals in Europe put great pressure on the budgets of public-service broadcasters as government subsidies and license revenues began to decline. Attempts to justify increased public expenditures to support these beleaguered institutions were met with challenges from groups who traditionally were marginalized by national networks. Women's organizations, labor unions, peace groups, environmental advocates, and ethnic and regional political movements all criticized state broadcast institutions for focusing on mass audiences and failing to represent a diverse range of perspectives.

This crisis of legitimacy came at the very moment when transnational entrepreneurs with access to new sources of capital began to develop satellite/cable services that fell outside the domain of national broadcast regulation. Business leaders supported these initiatives since it would expand the availability of television advertising time and diminish government control over the airwaves. The resulting licenses for new commercial channels initially targeted two groups: transnational niche viewers (e.g., business executives, sports enthusiasts, and music video fans) and subnational niche groups who were not being served by public broadcasters (e.g., regional, local, or ethnic audiences). Similar trends emerged outside of Europe in countries such as India, Australia, and Indonesia. Meanwhile, in the countries dominated by commercial broadcasting systems, market forces drove the development of new services as the number of satellite/cable channels began to expand rapidly, challenging the hegemony the existing national broadcast oligopolies.

During this era of change, a new generation of corporate moguls—such as Rupert Murdoch (News Corp.), Ted Turner (CNN), and Akio Morita (Sony)—aspired to build media empires that realized global synergies through horizontal and vertical integration of their television, music, motion picture, video game, and other media enterprises. These new conglomerates aim to serve a wide variety of mass and niche markets in both information and entertainment. Although national audiences continue to play an important role in their calculations, companies such as News Corp. increasingly strategize about transnational and subnational audiences, hoping to find new markets and potential synergies among their diverse operations.

Besides contributing to the growth of global media conglomerates, this "neo-network era" of multiple channels and flexible corporate structures has also engendered new local services, such as Zee TV in India and Phoenix TV in China. It has also forced global television services to adapt their content for local and regional audiences. For instance, MTV now operates eight distinctive channels in Asia alone, offering various mixes of global, regional, and local programming.

Thus, globalization has paradoxically fostered the production and promotion of transnational media products as well as localized niche products aimed at subnational audiences, such as teenage music fans. Unlike the classical network era, when television networks tended to focus exclusively on national mass audiences, media conglomerates today are flexibly structured to accommodate marketing strategies aimed at a variety of audiences, sometimes without regard to national boundaries. The scale and competitive power of these new television institutions have seriously undermined public broadcasting in some countries, such as Italy. But in other countries such as India, competition with satellite TV has encouraged Doordarshan—the public-service broadcaster—to improve program quality, conduct systematic audience research, and diversify its services, targeting new channels at local and niche viewers, many of whom were previously marginalized by the national broadcast monopoly. The globalization of television can in large part be explained by these changes in media institutions, audience configurations, and production practices. Yet it is also part of a broader historical transformation that has been going on for at least 500 years, beginning with the European voyages of discovery and conquest.

From a historical perspective, television is but one component of an ongoing process of globalization. This process refers on the one hand to the increasing speed and density of interactions among people and institutions around the world, a trend that manifests itself in the dynamic interdependence of global financial markets, the transnational division of labor, the interlocking system of nation-states, the establishment of supranational institutions, and the interconnection of communication and transportation systems. On the other hand, globalization also refers to changing modes of consciousness, whereby people increasingly think and talk about the world as an entity. Sociologist Roland Robertson suggests that rather than the world just being itself, we increasingly imagine the world being "for itself." We speak of global order, human rights, nuclear disarmament, and world ecology as shared experiences and collective projects. We reflect upon information from near and far and we often deliberate as if we have a stake in both domains. Not everyone joins in these conversations, and certainly all voices are not equal, but these discussions nevertheless span greater terrain and include more people than ever before and the outcomes of these interactions often have effects that transcend local and national boundaries.

All of the trends just outlined have accelerated in the past 150 years with the help of communication technologies like the telegraph, telephone, radio, cinema, television, and computer. Moreover, the development and deployment of these technologies have been linked to specific historical projects—European expansion and colonization, the cold-war-era struggle between the superpowers, and most recently neoliberal, supranational capitalism. This last project, which emerged after the decline of authoritarian communist regimes, is most centrally concerned with trade liberalization, as countries around the world are being pressed to eliminate import tariffs on goods and services, as well as cultural products. Consequently, no society today can confidently say that it stands outside the field of global financial markets and transnational corporate operations. A similar observation might be made about popular culture and television, since the commercial flow of goods and ideas around the world has escalated dramatically in recent times. Thus the globalization of television is part of a longer historical trajectory. It builds upon previous developments, yet it also has contributed significantly to the escalating pace of change.

Finally, from an intellectual perspective, one can see that debates about transnational flows of popular culture predate the emergence of global TV by almost a century. As early as the 1920s, national broadcast systems, such as the British Broadcasting Corporation (BBC), were put in place as a bulwark against foreign media influences, particularly Hollywood films and U.S. popular music. Throughout the 20th century, preserving and promoting national culture over the airwaves was characterized as a key element of national sovereignty in Europe, Latin America, and especially in the newly independent states of the postcolonial world, such as Ghana, Pakistan, and Indonesia. Scholars such as Herbert I. Schiller, Dallas Smythe, and Armand Mattelart were especially strong critics of U.S. TV exports, claiming that they played an important role in sustaining an international structure of economic and political domination. They furthermore contended that the huge flood of media messages exported from the core industrialized countries specifically served the interests of a Western ruling class by squeezing out authentic local voices and instead promoting a culture of consumption that sustains the profitability of capitalist enterprise. This media imperialism thesis emerged in the 1960s and prevailed through the end of the 1980s. Although many scholars still adhere to its central tenets, others have commented upon significant changes in television institutions, audiences, and programs since the 1980s.

Joseph Straubhaar, for example, questions the emphasis on Western dominance of TV schedules around the world by pointing out that in Latin American countries and the Caribbean, national or local programs generally tend to draw larger audiences than imported products. Even though Hollywood continues to be the world's dominant exporter of television programs, most U.S. shows are broadcast in off-peak hours, with the heart of prime time reserved for local productions. Moreover, scholars point to the increasing amount of television trade within particular regions of the world, and note that when audiences tune to a foreign program, they generally prefer a show that has been imported from a country with a similar language and/or culture. In Venezuela, for example, viewers are most likely to prefer a show imported from a regional producer like Mexico's Televisa or Brazil's Globo rather than a Hollywood production. Likewise, Taiwanese audiences seem to prefer Japanese or Hong Kong serial dramas over Western fare, and Kuwaiti audiences prefer dramas from producers in Cairo. In recent years, the one-way program flows from Hollywood to the rest of the world have been displaced by more complicated patterns of distribution.

One indication of these new patterns of TV flow can be gleaned from the emergence of global media capitals, such as Bombay, Cairo, and Hong Kong. Such locales have become centers of the global television industry that have specific logics of their own, ones that do not necessarily correspond to the geography, interests, or policies of particular nation-states. For example, Hong Kong television is produced, distributed, and consumed in Taipei, Beijing, Amsterdam, Vancouver, Bangkok, and Kuala Lumpur. The central node of all this activity is Hong Kong, but the logics that now motivate the development of the Hong Kong television are not necessarily governed by the interests of the Chinese state or even the Special Administrative Region. Likewise, Bombay, once the home of the national Indian film industry, is now the center for transnational enterprises that operate across the film, television, and music industries. For example, Zee TV—South Asia's most popular Hindi-language commercial satellite channel—also provides a satellite service to Europe, distributes music videos in Los Angeles, and mounts film productions targeted at audiences around the globe. As numerous critics have noted, Bollywood has gone global, seeking out new audiences, new financing, and fresh sources of creative talent. Although U.S. programs continue to play a powerful role in media markets around the world, their long-term domination of global markets is far less certain given the emergence of competing media capitals.

Moreover, even in countries where Hollywood programs make their way into prime time, their impact on viewers is uncertain. Cultural studies researchers such as David Morley, Ien Ang, Marie Gillespie, and James Lull have shown how audiences make unanticipated uses of television programming, often reworking the meanings of transnational texts to accommodate the circumstances of their local social context. These findings raise questions about the presumed ideological effects of Hollywood television programs as they circulate around the world. Rather than simply absorbing U.S. capitalist ideology, "active audiences" fashion meanings and identities that are hybrid and complex. It is therefore difficult to argue that the medium is little more than an instrument of capitalist domination. Moreover, investigations of the institutional practices of media organizations find that, contrary to widespread anxieties about cultural homogenization, television services around the world increasingly compete with Hollywood imports by developing programming that is adapted to the needs and interests of specific local audiences.

The media imperialism thesis has been challenged on other accounts as well. Critical studies of nationalism delineate the historical and contested qualities of modern nation-states, showing how power relations *within* countries are often as exploitative as power relations *between* countries. Consequently, the media imperialism thesis, which tends to venerate national media, may rush too quickly to the defense of countries with internal politics deserving of greater scrutiny. National media systems have often been insensitive to the interests of minority groups. In India, for example, Doordarshan, the national media monopoly, provided few benefits to Tamil or Telugu or Muslim populations prior to the introduction of satellite TV competitors. Indeed, pressures of globalization unexpectedly opened the door to new services, voices, and contexts for public deliberation. Likewise, in mainland China, the national television system has grown more responsive to local cultures and languages as it attempts to respond to the pressures of transnational television flows.

Finally, although the media imperialism thesis claims that "authentic" local cultures are disappearing under the avalanche of American popular culture, recent research in the humanities and social sciences—especially in the field of anthropology—questions the prior existence of "pure" or "authentic" cultures. Even before the advent of modern mass media, cultures were always in flux and often shaped, albeit more slowly, by outside influences. Rather than portraying local culture as an integrated, organic way of life that has only recently been violated by the intrusion of global television, recent scholarship suggests that it is more productive to understand culture as a dynamic site of social contest and interaction. Thus television should be understood as a site of struggle between competing social factions and forces. It is a terrain of interaction in which power relations clearly manifest themselves, yet it is also a dynamic sphere of discourse and social practice, with complex and often unintended outcomes. Consequently, careful attention must be paid to the diverse local contexts of television programming and institutions around the world.

These challenges to the media imperialism thesis have formed the foundation of globalization studies of television, while opening the door to new critical perspectives. John Tomlinson suggests, for example, that a critique of global capitalist modernity is perhaps a more salient analytical project for television scholars. Such an approach would still be alert to questions of power and dominance, but it would no longer fetishize local cultures of the pretelevision era, nor would it make sweeping assertions about the function of the medium as an unqualified tool of capitalist domination. Television does not instrumentally shape or homogenize human consciousness; rather, it alters the ways in which we reflect upon our environment—near and far—and the quotidian choices that we make. Tomlinson contends that the emergence of a "glocal" of popular culture may in fact lay the foundations for nascent transnational political movements around issues such as labor, ecology, and human rights.

Similarly, Ien Ang advocates television research that explores the global/local dynamics of the medium, arguing that the very indeterminacy of communication processes in a world of media conglomerates is perhaps the central question that researchers must address. The play of power in global television is to be found in the ways that media conglomerates attempt to set structural limits on the production and circulation of meaning and contrarily on the ways in which viewers both comply with and defy these semiotic limits. This play of power requires an understanding of industries and audiences, as well as the diverse social contexts in which the contest over meaning arises.

In conclusion, the study of global TV invites us to examine the emergence of transnational programming, audiences, and institutions, but it also encourages us to consider the longer trajectory of globalization as a social process and to reflect upon the relatively recent human encounter with a global communication medium. During the 1960s, Marshall McLuhan hyperbolically heralded the arrival of a "global village." Perhaps more modestly, one might suggest that television facilitates a process whereby villages around the world increasingly perceive their circumstances in relation to global issues, forces, and institutions, as well as local and national ones.

MICHAEL CURTIN

See also **McLuhan, Marshall; Murdoch, Rupert K.; News Corporation, Ltd.; Satellite; Television Studies; Turner, Ted**

Further Reading

Ang, Ien, *Living Room Wars: Rethinking Media Audiences for a Postmodern World,* London: Routledge, 1996

Curtin, Michael, "Media Capitals: Cultural Geographies of Global TV," in *The Persistence of Television: From Console to Computer,* edited by Jan Olsson and Lynn Spigel, Durham, North Carolina: Duke University Press, 2002

Gillespie, Marie, *Television, Ethnicity and Cultural Change,* London: Routledge, 1995

Gripsrud, Jostein, *The Dynasty Years: Hollywood Television and Critical Media Studies,* London: Routledge, 1995

Mankekar, Purnima, *Screening Culture, Viewing Politics,* Durham, North Carolina: Duke University Press, 1999

Lull, James, *China Turned On: Television, Reform, and Resistance,* London: Routledge, 1991

Morley, David, *Home Territories: Media, Mobility, and Identity,* London: Routledge, 2000

Morley, David, and Kevin Robins, *Spaces of Identity: Global Media, Electronic Landscapes and Cultural Boundaries,* London: Routledge, 1995

Schiller, Herbert I., *Mass Communications and American Empire,* Boulder, Colorado: Westview, 1969, 1992

Robertson, Roland, *Globalization: Social Theory and Global Culture,* Thousand Oaks, California: Sage, 1992

Straubhaar, Joseph, "Beyond Media Imperialism: Asymmetrical Interdependence and Cultural Proximity," *Critical Studies in Mass Communication* 8 (1991): 1–11

Tomlinson, John, *Globalization and Culture,* Chicago: University of Chicago Press, 1999

Godfrey, Arthur (1903–1983)

U.S. Variety Show Host

Arthur Godfrey ranks as one of the important on-air stars of the first decade of American television. Indeed, prior to 1959 there was no bigger TV luminary than this freckled-faced, ukulele-playing host and pitchman. Through most of the decade of the 1950s, Godfrey hosted a daily radio program and appeared in two top-ten prime-time television shows, all for CBS. As the new medium of television was invading U.S.

Arthur Godfrey, 1951.
Courtesy of the Everett Collection

households, there was something about Godfrey's wide grin, his infectious chuckle, his unruly shock of red hair that made millions tune in, not once, but twice a week.

To industry insiders, Godfrey was television's first great master of advertising. His deep, microphone-loving voice delivery earned him a million dollars a year, making him one of the highest-paid persons in the United States at the time. He blended a southern folksiness with enough sophistication to charm a national audience measured in the millions through the 1950s. For CBS-TV in particular, Godfrey was one of network television's most valuable stars, generating millions of dollars in advertising billings each year, with no ostensible talent save being the most congenial of hosts.

After more than a decade on radio, Godfrey ventured onto prime-time TV in December 1948 by simply permitting the televising of his radio hit *Arthur Godfrey's Talent Scouts.* The formula for *Talent Scouts* was simple enough. "Scouts" presented their "discoveries" to perform live before a national radio and television audience. Most of these discoveries were in fact struggling professionals looking for a break, and the quality of the talent was quite high. The winner, chosen by a fabled audience applause meter, often joined

Godfrey on his radio show and on *Arthur Godfrey and His Friends* for some period thereafter.

Through the late 1940s and 1950s Godfrey significantly assisted the careers of Pat Boone, Tony Bennett, Eddie Fisher, Connie Francis, and Patsy Cline. An institution on Monday nights at 8:30 P.M., *Arthur Godfrey's Talent Scouts* always functioned as Godfrey's best showcase and through the early 1950s was a consistent top-ten hit.

A month after the December 1948 television debut of *Arthur Godfrey's Talent Scouts* came the premiere of *Arthur Godfrey and His Friends.* In that program Godfrey employed a resident cast that at times included Julius La Rosa, Frank Parker, Lu Ann Simms, and the Cordettes. Tony Marvin was both the announcer and Godfrey's "second banana," as he was on *Arthur Godfrey's Talent Scouts.* The appeal of *Arthur Godfrey and His Friends* varied, depending on the popularity of the assembled company of singers, all clean-cut young people lifted by Godfrey from obscurity. Godfrey played host and impresario, sometimes singing off-key and strumming his ukulele, but most often leaving the vocals to others.

As he had done on radio, Godfrey frequently kidded his sponsors, but always "sold from the heart," only hawking products he had actually tried or regularly used. No television viewer during the 1950s doubted that Godfrey really did love Lipton Tea and drank it every day. He delighted in tossing aside prepared scripts and telling his audience: "Aw, who wrote this stuff? Everybody knows Lipton's is the best tea you can buy. So why get fancy about it? Getcha some Lipton's, heat the pot with plain hot water for a few minutes, then put fresh hot water on the tea and let it just sit there."

Godfrey perfected the art of seeming to speak intimately to each and every one of his viewers, to sound as if he were confiding in "you and you alone." Despite all his irreverent kidding, advertisers loved him. Here was no snake-oil salesman hawking an unnecessary item, merchandise not worth its price. Here was a friend recommending the product. This personal style drove CBS efficiency experts crazy. Godfrey refused simply to read his advertising copy in the allocated 60 seconds. Instead he talked—for as long as he felt necessary to convince his viewers of his message, frequently running over his allotted commercial time.

CBS owner William S. Paley detested Godfrey but bowed to his incredible popularity. CBS president Frank Stanton loved Godfrey because his shows were so cheap to produce but drew consistently high ratings. In 1955 when *Disneyland* cost $90,000 per hour, and costs for a half hour of *The Jack Benny Show* totaled more than $40,000, *Arthur Godfrey's Talent Scouts* cost but $30,000. This figure was more in line with the production of a cheap quiz program than fashioning a pricey Hollywood-based show on film.

In his day Godfrey accumulated a personal fortune that made it possible for him to own a vast estate in the Virginia horse country, maintain a huge duplex apartment in Manhattan, and fly back and forth in his own airplanes. In 1950 he qualified for a pilot's license; the following year he trained to fly jets. Constantly plugging the glories of air travel, Godfrey, according to Eddie Rickenbacker, did more to boost aviation than any single person since Charles Lindbergh.

Godfrey's end symbolized the close of the era of experimental, live television. But he should be remembered for more than his skill in performing for live television. Perhaps even more significant is that he taught the medium how to sell. In terms of the forces that have shaped and continue to shape the medium of television, Godfrey's career perfectly illustrates the workings of the star system. Here was a person who seemed to have had "no talent" but was so effective that through most of the 1950s he was "everywhere" in the mass media. In the end, times and tastes changed. In 1951 Arthur Godfrey stood as the very center of American television. Eight years later, he was back on radio, a forgotten man to all but the few who listened to the "old" medium.

DOUGLAS GOMERY

See also Arthur Godfrey Shows; Dann, Michael

Arthur Godfrey. Born in New York City, August 31, 1903. Educated at Naval Radio School, 1921; Naval Radio Materiel School, 1929; various correspondence courses. Married: Mary Bourke, 1938; children: Richard (from previous marriage), Arthur Michael, Jr., and Patricia Ann. Served in the U.S. Navy, receiving radio training and becoming a radio operator on destroyer duty, 1920–24; served in the U.S. Coast Guard, 1927–30. Radio announcer and entertainer, WFBR, Baltimore, Maryland, 1930; staff announcer, NBC, Washington, D.C., 1930–34; freelance radio entertainer, from 1934; joined CBS Radio, 1945; CBS television host, *Arthur Godfrey's Talent Scouts,* 1948–58; television host, *Arthur Godfrey and His Friends,* 1949–59; national radio host, *Arthur Godfrey Time,* 1960–72; starred in films, 1963–68. Member: National Advisory Committee on Oceans and Atmosphere, and Citizen's Advisory Committee on Environmental Quality. Died in New York City, March 16, 1983.

Television Series

1948–58	*Arthur Godfrey's Talent Scouts*
1949–59	*Arthur Godfrey and His Friends*

Films

Four For Texas, 1963; *The Glass Bottom Boat,* 1966; *Where Angels Go...Trouble Follows,* 1968.

Radio

Arthur Godfrey's Talent Scouts, 1945–48; *Arthur Godfrey Time,* 1960–72.

Goldbergs, The

U.S. Domestic Comedy

In many ways, the program that Gertrude Berg devised in 1928 and sold to NBC radio the following year was unique. No other daily serial drama reflected so explicitly its creator's own ethnic background, and few other producers retained such close control over their work. Until the late 1930s, Berg herself wrote all the scripts, five to six 15-minute stories per week, and even after hiring outside writers continued to act as producer; she performed the role of the main character herself throughout the show's 30-year history on radio and television.

The Rise of the Goldbergs began as skits produced at her family's Catskills hotel for the rainy-day entertainment of guests. Originally centered around the comic character Maltke Talzinitsky, Maltke became Molly and Talzinitsky modulated to Goldberg, while Berg herself ventured into writing theatrical and commercial continuities. On November 20, 1929, the first episode of *The Rise of the Goldbergs* aired as a sustaining program on WJZ, flagship of the NBC Blue network, no doubt building on the success of radio's first network dramatic serial, *Amos 'n' Andy,* introduced in August 1929. Early scripts concerned themselves explicitly and intimately with an immigrant Jewish family's assimilation into American life. The cast consisted of "Molly" herself, playing the wise and warmhearted wife of Jake (James R. Waters) and mother of Rosalie (Roslyn Silber) and Sammy (Alfred Ryder/Alfred Corn). Uncle David (Menasha Skulnik) filled the role of resident family patriarch. Molly, Jake, and Uncle David spoke with heavy Yiddish accents, while the children favored standard American with a goodly dash of the Bronx. Much humor derived from Molly's malapropisms and "Old World" turns of phrase, drawing on the vaudeville ethnic dialogue tradition. The first season's scripts deal with such issues as the difficulties of raising children in an American environment that sometimes clashed with old world traditions, and the immigrant family's striving for economic success and security. Molly's conversations up the airshaft with her neighbor ("Yoo hoo, Mrs. Bloo-oom") and frequent visitors in their small apartment vividly invoke New York tenement life. The success of this slice of specifically ethnic, but far from atypical, American experience resulted in 18,000 letters pouring into NBC's office when Berg's illness forced the show off the air for a week.

The Rise of the Goldbergs aired sporadically for its first few seasons, then more regularly from 1931 to 1934, sponsored by Pepsodent and appearing from 7:45 to 8:00 every day except Sunday. After a hiatus, it returned in 1936 as a late afternoon serial, running five days a week from 5:45 to 6:00 on CBS under the sponsorship of the Colgate-Palmolive-Peet company via the Benton and Bowles agency. At this point, it was renamed simply *The Goldbergs.* Procter and Gamble took over the program in 1938.

In 1939 the show's setting shifted from the Bronx to the Connecticut town of Lastonbury, in keeping with its narrative of American assimilation. Yet Berg never lost sight of the specifically Jewish ethnic background that made the Goldbergs unique in network radio and television. One memorable episode, aired April 3, 1939, invoked Krystallnacht and the worsening situation in Nazi Germany as the Goldberg's Passover Seder was interrupted by a rock thrown through their living room window. Other stories referred to family members or friends trying to escape from Eastern Europe ahead of the Holocaust. Most plot lines, however, avoided head-on discussion of anti-Semitism or world politics, concentrating instead on family and neighborhood doings, with the occasional crime or adventure story to liven up the action. Molly continued to supervise her family's activities, Jake experienced business

Goldbergs, Larry Robinson, Gertrude Berg, Arlene McQuade, 1949–55; 1952 episode.
Courtesy of the Everett Collection

setbacks and successes, Rosalie and Sammy grew up, got married, and went off to war, as American families in the show's loyal listening audience followed a similar trajectory.

In 1946 the show suspended production, during which time Berg adapted it to the Broadway stage as a play called *Me and Molly,* which ran for 156 performances. In 1949 *The Goldbergs* moved to television with a new cast (except Molly), sponsored on CBS by General Mills' Sanka Coffee, which dropped the program in 1951 when Philip Loeb, then playing Jake, was blacklisted in the infamous Red Channels purge. Reappearing without Loeb and with a different sponsor and network in 1952, the television Goldbergs ran on NBC from February 1952 through September 1953, then on DuMont from April to October 1954. These early seasons were all performed live and featured the Goldberg family back in the Bronx (with the children once again teenagers). In 1955 they moved to the New York suburb of Haverville in a version filmed for syndication; this lasted one season.

Combining aspects of the family comedy and the daytime serial, *The Goldbergs* pioneered the character-based domestic sitcom format that would become television's most popular genre. Its concern with ethnicity, assimilation, and becoming middle class carried it through the first three decades of broadcasting and into the postwar period but ultimately proved out of place in the homogenized suburban domesticity of late 1950s TV.

MICHELE HILMES

See also **Berg, Gertrude; Family on Television; Gender and Television; Racism, Ethnicity and**

Television

Cast

Molly Goldberg	Gertrude Berg
Jake Goldberg (1949–51)	Philip Loeb
Jake Goldberg (1952)	Harold J. Stone
Jake Goldberg (1953–56)	Robert H. Harris
Sammy Goldberg (1949–52)	Larry Robinson
Sammy Goldberg (1954–56)	Tom Taylor
Rosalie Goldberg	Arlene McQuade
Uncle David	Eli Mintz
Mrs. Bloom (1953)	Olga Fabian
Dora Barnett (1955–56)	Betty Bendyke
Carrie Barnett (1955–56)	Ruth Yorke
Daisy Carey (1955–56)	Susan Steel
Henry Carey (1955–56)	Jon Lormer

Producers

Worthington Miner, William Berke, Cherney Berg

Programming History
CBS
January 1949–February 1949   Monday 8:00–8:30

March 1949–April 1949	Monday 9:00–9:30
April 1949–June 1951	Monday 9:30–10:00
NBC	
February 1952–July 1952	Monday, Wednesday, Friday 7:15–7:30
July 1953–September 1953	Friday 8:00–8:30
DuMont	
April 1954–October 1954	Tuesday 8:00–8:30
First-run syndication	
1955–56	

Further Reading

Berg, Gertrude, *Molly and Me,* New York: McGraw-Hill, 1961

Hilmes, Michele, *Radio Voices: American Broadcasting 1922–1952,* Minneapolis: University of Minnesota Press, 1997

Lipsitz, George, *Time Passages: Collective Memory and American Popular Culture,* Minneapolis: University of Minnesota Press, 1990

Stedman, Raymond W., *The Serials,* Norman: University of Oklahoma Press, 1971

"Golden Age" of Television Drama

The "Golden Age" of American television generally refers to the proliferation of original and classic dramas produced for live television during the United States' postwar years. From 1949 to approximately 1960, these live dramas became the fitting programmatic complements to the game shows, westerns, soap operas, and "vaudeo" shows (vaudeville and variety acts on TV) that dominated network television's prime-time schedule. As the nation's economy and population expanded, and demographic patterns shifted, television and advertising executives turned to dramatic shows as a programming strategy to elevate the status of television and attract the growing and increasingly important suburban family audience. Golden Age dramas quickly became the ideal marketing vehicle for major U.S. corporations seeking to display their products favorably before a national audience.

In the early years, Golden Age drama programs such as *The Actors' Studio* (ABC/CBS, 1948–50) originated from primitive but innovative two-camera television studios located primarily in New York City, although some broadcasts, such as *Mr. Black* (ABC, 1949), a half-hour mystery anthology series, were produced in Chicago as well. Ranging in duration from 30 minutes to an hour, these live dramas were generic hybrids uniquely suited to the evolving video technology. Borrowing specific elements from the stage, network radio, and the Hollywood film, the newly constructed dramas on television ("teledramas") fashioned a dynamic entertainment form that effectively fused these high- and low-cultural expressions.

From radio these teledramas inherited the CBS and NBC network distribution system, sound effects, music, theme songs, and the omniscient narrator, who provided continuity after commercial message breaks. From film, teledramas borrowed aging stars and emerging personalities, camera stylistics, mobility, and flexibility. Imported from the theater were Broadway-inspired set designs; contemporary stage acting techniques (i.e., realist and "method" acting), which imparted a sense of immediacy and reality to small-screen performances; and, finally, teleplay adaptations of classic and middle-brow literature. In a statement that clearly expresses the debt owed by television dramas to the stage, Fred Coe, producer of the weekly *NBC Television Playhouse* (1948–55), remarked that "all of us were convinced it was our mission to bring Broadway to America via the television set."

Ironically, however, it was live teledramas that helped television to displace radio, the stage, and film as the favorite leisure-time activity for the nation's burgeoning suburban families in the late 1940s to the mid-1950s. This postwar demographic shift from urban to suburban centers is often credited with creating the new mass audience and the subsequent demand for the home-theater mode of entertainment that network television, boosted by the high-quality drama programs, was uniquely capable of satisfying.

The first so-called Golden Age drama program to appear was the *Kraft Television Theatre,* which premiered on May 7, 1947, on the NBC network. The *Ford Theater* (CBS/NBC/ABC, 1948–57), *Philco and Goodyear Television Playhouses* (NBC, 1948–55), *Studio One* (CBS, 1948–58), *Tele-Theatre* (NBC, 1948–50), and *Actors Studio* (ABC/CBS, 1948–49) followed the very next year. In 1951 network television was linked coast to coast, and in 1950 *Hollywood Theater Time* (ABC) became one of the first dramatic anthology shows to originate from the West Coast (although transmitted to the East Coast via kinescopes— inferior copies of shows filmed directly from the television screen).

Several important factors contributed to the rise of Golden Age dramas by the mid-1950s. First, the U.S. Congress issued more station licenses and allocated more airtime and frequencies to the nation's four networks, NBC, CBS, ABC, and DuMont. Consequently, this major expansion of the television industry necessitated a rapid increase in the number of new shows. Because this early video era preceded the advent of telefilm and videotape, the live television schedule was a programming vortex with an inexhaustible demand for new shows, 90 percent of which were broadcast live. The remaining dramas were transmitted (usually from the East Coast to the West Coast) via kinescopes. Location on the television schedule was also a key element in the success of anthology dramas during this early phase. Because the sponsors, and not the networks, generally controlled the programs, teledramas were not restricted to a particular network or time schedule. As a result of this programming flexibility, it was not unusual for shows either to rotate around the dial or to remain firmly entrenched, all in search of the best possible ratings. In 1953 the *Kraft Television Theatre* aired at 9:00 P.M. on Wednesdays over the NBC

network and aired a second hour under the same series title on Thursdays at 9:30 P.M. on ABC. The venerable *Ford Television Theater* appeared on all three networks during its nine-year run. The anthology format itself, which demanded a constant supply of actors, writers, directors, and producers, and was quite different from the episodic series structure featuring a stable cast, always offered something new to viewers. And since anthology dramas provided plenty of work to go around, many actors got their first starring roles in live dramas, while others gained national exposure that was not possible on the stage or eluded them on the big screen.

This rotating system of anthology-drama production resulted in a creative environment for television that many television historians consider as yet unsurpassed. The fact that these shows dramatized many high-quality original works as well as adaptations of high- and middlebrow literature gave advertisers cost-effective reasons for underwriting the relatively high production values that characterized many of the top-notch anthology programs. Many, in fact, were consistent Emmy Award winners. The *Texaco Star Theater* won the 1949 Emmy for "Best Kinescope Show." *U.S. Steel Hour* won two Emmys in 1953, its debut year, and *Studio One* received three Emmys during the 1955 season for its production of *Twelve Angry Men.*

As the genre matured and traded its amateur sets for professionally designed studios, it looked good, and by extension, so did its sponsors. Accordingly, the growing prestige of live dramas enabled established and fading stars from the Broadway stage and Hollywood films to be less reticent about performing on television, and many flocked to the new medium. In fact, some actors even lent their famous names to these anthology drama programs. *Robert Montgomery Presents* (ABC, 1950–57) was one of the first anthology series to rely on Hollywood talent. Montgomery's star-driven program was later joined by the *Charles Boyer Theater* (1953), and in 1955 silent film star Conrad Nagel hosted his own syndicated anthology drama entitled *The Conrad Nagel Theater.* Bing Crosby Enterprises produced *The Gloria Swanson Show* in 1954, with Swanson as host and occasional star in teleplays produced for this dramatic anthology series. More commonly, however, it was the sponsor's name that appeared in the show titles, with stars serving as narrators or hosts. For example, from 1954 to 1962 Ronald Reagan hosted CBS's *General Electric Theater.*

As crucial as these elements were, perhaps the most important reason leading to the success of this nascent television art form was the high caliber of talent on both sides of the video camera. Whereas many well-known actors from the stage and screen participated in live television dramas as the 1950s progressed, it was the obscure but professionally trained theater personnel from summer stock and such university theater programs as Yale's Drama School who launched the innovative teletheater broadcasts that we now refer to as television's Golden Age.

In 1949, 24-year-old Marlon Brando starred in *I'm No Hero,* produced by the *Actors' Studio.* Other young actors, such as Susan Strasberg (1953), Paul Newman (1954), and Steve McQueen, made noteworthy appearances on the *Goodyear Playhouse.* Among some of the most prominent writers of Golden Age dramas were Rod Serling, Paddy Chayefsky, Gore Vidal, Reginald Rose, and Tad Mosel. Serling stands out for special consideration here because, in addition to winning the 1955 Emmy for "Best Original Teleplay Writing" (*Patterns* on *Kraft Television Theatre*), he also won two teleplay Emmys for *Playhouse 90* (1956 and 1957), as well as three "Outstanding Writing Achievement in Drama" Emmys: two for *Twilight Zone* (1959 and 1960) and one for *Chrysler Theater* in 1963. Serling's six Emmys for four separate anthology programs over two networks unquestionably secures his position at the top of the Golden Age pantheon. For television, it was writers like Serling and Chayefsky who became the auteurs of its Golden Age. Gore Vidal sums up the opportunity that writing for television dramas represented in this way: "one can find better work oftener on the small gray screen than on Broadway." Chayefsky was more sanguine when he stated that television presented "the drama of introspection," and that "television, the scorned stepchild of drama, may well be the basic theater of our century."

In addition to actors and writers, some of the most renowned Hollywood directors got their big breaks on television's anthology dramas. John Frankenheimer directed for the *Kraft Television Theatre,* Robert Altman for *Alfred Hitchcock Presents,* Yul Brynner and Sidney Lumet for *Studio One,* Sidney Pollack for *The Chrysler Theater* (1965 Emmy for "Directorial Achievement in Drama"), and Delbert Mann for *NBC Television Playhouse.* These are but a few major directors who honed their skills during television's Golden Age.

By 1955 Golden Age dramas had proven so popular with national audiences that they became important staples of the network television schedule. Some of the anthologies were now produced on film, but they maintained the aesthetic and psychological premises of the live productions that tutored their creators and their audiences. These drama series aired on the networks each day except Saturdays, and on some days, there were up to four separate anthology shows airing on one evening's prime-time schedule. One instance of such a programming pattern occurred on Thursday nights during the 1954–55 TV season. In one single

evening, viewers could choose between *Kraft Television Theatre* (ABC, 1953–55), *Four Star Playhouse* (CBS, 1952–56), *Ford Theater* (NBC, 1952–56), and *Lux Video Theater* (NBC, 1954–57). Dramatic anthologies came in various generic formats as well, including suspense (*Kraft Suspense Theatre* [NBC, 1963–65] and *The Clock* [NBC/ABC, 1949–51]); mystery (*Mr. Arsenic* [ABC, 1952] and *Alfred Hitchcock Presents* [CBS/NBC, 1955–65]); psychological (*Theater of the Mind* [NBC, 1949]); legal (*They Stand Accused* [DuMont, 1949–54]); science fiction (*Twilight Zone* [CBS, 1959–64]); military (*Citizen Soldier* [syndicated, 1956]); and reenactments (*Armstrong Circle Theater* [NBC/CBS, 1950–63]).

As these various titles suggest, the dramas staged on these anthology programs were remarkably diverse—at least in form, if not in substance. In this regard, critics of the so-called Golden Age dramas have noted what they consider to be major problems inherent in the staging of plays for the commercial television medium.

Much of the criticism of these live television dramas concerned the power sponsors often exerted over program content. Specifically, the complaints focused on the mandate by sponsors that programs adhere to a "dead-centerism." In other words, sponsored shows were to avoid completely socially and politically controversial themes. Only those dramas that supported and reflected positive middle-class values, which likewise reflected favorably the image of the advertisers, were broadcast. Critics charge the networks with pandering to the expectations of southern viewers in order not to offend regional sensibilities. Scripts exploring problems at the societal level (e.g., racial discrimination, poverty, and other social ills) were systematically ignored. Instead, critics complain, too many Golden Age dramas were little more than simplistic morality tales focusing on the everyday problems and conflicts of weak individuals confronted by personal shortcomings such as alcoholism, greed, impotence, and divorce. While there is no doubt that teleplays dealing with serious social issues were not what most network or advertising executives considered appropriate subject matter for predisposing viewers to consume the advertised products, it is important to note that the Golden Age did coincide with the cold war era and McCarthyism, and that cold war references, including many denigrating communism and celebrating the United States, were frequently incorporated in teleplays of the mid- to late 1950s.

Most of the scripts in the live television dramas, however, were original teleplays or works adapted from the stage, ranging from Arthur Miller's *Death of a Salesman* and Eugene O'Neill's *The Iceman Cometh* to Shakespeare's *Romeo and Juliet* and *Othello,* among many others. This menu of live television dramas, especially when compared with popular Hollywood films, the elite theater, or commercial radio, presented American audiences with an extraordinary breadth of viewing experiences in a solitary entertainment medium. Moreover, this cultural explosion was occurring in the comfort of the new mass audience's brand-new suburban living rooms. While the classics and the writings of some contemporary popular authors provided material for the teleplays, these sources were not enough for the networks' demanding weekly program schedules. Moreover, the television programmers were often thwarted by Hollywood's practice of buying the rights to popular works and refusing to grant a rival medium access to them, thereby foreclosing the television networks' ability to dramatize some of the most popular and classic plays. In response, the networks began cultivating original scripts from young writers. Thus, the majority of the dramas appearing on these anthology shows were original works.

Perhaps the quintessential Golden Age drama is Chayefsky's *Marty.* On May 24, 1953, Delbert Mann directed Chayefsky's most renowned teleplay for NBC's *Philco Television Playhouse.* Starring Rod Steiger and Nancy Marchand as the principals, *Marty* is a love story about two ordinary characters and the mundane world they inhabit. *Marty* is important because its uncomplicated and sympathetic treatment of Marty, the butcher, and his ability to achieve independence from his demanding mother and embrace his uncertain future, resonated with many suburban viewers, who were, themselves, facing similar social and political changes in postwar American society. *Marty* was an ideal drama for the times, leading one reviewer to write that it represented "the unadorned glimpse of the American middle-class milieu." The suburban viewers, like the fictional "Marty" they welcomed into their living rooms, had become willing participants in an emerging national culture no longer distinguishable by intergenerational and interethnic differences. What further distinguishes *Marty* is the fact that it signaled a trend in the entertainment industry whereby teleplays were increasingly adapted for film. Shortly after its phenomenal television success, *Marty* became a successful feature film.

Some of the most successful and critically acclaimed dramatic anthology programs of the Golden Age were *Armstrong Circle Theater* (13 seasons), *Kraft Television Theatre* (11 seasons), *Alfred Hitchcock Presents* (10 seasons), *Studio One* (10 seasons), *The U.S. Steel Hour* (10 seasons), *General Electric Theater* (9 seasons), *Philco Television Playhouse* (7 seasons), *Goodyear Playhouse* (6 seasons), *Playhouse 90* (4 seasons), and *Twilight Zone* (4 seasons, revived from 1985 to 1988). In present times, only *Hallmark Hall of Fame* (first broadcast in 1951) survives from the heyday of television's Golden Age. With the advent of videotape and telefilm, the shift to Hollywood studios as sites of program production, and the social upheavals of the 1960s, live anthology dramas fell victim to poor ratings and changing social tastes.

ANNA EVERETT

See also **Advertising, Company Voice; Anthology Drama: Chayefsky, Paddy; Coe, Fred; Frankenheimer, John;** *Goodyear Playhouse; Kraft Television Theatre;* **Mann, Delbert;** *Playhouse 90;* **Programming; Rose, Reginald; Serling, Rod;** *Studio One*

Further Reading

Averson, Richard, and David Manning White, editors, *Electronic Drama: Television Plays of the Sixties,* Boston: Beacon Press, 1971

Brooks, Tim, and Earle Marsh, editors, *The Complete Directory to Prime Time Network TV Shows: 1946–Present,* New York: Ballantine, 1979; 5th edition, 1992

Gianakos, Larry James, *Television Drama Series Programming: A Comprehensive Chronicle, 1947–1959,* Metuchen, New Jersey: Scarecrow Press, 1980

Gitlin, Todd, *Inside Prime Time,* New York: Pantheon, 1985; revised edition, 1994

Hawes, William, *The American Television Drama: The Experimental Years,* University: University of Alabama Press, 1986

Kindem, Gorham, editor, *The Live Television Generation of Hollywood Film Directors: Interviews with Seven Directors,* Jefferson, North Carolina: McFarland, 1994

MacDonald, J. Fred, *One Nation under Television: The Rise and Decline of Network TV,* New York: Pantheon, 1990

McNeil, Alex, *Total Television: A Comprehensive Guide to Programming from 1948 to 1980,* Harmondsworth, England, and New York: Penguin Books, 1980; 4th edition as *Total Television: A Comprehensive Guide to Programming from 1948 to the Present,* New York: Penguin Books, 1996

Miner, Worthington, *Worthington Miner,* Los Angeles: Directors Guild of America, and Metuchen, New Jersey: Scarecrow Press, 1985

Newcomb, Horace, editor, *Television: The Critical View,* New York: Oxford University Press, 1976; 4th edition, 1987

Skutch, Ira, *Ira Skutch: I Remember Television: A Memoir,* Metuchen, New Jersey: Scarecrow Press, 1989

Stempel, Tom, *Storytellers to the Nation: A History of American Television Writing,* New York: Continuum, 1992

Sturcken, Frank, *Live Television: The Golden Age of 1946–1958 in New York,* Jefferson, North Carolina: McFarland, 1990

Wicking, Christopher, and Tise Vahimagi, *The American Vein: Directors and Directions in Television,* New York: Dutton, 1979

Wilk, Max, *The Golden Age of Television: Notes from the Survivors,* New York: Delacorte Press, 1976

Golden Girls, The

U.S. Situation Comedy

The popular song "Thank You for Being a Friend" was not only the weekly thematic prelude to the situation comedy *The Golden Girls;* its title/opening line also came to represent the sensibility that sprang from the heart of this delightful program. With *The Golden Girls,* NBC brought to television one of the first representations of senior women coming together to create a circle of friends that functioned as a family. The program centers around four main characters: Dorothy Zbornak (Bea Arthur), a divorced schoolteacher; Sophia Petrillo (Estelle Getty), Dorothy's elderly, widowed mother; Blanche DeVereaux (Rue McClanahan), a widow and owner of the Miami home in which all of the women live; and Rose Nylund (Betty White), a widow and an active volunteer in the community. Aside from the mother-daughter relationship between Dorothy and Sophia, no other family relations exist between the women, yet they share their daily lives, dreams, fears, and dilemmas as a unit. The group life of the characters enables expression of diverse opinions and approaches to problems the women face as individuals.

The south Florida setting adds a warmth and lightness to the show, reflected in the tropical furniture and clothing favored by the women. The vivid colors and the light that floods the production visually represents the vibrancy of the lives of the characters.

On *The Golden Girls,* the main characters are in their late-middle age or beyond, but they are presented as full of life, working, capable, and energetic. Even Sophia, the elderly mother, is often in plays, taking trips, going on dates, and doing charity work. Blanche, the youngest of the women, is known for her fondness for men. (Blanche's sexual adventures are always a topic of conversation, but they are never actually portrayed on the program.) Rose, the storyteller of the group, boasts about her roots in St. Olaf, Minnesota, and is presented as much more conservative than the passionate Blanche. Much of the comedy in the program stems from the absurdity of Rose's stories of her "simple" hometown. These rambling narratives are often utterly inane, but eventually—after the no-nonsense Dorothy shouts in frustration, "The point, Rose, get to the point!"—the story offers warmhearted

advice or a perceptive viewpoint on the problem at hand. Sophia often aims her sharp and sarcastic wit at Rose's stories, making fun of her in a critical, but kind, way. Dorothy, the working schoolteacher and the voice of reason, generally plays against the more extreme, often comical perspectives of the other women. Despite individual eccentricities, each woman is wise in her own way, and each values the others' experiences and sage advice. Each plays her part in the maintenance of friendships and family bonds that result from their cohabitation.

The Golden Girls valued women and put special emphasis on the importance of women's networks, friendships, and experiences. The series was inclusive enough to showcase the concerns and escapades of

The Golden Girls.
Courtesy of the Everett Collection

four distinctive, aging women, yet balanced enough to combine their individual experiences into a positive picture of four senior citizens functioning together to make the most of life.

Despite the success of the program, NBC dropped *The Golden Girls* from the prime-time lineup at the end of the 1992 season, when Bea Arthur decided to leave the show. CBS picked up the program and renamed it *The Golden Palace,* setting it in a hotel run by Blanche, Rose, and Sophia. It was a failure, and after its swift cancellation, the character Sophia returned to NBC to do occasional walk-ons on *Empty Nest,* a *Golden Girls* spin-off.

DAWN MICHELLE NILL

See also **Arthur, Beatrice; Harris, Susan; Thomas, Tony; Witt, Paul Junger**

Cast

Dorothy Zbornak	Bea Arthur
Rose Nylund	Betty White
Blanche Devereaux	Rue McClanahan
Sophia Petrillo	Estelle Getty

Producers

Paul Junger Witt, Tony Thomas, Susan Harris

Programming History

180 episodes
NBC

September 1985–July 1991	Saturday 9:00–9:30
August 1991–September 1992	Saturday 8:00–8:30

Further Reading

Gold, Todd, "*Golden Girls* in Their Prime," *Saturday Evening Post* (July–August 1986)

"*Golden Girls* Gets Golden Price in Syndication," *Broadcasting* (June 6, 1988)

Kaler, Anne K., "*Golden Girls:* Feminine Archetypal Patterns of the Complete Woman," *Journal of Popular Culture* (Winter 1990)

Walley, Wayne, "Golden Girl of Sitcoms; Susan Harris Helps TV Catch Up to Real," *Advertising Age* (January 30, 1986)

Waters, Harry F., "A New Golden Age: The Over-55 Set Flexes Its Wrinkles on Prime Time," *Newsweek* (November 18, 1985)

Goldenson, Leonard (1905–1999)

U.S. Media Executive

As the founder of a major U.S. network, Leonard Goldenson is perhaps not as famous as David Sarnoff of NBC or William S. Paley of CBS. Starting in 1951, over a 30-year period, Goldenson created the modern ABC (American Broadcasting Company) television network. He did not have the advantage of technological superiority, as NBC had from its owner, Radio Corporation of America (RCA). He did not have the advantage of an extraordinary talent pool, as CBS did from its radio contract. Yet Goldenson should be given credit as one of the modern corporate chieftains who shaped and led television in the United States into the network era, and beyond. The last of the old TV network tycoons, Leonard Goldenson snatched ABC from the brink of irrelevance as a minor radio network and by the 1980s had transformed the company into one of the top broadcasting networks and a leading site for advertising in the world. Goldenson's considerable accomplishments include luring the big Hollywood movie studios into the TV production business;

repackaging sports and making it prime-time fare with *Monday Night Football* and Olympic coverage; and leading the networks into the era of made-for-TV movies and miniseries.

After graduating from the Harvard Business School in 1933, Goldenson was hired to help reorganize the then near-bankrupt theater chain of Hollywood's Paramount Pictures. So skillful was his work at this assignment that Paramount's chief executive officer, Barney Balaban, hired Goldenson to manage the entire Paramount chain. In 1948, when the U.S. Supreme Court forced Paramount to choose either the theater business or Hollywood production and distribution, Balaban selected the Hollywood side and handed over the newly independent United Paramount theater chain to Goldenson. Goldenson then sold a number of movie palaces. Looking for a growth business in which to invest these funds, he selected ABC.

Goldenson finalized the ABC takeover in 1953, which came with a minor network and five stations.

Given the ownership restrictions defined by the Federal Communication Commission's Sixth Report and Order, Goldenson worked from the assumption that only three networks would survive. Only in 1955, with the failure of the DuMont television network, was ABC really off on what would become its successful quest to catch up with industry leaders, CBS and NBC.

As late as 1954, only 40 of the more than 300 television stations then on the air were primarily ABC-TV affiliates. More affiliates for ABC-TV were so-called secondary accounts, an arrangement through which an NBC or CBS affiliate agreed to broadcast a portion (usually small) of the ABC-TV schedule. When DuMont went under, ABC-TV could claim only a tenth of network advertising billings; NBC and CBS split the rest.

Goldenson developed a specific tactic: find a programming niche not well served by the bigger rivals and take it over. Thus, for a youth market abandoned by NBC and CBS, ABC set in motion *American Bandstand, Maverick,* and *The Mickey Mouse Club.* Goldenson found early ABC stars in Edd "Kookie" Byrnes, James Garner, and Ricky Nelson. Controversy came with the premiere of *The Untouchables,* as critics jumped on an apparent celebration of violence, but Goldenson rode out the criticism and lauded the high ratings to potential advertisers.

When necessary, Goldenson would also copy his competition. In the 1950s there was no greater hit than CBS's sitcom *I Love Lucy.* Goldenson signed up Ozzie Nelson and Danny Thomas, and in time *The Adventures of Ozzie and Harriet* would run 435 episodes on ABC, whereas Danny Thomas's *Make Room for Daddy* would air 336.

Goldenson was able to convince Hollywood, in the form of Walt Disney and Warner Brothers, to produce shows for ABC. A turning point—for the network and for all of television—came when Walt Disney agreed to supply ABC with TV shows. In exchange ABC sold its movie palaces and loaned the money to Disney to build a new type of amusement park. Disney had approached any number of banks, but he could not convince their conservative officers that he really did not want to build another "Coney Island." Repeatedly, the financial institutions passed on "Disneyland." So, too, did NBC and CBS, thus missing out on the opportunity to program *The Mickey Mouse Club* and *The Wonderful World of Disney.*

ABC's first Disney show went on the air on Wednesday nights beginning in October 1954; the program moved to Sunday nights in 1960 and would remain a Sunday night fixture for more than two decades. ABC-TV had its first top-20 ratings hit and made millions from its investment in Disneyland. In particular, a De-

Leonard Goldenson, 1984.
Courtesy of the Everett Collection

cember 1954 episode entitled "Davy Crockett" created a national obsession, fostering a pop music hit, enticing baby boomers to beg their parents for coonskin caps, and making Fess Parker a TV star.

With the Warner Brothers shows (*Cheyenne, 77 Sunset Strip, Surfside 6,* and *Maverick*) the ABC television network began making a profit for the first time. By the early 1960s ABC was airing the top-rated *My Three Sons, The Real McCoys,* and *The Flintstones,* which was television's first animated prime-time series. In the more turbulent late 1960s, ABC-TV mixed the traditional (*The FBI* and *Marcus Welby, M.D.*) with the adventuresome (*Mod Squad* and *Bewitched*). But it was not until the 1976–77 season that ABC-TV finally rose to the top of the network ratings; its prime-time hits that season were *Happy Days, Laverne and Shirley,* and *Monday Night Football.*

In sports telecasting ABC-TV soon topped NBC and CBS as a pioneer. ABC led the way with not only its Monday night broadcasts of National Football League games but also with *ABC Wide World of Sports* and coverage of both the summer and winter Olympics. In the late 1970s ABC's miniseries *Roots* set ratings records and acquired numerous awards for its 12 hours of dramatic history. The TV movie was also an innovation of ABC-TV, and in time the "alphabet" network received top ratings for airing *Brian's Song, The Thorn Birds,* and *The Winds of War.*

By the mid-1980s Leonard Goldenson had passed his 80th birthday and wanted out of the day-to-day grind of running a billion-dollar corporation. In 1986 Capital Cities, Inc., backed by Warren Buffett's Berkshire Hathaway investment group, bought ABC for $3.5 billion. Capital Cities, Inc., had long been an award-winning owner of a group of the most profitable television stations in the United States. "Cap Cities" chief executive officer, Thomas Murphy, inherited what Leonard Goldenson had wrought. Leonard Goldenson then gracefully retired. On December 27, 1999, Goldenson died at his home in Longboat Key, Florida, near Sarasota. At age 94, having written his autobiography, he was honored with obituaries in all major media as a founder of modern television in the United States.

Douglas Gomery

See also **American Broadcasting Company; Disney, Walt; Networks;** *Warner Brothers Presents*

Leonard Goldenson. Born in Scottsdale, Pennsylvania, December 7, 1905. Educated at Harvard College, B.S., 1927; Harvard Law School, LL.B., 1930. Married: Isabelle Weinstein, 1939; children: Genise Sandra, Loreen Jay, and Maxine Wynne. Served as law clerk to a railroad attorney, early 1930s; worked in reorganization of Paramount's New England theaters, 1933–37; assistant to the executive in charge of Paramount theater operations, 1937; head, Paramount theater operations, 1938; vice president, Paramount Pictures, Inc., 1942; president and director, Paramount Theatres Service Corporation, 1944; president, chief executive officer, and director, United Paramount Pictures, Inc., 1950, and American Broadcasting-Paramount Theatres, Inc., 1953; chair of the board and chief executive officer, American Broadcasting Companies, Inc., until 1986; chair of the executive committee and director, Capital Cities/ABC, Inc., from 1972. Honorary chair of the Academy of TV Arts and Sciences. Member: International Radio and Television Society; National Academy of Television Arts and Sciences; Broadcast Pioneers; Motion Picture Pioneers; graduate director of the Advertising Council, Inc.; director, Research America; trustee emeritus, Museum of Broadcasting. Died in Longboat Key, Florida, December 27, 1999.

Publication

Beating the Odds: The Untold Story behind the Rise of ABC: The Stars, Struggles, and Egos That Transformed Network Television by the Man Who Made It Happen (with Marvin J. Wolf), 1991

Further Reading

Auletta, Ken, *Three Blind Mice: How the TV Networks Lost Their Way,* New York: Random House, 1991

Benesch, Connie, "Giving Golden Opportunities: Hollywood Luminaries Tell of Support, Creative Vision," *Variety* (December 5, 1994)

Carter, Bill, "Networks' Last Patriarch Offers a Survival Strategy," *New York Times* (February 25, 1991)

Quinlan, Sterling, *Inside ABC: American Broadcasting Company's Rise to Power,* New York: Hastings House, 1979

Sugar, Bert Randolph, *"The Thrill of Victory": The Inside Story of ABC Sports,* New York: Hawthorn, 1978

Williams, Huntington, *Beyond Control: ABC and the Fate of the Networks,* New York: Atheneum, 1989

Wolf, Marvin J., "The Lion in Winter: Vision, Risk-Taking Defined Legendary Career of ABC's Chief Architect," *Variety* (December 5, 1994)

Yanover, Neal S., "Museum Is Monument to Media Maverick," *Variety* (December 5, 1994)

Goldie, Grace Wyndham (1900–1986)

BBC Television Producer

Long considered the first lady of British television, Goldie had transferred from BBC Radio to the BBC Television Service in 1948. She was working on BBC's popular Third Program but soon became responsible for the advent of news and public-affairs programming at the "Television Service." Goldie became the first woman to head a television production department and later became head of BBC Talks and Current Affairs. News-related programs like *Tonight, Monitor, Panorama,* and the highly controversial *That*

Was the Week That Was were projects headed by Goldie and her staff. As early as 1937, Grace Wyndham Goldie had written that television had a decided advantage over radio as a broadcast medium. She wrote, "Television has a vividness which you cannot get from radio broadcasting and a combination of reality and intimacy which you cannot get from cinema." She further exemplified her excitement over television's possibilities when she told members of Parliament that television was "a bomb about to burst" shortly after her appointment to the Television Service.

As a rule, the Television Service had not offered news programming to its audiences. Then director-general of the BBC, Sir William Haley did not believe that television was a good enough medium for news. Prime Minister Clement Attlee disliked television in general, as did Sir John Reith, grand architect of the BBC. Before Goldie's influence, the only televised offering was *Television Newsreel,* which began broadcasting after World War II. The program relied upon the style of the cinema newsreels, a format moviegoing Britons were familiar with. Since the programs were not topical, the same show would repeat weekly. Goldie's subsequent decisions on news content and focus often tested the Service's relationship with management, Parliament, the prime minister, and audiences.

Goldie is remembered for her initiation of the first televised General Elections. Election broadcasts had begun on radio in 1924, but the BBC had determined parties were not interested in using television. In February 1950 Goldie managed to convince the Television Service to let her create a program that would report election results as they came in. She worked closely with future BBC 1 controller Michael Peacock and well-known broadcaster Richard Dimbleby. The main presenter of the program was Chester Wilmot, who had come from radio. For commentary on the overall process, Grace Wyndham Goldie relied upon Oxford academic R.B. McCallum who had written a book on the 1945 election. In an era when the government regulated television's hours of broadcasting, the elections became one of the few occasions when Britons had overnight to breakfast-time television.

With increased immigration from the West Indies after World War II, race was rapidly becoming a major social issue in England. In response to this timely issue, Goldie organized a series of "Race Programs" for the BBC in 1952. The first program in the series would study scientific misconceptions about racial differences. The presenter of the program, Ritchie Calder, would interview scientists conducting anthropological research in Africa. The program entitled "The Scientists Look at Race" included examinations of "Jews, Negroes, Latins, and Ayrians, the Island race (British)

and European (as opposed to non-European)." As with other aspects of Goldie's career, the program was highly controversial.

In 1953 Her Majesty the Queen was intrigued by the idea of televising her coronation, against the wishes of the cabinet. Goldie oversaw the project. In this same year, Goldie began a program in which journalists interviewed leading politicians, called *Press Conference.* Cabinet ministers had to get permission from the prime minister to appear on it. Another program called *Panorama* appeared in the schedules, featuring some political discussions in between arts reviews. Critics panned the program, yet *Press Conference* featured a "who's who" of politicians and newsmakers.

Near the end of 1956, the government ended the practice of blanking television screens between six and seven every evening so that parents could put their children to bed (the "Toddler's Truce"). In February 1957 Goldie used this time slot to launch *Tonight.* Hosted by Cliff Michelmore, *Tonight* came on at ten to seven every weekday evening and soon developed an audience of 8 million viewers. On Sunday, February 2, 1958, another Grace Wyndham Goldie news program went on the air, *Monitor.* The program, which relied heavily upon filmed interviews and documentaries, employed neophyte film directors like John Schlesinger, Ken Russell, and others.

Though Goldie retired in 1965, she continued to serve the BBC as Special Advisor to the Director of Television. As a vanguard of public information, she was often a harsh critic of contemporary television programming. In two newspaper articles published in 1967, Goldie assailed the docudrama genre (aka documentary drama form). Her principal concern was that audiences would blur the lines between factual events and melodrama. She especially targeted the family drama *Cathy Come Home* that addressed mothers on public assistance.

In 1973 the 27th British Film Awards awarded Goldie with an Academy Fellowship based upon her service and commitment to the field. In 1977 Goldie published the book *Facing the Nation Television & Politics 1936–76.* The work is considered to be an excellent "insider's look" at the Service and underscores Goldie's commitment to public information. Goldie also continued to serve as a member of the Association of Charity Affairs for the United Kingdom.

Shortly after her death in 1986, the BBC established a trust fund in her name. The fund offers financial assistance to those who have worked in radio or television, and his or her dependents. The largest grants pay a portion of children's education costs, including travel, school books, and clothing.

DARRELL MOTTLEY NEWTON

See also **British Television**

Grace Wyndham Goldie. Born in England's Western Highlands, March 3, 1900. Her family was headed by her father, a Scots engineer who worked in railroading. She spent a great deal of her childhood living in Egypt before attending a French school in Alexandria. Later she attended the prestigious Cheltenham Ladies' College and Somerville. She married famed British actor Frank Wyndham Goldie and worked with the Board of Trade before accepting a positioning with the BBC in 1944. Died June 3, 1986.

Further Reading

Briggs, Asa, *The BBC: The First Fifty Years,* Oxford: Oxford University Press, 1985

Briggs, Asa, *The History of Broadcasting in the United Kingdom,* Oxford and New York: Oxford University Press, volumes 1–5, 1961, 1965, 1970, 1979, 1995

Carpenter, Humphrey, *The Envy of the World: Fifty Years of the BBC Third Programme and Radio Three,* London: Weidenfeld and Nicolson, 1996

Crisell, Andrew, *An Introductory History of British Broadcasting,* New York: Routledge, 1997

Crossman, Richard, *The Diaries of a Cabinet Minister: Volume One: Minister of Housing 1964–1966,* London: Hamish Hamilton, 1975

Goldie, Grace Wyndham, "Looking Forward, A Personal Forecast of the Future of Television," (London) *Radio Times* (October 29, 1936)

Goldie, Grace Wyndham, "The Story Behind the Challenge of Our Time," in *The Challenge of Our Time: A Series of Essays,* by Arthur Koestler et al., London: Percival Marshall, 1948

Goldie, Grace Wyndham, *Facing the Nation: Television and Politics, 1936–1976,* London: Bodley Head, 1977

Laws, Fredrick, Ralph Hill, Grace Wyndham Goldie, et al., *Made for Millions: A Critical Study of the New Media of Information and Entertainment,* London: Contact Publications, Ltd., 1947

Miall, Leonard, *Inside the BBC: British Broadcasting Characters,* London : Weidenfeld and Nicolson, 1994

Paulu, Burton, *British Broadcasting in Transition,* Minneapolis: University of Minnesota Press, 1961

Reith, Baron John Charles Walsham, *Broadcast Over Britain,* London: Hodden and Stoughton, Ltd., 1924

Wedell, E. G., *Broadcasting Policy in Britain,* London: Michael Joseph, 1968

Whitehouse, Mary, *Who Does She Think She Is?,* London: New English Library, 1971

Good Times

U.S. Domestic Comedy

Evictions, gang warfare, financial problems, muggings, rent parties, and discrimination were frequent elements in the television program *Good Times,* which aired on CBS from February 1974 to August 1979. The program was created by Norman Lear and Bud Yorkin, a highly successful team of independent producers who enjoyed unmitigated success during the 1970s and 1980s with a number of hit television shows including *Maude, Sanford and Son, The Jeffersons,* and one of television's most controversial sitcoms, *All in the Family.*

Good Times was a spin-off show of *Maude.* On *Maude* Esther Rolle played the title character's black maid/housekeeper, Florida, whose family became the center of *Good Times.* In addition to Florida, the spin-off featured her unemployed but always looking-for-work husband, James Evans (John Amos); their teenaged son, J.J. (Jimmy Walker); a daughter, Thelma (BernNadette Stanis); and a younger son, Michael (Ralph Carter). The Evans' neighbor, a 40ish woman named Willona (Ja'net DuBois), made frequent appearances. A very young Janet Jackson later joined the cast as Willona's adopted daughter, Penny.

Good Times earned its place in television history for a number of reasons. The program is significant for its decidedly different view not only of black family life but of American family life in general. Unlike the innocuous images served up in early televisions shows such as *Father Knows Best* and *Julia, Good Times* interjected relevancy and realism into prime-time television by dealing with the pressing issues of the day.

Good Times was also noteworthy in its portrayal of an African-American family attempting to negotiate the vicissitudes of life in a high-rise tenement apartment in an urban slum—the first show to tackle such a scenario with any measure of realism. The program ex-

Good Times, Ralph Carter, BernNadette Stanis, Ja'net DuBois, John Amos, Esther Rolle, Jimmie Walker, 1974–79. Courtesy of the Everett Collection

ploited, with comic relief, such volatile subject matter as inflation, unemployment, and racial bigotry. Along with *The Jeffersons, Good Times* was one of the first television sitcoms featuring a mostly black cast to appear since the controversial *Amos 'n' Andy* show had been canceled some 20 years previously.

Good Times was initially successful in that it offered solace for both blacks and whites, who could identify with the difficulties the Evans family faced. The program appeared on prime-time television in a period of history that included the Watergate scandal, the atrocities of the Vietnam War, staggeringly high interest rates, and growing unemployment. The James Evans character made clear his dissatisfaction with current government policies, and the show became a champion for the plight of the underclass.

The show also highlighted the good parenting skills of James and Florida. In spite of their difficult situation, they never shirked from their responsibility to teach values and morality to their children. The younger son, Michael, was thoughtful, intelligent, and fascinated with African-American history. He frequently participated in protest marches for good causes. J.J. was an aspiring artist who dreams of lifting his family from the clutches of poverty. In one episode, the family's last valuable possession, the television set, was stolen from J.J. on his way to the pawn shop to obtain a loan that would pay the month's rent. Somehow the Evans family prevailed, and they did so with a smile. Their ability to remain stalwart in the face of difficult odds was an underlying theme of the show.

Good Times is also significant for many layers of controversy and criticism that haunted its production. Both stars, Rolle and Amos, walked away and returned as they became embroiled in various disputes surrounding the program's direction. A major point of disagreement was the J.J. character, who metamorphosed into a "coon" stereotype reminiscent of early American film. His undignified antics raised the ire of the black community. With his toothy grin, ridiculous strut, and bug-eyed buffoonery, J.J. became a featured character with his trademark exclamation, "DY-NO-MITE!" J.J. lied, stole, and was barely literate. More and more episodes were centered around his exploits. Forgotten were Michael's scholastic success, James's search for a job, or anything resembling family values.

Both Rolle and Amos objected to the highlighting of the J.J. character. When both stars eventually left the program in protest, abortive attempts were made to soften the J.J. character and continue the program without James and Florida. "We felt we had to do something drastic," Rolle said later in the *Los Angeles Times,* "we had lost the essence of the show."

Even with a newly fashioned (employed and mature-acting) J.J. character, ratings for *Good Times* plummeted. With some concessions, Rolle rejoined the cast in 1978, but the program failed and the series was canceled. The program went on to enjoy success in syndication.

Good Times, with its success and its critics, remains an important program in television history. As the product of the highly successful Lear-Yorkin team, it stretched the boundaries of television comedy, while breaking the unspoken ban on television shows with mostly black casts.

PAMALA S. DEANE

See also **Lear, Norman;** *Maude;* **Racism, Ethnicity and Television**

Cast

Florida Evans (1974–77, 1978–79)	Esther Rolle
James Evans (1974–76)	John Amos
James Evans, Jr. (J.J.)	Jimmie Walker
Willona Woods	Ja'net DuBois
Michael Evans	Ralph Carter
Thelma Evans Anderson	BernNadette Stanis
Carl Dixon (1977)	Moses Gunn
Nathan Bookman (1977–79)	Johnny Brown
Penny Gordon Woods (1977–79)	Janet Jackson
Keith Anderson (1976–79)	Ben Powers
Sweet Daddy (1978–79)	Theodore Wilson

Producers

Norman Lear, Allan Mannings, Austin Kalish, Irma Kalish, Norman Paul, Gordon Mitchell, Lloyd Turner, Sid Dorfman, George Sunga, Bernie West, Dohn Nicholl, Viva Knight

Programming History

120 episodes
CBS

February 1974–September 1974	Friday 8:30–9:00
September 1974–March 1976	Tuesday 8:00–8:30
March 1976–August 1976	Tuesday 8:30–9:00
September 1976–January 1978	Wednesday 8:00–8:30
January 1978–May 1978	Monday 8:00–8:30
June 1978–September 1978	Monday 8:30–9:00
September 1978–December 1978	Saturday 8:30–9:00
May 1979–August 1979	Wednesday 8:30–9:00

Further Reading

Bogle, Donald, *Blacks, Coons, Mulattoes, Mammies, and Bucks: An Interpretive History of Blacks in American Film,* New York: Viking Press, 1973; 4th edition, New York: Continuum, 2001

Bogle, Donald, *Blacks in American Television and Film: An Encyclopedia,* New York: Garland, 1988

Friedman, Lester D., *Unspeakable Images: Ethnicity and the American Cinema,* Urbana: University of Illinois Press, 1991

Gray, Herman, *Watching Race: Television and the Struggle for "Blackness,"* Minneapolis: University of Minnesota Press, 1995

MacDonald, J. Fred, *Blacks and White TV: Afro-Americans in Television since 1948,* Chicago: Nelson-Hall Publishers, 1983; 2nd edition, 1992

Marc, David, and Robert J. Thompson, *Prime Time, Prime Movers: From I Love Lucy to L.A. Law—America's Greatest TV Shows and the People Who Created Them,* Boston: Little, Brown, 1992

Taylor, Ella, *Prime-Time Families: Television Culture in Postwar America,* Berkeley: University of California Press, 1989

Goodson, Mark (1915–1992), and Bill Todman (1918–1979)

U.S. Producers

Mark Goodson and Bill Todman were among television's most successful producers of game shows. They refined celebrity panel quizzes with *What's My Line?* and *I've Got a Secret* and created games that lasted for years. Some, like *The Price Is Right,* became even more popular in revived versions. Many of their shows have been adapted for production in television systems outside the United States.

In 1939 Goodson created his first game, *Pop the Question,* for San Francisco radio station KFRC. In *Pop the Question,* players threw darts at balloons to collect prizes inside. Goodson left for New York City in 1941, with an introduction from Ralph Edwards, an alumnus of University of California, Berkeley, where Goodson was also educated. While working several announcing and writing jobs, Goodson met Todman, a radio writer, director, and advertising copywriter. The two found a shared love of games and set to work on their first quiz show. They developed the methods that would serve them throughout their careers: Goodson refined the format, while Todman tested possible flaws in the rules and worked out the financial angles. CBS Radio finally picked up the game, *Winner Take All,* after World War II, and the two also partnered to create four local radio quizzes: *Hit the Jackpot, Spin to Win, Rate Your Mate,* and *Time's a Wastin'. Winner Take All* used a lockout buzzer system and was the first quiz show to pit two contestants against each other, rather than against the quizmaster one at a time. It was also first to have winners return each week until they were defeated. *Winner Take All* became the first Goodson and Todman show on CBS's new television network, debuting July 8, 1948.

Quiz shows had been popular on radio through the 1940s, and they were equally popular with TV executives: they cost little to produce, and merchandise prizes, so scarce during the war, were furnished free by manufacturers in return for plugs. An oft-repeated story had the partners carrying prizes for *Winner Take All* from their office to the studio. Todman slipped, sending small appliances clattering to the sidewalk. Writer Goodman Ace witnessed the accident and shouted, "Hey, Todman, you dropped your script!"

Most popular radio quizzes did not survive on television. Straight quizzes proved visually dull and failed to involve the audience. Before the rise and fall of the big-money shows, Goodson and Todman found their success by going in two different directions: celebrity panel shows and celebrations of ordinary people.

Their first panel show began in 1949 with Bob Bach, a staffer who had bet the partners that he could deduce the occupations of total strangers. This wager inspired a proposal called "Occupation Unknown," which CBS bought in 1950 and renamed *What's My Line?* Bach became its associate producer as a reward for creating the basic concept for the program, a custom that continued at Goodson-Todman. *What's My Line?* brought tuxedo-wearing bon vivants into viewers' homes for parlor games. These wits seemed amazed and amused by the occupations of ordinary working people. There was also a chance for suggestive exchanges: when questioning a guest whose "line" was "sells mattresses," Arlene Francis innocently provoked gales of laughter by asking, "If Bennett Cerf and I had your product, could we use it together?"

Beat the Clock, meanwhile, let ordinary folk attempt difficult, wacky stunts, which often involved whipped cream, mashed potatoes, or water balloons. This was the only Goodson-Todman show to join the trend in "big-money" games, as the prize for completing the stunts rose from $100 to $5,000 by 1958.

In 1950 CBS gave Goodson and Todman a shot at live drama when the producers of the popular anthology *Suspense* abruptly announced they were taking a summer hiatus. With just four weeks to the first air date, their studio put together *The Web,* an anthology of stories focused on people caught in a "web" of situations beyond their control. The show stayed on the air until 1954, and, like many New York–produced dramas, it featured several future Hollywood stars. James Dean made his television debut on *The Web* and later worked as a "stunt tester" for *Beat the Clock.* He proved so well coordinated, however, that his times at completing stunts could not be used to gauge average contestants. Dean was obliged to seek his fortune elsewhere. Goodson and Todman made a few other forays

Bill Todman (right) and Mark Goodson.
Photo courtesy of Mark Goodson Productions

into drama, with the westerns *Jefferson Drum, The Rebel,* and *Branded.* They also produced *Philip Marlowe* and a repertory anthology, *The Richard Boone Show.*

In its second season, the format and panelists of *What's My Line?* jelled, and CBS had a hit that would last for 18 seasons, the longest-running game show in prime time. Goodson and Todman continued to prepare more panel shows, such as *The Name's the Same* (ABC; 1951–55), in which celebrity panelists met ordinary people with famous or unusual names (e.g., George Washington, Mona Lisa, A. Garter).

Two unemployed comedy writers, Allan Sherman and Howard Merrill, created *I've Got a Secret* for Goodson-Todman, and when it debuted in 1952, Sherman became its producer. He managed prodigious booking feats such as locating the nearest phone to Mt. Everest in order to be the first to contact Edmund Hillary following his historic ascent. He requested the U.S. Air Force to attempt to break the flight speed record from Los Angeles to New York on a Wednesday so the pilot could be a guest that evening; that stunt gave audiences their first look at John Glenn.

I've Got a Secret caught a whiff of the quiz show scandals with its celebrity segment: since few celebrities in those days wanted to admit their real secrets, the writing staff created some of them. Thus, Boris Karloff's "secret" was that he was afraid of mice, whereas Monty Wooley "revealed" that "I sleep with my beard under the covers." Asked by Henry Morgan whether that was really true, Wooley shot back, "Of course not, you bloody idiot! Some damn fool named Allan Sherman told me to say so." (Sherman later became famous for his song parodies, especially "Hello Muddah, Hello Fadduh!")

The third of Goodson and Todman's long-running panel shows, *To Tell the Truth,* was created in December 1956 by Bob Stewart, a former advertising agency man, who later packaged game shows on his own, including *The $10,000 Pyramid.* Stewart also contributed *Password* in 1961, the first quiz show in which "civilians" teamed up with celebrities. In total airtime, however, Stewart's most enduring creation has been *The Price Is Right.* When *Price* debuted in 1956, it was a sponsor's dream. Contestants won fabulous prizes as rewards for knowing their retail prices, a skill prized in the 1950s consumption-oriented society. During the quiz show probes, it was revealed that contestants were sometimes furnished with ceiling prices over which they should not bid, but all the contestants had shared the information. *The Price Is Right* continued in daytime until 1965 and ran in prime time from 1957 to 1964. When the show was revived in 1972, it put contestants through several flashy games, but with the same object of guessing prices. *The New Price Is Right* continues to this day (now just called *The Price Is Right*), an hour each weekday on CBS, and it has spun-off syndicated versions.

By 1956 Goodson-Todman Productions was the biggest producer of game shows in the United States, but after the quiz show scandals, the thirst for new games had cooled considerably, and they were coasting on earlier successes. Their last winner in that period was another celebrity panel show, *The Match Game.* The prime-time audiences for *What's My Line?, I've Got a Secret,* and *To Tell the Truth* had grown older, and CBS retired the shows in 1967. By 1970 the networks swept nearly all their game shows from their daytime lineups as well.

A new window opened in 1971 with the implementation of the Prime-Time Access Rule, and Goodson-Todman produced new syndicated versions of nearly all their old shows. They even purchased *Concentration* from Barry and Enright after NBC canceled it in 1973 and issued a syndicated edition.

The New Price Is Right was part of the networks' attempt to return to daytime game shows in the early

1970s. Most shows of the period used more lights, flashy scoreboards, and high-tech, moving sets, but substance was lacking and the shows had short runs. Goodson-Todman had its share of gadget-filled failures, but they also struck gold with *Family Feud* and *Card Sharks.*

Goodson and Todman sold *What's My Line?* to CBS in 1958, and *I've Got a Secret* to CBS and program host Garry Moore in 1959. The sales helped reduce their capital gains tax burden and netted $3 million. They established the Ingersoll Newspaper Group, a chain of 8 dailies and 25 weeklies, and served as vice presidents.

The partnership continued until Todman's death in 1979, after which time the company was renamed Mark Goodson Productions. Goodson died in 1992, and his son, Jonathan, succeeded him as president and chief executive officer of Mark Goodson Productions, while Howard Todman served as treasurer. In December 1994 the company joined with Merv Griffin Enterprises to launch the Game Show Network, a cable outlet offering old game shows from a library of 41,000 episodes, and new shows allowing home viewers to play along for prizes via interactive controllers.

MARK R. McDERMOTT

See also **Quiz and Game Shows**

Mark Goodson. Born in Sacramento, California, January 24, 1915. Educated at the University of California at Berkeley, B.A. 1937. Married: 1) Bluma Neveleff, 1941; children: Jill and Jonathan; 2) Virginia McDavid; children: Marjorie; 3) Suzanne Waddell. Acted in small amateur theater productions as a child; worked in the Lincoln Fish Market, Berkeley, mid-1930s; disc jockey, KJBS in San Francisco, 1937–39; announcer, newscaster, and station director, Mutual Broadcasting System's KFRC station in San Francisco, 1939–41; freelance radio announcer, New York City, 1941–43; created the ABC dramatic series *Appointment with Life,* 1943; directed the U.S. Treasury Department's war bond–selling show *The Treasury Salute,* 1944–45; cofounder, Goodson-Todman Productions, 1946 (renamed Mark Goodson Productions after partner William Todman's death, 1979); with Todman, created and marketed radio shows, 1946–50; served as producer on television series, including *The Rebel* and *Branded.* Trustee, Museum of Broadcasting (now Museum of Television and Radio), from 1985. Member, board of directors, American Film Institute from 1975. Member: Academy of TV Arts and Sciences. Recipient: Emmy Awards, 1951 and 1952; Great Britain's National TV Award, 1951. Died in New York City, December 18, 1992.

William S. Todman. Born in New York City, July 31, 1918. Graduated from Johns Hopkins University, Baltimore, Maryland, 1938. Married: Frances Holmes Burson; one daughter and one son. Freelance radio writer following college; writer and producer, radio station WABC, New York; cofounder, with Mark Goodson, Goodson-Todman Productions, 1946, which produced game shows for television; expanded Goodson-Todman enterprises to form Capital City Publishing, which included Ingersoll newspaper group and other publishing holdings. Died in New York City, July 29, 1979.

Television Series (selected)

1948–50	*Winner Take All*
1950–54	*The Web*
1950–67	*What's My Line?*
1951–54	*It's News to Me*
1951–55	*The Name's the Same*
1952–67	*I've Got a Secret*
1953–54	*Two for the Money*
1956–67	*To Tell the Truth*
1956–72, 1974	*The Price Is Right*
1958–59	*Jefferson Drum*
1958–63	*Play Your Hunch*
1958–73	*Concentration*
1959–60	*Phillip Marlowe*
1959–61, 1962	*The Rebel*
1962–67	*Password*
1963–64	*The Richard Boone Show*
1965–66	*Branded*
1972–75	*The New Price Is Right*
1973–79	*The Match Game*
1974–78, 1982–84	*Tattletales*
1977–85, 1988–	*Family Feud*
1984–85	*Now You See It*

Radio (Goodson)

Pop the Question, 1939–40; *The Jack Dempsey Sports Quiz,* 1941; *The Answer Man,* 1942; *Appointment with Life; Battle of the Boroughs,* 1945–46; *Stop the Music.*

Radio (Todman)

Connie Boswell Presents; Anita Ellis Sings; Treasury Salute Dramas.

Radio (Goodson and Todman)

Winner Take All, 1946; *Time's a Wastin',* 1948; *Spin to Win,* 1949.

Further Reading

Blumenthal, Norman, *The TV Game Shows,* New York: Pyramid Communications, 1975

Doan, Richard K., "End of the Line: Why the Granddaddy of the TV Game Shows Is Finally Finished," *TV Guide* (June 1967); reprinted in *TV Guide: The First 25 Years,* edited by Jay S. Harris, New York: Simon and Schuster, 1978

Fabe, Maxene, *TV Game Shows,* Garden City, New York: Doubleday, 1979

Graham, Jefferson, *Come on Down!!!: The Game Show Book,* New York: Abbeville Press, 1988

Holbrook, Morris B., *Daytime Television Game Shows and the Celebration of Merchandise: The Price Is Right,* Bowling Green, Ohio: Bowling Green State University Press, 1993

Johnson, Steve, "Scrambled Picture," *Chicago Tribune* (August 21, 1995)

Schwartz, David, et al., *The Encyclopedia of TV Game Shows,* New York: Zoetrope, 1987

Sherman, Allan, *A Gift of Laughter,* New York: Atheneum, 1965

Stern, Jane, and Michael Stern, "Game Shows," *The Encyclopedia of Bad Taste,* New York: HarperCollins, 1990

Goodyear Playhouse

U.S. Dramatic Anthology

Goodyear Playhouse, a highly prestigious American program of live, one-hour plays, appeared on NBC from 1951 to 1957. Its original title, *Goodyear TV Playhouse,* was changed in 1955. The program shared its time slot in alternating weeks with *Philco Television Playhouse* and later with *The Alcoa Hour.* The varying titles referred to specific corporate sponsorship from week to week, but all three series were produced by the same people, and at times all three series were referred to simply as NBC's *Television Playhouse.*

Goodyear Playhouse was among several anthology dramas that many television critics associate with television's "Golden Age." Like other anthology programs, each episode of *Goodyear Playhouse* featured different actors and stories, many of which were developed from Broadway plays and short stories. New stories were also written especially for *Goodyear Playhouse* by writers who had little or no previous television experience. Because programs were produced live, on small sets, and for 9-inch television screens, they tended to rely upon close-ups and dialogue for dramatic impact. Stories necessarily took place indoors so that sets would seem more realistic. Partly because of such constraints, the plays usually had a strong psychological emphasis, concentrating upon characters rather than action.

During its brightest years (1951–55), *Goodyear Playhouse* was produced by Fred Coe, who had made a name for himself in experimental television productions in the late 1940s. Coe encouraged several young authors to write for the series, allowing them an un-

usual amount of freedom in their scripts. The writers included Paddy Chayefsky, Tad Mosel, Robert Alan Arthur, Horton Foote, David Shaw, and Gore Vidal, each of whom continued to write for other media as well as television. Similarly, because the series was performed in New York, Coe made ample use of stage actors who later became well-known television and screen stars, Grace Kelly, Rod Steiger, and Leslie Nielsen among them. Although neither actors nor writers were paid much for performing on *Goodyear Playhouse,* many enjoyed the excitement of live television and the national exposure the series offered. Coe also trained many directors, including Delbert Mann, Arthur Penn, and Sidney Lumet, who would later make names for themselves in television and film.

Although *Goodyear Playhouse* and other anthology dramas received more critical praise than most television fare of the day, they—like all commercial television productions—were constrained in their content and production styles by desires of advertisers, who were careful not to sponsor anything that might offend consumers. Hence, rather than suggest that the source of postwar problems was found in social inequities, television plays rooted problems within individual characters, who usually managed to overcome their problems by the denouement. Furthermore, television plays were bound by temporal limitations inherent in commercial television. While Coe argued that two commercial breaks were beneficial in that they allowed actors to rest and also simulated stage theater's three-act structure, the 60-minute format meant that the timing of productions was to a large extent predetermined.

Despite their limitations, the stories presented on *Goodyear Playhouse* were often impressive, featuring strong acting and direction. The most famous of this anthology's plays was Paddy Chayefsky's *Marty* (May 24, 1953), starring Rod Steiger as a middle-aged, lonely butcher, and Nancy Marchand as an unattractive schoolteacher whom he meets at a dance. *Marty* was perfectly attuned to the limitations placed upon live television drama, subtly and sensitively exploring the emotions of a man torn between family commitments and his need for personal maturation. *Marty* was later made into an Oscar-winning film starring Ernest Borgnine. In addition to *Marty,* other notable *Goodyear Playhouse* premiers include Chayefsky's *The Bachelor Party* (1955) and Gore Vidal's *Visit to Small Planet* (1955).

In 1954 and 1955 anthology sponsors began to demand more control of their programs. Gloomy personal problems faced by anthology characters did not seem to mesh with bright, optimistic commercials. Sponsors were increasingly turning to series television productions filmed in Hollywood. These factors signaled the demise of anthology programs, including *Goodyear Playhouse.* Fred Coe left NBC when his ideas no longer generated sponsor interest.

When Coe left the series in 1955, ratings dropped, and *Goodyear Playhouse* was canceled two years later. The series was reprised somewhat from 1957 to 1960 by a half-hour, taped program called the *Goodyear Theater. Goodyear Theater* was similar in content to its predecessor and again alternated with *Alcoa Theater* on NBC.

Goodyear Playhouse, along with other live anthology series such as *Omnibus* and *Playhouse 90,* set a standard for excellence in television production despite industrial limitations placed upon these programs. Just a few years after the end of *Goodyear Playhouse,* television writers, directors, and critics lamented the loss of the creative freedom that anthology dramas offered in contrast to series television. Today, complaints continue to made by television reformers who contrast present programming with television's Golden Age.

WARREN BAREISS

See also **Anthology Drama; Chayefsky, Paddy; Coe, Fred; "Golden Age" of Television;** *Philco Television Playhouse*

Programming History
NBC

October 1951–September 1957	Sunday 9:00–10:00
September 1957–September 1960	Monday 9:30–10:00

Further Reading

Barnouw, Erik, *Tube of Plenty: The Evolution of American Television,* New York: Oxford University Press, 1975; 2nd revised edition, 1990

Boddy, William, *Fifties Television: The Industry and Its Critics,* Urbana: University of Illinois Press, 1990

Bourjaily, V., "The Lost Art of Writing for Television," *Harper's* (September 1959)

Brooks, T., and E. Marsh, *The Complete Directory to Prime-Time Network TV Shows: 1946–Present,* New York: Ballantine Books, 1979; 4th edition, 1988

Coe, F., "TV Drama's Declaration of Independence," *Theatre Arts* (June 1954)

Gianakos, L.J., *Television Drama Series Programming: A Comprehensive Chronicle, 1947–1959,* Metuchen, New Jersey: Scarecrow Press, 1980

"Grownups' Playhouse," *Newsweek* (April 20, 1953)

Hey, K., "Marty: Aesthetics vs. Medium in Early Television Drama," in *American History/American Television,* edited by J.E. O'Connor, New York: Ungar, 1983

Grade, Lew (1906–1998)

British Television Producer, Executive

The eldest of three brothers, Lew Grade (originally Louis Winogradsky) emigrated with his parents to Britain from Russia in 1912, when he was six, and settled in London's East End, where his father set up as a tailor. He and his younger brother Boris (later the theatrical manager Baron Bernard Delfont of Stepney) went on to establish a reputation initially as dancers, Lew becoming World Charleston Champion in 1926 and subsequently turning professional. In 1933 he became an agent for European circus acts and switched

Lew Grade.
Courtesy of the Everett Collection

to a new career in theatrical management. Together with his youngest brother, Leslie, he set up his own theatrical agency and subsequently managed many of the most popular variety acts of the 1940s and 1950s. Stars represented by the Grades included such luminaries as Laurence Olivier, John Gielgud, Ralph Richardson, Norman Wisdom, and Morecambe and Wise.

Grade gave up his agency work in 1955, by which time he had recognized the possibilities of the emerging commercial television industry. He formed a consortium to bid for one of the ITV franchises then on offer and his company, called Associated Television (ATV), won Midlands weekday and London weekend ITV contracts and came to dominate the ITV network from the 1950s to the 1970s. He also set up the Independent Television Corporation (ITC) to produce films to be screened by ATV and to be sold to other networks.

An ebullient and irrepressible character, instantly recognizable with his bald head and ever-present trademark ten-inch cigar, Grade was a pioneer of commercial television in the United Kingdom and exerted a massive influence over early television scheduling through ATV and ITC. Grade never pretended that he had a mission to educate or "improve" his public. His sole ambition was to provide the kind of entertainment

he instinctively understood viewers wanted, which led to the development of a schedule largely based on a mixture of popular variety shows, action adventure series, and soap operas. He realized from the outset that the key to international and financial success lay in making programs that would appeal to both British and U.S. networks, and many of his most successful series, churned out on a "factory" basis modeled on U.S. practice, were of a deliberately transatlantic character.

Grade's first major international success came early, with *The Adventures of Robin Hood,* starring Richard Greene, Britain's first costume adventure series and the first of Grade's programs to be sold in the United States. Over the ensuing decades he worked much the same formula over and over again, producing adventure series that would appeal to audiences throughout the English-speaking world. Such series as *The Saint,* which was based on the thrillers of Leslie Charteris and starred a suave Roger Moore as the eponymous hero Simon Templar, *The Avengers,* and the puppet action adventures of Gerry Anderson (notably *Thunderbirds*) were huge commercial successes and are now regarded as enduring classics. Others, such as *The Baron, Man in a Suitcase,* and *The Persuaders* failed to make much of an impact with U.S. audiences and are now largely forgotten, despite changes made to introduce U.S. characters and contexts. (In *The Baron,* for instance, the aristocratic reformed English gentleman-thief of the original John Creasey novels on which the series was based was transformed into a Texan-born ranch owner based in London.)

As well as promoting early adventure series with appeal to transatlantic audiences, Grade also oversaw the screening of television's first medical soap opera, *Emergency Ward 10,* which started in 1957 and (broadcast twice weekly) ran for ten years. The series pioneered the mix of surgery, melodrama, and romance that was to provide the staple fare of numerous similar series in the future. Grade decided to axe *Emergency Ward 10* in 1967 because of a drop in ratings, but later identified this as one of his biggest mistakes and in 1972 attempted (though with only modest success) to revive the series in the form of the inferior *General Hospital.* Another major foray into soap opera was the long-running *Crossroads,* which ran for 24 years—despite criticisms of the acting and the sets—and was subsequently revived.

Other programs from the Grade organization ranged from the enigmatic cult series *The Prisoner,* which Grade axed after just 17 of a planned 36 episodes (either because of the cost or because of controversy aroused over drug references), and the historical drama series *Edward the Seventh,* which was filmed in various royal locations with permission of the Queen, to

The Muppet Show and adaptations of the romantic novels of Barbara Cartland. The success of many of these projects was a testament to Grade's personal judgment and understanding of what would work: several series were commissioned, and indeed sold, by him on the strength of a synopsis or a few brief rushes.

Perhaps Grade's greatest success was the two-part film *Jesus of Nazareth,* directed by Franco Zeffirelli. The pope himself had suggested the idea to Grade (a Jew), when introduced to the latter and his wife (a Christian). Kathie Grade nagged her husband to make the film and he agreed, on condition that it would be equally accessible to people of all religions. Starring Robert Powell as Jesus, Laurence Olivier, Ralph Richardson, Peter Ustinov, Rod Steiger, James Mason, and Olivia Hussey, it cost £9 million and was nicknamed "The Most Expensive Story Ever Told." Few expected it to be good, but it won wide critical acclaim, and Grade himself called it "the best thing I will ever do." With a repeated airing in the 1980s, it was estimated to have been seen by approximately 500 million people worldwide.

Always energetic and hardworking, Grade was Britain's most celebrated postwar showbiz mogul. His friendly and disarming, persuasive manner meant he had few, if any, enemies. He was also a dominant figure in theater and film, in which he became increasingly active from the 1970s. Concentrating on feature films that would appeal to family audiences, he had his successes, but on the whole his career in cinema was less lucrative than it might have been. His most expensive flop on the big screen was *Raise the Titanic,* a hugely ambitious project that cost $36 million to make but returned only $8 million on release, prompting Grade's famous quip "It would have been cheaper to lower the Atlantic." Undaunted by increasing financial difficulties, he carried on making films for both the large and small screens until his death at the age of 91. His nephew is the television executive Michael Grade (son of Leslie), who became director of programs at the BBC (1986–88), then chief executive officer of Channel 4 (1988–97).

DAVID PICKERING

See also Avengers, The; **Grade, Michael;** *Muppet Show, The; Prisoner, The; Thunderbirds*

Lew Grade (Baron Grade of Elstree). Born Louis Winogradsky in Tokmak, near Odessa, Ukraine, December 25, 1906. Emigrated to Great Britain, 1912. Attended Rochelle Street School, London. Married Kathleen Sheila Moody, 1942; children: one adopted son, Paul. Worked as a music hall dancer, 1926–34, before embarking on a career as a theatrical agent and impresario, moving into television in 1955. Joint managing director, Lew and Leslie Grade Ltd., until September 1955; chairman and managing director, Independent Television Corporation (ITC) Entertainment Ltd., 1958–82; managing director, Associated Television (ATV), 1962; Chairman, Stoll Moss Theatres Ltd., 1969–82; chairman and chief executive, Associated Communications Corporation Ltd., 1973–82; president, ATV, 1977–82; chairman, Bentray Investments Ltd., 1979–82; chairman and chief executive, Embassy Communications International Ltd., 1982–85; chairman, The Grade Company, from 1985; director, Euro Disney SCA, Paris, 1988. Governor, Royal Shakespeare Theatre. Fellow, BAFTA, 1979. KCSS, 1979. Knighted, 1969; created baron, 1976. Died December 13, 1998.

Television Series (selected)

1955–60	*The Adventures of Robin Hood*
1955–67	*Sunday Night at the Palladium*
1957–67	*Emergency Ward 10*
1961–69	*The Avengers*
1963	*The Plane Makers*
1963–68	*The Saint*
1964–88	*Crossroads*
1965	*The Power Game*
1965–66	*Secret Agent*
1965–66	*Thunderbirds*
1966	*Mrs. Thursday*
1966–67	*The Baron*
1967	*The Prisoner*
1967–68	*Man in a Suitcase*
1969	*Secret Service*
1969	*The Englebert Humperdinck Show*
1969–71	*This Is Tom Jones*
1971–72	*The Persuaders*
1972–74	*The Protectors*
1972–79	*General Hospital*
1974	*Moses the Lawgiver*
1974–76	*Space 1999*
1975	*Edward the Seventh*
1976	*Clayhanger*
1976	*George and Mildred*
1976–81	*The Muppet Show*
1977	*Jesus of Nazareth*
1978	*Will Shakespeare*

Films (selected)

Journey to the Far Side of the Sun, 1969; *The Possession of Joel Delaney,* 1971; *The Tamarind Seed,* 1974; *Return of the Pink Panther,* 1975; *Farewell My Lovely,* 1975; *Voyage of the Damned,* 1976; *March or Die,* 1977; *The Cassandra Crossing,* 1977; *Autumn Sonata,* 1978; *The Medusa Touch,*

1978; *The Boys from Brazil,* 1978; *Movie Movie,* 1978; *Firepower,* 1979; *The Muppet Movie,* 1979; *From the Life of the Marionettes,* 1980; *The Legend of the Lone Ranger,* 1980; *Raise the Titanic,* 1980; *Green Ice,* 1981; *On Golden Pond,* 1981; *Sophie's Choice,* 1982; *Something to Believe In,* 1998.

Publications

Still Dancing (autobiography), 1987

Grade, Michael (1943–)

British TV Executive

Unlike most of his contemporaries in the top executive positions of British television, Michael Grade did not progress through the usual route of program making, but rather through the entertainment business, which colored his approach to the commissioning and scheduling of programs, at which he was the acknowledged master.

Grade came from a family steeped in show business. His uncles were Lew Grade, the flamboyant businessman who ran the ITV franchise ATV among many entertainment interests, and Bernard Delfont, the theatrical impresario who ran the London Palladium. His father, Leslie Grade, was a talent agent. It was into this branch of the family business that Michael first moved, after a brief career as a sports journalist with the *Daily Mirror* in the early 1960s.

It was in this capacity that Michael Grade came into contact with the world of television, learning a great deal about the business from the sidelines. He worked with the Grade Organisation from 1966 to 1969 and with London Management and Representation, where he was joint managing director, from 1969 to 1973. His job included negotiating with TV entertainment controllers, including Bill Cotton, Jr., at the BBC. Indeed, Cotton was an old family friend, as Grade's father had been Cotton's father's agent, and Cotton was to play a significant role in bringing Grade to the BBC later in his career.

It was therefore no surprise when he moved into television entertainment himself, becoming deputy controller of programs (Entertainment) at London Weekend Television in 1973, later moving to the post of director of programs (and board member) from 1977 to 1981. Grade's big problem at LWT was that, as the London weekend franchise holder, LWT was responsible for only three nights a week, and those nights, especially Saturday, were the ones on which the

BBC was at its strongest. Although he gained his reputation for populism and entertainment at LWT, it should not be forgotten that, as director of programs, he also initiated the arts series *The South Bank Show,* which remains ITV's most important contribution to arts programming.

In 1981 Michael Grade moved to Hollywood, as president of Embassy Television, the independent Hollywood production company founded by Norman Lear, but the experience was not a happy one. He found American television too economically competitive, and he eagerly returned to Britain in a key role at the BBC in 1984.

He became controller of BBC 1 at a time when the corporation was losing the ratings war with ITV, using his scheduling skills and inside knowledge of ITV to turn the situation around to the BBC's advantage. The scheduling and success of the soap opera *Eastenders* was the most vital pillar in Grade's strategy. In 1986 Grade became BBC TV director of programs, with responsibility for rejuvenating the schedule across both networks. Again, despite his reputation is as a populist, the period also saw some of the BBC's most respected landmarks, including the drama series *Edge of Darkness* and *The Singing Detective,* as well as controversy over the World War I drama *The Monocled Mutineer,* which Grade wrongly defended as factually correct. However, the act for which he is most remembered in some circles is the cancellation of the cult sci-fi institution *Doctor Who.*

In 1987 Grade was interviewed for the job of BBC director-general but lost out to Michael Checkland. Checkland brought in John Birt as his deputy and it was the expansion of Birt's influence, at Grade's expense, which led Grade to leave the BBC.

At the beginning of 1988 he became the second chief executive of Channel 4. It was a surprise appointment, because Grade's reputation for populism did not seem to fit Channel 4's intellectual and minority image. Indeed, the channel's outgoing first chief executive, Jeremy Isaacs, was publicly critical of Grade's appointment and famously threatened to "throttle" him if he altered the channel's remit.

Yet again, Grade's populism was tempered by his commitment to quality and public service. His approach at Channel 4 was to apply the remit for innovation to entertainment and comedy, introducing programming like *Vic Reeves' Big Night Out.* Grade's Channel 4 also maintained its reputation for controversy, with strands like *Eurotrash* and *The Word,* and the sexual nature of some of the more high-profile offerings led the conservative tabloid newspaper, the *Daily Mail,* to dub him "Britain's pornographer-in-chief." Nevertheless, dramas like *Traffik* maintained Channel 4's reputation for quality.

The most important change, however, was organizational. Having previously proposed the privatization of the channel while at the BBC, Grade found himself on the other side of the argument when the 1990 Broadcasting Act considered Channel 4's future funding method. The eventual solution—Channel 4 became a public corporation selling its own airtime and with a renewed remit for innovation and minority programming—suited Grade's approach of maximizing audiences with innovative programming and scheduling. The 1990s were a time of great expansion for the channel under his leadership.

Grade left Channel 4 in 1997 and took on a variety of jobs outside television, notably with National Lottery organizer Camelot, but rumors regularly link him with top television jobs; his career in the medium cannot be said to be over.

STEVE BRYANT

See also **Channel 4; Grade, Lew**

Michael Ian Grade. Born March 8, 1943. Married: 1) Penelope Jane Levinson, 1967 (divorced, 1981); one son and one daughter; 2) Sarah Lawson, 1982 (divorced, 1991). Trainee journalist, *Daily Mirror,* 1960; sports columnist, 1964–66; theatrical agent, Grade Organisation, 1966–1969; joint managing director, London Management and Representation, 1969–73; deputy controller of programs (Entertainment), LWT, 1973–77; director of programs, LWT, 1977–81; president, Embassy Television, 1981–84; controller, BBC1, 1984–86; director of programs, BBC TV, 1986–87; chief executive, Channel 4, 1988–97.

Grandstand

British Sports Program

The BBC's flagship sports program, *Grandstand* has been broadcast in Britain since the autumn of 1958. This enduring and resourceful program runs for approximately five hours every Saturday afternoon, pulling together discrete sporting events under one program heading.

Grandstand was conceived by Bryan Cargill, then a sports producer within the BBC, with the idea of unifying the corporation's live Outside Broadcasts within a single sports omnibus. The sports magazine format had its precedents in both BBC radio and television, and *Grandstand* joined its sister programs *Sportsview* (a midweek sports magazine that was presented by Peter Dimmock from 1954 and later became known as *Sportsnight*) and *Sports Special* (a Saturday evening program of filmed highlights, presented by Kenneth Wolstenholme, which aired from 1955 to 1964, when it was replaced by *Match of the Day,* a program exclusively dedicated to soccer). These provided a comprehensive sports portfolio without comparison among the ITV companies.

It was Dimmock, then the head of BBC Television Outside Broadcasts, who presented the initial two programs. He was soon replaced by the sports journalist David Coleman, who from 1958 to 1968 brought a vibrant style and meticulous sporting knowledge to the program in a decade that saw televised sport in Britain come of age. The role of the anchor has been central to the success of *Grandstand,* whose structure changes from week to week and, on occasion, hour to hour, or even minute by minute. As the public end of a finely tuned production team, the anchor knits together and makes coherent the live and recorded material that alternates between various sports and locations. Since

Coleman left the program in 1968 it is a role only a few broadcasters have been privileged to undertake: Frank Bough (1968–83); Desmond Lynam (1983–93), Steve Ryder (1993–), Ray Stubbs (1996–), and ex-tennis star Sue Barker (1999–).

One of the guiding principles of *Grandstand* has been to appeal to a family audience, despite being male dominated in terms of its selection of presenters, commentators, and sports covered. Indeed, it is between the dichotomy of the sports fan (viewed as predominantly male) and the casual viewer (the family audience) that the presenters and commentators seek to appeal, and their efforts have given the aforementioned anchors of the program recognition as talented broadcasters beyond the genre of televised sport. Similarly, the sports commentators, many of whom joined the BBC in the 1950s and 1960s, have become household names in Britain: Peter O'Sullivan (horse racing), Murray Walker (motor racing), Bill McLaren (rugby union), Peter Allis (golf), Richie Benaud (cricket), John Motson (soccer), David Coleman (athletics), Ted Lowe (snooker), Dan Maskell (tennis), and Harry Carpenter (boxing). These commentators are among the most enduring names in British broadcasting, and although the latter three practitioners of the lip microphone retired from broadcasting in the early 1990s, all remain familiar to the armchair sports fan.

The individuals who have taken on the challenge of presenting the program have been aware of the need to produce the illusion of a seamless flow of sports entertainment, with continuity and slickness being key production values. Without any definitive script, without knowing what is going to happen next, the fronting of *Grandstand* is recognized as one of the toughest jobs in British television. Yet the complexity of directing several Outside Broadcasts in one afternoon, mixing events and making sure everything significant is captured, has been made to look easy.

Although soccer does not feature as one of the alternating live Outside Broadcasts, due to a historical fear on the part of the soccer authorities that live coverage would affect actual attendance on Saturday afternoons, the sport does figure strongly within the overall news values of the program. Starting with "Football Focus," a review and analysis of the previous week's games and an outlook toward the afternoon's matches, *Grandstand* provides a continual update of the latest scores for its viewers. "Final Score," which concludes the program, provides a soccer results service that emphasizes up-to-the-minute production values, formatively utilizing the technology of what affectionately became known as the "teleprinter" (later replaced by the "videprinter"). "Final Score" was introduced to the program not only as a means of informing soccer fans

of their teams' success or failure on a particular Saturday afternoon but also to provide news of success or failure to the hundreds of thousands of British people who gamble on the football pools. In this respect, *Grandstand* was the first television program to take the sports gambler seriously, specifically with regard to horse racing, which is a staple diet of the program. The show combines the coverage of racing events with analysis of race form, betting odds, and results.

Between 1965 and 1985 *Grandstand* had to compete with ITV's sports magazine program *World of Sport.* Initially launched in a joint operation between ATV and ABC, and subsequently produced by LWT, *World of Sport* took up the same scheduling time as *Grandstand.* Instead of alternating between Outside Broadcasts, it televised sports within a far more structured approach. Its demise was due to the problem of overcoming the regional system of the ITV network and its failure to encroach on the BBC's stranglehold on the television rights to the main sporting events. Of central importance here has been the BBC's predominance in the coverage of the "Listed Events": a set of sporting occasions that have been sidelined since 1954 by the postmaster general to maintain nonexclusivity in the broadcasting of Wimbledon tennis, the FA Cup Final, the Scottish Cup Final, the Grand National, the Derby, Test Cricket in England, the Boat Race, soccer's World Cup Final, the Olympic Games, and the Commonwealth Games. *Grandstand* has been the vehicle for the coverage of all these events. Therefore, not only has the program established Saturday as a day of televised sport, it has also created a seasonally shifting, broadcasting calendar of sport, ubiquitously known and familiar throughout the nation.

With the introduction of satellite and cable delivery systems in Britain, and the emergence of sports narrowcasting (most notably Sky Sports), the BBC has found it increasingly difficult to compete for television rights to sport as prices inflate. The loss of Formula One motor racing and the Saturday-evening highlights package of the FA Premier League to rivals ITV and, most dramatically, the loss of TV rights to English Test Cricket to Channel 4 from 2000 have severely damaged the BBC's reputation as the number one broadcaster of sports. However, the BBC has maintained its commitment to sports and introduced *Sunday Grandstand* (originally called *Summer Grandstand* when it began in 1981) as a means of extending its scheduled hours of sport, under a title that has become synonymous with quality sports programming. Additionally, the growth of BBC Online has given the corporation's coverage of sport a new lease of life, providing background information to *Grandstand* and other areas of BBC sports programming.

RICHARD HAYNES

See also **Sports on Television**

Anchors
David Coleman (1958–68)
Frank Bough (1968–83)
Desmond Lynham (1983–93)
Steve Ryder (1993–)
Ray Stubbs (1996–)
Sue Barker (1999–)

Programming History
BBC
1958–   Saturday afternoons, non prime time

Further Reading

Barnett, Steven, *Games and Sets: The Changing Face of Sport on Television,* London: British Film Institute, 1990
Bough, Frank, *Cue Frank!,* London: MacDonald Futura, 1980
Whannel, Garry, *Fields in Vision: Television Sport and Cultural Transformation,* London: Routledge, 1992
Whannel, Garry, "*Grandstand,* the Sports Fan, and the Family Audience," in *Popular Television in Britain: Studies in Cultural History,* edited by John Corner, London: British Film Institute, 1991

Grange Hill

British Children's Serial Drama

Grange Hill is a successful children's soap opera set in a fictional East London comprehensive school. More controversial than traditional BBC children's dramas, *Grange Hill* examines how social and political pressures directly affect Britain's schoolchildren, rupturing cherished and long-held images of sheltered youth and innocence.

The first two seasons concentrated on the lives of a group of mostly working-class 11-year-old students who started at Grange Hill Comprehensive in 1978. Bad boy Tucker Jenkins (Todd Carty) was the show's working-class antihero. His best friend, Benny Green (Terry Sue Patt), a sweet-tempered black boy, battled with the dual problems of racial prejudice and poverty (his father was unemployed as a result of an industrial injury). Although he was a skilled footballer, Benny was stigmatized by poverty as teachers constantly reprimanded him for wearing the wrong school uniform or old gym shoes.

When Tucker and friends reached their third year in school, a new generation of children entered Grange Hill. Every two years after this, a new class of younger students would share the limelight with their veteran classmates. The second group of Grange Hill pupils included another antihero, Zammo, the Tucker of his generation. A few years later, in the midst of national panic about drug abuse in schools, Zammo became addicted to drugs and engaged in glue-sniffing. This narrative was conceived in conjunction with a national antidrugs awareness scheme, which was featured on other BBC children's programs such as *Blue Peter* to educate children on the dangers of illegal drugs.

Generally, *Grange Hill* was not well received by parents or critics, who condemned its images of worldly, disrespectful, and disillusioned students. Children, on the other hand, found the series a little too idealistic. After the first season, producer Phil Redmond changed the tone of the show in response to children who complained that "things weren't tough enough." In all probability, the show would have been controversial as it engaged with an issue at the forefront of public debate: comprehensive schools. Labour government policy mandated that these mixed-ability schools would replace the two-tier system of grammar and secondary modern schools by 1980. Comprehensive schools came to represent both utopian and dystopian visions of the nation's future. At the center of it all were the children, a disenfranchised group unable to participate in the molding of their future. Throughout the years, *Grange Hill* has explored this theme, the idea that children engage with and are affected by politics even though the public tries to protect them or deny their interest in social matters.

Redmond's *Grange Hill* spin-offs continued to explore how government policy affected Britain's youth. *Tucker's Luck* (BBC 2, 1983–85) was aimed at slightly older children and teenagers and dealt with the problems facing working-class youth with few academic qualifications (like Tucker and his friends) in a world of growing unemployment. This series was neither as popular as nor as controversial as *Grange Hill,* largely because it was shown against the early evening news on both BBC 1 and ITV.

MOYA LUCKETT

See also **Redmond, Phil**

Producers

Anna Home, Colin Cant, Susi Hush, Kenny McBain, Ben Rea, Ronald Smedley, David Leonard, Albert Barber

Creator

Phil Redmond

Programming History

BBC1
Feb. 8, 1978–   various times

Further Reading

Messenger, Maire, "Tough Kids," *The Listener* (February 15, 1979)

Great Performances

U.S. Performing Arts Program

Great Performances is the longest-running performing arts series in the history of television. Produced by the public television station WNET (Channel 13 in New York), *Great Performances* debuted on the Public Broadcasting System (PBS) in 1972 as an on-air venue for opera and concerts; before long, theater, dance, adaptations of literary works in short-form series, and (more recently) documentary portraits of filmmakers and other artists came under its umbrella, as well. Still one of public television's most popular programs, *Great Performances* has been around almost as long as PBS, and, in many ways, its history reflects the broader history of public television in the United States.

Great Performances' executive producer, Jac Venza, started his career as a theater designer in New York City in the 1940s. In the 1950s he moved into designing for television at CBS, eventually producing and directing, too. In 1964 Venza left CBS to work for the Ford Foundation–funded alternative to commercial television known as National Educational Television (NET), becoming the broadcasting system's executive in charge of drama and dance. After the passage of the Public Broadcasting Act of 1967 and the creation of the Corporation for Public Broadcasting (CPB)—and then PBS—NET became WNET, a giant among local public television stations and a major producer of programs for PBS. Through the late 1970s, WNET provided more than half of the programming for public television in the United States.

As WNET's executive producer of cultural pro-grams, Venza was in a position to define the role of the arts on public television. Whereas the old educational television approach would have been to interview an artist about his or her work, Venza was determined to show the work itself, to broadcast theater, opera, dance, and concerts in performance. He insisted that television's cultural offerings could be entertaining as well as educational. Through *Great Performances,* viewers across America would see the best of performance from New York City and around the world, and regional American companies would reach a broader audience.

Highlights over the years have included: *The Rimers of Eldritch* (1972), a play by Lanford Wilson starring Rue McClanahan, Susan Sarandon, and Frances Sternhagen, initiating a tradition of showcasing American plays for public television; *Dance in America: Choreography by Balanchine, Parts III and IV* (1978), featuring Mikhail Baryshnikov; *Brideshead Revisited* (1982), an 11-part adaptation of Evelyn Waugh's novel; *Koyaanisqatsi* (1985), a performance of Philip Glass's avant-garde film score; *Tosca from Rome* (1993), with Placìdo Domingo and Catherine Malfitano; and *Chuck Jones: Extremes and In-Betweens, A Life in Animation* (2000), a celebration of the legendary Warner Brothers cartoonist, to name just a few.

Great Performances had its beginnings in the Great Society idealism of the 1960s, a moment when American culture—high as well as popular—captivated the world, and the government professed a renewed sense of responsibility for funding a variety of social initiatives, including public television and the arts. And the series has evolved over the years along with public television's changing circumstances. *Great Performances* is an expensive series to produce; it is also one of PBS's most popular. From the beginning, public television has not received enough federal and state funds to support even a fraction of its programming, and corporate sponsors have been an important funding source and an influential factor in the development of individual programs. *Great Performances* has relied on several different corporate sponsors over the years. For their part, these sponsors have tended to see *Great Performances* as an ideal vehicle for their ultimate purpose in supporting public broadcasting: to access an elite, affluent audience they might not reach through advertising on commercial television. Venza has always asserted that attention to quality, not ratings, should determine what sorts of arts programs are produced for television. In a sense, this attitude jibes perfectly with that of corporate sponsors, who, at least from the 1980s onward, have been less interested in reaching the widest possible audience than they have been in reaching a smaller, "quality" audience—one understood to gravitate to opera, classical music, theater, and literature—with greater spending power.

With such a great portion of its funding coming from corporate sponsors, *Great Performances'* fate has been forever dependent, to a degree, on the whims of the market and the prejudices of corporate executives. In 1986 Exxon, which had been a major sponsor since the series' inception, announced that it would begin phasing out its support for *Great Performances* due to a decline in oil industry profits. In 1992 another sponsor, Texaco, ended its corporate underwriting, citing the series' move away from traditional classical programming and toward more contemporary music and drama. At the time, some speculated that this decision was based at least in part on *Great Performances'* decision to broadcast an adaptation of David Leavitt's *The Lost Language of Cranes,* a novel with a homosexual theme. Though Texaco executives and *Great Performances'* producers denied the latter explanation, it was nevertheless clear that *Great Performances'* funding did rely, to an extent, on its sponsors' approval of the program's content.

Another important source of funding for *Great Performances* has been individual viewers, to whom public television stations reach out during pledge drives. The average donor is understood to be cautious and conservative, with middlebrow tastes. Over the years, some of *Great Performances'* programs have been criticized as pandering to this profile. Thus, on one side, critics charge that the program is elitist, attending to the highbrow tastes of a tiny minority with avant-garde material; on the other, critics reproach *Great*

Courtesy of the Everett Collection

Performances for "dumbing down" its offerings to garner pledges. What is more important—serving a minority of (elite) viewers who might not find what they're looking for elsewhere, or reaching out to the widest and most diverse audience possible? This question has been with *Great Performances*—and public television—from the start.

BETH KRACKLAUER

See also **Public Television**

Executive Producer
Jac Venza

Programming History
PBS
1972–   More than 600 episodes

Further Reading

Carter, Bill, "Texaco Ends a Sponsorship," *The New York Times* (April 2, 1992)

Day, James, *The Vanishing Vision: The Inside Story of Public Television,* Berkeley: University of California Press, 1995

Hoynes, William, *Public Television for Sale: Media, the Market and the Public Sphere,* Boulder, Colorado: Westview, 1994

LaFave, Kenneth, "Delicate Balance for PBS Raising Revenue, Devotion to High Art Sometimes Clash," *The Arizona Republic* (April 11, 1999)

Morgan, Thomas, "Exxon Cuts Financing to Great Performances," *The New York Times* (June 19, 1986)

Ouellette, Laurie, *Viewers Like You? How Public TV Failed the People,* New York: Columbia University Press, 2002

Stern, Christopher, "Non-commercial Breaks," *Variety* (November 1–7 , 1999)

Unger, Arthur, "Who Watches 'Live Performance TV?' And Who Will Pay for It?" *Christian Science Monitor* (April 2,1981)

Zahed, Ramin, "Event Programs Keep PBS Ahead of Pack," *Daily Variety* (August 28, 1998)

Greece

Television arrived late in Greece. Although private experiments in television transmission took place in the 1950s, the first public station was established by the state broadcaster, Hellenic Radio Foundation (EIR), in 1965. At about the same time, the Greek Armed Forces started its own television broadcasting in Athens. It had greater success than EIR, because it used army film crews and facilities and was given technical assistance by the U.S. government.

The first official telecasts by EIR started in 1966, consisting of news and travelogues. Meanwhile, Armed Forces Radio expanded its television broadcasts to three nights per week. This station inaugurated the practice of selling time to producers whose programs included commercials. The station's first sponsored program was *Mission Impossible.*

When the military took over the government in 1967, one of the first buildings to be seized was the EIR building. The junta realized the medium's propaganda potential and started developing a more extensive television network to help it gain public support. Regular nightly programming was started in November 1968 by the armed forces, and in April 1969 by EIR.

In 1970 the junta replaced EIR with the Hellenic Radio-Television Foundation (EIRT). The same year, it created the Armed Forces Information Service (YENED) to take over armed forces broadcasting and to provide "national, moral, and social education" to the armed forces and the public. The junta wanted to " reeducate" the Greek public; to that end it controlled all broadcasting.

From 1968 to 1973, YENED had the more popular and profitable television station, as it carried popular commercial programs, as well as propaganda. On the other hand, EIRT had budget deficits, while its programming was more informative. In 1974 civilian rule was once again restored, and a new constitution was put in place, which put radio and television "under the immediate control of the state." Furthermore, the constitution states that

> Radio and television shall aim at the objective transmission, on equal terms, of information and news reports as well as works of literature and art; The qualitative level of programs shall be assured in consideration of their social mission and the cultural development of the country.

At the same time a new broadcasting law (230/1975) created Hellenic Radio Television (ERT) to replace EIRT. As a public corporation, ERT's activities are supervised by an administrative council. However, the true authority of ERT rests with the government.

The purpose of ERT is to provide "information, education, and recreation for the Greek people (through) the organization, operation and development of radio and television." Law 230/1975 states that "ERT programs must be imbued with democratic spirit, awareness of cultural responsibility, humanitarianism and objectivity, and must take into account the local situation." Finally, the law states that "The transmission of sound or pictures of any kind by radio or television by any natural person or legal entity other than ERT and the Armed Forces Information Service shall be prohibited." This brought an end to private broadcasting in Greece. Meanwhile, color arrived to Greek television in 1979, as the government selected the French SECAM system for use.

The legal structure of ERT was one of the targets of the opposition socialist party, PASOK, before it came to power in 1981. It promised to change this structure, because it was used to promote only the party in power. However, following its election PASOK merely made more airtime available to other political parties.

In 1982 PASOK enacted law 1288/1982, which took away the broadcasting privileges of the armed forces. It transformed YENED into ERT-2, and ERT into ERT-1. In 1987 law 1730/1987 unified all broadcasting operations under the Hellenic Radio-Television (ERT). ERT is made up of Hellenic Television 1 (ET-1), formerly ERT-1; Hellenic Television 2 (ET-2), formerly ERT-2; and Hellenic Radio (ERA). This law established ERT as a public, state-owned, nonprofit corporation. ERT's purpose is to provide "information, education and entertainment to the Greek people." It is governed by an administrative council, whose president is the company's chief executive officer, but the company is under the jurisdiction of the minister of the press and mass media. Each successive government, until very recently, had been unwilling to distinguish between what the Constitution provides—broadcasting under "the immediate control of the state" to be used for the common good—and what actually takes place, namely, broadcasting under the immediate control of the party in power.

In 1989 a coalition government made up of conservatives and leftists enacted law 1866/1989, which allowed for the establishment of private television stations. This law also created the National Radio-Television Council (NRTVC) as the means through which the state controls broadcasting. The council is also charged with facilitating freedom of expression and promoting quality broadcasting.

However, even with the creation of NRTVC, the government has not been willing to hand over its authority over broadcasting, and the powers of the council remain primarily advisory. The council can levy penalties on those violating broadcast laws, but it can only make recommendations to the minister of press and mass media on other important matters. For example, the NRTVC must approve license applications for private radio and television stations, but licenses are granted by the ministry. Furthermore, each succeeding government changed the composition and even the number of members of the council, so that their own supporters would have the majority vote. Currently, the NRTVC has 9 voting members selected by a special parliamentary committee from a list of 18 proposed by the minister.

In 1991 the NRTVC established a Code of Journalism Ethics, Programming and Advertising Standards. This code deals with purposes of broadcast programming, crime and terrorism coverage, news coverage of political demonstrations, quiz and game shows, arousal of panic and fear, news objectivity, protection of children, and violence.

Broadcast law 1866/1989 allowed the establishment of private television stations, but did not deal with the important issue of the number of frequencies available. The law stated that the government, with the consent of the NRTVC, may grant corporations and local governments the right to operate television stations. The law further stated that corporate owners of TV stations must publish the names of all their shareholders. Furthermore, no one shareholder or family may own more than 25 percent of the shares of such corporation, nor more than one license.

According to law 1866/1989, television station licenses are renewable every seven years and granted only after consideration is given to the applicant's character, experience, and to the quality and variety of proposed programs. Licenses can be revoked by the NRTVC for law violations, and private stations must adhere to limits on advertising and to political campaign guidelines that also apply to ERT.

Another relevant law (1941/1991) outlined penalties for violation of broadcast laws, for operating without a license, and for interfering with air transport frequencies. Even this law, however, was amended later in 1991, to require NRTVC's consent in fines and license revocations. Nevertheless, this and other relevant laws are not strictly enforced.

By early 2002, a legal framework for permanent licensure had not yet been implemented. The government has indicated that there are 108 TV frequencies available for 150 competing private channels. Six licenses will be granted for nationwide coverage, even though in 2002 there were at least eight private channels broadcasting nationwide. Part of the reason for the government's inaction has been its inability to decide which strong political and/or economic interests will be denied a broadcasting license.

The introduction of private television to Greece was not only an event of economic importance, but one with great political importance as well. Those who built the first major television stations were allowed to do so because they wielded great political and economic power. The owners of the first private television station, Mega Channel, represent powerful interests in shipping, construction, and/or the media industries. The other major private television station, Antenna TV, is principally owned by M. Kyriakou, whose main business is shipping. Generally, broadcast station owners have used their stations for political leverage in gaining favor with the government for their other businesses. Law 2328/1995 attempted to solve this problem by prohibiting station stockholders from having interests in other companies doing business with the government. However, this ban is very broad and unenforceable. In 2002 the government considered prohibiting only those who have at least a 5 percent stake in a broadcast company from doing business with the government.

The first station completely controlled by a political party was 902-TV. This Communist Party–owned station went on the air in November 1991 and carries mostly news and information, as well as cultural programs.

In addition to Mega and Antenna, there are three other private stations and three ERT stations broadcasting nationwide. In 1988 ERT established ET-3 as a regional service for northern Greece, but it slowly became a national channel. Besides the stations already mentioned, there are at least 18 other channels currently broadcasting in the Athens area. These include stations Tempo, Alter, Polis, Alpha, Extra, Star, MAD, Tileora, Seven, and the Cyprus Radio Foundation's (RIK) station, which retransmits in Athens. Under a reciprocal agreement, ET-1 is also being retransmitted in Cyprus. In addition, a handful of satellite channels are being retransmitted terrestrially in the Athens area, such as RAI, Eurosport, CNN, and MTV. ERT has an agreement with U.S. satellite channels MTV and

CNN, which allows it to retransmit them without remuneration. Similarly, ERT stations, Mega, and Antenna are available via satellite in North America and Australia.

In Greece's second-largest city, Thessaloniki, there are a number of private stations broadcasting besides the ERT channels, RIK, and the major Athenian channels. The major local channel is Makedonia TV. Overall, it is estimated that more than 180 private and municipal television stations are operating throughout the country.

Furthermore, two digital television subscription services serve the nation. They also make their main signal and an additional package of stations available on satellite for the relatively few DBS subscribers in Greece. Nova Digital offers viewers the main terrestrial stations, Cartoon Network, CNN, Discovery Channel, and its own channels devoted to movies, sports, and children's programs. Alpha Digital's offerings include sports channels, CNBC Europe, Playboy Channel, Reality, and Spice.

In 2002 the three ERT stations had a smaller audience than in the past. Although initially they tried to compete with private channels through more popular programming, since 1997 they have attempted to become more quality television stations. Generally, ET-1 offers the more diverse programming, broadcasting almost 24 hours daily. It carries sitcoms, soap operas, informational and cultural programs in the early evenings, followed by news, series, and Greek movies and foreign movies.

ET-2, which was renamed New Hellenic Television (NET) in 1997, is the serious television alternative for Greek audiences. It broadcasts about 24 hours daily carrying children's educational programs, documentaries, news and information, and other cultural programs. ET-3 has a more limited program schedule starting around noon each day. Its focus is northern Greece, and it carries a variety of programs, including news, informational, and cultural programs.

Greek television has historically offered a variety of television programming, much of it imported. Generally, the public channels imported about one-third of their programs. American programs traditionally took up the bulk of foreign programming, sometimes making up over 60 percent of all entertainment programs. In the last few years, however, the public stations have decreased their appetite for foreign programs.

Nevertheless, Greek television in general has much more foreign programming, simply because there are many more stations, and the demand for inexpensive programming cannot be satisfied by Greek producers. At the same time, there are no limits as to the amount of imported programs, other than European Union directives, which are not enforced. As such, most major private stations carry an extraordinary amount of foreign programming, although less so during prime time.

The two major private stations broadcast primarily entertainment programs. Over 60 percent of the programming on both channels consists of movies, reality and game shows, and series/serials. Most private stations also carry political discussion programs.

Provincial stations broadcast from late afternoon until midnight each day. They carry mostly information programs, interview shows, news, and movies. Many of the movies shown are low-budget Greek video movies. Furthermore, even news clips they broadcast are often taken off satellite channels without permission.

There are three television audience measurement companies in Greece: AGB Hellas, Focus, and Icap Hellas. AGB uses the people meter in the Athens and Thessaloniki areas. Focus surveys the whole nation for television viewing by half-hour segments.

The most popular Greek television programs have traditionally been Greek movies, sports, Greek series, and one or two foreign (usually American) series or serials. In 2001 the most popular show on Greek television was the reality series *Big Brother*.

Sports programs have also historically been very popular on Greek television, and the emergence of two powerful private channels has created competition for this type of programming as well. Up until 1990, ERT had a monopoly over televised sporting events. However, the traditional popularity of sports in general, and the emerging popularity of basketball in the 1980s in particular, made sports a great target for private stations. Generally, Greeks watch about 3.5 hours of television per day. Heavy viewers are those over 45 years old and those who live in the provinces.

The introduction of new media in Greece also introduced piracy. Not only are videotapes pirated, but television stations broadcast illegally obtained programs. In the past, new television stations sometimes simply rented a tape from their local video club and broadcast it. The Motion Picture Association of America (MPAA) estimates its damages are about $23 million from pirated videotape rentals, and $12 million for over-the-air piracy. It is estimated that about 45 percent of all videotapes rented in the Athens area and 65 percent in Greek provinces are pirated tapes. In 2001 Greece and the United States signed an agreement that obligates the Greek government to provide adequate legal protection for intellectual property and to actually enforce recently enacted Greek copyright laws.

Greek private television stations are financed primarily through advertising, although some industrialists subsidize their stations because of the political power they yield. Advertising expenditures are increasing parallel to the increase in the number of multinational advertising agencies in the country. Over 60 percent of all advertising expenditures go to multinational advertising agencies, while advertising expenditures increased at a yearly rate of 25 percent from 1980 to 1995. As advertising expenditures increased, so did television's share of these expenditures. During 2001 television's share of total advertising expenditures was 45 percent, down from a high of 60 percent in 1991.

The only items not advertised on Greek television are tobacco products. The nation has adopted the European Union's limits on advertising minutes and commercial interruptions. Periodically the NRTVC levies fines on stations that violate such guidelines, but the council's small staff cannot adequately regulate Greek broadcasting.

Despite increasing advertising revenues, most private stations today are losing money, except possibly for Mega Channel and Antenna TV. ERT stations have also been losing money, not only because of the new competition, but also because of their responsibilities as public stations. For example, they provide free advertising for public welfare campaigns. However, as public bureaucracies, they often mismanage advertising traffic and have additional waste and fraud.

The financial status of ERT is troublesome to the government. ERT television receives most of its revenues from a special fee collected from all households through monthly electricity bills. The average household pays about $2.50 per month for ERT radio and TV, while ERT also receives periodic government subsidies. Generally, the infrastructure of ERT is weak. It has too many employees, is not well organized, and is a victim of the political patronage system, resulting in a heavy bureaucracy and a civil service mentality by many of its employees.

Although the finances and the quality of Greek state television has stabilized following the financial and ratings dive after the introduction of private television, its future is uncertain. Periodic big events it broadcasts, such as the Olympics and World Cup Soccer, give it a financial boost, but it cannot count on ongoing subsidies. It may be that three television channels are too many for the state to afford.

The future of private television in the country will necessarily reach some form of maturation. From a financial perspective, the country of 11 million people cannot afford so many television stations. At some point, political leaders will find the will to create an adequate infrastructure and to enforce relevant laws and regulations regarding television. The country is being transformed in order to successfully host the 2004 Olympics. Toward that end, all elements of society are being reorganized and updated, and television is no exception.

THIMIOS ZAHAROPOULOS

Further Reading

Doulkeri, T., and P. Dimitras, "Greece," in *Electronic Media and Politics in Western Europe,* edited by H. J. Kleinsteuber, D. McQuail, and K. Sione, Frankfurt, Germany: Campus Verlag, 1986

McDonald, R., *The Pillar and the Tinderbox: The Greek Press and the Dictatorship,* New York: Marion Boyars, 1983

Vlachos, H., "The Colonels and the Press," in *Greece under Military Rule,* edited by R. Clogg and G. Yannopoulos, New York: Basic Books, 1972

Zaharopoulos, T., *Mass Media in Greece: Power, Politics and Privatization,* Westport, Connecticut: Praeger, 1993

Green Acres

U.S. Situation Comedy

Green Acres (1965–71, CBS) is, in the words of author David Marc, "as utterly self-reflexive as any program ever aired on network TV." The product of television mastermind Paul Henning, who made his name and fortune on *The Beverly Hillbillies, Green Acres* was a spin-off created in conjunction with Jay Sommers, based on his original radio series *Granby's Green Acres.* Despite its folksy origins, and in an age that routinely produced garrulous nags, crusty aliens, flying nuns, suburban witches, maternal jalopies, and coconut-powered shortwaves, *Green Acres* stands proudly as the furthest point on the edge of television's psychedelic era.

Green Acres reversed the narrative hook of *The*

Beverly Hillbillies, which was that of city folks moving to the country. Prestigious lawyer Oliver Wendell Douglas (Eddie Albert) and his socialite wife, Lisa (Eva Gabor), trade in their exhausting Park Avenue existence for the simple country pleasures, which they imagine await them wrapped in a cloak of Jeffersonian idealism, glorious sunrises, and the smell of new-mown hay. What they find instead is a consensus reality that flies in the face of Cartesian logic, Newtonian physics, and Harvard-sanctioned positivism. Albert, who made his film debut in *Brother Rat* opposite Ronald Reagan, takes refuge in the same reductionist platitudes his former costar eventually learned to trade on quite deftly, but those platitudes ultimately prove no match. Meanwhile, Gabor (who with her sisters Zsa Zsa and Magda had by this time been dubbed "mythological" by Dorothy Parker) embraces this new order with a circular instinct worthy of Gracie Allen herself (Henning's longtime employer). Against all odds, Lisa flourishes, coaxing the chickens to lay square eggs, bringing a world-class symphony conductor to Hooterville, establishing a state-of-the-art beauty salon in Sam Drucker's General Store, and, of course, perfecting her signature biological weapons-grade hotcakes.

Also populating this wrinkle in critical reason are a healthy cross section of supporting eccentrics. These include Mr. Haney (Pat Buttram), the hornswoggling con man whose bargains invariably cost the Douglases several times their face value. Buttram once served as Gene Autry's sidekick and claimed he based his character loosely on Colonel Tom Parker, Elvis Presley's legendary shadowy manager, whom he had known as a carnival entrepreneur in the 1940s, where he ran a booth featuring dancing chickens. County agent Hank Kimball's "discourses on plant and animal husbandry rival those of a semiotics professor" (according to Marc), and this character played by Alvy Moore personifies a kind of infinite regress, where every empirical statement branches into multiple statements that in turn preclude it, spiraling each new observation back and away from itself like an inductive Escherism. Fred and Doris Ziffle (Hank Patterson and Barbara Pepper; later Fran Ryan) are the beaming parents of Arnold, a 250-pound adolescent pig, which watches television, is writing a book, visits Washington on scholarship, and ultimately falls in love with Mr. Haney's pet basset hound.

Green Acres was canceled in 1971 when CBS consciously targeted a younger demographic audience and purged its so-called rural comedies. Its user-friendly absurdism became one of the cornerstones of the mock-patriotic revivalism of the Nickelodeon Channel's "Nick at Nite" lineup in the early 1990s.

PAUL CULLUM

Cast

Oliver Wendell Douglas	Eddie Albert
Lisa Douglas	Eva Gabor
Mr. Haney	Pat Buttram
Eb Dawson	Tom Lester
Hank Kimball	Alvy Moore
Fred Ziffel	Hank Patterson
Doris Ziffel (1965–69)	Barbara Pepper
Doris Ziffel (1969–70)	Fran Ryan
Sam Drucker	Frank Cady
Newt Kiley (1965–70)	Kay E. Kuter
Alf Monroe (1966–69)	Sid Melton
Ralph Monroe (1966–71)	Mary Grace Canfield
Darlene Wheeler (1970–71)	Judy McConnell

Producers

Paul Henning, Jay Sommers

Programming History

170 episodes
CBS

September 1965–September 1968	Wednesday 9:00–9:30
September 1968–September 1969	Wednesday 9:30–10:00
September 1969–September 1970	Saturday 9:00–9:30
September 1970–September 1971	Tuesday 8:00–8:30

Further Reading

Marc, David, *Demographic Vistas: Television in American Culture,* Philadelphia: University of Pennsylvania Press, 1984; 2nd edition, 1996

Marc, David, *Comic Visions: Television Comedy and American Culture,* Boston: Unwin Hyman, 1989; 2nd edition, Malden, Massachusetts: Blackwell Publishers, 1997

Marc, David, and Robert J. Thompson, *Prime Time, Prime Movers: From I Love Lucy to L.A. Law—America's Greatest TV Shows and the People Who Created Them,* Boston: Little, Brown, 1992

Story, David, *America on the Rerun: TV Shows That Never Die,* Secaucus, New Jersey: Carol, 1993

Greenberg, Harold (1930–1996)

Canadian Media Executive

Harold Greenberg was one of Canada's leading television and film entrepreneurs. As chief executive officer and majority owner of Montreal-based Astral Communications, a leading provider of specialty television services, he was responsible for some of Canada's most significant successes in television and film production, processing, and delivery.

Starting in the photofinishing business, Greenberg moved into film processing and sound production through an acquisition of Canada's largest motion picture laboratory in 1968. The processing laboratories, Astral Bellevue-Pathe, established strong ties to major U.S. studios. This purchase represented the beginnings of the diversified structure of Greenberg's operations as well as its links to Hollywood. First forays into film production range from the faux-American *The Neptune Factor* (Daniel Petrie, 1973) to the critically acclaimed *The Apprenticeship of Duddy Kravitz* (Ted Kotcheff, 1974). Greenberg also produced *Porky's* (Bob Clark, 1981), still Canada's highest-grossing film of all time. After producing over 30 motion pictures, Greenberg became interested in developing a Canadian pay-TV movie channel. In this way, Greenberg came to television via photo and film processing and production, all of which still play a central role in Astral's diversified interests.

Astral Communications is a vertically integrated corporation, involved in production, processing, duplication, and distribution of film, television, and video. It plays a leading role in Canadian specialty channels. Its first were two premium film channels, the Movie Network (formerly First Choice) and the French-language Super Ecran in 1983. Since then Astral's English-language broadcasting ventures in Canada have come to include Viewer's Choice Canada Pay Per View, the Family Channel, and MoviePix, a pay-TV venue featuring films of previous decades. French-language broadcasting includes Le Canal Famille, Canal Vie, and Canal D, which offers arts and entertainment programming. The company also owns 50 percent of two French-language music channels, MusiquePlus and MusiMax. Astral's involvement in radio includes nine FM and three AM stations in Quebec. These cross-media interests are expected to expand with further acquisitions and plans for additional specialty channels. Astral continues to provide an array of postproduction and technical services, including dubbing, processing, and printing of film, video, and compact discs. In 1994 Astral opened a compact disc and video replication plant in Florida. The company has duplication and distribution agreements with Buena Vista, HBO, and Barney Home Video for Canada and French-language markets. Distribution deals with U.S. majors have made Astral the Canadian distributor for some popular U.S. programs. Astral has historically used its Montreal location as a way to bridge both English- and French-language markets, eventually giving the company a credible foothold in European ventures (e.g., coproduction agreements with TF-1, France 3, and Canal Plus in France; RAI-2 in Italy; and Europool in Germany, in addition to a minority holding in France's Canal Enfants).

Despite his internationalist outlook, Greenberg was chair of the Canadian Communications and Cultural Industries Committee, a lobby group of industry leaders who view their operations as fundamental to Canadian cultural sovereignty. In this capacity, Greenberg repeatedly supported the cultural exemption clause for Canada in the North American Free Trade Agreement. This brought him into conflict with some U.S. industry figures, including Jack Valenti, president of the Motion Picture Association of America. Astral's interest in ExpressVu, a Canadian direct-to-home satellite service, echoed Greenberg's corporate nationalism. Greenberg claimed that support for the Canadian service over offerings from Power DirectTV, a subsidiary of the U.S. DirectTV service, was fundamental to the protection of Canadian cultural interests. After a brief period of monopoly for ExpressVu, granted by the Canadian Radio-Television and Telecommunications Commission (CRTC), Parliament overturned the federal regulator's decision in April 1995 and opened the way for competition in the direct-to-home market, potentially from U.S.-controlled services.

Before his death, Greenberg received numerous awards and honors, including the Order of Canada and France's *Chevalier de la Legion d'honneur.* The

Harold Greenberg Fund, established in 1986, offers loans and equity investments to Canadian film production and script development and has been an important source of support for the Canadian film industry. Astral Media is a distinct example of contemporary convergence in the film and television sectors, as well as the synergy developing between broadcasting and theatrical production in Canada.

CHARLES ACLAND

Harold Greenberg. Born in Montreal, Quebec, January 11, 1930. Quit school at 13 to work in uncle's camera store; purchased half of Pathé Humphries Laboratory, 1966; took over Astral Films with help from the Bronfmans and merged them into Astral Bellevue Humphries, a communications empire of production, distribution, and pay-TV, 1974; producer and executive producer, pay-TV and films; chair of the board, First Choice Canadian Communications Corp. and Premier Choix TVEC. Recipient: Presidential Proclamation Award, SMPTE, 1985; International Achievement Award, World Film Festival, 1989; Air Canada Award, Academy of Canadian Cinema and Television, 1990; Golden Reel Award. Died in Montreal, July 1, 1996.

Television Series (selected)

1982	*Mary and Joseph*	(coexecutive producer)
1983	*Pygmalion*	(coexecutive producer)
1983	*Draw!*	(coexecutive producer)

Television Miniseries

1978	*A Man Called Intrepid*	(coexecutive producer)

Films

City on Fire (coexecutive producer), 1978; *Terror Train* (producer), 1979; *Death Ship* (coproducer), 1979; *Tulips* (coexecutive producer), 1980; *Hard Feelings* (coexecutive producer/producer), 1980; *Hot Touch* (coexecutive producer/producer), 1980; *Porky's* (executive producer), 1981; *Tell Me That You Love Me* (coexecutive producer), 1982; *Porky's II* (coexecutive producer), 1982; *Porky's Revenge* (executive producer), 1984.

Further Reading

Ellis, David, *Split Screen: Home Entertainment and the New Technologies,* Toronto: Lorimer, 1992

Magder, Ted, *Canada's Hollywood: The Canadian State and Feature Films,* Toronto: University of Toronto Press, 1993

Greene, Lorne (1915–1987)

Canadian Actor

Long before millions of Americans knew Lorne Greene on the popular western series *Bonanza,* he was known to Canadians as the "Voice of Doom," an epithet he acquired as the chief radio announcer for CBC Radio from 1939 to 1942, the height of Canada's darkest days of World War II.

Greene's interest in acting and media began in his hometown of Ottawa and gained further impetus when he joined a drama club while studying engineering at Queen's University in Kingston, Ontario. Always seeking a challenge, he joined CBC Radio, where his distinctive voice soon propelled him into newscasting. After finishing his military service in 1945, he decided not to return to his job as chief announcer at CBC Radio and pursued other interests, which eventually led him to cofound the Academy of Radio Arts in Canada and the Jupiter Theatre.

In 1953, like many of his contemporaries, Greene migrated south to pursue his acting career in the burgeoning television industry. He made numerous appearances on various U.S. telecasts such as *Studio One, Climax,* and *Playhouse 90.* He also made three movies, *The Silver Chalice, Tight Spot,* and *Autumn Leaves.* After a role in the Broadway production of *The Prescott Proposals,* he was offered the part in the movie *The Hard Man* in 1957. In spite of his friends' concerns that a western would limit his appeal, he accepted the role as a way of exploring the genre. It quickly led to another western, *The Last of the Fast Guns,* and eventually to the small screen and *Wagon Train.* It was after seeing him in *Wagon Train* that producers selected him to play Ben Cartwright in the pilot episode of *Bonanza.*

The show became a hit despite formidable competi-

Lorne Greene.
Courtesy of the Everett Collection

tion. A Sunday night standout on NBC for 14 years, from 1959 to 1973, *Bonanza* rode the television western's biggest wave of popularity. Its stories focused on the lives of widower Ben Cartwright and his three sons (all with different mothers) Adam (Pernell Roberts), Hoss (Dan Blocker), and Little Joe (Michael Landon). Each week the family would defend the Ponderosa, the most prosperous ranch outside Virginia City, or some helpless person against unscrupulous outsiders. The formula was common in U.S. television westerns, though *Bonanza* did differ somewhat from its competitors. Indeed, many critics consider the series to be more a "western soap opera" since it downplayed the violent action and moral ambiguity that characterized "adult westerns" such as *Gunsmoke* or *Cheyenne*.

Bonanza was engaging and had a large following, particularly among women, who could perhaps find among the Cartwrights a man to appeal to all types. Ben Cartwright was a tough yet wise father who exuded a balance between ruggedness and compassion. Adam was a suave lady's man. The huge Hoss was dim-witted but lovable. All three kept an ever watchful eye on the fresh-faced and hot-tempered Little Joe. It was a suc-

cessful pattern that outdrew audiences for dozens of competing shows. *Bonanza*'s "family-oriented" themes also made it popular when the medium was under criticism during congressional hearings on TV violence.

After the end of *Bonanza* and the collapse of the western's television popularity, Greene starred briefly in 1978 in the ill-fated *Battlestar Galactica,* a science-fiction television series about a flotilla of human refugees voyaging to Earth while hunted by the evil Cylons. Despite the interest generated by *Star Wars,* the series failed to catch on. In the 1980s Greene devoted his energies to wildlife and environmental issues. He collaborated with his son Charles and hosted a television series, *Lorne Greene's New Wilderness,* to promote environmental awareness.

MANON LAMONTAGNE

See also **Bonanza; Westerns**

Lorne Greene. Born in Ottawa, Ontario, February 12, 1915. Educated at Queen's University, Canada; studied on fellowship at Neighborhood Playhouse, New York. Married: 1) Rita Hands, 1940 (divorced, 1960); two children; 2) Nancy Deale, 1961. Joined Canadian Broadcasting Corporation, 1939; principal radio news reader, 1939–42; established the Academy of Radio Arts and the Jupiter Theatre; actor, U.S. television series, from 1950s. Recipient: NBC Radio Award, 1942; Canadian Man of the Year, 1965; Order of Canada, 1969; Outstanding Service Award, International Fund for Animal Welfare, 1983. Died in Santa Monica, California, September 11, 1987.

Television Series

1953–81	*Newsmagazine* (host)
1957	*Sailor of Fortune*
1959–73	*Bonanza*
1973–74	*Griff*
1978–79	*Battlestar Galactica*
1981–82	*Code Red*
1981–86	*Lorne Greene's New Wilderness* (executive producer and host)

Television Miniseries

1976	*The Moneychangers*
1977	*Roots*
1977	*The Trial of Lee Harvey Oswald*

Made-for-Television Movies

1969	*Destiny of a Spy*
1971	*The Harness*
1975	*Nevada Smith*
1977	*SST: Death Flight*
1980	*A Time for Miracles*

1980   *Conquest of the Earth*
1981   *Code Red*
1987   *Alamo: Thirteen Days to Glory*

Television Documentary
1974–79   *Lorne Greene's Last of the Wild* (host)

Films (selected)
The Silver Chalice, 1954; *Tight Spot,* 1955; *Autumn Leaves,* 1956; *The Hard Man,* 1957; *Peyton Place,* 1957; *The Last of the Fast Guns,* 1958; *The Gift of Love,* 1958; *The Buccaneer,* 1958; *The Trap,* 1959; *Nippon Chinbotsu (Japan Sinks),* 1973; *Earthquake,* 1974; *Klondike Fever,* 1980; *Ozu no Mahot-sukai (The Wizard,* U.S. version only, voice); *Vasectomy: A Delicate Matter,* 1986.

Stage (selected)
The Prescott Proposals; Julius Caesar; Othello.

Further Reading

MacDonald, J. Fred, *Who Shot the Sheriff?: The Rise and Fall of the Television Western,* New York: Praeger, 1987
West, Richard, *Television Westerns: Major and Minor Series, 1946–1978,* Jefferson, North Carolina: McFarland, 1987
Yoggy, Gary A., *Riding the Video Range: The Rise and Fall of the Western on Television,* Jefferson, North Carolina: McFarland, 1995

Griffin, Merv (1925–)

U.S. Talk Show Host, Producer

Merv Griffin had a series of overlapping careers in show business as a singer and band leader, then as a talk show host and developer of game shows for television. Griffin's career as a television talk show host was associated from the beginning with that of Johnny Carson, the reigning "king of late-night talk" from the 1960s through the 1980s. Griffin's first daytime talk show on NBC began the same day as Carson's reign on *The Tonight Show,* and if Carson was consistently rated number one as national talk show host, Griffin was for significant periods of time clearly number two.

Carson's approach to the television talk show had been forged in the entertainment community of Los Angeles in the mid-1950s. Griffin, who came to New York to sign a record contract with RCA in the early 1950s, was subject to other influences. He watched such shows as Mike Wallace's *Night Beat* and David Susskind's *Open End* and socialized with New York's theater crowd. On his own first ventures into network talk in the mid- and late 1960s, Griffin capitalized on the ferment of the era. As surprising as it might be to those who knew him only from his later tepid shows on Metromedia, the Merv Griffin of the 1960s and early 1970s thrived on controversy. Broadcast historian Hal Erickson may have been somewhat hyperbolic when he credited Griffin with using his "aw-shucks style to accommodate more controversy and makers of controversy than most of the would-be Susskind's combined," but it is true that Griffin booked guests such as journalist Adele Rogers St. John, futurist Buckminster Fuller, writer Norman Mailer, critic Malcolm Muggeridge, and a number of controversial new comedians, including Dick Gregory, Lily Tomlin, Richard Pryor, and George Carlin. In a 1965 Griffin special aired from London, when English philosopher Bertrand Russell issued the strongest indictment up to that time of the growing U.S. involvement in Vietnam, Griffin chided the audience for booing and not letting the English war critic be heard.

As the late-night television talk show wars heated up between Carson, Joey Bishop, Dick Cavett, and David Frost, Griffin entered the fray in 1969 as CBS's candidate to take on Carson in his own time slot. Griffin immediately ran afoul of network censors with controversial guests and topics. Concerned with the number of statements being made against the war in Vietnam in 1969, CBS lawyers sent Griffin a memo: "In the past six weeks 34 antiwar statements have been made and only one pro-war statement, by John Wayne." Griffin shot back: "Find me someone as famous as Mr. Wayne to speak in favor the war and we'll book him." As Griffin recalls in his autobiography, "The irony of the situation wasn't wasted on me; in 1965 I'm called a traitor by the press for presenting

Bertrand Russell, and four years later we are hard-pressed to find anybody to speak in favor of the Vietnam war." In March 1970 antiwar activist Abbie Hoffman visited the show wearing a red, white, and blue shirt that resembled an American flag. Network censors aired the tape but blurred Hoffman's image electronically so that his voice emanated from a "jumble of lines." The censors interfered in other ways as well, insisting Griffin fire sidekick Arthur Treacher because he was too old, or that he not use 18-year-old Desi Arnaz, Jr., as a guest host because he was too young. In each case Griffin resisted the censors, but the effort took its toll.

By the beginning of 1972, Griffin had had enough. He secretly negotiated a new syndication deal with Metromedia, which gave him a daytime talk show in syndication the first Monday after any day he was fired. (In addition, a penalty clause in his contract with CBS would give him $1 million if he were fired.) With his ratings sagging, CBS predictably lowered the boom, and Griffin went immediately to Metromedia where his daytime talk show ran for another 13 years. In 1986 he retired from the show to devote his time to highly profitable game shows.

Having learned some hard lessons about controversy, it was in the second arena of the daytime game show that Merv Griffin once again exerted a major influence on commercial television. A self-proclaimed "puzzle freak" since childhood, he began to establish his reputation as a game show developer soon after he launched his network talk show career. *Jeopardy!,* produced by Griffin's company for NBC in March 1964, became the second-most-successful game show on television. The most successful game show on television, with international editions licensed by Griffin in France, Taiwan, Norway, Peru, and other countries by the early 1990s, was *Wheel of Fortune.*

Wheel premiered in January 1975. It is a game show in which three contestants take turns spinning a large wheel for the chance to guess the letters of a mystery word or phrase. The show's first host was Chuck Woolery. Pat Sajak took over in 1982, assisted by Vanna White. Sajak and White have gone on to become household names in the world of television game shows.

In a largely unflattering portrait, biographer Marshall Blonsky describes Griffin as a financially successful but artistically limited individual. The key to Griffin's character, according to Blonsky, is a desperate drive to be accepted by the rich and powerful, and much of his financial success he owes to his financial manager, Murray Schwartz, whom he has never credited and with whom he parted ways in the late 1980s.

The Merv Griffin Show, Merv Griffin, 1962–86.
Courtesy of the Everett Collection

However that may be, Merv Griffin did provide controversy and significant competition for Carson and other talk show hosts during his long career on television and has demonstrated what even Blonsky acknowledges to be a genius for creating game shows for television.

BERNARD M. TIMBERG

See also **Format Sales; Quiz and Game Shows; Talk Shows**

Merv Griffin. Born in San Mateo, California, July 6, 1925. Educated at San Mateo Junior College and the University of San Francisco, 1942–44. Married Juliann Elizabeth Wright, 1958 (divorced, 1976); child: Anthony Patrick. Singer, San Francisco radio station KFRC, 1945–48; vocalist, Freddy Martin's Orchestra, 1948–51; appeared in motion pictures for Warner Brothers, 1953–54; headlined quarter-hour, twice-weekly musical segments, CBS, 1954–55; hosted CBS's *Look Up and Live,* 1953; radio show host, ABC, 1957; host of daytime game show *Play Your Hunch,* 1958–61, host of *Merv Griffin Show,* 1962–63; founded Merv Griffin Enterprises, which began producing *Jeopardy!,* 1964, and the Griffin-hosted *Word* *for Word,* 1963; hosted the *Merv Griffin Show* for Westinghouse, 1965–69, CBS, 1969–72, and syndication, 1972–86; sold production company, Merv Griffin Enterprises, to Columbia Pictures for $250 million, 1986, while retaining title as executive producer of *Wheel of Fortune* and *Jeopardy!* Chairman of the Griffin Group, which owns hotels, clubs, spas, Merv Griffin Entertainment, and Merv Griffin Productions (producer of special events and parties). Recipient: 15 Emmy Awards; inducted in Broadcast and Cable Hall of Fame, 1994. Honorary L.H.D. from Emerson College, 1981.

Television Series

1951	*The Freddy Martin Show*
1953	*Look Up and Live*
1954	*Summer Holiday* (regular)
1958–61	*Play Your Hunch*
1959–60	*Keep Talking*
1962–63	*Merv Griffin Show*
1963	*Word for Word*
1963	*Talent Scouts*
1964–75, 1978–79, 1984–	*Jeopardy!* (creator and executive producer)
1965–69	*Merv Griffin Show* (Westinghouse)
1969–72	*Merv Griffin Show* (CBS)
1972–86	*Merv Griffin Show* (syndicated)
1975–	*Wheel of Fortune* (executive producer)
1979–87	*Dance Fever* (producer)
1990	*Monopoly* (producer)

Television Specials

1960	*Biography of a Boy*
1968	*Merv Griffin's Sidewalks of New England*
1968	*Merv Griffin's St. Patrick's Day Special*
1973	*Merv Griffin and the Christmas Kids*
1989	*The 75th Anniversary of Beverly Hills*
1991	*Merv Griffin's New Year's Eve Special*

Films

By the Light of the Silvery Moon, 1953; *So This Is Love,* 1953; *Boy from Oklahoma,* 1953; *Phantom of the Rue Morgue,* 1954; *Hello Down There,* 1968; *Two Minute Warning,* 1976; *Seduction of Joe Tynan,* 1979; *The Man with Two Brains,* 1983; *The Lonely Guy,* 1984; *Slapstick of Another Kind,* 1982.

Publication

Merv: An Autobiography, with Peter Barsocchini, 1980

Further Reading

Blonsky, Marshall, *American Mythologies,* New York: Oxford University Press, 1992

Griffith, Andy (1926–)

U.S. Actor

Andy Griffith is one of television's most personable and enduring of star performers. He is perhaps best known as Andy Taylor, the central character in *The Andy Griffith Show,* which aired on CBS from 1960 to 1968 and consistently ranked among the top-ten shows in each of its eight seasons. As a "down home" attorney in the even longer running *Matlock* (1986–95), Griffith added another memorable character to television Americana.

The Andy Griffith Show began as a "star vehicle" for Griffith, who had achieved his initial success with recordings of humorous monologues based on a "hillbilly" persona (*What It Was Was Football, Romeo and Juliet*), which led to an appearance on *The Ed Sullivan Show.* He next played the leading role in the Broadway production of *No Time for Sergeants,* as well as in the film and TV versions. His film debut was in the critically acclaimed *A Face in the Crowd* (1957), directed by Elia Kazan, followed by *Onionhead* and the film version of *Sergeants* (both in 1958).

Having informed the William Morris Agency that he was ready to try television, Griffith was put in contact with Sheldon Leonard, producer of *The Danny Thomas Show.* A *Danny Thomas* episode was built around Thomas getting stopped for speeding by Griffith, and this show served as the pilot episode for the

Andy Griffith.
Courtesy of the Everett Collection

Griffith show. Astutely, Griffith negotiated for 50 percent ownership of the new program, which enabled him to be a major player in the program's creative development. Griffith's creative vision inspired him to take a very distinctive approach to TV comedy, in which place, pace, and character were equal and essential contributors to the overall effect. Scenes were allowed to play out with almost leisurely timing, with character development occurring alongside the humor. Another key element to the program's success was the casting of Don Knotts as Deputy Barney Fife. As the inept but lovable sidekick, Knotts took on the key comic role, enabling Griffith to play a more interesting and useful "straight man" role. In this capacity, Griffith's "Lincolnesque" character was allowed to develop—a character more appropriate to the role of single-parent father and, by extension, father to the small town of Mayberry. The Griffith-Knotts team became the driving comic relationship of the show, and the writers built most of the humorous situations around it.

Griffith left the show in 1968, feeling that he had contributed all he could to the character of Andy Taylor. Ironically, the program reached the number one

position that year. The show's sponsor, General Foods, was not ready to relinquish the successful vehicle, however, and a transitional program aired, introducing a new lead character and a new name: *Mayberry, RFD.* Griffith remained as a producer, and the ratings strength continued as several of the supporting characters stayed on. The program was canceled in 1971, when CBS decided to abandon its rural programming for more "relevant" shows targeted at younger viewers.

Griffith's career subsequently stalled. Two series attempts, *The Headmaster* and *The New Andy Griffith Show,* did not make it past their initial runs. A number of made-for-TV movies followed, many of which involved crime scenarios (and some in which he even played the villain). In 1981 Griffith received an Emmy nomination for *Murder in Texas,* in which he played a father who presses a court case against the son-in-law accused of murdering his daughter. Griffith played a prosecuting attorney in the miniseries *Fatal Vision* (1984), a performance that so impressed NBC's Brandon Tartikoff that a series was proposed utilizing an attorney as the main character. A pilot film for the show, *Diary of a Perfect Murder,* aired on NBC on March 3, 1986, and *Matlock* began airing in September 1986. Griffith played Ben Matlock in the hour-long crime drama, a criminal defense lawyer whose folksy demeanor belies his considerable investigative and courtroom abilities. Many of the regulars from *The Andy Griffith Show* made appearances on *Matlock,* continuing a Mayberry legacy spanning over 30 years. *Matlock* ran for 195 episodes, ending in 1995.

JERRY HAGINS

*See also **Andy Griffith Show***

Andy Griffith. Born Andrew Samuel Griffith in Mount Airy, North Carolina, June 1, 1926. University of North Carolina, B.A. in music 1949. Married: 1) Barbara Edwards, 1949 (divorced); children: Sam and Dixie Nan; 2) Cindi Knight, 1983. Teacher and variety performer, 1949–51; recorded hit comedy monologue *What It Was Was Football,* 1953; debuted as monologist on television's *Ed Sullivan Show,* 1954; debuted on Broadway in *No Time for Sergeants,* 1955; also in the television version and the film version, 1958; films debut *A Face in the Crowd,* 1957; appeared in commercials for Ritz Crackers and AT&T; various television series, guest appearances, since 1960, including star, *The Andy Griffith Show,* 1960–68; *Matlock* series and made-for-television movies, 1986–95. Recipient: Theater World Award; Tarheel Award, 1961; Distinguished Salesman's Award, 1962; Advertising Club of Baltimore's Outstanding TV Personality of the Year, 1968.

Television Series

1960–68	*The Andy Griffith Show*
1968–71	*Mayberry, R.F.D.* (executive producer)
1970–71	*The Headmaster*
1970	*The New Andy Griffith Show*
1979	*Salvage One*
1986–95	*Matlock*

Television Miniseries

1977	*Washington Behind Closed Doors*
1978	*Centennial*
1979	*From Here to Eternity*
1979	*Roots: The Next Generations*
1984	*Fatal Vision*

Made-for-Television Movies

1972	*Strangers in 7A*
1973	*Go Ask Alice*
1974	*Pray for the Wildcats*
1974	*Savages*
1974	*Winter Kill*
1976	*Street Killing*
1977	*Deadly Game*
1979	*Salvage*
1981	*Murder in Texas*
1982	*For Lovers Only*
1983	*Murder in Coweta County*
1983	*The Demon Murder Case*
1985	*Crime of Innocence*
1986	*Diary of a Perfect Murder*
1986	*Return to Mayberry*
1986	*Under the Influence*
1987	*Matlock: The Power Brokers*
1987	*Matlock: The Billionaire*
1989	*Matlock: The Thief*
1990	*Matlock: Nowhere to Turn*
1991	*Matlock: The Witness Killings*
1991	*Matlock: The Suspect*
1991	*Matlock: The Picture*
1992	*Matlock: The Vacation*
1992	*Matlock: The Fortune*
1993	*Matlock: The Kidnapping*
1993	*Matlock: The Fatal Seduction*
1994	*Matlock: The Idol*

1994	*Gift of Love*
1995	*Gramps*
1998	*Scattering Dad*
2001	*A Holiday Romance*

Television Specials

| 1965 | *The Andy Griffith-Don Knotts-Jim Nabors Show* |
| 1993 | *The Andy Griffith Show Reunion* |

Films

A Face in the Crowd, 1957; *No Time for Sergeants,* 1958; *Onionhead,* 1958; *Second Time Around,* 1961; *Angel in My Pocket,* 1969; *Adams of Eagle Lake,* 1975; *The Treasure Chest Murder,* 1975; *Hearts of the West,* 1975; *The Girl in the Empty Grave,* 1977; *Rustler's Rhapsody,* 1985; *Spy Hard,* 1996; *Daddy and Them,* 2001.

Stage (selection)

No Time for Sergeants, 1955; *Destry Rides Again,* 1959–60.

Further Reading

Castleman, Harry, and Walter J. Podrazik, *Watching TV: Four Decades of American Television,* New York: McGraw-Hill, 1982

Eliot, Marc, *American Television: The Official Art of the Artificial,* Garden City, New York: Anchor Press/Doubleday, 1981

Hamamoto, Darrell Y., *Nervous Laughter: Television Situation Comedy and Liberal Democratic Ideology,* New York: Praeger, 1989

Kelly, Richard, *The Andy Griffith Show,* Winston-Salem, North Carolina: John F. Blair, 1981; revised, 1993

McNeil, Alex, *Total Television: A Comprehensive Guide to Programming from 1948 to 1980,* Harmondsworth, England, and New York: Penguin Books, 1980; 4th edition as *Total Television: A Comprehensive Guide to Programming from 1948 to the Present,* New York: Penguin Books, 1996

O'Neil, Thomas, *The Emmys: Star Wars, Showdowns, and the Supreme Test of TV's Best,* New York: Penguin Books, 1992

Story, David, *America on the Rerun,* New York: Citadel, 1993

Winship, Michael, *Television,* New York: Random House, 1988

Griffiths, Trevor (1935–)

British Writer

Trevor Griffiths is one of Britain's most politically incisive television dramatists. He has combined television and film writing with a highly regarded theater career because he has wanted to reach the maximum possible audience with his socialist values.

Never a political propagandist or polemicist, Griffiths has been the leading international television proponent of "critical realism." This distinguishes between what Griffiths calls the "materialism of detail" (the surface appearance of the world) and the "materialism of forces" (the dynamic structure of a world determined by differences of power between genders, classes, and ethnicities). Thus, for example, in his miniseries *The Last Place on Earth* (or *Scott of the Antarctic,* screened on commercial television in Britain), Griffiths incorporated the familiar surface details of the competitive quest between Robert Falcon Scott and Roald Amundsen to reach the South Pole, within the deep structure of what his script calls the "historical conjuncture" of 1910. On the one hand, Griffiths imagines Scott's journey as among the dying throes of a failing British Empire (with parallels between the "heroic defeats" of Scott and the World War I fields of Flanders and Gallipoli). On the other hand, Amundsen's journey is related to the nationalism of a newly independent nation constructing its identity out of its successful explorers.

Griffiths's commitment has always been to reinventing form (the country house, hospital, and "high art" genres, for example), while at the same time revealing the real agencies and structures of history. This genuinely creative radicalism has led to many conflicts with Hollywood (he came close to taking his name off the feature film *Reds* after disagreements with cowriter/producer/director/star Warren Beatty), as well as to differences of opinion with other socialist television workers (Ken Loach). However, in a group of extraordinarily and critically creative British television dramatists who began work in the 1960s, Griffiths is unquestionably paramount in the systematic intelligence with which he has blended critical theory and popular television.

The intellectual clarity of Griffiths's work has also offered television scholars the unusual opportunity of tracing the quite specific transformations this dramatist's work undergoes as it encounters the generally more conservative and conventional work practices of set and costume designers, directors, producers, and so on. The analysis of the production of Griffiths's adaptation of D.H. Lawrence's *Sons and Lovers* by Mike Poole and John Wyver, for example, indicates the way in which Griffiths's counterreading of Lawrence's classism was itself subverted by the unthinkingly naturalistic assumptions of costume design, as well as the "high art" visual flourishes of directors making "BBC classics" (see Poole and Wyver). Similarly, Tulloch, Burvill, and Hood have explored the problematic path of Griffiths's adaptation of Anton Chekhov's *The*

Trevor Griffiths.
Photo courtesy of Trevor Griffiths

Cherry Orchard through conventions of acting, lighting, and set design.

During the late 1980s and 1990s, an increasingly conservative British institutional establishment made it harder for Griffiths to bring his projects to air. Also, the fragmentation of television through pay-TV and the proliferation of channels led to some change in his view that television was the vehicle of mass public education. In response, Griffiths worked less for television and made important returns to the theater (with formally innovative plays about the Gulf War and Margaret Thatcher's Britain). However, he continued to work in television, with a play on Danton, *Hope in the Year Two,* using the moment of the play's production (the breakdown of communism) as a stimulus to rethink issues of socialism by going back beyond "one revolutionary wave" (the Russian Revolution, where he focused some of his earlier works) to another, the French Revolution. This resistance to the stale "common sense" conventions of the media via new historical and formal exploration is typical of Griffiths. Like his unflinchingly tough lead character of *Comedians,* Gethin Price, Trevor Griffiths retains an undiminished energy for investing any interstices within popular culture with new and unsettling forms. As such, he continues to be a master of "strategic penetration" as politics, media institutions, and television genres continuously change their historical forms.

JOHN TULLOCH

Trevor Griffiths. Born in Manchester, Lancashire, England, April 4, 1935. Attended St. Bede's College, Manchester, 1945–52; Manchester University, 1952–55, B.A. in English and literature 1955; studied for external M.A. from 1961. Served in the Manchester Regiment, British Army, 1955–57. Married: Janice Elaine Stansfield, 1960 (died, 1977); one son and two daughters. Taught English and games at private school in Oldham, Lancashire, 1957–61; lectured in liberal studies at Stockport Technical College, Cheshire, 1962–65; co-editor, *Labour's Northern Voice,* 1962–65, and series editor, Workers Northern Publishing Society; further education officer, BBC, Leeds, 1965–72; debut as writer for stage, 1969; television debut, 1972. Recipient: British Academy of Film and Television Arts Writer's Award, 1982.

Television Series

1972	*Adam Smith* (under pseudonym Ben Rae)
1976	*Bill Brand*
1981	*Sons and Lovers* (adapted from D.H. Lawrence's novel)
1985	*The Last Place on Earth*

Television Plays

1973	*The Silver Mask* (part of *Between the Wars* series)
1974	*All Good Men*
1974	*Absolute Beginners* (part of *Fall of Eagles* series)
1975	*Don't Make Waves* (part of *Eleventh Hour* series, with Snoo Wilson)
1975	*Through the Night*
1977	*Such Impossibilities*
1979	*Comedians*
1981	*The Cherry Orchard* (adapted from Anton Chekhov's play)
1981	*Country: A Tory Story*
1982	*Oi for England*
1988	*The Party*
1994	*Hope in the Year Two*
1997	*Food for Ravens* (also director)

Films

Reds, with Warren Beatty, 1981; *Fatherland,* 1986; *Oeroeg (Going Home),* 1993.

Radio

The Big House, 1969; *Jake's Brigade,* 1971.

Stage

The Wages of Thin, 1969; *The Big House,* 1975; *Occupations,* 1970; *Apricots,* 1971; *Thermidor,* 1971; *Lay By* (with others), 1971; *Sam, Sam,* 1972; *Gun,* 1973; *The Party,* 1973; *Comedians,* 1975; *All Good Men,* 1975; *The Cherry Orchard,* 1977; *Deeds* (with others), 1977; *Oi for England,* 1982; *Real Dreams,* 1984; *Piano,* 1990; *The Gulf between Us: The Truth and Other Fictions,* 1992; *Thatcher's Children,* 1993; *Who Shall Be Happy?,* 1996.

Publications (selected)

The Big House/Occupations, 1972
The Party, 1974
Comedians, 1976
All Good Men/Absolute Beginners, 1977
Through the Night/Such Impossibilities, 1977
The Cherry Orchard, 1978
Apricots/Thermidor, 1978
Occupations, 1980
Sons and Lovers, 1981
Oi for England, 1982
Judgment over the Dead: The Screenplay of the Last Place on Earth, 1986
Fatherland, 1987

Real Dreams, 1987
Collected Plays for Television, 1988
Piano,, 1990
The Gulf between Us: The Truth and Other Fictions,
  1992
Hope in the Year Two, 1994
Thatcher's Children, 1994
Food for Ravens, 1998

Further Reading

Garner, Stanton, *Trevor Griffiths: Politics, Drama, History,* Ann
  Arbor: University of Michigan Press, 1999
Poole, Mike, and John Wyver, *Powerplays: Trevor Griffiths in
  Television,* London: British Film Institute, 1984
Tulloch, John, *Television Drama: Agency, Audience, and Myth,*
  London: Routledge, 1990
Wolff, Janet, et al., "Problems of Radical Drama: The Plays and
  Productions of Trevor Griffiths," in *Literature, Society and
  the Sociology of Literature,* edited by Francis Barker et al.,
  Colchester, England: University of Essex, 1977

Grundy, Reg (1923–)

Australian Media Executive

Australia has produced few media moguls, and even fewer who are known beyond Australia. The most remarkable has undoubtedly been Rupert Murdoch, but not far behind is the figure of Reg Grundy. Like Murdoch, Grundy found that global expansion could turn a media kingdom into an empire. Born in Sydney, he worked in commercial radio as a sporting commentator, station personality, and time salesman. Grundy developed a radio game show, *Wheel of Fortune,* which he adapted to television in 1959. As with the radio version, he worked as both master of ceremonies and producer on this first TV venture. Despite the coincidence of sharing this title with a U.S. counterpart, *Wheel of Fortune* was Grundy's own invention. However, he quickly discovered that he did not have the time or capacity to develop new quiz programs. Instead, realizing that U.S. network television could serve as a ready source of ideas, he began adapting programs such as *Concentration* and *Say When* for Australian television. However, in the 1960s he twice suffered simultaneous cancellation of all his shows.

But by around 1970, he had rebounded. Selling to all three commercial networks, the business empire was taking shape. Game shows were the foundation, and the advent of stripped nightly programs such as *Money Movers* and *Great Temptation* in 1971–72 meant that his company was starting to turn a handsome profit. For Reg Grundy Enterprises, the economies of television game shows were such that it was possible to sell variants of a show on a regional or state basis as well as on a national basis. By now Grundy was displaying the two qualities that made him

unique among Australian television packagers. The first was a capacity to spot and hire talented workers who would serve him well as managers and producers. As his company grew, he turned much of the day-to-day concerns over to them.

The second element of his business genius lay in his ability to recognize the value of particular program formats so far as scheduling and audience appeal were concerned. Increasingly Grundy himself concentrated on quality control on current shows and on searching for new formats. As always, American television was the key source although he also began looking to the United Kingdom.

By the late 1970s international adaptation of program formats was becoming more regularized. Grundy established an ongoing relationship with the Goodson-Todman group in the United States and had first call on their many television game show formats for adaptation in Australia and the Pacific. By now, the company, now known as the Grundy Organization, began buying game show formats in its own right. Among the first was a mildly successful U.S. program from the 1960s, *Sale of the Century,* which Grundy was to adapt in over 20 territories worldwide, including 20 years on-air in Australia.

Meanwhile, from 1974, the company had also become established in drama. Its first effort was *Class of '74;* this was soon joined by a clutch of others including *The Young Doctors, The Restless Years, Prisoner, Sons and Daughters,* and *Neighbors.* Having this second cash cow made the company enormously secure and it began thinking of international expansion. Hav-

Reg Grundy.
Photo courtesy of Grundy Television Pty Ltd

ing long outgrown its Sydney base and produced game shows for broadcasters right across the continent, there seemed no reason why the company should not seek new markets overseas. After all, the fact that many of its game shows had come from elsewhere meant that the company always had an implicit internationalism. To facilitate world distribution, most especially for its drama serials and, more occasionally, documentaries and feature films, Grundy appointed an independent agent to this task and later set up its own distribution arm. Additionally, the company was also building up its catalogue of formats, both through purchase from elsewhere as well as those of its own devising.

The 1980s and the 1990s is the story of Grundy as an increasingly transnational organization. The company set up a production office in Los Angeles in 1979, and by 1982 had programs in production in the United States, Hong Kong, and Brunei. However, the establishment of permanent offices in multiple territories was not part of its long-term goal. After all, in Aus-

tralia, it had opened and closed offices in different centers as the demands of production dictated. The same logic operated internationally. Here, the key was ownership and control of formats both in game shows and drama serials. Typically, in any territory, the company sought a local production partner, as this coproduction strategy had several benefits. It allowed Grundy to act in a quality-control role; it helped guarantee a necessary "indigenisation" of a program format; and it enabled Grundy to retain control of the format for other territories. Meanwhile, distributing its large packages of drama serials, especially those produced in Australia, ensured that the company had a "calling card" when it looked to enter new territories.

Nevertheless the company found it important to establish central offices in key regions. In 1983 the organization was restructured with Grundy World Wide, headquartered in Bermuda, as the new parent. To serve its European operation—the most important sector of its activities—Grundy established a permanent office in London. It also set up offices in Chile to anchor its Latin American operation and one in Singapore that serviced Asia. Meanwhile, its Los Angeles office had a major function in developing new game show formats for the United States and elsewhere.

But where was Reg Grundy himself in all of this? Until very recently he was the driving force behind the very highest officers in his company, always aware that good executives and new, attractive formats were the lifeline of his organization. Unlike Rupert Murdoch, however, he had no offspring to groom as a successor. Although his was a private company, some others did hold a minority of shares. Therefore, in 1995 he liquified this asset, selling Grundy World Wide to the Pearson International group for $386 million (U.S.). His executive team remained in place, continuing to expand the company inside Pearson. Although the larger organization has now become Fremantle Media, nevertheless the Grundy name remains in place for various branches, most especially in Australia, where it is known simply as Grundy Television.

Meanwhile, from his home in Bermuda, Reg Grundy continues as a very active (if remote) figure in Australian media through his private investment company, RG Capital. His private company owns several FM radio stations and has shares in others. He is also reported to have significant shares in Southern Star Endemol, ironically one of Grundy Television's main Australian rivals.

ALBERT MORAN

See also **Australia; Australian Production Companies; Australian Programming; Murdoch, Rupert K.;** *Neighbours; Wheel of Fortune*

Reg Grundy. Born in Sydney, Australia, 1923. Educated at St. Peter's College. Married: Joy Chalmers. Sports commentator and time salesman, Sydney radio station 2CH; host, radio quiz show, 1957, which he subsequently took to television TCN 9, 1959; founder, Reg Grundy Enterprises, 1960; leading producer of game shows in Australian television; expanded into production of drama serials, from 1973; company reorganized as Grundy Organization, 1978; opened its first overseas office in Los Angeles, 1979; Grundy relocated company to Bermuda, 1982; sold the television company to Pearson Television, United Kingdom, 1995.

Further Reading

Bielby, Peter, editor, *Australian TV.— The First Twenty Five Years,* Melbourne: Nelson, 1981

Dawtrey, Adam, "Media Magnet: Pearson Plays the Field" *Variety* (April 10, 1995)

Gelman, Morrie, "TV's Multinational Forces to Be Reckoned With," *Broadcasting and Cable* (January 23, 1995)

Hall, Sandra, *Supertoy: 20 Years of Australian Television,* Melbourne: Sun, 1976

McClellan, Steve, "Grundy Targets European Barter: Division will Develop Sponsored Programs," *Broadcasting* (August 24, 1992)

O'Regan, Tom, *Australian Television Culture,* Sydney: Allen and Unwin, 1994

Guilds. *See* Unions/Guilds

Gunsmoke

U.S. Western

Gunsmoke, America's longest-running television western, aired on CBS from 1955 to 1975. In 1956, its second season on the air, the series entered the list of top-ten programs on U.S. television and moved quickly to number one. It remained in that position until 1961 and in the top 20 until 1964. Following a shift in its programming time in 1967, *Gunsmoke* returned to prominence within the top 20 for the next seven years, dropping out only in its final year. From 1987 to the present there have been four *Gunsmoke* "reunion" programs, presented as two-hour, made-for-television movies. With the addition of more and more cable television channels, *Gunsmoke* continues to appear in reruns, introducing new generations of television viewers to the potential for powerful drama in generic fiction.

This exceptionally successful program is often referred to as the medium's first "adult western." The term is used to indicate differences between the Hollywood "B" westerns and versions of the genre designed for the small screen in the 1950s and 1960s. Without recourse to panoramic vistas, thundering herds of cattle, and massed charges by "Indians" or the United States Cavalry, the television western often concentrated on character relationships and tense psychological drama. *Gunsmoke* set the style and tone for many of these shows.

Set in Dodge City, Kansas, in the 1890s, the series focused on the character of United States Marshal Matt Dillon, played by James Arness. The part was designed for John Wayne, who chose not to complicate his still-successful film career with commitment to a long-term television contract. Wayne, who appeared on-air to introduce the first episode of *Gunsmoke,* suggested the younger actor for the lead role. The tall, rugged-looking Arness, who until this time had played minor film roles, became synonymous with his character during the next 20 years.

Surrounding Dillon were characters who became one of television's best-known "workplace families." Kitty Russell (Amanda Blake) owned and managed a local saloon, The Longbranch, and over the years developed a deep friendship with Dillon that always seemed to border on something more intimate. Doc Adams (Milburn Stone) represented science, rationality, and crusty wisdom. His medical skills were never questioned, and he patched up everyone on the show, often more than once. Dennis Weaver portrayed tenderhearted and gullible Chester Goode, deputy marshal. Chester's openness and honesty were often played against frontier villainy, and his loyalty to Dillon was unquestionable. When Weaver left the show in 1964 he was replaced by Ken Curtis as Festus Hagen, a character equally adept at providing humor in the often grim world of Dodge and a foil to the taciturn and sometimes obsessive professionalism of Dillon. Burt Reynolds appeared on *Gunsmoke* from 1962 to 1965 in the role of Quint Asper.

While *Gunsmoke* had its share of shoot-outs, bank robberies, cattle rustlings, and the like, the great strength of the program was the ongoing exploration of life in this community, with these people, in this place, at this time. In *Gunsmoke,* Dodge City stands as an outpost of civilization, the edge of America at the end of a century. It is one of the central images of the western in any of its media creations—a small town, a group of professionals, perhaps a school and a church, surrounded by the dangers of the frontier, its values of peace, harmony, and justice always under threat from untamed forces. Such a setting becomes a magnified experiment for the exploration of fundamental ideas about American culture and society. Issues faced by the characters and community in *Gunsmoke* ranged from questions of legitimate violence to the treatment of minority groups, from the meaning of family to the power of religious commitment. Even topics drawn from American life in the 1950s and 1960s were examined in this setting. The historical frame of the western and television's reliance on well-known, continuing characters allowed a sense of distance and gave producers the freedom to treat almost any topic.

The dramatic formula for the series, particularly in later years, was simple. Some type of "outsider"—a family separated from a wagon train, an ex-Confederate officer, a wandering theater troupe—entered the world of the regular characters. With the outsiders came conflict. With the conflict came the need for decision and action. If violence was called for, it was applied reluctantly. If compassion was the answer, it was available. Often, no solution so simple solved the problems. Many sides of the same issue could be presented, especially when moral problems, not action and adventure, were the central concerns. In such cases *Gunsmoke* often ended in ambiguity, requiring viewers to ponder the ideas and issues. As the series progressed into its last seasons, it became highly self-conscious of its own history. Characters explored their own motivations with some frequency, and memories became plot devices.

In the history of American popular culture, *Gunsmoke* has claimed a position of prominence. Innovative within traditional trappings, it testified to the breadth and resilience of the western genre and to television's ability to interweave character, idea, and action into narratives that could attract and compel audiences for decades.

HORACE NEWCOMB

See also **Gender and Television; Westerns**

Cast

Marshal Matt Dillon	James Arness
Dr. Galen (Doc) Adams	Milburn Stone
Kitty Russell (1955–74)	Amanda Blake
Chester Goode (1955–64)	Dennis Weaver
Festus Haggen (1964–75)	Ken Curtis
Quint Asper (1962–65)	Burt Reynolds
Sam, the bartender (1962–74)	Glenn Strange
Clayton Thaddeus (Thad) Greenwood (1965–67)	Roger Ewing
Newly O'Brien (1967–75)	Buck Taylor
Mr. Jones (1955–60)	Dabbs Greer
Louie Pheeters	James Nusser
Barney	Charles Seel
Howie	Howard Culver
Ed O'Connor	Tom Brown
Percy Crump	John Harper
Hank (1957–75)	Hank Patterson
Ma Smalley (1962–75)	Sarah Selby
Nathan Burke (1964–75)	Ted Jordan
Mr. Bodkin (1965–75)	Roy Roberts
Mr. Lathrop (1966–75)	Woody Chamblis
Halligan (1967–75)	Charles Wagenheim
Miss Hannah (1974–75)	Fran Ryan

Producers

Charles Warren, John Mantley, Phillip Leacock, Norman MacDonald, Joseph Drackow, Leonard Katzman

Programming History

233 half-hour episodes; 400 one-hour episodes
CBS

September 1955–September 1961	Saturday 10:00–10:30
September 1961–September 1967	Saturday 10:00–11:00
October 1961–June 1964	Tuesday 7:30–8:00

September 1967–September
1971   Monday 7:30–8:30
September 1971–September
1975   Monday 8:00–9:00

Further Reading

Barabas, SuzAnne, and Gabor Barabas, *Gunsmoke: A Complete History and Analysis of the Legendary Broadcast Series with a Comprehensive Episode-By-Episode Guide to Both the Radio and Television Programs,* Jefferson, North Carolina: McFarland, 1990

Fagen, Herb, *White Hats And Silver Spurs : Interviews with 24 Stars of Film and Television Westerns of the Thirties Through the Sixties,* foreword by Christopher Mitchum. Jefferson, North Carolina: McFarland, 1996

Fitzgerald, Michael G., and Boyd Magers. *Ladies of the Western: Interviews with Fifty-One More Actresses from the Silent Era to the Television Westerns of the 1950s and 1960s,* forewords by Kathryn Adams, Mala Powers, and Marion Shilling, Jefferson, North Carolina: McFarland, 2002.

Gordon, S., "*Gunsmoke's* Chester," *Look* (September 12, 1961)

Jackson, Ronald, *Classic TV Westerns: A Pictorial History,* Seacaucus, New Jersey: Carol, 1994

Lentz, Harris M., *Television Westerns Episode Guide: All United States Series, 1949–1996,* Jefferson, North Carolina: McFarland, 1997.

MacDonald, J. Fred., *Who Shot the Sheriff? The Rise and Fall of the Television Western,* New York: Praeger, 1987

Marsden, Michael T., and Jack Nachbar, "The Modern Popular Western: Radio, Television, Film and Print," in *A Literary History of the American West,* Fort Worth: Texas Christian University Press, 1987

Morhaim, Joe, "Why *Gunsmoke's* Amanda Blake, James Arness Won't Kiss," *TV Guide* (March 15, 1958)

Peel, John, *Gunsmoke Years: The Behind-The-Scenes Story: Exclusive Interviews with the Writers and Directors: A Complete Guide to Every Episode Aired: The Longest Running Network Television Drama Ever!,* Las Vegas, Nevada: Pioneer, 1989

West, Richard, *Television Westerns: Major and Minor Series, 1946–1978,* Jefferson, North Carolina: McFarland, 1987

Whitney, Dwight, "What's Gunsmoke's Secret," *TV Guide* (August 22, 1970)

Whitney, Dwight, "Why Gunsmoke Keeps Blazing," *TV Guide* (December 6, 1958)

Yoggy, Gary A., *Riding the Video Range: The Rise and Fall of the Western on Television,* Jefferson, North Carolina: McFarland, 1994

Yoggy, Gary A., editor, *Back in the Saddle: Essays on Western Film and Television Actors,* foreword by James Drury, introduction by Archie P. McDonald. Jefferson, North Carolina: McFarland, 1998

Gyngell, Bruce (1929–2000)

Australian Media Executive

Bruce Gyngell is best known by the general public in Australia for being the first face on television. When the commercial station Channel 9 in Sydney made its first broadcast in September 1956, Gyngell was the announcer who appeared to report the fact that television had arrived. His career was a remarkable and unique one in that he trained in the United States, operated in all spheres of the industry in Australia, and also played a significant role in television in the United Kingdom.

Gyngell's remarkable career cannot be understood without understanding the structure of television in Australia. From 1956 until 1980, when the national multicultural network SBS (Special Broadcasting Service) was established, the Australian television system was divided into two sectors. The ABC (Australian Broadcasting Commission, later Corporation) was modeled loosely on the BBC. A commercial sector first consisted of two networks (Nine and Seven) and later, in a controversial move, was joined by a third, the Ten

Network. Because Australia had a small population (then around 15 million) spread over a very large land mass, three commercial networks were thought to be too many to be viable. Two of the commercial systems were owned by print media barons from their beginnings, and in 1980 the third, Network Ten, also fell into the hands of a print media owner, Rupert Murdoch. While there was fierce competition among the three commercial networks, there was also collusion. For example, programs were acquired from U.S. suppliers in a manner that would not drive up prices for any individual broadcaster. Ultimately, Australia has been able to maintain all three commercial networks because traditionally there has been a high level—until recently, more than 50 percent—of imported programming. However, foreign programming does not by itself make for popularity. It has been the mix of local and overseas material that has led to strong ratings, and Gyngell's skill as a programmer contributed to the

Bruce Gyngell.
Photo courtesy of Bruce Gyngell

successes of the stations with which he was involved.

Having trained in the United States in the mid-1950s, Gyngell became programming director at Channel 9 Sydney in November 1956. Always the showman, he helped to make the Nine Network the dominant force in Australian commercial television. Gyngell's contribution was built upon a keen sense of audience tastes and an enthusiasm for catering to them. He scheduled a judicious mix of hit U.S. shows such as *I Love Lucy, The Mickey Mouse Club,* and *Father Knows Best* alongside such popular and long-running Australian-made programs as *Bandstand* and *In Melbourne Tonight.* Gyngell developed very strong links with U.S. program suppliers in those years, and his U.S. contacts and strong commercial instincts remained strong assets throughout his television career.

Gyngell became managing director of Channel 9 in 1966 and remained there until 1969, when a programming dispute with the owner, Sir Frank Packer, drove him to Network Seven. There he became managing director and led the so-called Seven Revolution, a programming strategy successfully designed to put his new network ahead of Nine in the ratings. In 1971, after three years at Seven and at the age of 42, he moved to the United Kingdom and became involved with Sir Lew Grade's ATV, then a leading U.K. company holding the lucrative Midlands franchise. Gyngell was also deputy managing director of ITC Entertainment, Grade's production company. From this position, Gyngell supported the production of the first episodes of *The Muppet Show,* which the U.S. network CBS was unwilling to finance wholly. Between 1975 and 1977 Gyngell was a freelance producer, working between the United States and Australia.

In 1977, in a move that was extremely controversial, Gyngell was appointed to be the first chair of a new broadcasting regulatory authority, the Australian Broadcasting Tribunal, established as a result of an inquiry organized by the conservative Fraser government. The former regulator, the Australian Broadcasting Control Board, had itself been replaced because it was seen to have been captured by the industry. Thus, Gyngell's complete identification with commercial television resulted in a great deal of criticism from observers worried about media concentration, the amount of Australian content, and the need for quality on television.

Gyngell was a controversial and high-profile chairman. Under his tenure the promotion of children's television improved—a committee to advise the tribunal on programs suitable for children was established and quotas for such programming reinforced. But Gyngell also presided over the award of the Ten Network to Rupert Murdoch, a bitterly contested decision. Because of Murdoch's already substantial media holdings, there was fear of his domination of both print and broadcasting media. Gyngell argued the legislation did not permit him to refuse approval of Murdoch's acquisition, but other commentators saw the incident as affirming Gyngell's closeness to commercial broadcasters and his disregard for the public interest. At the present time, there has been no sober reassessment of this period of Australian broadcasting history; the jury is thus still out on Gyngell's tenure as chair of the tribunal.

In 1980 Gyngell moved yet again to a new sector of the Australian broadcasting scene. Responding to determined "ethnic" lobbying, the Fraser government had established multicultural broadcasting in Australia in the late 1970s. When the first television station dedicated to this service was established in 1980, Gyngell was called upon to be its managing director. Given his lack of experience with either multicultural policy or public-service broadcasting, this was another controversial appointment.

The beginnings of the SBS, as the new service was called, were naturally fraught with difficulty. The ethnic communities and the government probably expected that the television station would be like the multiethnic radio station—an access channel for which ethnic groups could make their own programs. Gyngell had quite a different idea. Instead of a low-grade, well-meaning but amateurish channel, he envisioned a top-class station that would show the best of television from around the world. With programming skills well honed from watching hundreds of programs at the annual Los Angeles buying sprees, Gyngell set out to acquire programs mainly from European sources. He programmed SBS with quality programs from Italy, France, Germany, and Spain as well as from the Middle East and Asia. And he attempted as far as possible to match the nationality of the programs with the composition of the ethnic audience in Australia.

SBS television is generally deemed a success story, although its audience has never topped 2–3 percent. In its early days, its appeal was limited by its poor transmission conditions (a weak signal on UHF whereas all other television was on VHF), which made it accessible only to part of the population. Although it has remained controversial over the years, and although the very late advent of pay-TV in Australia in 1995 is likely to change its role considerably, the direction generally set by Gyngell has been adhered to and has led to SBS occupying a permanent place in Australia's broadcasting mix.

Bruce Gyngell's next big career move was to become managing director of Britain's first breakfast television service, TV-AM. The franchise was awarded to TV-AM in 1984, and at the end of its first year of operation, when Gyngell arrived, it had accumulated losses of £20 million. He applied the experience he had gained in the more competitive environment of Australian television and began trimming costs, which had the desired effect of turning around the financial fortunes of the service. However, Gyngell's tenure at TV-AM was as controversial as his ventures in Australia. Many observers saw the service's profitability being won at the expense of quality. There was no doubt that TV-AM was the most tabloidlike of any of the British franchises, but the material found a willing audience.

The controversy surrounding Gyngell deepened when, in 1987, he took on the broadcasting unions in much the same manner as his compatriot, Rupert Murdoch, had challenged the print unions. Needing to trim the coast of his regional studios, Gyngell wanted to replace workers with automated studios. The unions went on strike, and for many months Gyngell and other managers ran the service, replacing local programming with a high dose of repeat imported programs. Gyngell eventually broke the strike by installing automated equipment and recruiting new, untrained staff whom he trained quickly, winning in the process a Department of Industry Award for innovations in staff development. No doubt, these maneuvers were the basis of his reputed high standing with then-British prime minister Margaret Thatcher. When TV-AM failed to bid successfully for the breakfast franchise in the 1992 round of allocations, Thatcher sent Gyngell a personal letter of commiseration.

After TV-AM's removal from the British broadcasting scene, Gyngell returned to Australia to become executive chair of his old company, Network Nine. This position was largely ceremonial, however, and he returned to the United Kingdom in 1995 to become chair of the newly merged Yorkshire Tyne Tees service in Britain. He remained in this position until Yorkshire Television was taken over by Granada Media in 1997. In 1998 he was made Network Nine's international chairman, holding that post until his death from cancer in September 2000.

Bruce Gyngell was a consummate television executive who played a significant role in television in both Australia and Britain. He worked in both the commercial and public-service sectors and as a regulator. He was an influential figure in Australian television since its foundation and brought to it a showman's flair, a deep love of the medium, and a keen sense of how to please audiences. It is no accident that when pay-TV finally arrived in Australia in 1995, his was once again the first face to be seen. He was recalled from Britain to announce the arrival of a new era of television.

ELIZABETH JACKA

Bruce Gyngell. Born in Melbourne, Australia, July 8, 1929. Educated at Sydney Grammar School; studied medicine at Sydney University. Married: 1) Ann; two children; 2) Kathryn, 1986; children: Adam and Jamie. Pilot with the Citizen's Air Force. Trainee radio announcer, Australian Broadcasting Corporation, 1950; radio announcer, ABC, United States, 1950–55; in television at NBC and KGMB Hawaii, 1955–56; joined Sydney's TCN 9 as program manager, opening first commercial television broadcast in Australia, 1956; general manager, 1966–69; managing director, Seven Network, 1969–71; producer and programmer, ATV Network, 1971, deputy chairman and director, ATV Network, from 1973; manager of ITC Films U.K., from 1974; freelance producer, 1975–77; the first chair of the new regulatory body, the Australian Broadcasting Tribunal, 1977–80; chief executive of

Gyngell, Bruce

the new fifth Australian television channel, SBS Television, 1980–84; returned to London as managing director of TV-AM, 1984–92; returned to Australia as chief executive, TCN 9, from 1993 to 1995; director of Yorkshire Tynetees Television, England, from 1995. Member: Federation of Australian Commercial Television Stations. Died in London, September 7, 2000.

Further Reading

Bielby, Peter, editor, *Australian TV: The First Twenty-Five Years,* Melbourne: Nelson, 1981

Hall, Sandra, *Supertoy: 20 Years of Australian Television,* Melbourne: Sun, 1976

Jacka, Elizabeth, and Lesley Johnson, "Australia," in *Television, An International History,* edited by Anthony Smith, Oxford: Oxford University Press, 1995

O'Regan, Tom, *Australian Television Culture,* Sydney: Allen and Unwin, 1994

H

Hagman, Larry (1931–)

U.S. Actor

Larry Hagman is best known for his role as J.R. Ewing, the unscrupulous heir to a Texas oil fortune, in the long-running *Dallas,* the blockbuster night-time soap opera that still defines the genre. Less well known is the actor's earlier work in a variety of media.

The son of musical star Mary Martin, Hagman moved to England as a member of the cast of his mother's stage hit *South Pacific* after a variety of early theatrical experiences. He remained in England for five years, producing and directing shows for U.S. servicemen, before returning to the United States and appearing in a series of Broadway and off-Broadway plays.

Hagman's first television experience began with various guest appearances on such shows as *Playhouse 90*. He was then cast in the daytime soap opera *The Edge of Night,* in which he appeared for several years. In 1965, he became a television star playing Major Tony Nelson, astronaut and "master" to a beautiful blonde genie, in the comedy series *I Dream of Jeannie,* which ran from 1965 to 1970. He subsequently appeared in *The Good Life* and *Here We Go Again* and was a frequent guest star on a variety of television programs, until undertaking the career-making role of the crafty, silkily charming villain J.R. Ewing in 1978.

Hagman's role as the ruthless good old boy of Southfork would become indelibly associated with American cultural and economic life of the early 1980s. Over the course of 330 episodes, *Dallas* featured an American family beset by internal problems, many originating in the duplicitous schemes of its central figure, J.R. Ewing, who was a far cry from television's previous patriarchs. Viewers who tuned in could expect a weekly dose of greed, family feuds, deceptions, bribery, blackmail, alcoholism, adultery, and nervous breakdowns in the program that became, for a time, the second-longest-running dramatic hour in prime-time history (after *Gunsmoke*). The show's blended themes of sex, power, and money also sold well worldwide. When J.R. was shot in March 1980, the audience totaled 300 million in 57 countries.

Particularly noteworthy was the way in which *Dallas* made use of the cliff-hanger ending. With the "Who shot J.R.?" season-end cliff-hanger (the first ever in prime time), fans were left to speculate all summer over the fate of the man they loved to hate and ponder the question of which one of his many enemies might have pulled the trigger. The speculation grew to become an international cause célèbre, with the first show of the 1981 season generating Nielsen ratings comparable to *M*A*S*H*'s season finale, and pointing to the overlooked profitability of high-stakes serial narratives in prime time. Hagman's J.R. was influential in making greed and self-interest seem seductive, and the characterization inspired countless other portrayals (both male and female) on spin-off shows such as *Knots Landing,* and other night-time soap operas such as *Melrose Place.*

Since the end of the *Dallas* series, Hagman has reprised the role of J.R. in a couple of made-for-

Larry Hagman.
Courtesy of the Everett Collection

television movies about the further adventures of the Ewing clan, and he has acted in several other film and television projects. He has also been active in anti-smoking campaigns, producing a videotape entitled *Larry Hagman's Stop Smoking for Life,* whose proceeds went to the American Cancer Society. In 1995 the actor was diagnosed with a liver tumor and later underwent a successful liver transplant. In 2001 he published a memoir, *Hello Darlin'.*

DIANE M. NEGRA

See also **Dallas**

Larry Hagman. Born in Weatherford, Texas, September 21, 1931. Attended Bard College, Annandale-on-Hudson, New York. Married: Maj Axelsson, 1954; children: Heidi and Preston. Began career acting in Margo Jones Theatre in the Round, Dallas, Texas; later acted off-Broadway, then Broadway; motion picture debut in *Ensign Pulver,* 1964; starred in TV series *I Dream of Jeannie,* 1965–70, and *Dallas,* 1978–91.

Television Series

1956–84	*The Edge of Night*
1965–70	*I Dream of Jeannie*
1971–72	*The Good Life*
1973	*Here We Go Again*
1978–91	*Dallas*
1993	*Staying Afloat*
1996	*Orleans*

Television Miniseries

1977	*The Rhinemann Exchange*

Made-for-Television Movies

1969	*Three's a Crowd*
1971	*Vanished*
1971	*A Howling in the Woods*
1971	*Getting Away from It All*
1972	*No Place to Run*
1973	*What Are Best Friends for?*
1973	*Blood Sport*
1973	*The Alpha Caper*
1974	*Sidekicks*
1974	*Hurricane*
1974	*The Big Rip-Off*
1975	*Sarah T: Portrait of a Teenage Alcoholic*
1976	*Return of the World's Greatest Detective*
1977	*Intimate Strangers*
1978	*The President's Mistress*
1978	*Last of the Good Guys*
1982	*Deadly Encounter*
1986	*Dallas: The Early Years*
1993	*Staying Afloat* (also executive producer)
1994	*In the Heat of the Night: Who Was Geli Bendl?* (director)
1996	*Dallas: J.R. Returns* (also executive producer)
1997	*The Third Twin*
1998	*Dallas: The War of the Ewings* (also executive producer)
2000	*Doing Dallas* (documentary)

Films

Ensign Pulver, 1964; *Fail Safe,* 1964; *In Harm's Way,* 1965; *The Group,* 1966; *The Cavern,* 1965; *Up in the Cellar,* 1970; *Beware! The Blob* (also director), 1972; *Antonio,* 1973; *Harry and Tonto,* 1974; *Stardust,* 1975; *Mother Jugs and Speed,* 1976; *The Big Bus,* 1976; *Checkered Flag or Crash,* 1977; *The Eagle Has Landed,* 1977; *Superman,* 1978; *S.O.B.,* 1981; *Nixon,* 1995; *Primary Colors,* 1998; *Toscano,* 1999.

Stage

God and Kate Murphy, 1959; *The Nervous Set,* 1959; *The Warm Peninsula,* 1959–60; *The Beauty Part,* 1962–63.

Publications

"Hats Off to 10 Years of *Dallas!" People Weekly*
(April 4, 1988)
Hello Darlin', 2001

Further Reading

Adams, Leon, *Larry Hagman: A Biography,* New York: St.
Martin's Press, 1987

Kalter, Suzy, *The Complete Book of Dallas: Behind the Scenes
of the World's Favorite TV Program,* New York: Abrams,
1986
Masello, Robert, *The Dallas Family Album: Unforgettable Moments from the #1 Television Series,* New York: Bantam,
1980
Perlberg, Diane J., and Joelle Delourgo, *Quotations of J.R. Ewing,* New York: Bantam, 1980

Haley, Alex (1921–1992)

U.S. Writer

Alex Haley is best known as the author of the novel *Roots: The Saga of an American Family,* from which two television miniseries, *Roots* and *Roots: The Next Generation,* were adapted. The novels, loosely based on Haley's own family, presented an interpretation of the journey of African Americans from their homeland to the United States and their subsequent search for freedom and dignity. The novel was published in 1976, when the United States was celebrating its bicentennial.

During the last week of January 1977, the first *Roots* miniseries was aired by the American Broadcasting Company (ABC). Its phenomenal success surprised everyone, including Haley and the network executives who had "dumped" the program into one week, fearing the subject matter would not attract an audience. Instead, *Roots* garnered one of the largest audiences for dramatic television in the U.S. history of the medium, averaging a 44.9 rating and a 66 share.

The success of *Roots* went far beyond attracting a large audience, however. The miniseries, and Alex Haley, became a cause célèbre. In a cover story, *Time* magazine reported that restaurant and shop owners saw profits decline when the series was on the air. The report noted that bartenders were able to keep customers only by turning the channel selector away from basketball and hockey and tuning instead to those stations carrying *Roots.* Parents named their children after characters in the series, especially the lead character, Kunta Kinte.

The airing of *Roots* raised issues about the effects of television. There were debates about whether the television miniseries would ease U.S. race relations or exacerbate them. A *Time* magazine article explained that "many observers feel that the TV series left whites with a more sympathetic view of blacks by giving them a greater appreciation of black history." The same article, however, reported that white junior-high-school students were harassing African Americans and that black youths assaulted four white youths in Detroit, Michigan, while chanting, "Roots, roots, roots."

Haley began his writing career through assignments from *Reader's Digest* and *Playboy* magazine, for which he conducted interviews. During this time he met Malcolm X, then one of the followers of Elijah Muhammad, leader of the African-American Muslim organization the Nation of Islam. Later Haley was asked by Malcolm X to write his life's story. The result of that collaboration, *The Autobiography of Malcolm X,* was published in 1965 and sold 6 million copies.

Roots, Haley's next best-seller, was a fictionalized version of his own search for his ancestral past, which led him to the African village of Juffure, in Gambia. Haley described *Roots* as "faction," a combination of fact and fiction. Although criticized by some for taking too many liberties in the telling of his journey into his ancestral past, Haley maintained that "*Roots* is intended to convey a symbolic history of a people."

In the 1980s, Leslie Fishbein reviewed previous studies concerned with the inaccuracies found in both the book and television series and noted that Haley glossed over the complicity of Africans in the slave trade. Fishbein also analyzed an inherent contradiction in Haley's work—it centers on the family as an independent unit that isolates itself from the rest of the community and is thus unable to fight effectively the forces of slavery and racism.

Alex Haley.
Courtesy of the Everett Collection

Debates about *Roots* continued into the 1990s. Researchers Tucker and Shah have argued that the production of *Roots* by a predominantly white group led to decisions that resulted in an interpretation of race in the United States reflecting an Anglo-American, rather than an African-American, perspective. They also criticized the television version of *Roots* for transforming the African-American experience in the United States into an "immigrant" story, a narrative model in which slavery becomes a hardship, much like the hardships of other immigrant groups, which a people must experience before taking their place alongside full-fledged citizens. When slavery is simplified in this fashion and stripped of its context as a creation of social, economic, and political forces, they contended, those who experienced slavery are also stripped of their humanity.

The tremendous success of *Roots* can only be appreciated within its social context. The United States was moving away from what have come to be known as the "turbulent 60s" into an era when threats from outside forces, both real and imagined, such as the Organization of Petroleum Exporting Countries (OPEC, blamed for the mid-1970s oil crisis), and instability in Central America, especially Nicaragua, contributed to the need for a closing of ranks.

On one level, then, the program served as a symbolic ritual that helped bring African Americans into the national community. At another, more practical level, it represents the recognition on the part of television executives that the African-American community had become a significant and integral part of the larger mass audience. As Wilson and Gutiérrez have written, "In the 1970s, mass-audience advertising in the United States became more racially integrated than in any time in the nation's history." These writers point out that during this time blacks could be seen much more frequently in U.S. television commercials.

The importance of Alex Haley and the impact of his work on television history should not be underestimated. To fully appreciate the contribution he made to the medium, the African-American community, and the United States, his work must be examined within a context of changing demographics, historical events in the United States and elsewhere, and most importantly, the centuries-long struggle of a people to be recognized as full-fledged members of their national community.

RAUL D. TOVARES

See also **Roots**

Alex (Palmer) Haley. Born in Ithaca, New York, August 11, 1921. Attended Elizabeth City Teachers' College, North Carolina, 1936–37. Married: 1) Nannie Branch, 1941 (divorced, 1964); two children: Lydia Ann and William Alexander; 2) Juliette Collins, 1964; one daughter: Cynthia Gertrude. Served in the U.S. Coast Guard 1939–59, ship's cook during World War II, and chief journalist. On retirement from the Coast Guard, became fulltime writer, contributing stories, articles, and interviews to *Playboy, Harper's, Atlantic,* and *Reader's Digest;* based on interviews, wrote *The Autobiography of Malcolm X,* 1965; author, *Roots: The Saga of an American Family,* 1976, which was adapted as television miniseries, 1977. Recipient: Pulitzer Prize, 1977. Died in Seattle, Washington, February 10, 1992.

Television

1977	*Roots*
1980	*Palmerstown, U.S.A.* (producer)
1993	*Alex Haley's Queen*

Publications

The Autobiography of Malcolm X, with Malcolm X,
1965
Roots, 1976
A Different Kind of Christmas, 1988
Alex Haley's Queen: The Story of an American Family, 1993
The Playboy Interviews, 1993

Further Reading

Dates, Jannette L., "Commercial Television," in *Split Image: African Americans in the Mass Media,* edited by Jannette Dates and William Barlow, Washington, D.C.: Howard University Press, 1990
Fishbein, Leslie, "*Roots:* Docudrama and the Interpretation of History," in *American History, American Television: Interpreting the Video Past,* edited by John E. O'Connor, New York: Ungar, 1983
Gonzalez, Doreen, *Alex Haley: Author of Roots,* Hillside, New Jersey: Enslow, 1994
Shirley, David, *Alex Haley,* New York: Chelsea House, 1994
Tucker, Lauren R., and Hemant Shah, "Race and the Transformation of Culture: The Making of the Television Miniseries *Roots,*" *Critical Studies in Mass Communication* (1992)
Williams, Sylvia B., *Alex Haley,* Edina, Minnesota: Abdo and Daughters, 1996
Wilson, Clint C., and Félix Gutiérrez, *Minorities and Media: Diversity and the End of Mass Communication,* Newbury Park, California: Sage, 1985

Hallmark Hall of Fame

U.S. Anthology Drama

Created by Hallmark Cards to be a showcase around which to market its greeting cards, *Hallmark Hall of Fame* has become one of the most valued treasures in the history of quality television programming in the United States. *Hallmark Hall of Fame* made its debut on NBC on December 24, 1951, with *Amahl and the Night Visitors,* the first opera (by Gian-Carlo Menotti) to be commissioned for television, and continued as a weekly series until 1955. The half-hour series was called *Hallmark Television Playhouse* during its first two years. Sarah Churchill served as the host of the program during this early period.

Since 1955, *Hallmark Hall of Fame* has been a series of specials (appearing four to eight times a year throughout the 1960s, two to three times a year thereafter). *Hallmark Hall of Fame* has usually aired around holiday times, in order to coincide with the sale of greeting cards. These specials usually have been in 90-minute or 120-minute form, and many are adaptations of works by major playwrights and authors (e.g., William Shakespeare, Charles Dickens, and George Bernard Shaw), as well as original drama by established television writers such as Rod Serling. *Hallmark Hall of Fame* specials often have featured the leading stage actors and actresses from Great Britain and the Unites States (e.g., Maurice Evans, Dame Judith Anderson, Alfred Lunt, and Jessica Tandy).

Sarah, Plain and Tall, Christopher Walken, Glenn Close, 1991.
Courtesy of the Everett Collection

Hallmark Hall of Fame, 1951–present; James Donald, Julie Harris in *Pygmalion*, 1963.
Courtesy of the Everett Collection

Hallmark Hall of Fame ran exclusively on NBC from 1951 until 1979. The parting was a mutual one for NBC and Hallmark, as NBC was disappointed with the low ratings the specials routinely received, and Hallmark was disappointed with poor time slots allotted to it. With the promise of better time periods, *Hallmark Hall of Fame* moved to CBS for the 1979–80 season. Despite a brief switch to PBS in 1981, *Hallmark Hall of Fame* continues to air twice a year on CBS. In the 1988–89 season, *Hallmark Hall of Fame* made its appearance on ABC for the first time, thereby having appeared on all three of the major television networks, as well as PBS.

Hallmark Hall of Fame is one of the most honored programs in the history of U.S. television, having won more than 50 Emmy Awards, including 10 Emmys for best dramatic program of the year: *Little Moon of Al-* ban (1958–59), *Macbeth* (1960–61), *Victoria Regina* (1961–62), *The Magnificent Yankee* (1964–65), *Elizabeth the Queen* (1967–68), *Teacher, Teacher* (1968–69), *A Storm in Summer* (1969–70), *Love Is Never Silent* (1985–86), *Promise* (1986–87), and *Caroline?* (1989–90). In addition, Hallmark Cards has won the Trustees Award in 1960–61 and the ATAS Governors Award in 1981–82. Judith Anderson won her first Emmy for her portrayal of Lady Macbeth in the *Hallmark Hall of Fame* presentation of *Macbeth* in 1954 and would win again for the same role when *Hall* remade *Macbeth* in 1960–61. Also of note, in 1971, one month after he refused to accept his Academy Award for his portrayal of General Patton, George C. Scott accepted his Emmy for his performance in Arthur Miller's *The Price*.

Some other notable *Hallmark Hall of Fame* produc-

Amahl and the Night Visitors, Andrew McKinley, Leon Lishner, Chet Allen, 1951.
Courtesy of the Everett Collection

tions have included *Hamlet* (1953) with Maurice Evans, *Moby Dick* (1954) with Victor Jory, *Alice in Wonderland* (1955) with Elsa Lanchester, *Man and Superman* (1956) with Maurice Evans, *Twelfth Night* (1957) with Maurice Evans and Rosemary Harris,

Cyrano de Bergerac (1962) with Christopher Plummer and Hope Lange, *Inherit the Wind* (1966) with Ed Begley and Melvyn Douglas, *Anastasia* (1967) with Julie Harris, *The Man Who Came to Dinner* (1972) with Orson Welles and Lee Remick, *Beauty and the Beast* (1976) with George C. Scott and Trish Van Devere, *The Last Hurrah* (1977) with Carroll O'Connor, *Return Engagement* (1978) with Elizabeth Taylor, *Gideon's Trumpet* (1980) with Henry Fonda, *The Hunchback of Notre Dame* (1981) with Anthony Hopkins, *The Marva Collins Story* (1982) with Cicely Tyson, *My Name Is Bill W.* (1989) with James Garner and James Woods, *Decoration Day* (1990) with James Garner and Ruby Dee, and *Sarah, Plain and Tall* (1991) with Glenn Close and Christopher Walken. In 2001 Hallmark ventured into cable by purchasing the Odyssey cable network and renaming it the Hallmark Channel. This new venue provided an outlet for the vast library of previous Hallmark Hall of Fame telecasts, as well as reruns of many old network series.

MITCHELL E. SHAPIRO

See also **Anthology Drama; Rees, Marian**

Further Reading

McNeil, Alex, *Total Television: A Comprehensive Guide to Programming from 1948 to 1980,* Harmondsworth, England, and New York: Penguin, 1980; fourth edition, New York: Penguin, 1996

O'Connell, Mary C., *Connections: Reflections on 60 Years of Broadcasting,* New York: National Broadcasting Company, 1986

O'Neil, Thomas, *The Emmys: Star Wars, Showdowns, and the Supreme Test of TV's Best,* New York: Penguin, 1992

Hancock's Half Hour

British Comedy

Tony Hancock became the premier radio and TV comic of his generation, due mainly to the long-running radio and TV series that both bore the name *Hancock's Half Hour.* Hancock's career as a comedian began with performances when he was 16 and continued on radio the following year, before he joined the Royal Air Force in 1942. Following the war, he returned to the stage and eventually worked as resident comedian at the Windmill,

a famous London comedy and striptease club in which many of Britain's favorite comedians of the period worked. He reappeared on radio in 1950 in a famous variety series, *Variety Bandbox,* but it was the following year when he joined the cast of radio's *Educating Archie* that he really came to public notice. His success on the show eventually led to him being offered his own starring series on radio, from 1954, on *Hancock's Half Hour.*

Tony Hancock.
Courtesy of the Everett Collection

For *Hancock's Half Hour,* Hancock was paired with the script-writing team Ray Galton and Alan Simpson; with the comedian, they created one of Britain's best-loved and enduring comic characters. The Tony Hancock of the series was a slightly snobbish type with delusions of grandeur and a talent for self-deception. The sharp scripts were complemented by the contribution of the supporting cast (Hattie Jacques, Kenneth Williams, Bill Kerr, and Sid James) and immeasurably from Hancock himself. He proved a master of comic timing, instinctively knowing how long to hold a pause for maximum effect (similar to Jack Benny in the United States). In 1956 the show transferred to BBC Television, and Hancock went on to even greater success.

The television *Hancock's Half Hour* was a landmark in British television and became the yardstick by which all subsequent sitcoms were measured. On TV, many of the episodes were virtual double-handers between Tony Hancock and costar Sid James, who appeared as a down-to-earth type, though still a shady character always with an eye on the main chance. Their partnership proved enormously popular with viewers and critics alike. On TV, Hancock displayed a marvelous talent for facial comedy; by rolling his eyes, creasing his brow in deep concentration, sucking on his lips, or puffing out his cheeks, he could suggest any number of internal wranglings. When these expres-

sions were combined with his superb timing, he managed to wring big laughs from the thinnest of lines. But the lines were rarely thin; Galton and Simpson's writing was constantly improving, and the series, unlike many in the genre, continued to grow from strength to strength. After making 57 episodes of the TV series from July 6, 1956 to May 6, 1960, Hancock decided he wanted a change in the format. Always convinced he could do better, Hancock was rarely happy with the work he was doing. Against the advice of his writers and producer (Duncan Wood), he insisted that James be written out of the series because he thought they had fully explored the double-act potential. Finally, his position was accepted, and the series returned, now simply called *Hancock,* for six more episodes. To emphasize the change in format, the first episode featured Hancock alone in his room delivering a desperate rambling monologue as he struggled to pass the time.

Against all the odds, *Hancock* was a roaring success, and those six episodes stand out as the highlight of Hancock's career. One in particular, "The Blood Donor," is perhaps the best-remembered episode of any British sitcom. Hancock, however, remained unimpressed and finally split with his writers Galton and Simpson, complaining they were writing his character as being too poor, too hopeless. (Intriguingly, for their next major project, the writers went even further "down market" with the rag-and-bone man sitcom *Steptoe and Son.*)

Hancock never found the perfection he was seeking, and often sought solace in alcohol. After struggling to make his mark in films and other TV series, his bouts of depression deepened and eventually he committed suicide in Australia on June 25, 1968.

DICK FIDDY

Regular Performers
Tony Hancock
Sid James

Supporting Performers
Irene Handl
Warren Mitchell
Kenneth Williams
Hattie Jacques
Hugh Lloyd
Arthur Mullard
John Le Mesurier
Mario Fabrizi
Johnny Vyvyan
Frank Thornton
Patricia Hayes
June Whitfield

Patrick Cargill
Pat Coombes
Terence Alexander
Dick Emery

Producers
Duncan Wood, BBC; Tony Hancock, Alan Tarrant,
ATV

Programming History
BBC
July 1956–September 1956   6 episodes
April 1957–June 1957   6 episodes
September 1957–December 1957 12 episodes
December 1958–March 1959   13 episodes

September 1959–November 1959   10 episodes
March 1960–May 1960   10 episodes
May 1961–June 1961   6 episodes
ATV
January 1963–April 1963   13 episodes

Further Reading

Goddard, Peter, "Hancock's Half Hour: A Watershed in British Television Comedy," in *Popular Television in Britain: Studies in Cultural History,* edited by John Corner, London: British Film Institute, 1991
Hancock, Freddie, and David Nathan, *Hancock,* London: Kimber, 1969; 3rd edition, London: Ariel/BBC, 1986
Oakes, Philip, *Tony Hancock,* London: Woburn-Futura, 1975
Wilmut, Roger, *Tony Hancock—Artiste,* London: Methuen, 1978
Wilmut, Roger, *The Illustrated Hancock,* London: Queen Anne Press/Macdonald, 1986

Hanna, William (1910–2001), and Joseph Barbera (1911–)

U.S. Television Animators

The joint efforts of William Hanna and Joseph Barbera have had a powerful and lasting impact on television animation. Since the late 1950s, Hanna-Barbera programs have been a staple of television entertainment. Furthermore, a great many of the characters originally created by Hanna and Barbera for the small screen have crossed the boundaries into film, books, toys, and all manner of other media, becoming virtually ubiquitous as cultural icons.

The careers of comedy writer Bill Hanna and cartoonist Joe Barbera merged in 1940, when both were working in the Cartoon Department at MGM Studios. Their first joint effort was a Tom and Jerry cartoon entitled *Puss Gets the Boot* (1940). Dozens of Tom and Jerry episodes were to follow. When MGM closed its cartoon unit, nearly two decades after Hanna and Barbera began working there, the two decided to try their collaborative hand at creating material for television. In 1957, already having gained a solid reputation as animators working in film, the pair successfully approached Columbia's Screen Gems television studio with a storyboard for *Ruff and Reddy,* a cartoon tale about two pals, a dog and a cat.

The ensuing success of *Ruff and Reddy* as wraparound segments for recycled movie cartoons (including Tom and Jerry) proved to be the beginning of a lengthy partnership in television animation. In late 1958, Hanna and Barbera launched *Huckleberry Hound,* the first cartoon series to receive an Emmy Award. This half-hour syndicated program featured, in addition to the title character, such cartoon favorites as Yogi Bear, Pixie and Dixie, Augie Doggie, and Quick Draw McGraw. This latter character, like numerous others who began their "careers" in one Hanna-Barbera creation, went on to an enormously successful series of his own.

In 1960, when a survey revealed that more than half of *Huckleberry Hound*'s audience comprised adults, Hanna and Barbera turned their efforts toward creating a cartoon for prime time. The result was *The Flintstones,* a series that drew on and parodied conventions of popular live-action domestic sitcoms, most specifically in this case Jackie Gleason's *The Honeymooners.* The comical premise of a "typical" suburban family living in a cartoon "Stone Age," with home appliances represented as talking prehistoric animals and frequent

William Hanna (left) and Joseph Barbera.
Courtesy of the Everett Collection

celebrity guest stars (authentic voices with caricatured bodies) enabled *The Flintstones* to attract both child and adult audiences during its initial run on ABC (1960–66). *The Jetsons,* a "space-age" counterpart to *The Flintstones,* joined its predecessor in prime time in 1962.

Unlike *The Flintstones, The Jetsons* would last only one season in ABC's evening schedule. However, in the late 1960s both programs became extremely popular in Saturday morning cartoon line-ups and subsequently in syndication. The programs were so successful as reruns that in the 1980s, 51 new episodes of *The Jetsons* were produced, as were TV specials and movies based on both *The Flintstones* and *The Jetsons.* *Flintstones* spin-off series for children, including *Pebbles and Bamm-Bamm* (1971–72 and 1975–76), *The Flintstones Comedy Hour* (1972–74), and *The Flintstones Kids* (1986–90), also have appeared since the original series ceased production.

Other popular Hanna-Barbera series have included children's cartoons such as *Scooby-Doo, Where Are You?* (1969, plus a number of subsequent Scooby-Doo series); *The Smurfs* , a concept based on a Belgian car-

toon series and first brought to Hanna-Barbera by network executive Fred Silverman (1981); *Pac-Man* (1982); *Pound Puppies* (1986), and *Captain Planet* (1994).

A series of ownership changes began for Hanna-Barbera Productions in the 1990s. First, the company was acquired by Turner Broadcasting Systems (TBS) in 1991. TBS itself was then acquired by Time-Warner in 1995. As part of the huge media conglomerate that is now AOL Time-Warner, Hanna-Barbera has combined resources with its longtime rival Warner Bros., producers of Looney Toons cartoons. Hanna-Barbera and Looney Toons fare accounts for the bulk of the programming on the popular Cartoon Network cable service. Since the 1970s, Hanna-Barbera has produced, in addition to the cartoons, a number of films and specials for television, including *The Gathering* (1977), *The Stone Fox* (1987), and *Going Bananas* (1984), as well as live-action feature films, including *The Jetsons: The Movie* (1990), *The Pagemaster* (1994), *The Flintstones* (1994), and *The Flintstones in Viva Rock Vegas* (2000).

Prior to William Hanna's death in 2001, the long and productive partnership between him and Joseph Barbera yielded some of television's most successful and enduring programs. Cartoon series such as *The Flintstones, The Jetsons,* and *Huckleberry Hound* are as popular with audiences today as they were when first shown. While this is evidence of the timeless entertainment value of animated programming, it also reflects the astute business sense of Hanna and Barbera and their ability to recognize trends in the entertainment industry.

After decades of exposure to audiences worldwide, many individual Hanna-Barbera animated characters have become so familiar to audiences that they have to some extent transcended their original program contexts. An obvious example is the Flintstones characters, which have achieved international recognition through television series, specials, theatrical film, and their display on every imaginable consumer product (most licensed by Hanna-Barbera).

MEGAN MULLEN

See also **Cartoons;** *Flintstones, The*

William Denby Hanna. Born in Melrose, New Mexico, July 14, 1910. Studied journalism and engineering. Married: Violet Wogatzke, 1936; children: David William and Bonnie Jean. Engineer, California, 1931; story editor and assistant to Harman-Ising unit, Warner Brothers, 1933–37; director and story editor (Joseph Barbera was hired a few weeks later), MGM Studios, 1937; director, first animated film *Blue Monday,* 1938; began collaborating with Barbera as directors of animated shorts for Warners, making primarily Tom and Jerry shorts, 1940; co-head, with Barbera, animation department, 1955–57; cofounded Hanna-Barbera Productions, 1957, producing *The Flintstones,* the first-ever animated prime-time show, with half-hour storyline, which aired 1960–66; executive producer, *Once Upon a Forest,* a 20th Century-FOX release, 1993; directed the ABC specials *I Yabba-Dabba Do!* and *Hollyrock-A-Bye Baby;* executive producer, *The Flintstones* movie, 1994; director (his first solo directorial effort since 1941), Cartoon Network's *World Premiere Toons* project of the original cartoon short *Hard Luck Duck,* 1995. Charter member, Boy Scouts of America. Recipient: seven Oscars; eight Emmy Awards; Governor's Award, Television Arts and Sciences; Hollywood Walk of Fame Star, 1976; Golden IKE Award, Pacific Pioneers in Broadcasting, 1983; Pioneer Award, BMI (Broadcast Music Inc.), 1987; Iris Award–NATPE Men of the Year, 1988; Licensing Industry Merchandisers' Association Award for Lifetime Achievement, 1988; Academy of Television Arts and Sciences Governors Award, 1988; Jackie Coogan Award for Outstanding Contribution to Youth through Entertainment Youth in Film, 1988; Frederic W. Ziv Award for Outstanding Achievement in Telecommunications, Broadcasting Division, College-Conservatory of Music, University of Cincinnati, 1989; named to Television Academy Hall of Fame, 1991. Died in Los Angeles, March 23, 2001.

Joseph Barbera. Born in New York City, March 24, 1911. Attended American Institute of Banking. Children from first marriage: Jayne, Neal, and Lynn; married: Sheila. Banker, Irving Trust, New York City; changed career path after he sold drawing to *Collier's* magazine to earn extra money; sketch artist and storyboard writer, Van Buren Studio; animator, Terrytoons; moved from New York to Hollywood, 1937, and worked in animation department, MGM Studios, where he met William Hanna; started working with Hanna on their first collaboration, the cartoon *Puss Gets the Boot,* which led to the Tom and Jerry shorts; continued collaborating with Hanna as directors of animated shorts for Warners; co-head, MGM cartoon department, 1955–57; cofounded Hanna-Barbera Productions, 1957, which began to make cartoons directly for the small screen, launching its first production, *Ruff and Reddy,* 1957, and producing the first-ever animated prime-time family sitcom show, with half-hour storyline, *The Flintstones,* which aired 1960–66; creative consultant for animated feature film *Tom and Jerry: The Movie;* producer and executive producer for the syndicated Hanna-Barbera/FOX Children's Network show *Tom and Jerry Kids;* directed the Flintstones snorkassaurus Dino in two shorts, *Stay Out* and *The Great Egg-Scape,* for the World Premier Toons project (48 7-minute cartoon shorts), which began airing on Cartoon Network in 1995. Recipient: seven Oscars; eight Emmy Awards; Hollywood Walk of Fame Star, 1976; Golden IKE Award, Pacific Pioneers in Broadcasting, 1983; Pioneer Award, BMI (Broadcast Music, Inc.), 1987; Iris Award-NATPE Men of the Year, 1988; Licensing Industry Merchandisers' Association Award for Lifetime Achievement, 1988; Academy of Television Arts and Sciences Governors Award, 1988; Jackie Coogan Award for Outstanding Contribution to Youth through Entertainment Youth in Film, 1988; Frederic W. Ziv Award for Outstanding Achievement in Telecommunications, Broadcasting Division, College-Conservatory of Music, University of Cincinnati, 1989; named to Television Academy Hall of Fame, 1991.

Television Series (selected)

| 1957–60 | *Ruff and Reddy* |
| 1958–62 | *Huckleberry Hound* |

1959–62	*Quick Draw McGraw*
1960–66	*The Flintstones*
1960–62	*Snagglepuss*
1961–63	*The Yogi Bear Show*
1961–72	*Top Cat*
1962–63	*The Jetsons*
1964–65	*Jonny Quest*
1967–70	*Fantastic Four*
1969–93	*Scooby Doo*
1971–72, 1975–76	*Pebbles and Bamm-Bamm*
1972–75	*The Flintstones Comedy Hour*
1973–75	*Yogi's Gang*
1973–86	*Superfriends*
1978–79	*The New Fantastic Four*
1981–90	*The Smurfs* (coproduction with Sepp Int.)
1982–84	*Pac-Man*
1985	*The Jetsons*
1985	*Funtastic World of Hanna Barbera*
1986	*Foofur*
1986	*Pound Puppies*
1986–90	*The Flintstone Kids*
1986	*Wildfire*
1987	*Snorks*
1987	*Sky Commanders*
1987	*Popeye and Son*
1993	*Captain Planet*
1994	*The New Adventures of Captain Planet*

Made-for-Television Movies

1977	*The Gathering*
1979	*The Gathering, Part II*
1984	*Going Bananas*
1987	*The Stone Fox*

Animated Television Specials (selected)

1966	*Alice in Wonderland*
1967	*Jack and the Beanstalk*
1972	*The Last of the Curlews*
1974	*The Runaways*
1974	*Cyrano*
1979	*Caspar's First Christmas*
1979	*The Popeye Valentine Special: Sweethearts at Sea*
1982	*My Smurfy Valentine*

1982	*Yogi Bear's All-Star Comedy Christmas Caper*
1985	*Smurfily-Ever-After*
1986	*The Flintstones' 25th Anniversary Celebration*
1989	*Hagar the Horrible*
1993	*I Yabba-Dabba Do!*

Television Specials

1974	*The Crazy Comedy Concert*
1975	*Yabaa-Dabba Doo! The Happy World of Hanna-Barbera* (documentary, with Marshall Flaum)
1979	*Yabba-Dabba Doo!* (documentary, with Robert Guenette)

Films

Blue Monday, 1938; *Anchors Aweigh,* 1945; *Holiday in Mexico,* 1946; *Neptune's Daughter,* 1949; *Dangerous when Wet,* 1952; *Invitation to Dance,* 1956; *Hey There, It's Yogi Bear,* 1964; *A Man Called Flintstone,* 1966; *Project X,* 1967; *Charlotte's Web,* 1973; *Heidi's Song,* 1982; *Gobots: Battle of the Rock Lords,* 1986; *Jetsons: The Movie,* 1990; *The Pagemaster,* 1994; *The Flintstones,* 1994.

Publications

Hanna, William, and Joseph Barbera, with Ted Sennett, *The Art of Hanna-Barbera: Fifty Years of Creativity,* 1989

Barbera, Joseph, *My Life in "Toons": From Flatbush to Bedrock in Under a Century,* 1994

Hanna, William, *A Cast of Friends,* 1996

Further Reading

Cawley, John, and Jim Korkis, *Cartoon Superstars,* Las Vegas, Nevada: Pioneer, 1990

Erickson, Hal, *Television Cartoon Shows: An Illustrated Encyclopedia, 1949–1993,* Jefferson City, North Carolina: McFarland, 1995

Gelman, Morrie, "Hanna and Barbera: After 50 Years, Opposites Still Attract," *Variety* (July 12, 1989)

Maltin, Leonard, *Of Mice and Magic: A History of American Animated Cartoons,* New York: New American Library, 1987

Happy Days

U.S. Comedy

Happy Days originated in 1974 as a nostalgic teen-populated situation comedy centered on the life of Richie Cunningham (Ron Howard) and his best friend Potsie (Anson Williams), both students at Jefferson High School in 1950s Milwaukee, Wisconsin. The character of Arthur Fonzarelli, or Fonzie, with whom the show is now most associated, was originally only fifth-billed. But his leather-jacketed, "great with the girls," biker profile unexpectedly captured the imagination of viewers. Fonzie increased the popularity of the show and of the actor who portrayed him, Henry Winkler, and by 1980 "the Fonz" had achieved top billing.

The show presented a saccharine perspective on American youth culture of the 1950s. With rock and roll confined to the jukebox of Al's Diner, the kids worried over first loves, homecoming parades, and the occasional innocuous rumble. The Cunninghams represented the middle-class family values of the era. Minor skirmishes erupted between parents and children, but dinner together was never missed—prepared and served by mother, Marion (Marion Ross), or daughter, Joanie (Erin Moran). There was no inkling of the "generation gap" discourse that was beginning to differentiate youth from their parents in the 1950s, which exploded in the 1960s, and which was still active in the mid-1970s when the show was created.

One episode pits Richie and his friends against Richie's father, Howard (Tom Bosley), by virtue of the latter's support of a business plan that would send a freeway through the teen make-out spot, Inspiration Point. Civil disobedience is suggested by the teenagers' organization of petitions and picket signs to protest the plan. Fonzie even chains himself to a tree at the site. Yet generational harmony is restored when Richie makes Howard realize that he, too, participated in the culture of Inspiration Point when he was young.

Fonzie's lower-class status, his black leather clothes, motorcycle, propensity to get into fights, and apparent sexual exploits with multiple women take advantage of the code of delinquency that social scientists of the period fashioned under the rubric of deviancy studies. But again, Fonzie's representation had none of the hard edge or angst of a James Dean or Marlon Brandon character and was played more for laughs than social critique. Yet his popularity on the show may have tapped into deeper audience identifications.

His image of an impervious, highly testosteroned male, albeit with modicums of vulnerability and hyperbole as acted by Winkler, was overtly rewarded in the show. It took only a snap of his fingers to have women do his bidding or grown men cower in fear of being pummeled by an out-of-control Fonzarelli. So male-identified was his character that the men's restroom in Al's Diner was referred to as his "office." The Fonz's courting of many women at once meant he was never subject to the kind of romantic involvement and inevitable heartbreak that characterized Richie's relationships with women.

The Fonz's style, "my way" bravado, working-class ethos, and loner sensibility differed from the mainstream Cunninghams and was in direct opposition to the upwardly mobile, college-bound, leadership-quality Richie. Richie, audiences knew, would someday outgrow Milwaukee and leave it behind, but Fonzie had fewer choices and would stay. And perhaps the tension between these two worlds and life-directions kept audiences watching through the show's ten-year run, during which time Richie and his pals go to college, join the army, and even get married.

Despite these contrasts, however, Fonzie and the Cunningham family were never involved in overt conflict. Indeed, by the end of the show, Fonzie had moved into the Cunningham's garage apartment, and though the bemused Howard Cunningham often wondered what was happening "up there," Fonzie was, by this time, a thoroughly domesticated character. His role not only paralleled that of Mr. Cunningham, but those of countless sitcom fathers before him, and he was as likely to dispense careful, family-oriented wisdom as to suggest rebellion of the slightest sort. But this wisdom was always proffered with Winkler's parody-delinquent sense of style, a style that continues to appeal to youngsters in syndicated rerun throughout the world.

Happy Days stands as the first of a string of extremely successful spin-off comedies from producer Garry Marshall. *Laverne and Shirley, Mork and Mindy,* and other shows helped propel the ABC television network into first place in the ratings battles and enabled Marshall to move from television to feature-film direction.

LISA A. LEWIS

Happy Days, Ron Howard, Henry Winkler, Tom Bosley, Erin Gray, Marion Ross, 1974–84.
Courtesy of the Everett Collection

See also **Laverne and Shirley; Marshall, Garry**

Cast

Richie Cunningham (1974–80)	Ron Howard
Arthur "Fonzie" Fonzarelli	Henry Winkler
Howard Cunningham	Tom Bosley
Marion Cunningham	Marion Ross
Warren "Potsie" Webber (1974–83)	Anson Williams
Ralph Malph (1974–80)	Donny Most
Joanie Cunningham	Erin Moran
Chuck Cunningham (1974)	Gavan O'Herlihy
Chuck Cunningham (1974–75)	Randolph Roberts
Bag Zombroski (1974–75)	Neil J. Schwartz
Marsha Simms (1974–76)	Beatrice Colen
Gloria (1974–75)	Linda Purl
Wendy (1974–75)	Misty Rowe
Trudy (1974–75)	Tita Bell
Arnold (Matsuo Takahashi) (1975–76, 1982–83)	Pat Morita
Charles "Chachi" Arcola (1977–84)	Scott Baio
Lori Beth Allen Cunningham (1977–82)	Lynda Goodfriend
Eugene Belvin (1980–82)	Denis Mandel
Bobby (1980–84)	Harris Kal
Jenny Piccalo (1980–83)	Cathy Silvers
Roger Phillips (1980–84)	Ted McGinley
Flip Phillips (1982–83)	Billy Warlock
K.C. Cunningham (1982–83)	Crystal Bernard
Ashley Pfister (1982–83)	Linda Purl
Heather Pfister (1982–83)	Heather O'Rourke
Officer Kirk	Ed Peck

Producers

Garry Marshall, Thomas Miller, Edward Milkis, Lowell Ganz, Brian Levant, Fred Fox, Jr., Tony Marshall, Jerry Paris, William S. Bickley, Gary Menteer, Walter Kempley, Ronny Hallin

Programming History

256 episodes
ABC

January 1974–September 1983	Tuesday 8:00–8:30
September 1983–January 1984	Tuesday 8:30–9:00
April 1984–May 1984	Tuesday 8:30–9:00
June 1984–July 1984	Thursday 8:00–8:30

Harding, Gilbert (1907–1960)

British Television Personality

Gilbert Harding was an outspoken English panelist, quiz master, and broadcaster, known as "the rudest man in Britain." A former teacher, police constable, and journalist, he began working with the BBC's Monitoring Service in 1939 as a subeditor. In 1944, he went to Canada for three years to work with the BBC's

Toronto office. On returning to Britain in 1947, he began making appearances as a question master in the popular BBC radio panel game show *Round Britain Quiz.* He also introduced BBC radio's *The Brains Trust* and *Twenty Questions.* From 1951, he became part of the postwar British way of life with his appearances as a grumpy panelist in the highly successful, long-running television panel game show *What's My Line?* Every week he entertained and shocked viewers with his intellect, sharp wit, and rudeness. He often bullied innocent guests if they gave evasive answers or did not speak perfect English. After one clash between Harding and chair Eamonn Andrews, the BBC received more than 175 phone calls and 6 telegrams from viewers complaining about Harding's appalling behavior. For over a decade, *What's My Line?* was an institution on British television, and Harding became a national celebrity.

In 1960 Harding agreed to be interrogated by journalist John Freeman on a live television interview program called *Face to Face.* Harding was reduced to tears in front of millions of viewers when Freeman asked about the recent death of his mother. This was, in fact, a deliberate and tactless attempt to "out" him as gay at a time when homosexuality was still illegal in Britain. Harding admitted nothing, but clearly the interview was a distressing experience for him. He confessed on-screen that "my bad manners and bad temper are quite indefensible...I'm almost unfit to live with...I'm profoundly lonely...I should be very glad to be dead." John Freeman later admitted his lack of sensitivity, but Harding died shortly after the program's transmission. He was 53.

Owen Spencer Thomas described him on BBC Radio London's documentary *Gilbert Harding* in 1979 as "that enigmatic man...[he] was bad tempered and rude, yet his friends counted him as one of the kindest, and most generous."

STEPHEN BOURNE

Gilbert (Charles) Harding. Born in Hereford, Herefordshire, England, June 5, 1907. Attended Cambridge University. Taught English in Canada and France and worked as a police officer in Bradford, West Yorkshire, before settling in Cyprus as a teacher and *Times* correspondent; returned to England in 1936, and joined the BBC monitoring service in 1939, through his skills as a linguist; subsequently worked for BBC as overseas director in Toronto after World War II; host of and regular guest on radio and television panel shows, 1950s. Died November 16, 1960.

Television Series

1951–60	*What's My Line?*

Radio (as host)

Round Britain Quiz; The Brains Trust; Twenty Questions.

Publication

Along My Line (autobiography), 1953

Further Reading

Howes, Keith, *Broadcasting It: An Encyclopaedia of Homosexuality on Film, Radio, and TV in the UK 1923–1993,* London: Cassell, 1993

Medhurst, Andy, "Every Wart and Pustule: Gilbert Harding and Television Stardom," in *Popular Television in Britain: Studies in Cultural History,* edited by John Corner, London: British Film Institute, 1991

Rayburn, Wallace, *Gilbert Harding: A Candid Portrayal,* Brighton, England: Argus and Robertson, 1978

Harris, Susan

U.S. Writer, Producer

Watching television as she grew up in the 1950s in New York, Susan Harris concluded, as do many viewers, that "anybody could write this." Unlike most who make the claim, however, she persisted in preparing work for television, and by 1969 she found a way to present it to the creator of *Then Came Bronson,* a short-lived NBC series. The show needed a script and she sold one. In 1970 Garry Marshall brought her to the anthology series *Love, American Style,* for which she wrote ten scripts. There she met Norman Lear and ended up writing scripts for his breakthrough series *All in the Family,* taking her son with her to the story meetings. Following the U.S. Supreme Court's 1973 decision *Roe v. Wade,* which legalized abortion in the

Susan Harris.
Courtesy of Witt-Thomas-Harris Productions

United States, Lear decided to address the highly charged abortion issue in *Maude,* a spin-off from *All in the Family*. Susan Harris wrote the script for "Maude's Abortion," a sensitive and sensible examination of a married couple's choices in light of the court's decision. She received the Humanitas Award for her efforts. The Catholic Church, expectedly, disapproved of the story, not the last time Harris would hear from that institution.

During those years she met producers Paul Junger Witt and Tony Thomas, and with them formed an independent television production company, Witt/Thomas/Harris, in 1976. For the new company Harris created and wrote *Fay,* starring Lee Grant, a series essentially canceled by NBC before it aired. (Grant described the NBC executives as the mad programmers.) Harris's next effort was no less controversial, but far more successful. In 1977 she was the sole writer of the series *Soap,* which was attacked by *Newsweek* magazine, Southern Baptists, and Roman Catholics before any of them had seen it. The butler in *Soap* was spun off in a new series, *Benson,* and Harris then went on to create and write *I'm A Big Girl Now, Hail to the Chief, The*

Golden Girls, Empty Nest, and *Good and Evil.* After retiring from television, she commented in 1995 that her favorite series was *Soap.*

Harris recalled that on most of the shows with which she was associated before creating her own company, men were writing about women. *Maude,* she noted, had an all-male staff. By the time she received the Emmy Award for *The Golden Girls* in 1987, Harris had literally changed the face of television comedy. Her female characters were well defined and represented an array of personality types. Working alone, she sparked a revolution as a woman writing about women, while providing insight into male personalities as well. On the cutting edge, she drew the wrath of self-styled moralists even as she used wit, satire, and farce to provide a new kind of television.

Since its founding in 1976, Witt/Thomas/Harris has grown to become the largest independent producer of television comedy in the United States. Married to her partner, Paul Witt, Susan Harris is now active in community projects and an avid art collector.

ROBERT S. ALLEY

*See also **All in the Family; Golden Girls, The; Soap; Witt, Paul Junger***

Susan Harris. Born in Mount Vernon, New York. Married: Paul Junger Witt. Writer for various television series, from 1969; cofounder, Witt/Thomas/Harris TV production company, 1976; creator, writer, and producer, various TV series from 1977; assistant producer of film *Heart and Souls,* 1993. Recipient: Emmy Awards, 1986–87.

Television Series

1969–79	*Then Came Bronson* (writer for selected episodes)
1969–74	*Love, American Style*
1971–79	*All in the Family*
1977–81	*Soap*
1985	*Hail to the Chief* (also creator and producer)
1985–92	*The Golden Girls* (also creator and producer)
1988–95	*Empty Nest*
1991	*Good and Evil* (also creator and producer)
1991–94	*Nurses* (also creator and producer)
1992–93	*The Golden Palace* (also creator and producer)
1993–94	*Brighton Belles*
1995	*Platypus Man* (script supervisor)
1998	*The Secret Lives of Men* (producer)

Have Gun—Will Travel

U.S. Western

Have Gun—Will Travel transplanted the chivalric myth to television's post–Civil War West. The hit CBS series aired from 1957 to 1963 and was centered on Paladin, an educated knight-errant gunslinger who, upon payment of $1,000, would leave his well-appointed suite in San Francisco's Hotel Carlton to pursue whatever mission of mercy or justice a well-heeled client commissioned. Paladin was played by Richard Boone, an actor who had risen to TV fame in 1954 with his intense portrayal of Dr. Konrad Styner, the host/narrator of the reality-based hospital drama *Medic*.

Have Gun was created by Sam Rolfe and Herb Meadow, two innovative ex-radio writers who had been tipped that CBS was in the market for a cowboy show with a "different" twist. They thereupon fashioned the first truly adult TV Western—a story centered on a cultured gunfighter who had named himself Paladin after the legendary officers of Charlemagne's medieval court. A gourmet and connoisseur of fine wine, fine women, and Ming Dynasty artifacts, Paladin would quote Keats, Shelley, and Shakespeare with the same self-assurance that he brought to the subjugation of frontier evildoers.

Because the concept revolved entirely around Paladin, its success hinged on the ability of the actor portraying him to, in creator Rolfe's words, "play a high-I.Q. gunslinger and get away with it" (see Edson). When Western movie icon Randolph Scott (the first choice for the role) was unavailable, the producers turned to Richard Boone who, they were overjoyed to find, actually could ride a horse. Boone's intimidating growl, prominent nose, and pock-marked visage physically distanced him from the standard fresh-faced cowboy hero in the same way that his character's cultured background distinguished him from those prairie-tutored rustics. After watching Paladin muse about Pliny and Aristotle, one television critic marveled, "Where else can you see a gunfight and absorb a classical education at the same time?" (see Edson).

The show's identifying graphic was Paladin's calling card—bearing an image of the white knight chess piece and the inscription, "Have Gun—Will Travel...Wire Paladin, San Francisco." The responses that these cards generated were brought to Paladin by the show's only other continuing character—an Asian hotel minion named Hey Boy (Hey Girl in 1960–61 when actress Lisa Lu temporarily replaced actor Kam Tong who had moved to another series). Without an ensemble cast, the entire weight of the series rested on Richard Boone's shoulders. Paladin's mannerisms and motivations had to be what propelled and interlocked the show's episodes from week to week and season to season.

A descendent of Kentucky frontiersman Daniel Boone, method actor Richard successfully met this challenge both on camera and off, directing several dozen of the later episodes himself. The sophisticated elegance of his character also brought him more loyal fan mail from females than was received by any of his more photogenic cowboy contemporaries. The show's off-beat quality was further enhanced by its practice of

Have Gun—Will Travel, Richard Boone, 1957–63.
Courtesy of the Everett Collection

using mainly new writers who had not been drilled in conventional saddle-soap story lines. *Have Gun* became an immediate hit, ranking among the top five shows in its first season, and was the consistent number three program from 1958 to 1961. By early 1962, however, Boone was growing weary of the project and felt it had run its course. "Every time you go to the well, it's a little further down," he lamented to a *Newsweek* reporter. "It's sad, like seeing a [Sugar] Ray Robinson after his best days are past. You wish he wouldn't fight any more, and you could just keep your memories."

Have Gun's distinctive inversion of the television horse opera provided many memories to keep. In virtually every episode, Paladin would be seen in ruffled shirt, sipping a brandy or smoking a 58¢ cigar before or after embarking on his latest paid-in-advance assignment to the hinterland. Like Captain Marlowe from Joseph Conrad's *Heart of Darkness,* he was always the brooding observer as well as the valiant, if somewhat vexed, participant. Unlike the archetypal Western hero, Paladin wore black rather than white, complete with an ebony hat embellished by a band of silver conches and a holster embossed with a silver chess knight. He sported a villain's mustache and was not enamored of his horse, declining even to justify its existence with an appealing name. And he seemed to relish the adventures of the mind—his chess matches and library—far more than the frontier confrontations from which he drew his livelihood.

As articulator of *Have Gun*'s central premise, its theme song, "The Ballad of Paladin," became a success in its own right. Sung by the aptly-named Johnny Western and written jointly by Western, Boone, and series creator Rolfe, the tune was a hit single in the early 1960s. The first lines of the lyric encapsulated both the show's motivating graphic and the chivalric roots of its central character: "*Have gun, will travel* reads the card of a man, A knight without armor in a savage land."

Occasionally, this unshielded self-sufficiency would cause Paladin (again like Conrad's Marlowe) to turn on his employers when he determined them to be the unjust party. For a nation that, in 1957, was just becoming politically aware of cowering conformity's injustices, this may have been *Have Gun's* most potent, if most understated, element.

PETER B. ORLIK

See also **Boone, Richard; Westerns**

Cast
Paladin	Richard Boone
Hey Boy (1957–60; 1961–63)	Kam Tong
Hey Girl (1960–61)	Lisa Lu

Producers
Frank Pierson, Don Ingalls, Robert Sparks, Julian Claman

Programming History
156 episodes
CBS
September 1957–
September 1963   Saturday 9:30–10:00

Further Reading

Brooks, Tim, and Earle Marsh, *The Complete Directory to Prime Time Network TV Shows: 1946–Present,* New York: Ballantine, 1979

Edson, Lee, "TV's Rebellious Cowboy," *Saturday Evening Post* (August 6, 1960)

MacDonald, J. Fred, *Who Shot the Sheriff? The Rise and Fall of the Television Western,* New York: Praeger, 1987

Shulman, Arthur, and Roger Youman, *How Sweet It Was,* New York: Bonanza, 1966

West, Richard, *Television Westerns: Major and Minor Series, 1946–1978,* Jefferson, North Carolina: McFarland, 1987

"…Will Travel," *Newsweek* (January 22, 1962)

Yoggy, Gary A., *Riding the Video Range: The Rise and Fall of the Western on Television,* Jefferson, North Carolina: McFarland, 1994

Have I Got News For You

British Political Quiz Show

Having made their television breakthrough with Channel 4's improvisational comedy *Whose Line Is It Anyway?,* Hat Trick Productions steamrolled into mainstream popular culture in Britain with a glut of lucrative and long-running comedic game shows. Without a doubt, the granddaddy of them all is *Have I Got*

News For You, a panel quiz show focusing on politics and current events. However, rather than a serious competition, the primary point of the program is to lob as many cutting comments as possible at figures in the news, the guest participants, and even the regular host and panel members.

Have I Got News for You was originally hosted by Angus Deayton, with Ian Hislop and Paul Merton acting as regular panel members and opposing "team captains." Hislop and Merton are each joined by a new guest participant every week, thus forming two teams. The guests are generally familiar figures from British popular culture: politicians, musicians, actors, or comedians.

The show is always recorded the night before transmission for maximum retention of essential topicality (older programs are rerun under the title *Have I Got Old News For You*). The format was gleefully lifted from Radio 4's *The News Quiz* and given an anarchic make-over. The show presents a no-holds-barred attack on the powerful, famous and simply famously irritating. The modern-day equivalent of a traditional, grotesque-laden political cartoon, the show delights in the most base and insulting comment. Indeed, the oft-repeated and feebly inapt tag-line of "allegedly!" after the most nearly libelous comments has not only become a by-word for the program, but has seeped into the national consciousness.

Scripted and mocked proceedings were steered through the muddy waters of political intrigue and scandal by the host Angus Deayton until October 2002. He adopted a pseudo-John Cleese loftiness, and his quick comic manner is not averse to the odd, spontaneous gem. During an episode first aired in 1995, when the discussion lightly turned to thoughts of a possible Beatles reunion, Member of Parliament Teresa Gorman commented on the stupidity of the story: "isn't one of them dead?". Looking directly into the camera, Deayton muttered: "You heard it here first!"

The rival team captains are Ian Hislop, editor of the satirical magazine *Private Eye,* and Paul Merton, who had performed impressively on Hat Trick's *Whose Line Is It Anyway?* Merton was given his own Channel 4 sketch show and, for a brief period in 1996, was tempted away from the program entirely.

The rounds are designed to allow for as much mocking of political figures and events as possible; actual score-keeping is a secondary concern. Innuendo, implication, and mockery of Deayton himself were high on the agenda, with the missing-word round having produced such Merton quotable classics as "Queen Beats Spice Girls in Lesbian Mud Bath" and "Any Fool Can Host a TV News Quiz." In later seasons, the mix has been boosted with the regular feature of "this week's guest publication" which could deal with anything from egg-cup collecting to pig farming.

Politicians and celebrities in the news are not the only objects of ridicule. Perhaps the most hard-hitting (and, in terms of viewing figures, attractive) element of the program is the unbridled lampooning of the guest panelists themselves. The guest players generally divide into two clear camps: the professional wag, and the newsworthy target. Journalists and critics valiantly attempt to beat the regulars in the laughter-generating competition, sometimes with breath-taking and dexterous results. The newsworthy targets, on the other hand, are simply sacrificial lambs, there for the sake of a joke. Almost immediately cut down to size by Merton's charming, lackluster observations or Hislop's less complicated, forthright abuse, they are ritually humiliated throughout the program. Some, such as Princess Diana's beau James Hewitt, survive by charm and polite manners, while others, such as Sir Elton John, avoid humiliation by not turning up at all. However, these guests then risk facing the equally humiliating situation of a hired look-a-like to sit in his place and play the game. The show's most celebrated and lauded guest of this type was the infamous tub of lard which replaced the Labour Member of Parliament Roy Hattersley, who got cold feet at the last minute and cancelled his planned June 4, 1993 appearance on the show. The presence of the tub of lard as a stand-in for Hattersley was explained as logical, because "they possessed the same qualities and were liable to give similar performances." Finally, some guests, such as the late Paula Yates, miss the satirical slant of the show completely, and take it far too seriously (her furious condemnation of Hislop as the "sperm of the devil" has passed into television history).

In 2002, host Angus Deayton became the recipient of the most mockery when it was widely reported that he had engaged in drug use with prostitutes. Hislop and Merton teased Deayton mercilessly on the show, and in October of that year he was asked to resign. The show has been hosted by a different guest each week since Deayton's departure.

ROBERT ROSS

Programming History

A Hat Trick Production, produced by Harry Thompson.

Two series of 8 episodes per year.

BBC2

September 1990–September 2000

BBC1

October 2000–   Friday, 9:30–10:00

Further Reading

Deayton, Angus, Ian Hislop, Paul Merton, Colin Swash, and Harry Thompson, *Have I Got News For You,* London: BBC Books in association with Hat Trick Productions, 1994

Deayton, Angus, Ian Hislop, Paul Merton, Mark Burton, Robert Fraser Steele, John O'Farrell, and Colin Swash, *Have I Got 1997 For You,* London: BBC Books in association with Hat Trick Productions, 1997

Hawaii Five-O

U.S. Police Drama

Hawaii Five-O ran continuously on the CBS network from September 1968 to April 1980, making it the longest-running police drama in U.S. TV history. The program also ran in 80 countries, and is still often shown on cable and satellite TV services.

Hawaii Five-O was shot almost entirely on location in the Hawaiian islands, and it had much of the same cast throughout all twelve seasons. The "Five-O" police squad was headed by the hands-on, no-nonsense police detective Steve McGarrett, played (with never a shirt untucked or a hair out of place) by Jack Lord (born John Joseph Patrick Ryan in Brooklyn, N.Y. in 1920), with James MacArthur as his sidekick Danny ("Danno") Williams. It also featured what were arguably the most compelling opening credits in the history of television.

The opening credits to *Hawaii Five-O* commenced with a perfectly breaking wave from a Hawaiian surfing spot, accompanied by traditional Islander drums and Western drums and cymbals. The soundtrack then introduces multiple brass instruments, as trumpets riff on a high-tempo beat, backed by a string accompaniment that provides a counterpoint to the brass section. Visually, the opening credits offer a series of images that became synonymous with Hawaii for audiences worldwide: surfers catching 20-foot waves, Islander men vigorously paddling a straw canoe, dancing women with floral leis around their necks and rapidly gyrating hips, and Steve McGarrett (Jack Lord) atop a beachside high-rise apartment balcony.

The musical score for the opening credits was composed by Morton Stevens, who also composed much of the incidental music for the early series. Stevens also composed the theme music for TV series such as *The Man From U.N.C.L.E.* (1964), *Police Woman* (1977), *Knight Rider* (1982), and *Matlock* (1986). But none of these were as evocative as the *Hawaii Five-O* theme music, covered by artists as diverse as comedian

Bill Murray (as Nick the Lounge Singer on *Staurday Night Live* in 1977), to the Australian punk band Radio Birdman, whose 1978 single "Aloha Steve and Danno" was a paean to the program, marked by a remarkable section where the band do a guitar-based rendition of the theme music.

The Radio Birdman song ends with repetition of the line "Book him Danno. Murder one," which is apt, because after the opening credits, it is this closing line that most people remember about the program. In terms of classical narrative theory (Kozloff 1992), *Hawaii Five-O* had an extremely regular and predictable narrative structure. The first third of the program established the presence of criminality on the island, frequently arising from someone arriving in Hawaii from elsewhere, such as the U.S. mainland or a communist state. The second third of the program would involve McGarrett establishing the presence of criminality on the island, and developing a strategy (usually unsuccessful) to stake out the criminals, such as the ever-popular A.P.B. (All Points Bulletin). In the final third of the program, tragedy would often ensue for gullible locals who got caught up in the criminals' schemes, as Steve and Danno pursued and apprehended the criminals, leading to the famous final line "Book him Danno. Murder one."

Although *Hawaii Five-O* was produced throughout the 1970s, it never adopted the character-driven style of police dramas such as *Hill Street Blues* that emerged shortly after. Its focus was essentially plot-driven rather than character-driven. The only thing that the audience needed to know about Steve McGarrett was that he is responsible for enforcing the law in Hawaii. If one were to use the language of Lacanian psychoanalysis, McGarrett *is* the law in Hawaii, which is perhaps why criminality is so often presented on *Hawaii Five-O* as arriving from outside the islands.

Hawaii Five-O was a highly progressive program

in the late 1960s in terms of its commitment to racial and ethnic diversity. It had characters of Hawaiian Islander background as members of the police force, such as Gilbert Kauhi (Zulu) who played Kono, and it also acknowledged Hawaii's large Chinese community, with characters such as Detective Chin Ho, played by actor Kam Fong. However, its racial and ethnic diversity was not matched by any commitment to gender equality: after a brief period in the first series where there was a female detective, the detectives of *Hawaii Five-O* remained resolutely male.

After the final episode of *Hawaii Five-O* screened on U.S. television on April 5, 1980, Jack Lord remained in Hawaii, which had become his adopted home, and which had certainly adopted him and the program. When he died on January 22, 1998, Stanley Fong, President of the Hawaiian Chamber of Commerce, observed that "It was the original TV show that brought Hawaii to the fore of people who wanted to visit....It was a marketing bonanza for us" (quoted in Adams 1998). *Hawaii Five-O*'s ongoing significance lies in the unique way in which it packaged Hawaii as a site of cultural consumption for global audiences, its regularized narrative structure, and its compelling opening credits and theme music.

TERRY FLEW

See also **Hill Street Blues; Police Programs**

Cast

Steve McGarrett	Jack Lord
Danny ("Danno") Williams	James MacArthur
Kono Kalakaua	Zulu (Gilbert Kauhi)
Chin Ho Kelly	Kam Fong
The Governor	Richard Denning
The Attorney-General	Morgan White
Ben Kokua	Al Harrington
Edward (Duke) Lukela	Herman Wedemeyer
Wo Fat	Khigh Dheigh

Producers

Franklin Barton, Bill Finnegan, Leonard Freeman, Joseph Gantman, Douglas Green, Stanley Kallis, Leonard Kaufman, Philip Leacock, Sidney Marshall, Richard Newton, William Phillips, Bob Sweeney.

Programming History
CBS

September–December 1968	Thursday 8:00–9:00
December 1968–September 1971	Wednesday 10:00–11:00
September 1971–September 1974	Tuesday 8:30–9:30
September 1974–September 1975	Tuesday 9:00–10:00
December 1975–November 1979	Thursday 9:00–10:00
December 1979–January 1980	Tuesday 9:00–10:00
March–April 1980	Saturday 9:00–10:00

Further Reading

Adams, Wanda, "Show 'Brought Hawaii to the Fore,'" *Honolulu Advertiser,* January 22, 1998

Kozloff, Sarah, "Narrative Theory and Television," in Channels of Television, Reassembled, edited by Robert C. Allen, London: Routledge, 1992

Hazel

U.S. Situation Comedy

Hazel, starring Shirley Booth as Hazel Burke, the live-in housekeeper of the Baxter family, premiered on NBC in 1961. For the program's first four seasons, Hazel worked for lawyer George Baxter, his wife Dorothy, and their son Harold. In the fifth and final season, Hazel began to work for George's brother and his family (George and Dorothy were "transferred" to the Middle East for George's work), taking Harold with her from one household to another and from NBC to CBS.

Critics generally found *Hazel* mildly amusing, though they complained that it was often contrived and repetitive. Despite the mixed reviews, the program stayed in the top 25 for the first 3 years of its 5-year

Hazel, Don DeFore, Whitney Blake, Shirley Booth, 1961–65;
'Hazel and the Stockholder's Meeting.'
Courtesy of the Everett Collection

run. It ranked number 4 in 1961–62; number 15 in 1962–63; and number 22 in 1963–64. It also held some value with at least a few network producers, since after NBC dropped the show, CBS quickly picked it up. Perhaps CBS was relying too much on the capabilities of stage actress Booth. Nevertheless, *Hazel* held the attention of the American public.

Based upon the popular *Saturday Evening Post* cartoon strip, *Hazel* presents stories of Hazel's humorous involvement in both the professional and household business of George Baxter. In the television version, Hazel becomes the figure who, though seemingly innocuous, ultimately holds the household together: the servant, though in a marginalized position, is at the same time central to marking the well-being of the nuclear family. George, the father figure, competes with Hazel, who often ending up being "right." Dorothy, described by one critic as "dressing like and striking the poses of a high fashion model," follows in the tradition of glamorous TV moms living in homes where the housework often gets done by the maid. Also keeping with television tradition is Harold, who plays the part of the "all-American" kid. Completing this family

portrait is Hazel. She is characterized as "meddling" and as causing "misadventures" in her attempts to run the household, but ultimately it is her job to keep order, both literal and ideological, in the house.

Following in the footsteps of *Leave It to Beaver* and *Father Knows Best, Hazel* also proffers an American tale of the suburban family. Furthermore, in the decade that saw more American families bring televisions into their homes than any other, perhaps *Hazel* brought a sense of stability and appeasement, for this was also a decade of great civil and women's rights advancements.

Throughout television history (as well as the history of film), the representation of the American family is often made "complete" by the presence of the family housekeeper figure. Generally, the "American" family is specifically white American, although a few exceptions have existed, such as *The Jeffersons* and *Fresh Prince of Bel Air,* in which African-American families employ an African-American maid and an African-American butler, respectively. For the most part, however, "family" has been portrayed as white and therefore the ideology of the family has also been conceived in terms of dominant, white social values. The presence of a household servant, therefore, serves to reinforce the status (i.e., both economic and racial) of the family within society.

The significance of *Hazel,* then, is that it stands in a long history of television programs focused on American families and including their household servants. Beulah in *Beulah,* Mrs. Livingston in *The Courtship of Eddie's Father,* Hop Sing in *Bonanza,* Florida in *Maude,* Alice in *The Brady Bunch,* Nell in *Gimme a Break,* Mr. Belvedere in *Mr. Belvedere,* Dora in *I Married Dora,* and Tony in *Who's the Boss?* are all characters who occupy the servant's role. Differences in connotation among the various television servants serves to mark the status of the family for whom they work. More specifically, there are differences between a British butler and an Oriental houseboy, between a Euro-American nanny and a woman of color working as a domestic, marking subtle lines of hierarchy within the family and, ultimately, within the larger community. *Hazel* is yet another program in which the household servant demarcates the different roles played within the family according to such factors as gender, age, race, and class.

A popular program of the 1990s, *The Nanny* continued this tradition. In this series a Jewish-American woman worked for a wealthy British man and his three children living in New York City. Unlike either maids of color or white maids older than their employers, this household servant was portrayed as fashionable, attractive (though still a bit loud), and more significantly, as a potential mate for her employer (indeed, the nanny and her employer were married and had a child by the series finale). It will be interesting to observe and analyze the continuing representation of servants in American television, because, although shifting in form and style, the servant continues to mark the status of a house and the roles of the people working and living under its roof.

LAHN S. KIM

Cast

Hazel Burke	Shirley Booth
George Baxter (1961–65)	Don DeFore
Dorothy Baxter (1961–65)	Whitney Blake
Rosie	Maudie Prickett
Harvey Griffin	Howard Smith
Harold Baxter	Bobby Buntrock
Harriet Johnson (1961–65)	Norma Varden
Herbert Johnson (1961–65)	Donald Foster
Deidre Thompson (1961–65)	Cathy Lewis
Harry Thompson (1961–65)	Robert P. Lieb
Mona Williams (1965–66)	Mala Powers
Millie Ballard (1965–66)	Ann Jillian
Steve Baxter (1965–66)	Ray Fulmer
Barbara Baxter (1965–66)	Lynn Borden
Susie Baxter (1965–66)	Julia Benjamin

Producers
Harry Ackerman, James Fonda

Programming History
154 episodes
NBC

September 1961–July 1964	Thursday 9:30–10:00
September 1964–September 1965	Thursday 9:30–10:00
CBS	
September 1965–September 1966	Monday 9:30–10:00

Further Reading

Brooks, Tim, and Earle Marsh, *The Complete Directory to Prime Time Network TV Shows, 1946–Present,* New York: Ballantine Books, 1992

"It's Good-By, Mr. B . . . . As Hazel Adopts a New Family," *TV Guide* (August 14, 1965)

HBO. *See* Home Box Office

HDTV. *See* High-Definition Television

Heartbreak High

Australian Drama Series

An Australian drama series, *Heartbreak High* aired on the Ten Network from 1994 to 1995 and the Australian Broadcasting Corporation (ABC) from 1997 to 1999.

It also appeared on television systems in more than 30 other countries, including Britain, France, Germany, the Scandinavian countries, South Africa, Indonesia, and Israel. The series was particularly successful in Europe, where it gained a loyal fan base.

Heartbreak High was notable for breaking with the established formula for successful Australian audiovisual exports. Unlike feature films such as *The Man from Snowy River* and *Crocodile Dundee,* or television dramas such as *A Country Practice* and *Neighbours,* the series did not employ the themes of a perceived Australian innocence and harmonious community. It emerged from an early 1990s shift in Australian film and television toward the presentation of a grittier, urban, multicultural picture of contemporary Australian life.

The series was a television spin-off of the feature film *The Heartbreak Kid* (1993) by the same production company (Ben Gannon Productions). Like *The Heartbreak Kid, Heartbreak High* was set in an ethnically diverse inner-city high school and explored the pleasures and problems of young people growing up in such an environment. It was the first Australian television drama to make a central feature of multiculturalism and so extend to television a trend developed in films such as *Death in Brunswick, The Big Steal,* and *Strictly Ballroom,* as well as *The Heartbreak Kid.*

Set in Hartley High, a fictional school in suburban Sydney, *Heartbreak High* interwove narratives based on teen romance, conflicts of young people with teachers and parents, and social problems such as racism, teenage pregnancy, alcohol abuse, gay bashing, and abortion. A key character in early episodes was Nick (Alex Dimitriades), an impulsive teenage "heartthrob" from a Greek family background. Nick was a central romantic interest but also faced problems such as grief over the loss of his mother in a car accident.

Other major characters were Jodie (Abi Tucker), who came from a broken home but was a talented singer with ambitions to develop a career in the music industry; Rivers (Scott Major), a disruptive, anti-authority figure among the students; Con (Salvatore Coco), a "joker" who provided a comic focus; Steve (Corey Page), who found that he had been adopted and set out to find his birth mother; and Danielle (Emma Roche) who had an affair with Nick after he broke up from a longer relationship with Jodie. Among the teachers, the key characters were Yola Futoush (Doris Younane), the school counselor, who became closely involved with her students as she helped them overcome problems; and Bill Southgate (Tony Martin), a conservative authoritarian figure against whom the students rebelled. In the second series, these teachers were joined by Vic (Ernie Dingo), an Aboriginal teacher in media studies. Popular with the students, he taught them about more than the content of the official curriculum.

Stylistically, *Heartbreak High* was a fast-paced, realist drama that employed naturalistic dialogue. While teenage romance was an important narrative element, it was structured into rapid sequences and frequently intercut with "harder" content that maintained a strong sense of immediacy and action. Similarly, the series' emphasis on contemporaneity and relevance to a youth audience was rarely openly stated or didactic. Its topicality rested more on capturing the texture of life of young people than a fictionalization of issues taken directly from news or current affairs.

In its rhythm and editing techniques, *Heartbreak High* took its reference from the American-produced action or situation comedy genres, while at the same time taking on more "serious" content generally associated with the slower-paced genres of British or more traditional Australian television drama. *Heartbreak High* might therefore be seen as a "hybrid" televisual product that achieved commercial success while presenting a picture of an urban, multicultural Australia that had not previously had widespread international exposure.

Although successful internationally, *Heartbreak High* always struggled to gain solid backing from Australian broadcasters. A patchy programming history made it difficult to build consistent ratings. Production of the program ceased in 1998 after a decision by the ABC not to commit to further investment.

MARK GIBSON

See also **Australian Production Companies; Australian Programming; Dingo, Ernie**

Cast

Ruby	Jan Adele
Graham	Hugh Baldwin
Lucy	Alexandra Brunning
Hilary Scheppers	Tina Bursill
Effie	Despina Caldis
Con	Salvadore Coco
Anita Scheppers	Lara Cox
Nick	Alex Dimitriades
Charlie Byrd	Sebastian Goldspink
Ronnie Brooks	Deni Gordon
Helen	Barbara Gouskos
Chaka	Isabella Gutierrez
Rose	Katherine Halliday
Ryan Scheppers	Rel Hunt
Roberto	Ivor Kants
George	Nick Lathouris
Mai Hem	Nina Liu
Rivers	Scott Major
Southgate	Tony Martin
Sarah Lambert	Christina Milano
Drazic	Callan Mulvey
Jack	Tai Nguyen
Katerina	Ada Nicademou
Deloraine	Stephen O'Rourke
Steve	Corey Page

Matt	Vince Poletto
Danielle	Emma Roche
Les Bailey	Peter Sumner
Stella	Peta Toppano
Jodie	Abi Tucker
Irini	Elly Varrenti
Sam	Kym Wilson
Yola	Doris Younane
Vic	Ernie Dingo

Producers
Ben Gannon, Michael Jenkins

Programming History

Ten Network	
February 1994–May 1994	Sunday 6:30–7:30
June 1994–November 1994	Wednesday 7:30–8:30
May 1995–November 1995	Sunday 5:30–6:30
Australian Broadcasting Corporation	
February 1997–November 1999	Monday 6:00–7:00

Hemsley, Sherman (1938–)

U.S. Actor

African-American actor Sherman Hemsley is recognized mainly for his portrayal of the feisty George Jefferson character in the hit television show *The Jeffersons,* a program in which he starred for ten years. Earlier in his life, Hemsley aspired to be an actor, but he was too level-headed to quit his job as a postal worker to pursue his craft exclusively. Holding on to his job, he managed to maintain affiliations with local dramatic organizations, appearing in various children's theater productions. Eventually, Hemsley obtained a transfer to a position with the post office in New York. Here, he became a member of the famed Negro Ensemble Company. He began taking acting lessons, but became discouraged at his lack of progress. Then, in 1969, he earned the plum role of Gitlow in the highly successful musical version of *Purlie Victorious.*

In 1973 Hemsley was Cat in the successful stage play *Don't Bother Me, I Can't Cope.* It was during the run of this show that he was "discovered" by independent producer Norman Lear. Lear, along with his collaborator Bud Yorkin, produced a string of hit television shows during the 1970s, including *Maude, Good Times,* and the decade's most notable U.S. sitcom, *All in the Family.*

In 1973 Lear cast Hemsley to play the part of Archie Bunker's upwardly mobile and militantly black neighbor, George Jefferson, in the series *All in the Family.* The response to this character was so favorable that two years later, Hemsley was cast in the spin-off series *The Jeffersons.* That series became a top-rated television program, which aired in prime time for ten years.

The program focused on the lives of a successful African-American couple, George and Louise Jefferson. A thriving businessman, a millionaire, and the owner of seven dry-cleaning stores, George lived with Louise in a ritzy penthouse apartment on Manhattan's fashionable and moneyed East Side.

Along with *Good Times* and *Sanford and Son, The Jeffersons* was one of three highly successful 1970s television sitcoms to star African Americans at the head of mostly black casts—the first such series since *Amos 'n' Andy* in the 1950s. Conceptualized as a black equivalent of Archie Bunker, George was intolerant, rude, and stubborn; a bigot, he referred to white people as "honkies."

Hemsley as a person is quite unlike the high-strung characters he popularized on television. He is a private individual who has managed, even with success, to keep his life away from the glare of public scrutiny. During the height of *The Jeffersons'* popularity, he spoke of his sudden fame, simply stating that he was "just getting paid for what I did for free in Philadelphia."

When *The Jeffersons* was canceled in 1985, Hemsley went on to star in the 1986 sitcom *Amen.* In typical Hemsley style, he portrayed a feisty Philadelphia church deacon, Ernest Frye. Like George Jefferson, the Frye character was loud, brash, and conceited. *Amen* lasted five years on prime-time television, and Hemsley continues to be active as a performer. He was the lead in the short-lived sitcom *Goode Behavior* in 1996 and has appeared as an occasional character or guest in several television programs, including the long-

Sherman Hemsley.
Photo courtesy of Sherman Hemsley

running *Family Matters*. He has also acted in a number of films and been a commercial spokesman for Old Navy clothing stores and the Denny's restaurant chain, appearing in these ads as a George Jefferson-like character opposite the actress who portrayed George's wife, Louise (Isabel Sanford).

Although known mostly for his television work, Hemsley's acting credits include the motion picture *Love at First Bite* (1979) and the made-for-TV version of *Purlie* (1981). Years after its cancellation, *The Jeffersons* still enjoys success in syndication.

PAMALA S. DEANE

See also All in the Family; Amen; Jeffersons, The

Sherman Hemsley. Born in Philadelphia, Pennsylvania, February 1, 1938. Educated at the Philadelphia Academy of Dramatic Arts; studied with Lloyd Richards in New York. Served in the U.S. Air Force. Worked eight years for the U.S. Postal Service; active in the advanced workshop Negro Ensemble Company, New York City; appeared in various stage productions; starred in local television comedy series *Black Book*, Philadelphia; Broadway debut in *Purlie*, 1970; star, several television series, and motion pictures, since 1979; owner, Love Is, Inc., production company. Recipient: National Association for the Advancement of Colored People (NAACP) Image Award, 1976 and 1987; Golden Globe Award.

Television Series

1973–75   *All in the Family*
1975–85   *The Jeffersons*
1986–91   *Amen*
1991–94   *Dinosaurs* (voice)
1996   *Goode Behavior*

Made-for-Television Movies

1981   *Purlie*
1985   *Alice in Wonderland*
2000   *Up, Up, and Away!*

Films

Love at First Bite, 1979; *Stewardess School*, 1987; *Ghost Fever*, 1987; *Mr. Nanny*, 1993; *Home of Angels*, 1994; *The Miserly Brothers*, 1995; *Sprung*, 1997; *Senseless*, 1998; *Screwed*, 2000.

Stage (selected)

The People vs. Ranchman, 1968; *Alice and Wonderland*, 1969; *Purlie Victorious*, 1970; *Don't Bother Me, I Can't Cope*, 1973; *I'm not Rappaport*, 1987.

Henning, Paul (1911–)

U.S. Producer

Throughout the 1960s, Paul Henning was the creative mastermind behind three of the most successful sitcoms then on television—*The Beverly Hillbillies* (1962), *Petticoat Junction* (1963), and *Green Acres* (1965)—all of which shared narrative characteristics, and the first of which was perhaps the most successful network series on U.S. television. A perpetual Midwesterner who spent 30 years in Hollywood in both radio and television, Henning's basic country mouse/city mouse formula never veered far from his rural roots. Once those roots were deemed passé by the demographics avatars, his exile from television was both sudden and emphatic.

When a radio spec script Henning had written on a whim was accepted by *Fibber McGee and Molly,* he began a 15-year career as a series staff writer, culminating with *Burns and Allen* on radio and then television, where he became a protégé of future *Tonight Show* director Fred de Cordova. On TV Henning launched both *The Bob Cummings Show* (1955–59, all three networks), in which a pre-*Dobie Gillis* Dwayne Hickman assimilates the Southern California decadence of his starlet-addled bachelor uncle through a filter of Midwestern verities.

But he made both his name and fortune with *The Beverly Hillbillies* (1962–71, CBS). Equal parts John Steinbeck and absurdism, the nouveau-riche-out-of-water Clampetts populated the top-rated program of their premier season, remained in the top ten throughout the rest of the decade, and had regular weekly episode ratings that rivaled those of Super Bowls.

The Clampett clan initially hailed from an indeterminate backwoods locale somewhere along (in author David Marc's words) "the fertile crescent that stretches from Hooterville to Pixley and represents Henning's sitcomic Yoknapatawpha." As explained in the opening montage and theme song, Lincolnesque patriarch Jed (Buddy Ebsen) inadvertently stumbles onto an oil fortune languishing just beneath his worthless tract of scrub oak and brambles and pursues his destiny westward to swank Beverly Hills, California, in the interest of finding suitable escorts for daughter Elly May (Donna Douglas) and employment prospects for wayward nephew Jethro (Max Baer, Jr.). In tow (in a sight gag from *The Grapes of Wrath,* no less) is Granny (Irene Ryan), carried out to the truck at the last second in her favorite rocker. In this way, the Clampetts inadvertently echoed the fascination of a rural population newly wired for television with the purveyors of TV's content—at least partially accounting for their own corresponding popularity.

Meanwhile, Henning quickly moved to fashion several spin-offs with characters in common. *Petticoat Junction* (1963–70, CBS) featured long-time Henning player Bea Benaderet as Kate Bradley, proprietress of the Shady Grove Hotel, a homey inn situated along a railroad spur between Hooterville and Pixley, with her three growing daughters providing ample latitude for farmer's daughter jokes. The show was canceled in 1970 following Benaderet's death.

Then, into this homespun idyll, Henning dropped *Green Acres* (1965–71, CBS), a flat-out assault on

Paul Henning.
Photo courtesy of Paul Henning

Cartesian logic, Newtonian physics, and Harvard-centrist positivism. Lawyer Oliver Wendell Douglas (Eddie Albert) and his socialite wife Lisa (Eva Gabor) come to Hooterville in search of the greening of America and a lofty Jeffersonian idealism. What they discover instead is a virtual parallel universe of unfettered surrealism, rife with gifted pigs, square chicken eggs, and biogenetic hotcakes—a universe that Lisa intuits immediately, but by which Oliver is constantly bewildered.

In their later stages, these three worlds were increasingly interwoven, so that by the time of the holiday episodes where the arriviste Clampetts return to Hooterville to visit kith and kin, including the laconic Bradleys, and intersect with the proto-revisionist Douglases—using Sam Drucker's General Store as their narrative spindle—television had perhaps reached its self-reflexive pinnacle.

Despite high ratings, both *The Beverly Hillbillies* and *Green Acres* were canceled in 1971 by CBS president James Aubrey in the same purge that claimed *Mayberry RFD* and shows starring Jackie Gleason and Red Skelton (which aired for a final season on NBC). The push to cultivate a consumer base of advertising-friendly 18- to 34-year-olds was the same one that ushered in *M*A*S*H, All in the Family, The Mary Tyler Moore Show* and, ostensibly, political conscience.

Yet, viewed in retrospect, the canceled shows perhaps perfectly mirrored the times. A pervasive argument against television has always been that its hermetic nature removes it from a social context: idealized heroes or families and their better-mousetrap worlds seem all but impervious to the greater ills of the day. Nowhere is this more evident or egregious (so the argument goes) than in 1960s sitcoms, where a decade that was a watershed in politics and society elicited programming that seemed downright extraordinary in its mindlessness. But who better than garrulous nags, crusty aliens, maternal jalopies, suburban witches, subservient genies, gay Marines, or bungling Nazis to dramatize the rend in the social fabric, or typify the contradictions of the age? If so, no one was more adept at manipulating this conceit, nor pushed the envelope of casual surrealism further, than Henning.

PAUL CULLUM

See also **Beverly Hillbillies, The; Green Acres**

Paul Henning. Born in Independence, Missouri, September 16, 1911. Graduated Kansas City School of Law, 1932. Married: Ruth Margaret Barth, 1939; children: Carol Alice, Linda Kay, Paul Anthony. Began career as staff member at radio station KMBC Kansas City, 1933–37; writer and co-writer of radio programs 1937–50; writer-producer of television programs 1950–71; writer of feature films, 1961–88.

Television

1950–58	*The George Burns and Gracie Allen Show* (writer)
1952	*The Dennis Day Show* (writer)
1953	*The Ray Bolger Show* (writer)
1955–59	*The Bob Cummings Show* (writer and producer)
1962–71	*The Beverly Hillbillies* (creator, writer, and producer)
1963–70	*Petticoat Junction* (creator and producer)
1965–71	*Green Acres* (executive producer)

Films (writer)

Lover Come Back, 1961; *Bedtime Story,* 1962; *Dirty Rotten Scoundrels* (co-writer), 1988.

Radio

Fibber McGee and Molly (writer), 1937–39; *The Joe E. Brown Show,* 1939; *The Rudy Vallee Show,* 1940–51; *The Burns and Allen Show* (writer).

Further Reading

Marc, David, *Demographic Vistas: Television in American Culture,* Philadelphia: University of Pennsylvania Press, 1984; 2nd edition, 1996

Marc, David, *Comic Visions: Television Comedy and American Culture,* Boston: Unwin Hyman, 1989; 2nd edition, Malden, Massachusetts: Blackwell Publishers, 1997

Marc, David, and Robert J. Thompson, *Prime Time, Prime Movers: From I Love Lucy to L.A. Law—America's Greatest TV Shows and the People Who Created Them,* Boston: Little, Brown, 1992

Story, David, *America on the Rerun: TV Shows That Never Die,* Secaucus, New Jersey: Carol, 1993

Hennock, Frieda Barkin (1904–1960)

U.S. Attorney, Media Regulator

Frieda Barkin Hennock served as a Federal Communications Commissioner from 1948 to 1955. Appointed by President Harry S Truman, she was the first woman to serve as a commissioner on the Federal Communications Commission (FCC). In this position she was instrumental in securing the reservation of channels for noncommercial television stations, an FCC decision that enabled the development of the system of public broadcasting that exists in the United States today.

Before her nomination to serve on the FCC, Hennock had been practicing law in New York City. She had, as she told the Senate Committee during her confirmation hearings, no experience in broadcasting other than using radio to raise money for the political campaigns of Franklin Roosevelt and other Democratic candidates. After her confirmation in 1948, she quickly began to study the technical questions and policy issues facing the FCC, issues that would shape the future of the broadcast industry. Several systems for broadcasting color television were vying for FCC approval. Plans to use UHF frequencies were under discussion. Interference was being reported between signals from the 16 television stations already on the air. It was clear that more formal allocation plans were needed to ensure that all parts of the country would have access to television broadcasts. To allow time to study these issues and others, the FCC announced a freeze on awarding television licenses.

In addition to the technical issues she faced as a commissioner, Hennock became convinced that television had the power to serve as an important educational tool. As the proposed table of television channel assignments was developed during the freeze, however, there were no assignments reserved for educational stations. Hennock was determined that the opportunity to use television for educating the audience not be lost. She wrote a strong dissenting opinion and became an outspoken advocate for channel set-asides.

Anticipating that commercial interests would quickly file for all the available television licenses, Hennock understood the need to alert the public. She consulted with members of the Institute for Education by Radio and the National Association of Educational Broadcasters. She accepted invitations to speak to many civic groups and wrote articles for *The Saturday Review of Literature* and other publications. After she appeared on radio and television programs to discuss the importance of using television for educational purposes, listeners and readers responded with a flood of letters supporting her position. Educators formed the Joint Committee on Education Television and prepared to testify at the FCC hearings.

Hearings on the television allocation plan were held in the fall of 1950. Commercial broadcasters testified that reservations for noncommercial stations were not needed because the commercial programs served the educational needs of the audience. Educators produced the results of studies monitoring those programs. The studies found few programs that could be considered educational except in superficial ways.

Hennock was able to use these monitoring studies and other evidence presented during the hearings to build a strong case for channel reservations. When the FCC published its notice of rule-making in March 1951, it included channel reservations for education. Still, it was not clear that these were to be permanent. Hennock wrote a separate opinion urging that reservations for noncommercial stations should be permanent.

In June 1951 President Truman nominated Hennock for a federal judgeship in New York. The nomination proved to be controversial. In spite of strong support from her fellow FCC commissioners and several bar

Frieda B. Hennock.
Photo courtesy of Schlesinger Library, Radcliffe Institute, Harvard University

associations, confirmation by the Senate seemed unlikely and Hennock asked that her name be withdrawn.

Back at the FCC, Hennock renewed her commitment to educational television. When the FCC issued the Sixth Report and Order in April 1952, the allocation plan included 242 specific channel reservations for noncommercial stations. Hennock encouraged universities and communities to apply for these noncommercial licenses. She provided guidance on procedural matters, suggested ways to gain the support of community leaders and organizations, and enlisted the cooperation of corporations in providing grants to help these new stations buy equipment. Her belief in educational broadcasting was being realized. In June 1953 the first educational television station began to broadcast. KUHT-TV in Houston, Texas, invited Hennock to speak during its inaugural program. By mid-1955, 12 educational stations were on the air and more than 50 applications for noncommercial licenses had been filed.

Hennock was not surprised when her term as FCC commissioner was not renewed. Many of the positions she had taken were unpopular with powerful broadcasters. An outspoken critic of the practices of commercial networks, she criticized violence in television programming and warned about the growth of monopolies in the broadcast industry. She wrote many dissenting opinions questioning FCC actions. However, as her assistant Stanley Neustadt told oral historian Jim Robertson, when she took a position on an issue, "she was ultimately—sometimes long after she left the Commission—ultimately shown to be right." At the end of her term as FCC commissioner, Hennock returned to private life and private law practice.

LUCY A. LIGGETT

See also **Allocation; Federal Communications Commission; Educational Television; National Education Television Center**

Frieda Barkin Hennock. Born in Kovel, Poland, December 27, 1904. Educated at Brooklyn Law School, LL.B. 1924. Self-employed criminal lawyer, 1926–27; corporate lawyer, law firm of Silver and Hennock, 1927–34; independent lawyer and assistant counsel of the New York State Mortgage Commission, 1935–39; lawyer for Choate, Mitchell, and Eli, 1941–48; served as first woman member of the Federal Communica-

tions Commission, 1948–55; private practitioner in Washington, D.C., 1955–60. Died June 20, 1960.

Publications

"The Free Air Waves: An Administrative Dilemma," *Women Lawyers Journal* (Fall 1950)
"TV 'Conservation'," *The Saturday Review of Literature* (December 9, 1950)
"TV—Problem Child or Teacher's Pet?" *New York State Education* (March 1951)
"Educational Opportunities in Television," *The Commercial and Financial Chronicle* (March 15, 1951)
"Television and Teaching," *Educational Outlook* (May 1951)

Further Reading

"First Woman Member of FCC Makes Impression on Senators with Frankness," *Washington Post* (July 6, 1948)
"Frieda Hennock," *Current Biography: Who's News and Why 1948,* New York: H.W. Wilson, 1949
"Frieda Hennock Simons Dead," *New York Times* (June 21, 1960)
"Glamour at the Inquiry," *New York Times* (April 4, 1958)
Morgenthau, Henry, "Doña Quixote: The Adventures of Frieda Hennock," *Television Quarterly* (1992)
Powell, John Walker, *Channels of Learning: The Story of Educational Television,* Washington, D.C.: Public Affairs Press, 1962
Public Television's Roots Oral History Project, Madison: State Historical Society of Wisconsin, 1982
Robertson, Jim, *TeleVisionaries,* Charlotte Harbor, Florida: Tabby House, 1993

Henry, Lenny (1958–)

British Comedian, Actor

In 1976, at the age of sixteen, Lenny Henry won the British television talent show *New Faces,* as a comic and impressionist, and he became one of Britain's best-known personalities. The transitions in his career are indicative both of his personal development and of the changing cultural climate in Britain since his emergence. Henry began with stand-up comedy which often included racist jokes and impressions. Managed by Robert Luff, he entered the British variety circuit, touring with *The Black and White Minstrel Show* and the comedy duo *Cannon and Ball.* Although this was good

show-business experience, the press tended to focus more on the "novelty value" of Henry's blackness rather than on his actual stage performances.

In 1976, Henry was offered a part in *The Fosters* (LWT 1976–77), British television's first black television situation comedy. Working alongside established black actors such as Norman Beaton, Carmen Munroe, and Isabelle Lucas, Henry learned more about acting and the dynamics of television. When Henry began to make regular appearances on the Saturday morning children's program *Tiswas* and its adult equivalent

OTT (Over the Top), his anarchic, irreverent style of comedy gained popularity. Henry was recruited by BBC producer Paul Jackson for a prime-time sketch show *Three of a Kind* (1981–83), in which he appeared with Tracey Ullman and David Copperfield.

By the 1980s, Henry's gift for creating comic characters and witty vignettes of West Indian life in Britain was firmly established. The nuances of his comedy were gradually changing from straight jokes and blatant impressions to more farcical and chaotic comedy. This was partly influenced by other young rising comics of the time such as Alexei Sayle, Adrian Edmondson, Rik Mayall, and Dawn French. At this time, however, Henry was best known for his caricatures such as the African television host Josh Arlog, the cartoonish Rastafarian Algernon, and black politician Fred Dread, all with widely-imitated catch phrases. Many of Henry's character creations caused controversy and raised the question of whether Henry, as a black comedian, was actually reinforcing already-existing stereotypes of black people. Henry admits that some of the material he was doing at the time "was very self-deprecating, very self-detrimental."

Henry created a myriad of familiar caricatures but the most popular one earned him his own series, *The Lenny Henry Show* (BBCTV 1984–88). Set in a pirate radio station, the series featured Delbert Wilkins, a Brixton wide-boy, a character created at the same time as the real-life Brixton riots. Henry was influenced by comedians from the United States such as Richard Pryor, Steve Martin, and Bill Cosby, and became the first British comedian to make a live stand-up comic film, *Lenny Henry Live and Unleashed* (1989), in the tradition of U.S. comics such as Robin Williams and Eddie Murphy. His live tours are renowned for being chaotic, noisy, and daring, but also for relying on the same collective of characters such as the extravagant soul singer Theophilus P. Wildebeeste and the old West Indian man Grandpa Deakus.

By the late 1980s, Lenny Henry began to broaden his repertoire even further. He became increasingly interested in "serious" acting roles and starred in the BBC's Screen Two production *Coast to Coast.* In 1990, he was signed by Disney on a three-film deal, the first of which was *True Identity* (1991), a comic-drama about mistaken identity. Later that year, Henry starred in *Alive and Kicking,* a BBC drama in which he played a drug dealer alongside Robbie Coltrane as a drug counselor. The film was awarded the Monaco Red Cross and the Golden Nymph Award at the Monte Carlo Television Festival in February 1992.

Henry has extended his ambition to other areas, including his own production company, Crucial Films. The company was established to launch film and comedy projects, but particularly to encourage black performers and film practitioners. He initiated "Step Forward" comedy-writing workshops in conjunction with the BBC, which led to the comedy series *The Real McCoy,* consisting of selections of sketches and songs and stand-up comedy from a black perspective. Crucial Films also led to a series of ten-minute dramas entitled *Funky Black Shorts.*

In the 1990s, Henry created and starred in *Chef!* (BBC, 1993–1996), an exceptional series in which he played the erratic Head Chef Gareth Blackstock. The series has been highly critically acclaimed for its production values, its comic-drama scripts and its lead performances. Henry plays a character that also just "happens to be black" and is married to a black woman; the fact of their blackness does not limit either the narrative or the audience the series reached. A similar level of success and critical acclaim was gained through Henry's next television venture, *Hope and Glory* (BBC, 1999) in which he played head teacher Ian George, in an inner-city comprehensive school. After this relatively "straight" role, Henry returned to his comedy roots with his sketch show, *Lenny Henry in Pieces* (BBC, 2000–2002), in which he presented a range of comic characters. The comedy series won the Golden Rose of Montreux Award at the 2000 Montreux Television Festival.

Since the mid-1970s, Lenny Henry has risen from being a talent-show hopeful to being the most popular black British light entertainer. He has won numerous awards including the Radio and Television Industry Club Award for BBC Personality of the Year in 1993, and the Edric Connor Inspiration to Black People Award in 2002. Although Henry does not see himself as a specifically black comedian, he does believe that being black enriches his work. The development in his work and the breadth of his appeal signifies the different contexts within which he has managed to sustain his popularity and credibility as one of the key players in British entertainment.

Sarita Malik

See also **Beaton, Norman; Munroe, Carmen;** *Tiswas*

Lenny (Lenworth George) Henry. Born in Dudley, England, August 29, 1958. Attended Bluecoat Secondary Modern School; W.R. Tewson School; Preston College. Married: Dawn French, 1984; child: Billie. Made television debut on *New Faces* at the age of 16, 1975; subsequently established reputation as popular stand-up comedian and as character comedy actor; head of Crucial Films independent production company.

Television Series

1975	*Tiswas*
1976–77	*The Fosters*
1981–83	*Three of a Kind*
1982	*OTT*
1984, 1985,	
1987, 1988,	
1995	*The Lenny Henry Show*
1986	*Lenny Henry Tonite*
1993–96	*Chef!*
1999	*Hope and Glory*
2000–02	*Lenny Henry in Pieces*

Made-for-Television Movies (selection)

1984	*Coast to Coast*
1990	*Alive and Kicking*

Films

The Secret Policeman's Third Ball, 1987; *Lenny Henry Live and Unleashed,* 1989; *Double Take,* 1984; *Work Experience,* 1989; *True Identity,* 1990

Publications

Quest for the Big Woof, 1991
Charlie and the Big Chill, 1995
Charlie, Queen of the Desert, 1996

Recording

Stand Up, Get Down.

Henson, Jim (1936–1990)

U.S. Muppeteer, Producer

Jim Henson's most significant contribution to television culture was his imaginative ability. His creative talents are responsible for some of the most recognizable and beloved television characters in television history, the puppet/marionette hybrids better known as the Muppets. For more than four decades, the Muppets have entertained children and adults in myriad pop culture arenas; however, they are most associated with the television program known as *Sesame Street.*

As an adolescent, Henson was fascinated with television. His desire to work for the blossoming industry was inadvertently realized through the craft he considered a mere hobby—puppetry. His first puppet creations premiered on a local television station, an NBC affiliate in Maryland, which picked up Henson's five-minute puppet show and ran it prior to *The Huntley-Brinkley Report* and *The Tonight Show.* This exposure proved to be a tremendous opportunity.

Henson developed an innovative art form that was perfectly suited for television. His Muppets (some say this name is derived from a combination of the words "marionette" and "puppet") were ideal for the new medium because they perpetuated its "seamlessness." Muppets are stringless (unlike marionettes) and appear to move on their own (unlike traditional hand-puppets). This characteristic of "realness" made the Muppets readily accepted by the television audience.

Sam and Friends, Henson's first network program, aired for several years. The Muppets amassed a loyal following by appearing in commercials and performing in popular venues such as *The Ed Sullivan Show.* However, it was the character of Rowlf the Dog (a regular on *The Jimmy Dean Show*) that propelled the popular fascination with Henson's creations.

It was not until 1969 (and the commencement of a public television experiment called *Sesame Street*) that Henson and his Muppets became well known. *Sesame Street* was the brainchild of Joan Ganz Cooney. Frustrated by the lack of quality children's programming, Cooney proposed a television program especially for preschoolers that would incorporate the stylistic devices of advertisements (such as jingles) to "sell" learning. Although *Sesame Street* was designed for all preschool children, it was particularly targeted at inner-city youths. In many ways the program symbolized the idea of a televisual panacea, an entertainment offering with an educational and pro-social agenda.

It was Jon Stone, the first head writer for *Sesame Street,* who suggested Henson's Muppets for the project, and it has been suggested that if there were no Muppets, there would be no *Sesame Street.* The Muppets are largely responsible for the colossal success of this program. In skits, songs, and other performances, they have epitomized the social skills fundamental to

Sesame Street's mission—cooperation, understanding, tolerance, and respect.

Henson's Muppets are abstractions: most are animals, some are humans, and others a combination of both, all of different sizes, shapes, and colors. Their appearances are foreign, but their personalities are very familiar. Each member of the *Sesame Street* ensemble personify characteristics inherent in preschoolers. Through Ernie's whimsy, Big Bird's curiosity, Oscar's grouchiness, Grover's timidity, or the Cookie Monster's voracity, children experience an emotional camaraderie. However, Kermit the Frog (often referred to as Jim Henson's alter ego) is the Muppet most representative of the human spirit. Kermit's simple reflections often echo the philosophical complexities of everyday life.

Jim Henson's Muppets are a global phenomenon. The internationalization of *Sesame Street* is indicative of their cross-cultural appeal. *Sesame Street* is an anomaly within the realm of American children's television, and the unique qualities of the Muppets are somewhat responsible for this distinction.

Still, the immediate success of *Sesame Street* was a bitter-sweet experience for Henson. He felt stymied that the Muppets were branded "children's entertainment." He knew the wit and charm of the Muppets transcended all questions of age. In 1976, owing much to the implementation of the Financial Interest and Syndication (Fin-Sin) Rules, the syndicated variety program *The Muppet Show* began and offered a venue more in keeping with Henson's larger vision for his creations. The Fin-Sin Rules opened time slots in local television markets for non-network programming. Henson quickly took advantage of this need for syndicated programming with his new production. The half-hour show featured celebrity guests who participated in the Muppet antics. *The Muppet Show* was hosted by Kermit the Frog, the only *Sesame Street* character permitted to cross genre boundaries (except for guest appearances and/or film cameos). The series spawned a new generation of characters for its predominantly adult demographic. "Animal," "Doctor Teeth," "The Swedish Chef," and "Fozzie Bear" still appealed to both children and adults, but now the Muppets were more sophisticated and less pedagogical. The romantic relationship between Kermit and a porcine diva known as "Miss Piggy" established the dramatic potential of the Muppets. Miss Piggy was inspired by Frank Oz, Henson's lifelong colleague.

The success of *The Muppet Show* provoked Henson to explore the medium of film. His cinematic endeavors include *The Muppet Movie, The Great Muppet Caper, The Muppets Take Manhattan,* and *Treasure Island.*

The Muppets have permeated all media: television, film, animation, music, and literature. Their generative ability is notably manifest in a variety of past and present TV series, such as *Fraggle Rock, The Muppet Babies, Dinosaurs,* and *Bear in the Big Blue House.* The empire known as Jim Henson Productions has spawned numerous production companies—all infused with the imaginative potential of their creator. It is interesting to note that Henson's "Muppet-less" projects, feature films such as *The Dark Crystal* and *Labyrinth,* were not widely successful. Perhaps this is because they lacked the cheerfulness that has defined most of Henson's work.

Jim Henson died on May 16, 1990, from an untreated bacterial infection. His vision and creative spirit are immortalized by the Muppets and the future projects his legacy inspires.

SHARON ZECHOWSKI

See also **Children and Television; Cooney, Joan Ganz;** *Muppet Show, The; Sesame Street;* **Sesame Workshop; Tillstrom, Burr**

Jim (James Murry) Henson. Born in Greenville, Mississippi, September 24, 1936. Educated at the University of Maryland, B.A. 1960. Married: Jane Anne Nebel, 1959; children: Lisa, Cheryl, Brian, John, and Heather. Producer-performer, *Sam and Friends,* Washington, D.C., 1955–61; creator of the Muppets, combination marionettes and puppets, 1959; regular appearances on *The Jimmy Dean Show,* 1963–66; *Sesame Street,* from 1969; *The Muppet Show,* 1976–81; creator, *Fraggle Rock,* 1983–90; writer, producer, director, and muppeteer of various films, 1979–90. Member: Puppeteers of America (president, 1962–63), AFTRA, Directors Guild of America, Writers Guild of America, National Academy of Television Arts and Sciences, Screen Actors Guild, American Center of Union Internationale de la Marionette (president, board of directors), 1974. Recipient: Emmy Awards, 1958, 1973–74, 1975–76; Entertainer of the Year Award; American Academy of Television Arts and Sciences Award, 1978; Peabody Awards, 1979 and 1987; Grammy Award, 1981; President's Fellow Award, Rhode Island School of Design, 1982. Died in New York City, May 16, 1990.

Television Series

1955–61	*Sam and Friends* (muppeteer)
1969–	*Sesame Street* (muppeteer)
1976–81	*The Muppet Show* (muppeteer, producer)
1983–90	*Fraggle Rock* (creator)
1984–	*The Muppet Babies* (producer)
1987	*The Storyteller* (producer)

Television Specials

1977	*Emmet Otter's Jug-Band Christmas* (muppeteer, director, producer)
1986	*The Tale of the Bunny Picnic* (muppeteer, director, producer)
1990	*The Christmas Toy* (muppeteer, producer)

Films

The Muppet Movie, 1979; *The Great Muppet Caper,* 1981; *The Dark Crystal,* 1982; *The Muppets Take Manhattan,* 1984; *Into the Night,* 1985; *Sesame Street Presents Follow That Bird,* 1985; *Labyrinth* (also writer), 1986; *Muppet*vision 3-D,* 1991.

Publications

The Sesame Street Dictionary: Featuring Jim Henson's Sesame Street Muppets, 1980

The World of the Dark Crystal, 1982
In and Out, Up and Down, 1982
Muppets, 1986
Favorite Songs from Jim Henson's Muppets, 1986
Baby Kermit and the Dinosaur, 1987

Further Reading

Blau, E., "Jim Henson, Puppeteer, Dies: The Muppets Creator Was 53," *New York Times* (May 17, 1990)

Culhane, John, "Unforgettable Jim Henson," *Reader's Digest* (November 1990)

Finch, Christopher, *Of Muppets and Men: The Making of the Muppet Show,* New York: Knopf, 1981

Finch, Christopher, *Jim Henson: The Works, The Art, the Magic, the Imagination,* New York: Random House, 1993

"Jim Henson: Miss Piggy Went to Market and $150 Million Came Home (Jim Henson Sells Muppet Empire to Walt Disney Co.)," *American Film* (November 1989)

Herskovitz, David. *See* Zwick, Edward, and Marshall Herskovitz

---

Hewitt, Don (1922–)

U.S. Producer

Don Hewitt is a genius at what he does, and he does *60 Minutes.* However, Hewitt has done more in his TV career than act as the founder and executive producer of that enormously successful program. It was Hewitt who directed Edward R. Murrow's early TV experiment of bridging the U.S. continent with television. It was Hewitt who, while producing and directing the first Kennedy-Nixon debate in 1960, attempted to advise Nixon to use appropriate make-up to cover his wan appearance. Nixon did not listen, lost the debate, and lost the election. Thirty-three years later, Hewitt ventured (unsuccessfully) into cable-based home shopping.

Hewitt began his work in the world of print journalism, but he quickly moved to CBS TV, where he has spent the entirety of his career. He not only produced and directed *Douglas Edwards with the News* from 1948 to 1962 but also the first year (1962–63) of the trendsetting *CBS Evening News with Walter Cronkite.* These two programs had a tremendous influence on the general development of television news programming, as well as on CBS's own nightly news. Hewitt was also responsible for CBS's coverage of the national political conventions between 1948 and 1980, and he directed *Conversations with the President* (with Presidents Kennedy and Johnson), programs that were pooled for all three networks. Among this significant body of work, however, his most notable, profitable, and successful venture was the creation of *60 Minutes* in 1968.

60 Minutes has been one of the premier programs produced by CBS, which counts the profits from this show to be significantly in excess of $1 billion. Such profits bring independence and power to Hewitt. He does not hesitate to attack network executives as being deficient in foresight and fortitude, and he reportedly has the most favorable employment contract in the history of U.S. network broadcasting.

The unparalleled success of Hewitt's *60 Minutes* has led to considerable speculation regarding the programming strategies that have allowed the series to achieve high ratings. Some surmise that the program benefited from following National Football League (NFL) games on CBS for so many years. However, when the NFL moved to the FOX television network in 1994, *60 Minutes* continued to flourish (as it had in the seasons before it followed the games). Reuven Frank, formerly of NBC, who clearly suffered under the success of Hewitt's *60 Minutes,* called the show "star journalism," a form in which reporters such as Mike Wallace are the heroes whose questions are more important than the subsequent answers. The Prime Time Access Rule (PTAR) of the Federal Communication Commission (FCC) has also been credited with contributing to *60 Minutes'* success. The PTAR limited network offerings from 7:00 to 8:00 P.M. (EST) on Sunday to public affairs or children's programming. When Hewitt's program moved to this time slot in 1975, the argument goes, there was no real competition from entertainment programming, and CBS began raking in huge audiences, hungry advertisers, and giant profits. Most observers, however, give Hewitt the credit for the success of *60 Minutes.* As Peter Jennings of ABC put it, the success of *60 Minutes* is a "testimony to Don Hewitt's imagination and his editing."

Hewitt has an extraordinary news judgment and editing ability. He creates stories in a manner that appeals to the average person. He admits he is not college educated, is not especially intellectual in his inclinations, and that he identifies with the middle-of-the-road American. He knows what the average person likes to watch on TV. His formula for *60 Minutes* stories is not complex. He simply understands that the audience wants the hero (for example, Mike Wallace) to drive the bad guys out of town. These people have been known in the TV industry as Hewitt's "anchor monsters."

Despite these formidable skills, Hewitt is not always known as a nice or likeable person. His handling of *60 Minutes* producers and staff is, at best, volatile and heavy-handed. When Harry Reasoner, one of the first and best-liked anchors of the program, was dying of cancer, Hewitt reportedly removed him from the program with little apparent sensitivity to Reasoner or

Don Hewitt.
Photo courtesy of Don Hewitt

other staff. On the other hand, as Andy Rooney of *60 Minutes* has observed of Hewitt, "I don't think the show would last without him."

Hewitt's accomplishments have earned him countless honors and awards, including a place in the Television Hall of Fame. Perhaps the greatest recognition came from one of his colleagues, who said, Don Hewitt "invented the wheel" in the business of television news.

CLAYLAND H. WAITE

See also **CBS;** *60 Minutes*

Don Hewitt. Born in New York City, December 14, 1922. Attended New York University, 1941. Married: 1) Mary Weaver (died, early 1960s); 2) Frankie Hewitt (divorced); children: Jeffrey, Steven, Jill, and Lisa; 3) Marilyn Berger, 1979. Served as merchant marine correspondent and war correspondent for *Stars and Stripes* during World War II. Office boy and head copy boy, New York *Herald Tribune,* 1941; night editor, Associated Press, Memphis, Tennessee; editor, Pelham *Sun,* New York, 1946; night telephoto editor, Acme News Pictures, 1947; associate director, *CBS TV News,* 1948; sole producer-director, *Douglas Edwards with the*

News, 1948–62; executive producer, *CBS Evening News with Walter Cronkite,* 1962–63; produced CBS documentaries, 1965–68; creator and executive producer, *60 Minutes,* since 1968. Recipient: eight Emmy Awards; numerous honorary degrees; gold medal, International Radio and TV Society, 1988; Broadcaster of the Year Award, 1980; Peabody Award, 1989; named to Hall of Fame, National Academy of Television Arts and Sciences, 1990; Producers Guild of America Lifetime Award, 1993; Founders Emmy of the International Council of the National Academy of Television Arts and Sciences, 1995; the Fred Friendly First Amendment Award, Quinnipiac College, 2000; the Carr Van Anda Award (for contributions to journalism) of the E.W. Scripps School of Journalism, Ohio University, 2001; the Director's Guild Association Honor for contributions to American culture, 2002; the Spirit Award (a lifetime achievement award from the National Association of Broadcasters), 2003; the American Federation of Television and Radio Actors George Heller Lifetime Achievement Award, 2003.

Television Series (producer)

1948–62   *Douglas Edwards with the News*

1962–63   *The CBS Evening News with Walter Cronkite*
1968–   *60 Minutes*

Publications

Minute by Minute, 1985
Tell Me a Story: 50 Years and 60 Minutes in Television, 2002

Further Reading

Campbell, R., *60 Minutes and the News,* Urbana: University of Illinois Press, 1991
Coffey, Frank, *Sixty Minutes: 25 Years of Television's Finest Hour,* Santa Monica, California: General Publishing Group, 1993
Fairchild, Ken, *Sunday Showdowns with 60 Minutes,* Morris Publishing, 1998
Flander, J., "Hewitt's Humongous Hour," *Washington Journalism Review* (April 1991)
Madsen, A., *60 Minutes: The Power and the Politics of America's Most Popular TV News Show,* New York: Dodd, Mead, 1984
Wallace, Mike, and G.P. Gates, *Close Encounters: Mike Wallace's Own Story,* New York: William Morrow, 1984

Hey Hey It's Saturday

Australian Variety Program

Hey Hey It's Saturday, a variety program, began as a Saturday morning children's show, but, like other children's shows in Australia, it developed a curious adult following and became a durable feature of Australian television history. Programmed on Saturday nights from 6:30 to 8:30, it was a consistent ratings winner for Network Nine, outlasting almost every challenge the other networks threw at it until it ended in 1999. By that time the show was finally showing signs of tiredness, becoming a little repetitive and suffering from the loss of such key comic characters as Ossie Ostrich.

Television variety such as *Hey Hey* emerges from Australia's robust history of music hall, vaudeville, and revue on the stage and in radio. Vaudeville featured singers, dancers, comedians, acrobats, magicians, ventriloquists, male and female impersonators, and animal acts. In revue, a thin storyline was used to connect a series of comedy sequences, backed by song-and-dance numbers. It included an orchestra, ballet dancers and showgirls, and a comedienne. But the comedian was always the star of the show.

From such traditions great comedians, such as George Wallace and the legendary "Mo" (Roy Rene), emerged before the days of television. Australia's greatest TV comedian, Graham Kennedy, in his long-running variety program *In Melbourne Tonight,* adapted such vaudeville traditions for television, where they continued to thrive in specifically televisual terms. The compere of *Hey Hey It's Saturday* was Darryl Somers, a comedian who was perhaps the successor to Graham Kennedy on Australian television. While he may not have been so much a king of comedy, he remained a noteworthy lord of misrule. One of Kennedy's writers at *In Melbourne Tonight,* Ernie Carroll, provided another connection between *Hey Hey It's Saturday* and the earlier tradition. He became the producer of *Hey Hey* and also the arm and voice for its resident puppet figure, Ossie Ostrich, retained from the children's show version.

Hey Hey differed from 19th- and 20th-century vaudeville in not having showgirls or animal acts. It did for a period have a character called Animal, who silently wandered about the set, a walking icon of a crazy world, purely visual signifier of the ludic, of a world upside-down. The show did continue vaudeville and revue tradition in having an orchestra (a rock band) and, for a long period, a resident comedienne, Jacky MacDonald. She portrayed an apparent naïf, telling sly risqué jokes with wide innocent eyes.

Although Darryl Somers, with Ossie Ostrich sitting beside him, guided the show, *Hey Hey* was decentered comedy, dispersed through the various figures and performers, who often include the production crew. The show also contained various (changing) segments. "Media Watch" presented mistakes in TV commercials, or funny items, usually taken from the provincial press. "Red Faces" offered amateur acts. "Ad Nauseum" invented a quiz show with questions about TV ads. "What Cheeses Me Off" was a complaints column, and "Beat It" a music quiz.

Hey Hey used all the technical and audiovisual resources of TV itself to make everyone and everything in the show part of the comedy. For example, viewers rarely saw John Blackman, but he was a regular voice off-screen, doing impersonations, being ironic and sarcastic about guest acts and cast members, or making dry jokes and performing "insult comedy." This visual "absence" was countered by the highly visual cartoon jokes flashed on the screen at any moment. When "Media Watch" speculated on possible mistakes in TV commercials, a camera might suddenly focus on a producer. Surrounded by cameras and cords, he held a microphone and said what he thought, though he would earn derision if the others thought he got it wrong. Puppet Ossie Ostrich would comment on everything dryly and ironically. The other puppet, Little Dickie (a blue head held on a stick, with a raspy voice provided by John Blackman), might suddenly rush forward and be rude about someone or something. In turn, in one show Ossie commented of Little Dickie that his stick had "terminal white ant."

The show reveled in the festive abuse that Mikhail Bakhtin has identified as a feature of carnival in early modern Europe. In a society where, he suggests, people were "usually divided by the barriers of caste, property, professions, and age," festive abuse overturned hierarchy in social relations, creating an atmosphere of equality, freedom, and familiarity—*Hey Hey* exactly.

In *Hey Hey* all was chaos and anarchy, the reverse of structured sequences guided by the straight person and

chief comedian. Darryl Somers as compere was, instead, a relatively still space across which all the mad traffic of jokes, the different comic contributions and voices, traversed and clashed and commented on each other. If he maintained an ongoing program, he was never a central voice of authority, a ringmaster. His strength was in his alertness to what was going on about him as much as in his own comic contributions.

Traditional stage variety entertainment thrived on familiarity and audience involvement. Similarly, *Hey Hey* actively drew on the vast and intimate knowledge that its audience (in the studio and at home) had of the media, of the rest of popular commercial TV. Like *Monty Python's Flying Circus* in the early 1970s, *Hey Hey* was variety for the electronic age. The media were often the material for the comedy: parodying Lotto in "Chook Lotto," the media in "Media Watch," talent shows in "Red Faces," or testing knowledge of pop music in "Beat It."

Involvement by the studio audience was always encouraged. If, for example, a show was declared a 1960s or a Science Fiction night, Darryl and Jacky and Ossie would wear extravagant uniforms and masks. The audience would also dress up—a touch of the masks and disguises of carnival of old, taking people out of their ordinary life and circumstances. In "Red Faces," perennially one of *Hey Hey's* most popular segments, the audience could override Red's gong if it liked an act.

Clearly, in *Hey Hey* there was an extreme self-reflexivity; viewers saw camera people with their cameras and crew with mikes and cords going everywhere. For television culture, this built on a very long tradition of self-reflexivity in popular culture and theater. The festive abuse of *Hey Hey* reminded viewers that a great deal of popular culture, from carnival in early modern Europe to music hall and vaudeville in the 19th century and into the 20th, featured parody and self-parody. This was more than a way of mocking received attitudes and official wisdom. It was a philosophical mode, a cosmology, a way of questioning all claims to absolute truth—including its own. To the degree that our own "wisdom" is drawn from and dependent upon the media, *Hey Hey It's Saturday* suggested we should look on that knowledge with a wary eye.

JOHN DOCKER

See also **Australian Programming;** *Monty Python's Flying Circus*

Hosts
Darryl Summers
"Ozzie Ostrich"/Ernie Carroll (1971–94)

Producers
Bob Phillips, Pam Barnes

Programming History
Nine Network

October 1971–	
September 1973	Saturday 8:30–11:30 A.M.
October 1973–	
December 1977	Saturday 8:00–11:00 A.M.
March 1979–	
December 1983	Saturday 8:00–11:00 A.M.
March 1984–May	
1985	Saturday 9:30 P.M.-12:00 midnight (as *Hey Hey It's Saturday Night*)
June 1985–November	
1999	Saturday 6:30–8:30 P.M. (with title reverting to *Hey Hey It's Saturday*)

Further Reading

Bakhtin, Mikhail, *Rabelais and His World,* Bloomington: Indiana University Press, 1984

Docker, John, "In Defence of Popular TV: Carnivalesque v. Left Pessimism," *Continuum* (1988)

McDermott, Celestine, "National Vaudeville," in *The Australian Stage,* edited by Harold Love, Sydney: New South Wales University Press, 1984

Turner, Graeme, "Transgressive TV: From *In Melbourne Tonight* to *Perfect Match,*" in *Australian Television: Programs, Pleasures, and Politics,* edited by John Tulloch and Graeme Turner, Sydney: Allen and Unwin, 1989

High-Definition Television

High-Definition Television (HDTV) is an arbitrary term that applies to any television production, transmission, or reception technology with a scanning rate that exceeds the 525 lines of the present U.S. NTSC standard or the 625 lines of the PAL or SECAM standards. Most U.S. HDTV television displays have at least 720 scanning lines, a wide-screen 16:9 image aspect ratio, and six-channel audio capability. When viewed on a large television tube, a flat-screen display, or projected on a wall screen, digital HDTV images are demonstrably sharper than that of conventional analog television displays.

The first commercial HDTV system was Hi-Vision/MUSE developed by NHK laboratories in Japan in the 1970s. After abortive Japanese attempts to have High-Vision/MUSE adopted as a de facto world television standard in 1986, a European consortium developed an alternative incompatible standard with 1,250 scanning lines.

In 1987, the U.S. Federal Communications Commission (FCC) created an Advisory Committee on Advanced Television Service (ACATS) to conduct a testing program to select an American HDTV standard. After eight years of development and testing, the FCC adopted a digital scheme that includes 18 types of advanced television production and transmission technology. American broadcasters will be able to transmit both HDTV and SDTV (lower-quality Standard Definition) programming via terrestrial towers, over cable television systems, and from broadcast satellites.

The FCC mandated a ten-year conversion period (1997–2006) for the transition from terrestrial analog broadcasting to a system based on all-digital technology. Most large market television stations are transmitting their programming in both analog and digital formats, but many small-market stations and public broadcaster affiliates have yet to make the conversion.

U.S. television networks are simulcasting prime time programming in both analog and digital HDTV formats. Cable television and satellite services are increasing the amount of HDTV programming they transmit as the number of digital television sets sold to consumers increases. A key driver of set sales and cable/satellite HD programming subscriptions are sporting events and feature films transmitted in high-definition. HDTV sets are available at retail prices between $1,000 and $2,000, and prices continue to fall as more consumers purchase advanced television models.

Japan is also making the conversion to digital broadcasting, but HDTV adoption is proceeding more slowly in Europe and other regions of the world. The future of global television technology features digital production and transmission with increasing use of wide-screen displays and multi-channel audio playback that replicates that found in motion picture theaters. Home theaters featuring HDTV image and sound technology will be commonplace in the United States as the technology is adopted by viewers of all socio-economic groups. It is uncertain if the FCC's deadline of 2006 for full digital conversion will be met, but HDTV technology will continue to make gradual but steady gains in adoption as users make the decision to switch to the new viewing option.

PETER B. SEEL

See also **Digital Television; Television Technology**

Hill, Benny (1925–1992)

British Comedian

Benny Hill was born in Southampton in the south of England in 1925. His family was lower-middle class; Hill's father was the manager of a medical appliance company. Hill was attracted early to the stage and saw many live stage shows at the two variety theatres in Southampton. Hill served in the army in the later years of World War II; it was there that he began to perform as a comedian. After demobilization, Hill began working in variety theater, where he slowly learned his craft. In 1956, Hill starred in the feature film comedy *Who Done It?* (Ealing Studios) as a hapless, bungling private detective. The film was only mildly funny, although Hill did display touches of the comic slapstick and characterization that were to become part of his genius. The film was moderately successful but did nothing to further Hill's career. Instead, it was in the new medium of television that he was to shine.

Hill's career as a British comedian fits between that of earlier figures such as Tony Hancock and later performers such as Frankie Howerd. Whereas Hancock established his definitive comic persona in radio and then extended this to television, Hill was created by television. Yet Hill was also the most traditional of comedians and his programs had strong roots in variety theater, revolving around comic songs, routines, and sketches rather than an on-going comic characterization and situation. And although Hill had his own show on the BBC as early as 1955, his career was actually launched by the 1960s vogue for comedy on British television. Other British comedians such as Ken Dodd, Charlie Drake, and Frankie Howerd also gained their own shows around the same time, but none had the comic genius and stamina of Hill.

Part of this genius lay in his writing. Hill wrote all his own material, a grueling task that helps explain the relatively small number of programs produced. Under his later contract with Thames Television, Hill was given full control of his program, allowing him to delay making a program until, in his opinion, he had accumulated enough comic material. Hill also had a hand in producing some of the offshoots of *The Benny Hill Show* such as the 1970 half-hour silent film *Eddie in August*.

Although all his material was original, Hill nevertheless owed a comic debt to U.S. entertainer Red Skelton. Like Skelton, Hill worked in broad strokes and sometimes in pantomime with a series of recurring comic personae. Hill even adopted Skelton's departing line from the latter's show that ran on network television from 1951 to 1971: "Good night, God bless." However, Hill was without Skelton's often-maudlin sentimentality, substituting instead a ribald energy and gusto. Hill's humor was very much in a broad English vaudeville and stage tradition. The Socialist writer George Orwell once drew attention to the kind of humor embodied in the English seaside postcard—henpecked and shrunken older men and randy young men, both attracted to beautiful young women with large breasts, and an older, fatter, unattractive mother—and some of these archetypes also fed into Hill's television comedy, just as it was to feed into the *Carry On* feature films.

While Hill's publicity often portrayed him as a kind of playboy who liked to surround himself with beautiful, leggy showgirls, this was an extension of his television persona and had nothing to do with his private life. In fact, Hill never married and lived alone in what would have been a lonely life had it not been for the heavy work demands imposed by the television show.

Hill's humor, with its reliance upon vulgarity and double-entendres, was never entirely acceptable to the moral standards of some, and his sexism made him

Benny Hill.
Courtesy of the Everett Collection

See also **Benny Hill Show, The**

Benny Hill. Born Alfred Hawthorn Hill in Southampton, Hampshire, England, January 21, 1925. Attended local schools in Southampton. Served with Royal Engineers during World War II. Began as amateur entertainer in Southampton, while also working in shops and as milkman; assistant stage manager and actor, East Ham Palace, London, 1940; made TV debut, 1949; became popular radio guest, early 1950s; had his own BBC television show, 1955; made film debut, 1956; comedy star of his own long-running comedy sketch show; moved from BBC to Thames Television, 1969–89. Recipient: *Daily Mail* TV Personality of the Year, 1954; *TV Times* Hall of Fame, 1978–79; *TV Times* Funniest Man on TV, 1981–82; Charlie Chaplin International Award for Comedy, 1991. Died in Teddington, London, April 19, 1992.

Television Series

1949	*Hi There*
1952	*The Service Show*
1953	*Show Case*
1955–89	*The Benny Hill Show*

Films

Who Done It?, 1956; *Light Up the Sky*, 1960; *Those Magnificent Men in Their Flying Machines*, 1965; *Chitty Chitty Bang Bang*, 1968; *The Italian Job*, 1969; *The Waiters*, 1969; *The Best of Benny Hill*, 1974; *To See Such Fun*, 1977; *Benny Hill: The Motion Picture*, 1979; *The Unedited Benny Hill*, 1983; *Le Miracule*, 1986; *The Benny Hill Special*, 1987.

Radio

Educating Archie; Archie's the Boy.

Stage (selection)

Stars in Battledress, 1941; *Paris by Night; Fine Fettle.*

Recording

Ernie (the Fastest Milkman in the West), 1971.

Further Reading

Johnson, Terry, *Dead Funny*, London: Methuen Drama, 1994
Smith, John, *The Benny Hill Story*, New York: St. Martin's Press, 1989

seem increasingly old-fashioned. The forces of political correctness finally had their way in 1989, when Thames Television canceled the program due not only to complaints about its smuttiness, but also because its old-fashioned sexism had become increasingly intolerable. In his last television appearance, in 1991, he appeared as himself, the subject of the BBC arts documentary series, *Omnibus*. Although over the last three years of his life, Hill talked in interviews about a comeback, it was the end of his career. He died in hospital, suffering from a chest complaint, in 1992. Benny Hill once told an interviewer that, like Van Gogh, he would be appreciated in 100 years' time. The statement implied that he was not recognized as a great comedian and was belied by the enormous international popularity of his program and by the fact that in the 1970s and 1980s he was several times voted the Funniest Man in the World by the British television audience.

ALBERT MORAN

Hill Street Blues

U.S. Police Procedural/Melodrama

Hill Street Blues, one of the most innovative and critically acclaimed television series in recent television history, aired on NBC from 1981 to 1987. Although never highly rated, NBC continued to renew *Hill Street* for its "prestige value" as well as the demographic profile of its fiercely loyal audience. Indeed, *Hill Street* is perhaps the consummate example of the complex equation in U.S. network television between "quality programming" and "quality demographics." *Hill Street Blues* revolutionized the TV cop show, combining with it elements from the sitcom, soap opera, and *cinéma vérité*-style documentary. In the process, it established the paradigm for the hour-long ensemble drama: intense, fast-paced, and hyper-realistic, set in a densely populated urban workplace, and distinctly Dickensian in terms of character and plot development.

Hill Street's key antecedents actually were sitcoms, and particularly the half-hour ensemble workplace comedies of the 1970s such as *M*A*S*H, The Mary Tyler Moore Show,* and *Barney Miller. M*A*S*H* was influential not only as a medical series set in a literal "war zone" (versus the urban war zone of *Hill Street*), but also for the aggressive cinematic style adapted from Robert Altman's original movie version. *The Mary Tyler Moore Show*'s influence had to do primarily with its "domesticated workplace," a function of Mary's role as nurturer as well as the focus on the personal as well as the professional lives of the principals. The influence of *Barney Miller,* an ensemble sitcom set in a police precinct, was more direct. In fact the genesis of *Hill Street* resulted from NBC's Fred Silverman suggesting that the network develop an hour-long drama blending *Barney Miller* and the documentary-style anthology drama, *Police Story.*

To develop the series, NBC turned to Grant Tinker's MTM Enterprises, which in the early 1970s had specialized in ensemble sitcoms (*The Mary Tyler Moore Show, Bob Newhart,* and others) before turning to the hour-long ensemble drama in 1977 with *Lou Grant. Hill Street* was created by Steven Bochco and Michael Kozoll, two veteran TV series writers with extensive experience on various crime series. The two had collaborated on the short-lived police drama *Delvecchio* in 1976–77 before joining MTM, and they had little interest in doing another cop show unless they were

given considerable leeway to vary the form. NBC agreed, and *Hill Street* debuted as a mid-season replacement in January 1981.

The basic *Hill Street Blues* formula was simple enough. The series was set in the Hill Street station, a haven of controlled chaos in a crime-infested, racially torn ghetto within an unnamed industrial metropolis. Each episode invariably charted a "day in the life" on the Hill, from the early-morning "roll call" to a late-night rehash of the day's events.

In the hands of Bochco and Kozoll, who teamed for much of the writing in the first two seasons, this formula provided the framework for a remarkably complex and innovative series—qualities which were evident from the opening roll call. This daybreak ritual was conducted "below decks" in the precinct house by the desk sergeant—most memorably Sgt. Phil Esterhaus (Michael Conrad from 1981 until his death in 1984), who always closed with the trademark line: "Let's be careful out there."

A deft expositional stroke, the roll call served a range of narrative functions. It initiated the day-long trajectory; it provided an inventory not only of the current precinct case load but also the potential plot lines for the episode; it reintroduced most of the principal characters, whose commentary on the cases reestablished their individual personalities and professional attitudes. And technically, it set *Hill Street*'s distinctive *vérité* tone with its hand-held camera, continual reframing instead of cutting, multi-track sound recording, and edgy, improvisational feel.

After the roll call, the cops filed upstairs to begin their assignments, which set the episode's multiple crime-related plot lines in motion. Most of the series regulars who worked "out there" on the streets were partners: Hill and Renko (Michael Warren and Charles Haid), Coffey and Bates (Ed Marinaro and Betty Thomas), LaRue and Washington (Kiel Martin and Taurean Blacque). Other notable street cops were Lt. Howard Hunter (James Sikking), the precinct's SWAT team leader; Mick Belker (Bruce Weitz), a snarling, perpetually unkempt undercover detective; and Norm Buntz (Dennis Franz), an experienced, cynical, street-wise detective prone to head-strong, rule-bending tactics.

Hill Street Blues, Michael Conrad, Daniel J. Travanti, Veronica Hamel, 1981–87.
Courtesy of the Everett Collection

With the episode thus set in motion, the focus shifted to Captain Frank Furillo (Daniel Travanti), the professional touchstone and indisputable patriarch of the precinct work-family, and the moral center of *Hill Street*'s narrative universe. Furillo adroitly orchestrated his precinct's ceaseless battle with the criminal element. He also did battle with bureaucrats and self-serving superiors, principally in the character of Chief Fletcher Daniels (Jon Cypher). And on a more personal level, he battled his own demons (alcoholism, a failed marriage) and the human limitations of his officers, ever vigilant of the day-to-day toll of police work in a cesspool of urban blight whose citizenry, for the most part, was actively hostile toward the "police presence."

Furillo also battled Joyce Davenport (Veronica Hamel), a capable, contentious lawyer from the Public Defender's office. Their professional antagonism was countered, however, by an intimate personal relationship—the two were lovers. Their affair remained clandestine until the third season, when they went public and were wed. And through all this, Furillo also maintained a troubled but affectionate rapport with his ex-wife, Fay (Barbara Bosson).

The Furillo-Davenport relationship was *Hill Street*'s most obvious and effective serial plot, while also giving a dramatic focus to individual episodes. As professional adversaries, they endlessly wrangled over the process of law and order; as lovers they examined these same conflicts—and their own lives—in a very different light. Most episodes ended, in fact, with the two of them together late at night, away from the precinct, mulling over the day's events. This interplay of professional and personal conflicts—and of episodic and serial plot lines—was crucial to *Hill Street*'s basic narrative strategy. Ever aware of its "franchise" as a cop show, the series relied on a crime-solution formula to structure and dramatize individual episodes, while the long-term personal conflicts raised the dramatic stakes and fueled the serial dimension of the series.

Hill Street's narrative complexity was reinforced by its distinctive cinematic technique. As Todd Gitlin suggests, "*Hill Street*'s achievement was, first of all, a matter of style." Essential to that style was the "density of look and sound" as well as its interwoven ("knitted") plot lines, which created *Hill Street*'s distinctive ambience. "Quick cuts, a furious pace, a nervous camera made for complexity and congestion, a sense of entanglement and continuous crisis that matched the actual density and convolution of city life." *Hill Street*'s realism also extended to controversial social issues and a range of television taboos, particularly in terms of language and sexuality.

This realism was offset, however, by the idealized portrayal of the principal characters and the professional work-family. Whatever their failings and vulnerabilities, Furillo and his charges were heroic—even tragic, given their fierce commitment to a personal and professional "code" in the face of an insensitive bureaucracy, an uncaring public, and an unrelenting criminal assault on their community. But the Hill Street cops found solace in their work and in one another—which, in a sense, was all they had, since the nature of their work precluded anything resembling a "real life."

Not surprisingly, considering its narrative complexity, uncompromising realism, and relatively downbeat worldview, *Hill Street* fared better with critics than with mainstream viewers. In fact, it was among TV's lowest-rated series during its first season but was renewed due to its tremendous critical impact and its six Emmy Awards, including Outstanding Drama Series. *Hill Street* went on to win four straight Emmys in that category, while establishing a strong constituency among upscale urban viewers. It also climbed to a respectable rating, peaking in its third season at number 21; but its strength was always the demographic profile rather than the sheer size of its audience.

Thus *Hill Street* paid off handsomely for NBC, and its long-term impact on TV programming has been equally impressive. In a 1985 *TV Guide* piece, novelist Joyce Carol Oates stated that the series was as "intellectually and emotionally provocative as a good book," and was positively "Dickensian in its superb character studies, its energy, its variety; above all, its audacity." Critics a decade later would be praising series like *NYPD Blue, Homicide, ER, Chicago Hope,* and *Law and Order* in precisely the same terms, heralding a "new golden age" of television drama—a golden age which owes a considerable debt to *Hill Street Blues.*

THOMAS SCHATZ

See also **Bochco, Steven**

Cast

Capt. Frank Furillo	Daniel J. Travanti
Sgt. Phil Esterhaus (1981–84)	Michael Conrad
Officer Bobby Hill	Michael Warren
Officer Andy Renko	Charles Haid
Joyce Davenport	Veronica Hamel
Det. Mick Belker	Bruce Weitz
Lt. Ray Calletano	Rene Enriquez
Det. Johnny (J.D.) LaRue	Kiel Martin
Det. Neal Washington	Taurean Blaque
Lt. Howard Hunter	James Sikking
Sgt./Lt. Henry Goldblume	Joe Spano
Officer/Sgt. Lucille Bates	Betty Thomas
Grace Gardner (1981–85)	Barbara Babcock
Fay Furillo (1981–86)	Barbara Bosson
Capt. Jerry Fuchs (1981–84)	Vincent Lucchesi
Det./Lt. Alf Chesley (1981–82)	Gerry Black
Officer Leo Schnitz (1981–85)	Robert Hirschfield
Officer Joe Coffey (1981–86)	Ed Marinaro
Chief Fletcher P. Daniels	Jon Cypher
Officer Robin Tataglia (1983–87)	Lisa Sutton
Asst. D.A. Irwin Bernstein (1982–87)	George Wyner
Jesus Martinez	Trinidad Silva
Judge Alan Wachtel	Jeffrey Tambor
Det. Harry Garibaldi (1984–85)	Ken Olin
Det. Patricia Mayo (1984–85)	Mimi Kuzyk
Mayor Ozzie Cleveland (1982–85)	J.A. Preston
Sgt. Stanislaus Jablonski (1984–87)	Robert Prosky
Lt. Norman Buntz (1985–87)	Dennis Franz
Celeste Patterson (1985–86)	Judith Hansen
Sidney (The Snitch) Thurston (1985–87)	Peter Jurasik
Officer Pagtrick Flaherty (1986–87)	Robert Clohessy
Officer Tina Russo (1986–87)	Megan Gallagher
Officer Raymond (1987)	David Selburg

Producers
Steven Bochco, Michael Kozoll, Gregory Hoblit, David Anspaugh, Anthony Yerkovich, Scott Brazil, Jeffrey Lewis, Sascha Schneider, David Latt, David Milch, Michael Vittes, Walon Green, Penny Adams

Programming History
NBC

January 1981	Thursday/Saturday 10:00–11:00
January 1981–April 1981	Saturday 10:00–11:00
April 1981–August 1981	Tuesday 9:00–10:00
October 1981–November 1986	Thursday 10:00–11:00
December 1986–February 1987	Tuesday 9:00–10:00
March 1987–May 1987	Tuesday 10:00–11:00

Further Reading

Bedell, Sally, *Up the Tube: Prime-Time TV and the Silverman Years,* New York: Viking, 1983

Deming, Caren J., "*Hill Street Blues* as Narrative," *Critical Studies in Mass Communication* (March 1985)

Feuer, Jane, Paul Kerr, and Tise Vahimagi, editors, *MTM: "Quality Television,"* London: British Film Institute, 1984

Gitlin, Todd, *Inside Prime Time,* New York: Pantheon, 1983

Marc, David, "MTM's Past and Future," *Atlantic Monthly* (November 1984)

Newcomb, Horace, and Robert S. Alley, *The Producer's Medium,* New York: Oxford University Press, 1983

Anita Hill–Clarence Thomas Hearings

The Hill–Thomas Hearings, conducted by the U.S. Senate Judiciary Committee to investigate Professor Anita Hill's allegations of prior sexual harassment by Supreme Court nominee Clarence Thomas, were televised nationally on American television from October 11 to October 13, 1991. Although the hearings themselves had no legal significance, to many observers they symbolized a public referendum on sexual harassment and other gender inequities in late 20th-century America. As such, they have been widely credited with increasing public awareness about gender discrimination, and with motivating female voters during the 1992 congressional elections.

As President George Bush's nominee to replace Thurgood Marshall on the Supreme Court, Thomas had been the subject of confirmation hearings in September 1991; however, the Senate Judiciary Committee was unable to make a recommendation to the full Senate after these hearings. Thomas's appointment seemed further jeopardized by reports in *Newsday* and on National Public Radio on 6 October that he allegedly sexually harassed a co-worker from 1981 to 1983. These charges, made by Anita Hill during interviews with the FBI, were apparently leaked to the press just days before the Senate's final vote on Thomas' appointment. Responding to demands from feminist organizations and seven female Democratic members of the House of Representatives, the Senate delayed the vote in order to hear more about Hill's allegations.

During the three days of televised hearings, the senators and the viewing public heard testimony from both Hill and Thomas, as well as their supporters. Hill referred to specific incidents of Thomas's behavior, including repeated requests for dates and references to pornographic material. Thomas vehemently denied Hill's allegations and responded with outrage, at one point calling the hearings "a national disgrace...a high-tech lynching for uppity blacks who in any way deign to think for themselves, to do for themselves." So adamant was each sides' accounts that many observers in the press labeled the hearings an example of "He Said, She Said," with both parties offering such vastly differing recollections of events that many wondered if the hearings could ever reveal the truth.

Two days after the hearings ended, with no clear resolution of the discrepancies between Hill's and Thomas's accounts, the Senate voted on Thomas's confirmation. Due to the media coverage of the hearings, public interest in the vote was unusually high, as evidenced by a barrage of phone calls and faxes sent to the capital on this issue. Although opinion polls reported evidence of debate and division among minority groups, including African Americans and women, they also indicated that a majority of voters supported Thomas. Ultimately, the Senate voted 52 to 48 in favor of Thomas's confirmation.

The visual imagery and political symbolism of the hearings may be their most important legacy. In this regard the hearings take their place alongside other

Anita Hill.
©*CJ Contino/Everett Collection*

memorable television events, including the Army–McCarthy Hearings and the Watergate Proceedings. These events exemplify television's ability to galvanize a national audience around matters of crucial social significance, and often they stand as historical markers of significant social and cultural shifts.

Indeed, many feminist groups refer to Anita Hill as the mother of a new wave of awareness of gender discrimination, particularly given the attacks on her credibility that she withstood from the white male senators. To witness a composed, articulate law professor being questioned about her mental state (some senators and Thomas supporters had theorized that Hill was "delusional") offended many female viewers who themselves had experienced sexual harassment. Harriett Woods, then president of the National Women's Political Caucus, commented that "Anita Hill focused attention on the fact that there were no women in that Senate panel making decisions about people's lives."

As is true for so many cultural memories in the United States, the televised Hill-Thomas hearings etched some clear and unforgettable images into the minds of the American public. To those observers who did not believe Hill's claims, the hearings represented the gravity of such allegations in a society where gender politics can be divisive. To Hill's sympathizers, the memory of a lone woman reluctantly speaking out about past painful experiences to a room full of bewildered and unsympathetic men may have been one reason why an unprecedented 29 women were elected in the subsequent congressional elections.

VANESSA B. BEASLEY

See also **U.S. Congress and Television**

Further Reading

Cohn, Bob, "Dirt Trail," *New Republic* (January 6, 1992)

Corry, John, "Playmates of the Month," *American Spectator* (January 1995)

Chrisman, Robert, and Robert L. Allen, editors, *Court of Appeal: The Black Community Speaks Out on the Racial and Sexual Politics of Clarence Thomas vs. Anita Hill,* New York: Ballantine, 1992

Danforth, John, *Resurrection: The Confirmation of Clarence Thomas,* New York: Viking, 1994

Garment, Suzanne, "Afterword: On Anita Hill and Clarence Thomas," in her *Scandal: The Culture of Mistrust in American Politics,* New York: Times Books, 1992

Mayer, Jane, *Strange Justice: The Selling of Clarence Thomas,* Boston: Houghton Mifflin, 1994

Morrison, Toni, editor, *Race-ing Justice, En-Gendering Power: Essays on Anita Hill, Clarence Thomas, and the Construction of Social Reality,* New York: Pantheon, 1992

Phelps, Timothy M., *Capitol Games: Clarence Thomas, Anita Hill, and the Story of a Supreme Court Nomination,* New York: Hyperion, 1992

Smith, Christopher E., *Critical Judicial Nominations and Political Change: The Impact of Clarence Thomas,* Westport, Connecticut: Praeger, 1993

Smitherman-Donaldson, Geneva, editor, *African American Women Speak Out on Anita Hill–Clarence Thomas,* Detroit, Michigan: Wayne State University Press, 1995

Steenland, Sally, "On Trial: Courtroom Television," *Television Quarterly* (Winter 1992)

Thompson, David, "Our Process (Our Show)," *Film Comment* (January–February 1992)

United States Congress Committee on the Judiciary, *The Complete Transcripts of the Clarence Thomas–Anita Hill Hearings,* Chicago: Academy Chicago Publishers, 1994

Hillsborough

British Docudrama

Hillsborough was a highly acclaimed docudrama about the 1989 Hillsborough soccer stadium disaster, which claimed the lives of 96 football fans. Scripted by the renowned writer Jimmy McGovern, the 1996 program was a searing criticism of the police in charge at the time of the disaster, and a trenchant attack on the establishment for its appalling handling of the victims' families and their demands for justice in the aftermath. Described by the TV reviewer Stuart Jeffries as "one of the most upsetting two hours of television you are likely to see," the program won several international awards and was heralded as a crucial factor in the government's decision to order a new judicial inquiry into the event.

The tragedy itself took place on Saturday April 15, 1989 when fans descended on Sheffield Wednesday's Hillsborough soccer stadium for the Football Association (FA) Cup semi-final between teams Liverpool and Nottingham Forest. As crowds built up in the stadium, there was a late surge of Liverpool supporters entering the back of a standing area, causing those at the front to be pushed against the wire fence separating them from the pitch; 96 fans were killed. Both the soccer community and the city of Liverpool were stunned by the event, and in the week that followed around a million people filed through the gates of Liverpool's football ground to leave flowers, football scarves, and messages.

In the immediate aftermath, police in charge of crowd control at the match blamed the disaster on drunken Liverpool fans, and this was reported in sections of the tabloid press. In the following coroner's inquest a verdict of "accidental death" was recorded on the victims, and the public inquiry set up to investigate the event, though critical of crowd management, failed to indict the police officers in charge at the time.

The idea to dramatize the event for television evolved after McGovern had touched on the tragedy in a storyline for Granada Television's psychological police fiction series *Cracker* (1993–96). In a three-part episode titled "To Be a Somebody," the actor Robert Carlyle played a man driven to murder in revenge for the Hillsborough disaster. Concerned that the fictional depiction of a survivor's reaction might cause distress, the TV company arranged a special screening for victims' families. The response was very positive and the Hillsborough Families Support Group (HFSG), which had been campaigning for justice after the event, invited McGovern to tackle the subject head on.

With a commission from Granada (a company known for investigative journalism and groundbreaking drama) and the help of a team of researchers, McGovern set about writing the drama based on documented evidence and witness statements. A former schoolteacher from Liverpool, McGovern was no stranger to controversial subject matter, having tackled homosexuality in the Catholic church in *Priest* (1994), and discord in education in *Hearts and Minds* (1995). With *Hillsborough* he set out to do two things: to show that it had been police incompetence that had led to the disaster, and not drunken fans; and to show the grievous injustice the families of the deceased had suffered after the event. Contentiously, the program claimed to provide new evidence, notably that CCTV video tapes which would have demonstrated police failings had gone missing, and that police officers had changed statements and interfered with witnesses.

Yet it was the human drama that made Hillsborough such compelling and upsetting viewing. The story focused on three families who lost teenage children in the disaster, including Trevor Hicks—who went on to become chairman of the HFSG—and his wife Jenni, who lost their two teenage daughters, Sarah, aged 19, and Vicki, aged 15.

The program started with families seen joyfully receiving their tickets, and then the drama quickly moved to the match day itself. As Stuart Jeffries suggests, McGovern's consummate skill as a scriptwriter made even the advertisement breaks work for him. The first break was placed just as the crowds began to build up at the stadium. Immediately after the break, a father of one of the dead says to camera, "All they had to do was close off the tunnel like they normally did and we would have all had to go round the sides into the pens with plenty of space." This had the double impact of pointing the finger of blame, while at the same time avoiding a harrowing reconstruction of the crush itself.

Hillsborough followed the families learning the news of the tragedy, the horror of identifying bodies, and the insensitivity of police questioning. The rest of the two hours was filled with the painful aftermath, and the costs of bereavement, including the separation of Trevor and Jenni Hicks, the families' fight for justice, and the frustration, pain, and anger at the coroner's inquest and public inquiry.

Hillsborough featured a strong cast, including Ricky Tomlinson and Christopher Eccleston, a regular of McGovern's dramas. It was directed by Charles Mc-Dougall, who had not only previously made an award-winning football-related short film, *Arrivederci Millwall* (1990), but had also been on the terraces with the Liverpool fans on the day of the tragedy. Members of the cast met with the families before shooting, and the families themselves watched the completed program prior to broadcast, in private screenings.

The first transmission, on December 5, 1996, was watched by approximately 7 million people and made for difficult viewing. It had been sympathetically trailed in the press beforehand and was critically applauded afterwards. The docudrama reinvigorated public debate about the event, and the following summer, after the election of a new Labour government, a judicial inquiry was announced to look at the issues and evidence raised by the campaigners and the program. *Hillsborough* went on to win a clutch of awards from the Royal Television Society, the British Academy, and won the grand prize at the Banff Television Festival. It also won a prize of £18,000 at the Munich Film Festival; Granada pledged the money to the appeal for the victim's families.

In February 1998 the government declined a new public inquiry after a judge ruled that the supposed new evidence put forward by campaigners and the program did not add anything significant to the material available at the original inquiry.

ROB TURNOCK

See also **Cracker; Docudrama; McGovern, Jimmy**

Cast

Trevor Hicks	Christopher Eccleston
John Glover	Ricky Tomlinson
Jenni Hicks	Annabelle Apsion
Theresa Glover	Rachel Davies
Eddie Spearritt	Mark Womack
Jan Spearritt	Tracey Wilkinson
Joe Glover	Scot Williams
Chief Supt. David	
Duckenfield	Maurice Roëves
Sarah Hicks	Sarah Graham
Victoria Hicks	Anna Martland

Producer

Nicola Shindler

Programming History

ITV December 5, 1996	9:00–10:00, 10:40–11:40
ITV February 24, 1998	Unscheduled repeat

Further Reading

Duncan, Andrew, interview with Jimmy McGovern, *Radio Times,* November 30–December 6, 1996

Jeffries, Stuart, "Last Night's TV: A Walk Through the Storm," *The Guardian,* December 6, 1996

McDougall, Charles, "Inside Story: *Hillsborough:* Back to the Nightmare," *The Guardian,* December 2, 1996

Paget, Derek. *No Other Way to tell It: Dramadoc/Docudrama on Television,* Manchester: Manchester University Press, 1998

Hird, Thora (1911–2003)

British Actor

Dame Thora Hird was one of Britain's finest character actors. Her career spanned nearly 90 years, from her earliest stage appearance at the age of 8 weeks to her death in 2003; it encompassed work in a range of media, including radio broadcasting and appearances in more than 100 films. In television, she appeared both in her capacity as actress, and as presenter of the popular *Your Songs of Praise Choice* (later renamed *Praise Be!*). She also wrote her autobiography, as well as a number of books on prayer.

Hird's durability was due to both her versatility, revealed by her work in a number of television genres, and paradoxically, her ability to remain distinctly unique and individual. Her work for television included an early drama for BBC TV, *The Queen Came By,* about life in a draper's store, set in Queen Victoria's jubilee year. In the play, her characterization of Emmie Slee proved very popular. She also appeared as the long-suffering wife in the comedy series *Meet the Wife,* with Freddie Frinton; the nurse in *Romeo and Juliet* for the BBC in 1967; Billy's overbearing mother in the situation comedy *In Loving Memory* (1979–86), set in a funeral parlor; and the tragicomic character in *A Cream Cracker under the Settee,* one of the acclaimed series of *Talking Heads* monologues written by Alan Bennett, and broadcast in 1988. Hird also starred in one of the second series of Bennett's *Talking Heads* monologues, *Waiting for the Telegram* (1998), and she played leading roles in ITV's *Wide-Eyed and Legless* (1994) and its sequel *Lost for Words* (1999). In 2001 Hird was visible on British television in a nonacting capacity, serving as spokeswoman in a public service campaign encouraging pensioners to request their full government entitlements.

Many of her television roles offered Hird the opportunity to exercise her particular brand of Lancastrian wit, which was firmly located within the music-hall-based tradition of northern, working-class comedy, characteristically "down to earth," anecdotal, and always constructed in opposition to the "pretentious and privileged" south of England. In much the same vein as the seaside postcards of her Morecambe birthplace, Hird's typical roles were as an all-seeing boarding-house landlady, a gossiping neighbor, or a sharp-tongued mother-in-law, in each case the "eyes and ears" of the (female) community. And, just as the veneer of the garishly painted seaside piers cracks to reveal the old and slightly rotten wood beneath, so Hird's skillful characterizations offered a hint of the underlying sadness and pathos that is often found beneath the proud facade.

Hird earned considerable recognition and respect within her profession, as well as critical and audience acclaim for many of her roles, and she was the subject of a *South Bank Show* monograph in 1995. However, her contributions to television have not been the subject of significant scholarly attention. This neglect may be due to the fact that she tended to play roles that are located within genres such as situation comedy, which is afforded a lowly status in many aesthetic and critical hierarchies. Potentially, however, there is much critical currency in exploring how these roles or types represent working-class women, and indeed, how older actresses may often be subject to typecasting.

NICOLA STRANGE

Thora Hird. Born in Morecambe, Lancashire, England, May 28, 1911. Attended the Misses Nelson's Preparatory School, Morecambe. Married: James Scott, 1937 (died, 1994); child: Janette. Followed parents into the theater as a child; gained early experience with the Royalty Theatre Repertory Company, Morecambe, before establishing name on London stage in *Flowers for the Living,* 1944; film debut, 1940; subsequently played a range of classical and contemporary roles on the stage and also acted in films and on television, starring in several comedy series. Honorary D.Litt., University of Lancaster, 1989. Officer of the Order of the British Empire, 1983; Dame Commander of the Order of the British Empire, 1993. Recipient: Pye Female Comedy Star Award, 1984; British Academy of Film and Television Arts Awards, 1988, 1994, 1999, 2000. Royal Television Society Awards, 1999 and 2000. International Emmy Award, 1999. Died March 15, 2003, Brinsworth House, Twickenham, England, following a stroke.

Television Series (selected)

1956	*The Jimmie Wheeler Show*
1964–66	*Meet the Wife*
1968–69	*First Lady*
1969–70	*Ours Is a Nice House*
1979–86	*In Loving Memory*
1980	*Flesh and Blood*
1983–84	*Hallelujah*
1986	*The Last of the Summer Wine*
1993	*Goggle Eyes*
1998	*The Queen's Nose* (mini-series)

Television Plays (selected)

1962	*A Kind of Loving*
1966	*Who's a Good Boy Then?*
1967	*Romeo and Juliet*
1975	*When We Are Married*
1977	*The Boys and Mrs B*
1979	*Afternoon Off*
1982	*Say Something Happened*

1982	*Intensive Care*
1988	*Talking Heads: A Cream Cracker under the Settee*
1992	*Memento Mori*
1994	*Wide-Eyed and Legless*
1994	*Pat and Margaret*
1998	*Talking Heads: Waiting for the Telegram*
1999	*Lost for Words*

Films

Spellbound, 1940; *The Black Sheep of Whitehall,* 1941; *The Foreman Went to France,* 1941; *Next of Kin,* 1942; *The Big Blockade,* 1942; *Went the Day Well?,* 1942; *Two Thousand Women,* 1944; *The Courtneys of Curzon Street,* 1947; *My Brother Jonathan,* 1948; *Corridor of Mirrors,* 1948; *The Weaker Sex,* 1948; *Portrait from Life,* 1948; *Once a Jolly Swagman,* 1948; *A Boy, a Girl and a Bike,* 1949; *Fools Rush in,* 1949; *Madness of the Heart,* 1949; *Maytime in Mayfair,* 1949; *Boys in Brown,* 1949; *Conspirator,* 1949; *The Cure for Love,* 1950; *The Magnet,* 1950; *Once a Sinner,* 1950; *The Galloping Major,* 1951; *The Frightened Man,* 1952; *Emergency Call,* 1952; *Time Gentlemen Please!,* 1952; *The Lost Hours,* 1952; *The Long Memory,* 1952; *The Great Game,* 1953; *Background,* 1953; *Turn the Key Softly,* 1953; *Personal Affair,* 1953; *Street Corner,* 1953; *A Day to Remember,* 1953; *Don't Blame the Stork; For Better,* 1954; *For Worse,* 1954; *The Crowded Day,* 1954; *One Good Turn,* 1954; *Love Match,* 1955; *The Quatermass Experiment,* 1955; *Tiger by the Tail,* 1955; *Lost,* 1955; *Women without Men,* 1955; *Sailor Beware!,* 1956; *Home and Away,* 1956; *The Good Companions,* 1957; *These Dangerous Years,* 1957; *Further Up the Creek,* 1958; *The Entertainer,* 1960; *Over the Odds,* 1961; *A Kind of Loving,* 1962; *Term of Trial,* 1962; *Bitter Harvest,* 1963; *Rattle of a Simple Man,* 1964; *Some Will, Some Won't,* 1969; *The Nightcomers,* 1971; *Consuming Passions,* 1988; *Julie and the Cadillacs,* 1999.

Stage (selected)

No Medals, 1944; *Flowers for the Living,* 1944; *The Queen Came by,* 1948; *Tobacco Road,* 1949; *Dangerous Woman,* 1951; *The Happy Family,* 1951; *The Same Sky,* 1952; *The Trouble-Makers,* 1952; *The Love Match,* 1953; *Saturday Night at the Crown,* 1957; *Come Rain Come Shine,* 1958; *Happy Days,* 1958; *Romeo and Juliet; No, No, Nanette; Me, I'm Afraid of Virginia Woolf; Afternoon Off.*

Publications

Scene and Hird (autobiography), 1976
Thora Hird's Praise Be! Notebook, 1991
Thora Hird's Praise Be! Year Book, 1991
Thora Hird's Praise Be! Christmas Book, 1991
Thora Hird's Praise Be! Book of Prayers, 1992
Thora Hird's Praise Be! I Believe, 1993

Happy Days: A Thought for Every Day, 1994
Thora Hird's Little Book of Home Truths, 1994
Sing with Praise!: Hymns, Prayers and Readings for Help the Aged, 1995
Is It Thora? My Autobiography, 1996
Thora Hird's Book of Bygones, 1998
Not in the Diary (autobiography), 2000

History and Television

As a productive cultural force, television is involved in projecting new modes and forms of historical understanding. These forms do not always follow from traditional scholarly or professional ideas about history. On the contrary, for a number of reasons, television has been widely seen as contributing to the disappearance or loss of history in the contemporary postmodern condition. The emphasis on television's "liveness," based in its technology and its common discursive and rhetorical strategies, has led some theorists to the conclusion that television plays a central role in erasing a sense of the past, and eliminating a common, coherent linear sense of cultural and social development.

It is certainly the case that conventional history is increasingly hard to identify in mass culture, especially in the form of coherent linear narratives, a clear set of major historical players, or readily identifiable class struggles. At the same time, however, television seems obsessed with defining itself in relation to history. Television's ubiquity suggests that its conceptions of history—both its representations of specific events and its appropriation of history as a way of understanding the world—must be taken seriously. Television does not supplant, but rather coexists with, familiar ideas about how we know the past, what we know of the past, and the value of such knowledge. In the process, television produces everyday forms of historical understanding.

As a result, it is probably more accurate to propose that television is contributing to a significant transformation and dispersion of how we think about history, rather than to the loss of historical consciousness. Television offers forms of history that are simultaneously more public than traditional professional history, and more personal and idiosyncratic. This is because the medium's historical narratives are available to mass viewing publics, but also engage viewers in diverse, and even highly idiosyncratic ways. While history may be conceived in both broadly social and intensely personal terms, television has transformed the ways in which individuals understand and position themselves in relation to either of these definitions.

In the case of the United States, it is nearly impossible to think about American culture and its global influence today without including everyday media culture as an integral part of this history. Significant historical events and conjunctures of postwar 20th-century American history—the Vietnam war, the assassination of John F. Kennedy, civil rights and student protests, the Challenger explosion, the first Persian Gulf War, September 11, 2001, the "War on Terrorism"—can hardly be imagined without the television images which carried them into American (and other) homes. Similar conditions, events, and moments, such as the collective memory of the 1953 coronation of Queen Elizabeth for British viewers, exist in other nations of the world which have also had a long experience with television. As these examples suggest, for some established nation-states television can actually connote national identity through a televisual history. Other nations and regions, particularly in the postcolonial world, have yet to see representations of their national identity consistently emerge on their television screens. And yet another group of nations and regions, such as post-apartheid South Africa, are experiencing a transformation of the historical representation of their televisual national identity.

At the beginning of the new millennium, the idea of "video diplomacy" also has increasing importance in a world linked by telecommunications technology and covered by international television news organizations. Indeed, television news—with its emphasis on being live and up to date—is one of the key places where television most insistently promotes its historical role. The rapid growth of television in the postcolonial world, coincident with the end of the Cold War (since 1989, sets in use worldwide have doubled, with most of that growth in the postcolonial world) suggests that the impact of televisual history first experienced in the United States will now be seen on a world scale. The live televising of coups and crises in post-Soviet Russia is one example of the globalizing trend of television and historical consciousness. Other indicators include the unprecedented global circulation of war reporting, of political journalism, and of the lives and misfortunes of celebrities.

In other contexts, television links history to world-historical events, often before they have even begun. The term "history" is regularly used to designate events before, during, and after they occur. In this vein, television casts all sorts of events as history, including the Middle East peace summit in Madrid; the fall of the Berlin Wall; the annually occurring World Series (baseball); Michael Jordan's return to basketball; the O.J. Simpson trial; the impeachment proceedings against U.S. President Bill Clinton; and the primetime airing of the final episode of *Seinfeld*. From the apparently sublime to the apparently inexplicable, "history" is a term and a conceptual field that television often bandies about with surprising frequency and persistence. In the process conventional ideas of history as a distinctive temporal and narrational discourse are dispersed. "History" becomes a process wherein events and people in the present (and future) are simultaneously implicated in a social, political, and cultural heritage.

Television routinely correlates liveness and historicity in the form of equivalence, alibi, reversals, and identity, especially in the area of news and public affairs/documentary programming. In the context of news coverage, especially events that warrant live coverage, it is not unusual to hear that the events thus presented are "historic." At the same time, the very presence of television at an event constitutes a record for posterity. In this sense, television acts as an agent of history and memory, recording and preserving representations to be referenced in the future. The institution of television itself becomes the guarantor of history, even as it invokes history to validate and justify its own presence at an event.

Another factor at work in this array is the long-term search by broadcasters for a recognition of their own legitimacy as social institutions. Many critics of television have linked the rise of a televisual historical consciousness and the aggressive self-promotion of the broadcasting industry when criticizing television for its supposed failure to fully advance public ideals. Even while driven by the lure of significant profit, American television broadcasters are often desperate to dissociate themselves from discourses presenting television as a vast wasteland. As part of a spirited defense against their many detractors they point to their unique ability to record and represent history. The "high culture–low culture" debate, so prevalent in analyses of American media, has sunk its roots into this issue as well.

In much of the rest of the world, by contrast, government investment in broadcasting has meant that questions of legitimation, and subsequent defense through claims of unique historical agency, have been less urgent. However, following the worldwide wave of privatization of media outlets, which began in the 1980s, television broadcasters throughout the world may begin to mimic their American predecessors. They, too, may protect their self interests by turning the production of "history on television" and "television as history" into a useable past.

As a result of all these activities, it is possible to see how forms of historical consciousness purveyed by television get transformed in the process of representing current events that are all equally "historic." Television promotes ideas about history that involve heterogeneous temporal references—past, present, and future. But actual historical events are unstable combinations of public and private experiences, intersecting both global and local perspectives. By proposing combinations and permutations of individual memory and official public document, television produces a new sense of cultural and social identity among its viewers.

For example, in relation to past events, television frequently addresses viewers as subjects of a distinctive historical consciousness: Americans of various ages are all supposed to remember where they were when they first heard and saw that John F. Kennedy was shot, that the space shuttle *Challenger* had exploded, or when the first plane hit the north tower of New York's World Trade Center on September 11, 2001. The drama of the everyday can be similarly historicized when, for example, television promotes collective memories of Kathy Fiscus for one American generation or Baby Jessica for another. By addressing viewers in this way, television confirms its own central role as the focal point of the myriad individual experiences and memories of its individual viewers. In the process the medium brings sentimental domestic drama into direct relation with public, domestic, and global histories.

In all these instance, television's ideas of history are intimately bound up with the history of the medium itself (and indirectly with other audiovisual recording media), and with its abilities to record, circulate, and preserve images. In other words, the medium's representations of the past are highly dependent on events that have been recorded on film or video, such that history assumes the form of television's self-reflection. The uses of available still photography and audio recordings can also, on occasion, play a significant role in this regard. The medium's own mechanisms—its prevailing technologies and discourses—become the defining characteristics of modern historiography. Similarly, the television journalist—particularly the news anchor—can become an embodied icon of television's ability to credibly produce and represent history. Many nations have (or have had) a number of individuals achieve this status typically associated with an American reporter like Walter Cronkite. Now television journalists seem on the cusp of achieving this at transnational and transcultural levels. Television may in the process also begin to produce a new sense of global histories, along with national and personal histories.

This self-reflective nature of television's historiography develops in relation to both public events and in relation to the medium's own programming. American television routinely celebrates its own past in an array of anniversary, reunion, and retrospective shows about its own programs, and even in "bloopers" specials which compile outtakes and mistakes from previously aired programs. Programs of this ilk serve multiple functions, and have various implications with regards to ideas of history. Self-promotion, in the form of inexpensive, recycled programming, is one obvious motivation for these shows, especially as the multi-channel environment means that more "old" shows are rerun on broadcast and cable services. This also becomes a kind of self-legitimation, by means of retrospective logic. For if American programs such as *The Tonight Show, The Brady Bunch,* or *Laverne and Shirley* warrant celebratory reunion or retrospective celebration, even years after they are no longer in production, this could mean they are important cultural artifacts/events.

Television thus continually rewrites its own past in the form of "history" as a way of promoting itself and its ongoing programming as a significant, legitimate part of culture. In the process, postwar American popular culture is held up as the measure of social-cultural history more generally. All viewers are enjoined to "remember" this heritage, whether they experienced it first-hand, in first-run, or not. This can even lead to the production of instant nostalgia, when special programs herald popular series' final episodes (such as occurred with *Cheers* and *Friends*), just as those final new episodes air in primetime. This sort of self-promotional and self-reflective hype (in network

specials, as well as on talk shows, entertainment news programs, and local news programs around the country) proposes that these programs have been absorbed into a common popular cultural historical heritage from the very moment they are no longer presenting new episodes in primetime.

Programming schedules and strategies in themselves adopt and offer these new ideas about history, especially in terms of popular culture. This is increasingly apparent in the multi-channel universe, as television becomes something of a cultural archive, where movies and television programs from the past are as readily accessible as new programs. This can even be made self-conscious, as in the case of Nick at Nite (a programming subdivision of Nickelodeon, an American cable network), which features American sitcoms from the 1960s and 1970s, and promotes itself as "celebrating our television heritage." In 1995 Nickelodeon developed a second network, called TV Land, programmed exclusively with old television shows. Once again, the history in question is the medium's own history, self-referentially reproducing itself as having cultural value and utility.

Beyond these strategic constructions of the historical significance of television as medium, a specific sense of history also pervades television's fiction programs. Because of the nature of American commercial television programming, individual programs develop and project a sense of history in direct proportion to their success—the longer they stay on the air, the more development there is over time. Characters and the actors who portray them not only age, but accrue a sense of density of experience, and viewers may establish variable relationships with these characters and their histories. This sense of continuity and history, linking and intersecting fictive worlds with the lives of viewers, seems strongest and most explicit in serial melodrama, but equally affects any successful, long-running series. It is also complicated by the question of syndication and reruns where the interplay of repetition and development, seriality and redundancy leads to the sense that history is malleable and mutable, at least at the level of individual, everyday experience. While many European television programs intentionally have a limited run of episodes, other long-running programs, such as *East-Enders,* indicate that this tendency toward openendedness is not unique to American television. Furthermore, complicated historical issues can certainly be involved in limited-run series, as suggested by mini-series such as *Roots* in the United States or *Yearnings* in China.

As suggested above, many of these ideas about history are powerfully played out in the context of serial melodrama, a genre which may seem as far removed from "history" in the conventional sense as anything on television. These "soap operas" offer stories that may continue for decades, maintaining viewer allegiances in the process, even though the stories are punctuated by redundancies on the one hand, and unanticipated reversals on the other. These narrative conventions are some of the very things for which the genre is often derided—slow dramatic progress, the ongoing breakups of good relationships, the routine revival of characters presumed dead, and sudden revelations that characters were switched at birth, or the product of previously unrevealed affairs, leading to major reconstructions of family relations. These characteristic narrative strategies also produce a subtle and sophisticated sense of historicity and temporality, in the context of the accumulation of a long-term historical fiction and long-term viewing commitments. Among other things, they encourage a persistent reexamination of conventional assumptions and attitudes in patriarchal culture about lineage, and about family and community relations. In the process, they also offer a sense that the force and weight of the past is important, but not always readily transparent, requiring the active interpretive involvement and participation of the most ordinary people, including soap-opera viewers. Complex and contradictory ideas about temporality and narrative contribute to a popular historical consciousness because they have everything to do with individuals' actual relations to and ideas about historicity. One example is found in the various *telenovelas* produced and aired in Brazil during the downfall of the Collor presidency in 1992; these *telenovelas* were read by audiences as socio-political texts imbued with the twists and turns that eventually led to Collor's resignation.

Television also produces ideas about history through historical fictions, in particular in primetime dramas and historical miniseries. These offer particular revisions and interpretations of the past, often inflected by a sense of anachronism. It is not surprising that many controversial social issues continue to be readily explored in the context of historical narrative. For viewers, the historical fictions provide the alibi of a safe distance and difference in relation to situations they might encounter in the present. A range of programs have thus explored ideas about race, gender, and multiculturalism in anachronistic historical contexts, allowing the past to become the terrain for displacing and exploring contemporary social concerns. In this way, particular historical moments, however fictionalized, may be revivified in conjunction with contemporary social issues. This occurred, for example, in such programs as *Dr. Quinn, Medicine Woman, I'll Fly Away,* and *American Dreams.*

While these historical frames permit an opportunity for exploring issues that might otherwise be consid-

ered overly controversial (especially in the present), they also propose that the issues are not necessarily of current or topical concern, since they are retrospectively projected into the past. In this context, it is also interesting to examine which periods of the past become fertile territory for reexamination. Television often focuses on periods that are based in the recent past and thus overdetermined in their familiarity; or, the chosen moments are widely recognized as eras of national transition or upheaval, providing opportunity for the exploration of many socially charged topics. Even within particular programs dealing with these particular periods, however, the idea of a stable linear historicity is not necessarily the rule.

In various ways, then, television situates itself at the center of a process wherein it produces and reconstructs history for popular consumption. For if the things it reports are historic, sometimes before they have even occurred, and if early television programs are our common cultural heritage, then the medium itself is the agent of historical construction. This reaches extremes when the medium's presence at an event becomes the "proof" of the event's historical importance, a tautological process that tends to encourage self-absorption, self-referentiality, and self-legitimation. Watching television and being on television become twin poles of a contemporary cultural experience of historicization. Viewers are likely to get caught up in this process.

There is, for example, the case of a young woman standing in a crowd on an L.A. freeway overpass in the summer of 1994, waiting for O.J. Simpson to pass by in a white Ford Bronco, trailed by police who were trying to arrest him. A reporter from CNN asked her why she was there. She explained that she had been watching it all on television, and realized that O.J. would pass near her house and, she said, "I just wanted to be a part of history." In the logic of contemporary television culture she achieved her goal, because she was on television and was able to write history in her own voice, live, with her presence and participation in a major televised event.

Mimi White and James Schwoch

See also **Civil Rights Movement and Television, Kennedy, John F.: Assassination and Funeral; Vietnam on Television; War on Television**

Further Reading

Boddy, William, *Fifties Television: The Industry and Its Critics,* Urbana: University of Illinois Press, 1990

Caldwell, John Thornton, *Televisuality: Style, Crisis, and Authority in American Television,* New Brunswick, New Jersey: Rutgers University Press, 1995

Dayan, Daniel, and Elihu Katz, *Media Events: The Live Broadcasting of History,* Cambridge, Massachusetts: Harvard University Press, 1992

Freehling, William W., "History and Television," *Southern Studies: An Interdisciplinary Journal of the South* (Spring 1983)

Jameson, Frederic, *Postmodernism, or, The Cultural Logic of Late Capitalism,* Durham, North Carolina: Duke University Press, 1991

Jenkins, Henry, III, "Reading Popular History: The Atlanta Child Murders," *Journal of Communication Inquiry* (Summer, 1987)

Lipsitz, George, *Time Passages: Collective Memory and American Popular Culture,* Minneapolis: University of Minnesota Press, 1990

McChesney, Robert, and William Solomon, editors, *Ruthless Criticism: New Perspectives in U.S. Communication History,* Minneapolis: University of Minnesota Press, 1993

Monaghan, David, "Em-Bodying the Disembodied: Tumbledown, Resurrected, and Falklands War Mythology," *Works and Days: Essays in the Socio-Historical Dimensions of Literature and the Arts* (Fall, 1993)

O'Connor, John E., editor, *Image as Artifact: The Historical Analysis of Film and Television,* Washington, D.C.: American Historical Association, 1990

Pilgrim, Tim A., "Television and the Destruction of Democracy: Blurring of Fiction and Fact as a Hegemonic Tool," *Studies in Popular Culture* (1992)

Rønning, Helge, and Knut Lundby, *Media and Communication: Readings in Methodology, History, and Culture,* Oxford: Oxford University Press, 1991

Schudson, Michael, *The Power of News,* Cambridge, Massachusetts: Harvard University Press, 1995

Schwoch, James, Mimi White, and Susan Reilly, *Media Knowledge,* Albany: State University of New York Press, 1992

Spigel, Lynn, *Make Room for TV,* Chicago: University of Chicago Press, 1992

Winston, Brian, *Misunderstanding Media,* Cambridge, Massachusetts: Harvard University Press, 1986

Hitchhiker's Guide to the Galaxy, The

British Science Fiction Comedy

The Hitchhiker's Guide to the Galaxy is a book, television program, radio series, record, cassette, video, and proposed feature film. The six-part BBC Television adaptation of its own original radio comedy is only one small part of a whole universe of merchandising that has sprung from this saga of angst and despair—from illustrated book versions to T-shirts and towels.

The story centers on an Earthman, Arthur Dent, one of a handful of survivors who remain when the planet is demolished to make way for a hyperspace bypass. Arthur travels through the galaxy with a group of companions: his friend Ford Prefect; Zaphod Beeblebrox, two-headed ex-president of the galaxy; a pretty young astrophysicist called Trillian; and a copy of *The Hitchhiker's Guide to the Galaxy,* a woefully inaccurate electronic tourist guide.

The tale is a despair-ridden one. Our world, traditionally the center of our "Earthnocentric" view of the universe, becomes "an utterly insignificant blue/green planet," orbiting a "small, unregarded sun at the unfashionable end of the Western spiral arm of the galaxy." Indeed, the entire *Hitchhiker's Guide* entry for "Earth" says nothing more than "Mostly Harmless." In the course of the plot, it is repeatedly made clear just how meaningless the universe is. For example, when Deep Thought, the greatest computer of all time, discovers the answer to "Life, the Universe, and Everything," it turns out to be "Forty-Two." Indeed, Earth is in fact a huge computer, built to discover the real Question of Life, the Universe, and Everything to which "Forty-Two" is the answer. On discovering this, Arthur Dent exclaims that this explains the feeling he has always had, that there is something going on in the universe which nobody would tell him about. "Oh no," says Zaphod Beeblebrox, "That's just perfectly normal paranoia. Everyone in the universe has that." This whole tone of angst is emphasized by the title sequence of the television program: a single spaceman falls, isolated, against a backdrop of distant stars, while a melancholy mandolin plays in the background.

The form of all the incarnations of this story, not least the television version, is comedy-science fiction. A sparsely populated category even in literature, it is even rarer to find films or television programs that twist the logic of the genres involved to provide innovative science fiction that is also very funny. Films such as *Spaceballs,* for example, take rules from established comedy genres (in this case, satire) and use a science fiction iconography as little more than a backdrop. *Red Dwarf,* the BBC's other successful science

The Hitchhiker's Guide to the Galaxy.
Copyright © BBC Photo Library

fiction comedy, relies on well-known science fiction standard scenarios done over as comedy. None of these, were the comedy removed, would stand as notable science fiction in their own right.

Removing the comedy from *Hitchhiker* would also be harmful, but this is because it is a part of the science fiction context, and vice versa. The humor in the program comes from puncturing portentous science fiction themes. For example, there are extraterrestrial beings, but far from being all-knowing or enlightened, they are concerned mainly with drinking and sex. Similarly, Earth is under threat from aliens, not for reasons of power or resources, but simply because it is in the way of a planned bypass.

This comic deflation is an important part of the program's feeling of despair. The jokes build up expectations of transcendent truths, then knock them down with the realization that everything is meaningless after all. *Hitchhiker's* is a consistently comic dystopia.

It is also worth noting that the only constant name through all the manifestations of *Hitchhiker* was one of its original authors, Douglas Adams, who died in 2001. It is possible to make an auteur reading of the program in terms of Adams's other work. He was also a script editor of the BBC's long-standing science fiction series *Doctor Who*. Over the 26 seasons of that program, its style changed considerably, according to its producer and script editor: from space opera to gothic horror, adventure program to serious science fiction. While Adams was working on the program, he edited and wrote some of the most explicitly humorous episodes in that program's history. "City of Death," for example, features an alien creature forcing Leonardo da Vinci to paint multiple copies of the *Mona Lisa* to be sold on the black market; "Shada" was written almost as sitcom, with lines such as, "I am Skagra and I

want the globe!—Well, I'm the Doctor, and you can't have it."

Focusing on Adam's authorship underlines other aspects of *Hitchhiker*. The story has been reused across several different formats. The great efficiency of Adams's recycling is also evident in his earlier work—material from his *Doctor Who* stories "Shada" and "City of Death," for example, is brought wholesale into his other major enterprise: mystery stories about a "holistic" detective called Dirk Gently.

The most distinctive things about the television production of *Hitchhiker* are the sections of the program that come from "the book"—the fictional *Hitchhiker's Guide* itself. As Arthur encounters the various wonders of the Universe, the live action stops and there are short sections of what is essentially comic monologue—the disembodied voice of the *Guide* talks, while its comments are illustrated by "computer graphics" (illustrated line drawings). The structure of these programs is somewhat like that of the musical, in that the narrative stops for a short performance. This gives a unique comic feel to the program.

Ultimately, the most impressive fact about *The Hitchhiker's Guide to the Galaxy* is that so much has so repeatedly been made of so little. This is not to belittle the program in any way, but simply to point out that basically the same narrative was reworked and reissued over more than a decade, consistently finding, with new media, new audiences. This is surely worthy of some respect if for nothing else than being an impressive feat of environmentally sound narrative recycling.

ALAN MCKEE

Cast

The Book	Peter Jones (voice)
Arthur Dent	Simon Jones
Ford Prefect	David Dixon
Trillian	Sandra Dickinson
Zaphod Beeblebrox	Mark Wing-Davey
Marvin	Steven Moore

Producer
Alan Bell

Programming History
Six 35-minute episodes
BBC
January 5, 1981–February 9, 1981

Further Reading

Adams, Douglas, *The Illustrated Hitchhiker's Guide to the Galaxy,* New York: Harmony, 1994

Gaiman, Neil, *Don't Panic: The Official "Hitchhiker's Guide to the Galaxy" Companion,* New York: Pocket Books, 1988

Hockey Night in Canada

Canadian Sports Program

Hockey Night in Canada (*HNIC*) is one of sports broadcasting's longest-running and most groundbreaking programs. The contractual foundation for the series was established on an Ontario golf course in 1929 with a handshake between Toronto Maple Leafs boss Conn Smythe and advertising agency owner Jack MacLaren. The agreement granted MacLaren and his General Motors client the radio rights to Leafs games once Maple Leaf Gardens had been built. The inaugural *General Motors Hockey Broadcast* subsequently aired on November 12, 1931, soon after the Gardens was completed, with Foster Hewitt calling a Leafs/Chicago Black Hawks match-up. That same night, a Montreal contest between the Canadiens and the New York Rangers was also transmitted. By the start of 1933, a 20-station hook-up relayed broadcasts in English from both Toronto and Montreal. A telephone survey estimated the combined per-game audience at just under 1 million—in a country of less than 10 million people, many of whom did not even own radio sets. A coast-to-coast ad hoc network for the program was in place by the end of the 1933–34 season.

From 1936 to 1937, Imperial Oil (another MacLaren client) replaced General Motors when GM of Canada's new president, freshly transferred from the United States, declared that he "did not believe hockey would sell cars." Meanwhile, on January 1, 1937, the Canadian Broadcasting Corporation (CBC) was launched as a public network and assumed national carriage of the program. Sometime thereafter, the series began to be identified as *Hockey Night in Canada*.

HNIC's first publicly televised game originated from Montreal on October 11, 1952. The initial Toronto telecast followed on November 1. The Toronto broadcasts were supervised by George Retzlaff, a 30-year-old technical director from Winnipeg, Manitoba, who had just finished his CBC cameraman's training when he was named head of CBC Sports and producer of *HNIC*. Retzlaff's flair for cogent camera angles and sensitivity to the sound factors of a telecast proved to be vital assets in his new job. Meanwhile, Gerald Renaud, a 24-year-old newspaper sports editor from Ottawa, Ontario, taught himself television and secured the job of Montreal sports producer. Renaud remarked, "The basic principle for the camera positions I wanted to have was an ideal seat from which to watch the game." *HNIC* broadcasts originally utilized three overhead cameras. In 1956 Renaud introduced a fourth "goal camera" at ice level to catch the action around one of the nets. This was a natural extension of his daring method for shooting a game and pioneered a tighter, more adventurous school of hockey directing. Toronto's Retzlaff was an innovator as well. Anticipating the videotape replay, he used a new "hot processor" in 1955–56 to develop a kinescope (film) recording of a goal within 30 seconds for "almost instant" replay. Separately, and in their own ways, Retzlaff and Renaud taught telecasters how to convey the hockey drama. In these early years, Retzlaff was also a master at keeping both the CBC and MacLaren Advertising happy—an essential factor in *HNIC*'s fiscal stability.

Throughout the 1950s the national feed game alternated weekly between Toronto and Montreal, with the opposite game downgraded to regional status for airing within Ontario or Quebec respectively. Because there was no real liaison between the two units, tensions and differences in coverage styles developed. In 1966, therefore, Ted Hough (whose MacLaren vice presidency made him administrative head of *HNIC*) hired TV football director Ralph Mellanby to be executive producer of all *HNIC* telecasts. To make the coverage more interesting, Mellanby began by requiring staff to ledger every stoppage in play and justify what the production featured during each stoppage. He introduced dramatic scripted openings to sell the personality of each particular game in the same way that teasers were used in entertainment series. Mellanby also brought in directional microphones to catch the sounds of crunching bodies and ricocheting pucks and (once colorcasting began after a March 1965 test) put the home team in white uniforms so that succeeding weeks' matches would benefit from the changing hues of different visitors' bright road jerseys.

For many years the television production of *HNIC* dovetailed with the radio coverage. Thus, the series aired on Saturday evenings (with some regional Wednesday games continuing into the 1970s) until Stanley Cup playoff time, when coverage could be almost nightly. However, because of CBC scheduling constraints, the early telecasts did not begin until 9:00 P.M.—the middle of the games' second period. In

Hockey Night in Canada.
Photo courtesy of CBC Sports

1963–64, sign-on was moved up to 8:30 (near the first period's end) and in 1967–68, an 8:00 start inaugurated full-game coverage. In 1995 a Saturday doubleheader pattern began, featuring two regional matches at 7:30 followed by a 10:30 nationwide feed from a western venue.

Financial aspects of the series also evolved. In 1958, the Molson family bought controlling interest in the Montreal Canadiens and used this as leverage to acquire part of the *HNIC* sponsorship for their Molson Breweries. By 1963 their sponsorship share equaled that of Imperial Oil. Ford of Canada also came aboard, initially to air "cover" commercials in provinces where beer advertising was prohibited. Imperial Oil pulled out of partner sponsorship in 1976, as oil shortages made advertising redundant (though it left behind the postgame ritual of picking the "three stars"—a practice begun to promote Imperial's "Three Star" brand of gas). The CBC then assumed Imperial's equity, creating a struggle for control with MacLaren's Canadian Sports Network, the entity that actually produced *HNIC*. Ultimately, Molson chose to eliminate the MacLaren middleman, setting the stage for a 1988 Molson/CBC pact that kept the series out of the hands of eager independent network CTV, and officially retitled it *Molson Hockey Night in Canada on CBC*. The CBC thereby solidified its technical and transmission control of the series while Molson subsidiary Molstar Communications strengthened its role as the proprietary producer and holder of exclusive contracts with the key on-air personalities. Ten years later, brewer Molson's archrival supplanted it as lead sponsor and the program became *Labatt Hockey Night in Canada on CBC*.

Over the years, *HNIC*'s air talent have been among the most famous people in Canada. Pioneering sportscaster Foster Hewitt was joined by son Bill when television coverage was added. Once *HNIC* outgrew radio-TV simulcasts, the elder Hewitt let his son handle the bulk of the TV side while he concentrated on his first love, radio. Foster Hewitt's ability to call a play and anticipate where it was going set the standard for the *HNIC* personalities who have followed him. Among them is Bob Cole, who replaced the ailing Bill Hewitt in 1973. Cole's style is to build his voice in a compelling series of plateaus as a play develops to its climax. Another broadcaster, former Vancouver and Detroit coach Harry Neale, inserts pithy lines into his games ("Turnovers in your own end are like ex-wives. The more you have, the more they cost you"). Dick Irvin, Jr., whose father coached both the Maple Leafs and the Canadiens to Stanley Cups, imbues the broadcasts with a genteel sense of heritage. And commentator and ex-coach Don Cherry is a volatile legend himself. Together with adroit foil and master punster Ron MacLean, Cherry's between-periods *Coach's Corner* often attracts more audience than the game itself, as he rails against the "pukes" and "LA-LA land sissies" who would outlaw on-ice fighting and as he draws blustery, unfavorable comparisons between European players and "good Canadian boys who play hockey the way it's supposed to be played."

PETER B. ORLIK

See also **Sports and Television**

Hosts/Announcers/Commentators
Ward Cornell (1959–72)
Steve Armitage
Dave Hodge (1972)
Ron MacLean (1986–)
Scott Russell (1989–)
Don Cherry (1980–)
Bob Cole (1973–)
Marc Crawford
Chris Cuthbert
John Davidson (1984–86, 1999–)
Patrick Flatley
Danny Gallivan
Foster Hewitt
Kelly Hrudey
Dick Irvin, Jr. (1967–)
Mark Lee

Harry Neale (1977–)
Scott Oake
Don Wittman (1979–)
Bill Hewitt
Greg Millen

Programming History
CBC
October 11, 1952–

Further Reading

Benedict, Michael, and D'Arcy Jenish, *Canada on Ice: 50 Years of Great Hockey,* Toronto: Penguin, 1998
Dryden, Steve, "Harry Neale's Off-Ice Gag Lines and Punch Lines," *The Hockey News* (November 25, 1994)
Duplacey, James, and Joseph Romain, *Toronto Maple Leafs: Images of Glory,* Toronto: McGraw-Hill Ryerson, 1990
Hockey Hall of Fame Magazine: Inaugural Issue (1993)
Young, Scott, *The Boys of Saturday Night,* Toronto: Macmillan, 1990

Hodge, Patricia (1946–)

British Actor

Patricia Hodge is a versatile and familiar face in British television comedy and drama. Her credits extend from the situation comedy *Holding the Fort* to supporting roles in long-running drama serials, such as *Rumpole of the Bailey,* and leading parts in specials and miniseries like *The Life and Loves of a She-Devil.*

Hodge's abilities as an actress were evident even before she completed her training at the London Academy of Music and Dramatic Art, where she won the Eveline Evans Award for Best Actress. Prior to establishing herself in television and film, she gathered valuable stage experience, appearing in major productions of plays as varied as *Rookery Nook, Two Gentlemen of Verona, Hair,* and *Look Back in Anger.* With her vivacious good looks, half-closed eyes, and distinctive sharp-lined mouth, she proved herself equally adept at playing sultry temptresses and outraged harpies with a cruel streak, among other contrasting roles. The one factor common to the majority of her characters has been their patently aristocratic birth.

As a television performer, Hodge was warmly received as well-spoken barrister Phyllida Trant in support of a rascally Leo McKern in *Rumpole of the Bailey,* a role in which she reappeared many times. Her first starring parts came in the situation comedies *The Other 'Arf,* in which she was Member of Parliament John Standing's snobbish, spurned partner Sybilla Howarth, and *Holding the Fort,* a somewhat lackluster series in which she was paired with Peter Davison as a newly married young mother experimenting with role reversal, going back to work while her restless husband stayed at home to do the chores.

By now established as a player of ladies of distinctly elevated backgrounds, Hodge was an obvious choice for Lady Antonia Fraser's aristocratic amateur sleuth Jemima Shore in *Jemima Shore Investigates,* sniffing out crimes among the nobility. Hodge's playing was widely recognized as the best feature of an otherwise very ordinary effort, which, despite her contribution, was fated to be only short-lived. Also wealthy and well-connected was her character in Fay Weldon's far more successful *The Life and Loves of a She-Devil:* the arrogant and man-stealing best-selling novelist Mary Fisher finally brought low by the vengeful Ruth Patchett (played by Julie T. Wallace). Also worthy of note have been her performances as Julia Merrygrove in *Rich Tea and Sympathy* and guest appearances in shows ranging from *Softly, Softly, The Adventures of Sherlock Holmes,* and *Inspector Morse,* to *Victoria Wood: Staying In* and *The Full Wax,* in which she showed a refreshing readiness to allow herself to be made the target of jokes.

DAVID PICKERING

See also **Naked Civil Servant, The; Rumpole of the Bailey**

Patricia Hodge. Born in Cleethorpes, Lincolnshire, England, September 29, 1946. Attended Wintringham Girls' Grammar School, Grimsby; St. Helen's School, Northwood, Middlesex; Maria Grey College, Twickenham; London Academy of Music and Dramatic Art. Married: Peter Owen, 1976; children: Alexander and Edward. Worked as a teacher; stage debut, Traverse

Patricia Hodge.
Courtesy of the Everett Collection

Theatre, Edinburgh, 1971; popular leading lady in television drama series.

Television Series

1978–90	*Rumpole of the Bailey*
1978	*Edward and Mrs. Simpson*
1979–82	*Holding the Fort*
1979–80, 1981	*The Other 'Arf*
1980	*Nanny*
1981	*Winston Churchill: The Wilderness Years*
1982	*Jemima Shore Investigates*

1986	*The Life and Loves of a She-Devil*
1991	*Rich Tea and Sympathy*
1992	*The Cloning of Joanna May*
1996	*The Legacy of Reginald Perrin*
2003	*Sweet Medicine*

Television Specials

1975	*The Girls of Slender Means*
1975	*The Naked Civil Servant*
1978	*The One and Only Phyllis Dixey*
1984	*Hay Fever*
1985	*The Death of the Heart*
1986	*Hotel du Lac*
1988	*Heat of the Day*
1989	*The Shell Seekers*
1989	*Spymaker: The Secret Life of Ian Fleming*
1996	*The Moonstone*
1999	*The People's Passion*
2002	*The Falklands Play*

Films

The Disappearance, 1978; *Rosie Dixon—Night Nurse*, 1978; *The Waterloo Bridge Handicap*, 1979; *The Elephant Man*, 1980; *Heavy Metal*, 1981; *Riding High*, 1981; *Betrayal*, 1983; *Behind Enemy Lines*, 1985; *Dust to Dust*, 1985; *Skin*, 1986; *The Second Stain*, 1986; *92 Grosvenor Street*, 1987; *Sunset*, 1987; *Falcon's Maltester*, 1987; *Thieves in the Night*, 1988; *Just Ask for Diamond*, 1988; *The Leading Man*, 1996; *Jilting Joe*, 1997; *Lies and Whispers*, 1998; *Before You Go*, 2002.

Stage

No-One Was Saved, 1971; *Rookery Nook*, 1972; *Popkiss*, 1972; *Two Gentlemen of Verona*, 1973; *Pippin*, 1973; *Hair*, 1974; *The Beggar's Opera*, 1975; *Pal Joey*, 1976; *Look Back in Anger*, 1976; *Then and Now*, 1979; *The Mitford Girls*, 1981; *As You Like It*, 1983; *Benefactors*, 1984; *Lady in the Dark*, 1988; *Noël and Gertie*, 1989–90; *Shades*, 1992; *Separate Tables*, 1993; *The Prime of Miss Jean Brodie*, 1994; *A Little Night Music*, 1995; *Heartbreak House*, 1997; *Money*, 1999; *Summerfolk*, 1999.

Holbrook, Hal (1925–)

U.S. Actor

Hal Holbrook is a highly respected actor whose career in the television medium began in the 1950s when he appeared on daytime soap operas. However, his creation of the stage play *Mark Twain Tonight!* in 1954 was the endeavor that really admitted him into a highly respected career as a television, film, and stage actor. He has since performed onstage as Twain more than 2,000 times.

Holbrook is known to many TV viewers for his regular supporting role in *Evening Shade,* in which he played a cantankerous older man, a newspaper editor whose son-in-law was played by Burt Reynolds. Holbrook is also known for his portrayal of the cunning lawyer Wild Bill McKenzie in the NBC made-for-TV *Perry Mason Mystery* movies of the 1990s. In these movies, Perry Mason is out of town, and Holbrook's McKenzie handles court cases for him. Another regular recurring role introduced Holbrook to television audiences as Reese Watson, boyfriend of the rambunctious Julia Sugarbaker on *Designing Women* (1986–93). Dixie Carter, who portrayed Julia, is Holbrook's wife. However, Holbrook's acting experience is much more expansive than these television excursions indicate.

Holbrook began his acting career on Broadway in the 1950s, when his characterization of Mark Twain won him international recognition. The one-man drama *Mark Twain Tonight!* premiered on Broadway in 1959, and Holbrook won a Tony Award for the play in 1966. He performed the act on network TV and has continued its performance. He also has acted in many other plays and locations. In 1993, for example, he played Shakespeare's *King Lear* at the Old Globe Theatre in San Diego, California, winning both critical and popular acclaim. While touring with *Mark Twain Tonight!*, Holbrook began acting in cinema. He first appeared in *The Group* (1966) and *Wild in the Streets* (1968).

Holbrook began acting on TV as he simultaneously toured *Mark Twain Tonight!* and acted in film. In 1969 he appeared in the made-for-TV movie *The Whole World Is Watching.* This was followed by a quick succession of other TV movies, such as *A Clear and Present Danger, Travis Logan, D.A., Suddenly Single, Goodbye, Raggedy Ann,* and *That Certain Summer.* Most of his best acting on TV has been in single appearances rather than in series. Many of these performances have been based on historical figures (such as Twain, Lincoln, and Commander Lloyd Bucher of the ship *Pueblo*). He has won Emmy Awards for *The Senator, Pueblo,* and *Sandburg's Lincoln.* His TV credits include working as the sometime-host of *Omnibus* and acting in miniseries such as *North and South.*

Holbrook's work in the theater has been of enormous benefit to his TV performances. He has learned the craft of acting primarily on the stage. In theater, says Holbrook, the actor is responsible for his/her success or failure. Thus, Holbrook's acting has improved

Hal Holbrook.
Courtesy of the Everett Collection

over several decades due to his professional theater work. However, he has consistently come back to the mass medium of TV to entertain audiences in movies and historical dramas, bringing well-crafted acting, intelligent characterizations, and award-winning performances. As he continues his work in TV and film, he also receives acclaim for his work on stage, winning, for example, the 1998 William Shakespeare Award for Classical Theater.

CLAYLAND H. WAITE

Hal (Harold Rowe, Jr.) Holbrook. Born in Cleveland, Ohio, February 17, 1925. Educated at Suffield Academy, 1933–37, Culver Military Academy, 1938–42; Denison University, B.A. with honors, 1948. Married: 1) Ruby Elaine Johnson, 1945 (divorced), children: Victoria and David; 2) Carol Rossen (divorced), child: Eve; 3) Dixie Carter, 1984. Early career in summer stock; developed solo performance, *Mark Twain Tonight!*, 1954; has toured widely in the United States and abroad; in film and television since 1960s. Member, Committee on International Cultural Exchange; National Council of Arts and Government; Mark Twain Memorial Association. Recipient: Vernon Rice Memorial Award, 1959; Outer Circle Award, 1959; Special Citation, New York Drama Critics Circle, 1966; Tony Award, 1966; Torch of Liberty Award, Anti-Defamation League, B'nai Brith, 1972; Emmy Awards, 1970, 1973, 1975; William Shakespeare Award, Shakespeare Theater, Washington, D.C., 1998.

Television Series

1954–59	*The Brighter Day*
1970–71	*The Senator*
1986–93	*Designing Women*
1990–94	*Evening Shade*
2003	*The Street Lawyer*

Television Miniseries

1974	*Sandburg's Lincoln*
1984	*George Washington*
1984	*Celebrity*
1985	*North and South*
1986	*North and South II*
1988	*Mario Puzo's "The Fortunate Pilgrim"*
1997	*Lewis and Clark: The Journey of the Corps of Discovery* (documentary narrator)
2001	*Founding Fathers*

Made-for-Television Movies

1966	*The Glass Menagerie*
1969	*The Whole World Is Watching*
1970	*Travis Logan, D.A.*
1970	*A Clear and Present Danger*
1971	*Suddenly Single*
1971	*Goodbye, Raggedy Ann*
1972	*That Certain Summer*
1973	*Pueblo*
1978	*The Awakening Land*
1979	*When Hell Was in Session*
1979	*Murder by Natural Causes*
1979	*The Legend of the Golden Gun*
1980	*Our Town*
1980	*Off the Minnesota Strip*
1981	*The Killing of Randy Webster*
1984	*The Three Wishes of Billy Grier*
1985	*Behind Enemy Lines*
1986	*Under Siege*
1986	*Dress Gray*
1987	*Plaza Suite*
1988	*I'll Be Home for Christmas*
1988	*Emma: Queen of the South Seas*
1989	*Sorry, Wrong Number*
1989	*Day One*
1990	*A Killing in a Small Town*
1993	*Bonds of Love*
1994	*A Perry Mason Mystery: The Case of the Lethal Lifestyle*
1994	*A Perry Mason Mystery: The Case of the Grimacing Governor*
1995	*She Stood Alone: The Tailhook Scandal*
1995	*A Perry Mason Mystery: The Case of the Jealous Jokester*
1996	*Innocent Victims*
1997	*All the Winters That Have Been*
1997	*The Third Twin*
1998	*Beauty*
1999	*My Own Country*
2000	*A Place Apart*
2001	*Haven*
2001	*The Legend of the Three Trees* (voice only)

Television Special (selected)

1967	*Mark Twain Tonight!*

Films (selected)

The Group, 1966; *Wild in the Streets*, 1968; *The People Next Door*, 1970; *The Great White Hope*, 1970; *They Only Kill Their Masters*, 1972; *Magnum Force*, 1973; *Jonathan Livingston Seagull*, 1973; *The Girl from Petrovka*, 1974; *Midway*, 1976; *All the President's Men* (voice), 1976; *Julia*, 1977; *Rituals*, 1978; *Capricorn One*, 1978; *Natural Enemies*, 1979; *The Kidnapping of the President*, 1980; *The*

Fog, 1980; *Creepshow,* 1982; *The Star Chamber,* 1983; *Girl's Night Out,* 1984; *Wall Street,* 1987; *The Unholy,* 1988; *Fletch Lives,* 1989; *The Firm,* 1993; *Cats Don't Dance* (voice), 1996; *Carried Away,* 1996; *Hercules* (voice), 1997; *Eye of God,* 1997; *Operation Delta Force,* 1997; *Hush,* 1998; *Judas Kiss,* 1998; *The Florentine,* 1999; *The Bachelor,* 1999; *Waking the Dead,* 2000; *Men of Honor,* 2000; *The Majestic,* 2001; *Purpose,* 2002; *Shade,* 2003.

Stage (selected)

Mark Twain Tonight!, 1954–; *Do You Know the Milky Way,* 1961; *After the Fall,* 1964–65; *Marco Millions,* 1964; *Incident at Vichy,* 1964–65; *Tartuffe,* 1965; *The Glass Menagerie,* 1965; *Man of La Mancha,* 1965–71; *The Apple Tree,* 1966–67; *I Never Sang For My Father,* 1968; *Does a Tiger Wear a Necktie?,* 1969; *King Lear; An American Daughter,* 1997.

Publication

Mark Twain Tonight: An Actor's Portrait, Selections from Mark Twain, 1959

Further Reading

Richards, David, "Secret Sharers: Solo Acts in a Confessional Age," *New York Times* (April 14, 1991)

Hollywood and Television

The history of the vital relationship between Hollywood and television began in the 1920s, as radio broadcasting created new opportunities for showmanship and entertainment. Film entrepreneurs eagerly pursued the possibilities that radio awoke for various aspects of the film business, including production, promotion, and exhibition. One of the earliest pioneers was Samuel L. Rothafel, manager of the Capitol Theater in New York City, owned by the Loews Corporation. "Roxy," as he was known, took to the air on November 19, 1922, over WEAF as host of *The Capitol Theater Gang,* a regular Sunday night broadcast of the Capitol Theater's prefeature stage show. Roxy soon became one of radio's first celebrity personalities, and Loew's flagship theater and films received the benefit of national promotion as WEAF became the central hub of the fledgling NBC network. This mutual publicity and benefit showed what a strategic alliance of the two media could accomplish.

Samuel L. Warner parlayed his interest in sound-film technology into a Warner Brothers radio station, KFWB, in 1925, proposing that other studios recognize the potential in this new medium as well. Loew's New York station, WHN, provided one of the few consistent venues for black jazz musicians in the 1920s and early 1930s. Despite some exhibitors' objections, both Paramount and MGM announced their intention to form radio networks in the late 1920s. Paramount eventually became half-owner of CBS, until the studio was forced to sell back its stock in 1932; MGM went on to participate in radio program origination with *The Maxwell House Showboat* in the 1930s; and in a reversal of this pattern RCA, parent of NBC, acquired its own film studio, RKO, in 1929.

With the entry of advertising agencies into radio production in the early 1930s, the somewhat stuffy "potted-palm" aesthetic of NBC gave way to Hollywood-based showmanship, and film stars and film properties made up an increasing proportion of radio's daily schedules. Hollywood became a major broadcast production center in the mid-1930s, with such programs as *Hollywood Hotel,* the *Lux Radio Theater* (hosted by Cecil B. DeMille), and most major variety shows featuring Hollywood talent originating from the West Coast studios of NBC, CBS, and major agencies.

In turn, as radio developed its own roster of stars, the studios capitalized on a long series of radio pictures, from Amos and Andy's *Check and Double Check* in 1932 and the *Big Broadcast* films to the Bob Hope and Bing Crosby "road" movies of the 1940s. The studios also capitalized on the promotional capacity of radio in the form of spot advertising, using audio-only trailers as an important part of film promotion.

This lucrative and mutually beneficial relationship, combined with Federal Communications Commission

(FCC) regulation, kept Hollywood from developing its potential for competition with network broadcasting by restricting the use of recorded material for syndication. Not until the advent of television did film itself present a strong alternative to provision of live programming via networks. Paramount, Warner Brothers, Loew's-MGM, and 20th Century-FOX had all opened stations or applied for television station licenses in the late 1940s, but indications from the FCC that movie studios would not be looked upon favorably in postfreeze allocations led to experimentation with other methods of capitalizing on the television medium.

Hollywood studios plunged into television on three fronts: first, in the development of pay television systems in the late 1940s, designed to provide feature films on a box-office basis; second, in experiments with theater television, a method for projecting television onto movie theater screens; and third, in direct production for television, both network and syndicated. Paramount experimented with its Telemeter pay-per-view system, along with Zenith's Phonevision and the Skiatron Corporation's over the air technology; FCC discouragement of this potentially powerful competition to network broadcasting prevented pay television from becoming a reality and allowed the cable industry to find a foothold. Both FOX and Paramount attempted to develop theater television, but the expansion of individual TV set sales, combined with the FCC's refusal to allocate part of the mostly unused UHF band for transmission, brought this shortlived technology to a halt. By the early 1950s the studios had turned to television production, led by Hollywood independents but culminating in the Disney/ABC alliance that produced *Disneyland* in 1954. Warner Brothers and MCA/Universal followed, as network expansion and consolidation allowed a shift from live programming to filmed series. By 1960, 40 percent of network programming was produced by the major Hollywood studios and the proportion continued to grow.

The FCC's institution of the Financial Interest and Syndication (Fin-Syn) Rules in the mid-1970s finally allowed the production companies to break free of network dominance of the lucrative syndication market. Combined with the growth of cable, where the federal Must-Carry Rule helped provide new audiences for independent stations, the market for Hollywood-produced series, specials, miniseries, and movie packages skyrocketed in the 1980s. Pay-cable companies such as HBO and Showtime provided new funds for production capital.

By the late 1980s, history had come full circle, as Rupert Murdoch's vertically integrated Twentieth Century-FOX corporation formed the first successful fourth network in U.S. broadcasting history. The new FOX network capitalized on a ready supply of in-house programming, newly powerful independent stations, niche marketing to youth, and favorable FCC regulation in order to prove that the Hollywood film industry and network television broadcasting had only remained separate for 40 years as a result of heavy legislative intervention.

Paramount and Warner Brothers were not slow to take heed, starting up two new networks, the United Paramount Network (UPN, which drew on the success of the syndicated *Star Trek* series) and the WB (geared primarily to adolescent audiences), in January 1995. That same year, a wave of mergers hit the industry as Westinghouse Corporation bought the CBS network and Time Warner merged with Turner Broadcasting. Disney's purchase of ABC in 1996 confirmed the studio-network alliance. This alliance also relied on the rewriting of ownership rules in the Telecommunications Act of 1996, which loosened caps on the number of stations an individual or company could own.

By the late 1990s, as cable, telephone, computer and broadcasting companies struggled for favorable alliances with Hollywood-based creative organizations, the relationship of Hollywood and television continued its cruise at warp speed into the integrated and interactive sphere of cyberspace. Upstart Internet provider America OnLine (AOL) purchased entertainment behemoth Time Warner to become AOL Time Warner, a merger which ultimately failed. The potential for high-speed cable access at least partially drove the deal; AOL controlled 54 percent of the Internet access market, while Time Warner Cable reached over 20 percent of the U.S. public with valuable broadband connections. Viacom Corporation, the cable, film, and television production empire and parent of Paramount, purchased CBS in 1999, finally bringing CBS and Paramount together in the networking business again. However, since ownership of more than one television network was illegal under current ownership restrictions, Viacom (which already owned UPN) at once set about lobbying for a further relaxation of the rules, and in 2001 it received permission from the Federal Communications Commission to own both entities. Networks vied for the most prominent web presence, from Warner Brothers' leading position on AOL to Disney's purchase of the web portal SNAP in 1998, and ABC/Disney's creation of the Go Network, a new portal launched in 1999. However, both Warner and Disney had retreated from the portal business by 2001, even as the new synergy produced glossy websites featuring current film and television productions.

Synergy could have unanticipated results. For example, Twentieth Century-FOX attracted notoriety early in 2000 when it sought to curb websites featuring its popular series *Buffy the Vampire Slayer, The Simpsons,* and *The X Files,* as fans began to circulate their own video clips, audio segments, and transcripts of the show. These and many other ownership, copyright, and competitive issues promised to trouble the now fully integrated film and television industries of the United States in the 21st century, even as those industries continue to expand across the globe.

MICHELE HILMES

See also **FOX Broadcasting Company; Time Warner; UPN Television Network; WB Network**

Further Reading

Anderson, Christopher, *Hollywood TV: The Studio System in the Fifties,* Austin: University of Texas Press, 1994
Balio, Tino, editor, *Hollywood in the Age of Television,* Boston: Unwin Hyman, 1990
Hilmes, Michele, *Only Connect: A Cultural History of Broadcasting in the United States,* Belmont, California: Wadsworth, 2001

Holocaust

U.S. Miniseries

Holocaust first aired on NBC from April 16–19, 1978. The most obvious comparison for this nine-and-a-half-hour, four-part series was with *Roots,* which had aired on ABC a year earlier and on which *Holocaust*'s director, Marvin Chomsky, had worked. Like *Roots*' saga of American slavery, *Holocaust*'s story of Jewish suffering before and during World War II apparently flew in the face of network programming wisdom, which advised against presenting tales of virtually unrelieved or inexplicable misery. While *Holocaust* was a smaller ratings success than was *Roots* (it drew a 49 audience share to *Roots*' 66), NBC estimated after the 1979 rebroadcast that as many as 220 million viewers in the United States and Europe had seen *Holocaust.*

Produced by Herbert Brodkin, *Holocaust* contrasts the interlocking fates of two German families, the Jewish Weisses and the Nazi Dorfs. At the time of the series' first airing, critics sniped at the improbability of the proposition that so small a cast of characters would be witnesses to so great a number of the major milestones in the destruction of European Jewry, among them the confabulations of the architects of Hitler's Final Solution, the slaughter at Babi Yar, the Warsaw Ghetto uprising, and the liberation of Auschwitz. In another sense, however, this emphasis on blood ties conforms to this drama's major artistic strategy, the employment (overemployment, James Lardner complained in the *New Republic*) of symbol and archetype. Thus, the Holocaust is, in this conception, the destruction of a family within Europe, just as the infamous smokestacks of the death camps may be emblematized by a moment when the small daughter of Nazi bureau-

crat Erik Dorf stuffs a sheaf of Weiss family photographs into the parlor stove and shuts the door firmly upon them.

On its U.S. debut, *Holocaust* met with a generally positive response but not with unanimous approbation. Holocaust survivor Elie Wiesel protested in the *New York Times* that it was "untrue, offensive, cheap." Reviewers generally applauded the cast (which included Meryl Streep, Ian Holm, Fritz Weaver, Rosemary Harris, and Michael Moriarty, who won an Emmy for his portrayal of Dorf) and praised Gerald Green's script, an overnight best-seller when published in novel form as a tie-in. Still, several critics described a curious "emptiness" at the drama's heart, emanating from what they identified as excessive melodrama and flat characters who seemed designed to represent particular classes and types more than individuals. Moreover, many viewers were particularly dismayed by the content of the commercial interruptions, which at best seemed to strike a cheerfully vulgar note inappropriate to the subject matter of the series and at other times appeared, horrifyingly, to parody it, as in the juxtaposition of a Lysol ad alerting viewers to the need to combat kitchen odors, with a scene in which Adolf Eichmann complains that the crematoria smells make dining at Auschwitz unpleasant.

When the series aired in West Germany on the Third (Regional) Network in January 1979 (a forum apparently designed to lessen its impact), however, viewer response was little short of stunning. According to German polls intended to measure audience reaction before, immediately after, and several months after

Holocaust, Meryl Streep, 1978.
Courtesy of the Everett Collection

Holocaust appeared, this single television event had a significant effect on West Germans' understanding of this episode in the history of their country. Despite strong opposition to the broadcast before it aired, some 15 million West Germans (roughly half the adult population) tuned in to one or more episodes, breaking what Judith Doneson calls "a thirty-five-year taboo on discussing Nazi atrocities." Among those who saw the series, the number favoring the failed German-resistance plot of 20 July 1944 to assassinate Hitler rose dramatically. *Variety* reported that "70 percent of those in the 14 to 19 age group declared that they had learned more from the shows about the horrors of the Nazi regime than they had learned in all their years of studying West German history." Such was the public response that the West German government promptly canceled the statute of limitations for Nazi war crimes, formerly scheduled to expire at the end of 1979.

The mixture of prime-time commercialism and emotional commitment that informed *Holocaust* goes far to explaining both its wide appeal (and, often, powerful effect) and the disappointment it represented for its detractors. Filmed, unlike *Roots,* on location—in Mauthausen concentration camp, among other places—and reportedly a shattering experience for those who made

it, especially for the actors portraying Nazis, the series allowed its producers to take pride in the quality of the research involved; they were creating, they noted, a major television event designed to shape the historical perceptions of millions. But ultimately, it would seem, the critiques of the series arise from the fact that it is no more than the "major television event" that NBC assuredly achieved.

ANNE MOREY

See also **Docudrama; History and Television; Racism, Ethnicity, and Television**

Cast

Adolph Eichmann	Tom Bell
Rudi Weiss	Joseph Bottoms
Helena Slomova	Tovah Feldshuh
Herr Palitz	Marius Goring
Berta Weiss	Rosemary Harris
Heinrich Himmler	Ian Holm
Uncle Sasha	Lee Montague
Erik Dorf	Michael Moriarty
Marta Dorf	Deborah Norton
Uncle Kurt Dorf	Robert Stephens
Inga Helms Weiss	Meryl Streep
Moses Weiss	Sam Wanamaker
Reinhard Heydrich	David Warner
Josef Weiss	Fritz Weaver
Karl Weiss	James Woods
Hoefle	Sean Arnold
Hans Frank	John Bailey
Anna Weiss	Blanche Baker
Frau Lowy	Kate Jaenicke
Dr. Kohn	Charles Kovin

Producers

Herbert Brodkin, Robert "Buzz" Berger

Programming History

NBC

April 16, 1978	8:00–11:00
April 17, 1978	9:00–11:00
April 18, 1978	9:00–11:00
April 19, 1978	8:30–11:00

Further Reading

Doneson, Judith E., *The Holocaust in American Film,* Philadelphia, Pennsylvania: Jewish Publication Society, 1987
Guild, Hazel, "Germany and the TV *Holocaust,*" *Variety* (May 23, 1979)
Langer, Lawrence, "The Americanization of the Holocaust on Stage and Screen," in *From Hester Street to Hollywood,*

edited by Sarah Blacher Cohen, Bloomington: Indiana University Press, 1983

Lardner, James, "Making History," *New Republic* (May 13, 1978)

Morrow, Lance, "Television and the Holocaust," *Time* (May 1, 1978)

Neusner, Jacob, *Strangers at Home: "The Holocaust," Zionism, and American Judaism,* Chicago: University of Chicago Press, 1981

Rich, Frank, "Reliving the Nazi Nightmare," *Time* (April 17, 1978)

Rosenfeld, Alvin H., "The Holocaust in American Popular Culture," *Midstream* (June–July 1983)

Waters, Harry F., and Betsy Carter, "*Holocaust* Fallout," *Newsweek* (May 1, 1978)

Wiesel, Elie, "Trivializing the Holocaust: Semi-Fact and Semi-Fiction," *New York Times* (April 16, 1978)

Home Box Office

In the mid-1980s, FOX Broadcasting's Barry Diller announced somewhat hyperbolically that if someone didn't do something soon, Home Box Office (HBO) would take over Hollywood. Former HBO executive George Mair describes the company as "The Cash Cow That Almost Ate Hollywood." How did a pay cable company, which did not exist fifteen years before, suddenly come to this position of power in the century-old American audio-visual entertainment industry?

Home Box Office, now a subsidiary of AOL Time Warner, currently delivers movies, sports, and original series programming to 35 million households in the United States. This is about a third of the audience for broadcast network television, which currently reaches approximately 100 million households. The difference, however, is that the HBO households pay over $10 per month for the service, generating some $4 billion in revenue every year. For this reason, HBO is able to finance a tremendous percentage of Hollywood films each year.

In addition, HBO produces some of the highest-gloss series in the history of American television, including its break-out sitcoms (*The Larry Sanders Show, Sex and the City,* and *Curb Your Enthusiasm*) and hour-long dramas (*Oz, The Sopranos,* and *Six Feet Under*). HBO's in-house programming ranges from high-profile miniseries (*From the Earth to the Moon* and *Band of Brothers*) to Made-For-TV movies (*Conspiracy, The Laramie Project*). Along with PBS's *Frontline,* HBO represents the industry standard in documentaries. Under the direction of Sheila Nevins, HBO's "America Undercover" series provides American documentary filmmakers with a showcase for their work. HBO's sports documentary shows—*On the Record with Bob Costas* and *Real Sports with Bryant Gumbel*—represent the only critical examinations of sports in American life on American televi-

sion. With the departure of ABC's *Wide World of Sports,* boxing coverage on HBO (and pay-cable rival Showtime) is a remaining remnant of what used to be a centerpiece of American broadcasting. HBO's long-standing commitment to stand-up comedy is maintained via stand-up performance records of all major American comedians (including Jerry Seinfeld, Larry David, and Ellen DeGeneres) and *The Dennis Miller Show.*

The basic idea for what has become the HBO empire began with Chuck Dolan, owner of Sterling Manhattan Cable, who believed he could deliver movies and sports programming to cable subscribers via what he then called "the Green Channel." In November 1972, under the direction of Gerald Levin, this dream came to fruition, when HBO delivered a National Hockey League game broadcast from Madison Square Garden and the 1971 Paul Newman film, *Sometimes a Great Notion,* to a handful of cable subscribers in Wilkes-Barre, PA. In the early 1970s, as a program broker (delivering Hollywood films from the studios to cable subscribers), HBO struggled, relying on the few films it could afford, playing them repeatedly throughout each month of service. As a result, HBO's business model was crippled by "churning," a term describing the high turn-over rate for dissatisfied subscribers. For every two new subscribers HBO would sign on, only one would remain at the end of the month.

The turning point came in September 1975, when the company was the first to effectively make use of satellite technology for program delivery. HBO revolutionized the industry by using the RCA satellite, SATCOM I, to deliver "The Thrilla in Manila" (the World Heavyweight title fight between Joe Frazier and Muhmmad Ali, fought in Manila) to a national audience in the United States. Previously, network television had to film such a sporting event, fly the film to the United States, and broadcast it days later. With the satellite technology, the cable programmer was able to deliver the Ali-Frazier fight live.

The prescient use of satellite technology rapidly pushed HBO to prominence. In October 1977, HBO turned its first profit for its parent company, Time Inc. With a stable financial position, the cable network began shifting its business model from one of program brokering to program development and production. As early as 1975, HBO had begun original television programming, with its innovative comedy shows, *Standing Room Only* and *On Location,* which gave stand-up comics Robin Williams and Steve Martin their early breaks. In 1978, HBO began "pre-buy" financing of Hollywood movies, which entailed providing significant production up-front financing to independent film producers, with the proviso that HBO would have exclusive rights to the film's run on pay cable television. Using this business model, HBO has become the single largest financier of movies in Hollywood.

In the 1980s, HBO's financial position was threatened by the increasing market penetration of the videocassette recorder. Earlier release dates of Hollywood films to videotape, available for rental at local video stores, threatened to render HBO, primarily a movie supplier, obsolete. Rather than fight the trend, as did most of the other players in Hollywood, HBO rebuilt its business model to incorporate home video to its advantage. First, HBO intensified its role in production of feature-length films. In 1983, HBO produced *The Terry Fox Story,* the first made-for-pay-TV movie. Secondly, HBO moved into the video business itself, as a way of releasing its original productions. Third, HBO began to intensify its role in original series television production.

It is this last strategy that became most noteworthy in the 1990s. HBO began such original series programming with sitcoms, the staple genre of American network television. *Dream On* premiered in July 1990, but it was with *The Larry Sanders Show* (1992–98) that HBO achieved, in Deborah Jaramillo's words, its "flagship series." Coupled with its increasing prominence in made-for-pay-television movies (including *Barbarians at the Gate* and *Stalin*), HBO won 17 Emmys in 1993 (the second-highest awarded network that year, NBC, received 16).

HBO's strategy for competing with network television sitcoms first involved summer counter-programming. *Dream On*'s 1990 first season ran from July to October, and *The Larry Sanders Show*'s 1993 second season ran from June to September, thus exhibiting new episodes against the network's summer re-runs.

By the late 1990s, HBO had perfected a full-blown counter-programming strategy, featuring seasons with 13 episodes only. Equally important, HBO series explicitly featured content not available on network television, as in the frank sexuality of *Sex and the City.*

In July 1997, HBO premiered its first foray into hour-long drama, with Tom Fontana's *Oz,* a violent and graphic depiction of life inside a prison. It was with *The Sopranos,* however, that HBO solidified its reputation in hour-long drama. Debuting in January 1999, *The Sopranos* brought a cinematic genre—the gangster film—to television, hybridizing this with a melodrama about the private lives of a mafia family. HBO used the break-out success of the show to announce itself as delivering a product distinct from network television, best exemplified in their motto, "It's Not TV, It's HBO."

Under Chris Albrecht, head of original programming, HBO continues to glean tremendous critical acclaim for its series television. At the 2000 Emmy awards, 42 percent of all nominations went to HBO shows. In October 2000, *Curb Your Enthusiasm* featured Larry David, the co-creator of *Seinfeld,* in an experimental mockumentary sit-com format, replaying in his "real" life the comedic situations that had formed the central narrative content of *Seinfeld.* In the summer of 2001, HBO debuted its third hour-long drama, *Six Feet Under,* filmmaker Alan Ball's melodrama about a family living and working in a funeral home.

The fact of the matter is that these shows are much more complexly linked to network television than HBO's marketing scheme suggests. The shows are outstanding sitcoms and dramas, comparable to such historically significant programs as *Hill Street Blues* and *St. Elsewhere,* and defined by academic critics as "quality television." However, HBO exploits its difference from network television as an issue of quality only when it is critically advantageous to do so. In other venues—as in the soft-core porn series *G-String Divas*—such a distinction is used for titillation. This is not to say that *Divas,* which represents the lives of pole-dancing strippers, is indefensible. Unlike puritanical network television, the women on *Divas* refreshingly discuss sexuality-as-performance in straightforward, non-censorious terms.

However, most of the HBO original series—most crucially *Sex and the City*—are caught in this contradiction. On the one hand, the series is a continuation of the strain of television melodrama begun by Darren Star on FOX's critically reviled *Melrose Place.* Yet despite *Sex and the City*'s requisite featuring of breasts and unbridled sexual activity, the show does examine, in complex ways, a post-feminist, consumerist female community of friends.

Thus, HBO offers programs as interesting as anything on network television (but not necessarily more so). Delivered without commercials, the programs perhaps seem of higher quality, less poisoned by the crass commercialism of their network peers. The fact that one is paying over $10 a month for the privilege of viewing these television shows is, of course, the repressed term in this equation.

WALTER METZ

See also **Cable Networks; Pay Cable;** *Sex and the City; Sopranos, The*

Further Reading

Gershon, Richard A., "Pay Cable Television: A Regulatory History," *Communications and the Law* 12 (1990)

Jaramillo, Deborah L., "The Family Racket: AOL Time Warner, HBO, The Sopranos, and the Construction of a Quality Brand," *Journal of Communications Inquiry* 26/1 (January 2002)

Mair, George, *Inside HBO: The Billion Dollar War between HBO, Hollywood, and the Home Video Revolution,* New York: Dodd, Mead, 1988

Mullen, Megan, "The Pre-History of Pay Cable Television: An Overview and Analysis," *Historical Journal of Film, Radio, and Television* 19/1 (March 1999)

Wasko, Janet, *Hollywood in the Information Age: Beyond the Silver Screen,* Austin: University of Texas Press, 1994

Home Shopping

The concept of home shopping originated in 1977 by chance. An advertiser on WWQT, an AM radio station in Clearwater, Florida, could not pay his bill and, in lieu of cash, the station owner agreed to accept 112 electric can openers, which he auctioned off on the air. The can openers sold out quickly, and the station realized they were onto something. WWQT was owned by Lowell "Bud" Paxson, who created a regularly scheduled radio show that, in 1981, gave birth to a Tampa Bay-based cable access television show called the Home Shopping Channel. In 1982, the Home Shopping Channel held a permanent spot on the Tampa Bay television system. By 1986, the Home Shopping Channel evolved into the publicly traded Home Shopping Network and a muti-billion dollar industry.

The key to the success of the Home Shopping Network and its competitors, QVC and Value Vision, is that they are experts at selling materials to people, said Jack Kirby, president of HSNi (the interactive division of the Home Shopping Network). Josh Bernoff, a principal analyst at Forrester Research, says that the home shopping networks use hosts who are successful salespeople, appealing and effective screen layouts, reasonable and accurate pricing, and techniques that are very effective at turning viewers into buyers.

A particular challenge for the television retailer is to convince a viewer to buy. Doug Rose, vice president of brand merchandising and development for QVC, says the real task is to create trust between the viewer, the host, and the network. The customer needs to be confident they will like the item once they receive it at home. Rose stresses that home shopping networks need to be advocates for consumers. Quality assurance processes, fact-checking items and torture-testing items to make sure they will stand up to their warranties is absolutely vital to a home shopping industry. This means that creating a level of trust with the consumers can turn them into repeat customers. Of course, offering an interesting selection of goods and creative packaging is also important.

Home Shopping Network (HSN), QVC, and Value Vision are the three largest networks in home shopping. The sales figures for these three networks combined are approximately $5 billion, and they reach more than 250 million households worldwide.

HSN is a division of USA Networks Inc's Interactive Group. Barry Diller is USA Networks' Chairman and CEO. In 2001, HSN celebrated its 25th anniversary. Today, HSN is a multi-channel retailer with a thriving television, catalog, and web business (at www.hsn.com). The company's e-commerce website, launched in September 1999, became profitable within three months by giving consumers an incremental shopping platform to the already existing television and direct mail channels.

HSN has international networks in Spain, Germany, France, Italy, the Netherlands, and the United Kingdom.

HSN offers products in the following categories: home and entertainment, health and beauty, fashion and jewelry, and electronics. They have also formed

Home Shopping Network.
Courtesy of the Everett Collection

partnerships and strategic alliances to offer customers a greater variety of goods. The alliances include: sports (NFL, NBA, NASCAR, PGA); entertainment (Nickelodeon, Universal); technology (Intel, IBM, Sharp, Sony, Hewlett Packard); fashion (Marie Claire, Randolph Duke); and media services (Vica, MCI, Time, Inc).

The second home shopping network to appear on television was QVC, Inc. Joseph Segel, founder of the Franklin Mint, founded the company in 1986. QVC established a new record in American business history for first full year fiscal sales by a new public company, with revenues over $112 million. By 1993, QVC, based in West Chester, Pennsylvania, had become the number one televised shopping service in sales and profits in the United States by reaching over 80 percent of all U.S. cable homes and three million satellite dishes. By 2000, its turnover had reached more than $3.5 billion. QVC claims to be the world's largest electronic retailer.

QVC is a virtual shopping mall, where customers can and do shop at any hour, at the rate of two customers per second. Themed programs are broadcast live 24 hours a day, seven days a week to 77 million households in the United States. Related channels in the group also broadcast to some 8.2 million households in the United Kingdom and the Republic of Ireland, and more than 27 million households in Germany.

QVC employs more than 100 buyers source new products from around the world—at least 250 new products are introduced on air each week. The channels' categories include home and kitchen goods, consumer electronics, and jewelry—the latter category accounts for 32 percent of screen time, and has made QVC one of the largest retailers of gold and silver jewelry in the world.

QVC's current customer base spans all socioeconomic groups, linked only by the fact that they have a cable service subscription. Because the audience for each QVC program is driven by product, demographics vary significantly from one hour to the next. The total customer base is about 20 million people in four countries.

Value Vision is currently the third-largest home shopping network, and is based in Minneapolis. In 1999 it recorded sales of $274.8 million, reaching £470 million in 2001. In 1997, NBC bought a 36 percent stake in the company, becoming Value Vision's negotiator with cable operators. Since Value Vision's reach is less than half of QVC's, the company relies on affiliating with a local broadcaster to take advantage of the must-carry provision of the 1992 Cable Act. The must-carry rules require cable operators to carry all stations within their community that meet certain required criteria, which includes historic carriage of the station on the system, a station's local service to the cable community, carriage of other similar stations in the market, and evidence of viewership in the community.

Cable operators, which use analog systems with limited available space, argued that home shopping channels were not operating in the public interest. Because of this, they contended that these local broadcast stations, which for the most part had weak signals and small audiences, did not qualify for must-carry status. The FCC ruled that stations carrying home shopping channels—assuming they deliver the requisite signal strength and meet all the other requirements for must-carry—were operating in the public's interest and were eligible for carriage.

In June 2001, Value Vision was renamed SHOPNBC. NBC announced a deal with Wink Communications, Inc. that gives viewers the option to buy merchandising by clicking their remote control any time of the day or night, activating a purchase using a pre-authorized credit card. SHOPNBC pays Wink a fee for each transition. It is up to Wink to determine how it shares that cut with its direct-broadcast satellite or cable-operator affiliates. This interactive-television partnership is currently available in more than 3 million homes, the majority of which are DirecTV Inc. subscribers. DirecTV does not presently handle commerce purchases in real time, so SHOPNBC does not make all of its items available for purchase via remote.

The Enhanced Broadcast Technologies group at SHOPNBC has also produced interactive content for programs on the NBC broadcast network, including *The Tonight Show* and *Will & Grace*. NBC also produces blocks of programming for companies that want to sell products themselves, presumably going after existing NBC advertisers.

IN 2002, SHOPNBC bought FanBuzz, which will move the network into sports-merchandise sales. FanBuzz operated the website www.teamstore.com and the CustomFan service, allowing online sales of sports clothing. About 90 percent of the business was in fulfillment sales for other clients, including ESPN, CNN, *Sports Illustrated* and the *Los Angeles Times.*

When the World Wide Web emerged in the mid-1990s, home shopping channels were fearful that the television retailing business would decrease. However, the networks found that the television growth rate accelerated as a result of Internet sales, and both modes of selling have become profitable. The core of the business, however, remains television.

The largest expenses for the home shopping networks are the payments to cable operators and marketing expenses. In 2001, these networks paid an average of $4.1 million to cable operators, which increased to $35.9 million in 2002.

GAYLE M. POHL

Further Reading

Advanstar Communications, "E-Retailing: A Brave New Money-Making World," *Global Cosmetic Industry,* June 1999

Broadcasting Publications, "When a Network is not a Network—FCC Rules that Univision, HSN are not Networks," *Broadcasting,* March 1989

Cahners Business Information, "Value Vision Network becomes SHOPNBC," *Broadcasting & Cable,* March 2001

Cahners Business Information, "USA networks to take $100M charge," *Multichannel News,* March 2002

Cahners Business Information, " Home Shopping Network," *Multichannel News,* March 1999

Cahners Business Information "Cash Flow Up 15% at USA," *Multichannel News,* February 1999

Dempsey, J., "What Diller Hath Wrought," *Variety,* December 2001

Economist Newspaper Ltd. "Home Alone? Home Shopping," *The Economist,* October 1996

EPM Communications, "HSN and ABC Market Soap-Opera Jewelry," *Marketing to Women: Addressing Women and Women's Sensibilities,* " September 2001

Farrell, M., "Value Vision Gets Sporty with FanBuzz Purchase," *Multichannel News,* March 2002

Gorham, J., "Yell and Sell," *Forbes,* October 2001

Grotticelli, M., and K. Kerschbaumer, " Slow and Steady," *Broadcasting & Cable,* July 2001

Hogan, M., "SHOPNBC Winks at ITV," *Multichannel News,* June 2001

McAdams, D. "Not Just Cubic Zirconium," *Broadcasting & Cable,* April 2000

Mack, A., "Roxy.com TV Programs to Debut this Week," *Media Week,* April 2000

Petrozzello, D., "HSN, Univision Go Shopping; Two Companies will Launch Spanish-Language Shopping Channel," *Broadcast & Cable,* November 1997

Sullivan, S., " Shopping Channels: Less of a Hard Sell," *Broadcasting & Cable,* November 2000

United Press, "Homeshopping Network Goes to China," *United Press International,* July 2000

United Press, " AM Minnesota Report/Take Two," *United Press International,* September 1999

Home Video

In the early 1960s, major players in the U.S. electronics and entertainment industries began making plans to develop some form of home video system. All of these projects conceived of home video as a playback-only system, employing some kind of disc. The basic assumption was that consumers would purchase copies of programs on videodiscs just as they purchased phonograph records. In this way, the program producers could retain strict control over the duplication and sale of their copyrighted material. A machine that recorded could only mean one thing: piracy of valuable rights. To U.S. interests, videotape was strictly a professional medium.

Japanese corporations, however, sought to develop video recorders for consumer use. Sony was the leader in this effort, making brief attempts to open the home market with open-reel videotape recorders (VTRs) in the mid-1960s, and 3/4-inch U-Matic video cassette recorders (VCRs) in the early 1970s. These formats had been developed with home video in mind, and although they were either too crude, complex, cumbersome, or costly to catch on with consumers, both were successes in educational and industrial markets, allowing Sony to continue development work.

The U.S. video ventures tended to be over-promoted and under-engineered—more hype than substance. RCA began making grand pronouncements about its soon-to-be released videodisc in 1969, yet the device did not reach the market until 1981. One of the factors that plagued the development of videodisc systems was the chicken-and-egg nature of the relationship between software and hardware. Hardware producers were unwilling to invest major efforts if software was not available, and software producers were unwilling to commit production to an untried system.

Sony did not have this problem. Sony CEO Akio Morita had long contended that video's consumer potential lay in its ability to free viewers from the rigid time constraints of the broadcast schedule. "People do not have to read a book when it's delivered," he argued, "Why should they have to see a TV program when it's delivered?" In 1975 Sony introduced the Betamax VCR with an ad campaign positioning it as a product with a unique single purpose: time-shift viewing.

Sony did not suggest that viewers might then save the tapes, and begin building a library of programs.

However, this prospect occurred almost immediately to MCA president Sidney Sheinberg when he saw the first Betamax ads. MCA, the parent company of Universal studios, was a major entertainment copyright holder—and was also seeking to develop its own videodisc system. MCA sued Sony, arguing that the Betamax encouraged copyright infringement, and seeking to have the VCRs withdrawn from the market.

The Betamax VCR system soon faced opposition in the market as well. Sony's more powerful Japanese competitors, Matsushita (the parent company of Panasonic) and Hitachi, developed their own video cassette recording devices, this time using the VHS system, a format that was developed by JVC and was incompatible with the Sony system.

Although early VCRs in any format were expensive luxury items restricted mainly to the relatively well-to-do, they sold well enough for the manufacturers to expand production, and worry the domestic videodisc forces. In 1978, inside buzz in the consumer electronics industry held that RCA was about to ship disc players with prices so cheap, and with so much software and marketing power behind them, that the Japanese upstarts would be sent packing, and VCRs would go the way of 8-track tape players. It did not happen. Instead, RCA, General Electric, Magnavox, and other domestic companies entered the video business by marketing VCRs manufactured by Matsushita and Hitachi. These companies were willing to slap U.S. brand names on their machines because they could garner significant sales without spending large sums on promotion or establishing new dealer networks.

The verdict in the original Betamax case was delivered in 1979. Sony won. MCA appealed, backed by the larger forces of the Motion Picture Association of America and a coalition of copyright holders in other media. In 1981 the U.S. Court of Appeals reversed the earlier decision, but it did not order the Betamax withdrawn, leaving the matter of penalty to be decided later. Although still not common household items, VCRs had by this time won enough favor with the public that it would have been politically unwise to prohibit them. No action was taken, pending Sony's appeal to the U.S. Supreme Court.

When RCA finally released its long-awaited videodisc player that same year, the cost was near that of a VCR, the picture was mediocre, and the discs began to wear out after a number of plays. The public reacted with a collective yawn. The RCA videodisc was the only home video product created directly by a major U.S. corporation ever to reach the market.

Although a number of bills dealing with VCR development and use had been introduced in Congress, none passed. In 1984 the Supreme Court reversed the Appeals Court decision in the Betamax case, ruling in Sony's favor on the grounds that home video recording fell under the "fair use" provisions of copyright law. However, Sony's legal triumph was tempered by setbacks in the market. Almost all the U.S. companies marketing VCRs had opted for the VHS format, and Betamax machines had steadily lost market share.

VCR use continued to move away from mere time-shifting, and in the format wars between the Beta and VHS systems, software was the deciding factor. And software in this case meant movies. When the Betamax appeared, the movie industry had little interest in releasing old films on videocassette. After all, the studios and trade organizations were supporting the suit to get rid of the Betamax, and still had visions of videodiscs dancing in their heads.

Nevertheless, a Michigan entrepreneur named Andre Blay decided to start a pre-recorded videocassette business. He began soliciting the studios, seeking to purchase the rights to distribute films on tape. All but one rejected him. Strapped for cash at the time, Twentieth Century Fox signed on, and in late 1976 Blay began selling tapes through a video club arrangement advertised in *TV Guide*. The promotion was an instant success. Blay and Fox made more money than they had imagined, and the other film companies slowly but surely followed them to this new source of profit.

Because the first films on video were prepared for an untested market, they were produced on a small scale and were quite expensive. Like the first VCRs, they seemed to be luxury items with a limited market. However, another entrepreneur struck on the idea of acquiring a library of tapes and renting them out for a reasonable fee. This seemed like a good idea to many would-be small businesspeople, and video rental businesses quickly spread across the United States. "Mom and pop" video shops seemed to appear on every local corner.

For all the power of the large corporations that created the hardware, this grassroots phenomenon of tape rental was the key to the diffusion of the VCR. With inexpensive software readily available for rent, VCR ownership became more desirable. Rising VCR sales drew more video titles into release and lowered rental prices, which helped VCR sales grow again, and so on. Unfortunately for Sony, the fact that a majority of VCR sales were VHS units led video-shop owners to

stock more VHS titles, which led to even more VHS sales. The Beta format was left on the wrong end of the economic spiral. By 1986, with basic models priced under $200 in discount stores, the VCR was no longer a luxury, but a household staple, a piece of the common culture. As the decade turned, Sony quietly folded Beta production and began manufacturing VHS machines.

Ironically, perhaps, most VCR owners in North America rarely use the machines for time-shifting (and their VCR clocks will do nothing but blink "12:00" on into eternity). Instead, consumers there use VCRs primarily for the purpose intended for the failed disc players—that is, to play back pre-recorded material. Another irony is that, despite all the entertainment industry's fears of piracy, prerecorded videocassette sales proved to a major source of revenue; the VCR helped save the studios instead of helping destroy them. The Japanese triumph in the video wars was the last straw in the collapse of the U.S. consumer electronics industry and signaled the development of new global relations in the entertainment business. A final irony was that in the early 1990s Matsushita purchased MCA (only to sell it in 1995, perhaps an indication that the manufacturer is a stronger force in the creation of hardware than software).

The cultural impact of home video is not as easy to gauge as the economic. When the VCR first arrived, some social thinkers enveloped it in utopian promise. By putting technology in the hands of the people, their argument went, humans finally had the mechanism to enable true media diversity that would replace an imposed, top-down mass culture. Indeed, videotape distribution does not require the economies of scale necessary for large-scale network or even local broadcasting. Thus, theoretically, home video opens the television medium to a host of small, noncorporate voices. The utopian promise grew with the advent of portable VCRs and video cameras, later refined into the low-cost compact camcorder. With this technology almost anyone could become a producer!

Yet home video did not lead to a great democratic decentralization of television. In the early days of the video business, a number of tapes from non-mainstream producers became widely available, but these were largely pornography and low-grade slasher films. Even these disappeared as the mom and pop video stores were displaced by the clean corporate hegemony of Blockbuster Video and other chain distributors. The pre-recorded tapes most VCR users pop into their machines are mainstream products of an increasingly monopolized culture industry. What home video *has* enabled is the phenomenon of "cocooning," the ability to participate in cultural consumption without going out in public. Even the camcorder remains a largely private phenomenon, restricted by most users to home movies of family events (with all cute-kid outtakes shipped off to *America's Funniest Home Videos,* of course).

In the late 1990s, new technology enabled consumers to enhance their home-video cocoons in several ways. DVD players began to achieve wide acceptance. The DVD format delivers much better video quality than VHS tapes, and DVD releases of feature films are generally offered "letter-boxed" in the original widescreen aspect ratio, rather than the "pan-and-scan" maskings used in most VHS releases, which cut off the edges of the original image in order to fill the TV frame. The premise behind letter-boxing is that viewers will have large-screen sets, and, indeed, TV sets have gotten bigger. In the 1980s, 20" sets were most common, and a 27" set was considered large. At the turn of the 21st century, however, 27" sets are the norm and large TVs run 35" or more. DVDs also generally have soundtracks engineered for 5-speaker surround-sound. Surround-sound audio systems allow a film's sound to appear to come from all sides and even behind the viewer, and include a subwoofer for seat-rattling bass effects. The advent of bigger screens and sophisticated audio playback systems must be attributed more to desires stemming from home video use than from viewing broadcast television. Watching *Star Wars* at home is clearly a different matter than watching a situation comedy or talk show. High-tech "home theater" rooms go hand in hand with a mainstream cinema ever more dependent on spectacle and special effects.

Still, while home video has had no revolutionary effect on the cultural mainstream, it has enabled new activity at the margins. Independent, experimental, or alternative tapes of all sorts do get made and distributed. For example, *Cathode Fuck* and other scabrous works of culture-criticism-on-video circulate more freely and widely than the avant-garde films from which they descended. On another front, DVDs are allowing viewers a deeper engagement with the mainstream, in that DVD releases often contain "bonus features" such as behind-the-scenes documentaries, storyboards, and audio commentary tracks by the director. These materials can provide fascinating glimpses into both the "why" and "how" of filmmaking and offer new pleasures to movie fans and film scholars alike.

In all, the history of home video indicates that technology does not so much change society as better enable people to pursue their existing interests, be it the few who experiment with media alternatives, or the many who seek Hollywood thrills and romance from the comfort of their living room sofas.

DAVID J. TETZLAFF

Further Reading

Lardner, James, *Fast Forward: Hollywood, the Japanese, and the Onslaught of the VCR,* New York: Norton, 1987

Levy, Mark R., editor, *The VCR Age: Home Video and Mass Communication,* Newbury Park, California: Sage, 1989

Levy, Mark R., and Barrie Gunter, *Home Video and the Changing Nature of the Television Audience,* London: Libbey, 1988

Lyman, Peter, *Canada's Video Revolution: Pay-TV, Home Video, and Beyond,* Toronto: J. Lorimer, 1983

The Video Age: Television Technology and Applications in the 1980s, White Plains, New York: Knowledge Industry Publications, 1982

Wasko, Janet, *Hollywood in the Information Age: Beyond the Silver Screen,* Austin: University of Texas Press, 1995

Homicide

Australian Crime Series

Homicide was one of the first drama series produced in Australia, and one of its most historically significant and successful. First broadcast in 1964, *Homicide* ran for 509 episodes until production ceased in 1975, establishing the police drama as a staple of Australian-made TV in the 1960s and 1970s, and revealing an enthusiasm among Australian TV viewers for local programming, of which there had been very little prior to the success of *Homicide.*

Homicide was produced for the Seven Network by the Melbourne-based Crawfords Productions, whose founder Hector Crawford has been a pivotal figure in Australian radio and television. With *Homicide,* Crawfords pioneered long production runs for serialized

Homicide.
Photo courtesy of Crawford Productions Pty. Ltd.

drama on modest budgets, and established the importance of the external production house as a source of local drama material for the commercial networks. Crawfords also pioneered outdoor location filming in Australia, which was an important part of *Homicide*'s popularity with Australian audiences, who for the first time saw drama taking place in familiar urban locations.

Homicide was an episodic crime drama, invariably involving a murder, with most episodes following closely a narrative structure in which the detective team investigates and, in the final segments, resolves the murder and arrest the perpetrators. The program was thus "realist" in both narrative and visual representation. Still, the team of male detectives was detached from their social environment. They were always presented as part of a stable hierarchy; they were bound by thorough professionalism, and no consideration was given to their private lives. These factors place *Homicide* in an older tradition of TV police drama. Here dichotomies between law and crime, the police and the society in which they operate, their professional work and private lives, and the relationship of hierarchical authority to individual initiative remain stable and largely uncontested. *Homicide* can be seen as a program that defined the generic conventions of police drama in Australia, drawing upon the codes and conventions established in police dramas such as *Dragnet* in the United States and *Z Cars* in Britain, with more emphasis upon the narrative of crime-solving than on the development of character and the generation of conflict.

The peak years of *Homicide* were also the peak years of police drama on Australian TV, with it and other similar programs consistently rating highly with local, particularly male audiences. When production of *Homicide* ceased in 1975, the police drama had already declined in significance in programming schedules and popularity, giving way to the rise of the serial drama and, later, the miniseries.

The significance of *Homicide* to Australian television perhaps lies less in its textual innovations than in certain institutional factors. It demonstrated a capacity to present familiar environments and character types to Australian audiences on TV for the first time. It created an environment more conducive to policy measures that promoted local drama production and restricted imported material. And it exemplified the innovations in program production necessitated by the need to produce an on-going drama series. In many ways, the program demonstrates that Australia's international reputation as a country with a competitive advantage in low-budget strip programming has its origins in the production techniques developed at Crawfords in the 1960s.

TERRY FLEW

See also **Australian Production Companies; Australian Programming; Crawford, Hector**

Cast

Inspector Jack Connoly	John Fegan
Detective Frank Bronson	Terry McDermott
Detective Rex Fraser	Lex Mitchel
Senior Detective David Mackay	Leonard Teale
Senior Detective Bill Hodson	Leslie Dayman
Senior Detective Peter Barnes	George Malleby
Senior Detective Bert Costello	Lionel Long
Inspector Colin Fox	Alwyn Kurts
Senior Detective Jim Patterson	Norman Yamm
Senior Detective Bob Delaney	Mike Preston
Senior Detective Phil Redford	Gary Day
Inspector Reg Lawson	Charles Tingwell
Senior Detective Pat Kelly	John Stanton
Senior Detective Harry White	Don Barker
Senior Detective Mike Deagan	Dennis Grosvenor

Producers

Ian Crawford, Paul Eddey, Paul Karo, Nigel Lovell, David Stevens, Igor Auzins, Don Battye

Programming History

507 one-hour episodes

2 ninety-minute episodes
1 two-hour episodes
1 ninety-minute documentary
Seven Network

October 1964–January 1977	Tuesday 7:30–8:30
October 21, 1975	Tuesday 7:30–9:00
February 5, 1976	Tuesday 7:30–9:00
June 5, 1976	Tuesday 7:30–9:30

November 21, 1970
(documentary)   Tuesday 7:30–9:00

Further Reading

Hall, Sandra, *Supertoy: 20 Years of Australian Television,* Melbourne: Sun Books, 1976

Moran, Albert, *Images and Industry: Television Drama Production in Australia,* Sydney: Currency Press, 1985

Moran, Albert, *Moran's Guide to Australian TV Series,* Sydney: AFTRS/Allen and Unwin 1993

Homicide: Life on the Street

U.S. Police Drama

Airing on NBC from 1993–1999, *Homicide* emerged in the middle of the cycle of gritty, urban police dramas inaugurated by *Hill Street Blues,* and became one of the most acclaimed series in the history of the genre in the United States. Loosely based on the true-crime book, *Homicide: A Year on the Killing Streets* by David Simon (a former crime reporter for *The Baltimore Sun*), *Homicide* was an ensemble drama built around a group of detectives in the Baltimore police department's homicide unit and shot on location in Baltimore. Through a unique blend of documentary realism and the pseudo-avant-garde stylings of MTV, the series charted a heady and daring course, challenging the cop genre's narrative obsession with moral authority as well as its devotion to a narrow stylistic realism. *Homicide* also illuminates the ever-present tensions between creativity and commerce in the current media landscape, and demonstrates how the strategies for developing and maintaining series have changed at the networks over the past two decades.

Homicide was first introduced to the viewing public immediately following the 1993 Super Bowl—a strategy designed to announce the series as a significant television event. NBC's initial promotion of the series emphasized its cinematic pedigree: namely, the presence of Academy Award winning director (and Baltimore native) Barry Levinson as one of the executive producers, and director of the pilot episode. In addition, screenwriter Paul Attanasio (*Quiz Show, Donnie Brasco*), was commissioned to write the pilot episode and was credited as the series creator. The correlation between Hollywood and *Homicide* continued to be fruitful over the years, as an impressive number of feature film directors and actors appeared both behind and in front of the cameras. The series also boasted impressive television credentials, particularly in the person of Tom Fontana. Fontana, already a veteran writer and producer whose previous experience included NBC's critically acclaimed drama *St. Elsewhere,* was brought in to oversee the daily operations of production, and emerged as the major creative force behind the series as a whole.

Though the exigencies of network television precluded the series from attacking its subject matter with the same kind of daunting grit and detail found in David Simon's lengthy account, the series always strove to chart the same territory as that of the book: the cynical squad room digressions; the morbid corpse-side manner adopted as a defense mechanism, and the small personal and interpersonal battles waged by the detectives as they faced the brutal realities of life and death in the inner city. The series was shot entirely on location in Baltimore, and the city itself also played a crucial role in the narrative, lending it a richness and flavor not often found in studio back lots.

No real formula ever emerged over the course of the series. Like *Hill Street Blues,* each episode was a mixture of episodic plotlines and cumulative narratives. Individual cases provided the basic contours of each episode, but were always set against a range of ongoing personal and professional conflicts being faced by the detectives and their partners. The increasingly close partnership between detectives Tim Bayliss (Kyle Secor) and Frank Pembleton (Andre Braugher) quickly became the centerpiece of the series—described by Tom Fontana, with some hyperbole, as the "greatest love story in the history of television." Bayliss's arrival on the squad marked the beginning of the series, and his growth, both professional and personal, comprised the primary arc of the serial narrative. Pembleton was perhaps the brightest and most enigmatic detective on the squad, known for the artistry of his interrogation technique, his philosophical approach to policing, and his strained Catholicism. Other pairs from the first season included Bolander and Munch (Ned Beatty and Richard Belzer), Felton and Howard (Daniel Baldwin and Melissa Leo), and Lewis and Crosetti (Clarke Johnson and Jon Polito). The squad was overseen by Lieutenant Al Giardello (Yaphet Kotto), described by Tod Hoffman as "sometimes moved to rage, often frustrated, but frequently just bemused." In this sense, Giardello's character was emblematic of the series as a whole.

But unlike most police series, *Homicide* was a show as much about its victims as its heroes. Quite often, the victims whose names hung in red and black on "the board" in the squad room were the dealers, thieves, and pushers that have bedeviled the genre from the beginning. But rather than revel in their untimely demise, the series worked to place their lives and deaths in the larger context of a society at odds. The process of investigation typically provided more questions than answers, and arrests rarely served as resolutions to the bigger problems at hand, especially when it came to issues of race. As Christopher Campbell has suggested, *Homicide* was frequently at its best when it placed race on the center stage and then refused to give easy answers, "leaving audiences to grapple with the subtleties and impact of contemporary racism."

Audiences were also left to grapple with the style of *Homicide,* which took a complicated approach to the realist aesthetic so important to the police genre. The look of *Homicide* was a complex blend of stylistic and cultural references working together both to set the series apart in the crowded market of prime-time drama, and to sharpen its critical edge. As if springing forth from the unlikely union of Frederick Wiseman and MTV, the series used elements of montage (jump-cuts and rapid repeat cuts) along with a swooning hand-held camera to both heighten the documentary feel of the series and to self-reflexively call attention to the highly constructed quality of all media images, especially those found on the evening news or on "reality" shows such as *COPS.*

Alongside its camerawork and editing, *Homicide* was also known for its use of popular music as a central narrative and stylistic tool. Like *Miami Vice* in the

Homicide.
Photo courtesy of Crawford Productions Pty. Ltd.

1980s, *Homicide* frequently used popular music to supply a certain amount of stylistic energy. And in both series the music also underscored important points in the story, often complicating the narrative by offering a second level of commentary on the action. But the music in *Homicide* often acted as a critical reversal of the documentary aesthetic as well: an ironic counterpoint to the claims to realism presented by the *vérité* style.

Perhaps because of its flamboyant style, the series never achieved widespread popular appeal, never appearing in the top 20 shows during its seven seasons. But it did enjoy nearly universal praise from media critics. Most impressively, perhaps, the series received an unprecedented three Peabody Awards (1993, 1995, and 1997), making it the most decorated dramatic program in the history of that award. Despite the Peabody accolades, however, the industry itself was slightly less generous. Though the series, along with its cast and crew, were regularly nominated for Emmys, *Homicide* actually won only three Emmy Awards in any category over the course of its seven seasons.

While its daring stylistic and narrative approach may have puzzled viewers, the lack of high ratings for the series may also be attributed to network programming strategies. When *Homicide* first appeared, NBC was mired in third place behind CBS and ABC and approached the series in a somewhat guarded fashion. As a testament to NBC's ongoing indecision and apprehension regarding the series, *Homicide*'s first two seasons consisted of a mere 13 episodes combined (nine in the first and four in the second). Additionally, the show was moved from Sunday to Wednesday and then to Thursday in this short span, and was simply difficult to locate or anticipate on the schedule until it finally settled on Fridays for its third season. The third season consisted of 20 episodes, but after it proved a ratings disappointment, the cast and crew were forced to wait until May to find out whether or not they would be back for a fourth the following fall.

Once the network's fortunes began to turn in the mid-1990s, the under-performing *Homicide* was placed under much less pressure to generate revenue. Even though the series continued to finish third in its time-slot, behind ABC's *20/20* and CBS's *Picket Fences,* the network responded with a full order of 22 episodes for the fourth season, and then granted the series a two-year lease for its fifth and sixth seasons (1996–97 and 1997–98). But while the series managed to survive the lean years, the network's generosity always came with a mandate to clean up the series look (including the cast) and to focus more expansive and dramatic stories built around "red balls"—cases and situations that demanded the attention and effort of the entire squad.

The end finally came for *Homicide* after the seventh season (1998–99). NBC held off making its final decision until after the production company had wrapped up shooting for the season and, consequently, the final episode was shot with two possible endings: a season finale and a series finale. The multiple endings seem fitting for a series perpetually threatened with cancellation, and for which the end was always in sight, but repeatedly deferred.

As a final testament to *Homicide*'s troubled relationship to the increasingly unstable fortunes of the network, NBC brought *Homicide* back for a two-hour movie during March sweeps in 2000. The series that existed perpetually on the cancellation bubble, unable to attract a significant audience for advertisers, and continually finishing third in its time slot, was brought back to represent the network in the sweeps battle that helps determine advertising rates. On the one hand, bringing the series back for a 2-hour movie allowed the producers to wrap up some of the most important narrative arcs, something they were unable to do previously, given the cloud of uncertainty that haunted the final season. But, perhaps more significantly, NBC's actions regarding *Homicide* were a telling indication of the chaotic state of network programming at the turn of the century.

JONATHAN NICHOLS-PETHICK

See also **Detective Programs; Fontana, Tom;** *Hill Street Blues;* **Police Programs**

Cast

Det. Tim Bayliss	Kyle Secor
Det. John Munch	Richard Belzer
Det. Meldrick Lewis	Clarke Johnson
Lt. Al Giardello	Yaphet Kotto
Det. Frank Pembleton (1993–98)	Andre Braugher
Det./Sgt. Kay Howard (1993–97)	Melissa Leo
Det. Stanley Bolander (1993–95)	Ned Beatty
Det. Beau Felton (1993–95)	Daniel Baldwin
Det. Steve Crosetti (1993–94)	Jon Polito
Lt. Capt. Meghan Russert (1994–96)	Isabella Hoffman
Det. Mike Kellerman (1995–98)	Reed Diamond
J.H. Brodie (1995–97)	Max Perlich
Dr. Julianna Cox (1996– 98)	Michelle Forbes
Det. Laura Ballard (1997–99)	Callie Thorne
Det. Paul Falsone (1997–99)	Jon Seda
Det. Terri Stivers (1997–99)	Toni Lewis
Det. Stuart Gharty (1997–99)	Peter Gerety
Det. Rene Sheppard (1998–99)	Michael Michele
Agent Mike Giardello (1998–99)	Giancarlo Esposito
Dr. Scheiner (1993–97)	Ralph Tabakin
Dr. Carol Blythe (1993–94)	Wendy Hughes
Dr. Alyssa Dyer (1994–97)	Harlee McBride
ASA Ed Danvers	Zeljko Ivanek
Col. George Barnfather	Clayton LeBoeuf
Det./Capt. Roger Gaffney (1994–99)	Walt MacPherson
Mary Wheaton Pembleton (1993–99)	Amy Brabson
Beth Felton (1995)	Mary B. Ward

Producers

Barry Levinson, Tom Fontana, Henry Bromell, David Simon, Julie Martin, James Yoshimura, Jim Finnerty, Gail Mutrux, Debbie Sarjeant, Eric Overmeyer, Anya Epstein, Lori Mozilo, Jorge Zamacona.

Programming History

NBC

January 1993	Sunday 10:25–11:25

February 1993–March 1993 Wednesday 9:00–10:00
January 1994 Thursday 10:00–11:00
October 1994–August 1999 Friday 10:00–11:00

Further Reading

Caldwell, John Thornton, *Televisuality: Style, Crisis, and Authority in American Television,* New Brunswick, New Jersey: Rutgers University Press, 1995

Campbell, Christopher, "A Post-Mortem Time for Racial Imperialism," *Television Quarterly* (Winter 2000)
Hoffman, Tod, *Homicide: Life on the Screen,* Toronto: ECW Press, 1998
Nichols-Pethick, Jonathan, "Lifetime on the Street: Textual Strategies of Syndication," *The Velvet Light Trap* (Spring 2001)
Thompson, Robert J., *Television's Second Golden Age: From* Hill Street Blues *to* ER, New York: Continuum, 1996

Homosexuality. *See* **Sexual Orientation and Television**

Honey West

U.S. Detective Program

Honey West is significant as the first American network television series in which a woman detective appears as the central character. While women had portrayed investigators, police reporters, FBI agents, and undercover operatives in crime drama formats from the earliest days of television, they typically shared billing as sidekick characters, worked at occupations more commonplace than detective, or were cast in secondary roles. Examples would include, among others, journalist Lorelei Kilbourne in the series *Big Town* (1950–56), international art gallery owner turned sleuth, Mme. Lui-Tsong, in *The Gallery of Mme. Lui-Tsong* (1951), and girl Friday Maggie Peters in *The Investigators* (1961). Honey West took this activity to another level. Her principal work was operating a detective agency and, unquestionably, she was the star of her show. Featuring actress Anne Francis in the title role, the ABC series was broadcast for one season (1965–66) and broke ground for other female detective/spy programs to follow, such as *The Girl from U.N.C.L.E.* (1966–67), *Get Christie Love* (1974–75), and *Police Woman* (1974–78).

The character of Honey West was created by husband-and-wife writing team Skip and Gloria Fickling (also known as G.G. Fickling) in a series of novels published in the late 1950s to early 1960s. On April 21, 1965, the character was introduced to television audiences in a *Burke's Law* episode, "Who Killed the Jackpot?," and, true to form, Honey outwitted the dapper detective played by Gene Barry. Producer Aaron Spelling spun the character off into a separate series of 30-minute episodes that premiered September 17, 1965.

Operating her late father's detective agency, Honey West used many talents in her fight against crime. She was expert at judo and held a black belt in karate. Beautiful and shapely, her feminine wiles were accentuated by form-fitting black leather jumpsuits, a sexy mole on her right cheek, tiger coats, and "Jackie O" sunglasses. Like James Bond, she also owned an arsenal of weapons filled with "scientific" gadgets, including a specially modified lipstick tube and martini olives that camouflaged her radio transmitters.

For undercover work, Honey and her admiring partner, Sam Bolt (John Ericson), drove a specially equipped van labeled "H.W. Bolt and Co., TV Ser-

Honey West, Anne Francis, 1965–66.
Courtesy of the Everett Collection

blonde wig was quite obviously wheeled in to do the stunts."

Often compared to Emma Peel, the character played by Diana Rigg in the British series *The Avengers* from 1965–67, Honey West simply did not have Miss Peel's style or longevity and lasted a total of 30 episodes. Providing a notable change to the male-dominated detective genre so prevalent from the earliest days of network television, *Honey West* broadcast its last original show on April 8, 1966.

JOEL STERNBERG

Cast

Honey West	Anne Francis
Sam Holt	John Ericson
Aunt Meg	Irene Hervey

Producers

Jules Levy, Arthur Gardner, Arnold Laven, Alfred Perry, Richard Newton, Mort Warner, William Harbach

Programming History

30 episodes
ABC
September 1965–September 1966   Friday 9:00–9:30

Further Reading

Brooks, Tim, and Earle Marsh, *The Complete Directory to Prime Time Network TV Shows 1946–Present,* New York: Ballantine, 1992

Fickling, Skip, "Take It Seriesly!" *The Writer* (May 1966)

Finnegan, Maggie, "From Spurs to Silk Stockings: Women in Prime-Time Television, 1950–1965," *UCLA Historical Journal* (1991)

Gianakos, Larry James, *Television Drama Series Programming: A Comprehensive Chronicle, 1959–1975,* Metuchen, New Jersey: Scarecrow, 1978

Lewis, Jon E., and Penny Stempel, *Cult TV: The Essential Critical Guide,* London: Pavilion, 1993

Marc, David, and Robert J. Thompson, *Prime Time, Prime Movers: From I Love Lucy to L.A. Law—America's Greatest TV Shows and the People Who Created Them,* Boston: Little, Brown, 1992

Nelson, Craig, *The Very Best of the Very Worst Bad TV,* New York: Delta, 1995

"Spelling, Aaron," *Current Biography Yearbook 1986,* New York: Wilson, 1987

Terrace, Vincent, *The Complete Encyclopedia Of Television Programs 1947–1979, Volume 1, A–Z,* New York: Barnes, 1979

Terrace, Vincent, *Television Character and Story Facts: Over 10,000 Details from 1,008 Shows, 1945–1992,* Jefferson, North Carolina: McFarland, 1993

vice." Her principal base of operation was her Los Angeles apartment, complete with secret office behind a fake living-room wall. Bruce, her pet ocelot, and Meg West (Irene Hervey), her sophisticated aunt, also lent assistance and comfort as necessary.

Honey West premiered to reasonably good reviews. Citing the show's sensual aspects, smooth production values, and Honey's ability to bounce Muscle Beach types off the wall with predictable regularity, *Variety's* 1965 evaluation predicted some success "as a short-subject warm-up to *The Man from U.N.C.L.E.*" Season-opening Nielsen ratings ranked the show in a tie for 19th place, but this level of viewership proved short-lived, as the show's CBS competition, *Gomer Pyle,* knocked it quickly out of the top 40.

Contrasted with *Variety's* review, Jon Lewis and Penny Stempel note that while the "*Honey West* concept was good and the character deserves credit for working in a man's world, the series suffered from unimaginative plots and poor production quality." In fact, say Lewis and Stempel, *Honey West* is "mostly memorable for the fight scenes in which a man with a

Honeymooners, The

U.S. Situation/Sketch Comedy

The Honeymooners is one of U.S. network television's most beloved and influential series. Although *The Honeymooners* ran for only one season as a half-hour situation comedy (during the 1955–56 season on CBS), Jackie Gleason presented the sketch numerous times during his various variety series. In fact, perhaps no premise has been seen in so many different guises in the history of U.S. television—aired live, on film, and on tape; in black-and-white and color; as sketch comedy, situation comedy, and musical. It has succeeded on network, syndicated, and cable television. Whatever the form, audiences have continued to embrace the loudmouthed bus driver Ralph Kramden, Gleason's most resonant creation, as an American Everyman, a dreamer whose visions of upward mobility are constantly thwarted.

The Honeymooners stands in stark contrast to the prosperous suburban sitcoms of the 1950s. The battling Brooklynites, Kramden and his sarcastic wife Alice (Audrey Meadows, the best known of the several women who played the role), are trapped on the treadmill of lower-middle-class existence. Their spartan apartment is one of the most minimal and recognizable in television design. A functional table, a curtainless window, and an antiquated ice box signal their impoverishment. Most of the comedy revolves around Ralph's schemes to get rich quick (such as his infomercial for the Handy Housewife Helper in "Better Living through TV"). The tempestuous Ralph is assisted by his friend and upstairs neighbor Ed Norton (agilely and always played by Art Carney), a dimwitted sewer worker. *The Honeymooners* quartet is rounded out by Trixie Norton (most notably played by Joyce Randolph), Ed's loyal wife and Alice's best friend. Unlike most couples in situation comedy, both the Kramdens and the Nortons were childless, and rarely talked about their situation in a baby-booming United States.

Gleason introduced "The Honeymooners" sketch on October 5, 1951, during his first variety series, *Cavalcade of Stars,* broadcast live on the DuMont network. Kramden directly reflects the frustrations and yearning of Gleason's upbringing; the Kramdens' address on Brooklyn's Chauncey Street was the same as the star's boyhood home. *The Honeymooners* began as a six-minute sketch of marital combat. The battered wife was realistically played by veteran character actress Pert Kelton. A cameo was provided by Art Carney as a policeman. Viewers immediately identified with Ralph and Alice's arguments, and further sketches were written by Harry Crane and Joe Bigelow. Early on, they added the Nortons; Trixie was first played by Broadway actress Elaine Stritch. These early drafts were a starkly realistic insight into the compromises of marriage, a kind of kitchen-sink comedy of insult and recrimination.

In September 1952 Gleason and his staff were lured to CBS by William Paley to star in a big-time variety series, again on Saturday night. Audrey Meadows, who performed with Bob and Ray, replaced Kelton, who suffered from heart problems and political blacklisting. "The Honeymooners" sketches were mostly less than ten minutes during the first CBS season. During the next two years, the routines grew increasingly longer, many over 30 minutes. Most were marked with the familiar catchphrases—Ralph's blustery threats ("One of these days, Pow! Right to the Kisser!") and the assuring reconciliations with Alice at the end ("Baby, you're the greatest").

For the 1955–56 season, Gleason was given one of the largest contracts in show business history to produce *The Honeymooners* as a standard situation comedy. Gleason formed his own production company and experimented with the Electronicam technology, which enabled him to film and edit a live show with several cameras, a precursor of three-camera videotape recording. Gleason filmed two shows a week at the Adelphi Theater in New York, performing to more than 1,000 spectators. Gleason's stable of writers felt hemmed in by the regular format, and Gleason noticed a lack of fresh ideas. When the ratings of *The Honeymooners* sitcom plummeted out of the top ten shows (in the previous season, *The Jackie Gleason Show* ranked number two), Gleason decided to return to the variety format. Gleason later sold these "classic" 39 films of *The Honeymooners* to CBS for $1.5 million, and they provided a bonanza for the network in syndication.

The Honeymooners, Jackie Gleason, Audrey Meadows, Art Carney, Joyce Randolph, 1952–70. *Courtesy of the Everett Collection*

"The Honeymooners" remained a pivotal sketch during Gleason's variety show the following season. The writers created a few new wrinkles, including a musical trip to Europe that covered ten one-hour installments. When Carney left the show in 1957, Gleason dropped the sketch entirely.

He resurrected his big-time variety show in 1962 and moved the production permanently to Miami Beach, Florida, in 1964. He sporadically revived "The Honeymooners" when Carney was available. Since Meadows and Randolph did not want to relocate, Sue Ann Langdon (Alice) and Patricia Wilson (Trixie) took over as the wives. Meadows returned for a one-time special reenactment of "The Adoption," a 1955 sketch in which Ralph and Alice discuss their rarely heard feelings about parenthood. During the 1966–67 season, Gleason decided to remake the "Trip to Europe" musicals into color spectaculars with 40 new numbers. Sheila MacRae and Jean Kean were recruited for the roles of Alice and Trixie.

Gleason's variety show ended in 1970, but he was reunited with Carney and Meadows for four one-hour *Honeymooners* specials during the late 1970s. The specials, broadcast on ABC, revolved around such family celebrations as wedding anniversaries, Valentine's Day, and Christmas. With Jean Kean as Trixie, *The Honeymooners* remained two childless couples, the most basic of family units on television.

The filmed episodes of *The Honeymooners* have been one of the great financial successes in syndication. A local station in New York played them every night for over two decades. The 39 programs, with their almost ritualistic themes and incantatory dialogue, have inspired cultic worship, most notably the formation of the club RALPH (Royal Association for the Longevity and Preservation of the Honeymooners). For years, the live sketches were considered lost. When the Museum of Broadcasting discovered four complete variety programs featuring the Kramdens and the Nortons, Gleason revealed that he had more than 80 live versions in his Miami vault. He sold the rights of the "lost episodes" to Viacom and the live *Honeymooners* found an afterlife on cable television and the home video market. In 2001 museum screenings and network specials marked the 50th anniversary of the program.

The Honeymooners remain one of the touchstones of American television, enjoyable on many levels. Critics have compared the richness of Gleason's Ralph Kramden to such literary counterparts as Don Quixote, a character from Charles Dickens, or *Death of a Salesman*'s Willy Loman. Although *The Honeymooners* did not tackle any social issues throughout its many incarnations, the comedy evokes something very essential to the national experience. The Kramdens and Nortons embody the yearnings and frustrations of the postwar, urban United States—the perpetual underdogs in search of a jackpot. When such producers as Norman Lear in *All in the Family* or Roseanne in her own series have sought to critique the flipside of the American Dream, *The Honeymooners* has been there as a source of inspiration.

RON SIMON

See also **Carney, Art; Gleason, Jackie**

Cast (the series)

Ralph Kramden	Jackie Gleason
Ed Norton	Art Carney
Alice Kramden	Audrey Meadows
Trixie Norton	Joyce Randolph

Producers

Jack Philbin, Jack Hurdle

Programming History

39 episodes
CBS

October 1955–February 1956	Saturday 8:30–9:00
February 1956–September 1956	Saturday 8:00–8:30

Further Reading

Bacon, James, *The Jackie Gleason Story,* New York: St. Martin's Press, 1985

Bishop, Jim, *The Golden Ham: A Candid Biography of Jackie Gleason,* New York: Simon and Schuster, 1956

Cresenti, Peter, and Bob Columbe, *The Official Honeymooners Treasury,* New York: Perigee, 1985

Henry, William, *The Great One: The Life and Legend of Jackie Gleason,* New York: Doubleday, 1992

Jackie Gleason: "The Great One," New York: Museum of Broadcasting, 1988

McCrohan, Donna, *The Honeymooners' Companion,* New York: Workman, 1978

McCrohan, Donna, and Peter Cresenti, *The Honeymooners Lost Episodes,* New York: Workman, 1986

Meadows, Audrey, *Love, Alice: My Life As a Honeymooner,* New York: Crown, 1994

Waldron, Vince, *Classic Sitcoms,* New York: Macmillan, 1987

Weatherby, W.J., *Jackie Gleason: An Intimate Portrait of the Great One,* New York: Pharos, 1992

Hong Kong

With the potential to articulate identities, to provide information, to serve as a foundation for political exchange, or to operate as an industry, television in Hong Kong appears more dominated by economic factors than its political, social, or cultural possibilities. At this juncture in Hong Kong's history, television maintains its position as a profitable commercial venture and as a dominant social force in a new era of People's Republic of China (PRC) governance, just as it had during British colonial rule.

Television continues to be one of the most popular forms of leisure in Hong Kong. In the territory, almost all homes have at least one television, and on a typical evening, about one-third of the population watches prime-time programming. Dramas appear to be the most popular genre for Hong Kong viewers. Most television programming is produced in Hong Kong and broadcast in Cantonese, the dialect of Chinese spoken in Hong Kong and southern China. Local programming helps to perpetuate a sense of local Hong Kong identity, at times distinct from and at times integrated with a larger identification with a Chinese community. Most residents see this cultural identification with a Chinese community separately from their political identification with the PRC.

The pervasive influence of television in Hong Kong

was evident in the mediated political transition from the territory's colonial status as a subject of the British empire to its current status as a Special Administrative Region (SAR) within the PRC. Most Hong Kong residents participated in this hand-over at midnight on July 1, 1997 through viewing the ceremonies on television. The ceremony itself, orchestrated carefully for media coverage, moved from Prince Charles, declaring Britain's responsibilities to Hong Kong, to President Jiang Zemin, pronouncing Hong Kong's need for a strong PRC government. Hong Kong itself was remarkably absent from this televised account. No representative from Hong Kong, as a third party, graced the stage with British and Chinese dignitaries, neatly divided as outgoing and incoming political administrations. No flag of Hong Kong flew separately, but instead only in tandem with British and Chinese flags. Moreover, not a word of Cantonese entered this official ritual. English and Mandarin, languages representing the former colonial and current political powers, dominated the ceremony. Hong Kong media coverage of the event hinted at the mixture of pride and concern felt by many viewers, who felt aligned with a cultural Chinese community but at odds with the particular political regimes purporting to represent them.

This political transition, on the surface a rather peaceful, televised event, structures the more formal political boundaries within which Hong Kong residents must work. According to policies established prior to this historical event, Hong Kong should be administered by the PRC's "one country, two systems" policy, as stipulated in the 1984 Sino-British Joint Declaration. Prior to this transition, Hong Kong served as a British colony for more than 150 years. As a result of the Anglo-Chinese wars in the mid-19th century, Hong Kong Island and the southern tip of the Kowloon peninsula were ceded by China to Britain through the Treaty of Nanking in 1842 and the Convention of Peking in 1860; northern Kowloon was then leased to the British government for 99 years in 1898.

The television industries in Hong Kong have continued to prosper, despite economic difficulties experienced in the late 1990s. Although Hong Kong's official governance system is contingent upon the PRC as its dominant political authority, Hong Kong's economic status as an arena favoring private enterprise and free trade has not diminished. In keeping with the capitalist economic climate of the territory, all television stations continue to be run as commercial enterprises.

Subsequent to the transition to PRC rule, broadcasting regulation has actually become more laissez-faire, rather than less. Focusing on attracting investment, particularly in response to losing some international televi-

sion providers to Singapore, current broadcasting ordinances have relaxed previous rules regarding nonresident and cross-media ownership. In addition, prior royalties on subscription and advertising profits are no longer being charged to television service providers. Many more applicants are being awarded pay-television licenses as well, thus creating the possibilities for many more pay-television services.

Free television in Hong Kong has remained in the hands of two terrestrial television stations, Asia Television Limited (ATV) and Television Broadcasts Limited (TVB). Each of the terrestrial stations transmits two channels. TVB broadcasts the Jade channel in Cantonese and the Pearl channel mostly in English, while ATV broadcasts the Home channel in Cantonese, and the World channel mostly in English. On the English-language stations, movies (on TVB Pearl) and documentaries (on ATV World) attract more viewers than other types of programming. Together, these stations produce 550 hours of television each week, reaching 6.5 million viewers. Controlled by a private corporation, the Lai Sun Group, ATV offers a service similar to that of its competitor, although its programming is not as popular, nor the station as wealthy, as TVB.

TVB is by far the dominant station within the Hong Kong community. During prime-time hours, it is estimated that TVB's two stations, Jade and Pearl, command more than three-quarters of the market share of Hong Kong's viewing public. Jade, producing most of its own programming in the local language, enjoys by far the greater part of this popularity. Initiating broadcasting in 1967, TVB was the first television station in the territory. In 1971 TVB produced its first local television program in color, a musical variety show known as *Enjoy Yourself Tonight.* Since then, the station has developed its technological capacity to improve the appeal of foreign programming to the Hong Kong audience. TVB operates its own Chinese character generator for subtitling and has employed a localized NICAM (Near Instantaneously Compounded Audio Multiplex) system since 1991, offering viewers with equipped television sets the choice of viewing designated programs in different languages (typically, Cantonese, Mandarin, or English).

TVB not only produces most of the programming for its Jade channel but also distributes Chinese-language programs globally. TVB claims to be the largest producer of Chinese-language television programming in the world, distributing its products to more than 30 countries. This company has also invested in satellite broadcasting systems (a joint venture with MEASAT Broadcast Systems), in Internet ventures (TVB.com Limited), and in cable news services, particularly popular in Taiwan. TVB, like other television companies, is also looking toward mainland China as a future profitable market.

The government of Hong Kong does not have its own television station, but instead requires the two terrestrial stations, TVB and ATV, to carry programming and advertisements in the public interest (APIs) that its agency, Radio-Television Hong Kong (RTHK), produces. RTHK stipulates the blocks of time within which these public programs and APIs must be aired. RTHK attempts to maintain editorial independence in its programming. Its shows tend to be informative in nature, illustrated in programs such as *Media Watch* and *The Week in Politics.*

Although the free domestic television services have remained relatively constant, pay-television options have expanded a great deal. The Hong Kong Broadcasting Authority (BA) has granted licenses to five domestic pay-television services and six nondomestic pay-television services. Among the domestic services, Hong Kong Cable TV Limited carries 31 channels on fiber-optic service and another 16 on microwave service, including news, films, sports, and other channels. More than half a million households subscribe to this cable service. Nielsen ratings estimate about 1.4 million viewers of cable television during prime-time hours. Most cable programming is transmitted in Cantonese, or subtitled in Chinese if produced in another language.

Other domestic services include a video-on-demand channel (through PCCWW VOD); satellite television (Galaxy Satellite Broadcasting Limited) through TVB, including entertainment channels in both Cantonese and Mandarin; and two digital television services (Pacifica Digital Media [HK] Corp Limited and Yes [HK] Television Limited). The Pacific Century Cyberworks (PCCW) illustrates a growing trend toward integrating different media services. Initiated by Richard Li, PCCW is attempting to create a satellite-based broadband Internet network with television services, beginning by broadcasting satellite television channels with web content.

Other licenses have been awarded to nondomestic pay-television service providers (such as Galaxy, APT Satellite Glory Ltd., Starbucks [HK] Ltd., Asia Plus Broadcasting Ltd., and MAT Limited), the most prominent being Star TV. Hutchinson Whampoa launched this commercial system in 1991, mostly as an English-language service to the Asian region. When Rupert Murdoch's News Corporation purchased this station in 1993, approximately one-fifth of the households in Hong Kong had the capability to receive these

satellite television services. Star TV's popularity grew as more local programming was introduced. From its base in Hong Kong, Star TV reaches approximately 38 countries from Egypt to Japan, and from Indonesia to Siberia. In Hong Kong, approximately 700,000 viewers watch Star TV prime-time programming, according to recent Nielsen ratings. Star TV offers Chinese programming (from Hong Kong, Taiwan, the PRC, and Japan), sports, entertainment (mostly Western programs), and a music video channel. Originally, an Asian version of Music Television (MTV) was part of the Star TV package, but this was later replaced by a local Asian broadcast known as Channel V, which divided into a Mandarin-dominated music video service for northern Asia and a Hindi-dominated music video service for western Asia. In addition to broadcasting regional productions, Channel V broadcasts videos supplied by global corporations, such as Warner Music, EMI, PolyGram, Sony, and BMG.

Star TV had also offered the British Broadcasting Corporation (BBC) World News Service, but this channel was dropped subsequent to Murdoch's purchase, reflecting both Murdoch's bitter rivalry with the BBC in Britain and the objections raised by the PRC over a documentary the BBC had produced about the reign of Mao Zedong. Broadcast in Britain in 1993, this documentary addressed sufferings caused by Mao's failed economic policies, as well as his alleged relations with young girls. In response, the PRC government extended new restrictions on BBC operations within China. Moreover, this film was not broadcast on television in Hong Kong, despite being purchased by TVB and being approved by public censors representing the Hong Kong Film Censorship Ordinance (even though this very ordinance prohibits screening films that might damage relations with other countries). Instead, private organizations broadcast this documentary to community groups within the territory.

In addition to canceling the BBC news channel, Murdoch's News Corporation has made other overtures toward the PRC government. It invested in the PRC's central newspaper, the *People's Daily,* in 1995, and a few years later forced its subsidiary Harper-Collins to withdraw its contract to publish former Hong Kong governor Chris Patten's book, which was to include a critique of the PRC government. In addition, the Star TV service is carried through Asiasat, which serves as a source of income for the PRC government. With these political concessions News Corporation intends to ensure entry into a potentially profitable market.

Echoing Star TV's strategy toward appeasing the state in the interest of profit, TVB has advocated similarly politically cautious approaches to its programming. In addition to choosing not to air the controversial BBC documentary on Mao it had purchased, TVB produced and broadcast a documentary chronicling Hong Kong's history that was sympathetic to PRC interests. In contrast to more politically direct programming in Taiwan, TVB programming in Hong Kong tends to avoid controversial subject matter. These strategies may be designed to pacify the government with control over potential revenue. Although many local cable operators in southern China are able to receive and relay popular TVB broadcasts, they tend to substitute local advertisements to generate local revenue. TVB's attempts to gain access to licensing and advertising fees from their broadcasts in southern China may be contingent upon a good working relationship with PRC government authorities.

It is important to note that not all stations are as uniformly receptive to perceived political interests. In 1994 ATV news staff resigned over a battle with their management concerning the screening of a Spanish documentary that included coverage of the 1989 Tiananmen Square massacre; this program was aired as scheduled following this well-publicized disagreement. This sort of political debate was particularly significant given the PRC's demonstrated commitment to controlling content within mainland television's industries. Regarding the mainland's own local television, PRC government officials have warned that programs ought to promote patriotism, collectivism, and socialism, but not consumerism. Although many homes (some estimate almost two-thirds of households in the southern area of China's Guangzhou province) have access to cable television services, satellite dishes are officially banned for personal use. The PRC attempts to control the influence of foreign culture by limiting the importation of foreign media; whether Hong Kong media are to be viewed as domestic or foreign is still uncertain in policy and in practice in mainland China.

While a significant proportion of Hong Kong television is produced locally, many programs are imported from other countries, dubbed into Cantonese or subtitled in Chinese characters. Aside from importing news, entertainment series, and films from the West, most animated programs are imported from Japan, and several popular fictional series are imported from Taiwan. Some of the more popular imported programming include movies, news, and the Discovery channel.

Although the primary objective within the Hong Kong television industry is profit, programming is monitored for "taste and decency" through the Hong Kong government's Television and Entertainment Licensing Authority and Broadcasting Authority. The BA meets monthly to review complaints raised by the public. This agency issues warnings and imposes fines against violations of license conditions. Programming standards dictate content concerning social issues, such as crime, family life, and violence, as well as suitable presentations of cigarettes and alcohol. Regulations also define permissible commercial advertising and sponsorship of programs. Recent reprimands to television stations have addressed placing advertisements for alcohol in early viewing hours, presenting factual errors, and showing corporate logos within program content. In one recent instance, TVB was fined for airing an advertisement of a driver kicking his car angrily, as depicting violence without justification and thereby constructing vandalism as an acceptable practice.

A central feature of Hong Kong's new regulatory environment addresses the convergence of media services. Current policies encourage, rather than prohibit, cross-media ownership and attempt to establish new digital standards for high-definition television. Consequently, television broadcasters are working more closely with telecommunications companies in creating new pay-television services, such as an interactive iTV multimedia service and DTV digital entertainment service through Star TV. Recent negotiations between government officials and industry representatives aim to support a shift toward digital service that would be compatible with similar shifts in mainland China.

While Hong Kong may be reunited with a larger "cultural China" through formal political ties, the island's economic system functions quite separately from that of the mainland. In this instance, the state apparatus chooses to privilege television's place in a market economy above its role as a political tool.

KARIN GWINN WILKINS

Further Reading

Curtain, Michael, "Images of Trust, Economies of Suspicion: Hong Kong Media after 1997," *Historical Journal of Film, Radio, and Television* 118/2 (June 1998)

Lee, Chin-Chuan, editor, *Power, Money, and Media: Communication Patterns and Bureaucratic Control in Cultural China*, Evanston, Illinois: Northwestern University Press, 2000

Hood, Stuart (1915–)

British Media Executive, Producer, Educator

Stuart Hood has had a considerable impact upon the development of television production, news broadcasts, program scheduling, and programming policy in the United Kingdom. He has also acted as an adviser and consultant to various countries, Israel being the most notable, as they established their national television broadcasting potential. He has also contributed significantly to the practice of higher education for the television profession and as an academic writer on broadcasting.

Hood's life has been a mixture of involvement with broadcasting, the media, politics, education, and literature. The significance of his contribution to television has been a product of his scholarship, the range of his interests, and his creative drive, rather than any narrow dedication to the medium. He was born in the village of Edzell, Angus, Scotland, the son of a village schoolmaster. After graduating in English literature from Edinburgh University, he taught in secondary schools until World War II.

During the war, Hood served in Italian East Africa and the Middle East as an infantry officer, then as a staff officer on operational intelligence with the German Order of Battle. He was captured in North Africa and then spent time as a prisoner of war in Italy. He escaped at the time of the Italian Armistice in September 1943 and lived at first with the peasants. He then joined the partisans in Tuscany. His account of this period, *Pebbles from My Skull,* is a major piece of 20th-century war writing. He saw further military service in Holland, then at the Rhine crossing with the U.S. Ninth army. In the final years of the war, Hood did political intelligence work in Germany.

These biographical details are important for two reasons. The first is that the war took Hood and a whole generation of young, talented graduates and offered them, among other things, an apprenticeship in the farces, tragedies, and innovations of military administrative matters. The second is that the war has had a lasting impact on Hood's literary output as well as providing him with a lasting contempt for cant and superficiality.

Fluent in German and Italian, Hood joined the BBC German Service at the end of the war. He went on to become head of the BBC Italian Service and then of the 24-hour English-language service for overseas. After a period as editor-in-chief of BBC Television News, he became controller of programs for BBC Television. Ten years working as a freelancer was followed, in 1974, by an invitation to become professor of film and television at the Royal College of Art in London. During the next four years, Hood was not always happy with his role as a senior educator. His approach to higher education was not always greeted with enthusiasm by his peers. He gave students the chance to be involved in the decision-making process in relation to both their own work and general staffing and administrative matters during his period at the Royal College of Art.

Hood has always been politically liberal. For several years he was vice president of ACCT, the film and television union in the United Kingdom. His politics might have placed him, as a senior manager, in something of a difficult position. He has never shirked responsibility, however, and has worked rather to make positive and productive use of his management positions. He was responsible, in large part, for the break between radio and television news, and was the first to employ a woman newsreader at the BBC. He worked under Carleton Greene at the BBC and was encouraged to seek to test the limits of viewer tolerance and interest. This resulted in series such as the now legendary satirical program *That Was the Week That Was.* In relation to television drama, Hood also did all he could to encourage the work of innovative writers such as David Mercer. Hood has publicly expressed his disgust at the fact that the BBC had denied for many years that MI5 routinely vetted BBC staff. On some things, he had to remain silent, and as a result of this he developed something of a reputation as an enigmatic character.

As a director and producer in his own right, Hood was responsible for such innovative programs as *The Trial of Daniel and Sinyavsky* (Soviet dissidents) and a program on the trial of Marshal Petain entitled *A Question of Honor.* Hood has made a unique contribution to broadcasting through the diversity of his interests and talents. He has demonstrated, through his literary output, that senior administrators in broadcasting are not necessarily outside the world of direct productive activity. He has also made a significant contribution to writing about broadcasting, and his *On Television* is a classic in the field. Hood's major contribution to television has been to demonstrate that both production and management can be enhanced and enriched by scholarship and astute political awareness.

ROBERT FERGUSON

Stuart Hood. Born in the Edzell, Angus, Scotland, 1915. Educated at Edinburgh University. Served as an intelligence officer in the British army during World War II; worked with Italian partisans, 1943–44. Briefly joined the Workers' Revolutionary Party; writer, first achieving widespread recognition in the United Kingdom, 1960s; media career began at the BBC World Service; controller of programs, BBC-TV, 1962–64; independent filmmaker; involved with the Free Communications Group, from 1968; vice president, ACTT; continued writing, from mid-1980s; professor of film, Royal College of Art.

Publications

The Circle of the Minotaur, 1955
Pebbles from My Skull, 1963 (republished as *Carlino,* 1985)
A Survey of Television, 1967
The Mass Media, 1972
In and Out the Windows, 1974
Radio and Television, 1975
On Television, 1980; 4th edition, 1997
A Storm from Paradise, 1985
The Upper Hand, 1987
The Brutal Heart, 1989
Questions of Broadcasting, with Garret O'Leary, 1990
A Den of Foxes, 1991
Fascism for Beginners, 1993; second edition as *Fascism and Nazism for Beginners,* with Litza Jansz, 2000
Behind the Screens: The Structure of British Programming in the 1990s, 1994
The Book of Judith, 1994
Marquis de Sade for Beginners, with Graham Crowley, 1995

Hooks, Benjamin Lawson (1935–)

U.S. Media Regulator

Benjamin Lawson Hooks was nominated as a member of the Federal Communications Commission (FCC) by President Richard M. Nixon in 1972. Shortly thereafter the U.S. Senate confirmed the nomination, and Hooks became the first African American to be appointed to the commission. He served as a member of the FCC until July 27, 1977.

During his tenure on the commission, Hooks actively promoted the employment of African Americans and other minorities in the broadcast industry as well as at the FCC offices. He also encouraged minority ownership of broadcast properties. Hooks supported the Equal Time provision and the Fairness Doctrine, both of which he believed were among the few avenues available to minorities to gain access to the broadcast media.

Hooks received his undergraduate degree from LeMoyne College in his hometown of Memphis, Tennessee. However, because Tennessee at that time prohibited blacks from entering law school, he attended

DePaul University in Chicago. He returned to Tennessee to serve as a public defender in Shelby County. From 1964 to 1968 he was a county criminal judge.

The nomination and confirmation of Hooks to the FCC represented the culmination of efforts by African-American organizations such as Black Efforts for Soul on Television (BEST), to have an African American appointed to one of the seven seats on the commission. Before Hooks's appointment, there had been no minority representation on the commission and only two women, Frieda Hennock and Charlotte Reid, had been appointed up to that time.

Riding a wave created by the Report of the National Advisory Commission on Civil Disorders (1968), otherwise known as the Kerner Commission, which itself was a reaction to the civil unrest of the 1960s, African-American organizations such as BEST lobbied aggressively for an African-American appointment to the Federal Communications Commission. Under a section titled "The Negro in the Media," the Kerner Commission urged that African-Americans be integrated "into all aspects of televised presentations." African-American organizations knew that in order to achieve such a goal, representation on the policy-making body that governed broadcasting was critical. However, when it was announced that Benjamin Hooks was one of three African Americans considered for a seat on the FCC, BEST expressed some strong reservations about his candidacy. Leaders of the organization did not believe that Hooks was qualified to serve on the commission and instead favored the appointment of Ted Ledbetter, a Washington, D.C., communications consultant. The third candidate considered for the position was Revius Ortique, an attorney from New Orleans. Although there are no set criteria for qualifying as a candidate for the FCC, it was believed by BEST that Hooks did not have the experience or expertise in broadcasting necessary to be an effective commissioner. However, while far from being an industry insider, Hooks was not entirely new to broadcasting.

In addition to being a lawyer and minister, Hooks had been a popular local television personality before being considered for the FCC post. He hosted a weekly half-hour program, *Conversations in Black and White,* on the station WMC-TV in Memphis. He had also appeared as a panelist on a broadcast of the program *What Is Your Faith?,* which aired on WREC-TV in Memphis. The presence of Hooks on the commission meant that organizations previously outside the policy-making process in broadcasting finally had access. The National Media Coalition, Citizens Communications Center, and the United Church of Christ all felt that their cases would at least get a fair hearing, because of Hooks.

Although he was a spokesman for the perspectives of blacks, women, and Latinos with respect to broadcasting policies, relations between Hooks and these groups were not always friendly. Two of his decisions while on the commission stand out as especially difficult for Hooks. The first was his vote to uphold the First Amendment and not censor a political candidate for the U.S. Senate in the Georgia primary. As part of his political campaign, senatorial candidate J.B. Stoner produced and aired television and radio spots that referred to African Americans as "niggers." Understandably, African Americans and other groups wanted the spots banned by the FCC. Hooks, however, felt that supporting freedom of speech was more important than banning the spots. In a *New York Times* interview, he suggested that "even if it hurts sometimes, I'm a great believer in free speech and would never do anything to tamper with it." He argued that in the long run, banning the spots would prove more detrimental to blacks and other groups than allowing them to air.

Benjamin L. Hooks.
Photo courtesy of Broadcasting & Cable

The second major decision that proved controversial during his stint on the FCC involved broadcasters and the rules related to Equal Employment Opportunities (EEO). Prior to 1976, stations with five or more employees were required to file a statistical report, including the number of employees by race and gender, with the commission. In 1976 the commission proposed to raise the number that would trigger this reporting requirement. It also proposed that such stations should have an EEO-approved strategy for increasing minority representation at the stations. Citizens' groups felt the FCC was easing its restrictions regarding minority hiring practices on smaller stations. They asked Commissioner Hooks not to support the new policy. Hooks decided that the new rules would have an overall positive impact on the hiring of minorities and women, so he supported the new policies, except for the section no longer requiring stations with fewer than 50 employees to file EEO programs.

While Hooks served on the commission, broadcast ownership groups that included minorities were given preferential treatment by the FCC, an office of Equal Employment Opportunity was set up, and the employment of blacks by the Federal Communications Commission offices increased. After serving five years of his seven-year term, Hooks resigned from the FCC to become the head of the National Association for the Advancement of Colored People (NAACP). His plans were to establish a communications department in the NAACP in order "to see how we can make television more responsive to the people, black and white."

The appointment of Hooks to the FCC must be seen as one part of a long history of demands for access to the broadcast media by African Americans. While African Americans had at times been included in the "television family," their roles had too often been limited to stereotypical portrayals that were thought to contribute to distorted images of the black experience. Organizing and lobbying for an African-American appointment to the FCC was a continuation of a political and social process. The appointment of Benjamin Hooks symbolized a crystallization of those efforts, and while it would be incorrect to state that with his appointment all barriers to minority access were knocked down, it would be equally incorrect not to recognize that the appointment of Benjamin Hooks did lead to increased access for African Americans and other minorities in the field of broadcasting.

RAUL D. TOVARES

See also **Federal Communications Commission**

Benjamin (Lawson) Hooks. Born in Memphis, Tennessee, January 31, 1935. Studied at LeMoyne College, Memphis, 1941–43; Howard University, Washington, D.C., 1943–44; De Paul University, Chicago, J.D. 1948. Married: Frances Dancy, 1951; one daughter. Admitted to the Tennessee Bar, 1948; private law practice, Memphis, 1949–65; ordained minister, from 1956; assistant public defender, 1961–64; judge, Division IV, Criminal Court of Shelby County, Tennessee, 1966–68; appointed as first African-American commissioner, Federal Communications Commission, 1972–78; executive director, National Association for the Advancement of Colored People (NAACP), 1978–93; television producer, *Con-*

versations in Black and White; co-producer, *Forty Percent Speaks;* television panelist, *What Is Your Faith?.* Member: Board of directors, Southern Christian Leadership Conference, Tennessee Council on Human Relations, Memphis and Shelby County, Tennessee Human Relations Commission; Martin Luther King, Jr., Federal Holiday Commission; president, National Civil Rights Museum, Memphis, Tennessee; senior vice president, Chapman Company, Memphis, Tennessee, from 1993. Member, American Bar Association, National Bar Association (judicial council member), Tennessee Bar Association. Recipient: Springarn Award, NAACP, 1986.

Publications

"Hooks Calls For Return To 'Bad Old Days.'" *Broadcasting* (23 January 1989)
"In the Matter of Clarence Thomas," *The Black Scholar* (Winter 1991)
"Excerpts from Some of Dr. Hooks' Speeches," *The Crisis* (January 1993)

Further Reading

Dates, Jannette L., "Public Television," in *Split Image: African Americans in the Mass Media,* edited by Dates and William Barlow, Washington, D.C.: Howard University Press, 1990
Flannery, Gerald V., editor, *Commissioners of the FCC: 1927–1994,* Lanham, Maryland: University Press of America, 1995
Henry, Diane, "Sophisticated 'Country Preacher,'" *New York Times* (8 November 1976)
Higgins, Chester A., Sr., "Meet Benjamin Lawson Hooks—A Passionate Fighter for Justice," *The Crisis* (January 1993)
Leavy, Walter, "Black Leadership at the Crossroads," *Ebony* (February 1984)
Williams, James D., "Dr. Hooks Heats Up the 83rd NAACP Convention and Bids Farewell," *The Crisis* (August–September 1992)

Hope, Bob (1903–2003)

U.S. Comedian

Bob Hope was one of television's most renowned comedians and actors. He also worked in vaudeville, radio, and film, and, for the last eight decades of his long life, made audiences laugh at themselves, their contemporary culture and its foibles, their politics and

politicians. For his efforts he received numerous awards and accolades. He was perhaps equally well known, and certainly equally applauded, for his efforts in entertaining U.S. soldiers overseas.

Hope began his career in 1914 when he won a Charlie Chaplin imitator contest. He then made his way into vaudeville in the 1920s and his Broadway acting and musical debut in 1933, when he appeared in *Roberta*. Hope moved to Hollywood in 1938 after appearing in several short films and on radio. He made his film acting debut in the full-length film *The Big Broadcast of 1938*, where he first sang his signature song, "Thanks for the Memory," with Shirley Ross. In 1940 Hope made the first of seven "Road" films, *The Road to Singapore*, with Bing Crosby and Dorothy Lamour. He became a showbiz wizard by playing on his rapid-fire wisecracking technique in the "Road" films that followed. The best-known and probably most televised of these films, *The Road to Utopia*, was made in 1945. Hope regularly starred as a comic coward, caught in comic-adventurous situations, but he generally wound up winning the hand of the leading lady. In addition to the "Road" films, he also appeared in many other movies. He made his last "Road" film, *The Road to Hong Kong*, in 1962, and his film career virtually ended in the early 1960s.

Hope was one of the biggest names in show business when television began to develop. Unlike some of his fellow stars, he jumped into the new medium, making his debut on Easter Sunday in 1950. On a regular basis he was seen on two budget variety shows, *Chesterfield Sound Off Time* and *The Colgate Comedy Hour*. In 1953 NBC broadcast the first annual *Bob Hope Christmas Special*. These specials were usually filmed during his regular tour to entertain the troops overseas. He also began a series of comedy specials for NBC-TV, where he became known for his marvelous comic timing, his stunning array of guest stars, and his ease with both studio audiences and the camera. His guests regularly included top stars from film, stage, television, and the music industry. He was usually surrounded by Hollywood starlets and athletic figures. His humor poked gentle fun at the world of politics, usually leaning toward the conservative. He also made numerous guest appearances on various comedy shows such as *I Love Lucy, The Danny Thomas Show*, and *The Jack Benny Show*, where he was applauded for his wisecracking ability to throw new comic wrenches into already hilarious situations. In most cases, Hope simply played himself, and his appearance as a guest star was a guarantee of a larger audience. His ability to make both the audience and his costars feel at ease, eager for the wry comment that would put a new spin on any situation, was performance enough.

In commemoration of the 50th anniversary of end of World War II, NBC broadcast an hour-long Bob Hope special chronicling the comedian's camp tours during the war. Hope, at the age of 92, narrated *Mem-*

Bob Hope.
Courtesy of the Everett Collection

ories of World War II. The special was crafted from a video and CD collection originally produced for retail sales. An additional 20 minutes shows Bob Hope and his wife Dolores talking with friends and coworkers, including Charlton Heston, Dorothy Lamour, and Ed McMahon, about special photos and remembrances about the war, the entertainment, and their efforts to build and maintain morale. Many scenes extol Hope's comic abilities, patriotism, and human compassion. The recollections range from outrageously funny to heartfelt to harrowing. Still, some critics saw the special as self-congratulatory, inept, and awkward. Mike Hughes, a critic for the Gannett News Service, declared, "This doesn't mean Hope isn't a fine person. It doesn't mean the war effort wasn't worthy. It simply means that bad is bad, no matter the motivation." By this point in his long career, Hope seemed at times anachronistic, a reminder of a different world, and a different sort of television.

In spite of such commentary, Bob Hope remained an American institution in the entertainment world, a quick-witted master of comic response, until his death on July 27, 2003, less than two months after his 100th birthday. He will be remembered as one of the foundational figures of U.S. television in the network era, and one of the kings of television comedy.

GAYLE M. POHL

Bob Hope. Born Leslie Townes Hope in Eltham, London, May 29, 1903; emigrated with family to the United States, 1908, became U.S. citizen, 1920. Attended Fairmont High School, Cleveland, Ohio. Married: Dolores Reade, 1933; children: Linda, Anthony, Kelly, and Nora. Entered vaudeville, 1922; Broadway debut, *The Sidewalks of New York,* 1927; film debut, *Going Spanish* (short), 1934; radio debut, 1935, *The Bob Hope Pepsodent Show,* 1939–48; began overseas tours to entertain U.S. troops, early 1940s, continued until 1994; host and occasional star, various shows, NBC-TV; host of numerous television specials, 1970s–90s. Honorary Knight Commander, Order of the British Empire. More than 40 honorary degrees. Recipient: Honorary Academy Awards, 1940, 1944, 1952, 1959, 1965; Emmy Award; three People's Choice Awards for Best Male Entertainer; Congressional Gold Medal awarded by President John F. Kennedy; Medal of Freedom awarded by President Lyndon B. Johnson; People to People Award presented by President Dwight D. Eisenhower; George Foster Peabody Award; Jean Hersholt Humanitarian Award; Criss Award; Distinguished Service Medals from all branches of U.S. Armed Forces; Poor Richard Award; Kennedy Center Honors Award; Fellow, Westminster (New Jersey) Choir College; Most Decorated Entertainer (*Guinness Book of Records*); Honored Entertainer (*The Guinness Book of Records*). Died in Toluca Lake, California, July 27, 2003.

Television Series
1951–52	*Chesterfield Sound Off Time* (host)
1952–53	*The Colgate Comedy Hour* (host)
1963–67	*Bob Hope Presents the Chrysler Theatre* (host)

Made-for-Television Movie
| 1986 | *A Masterpiece of Murder* |

Television Specials
| 1950–95 | More than 270 specials |

Films
Going Spanish, 1934; *The Big Broadcast of 1938,* 1938; *College Swing,* 1938; *Some Like It Hot,* 1939; *Never Say Die,* 1939; *The Cat and the Canary,* 1939; *The Road to Singapore,* 1940; *The Ghost Breakers,* 1940; *Louisiana Purchase,* 1941; *The Road to Zanzibar,* 1941; *Nothing but the Truth,* 1941; *Caught in the Draft,* 1941; *Star Spangled Rhythm,* 1942; *The Road to Morocco,* 1942; *My Favorite Blonde,* 1942; *They Got Me Covered,* 1943; *Let's Face It,* 1943; *The Princess and the Pirate,* 1944; *The All-Star Bond Rally,* 1945; *The Road to Utopia,* 1946; *Monsieur Beaucaire,* 1946; *Where There's Life,* 1947; *Variety Girl,* 1947; *The Road to Rio,* 1947; *My Favorite Brunette,* 1947; *The Paleface,* 1948; *Sorrowful Jones,* 1949; *The Great Lover,* 1949; *Fancy Pants,* 1950; *My Favorite Spy,* 1951; *The Lemon Drop Kid,* 1951; *Son of Paleface,* 1952; *The Road to Bali,* 1952; *The Greatest Show on Earth,* 1952; *Off Limits,* 1953; *Here Come the Girls,* 1953; *Casanova's Big Night,* 1954; *The Seven Little Foys,* 1955; *That Certain Feeling,* 1956; *The Iron Petticoat,* 1956; *Beau James,* 1957; *Paris Holiday,* 1958; *Alias Jesse James,* 1959; *The Facts of Life,* 1960; *Bachelor in Paradise,* 1961; *The Road to Hong Kong,* 1962; *Critic's Choice,* 1963; *Call Me Bwana,* 1963; *A Global Affair,* 1964; *I'll Take Sweden,* 1965; *Boy, Did I Get a Wrong Number!,* 1966; *The Private Navy of Sgt. O'Farrell,* 1968; *How to Commit Marriage,* 1969; *Cancel My Reservation,* 1972; *The Muppet Movie,* 1979; *Spies Like Us,* 1985.

Radio (selected)
Capitol Family Hour, 1932; *Woodbury Soap Show,* 1937; *Your Hollywood Parade,* 1938; *The Bob Hope Pepsodent Show,* 1939–48.

Stage (selected)
Sidewalks of New York, 1927; *Ballyhoo,* 1932; *Roberta,* 1933; *Say When,* 1934; *Ziegfeld Follies,* 1935; *Red, Hot, and Blue,* 1936; *Smiles,* 1938.

Publications
They Got Me Covered, 1941
I Never Left Home, 1944
So This Is Peace, 1946
Hollywood Merry-Go-Round, 1947
Have Tux, Will Travel (as told to Pete Martin), 1954
I Owe Russia $1,200, 1963
Five Women I Love: Bob Hope's Vietnam Story, 1966
The Last Christmas Show (as told to Pete Martin), 1974
The Road to Hollywood: My Forty Year Love Affair with the Movies, with Bob Thomas, 1977
Confessions of a Hooker: My Lifelong Love Affair with Golf (as told to Dwayne Netland), 1985

Don't Shoot, It's Only Me, with Melville Shavelson, 1990

Have Tux, Will Travel: Bob Hope's Own Story, with Pete Martin, 2003

Further Reading

Angelo, Bonnie, "Thanks for the Memory" (interview), *Time* (June 11, 1990)
Egan, Jack, "The Midas of Comedy," *U.S. News and World Report* (May 6, 1991)

Faith, William, *Bob Hope: A Life in Comedy,* New York: Putnam, 1982 (reprint, 2003)
Fox, Sally, "The Bob Hope Special You Can't Turn Off," *Harper's Magazine* (December 1991)
Kaplan, P.W., "On the Road with Bob Hope," *Film Comment* (January–February 1978)
Manchel, Frank, *The Box Office Clowns: Bob Hope, Jerry Lewis, Mel Brooks, Woody Allen,* New York: F. Watts, 1979
Marx, Arthur, *The Secret Life of Bob Hope: An Unauthorized Biography,* Fort Lee, New Jersey: Barricade, 1993
Thompson, Charles, *Bob Hope: Portrait of a Superstar,* New York: St. Martin's Press, 1981

Hopkins, John (1931–1998)

British Writer

John Hopkins was one of the great pioneers of British television drama whose considerable output as a writer includes the award-winning play quartet *Talking to a Stranger,* described by one critic as "the first authentic masterpiece written directly for television." Hopkins's career in television began first as a studio manager in the 1950s, but he was soon turning his attention to writing and putting his earlier experience to good use in his plays. Few other writers have exploited so effectively the potential of the multi-camera studio in their work. After serving an apprenticeship with single plays, Hopkins rapidly established himself as a key writer for the popular BBC crime series *Z Cars* and, between 1962 and 1964, he wrote 53 episodes for the program. He went on to write noted single plays, such as *Horror of Darkness* (1965) and *A Story to Frighten the Children* (1976), and also to adapt Dostoevsky's *The Gambler* (1968), and John Le Carré's *Smiley's People* with the novelist (1982). The pinnacle of Hopkins's achievement, however, is undoubtedly his 1966 series, *Talking to a Stranger,* directed by Christopher Morahan and shown on BBC 2.

The 1960s in Britain provided a golden age for writers of TV drama, with well over 300 hours a year available in the schedules for original work. The 1964 launch of BBC 2, in particular, opened up opportunities for serious TV drama and exploration of television as an art. Experimentation with form was being discussed openly by writers, and Troy Kennedy-Martin, the originator of the *Z Cars* series, produced a manifesto for a new TV drama free from the conventional

spatial and temporal constraints of naturalist theater. *Talking to a Stranger,* especially in its free-floating use of time, sets up a similar experimental agenda, but in other respects this program remains rooted in a familiar naturalism and the close-up observation of ordinary people.

Nothing could be more mundane than the basic situation at the center of this family drama. A grown-up daughter and her brother go back home to visit their aging father and mother, but the emotional collisions that arise provoke unexpected tragedy—the suicide of the mother. Some of the same events are repeated from one play to the next, but the viewpoint changes as each play focuses on a different character. In this way, the series provides a sustained opportunity to explore subjective experience. The self-absorption of the characters is enhanced by the use of experimental devices that include extended monologues, overlapping dialogue, lingering reaction shots, and film flashbacks in time.

Hopkins's vision of human loneliness and alienation may be an uncompromisingly bleak and pessimistic one, but it is made compelling through his artistic manipulation of the television medium. As a family drama, *Talking to a Stranger* bears comparison to Eugene O'Neill's great stage play *A Long Day's Journey into Night.* In relation to the development of the art of television, Hopkins's successful pioneering of the short series for serious drama established an important precedent in Britain, and writers of the stature of Dennis Potter and Alan Bleasdale subsequently followed in his example to produce some of their most distinctive work.

BOB MILLINGTON

See also **Z Cars**

John Richard Hopkins. Born in London, January 27, 1931. Attended Raynes Park County Grammar School; St. Catharine's College, Cambridge (B.A. in English). Served in the British Army, 1950–51. Married: 1) Prudence Balchin, 1954; 2) Shirley Knight, 1970; two daughters. Began career as television studio manager; worked as writer for BBC Television, initially as first scriptwriter of *Z Cars*, 1962–64; freelance from 1964. Recipient: two Screenwriters' Guild Awards. Died in Woodland Hills, California, August 23, 1998.

Television Series

1961	*A Chance of Thunder*
1962–65	*Z Cars*
1964	*Parade's End*
1966	*Talking to a Stranger*
1968	*The Gambler*
1977	*Fathers and Families*
1982	*Smiley's People* (co-writer, with John Le Carré)

Television Specials

1958	*Break Up*
1958	*After the Party*
1959	*The Small Back Room*
1959	*Dancers in Mourning*
1960	*Death of a Ghost*
1961	*A Woman Comes Home*
1961	*By Invitation Only*
1962	*The Second Curtain*
1962	*Look Who's Talking*
1963	*A Place of Safety*
1964	*The Pretty English Girls*
1964	*I Took My Little World Away*
1964	*Time Out of Mind*
1964	*Houseparty*
1965	*The Make-Believe Man*
1965	*Fable*
1965	*Horror of Darkness*
1965	*A Man Like Orpheus*
1966	*Some Place of Darkness*
1966	*A Game—Like—Only a Game*
1969	*Beyond the Sunrise*
1970	*The Dolly Scene*
1971	*Some Distant Shadow*
1972	*That Quiet Earth*
1972	*Walk into the Dark*
1972	*The Greeks and Their Gifts*
1976	*A Story to Frighten the Children*
1976	*Double Dare*
1987	*Codename Kyril*
1995	*Hiroshima*

Films

Two Left Feet, with Roy Baker, 1963; *Thunderball,* with Richard Maibaum, 1965; *The Virgin Soldiers,* with John McGrath and Ian La Frenais, 1969; *Divorce—His, Divorce—Hers,* 1972; *The Offence,* 1973; *Murder by Decree,* 1980; *The Power,* with John Carpenter and Gerald Brach, 1983; *The Holcroft Covenant,* with George Axelrod and Edward Anhalt, 1985; *Torment,* with Samson Aslanian (also codirector and producer), 1986; *Runaway Dreams,* 1989.

Stage

This Story of Yours, 1968; *Find Your Way Home,* 1970; *Economic Necessity,* 1973; *Next of Kin,* 1974; *Losing Time,* 1979; *Valedictorian,* 1982; *Absent Forever,* 1987.

Publications

Talking to a Stranger: Four Television Plays, 1967
"A Place of Safety," in *Z Cars: Four Scripts from the Television Series,* edited by Michael Marland, 1968
"A Game—Like—Only a Game," in *Conflicting Generations: Five Television Plays,* edited by Michael Marland, 1968
This Story of Yours, 1969
Find Your Way Home, 1971
Losing Time, 1983

Further Reading

Bakewell, Joan, and Nicholas Garnham, *The New Priesthood: British Television Today,* London: Allen Lane, 1970
Brandt, George, editor, *British Television Drama,* Cambridge: Cambridge University Press, 1980
Kennedy-Martin, Troy, "Nats Go Home: First Statement of a New Drama for Television," *Encore* (March–April 1964)

Hour Glass

U.S. Variety Program

Hour Glass was a seminal, if now largely forgotten, variety program airing on NBC-TV from May 1946 to February 1947. It is historically important because it exemplified the issues faced by networks, sponsors, and advertising agencies in television's formative years. The program was produced by the J. Walter Thompson agency on behalf of Standard Brands for their Chase and Sanborn and Tenderleaf Tea lines. The sponsor and agency took several months to decide on the show's format, eventually choosing variety for two reasons: it allowed for experimentation with other forms (comedy sketches, musical numbers, short playlets, and the like), plus Thompson and Standard Brands had previously collaborated on the successful radio show *The Chase and Sanborn Hour.*

The lines of responsibility were not completely defined in those early years, and the nine-month run of *Hour Glass* was punctuated by frequent squabbling among the principals. Each show was assembled by seven Thompson employees working in two teams, each putting together a show over two weeks in a frenzy of production. Using a format that was familiar to *Chase and Sanborn Hour* listeners, the program accentuated star power as the means of drawing the largest audience. *Hour Glass* featured different performers every week, including Peggy Lee and, in one of the first examples of a top radio star appearing on network television, Edgar Bergen and Charlie McCarthy, who appeared in November 1946. The show also showcased filmed segments produced by Thompson's Motion Picture Department; these ranged from short travelogues to advertisements. Every episode also included a ten-minute drama, which proved one of the more popular portions of the show.

It must have been the curiosity factor that prompted some stars to appear on the show because they certainly were not paid much money. *Hour Glass* had a talent budget of only $350 a week, hardly more than enough to pay scale wages for a handful of performers. Still, Standard Brands put an estimated $200,000 into the program's nine-month run, by far the largest amount ever devoted to a sponsored show at that time.

Although Thompson and Standard Brands representatives occasionally disagreed over the quality of individual episodes, their association was placid compared to the constant sniping that was the hallmark of the agency's relationship with NBC. It started with unhappiness over studio space, which Thompson regarded as woefully inadequate, and escalated when the network insisted that an NBC director manage the show from live rehearsals through actual broadcast. The network was similarly displeased that Thompson refused to clear their commercials with NBC before air time.

In February 1947 Standard Brands canceled *Hour Glass.* They were pleased with the show's performance in terms of beverage sales and its overall quality, but they were leery about continuing to pour money into a program that did not reach a large number of households (it is unclear if the show was broadcast anywhere other than NBC's interconnected stations in New York and Philadelphia). The strain between NBC and Thompson also played a role in the decision to cancel the program. Still, *Hour Glass* did provide Thompson with a valuable blueprint for the agency's celebrated and long-running production *Kraft Television Theatre.*

MICHAEL MASHON

See also **Advertising, Company Voice; Advertising Agency;** *Kraft Television Theatre;* **Variety Programs**

Emcees
Helen Parrish (1946)
Eddie Mayehoff

Producer
Howard Reilly

Programming History
NBC
May 1946–March 1947   Thursday 8:00–9:00

Howdy Doody Show, The

U.S. Children's Program

The Howdy Doody Show was one of the first and easily the most popular children's television show of the 1950s in the United States, and a reflection of the wonder, technical fascination, and business realities associated with early television. While Howdy and his friends entertained American children, they also sold television sets to American parents and demonstrated the potential of the new medium to advertisers.

The idea for *Howdy Doody* began on the NBC New York radio affiliate WEAF in 1947, with a program called *The Triple B Ranch*. The three Bs stood for Big Brother Bob Smith, who developed the country-bumpkin voice of a ranch hand and greeted the radio audience with, "Oh, ho, ho, howdy doody." Martin Stone, Smith's agent, suggested putting Howdy on television and presented the idea to NBC Television programming head Warren Wade. With Stone and Roger Muir as producers, Smith launched *Puppet Playhouse* on December 17, 1947. Within a week the name of the program was changed to *The Howdy Doody Show.*

Children loved the Doodyville inhabitants, a skillfully created, diverse collection of American icons. The original Howdy marionette was designed by Frank Paris and, in keeping with Smith's voice, was a country bumpkin; however, in a dispute over licensing rights, Paris left the show with the puppet. The new Howdy, who premiered in March 1948, was an all-American boy with red hair, 48 freckles (one for each state in the United States at that time), and a permanent smile. Howdy's face symbolized the youthful energy of the new medium and appeared on the NBC color test pattern beginning in 1954.

Smith treated the marionettes as if they were real, and as a result, so did the children of America. Among the many unusual marionettes on the show was Phineas T. Bluster, Doodyville's entrepreneurial mayor. Howdy's grumpy nemesis, Bluster had eyebrows that shot straight up when he was surprised. Bluster's naive, high-school-aged accomplice was Dilly Dally, who wiggled his ears when he was frustrated. Flub-a-Dub was a whimsical character who was a combination of eight different animals. In *Howdy and Me,* Smith notes, "Howdy, Mr. Bluster, Dilly, and the Flub-a-Dub gave the impression that they could cut their strings, saunter off the stage, and do as they pleased."

Although the live characters, particularly the Native Americans Chief Thunderthud and Princess Summerfall Winterspring, were by modern standards stereotypical and often clownish, each had a rich heritage interwoven into the stories. These were prepared by Eddie Kean, who wrote the scripts and the songs until 1954, and Willie Gilbert and Jack Weinstock, who wrote scripts and song lyrics thereafter. For example, Smith (born in Buffalo, New York) was transformed into Buffalo Bob when he took his place in the story as the great white leader of the Sigafoose tribe. Chief Thunderthud (played by Bill LeCornec) of the mythical Ooragnak tribe ("Kangaroo" spelled backward) introduced the word "Kowabonga," an expression of surprise and frustration, into the English language. One of the few female characters in the cast was the beloved Princess Summerfall Winterspring of the Tinka Tonka tribe, who was first introduced as a puppet, then transformed into a real, live princess, played by Judy Tyler.

The Howdy Doody Show also reflected Americans' fascination with technology. Part of the fun and fantasy of Doodyville were crazy machines such as the Electromindomizer, which read minds, and the Honkadoodle, which translated Mother Goose's honks into English. Television's technical innovations were also incorporated into the show. On 23 June 1949 split-screen capabilities were used to join Howdy in Chicago with Buffalo Bob in New York, one of the first instances of a cross-country connection. Howdy also ushered in NBC's daily color programming in 1955.

The Howdy Doody Show was immediately successful and was NBC's first daily show to be extended to five days a week. In 1952 NBC launched a network radio program featuring Howdy, and in 1954 *Howdy Doody* became an international television hit with a Cuban and a Canadian show, using duplicate puppets and local talent, including Robert Goulet as the Canadian host Timber Tom.

As amazing as it may now seem, there were published concerns over violent content in *Howdy Doody,* but although the action in Doodyville often involved slapstick, parents generally supported the show. Much of the mayhem was perpetrated by a lovable, mis-

The Howdy Doody Show, 1947–60; Howdy Doody, Buffalo Bob Smith, 1950s.
Courtesy of the Everett Collection

chievous clown named Clarabell Hornblow. Clarabell was played until 1953 by Bob Keeshan, who later become Captain Kangaroo. The clown's pratfalls were generally accidents, and the most lethal weapon on the show was his seltzer bottle. Moreover, educational material was consciously incorporated both into the songs and the stories; for example, young viewers received a lesson in government when Howdy ran for president of the kids of America in 1948. The educational features of the program made the Doodyville characters attractive personal promoters both for the show and for the sale of television sets.

In an era before the advent of the Nielsen ratings, *Howdy Doody* demonstrated its ability to draw an audience both for NBC and for possible advertisers. In 1948 children's shows were often provided as a public service either by the networks or the stations. When Howdy ran for president of all the kids, Muir suggested that the program offer free campaign buttons. It received 60,000 requests, representing one-third of American homes with television sets at that time. Within a week the program's advertising time was sold out to major advertisers, such as Colgate Palmolive Peet Company. Although the producers were careful about what they advertised, they were very aggressive about marketing products they selected, incorporating product messages into songs and skits.

The producers also recognized the potential for merchandising. In 1949 the first Howdy Doody comic book was published by Dell and the first Howdy Doody record was released, selling 30,000 copies in its first week. There were also Howdy Doody wind-up toys, a humming lariat, a beanie, and T-shirts, among other licensed products.

Although extremely popular, the demise of *The Howdy Doody Show* demonstrated the financial realities of the new medium. In 1956 the early-evening timeslot became more attractive to older consumers, and the show was moved to Saturday morning. Although it continued to receive high ratings, the expense of producing it was eventually its downfall, and *The Howdy Doody Show* was taken off the air on September 24, 1960, after 2,343 programs.

The most famous moment in the history of *The Howdy Doody Show* came during the closing seconds of the final show, when Clarabell, who had never before spoken but communicated through pantomime and honking his horns, surprised the audience by saying, "Good-bye, kids." Today, the rich, live-action performances that filled early children's programming are considered too costly for modern, commercial television in the United States. The show was briefly brought back to television as *The New Howdy Doody Show* in August 1976, but it was canceled in January 1977, after only 130 episodes.

SUZANNE WILLIAMS-RAUTIOLLA

See also **Children and Television**

Cast

Buffalo Bob Smith	Bob Smith
Clarabelle Hornblow (1947–53)	Bob Keeshan
Clarabell Hornblow	Henry McLaughlin
Clarabell Hornblow	Bob Nicholson
Clarabell Hornblow	Lew Anderson
Story Princess	Arlene Dalton
Chief Thunderthud	Bill Lecornec
Tim Tremble	Don Knotts
Princess Summerfall Winterspring	Judy Tyler
Princess Summerfall Winterspring	Linda Marsh
Bison Bill (1954)	George "Gabby" Hayes
Howdy Doody (voice)	Bob Smith
Howdy Doody (voice, 1954)	Allen Swift
Phineas T. Bluster (voice)	Dayton Allen

Double Doody (voice)	Bob Smith	
The Flubadub (voice)	Dayton Allen	
Traveling Lecturer	Lowell Thomas, Jr.	

Puppeteers
Rhoda Mann, Lee Carney, Rufus C. Rose

Producers
Martin Stone, E. Roger Muir, Simon Rady

Programming History
2,343 episodes

NBC
December 1947–September 1960   Non-prime-time

Further Reading

Davis, Stephen, *Say Kids! What Time Is It?,* Boston: Little, Brown, 1987
Davis, Stephen, "It's Howdy Doody Time," *Television Quarterly* (Summer 1988)
Fischer, Stuart, "Howdy Doody," in *Kids TV: The First Twenty-Five Years,* New York: Facts on File, 1983
Grossman, Gary H., *Saturday Morning TV,* New York: Dell, 1981
Smith, Buffalo Bob, and Donna McCrohan, *Howdy and Me,* New York: Penguin, 1990

Howerd, Frankie (1922–1992)

British Comedian

Frankie Howerd was a popular postwar stand-up comedian, who survived many changes in the humor tastes of the British nation to remain a television favorite until his death in 1992. From an early age, he decided he wanted to be an actor, despite bouts of nervousness and a recurring stammer, but after suffering rejection from the Royal Academy of Dramatic Arts, he decided instead to become a stand-up comic. However, this route seemed equally closed to him as he failed numerous auditions. During World War II he joined the army but failed to impress as an entertainer and was turned down by the military entertainment organization, ENSA (Entertainments National Service Association—but better known by the troops as Every Night Something Awful). This rejection, however, did not deter Howerd, who still performed for his comrades in arms, learning to control his stammer and develop a line of patter. Following the war, Howerd's rise was dramatic. He toured the provinces in a stage show, *For the Fun of It,* in 1946, and although placed at the bottom of the bill, he hit upon the clever ruse of changing his name from Howard to Howerd. This meant that his name was more noticeable simply because people assumed it was a misprint. And if the name was spelt incorrectly as the more normal Howard (an easy mistake), the comedian could complain and get some appeasement, perhaps larger lettering on the next poster or a longer spot, or even extra money.

In 1947 Howerd presented his comedy act in the radio series *Variety Bandbox* and soon became a hit with the listening public. His comic persona was becoming defined. Influenced by the comedians of his time, especially his great idol Sid Field (one of Britain's greatest comic talents from the 1930s to his death in 1950), Howerd had, by the end of the 1940s, developed a strong style of his own. His tactic was to deliver jokes and appear in sketches almost reluctantly, as if forced there by circumstance. It was as if he had something better to do, and if the audience did not respond to the lines in the right way, then he did not care. Indeed, his offhand statement to such indifference, "Oh please yourself," became one of his great catchphrases, getting a huge laugh as the audience identified with the character.

Success on radio increased Howerd's standing in the stage world, but many of the venues were shutting their doors as the era of music hall was drawing to an end. Sadly, as his stock rose, the circuit itself was closing down. Many of his comic contemporaries were crowding the radio waves, and some (such as Charlie Chester and Terry-Thomas) had even landed their own shows on the increasingly popular medium of television. In 1952 Howerd got his first television series, *The Howerd Crowd,* an hour-long entertainment with scripts by Eric Sykes. Howerd had a good face for television, long and lugubrious, and the small screen en-

Frankie Howerd (right).
Courtesy of the Everett Collection

abled him to use his exaggerated facial expressions to good effect. He appeared a few more times in that period, but he was about to enter one of the quiet phases of his career.

Howerd made his feature film debut in 1954, a major role in *The Runaway Bus,* and he had a small but memorable part in *The Ladykillers* the following year; it was such film roles and occasional radio appearances that kept him occupied throughout the rest of the 1950s. His television career throughout this period was in the doldrums and, with each year bringing in less work than the year before, he seemed to be on a familiar path that led to obscurity. Then, in 1962, Howerd's career was suddenly and dramatically resurrected when he did a stand-up routine for Peter Cook's Establishment Club, an American-style comedy cabaret club specializing in satire. With a script by Johnny Speight, Howerd was a big hit. It seemed his style of innuendo and ad-libbed asides had a place in the new world of anti-establishment comedy. The following year, Howerd consolidated his revitalized reputation with an appearance on the BBC's controversial and ground-breaking satire series *That Was the Week That Was.* In the space of a year, he was reestablished as a major comedy star and became a familiar face on television as a guest star or leading artist in variety shows. He headlined his own show again, *Frankie Howerd* (1964–66), this time with scripts from Galton and Simpson, mixing an introductory stand-up routine with a long-form sketch that continued the same theme. Later, the series *The Frankie Howerd Show* (1969) was made by ATV for the ITV network, and Howerd also appeared in one-off entertainments such as *The Howerd Hour* (1968) made by ABC for the ITV network.

In 1970 Howerd had his biggest TV success with *Up Pompeii!* (BBC 1970), a period-piece sitcom set in ancient Pompeii and inspired by the American stage musical *A Funny Thing Happened on the Way to the Forum,* in which Howerd had appeared (as Prologus and Pseudolus) in its British stage production. In 1969 a pilot episode of *Up Pompeii!* raised enough interest for the series to continue the following year. Howerd played the slave Lurcio, who commented on and got involved in the various comings and goings in his master's household. His master was Ludricrus Sextus, and most of the main characters in the plots had punnish names, such as Ammonia, Erotica, Nausius, and Prodigus. The shows (scripted by Talbot Rothwell, one of the writers of the bawdy *Carry On ...* film series) were peppered with innuendo and smutty references and also allowed Howerd free rein to talk directly to camera and deliver his typically weary asides about how awful the show was. This method of combining a pseudo-stand-up routine with plot—coupled with Howerd's conspiratorial relationship with the viewing audience, which allowed him to step in and out of character—gave the series a unique, almost theatrical feel that lingered long in the public psyche despite the fact that only 13 episodes were made (14 including the pilot). Such was its popularity that an Easter special, *Further Up Pompeii!*, aired on the BBC in 1975 and a revival, also called *Further Up Pompeii!*, was made by the commercial London Weekend Television in 1991. It also spawned a feature film version in 1971 (followed by two others on similar themes, a medieval romp, *Up the Chastity Belt*, in 1971, and a World War I version, *Up the Front*, in 1973). On TV the format was reworked as *Frankie Howerd in Whoops Baghdad* (BBC, 1973), which ran for six episodes and featured Howerd as Ali Oopla, bondservant to the Wazir of Baghdad.

Howerd actually improved with age. His face, lined and wrinkled with doleful bags under his eyes, became even more expressive, allowing him to suggest any number of things with a raise of the eyebrow, his impossibly deep frown, or his wide-eyed aghast look. The face was perfectly fitted to his camp delivery, and his confidential asides and world-weary looks were given added authenticity. In 1975 Howerd appeared in an abortive pilot *A Touch of the Casanovas* for Thames TV, and he made the series *The Howerd Confessions* for the same company the following year. But British tastes were changing. The anarchic comedy wave that emerged in the wake of the punk rock phenomenon began to be taken seriously by television companies in the early 1980s, and there was a backlash against Howerd's sexual-innuendo style of humor in favor of full-frontal comedy attacks on taboo subjects. After his Yorkshire TV series *Frankie Howerd Strikes Again* (1981), Howerd once again found it harder to come by work. His 1982 sitcom *Then Churchill Said to Me* was made but shelved by the BBC; in 1985 he was chosen as front-man in an ill-fated and ill-timed attempt to make *The Gong Show* (Gambit productions for C4), a British version of the successful U.S. show.

However, some of the younger audiences began to rediscover and reassess the old comedians, and How-erd once again found himself back in favor—achieving success appearing before rapturous college students comparable to that which he had earlier enjoyed at the Establishment Club. Indeed, evidence of Howerd's regained popularity can be found from his appearance in 1987 on LWT's live new-wave comedy showcase *Saturday Live;* it meant that the producers considered Howerd "hip" enough for their audience. Although this appearance did not have the sort of impact his previous comeback (on TW3) had had, it nonetheless heralded another revival, and he again was a regular face on TV as he appeared in the young people's sitcom *All Change* (Yorkshire TV, 1989). A series of his concerts were filmed for television, the most revealing of which was *Live Frankie Howerd on Campus* (LWT, 1990). Howerd, back in demand, was as busy as ever.

Two revealing TV documentaries contain much of the essence of Howerd's style and craft: 1990's *Ooh Er, Missus—The Frankie Howerd Story from Arena* (the BBC's art documentary series) and Thames Television's *Heroes of Comedy—Frankie Howerd* (1995).

DICK FIDDY

Frankie Howerd. Born Francis Alex Howard in York, England, March 6, 1922. Attended schools in Woolwich, London. Made stage debut, as an amateur, at the age of 13; insurance clerk; performed in camp concerts during World War II, in which he served in the Royal Artillery; after the war became a favorite on radio's *Variety Bandbox;* first television show, 1952; made film debut, 1954; star of revue, stage, and television comedy, pantomime, and film. Officer of the Order of the British Empire, 1977. Recipient: Variety Club of Great Britain Showbusiness Personality of the Year Award (twice). Died in London, April 19, 1992.

Television Series (selected)

1952	*The Howerd Crowd*
1969	*The Frankie Howerd Show*
1970	*Up Pompeii!*
1973	*Frankie Howerd in Whoops Baghdad*
1976	*The Howerd Confessions*
1981	*Frankie Howerd Strikes Again*
1982	*Frankie Howerd: Then Churchill Said to Me*
1989	*All Change*
1990	*Live Frankie Howerd on Campus*

Television Specials

1973	*Whoops Baghdad!*
1975, 1991	*Further up Pompeii!*

Films

The Runaway Bus, 1954; *An Alligator Named Daisy,* 1955; *The Ladykillers,* 1955; *Jumping for Joy,* 1956; *A Touch of the Sun,* 1956; *Further Up the Creek,* 1958; *Three Seasons,* 1961; *Watch It Sailor!,* 1961; *The Fast Lady,* 1962; *The Cool Mikado,* 1962; *The Mouse on the Moon,* 1963; *The Great St. Trinian's Train Robbery,* 1966; *Carry On Doctor,* 1967; *Carry On Up the Jungle,* 1969; *Up Pompeii!,* 1971; *Up the Chastity Belt,* 1971; *Up the Front,* 1972; *The House in Nightmare Park/Crazy House,* 1973; *Sergeant Pepper's Lonely Hearts Club Band,* 1978; *Trial by Jury,* 1983.

Radio

Variety Bandbox, 1946–52.

Stage

For the Fun of It, 1946; *Ta Ra Rah Boom De Ay,* 1948; *Out of This World,* 1950; *Dick Whittington; Pardon My French; Way Out in Picadilly; Wind in the Sassafras Trees; Charley's Aunt; A Midsummer Night's Dream; Mr. Venus,* 1958; *A Funny Thing Happened on the Way to the Forum,* 1962.

Publications

On the Way I Lost It (autobiography), 1976
Trumps, 1982

Huggins, Roy (1914–2002)

U.S. Writer, Producer

Roy Huggins was a prolific and influential producer who created several of the most enduring dramatic series in the history of U.S. television, including *Maverick* (1957–62), *77 Sunset Strip* (1958–64), *The Fugitive* (1963–67), and *The Rockford Files* (1974–80). Huggins spent much of his career in television as a producer for two large studios, Warner Brothers and Universal. Working within these studios, Huggins served as producer or executive producer on made-for-television movies, miniseries, and more than 20 dramatic series. While Huggins supervised a wide range of projects, many of which were simply studio assignments, he was one of the first writer-producers to emerge once television production shifted to Hollywood in the 1950s. Many of his series bear the distinctive stamp of his irreverent, self-deprecating wit and his fondness for characters who operate on the margins of society.

As a civilian employee of the U.S. government during the war, Huggins spent his spare time writing hard-boiled crime fiction, inspired by the work of Raymond Chandler. In 1946 his first novel, *The Double Take,* was published. Huggins sold several serialized mysteries to *The Saturday Evening Post* and soon published two more novels, *Too Late for Tears* and *Lovely Lady, Pity Me.* When Columbia Pictures purchased the rights to *The Double Take* in 1949, Huggins recognized an opportunity for more steady employment, and signed on to adapt the script. From here he entered the movie industry, working as a contract writer at Columbia and RKO. In 1952 he wrote and directed the feature film *Hangman's Knot,* a Randolph Scott western produced by independent producer Harry Joe Brown for Columbia. Afterwards, he signed a contract with Columbia, where he worked as a staff writer until 1955.

Huggins made the transition to television in April 1955, when Warner Brothers hired him as a producer for its inaugural television series, *Warner Brothers Presents,* an omnibus series that featured three alternating dramas, *King's Row, Casablanca,* and *Cheyenne.* Huggins agreed to produce *King's Row,* but after creating the series he was reassigned to *Cheyenne* in order to salvage the faltering series, which faced withering reviews from both critics and sponsors. Huggins rescued *Cheyenne* by recycling scripts from Warner Brothers movies such as *Treasure of the Sierra Madre* (1948), often simply inserting the character of Cheyenne Bodie (Clint Walker) into familiar stories from the studio vaults. These changes brought the series a measure of respect as an "adult" western and made it the studio's first full-fledged hit.

Huggins immediately moved from *Cheyenne* to *Conflict* (1956–57), a short-lived anthology series that

Roy Huggins in the 1960s.
Courtesy of the Everett Collection/CSU Archives

alternated with the western. During the production of *Conflict,* Huggins met James Garner, an actor who perfectly embodied his wry sense of humor. When Warner Brothers asked Huggins to create a new series, he thought immediately of Garner and tailored *Maverick* as a star vehicle for him. In a crowded field of TV westerns, *Maverick* quickly moved into the top ten and won an Emmy for Best Western in 1958.

Maverick was a refreshing antidote to the strained seriousness of so many westerns, including *Cheyenne,* but it was also ground-breaking because it redefined the heroic protagonist and brought a sly self-mockery to television drama. For the first time, Huggins built a series around a flawed central character, a reluctant hero who lives on the fringes of society. Huggins wanted Bret Maverick to have none of the "irritating perfection" of TV's typical western heroes. Instead, Maverick is a much more complicated character than those found at the center of most dramatic series up to that time. Although obviously charming, he is an unrepentant rascal whose moral code is molded by expediency, greed, and the need for self-preservation. As Garner and costar Jack Kelly, who played brother Bart Maverick, proved adept at balancing a subtle blend of adventure and comedy, Huggins guided the series in the direction of comedy. While generally sending up the entire western genre, Maverick soon began to nee-

dle its more serious competitors, offering razor-sharp parodies of *Gunsmoke* and *Bonanza.* The touch of irony that Huggins brought to the western genre in *Maverick*—an irreverent blend of drama and comedy—has become one of the defining characteristics of dramatic series in the subsequent years.

During the second season of *Maverick,* Huggins created the detective series *77 Sunset Strip,* which was based loosely on his novel *Lovely Lady, Pity Me.* It was *77 Sunset Strip* that revived the crime drama on U.S. television, much as *Maverick* had revived the western, by injecting a healthy dose of humor into a genre trapped in grim rites of law and order. In place of the stolid cops who governed most crime series, *77 Sunset Strip* brought the hard-boiled private detective into the endless summer of Los Angeles circa 1958. Starring Efrem Zimbalist, Jr., and Roger Smith as private detectives Stuart Bailey and Jeff Spenser, the series defined Sunset Boulevard as the epicenter of hipness on television, a sun-drenched world of cocktails, cool jazz, and convertibles.

77 Sunset Strip lacked the satirical edge of *Maverick,* because after producing the pilot episode Huggins had no responsibility for the series. Nor did he have anything to do with the clones generated by the Warner Brothers management: *Hawaiian Eye* (1959–63), *Bourbon Street Beat* (1959–60), and *Surfside 6* (1960–62). Huggins also stopped producing *Maverick* after the second season, wearied by the pace of production at Warner Brothers and by the studio's tight-fisted finances. As a matter of policy, Warner Brothers refused to share profits with its television personnel—including Huggins, its most gifted and indispensable producer. Huggins was directly responsible for the studio's three most successful series, but he was not even given credit for having created *Maverick* and *77 Sunset Strip,* which studio executives claimed had been based on properties already owned by the studio.

Huggins left Warner Brothers and in October 1960 became the vice president in charge of television production at 20th Century-FOX. This proved to be a strange interlude in his career, because while he was only able to place one series in prime time, that series stirred up an inordinate amount of controversy. *Bus Stop* (1961–62), adapted from the play by William Inge, was set in a small town in Colorado, a way-station on an otherwise endless highway. The central location served as the premise for an anthology series featuring the stories of wandering, disenfranchised characters who passed through the bus stop. The program gained national notoriety when an episode titled "A Lion Walks among Us" starred pop icon Fabian as a charismatic psychopath who commits several cold-blooded murders. In the climate of criticism that was soon crystallized in a speech by Newton Minow, the chair of the Federal Communications Commission (his "Vast Wasteland" speech), the episode became a target of television critics and politicians, who seized upon it in order to decry television's degrading influence on American culture.

Stung by the criticism of the series, 20th Century-FOX placed Huggins in a kind of administrative limbo by refusing to allow him to develop other series and essentially waiting for his contract to expire. Huggins used the unexpected free time to write a stinging rebuttal of Minow that appeared in *Television Quarterly*. In writing the article, Huggins became one of the few members of Hollywood's creative community to defend the artistic merit of commercial, popular culture and to question Minow's essentially elitist criticism of television. He criticized Minow and other cultural elitists for allowing their contempt for kitsch ("their dread of being caught in a profane mood") to cloud their judgment. Huggins's essay amounted to a sophisticated and subtle defense of popular culture in an era when television producers did not make artistic claims for their work. "The public arts," he wrote, "are created for a mass audience and for a profit; that is their essential nature. But they can at times achieve truth and beauty, and given freedom they will achieve it more and more often."

After the debacle at FOX, Huggins returned to graduate school at University of California, Los Angeles, determined to get his Ph.D. and to leave television behind. He needed a bankroll and came up with the idea of creating a series that he could sell to another producer, then sit back and watch the residuals roll in. This series was *The Fugitive,* which he sold to independent producer Quinn Martin after overcoming ABC's initial resistance to a series with an escaped convict as its central character. The story of Dr. Richard Kimble (David Janssen), suspected of murdering his wife and forced to flee the police while in pursuit of the actual killer, carried the mythic resonance of quest narratives from *The Odyssey* to *Les Miserables*. Huggins wanted to update the western by placing its wandering hero in a contemporary setting. In transposing the stock figure of the wanderer from the mythic landscape of the West to the landscape of 1960s America, he created a new and unsettling dramatic hero for television, a rootless, paranoid loner, the most unsettled character on the New Frontier of Kennedy-era America. The quest—the ongoing tension between pursuit and capture—was new to prime-time series and gave *The Fugitive* a powerful narrative momentum that paid off in the record-setting ratings for the final episodes. *The Fugitive* did not exhibit Huggins's characteristic sense of humor, but it developed his fas-

cination with heroic outcasts and revealed his skepticism toward what he considered the American "cult of optimism."

In 1963 Huggins gave up his plans of graduate school and accepted a job as a vice president in the television division at Universal, where he spent the next 18 years. During this period, Universal became the predominant creator of dramatic series, often accounting for much of the NBC schedule throughout the 1960s. Huggins adapted to the programming formats that evolved over the years at Universal, producing series, made-for-TV movies, and miniseries. He began by producing *The Virginian* (1962–71) and *Kraft Suspense Theater* (1963–65). He created and produced *Run for Your Life* (1965–68), a variation on *The Fugitive* in which attorney Paul Bryan (Ben Gazzara) sets off on adventurous journey after discovering that he has a mysterious fatal illness and only two years to live.

In 1969 Huggins set up an independent production company, Public Arts, at Universal and began a series of coproductions with the studio. He created the segment "The Lawyers" of the omnibus series *The Bold Ones* (1969–73) and produced several other series, including *Alias Smith and Jones* (1971–73), *Toma* (1973–74), and *Baretta* (1975–78). The crown jewel of Huggins's period at Universal is certainly *The Rockford Files,* which he cocreated with Stephen J. Cannell. Huggins produced *The Rockford Files* for only two seasons, but his influence is unmistakable in the self-deprecating, slightly disreputable private eye played by James Garner.

In the late 1970s Huggins turned to producing miniseries, including *Captains and Kings* (1976) and *Arthur Hailey's Wheels* (1978). His association with Universal ended in 1980, when he left to concentrate on writing. In 1985 he returned to television at the request of his former protégé Stephen J. Cannell to produce *Hunter* (1984–91), and he served as co-executive producer for a new television version of *The Fugitive* (2000–01). That series did not fare well, but feature-film versions of *The Fugitive* (1993) and *Maverick* (1994) were successes at the box office. Their success is a tribute to Huggins's lasting importance as one of television's great storytellers. Huggins died on April 3, 2002.

CHRISTOPHER ANDERSON

See also **Fugitive, The; Maverick; Rockford Files, The**

Roy Huggins. Born in Littlefield, Washington, July 18, 1914. Educated at the University of California, Los Angeles, 1935–41. Married: Adele Mara. Worked as a special representative of the U.S. Civil Service, 1941–43; industrial engineer, 1943–46; screenwriter,

1952–55; producer, Warner Brothers Television, 1955–60; vice president of 20th Century-FOX Television, 1960; producer, MCA Revue, Universal Television, 1963–80; president of production company, Public Arts, Inc., Universal City, California; writer, director, and producer for television from 1968. Died in Santa Monica, California, April 3, 2002.

Television Series (producer)

1955–56	*Warner Brothers Presents: King's Row* (creator)
1955–63	*Warner Brothers Presents: Cheyenne*
1956–57	*Conflict*
1957–62	*Maverick* (creator)
1957–60	*Colt .45* (creator)
1958–64	*77 Sunset Strip* (creator)
1961–62	*Bus Stop*
1962–71	*The Virginian*
1963–67	*The Fugitive* (also creator)
1963–65	*Kraft Suspense Theater*
1965–68	*Run For Your Life* (also creator)
1969–73	*The Bold Ones*
1971–73	*Alias Smith and Jones*
1973–74	*Toma*
1974–80	*The Rockford Files* (creator)
1975–78	*Baretta*
1976	*City of Angels* (creator)
1984–91	*Hunter*
2000–01	*The Fugitive* (co-executive producer)

Made-for-Television Movies (selected)

1973	*Drive Hard, Drive Fast*
1974	*This Is the West That Was*
1974	*The Story of Pretty Boy Floyd*
1976	*The Invasion of Johnson County*
1976	*The November Plan*
1977	*The Three-Thousand Mile Chase*

Television Miniseries

1976	*Captains and Kings*
1977	*Aspen*
1978	*Arthur Hailey's Wheels*

Films

Pushover (writer), 1954; *Fuller Brush Man* (writer), 1948; *Good Humor Man* (writer), 1950; *Sealed Cargo* (writer), 1951; *Woman in Hiding* (writer), 1949; *Hangman's Knot* (writer), 1952; *Gun Fury* (writer), 1953; *A Fever in the Blood* (producer), 1961; *The Fugitive* (executive producer), 1993; *U.S. Marshals* (executive producer), 1998.

Publications

The Double Take (novel), 1946
Too Late for Tears (novel), 1947
Lovely Lady, Pity Me (novel), 1949
"The Bloodshot Eye: A Comment on the Crisis in American Television," *Television Quarterly* (August 1962)

Further Reading

Anderson, Christopher, *Hollywood TV: The Studio System in the Fifties,* Austin: University of Texas Press, 1994
Marc, David, and Robert J. Thompson, *Prime Time, Prime Movers: From I Love Lucy to L.A. Law—America's Greatest TV Shows and the People Who Created Them,* Boston: Little, Brown, 1992

Hungary

During the socialist era, Hungarian television boasted more channel diversity and more openness to foreign broadcasts, including Western channels, than any other Eastern bloc nation. Yet ironically, commercial television arrived in Hungary only in late 1997, much later than in other Central European nations. The explanation for this irony lies in uncertainties about commercial broadcasting and disagreements about the proper role of television in the newly democratic nation.

Today, Hungarian television includes three state-run channels, two national commercial broadcasters, several commercial cable and satellite channels, and a number of local and regional non-profit broadcasters. Magyar Televízió (MTV), the premier state broadcaster, enjoys a nationwide reach, while a second public channel, MTV2, is carried on satellite and cable. State-funded Duna Televízió operates a second satellite channel that targets the more than three million Hungarian speakers who live in neighboring countries. Hungarian public broadcasting is a mixed system, funded by a combination of license fees and advertising.

The two national commercial channels are RTL-Klub, which broadcasts on the channel formerly occupied by MTV2, and TV2, which took over the former Soviet channel. Both RTL-Klub and TV2 are run by a media consortium headed by Western investors. RTL-Klub is owned by Luxembourg-based CLT-Ufa (49 percent), the Hungarian telephone monopoly MATÁV (25 percent), the British media group Pearson (20 percent), and the Austrian bank group Raiffeisen (6 percent), while TV2 is owned by Scandinavian-based SBS (49 percent), Hungarian production company MTM Kommunikációs Rt. (38.5 percent), and German production company Tele-München Fernseh (12.5 percent).

Cable penetration in Hungary is high, and DTH services are growing. Estimates project that in 2002, 52 percent of Hungary's 3.8 million television homes subscribed to cable, while DTH penetration was 20 percent. Cable and satellite broadcasters include both niche and general entertainment channels. Among the most popular of these channels are HBO Hungary, the American movie channel's first international venture (begun in 1991), and the general entertainment channel ViaSat, owned by the Swedish media group Modern Times. TV3, a general entertainment cable channel owned by U.S.-based Central European Media Enterprises (CME), a media powerhouse in the region, went bankrupt in 2000, after three years on the air.

Hungary boasts one of the fastest-growing advertising industries in the region, with revenues climbing more than 500 percent between 1997 and 2002, and projected to nearly double again in the next five years. For the first four months of 2002, RTL-Klub was the top-ranked broadcaster, averaging a 33 rating in all demographics, followed closely by TV2 with an overall 30 rating. MTV, meanwhile, attracted 12.7 percent of overall viewers during the same period. While imported programming from the United States and Western Europe, particularly Germany, make up a significant portion of the Hungarian television landscape, local production is growing. ViaSat scored good ratings with its local version of the reality series *Bár (The Bar),* especially among 18- to 49-year-olds, while RTL-Klub has had success with the homegrown melodrama *Barátok közt (Among Friends).* In addition, Latin American telenovelas have proved quite popular, leading to the formation of the Romantica cable channel devoted exclusively to the genre.

Television broadcasting in Hungary began on May 1, 1957, with a live broadcast of May Day ceremonies from Hero's Square. The Rome Olympics in 1960 greatly helped accelerate adoption rates of the new medium, nearly doubling the number of sets to 100,000 by the end of the year. In order to understand the character of Hungarian television during socialism, it is necessary to examine briefly the political conditions surrounding broadcasting. In 1956, Hungarian reformers overthrew the socialist government, and were suppressed only through Soviet military intervention. Thereafter the new party secretary, János Kádár, implemented a series of political and economic reforms—often referred to as "goulash communism"—designed to redress or placate many of the reformers' concerns. Openness to the West, including unrestricted travel for Hungarians, was an important part of these reforms, and this openness extended to imported Western programming and television channels. Sparks and Reading (1992) report that nearly 70 percent of MTV's programming in 1986 was imported from Western nations, in particular the UK and West Germany. Viewers were also given a degree of choice in entertainment and current affairs programming with the introduction of MTV2 in the mid-1970s. One of the most popular and enduring programs of this period was the amateur talent-variety show *Ki mit tud?(What Can You Do?),* begun in 1962, which launched the careers of several musicians, actors, and entertainers.

In 1984, Hungary became the first Eastern bloc nation to introduce community cable television, reaching upwards of 200,000 homes by 1988. Run by the Hungarian Post Office, these cable systems carried public television broadcasts from West Germany and France. Also under the 1984 media laws, the legality of private television productions, the reception of satellite and terrestrial broadcasts from abroad, and the purchase of VCRs and videotapes were affirmed. The relative openness of television during this period kept the media from losing popular confidence, which also helped insulate them from radical changes when the socialist regime collapsed in 1989.

Although the transition in Hungary from the socialist regime to a democratic form of government occurred peacefully, the same cannot be said for the transition from socialist state broadcasting to the current public-private system. From the collapse of the ruling socialist party in 1989 until the passage of the new media law in late 1995, the various factions of the Hungarian political scene carried out a highly publicized "media war" over the future of broadcasting. In the 1990 elections, a conservative coalition led by the nationalist Hungarian Democratic Forum (MDF) came to power, with the opposition led by the liberal Alliance of Free Democrats (SZDSZ) and the re-christened Hungarian Socialist Party (MSZP). The media wars stemmed from different political philosophies regarding broadcasting. Sensitive to criticism, the MDF tried to install its own members in positions of power at MTV under the guise of purging the broadcaster of leftovers from the socialist period. The opposition, meanwhile, hoped to place the state broadcaster beyond governmental control in order to keep MTV from falling under the majority's influence.

Because neither side could muster the two-thirds majority required to pass broadcasting legislation, they agreed to appoint a compromise candidate, Elemér Hankiss, to head Hungarian television until the details of the new law could be hammered out. Hankiss drew the ire of the MDF when he removed its appointees from positions of power in an effort to make television news more objective, and the MDF fought back by invoking a 1974 decree that gave the prime minister the authority to dismiss media presidents. The decree was sent to the president, opposition leader Árpád Göncz, for his signature, but Göncz refused to sign, sending the matter to the Constitutional Court. The Court held in favor of the president's right to refuse to sign legislation that he deemed undemocratic, and also required parliament to pass new legislation by the end of 1992.

The 1992 deadline came and went with various drafts of the new laws stalled in parliament. Weary of battling the MDF, Hankiss formally resigned, along with his counterpart at Hungarian Radio. The MDF quickly took control of MTV and turned it into a party mouthpiece, firing or reassigning numerous journalists and launching a concentrated attack against the MSZP, which was then leading in election polling. Their efforts, however, proved unsuccessful, as the MSZP emerged victorious and formed a majority coalition with the SZDSZ. Most importantly for its impact on broadcasting, the MSZP-SZDSZ coalition held 72 percent of parliamentary seats, more than the two-thirds required to pass a media law. In spite of the change in government, cronyism continued at MTV and political wrangling delayed the new media law until late 1995. The ruling coalition appointed a new president of MTV, who subsequently fired conservative personnel appointed by the MDF and replaced them with liberals and socialists, leaving many to wonder whether anything had changed with the new government. The liberal-socialist coalition also squabbled internally about how best to design a public-private broadcasting industry. At issue was the fate of the public channel MTV2, which the socialists wanted to keep in public possession, and the liberals wanted to privatize to help pay off foreign debts. Ultimately, a compromise was reached that privatized the second channel and placed MTV2 on satellite.

The 1996 Radio and Television Services Act established an oversight commission for public broadcasting, the Országos Rádió és Televízió Testület (National Radio and Television Commission, ORTT) made up of nominees from each party represented in parliament. In addition, the Board of Trustees of the Public Television Foundation, which oversees the operations of MTV, consists of representatives from a variety of social, ethnic, and religious groups. Other key features of the new law include advertising caps, foreign and domestic ownership regulations, domestic content regulations, and the process for soliciting bids and awarding Hungary's two 10-year commercial television broadcasting licenses. The new commercial channels, RTL-Klub and Channel 2, began broadcasting in October 1997.

Although the long-awaited law was passed, one final chapter in the Hungarian media wars remained to be written. After the awarding of licenses, rumors began to circulate that CME had, in fact, outbid competitors, but had been denied the license because of its American ownership and its hegemonic position as a commercial broadcaster in the region. CME filed suit in Hungarian court claiming that RTL-Klub's bid had arrived after the deadline, and was therefore illegal. The case made its way to the Supreme Court, which in January 2000 ruled against the ORTT and RTL-Klub, but stopped short of directing the ORTT to pull the plug on RTL-Klub. Instead, the Court claimed it lacked the authority to compel the ORTT to act, because the ORTT answered only to parliament. Many in the Western television industries held their breaths to see whether the ORTT would, in fact, be forced to remove RTL-Klub from the airwaves after more than two years of broadcasting, but the directive from parliament never came.

Private, multichannel television was slow in coming to Hungary for a variety of reasons, not least uncertainties about the impact of commercialization on the public sphere and different political philosophies about the merits of corporate capitalism. After spending seven years pacing the sidelines, the forces of international television entered the television game in Hungary with vehemence. Concerns about cultural decay have since become commonplace among Hungarian scholars, but the initial fascination with all things Western among everyday Hungarians seems to be wearing off. While it remains to be seen how the forces of international capital will reshape the Hungarian television market and what the cultural consequences will be, it is certain that Hungarians today find themselves rather suddenly at the confluence of numerous transnational television flows from North America, Western Europe, Eastern Europe, Australia, and Latin America.

TIM HAVENS

Further Reading

Boyle, Maryellen, "The Public Sphere After Communism in Central Europe: Television and the New Political Class," *Research in Political Sociology* 7 (1995)

Downing, John, *Internationalizing Media Theory: Transition, Power, Culture—Reflections on Media in Russia, Poland and Hungary 1980–95*, London and Thousand Oaks, California: Sage, 1996

Koreny, János, Gábor Heckenast, and András Polgár, *A Magyar Televízió története kezdetektol—napjainkig* (*The History of Hungarian Television from the Beginning Until the Present*), Budapest: Ajtósi Dürer Könyvkiadó, 1995

Kosztolányi, Gusztáv, "'No One's Jamming Their Transmission:' TV Broadcasting in Hungary," *Central European Review* 1 (1999)

Kosztolányi, Gusztáv, "Screen Test: TV Broadcasting in Hungary," *Central European Review* 1 (1999)

Lánczi, András, and Patrick H. O'Neil, "Pluralization and the Politics of Media Change in Hungary," in *Post-Communism and the Media in Eastern Europe*, edited by Patrick H. O'Neil, London. F. Cass, 1996; Portland, Oregon: F. Cass, 1997

Sparks, Colin, and Anna Reading, *Communism, Capitalism, and the Mass Media*, London and Thousand Oaks, California: Sage, 1998.

Sparks, Colin, "Media Theory After the Fall of European Communism: Why the Old Models from East and West Won't Do Any More," in *De-Westernizing Media Studies*, edited by James Curran and Myung-Jin Park, London and New York: Routledge, 2000

Szekfü, András, "Intruders Welcome? The Beginnings of Satellite Television in Hungary," *European Journal of Communication* 4 (1989)

Huntley, Chet (1911–1974)

U.S. Broadcast Journalist

Chet Huntley is most famous for his role as co-anchor of the critically acclaimed and highly rated *Huntley-Brinkley Report*. This evening newscast, which first appeared in October 1956 on NBC, ushered in the modern era for television evening news. *The Huntley-Brinkley Report* introduced an innovative broadcast style, cutting between Huntley in New York and David Brinkley in Washington, D.C. The energy, pace, and style of the program was clearly a step beyond the more conventional work of the "news readers" who had preceded the new format.

Huntley's rise to broadcast news stardom began during his senior year at the University of Washington, when he landed his first broadcasting job, at Seattle's KPCB radio. His roles for the station ranged from writer and announcer to salesman, and his salary was a mere $10 a month. These modest beginnings led to several short stints at radio stations in the northwest, but by 1937 Huntley settled in Los Angeles. He worked first at KFI Los Angeles, and then at CBS News in the west. He stayed with CBS for 12 years until he was lured to ABC in 1951. His tour of the networks was complete when NBC enticed him to New York in 1955 with talk of a major TV news program.

Huntley first worked with Brinkley in 1956 while co-anchoring the Republican and Democratic national conventions of that year. The NBC duo successfully garnered the largest share of the convention television audience, and as a result, the Huntley-Brinkley team was born. *The Huntley-Brinkley Report*'s audience was estimated at 20 million, and in 1965, a consumer research company found that, as a result of their hugely successful news program, both Huntley and Brinkley were more recognizable to American adults than such famous stars as Cary Grant, James Stewart, or the Beatles.

Throughout his impressive career, however, Huntley developed a reputation for airing his personal opinions on-air, and he was once accused of editorializing with his eyebrows. In the 1950s, he candidly criticized Senator Joseph McCarthy's outrageous allegations of Communist sympathy among government officials and members of Hollywood's film industry.

As a cattle owner in his native Montana, Huntley's endorsements for the beef industry during the 1960s again brought criticism from other professionals. His only apparent disagreement with his partner came during 1967, when Huntley crossed an American Federation of Television and Radio Artists' picket line, claiming that news anchors did not belong in the same union as "actors, singers, and dancers."

Despite his critics, Huntley received an estimated

Chet Huntley.
Courtesy of the Everett Collection

$200,000 salary from NBC during the height of *The Huntley-Brinkley Report*'s time on the air. He also earned several prestigious news industry awards. He was named the International Radio and Television Society's "Broadcaster of the Year" in 1970.

The Huntley-Brinkley Report's ceremonial closing ("Good night, David," "Good night, Chet") would have been heard for the last time on August 1, 1970, when Huntley retired from broadcasting, but Brinkley altered his words to "Good-bye, Chet." As he signed of, Huntley left his audience with one final plea: "Be patient and have courage—there will be better and happier news some day, if we work at it."

Huntley retired to his native Montana, where he worked to develop the Big Sky resort. His love for the state and its people is evident in his memoir, *The Generous Years: Remembrances of a Frontier Boyhood.*

JOHN TEDESCO

See also **Anchor; Brinkley, David**

Chet Huntley. Born in Cardwell, Montana, December 10, 1911. Educated at the University of Washington. Married: 1) Ingrid Rolin (divorced 1959); children, two daughters; 2) Tipton Stringer. Began career as a radio announcer, KPCB, Seattle, Washington; announcer, disc jockey and writer, Spokane, Washington and Portland, Oregon; joined KFI, Los Angeles, 1937; CBS News, Los Angeles, 1939–51; newscaster and correspondent, ABC television, 1951–55; newscaster and correspondent, NBC television, 1955–70; teamed with David Brinkley as co-anchor, *The Huntley-Brinkley Report* 1956–70; retired to Montana, 1970, to pursue business interests. Recipient: Alfred I. DuPont Award, George Polk Memorial Award, two Overseas Press Club Awards; eight Emmy Awards, with Brinkley. Died March 20, 1974.

Television

1956–70	*The Huntley-Brinkley Report*

Publication

The Generous Years: Remembrances of a Frontier Boyhood, 1964

Further Reading

Fensch, Thomas, editor, *Television News Anchors: An Anthology of Profiles of the Major Figures and Issues in United States Network Reporting,* Jefferson, North Carolina: McFarland, 1993
Frank, Reuven, *Out of Thin Air: The Brief Wonderful Life of Network News,* New York: Simon and Schuster, 1991

I

I, Claudius

British Historical Serial

I, Claudius, a 13-episode serial produced by BBC/London Film Productions and first aired on BBC 2 in 1976, made its U.S. debut on the Public Broadcasting Service (PBS) in November 1977 as an installment of *Masterpiece Theatre,* sponsored by Mobil Corporation. The production was based on two novels by poet and essayist Robert Graves, *I, Claudius: From the Autobiography of Tiberius Claudius, Born B.C. X, Murdered and Deified A.D. LIV* (1934), and *Claudius the God and His Wife Messalina* (1935). Adapted for television by Jack Pulman, *I, Claudius* chronicles the slide of Roman civilization in the 1st century A.D. into unrelenting depravity during the reigns of the four emperors who succeeded Julius Caesar: Augustus, Tiberius, Caligula, and Claudius. The program's representations of decadence (which included brutal assassinations, sadistic gladiatorial contests, incest, forced prostitution, adultery, nymphomania, and homosexuality) and its scenes of nudity and orgiastic violence, including a gruesome abortion, while toned down somewhat from the BBC original, nevertheless pushed the limits of moral acceptability on American television at the time.

Anchored firmly in the genre of fictional history, *I, Claudius* portrayed real historical figures and events, but, according to C. Vann Woodward, "with the license of the novelist to imagine and invent." While Graves drew extensively from Claudius's biographer Suetonius, among others, for the historical material in the novels, he framed the story by using Claudius himself as the autobiographical narrator of his 13-year reign as emperor and the reigns of his three predecessors. At the outset of the TV drama, Claudius is seen as a lonely old man perusing various incriminating documents from which he is constructing his "history." His project was prophesied by the Cumaen sibyl many years earlier when Claudius visited her and was told to write the work, seal and bury it where no one will find it. Then, according to the sibyl, "1,900 years from now and not before, Claudius shall speak." The remainder of the serial is back-story, recounting the unbridled ambition, domestic intrigue, bloodlust and sexual dysfunction of Rome's ruling elite.

Claudius is among the most fascinating dramatis personae of Roman history. A weak and sickly youth, repressed by a stern tutor as a child, physically deformed and suffering from a severe stammer, he was an outsider in the royal family, considered an idiot and, as Otto Kiefer puts it, "utterly unsuited for all the duties expected of him as a young prince." As an adult, he was never taken seriously as a future ruler of Rome. Ironically, however, Claudius was ostensibly the most intelligent of the lot. A shy man of considerable culture and inclined toward a life of quiet scholarship, he knew Greek well and wrote several works on history (now lost), including two on the Etruscans and the Carthaginians. In the imperial Rome of his day, however, which was obsessed with the exercise of power

I, Claudius, Derek Jacobi, 1976.
Courtesy of the Everett Collection

through treachery and brute force, such preoccupations of the mind were considered little more than idle pastimes.

While Claudius was wise in matters of history, he was apparently far less so in matters requiring discernment of human character. His repression as a child led to his weak reliance on other people as an adult, especially the ruthless women in the imperial family. Nevertheless, Claudius was not the "complete idiot." He was consul under Caligula; and when chosen by the soldiers to be emperor, following Caligula's murder, he demonstrated many excellent administrative qualities. He annexed Mauretania, and in 43 he landed in Britain, which he made a Roman province. During his reign the kingdoms of Judea and Thrace were reabsorbed into the empire.

The character of Claudius (played with great intelligence and wit by Derek Jacobi) is clearly the linchpin that provides dramaturgical continuity throughout the serial, serving as both historical actor and observer/commentator. If one were to assume for a moment that *I, Claudius* is history (which it is not), a professional historian would question Claudius's motivation for presenting his "history" as he has done here. Self-interest might be a driving force for Claudius's portraying himself in the best possible light, given the less-than-savory historical epoch in which he played a major role.

In fact, *I, Claudius* does present its main character in a positive manner. Claudius is the much misunderstood and frequently mocked "good guy" (the "holy fool") amid a rogue's gallery of psychopaths, most notably Livia (played to fiendish perfection by Siân Phillips), the scheming wife of Augustus, and Claudius's grandmother, who methodically poisons all possible candidates who might assume upon Augustus' death the emperor's throne instead of her weak son Tiberius; and the ghoulish and crazed Caligula (played by John Hurt, whose memorably hyperbolic performance might be classified as a caricature if the subject were anyone but Caligula). Set against the likes of such characters, Claudius comes off looking like a saint. But was he in reality?

While reviewers generally accepted the presentation as accurate, the actual biography seems quite different. Suetonius's treatment of Claudius, while questioned by some modern scholars as likely exaggerated in some details, is nevertheless accepted in large measure as an accurate reflection of the man. According to Suetonius, Claudius "overstepped the legal penalty for serious frauds by sentencing such criminals to fight with wild beasts." He "directed that examination by torture and executions for high treason should take place in full before his eyes.... At every gladiatorial game given by himself or another, he ordered even those fighters who had fallen by accident...to have their throats cut so that he could watch their faces as they died." This sadistic streak in Claudius, which Suetonius also notes in other passages, is absent from the BBC serial, and for good reason, for it would make the character far less sympathetic and thereby subvert the melodramatic "good vs. evil" contrast established throughout.

In another area, that of sexuality, the historical record again comes into conflict with the fictional treatment. According to Suetonius, Claudius's "passion for women was immoderate." In the television version, Claudius is clearly portrayed more as a hapless victim of duplicitous women (and a staunch protector of virtuous women) than as a lecher.

The historical record does, however, include the positive side of Claudius's character so much in evidence in the BBC presentation. He often appears as "a gentle and amiable man," as when he published a decree that sick and abandoned slaves should have their freedom and that the killing of such a slave should count as murder.

Claudius was a man grounded in his cultural milieu. His sadism, though tempered by erudition and amiability, should nonetheless be acknowledged. At the same time, his behavior can properly be contextualized by noting that not only in imperial Rome but also in the republic preceding it (which Claudius held in high regard), criminals, when condemned to death, were routinely taken to the amphitheater to be torn to pieces by wild beasts as a public show.

The historical character Claudius was a complex man full of contradictions, and, one could reasonably argue, dramatically more resonant than the sanitized emperor offered readers of Graves's novels and viewers of *I, Claudius*. The BBC production is, nevertheless, excellent entertainment featuring superb ensemble acting and Herbert Wise's expert direction. Its treatment of deviant behavior is sensitive, seeking to avoid the titillation evidenced in so much of today's violent Hollywood fare. Its scenes of debauchery and carnage seem safely distanced (by 2,000 years) from our present milieu and may even allow us to feel good that the contemporary world seems less debased by comparison—if we bracket out such collective barbarity as Nazi and Khmer Rouge genocide. However, the nagging issue of historical veracity remains.

While the BBC production is simply a dramatization of Graves's novels (in which the naturally self-promoting stance taken by Claudius as the first-person narrator is made plain), and not an independent attempt to present a historically verifiable picture, a potential problem is that viewers of the TV version, perhaps not familiar with the conventions within which Graves worked, might be inclined to view it as having a more documentary basis. As Woodward points out, it is from the popular media that the broad public "mainly receives whatever conceptions, impressions, fantasies, and delusions it may entertain about the past." As a consequence, the general populace may not only internalize a distorted picture of historical persons and events but also be deprived of the invaluable opportunity to better understand its collective past and apply that knowledge critically and constructively to the present. People today, in the thrall of the media popularizers of history, are less likely than their forebears to read the work of professional historians, whose scholarly ethics require them to "disappoint" those among the laity or designing politicians who would "improve, sanitize, gentrify, idealize, or sanctify the past; or, on the other hand…discredit, denigrate, or even blot out portions of it." Thus, the door is left open to the demagoguery of self-interested revisionist history.

Predictably, discussion of *I, Claudius* in the popular press prior to its U.S. television debut focused not on such questions of historical veracity, but rather on how American audiences might react to its presentation of sex and violence. As Les Brown noted, the serial "is a chancy venture for American public television and one that got on the national service…on sheer merit." Mo-

bil Corporation, the *Masterpiece Theatre* sponsor, was informed by WGBH-TV, the Boston public station that puts together the *Masterpiece Theatre* package, that some scenes might cause audience discomfort. Mobil spokespeople responded that they had no reservations about the program and understood *I, Claudius* to be television of "extraordinary quality." Nonetheless, WGBH did make selective edits for the U.S. version without prompting by Mobil. These included shortening a scene featuring bare-breasted dancers, and eliminating what might be considered a blasphemous comment by a Roman soldier on the Virgin birth, some gory footage of an infant being stabbed to death, and bedroom shots featuring naked bodies making love. WGBH defended these and other excisions by arguing that viewers in some parts of the United States would be disturbed by their inclusion.

I, Claudius became one of the more critically acclaimed *Masterpiece Theatre* offerings and attracted a loyal following, which today can revisit the fictionalized life and times of Emperor Tiberius Claudius Drusus Nero Germanicus, a.k.a. Claudius I, on video, DVD, and occasional cable repeats.

HAL HIMMELSTEIN

See also **History and Television**

Cast

Claudius	Derek Jacobi
Augustus	Brian Blessed
Livia	Siân Phillips
Tiberius	George Baker
Caligua	John Hurt
Sejanus	Patrick Stewart
Piso	Stratford Johns
Herod	James Faulkner
Germanicus	David Robb
Agrippina	Fiona Walker
Messalina	Sheila White
Drusilla	Beth Morris
Antonia	Margaret Tyzack
Drusus	Iain Ogilvy
Castor	Kevin McNally
Macro	Rhys Davies
Nero	Christopher Biggins
Gratus	Bernard Hill
Pallus	Bernard Hepton
Narcissus	John Carter
Marcellus	Christopher Guard
Agrippa	John Paul
Julia	Frances White
Octavia	Angela Morant
Vipsania	Sheila Ruskin
Thrasyllus	Kevin Stoney

Young Claudius	Ashley Knight	Marcus	Norman Eshley
Pylades	Guy Siner	Domitia	Moira Redmond
Livy	Denis Carey	Plautius	Roger Bizley
Plautius	Darian Angadi	Xenophon	John Bennett
Livilla	Patricia Quinn	Agrippinilla	Barbara Young
Lucius	Simon MacCorkindale	Caractacus	Peter Bowles
Postumus	John Castle	Britannicus	Graham Seed
Praxis	Alan Thompson	Octavia	Cheryl Johnson
Placina	Irene Hamilton		
Domitius	Esmond Knight		
Sergeant	Norman Rossington		
Titus	Edward Jewesbury		
Lollia	Isabel Dean		
Monatanus	James Bree		
Pollio	Donald Eccles		
Junius	Graham Rowe		
Gershom	George Pravda		
Vitellius	Roy Purcell		
Calpurnia	Jo Rowbottom		
Cestius	Neal Arden		
Martina	Patsy Byrne		
Sabinus	Bruce Purchase		
Helen	Karin Foley		
Gallus	Charles Kay		
Silius Caecina	Peter Williams		
Varro	Aubury Richards		
Poppaea	Sally Bazely		
Caesonia	Freda Dowie		
Silanus	Lyndon Brook		
Asprenas	James Fagan		

Producer

Martin Lisemore

Programming History

1 100-minute episode; 11 50-minute episodes
BBC
September 20, 1976–December 6, 1976

Further Reading

Brown, Les, "TV's *I, Claudius* Will Test the Boundaries of Public Broadcasting," *New York Times* (November 6, 1977)

Graves, Robert, *I, Claudius: From the Autobiography of Tiberius Claudius, Born B.C. X, Murdered and Deified A.D. LIV,* New York: Vintage, 1934

Graves, Robert, *Claudius the God and His Wife Messalina,* New York: Vintage, 1935

Kiefer, Otto, *Sexual Life in Ancient Rome,* New York: Dorset, 1993

O'Connor, John J., "TV: Tour of Rome With *I, Claudius*," *New York Times* (November 3, 1977)

Woodward, C. Vann, *The Future of the Past,* New York: Oxford University Press, 1989

I Love Lucy

U.S. Situation Comedy

I Love Lucy debuted on CBS in October 1951 and was an immediate sensation. It spent four of its six prime-time seasons as the highest-rated series on U.S. television and never finished lower than third place. Dwight Eisenhower's presidential inauguration in January 1953 drew 29 million viewers; when Lucy gave birth to Little Ricky in an episode broadcast the next day, 44 million viewers (72 percent of all U.S. homes with TV) tuned in to *I Love Lucy.* When it ceased production as a weekly series in 1957, *I Love Lucy* was still the number-one series in the country. And its remarkable popularity has barely waned in the subsequent de-

cades. Since passing into the electronic museum of reruns, *I Love Lucy* has become the *Mona Lisa* of television, a work of art whose fame transcends its origins and its medium.

Television in the 1950s was an insistently domestic medium, abundant with images of marriage and family. The story of *I Love Lucy*'s humble origins suited the medium perfectly, because it told of how a television program rescued a rocky marriage, bringing forth an emotionally renewed and financially triumphant family. After a relatively successful career in Hollywood, Lucille Ball had spent three years with actor

Richard Denning in a CBS radio sitcom, *My Favorite Husband.* When CBS asked her to move into television, she agreed—but only if her real husband, Desi Arnaz, were allowed to play her TV husband. Arnaz, a one-time contract performer at RKO Pictures, was a moderately successful musician and orchestra leader who specialized in Latin pop music. His touring schedule placed a tremendous strain on the marriage, and they wanted to be together in order to raise a family. The network and prospective sponsors balked at the casting of Arnaz, fearing that his Cuban accent—his ethnic identity—would alienate television viewers. To dispel doubts, Ball and Arnaz created a nightclub act and toured during the summer of 1950. When the act proved to be a huge success, CBS agreed to finance a pilot starring husband and wife.

In 1951 agent Don Sharpe negotiated a contract with CBS and sponsor Philip Morris cigarettes for Desilu, the couple's new production company, to produce *I Love Lucy.* CBS and the sponsor insisted that the program be broadcast live from New York, to take advantage of network production facilities in what was still predominately a live medium. Ball and Arnaz wanted to stay in Hollywood for personal reasons, but they also wanted to be there in order to take advantage of movie industry production facilities and to ensure the long-term value of their series by capturing it on film. Syndication of reruns had not yet become standard procedure, but television's inevitable growth meant that the return on serious investment in a television series was incalculable. The network finally agreed to the couple's demands, but as a concession asked Ball and Arnaz to pay the additional cost of production and to accept a reduced fee for themselves. In exchange Desilu was given 100 percent ownership of the series—a provision that quickly turned Ball and Arnaz into the first millionaire television stars.

I Love Lucy reflected the couple's own family life in the funhouse mirror of a sitcom premise. To this extent, *I Love Lucy* resembled several other vaguely autobiographical showbiz family sitcoms of the 1950s, such as *The George Burns and Gracie Allen Show* (1950–58), *The Adventures of Ozzie and Harriet* (1952–66), and *The Danny Thomas Show* (1953–64). Lucille Ball and Desi Arnaz played Lucy and Ricky Ricardo, a young married couple living in a converted brownstone on the upper east side of Manhattan. Ricky is the orchestra leader for the Tropicana nightclub; Lucy is a frustrated housewife who longs to escape the confinement of her domestic role and participate in a larger public world, preferably to join Ricky in show business. They were joined by Vivian Vance and William Frawley, who played Ethel and Fred Mertz, former vaudeville performers who are the Ricardos' landlords.

Conflicts inevitably arise when Lucy's fervent desire to be more than a housewife run up against Ricky's equally passionate belief that such ambitions in a woman are unseemly. This dynamic is established in the pilot episode—when Lucy disguises herself as a clown in order to sneak into Ricky's nightclub act—and continues throughout the entire series. In episode after episode Lucy rebels against the confinements of domestic life for women, the dull routines of cooking and housework, the petty humiliation of a wife's financial dependence, the straightjacket of demure femininity. Her acts of rebellion, whether taking a job, performing at the club, concocting a money-making scheme, or simply plotting to fool Ricky, are meant to expose the absurd restrictions placed on women in a male-dominated society. Yet her rebellion is forever thwarted. By entering the public sphere she inevitably makes a spectacular mess of things and is almost inevitably forced to retreat, to return to the status quo of domestic life that will begin the next episode.

It is possible to see *I Love Lucy* as a conservative comedy in which each episode teaches Lucy not to question the social order. In a series that corresponded roughly to their real lives, it is notable that Desi played a character very much like himself, while Lucy had to sublimate her professional identity as a performer and pretend to be a mere housewife. The casting decision seems to mirror the dynamic of the series; both Lucy Ricardo and Lucille Ball are domesticated, shoehorned into an inappropriate and confining role. But this apparent act of suppression actually gives the series its manic and liberating energy. In being asked to play a proper housewife, Ball was a tornado in a bottle, an irrepressible force of nature, a rattling, whirling blast of energy just waiting to explode. The true force of each episode lies not in the indifferent resolution, the half-hearted return to the status quo, but in Lucy's burst of rebellious energy that sends each episode spinning into chaos. Lucy Ricardo's attempts at rebellion are usually sabotaged by her own incompetence, but Ball's virtuosity as a performer perversely undermines the narrative's explicit message, creating a tension that cannot be resolved. Viewed from this perspective, the tranquil status quo that begins and ends each episode is less an act of submission than a sly joke; the chaos in between reveals the folly of ever trying to contain Lucy.

Although *I Love Lucy* displayed an almost ritualistic devotion to its central premise, it also changed with each passing season. The first season presented the Ricardos as a young couple adjusting to married life and to Lucy's thwarted ambitions. The second and third seasons brought the birth of Little Ricky and focused more often on the couple's adjustment to being parents—particularly the question of how motherhood would affect Lucy's ambition. The fourth season saw Ricky courted by a Hollywood studio. The Ricardos and Mertzes took a cross-country automobile tour and eventually landed in Hollywood, where Lucy wreaked havoc in several hilarious encounters with celebrity guest stars. During the fifth season the Ricardos returned to New York but then soon left for a European tour—a sitcom variation of *Innocents Abroad*. The sixth and final season found the Ricardos climbing the social ladder as the series shifted toward family issues. Ricky bought the Tropicana nightclub, renaming it Club Babalu. Plots began to revolve around five-year-old Little Ricky (Richard Keith). Finally, the Ricardos joined the exodus to the suburbs, abandoning New York for a country home in Connecticut, where they were joined by the Mertzes and by new neighbors Betty and Ralph Ramsey (Mary Jane Croft and Frank Nelson).

The creative team behind *I Love Lucy* was remarkably consistent over the years. Writers Jess Oppenheimer, Madelyn Pugh, and Bob Carroll, Jr., had written *My Favorite Husband* on radio, and they accompanied Ball to television. Oppenheimer served as the series producer, while Pugh and Carroll were the writers. Together the three would sketch out episode ideas—many of which were based on scripts from the radio series. Pugh and Carroll would write the script, and Oppenheimer would edit it before production. This pattern continued, regular as clockwork, for four entire seasons in which the trio wrote each and every episode—an incredible achievement, considering the pace of television production. In the fifth and sixth seasons, Bob Schiller and Bob Weiskopf joined as a second writing team. Oppenheimer left to take a job at NBC after the fifth season, and Desi Arnaz, who had served as executive producer since the beginning, stepped in to replace him as producer. While in production as a weekly series, *I Love Lucy* had only three directors: Marc Daniels (1951–52), William Asher (1952–55, 1956–57), and James V. Kern (1955–56). Much of the quality of the series is a result of this unusually stable production team.

The production process was unusual for filmed television at that time. Recognizing the economic importance of the work they produced, Arnaz and Ball still faced the difficulty that shooting the series on film generally meant shooting with one camera on a closed soundstage. But they also wanted to capture the spontaneity of Ball's comic performances, her interaction with other performers and her rapport with a live audience. Arnaz recruited famed cinematographer Karl Freund to help solve the problem. Freund was a respected Hollywood craftsman who had begun his career in Germany working with directors Robert Weine

and Fritz Lang. In the United States he had a long career at MGM, where he shot several films with Greta Garbo and won an Academy Award in 1937 for *The Good Earth*. Freund adapted the live-TV aesthetic of shooting with multiple cameras to the context of film production—a technique already used with limited success by others in the telefilm industry. Freund developed a system for lighting the set from above, since it would not be possible to change the lighting during a live performance. With three cameras running simultaneously in front of a studio audience, *I Love Lucy* was able to combine the vitality of live performances with the visual quality of film. Although the technique was not generally used outside of Desilu until the 1970s, it is now widely used throughout the television industry.

During the network run of *I Love Lucy*, Desilu became the fastest-rising production company in television by capitalizing on the success of *I Love Lucy*, which earned over $1 million a year in reruns by the mid-1950s. From this foundation, Desilu branched out into several types of production, a process of expansion that began with an investment of $5,000 in 1951 and saw the staff grow from 12 to 800 in just 6 years. Desilu produced series for the networks and for syndication (*December Bride, The Texan*) and contracted to shoot series for other producers (*The Danny Thomas Show*). In October 1956 Desilu sold the rights to *I Love Lucy* to CBS for $4.3 million. With the help of this windfall profit, Desilu purchased RKO studios (the studio at which Ball and Arnaz had once been under contract) for $6.15 million in January 1958. The success of *I Love Lucy* created one of the most prolific and influential television production companies of the 1950s.

By 1957 Arnaz, Ball, and the entire production team had grown weary of the grinding pace of series production. Desilu ceased production of the weekly series after completing 179 episodes. The familiar characters stayed alive for three more seasons through thirteen one-hour episodes, many of which appeared as installments of the *Westinghouse-Desilu Playhouse* (1958–60).

CHRISTOPHER ANDERSON

See also **Arnaz, Desi; Ball, Lucille; Comedy, Domestic Settings; Family on Television**

Cast

Lucy Ricardo	Lucille Ball
Ricky Ricardo	Desi Arnaz
Ethel Mertz	Vivian Vance
Fred Mertz	William Frawley
Little Ricky (1956–57)	Richard Keith
Jerry	Jerry Hausner

Mrs. Trumbull	Elizabeth Patterson	
Caroline Appleby	Doris Singleton	
Mrs. MacGillicuddy	Kathryn Card	
Betty Ramsey (1957)	Mary Jane Croft	
Ralph Ramsey (1957)	Frank Nelson	

Producers

Jess Oppenheimer, Desi Arnaz

Programming History

179 episodes
CBS

October 1951–June 1957	Monday 9:00–9:30
April 1955–October 1955	Sunday 6:00–6:30
October 1955–April 1956	Sunday 6:30–7:00
September 1957–May 1958	Wednesday 7:30–8:00
July 1958–September 1958	Monday 9:00–9:30
October 1958–May 1959	Thursday 7:30–8:00
July 1959–September 1959	Friday 8:30–9:00
September 1961	Sunday 6:30–7:00

Further Reading

Anderson, Christopher, *Hollywood TV: The Studio System in the Fifties,* Austin: University of Texas Press, 1994
Andrews, Bart, *The "I Love Lucy" Book,* New York: Doubleday, 1985
Doty, Alexander, "The Cabinet of Lucy Ricardo: Lucille Ball's Star Image," *Cinema Journal* (1990)
Mellencamp, Patricia, "Situation Comedy, Feminism and Freud: Discourses of Gracie and Lucy," in *Studies in Entertainment,* edited by Tania Modleski, Bloomington: Indiana University Press, 1986
Schatz, Thomas, "Desilu, I Love Lucy, and the Rise of Network TV," in *Making Television: Authorship and the Production Process,* edited by Robert J. Thompson and Gary Burns, New York: Praeger, 1990
Spigel, Lynn, *Make Room for TV: Television and the Family Ideal in Postwar America,* Chicago: University of Chicago Press, 1992

I Spy

U.S. Adventure/Espionage Program

I Spy, which ran on NBC from 1965 to 1968, was a Sheldon Leonard Production chronicling the exploits of fictional characters Kelly Robinson (Robert Culp) and Alexander Scott (Bill Cosby). Robinson and Scott, who posed as a professional tennis player and his personal trainer, were in reality spies for the United States. *I Spy* was a whimsical adventure show with a hip wit characteristic of the espionage genre in the 1960s. But rather than being drawn in the cartoonish James Bond-like style, Robinson and Scott were fully realized characters who displayed a range of feelings and concerns uncharacteristic of television spy heroes. They bled, got headaches, and often doubted themselves and their role in global affairs.

The Cold War has often been considered a generative force for television espionage programs. The genre of spy fiction, which arguably began its 1960s cinematic history with *Dr. No,* made its way to television in 1964 with *The Man from U.N.C.L.E.* Many imitators followed, but *I Spy* was a departure from the style established in earlier shows. In this series, Robinson and Scott did not battle against shadowy or-

ganizations of global evil, such as THRUSH from *The Man from U.N.C.L.E.* or SPECTRE from the James Bond films. Rather, the show recognized the political tensions of the day. *I Spy* unashamedly acknowledged the role of the United States in the arena of world espionage.

Virtually the entire first season was filmed on location in Hong Kong and other Asian locales. Leonard, as well as producers David Friedkin and Morton Fine, had no qualms about spending money to avoid a "back-lot" look to the show. Associate producer Ron Jacobs and location manager Fuad Said worked with both their own "Cinemobile" and film crews from NBC News Asian bureaus to get much of the location footage used in that first season. The second season was filmed almost exclusively in Greece, Spain, and other Mediterranean locations, using similar techniques.

However, the series did not depend exclusively on exotic location and "realism" for its narratives. It also looked at the personal side of espionage and the toll it could take on those who practiced it. The characters

I Spy, Robert Culp, Bill Cosby, 1965–68.
Courtesy of the Everett Collection

Television Series between 1965 and 1968. Originally, the role of Alexander Scott was to have been that of a bodyguard for Kelly Robinson. Both Cosby and Culp conferred with the three producers (Leonard, Friedkin, and Fine), and the decision was made to portray Robinson and Scott as equals. Cosby also stated that racial issues would not be dealt with on *I Spy*. This "color-blind" approach freed the show from having to impart a message each week and instead allowed it to succeed by emulating the conventions of the genre of espionage adventure. *I Spy* also showcased the talents of other African-American actors of the time, including Godfrey Cambridge, Ivan Dixon, and Eartha Kitt. As a result of its ostensible neutrality on race relations, African Americans could be portrayed as heroes or villains with a minimum of political overtones.

Though never a top-20 show, *I Spy* enjoyed three successful years on NBC. Cosby in particular enjoyed very high Q ratings (audience-appreciation ratings) for the run of the show. In 1994 an *I Spy* reunion movie was broadcast.

JOHN COOPER

See also **Cosby, Bill; Leonard, Sheldon; Spy Programs**

Cast

Kelly Robinson	Robert Culp
Alexander Scott	Bill Cosby

Producers
Sheldon Leonard, David Friedkin, Mort Fine

Programming History
82 episodes
NBC

September 1965– September 1967	Wednesday 10:00–11:00
September 1967– September 1968	Monday 10:00–11:00

Further Reading

Barnouw, Erik, *Tube of Plenty: The Evolution of American Television,* New York: Oxford University Press, 1975; 2nd revised edition, 1990
Leonard, Sheldon, *And the Show Goes on: Broadway and Hollywood Adventures,* New York: Limelight Editions, 1995
MacDonald, J. Fred, *Blacks and White TV: Afro-Americans in Television since 1948,* Chicago: Nelson-Hall Publishers, 1983; 2nd edition, 1992

would often admit and lament the fact that they had to fight the forces of evil on their opponents' level. Unlike many shows of the genre, *I Spy* dealt with agents dying cruel deaths, burning out on the spy game, and often even doubting the nature of orders from superiors. This questioning of authority was more typically found in programming based on the "counterculture" and pitched toward the youth of the times. Cosby and Culp, however, more often than not straddled the fence between rebellion and allegiance, despite the fact that after the premiere of *I Spy, New York Times* television critic Jack Gould called it a show "looking for a style and attitude."

I Spy was one of the first dramatic shows to feature an African-American male as a leading character. Producer Leonard was certain of Cosby's talents, but the network had grave doubts about casting an untested stand-up comedian in a dramatic lead. The network's concerns were quickly dispelled by Cosby's deft and multifaceted talent—a talent that garnered him three consecutive Emmys as Best Male Actor in a Dramatic

Iceland

Iceland, a country comprising a small population on a large mountainous island, situated between North America and Western Europe in the middle of the Atlantic Ocean, belongs culturally and historically to the Nordic countries, having been settled almost exclusively by emigrants from Scandinavia since the island's first discovery in the 9th century. Iceland has very small population of approximately 280,000 people, about half of whom reside in the capital city, Reykjavík. Following the example of the Scandinavian countries, Iceland maintained a state-run public service television monopoly until the mid-1980s, when deregulation introduced private commercial television services. In recent years increased competition has been rapidly transforming the landscape of Icelandic broadcasting. Today, Iceland has acquired all the main characteristics of any other television market in Europe and has national, regional and local television channels.

The Icelandic National Broadcasting Service, RUV, was established in 1930. Public service radio broadcasting was launched with a programming policy characterized by cultural conservatism and a strong emphasis on cultural heritage. The radio monopoly was broken in 1951 when the American NATO forces stationed at the Keflavik military base started a radio service, mainly offering popular music. In 1955 a television broadcast was added to their service. Although the broadcast was intended for the service members and their families, Keflavik is situated close to the capital city and the signal could also be enjoyed by a considerable number of the Icelandic population outside the NATO base. Thus, Icelanders were introduced to the new medium of television by the American military and the programming consisted largely of popular American entertainment and children's programs. The existence of an American television station in Keflavik became a significant political issue and added to a debate focused both on the military presence in the country and the preservation and future of an independent national culture.

Because of their geographical isolation and strong literary tradition, Icelanders have managed to preserve their language intact, and any threat to the purity of the language by a foreign mass media has been met with resistance, and an accompanying idealization of the national culture. By the mid-1960s, however, Icelanders had already been buying television sets for a decade, and the American broadcasts had become popular with a proportion of the public, who enjoyed watching shows such as *I Love Lucy*. Therefore, the decision to establish an Icelandic television service was prompted by a fierce debate about foreign cultural influences, and the Icelandic Broadcasting Company Service (RUV) began television broadcasting in 1966, partly as a response to what was considered a cultural invasion. In the beginning, RUV broadcast for a few hours a day, three days a week, but soon it increased its programming to six days a week. However, until 1983 the month of July was without television, and until 1987 there was no television on Thursdays. The television-free day was meant to protect the traditional social and cultural life of the nation.

RUV is a national public broadcasting service formally owned by the Icelandic state, but it is a financially independent organization. It is required to provide universal penetration and sees its role first and foremost as a public service television station. From the beginning RUV's sources of income have been license fees, as was the case in most other Northern and Western European countries. Some additional funds came from advertising revenue because license fees from such a small population base provide a limited financial foundation, but all incoming revenue may only be used for broadcasting. Since it is owned by the Icelandic state, decisions on policy and strategy are partly made in the political arena and RUV is subject to control by the Broadcasting Council appointed by Parliament. The Council's role is to make policy decisions on programming within the framework of RUV's budget.

RUV is required by law to preserve and further Icelandic culture and the Icelandic language, as well as to promote awareness of Icelandic history and cultural heritage. It is also required to observe basic democratic rules and to uphold human rights and freedom of speech and opinion, to provide a general news service and act as a forum for diverse points of view, and to broadcast diverse entertainment suitable for individuals of all ages with particular emphasis placed on the needs of children. Further, RUV must offer a variety of material in the field of art, literature, science, history, and music as well as providing general education material. RUV has traditionally presented high-brow culture, but as a response to the current commercial market influences has also imported popular shows, such as (among the U.S. titles) *The West Wing, The Sopranos, Sex and the City, Alias, Frasier,* and *ER.*

Until 1986, RUV held exclusive rights to both radio and television broadcasting in the country. The monopoly was ended in that year by a deregulation of the Broadcasting Act. A Broadcasting Committee elected by Parliament now regulates the private broadcasting sector and issues broadcasting licenses. The Icelandic broadcasting market is considered among the most deregulated in Europe, with almost no restrictions on ownership, and little regulation on programming in the private sector. Nevertheless, according to the Broadcasting Act, both private and public television are intended to play an important cultural role. All television stations in Iceland are required to uphold basic fundamental democratic principles and should ensure that diverging opinions and views of controversial matters are aired. They should strive to strengthen the Icelandic language, promote general cultural advancement, and make an effort to broadcast Icelandic and European material. Foreign language programs should in general be subtitled or dubbed with Icelandic dialogue.

After the demise of RUV's monopoly, and despite a lack of a financial foundation for commercial television, Stod 2 (Channel 2) was launched in 1986 and has become a well-established major television channel with a full-fledged programming schedule, offering traditional commercial programming with a limited production of national news, current affairs and entertainment. The main part of the programming consists of Anglo-American series, films, sitcoms, and dramas, and the channel has remained popular for airing shows such as *60 Minutes, Friends, Seinfeld,* and *Oprah.* Stod 2 is owned by the Icelandic Broadcasting Company Ltd., a subsidiary of the multi-media company Northern Lights Corporation Ltd. Stod 2 derives its income from a subscription fee, advertising revenue and sponsorship of individual shows. Since the mid-1990s, Stod 2 has had almost universal penetration and the number of subscribers has remained fairly stable, creating to a certain extent a duopoly between RUV and Stod 2. In 1990 the Northern Lights Corporation bought the rights to another television channel, Syn (Vision), the sole purpose of the transaction seeming to have been the elimination of competition. Syn is also funded by subscriptions and advertising revenue but the programming is limited to sports and American films.

In 1993, amendments were made to the Broadcasting Act allowing the programs of foreign television channels to be aired without having to translate the text into Icelandic, thus paving the way for redistribution of international satellite channels. In 1994 the Northern Lights Corporation added a redistribution service of international satellite channels and now offers a package of 14 channels that are predominantly in English. In 1998 they added yet another television channel to their service, Biorasin (The Movie Channel), which offers feature films 24 hours a day. Subscription to all these services is offered as a part of a package deal including the Icelandic channels Stod 2 and Syn. Also, in 1998 Icelandic Telecom Ltd. Began to distribute, via fiber optic broadband network, international satellite channels offered in subscription package deals. However, international television channels play an insignificant role on the Icelandic television market and have never been met with real enthusiasm from the Icelandic public. Other minor private television channels also exist but are not significant in Icelandic broadcasting. In 2003 ten television stations were on the air, most of them aiming toward local or niche markets, such as a religious channel and a music video channel.

In 1999 a new independent commercial television station, owned by the Icelandic Television Corporation, was launched under the name of Skjar 1 (Screen 1). It is the first Icelandic channel to be entirely financed from advertising revenue and became a real financial challenger to Stod 2 and RUV, who all compete for the same small market of advertisers. Today the signal reaches close to 90 percent of the population. Skjar 1 is heavily entertainment oriented prime-time television aimed at the younger audience. The programming consists of, on the one hand, popular American series, sitcoms, and reality-shows such as *Will & Grace, Malcolm in the Middle, The Practice, Jay Leno, Survivor,* and *The Bachelor,* and on the other hand, domestic in-house production of talk shows, lifestyle programs, a dating show, and current affairs analysis. The original agenda of Skjar 1 was to increase the production of national programming and create Icelandic television for Icelanders; however, Skjar 1 has had to lessen the emphasis on original programming due to costs. In 2003 the owners of Skjar 1 launched a new subscription channel, Skjar 2 (Screen 2), delivered through broadband. The programming is limited to American films and entertainment.

A characteristic feature of Icelandic television is the remarkably small proportion of Icelandic programming. Iceland has the lowest proportion of nationally produced programs in Europe. The reason is simply due to the low population and the small size of the market, which financially hinders original Icelandic programming. RUV has consistently devoted approximately one third of the schedule to Icelandic material, but had gradually increased the proportion to 50 percent of its programming by 2002. RUV is ambitious about national production and offers diverse material including Icelandic documentaries, movies, dramas, plays, and talk shows on various subjects. Stod 2 offers 10–20 percent national programming but has found it important to build a serious news service and also provides an extensive supply of children's programs dubbed with Icelandic voices. National production make up about 30 percent of Skjar 1 programming, mainly consisting of low budget in-house productions. The imported programs on the channels are almost entirely of British and American origin. The exception is RUV, which offers approximately one third of their programming from other language areas, mostly European.

The Icelandic television market is highly concentrated, and largely dominated by RUV and Stod 2, although in a short time Skjar 1 has carved out an impressive share of the market. In 2003, RUV was the obvious market leader with 46 percent share of ratings, while Stod 2 holds a strong position of 32 percent share and Skjar 1 has won over 13 percent of the market. The introduction of Skjar 1 in 1999 has intensified the competition on the tiny market and has subjected Stod 2 to a loss of subscribers and advertising revenue, while RUV has been able to hold on to its role as the primary television service in the country. In this small society any attempt at setting up a broadcasting service is burdened with financial difficulties. Even considering RUV's license fees and Stod 2's subscription fees and the added income of commercials it is difficult to maintain three fully fledged television services in such a small market.

Penetration of television sets is universal and the supply of television channels and hours broadcast seems already to outweigh the demand of the Icelandic audience. As a response to increased competition RUV has more than doubled the transmission of hours since 1986 and broadcasts approximately 9 hours a day. Stod 2 provides 19 hours of programming daily, and Skjar 1 broadcasts 9 hours of programming daily, and nonstop music videos at other hours. Viewing habits have remained relatively consistent in recent years despite the increase in supply of television broadcasting. Television viewing in Iceland is a daily activity and the reach is among the highest in Europe, but when television consumption is considered in terms of viewing time per person, Iceland ranks among the lowest in Europe. Viewers usually tune into prime time, and the evening news remains the most popular programming with the highest ratings. In terms of financial turnover, the broadcasting industry is the second most important media and cultural industry in the country, next to newspapers and the printing press, which holds its top position owing to the strong literary tradition.

The television environment has become increasingly commercialized, and at the political level there is an ongoing discussion regarding RUV's public service role and the future of public broadcasting. However, RUV takes its role as a national institution seriously and strives to offer diverse programming. How the turmoil on the present Icelandic television market will play out remains to be seen and will depend upon technical, political, and economic factors.

HANNA BJÖRK VALSDOTTIR

Further Reading

Broddason, Thorbjorn, *Television in Time: Research Images and Empirical Findings,* Lund: Lund University Press, 1996
Carlsson, Ulla *et al.,* editors, *Media Trends 2001 in Denmark, Finland, Iceland, Norway and Sweden: Statistics and Analysis,* Gothenburg: Nordicom, 2001
Karlsson, Ragnar, Hilmar Thor Bjarnason, and Thorbjorn Broddason, "The Icelandic Media Landscape: Structure, Economy and Consumption," in *Media Trends 2001 in Denmark, Finland, Iceland, Norway and Sweden: Statistics and Analysis,* edited by Ulla Carlsson *et al.,* Gothenburg: Nordicom, 2001
Karlsson, Ragnar, Hilmar Thor Bjarnason, Thorbjorn Broddason, and Margret L. Gudmundsdottir, "Performance of Public and Private Television in Iceland 1993–1999: An Assessment," *Nordicom Review* 21/1 (2000)

Iger, Robert A. (1951–)

U.S. Television Executive

In January 2000, Robert Iger was named president and chief operating officer of ABC's corporate parent, the Walt Disney Company, making him second-in-command to Disney chairman Michael Eisner. The promotion capped a remarkably steady 25-year ascent of the corporate ladder at ABC, where Iger had thrived even as ABC was absorbed twice by outside firms—first by Capital Cities Communications in 1985 and then by Disney in 1995. In both cases—and particularly after the Disney purchase—Iger was given a large measure of responsibility for merging the operations of ABC with those of a new parent company, which required not only a talent for softening the collision of corporate cultures, but also the discipline and tact needed to carry out sweeping change.

Iger is widely recognized as a steady, patient leader with the diplomatic skills for managing egos in a supremely competitive environment. However, given that ABC has struggled mightily in the decade following the Disney merger, his legacy remains unclear. Iger's ascendance may say less about his leadership than about his skills as a master politician whose greatest accomplishment may be his own survival, particularly when considering how many colleagues have exited through the revolving door of Disney's executive suite while Iger has persevered. Although Iger has risen to become second-in-command to Michael Eisner, one should be careful not to assume that he is Eisner's successor; indeed, it is difficult to predict where he will be in the years to come.

Robert Iger was born in 1951 and raised in a middle-class household on Long Island. He attended Ithaca College in upstate New York, where he graduated with a degree in communications. His career at ABC began in 1974 when he moved to New York City and became a studio supervisor for soap operas and game shows.

In 1976 he joined ABC Sports, where he received six promotions over the next twelve years and advanced through a series of increasingly significant positions. For several years he managed program planning for ABC's flagship sports program, *Wide World of Sports.* In 1985 he became vice president of programming for ABC Sports, where, among other duties, he helped to coordinate Olympic coverage and was responsible for setting the schedule of events at the 1988 Calgary Winter Olympics. Iger's grace under fire during the Calgary Olympics brought him to the attention of Capital Cities president Dan Burke. Warm weather in Calgary, followed by melting snow and ice at the Olympic sites, played havoc with ABC's schedule. With millions of dollars in advertising revenue on the line and others panicking, Iger kept his cool and juggled the schedule. An impressed Burke anointed Iger as a future leader of ABC and placed him on the corporate fast track.

Iger was made executive vice-president of the ABC television network group in 1988, where he learned the intricacies of network business affairs, negotiated contracts for prime-time programming, and resolved scheduling conflicts arising between the entertainment, sports, and news divisions at ABC. Iger had held this position for only seven months when Burke and Capital Cities chairman Tom Murphy made him the surprise choice to succeed Brandon Stoddard as the president of ABC entertainment in March 1989.

Iger made a strong impression by making series commitments to two of the most radical dramas in television history, both developed by Brandon Stoddard: *Twin Peaks,* produced by David Lynch and Mark Frost, and the musical police drama *Cop Rock,* produced by Steven Bochco. In championing *Twin Peaks* (which lost viewers and was cancelled after its second season) and *Cop Rock* (which was cancelled after only a few episodes, resulting in huge financial losses for ABC), Iger sent a message to the Hollywood creative community that ABC was prepared to take risks and grant creative freedom—without the smothering network oversight so typical of television production. For the first time ever, Emmy-winning writers and producers and Hollywood filmmakers came to ABC with ambitious projects. Producer James L. Brooks, who had a hand in the creation of *The Mary Tyler Moore Show, Taxi,* and *The Simpsons,* signed a lucrative development deal with ABC. In this supportive environment, Stephen Bochco bounced back from the disappointment of *Cop Rock* to deliver two successful series, *Doogie Howser, M.D.,* and the critically acclaimed *NYPD Blue.*

Iger's four years at the head of ABC Entertainment kicked off the network's last great period of ratings dominance. Iger inherited *thirtysomething* and *Roseanne* from the regime of Brandon Stoddard and added several other series that became long-running hits: *Family Matters, Full House, America's Funniest Home Videos,* and *Home Improvement.* In the target market of 18- to 49-year-old adults, ABC won the prime-time ratings race three times during Iger's tenure. This period of success for ABC continued as Iger was elevated up the corporate ladder: first as president of the ABC Network Group in 1993, then as president and chief operating officer of the parent company, Capital Cities/ABC in 1994. ABC moved into first place in the network ratings for the 1994–95 season and saw tremendous growth in other areas as well, including far-sighted investments in cable networks, A&E, The History Channel, Lifetime, and ESPN.

When Disney acquired Capital Cities/ABC in August 1995, Iger had been six months away from succeeding Tom Murphy as the CEO. Michael Eisner asked Iger to stay on board as president and chief operating officer of ABC, giving him responsibility for all of the Capital Cities operations as well as Disney's syndication and cable businesses. Iger was essentially the point man for the merger, charged with actually creating the vaunted synergy that justified Disney's acquisition of a television network in the first place. At first glance, the integration of Disney and ABC, following the FCC's early 1990s decision to allow television networks to produce their own prime-time programs once again, made Disney the model of the fully integrated media company of the future.

But shortly after Disney's takeover, the ratings for ABC began a downhill slide with no end in sight. In just two seasons after the Disney merger, ABC fell from first to third in the ratings, losing 23 percent of its target 18- to 49-year-old adult viewers, 35 percent of teens, and 45 percent of children aged 2–11. Unable to deliver its promised ratings, ABC has been forced to compensate advertisers with extra airtime, which cuts deeply into network profits. Operating income dropped from $400 million to $100 million in the first two years, and the network has seen its first losses continue in subsequent years. Except for the one season of 1999–2000, when the surprise hit *Who Wants To Be a Millionaire?* (scheduled as many as four times a week) carried the network into first place, ABC's prime-time ratings have not yet recovered their form of the early 1990s—in part because the network has failed to use opportunities such as the fluke success of *Millionaire* to develop new hits. As ABC has dropped into fourth place in the ratings, industry commentators have begun talking about a two-network universe, in which only NBC and CBS are capable of actually winning the ratings race.

Management strategies dictated by Eisner and carried out by Iger are largely responsible for ABC's steep decline. The demand for synergy, which was introduced by Disney, has skewed network practices, distorting the most fundamental goals of identifying talented writers, producers, and performers in order to develop programs that are attractive to viewers. The goal of supplying ABC with Disney productions, for instance, has been an unmitigated disaster. The network has suffered in attempting to stock its schedule with Disney-produced programs; no Disney series has survived long enough to make it into syndication since *Home Improvement,* which debuted well before the takeover. In 1999 Iger supervised the formation of the ABC Entertainment Television Group, which formally united Disney's television production—Touchstone, Walt Disney Television Studios, and Buena Vista Television Productions—with ABC's prime-time division and gave ABC responsibility for television production. The goal was to save money while achieving the goals of a fully integrated media company, but the operation has not yet proven capable of solving the riddle of synergy.

ABC's management of prime time has been equally disastrous, characterized by confusion and an almost ritualistic semi-annual sacrifice of programming chiefs. The chaos began when Iger hired Jamie Tarses as head of programming after she had helped to develop comedies such as *Friends* at NBC. Tarses alienated some of ABC's most loyal producers, who left the network for production deals elsewhere; Eisner tried to replace Tarses by recruiting Marcy Carsey, the producer of *Roseanne* and *The Cosby Show;* Iger made an expensive, two-year commitment to *Lois and Clark* just before its ratings collapsed; Eisner vetoed development deals negotiated by Iger.

In spite of these apparent failures, Iger was promoted in February 1999 to a new position as chairman of the ABC Group and President of Walt Disney International, where he was expected to work toward establishing the Disney brand on a worldwide basis and to coordinate the leadership of Disney's international operations. While no one doubted Disney's commitment to international expansion, some industry observers wondered whether Iger had been given an impressive-sounding demotion that removed him from the day-to-day operations at ABC. Otherwise, why would Eisner reward Iger for failing to turn ABC around? The answer could be that, while prime time floundered, the larger ABC organization had achieved some notable successes under Iger's leadership. ESPN became the world's most valuable network, generating more than $500 million per year and establishing a brand name that has led to the creation of additional ESPN cable channels, ESPN magazine, and ESPN Zone restaurants. Several of ABC's other cable networks, including the Disney Channel, A&E, and Lifetime (often the most watched cable network in prime time) have seen steady growth in revenues and profits. Synergy has worked in children's programming, at least, where Disney series fill ABC's Saturday morning schedule and promote the entire range of Disney products.

In January 2000 Iger was named president and chief operating officer, positions vacant since the resignation of Michael Ovitz in the mid-1990s, and was asked to join the board of directors and executive management committee of the Walt Disney Company. With Disney and Eisner seemingly always targets for criticism, Iger also has emerged as Disney's chief diplomat in controversial situations—testifying before Congress about violence in the media, negotiating a dispute with the Echostar cable system over its initial refusal to carry the Disney Family Channel, dealing with the fallout of a dispute with Time Warner over the transmission of Disney channels on its cable systems, and smoothing ruffled feathers at ABC's news division when word leaked that the network had attempted to lure David Letterman to replace *Nightline.*

Although Iger has an enormous portfolio as Disney president, it would appear that his future will involve reviving the flagging fortunes of the ABC network—or at least redefining the long-term value of a broadcast network in a digital environment. In the short term, he has taken a much more active role in prime time since appointing Susan Lyne as president of ABC Entertainment in 2002. But, more importantly, he is involved in the strategic decisions about how ABC should compete in the world of digital television. Iger believes that there is a synergistic value in having a broadcast network that outweighs its cost to a diversified media conglomerate. Only time will tell whether Disney remains in the network television business or whether Iger remains at Disney.

CHRISTOPHER ANDERSON

See also **Eisner, Michael**

Robert A. Iger. Born in New York City, February 10, 1951. Education: Ithaca College, B.A. in communication, 1973. Began career at local TV station in Ithaca, NY, 1973; studio supervisor at ABC TV in New York, 1974–76; held various positions at ABC Sports, 1976–85; vice president, program planning, development, and acquisition, ABC Sports, 1985–88; executive vice president, ABC TV Network Group, 1988–89; president, ABC Entertainment, 1989–92; president, ABC TV Network Group, 1993–94; president and chief operating officer, Capital Cities/ ABC, 1994–96; president, ABC Television Group of the Walt Disney Company, 1996–99; chairman, ABC Television Group and president, Walt Disney International, 1999–2000; president and chief operating officer, the Walt Disney Company, 2000– .

Further Reading

Gunther, Marc, "Can He Save ABC?" *Fortune* (June 23, 1997)
Gunther, Marc, "Bob Iger Gets Serious About Fixing ABC," *Fortune* (June 22, 1998)
Masters, Kim, *Keys to the Kingdom: How Michael Eisner Lost His Grip,* New York: William Morrow, 2000
Mermigas, Diane, "Iger Bullish on ABC," *Electronic Media* (January 11, 1999)
Orwall, Bruce, "When the Mouse Squeaks, Disney Calls on Bob Iger," *Wall Street Journal* (March 8, 2002)
Siklos, Richard, and Grover, Ronald, "What ABC Needs Is Home Improvement," *Business Week* (December 14, 1998)

Independent Production Companies

The beginning of the 21st century marks a pivotal moment in the history of independent television production. Once the leading source for most prime-time network programming in many countries, independent production companies now compete for access to these coveted spots with program production arms owned by the networks themselves. Under these conditions, the very meaning of independent production has been transformed.

Traditionally, "independent" referred to companies producing programming independent of network ownership or control. By this standard, the autumn 2003 network primetime schedule in the United States included only one new program *(Dinotopia)* produced entirely independently of a network or its parent company. Of the nine new shows in ABC's 2003 season lineup, seven programs were produced by Touchstone movie studios, owned by the network's parent company, Disney.

But some of the very strongest independent voices of television's past in the United States have joined a broad-based movement to ensure a future for independent production companies. Norman Lear, Grant Tinker, David W. Rintels, John Gay, Greg Strangis, Allan Burns, Diane English, and others responsible for some of the most pioneering programs in U.S. television history are leading figures in opposing the most recent Federal Communications Commission (FCC) push to lift caps on media ownership even higher. Five horizontally and vertically integrated media conglomerates (Time Warner, Disney, Viacom, General Electric, and News Corporation) now own nearly 90 percent of American media outlets. Independent producers widely agree that getting a show on the air requires aligning with the networks in ways that undermine their independence. Networks now enjoy greater financial interest and greater ownership stake in independently produced programs, through perpetual license terms, repurposing rights, and backend profits. In the process, they have gained an unprecedented say in everything from programming creation to casting. In this context of consolidation, the amount of programming supplied by independent production companies has diminished to roughly 15–20 percent of all network programming, compared to 85 percent just over a decade ago. To offset the consequences of consolidation, Lear,

Tinker, and the rest are calling upon the FCC to require the four major networks to purchase at least 50 percent of their prime-time programming from independent producers that are "not wholly or partially owned by a company affiliated with the producing or distributing company."

This call by independent producers is part of a larger public protest against a controversial June 2003 ruling by the FCC which raises the limits on how much media companies can own. The new rules would allow a company in major markets (the size of New York or Los Angeles) to own up to three local television stations. Across the country, the rule would permit a single company to own stations that reach 45 percent of TV households—a ten percent increase on the previous ownership cap. A brief historical overview of media ownership deregulation and its consequences for television programming will help explain what is currently at stake for independent production companies in the United States, and why they are joining the effort to oppose this FCC ruling.

The diminishing presence of independently produced television programming in U.S. prime time is rooted in a series of successive deregulatory moves during the last decades of the 20th century. In 1993, the financial interest and syndication rules (fin-syn) expired. These rules, established by the FCC in the 1970s when ABC, CBS, and NBC commanded 95 percent of viewing households, barred the major networks from producing, owning, or syndicating their own prime-time programs. What followed were two decades in which a thriving independent production industry provided the bulk of programming for the networks. When fin-syn expired in 1993, the FCC determined that the rise of cable and the emergence of a fourth network (FOX) made such safeguards against network monopoly unnecessary. At the time, the FCC was also considering lifting regulatory obstacles to mergers among media corporations that promised to secure dominance of U.S.-based media in an emerging global media market. Even before the fin-syn rules were repealed, the deal that resulted in the acquisition of ABC by Disney was already taking shape.

While the networks maintained that their entry into production would inspire more, not less, programming diversity, critics of the repeal were quick to warn of an ensuing consolidation among media companies that would shore up network control over the airwaves and squeeze out independent producers. For the first time, it became possible for a single parent company to own broadcast programming, created by its own movie studio, which could then be directly repurposed for one of its cable networks just days after its prime-time premiere. As the networks' increasingly preferred prime-time programming in which they held a direct financial interest, independent production companies faced new and formidable obstacles to prime-time access. With few exceptions, a spot in the network prime-time schedule has come to require independents to concede to the networks not only greater revenues, but rights to syndication as well.

While the repeal of fin-syn in 1993 undermined independent television production companies, political and economic conditions did even more damage. The Telecommunications Act of 1996, signed into law by President Clinton, lifted important restrictions on ownership and control of media and opened the gates to further industry concentration. As once-discrete media operations were consolidated under a single corporate umbrella at a feverish pace, independent production companies faced new uncertainties.

The Telecommunications Act of 1996 is widely considered the most significant piece of media ownership legislation in the recent history of American telecommunications. The 1996 act fundamentally overhauled laws governing media ownership. Until the passage of this act, no single corporation could own more than 12 television broadcast stations with a combined reach of 25 percent of the nation's television households. Passage of the Telecommunications Act raised the limit to 35 percent, clearing the way for some of the biggest media mergers in history. Before passage of the act, negotiations between CBS and Westinghouse were already underway, as was a deal between Gannett and Multimedia. Its passage ushered in nothing less than a tidal wave of more than $10 billion in TV station transactions. Leading the way was Disney, with its acquisition of Capital Cities/ABC, and FOX TV with its purchase of the New World TV group. Lifting the cap on station ownership has favored the formation of many group-owned stations. This has not been beneficial to independent writers and producers, for whom consolidation means fewer outlets in which to sell their programs.

The concerns of independent production companies have taken on new urgency since the 1996 Telecommunications Act, which directed the FCC to conduct a biennial review of media ownership rules. When the FCC began this review process in September 2002, media conglomerates Viacom (owner of CBS and UPN), General Electric (owner of NBC), and News Corporation's FOX Entertainment Group were quick to file a request that the Commission use the review process as an opportunity to abolish the remaining media ownership rules. According to the conglomerates, in the age of the Internet, with so many new channels of communication, concerns about concentration of ownership are baseless.

While the FCC did not entirely eliminate ownership caps, it did vote to raise the limit from 35 percent to 45 percent of the national television household audience. The aftermath of this decision has been marked by one of the greatest public outcries against the corporate consolidation of media in the United States. The future of independent television production is bound up in its (as yet) undetermined outcome. If the FCC decision holds, independent television production companies will have even fewer stations willing to buy their programming. However, many cling to the possibility that the federal government will overturn the new ownership rules and create conditions favorable to a revitalized arena for independent production.

Fallout over the FCC decision has provided an opportunity for clarification of what constitutes an independent company. A brief filed with the FCC by a coalition of writers and producers defines an independent company as "one not owned or controlled by or affiliated with the same entity owning or controlling the national program service." It was much less complicated, in the early decades of television, to identify an independent production company. Today very few companies fit this definition of a "pure" independent. Many of the one-time giants who helped define the independent production company—MTM, Cannell Studios, Reeves, Rysher, New World, Lorimar, SEE, Witt-Thomas, Miller-Boyett, Orion, Republic, ITC—have either closed down or are struggling to stay afloat. Others have been acquired by the networks.

Independent production companies emerged during the mid-1950s out of the struggles for control over programming between networks and sponsors. At that time, sponsors both owned and produced the majority of programs, as well as the network time slots in which their shows played. Networks found their situation improving as television slowly won over more advertisers to the medium. The possibility of multiple sponsorships curtailed the control that any one sponsor could wield over a program, and the result was increased profits and power for networks. At the same time, networks were reassessing their reliance on costly live programming (the standard fare) and began adopting new cost-saving practices of broadcasting previously filmed shows, or telefilms. The independent production companies were the primary source of telefilms. Thus, networks enjoyed new freedom from the financial outlays for live programming and the independents enjoyed access to a promising new market for their programming beyond the movie theaters.

Scholars have noted, however, that independence should not be confused with autonomy. As long as independent producers relied on funding from sponsors, programs remained subject to the imprint of the sponsor's interests. Few companies have had the benefit of operating entirely independently of the networks. For the capital required to develop their pilot episodes, independents commonly bargained away some rights and financial interest to the networks in exchange for production dollars. The first independent producer to develop a show along these lines was Hal Roach, Jr., in 1953. In the 1950s, programming was also shaped by Frederick W. Ziv, whose experiences over the course of the decade help illustrate the tensions between independence and network control. Ziv left his mark in the first-run syndication market, without the help of the major networks or national sponsors, opting instead for local and regional sponsors who positioned his series on local stations, mostly in non-prime-time slots. This approach proved successful for several of Ziv's series, including *The Cisco Kid* (1949–56), *Highway Patrol* (1955–59), and *Sea Hunt* (1957–61).

But by mid-decade, Ziv found the market for first-run syndication contracting as networks began to sell their own prime-time programs that had already proven successful for syndication to local markets. These deeply discounted reruns sharply undercut independents' bids for first-run syndication, as local stations favored the less-expensive programs that already had established audiences. Between 1956 and 1964, the number of first-run syndicated programs on air withered from 29 to just one. As his opportunities in first-run syndication dwindled, Ziv reversed tack and began making programs to sell to networks, including *West Point* (1956–57) for CBS. Although he had several successful network series, Ziv sold off his company to United Artists in 1960, citing the incursions of the networks into both the creative process and the profits: "I didn't care to become an employee of the networks."

The sentiment expressed by Ziv is echoed today by independent producers and writers in their current struggle to oppose the FCC's new ownership rules. Letters from award-winning writers and producers of independent programming are among the hundreds of thousands of letters send to the Senate Commerce, Science, and Transportation Committee to protest the FCC's decision. When Norman Lear, one of the protesting voices, brought *All in the Family, The Jeffersons,* and *Good Times* to television, he did so under what he calls "the watchful eye of an FCC that was committed to keeping the playing field even, protecting against vertical integration of the major broadcasting networks that would, if they had been allowed, have forced independent companies...to take a minority interest in the very shows we had created, giving majority ownership to the network in order to get on the air."

The letters from Lear and others who did so much to build the independent production industry in the last decades of the 20th century speak of the "near extinction," "peril," and "jeopardy" of these companies. As Emmy Award-winning producer David Rintels describes it, independent writers and producers "now live and work in a business where a few enormously powerful companies control virtually every aspect of the work—not just who gets to write and produce the programs, but the subjects and treatment, and who can direct and who can act, who can photograph and who can write the music." Rintels is known for television dramas that engage controversial issues of politics (*Washington: Behind Closed Doors,* 1977), law (*Fear on Trial,* 1975), and war (*Day One,* 1989), and a longtime critic of network television for avoiding programs that deal with controversy.

Independent television producers are deeply familiar with the issues of ownership and control that are at the core of the FCC controversy. In her letter addressed to the senators, Diane English, the creator of *Murphy Brown,* recounts her struggles with CBS over everything from character to casting to comedic content. Murphy Brown reached prime time only after English battled relentlessly to retain creative authority over the program. Had the network prevailed, *Murphy Brown* would have been an entirely different program; the character of Murphy would have been at least twenty years younger, and played by Heather Locklear rather than Candice Bergen. CBS also suggested cutting from the script the show's defining political satire, because the humor would be lost on viewers who did not follow current events, or alternatively, might offend audiences. Of her ultimate success to preserve her creative control over *Murphy,* English states that "in 1988 CBS let me do it my way because I could take the show across the street if I wasn't happy.... In 2003, forget it. They own it and you're stuck."

The pending rule changes are seen by many as potentially the decisive blow to the "true" independent producer, already "disappearing from the marketplace." In comments filed by the president of the Writers' Guild of America west, Victoria Riskin called upon the FCC "to establish a safety net for the small entrepreneur producer and independent producers and writer-creators who brought American audiences such classics as *The Mary Tyler Moore Show, All In the Family,* and *The Cosby Show.*" Specifically, the Guild calls upon the FCC to redress a dramatic shift that has occurred since the elimination of fin-syn rules in 1993. According to Guild data, in that decisive year, only 15 percent of new prime-time series, and 25 percent of new and returning prime-time series, were produced by the major networks in-house. Ten years later, 77 percent of new prime-time series, and 69 percent of all new and returning prime-time series were produced by

the networks' own studios. To reverse the trend that has made prime-time more inaccessible to independents than ever before, the Guild entreats the FCC to direct national program services to "purchase at least 50 percent of their prime-time programming from independent producers that are not wholly or partially owned by a company affiliated with the producing or distributing company."

No such mandate will come from the FCC alone. But independent production companies are hopeful for an outcome that favors their survival. In a historic move, just one month after the FCC decision, the House of Representatives voted 400–21 to prevent the Commission from raising ownership limits to 45 percent by freezing the funding necessary for such a move. Although the House reversal brought a threat of veto from President Bush, a number of other legal moves have effectively thwarted the enactment of the new cap. In September 2003, in another move that portends well for independent production companies, the Senate invoked a rarely used Congressional Review Act veto to reject the FCC's decision.

A growing public awareness of the consequences of media consolidation has brought positive attention to the meaning and value of independent television production companies. Independent producers and writers, who have long fought to secure a space for their programming on the airwaves, are joined by a vast coalition of interests hoping to help shape the outcome of this debate.

LORA TAUB-PERVIZPOUR

See also **Financial Interest and Syndication Rules; U.S. Policy: Telecommunications Act of 1996**

Further Reading

Barnouw, Erik, *Tube of Plenty.* New York: Oxford University Press, 1975; revised edition, 1990

Bettig, Ronald V., and Jeanne Lynn Hall, *Big Media, Big Money: Cultural Texts and Political Economics,* Lanham, Maryland: Rowman and Littlefield, 2003

Boddy, William, *Fifties Television,* Urbana: University of Illinois Press, 1993

Gitlin, Todd, *Inside Prime Time,* New York: Pantheon, 1985

MacDonald, J. Fred, *One Nation Under Television,* New York: Pantheon Books, 1990

Marc, David, and Robert J. Thompson, *Prime Time Prime Movers,* Boston, Massachusetts: Little, Brown, 1992

McChesney, Robert, and John Nichols, *Our Media Not Theirs: The Democratic Struggle Against Corporate Media,* New York: Seven Stories Press, 2002

Newcomb, Horace, and Robert S. Alley, *The Producer's Medium: Conversations with Makers of American TV,* New York: Oxford University Press, 1983

Wasco, Janet, *Hollywood in the Information Age,* Austin: University of Texas Press, 1994

Independent Television Service

In 1988 the U.S. Congress amended the Public Broadcasting Act by creating a separate fund for independent productions called the Independent Television Service (ITVS). ITVS was merely the latest attempt to implement some of public broadcasting's earliest goals: that public television would be independent of commercial interests and would become, in the words of the Carnegie Commission in 1967, "the clearest expression of American diversity, and of excellence through diversity." By 1988, however, many had come to view the Public Broadcasting Service (PBS) as neither independent nor diverse.

The very organizing logic of network television in the United States—that it act for Americans in the public interest, operate under government regulation, and define itself economically by the "mainstream"—has meant that television encouraged a consensual cultural "inside" and a marginalized "outside." By delegating to television the authority to provide a balanced view of the world and to serve the mass audience, many individual and cultural voices have been underrepresented. While intellectual and artistic cultures, in postures of voluntary cultural exclusion, have demeaned television's mass mentality from the medium's start, it was the civil rights crisis in the 1960s, by contrast, that highlighted television's involuntary forms of ethnic, racial, and gender bias. Even as underground filmmakers, newsreel activists, and video artists at the time forged the notion of "independent" media as an alternative to the networks, a more public crisis over television's exclusionary practices challenged the government to recast its relationship to broadcasting. The formation of National Educational Television (NET); its successor, the Public Broadcasting Service; and the funding arm, the Corporation for Public Broadcasting (CPB) were all attempts to correct the narrow interests that democratically minded critics saw at the foundation of network television. Public television's mandate was to open up and diversify television in both an aesthetic and a social sense. Different types of stories and perspectives on American culture were to emerge, even as the very notion of an independent perspective would be part of the PBS niche that followed.

Yet, by the late 1980s, many liberal critics complained that PBS had failed in its mission to diversify television and to give voice to those without one. The presence of advertising spots in major PBS affiliate stations, Fortune 500 corporate sponsorship of programs, and the generic monotony that came from a limited diet of nature documentaries, high-culture performing, and British imports proved to such critics that, far from fulfilling its function, PBS represented rigid class interests of the most limited type—that this was in fact corporate, rather than independent, television. A direct result of this organized critique was the formation of ITVS.

With advocacy from the Association of Independent Video and Filmmakers and its publication *The Independent,* a coalition of independent producers from major cities across the United States publicly criticized contradictions at the root of public broadcasting's "failure": administrative overheads at PBS and CPB consumed the lion's share of public subsidies from the government; panels that awarded program development and production funds were ingrown networks; and PBS affiliate stations, along with a select group of insider companies, now fulfilled the role of "independents." Apart from token programming ghettos (such as the TV "labs" and new artists "workshops" at WNET and WGBH, segment-producing spots on *Frontline,* and half-hour anthologies of experimental work on affiliates WTTW, WNED, and KQED), independent work that engaged radical political, racial, or sexual politics was essentially absent from public television. PBS seemed unresponsive to such issues, and ITVS organizers took their critique directly to the source of PBS subsidies: Congress.

The resulting federal mandate required that CPB negotiate directly with the National Coalition of Independent Public Broadcasting Producers (NCIPBP) to develop programs through ITVS. ITVS's $6 million yearly budget was to be allocated without oversight or interference by any existing funding entity, including CPB and PBS. However, the independence guaranteed by direct-to-producer subsidies also brought with it a lasting complication for ITVS: freed of PBS/CPB intrusions into program development, ITVS also lost any guarantee of final broadcast on PBS stations. While public broadcasters protested that federal funds would now go to programs that had little chance of carriage on the stations that they controlled, ITVS countered that up-front development money, not carriage, had always been the historic problem for independents.

By May 1990, complications arose on both sides. Spun as an "overhead-versus-production funding" struggle, CPB complained of NCIPBP's unrealistic assumptions about support; ITVS criticized CPB's refusal to cover basic postproduction, packaging, and promotion costs. Many others noted that very little television had actually been developed by ITVS—and none broadcast.

From St. Paul, Minnesota, ITVS aimed to develop "innovative" series and single programs. Topics were identified, professional panels constituted, and "requests for proposals" announced. Open calls received as many as 2,000 submissions; focused topics were as few as 75. By 1993–94, numerous series were finally in production or distribution. *Declarations* collaged video essays around ITVS's charter notion of free speech; *TV Families* serialized family diversity as an antidote to network television's one-dimensional paradigm; *Stolen Moments* tackled AIDS in the context of urban street culture, hip-hop, and jazz; and *The United States of Poetry* and *Animated Women* brought their artistic subcultures to after-prime PBS affiliate audiences.

While some ITVS programs were picked up by many PBS stations, others were less successful. ITVS's quarterly *Buzzwords,* however, defended the organization's uneven successes by pointing to the critical acclaim given some individual works, such as Marlon Riggs's *Black Is...Black Ain't* at the Berlin, San Francisco, and Sundance film festivals.

Two complications built into ITVS from the start continue to dog the organization's future: carriage and overhead. Despite a new rhetoric of "audience-driven programming," ITVS remains weakest in its ability to deliver programming to a national audience. Second, although ITVS was designed to prevent the overhead and administrative skimming that characterized CPB/PBS, many independents by 1995 began to question the ability of ITVS to deal with such problems as the "identity politics" that skewed awards, or the "insiders" that comprised funding panels. The criticism

that ITVS is simply a re-emergent bureaucracy that constrains independence is exacerbated by the fact that its $7 million yearly budget for program development is minuscule by commercial industry standards.

Statistically and economically, then, ITVS cannot possibly represent the thousands of independents that were publicly linked to it by NCIPBP and Congress. Dissension and broadcaster resistance alike may pale, however, before political threats to ITVS funding. ITVS has been resilient in responding to its critics and has continued to refine its effectiveness in several ways: first, by redefining its mission as an attempt to "reach minority filmmaking communities"; second, by establishing its "LinCS" program to co-produce minority independents with local PBS stations; third, by marketing itself as a "service" or "bridge" (that provides "comprehensive" development, marketing, educational outreach, and ancillary Internet activities) rather than as a broadcaster; and, finally, by providing extensive materials that teach the funding-and-development process to new producers and ITVS applicants.

By 2002 approximately two-thirds of ITVS-funded shows went to stations through PBS subscription services such as NPS, PBS Plus, *POV,* or *Frontline,* and producers maintain (with CPB oversight) many ancillary rights for subsequent markets and distribution. The creative history of ITVS during the previous decade shows the difficulties and challenges inherent in attempts to fulfill with limited funding and lack of governmental will the Carnegie Commission's defining notions of independence and diversity.

JOHN THORNTON CALDWELL

Further Reading

Buzzwords (quarterly newsletter of the Independent Television Service), 1991–
The Independent (periodical of the Foundation for Independent Video and Film), 1978–

India

The Indian television system is one of the most extensive in the world. Terrestrial broadcasting, which has until recently been the sole preserve of the government, provides television coverage to over 90 percent of India's population, which stood at 1.027 billion in March 2001. By the end of 2003, nearly 80 million households had television sets. International satellite broadcasting, introduced in 1991, has swept across the country because of the rapid proliferation of small-scale cable systems. By the end of 2003, Indians could view around 60 foreign and local channels, and the competition for audiences and advertising revenues is one of the hottest in the world. In 1995, the Indian Supreme Court held that the government's monopoly over broadcasting was unconstitutional, setting the stage for India to develop into one of the world's largest and most competitive television environments.

Broadcasting began in India with the formation of a private radio service in Madras in 1924. In the same year, the British colonial government granted a license to a private company, the Indian Broadcasting Company, to open radio stations in Bombay and Calcutta. The company went bankrupt in 1930, but the colonial government took over the two transmitters, and the Department of Labour and Industries started operating them as the Indian State Broadcasting Corporation. In 1936, the corporation was renamed All India Radio (AIR) and placed under the Department of Communications. When India became independent in 1947, AIR was made a separate department under the Ministry of Information and Broadcasting.

The early history of radio broadcasting in independent India is important because it set the parameters for the subsequent role of television in the country. At independence, the Congress government under Jawaharlal Nehru planned to achieve political integration, economic development, and social modernization. Broadcasting was expected to play an important role in all three areas. The most important challenge the government faced at independence was that of forging a nation out of the diverse political, religious, geographic, and linguistic entities that composed independent India. In addition to the territories ruled directly by the British, over 500 "independent" princely states had joined the new nation, some quite reluctantly. The country immediately found itself at war with Pakistan over one of those states, Kashmir. The trauma of the partition of the country into India and Pakistan, and the violence between Hindus and Muslims, had further weakened the political stability of the country. Broadcasting was harnessed for the task of political nation building. National integration and the development of a "national consciousness" were among the early objectives of All India Radio.

Broadcasting was organized as the sole preserve of the chief architect of this process of political integration—the state. The task of broadcasting was to help in overcoming the immediate crisis of political instability that followed independence, and to foster the long-term process of political modernization and nation-building that was the dominant ideology of the newly formed state. Broadcasting was also charged with the task of aiding in the process of economic development. The Indian Constitution, adopted in 1950, mandated a strong role for the Indian state in the economic development of the country. The use of broadcasting to further the development process was a natural corollary to this state-led developmental philosophy. Broadcasting was especially expected to contribute to the process of social modernization, which was considered an important pre-requisite of economic development. The dominant development philosophy of the time identified the problems of development as being primarily internal to developing countries. These endogenous causes, to which communications solutions were thought to exist, included traditional value systems, lack of innovation, lack of an entrepreneurial culture, and lack of a national consciousness. In short, the problem was one of old ideas hindering the process of social change and modernization and the role of broadcasting was to provide an inlet for the flow of modern ideas.

It was in the context of this dominant thinking about the role of broadcasting in India that television was introduced in 1959. The government had been reluctant to invest in television until then because the general consensus was that a poor country like India could not afford the medium. Television had to prove its role in the development process before it could gain a foothold in the country. Television broadcasts started from Delhi in September 1959 as part of All India Radio's services. Programs were broadcast twice a week for an hour a day on such topics as community health, citizens' duties and rights, and traffic and road sense. In 1961 the broadcasts were expanded to include a school educational television project. In time, Indian films and programs consisting of compilations of musical numbers from Indian films joined the program lineup as the first entertainment programs. A limited number of old U.S. and British shows were also telecast sporadically.

The first major expansion of television in India began in 1972, when a second television station was opened in Bombay (now Mumbai). This was followed by stations in Srinagar and Amritsar (1973), and Calcutta, Madras (now Chennai), and Lucknow in 1975. Relay stations were also set up in a number of cities to extend the coverage of the regional stations. In 1975, the government carried out the first test of the possibilities of satellite-based television through the SITE program. SITE (Satellite Instructional Television Experiment) was designed to test whether satellite-based television services could play a role in socioeconomic development. Using a U.S. ATS-6 satellite and up-link centers at Ahmedabad and Delhi, television programs were beamed down for about 4 hours a day to about 2,400 villages in 6 states. The programs dealt mainly with in- and out-of-school education, agricultural issues, planning, and national integration. The experiment was fairly successful in demonstrating the effectiveness of satellite-based television in India, and the lessons learnt from SITE were used by the government in designing and utilizing its own domestic satellite service INSAT, launched in 1982.

In these early years, television, like radio, was considered a facilitator of the development process, and its introduction was justified by the role it was asked to play in social and economic development. Television was institutionalized as an arm of the government, since the government was the chief architect of political, economic and social development in the country.

By 1976, the government found itself running a television network of eight television stations covering a population of 45 million spread over 29,000 square miles (75,000 square kilometers). Faced with the difficulty of administering such an extensive television system as part of All India Radio, the government constituted Doordarshan, the national television network, as an attached office under the Ministry of Information and Broadcasting—a half-way house between a public corporation and a government department. In practice, however, Doordarshan, whose director general was appointed by the ministry, operated much like a government department, at least as far as critical issues of policy, planning and financial decision-making were concerned.

Television went though major changes under what has been called, in the official language, *The Special Expansion Plan for TV,* an important state initiative in (re)organizing television during the 1980s. In 1982 television began to attain national coverage and develop as the government's pre-eminent media organization. Two events triggered the rapid growth of television that year. INSAT-1A, the first of the country's domestic communications satellites became operational and made possible the networking of all of Doordarshan's regional stations. For the first time Doordarshan originated a nation-wide feed dubbed the "National Programme," which was fed from Delhi to the other stations. In November 1982, the country hosted the Asian Games and the government introduced color broadcasts for the coverage of the games. To increase television's reach, the government launched a crash program to set up low- and high-power transmitters that would pick up the satellite-distributed signals and re-transmit them to surrounding areas. In 1983 television signals were available to just 28 percent of the population; this had doubled by the end of 1985, and by 1990 over 90 percent of the population had access to television signals.

In 1976 a significant event in the history of Indian television occurred: the advent of advertising on Doordarshan. Until that time television had been funded through a combination of television licenses and allocations from the annual budget (licenses were later abolished as advertising revenues began to increase substantially). Advertising began in a very small way with less than 1 percent of Doordarshan's budget coming from advertising revenues in the 1976–77 season. But the possibility of reaching a nationwide audience made television look increasingly attractive to advertisers after the introduction of the "National Programme" in 1982. In turn, Doordarshan began to shift the balance of its programming from educational and informational programs to entertainment programs. The commercialization of Doordarshan saw the development of soap operas, situation comedies, dramas, musical programs, quiz shows, and the like. By 1990, Doordarshan's revenues from advertising were about $300 million, accounting for about 70 percent of its annual expenditure.

By 1991, Doordarshan's earlier mandate to aid in the process of social and economic development had clearly been diluted. Entertainment and commercial programs had begun to take center stage in the organization's programming strategies, and advertising had come to be Doordarshan's main source of funding. However, television in India was still a modest enterprise, with most parts of the country receiving just one channel, and the major cities receiving two. But 1991 saw the beginnings of international satellite broadcasting in India, and the government launched a major economic liberalization program. Both these events combined to change the country's television environment dramatically.

International satellite television was introduced in India by CNN, through its coverage of the First Gulf War in 1991. Three months later, Hong Kong-based Star-TV (now owned by Rupert Murdoch's News Corporation) started broadcasting five channels into India using the ASIASAT-1 satellite. By early 1992, nearly half a million Indian households were receiving Star-TV telecasts. A year later the figure was close to 2 million, and by the end of 1994, an estimated 12 million households (a little less than one-fourth of all television households) were receiving satellite channels. This increase in viewership was made possible by the 60,000 or so small-scale cable system operators who mushroomed across the country. These systems redistributed the satellite channels to their customers at rates as low as $5 a month. Taking advantage of the growth of the satellite television audience, a number of Indian satellite-based television services were launched between 1991 and 1994, prominent among them ZeeTV, the first Hindi satellite channel. By the end of 1994 there were 12 satellite-based channels available in India, all of them using a handful of different satellites.

By the end of 2003, Indian viewers were exposed to more than 50 satellite-based channels, with a number of Indian programmers and international media companies such as Turner Broadcasting, Time-Warner, ESPN, CANAL 5, and Pearsons seriously considering the introduction of new satellite television services for India. The steep rise in channel availability has led to a major increase in software and program production from both local Indian and multinational corporations.

The proliferation of channels has put great pressure on the Indian television programming industry. Already the largest producer of motion pictures, India is poised to become a sizable producer of television programs as well. With Indian audiences clearly preferring locally produced programs over foreign ones, the new television services are spending heavily on the development of indigenous programs. The number of hours of television programming produced in India has increased 800 percent between 1991 and 2003, and is expected to grow at an ever-faster rate in the future.

Despite the rapid growth in the number of television channels, television programming continues to be dominated by the Indian film industry. Hindi films are the staple of most national channels, and regional channels rely heavily on a mix of Hindi and regional-language films to attract audiences. Almost all Indian commercial films are musicals, and this allows for the development of inexpensive, derivative programs. One of Doordarshan's most popular programs, *Chitrahaar,* is a compilation of old film songs, and all the private channels, including ZeeTV and music video channels such as MTV India and Channel V, show some variation of *Chitrahaar.* A number of game shows are also based on movie themes. Other genres, such as soap operas, talk shows, and situation comedies are also gaining in popularity, but the production of these programs has been unable to keep up with demand, hence the continuing reliance on film-based programming.

International satellite programming has opened up competition in news and public affairs programming, with BBC and CNN International challenging Doordarshan's long- standing monopoly. Most of the other foreign broadcasters, for example, ESPN and the Discovery Channel, are focusing on special-interest programming. Only Star-TV's STAR Plus channel offers broad-based English-language entertainment programs. Most of its programs are syndicated U.S. shows, including soap operas such as *The Bold and the Beautiful* and *Santa Barbara* and talk shows such as *Donahue* and *Oprah.* However, STAR Plus has a very small share of the audience in India and even this is threatened by the launch of new channels.

Since 1996 the televisual "map" of India has undergone considerable shifts in structural terms and program production. The contemporary television system includes transnational satellite networks and channels, the state-run national network, several privately owned regional satellite channels, and numerous small and large-scale cable operators involved in creation and transmission of consumerist popular culture. An interesting feature has been the formation of a range of regional television networks like Gemini, Eenadu, Asianet, Sun, Udaya, Surya, Vijay that exist alongside the transnational networks like StarTV, Zee, Sony, MTV India, Channel V, CNN India, and the state-run television.

A peculiar development in television programming in India has been the use of hybrid English-Hindi program formats, popularly called "Hinglish" formats, which offer programs in Hindi and English on the same channel and even have programs, including news shows, that use both languages within a single telecast. This takes advantage of the audience for television (especially the audience for satellite television) which is largely composed of middle-class Indians who have some knowledge of English along with Hindi, and who colloquially speak a language that is primarily Hindi intermixed with words, phrases, and whole sentences in English. There are several other regional languages in which programs are produced that also mix English with various regional languages. This kind of hybrid program format and language-use has led to interesting phenomena that provides an ostensible cosmopolitan context to the programs.

Commercial competition has transformed Doordarshan as well, and it is scrambling to cope with the changed competitive environment. Satellite broadcasting has threatened Doordarshan's audiences, and self-preservation has spawned a new ideology in the network, which is in the process of reinventing itself, co-opting private programmers to recapture viewers and advertising rupees lost to ZeeTV and StarTV. In 1994, the government ordered Doordarshan to raise its own revenues for future expansion. This new commercial mandate has gradually begun to change Doordarshan's perception of who its primary constituents are, from politicians to advertisers.

But this change has been slow in coming. The government's monopoly over television over the years has resulted in Doordarshan being tightly controlled by successive governments. In principle, Doordarshan is answerable only to Parliament. Parliament lays down the guidelines that Doordarshan is expected to adhere to in its programming and Doordarshan's budget is debated and approved by Parliament. But the guidelines established by Parliament to ensure Doordarshan's political neutrality are largely ignored in the face of the majority that different ruling parties have held in Parliament. Doordarshan has been subject more to the will of the government than the oversight of Parliament. Successive governments and ruling political parties have used Doordarshan to further their political agendas, weakening its credibility as a neutral participant in the political process. There have been periodic attempts to reconstitute Doordarshan into a BBC-like public corporation, but governments have been reluctant to relinquish their hold on such a powerful medium.

The government bases its right to operate the country's broadcasting services as a monopoly from the Indian Telegraph Act of 1885, which empowered the government with the exclusive right to "establish, maintain and work" telegraph, and later wireless services. In addition, the Constitution lists broadcasting as falling solely within the domain of Parliament, effectively shutting out the state governments from making any laws with regard to television. Within the ambit of these provisions it was assumed that media autonomy or liberalization in any form was the prerogative of the government to grant. But the government's monopoly was challenged in the Indian Supreme Court in 1995. The court held that the government monopoly over broadcasting was unconstitutional, and while the government has the right to regulate broadcasting in the public interest, the Constitution forbids monopoly control over any medium by either individuals or the government. The court directed the government to establish an independent public authority for "controlling and regulating" the use of airwaves. The court's decision holds out the promise of significant structural changes in Indian broadcasting and the possibility that terrestrial television may finally free itself from governmental control.

It is evident that over time the control of the Indian state over television will continue to diminish. With changes in its revenue structure and the need to respond to increasing commercial pressures, the character of Doordarshan's programming has increasingly begun to reflect the demands and pressures of the marketplace. In the meantime, caught between the government and the market, Doordarshan continues to struggle to maintain its mandate of public-service programming. The Supreme Court's decision ordering the government to establish an independent broadcasting authority to regulate television in the public interest holds the promise of allowing Indian television to escape both the stifling political control of the state and the commercial pressures of the market. There are a number of other constituencies, such as state governments, educational institutions, non-governmental organizations, and social-service agencies who can participate in a liberalized broadcast system, in addition to private corporations. A number of technological factors, such as media convergence, broadband internet delivery, and Direct-to-Home (DTH) satellite transmissions will also be instrumental in the shaping of the future of India's television system. More importantly, the co-existence of state, domestic private, and multinational corporations—and the rapid rise of consumerist-oriented entertainment, religious-based programming, talk shows, game shows, news, and current affairs—indicates that the discourses of nationalism, globalization, and localization all remain powerful vectors for the televisual system and its audiences both within and outside the borders of the postcolonial Indian nation-state.

NIKHIL SINHA AND SANJAY ASTHANA

Further Reading

Chatterji, P.C., *Broadcasting in India,* New Delhi: Sage, 1991

Desai, M.V., *Communication Policies in India,* Paris: UNESCO, 1977

Mankekar, P., *Screening Culture, Viewing Politics: An Ethnography of Television and Nation in Postcolonial India,* Durham, North Carolina: Duke University Press, 1991.

Mehra, M., *Broadcasting and the People,* New Delhi: National Book Trust, 1976

Mehta, D.S., *Mass Communication and Journalism in India,* New Delhi: Allied, 1992

Rajagopal, A., "The Rise of National Programming: The Case of Indian Television," *Media, Culture and Society* (1993)

Rajagopal, A., *Politics after Television: Hindu Nationalism and the Reshaping of the Public in India.* Cambridge and New York: Cambridge University Press, 2001

Sinha, N., "India: Television and National Politics," in *Public Broadcasting for the Twenty-First Century,* edited by Marc Raboy, Montreal: World Radio and Television Council, 1996

Sinha, N., "Liberalization and the Future of Public Service Broadcasting in India," *Javnost* (1996)

Sinha, N., "Doordarshan, Public Service Broadcasting and the Impact of Globalization: A Short History" in *Broadcasting Reform in India: Media Law from a Global Perspective,* edited by Monroe E. Price and Stefaan Verhulst, Delhi: Oxford University Press, 1998

Inspector Morse

British Police Program

This lushly produced and melancholy series was made by Zenith for Central Independent Television, to critical and popular acclaim, between 1987 and 1993, with five occasional specials following between 1995 and 2000. In Britain, the series gained audiences of up to 15 million, and it has been widely exported, contributing internationally to the image of an England of dreaming spires, verdant countryside, and serious acting. *Inspector Morse* was also one of the first programs on British television to be commercially sponsored, in this case by the narratively appropriate "Beamish Stout," whose logo appeared on the later series. Originally based on detective novels by Colin Dexter featuring Chief Inspector Morse and Detective Sergeant Lewis, the series was developed to include Dexter's characters in new scripts by, among others, Julian Mitchell, Alma Cullen, Daniel Boyle, and Peter Buckman. Of the 28 films broadcast in the 1987 to 1993 run, nine are based on Dexter stories, as were some of the "return by popular demand" Morse "specials" (which followed the same format as the episodes in the original series) aired between 1995 and 2000.

Shot on film, in Oxford, the individual stories were broadcast in two-hour prime-time slots on British networked commercial television, contributing significantly to the reputation for quality garnered for independent television by series such as *Brideshead Revisited* and *The Jewel in the Crown* (both made by Granada). This reputation was enhanced by the increasing willingness of theatrical actors such as Janet Suzman, Sheila Gish, and Sir John Gielgud to guest in the series. However, the series also staked its claim to be "quality television" through continual high-cultural references, particularly the use of literary clues, musical settings, and Barrington Pheloung's theme music. Thus, the very first *Morse,* "The Dead of Jericho" (January 6, 1987), investigates the murder of a woman with whom Morse (no forename given until the 1997 special *Death Is Now My Neighbour*) has become romantically involved through their shared membership of an amateur choir. The opening titles intercut shots of Oxford colleges to a soundtrack of the choir singing, while Morse plays a competing baroque work loudly on his car stereo. Morse spends some large part of the film trying to convince the skeptical Lewis that

"Sophocles did it," after finding that the murdered woman has a copy of *Oedipus Rex* at her bedside and her putative son has damaged his eyes. Morse is, characteristically, wrong—but right in the end.

Almost symmetrically, but with the rather more splendid setting of an Oxford ceremony for the conferring of honorary degrees testifying to the success of the series, the final episode in the series, "Twilight of the Gods," not only uses a Wagnerian title but also weaves the opera through the investigation of an apparent assassination attempt on a Welsh diva. The significance of music in the series for both mise-en-scène and character (it is repeatedly shown to be Morse's most reliable pleasure, apart from good beer) can be seen at its most potent in the regular use of orchestral and choral works as the soundtrack to a very characteristic Morse shot, the narratively redundant crane or pan over Oxford college buildings. This juxtaposition, like Morse's old and loved Jaguar, insists that although the program may be about murder, it is murder of the highest quality. The plots, which frequently involve the very wealthy—and their lovely houses—tend to be driven by personal, rather than social factors. Morse's Oxford is full of familial and professional jealousies and passions rather than urban deprivation, unemployment, or criminal subcultures.

Inspector Morse, despite the skillful and repeated insertion of contemporary references, somehow seems to be set in the past, and is therefore cognate with *The Adventures of Sherlock Holmes* and Agatha Christie's Hercule Poirot and Miss Marple stories—in a genre we might call "retro-expo" crime—rather than with *Between the Lines* or *The Bill.* Within these relatively reliable and familiar parameters of a certain kind of Englishness, it is the casting of John Thaw as Morse that most significantly shapes the series. This has two main aspects, apart from the continuing pleasures of Thaw's grumpy, economical, and—in contrast to some of his guest costars—profoundly televisual performance. First, Thaw, despite a long television history, is best known in Britain as the foul-mouthed, insubordinate, unorthodox Inspector Regan of *The Sweeney,* a police show first broadcast in the 1970s and regarded as excessively violent and particularly significant in eroding the representational divide between law enforcers

Inspector Morse, John Thaw, 1987–2000.
Courtesy of the Everett Collection

and law breakers (an erosion in which, for example, Don Siegel's film with Clint Eastwood, *Dirty Harry,* was seen as particularly significant). That it should be Thaw who once again appears as "a good detective, but a bad policeman," but this time in a series that eschews instinct and action for intuition and deduction, offers a rich contrast for viewers familiar with *The Sweeney.* However, it is the partnership between Thaw and Kevin Whately (originally a member of the radical 7.84 theater group, and subsequently a lead in his own right as Dr. Jack Kerruish of *Peak Practice*) that drives the continuity of the series and offers pleasures to viewers who may not be at ease with Morse's high-cultural world. For if Morse, the former Oxford student and doer of crosswords, is the brilliant loner who is vulnerable to the charms of women of a certain age, it is Lewis, happily married with children, who, like Dr. Watson, does much of the legwork and deduction, while also nurturing his brilliant chief. However, it is also Lewis, a happy man who often fails to understand the cultural references ("So do we have an address for this Sophocles?"), who, in the most literal sense, brings Morse down to earth—to popular television.

CHARLOTTE BRUNSDON

See also **Miss Marple; Sherlock Holmes; Thaw, John**

Cast (selected)

Chief Inspector Morse	John Thaw
Detective Sergeant Lewis	Kevin Whately
Max	Peter Woodthorpe
Dr. Grayling Russell	Amanda Hilwood
Chief Superintendent Bell	Norman Jones
Chief Superintendent Strange	James Grout
Chief Superintendent Holdsby	Alun Armstrong

Producers

Ted Childs, Kenny McBain, Chris Burt, David Lascelles, Deirdre Keir

Programming History

28 120-minute episodes, plus 5 120-minute specials
ITV

January 6, 1987–January 20, 1987	3 episodes
December 25, 1987–March 22, 1988	4 episodes
January 4, 1989–January 25, 1989	4 episodes
January 3, 1990–January 24, 1990	4 episodes
February 20, 1991–March 27, 1991	5 episodes
February 26, 1992–April 15, 1992	5 episodes
January 6, 1993–January 20, 1993	3 episodes
November 29, 1995	*The Way through the Woods*
November 27, 1996	*The Daughters of Cain*
November 19, 1997	*Death Is Now My Neighbour*
November 11, 1998	*The Wench Is Dead*
November 15, 2000	*The Remorseful Day*

Further Reading

Sparks, Richard, "Inspector Morse: The Last Enemy (Peter Buckman)," in *British Television Drama in the 1980s,* edited by George Brandt, Cambridge: Cambridge University Press, 1993

Thomas, Lyn, "In Love with Inspector Morse: Feminist Subculture and Quality Television," *Feminist Review* (Autumn 1995)

Interactive Television

Television is typically perceived as a passive medium, its content and information flowing only in one direction, from provider to viewer. Almost since the beginning of the television age, however, there have been those—both providers and viewers—who have wanted more from television. In 1953, in one of the first instances of viewers actually interacting with television, *Winky Dink and You* allowed children to place a plastic sheet over the television screen and draw on it to complete puzzles and games shown on the screen. Today, the term "interactive television" represents several recent advances in new television technologies. The term is commonly used to refer to all of these technologies, but distinctions can in fact be made among personal television, enhanced television, and interactive television.

Personal television refers to technology that allows the viewer to manipulate live television content sent by the provider (over the air, cable, or satellite). One of the most popular of these technologies is known as the personal video recorder (PVR) or digital video recorder (DVR). The PVR acts much like a video cassette recorder in that it can record live shows to be watched at a later time (time-shifting). The difference lies in the fact that PVRs record the content to a hard disk instead of a cassette. PVRs also constantly record the stream of content the viewer is currently watching, providing the capability to pause, rewind and repeat, and even slow-motion-repeat live television. If viewers intentionally choose to begin viewing a program after the program has begun, they have the capability to rewind and start at the beginning of the show. This also affords the ability to fast forward until the recorded content "catches up" to the live stream. This process allows viewers to skip commercials, a capability that has started a vigorous debate among advertisers worried about the loss of attention to commercials. Most PVRs come assembled as a stand-alone device, or are bundled with devices such as a digital cable or satellite receiver already providing content, commonly referred to as set-top boxes. TiVo, ReplayTV, and Microsoft were among the first companies to introduce PVRs as stand-alone devices. Now many service providers, such as cable and satellite companies, are combining PVR functionality with their digital receivers. For this reason, many scholars believe this technology will spread rapidly.

One key aspect of the PVR, and central to most new television technologies, is the electronic program guide (EPG). This is a built-in television guide that downloads the television schedule for several days into the future. This allows viewers an easier means of searching for a program and commanding the PVR to record particular programs. The EPG also acts much like a database, able to catalog search terms such as actors, directors, plotlines, and titles, making it easier for viewers to find preferred content.

Enhanced television allows viewers not only to receive television programming, but also to receive additional information (enhancements) pertinent to the content being viewed. While watching a baseball game, for example, an icon appears on the television screen that can be selected and accessed via the remote control. Doing so may give the viewer individual player statistics, current wind conditions at the ballpark, or other information relevant to the game. Such enhancements could include actor biographies, director's comments, or a full list of program credits. Wink is a current company that provides this type of content and technology to service providers.

Many of these enhancements work via the Vertical Blanking Interval (VBI) contained in the transmission of data to a viewer's set-top box. The VBI is an extremely brief time interval occurring between different frames being scanned onto the television screen— comparable to the blank space between frames on film stock. The potential of VBI was understood more fully after engineers realized that closed captioning content could be sent through this VBI. The same concept works for Enhanced Television, but the VBI can carry content, including enhancements, other than video and audio. As an alternative to the VBI, some content providers also use telephone lines, which can be connected to the back of the set-top box, to send the enhancements.

A truer definition of interactive television takes the concept of enhanced television one step further. In fully interactive television, information between content provider and viewer flows both ways. There are two primary ways this takes place: either through the television setup itself, or through another device such as a computer. The route by which information is sent back to the content provider is called a back channel. The back channel can theoretically operate through the cable or satellite connection originally providing the content or independently through a separate phone line or modem (cable or DSL). This technology is not firmly in place in the United States, but is growing in popularity in Europe. A current concept of interactive television in the United States also allows viewers to use computers simultaneously with television to interact with content. The Game Show Network (GSN), for example, allows users to visit GSN's website on a home computer in order to play along with the contestants in a selected number of shows.

One element of interactive television developing in the United States is Video on Demand (VOD), an arrangement allowing viewers to order content from their video provider at random times and have it begin playing instantly. The customer searches through a catalogue of shows and chooses content that is then downloaded to their set-top box. Current VOD applications usually sell movies and sporting events but any type of content could theoretically be archived and catalogued. A version of this technology, Near Video On Demand (NVOD), also allows customers to purchase content, although the programming runs in blocks (perhaps beginning every 15 minutes) instead of beginning instantly. This is closer to the concept of the pay-per-view channels that are currently widely offered.

More interactive television designs in Europe allow viewers to use television, rather than a second device, as a back channel. Much like enhanced television, viewers can select items on screen with their remote controls and interact with the content. For example, pressing a button during Wimbledon allows the viewer to choose which match he or she wishes to see. Selecting a match other than that on the main video feed gives the viewer the feed and commentary from a different court.

The ability to send as well as receive information also means that business can be conducted over television, a practice already known as television commerce (t-commerce). In Europe, viewers can order a pizza from Domino's over their television service—during a commercial, the viewer uses the remote control to both order and pay for the pizza to be delivered. This is made possible by accessing what is known as a Walled Garden—viewers are allowed to go online, but only to sites sponsoring the programming or able to make money from the programming. The prospect is that the same t-commerce concept could be successful in the United States, which has much more advertiser-supported programming than Europe. Product placement in television shows could allow viewers to order that product through their remote controls.

In some ways, all these versions of interactive television are fundamental alterations of conventionally understood "passive" uses of the medium. It is unlikely, however, that they will completely supplant other practices, such as typical viewing of information and entertainment. They do make clear, however, that the ways in which television has been experienced for more than half a century are not determined by its technological features, which far exceed the uses that have become most familiar to most viewers.

KEVIN D. WILLIAMS

See also **Satellite; Technology, Television**

Further Reading

Gurian, Phil, *The Interactive Television Dictionary (Revised and Update Edition),* Spokane, Washington: Grand National Press, 2002

Swann, Phillip, *TV dot Com: The Future of Interactive Television,* New York: TV Books, 2000

International Telecommunication Union

The instantaneous transmission of news and information across the globe was made possible in the 1830s by the invention of the telegraph, the invention that gave rise to the word "telecommunications." The electric telegraph machine was created through efforts of Samuel Morse, Sir Charles Wheatstone, and Sir William Cooke, and telegraphy began in England in 1837. Today, pagers, mobile phones, remote control toys, faxes, aircraft and maritime navigation systems, satellite communications, e-mail, radio, television, wireless Internet, and many more daily communication tools function in the modern global communication network thanks in part to the work of the International Telecommunication Union (ITU).

In the early days of cross-national communication, messages were encoded on a telegraph machine and sent to the bordering country for transcription, usually by a national post office, and then sent to their destination. Messages could not be sent directly from a source in one country to a receiver in another country because a common code was not used.

The need for technical standardization was first recognized by Prussia and Austria, and in October 1849 these two countries made the first attempt to link telegraph systems with a common code. One year later, an agreement between these two countries, Bavaria, and Saxony created the Austro-German Telegraph Union. The success of this first union gave rise to additional regional unions, leading to the creation of the International Telegraph Union in 1865. The advent of radio communications at the end of the 19th century led to the first International Radiotelegraph Conference, held in Berlin in 1906, at which the International Radiotelegraph Convention was agreed in order to establish regulations and technical standards for cross-border wireless communication. In 1934, the International Telegraph Union expanded its remit to take in the 1906 convention, changing its name to the International Telecommunication Union. Today, the ITU is the sole regulating institution with power to regulate the transfer of data throughout the world.

In 1947 the ITU became an agency in the United Nations. According to a 1982 ITU Convention report, the purposes of the ITU are as follows: (1) to maintain and foster rational use of telecommunications and to offer technical assistance; (2) to promote and improve efficient use of technical equipment and operations; and (3) to coordinate and promote a positive world environment for the achievement of the above goals.

As the speed of telecommunications inventions increases, so does the importance of the ITU. The evolution of telecommunications technology during the 20th century is so great that telecommunications affects almost every aspect of life, and the role of the ITU continues to extend into new areas of concern. The three major areas of jurisdiction for the ITU are: (1) distribution of radio and satellite services and assignments; (2) establishment of international telecommunications standards; and (3) regulation of international information exchange such as telephony, telegraphy, and computer data. The ITU also plays a vital role in telecommunications assistance for developing countries. The ITU is divided into three major sectors—Radiocommunication (ITU-R), Telecommunication Standardization (ITU-T), and Telecommunication Development (ITU-D)—aimed at facilitating global discussion of the wide range of radio and telecommunication issues.

Some 160 countries within the United Nations (UN) have representatives in the ITU. Each of these countries gets one vote on ITU decisions. The general meeting of the ITU is held once every few years and is called the Plenipotentiary Conference. The chief objective of this conference is to review and revise the *ITU Convention,* which is the governing document of the union. The one-country, one-vote format often leads to voting blocks based on country alliances, and creates the political nature of the ITU.

The antagonisms between these voting blocks, in the light of the ever-increasing quantity of information being sent and received internationally, at times threaten the existence of the ITU. Many developing countries want to break the dominant flow of information from Northern industrialized countries to Southern developing countries. Broadly speaking, the North wants to continue the "free flow" of information while the South would like to be able to regulate the flow to enable them to maintain greater control of their own socio-cultural development.

A second factor that threatens the existence of the ITU is the fact that the speed at which technological changes now occur is greater than the ITU's international standards process can accommodate. Thus, several other standards organizations have developed, such as the T1 Committee of the Exchange Carriers Standards Association in the United States, the Telecommunications Technology Committee (TTC) in Japan, and the European Telecommunications Standards Institute (ETSI). These regional standards organizations (RSOs) offer a more homogeneous membership than the ITU, which makes the standardization process quicker.

In response to the RSOs, the ITU has streamlined its standards process and restructured its voting rules so that decisions can be made by ballot between Plenipotentiary Conferences. In 1996, the ITU convened the first World Telecommunication Policy Forum (WTPF) in an effort to promote discussion and harmony regarding telecommunication regulatory policies. For example, one of the more recent ITU debates focused on satellite and orbital space allocation for ITU members. Globally accepted standards are necessary for crossnational telecommunication and safety. The telecommunication industry is at the core of many global health, education, and food manufacturing and distribution services such as tele-medicine and distance learning. The ITU will most likely continue to play an important regulatory role in global communications, economics, and politics.

JOHN TEDESCO

See also **Standards and Practices**

Further Reading

Codding, George A., *The International Communication Union: An Experiment in International Cooperation,* New York: Arno, 1972

Codding, George A., with Anthony M. Rutkowski, *The International Telecommunication Union in a Changing World,* Dedham, Massachusetts: Artech, 1982

Global Communication in the Space Age: Toward a New ITU (report on an International Conference), New York: John and Mary R. Markle Foundation, 1972

Gutestam, Monica, "ITU—125 Years Old: At the Cutting Edge of Telecommunications," *UN Chronicle* (September 1990)

Irmer, Theodor, "Shaping Future Telecommunications: The Challenge of Global Standardization," *IEEE Communications Magazine* (January 1994)

Lauria White, Rita, and Harold M. White, Jr., *The Law and Reg-ulation of International Space Communication,* Boston: Artech, 1988

Leive, David M., editor, *The Future of the International Telecommunication Union: A Report for the 1973 Plenipotentiary Conference, American Society of International Law* (panel report on International Telecommunications Policy), Washington, D.C.: American Society of International Law, 1972.

MacLean, Donald J., "A New Departure for the ITU," *Telecommunications Policy* (April 1995)

Savage, James G., *The Politics of International Telecommunication Regulation,* Boulder, Colorado: Westview, 1989

International Television Program Markets

(MIDEM, MIPCOM, MIP-TV, MIP-ASIA, DISCOP, Asia Television Forum, and HK Filmart)

Television has always been traded, exchanged, bought, and sold. It would be fair to say, however, that for a good part of the history of this medium, commerce in television traveled along what Kaarle Nordenstreng and Tapio Varis called, in 1974, "a one-way street" from the United States (and, to a lesser extent, Great Britain) to the rest of the world (see Nordenstreng and Varis). Now, however, this situation is changing. The pressures of globalization, the spread of post-Fordist models of production, and the emerging dynamism of many alternative centers of production make the idea of "world television" less fanciful. A more appropriate metaphor for depicting international television might now be Michael Tracey's notion of a "patchwork quilt" (see Tracey, 1988). This image implies interconnectedness in a world system. One cause of this newer pattern of world television is the very practical need for cofinancing arrangements when it is impossible to fund high-end product domestically. A second factor in the newer arrangements is the continuing dependency of most programming services on some degree of imported television.

Today, then, there is a world market for television. The main players in this market are producers, distributors, and broadcasters. The subsidiary players are government agencies, financiers, packagers, and sales agents. The stages on which the players appear are the markets held several times a year in the United States, Europe, and more recently, Asia. The most well-observed markets are MIP-TV (held in April in Cannes, France), MIPCOM (held in October in Cannes), the American Film Market, or AFM (held in Santa Monica, California, in February), the Monte Carlo Television market, and the National Association of Television Programming Executives, NATPE (held in Los Vegas, Nevada, in January). Other markets of note are the Reed-Midem organized MILIA market for interactive television, held in Cannes in February; the Cannes Market (MIF); and the International Animated Film Market (MIFA), held in Annecy, France. However, the glut of such markets in Europe has led to a downturn in attendance in recent years. A recent addition to the international schedule, and one that is gaining momentum, is the DISCOP format market, first held in Lisbon in 2002. The nature of the DISCOP market is to generate sales of format ideas and establish relationships between format licensors, creators, producers, and investors. This is a significant development given that a number of major media organizations now see formats as integral to their internationalization strategies.

Some of the sales conventions are well established. The MIDEM organization, which runs the MIP events, started in the 1950s and is now owned by Reed International, the publishing company. The dominance of European and North American markets has in recent years been challenged by new events in the Asian region. MIP Asia was first held in December 1994 in Hong Kong. The market achieved mixed success in comparison with its European-based namesakes and was wound down after the 1999 MIP Asia, held in Singapore, being replaced by the Asia Television Forum, which is now held in early December and is organized by Reed Exhibitions and Television Asia. An Asian-based trade forum that has doubled its volume of sales since 1999 is the Hong Kong International Film and Television Market (HK Filmart). This market is organized by the Hong Kong Trade and Development Council, and is held in June. Also gathering momentum is the Shanghai International Film and TV Program Market, which follows the now-merged Shanghai TV and Shanghai Film festivals. It is also held in early June.

MIP-TV, the longest-running of the markets, attracted 1,205 exhibitors and 10,217 participants from 92 countries in 2002. MIPCOM (International Market for Television, Video, Cable and Satellite Films and Programs), which began life in the early 1980s as an "obscure sibling" to the long running MIP-TV in spring, is held in the northern fall, also in Cannes. It grew fast to become, by the late 1980s, the second-biggest event after MIP-TV, and it is now a huge meeting of the world's television buyers and sellers, with the established players dominant. The 2001 MIPCOM attracted 5,185 exhibitors and nearly 10,000 participants from dozens of countries. Xavier Roy, chief executive of the Reed-Midem organization, believes the event can accommodate expansion to 12–15,000 participants.

In these big markets, programming is often bought or rejected sight-unseen, in job lots, based on company reputation or distributor clout. Very broad, rough-and-ready genre expectations are in play. Decisions to purchase programs not central to the schedule are frequently made on such grounds, even though the choices seem arbitrary. Conversely, there is a tradition among some European public broadcasters of scrutinizing possible foreign acquisitions extremely closely. In this atmosphere, it is difficult for the new company, the off-beat product, or the unusual concept to be discovered. (For its first foray as a seller into MIPCOM in 1993, the U.S. documentary cable channel Discovery "tarted up" its profile by dressing its stall as a movie set. Actors were employed to create live action scenarios around a World War II theme to coincide with Dis-

covery's use of Normandy-landing documentaries as its flagship programs.)

These markets are the places where buyers can view the programs on sale from various producers, distributors, and sales agents. Just as crucially, markets are the places where the players can circle each other at screenings and parties in the attempt to set up or consolidate partnerships that can help to finance the next project. If there is one thing true about "world" television, it is that it works on a basis of personal contact. Experienced distributor Bruce Gordon, head of Paramount International, has described the international television market as a club. However, not all players in this club are equal. The most powerful are the U.S. networks; the representatives of the Hollywood studios; the major broadcasters, both commercial and public service, from the richest regions elsewhere (Japan and Europe); the emerging new pay services like Star TV, British Sky Broadcasting (BSkyB), and Canal Plus; and perhaps some of the biggest television distributors, such as Germany's Kirsch Group, whose large holdings of library material gave it considerable economic clout until the company was declared insolvent in 2002. Given the multiplication of television distribution channels throughout the world, it is likely that the international markets will continue to grow in importance. New participants will need to find ways to place themselves within the structures of power and exchange already controlled by these more established institutions and individuals.

STUART D. CUNNINGHAM

See also **Format Sales, International**

Further Reading

Nordenstreng, Kaarle, and Tapio Varis, "Television Traffic: A One-Way Street," *UNESCO Reports and Papers on Mass Communication* 70 (1974)

Tracey, Michael, "The Poisoned Chalice? International Television and the Idea of Dominance," *Daedalus* (Fall 1985)

Tracey, Michael, "Popular Culture and the Economics of Global Television," *Intermedia* (March 1988)

Varis, Tapio, "Global Traffic in Television," *Journal of Communication* (1974)

Varis, Tapio, "The International Flow of Television Programs," *Journal of Communication* (1984)

Ireland

The island of Ireland is made up of two nation-states. Northern Ireland consists of six counties of the province of Ulster and is part of the United Kingdom.

The terrestrial television service provided in its broadcast area is that of the BBC, Channel 4, Channel 5 and ITV. BBC Northern Ireland transmits many BBC programs originating in Britain, produces a significant number of its own programs, broadcasting its own versions of BBC 1 and BBC 2 as well as the Corporation's new digital TV channels BBC 3, BBC 4, and two channels of children's programs. Meanwhile, Ulster Television is the regional member of the ITV network. It acts both as a broadcaster of the ITV service and produces programs for inclusion in the local schedule.

To the south, Ireland is an independent republic and consists of the remaining 26 counties of the country. Hence, "Irish television" usually refers to the set-up that is viewed in the republic, although, as will become clear, the spillover service (now including BBC1, BBC2, UTV, Channel 4, Sky News, Sky Sports, Eurosport, the Movie Channel, Sky One, UK Gold, Cartoon Network and Discovery) has a strong determining role in that system.

Through the 19th and 20th centuries, the Irish state (whether operating from London or Dublin) has been characterized by a high degree of authoritarian control, both coercive and ideological. In 1926, shortly after the founding of the Irish Free State in 1922, the state itself assumed control of all broadcasting in the 26 counties. This was motivated by a desire to head off any attempt by the British Marconi Company to establish itself in the region. Ironically, to help in the ideological task of establishing a nationalist identity, the government decided to implement a British-style system of broadcasting monopoly. Until 1960, the state, through the agency of the Department of Posts and Telegraph (Radio Eireann) provided a broadcast service through a single radio network. Then as now, this public service was financed by a combination of license fee and advertising. Highly conservative in programming, Radio Eireann was only tolerated by most of its listeners. In fact, the service did not have an audience monopoly. Households on the east coast and near the northern border could also receive the BBC and Radio Luxembourg.

It was this proximity to British broadcasting in the 1950s that forced the Irish government's hand so far as the inauguration of television was concerned. BBC Northern Ireland had begun TV transmission in 1953 and had been joined by UTV in 1959. Hence, the Irish Broadcasting Act of 1960 legislated the establishment of a television service, which began the following year. Again, following the public-service monopoly model, the facility, consisting of a single national channel, was put under the control of Radio Telefis Eireann (RTE). A revamped version of the radio provider, RTE was an independent public authority. This was a significant move toward liberalization, in line with the government's own moves to "modernize" Ireland to make it attractive to transnational capital investment.

However, this has not lessened attempts by the state to keep a tight control on the nature of political debate on Irish television. In general, this has led to poor relations between RTE and most Irish politicians. For example, in 1969, following political unrest in Northern Ireland, the Irish government imposed direct censorship over RTE news and current affairs. When, in 1972, RTE interviewed a spokesperson for the Provisional Irish Republican Army (IRA), a paramilitary group defending Catholics in Northern Ireland, the government dismissed the RTE board and appointed its own members.

Meanwhile, aware of the necessity of a second RTE channel but hoping to save revenue, in 1978 the government considered allowing the BBC to broadcast across the nation. Instead, it bowed to public opinion and allowed RTE to begin a second television network. The broadcaster, however, was not allowed to increase license fees or advertising rates, so that its overall finances, and therefore its capacity to produce local programs, was significantly weakened.

Technological and ideological pressures have also been persistent, such that RTE's monopoly has now ended. Since 1970, the authority had operated its own cable network, RTE Relay, which was renamed Cablelink in 1986. Cablelink was at one point the largest cable operator in Europe and provided about two-thirds of television households in the Irish Republic with all the terrestrial channels broadcast in Britain, later complemented by the European services Superchannel and Sky. By the early 1990s, Cablelink was beginning to carry advertising, thereby diminishing RTE's potential revenue. In addition, there was also the possibility that Cablelink might be sold to a private operator, thereby providing direct competition to RTE's broadcast service. This came to pass when Cablelink was sold to NTL in 2000. New channels (such as National Geographic) continue to be added to NTL's roster, and old ones (such as Superchannel) are discontinued, with the overall number of channels available continuing an upward trend.

Generally, the government was also interested in weakening RTE's power. It saw further opportunity to do so with moves throughout Europe to open up broadcast television to other interests. The 1988 Broadcast and Wireless Telegraphy Act formally broke the television broadcast monopoly. A new broadcast body, the Independent Radio and Television Commission, was established to oversee the introduction of privately owned radio and television stations. Several commercial radio stations have since gone on the air. At the same time, a private commercial television station, TV3, was announced in 1990, although it did not go on the air until 1998. The delay was partially caused by the need for strong financial backing, which was finally secured by entering a partnership with CanWest Global Communications, a Canadian-based international broadcaster. Meanwhile, in 1996, an Irish language broadcaster, Telefís ne Gaeilge (TG4), was established under the statutory umbrella of RTE, although under the 2001 Broadcasting Act it is moving toward full statutory authority. Dedicated to the maintenance and development of the Irish language, programming is mostly in Gaelic. However, despite these legislative developments, RTE continues to have to supply TG4 with 365 hours of programming annually, at no cost to the newcomer.

Increased commercial competition, involvement in three public service networks, and the low revenue generated through the license fee has affected RTE's capacity to produce local content. In 1965, Irish programs constituted approximately 60 percent of material transmitted. This figure had fallen to around 36 percent by 1990 and is still falling. In a schedule dominated by imported programs, RTE's own programs, particularly those with mass appeal, are especially important as "flagship" programs in the schedule. In the past, these have included *Glenroe, Fair City,* and *Pat Kenny's The Late Show,* among others. *Glenroe* and *Fair City* are popular soap operas in a "public-service" tradition, while *Pat Kenny's The Late Show* is a talk show with a strong sense of community, and marked by a refusal to shy away from controversial issues.

However, given the external spillover and the internal commercial rivalry, RTE exists in an environment where it is no match for its opposition. To attempt to maintain its general ratings both for its imported programs and its local programs, RTE is forced to engage in a scheduling strategy of parallel programming with British television, especially the channel ITV. It buys some of the latter's most popular programs, such as *Coronation Street,* which it then schedules against the same program on ITV. Like other public broadcasters, RTE finds itself in an increasingly grim situation. The Irish state has charged RTE with the task of fostering an Irish cultural identity yet has, over the past 30 years, become ever more prone to withhold the resources that would enable RTE to carry out this mission more effectively. Cross-national transmission has always posed a fundamental threat to the service and recent developments in technology, ideology, and financial arrangements have made that task even more difficult.

ALBERT MORAN

See also **Scotland; Wales**

Isaacs, Jeremy (1932–)

British Producer and Executive

Jeremy Isaacs had one of the most distinguished careers in the history of British television, from producer to channel controller, yet the top job which many anticipated he would earn—the Director-Generalship of the BBC—ultimately eluded him.

From a humble background in Glasgow's Jewish community, he attended Merton College, Oxford, where he became President of the Oxford Union. Specializing in factual programming, his first television work was with Manchester-based Granada Television from 1958 to 1963, where he produced the long-running stalwarts *What the Papers Say* and *All Our Yesterdays,* the latter beginning the association with archive-based history programs which was to become such an important feature of his career.

In 1963 he moved to the London ITV franchise holder, Associated-Rediffusion, where he was a producer and editor on the flagship ITV current affairs program *This Week* for three years, covering major foreign and domestic issues of the time, from Vietnam and the assassination of President Kennedy to the reform of homosexuality and divorce legislation, and Beatlemania.

In 1965, he moved to the BBC as editor of the Corporation's current affairs flagship, *Panorama,* a position he held for the next two years, before returning to Associated-Rediffusion in 1967 as Controller of Features. In 1968, the company was succeeded by Thames Television as the ITV London weekday franchise holder, and Isaacs continued in the same role for the new company until 1974. Isaacs made Thames's factual output among the most admired in the British television landscape. He also continued to make programs himself, as producer and executive producer, and it was a project which became something of a personal crusade that was to become the undoubted highlight of his program-making career.

As series producer of *The World At War,* Isaacs oversaw an immensely talented group of writers, historians, and producers. The finished product, an extremely ambitious, 26-part history of World War II, set the standards that still apply today for the combined use of archive film and eye-witness testimony to tell the story of the past. Endlessly repeated down the years since its first appearance in 1973, *The World At War* remains a television classic. In a poll of TV industry professionals conducted by the British Film Institute in 2000, it was voted by a long margin the best factual program in British television history. It also remains a testament to the commitment to quality broadcasting that Isaacs instilled in the commercial company Thames Television.

Isaacs strengthened Thames's reputation as its Director of Programs from 1974 to 1978. One production in particular serves to illustrate his achievement: the drama *The Naked Civil Servant* (1975), directed by Jack Gold and starring John Hurt as Quentin Crisp, which not only stands as a milestone of British TV drama, but also helped to influence changing public attitudes to homosexuality.

In 1979, Isaacs was invited to give the prestigious James McTaggart Memorial Lecture, which opens the annual Edinburgh International Television Festival. The biggest debate in the television industry at the time surrounded the new Conservative government's plans for Britain's fourth television channel. Isaacs used the platform he was given to set out his own ideas about how the channel should be created and run. Channel 4 was eventually set up largely along the outlines he promoted: it which would be funded by the ITV companies, who would sell its advertising space and cross-promote it, an ingenious formula which allowed it to be given a strong public-service remit with a particular duty to be innovative and cater for minorities otherwise underserved by television. It was also to act as a publisher, rather than maker of programs, commissioning its output from independent companies. Isaacs was duly given the job of Channel 4's first Chief Executive, with the channel set to start transmission in 1982. In the meantime, he acted as consultant on another large, archive-based series, *Hollywood,* transmitted by Thames in 1980, and as series producer of *Ireland: A Television History,* made for the BBC in the same year. He then embarked on the adventure of creating a completely new television channel.

Channel 4 began broadcasting in November 1982 and immediately ran into a variety of troubles. It also changed the face of British television. The independent productions often had a raw edge not previously seen on the mainstream channels, the professional conventions of which were overdue for reconsideration. Programs for minorities included not only women and

ethnic groups, but trade unionists. Youth programming such as *Whatever You Want* and *The Tube* caused a stir for its sometimes unrestrained energy.

The controversies centered usually on matters of taste and language—with the channel's soap opera *Brookside* to the fore—or on the perceived ratings crisis. Isaacs knew what he was doing, however, and the channel certainly bore witness to his commitment to innovation and quality. The first night's programming included the filmed drama *Walter,* starring Ian McKellen as a mentally retarded man, which kicked off Channel 4's film-making strand *Film on Four,* later to be credited with reviving the British film industry, giving work to major talents like Mike Leigh and Peter Greenaway. Another early and emblematic triumph was the television version of the Royal Shakespeare Company's *The Life and Adventures of Nicholas Nickleby.* Probably the greatest success was the hour-long *Channel 4 News,* which combined a serious approach to news and in-depth analysis in a way that revolutionized the coverage of news on British television.

Channel 4 became a vital part of the British television landscape. The then comparatively staid BBC 2 (seen as its natural competitor, as BBC 1 was for ITV) was forced to respond, and the result was a rise in the quality of output unprecedented in British television history. Many see the 1980s as an era of great energy and renewal in British television, which can be attributed, for the most part, to Isaacs. When he handed the task of running the channel over to the populist Michael Grade in 1987, it was with a strong warning not to allow the quality of output to suffer in the search for ratings.

By then Isaacs had tried, and failed, to get the job he most coveted and which most industry professionals wanted him to have: Director-General of the BBC. British television was entering an era in which profits (or in the BBC's case, ratings), rather than quality, would be the prime moving force, and Isaacs was the first casualty of that sea change.

Isaacs turned away from television and took a job that reflected another of his passions, becoming General Director of the Royal Opera House, Covent Garden, from 1988 to 1997. Controversies followed him there also, no more so than when in 1996 he invited a television documentary crew to make a series on the opera house for the BBC, which produced a highly unflattering portrait of an institution in crisis.

He never completely severed his television links. From 1989 to 1998 he acted as the unseen interviewer in a revival of the classic *Face to Face* interview series, talking to the likes of Sir Peter Hall, Maya Angelou, Salman Rushdie, Norman Mailer, Stephen Sondheim, and Anthony Hopkins. Then, at the end of the 1990s, he returned once more to the large-scale archive history format as executive producer on the 24-part *The Cold War* for Turner Enterprises. Consciously modeled on *The World at War* (it was narrated by the classical actor Kenneth Branagh, for instance, as the earlier series had been narrated by Laurence Olivier), it included testimony from most of the major political figures of the second half of the twentieth century, and was first shown in 1999.

STEVE BRYANT

See also **World at War, The**

Jeremy Israel Isaacs. Born in Glasgow, Scotland, September 28, 1932. Married: 1) Tamara Weinreich (died 1986); one son, one daughter. 2) Gillian Widdecombe, 1988. Educated at Glasgow Academy and Merton College, Oxford. Producer, Granada Television, 1958–63. Producer and Editor, *This Week,* Associated-Rediffusion, 1963–65. Editor, *Panorama,* BBC, 1965–67. Controller of Features for Associated-Rediffusion, 1967–68, and for Thames Television, 1968–74. Director of Programmes, Thames Television, 1974–78. Chief Executive, Channel 4, 1981–87. Knighted 1996.

Further Reading

Isaacs, Jeremy, *Storm Over 4: A Personal Account,* London: Weidenfeld and Nicolson, 1989

Israel

Television did not arrive in Israel until 1968. Establishment opposition to television during the two preceding decades since the founding of the state had been strong enough to thwart earlier pro-television initiatives. It was feared that reading would decline; that newly developed Israeli culture and the Hebrew language, still in need of nurturing, would be overwhelmed by imported, mostly U.S. programs; that national integration would be weakened by entertainment; and that politics would become less ideological—that is, less oriented to issues, and more to charismatic personalities (Katz), should television become widely available.

All these considerations were overcome when, following the 1967 Six Day War, Israel found itself in charge of two million Palestinians in Gaza and the West Bank. The establishment of television was originally conceived by the government as a bridge to the Arab population in the occupied territories, which had previously been exposed only to broadcasts from Arab nations.

Until the introduction of television, radio was the central medium of national integration, serving as a Hebrew teacher to the masses of new immigrants, and providing a focus for the development of a shared Israeli culture, and for the celebration of holidays. Radio also played a crucial role in surveillance of the Arab-Israeli conflict. *Kol Yisrael* ("Voice of Israel") started transmitting illegally during the last years of British Mandatory Rule as a means of mobilizing for the national struggle. In 1965, however, Israel Radio became a public authority, modeled on the BBC, administered by a largely independent board, and financed by a user's license fee.

A decision to incorporate television into the existing authority for Public Broadcasting had a significant impact on its development. Television staff were recruited from radio, and moved into television with their already tenured positions. This caused a lack of mobility, and made it almost impossible to recruit new talent. Moreover, cultural conflicts added to these industrial problems. Israel Television's first challenge in this arena, brought by the National Religious Party over the violations of the Sabbath, was in the very fact of broadcasting on Friday nights and Saturdays. The controversy was overcome (in favor of broadcasting) in an appeal to the Supreme Court.

For the next 25 years Israel had only one television channel. During the day, it showed educational programs and public broadcasting initiatives, starting transmissions in the late afternoon, and ending with the national anthem at midnight. As with the radio service, television in Israel was modeled on the BBC, but number of significant deviations from the British model made it more politicized, and more dependent on Parliamentary control. In the U.K., the Queen, on the advice of the government, appoints the Board of Governors, who appoint the director general. In Israel, the government appoints the director general directly, on the recommendation of the Board of Governors.

Moreover, the Board of Governors in Israel consists of representatives of the various parties, and does not follow the British precedent according to which its members should represent "the great and the good." In Israel, the Ministry of Finance retains indirect control of the license fee (as it is in charge of approving Public Broadcasting's annual budget), decides on the amount of the license-fee increase (to keep up with inflation), and finances the budgetary deficits. Television's income also suffers from the tendency of Israelis (the number varies in different periods) to escape paying the license fee. Revenues from corporate-based "sponsorship" slowly crept into the system, but then decreased to almost nothing with the establishment of a second commercial channel.

The second television channel started its official existence only in 1991. Again following the British example, it was also public, but financed by advertising rather than by a license fee. Broadcasting on the second channel is divided among three companies, each of which broadcasts two days a week in rotation, and a news company, financed jointly by the three other companies.

Channel 2 functioned as a purely commercial channel, signaling the beginning of a new media era characterized by an explosion in the number of cable and satellite channels. Increased sales of video cassette recorders, the establishment of video rental libraries, the installment of roof satellite dishes to receive broadcasts from Europe and the U.S., and the infiltration of pirate cable channels, all offered easy alternatives to national television for segmented audiences. It also sped up the legislation of cable television, first established in 1990. By 2001, 90 percent of Israeli households were connected to cable television. Segmentation was further increased with the introduction of satellite television in 2000. The new technology facilitated interactive forms of consumable television (such as video games and "movies on demand"). A third nationwide commercial channel, Channel 10, was established in 2002, and presented as an alternative to the more mainstream offerings on the other channels (Channel 10 was modeled on the British Channel 4). However, it turned out to be little more than a pale copy of the commercial Channel 2, and has fared poorly in the ratings race.

By 2002, more than 90 percent of Israeli households were connected to multi-channel (cable or satellite) television services, offering altogether more than 50 channels. This positions Israel (with a population of 6 million) as second only to the U.S. (with its nearly 300 million) in the number of channels available to the majority of the population (Adoni and Nossek).

The numerous television and radio channels address various target audiences, dividing Israelis according to age, gender, culture/ethnicity, and nationality, and according to self-selective community categories. Thus, public broadcasting is viewed by older Israelis, the *telenovela* channel is viewed mostly by women, Russians view Russian-speaking channels, and so on. Channels for children, family, sports, films, science, and shopping are assembled by the local companies, who also provide Hebrew subtitles, announcements, promos, and originally produced programs. Local productions consist of sports, children's programs, documentaries, reality programs, soap operas, and drama series, and time is allocated for public access programs.

Channel 2, originally defined as public, has gradually distanced itself from this categorization and behaves like a commercial channel. In order to increase advertising profits, it started a ratings war with Channel 1 in which the latter, by its adherence to its aims as a public service, by inferior financing, and by increasing political control, was bound to be the loser.

By 2002, according to the data gathered by the Israel Audience Research Board, the multiplicity of channels resulted in the three nationwide channels together having only a 29 percent share of viewers: 17 percent went to Channel 2, 10 percent to Channel 1, and 2 percent to Channel 10. (The Russian-speaking Israel Plus channel, going on air in 2001, managed better than Channel 10, with a 2.2 percent share.)

A major consequence of the increased number of channels is the marginalization of television news. Until the establishment of the second channel, an evening news program was broadcast at 9:00 P.M., serving as the sole focus for prime-time viewing and providing a common agenda for public debate. Over 60 percent of Israelis watched regularly, and in consequence, the medium of television was regarded as supplying more information than entertainment (Katz, Haas, and Gurevitch). One side-effect of the focus on news production was that locally produced entertainment shows remained underfunded, and local drama was virtually nonexistent. This made the news even more central.

During the first 25 years of Israel Television, drama series consisted mainly of American, but also British, imports. Usually, only one such series was aired on prime time. *Kojak, Starsky and Hutch, Dallas,* and *Dynasty,* and the British dramatic serial *Upstairs, Downstairs,* were popular. *Dallas* exceeded all others in popularity (Liebes and Katz). British comedies *(Yes, Minister; Are You Being Served?)* and detective series *(Inspector Morse)* were popular, but imports of more highbrow series were stopped, following the failure in Israel of the prestigious *Brideshead Revisited,* based on the Evelyn Waugh novel. Programs such as *Hill Street Blues, The Cosby Show,* and *Northern Exposure,* representing a plurality of American television genres, were successfully shown. *Cheers* is the only program in the public channel's history which was rejected by the Israeli audience to the extent that it was taken off the screen.

American programs have gained more popularity than their British counterparts, as the abundance of American shows has increasingly socialized viewers to American conventions and styles of production. With the impoverishment of the public channel, new U.S. series (and new films) are now bought by the second channel and cable networks. Israel Television produced high-quality current-affairs programs *(Mabat Sheni)* often based on investigative reporting, and a few sitcoms (such as *Krovim krovim*), which were popular. Highlights in the history of Israel Television include the documentary series on the history of Zionist settlement in Israel, *Amud Haesh;* an inventive series of political satire, *Nikuy Rosh,* which drew heavy attack from the political establishment and launched the careers of a number of Israeli comedy stars; and made-for-television films, which touched on central controversies in Israeli society, notably by prize-winning television director Ram Levi (whose film *Hirbat Hiza,* showing Israeli soldiers evacuating an Arab village during the 1948 war, was broadcast only years after its production).

Beyond creating an integrative focus for daily life, Israel Television also took an active part in the shaping of holidays, creating secular alternatives to traditional rituals (for example, by showing a classic movie); complementing the traditional content (such as by dramatizing the Passover Seder); taking the viewers to the event (the public reading of the book of Esther on Purim, or the Holocaust observance ceremony); or by creating the event itself (such as the annual Bible Quiz, invented for the Day of Independence).

The ten most popular prime-time series broadcasting on the three nationwide channels in 2003 were all Israeli-made productions in a variety of genres: telenovelas, reality television, investigative reporting, soft-satire, and public folk-singing. The winner in a Channel 2 competition for the most popular program of the decade was *A Star is Born,* a series in which amateur singers competed for fame and recognition. Political or quasi-political talk shows, the most popular genre of the 1990s, had almost disappeared.

Throughout Israel's history, in moments of crisis, broadcasting has taken over the function of surveillance and social integration. Radio is still listened to in cars and public buses (in total silence at moments of crisis). It is used by the army (now as an adjunct to television) for fast mobilization of its reserve forces, and stands in for the outdated alarm system, announc-

ing when it is time to go to the air-raid shelters (the "sealed rooms" of the Gulf War).

While television took over as the ceremonial medium of integration, radio adapted itself by switching to open-ended programming, always interruptible by the latest news of any conflict, perhaps relaying regards from soldiers away from home to their families, perhaps instructing the people in Northern Kiriat Shmona to spend the night in shelters, perhaps summoning soldiers to their reserve units by reading out the appropriate code phrases for rehearsing an emergency mobilization, or for enacting a real one.

In critical moments, however, television also interrupts its schedule, switching to "open" live broadcasting, and becomes the focus for sharing national trauma, and for reflecting on its meaning. Thus, during the week following the assassination of Prime Minister Yitzhak Rabin, in November 1995, Israelis could not disconnect themselves from the television set. Television acted as a locus for sharing grief, pointed out the various "sacred" arenas for people who wanted to go out and mourn in public, and provided a forum for debating the ideological rift in which the assassination was rooted.

Television has also been a central factor in historic events which became landmarks in the collective memory of Israelis. The live broadcasting of Egyptian President Sadat's visit to Jerusalem in 1977 is the best example for illustrating the crucial part played by television in influencing public opinion (Liebes, 1997). The various stages of development toward achieving a lasting peace with Jordan and the Palestinians, from 1993 to 1995, were celebrated by media events which endowed them with (various degrees of) public legitimacy, reuniting the segmented television audience. By 2003, the dominant genre of live television was the "Disaster Marathon," in which the television schedule was interrupted following the latest terrorist attack (Liebes, 2002). Whereas at the time of the Oslo process these were the moments in which political debates flourished, and opposition voices were given the stage, in the early 21st century there was only the mourning with the victims, and the momentary creation of a personalized, apolitical, national unity.

TAMAR LIEBES

Further Reading

Adoni, H., and H. Nossek., *Readers' Voices: The Reading Public in the Multi Channel Media Environment in Israel,* 2004

Katz, E. "Television Comes to the People of the Book," in *The Use and Abuse of Social Science,* edited by Irving Louis Horowitz, New Brunswick, New Jersey: Transaction Books, 1971

Katz, E., H. Haas, and M. Gurevitch, "Twenty Years of Television in Israel: Are There Long-Run Effects on Values, Social

Connectedness, and Cultural Practices?" *Journal of Communication* 47 (1997)

Liebes, T., *Reporting the Arab-Israeli Conflict: How Hegemony Works,* London: Routledge, 1997

Liebes, T., *American Dreams, Hebrew Subtitles: Globalization from the Receiving End,* Hampton Press, 2002

Liebes, T., and E. Katz, *The Export of Meaning: Cross-Cultural Readings of* Dallas, Cambridge: Polity Press, 1992

Nossek, H., and H. Adoni, "Social Implications of Cable Broadcasting: Structuring Orientations towards Self and Social Groups," *International Journal of Public Opinion,* 1996.

Wolfsfeld, G., W.L. Bennett, and R.M. Entman, *Media and the Path to Peace,* Cambridge: Cambridge University Press, 2003

Italy

In the bars of Italy in the 1950s, television became popular when crowds of people, women as well as men, left their homes to meet after supper and watch the first huge success of Italian public television. The attraction was *Lascia o raddoppia* (*Double Your Money*), a quiz-show format imported from the United States by a young showman, Mike Bongiorno (who continued to host shows through the 1990s).

In August 1996, the board of administrations of RAI, the public radio and television company, made decisions concerning the directors and vice directors of all the news and programs departments in RAI—the third such change of executives in four years. For three days, all Italian newspapers dedicated their leading articles to the subject, and continued with two or three inside pages filled with comments, backgrounds, and feature stories. As on previous occasions, the nominations of RAI department directors were an important conversation topic. This level of attention in the press, and the concern for public opinion by RAI, would be seen as quite unusual in most countries; even in Italy, there is no similar interest with regard to other kinds of companies. Television is not only a conversation topic in terms of the content and programs it presents to audiences, but for itself.

Beginnings and Developments

The official history of Italian television began on January 3, 1954, at which time Radiotelevisione Italiana (RAI) was the only television network, transmitting news and prime-time programs. RAI had begun as a state-owned radio broadcasting entity in 1924, when it was called Unione Radiofonica Italiana (URI), and was heavily controlled by the national government, at that point a fascist regime. For years, and despite transformations in government, the same company remained a monopoly, simply changing its name—in 1924 URI, in 1927 Ente Italiano Audizioni Radiofoniche (EIAR), and in 1944 RAI (which originally stood for Radio Audizioni Italia; when TV broadcasts began ten years later its named changed, but retained the same acronym). From 1954 to 1976, the history of Italian television *is* the history of RAI, for the monopoly was extended to television, with the same concentration established during the radio era.

In 1954, the postwar reconstruction period ended and a new phase of industrialization began, with huge transformation of the country. Until the end of the 1960s millions of Italians relocated inside the country, from south to north, from small villages to large cities, from agriculture to industry. This was a period of great transformation. Television, contrary to the expectations of intellectuals and politicians, was an immediate success. At first, for most people, television viewing was public viewing: in the bars, the cinemas, the houses of the richest families. When a second channel began broadcasting on November 4, 1961, television reached a nationwide audience and family viewing at home began to be more common. In a country still characterized by a high level of illiteracy, television became the most widespread media, in contrast to the traditional low circulation of the daily press (among the lowest in the world) and the irregularity of school attendance (especially in the south).

The unexpected success of television, coincident with the unexpected great transformation of the country and the rapid growth of national income, explains why the medium became an important political issue. While private entrepreneurial groups tried to create alternatives to the state monopoly of radio and television, the Corte Costituzionale (the high court that oversees the Constitution), ruled on July 13, 1960, that the television monopoly was legal. Just a few years after the beginning of regular programming, then, "television" and RAI (as the only broadcaster and producer), became the makers of two different kinds of histories. One was the history of a new medium, which concerned technological evolution, the quantity and quality of programs produced and broadcast, and the audience reactions. The other was the history of the power struggles among political parties and businesses for the control both of legislation and the resources related to RAI—from the control of news and electoral campaigns, to the control of advertising, to the production of fiction, variety shows, and other forms of popular culture.

The Struggles for Television Power

Italian television has not only been a public-service institution, in the European tradition. It has also historically been a central means of power controlled by the Christian Democratic Party (until its dissolution in 1994) and the Catholic Church. It does not work as a self-supporting industry. Rather, it receives financial resources from both advertising and from fees paid by subscribers. Advertising is sold to firms at low prices and in a very discriminating way, depending on the political power of the organizations and institutions involved. Automobile advertising, for example, was forbidden because FIAT, the Italian automobile company, did not want other cars to be seen on the screen.

During the 1970s this situation began to change. On April 14, 1975, governmental reforms gave RAI a new regulatory structure. The main powers (nomination of the board of administration, and control over policies) were transferred from the government to parliament. Even more significantly, on July 28, 1976, the Corte Costituzionale issued a new ruling that allowed the transmission of radio and television programs at local level. With that decision the era of competition had begun and the media system entered a period of change that continued through the 1990s.

RAI no longer holds monopolies for radio or television: half of its radio audience has gone. Even within RAI itself, the organization is no longer monolithic. Radio and television channels have their own news departments, budgets, and political and cultural outlook. They compete among themselves and with private broadcasters for audience. Influence, power, resources, and audiences are broadly divided across three segments: the major portion goes to the Catholic sector, the second to the Socialists, the third part to the Communists. Meanwhile, in the private sector the greatest competition has come from the media empire created by Silvio Berlusconi.

Under the new legal structure permitting local broadcasting, Berlusconi was able to build a network of three channels: Canale 5, Italia 1, and Rete 4. These local and regional broadcasting systems were unified by a common management and strategy within Mediaset, which in turn was controlled by Fininvest, the holding company created to oversee Berlusconi's media operations. They were financially supported by Pubitalia, a firm specializing in the collection of advertising revenues. The extraordinary and very rapid success of private television in Italy was due mainly to one factor: a large number of new companies which had flourished in the roaring 1960s and 1970s had no way to reach Italian markets with their advertising, because of the restrictions described above. Yet after years of hard work, and of social and political unrest, consumers were ready to accept new styles of living and to enter the era of mass consumption. Berlusconi and his management understood this need and provided an answer—a private television system which for the first time in the European scene offered a scheduling and programming policy shaped by marketing philosophy.

The three channels were intended to be strong competitors with the public channels. Canale 5 was created as a general channel for mass audience, while Italia 1 was aimed at a younger audience, and Rete 4 at women. Successful programs included American films and American series and serials (such as *Dallas* and *Dynasty*), game shows, Latin American *telenovelas,* new formats of Italian variety shows, and Japanese cartoons for children. By the end of the 1980s, the competition between the private and public networks was at its height and the audience more or less divided in two equal parts. The financial resources coming from advertising grew seven-fold in about 12 years, and, although the greatest part went to the private network, the overall media system—RAI and daily press included—increased their revenues as well. While at the end of the 1970s advertising expenditure as a percentage of gross national product was the lowest among industrial countries, at the end of 1980s it reached 6 percent.

On August 6, 1990, after years of discussion and struggle among the main political parties, a new law was passed by parliament recognizing that a new television system had emerged from the rough competition between RAI and Fininvest. With the new law, private television systems, at both national and local levels, are obliged to transmit a news program in order to maintain their license. In the 1990s, then, competition began in the news arena. Twelve national channels were recognized by the 1990 law. But the six channels owned by the two main networks, RAI and Fininvest, shared 90 percent of the audience.

Television as a New Enemy

In the 1990s television became, even more than before, the centre of the Italian political scene. Silvio Berlusconi, the owner of Fininvest, made the decision to enter into the political arena, creating a new political movement called *Forza Italia (Forward Italy).* The coalition of leftist parties that had replaced the old Socialist and Communist parties, led by the Partita Democratica della Sinistra (PDS, Democratic Party of the Left), was furious. The two television networks were heavily engaged in the 1994 election campaign: RAI effectively on the side of the left coalition and Fininvest on the side of right coalition. To the surprise of most observers, the right coalition of Silvio Berlusconi won the elections of March 27, 1994 and Berlusconi became the head of the national government.

From the day of the Berlusconi victory, a war began. It was not only a war against Berlusconi but against television itself—the new enemy. Politicians, intellectuals, teachers, newspapers, began to organize public meetings and conventions against television. Some called to a national referendum against private television. Berlusconi became, for half of the country, the incarnation of evil, and was unable to resist the attacks—he resigned after only seven months. A temporary, technocratic government passed a law, which was not approved by parliament, dictating severe restrictions on the use of television in electoral campaigns (practically forbidding the use of television as a propaganda device). In the meantime, advertising revenues decreased rapidly and the entire media system entered a period of recession. Both RAI and Fininvest faced large debts and drastically reduced their investments in drama production, the most expensive segment of the television industry.

In spite of these views, a June 1995 national referendum on a number of questions to do with television—such as the quantity and placement of advertising, and whether one person should be allowed to own more than one private TV channel—ended in a low-turnout victory for Berlusconi, who had used his three channels to campaign vigorously for a "no-change" vote (such as by implying that favorite soap operas and *telenovelas* would no longer be available if the vote went against him), while the three RAI channels, by then headed by Berlusconi's own appointees from his 1994 stint as prime minister, remained neutral. The campaign against Berlusconi's domination of private television continued (and he was obliged to reduce his holding in Mediaset to below 50 percent), but began to resemble campaigns of the same kind occurring in other countries, focusing on the amount of violence and sex in programming, or on ways to protect children from television.

Scheduling: Programs and Audiences

Italian television is created from an original and changing mixture of five different kinds of content: American drama, Italian drama, Italian soccer and other sports, Italian songs and shows, Italian news and politics. Each one is bound to strong patterns of Italian culture.

The style of presentation has two main approaches. One is melodramatic, in the 19th-century tradition of melodrama and opera. The other is light and ironic, in the tradition of the commedia dell'arte and of the *avanspettacolo,* a form of popular theater variety show featuring comedians and girls.

The relationship of Italian television to American drama has specific characteristics. Even prior to television, American mass culture has been the model for Italian entertainment, mainly through films. Throughout the 1950s most American movies were imported into Italy, dubbed in Italian, and shown throughout the country in more than 11,000 cinemas. The first audiences for television, then, looked at television as a different form of movie, and indeed, American films have, for years, been the prime-time family viewing on Mondays. American films, and subsequently, American series and serials have provided a considerable part of the offering of Italian television channels. Among European channels, Italian television has dedicated more air time to American drama programs and to foreign films dubbed in Italian than any other.

Another important element of Italian television has been the production of a form of original drama series that has no real counterpart abroad. This is the *teleromanzo* (television romance) or *sceneggiato* (adaptation of novels). The stories are presented in six or eight episodes of two hours each, taken from the masterpieces of international literature. They are shot and played in a realistic setting in a mixed style between theater and film. One of their models is to be found in an Italian postwar invention, the *fotoromanzo* or novel with photographs—long-running series that sold weekly as magazines (and are still produced). Action is slow and all the stories are located in the past, mainly in the 19th century. Prime-time Sunday was for years dedicated to the family viewing of *teleromanzi.* Since the 1980s, however, this kind of drama production has no longer been produced in the same way. Since then, Italian drama has tried to adopt more standard formats, with stories now located in contemporary Italy. The most successful of these stories was *La Piovra* (The Octopus), a story about the Mafia. Begun in 1984 and still continuing, it is a kind of Italian-style serial comprising seven miniseries to date.

New Developments

The trend that began in the 1990s has been toward tighter television regulation. Antitrust rules, limits on advertising, establishment of national authorities and regional control bodies, regulation of access to media during election campaigns (introduced immediately following the fall of the first Berlusconi government), and programming and production quotas within the framework of the European directive "Television Without Frontiers": all these and other steps have been approved by Italian legislators after the establishment of the RAI-Mediaset duopoly. Law 122, passed in the spring of 1998 by the PDS-led government that succeeded Berlusconi's first period in office, established for the first time a quota of net revenues to be re-invested in national and European TV drama and movie production. Some 20 percent of the license fee from state television, and 10 percent of television advertising revenue from private television, went to this purpose. The intention was to help bring about a re-naissance in the television industry, setting aside a fig-ure estimated at around   400 million per annum.

This policy of production fund quotas, related to the much-debated issue of the "defence of national iden-tity" against the risks of Americanization, has had an immediately visible impact: the crisis that followed the massive import of foreign productions has been suc-ceeded by a remarkable recovery, and the schedules of both private and public television have since been filled with domestic drama, much appreciated by the viewer for its cultural proximity.

However, American series maintain a cadre of faith-ful fans. Normally shown outside prime time, they are generally able to guarantee audiences in accordance with the average share of the channels on which they appear. Only a tiny slice of American imports now have access to prime time on the Italian channels, which are dominated by domestic drama, and these imported offerings are mostly TV movies or a small number of series suitable for a family audience or young adults. The remaining American programming is spread over the daytime schedule, or, in the case of harder or more edgy products, late at night.

Satellite television arrived in Italy—where the cable infrastructure has never been highly developed—in the second half of the 1990s. It heralded the advent of a multi-channel environment that is still expanding thanks to digital technology and, even more signifi-cantly, to international operators who were allowed to enter the national market. Telepiù and Stream, the two satellite platforms operating in Italy, have been largely controlled by foreign capital from the beginning. Some 90 percent of Telepiù was owned by Vivendi Universal (Canal Plus), and Stream was owned jointly by Mur-doch's News Corporation and the former Italian mo-nopolist Telecom. In 2002 the two platforms merged into Sky, under Murdoch's total control. This develop-ment resulted from two factors. One was a conse-quence of the global alliance between Vivendi and News Corporation. The other was related to the fact that the Italian market proved too limited for two dif-ferent satellite-based entities, both of which went through a critical period, as did other European pay-television systems.

In spite of the "pull" of soccer, the penetration of satellite pay-TV is quite slow. Interestingly enough, the "television of the future" seems to have prompted Italians to rediscover the social and collective mode of television viewing, which in the past accompanied the beginnings of terrestrial TV when only a minority of households had a television set. Bars, sports clubs, and groups of friends and neighbors now take out a single subscription, from which tens of them can benefit at a much lower individual cost.

If the arrival of the multi-channel environment has not (or not yet) affected television audiences' habits and preferences, it *has* had an immediate impact on the programming structure of terrestrial television, drain-ing off quite large portions of premium content, partic-ularly sport and cinema, which have consequently resulted in a downswing in the supply afforded to tra-ditional television. On the RAI channels, for example, sports programs fell from 2,280 hours in 1998 to 1,426 in 2001, while in the same period showings of movies fell from 3,074 to 2,344 hours.

In recent years, RAI and Mediaset managed to ob-tain and maintain more or less equal positions in the Italian market, and their six channels (three each) hold a steady 90 percent. This balance is the result of two opposite trajectories: descending in the case of public and ascending in the case of private television, which year after year gains a small fraction of the market. From 1998 to 2003 the commercial networks share in-creased from 41 to 44 percent while that of the public networks decreased from 48 to 45 percent.

After 2000, these opposing trajectories accelerated. Mediaset got the advantage by exploiting the reality and game-show format (such as *Big Brother* and *Who Wants To Be A Millionaire?*) and its gain was further galvanized by the victory of the political coalition led by Berlusconi in 2001. RAI went through one of its pe-riodic phases of instability, due to changes in top man-agement and the redistribution of posts according to the spoils system of the new centre-right majority. In spite of this, public television has maintained a slight superiority, even though this was more difficult to achieve than in the past.

This was not the case as far as advertising is concerned. It Italy, as everywhere else, advertising revenue from television began to fall after 2001 because of the downswing in the telecommunications sector. Actually, the public and private television channels felt this to quite a different degree. RAI's revenue decreased dramatically, whereas Mediaset actually obtained a slight increase: an opposing trend which, it has been surmised, is not unrelated to the political landscape.

Speculation mushroomed in other circumstances as well. The wait for a third pole able to rupture the crystallized balance of the RAI-Mediaset duopoly has accompanied Italian national broadcasting history for more than ten years, since the duopolistic system was established and received legal recognition. During 2000 it seemed that the conditions for achieving this had finally come about, thanks to the purchase by Seat/Telecom of the two Telemontecarlo networks owned by the Cecchi Gori Group. Telemontecarlo had never managed to obtain more than a skimpy 2 percent of the market, but the new owners announced plans for expansion of the main network, renamed La7, and had successfully started an acquisition campaign of stars, managers and journalists taken from RAI and Mediaset as well as a fairly substantial advertising round-up. This decision could also be viewed as a progressive development, the creation of a new network, no matter how small, in the wake of the multimedia convergence between telecommunications, television and Internet.

On this premise, it is not surprising that what happened afterwards was traced back, in some circles, to a craftily orchestrated plot to neutralize the challenge of La7 to the supremacy of the duopoly. The hard facts are that in July 2001 the Pirelli and Benetton companies took over the controlling share of Olivetti from the Luxembourg financial enterprise Bell, in turn the major shareholder of Telecom. The new owners announced that they did not intend to risk a large investment in a television project that could not ensure results. The prospects of a third Italian television pole melted away into thin air. The cozy duopoly of the Italian television system is still alive and in good shape.

GIOVANNI BECHELLONI AND MILLY BUONANNO

Further Reading

Bechelloni, Giovanni, "Private Television in Italy: The Managerial Strategy of the Berlusconi Group," in *Economie et culture: 4e Conférence internationale sur l'économie de la culture, Avignon, 12–14 mai 1986,* edited by Xavier Dupuis and François Rouet, Paris: Documentation Française, 1987

Bechelloni Giovanni, "Mafia In The Italian Media," *Interfaces* 6 (1994)

Buonanno, Milly, editor, *Continuity and Change: Television Fiction in Europe,* Luton: University of Luton Press, 2000

Buonanno, Milly, editor, *Convergences: Eurofiction Fourth Report,* Naples: Liguori, 2002

Gundle, Stephen, "Television in Italy," in *Television in Europe,* edited by James Coleman and Brigitte Rollet, Exeter: Intellect, 1997

Mancini, Paolo, and Wolf Mauro, "Mass Media Research in Italy: Culture and Politics," *European Journal of Communication* (1990)

Mazzoleni, Gianpietro, "Italy," in *The Media in Western Europe,* edited by Bernt Stubbge Østergaard, London: Sage, 1992

Schlesinger, Philip, "The Berlusconi Phenomenon," in *Culture and Conflict in Postwar Italy,* edited by Zygmunt Baranski and Robert Lumley, New York: St. Martin's Press, 1990

Silj, Alessandro, editor, *East of Dallas: The European Challenge to American Television,* London: British Film Institute, 1988

It's Garry Shandling's Show/The Larry Sanders Show

U.S. Situation Comedies

Garry Shandling put aside a successful career as a stand-up comedian to venture into irreverent forms of fictional television with film producers and talent managers Bernie Brillstein (*Ghostbusters*) and Brad Grey. The trio created comedies in 1986 and 1992: the whimsical and warm *It's Garry Shandling's Show* and the darker *Larry Sanders Show.*

The first program began on the Showtime cable network in 1986. After a year, it reached critical success, and Shandling relinquished his role as one of Johnny

Carson's regular guest hosts on NBC's *The Tonight Show,* leaving Jay Leno as the primary alternate behind the desk. Shandling and Leno had replaced Joan Rivers as Carson's principal replacements in 1986 when Rivers began her own talk show—the initial program on the fledgling FOX Broadcasting Company network.

While still in first run on Showtime, *It's Garry Shandling's Show* was licensed by the new FOX Broadcasting Company as part of its second-season Sunday evening lineup. Although plagued by low ratings and hence unable to satisfy FOX's expectations, critics praised Shandling's tongue-in-cheek style. FOX reran the Showtime episodes and then contracted with "Our Production Company" for new installments until 1990.

The program, set in Shandling's condominium in Sherman Oaks, California, featured comic schtick. Shandling played a single man looking for the right woman. He spent his free time with his platonic friend Nancy (Molly Cheek), his best friend's family (Stanley Tucci and Bernadette Birkett), and his single mother. Much of the show mimicked Shandling's own life, including his actual home in Sherman Oaks and his romances (a girlfriend moved in with Shandling's "character" when his personal domestic life changed).

The program began with a monologue, introducing the show. Next came a silly theme song, performed by Randy Newman, including the lyrics "Garry called me up and asked if I could write it" and a whistling segment. The "dramatic action" in each episode was simple, built on such premises as Garry's bad dates, or his discovery of a nude photo of his mother from the 1960s. Each situation was resolved with warmth and whimsy, sometimes with the help of audience members.

Shandling's antics included "breaking the fourth wall"—acknowledgement and direct address of the audience, both in the studio and at home—as part of the show. In one episode, Garry told the audience to feel free to use his "apartment" (the set) while he was at a baseball game. Several people from the audience (perhaps extras) left their seats to read prop books and play billiards in front of the cameras as the program segued into its next scene.

It's Garry Shandling's Show often included guest stars. In the pilot, just after Garry's character moved into the condo, he was robbed. That night he dreamed of Vanna White (appearing on the show) giving away his good underwear and other personal belongings as prizes on *Wheel of Fortune*—for less value than he hoped. His most frequent visitor was his "next-door neighbor," rock musician Tom Petty. In one episode,

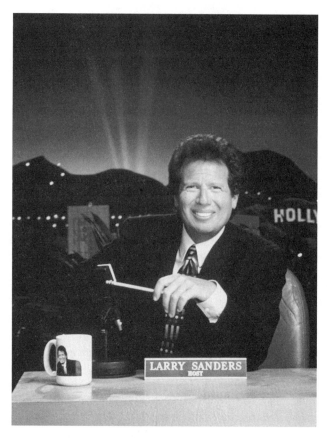

The Larry Sanders Show, Gary Shandling, 1992–98. *Courtesy of the Everett Collection*

Petty, who usually appeared with disheveled long hair, wearing loose shirts and tight pants, became part of a neighborhood quartet. He made his entrance walking in line with three middle-aged singers, all four wearing ugly matching plaid wool vests.

Shandling sometimes used other sight jokes, but most often he exploited running verbal gags. These included the unseen ceiling mirror inscribed with the typed motto, "Things may be larger than they appear." Another continuing joke involved Larry's ongoing consideration of what to do during the 41 seconds when theme music interrupted the action.

Some episodes, however, were more serious. One of these featured Gilda Radner near the end of her unsuccessful battle with cancer. This show also presented a Vietnam antiwar theme, detailing how one friend's conduct caused a man to become a prisoner of war. Although the program ended jovially, the action included a darkly lit battle sequence in which uniformed soldiers shot at each other and put holes into Radner's living room set.

Although each episode of the show was scripted, Shandling was known to improvise his lines. If a scene needed three takes, he often performed differently in each iteration, as though challenging himself to make each retake funnier than the prior one.

The Larry Sanders Show, which played its first-run episodes on HBO from 1992 until 1998, was the "Mr. Hyde" of Shandling's pair of comedies. The program, which mocked behind-the-scenes activities of post-prime-time talk shows, painted a more disturbing view of television as a status-bestowing medium. The technique included intertwining fictional characters with guest stars appearing as themselves. By 1995 the show had received Emmy nominations and Cable Ace Awards, but the audience was not large, both because the sophisticated content of the program was not universally attractive and because the program appeared on a premium cable channel with a limited viewership.

Shandling starred as Larry Sanders, a talk-show host competing with the larger networks' late-night programs. Although Larry is not the biggest fish in the chat pond, it is difficult to realize this from his interactions. He uses his power and position as a celebrity to control his office staff, show crew, and, at times, the general public as portrayed in this fictional world. Larry exposes his deep insecurities only to his executive producer, Artie (veteran character actor Rip Torn) and to his assistant, Beverly (Penny Johnson).

On screen, Larry is smooth and controlled, but behind the scenes, he is manipulative and disturbed, descending frequently into paranoia and tempter tantrums. His interactions with his office employees feature a peculiar style of communication. Each staff member or guest has a clear position in an invisible hierarchy. This situation is accepted because the strong office culture is dominated by constant job insecurity. People with greater clout are allowed to act abusively to those with less status. In one show, it seems clear that a staff member will be fired, but Larry cannot decide which person. Facing the tension mounting within the office, one writer breaks down with anxiety, creates several ugly scenes and—predictably—is chosen to lose his job.

Office relations are not the only storyline. Plots derived from typical talk show circumstances include contract renegotiations, strange sponsors needing odd on-air celebrity endorsements, marriages and relationships, problems with guests, and difficulty managing public images. During the program's run, Larry is married (to Megan Gallagher), divorced, and involved in a live-in arrangement with another ex-wife (Kathryn Harrold). These relationships exhibit little tenderness; instead, the unions are portrayed as fitting Larry's profession and lifestyle. If love blocks his career in any way, love ends.

Many of the show's elements focus on Larry's relationship with his sidekick, Hank Kingsley, played to perfection by Jeffrey Tambor. Hank is presented as an essentially talentless individual who has made an incredibly successful career by translating his position as hanger-on into hugely recognizable celebrity status. He makes additional money by endorsing cheap products; he gets dates because of his proximity to Larry; and he uses his status to bully other members of the show's staff. Larry tolerates Hank because he is, at once, confidante and pitch-man, as responsible for Larry's success as are Sanders's own skills.

In the final seasons of *The Larry Sanders Show,* questions about sexual preferences shaped absorbing storylines. "Everybody Loves Larry" hints that the *X-Files* star David Duchovny may be sexually attracted to Sanders. In the final episode, "Flip" (May 1988), this storyline plays out in a hotel room where Duchovny crosses and uncrosses his legs in homage to Sharon Stone's infamous scene in the film *Basic Instinct.* Duchovny declares that his feelings for Sanders are the same as his feelings for a woman, "It's definitely a heterosexual feeling, but it's directed at you." When Ellen DeGeneres announced she was gay, ABC used the incident to hype her sitcom, *Ellen. The Larry Sanders Show* parodied the fuss with "Ellen, or Isn't She?" In that episode, Sanders asks DeGeneres to come out on his program. The acting and writing in these episodes garnered accolades from television critics and earned an American Comedy Award for Duchovny.

While the program was in production, Shandling was twice involved in courtroom battles with persons linked to the show. In 1994, series regular Linda Doucett ended her seven-year personal relationship with Shandling and was subsequently fired from the program. In a lawsuit she charged him with sexual discrimination and harassment; the case eventually was resolved without litigation. When executive producer Brad Grey (who was also Shandling's manager) dropped Shandling as a client after 18 years, Shandling litigated, claiming conflict of interest for prior business arrangements. Grey countersued. Just before their scheduled court date, Grey and Shandling settled.

In addition to the subplot with Duchovny, the final episode of *The Larry Sanders Show* lampoons the legal activity in Shandling's own life, while ending several ongoing storylines on fictional Stage 11. The episode chronicles the end of Sanders's relationship with his talent agent, Stevie Grant—a smarmy, cocaine-snorting yuppie, and Shandling's ex-girlfriend Doucett appears briefly. A long list of Hollywood's top talents, including Carol Burnett, Jim Carrey, and Jerry Seinfeld, guest star, with country music star Clint Black singing a tribute reminiscent of Bette Midler's farewell on Johnny Carson's final episode of *The Tonight Show.*

Signing off the air as Sanders, Shandling gave a soliloquy about TV comedy. "Television is a risky business. You want to entertain. You want to try to do something new every night. You want to say something fresh. Nine times out of ten, you end up with *The Ropers* [a short-lived spin-off of the sitcom *Three's Company*]. Hopefully, occasionally, there are nights when we are not one of those nine."

The consistent quality of Shandling's two series translated into critical acclaim, and numerous wards and nominations. *It's Garry Shandling's Show* won Cable Ace honors for Best Comedy Program, Actor, and Writing. *The Larry Sanders Show*'s Rip Torn received the 1996 Emmy for Best Supporting Actor in a Comedy. The Academy of Television Arts and Sciences also recognized the series' final season with a writing award for Shandling and Peter Tolan, and honored Todd Holland for directing. In 1999 the program won the George Foster Peabody Award for outstanding achievement in broadcasting and cable.

Shandling used *It's Garry Shandling's Show* to push television to its whimsical extreme. With *The Larry Sanders Show,* he presented the funny side of television at its worst. In each case, he explored the medium intelligently and inventively, creating an arena to consider what television can be, rather than continuing the hackneyed stereotypes and norms.

JOAN STULLER-GIGLIONE

It's Garry Shandling's Show

Cast

Garry Shandling	Garry Shandling
Mrs. Shandling	Barbara Cason
Nancy Bancroft	Molly Cheek
Pete Schumaker	Michael Tucci
Jackie Schumaker	Bernadette Birkett
Grant Schumaker	Scott Nemes
Leonard Smith	Paul Wilson
Ian (1989–90)	Ian Buchanan
Phoebe Bass (1989–90)	Jessica Harper

Programming History
72 30-minute episodes

Showtime	
September 1986–May 1990	
FOX	
March 1988–July 1989	Sunday 9:00–9:30
July 1989	Sunday 9:30–10:00
July 1989–August 1989	Sunday 10:00–10:30
August 1989–March 1990	Sunday 10:30–11:00

The Larry Sanders Show

Cast

Larry Sanders	Gary Shandling
Hank Kingsley	Jeffrey Tambor
Producer Arthur	Rip Torn
Paula (1992–97)	Janeane Garofalo
Darlene (1992–94)	Linda Doucett
Jeannie Sanders (1992–93)	Megan Gallagher
Francine Sanders (1993–94)	Kathryn Harrold
Beverly Barnes	Penny Johnson
Phil	Wallace Langham
Jerry Capen (1992–93)	Jeremy Piven
Brian (1995–98)	Scott Thompson
Mary Lou (1996–98)	Mary Lynn Raiskub

Producers
Gary Shandling, Brad Grey, Peter Tolan, John Ziffren, Paul Simms

Programming History
89 episodes
HBO

August 1992–May 1998	Irregular schedule

Further Reading

Cohen, Noam, "Meta-musings: The Self-Reference Craze," *The New Republic* (September 5, 1988)

Gelman, Morrie, "Crystal, Shandling, HBO Take Home Handful of Aces," *Variety* (January 21, 1991)

Martel, Jay, "True Lies," *Rolling Stone* (September 8, 1994)

O'Connor, John J., "The Larry Sanders Show," *New York Times* (July 19, 1995)

Schleier, Curt, "The Open-and-Shut Life of Garry Shandling," *Emmy* (June 1995)

Shandling, Garry, and David Rensen, *Confessions of a Late Night Talk Show Host: The Autobiography of Larry Sanders,* New York: Simon and Schuster, 1998

Woolcott, James, "The Larry Sanders Show," *The New Yorker* (December 21, 1992)

I've Got a Secret

U.S. Game Show

Many radio and television game shows have their origin in parlor games, and it is no surprise to realize that *I've Got a Secret* was based on the game of "Secret, secret, who's got the secret." The format of the television program was simple but very durable. Sitting together on one side of a plain, unadorned set, each of four panelists took a 30-second turn questioning and then guessing a contestant's secret. The contestants were a mixture of ordinary people and celebrities, and the panelists were invariably celebrities. Each episode used four contestants and, in the American original, one contestant in each episode was a celebrity. Ordinary contestants received a small money prize if they stumped the panel. In the case of the celebrity contestant, the secret was very often related to some element of their fame. Thus, the first episode of *Secret* in 1952 featured the actor Boris Karloff's revelation was that he was afraid of mice.

The U.S. version of the program was among the longest-running and most popular game shows in the history of the genre. It began in June 1952 and ran on the CBS network until 1967. However, it was not quite an overnight success. The premiere episode used a courtroom as the set. Host Garry Moore was presented as a judge, the contestants as witnesses under cross-examination, and the panelists as the questioning lawyers. CBS canceled the program after its first season but almost immediately changed its mind, and the program resumed after its summer break. *Secret* became enormously popular and ran for 15 years on network television. By the late 1950s it was consistently in the top ten of U.S. television programs; it survived the quiz scandals of 1958–59; its popularity remained intact through the first part of the 1960s. The program was revived for syndication in 1972–73 and also played a short summer stint on CBS in 1976.

I've Got a Secret had three hosts in its time on U.S. television: Moore, Steve Allen, and Bill Cullen. Cullen, a long-time panelist, was made famous by the program, but many other panelists were already well known. Among them were Laraine Day, Orson Bean, Henry Morgan, Jayne Meadows, Faye Emerson, and Betsy Palmer. *Secret* featured several producers, including Allan Sherman, who was to have his own career in the early 1960s as a comic singer-cum-satirist.

The program was originated and produced by the inimitable Mark Goodson and Bill Todman. Their partnership in developing successful game-show formats had begun in radio in 1946, and *I've Got a Secret* was one of their earliest programs in television.

ALBERT MORAN

See also **Quiz and Game Shows**

Hosts
Garry Moore (1952–64)
Steve Allen (1964–67)
Bill Cullen (1976)

Panelists
Louise Allbritton (1952)
Laura Hobson (1952)
Walter Kiernan (1952)
Orson Bean (1952)
Melville Cooper (1952)
Bill Cullen (1952–67)
Kitty Carlisle (1952–53)
Henry Morgan (1952–76)
Laraine Day (1952)
Eddie Bracken (1952)
Faye Emerson (1952–58)
Jayne Meadows (1952–59)
Betsy Palmer (1957–67)
Bess Myerson (1958–67)
Pat Collins (1976)
Richard Dawson (1976)
Elaine Joyce (1976)

Producers
Mark Goodson, Bill Todman, Allan Sherman

Programming History
CBS
June 1952–June 1953   Thursday 10:30–11:00

July 1953–September 1961	Wednesday 9:30–10:00
September 1961–September 1962	Monday 10:30–11:00
September 1962–September 1966	Monday 8:00–8:30
September 1966–April 1967	Monday 10:30–11:00
June 1976–July 1976	Tuesday 8:00–8:30

Further Reading

Blumenthal, Norman, *The TV Game Shows,* New York: Pyramid, 1975

Fabe, M., *TV Game Shows,* Garden City, New York: Doubleday, 1979

Graham, J., *Come on Down!!!: The TV Game Show Book,* New York: Abbeville Press, 1988

Schwartz, D., S. Ryan, and F. Wostbrock, *The Encyclopedia of Television Game Shows,* New York: Zoetrope, 1987

J

Jackson, Gordon (1923–1990)

Scottish Actor

Gordon Jackson was one of the stalwarts of British television in the 1970s, although he also had extensive stage and screen experience going back to the 1940s. A Scot, he began his career playing small parts in a series of war films made by the Ealing Studios and others. Initially typecast as a weakling, Jackson gradually won recognition as a useful character actor, specializing in stern, well-mannered gents of the "stiff upper lip" variety, often lacking in a sense of humor. His rich Scottish accent, however, balanced this with a certain charm; it was this combination of sternness and warmth that characterized most of his roles on stage and screen.

During the 1950s, Jackson continued to develop his film career and was also busy in repertory theatre, making his debut on the London stage in the farce *Seagulls over Sorrento* in 1951. Other acclaimed roles on the stage included an award-winning Horatio in Tony Richardson's production of *Hamlet* in 1969, Tesman in Ibsen's *Hedda Gabler,* and Malvolio in *Twelfth Night.* In the cinema he gradually moved from young soldiers and juvenile leads in the likes of *Millions Like Us* (1943), *Whisky Galore* (1949), *Tunes of Glory* (1960) to major supporting parts in such films as *The Ipcress File* (1965), starring Michael Caine, and *The Prime of Miss Jean Brodie* (1969), which was adapted from the novel by Muriel Spark. By the 1960s, it was apparently automatic for Jackson's name to crop up whenever a genial, but crusty Scotsman was required,

whether the production under discussion was a wartime epic or something more homely.

As a television star, Jackson really came into his own in 1971, when he made his first appearances in the role of Hudson, the endearingly pompous butler in the classic period-drama series *Upstairs, Downstairs.* Over the next five years, Jackson, as one of the central characters in this hugely popular series about Edwardian life, became a household name—a status formally acknowledged in 1975 when he won the Royal Television Society's Best Actor Award (followed later by his being made an Officer of the British Empire). As Hudson, a character the actor himself professed to dislike, Jackson was in turn supportive and dependable and dour and infuriating, not least through his old-fashioned attitudes to the other servants and any inclination they showed to forget their station.

Not altogether dissimilar in this regard was Jackson's other most famous television role, the outwardly contrasting part of George "The Cow" Cowley in the action adventure series *The Professionals,* which was first seen in 1977. As Cowley, a former MI5 agent and now head of the specialist anti-terrorist unit CI5, Jackson combined a hard-bitten determination and impatience with his wayward operatives Bodie and Doyle (Lewis Collins and Martin Shaw) with genuine (if grudging) concern for their well-being when their lives were in danger. This show became favorite viewing for peak-time audiences in the 1970s, as much through the

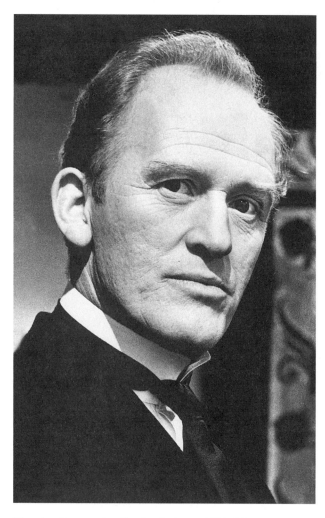

Upstairs, Downstairs, Gordon Jackson, 1971–75.
Courtesy of the Everett Collection

chemistry of the three main performers as through the somewhat formulaic car chases and action sequences that were included. The series did have its critics—many people protested at the violence of many episodes (leading the producers to limit explosions to two per story), and others refused to accept that Jackson, still firmly associated in their minds with the stuffy Mr. Hudson, could ever be convincing as a tough anti-terrorist chief, notwithstanding his early experience in the Ealing war films.

Also worthy of note were Jackson's always reliable appearances in other classic television programs, which ranged from *Doctor Finlay's Casebook* to the Australian-made *A Town Like Alice* and *Stars on Sunday* (as host).

DAVID PICKERING

See also **Upstairs, Downstairs**

Gordon Cameron Jackson. Born in Glasgow, Scotland, December 19, 1923. Attended Hillhead High School, Glasgow. Married: Rona Anderson; children: Graham and Roddy. Engineering draughtsman and actor, BBC radio, Glasgow, from 1939; film debut, 1942; debut on London stage, 1951; subsequently specialized in Scottish character roles in films and television and on the stage; best known to television audiences for the series *Upstairs, Downstairs* and *The Professionals*. Officer of the Order of the British Empire, 1979. Recipient: Clarence Derwent Award, 1969; Royal Television Society Award, 1975; Emmy Award, 1976. Died January 14, 1990.

Television Series

1971–74	*Upstairs, Downstairs*
1977–83	*The Professionals*

Made-for-Television Movies

1968	*The Soldier's Tale*
1977	*Spectre*
1979	*The Last Giraffe*
1981	*A Town Like Alice*
1986	*My Brother Tom*
1987	*Noble House*

Films

The Foreman Went to France, 1942; *Nine Men,* 1943; *Millions Like Us,* 1943; *San Demetrio—London,* 1943; *Pink String and Sealing Wax,* 1945; *The Captive Heart,* 1946; *Against the Wind,* 1948; *Eureka Stockade,* 1948; *Floodtide,* 1949; *Stop Press Girl,* 1949; *Whisky Galore,* 1949; *Bitter Springs,* 1950; *Happy Go Lovely,* 1951; *Lady with a Lamp,* 1951; *Castle in the Air,* 1952; *Death Goes to School,* 1953; *Malta Story,* 1953; *Meet Mr. Lucifer,* 1953; *The Love Lottery,* 1954; *The Delavine Affair,* 1954; *Passage Home,* 1955; *Windfall,* 1955; *The Quatermass Experiment,* 1955; *Pacific Destiny,* 1956; *Women Without Men,* 1956; *The Baby and the Battleship,* 1956; *Sailor Beware,* 1956; *Seven Waves Away,* 1957; *Let's Be Happy,* 1957; *Hell Drivers,* 1957; *The Black Ice,* 1957; *Man in the Shadow,* 1957; *Scotland Dances* (voice only), 1958; *Blind Spot,* 1958; *Rockets Galore,* 1958; *Three Crooked Men,* 1958; *Yesterday's Enemy,* 1959; *The Bridal Path,* 1959; *Blind Date,* 1959; *The Navy Lark,* 1959; *Devil's Bait,* 1959; *The Price of Silence,* 1960; *Cone of Silence,* 1960; *Snowball,* 1960; *Tunes of Glory,* 1960; *Greyfriars Bobby,* 1961; *Two Wives at One Wedding,* 1961; *Mutiny on the Bounty,* 1962; *The Great Escape,* 1963; *The Long Ships,* 1964; *Daylight Robbery,* 1964; *Those Magnificent*

Men in Their Flying Machines, 1965; *The Ipcress File,* 1965; *Operation Crossbow,* 1965; *Cast a Giant Shadow,* 1966; *Fighting Prince of Donegal,* 1966; *Night of the Generals,* 1966; *Triple Cross,* 1967; *Danger Route,* 1967; *Three to a Cell,* 1967; *Casting the Runes,* 1967; *Talk in Craig,* 1968; *The Eliminator,* 1968; *Negatives,* 1968; *On the Run,* 1969; *The Prime of Miss Jean Brodie,* 1969; *Run Wild Run Free,* 1969; *Wind v Polygamy,* 1969; *Hamlet,* 1970; *Scrooge,* 1970; *The Music Lovers,* 1970; *Singing Sands,* 1970; *Rain,* 1970; *Allergy,* 1970; *Dickens Centenary,* 1971; *Kidnapped,* 1971; *The Befrienders,* 1971; *Budgie,* 1971; *The Man from Haven,* 1972; *Madame Sin,* 1972; *Square of Three,* 1973; *Places Where They Sing,* 1973; *Places*

in History, 1974; *J.M. Barrie Lived Here,* 1975; *Russian Roulette,* 1975; *The Treasure,* 1976; *Supernatural,* 1977; *The Golden Rendezvous,* 1977; *The Medusa Touch,* 1978; *Captain Beaky,* 1980; *Father's Day,* 1982; *Strange but True,* 1983; *The Shooting Party,* 1984; *Shaka Zulu,* 1985; *The Masks of Death,* 1985; *The Whistle Blower,* 1986; *Gunpowder,* 1987.

Stage (selected)

Seagulls Over Sorrento, 1951; *Moby Dick,* 1955; *Macbeth,* 1966; *Hamlet,* 1969; *Hedda Gabler; What Every Woman Knows; Noah; Twelfth Night; Cards on the Table; Mass Appeal.*

Jackson, Michael (1958–)

British Television Executive

Michael Jackson, currently chair of Universal Television, was the first graduate of a media studies degree course to reach executive levels in British television. He was the BBC's youngest department head of all time, and shares with Michael Grade the distinction of having been in charge of both BBC Television and Channel 4.

He graduated in 1979 with the intention of becoming an independent producer. His dissertation on purchased programs enabled him to make contacts in the television industry, and he became the organizer of the Channel 4 Group, a campaign aimed at ensuring the planned fourth channel would provide extensive opportunities for independent production. When Channel 4 was established, a series on the 1960s developed and produced by Jackson was one of its first commissioned programs. The series *Open The Box,* coproduced by Jackson's company, Beat, and the British Film Institute, and his long-running magazine program *The Media Show* illustrated his interest in the culture industries. When he joined the BBC in 1988 he pursued this interest by establishing a long-running nightly arts review, *The Late Show,* producing *Rock Family Trees,* based on the book of elaborate charts of rock history by Pete Frame, and commissioning the media-based series *Naked Hollywood,* and *TV Hell.* With *The Late Show,* Jackson designed a program format that was self-consciously elusive, breaking television convention by dispensing

with fixed theme tune and title sequence, and attempting to ensure that the program could remain fresh and surprising. Its disappearance from the screen has left a gap yet to be filled.

Projects generated by and programs commissioned by Michael Jackson typically had a distinctive approach characterized by a marked degree of postmodern self-referentiality. Successes at the BBC included *Fantasy Football League, The Mrs. Merton Show, Changing Rooms,* and *This Life. Changing Rooms* was the first and most successful of a new genre of style transformation shows. After he moved to Channel 4, successes included *Da Ali G Show, Smack The Pony, The Valley, 1900 House, Staying Lost, Tina Goes Shopping,* and *So Graham Norton.* Several careers benefited from the success of these programs, which helped to establish the personalities of Frank Skinner and David Baddiel, Caroline Aherne, Graham Norton, and Ali G. *Queer As Folk* broke new ground in being a drama series based around gay relationships.

As chief executive, Michael Jackson steered Channel 4 in a more entrepreneurial direction, raising turnover 30 percent over four years, and establishing new channels Film Four and E4. Programming initiatives included the innovative coverage of Test Cricket, the re-launched seven-day Channel 4 News, and the British version of *Big Brother. Big Brother* attracted extensive attention from the audience and the media. The Internet site has attracted over 119 million hits and up to seven million votes were cast in the regular eviction contests. Channel 4 has been able to compete well in its niche, capitalizing on its ability to attract young affluent viewers and hence advertising revenue. Some critics have expressed concern that the repositioning engineered by Jackson has taken the channel away from its brief to be alternative and innovative. It would be fair to say that it has a metropolitan trendiness when compared to its closest competitor channel, BBC 2, and that the range of voices, a feature of the channel's early years, now seems narrower.

Throughout his career, a genuine concern with the quality of television, across program genres, has been evident. Jackson believes the scarcest commodity in television is good ideas, and his commissioning is based on a search for innovation in form as well as content. The frequent change of post and ceaseless quest for innovation might suggest a restless process of refocusing, but Jackson is also known to have dogged persistence, working with projects like *Rock Family Trees* and the drama *Our Friends in the North* for many years before they reached the screen. Michael Jackson has never been slow to take on a new challenge, and having held top jobs at two channels in the United Kingdom, is now working to make a mark in the United States. Many media observers expect him to return home eventually to become director general of the BBC. Typically, Jackson himself does not proclaim a desire for the post, but neither does he deny its potential appeal.

GARRY WHANNEL

See also **British Programming; Channel 4**

Michael Jackson. Born in Congleton, Cheshire, United Kingdom, in 1958. Attended King's School, Macclesfield. Earned degree in media studies at the Polytechnic of Central London, 1979. Organizer of the Channel 4 Group. Producer, *The Sixties* (Channel 4, 1982), *Whose Town Is It Anyway?* (Channel 4, 1984), *Open the Box* (Channel 4, 1986). Edited *The Media Show* for Channel 4, 1984–88. Joined the BBC in 1988 as founding editor of *The Late Show* (BBC, 1989–93). Named head of the music and arts department, 1990. Named controller of BBC 2, 1993. Named controller of BBC 1 and BBC's director of television, 1996. Named chief executive of Channel 4 Television, 1997. Moved to New York to become president and chief executive of USA Entertainment, 2001. Named chair of Universal Television, 2002. Nonexecutive director, EMI Group and chairman of London's Photographers' Gallery. Recipient: Hon DLitt, University of Westminster, 1995; Editor of *Absurdistan* 1991: British Film Institute Grierson Documentary Award. Executive producer of *Naked Hollywood* (BBC 2): British Academy of Film and Television Arts (BAFTA) Best Documentary Series Award, 1991. *The Late Show* BFI Television Award, 1989. Channel 4 voted UK Media Brand of the Year by *Media Week* magazine, 2001. At the 2001 BAFTA awards Channel 4 won 11 of the 19 awards, more than the BBC and ITV combined, and *The Valley* won the Prix Italia award.

Jaffrey, Madhur (1933–)

British Actor, Television Personality, Cookery Host

Madhur Jaffrey, born in India, has had a remarkably varied career encompassing acting, directing, and writing. In Britain she is most highly renowned and respected for her role as a presenter of television cookery programs.

Professionally, Jaffrey has worked largely in cinema, with prominent roles in films such as the Merchant Ivory Production *Shakespeare Wallah* (1965), for which she was awarded a prize at Venice, *The Assam Garden* (1985), and *Chutney Popcorn* (1999). Her most prolific role as an actor in recent British television has been the drama series *Firm Friends* (ITV,

1992 and 1994). Jaffrey played Jayshree Kapor, a cleaning lady turned business partner to white, middle-class Rose (Billie Whitelaw), in a show that was unusual in representing a racially mixed society without treating this as an issue. While many of the productions in which Jaffrey has performed draw on her cultural background, *Firm Friends* also unashamedly drew on her culinary image—the business Jayshree initiates is selling cooked foods.

Jaffrey as an actor has not surpassed her popularity as a food presenter. Jaffrey's route into presenting BBC food shows was less than orthodox. While a

While her shows have been educational from a culinary perspective, they have also proved influential within television culture, as Jaffrey seeks to contextualize the cookery by presenting it in the appropriate geographical location. In liberating cookery from the studio-bound format, these shows not only offer the viewing pleasures of a travel show but also work to redefine popular perceptions of Eastern cultures. Jaffrey focuses on the recipes and their ingredients by presenting a variety of people (mainly cooks, professional and otherwise) and by exploring a wealth of marketplaces, local lifestyles, and regional religions.

The gastronomic travelogue format may no longer be considered revolutionary, as it has developed into a television standard, but Jaffrey remains a guru of British culinary television. Her series are particularly noteworthy for their stylish and sophisticated production values and their attention to detail; for example, Madhur dresses to reflect the cultural background of specific recipes. The greatest appeal of her cookery shows lies in her vibrant approach and personality, with which she has spiced up British television. Jaffrey has argued that she sees no conflict in her professional double life, as she treats the presentation of food as a performance equal to any acting role.

NICOLA FOSTER

Madhur Jaffrey. Born in Delhi, India, August 13, 1933. Attended local schools in Delhi; Royal Academy of Dramatic Art, London. Married: 1) actor Saeed Jaffrey (divorced); three children: Zia, Meera, and Sakina; 2) violinist Sanford Allen. Settled in England to train as a drama student; subsequently appeared in numerous stage and film productions before establishing reputation as leading authority on Indian food, presenting her own cookery programs on television and writing best-selling cookbooks.

Television Series

1982	*Madhur Jaffrey's Indian Cookery*
1989	*Madhur Jaffrey's Far Eastern Cookery*
1992, 1994	*Firm Friends*
1995	*Madhur Jaffrey's Flavours of India*
1996	*The Peacock Spring*

Television Films

1986	*The Love Match*

Films (selected)

Shakespeare Wallah, 1965; *The Guru,* 1969; *Autobiography of a Princess,* 1975; *Heat and Dust,* 1982; *Saa-*

Madhur Jaffrey.
Courtesy of the Everett Collection

drama student at the Royal Academy of Dramatic Arts in London, she wrote to her mother in India, begging her to send simple recipes. Her mother obliged, and thus Jaffrey learned to cook by correspondence, although this was never intended as a career move. She was drawn into cooking as a business after friends implored her to write a cookery book. Her immense success and appeal may be attributed to her flamboyant yet sensitive style of presentation and the way she has revolutionized and demystified Indian cooking, a cuisine particularly favored by the British. By introducing authentic Indian cuisine to the British kitchen, Jaffrey radically altered the way British people cook, eat, and think about Indian food. Indeed, it is fair to suggest that the ready availability of oriental spices and other Indian ingredients in British supermarkets is a direct result of Jaffrey's television programs.

The inspirational presentation of food in the three BBC series—*Madhur Jaffrey's Indian Cookery* (1982), *Madhur Jaffrey's Far Eastern Cookery* (1989), and *Madhur Jaffrey's Flavours of India* (1995)—is equaled by the warmth and charm of its presenter.

gar, 1985; *The Assam Garden,* 1985; *The Perfect Murder,* 1990; *Six Degrees of Separation,* 1993; *Vanya on 42nd Street,* 1994; *Flawless,* 1999; *Chutney Popcorn,* 1999; *Cotton Mary,* 2000; *ABCD,* 2001.

Publications (selected)

An Invitation to Indian Cookery, 1973
Madhur Jaffrey's World-of-the-East Vegetarian Cooking, 1981
Madhur Jaffrey's Indian Cookery, 1982
Eastern Vegetarian Cooking, 1983
Seasons of Splendor: Tales, Myths, and Legends of India, 1985
Madhur Jaffrey's Cookbook: Food for Family and Friends, 1989
Madhur Jaffrey's Far Eastern Cookery, 1989

The Days of the Banyan Tree, 1990
Madhur Jaffrey's Quick and Easy Indian Cooking, 1993
Madhur Jaffrey's a Taste of the Far East, 1994
Madhur Jaffrey's Illustrated Indian Cooking, 1994
Entertaining with Madhur Jaffrey, 1994
Madhur Jaffrey's Flavours of India, 1995
Madhur Jaffrey's Spice Kitchen, 1995
Madhur Jaffrey's Market Days: From Market to Market Around the World, 1995
The Essential Madhur Jaffrey, 1996
Madhur Jaffrey Cooks Curries, 1996
Robi Dobi: The Marvellous Adventures of an Indian Elephant, 1997
Madhur Jaffrey's World Vegetarian, 1998
Madhur Jaffrey's Step by Step Cookery, 2000

Jaffrey, Saeed (1929–)

Indian Actor

Saeed Jaffrey is one of Britain's best-known and most experienced actors, playing a wide variety of roles in comedy and drama with equal enthusiasm. He started his performing career in India, setting up his own English theater company in Delhi after completing his postgraduate degree in history. His early theatrical work included roles in productions of Tennessee Williams, Fry, Priestly, Wilde, and Shakespeare. Having completed his studies at the Royal Academy of Dramatic Art in London, he went to the United States on a Fulbright scholarship and took a second postgraduate degree in drama from the Catholic University in Washington, D.C. From these firm foundations, Jaffrey set out as the first Indian actor to tour Shakespeare, taking his company across the United States and subsequently joining the Actor's Studio in New York, where he played the lead in off-Broadway productions of Lorca's *Blood Wedding,* as well as *Rashomon* and *Twelfth Night.* Jaffrey is an accomplished stage actor and has appeared on Broadway and at London's West End in a diverse range of characterizations.

His work in television has been just as varied. He appeared as Jimmy Sharma in Channel 4's first "Asian" comedy, *Tandoori Nights* and as the elegiac Nawah in Granada Television's adaptation of *The Jewel in the Crown.* It was arguably his performance as the smooth Rafiq in the BBC cult-classic *Gangsters* that brought him to national recognition, even though he had been acting in both theater and television for several years previously.

In some ways, Jaffrey's character types have been broadly similar and, like Clint Eastwood, he always plays himself playing a character. Jaffrey's impeccable English accent, his dapper style, and his catchphrases ("My dear boy") are part of his acting persona. His smooth charm is used to good effect whether he plays the archetypal oily, corrupt businessman or the kindly, knowing father figure. In 1994 he costarred with Norman Beaton in Michael Abbensett's new TV series, *Little Napoleons,* for Channel 4, playing once again a successful lawyer who wants political as well as economic power.

Jaffrey's career has spanned several decades, and it is still unfortunately the case that he is one of only a handful of Indian actors who is regularly employed, be it for radio, television, or the stage. Although this is good news for him, his prodigious success and his ability to talk the right language means that he is a hard

Saeed Jaffrey.
Courtesy of the Everett Collection

act to follow for younger talent trying to penetrate a hard-faced industry.

KAREN ROSS

Saeed Jaffrey. Born in Maler Kotla, India, 1929. Attended the University of Allahabad, M.A. in history; Staff Training Institute, All India Radio; Royal Academy of Dramatic Art, 1956; Catholic University, Washington, D.C., 1956–57, M.A. in drama; Actors' Studio, New York. Married: Madhur (divorced); three children. Radio director, All India Radio, 1951–56; began stage career in India as founder, Unity Theatre, New Delhi, 1951–56, as actor, 1954; performed with his own company in U.S. tour of Shakespeare, 1957; various stage performances and tours, 1960s; director of publicity and advertising, Government of India Tourist Office, United States, 1958–60; began U.S. television career with guest appearances, 1960s; began film career in *The Guru*, 1969, numerous film performances, including roles in *Gandhi*, 1982, *A Passage to India*, 1984, and *My Beautiful Laundrette*, 1986. Mem-

ber: Actors' Equity Association; Screen Actors Guild; American Federation of Television and Radio Artists.

Television Series

1975–76	*Gangsters*
1985	*Tandoori Nights*
1994	*Little Napoleons*
1999–	*Coronation Street*

Television Miniseries

| 1984 | *The Far Pavilions* |
| 1984 | *The Jewel in the Crown* |

Made-for-Television Movies

| 1979 | *The Last Giraffe* |
| 2003 | *The Inspector Lynley Mysteries: Deception on His Mind* |

Films

The Guru, 1969; *The Horsemen*, 1971; *The Man Who Would Be King*, 1975; *The Wilby Conspiracy*, 1975; *The Chess Players*, 1977; *Hullabaloo Over Georgie and Bonnie's Pictures*, 1979; *Sphinx*, 1981; *Gandhi*, 1982; *The Courtesans of Bombay* (documentary), 1982; *Pandit Nehru* (narrator), 1982; *Masoom*, 1983; *A Passage to India*, 1984; *The Razor's Edge*, 1984; *My Beautiful Laundrette*, 1986; *The Deceivers*, 1988; *Just Ask for Diamond*, 1988; *Partition*, 1988; *Manika*, 1988; *Dil*, 1990; *Masala*, 1991; *Bollywood*, 1994; *Kartavya*, 1995; *Uff! Yeh Mohabbat*, 1997; *Raja Ki Ayegi Barrat*, 1997; *Judaai*, 1997; *The Journey*, 1997; *Deewana Mastana*, 1997; *Achanak*, 1998; *Guru in Seven*, 1998; *Being Considered*, 2000; *Second Generation*, 2000; *Pyar Ki Dhun*, 2001; *Mr. In-Between*, 2001; *Albela*, 2001; *Pyarr Ki Dhun (The Song of Love)*, 2002; *Day of the Sirens*, 2002; *Cross My Heart*, 2003.

Stage

Othello; The Firstborn; A Phoenix Too Frequent; Under Milk Wood; Auto-Da-Fe; The Importance of Being Earnest; The Cocktail Party; and *Le Bourgeois Gentilhomme* (all with Repertory Company, Unity Theatre, New Delhi, India 1951–56); *The Eagle Has Two Heads*, 1954; *Blood Wedding*, 1958; *Twelfth Night*, 1960; *King of the Dark Chamber*, 1961; *India: A Dancer's Pilgrimage*, 1961; *A Passage to India*, 1962; *A Tenth of an Inch Makes the Difference*, 1962; *Nathan Weinstein, Mystic, Connecticut*, 1966; *Captain Brassbound's Conversion*, 1971.

James, Sid (1913–1976)

British Comedian

Sid James established himself as a nationally recognized figure in British broadcasting in a groundbreaking radio comedy, *Hancock's Half Hour* in the mid-1950s. But James was a ubiquitous supporting role actor. Appearing in more than 150 features during his career, he was best known as a regular character in some of the *Carry On* comedy films (1958–80). He acted in numerous stage comedies and starred in several television series. With the situation comedy, *Bless This House* (ITV, 1971–76), James secured his status as one of the most enduring figures of postwar British popular culture. Clever exploitation of a naturally heavily lined face to produce a variety of put-upon expressions endeared him to *Carry On* and television audiences alike. His "dirty" cackle of a laugh embodied a vein of "kiss-me-quick" bawdiness that runs deep in English humor.

Christened Sidney Joel Cohen, Sid James was a South African-born Jew whose parents worked in the music hall business. James joined a South African regiment of the British Army in 1939 and soon became a producer in its entertainment unit. As such, he was typical of a generation of British performers and writers who learned their trade while in the armed forces. After the service, James arrived in London on Christmas day 1946, looking to make a start in acting. He landed his first film role nine days later. His grizzled face led to typecasting as minor gangsters in his early film appearances. His career success came when he transformed himself into a quintessential Londoner, an ordinary "bloke," who drew sympathy from his audience despite playing a rascal in many of his roles.

His television credits include some dozen plays (including some drama) and several series. He made his television debut in 1948 in a two-part BBC drama, *Kid Flanagan,* as Sharkey Morrison and played the lead role of Billy Johnson in *The Front Page* (BBC) later the same year. In 1949 he played an American film director in a 30- minute play called *Family Affairs* (BBC). After significant supporting roles in films such as *The Lavender Hill Mob* (1951) and *The Titchfield Thunderbolt* (1952), his repertoire began to develop from gangsters into characters who lived just this side of the law in the austere conditions of 1950s Britain. Although he was best known for his comic roles, James rarely turned down dramatic work. His next television appearance was in *Another Part of the Forest* (BBC, 1954), one of an acclaimed *20th-Century Theatre* series.

Spotted by two scriptwriters, Ray Galton and Alan Simpson, James was cast as Tony Hancock's housemate in the BBC radio comedy *Hancock's Half Hour.* His ability as an actor to play off a lead was recognized by Hancock. When the show switched to television, Hancock insisted that all his supporting actors from the radio version be dropped except James. The 30-minute television show (1956–60) represented a defining moment in British situation comedy. The show developed huge audiences; BBC audience research estimates that 28 percent of the population watched at its peak. During this four-year period, James appeared as a pirate (Shanty Jack) in *The Buccaneers* (BBC, 1957) and played a character from the shadier side of London's Jewish community in a six-part series for ITV called

Sid James.
Courtesy of the Everett Collection

East End, West End (1958). James's dependency on the Hancock connection was broken at the start of the 1960s, when he began to appear in a highly successful series of *Carry On* films (*Carry On Constable* was his first in 1960). These quickly made film farces provided regular, almost annual income for its troupe of actors. James became one of the best-loved stars, appearing in almost 20 films, usually playing a hen-pecked husband desperate for extramarital sex with younger women.

James never worked with Hancock again, but he was immediately contracted by the BBC to star in a Galton and Simpson-scripted series called *Citizen James* (1960–62). In a series called *It's a Deal* (BBC, 1961), he played a working-class property dealer whose business partner was a Mayfair playboy (Dennis Price). Mismatched in class, the two characters were essentially similar rogues underneath, who found themselves reluctantly dependent on one another. Throughout the 1960s, James's television work was based on characters and plots that employed variations on this theme. In *Taxi!* (BBC, 1963–64), he played a London cabby who gets involved in the day-to-day problems of his fares and his fellow drivers. The 12 50-minute episodes were an uneven mix of drama and comedy that did not prove successful in the audience ratings. In *George and the Dragon* (ITV, 1966–68), James played a chauffeur (George) to John Le Mesurier (Colonel Maynard). Both men are dominated by the overbearing housekeeper character (the Dragon), played by Peggy Mount. The comedy came from James's challenge to her control of their social superior and employer. In *Two in Clover* (ITV, 1969–70) James played alongside Victor Spinetti in a series whose comic situation derived from transplanting a mismatched pair from the city to the country.

With *Bless This House*, James secured his position as a television sitcom actor of national acclaim. It also signaled a change in emphasis from his early film and *Carry On* types to one that suited his maturing years. He played Sid Abbott, a long-suffering father-husband to his wife Jean (Diana Coupland) and their two children, Mike and Kate. The key to his success was his ability to deliver lines for comic effect and react to those around him. His lined face testified to a lot of laughter. While his characters typically gave in to their fate, his distinctive dirty cackle erased any lingering pathos. James died suddenly in 1976, on stage in a comedy called *The Mating Game* after the prerecorded *Bless This House* series had just completed its run.

LANCE PETTITT

See also **Hancock's Half Hour**

Sidney James. Born in Johannesburg, South Africa, May 8, 1913. Attended schools in Johannesburg. Married: 1) Meg Williams; one daughter; 2) Valerie Ashton; one son and one daughter. Served in anti-tank regiment in Middle East during World War II. Worked as coal heaver, stevedore, diamond polisher, and professional boxer, South Africa, before World War II; gained first stage experience with wartime entertainment unit; settled in the United Kingdom, 1946, and entered repertory theater and films, playing character roles; with comedian Tony Hancock on radio and television, late 1950s; starred in 18 *Carry On* films; toward the end of his career appeared on television in situation comedies. Recipient: *TV Times* Funniest Man on Television Award, 1974. Died April 26, 1976.

Television Series

1956–60	*Hancock's Half Hour*
1958	*East End, West End*
1960–62	*Citizen James*
1961	*It's a Deal*
1963–64	*Taxi*
1966–68	*George and the Dragon*
1969–70	*Two in Clover*
1971–76	*Bless This House*

Television Plays

1948	*Kid Flanegan*
1948	*The Front Page*
1949	*Family Affairs*
1954	*Another Part of the Forest*
1958	*The Buccaneers*

Films

Black Memory, 1947; *The October Man*, 1947; *It Always Rains on Sunday*, 1947; *No Orchids for Miss Blandish*, 1948; *Night Beat*, 1948; *Once a Jolly Swagman/Maniacs on Wheels*, 1948; *The Small Back Room*, 1948; *Paper Orchid*, 1949; *The Man in Black*, 1949; *Give Us This Day/Salt to the Devil*, 1949; *Last Holiday*, 1950; *The Lady Craved Excitement*, 1950; *Talk of a Million/You Can't Beat the Irish*, 1951; *Lady Godiva Rides Again*, 1951; *The Lavender Hill Mob*, 1951; *The Magic Box*, 1951; *The Galloping Major*, 1951; *I Believe in You*, 1952; *Emergency Call/Hundred Hour Hunt*, 1952; *Gift Horse/Glory at Sea*, 1952; *Cosh Boy/The Slasher*, 1952; *Miss Robin Hood*, 1952; *Time Gentlemen Please!*, 1952; *Father's Doing Fine*, 1952; *Venetian Bird/The Assassin*, 1952; *Tall Headlines*, 1952; *The Yellow Balloon*, 1952; *The Titchfield Thunderbolt*, 1952; *The Wedding of Lili Marlene*, 1953; *Escape By Night*, 1953; *The Square Ring*, 1953; *Will Any Gentleman…?*, 1953; *The Weak and the Wicked/Young and Willing*, 1953; *Park Plaza*

605/Norman Conquest, 1953; *The Flanagan Boy/Bad Blonde*, 1953; *Is Your Honeymoon Really Necessary?*, 1953; *The Rainbow Jacket*, 1954; *The House Across the Lake/Heatwave*, 1954; *Seagulls Over Sorrento/Crest of the Wave*, 1954; *The Crowded Day*, 1954; *Orders Are Orders*, 1954; *Aunt Clara*, 1954; *For Better, For Worse/Cocktails in the Kitchen*, 1954; *The Belles of St Trinian's*, 1954; *Out of the Clouds*, 1955; *Joe Macbeth*, 1955; *The Deep Blue Sea*, 1955; *A Kid for Two Farthings*, 1955; *The Glass Cage/The Glass Tomb*, 1955; *A Yank in Ermine*, 1955; *It's a Great Day*, 1955; *John and Julie*, 1955; *Ramsbottom Rides Again*, 1956; *The Extra Day*, 1956; *Wicked As They Come*, 1956; *The Iron Petticoat*, 1956; *Dry Rot*, 1956; *Trapeze*, 1956; *Quatermass II/Enemy from Space*, 1957; *Interpol/Pickup Alley*, 1957; *The Smallest Show on Earth*, 1957; *The Shiralee*, 1957; *Hell Drivers*, 1957; *Campbell's Kingdom*, 1957; *A King in New York*, 1957; *The Story of Esther Costello/The Golden Virgin*, 1957; *The Silent Enemy*, 1958; *Another Time, Another Place*, 1958; *Next to No Time!*, 1958; *The Man Inside*, 1958; *I Was Monty's Double/Monty's Double*, 1958; *The Sheriff of Fractured Jaw*, 1958; *Too Many Crooks*, 1959; *Make Mine a Million*, 1959; *The 39 Steps*, 1959; *Upstairs and Downstairs*, 1959; *Tommy the Toreador*, 1959; *Desert Mice*, 1959; *Idle on Parade/Idol on Parade*, 1959; *Carry On Constable*, 1960; *Watch Your Stern*, 1960; *And the Same to You*, 1960; *The Pure Hell of St Trinian's*, 1960; *Double Bunk*, 1961; *A Weekend with Lulu*, 1961; *The Green Helmet*, 1961; *What a Carve Up!/No Place Like Homicide*, 1961; *Raising the Wind/Roommates*, 1961; *What a Whopper!*, 1961; *Carry On Regardless*, 1961; *Carry On Cruising*, 1962; *We Joined the Navy*, 1962; *Carry On Cabby*, 1963; *The Beauty Jungle/Contest Girl*, 1964; *Carry On Cleo*, 1964; *Three Hats for Lisa*, 1964; *The Big Job*, 1965; *Carry On Cowboy*, 1965; *Where the Bullets Fly*, 1966; *Don't Lose Your Head*, 1966; *Carry On Doctor*, 1967; *Carry On Up the Khyber*, 1968; *Carry On Again, Doctor*, 1969; *Carry On Camping*, 1969; *Carry On Up the Jungle*, 1969; *Carry On Loving*, 1970; *Carry On Henry*, 1970; *Carry On at Your Convenience*, 1971; *Tokoloshe, the Evil Spirit*, 1971; *Carry On Matron*, 1972; *Bless This House*, 1972; *Carry On Abroad*, 1972; *Carry On Girls*, 1973; *Carry On Dick*, 1974.

Radio

Hancock's Half Hour, 1954–59; *Educating Archie*.

Stage (selection)

Kiss Me Kate, 1951.

Further Reading

Goddard, Peter, "*Hancock's Half Hour:* A Watershed in British Television Comedy," in *Popular Television in Britain: Studies in Cultural History,* edited by John O'Connor, London: British Film Institute, 1991

Japan

In Japan today, there are six televisions for every ten people and a diffusion rate of 100 percent. TV is viewed by virtually every Japanese every day: 95 percent of the population according to a 2002 study (see Kamimura and Ida). This far exceeds other popular forms of information processing: newspapers (86 percent), cell phones (73 percent), and the Internet (27 percent). The average amount of personal viewing per day approaches 225 minutes and has constantly topped three hours since 1960. A recent European survey places the number in excess of four hours, ranking Japan third in the world. The figures are astounding and capture the centrality of television in Japanese society.

Political Dimensions

Japan was at the forefront of the technical development of television, conducting its first experimental broadcast in 1939. However, the Pacific war curtailed research and development and infrastructure expansion. Once renewed, television bore the imprimatur of SCAP, the American occupational army. Seeking to ensure that television could not so easily become a tool for government (as both radio and early TV had before and during the Pacific war), Article 3 of the 1952 broadcasting law specified that programming by domestic broadcasters must: (1) uphold public security, morals, and good behavior, (2) pursue political impartiality, (3) present news without distorting the facts, and (4) present the widest possible range of viewpoints when dealing with controversial issues. These are goals that are not always upheld, though, with the advent of opinion-oriented news programs critical of government and business institutions in the late 1980s, for instance, and the profound increase in "infotainment" as a communication style in all genres of television content in the late 1990s. This has worked to bring politics off the pedestal, where it has so often before resided, beyond the popular realm. By the millennium, "wide shows" made it a habit to explain terms and issues for viewers, evening news interviewed candidates, and western-style political spots became a staple of election campaigns. To date, strains at the edges of the broadcast law appear, but not in ways contemplated by Japan's American conquerors: that is, in ways such that the medium became hostage to government control.

Economic Dimensions

In the 1950s, television remained a luxury item, beyond the means of most citizens. That changed, however, with the "economic miracle" that sent domestic production booming and incomes soaring. In a two-year span in the late 1950s, television production quadrupled, and within the last half of that decade TV ownership increased 41-fold: from 165,666 to 6,860,472 sets. Content, however, was still heavily dependent on external sources. Reflective of political history and economic realities, content remained heavily dependent on American imports: in 1958, for instance, five of the nation's top ten programs were either made in the United States or were Japanese-made clones of popular U.S. programs. The following year, *Rawhide* was the number one show. Its immense success led to the importation of *Laramie* two years later. In the 1960s, however, Japan's networks began weaning themselves away from American programming, developing their own programming. By the 1980s, with a vital domestic economy, virtual economic independence, and a fully developed popular culture, import-dependence had all but dissipated. Like other large states such as the United States, China, India, and the Soviet Union, Japan filled less than 10 percent of its program time with imported material—albeit 90 percent of which still came from the United States.

Without doubt, the major factor sustaining Japanese television is the vibrant commercial culture that contains, infuses, characterizes, colors, and depends on it. Advertising outlays for TV (at 34.1 percent) outdistance all other media sources, with the closest alternative conduit being newspapers (19.9 percent). Japan's advertising market is the second largest worldwide, amounting to more than $223 million just for television, dedicated to 957,447 ads, consuming 6,016 broadcasting hours per year. As one might infer, advertising serves not only as a major motor for Japanese television; it also works as one of the major conduits of cultural communication. Through ads, television plays a powerful socializing and ideological function, narrowly and repetitiously re/producing images of gender, cultural values, history, nationalism, and political, social, and personal identity (among others).

Cultural Dimensions

Three of the top five leisure goods listed as "essential" are television-related: a TV, itself (ranked second behind "music system"), VCR (third) and video software (fifth). VCRs are now owned by 79.6 percent of the population. In terms of leisure activities engaged in, television viewing is not listed—likely because it is viewed as an endemic, if not essential, part of everyday life; video-viewing ranks 12th, drawing 36.5 percent of the population, and is the fourth-most subsidized activity. As an industry, video sale and rental are big business: rentals for the first half of 2003 topped $550 million, with sales in excess of $1 billion. In short, TV-centered leisure is not only a core way of life in contemporary Japan; it is a core economic enterprise.

Befitting a leisure lifestyle, television has long been held to be an entertainment medium. This is reflected in the fact that so much programming today—whether game shows, talk shows, and even news—is best characterized as "infotainment." Form, as well as content, is primed to mix information with pleasant packaging. Learning is coupled with stimulation and pleasure. Thus, it is not unusual to have a segment on the post-"golden hour" news featuring "person in the street" interviews critical of the faltering economy or the latest political scandal, followed up by an in-studio guest such as Sting performing an anti-war song or the popular Japanese singing duo Chage and Aska. So, too, is it common to have a quiz show in which entertainers test their acumen concerning places, peoples, and customs from around the world, or else view segments on an array of topics—domestic and foreign; political, moral, or cultural—and then weigh in with their opinions.

In this way, Japanese television is a medium for the reproduction of nation and the nurturing of nationalism. It is certainly a "globalizer" in terms of assisting the transcultural flow of exogenous practices and beliefs; yet, in the main, it is a heavy defender of indigenous cultural content. Numerous programs—from the annual New Year's "red-white" singing contest, to food shows (which are pervasive) to regular sporting events (baseball, golf, volleyball, and boxing) to (golden-hour and late-night) music shows to daily quiz shows—make Japan the unspoken referent. While foreigners or foreign countries often appear, it is the juxtaposition of oppositional elements that enables Japan to emerge as a unique, privileged place. This tendency is reinforced by the now decades-long practice of foreigners appearing on variety, quiz, and food shows. Although the emphasis might once have been on "the strange foreigner," this discursive trope has for more than a decade taken a back seat to the foreigner who "fits in"—the "half" or Western transplant who is fluent with Japanese language and customs.

No less important in the reproduction of nation has been Nippon Hoso Kyokai, or NHK, the publicly funded, viewer-subscribed network. It features two terrestrial stations (Sogo, which broadcasts news, cultural, and entertainment programs, and Kyoiku, which chiefly broadcasts educational programs), as well as three satellite-based stations. NHK is justly famous for the quality of its programming, although much of it adopts historical or culturally reproductive themes such as postwar reconstruction, samurai and period pieces, national baseball tournaments, and documentaries about daily contemporary life. NHK's dramas—which have been produced for over 50 years—can be immensely popular. *Oshin,* the 1983 serialized tale of a poor woman struggling to survive in the immediate postwar era, garnered viewer rates in excess of 60 percent and was exported for international consumption to countries as far-flung as Australia, China, Egypt, Iran, Poland, and Mexico. This drama was among the first, but far from the last, case of Japanese television products assisting the global transmission of culture.

Technological Dimensions

Sociocultural events have long been regarded as influencing institutional ecology. For instance, the Crown Prince's wedding in 1959 is often cited as providing a spur to domestic TV sales. So, too, did it precipitate the creation of complicated nationwide commercial networks. What emerged after a number of years were five key networks featuring a "key TV station": Nippon News Network (NTV), Japanese News Network (TBS), Fuji News Network (Fuji TV), All Nippon News Network (TV Asahi) and TX Network (TV Tokyo)—all based in Tokyo, with 30, 28, 28, 26, and 6 network members, respectively. Each network, privately owned and heavily commercial, is closely connected with a national newspaper.

Television diffusion was greatly influenced by the staging of the 1964 Tokyo Olympics. Just as significant, though, was this event's role in prompting technical innovation; for, like its predecessor, the canceled 1940 Olympiad, domestic engineers were inspired to solve transmission and delivery problems for audiences both local and international. For instance, NHK created an image pickup tube and equipment for satellite relay broadcasting, enabling one of the first satellite broadcasts in history. In addition, these games were the first to broadcast in color (albeit only eight events). Given the medium's central role, these games were dubbed "the TV Olympics."

Television tropes—no less than technical advances—have been shaped by external events. For instance, it was the Crown Prince's departure by ship to attend Queen Elizabeth's coronation in 1952 that led to the practice of remote broadcasts—a practice widely followed today on morning wake-up programs. It might even be suggested that the root trope of visuality (inherent in the technology itself) is spurred by the imperative of culture. Japanese written language, based on ideograms is but one indicator. Throughout Japanese society, the image reigns supreme. This truism finds expression in the increasingly common practice on TV today of writing dialogue out as subtitles, even in cases where the speakers are Japanese. This has the effect of binding audiences, filling in gaps, providing more information, and potentially engendering greater intimacy.

A final technological advance has been cable, which, although making inroads over the past decade, has been relatively slow to take hold. Indeed, Japanese television is still heavily broadcast-network centered. According to data published in 2001, the five commercial networks along with NHK receive more than 51.6 percent of all Japanese broadcasting and cable market revenue (which breaks down into 18.9 percent for NHK, 9.1 percent for Fuji TV, 8.3 percent for Nippon TV, 7.0 percent for TBS, 5.5 percent for TV Asahi, and 2.6 percent for TV Tokyo). For cable, the diffusion rate doubled in the latter half of the 1990s—from 11.0 percent in 1995 to 21.8 percent in 2000. As of 2002, premium cable in the form of "SkyPerfect TV" (a merged entity of former rival services) features sports, movies, and adult entertainment stations. It is far from heavily subscribed (with but 3 million households). Regular cable is faring better with almost 19 million households.

In terms of cable content, it may be of limited utility to speak about specific content (since the ebb and flow of global media products can easily render stations and content obsolete). Still, for the foreseeable future, it would be safe to identify the staples of current

Japanese cable as NHK's three stations: BS satellite 1 (which is world news-oriented), and 2 (which is entertainment- and events-oriented), and Hi-vision (which emphasizes programming that places the spotlight on this advanced visual technology). Other standbys include CNN, MTV, a (generally) Hollywood-centered movie channel, and a couple of 24-hour sports channels).

Social Dimensions

For many theorists Japan is viewed as a society in which the duality inside (*uchi*) and outside (*soto*) serves as a key organizing principle. In everyday life this has produced a complex set of social orientations, governing individual psychology and interpersonal behavior. The management of emotions under such terms is essential—separating interior, private faces from the external, public one. TV programming appears to understand that. Not only do television shows try to invite the (outside) viewer into the group inside the box, they strive to create what A.A. Painter calls "quasi-intimacy": programs "emphasiz(ing) themes related to unity (national, local, cultural, or racial) and unanimity (consensus, common sense, identity) in order to create an intimate and friendly atmosphere" (Painter, p. 198). In this way, television is exceptional at defining groups, often by juxtaposition (and implicit comparison): Japanese versus (foreign or ethnic) "others," women versus men, young versus old, economically developed versus underdeveloped, beautiful versus ugly.

This can take forms both positive and negative. In terms of the latter, Japanese television is highly gendered—and ideologically so. For instance, studies continue to show that women are outnumbered by men on screen by a ratio of two to one, and when on screen, they tend to be depicted in "traditional" roles such as housekeeping, shopping, or family nurturing. Their age range is also narrower than that of men. Other research indicates that women are generally evaluated in ways distinct from men, in particular as objects, subordinate, with low ability, and ensconced in the home.

Reflecting a long-standing cultural thread, Japanese television is surveillance oriented—in the last few years increasingly so. It has been said that "Japan was years ahead of the U.S. and Europe in pioneering 'reality TV', in which ordinary people are placed in extraordinary situations" ("Country Profile: Japan," *BBC News*). Now such shows are staple fare, featuring hidden cameras, "sting operations," and behind-the-scenes peeks at how everyday people live. A current favorite is "London Hearts," which features segments in which duplicitous women try to shake money out of

prospective suitors, and cads are baited into cheating on their lovers. The commentary by hosts and guests in a private booth is raucous and aims at besmirching the character of those spotlighted.

No less discomfiting are "boot camp"-like shows in which adults, buffeted by an increasingly severe economy, are forced to endure humiliations for possible job opportunities or monetary rewards. Their travails—laughed at and commented on by celebrity guests—are all in the name of "viewer entertainment." Add to this the recent wave of legal shows in which simulated cases (with a variety of alternately filmed conditions) draw celebrity and expert commentary and one can apprehend that, in the hands of television, contemporary Japan appears to be a conflictual, confrontational, controversy-riven society.

The Future

For a society that historically has been image-based, village-organized, information-centered, consumption-oriented, and technology-driven, what is the role of television in the years to come? While prognoses in the 1990s were often pessimistic, the same cannot be said of the new millennium. Those earlier concerns were based on the conservative nature of Japanese society, the internecine struggles between rival ministries over regulation and control of new media, and the slow diffusion of cable. But viewing societal changes, as well as the way image-based, television-like technologies have proliferated and become integrated into the fabric of everyday life, such dire projections are now difficult to maintain.

As indicated earlier, video rentals have become a staple of Japan's high-consumption, leisure lifestyle, providing uses for owners of VCRs and stoking electronic innovations such as digital video discs (DVDs). The explosion of cell phone use has exerted pressures on technology developers to churn out newer, better features. As of this writing, most of this competition is being played visually, with camera- and Internet-enabled phones that are able to send, receive, and play images—both stationary and animated. So, too, are TV-equipped cars becoming standard in Japan. These TV units are often part of an integrated satellite-assisted map (or "navi"). One can imagine such units enabling on-the-road Internet searches, which will result in downloadable video clips introducing hotel rooms, restaurants, and tourist attractions in various cities along one's route. Currently, desktop computers serve as hubs for TV viewing, recording, video editing, and photo production. In this way, the television-based technologies of the immediate future may encourage the Japanese to be less passive, assisting them in moving from mere reception toward personal expression.

TODD JOSEPH MILES HOLDEN

Further Reading

Asian Trade Gallery, http://www.asiatradehub.com/japan/general.asp (date last accessed October 20, 2003)

Berwanger, Dietrich, "The Third World," in *Television: An International History,* edited by A. Smith with R. Paterson, Oxford: Oxford University Press, 1998

Boddy, William, "The Beginnings of American Television," in *Television: An International History,* edited by A. Smith with R. Paterson, Oxford: Oxford University Press, 1998

"Broadcasting in Japan," NHK Broadcasting Culture Research Institute, http://www.nhk.or.jp/bunken/bcri-news/bnl-s-data.html (Summer 2000)

Cooper-Chen, A., *Mass Communication in Japan,* Ames: Iowa State University Press, 1997

"Country Profile: Japan," *BBC News,* September 22, 2003, http://news.bbc.co.uk/go/pr/fr/-/1/hi/world/asia-pacific/country_profiles/1258586.stm (date last accessed October 20, 2003)

"The Evolution of TV: A Brief History of TV Technology in Japan," NHK home page, p. 10, http://www.nhk.or.jp/strl/index-e.html (date last accessed October 25, 2003)

Japan: Profile of a Nation, Kodansha: 1995

Kamimura, Shuichi, and Mieko Ida. "Will the Internet Take the Place of Television? From a Public Opinion Survey on 'The Media in Daily Life,'" *NHK Culture Broadcasting Institute,* No.19 (New Year 2002), http://www.nhk.or.jp/bunken/bcri-news/bnl-s-feature.html

Nihon no Telebi Hensei (Japanese Television Compilation), Nihon Hoso Kyokai, 1976

Nippon Hoso Kyokai, *Fifty Years of Japanese Broadcasting,* Tokyo: Nippon Hoso Shuppan Kyokai, 1977

Painter, A.A., "Japanese Popular Daytime Television, Popular Culture, and Ideolog," in *Contemporary Japan and Popular Culture,* edited by J.W. Treat, Surrey, England: Curzon Press, 1996

Suzuki, M.F. "Women and Television: Portrayal of Women in the Mass Media," in *Japanese Women: New Feminist Perspectives on the Past, Present, and Future,* edited by K. Fujimura-Fanselow and A. Kameda, New York: Feminist Press, 1995

Jason, David (1940–)

British Actor

David Jason's career can be viewed in many respects as that of the archetypal modern television actor in Britain. Although he made forays into the theater in the 1970s and 1980s, and made occasional appearances on film, these fade into relative insignificance when compared to the steady stream of eye-catching and increasingly high-profile roles he created for television. As a result, his acting persona is circumscribed by the televisual medium. Nevertheless, such exposure, while making him a British "household name," did not make him into a celebrity, for Jason has largely eschewed the paraphernalia of television fame.

Jason's histrionic instincts are basically comic, and the majority of his roles have been in the situation comedy format. His earliest major television role was an elderly professor doing battle against the evil Mrs. Black and her gadgets in the surreal *Do Not Adjust Your Set* (1967), a comedy show whose ideas and personnel later fed into *Monty Python's Flying Circus.* But Jason first achieved note through his association with comic actor-writer Ronnie Barker, by supporting performances in the prison comedy *Porridge* and corner-shop comedy *Open All Hours,* both starring Barker. In the former, Jason played the dour wife-murderer Blanco; in the latter, and to great effect, he acted the boyish, downtrodden deliveryman and assistant to Barker's parsimonious storekeeper. *Open All Hours* cast Jason as a kind of embryonic hero-in-waiting, constantly dreaming of ways of escaping the provincial narrowness and boredom of his north-country life. The role provided the actor with an opportunity to develop his acting trademark—a scrupulous and detailed portrayal of protean ordinariness, sometimes straining against a desire to be something else.

A later series, *The Top Secret Life of Edgar Briggs,* toyed with this sense of ordinariness by having Jason as a Secret Service agent ineptly trying to combine his covert profession with suburban home life. But Jason's greatest success has been with several series of the comedy *Only Fools and Horses,* in which he played Del Trotter, the small-time, tax-evading "entrepreneur" salesman, living and working in the working-class council estates and street markets of inner-city London. Deftly written by John Sullivan—the series is regarded by some as a model for this kind of sitcom writing—the series cast Jason in a domestic situation in which he is quasi-head of an all-male family, responsible for both his younger brother and an elderly uncle. In the role, Jason cleverly trod a path between pathos and the quick-wittedness necessary to someone operating on the borderlines of legality. The character was, in many respects, a parody of the Thatcherite working-class self-motivator, complete with many of the tacky and vulgar accoutrements and aspirations of the (not-quite-yet) *nouveau-riche.* At the local pub, while others order pints of beer, Del seeks to distinguish himself from his milieu by drinking elaborate and luridly colored cocktails. The undertone, though, is salt-of-the-earth humanity and selflessness, called out in his paternal role to his younger brother, who eventually leaves the communal flat to pursue a life of marriage and a proper career. Jason's character is hemmed in by both the essential poverty of his situation but also by a deep-rooted sense of responsibility: though the plots of the individual episodes invariably revolve around one or either of Del's minor get-rich-quick or get-something-for-nothing schemes, the failure of these ventures often owes much to the character's inability to be sufficiently ruthless. Jason's skill was to interweave the opposing forces of selflessness and selfishness, working-class background and pseudo-middle-class tastes, brotherly condescension and "paternal" devotion into a successful balance. The character Del, exuding a deeper humanity as expressed in his ability to imbue the everyday with a well-judged emotional resonance and believability, ultimately embodied a rejection of aggressive materialism. The ultimate financial success of Del (he becomes a millionaire, ironically by accident rather than through one of his schemes) gave viewers a satisfying payoff. This comedy series has achieved a unique level of popularity in British television—one probably unrepeatable in the now-fragmented digital age—making Jason one of the most sought-after television actors.

Since *Only Fools and Horses,* Jason made moves away from overtly comic vehicles, pursuing variations on this rootedness in the everyday. In the adaptation of the satirical novel on Cambridge University life by Tom Sharpe, *Porterhouse Blue,* he played the sternly traditional porter Skullion, the acutely status-conscious servant of the college, dismayed by the liberalizing tendencies of the new master, and making determined efforts to turn back time. In *The Darling Buds of May,* his other great ratings success, he took the role of Pa ("Pop") Larkin, in these adaptations of the rural short stories of H.E. Bates. Such roles allowed him to develop the range and craftsmanship of his character performances.

In 1992 Jason ventured out of comedy altogether into the crime genre, as the eponymous Inspector Frost in *A Touch of Frost.* In this series, Jason's Frost is a disgruntled, middle-aged, loner detective, whose fractious, down-to-earth nature has not entirely endeared him to his superiors and therefore—we infer—has hindered his career prospects. In such respects the series is in the mold of the immensely successful adaptations of Colin Dexter's *Inspector Morse* novels. But whereas Morse's cantankerousness, as played by John Thaw, was epitomized by a certain snobbishness—his love of classical music, his vintage car, his instinctive aloofness—in the Oxford environment of Dreaming Spires, Frost's gradually unfolding history reveals a lower middle-class resentfulness of those with money, fortune, pretensions, and easily gained happiness. His own life has—as we find out gradually—rendered him increasingly a victim of misfortune (his wife has died, his house has burned down). While *Morse,* in effect, creates a world of evil-doing amid soft-toned college greens, country pubs, and semi-rural Englishness, the Frost series is nearer to the subgenre of the detective soaps, its principal character a distinctly unglamorous malcontent, whose ideas and experience are entirely provincial and suburban. The series, now achieving very large audiences, has witnessed an increasing sureness of touch in this respect by Jason. As the actor matures, it could well be that he is becoming one of those to make the successful transition from comic-oriented younger work to a memorable body of serious roles. *Inspector Frost,* along with his moving portrayal of a doomed World War I officer in *All the King's Men,* suggests he has the capacity to do just that.

MARK HAWKINS-DADY

David Jason. Born David White in Edmonton, London, England, February 2, 1940. Attended schools in London. Gained early stage experience as an amateur while working as an electrician before entering repertory theater; entered television through *Crossroads* and children's comedy program, *Do Not Adjust Your Set,* 1967; popular television comedy star. Officer of the Order of the British Empire, 1993. Recipient: BBC Television Personality of the Year, 1984; British Academy of Film and Television Arts Best Actor Award, 1988.

Television Series

1967	*Crossroads*
1967	*Do Not Adjust Your Set*
1968	*Two Ds and a Dog*
1969–70	*Hark at Barker*
1969–70	*His Lordship Entertains*
1969–70	*Six Dates with Barker*
1969–70	*Doctor in the House*
1971	*Doctor at Large*

1973–74	*The Top Secret Life of Edgar Briggs*
1974	*Doctor at Sea*
1974	*Mr. Stabbs*
1974–77	*Porridge*
1975, 1976, 1981–82	*Lucky Feller*
1985	*Open All Hours*
1978–81	*A Sharp Intake of Breath*
1981–91	*Only Fools and Horses*
1986	*Porterhouse Blue*
1988	*Jackanory*
1988–89	*A Bit of a Do*
1989	*Single Voices: The Chemist*
1990–93	*The Darling Buds of May*
1992, 1994	*A Touch of Frost*
1993–97, 1999, 2001–2003	*Inspector Frost*
1997, 2000	*David Jason in His Element* (documentary series)

Television Specials

1990	*Amongst Barbarians*
1998	*March in the Windy City*
1999	*All the King's Men*
2001	*Micawber*

2002	*Only Fools and Horses* (Christmas special)
2002	*The Quest*

Films

Under Milkwood, 1970; *White Cargo,* 1974; *Royal Flash,* 1974; *The Mayor of Strackentz,* 1975; *Doctor at Sea,* 1976; *The Odd Job,* 1978; *Only Fools and Horses,* 1978; *The Water Babies,* 1979; *Wind in the Willows* (voice only), 1980; *The B.F.G.,* 1989 (voice only); *The Bullion Boys,* 1993 (TV); *March in the Windy City,* 1998 (TV); *Father Christmas and the Missing Reindeer,* 1998 (TV, voice only); *All the King's Men,* 1999 (TV); *The Quest,* 2002 (TV).

Radio

Week Ending; Jason Explanation.

Stage (selected)

South Sea Bubble; Peter Pan; Under Milkwood, 1971; *The Rivals,* 1972; *No Sex Please... We're British!,* 1972; *Darling Mr. London,* 1975; *Charley's Aunt,* 1975; *The Norman Conquests,* 1976; *The Relapse,* 1978; *Cinderella,* 1979; *The Unvarnished Truth,* 1983; *Look No Hans!,* 1985.

Jeffersons, The

U.S. Domestic Comedy

The Jeffersons, which appeared on CBS television from 1975 to 1985, focused on the lives of a nouveau riche African-American couple, George and Louise Jefferson. George Jefferson was a successful businessman, millionaire, and owner of seven dry cleaning stores. He lived with his wife in a ritzy penthouse apartment on Manhattan's fashionable and moneyed East Side. "We're movin' on up!" intoned the musical theme of the show opener, which featured George, Louise, and a moving van in front of the entrance to "their de-luxe apartment in the sky."

The program was conceived by independent producers Norman Lear and Bud Yorkin. This team's creation of highly successful and often controversial sitcoms during the 1970s and early 1980s helped to change television history. Programs such as *Maude,*

Sanford and Son, and *Good Times* were frequently ranked among the top-ten most watched programs.

The Jeffersons was a spin-off of one of 1970s television's most notable television sitcoms, *All in the Family.* In 1973 Lear cast Sherman Hemsley in the role of George Jefferson, Archie Bunker's irascible and upwardly mobile black neighbor. This character was such a hit with viewers that Hemsley was soon cast in the spin-off series *The Jeffersons.*

George and Louise Jefferson led lives that reflected the trappings of money and success. Their home was filled with expensive furnishings; art lined the walls. They even had their own black housekeeper, a wise-cracking maid named Florence. The supporting cast comprised a number of unique characters, including neighbor Harry Bentley, an eccentric Englishman who

The Jeffersons, 1975–85, Berlinda Tolbert, Sherman Hemsley, Isabel Sanford, Franklin Cover, Roxie Roker, Marla Gibbs.
Courtesy of the Everett Collection

often made a mess of things; the Willises, a mixed-race couple with two adult children—one black, one white; and the ever-obsequious Ralph the Doorman, who knew no shame when it came to earning a tip. Occasional characters included George's mother, the elderly and quietly cantankerous "Mother Jefferson" (the actress, Zara Cully, died in 1978); and George and Louise's college-aged son, Lionel (who was portrayed during various periods by two different actors).

The George Jefferson character was conceptualized as an Archie Bunker in blackface. George was intolerant, rude, and stubborn; he referred to white people as "honkies." He was a short, mean, bigoted popinjay who balked at manners. Louise, his long-suffering wife, spent most of her time apologizing for her husband's behavior. Florence, the maid, contributed a great deal of comic relief, with her continuous put-downs of George. She was not afraid of his of angry outbursts and in fact had little regard for him or his tirades. She referred to him as "Shorty" and never missed a chance to put him in his place.

The program was enormously popular and remained on prime-time television for ten years. There are a num-ber of factors that position this program as an important facet of television history. First, *The Jeffersons* was one of three programs of the period to feature African Americans in leading roles—the first such programming since the cancellation of the infamous *Amos 'n' Andy* show in 1953. *The Jeffersons* was the first television program to feature an interracial married couple, and it offered an uncommon, albeit comic, portrayal of a successful African-American family. Lastly, *The Jeffersons* is one of several programs of the period to rely heavily on confrontational humor. Along with *All in the Family,* and *Sanford and Son,* the show was also one of many to repopularize old-style ethnic humor.

It also serves to examine some of the controversy that surrounded *The Jeffersons.* Throughout its ten-year run on prime-time television, the show did not go without its share of criticism. The range of complaints, which emanated from media scholars, television critics, and everyday black viewers, ranged from the show's occasional lapses into the negative stereotyping to its sometimes lack of ethnic realism. To some, the early Louise Jefferson character was nothing more than an Old-South Mammy stereotype. And George, though a millionaire businessman, was generally positioned as nothing more than a buffoon or the butt of someone's joke. Even his own maid had no respect for him. Some blacks questioned, "Are we laughing with George as he balks at convention, or at George as he continuously makes a fool of himself?"

Ironically, as the show continued into the conservatism of the Reagan years, the tone of the program shifted. Louise Jefferson's afro hairstyle disappeared and so did her poor English. There was no mention of her former life as a housekeeper. George's racism was toned down, and the sketches were rendered more palatable in order to appeal to a wider audience. As with *Amos 'n' Andy* some 20 years prior, America's black community remained divided in its assessment of *The Jeffersons.*

This period of television history was a shifting one for television programmers seeking to create a show featuring African Americans. Obvious stereotypes could no longer be sold, yet the pabulum of shows like *Julia* was equally as unacceptable. *The Jeffersons* joined other Lear-Yorkin programs in setting a new tone for prime-time television, exploring issues that TV had scarcely touched before; furthermore, the series proved that programs with blacks in leading roles could indeed be successful commodities.

PAMALA S. DEANE

*See also **All in the Family; Cosby Show; Good Times;** Hemsley, Sherman; Lear, Norman*

Cast

George Jefferson	Sherman Hemsley
Louise Jefferson	Isabel Sanford
Florence Johnston	Marla Gibbs
Helen Willis	Roxie Roker
Tom Willis	Franklin Cover
Lionel Jefferson (1975, 1979–81)	Mike Evans
Lionel Jefferson (1975–78)	Damon Evans
Jenny Willis Jefferson	Berlinda Tolbert
Harry Bentley	Paul Benedict
Mother Jefferson (1975–78)	Zara Cully
Ralph the Doorman	Ned Wertimer

Producers

George Sunga, Jay Moriarity, Mike Mulligan, Don Nichol, Michael Ross, Bernie West, Sy Rosen, Jack Shea, Ron Leavitt, David Duclon

Programming History

CBS

January 1975–August 1975	Saturday 8:30–9:30
September 1975–October 1976	Saturday 8:00–8:30
November 1976–January 1977	Wednesday 8:00–8:30
September 1977–March 1978	Monday 8:00–8:30
April 1978–May 1978	Saturday 8:00–8:30
June 1978–September 1978	Monday 8:00–8:30
September 1978–January 1979	Wednesday 8:00–8:30
January 1979–March 1979	Wednesday 9:30–10:00
March 1979–June 1979	Wednesday 8:00–8:30
June 1979–September 1982	Sunday 9:30–10:00
September 1982–December 1984	Sunday 9:00–9:30
January 1985–March 1985	Tuesday 8:00–8:30
April 1985	Tuesday 8:30–9:00
June 1985	Tuesday 8:30–9:00
June 1985–July 1985	Tuesday 8:00–8:30

Further Reading

Bogle, Donald, *Blacks, Coons, Mulattoes, Mammies, and Bucks: An Interpretive History of Blacks in American Film,* New York: Viking Press, 1973; 4th edition, New York: Continuum, 2001

Bogle, Donald, *Blacks in American Television and Film: An Encyclopedia,* New York: Garland, 1988

Friedman, Lester D., *Unspeakable Images: Ethnicity and the American Cinema,* Urbana: University of Illinois Press, 1991

Gray, Herman, *Watching Race: Television and the Struggle for "Blackness,"* Minneapolis: University of Minnesota Press, 1995

MacDonald, J. Fred, *Blacks and White TV: Afro-Americans in Television Since 1948,* Chicago: Nelson-Hall, 1983; 2nd edition, 1992

Marc, David, and Robert J. Thompson, *Prime Time, Prime Movers: From I Love Lucy to L.A. Law—America's Greatest TV Shows and the People Who Created Them,* Boston: Little, Brown, 1992

Taylor, Ella, *Prime-Time Families: Television Culture in Postwar America,* Berkeley: University of California Press, 1989

Jenkins, Charles Francis (1867–1934)

U.S. Inventor

Charles Francis Jenkins was a leading inventor and promoter of mechanical scanning television and was largely responsible for strong and passionate interest in television in the 1920s and early 1930s in the United States. His work in mechanical television paralleled the work of John Logie Baird in England. Jenkins also provided the first public television demonstration in the United States on June 13, 1925, less than three months after a somewhat similar demonstration by Baird in England. Jenkins's demonstration, using mechanical scanning at both the transmitting and receiving ends, consisted of crude silhouette moving images called "shadowgraphs." This early work in mechanical scanning television helped lay the foundation for later all-electronic television.

Jenkins was the archetype of the independent inventor. Without major corporate financial backing, he never received the recognition, success, or wealth that otherwise might have come to him. His numerous contributions and inventions covered a broad range of areas and uses. He co-invented and publicly demonstrated the first practical motion picture projector in the United States (1894), developed an automobile with the engine in the front instead of under the seat (1898), designed an early sight-seeing bus (1901), created an early automobile self-starter (1911), and developed significant improvements to the internal combustion engine (1912). He was granted more than 400 U.S. patents for inventions as diverse as an altimeter, an airplane brake, a conical paper drinking cup, and even a bean-shelling machine. In the area of communication and media technology, he developed the "prismatic ring" (circa 1915), designed to eliminate the need for film shutters in motion picture projectors by using a glass disk scanning apparatus. He later experimented with a variation of this concept for one of his mechanical television scanning systems. His work in facsimile in the early 1920s led to successful wirephoto transmissions by January of 1922 and radiophotos in May of that year. He was also involved in early wireless teletype transmission.

In 1916 Jenkins helped found the Society of Motion Picture Engineers, later renamed the Society of Motion Picture and Television Engineers (SMPTE), and was elected as the organization's first president. The idea of visual transmission interested Jenkins many years before his first demonstrations of facsimile and television. In the July 1894 issue of *Electrical Engineer,* he proposed a method for electrically transmitting pictures. In the September 1913 issue of *Motion Picture News,* he proposed a mechanism for television.

Jenkins's initial target market for television was radio amateurs and experimenters. He expected this market to quickly grow as a larger public became interested in television. The Federal Radio Commission (FRC) issued the first experimental television station license in the United States to Jenkins in 1927, and this station, W3XK, began transmitting on July 2, 1928, with regular broadcasts of "radiomovies," television images of motion pictures, from Jenkins's facility near Washington, D.C. In addition, his company provided information and instructions on how to build television receivers. In December 1928, the Jenkins Television Corporation was founded in New Jersey to sell Jenkins television equipment and operate television stations in order to promote the sale of receivers to the public and equipment for experimenters and other experimental stations. By mid-1929, the Jenkins Television Corporation was marketing receivers, named Radiovisors, to pick up signals from its transmitters in Washington, D.C., and New Jersey. The receivers were designed for easy use by people in their homes. The devices initially utilized a compact spinning-drum scanning mechanism that conserved space, energy, and weight. Unfortunately, picture quality was extremely limited, making the reception of television little more than a "quickly tiresome novelty." By 1931 the Jenkins Television Corporation was offering both factory-built Radiovisors and do-it-yourself kits. Because of the high cost of Radiovisors during the Depression, the lessening interest in the limited program offerings, mediocre image quality, and the pending introduction of all-electronic television, sales dropped precipitously by the end of the year. To make matters worse, the FRC had disallowed the broadcast of on-air advertisements promoting Jenkins receivers and receiver kits.

In October 1929, DeForest Radio acquired a majority interest in Jenkins Television. In March 1932, Jenkins Television was liquidated and its assets sold to DeForest Radio. Within months, DeForest Radio went into receivership and sold its assets, including its Jenkins holdings, to RCA, which then discontinued the Jenkins television operation owing to a notable lack of interest in, and support for, mechanical television. The limitations inherent in mechanical television's picture quality kept it from being able to compete with electronic scanning television systems, and it was therefore deemed a failure and doomed to quick obsolescence in the United States. The Jenkins Laboratories in Washington, D.C., continued television research but closed in 1934 with the death of Jenkins.

Perhaps Jenkins was shortsighted for concentrating on mechanical television and not moving ahead into electronic television. Perhaps he simply did not have the financial backing to move in this direction. Today, he has been almost forgotten by all but a few television historians. However, in the United States he was responsible for the advent of television and was the first pioneer to make television a reality. He was responsible for creating a great interest in television and its future among experimenters, amateur radio enthusiasts, the public, and business. He paved the way for television's future success, helping provide the incentive for support of television experimentation by "big business" such as RCA's support of Vladimir K. Zworykin; Crocker and later Philco's support of Philo T. Farnsworth; and General Electric's support of Ernst F.W. Alexanderson.

STEVE RUNYON

See also **Baird, John Logie; Television Technology**

Charles Francis Jenkins. Born in Dayton, Ohio, August 22, 1867. Attended Earlham College, Richmond,

Indiana. Married: Grace Love, 1902. Independent inventor, demonstrated the first practical motion picture projector, 1894; invented automobile with the engine in front instead of under the seat, 1898; designed an early sight-seeing bus, 1901; created an early automobile self-starter, 1911; developed significant improvements to the internal combustion engine, 1912; developed inventions in radiophotography, television, radiomovies, 1915–20s; founded the Society of Motion Picture Engineers, 1916; research vice president of Jenkins Television Corporation, 1928. Member: National Aeronautical Association, American Automobile Association. Recipient: Franklin Institute and the City of Philadelphia medal. Died in Washington, D.C., June 6, 1934.

Publications (selected)

"Transmitting Pictures by Electricity," *Electrical Engineer* (July 1894)

"Prismatic Rings," *Transactions of the SMPE* (1922)

"Radio Photographs, Radio Movies, and Radio Vision," *Transactions of the SMPE* (1923)

"Recent Progress in the Transmission of Motion Pictures by Radio," *Transactions of the SMPE* (1924)

Vision by Radio, Radio Photographs, Radio Photograms, 1925

"Radio Vision," *Proceedings of the IRE* (November 1927)

"The Drum Scanner in Radiomovies Receivers," *Proceedings of the IRE* (September 1929)

Radiomovies, Radiovision, Television, 1929

"Television Systems," *Journal of the SMPE* (October 1930)

The Boyhood of an Inventor, 1931

Jennings, Peter (1938–)

U.S. Broadcast Journalist

Very few names in broadcast journalism are as recognizable as that of Peter Jennings. His father, Charles, was the most prominent radio announcer for the Canadian Broadcasting Corporation (CBC). Thus, it seems perhaps predictable that Peter Jennings would have his own successful career in the news industry.

Jennings was ten years old when he received his first anchor job for *Peter's Program,* a Saturday morning radio show which showcased young talent. As a student, he exhibited little interest in formal education. However, his interests and talent in the area of news would demonstrate his capacity and willingness to learn. He began his professional career as a disc jockey and news reporter for a small radio station in Brockton, Ontario. Like many reporters who achieve major success, Jennings's opportunity to make a name for himself came with breaking news. In this case it was the story of a train wreck he covered for the CBC that brought attention. But the story got him a job with CTV, Canada's first private TV network, rather than with the public broadcaster. Elmer Lower, who identified Jennings's good looks and charm as elements that would sell to the American public, recruited Jennings

from CTV to ABC News. Shortly after, in 1964, Jennings joined ABC as an anchor for a 15-minute evening news segment.

A year later, in an unprecedented rise to the top, Jennings, at 27, became the youngest *ABC Evening News* anchor. His competition at the time—Walter Cronkite on CBS, and the team of Chet Huntley and David Brinkley on NBC—stood as the most credible anchors of their time. In this competitive environment, Jennings was unable to break through and establish a strong share for ABC News. In 1968 he left the anchor desk and was sent to Rome to become a foreign correspondent and sharpen his reporting skills. Jennings was credited with establishing the first American television news bureau in the Middle East and served for seven years as ABC News Bureau Chief in Beirut, Lebanon. After building a strong reputation for world-class reporting, Jennings was put back in an anchor position for *A.M. America,* the predecessor for *Good Morning America,* where he delivered five-minute newscasts from Washington, D.C.

The experience and contacts in the Middle East paid off for Jennings. He established a reputation as Anwar

Peter Jennings.
Courtesy of the Everett Collection

Sadat's favorite correspondent after completing a documentary on the Egyptian president, and in 1977, when Egypt and Israel were about to make peace, Jennings was called to the scene. In 1978, he was the first U.S. reporter to interview the Ayatollah Khomeini, then in exile in Paris. When the Ayatollah came to power in Iran, Jennings was the first reporter to be granted an interview and accompanied the Ayatollah on the plane back to Iran.

Shortly after, on July 10, 1978, the first *ABC World News Tonight* aired. Jennings was to become a star. His breadth of experience in national and international reporting served him well while he was a reporter for *World News Tonight,* and in 1983 he was named lead anchor.

During the late 1980s, Jennings anchored several highly acclaimed programs, including a live series called *Capital to Capital,* which broadcast communications between Soviet officials and members of the U.S. Congress. News specials on political volatility in China, Iran, and the former Soviet Union also won praise. His contributions include a live, via-satellite, town hall meeting between U.S. citizens and Soviet leaders Mikhail Gorbachev and Boris Yeltsin. This show, with its question-and-answer format, gave Americans unprecedented exposure to the Soviet leaders.

Although Jennings's political reports have won him the most praise at *World News Tonight,* they do not stand alone. Jennings also anchors *Peter Jennings Reporting.* These one-hour, prime-time specials address important issues facing the nation and the world. He has explored issues ranging from abortion, gun control, AIDS, and rape to funding for the arts and Ross Perot's presidential campaign. Jennings's accomplishments also include a series of news reports for children. In 1994, he served as moderator of a special question-and-answer broadcast from the White House in which American children questioned President Clinton about issues important to their lives.

For his work, Jennings has won several Emmy and Overseas Press Club Awards and the prestigious Alfred I. duPont-Columbia University Award for journalism. In 1989, a *Times-Mirror* poll found Jennings to be the most believable source of news. Jennings was also named Best Anchor by the *Washington Journalism Review* in 1988, 1989, 1990, and 1992.

Jennings teamed with Todd Brewster to develop three best-selling books and corresponding television series. *The Century* and *The Century for Young People* present a comprehensive, colorful, and impressive chronicle of 20th-century history. *In Search of America,* although conceptualized before September 11, 2001, gathers stories both inspiring and poignant, and focuses on diverse American issues and individuals.

JOHN TEDESCO

See also **Anchor; News, Network**

Peter (Charles) Jennings. Born in Toronto, Ontario, Canada, July 29, 1938. Attended Trinity College School and Carleton University, Ontario, and Rider College in New Jersey, United States. Married: 1) Valerie Godsoe (divorced), 2) Annie Malouf (divorced), 3) Kati Marton, 1979 (divorced, 1994); children: Elizabeth and Christopher. Began career in Canadian radio and television as news correspondent; parliamentary correspondent and network co-anchor, independent Canadian Television Channel (CTV); New York correspondent, ABC television, 1964; nightly news anchor, 1965–68; overseas assignment, 1968–1974; Washington correspondent, news anchor, A.M. *America,* 1975–76; chief foreign correspondent, 1977; foreign desk anchor, *World News Tonight,* 1978; anchor, senior editor, *ABC World News Tonight with Peter Jennings,* since 1983. Named Best Anchor in the United States, *Washington Journalism Review,* 1988, 1989, 1990, 1992. Member: International Radio and Television Society. Recipient: Alfred I. duPont-Columbia University Award; 12 Emmy Awards; several Overseas Press Club Awards; Harvard University's Goldsmith Career Award for Excellence; Radio and Television News Directors Paul White Award; George Foster Peabody Award.

Television Series

1964	*World News Tonight* (co-anchor)
1965–68	*World News Tonight* (anchor)
1975–76	*A.M. America* (news anchor)
1978	*ABC World News Tonight with Peter Jennings* (anchor)

Television Specials (selected)

1985	*45/85*
1988	*Drugs: A Plague Upon the Land*
1988	*Why This Plague?*
1989	*AIDS Quarterly*
1992	*Men, Sex and Rape*
1993	*President Clinton: Answering Children's Questions*
1994	*ABC Viewpoint: Whitewater: Underplayed? Overplayed?*

Publications

In Search of America, 2002
The Century, 1998
The Century for Young People, 1999

Further Reading

Attanasio, Paul, "Anchors Away: Good Evening, Dan, Tom and Peter. Now Buzz Off," *New Republic* (April 23, 1984)

Corliss, Richard, "Broadcast Blues," *Film Comment* (March–April 1988)

Fensch, Thomas, editor, *Television News Anchors: An Anthology of Profiles of the Major Figures and Issues in United States Network Reporting,* Jefferson, North Carolina: McFarland, 1993

Goldberg, Robert, and Gerald Jay Goldberg, *Anchors: Brokaw, Jennings, Rather, and the Evening News,* Secaucus, New Jersey: Carol, 1990

Goldenson, Leonard, *Beating the Odds,* New York: Scribner, 1991

Gunther, Marc, *The House That Roone Built: The Inside Story of ABC News,* Boston: Little, Brown, 1994

Kaye, Elizabeth, "Peter Jennings Gets No Self-Respect," *Esquire* (September 1989)

Moore, Mike, "Divided Loyalties: Peter Jennings and Mike Wallace in No-man's-land," *Quill* (February 1989)

Murphy, Ryan P., "Voted Most Trusted of the Anchormen," *Saturday Evening Post* (November 1988)

Jeopardy!

U.S. Game Show

Premiering in 1964 in a daytime slot on NBC, *Jeopardy!* was one of the first quiz shows to reintroduce factual knowledge, including knowledge of sports and entertainment trivia as well the arts, literature, and science, as the main source of questions. Seemingly reversing the logic of the big money quiz shows of the 1950s (e.g., *The $64,000 Question, Twenty-One*), producer Merv Griffin introduced a format in which the answers for questions are revealed and the contestants must phrase their response in the form of a question. *Jeopardy!* also made the competitions more challenging for contestants by deducting money for each incorrect answer from their winnings, making it possible to have negative scores.

Jeopardy! is played in three rounds: the "Jeopardy" round, the "Double Jeopardy" round, and the "Final Jeopardy" round. In the Jeopardy round, 30 "answers" in six categories are revealed on a large, upright game board, with the values in each category increasing according to their difficulty level. A "Daily Double" hidden behind one of the questions forces contestants to wager all or part of their winnings on the answer. The same pattern of play is repeated in the Double Jeopardy round, with the value of questions now doubled and two Daily Doubles hidden on the game board. The game ends after all answers have been revealed or when time runs out. In the Final Jeopardy round contestants again wager some or all of their winnings on one common question that has to be answered in 30 seconds. The contestant with the highest score at the end of Final Jeopardy becomes the champion and is allowed to return for a maximum of five appearances. All five-time champions and some of the highest scoring winners return for the "Tournament of Champi-

Jeopardy!
Photo courtesy of Steve Crise

ons," which is held once a year. *Jeopardy!* also regularly conducts other competitions, such as junior Jeopardy!, college tournaments, and celebrity shows.

The original version of *Jeopardy!,* hosted by Art Fleming, ran from 1964 to 1975. Prizes for individual answers ranged from $10 to $50 in the Jeopardy round and from $20 to $100 in the Double Jeopardy round. In this version, all contestants kept their winnings, and the overall champion returned for another show. A 1978 remake of the show entitled *All New Jeopardy!* returned with Art Fleming as the host. In this version, the lowest-scoring contestant was eliminated after the Jeopardy round, and only the top winner after the Double Jeopardy round went on to play the Super Jeopardy bonus round. This version of *Jeopardy!* was less popular than the original and was canceled after only five months. From 1974 to 1975, *Jeopardy!* also ran parallel to the NBC network version in syndication.

A new syndicated version of *Jeopardy!* premiered in September 1984 with Alex Trebek as host and has proved to be the most successful version of the program so far. While the rules of the game stayed essentially the same, the value of the questions in the Jeopardy round range from $100 to $500 and from $1,000 to $2,000 in the Double Jeopardy round. Only the winning contestant is allowed to keep the amount accumulated in the three rounds of competition. The two other contestants only receive consolation prizes. To add visual interest, *Jeopardy!* also added videotaped clues and celebrities reading answers.

The most recent spin-off from *Jeopardy!* is *Rock 'n' Roll Jeopardy,* broadcast on the cable music channel VH-1. The distinctive feature in this version is the focus on rock and pop music in the questions. Instead of the actual amount won during the three rounds of competition, the champion on *Rock 'n' Roll Jeopardy* wins $5,000, while the other contestants receive consolation prizes. Numerous rock musicians have appeared in celebrity editions of this show, playing for their favorite charity rather than personal gain. Jeff Probst, who went on to host *Survivor,* was the original host of *Rock 'n' Roll Jeopardy!*.

Unlike most other game shows from the 1960s to the mid-1990s, which focused on gambling, guessing, and consumption, *Jeopardy!* produced an appearance of serious competition and regard for education. The dramatically lit set and the dominance of blue in the color scheme add an impression of austerity on the show, serving to underline the pressure that the program attempts to create for the contestants. *Jeopardy!* avoids foregrounding consumerism and merchandise, as contestants generally only win cash prizes. At the same time, however, the large sums of cash that can be won on the program (up to $100,000 for one contestant) still reinforce a sense of materialism. Host Alex Trebek regularly emphasizes the intellectual abilities of the contestants, and popular magazines highlight the difficulty level of the questions on the show. However, the structure of the questions usually incorporates multiple clues to the correct answer and most questions do not require in-depth knowledge of a subject. Contestants can succeed on the program based on their ability to correctly identify clues within the question, so that only a surface familiarity with a given subject is necessary. The cultural competence required on *Jeopardy!* is closely aligned with "classical knowledge" and excludes marginal cultural groups and forms. As Michael Berthold points out, for example, literary authors used in questions are very likely canonized white male authors from the 19th and 20th centuries. Female and non-white authors rarely make an appearance. In other words, the game structure of *Jeopardy!* provides powerful financial incentives for being educated and accepting of the hierarchies of dominant culture.

OLAF HOERSCHELMANN

See also **Quiz and Game Shows**

Further Reading

Berthold, M., "Jeopardy!, Cultural Literacy, and the Discourse of Trivia," *Journal of American Culture,* 13 (1990)

Fabe, M., *TV Game Shows,* Garden City, New York: Doubleday, 1979

Fiske, J., *Television Culture,* London: Routledge, 1987

Graham, J., *Come on Down!!!: The TV Game Show Book,* New York: Abbeville Press, 1988

Schwartz, D., S. Ryan, and F. Wostbrock, *The Encyclopedia of Television Game Shows,* 3rd edition, New York: Facts On File, 1999

Shaw, P., "Generic Refinement on the Fringe: The Game Show," *Southern Speech Communication Journal,* 52 (1987)

Jewel in the Crown, The

British Serial Drama

The Jewel in the Crown is a 14-part serial produced by Granada Studios and first broadcast on British independent television in January 1984. A lavish prestige production, *The Jewel in the Crown* received immediate critical acclaim, going on to win several national and international awards and in the process confirming Britain's excellence in the field of television drama. In addition to receiving critical attention, the serial also proved popular with British audiences. The first run averaged eight million viewers a week, a significant figure for a "quality" drama on British television.

Based on Paul Scott's *Raj Quartet,* four novels published between 1966 and 1975, the serial focuses on the final years of the British in India. Set against the backdrop of World War II and using the rape of an English woman as its dramatic center, *The Jewel in the Crown* charts a moment of crisis and change in British national history.

The serial should be seen in the context of a cycle of film and television productions that emerged during the first half of the 1980s and that seemed to indicate Britain's growing preoccupation with India, the Empire, and a particular aspect of British cultural history. Notable examples from this cycle would include the films *A Passage to India* (1984) and *Heat and Dust* (1982), and the television drama *The Far Pavilions* (1984). These fictions were produced during, and indeed reflected, a moment of crisis and change in British life: mass unemployment and the arrival of new social and class configurations tied to emerging political and economic trends all conspired to destabilize and recast notions of national and cultural identity in the early 1980s. While often critical of Britain's past, these fictions nevertheless permitted a nostalgic gaze back to a golden age, presenting a vision of the Empire as something great and glorious. These fictions seemed to offer reassurance to the British public; as cultural fetish objects, they helped negotiate and manage a moment of social and political upheaval.

If these fictions were ultimately reassuring for certain sections of the British public, then *The Jewel in the Crown* has been seen by at least one commentator,

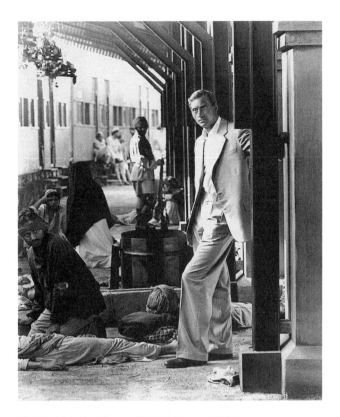

The Jewel in the Crown, Charles Dance, 1984.
Courtesy of the Everett Collection

Tana Wollen, to be the least nostalgic and most troubled text in the cycle. However, this "trouble" may have less to do with the serial's overt politics and more to do with its form and style. Paul Scott's *Raj Quartet* are fairly unconventional novels and were not wholly suited to the demands of serial form. Their use of multiple points of view and their elliptical, collage-like narratives were not easily adapted to a form based around linear progression, continuity of action and character, and the promise of eventual narrative resolution.

The television adaptation was necessarily a more conventional rendering of the story, the narrative now flattened out and the events subjected to a more chronological ordering. Nevertheless, *The Jewel in the Crown* managed to hold on to some of the formal complexity of the novels by employing voice-overs, flashbacks, and newsreel inserts—techniques that tend to arrest narrative development, giving the serial a heavy, ponderous quality. The adaptation, and Scott's novels, lacked the kind of character development and continuity that we have come to expect from the television serial. By the third episode, the serial's central character Daphne Manners is killed off and only one character spans all 14 episodes. This is the evil Ronald Merrick, who dies in episode 13 and appears in the final part

only through flashback. However, *The Jewel in the Crown* managed to maintain continuity through a series of echoes and motifs: images of fire, the repetition of certain actions and events, and the passing down of the lace christening gown all helped to provide the serial with a formal cohesion that seemed to be lacking at the level of character and plot development. All in all, *The Jewel in the Crown* proved to be a challenging text and demanded from its audience an unusually high degree of commitment and perseverance.

Although *The Jewel in the Crown* was broadcast in 1984, with a repeat screening the following year, by the late 1980s the serial still had a high public profile as it became embroiled in debates about television, quality, and the future of British broadcasting. This debate followed legislation calling for the deregulation of the British airwaves, which in turn kindled anxieties concerning the fate of public service and quality television. In this debate, as Charlotte Brunsdon has pointed out, *The Jewel in the Crown,* along with *Brideshead Revisited,* came to represent the "acme of British quality." Elsewhere, *The Jewel in the Crown* was being held up as the epitome of excellence. In 1990 the serial was screened at the National Film Theatre as part of a season called "Good-by to All This." Here *The Jewel in the Crown* was described as the "title everyone reaches for when asked for a definition of 'quality television.'" *The Jewel in the Crown* came to represent what was at stake in the deregulation of the British airwaves. It articulated fears over what could be lost in the transition from a regulated, public-service tradition in broadcasting to a more commercial, market-led system. Increasingly, *The Jewel in the Crown* was coming to represent the golden days prior to the deregulation of quality television.

This serial, then, had originally emerged as part of a cycle of texts dealing with anxieties over national identity. At a moment of radical change in British life, these texts may have offered viewers a nostalgic vision of a glorious past. By the late 1980s, the serial was referring to a more immediate past and a cultural identity bound to a broadcasting tradition of public service and quality drama. In both cases *The Jewel in the Crown* articulated and represented the anxieties and the sense of loss felt by sections of the British public who were faced with the decline of a particular idea of national and cultural identity.

PETER McLUSKIE

See also **Adaptations; British Programming; Miniseries**

Cast

Daphne Manners	Susan Wooldridge
Hari Kumar	Art Malik

Ronald Merrick	Tim Piggot-Smith
Barbie Batchelor	Peggy Ashcroft
Sophie Dixon	Warren Clarke
Guy Perron	Charles Dance

Programming History

1 120-minute episode; 13 60-minute episodes
ITV
January 9, 1984–April 3, 1984

Further Reading

Brandt, G., "*Jewel in the Crown:* The Literary Serial; Or the Art of Adaptation," in *British Television Drama in the 1980s,* edited by G. Brandt, Cambridge: Cambridge University Press, 1993

Brunsdon, Charlotte, "Problems with Quality," *Screen* (Spring 1990)

Robinson, A., "The Jewel in the Crown," *Sight and Sound* (winter 1983–84)

Rushdie, Salman, "Outside the Whale," *American Film* (January–February 1985)

Wollen, Tana, "Over Our Shoulders: Nostalgic Screen Fictions for the 1980s," in *Enterprise and Heritage: Cross Currents of National Culture,* edited by J. Corner and S. Harvey, London: Routledge, 1991

Johnson, Lamont (1922–)

U.S. Director

Lamont Johnson is an actors' director who is also a director's director. Acclaimed, respected, and superbly consistent, he is television's answer to William Wyler. Between his 1964 Emmy nomination and Directors Guild of America (DGA) Award for a *Profiles in Courage* episode ("The Oscar Underwood Story") and his 1992 Emmy nomination for the real-life disaster film *Crash Landing,* Johnson amassed 11 Emmy nominations (winning in 1985 for *Wallenberg: A Hero's Story* and in 1988 for *Gore Vidal's Lincoln*) and eight DGA nominations (winning four, plus a special award as the Most Outstanding TV Director of 1972). Although he has racked up admirable big-screen credits, too, such as *The Last American Hero* (a 1973 movie based on Tom Wolfe's profile of a stock-car racing champion, "The Last American Hero Is Junior Johnson. Yes!"), television is the medium that has allowed Johnson the most room to flex his creative muscles. His video credits list contains character portraits, period epics, theater pieces, and docudramas.

Employing what he learned in theater, radio, live TV, and feature films, Johnson imbues his TV movies with dramatic briskness and invention, vital sound, and visual dimension. His distinctive humane touch derives from his feeling for performers, who in some way become his true subject. Almost every year brings new additions to his gallery of unforgettable figures, from John Ritter's agonizingly frustrated Vietnam vet in the Agent Orange exposé *Unnatural Causes* (1986) to Annette O'Toole's Rose Fitzgerald—part stoic heroine, part religious maniac—in *The Kennedys of Massachusetts* (1988). The vibrant characters who populate his TV films would fill a small city—Johnsonville, USA—except his art encompasses the world. One of his most impressive accomplishments is *Wallenberg: A Hero's Story,* starring Richard Chamberlain, in which the Scarlet Pimpernel-like heroism of Raoul Wallenberg (the Swedish diplomat who saved tens of thousands of Hungarian Jews) puts the horror of the Holocaust in stark relief.

Gifted with a "roaring bass voice," Johnson turned pro as a radio actor at age 16 and financed his college education by working as a broadcast performer, news announcer, and disc jockey. After student theater experience (such as directing a production of *Liliom* in a women's gym), he moved from Los Angeles to New York with the aim of acting on the stage. He became a mainstay of radio soap operas and a Broadway understudy; on a USO tour through Europe, he befriended Gertrude Stein, who gave him rights to her play, *Yes Is for a Very Young Man.* His first professional directing job was to mount it, in 1948, at off-Broadway's Cherry Lane Theater, with a cast that boasted Anthony Fran-

Lamont Johnson.
Photo courtesy of Lamont Johnson

ciosa, Gene Saks, Michael V. Gazzo, Bea Arthur, and Kim Stanley.

Although he swore off directing after that—he could not bear the role of referee—Johnson came under its spell for good while acting for such broadcast luminaries as John Frankenheimer, Sidney Lumet, and Jack Smight. In 1955 Johnson made his TV directorial debut guiding Richard Boone through an adaptation of *Wuthering Heights* for the hour-long live drama series, *Matinee Theater.* (Johnson ended up doing 28 of those shows in two years.) In 1958 Boone gave Johnson the opportunity to break into filmed TV when the star insisted that Johnson be hired for six episodes of the second season of his hit western, *Have Gun—Will Travel.* In the late 1950s and early 1960s, Johnson went on to direct popular and innovative dramatic series such as *Peter Gunn, Naked City,* and *The Defenders.* He did a fistful of episodes for *The Twilight Zone,* including "Kick the Can" (which Steven Spielberg remade in his *The Twilight Zone: The Movie*). Four decades later, when *Felicity* creator J.J. Abrams decided to shake up his lethargic collegiate characters by dropping them in a latter-day *Twilight Zone,* he turned for direction to Johnson, who ended up reworking an episode he had directed in 1961: "Five Characters in Search of an Exit." More than a replica, the result was a unique hybrid that transformed the youthful self-absorption of the *Felicity* characters into something both eerie and hilarious.

It was a trio of collaborations with the producing-writing team of Richard Levinson and William Link that cemented Johnson's place in broadcast history. Levinson and Link smartly emphasized the plight of individuals while blazing trails in TV movies' depictions of race relations (*My Sweet Charlie,* 1970), homosexuality (*That Certain Summer,* 1972), and American military conduct (*The Execution of Private Slovik,* 1974). Coming fully into his own as a director, Johnson shaped performances with an emotional combustion to match the script's social conflagrations. Working on location whenever possible, he brewed alive and unpredictable atmospheres. It is rare to remember character bits and mood points from what are usually called "message movies," but what springs to mind from *My Sweet Charlie* is the edgy sheepishness of the fugitive northern black lawyer (played by Al Freeman Jr.) as he tries to persuade the pregnant southern runaway (Patty Duke) that he can impersonate a down-home black man. From *That Certain Summer,* one recalls the uncomfortable-looking figures of the gay hero (Hal Holbrook) and his teenage son (Scott Jacoby) as the father struggles to explain his lifestyle on a three-minute downhill walk. Picture *The Execution of Private Slovik*—the first docudrama TV movie—and a different trek pops into memory: the penetratingly sad, snow-blown death march for the only U.S. soldier to be executed for desertion after World War II. Though the writers received the lion's share of attention, and the scripts were solid and sensitive, Johnson's direction was the most artistic aspect of these ambitious projects, lending them delicacy as well as poignancy. In the capper to this spate of TV productivity, his 1975 *Fear on Trial* (based on a David W. Rintels script), Johnson's evocation of a frigid 1950s New York City winter overpowered the screenplay's conventional, simplistic anti-blacklisting theatrics; it looked as if the Cold War itself had set the city's temperature.

Johnson did astonishing work while constantly shuttling among media from the mid-1970s to the mid-1980s. In 1980 two of his favorite TV productions premiered. The first, *Paul's Case,* a 52-minute-long drama for the PBS *American Short Story* series (shot in ten days on a $180,000 budget), is a powerful, peculiar American tragedy about the downfall of a fragile escapist. Following Willa Cather's original story to the letter, Johnson led Eric Roberts to his best performance—he is splendidly off-kilter as a high school boy in 1905 Pittsburgh who is too far into his dream world of glamour and theatricality to come of out it alive. Johnson's TV-movie *Off the Minnesota Strip*, which aired just three months later, is a revelation of a contemporary adolescent limbo, with Mare Winningham as a teenage hooker, brilliantly conveying the interlocking social and sexual pressures that trap teenagers into self-destructive fantasies of "making it." Around the same time as these TV milestones, Johnson completed one of his finest feature films, *Cattle Annie and Little Britches* (not released until 1981), an offbeat western that explored Americans' need for pop mythology and turned the adventures of its young pulp heroines (stunningly played by Diane Lane and Amanda Plummer) into coming-of-age action poetry.

Pulling off three wildly different projects in a year would be admirable for the resident director of a repertory company or an anthology series; to do it by leapfrogging the worlds of network TV, PBS, and independent filmmaking would seem a feat. But not for Johnson. He has nurtured a robust, sane creativity by approaching the theatrical arts as a continuum—and creating an emotional spectrum that retains its intensity whether projected on a movie screen or transmitted via satellite and cable.

MICHAEL SRAGOW

Lamont Johnson. Born in Stockton, California, September 30, 1922. Educated at the University of California, Los Angeles, 1942–43; studied at Neighborhood Playhouse School of the Theatre. Married: Toni Merrill, 1945, children: Jeremy, Carolyn, Christopher Anthony. Stage producer and director, since 1948; founded UCLA Theater Group (now Centre Theater Group), 1959; television director, since 1950s; film director, since 1961. Recipient: numerous Directors Guild of American Awards; numerous Emmy Awards.

Television (actor)
1949	*Julius Caesar*
1952	*Aesop*
1953–54	*Prize Winner*

Television Series (director)
1956–58	*Matinee Theater*
1957–63	*Have Gun—Will Travel*
1958–63	*The Rifleman*
1958–61	*Peter Gunn*
1959–65	*Twilight Zone*
1959–60	*Johnny Ringo*
1960–63	*Naked City*
1961–65	*The Defenders*
2000	*Felicity*

Television Miniseries (director)
1985	*Wallenberg: A Hero's Story*
1988	*The Kennedys of Massachusetts* (aired 1990)
1988	*Gore Vidal's Lincoln*

Made-for-Television Movies (director)
1964	*Profiles in Courage*
1969	*Deadlock*
1970	*My Sweet Charlie*
1972	*That Certain Summer*
1974	*The Execution of Private Slovik* (also writer)
1975	*Fear on Trial*
1980	*American Short Story: Paul's Case*
1980	*Off the Minnesota Strip*
1981	*Escape from Iran: The Canadian Caper*
1981	*Crisis at Central High*
1982	*Life of the Party: The Story of Beatrice*
1982	*Dangerous Company*
1982	*Beatrice*
1982	*Two Plays by David Mamet*
1983	*Jack and the Beanstalk*
1984	*Ernie Kovacs: Between the Laughter*
1986	*Unnatural Causes*
1990	*Voices Within: The Lives of Truddi Chase*
1992	*Crash Landing: The Rescue of Flight 232*
1993	*The Broken Chain*
1995	*The Man Next Door*
1997	*All the Winters That Have Been*

Films (actor)
Sally and Saint Anne, 1952; *The Human Jungle*, 1954; *The Brothers Rico*, 1957; *One on One*, 1977; *Sunnyside*, 1979; *Death Wish II*, 1981; *The Five Heartbeats*, 1991; *Class Act*, 1992; *Fear of a Black Hat*, 1993; *Waiting to Exhale*, 1995; *The Great White Hype*, 1996; *Live Virgin*, 2000.

Films (director)
Thin Ice, 1961; *A Covenant with Death*, 1966; *Kona Coast*, 1968; *The McKenzie Break*, 1970; *A Gunfight*, 1971; *The Groundstar Conspiracy*, 1972; *You'll Like My Mother*, 1972; *The Last American Hero*, 1973; *Visit to a Chief's Son*, 1974; *Lipstick*, 1976; *One on One*, 1977; *Somebody Killed Her Husband*, 1978; *FM*, 1978; *Cattle Annie and Little Britches*, 1981; *Spacehunter: Adventures in the Forbidden Zone*, 1983.

Opera (director)

The Man in the Moon, 1959; *Iphigenie en Tauride,* 1962; *Orfeo,* 1990.

Stage (actor)

Manja, 1939; *Young Woodley,* 1946; *Yes Is for a Very Young Man,* 1948; *Macbeth,* 1948; *The Pony Cart,* 1954; *A Christmas Carol,* 1980–81.

Stage (director)

Yes Is for a Very Young Man, 1948; *The Potting Shed,* 1957; *The Man in the Moon,* 1957; *The Skin of Our Teeth,* 1958; *Under Milkwood,* 1959; *4 Comedies of Despair,* 1960; *The Egg,* 1961; *The Perfect Setup,* 1962; *'Tis a Pity She's a Whore,* 1963; *Iphigenia in Tauris,* 1964; *The Adventures of the Black Girl in Her Search for God,* 1969; *The Tempest,* 1978; *Popular Neurotics,* 1981; *California Dogfight,*

1983; *Nanawata,* 1985; *The Eighties,* 1988–89; *Orfeo,* 1990.

Publication

"The Director as Answerman," *DGA News* (October–November 1994)

Further Reading

Averson, Richard, and David Manning White, editors, *Electronic Drama: Television Plays of the Sixties,* Boston: Beacon Press, 1971

Avrech, Robert, and Larry Gross, "Lamont Johnson," *Millimeter* (May 1976)

Levinson, Richard, and William Link, *Stay Tuned: An Inside Look at the Making of Prime-Time Television,* New York: St. Martin's Press, 1981

Orner, Eric, "A-: Lamont Johnson," *Film Comment* (September–October 1977)

Jones, Quincy (1933–)

U.S. Musician, Producer

Quincy Jones's long career as a music composer lends insight into popular music's influence on the television and film media. In 1951 a teenaged Jones began working as a trumpet player and arranger for Lionel Hampton. During his early career, he played with some of the best-known names in black bebop and jazz, performers such as Count Basie, Clark Terry, Ray Charles, Billy Eckstine, Dizzy Gillespie, and Sarah Vaughan. He toured Europe, the Middle East, and South Africa during the 1950s. In 1957 he studied in Paris with Nadia Boulanger. During this period he also became a major publisher of music.

However, failed business ventures in 1959 forced him to sell his music publishing catalogue. Jones overcame this major financial setback by working as an executive at A and M Records and by working as an arranger for Dinah Washington in New York City. He became vice president of Mercury Records in 1964, the first African-American executive at a major record label.

In 1961, *Jet* magazine, a weekly entertainment periodical directed to an African-American readership, awarded Jones the title of best arranger and composer.

But despite honors from his African-American community and excellent critical reviews, he recognized that jazz music was not earning high record sales. He decided then to produce more commercial songs. In 1963, he branched out to develop the talent of a white teenage singer, Lesley Gore, with whom he recorded the pop hit "It's My Party." Jones continued to work with talented white artists such as Frank Sinatra, for whom he conducted and arranged *Sinatra: Live in Las Vegas at the Sands with Count Basie* (1966). By adapting to technological changes that gave more control to engineers and producers, Jones achieved commercial success in the music recording industry during the 1960s. Yet, he still desired to compose scores for motion pictures, and his success allowed him to pursue the small openings in media industries previously closed to African-American artists.

After Jones scored his first film, *The Boy in the Tree* (1960), he scored *The Pawnbroker* (1965) for director Sidney Lumet. Jones's first major Hollywood contract was with Universal Pictures. He became an African-American pioneer in film and television industries during the late 1960s, and he had few black colleagues. At

Quincy Jones.
Photo courtesy of Greg Gorman Photography

this time, television news reports were increasingly presenting images of the United States facing racial conflict. Amid the struggle for civil rights, Jones worked in Hollywood to help destroy the negative stereotypes of African Americans. In 1965 he was hired to score the film *Mirage,* starring Gregory Peck, and he scored *In the Heat of the Night* (1967), starring a top box-office star of the era, Sidney Poitier.

In 1967 Jones scored the pilot and eight episodes of the dramatic television series *Ironside.* In creating the *Ironside* theme, he was the first composer to utilize a synthesizer in the arrangement of a television score. During the same year, he composed the theme to the television movie *Split Second to an Epitaph.* Jones also wrote the theme song for Bill Cosby's first situation comedy, *The Bill Cosby Show* (NBC; 1970) and went on to score 56 episodes.

In a brief two-week period between film and television scores, Jones returned to record making with the jazz album *Walking.* The album won a Grammy for Best Jazz Performance by a Large Group in 1969.

In 1972 Jones wrote the theme to the *NBC Mystery Movie* series, and his momentum in the television industry continued to grow. During the same year, he scored 26 episodes of *The Bill Cosby Variety Series,* and in 1973 he composed the theme to the comedy

program *Sanford and Son,* starring comedian Redd Foxx.

In 1974, soon after his *Body Heat* album reached the top of the music charts, Jones suffered from health problems. A brain aneurysm required two surgical procedures and he had to stop playing the trumpet.

After a four-year hiatus, during which he concentrated on his own music productions, Jones returned to television in 1977 to score the ABC miniseries *Roots,* one of the highest-rated programs in television history. His score accented the exploration of African chants and rhythms as indigenous to American culture and garnered Jones an Emmy Award. Coinciding with this success in television, he scored *The Wiz* (1978), a Universal Pictures all-black version of *The Wizard of Oz,* starring Diana Ross and Michael Jackson.

Between 1963, when he entered the Hollywood film industry as a film composer, and 1990, Jones earned 38 film credits. Most notably, he coproduced the critically acclaimed film *The Color Purple* (1985) with director Steven Spielberg. In 1994 Jones was honored with an Academy Award for his achievements in the film industry.

Despite his success in television and film, Jones has never lost interest in spotting talent in black music. During the 1970s, he continued to cultivate new performers in this arena. He created technically advanced, funk-influenced albums for the Brothers Johnson, Chaka Kahn, and Rufus. In 1977 he produced Michael Jackson's *Off the Wall* album, which sold seven million albums (in the pre-MTV era). His production of Michael Jackson's record-breaking pop album *Thriller* (1984) became a musical landmark.

In 1981 Jones left A and M and formed his own Qwest label at Warner Brothers. The Qwest label produced hits for Patty Austin and James Ingram and captured Lena Horne's performance on Broadway; these recording projects earned Grammy Awards for Jones. In 1985 he produced the all-star recording of "We Are the World," to help performer Harry Belafonte's charity drive to raise world awareness of famine. From the song's popular music video, Jones became a recognizable face to the general public. He raised money for Jesse Jackson's historic run for the Democratic party's presidential nomination in 1988 and produced *The Jesse Jackson Show* in 1990, granting a forum to a high-profile black figure in U.S. politics.

Jones discovered a larger television audience by producing situation comedies. In 1990 *Fresh Prince of Bel-Air* premiered, starring a popular rap artist, Will Smith, and the series became a highly rated program on NBC. Also in 1990, Jones formed the multimedia entertainment organization Quincy Jones Entertainment Company and Quincy Jones Broadcasting, to acquire television and radio properties. Three years later he joined with David Salzman to create the production company QDE, which has produced the sitcom *In the House* (NBC and UPN, 1995–99) and the sketch comedy/variety series *Mad TV* (FOX, 1995–).

In 1994 Jones cofounded Qwest Broadcasting, a minority-owned company that would purchase television stations in Atlanta, Georgia, and New Orleans, Louisiana; five years later, Jones and his partners sold this company for around $270 million. In 1996 Jones was executive producer for the Academy Awards program. In 1998 he established the production company Quincy Jones Media Group, Inc., with the aim of producing projects for both film and television.

While overcoming racial barriers and redefining several genres in music composition, Jones's creative persistence in the music business helped to maneuver black music across the color line of the musical mainstream and into every form of media expression. Jones's body of work spans over half a century and has opened the door for the growth of successful black entrepreneurs in television, film, and music. Since Miles Davis's death, many critics cite Quincy Jones as the only remaining figure from the bebop era who has stayed contemporary and whose work continues to have an impact on these three closely integrated media industries.

MARLA L. SHELTON

Quincy (Delight) Jones. Born in Chicago, Illinois, March 14, 1933. Attended Seattle University, Seattle, Washington; Berklee School of Music, Boston; studied with Nadia Boulanger and Oliver Messiaen, Paris. Married: 1) Jeri Caldwell, 1957 (divorced), 2) Ulla Anderson, 1965 (divorced), 3) Peggy Lipton, 1974 (divorced); seven children. Began career as jazz trumpeter and arranger for numerous big bands and solo performers; music director, Mercury Records, 1961, vice president, 1964; composer, film and television music, from 1960s; founded Qwest recording company, 1981, QDE Productions, 1993, Qwest Broadcasting, 1994 (sold, 1999), and Quincy Jones Media Group, 1998; record producer for Barbra Streisand, Michael Jackson, and other artists; television producer, since 1990. Chairman, *Vibe* magazine, and co-owner *Spin* magazine, since 1992. Recipient: 26 Grammy Awards; Emmy Award, 1977; Polar Music Prize (Sweden), 1994; Academy Award, 1994.

Television Series (selected)

1966–67	*Hey, Landlord* (composer)
1967–75	*Ironside* (composer)
1967	*Split Second to an Epitaph* (composer)
1970	*The Bill Cosby Show* (composer)
1972	*The NBC Mystery Movie* (composer)
1972	*The Bill Cosby Variety Series* (composer)
1973	*Sanford and Son* (composer)
1977	*Roots* (composer)
1990	*The Jesse Jackson Show* (producer)
1990–96	*Fresh Prince of Bel-Air* (producer)
1995–99	*In the House* (producer)
1995–	*Mad TV* (producer)

Television Specials (selected)

1967	*Rodgers and Hart Today* (music director)
1971	*The Academy Awards* (conductor)
1971	*Merv Griffin Presents Quincy Jones* (performer)
1973	*Duke Ellington, We Love You Madly* (coproducer and conductor)
1973	*A Show Business Salute to Milton Berle* (music director)
1990	*Grammy Legends* (honoree)
1991	*Ray Charles: 50 Years of Music, Uh-Huh!* (cohost)
1996	*The Academy Awards* (executive producer)

Films

The Boy in the Tree, 1960; *The Pawnbroker,* 1965; *The Slender Thread,* 1965; *Mirage,* 1965; *Made in Paris,* 1965; *Walk Don't Run,* 1966; *The Deadly Affair,* 1967; *Enter Laughing,* 1967; *In Cold Blood,* 1967; *Banning,* 1967; *In the Heat of the Night,* 1967; *A Dandy in Aspic,* 1968; *Jigsaw,* 1968; *The Counterfeit Killers,* 1968; *For Love of Ivy,* 1968; *The Hell with Heroes,* 1968; *Mackenna's Gold,* 1969; *The Italian Job,* 1969; *The Lost Man,* 1969; *Bob and Carol and Ted and Alice,* 1969; *Cactus Flower,* 1969; *John and Mary,* 1969; *Blood Kin,* 1969; *The Out-of-Towners,* 1970; *They Call Me Mister Tibbs!,* 1970; *Eggs* (short), 1970; *Of Men and Demons* (short), 1970; *Up Your Teddy Bear,* 1970; *Brother John,* 1970; *The Anderson Tapes,* 1971; *Honky,* 1971; *$ (Dollars),* 1971; *The Hot Rock,* 1972; *The New Centurions,* 1972; *The Getaway,* 1972; *Killer by Night,* 1972; *Mother, Jugs, and Speed,* 1976; *The Wiz,* 1978; *Portrait of an Album* (also director), 1985; *Fast Forward,* 1985; *Lost in America,* 1985; *The Slugger's Wife,* 1985; *The Color Purple* (coproducer), 1985; *Heart and Soul,* 1988; *Listen Up: The Lives of Quincy Jones,* 1991; *A Great Day in Harlem* (narrator), 1994; *Austin Powers, International Man of Mystery,* 1997; *Steel* (producer), 1997.

Publication

Q: The Autobiography of Quincy Jones, 2001

Further Reading

Collier, Aldore, "After 40 Years, Fame and Fortune, Three Marriages, Brain Surgery and an Emotional Breakdown, Quincy Jones Finds Peace" (interview), *Ebony* (April 1990)

Gillen, Marilyn A., "Quincy's CD-ROM Explores Music's Roots," *Billboard* (May 20, 1995)

Nathan, David, "The Producer," *Billboard* (December 16, 1995)

Rowland, Mark, "Quincy Jones" (interview), *Billboard* (December 16, 1995)

Sanders, Charles L., "With Quincy Jones" (interview), *Ebony* (October 1985)

Shah, Diane K., "On Q," *New York Times Magazine* (November 18, 1990)

Stewart, Zan, "The Quincy Jones Interview," *Down Beat* (April 1985)

Journal, The. *See* National, The/The Journal

Julia

U.S. Domestic Comedy

Julia, a half-hour comedy premiering on NBC in September 1968, was an example of American network television's attempt to address race issues during a period of heightened activism and turmoil over the position of African Americans in U.S. society. The series was the first to star a black performer in the leading role since *Beulah, Amos 'n' Andy,* and *The Nat "King" Cole Show* all left the air in the early and mid-1950s. By the mid-1960s, a number of prime-time series began featuring blacks in supporting roles, but industry fears of mostly southern racial sensibilities discouraged any bold action by the networks to represent more fully African Americans in entertainment television. Series creator Hal Kanter, a Hollywood liberal and broadcasting veteran whose credits included writing for the *Beulah* radio show in the 1940s, initiated *Julia*'s challenge to what remained of television's color bar. Kanter had attended a luncheon organized by the National Association for the Advancement of Colored People (NAACP) and been inspired enough to propose the project to NBC. The network agreed to run the show, but programmers did not expect it to do well since it was scheduled opposite the hugely popular *Red Skelton Show. Julia* proved to be a surprise hit, however, jumping into the top-ten list of most-watched programs during its first year, and continuing to be moderately successful during its remaining two seasons on the air.

The series revolves around the lives of Julia Baker (Diahann Carroll), a widowed black nurse, and her young son, Corey (Marc Copage). Julia's husband has been killed in a helicopter crash in Vietnam, and the series begins with the now fatherless Baker family moving into an integrated apartment building in Los Angeles while Julia secures employment at the medical offices of Astrospace Industries. She works with a gruff but lovable elderly white physician, Dr. Chegley (Lloyd Nolan), and a homely but spirited white nurse, Hannah Yarby (Lurene Tuttle). Julia's closest friends are her white neighbors, the Waggedorns—Marie, a scatterbrained housewife; Len, a police officer; and Earl J. Waggedorn, their son and Corey's pal. While Julia lives in an almost exclusively white environment, she manages to find a series of impeccably refined African-American boyfriends. Paul Winfield played one of her more long-standing romantic partners. Performed with elegance and dignity by Carroll, Julia represented a completely assimilated—and thoroughly nonstereotyped—African-American image to prime-time viewers.

Julia, Diahann Carroll, Lloyd Nolan, Marc Copage, 1968–71.
©*20th Century Fox/Courtesy of the Everett Collection*

Julia's unthreatening respectability served as the basis for a great deal of heated debate during the series' initial run. In the midst of growing political militancy among many African Americans, some critics accused the show of presenting Julia as a "white Negro." Nothing in the Bakers' lives indicated that they were in any way connected to the rich tradition of black culture and history. Neither Julia nor Corey was ever the victim of racism. However, Hal Kanter emphasized that the show did attempt to stress the more "humorous aspects" of prejudice and discrimination, while focusing on how the black characters attempted "to enjoy the American dream." Humorous situations dealing with race tended to work to defuse anxieties about racial difference. For instance, in her initial telephone interview with Dr. Chegley in the series' pilot, Julia mentions that she is black. Chegley deadpans: "Have you always been black—or are you just being fashionable?" When little Earl J. Waggedorn sees Corey's mother for the first time, he points out, "Hey, your mother's colored." Corey replies, matter-of-factly, "Yeah, so am I." To which Earl responds: "You are?!"

The show was also criticized for presenting no male head of the family. While the Bakers were emphatically middle-class, living in a beautifully appointed apartment rather lavish for a nurse's salary, the fact that an unattached black mother ran the family appeared to perpetuate stereotypes about a "black matriarchy" in which black men had no place. A recurring problem in the Baker household was who would care for Corey while Julia was at work. Several episodes deal with Julia's dilemma in securing a mother's helper. Unwittingly and quite unself-reflexively, the show was echoing a painful aspect of the history of black women, many of whom had to leave their children unattended while they went off to care for white children and work as domestics in white establishments.

While these depictions of race relations generated objections, they also elicited praise from critics and viewers. *Ebony,* a mass-circulation magazine targeted at a middle-class black readership, lauded the series for giving viewers an alternative to the steady diet of ghetto riot images of blacks so pervasive on news programming. The show was also commended for representing black characters who were not thoroughly and exclusively defined by race.

Julia was an important moment in American broadcasting history as television programmers struggled to find a way to introduce African Americans into entertainment formats without relying on objectionable old stereotypes, but also without creating images that might challenge or discomfort white audiences.

ANIKO BODROGHKOZY

See also **Comedy, Domestic Settings; Racism, Ethnicity, and Television**

Cast

Julia Baker	Diahann Carroll
Dr. Morton Chegley	Lloyd Nolan
Marie Waggedorn	Betty Beaird
Corey Baker	Marc Copage
Earl J. Waggedorn	Michael Link
Melba Chegley	Mary Wickes
Sol Cooper	Ned Glass
Carol Deering (1968–69)	Allison Mills
Hannah Yarby (1968–70)	Lurene Tuttle
Eddie Edson	Eddie Quillan
Paul Cameron (1968–70)	Paul Winfield
Len Waggedorn	Hank Brandt
Steve Bruce (1970–71)	Fred Williamson
Roberta (1970–71)	Janear Hines
Richard (1970–71)	Richard Steele
Kim Bruce (1970–71)	Stephanie James

Producers

Hal Kanter, Harold Stone

Programming History
86 episodes
NBC
September 1968–January 1971   Tuesday 8:30–9:00
January 1971–May 1971   Tuesday 7:30–8:00

Further Reading

Gray, Herman, *Watching Race: Television and the Struggle for "Blackness,"* Minneapolis: University of Minnesota Press, 1995

MacDonald, J. Fred, *Blacks and White TV: Afro-Americans in Television Since 1948,* Chicago: Nelson-Hall, 1983; 2nd edition, 1992

Julien, Isaac (1960–)

British Filmmaker

Isaac Julien is one of Britain's most innovative and provocative filmmakers. Born in 1960, he comes from a black, working-class, East London background. Julien studied painting and film at St. Martin's School of Art in London. He was both writer and director for *Who Killed Colin Roach?*, a 1983 documentary about the controversial death of a young black man while in police custody. This was followed by *Territories* in 1984, an experimental video that examined policing at London's Notting Hill Carnival.

A cofounder of Sankofa Film and Video Collective, a pioneering group of young black British filmmakers, Julien has collaborated with them on several ground-breaking, radical dramas for film and television since the mid-1980s. With Sankofa, Julien co-wrote and codirected *The Passion of Remembrance* (1986), an ambitious feature-film drama that offered a fresh and revealing look at black feminism and black gay politics. This was followed by the award-winning short film *Looking for Langston,* in 1988. Set in Harlem in the 1920s, this homoerotic, hauntingly beautiful study of the black gay American poet Langston Hughes cleverly blended his words with those of the contemporary black gay poet Essex Hemphill. *Looking for Langston* received the Golden Teddy Bear for Best Gay Film at the Berlin Film Festival and was shown in Channel 4's innovative lesbian and gay television series *Out on Tuesday* in 1989.

In 1991 Julien directed *Young Soul Rebels,* a seductive, engaging, and challenging feature-film drama set in 1977, the year of Queen Elizabeth II's Silver Jubilee. Once again, Julien explored sexual and racial identities in a provocative way and walked off with the Cannes Film Festival's Critics' Week Prize.

In 1991 Julien was interviewed with other young black gay filmmakers in *Some of My Best Friends,* one of the programs featured in BBC Television's *Saturday Night Out,* an evening of programs devoted to lesbian and gay viewers. The following year, he directed *Black and White in Colour,* a two-part documentary for BBC Television that traced the history of black people in British television from the 1930s to the 1990s. Using archival footage and interviews with such black participants as Elisabeth Welch, Norman Beaton, Carmen Munroe, and Lenny Henry, *Black and White in Colour* was well received by the critics. It was also nominated for the British Film Institute's Archival Achievement Award, and the Commission for Racial Equality's Race in the Media Award.

Since making *Black and White in Colour,* Julien has directed a short film, *The Attendant,* and *The Dark Side of Black* (1994), an edition of BBC Television's *Arena* series. This compelling documentary examines the social, cultural, and political influences of rap and reggae music, with particular emphasis on its growing homophobic content. He also directed *Frantz Fanon: Black Skin, White Mask* (1995), a documentary about the noted theorist of anticolonial resistance, and has created several video-installation pieces, such as *Three* (1999), *The Long Road to Mazatlan* (1999), and *Vagabondia* (2000), which have been displayed in art galleries and museums worldwide. In August 2002, the Independent Film Channel (IFC), a U.S. cable channel, debuted his documentary, *Baadasssss Cinema,* on the history of "blaxploitation" films. Julien told the *New York Times* that this work was inspired by research he conducted to teach a course at Harvard University on the genre.

STEPHEN BOURNE

Isaac Julien. Born in London, England, 1960. Educated at St. Martin's School of Art, B.A., 1984. Began career as writer-director, *Who Killed Colin Roach?*, 1983; cofounder, Sankofa Film and Video Collective; visiting professor, Harvard University, 2000– ; research fellow, Goldsmiths College, University of London. Recipient: Golden Teddy Bear Award, Berlin, 1988; Cannes Film Festival Critics' Week Prize, 1991.

Television Specials

1988	*Looking for Langston*
1992	*Black and White in Colour*
1994	*The Dark Side of Black*
2002	*Baadasssss Cinema*

Films (selected)

Who Killed Colin Roach? 1983; *Territories*, 1984; *The Passion of Remembrance*, 1986; *Young Soul Rebels*, 1991; *The Attendant*, 1995; *Frantz Fanon: Black Skin, White Mask*, 1995.

Further Reading

Bourne, Stephen, *Black in the British Frame: Black People in British Film and Television 1896–1996*, London: Cassell, 1996; 2nd edition, London: Continuum, 2001

Hinson, Hal, "Birth of a Genre: The Black Hero Who Talks Back," *New York Times* (August 11, 2002)

Julien, Isaac, and Colin McCabe, *Diary of a Young Soul Rebel*, London: British Film Institute, 1991

Juneau, Pierre (1922–)

Canadian Media Executive

Pierre Juneau has held virtually every important position in the Canadian broadcasting hierarchy. His long career has been characterized by a sustained commitment to the principles of public broadcasting and ownership.

In 1949 Juneau joined the National Film Board of Canada (NFBC) as the Montreal district representative. In the 1950s, he became the Quebec assistant regional supervisor, then the chief of international distribution, the assistant head of the European office, and the NFBC secretary. In 1964 he took on the position of director of French-language production. He also pursued film interests only secondarily related to his official position. In 1959 Juneau cofounded the Montreal International Film Festival and served as its president until 1968.

In 1966 Juneau left the NFBC to become vice chair of the Board of Broadcast Governors (BBG), the federal broadcast regulatory agency. In 1968 Parliament enacted a new Broadcasting Act, which replaced the BBG with the Canadian Radio-television and Telecommunications Commission (CRTC) and Juneau was named its first chair, a position he held until 1975. As CRTC chair, Juneau is best remembered for promoting Canadian-content regulations in both radio and television, as well as in the growing medium of cable. The regulations, soon called "Cancon," helped create a permanent domestic market for Canadian music and television. They stipulate percentages of overall air time and specific time slots that must be devoted to material produced or performed by Canadians. These regulations met with widespread public support, and their principle remains essentially unchanged to the present day. Indeed, in 1971 the Canadian Academy of Recording Arts and Sciences (CARAS) named its annual ceremony the "Juno Awards" as a gesture toward both the CRTC chair and the Roman goddess.

In 1975 Liberal Prime Minister Pierre Trudeau appointed Juneau minister of communication, but he was defeated in the by-election of that year and resigned from the post. In 1978, still under Trudeau, Juneau became undersecretary of state and in 1980 deputy minister of communication. Trudeau appointed Juneau to a seven-year term as president of the Canadian Broadcasting Corporation (CBC) in 1982. These proved to be turbulent times, however, as the Trudeau government was defeated by the Conservative Party of Prime Minister Brian Mulroney. Although the CBC president enjoys an "arm's length" relationship with the government, relations between Juneau, who was closely iden-

Pierre Juneau.
Photo courtesy of CBC Television

as Parliament declined to cover all expenses. Under Juneau, the CBC consolidated its reputation for news and public affairs on both its French- and English-language networks, increased its Canadian content, brought in a new head of English-language programming, Ivan Fecan, and shifted toward independently produced dramatic content. In the 1980s, the CBC also scored some of its highest ratings successes ever. However, its dependence upon advertising revenue became more acute and its audience share fell. In 1995 Juneau was appointed to head the Mandate Review Committee of the CBC, NFB, and Telefilm Canada. Since that time, he has also become president of the World Radio and Television Council and of the Canadian Centre for International Studies and Cooperation, both based in Montreal.

PAUL ATTALLAH

Pierre Juneau. Born in Verdun, Quebec, Canada, October 17, 1922. Educated at Jesuit schools, College Sainte-Marie in Montreal, B.A., 1944, Sorbonne in Paris, France; graduated from the Institut Catholique, Paris, as a licenciate in philosophy, 1949. Married: Fernande Martin, 1947; children: Andre, Martin, and Isabelle. Joined National Film Board of Canada as Montreal district representative, 1949; assistant regional supervisor for the Province of Quebec; chief of international distribution, 1951; assistant head of the European office, London, 1952; secretary, National Film Board, 1954; cofounder and president, Montreal International Film Festival, 1959–68; senior assistant to the commissioner and director of French-language production, 1964–66, vice chair; named vice-chair, Board of Broadcast Governors, 1966; chair, Canadian Radio and Television Commission, 1968–75; Canadian minister of communications, 1975; adviser to Prime Minister Pierre Trudeau; appointed chair, National Capital Commission, 1976; undersecretary of state, 1978; deputy minister of communications, 1980; president, CBC, 1982–89; chair, CBC's mandate review committee, 1995; president, World Radio and Television Council and Canadian Centre for International Studies and Cooperation, 1995. Honorary doctorates: York University, 1973, Trent University, 1987, University of Moncton, 1988. Fellow: Royal Society of Canada. Recipient: Order of Canada, 1975; Officier de l'Ordre de la Pléiade (section canadienne de l'Assemblée parlementaire de la francophonie), 2001.

Publication

Making Our Voices Heard: Canadian Broadcasting and Film for the 21st Century (The Juneau Report) (editor), 1995

tified with the Trudeau Liberals, and the new government became strained as increasingly severe budget cuts were imposed upon the CBC. In 1988 the Mulroney government also revised the Broadcasting Act. It foresaw that Juneau's position would be split between a part-time president and a full-time chair, a move Juneau opposed. Simultaneously, throughout the 1980s, new television services were launched, and the CBC's audience share declined. Juneau defended both the ideal and the practical reality of public broadcasting and stated his intention to raise to 95 percent the amount of Canadian content on the CBC. Furthermore, in 1988 and 1989, he oversaw the launch of the CBC's all-news cable channel, Newsworld, on which he appeared as the first speaker on the last day of his mandate.

Like CBC presidents before him, Juneau campaigned for operating budgets, controlled by Parliament, covering five-year rather than one-year periods and refused to relinquish advertising revenue so long

Further Reading

"CBC Union Gets Juneau on Side: Former Chief To Appear Before CRTC," *Globe and Mail* (March 14, 1991)

Cuthbert, Pamela, and Leo Rice-Barker, "Juneau Report Debated," *Playback* (February 12, 1996)

"I Am Very Pessimistic" (interview) *Maclean's* (August 7, 1989)

"Juneau Joins Montreal University," *Globe and Mail* (November 23, 1989)

Levine, Allan, *Scrum Wars: The Prime Ministers and the Media,* Toronto: Dundurn, 1993

Raboy, Marc, *Missed Opportunities: The Story of Canada's Broadcasting Policy,* Montreal: McGill-Queen's University Press, 1990

"Reflecting Canada to Canadians," *Globe and Mail* (May 6, 1995)

"Report Fuzzy," *Playback* (February 12, 1996)

Rutherford, Paul, *When Television Was Young: Prime Time Canada, 1952–67,* Toronto: University of Toronto Press, 1990

K

Kate and Allie

U.S. Domestic Comedy

Kate and Allie, which ran on CBS from March 19, 1984, to May 22, 1989, was the brainchild of Sherry Coben, who came up with the idea for the series while attending a high school reunion. There she noticed that a couple of divorcées, who seemed unhappy and dissatisfied, found comfort in sharing with each other. Coben worked with this germinal notion and successfully pitched the resulting script, originally entitled, "Two Mommies," to Michael Ogiens, then head of New York program development at CBS. Ogiens liked the script because it contained fresh material that dealt with a real issue of the day: single parenthood.

The next step in the series' genesis was the location of actresses for the central roles. Susan St. James was, at the time, under contract to CBS. Although she was best known for romantic comedy, she liked the script and the part of Kate McArdle but stipulated her demands: production before a live audience and a New York shooting location. St. James's close friend Jane Curtin was soon convinced to accept the part of Allie Lowell. Producer-director-writer Bill Persky agreed to produce and direct six episodes, without committing to an entire series. He also insisted that Bob Randall be brought on board as producer-writer and supervisor. Reeves Communications, with executive producers Mort Lachman and Merrill Grant, undertook production of *Kate and Allie,* and the series debuted with a script by Coben setting the series' premise: two divorced women who have known one another since childhood decide to move in together and raise their three children as a family unit.

Kate and Allie was an instant success, ranking fourth the week it debuted, garnering consistently high ratings thereafter, and earning Jane Curtin two consecutive Emmys and Bill Persky, one. The characters and the issues addressed on the program obviously appealed to its audience.

St. James's character, Kate, is a woman recently divorced from her unstable and somewhat flighty part-time actor husband, Max. She has one daughter, 14-year-old Emma (Ari Meyers). Curtin's Allie is also recently divorced from her successful, but unfaithful doctor husband, Charles. She has a 14-year-old daughter Jennie (Allison Smith) and a 7-year-old son, Chip (Frederick Koehler). Neither Kate nor Allie have ruled out remarriage, but view their new situation as a provisional reprieve, a time for both women to come to know and appreciate themselves. On one level the series dealt with practical problems faced by divorced women with children: adjusting to a new lifestyle and to living closely with new people, dealing with children's issues, beginning to date again, securing financial stability.

On another level, however, the series addressed the larger issue of gender identity at a time when gender roles were in transition. Allie Lowell submerged her own identity into that of her husband, and most of the series' trajectory tracks her journey toward autonomy.

Kate and Allie, Jane Curtin, Susan Saint James, 1984–89.
Courtesy of the Everett Collection

Kate McArdle, on the other hand, has a stronger sense of her own identity, but she must constantly struggle for equality at work and for the assurance that her goals will be respected in any love relationship.

Key to the series' notion of women's development is same-sex friendship, and each episode is narratively structured to highlight the long-term, supportive friendship between the two main characters. Episodes begin with a conversation between Kate and Allie designed to enhance the audience's understanding of both women or to provide background information. Similarly, each episode ends with Kate and Allie discussing and bringing closure to the events just depicted. Their verbal intimacy both reflects and heightens their sustaining friendship. As the series evolved, the same kind of supportive friendship developed between the two daughters, who initially disliked being forced together.

After directing 100 episodes and having Allie accept the wedding proposal of likable character Bob Barsky, Bill Persky left the series, feeling that *Kate and Allie* had now fulfilled its premise. The needed respite had worked for Allie, who was now able to enter a meaningful heterosexual relationship as a fully autonomous individual, sure of herself and of her own goals. While Kate still had not met a man whose life goals matched her own, she and Allie owned a successful business, and the audience was sure that she would not succumb to a marriage that downplayed her personal desires.

Despite these developments, the series continued. Linda Day became the director, with Anne Flett and Chuck Ranberg as producers, but the new team did not meet with the same success as had the first. The decline of *Kate and Allie* illustrates an interesting aspect of television's capabilities in combining sociocultural issues with particular narrative strategies. With the series' premise fulfilled, plots lacked the same objective and lost the relevance and vitality of earlier episodes. In part to address this situation, early in the new season, the writers created a device to bring the two women together again: Kate moved out of the old apartment and in with Allie and Bob, who accepted a sportscasting job that would take him away on weekends. By this time, however, Emma was out of the series, ostensibly at college, and while Jennie remained an active and visible character, she too had moved out of the household to live in a university dorm. The friendship between Kate and Allie lost its earlier dynamism now that Allie was married. Kate appeared as an intrusion into the household, rather than a necessary part of it. Even though the series had not "solved" the social problems it addressed, its creators and performers had moved the main characters into a narrative situation that no longer seemed a workable fiction. After its sixth season, the series was not renewed.

CHRISTINE R. CATRON

See also **Comedy, Domestic Settings; Curtin, Jane; Gender and Television**

Cast

Kate McArdle	Susan St. James
Allie Lowell	Jane Curtin
Emma McArdle (1984–88)	Ari Meyers
Chip Lowell	Frederick Koehler
Jennie Lowell	Allison Smith
Charles Lowell (1984–86)	Paul Hecht
Ted Bartelo (1984–85, 1987–88)	Gregory Salata
Bob Barsky (1987–89)	Sam Freed
Lou Carello (1988–89)	Peter Onorati

Producers

Bob Randall, Mort Lachman, Merrill Grant, Bill Persky, Anne Flett, Chuck Ranberg

Programming History

122 episodes
CBS

March 1984–May 1984	Monday 9:30–10:00
August 1984– September 1986	Monday 9:30–10:00
September 1986– September 1987	Monday 8:00–8:30
September 1987– November 1987	Monday 8:30–9:00
December 1987–June 1988	Monday 8:00–8:30
July 1988–August 1988	Saturday 8:00–8:30

August 1988–	
September 1988	Monday 9:00–9:30
December 1988–March 1989	Monday 8:30–9:00
March 1989–June 1989	Monday 10:30–11:00
June 1989–September 1989	Monday 8:00–8:30

Further Reading

Brown, Mary Ellen, editor, *Television and Women's Culture: The Politics of the Popular,* Newbury Park, California: Sage, 1990

Horowitz, S., "Life with Kate and Allie—The Not-So-Odd Couple on TV," *Ms.* (1984)

Rabinovitz, L., "Sitcoms and Single Moms: Representations of Feminism on American TV," *Cinema Journal* (1989)

Shales, Tom, "Comedy with Class: The Creative Spark Behind CBS' *Kate and Allie*," *Washington Post* (March 19, 1984)

Spigel, Lynn, and Denise Mann, editors, *Private Screenings: Television and the Female Consumer,* Minneapolis: University of Minnesota Press, 1992

Keeshan, Bob (1927–2004)

U.S. Children's Television Performer

Bob Keeshan was the actor and producer responsible for the success of the long-running children's program, *Captain Kangaroo.* As the easy-going captain with his big pockets and his bushy mustache, Keeshan lured children into close engagement with literature, science, and especially music, adopting an approach that mixed pleasure and pedagogy. Children learned most easily, he argued, when information and knowledge became a source of delight. Keeshan's approach represented a rejection of pressures toward the increased commercialization of children's programming as well as a toning-down of the high volume, slapstick style associated with earlier kid show hosts, such as Pinky Lee, Soupy Sales, and *Howdy Doody*'s Buffalo Bob.

Keeshan was working as a receptionist at NBC-Radio's Manhattan office when Bob Smith started offering him small acting parts on his NBC-TV show, *Triple B Ranch,* and then, subsequently, hired him as a special assistant for *The Howdy Doody Show.* Although Keeshan's initial responsibilities involved supervising props and talking to the children who were to be program guests, he was soon pulled on camera, bringing out prizes. After appearing in clown garb on one episode to immense response, he took on the regular role of Clarabell, the mute clown who communicated by honking a horn. Leaving the series in 1952, he played a succession of other clown characters, such as Corny, the host of WABC-TV's *Time For Fun,* a noontime cartoon program, where he exerted pressure to remove from airplay cartoons he felt were too violent or perpetuated racial stereotyping. While at WABC-TV, he played an Alpine toymaker on *Tinker's Workshop,* an early morning program, which served as the prototype for *Captain Kangaroo.*

The CBS network was searching for innovative new approaches to children's programming and approved the *Kangaroo* series submitted by Keeshan and longtime friend Jack Miller. The series first aired in October 1955 and continued until 1985, making it the longest running children's series in network history. Keeshan not only vividly embodied the captain, the friendly host of the Treasure House, but also played a central creative role on the daily series, supervising and actively contributing to the scripts and ensuring the program's conformity to his conceptions of appropriate children's entertainment. Through encounters with Mr. Green Jeans and his menagerie of domestic animals, with the poetry-creating Grandfather Clock, the greedy Bunny Rabbit, the punning trickster Mr. Moose, and the musically inclined Dancing Bear, the captain opened several generations of children to the pleasures of learning. Unlike many other children's programs, *Captain Kangaroo* was not filmed before a studio audience and did not include children in its cast. Keeshan wanted nothing that would come between him and the children in his television audience and so spoke directly to the camera. He also personally supervised which commercials could air on the program and promoted products, such as Play-Dough and Etch-a-Sketch, which he saw as facilitating creative play, while avoiding those he felt purely exploitative.

Bob Keeshan.
Courtesy of Robert Keeshan

As his program's popularity grew, Keeshan took on an increasingly public role as an advocate for children, writing a regular column about children and television for *McCall's* and occasional articles for *Good Housekeeping, Parade,* and other publications. Keeshan wrote original children's books (as well as those tied to the *Kangaroo* program) and recorded a series of records designed to introduce children to classical and jazz music. He appeared at "tiny tot" concerts given by symphony orchestras in more than 50 cities, offering playful introductions to the musical instruments and the pleasure of good listening.

After his retirement, Keeshan became an active lobbyist on behalf of children's issues and in favor of tighter controls over the tobacco industry. A sharp critic of contemporary children's television, Keeshan long campaigned to participate in a new version of *Captain Kangaroo.* When a syndicated revival of the program began airing in 1997, Keeshan was not chosen to portray the Captain.

HENRY JENKINS

See also **Children and Television; Educational Television**

Bob Keeshan. Born in New York City, June 27, 1927. Attended Fordham University, 1946–49. Served in U.S. Marine Corps Reserve, 1945–46. Married: Anne Jeanne Laurie, 1950; children: Michael Derek, Laurie Margaret, and Maeve Jeanne. Began career as Clarabell for NBC-TV's *The Howdy Doody Show,* 1947–52; appeared as Corny the Clown (ABC-TV), 1953–55, and Tinker the Toymaker (ABC-TV), 1954–55; starred as Captain Kangaroo (CBS-TV), 1955–85; president, Robert Keeshan Associates, from 1955; appeared as Mr. Mayor and the Town Clown (CBS-TV), 1964–65; president, Suffolk County Hearing and Speech Center, 1966–71; director of Marvin Josephson Associates, Inc., New York, 1969–77; director, Bank of Babylon, New York, 1973–79; chair, board of trustees, College of New Rochelle, New York, 1974–80; director, Anchor Savings Bank, 1976–91; chair, Council of Governing Boards, 1979–80; commentator, CBS-Radio, 1980–82; television commentator, 1981–82. Member: Board of Education, West Islip, New York, 1953–58; board of directors, Good Samaritan Hospital, West Islip, New York, 1969–78. Honorary degrees: D. of Pedagogy, Rhode Island College, 1969; D.H.L., Alfred University, 1969; D.F.A., Fordham University, 1975; Litt.D., Indiana State University, 1978; L.L.D., Elmira (New York) University, 1980; D.L., Marquette University, 1983; D.P.S., Central Michigan University, 1984; D.H.L., St. Joseph College, 1987. Honorary Fellow: American Academy of Pediatrics. Recipient: Sylvania Award, 1956; Peabody Awards, 1958, 1972, 1979; American Education Award, Education Industries Association, 1978; Distinguished Achievement Award, Georgia Radio and TV Institute-Pi Gamma Kappa, 1978; Emmy Awards, 1978, 1981, 1982, 1983, 1984; TV Father of the Year, 1980; James E. Allen Memorial Award, 1981; Distinguished Service to Children Award, 1981; National Education Award, 1982; American Heart Association National Public Affairs Recognition Award, 1987; Frances Holleman Breathitt Award for Excellence, Kennedy Center for the Performing Arts, 1987; Clown Hall of Fame, 1990; AMA Distinguished Service Award, 1991; National Association of Broadcasters' Hall of Fame, 1998. Died January 23, 2004.

Television Series

1947–52	*The Howdy Doody Show*
1953–55	*Time for Fun*
1954–55	*Tinker's Workshop* (also producer)
1955–85	*Captain Kangaroo* (also producer)
1964–65	*Mr. Mayor* (also producer)
1981–82	*Up to the Minute, CBS News* commentator)
1982	*CBS Morning News* (commentator)

Radio

The Subject Is Young People, 1980–82.

Publications (selected)

Growing Up Happy, 1989
Family Fun Activity Book, 1994
Holiday Fun Activity, 1995
Books To Grow By, 1996
Alligator in the Basement, 1996
Hurry, Murry, Hurry, 1996
*Good Morning, Captain: 50 Years with Bob Keeshan,
   TV's Captain Kangaroo,* 1996

Further Reading

Blum, David, "Fighting Demotion to Mr. Marsupial" (interview), *New York Times* (June 14, 1995)
Deutschman, Alan, "Lessons from Dad," *Fortune* (January 29, 1990)
Kaye, Evelyn, *The ACT Guide to Children's Television: Or How To Treat TV with T.L.C.,* Boston: Beacon, 1979
Norton-Smith, Thomas M., and Linda L. Norton-Smith, "Two Conceptions of the Value of Individuals in Children's Programming," *Midwest Quarterly* (Autumn 1992)

Kelley, David E. *See* **Producer in Television; Workplace Programs**

Kellner, Jamie

U.S. Television Executive

Jamie Kellner is one of a select number of individuals responsible for dictating the terms by which television made its transition from broadcasting to narrowcasting. By helping to create both the FOX Broadcasting Network as well as the WB, Kellner played a crucial role in redefining how the networks do business. And by leading in the restructuring of the Turner Broadcasting System's entertainment properties, Kellner also improved the relationship between broadcast networks and cable channels. Although he is most often identified for his contributions to television sales, marketing, and distribution, Kellner has been equally central in shaping television programming for the last three decades.

Kellner began his career in the entertainment industry in the CBS executive training program in 1969. After working in a number of different departments at the company, he found a permanent position in the syndication division. When, in 1972, CBS was forced to dispose of this division due to antitrust considerations, Kellner remained with the spun-off group, which was renamed Viacom. He quickly moved up the ranks of Viacom's syndication and sales department to become vice president of first-run programming, development, and sales.

In 1978 Kellner moved from Viacom to the film and television producer-distributor, Filmways, where he shepherded a number of shows into syndication, including *Saturday Night Live.* When Orion Pictures took over the firm in 1982, Kellner was one of a handful of Filmways employees to stay on with the company. At Orion, Kellner was responsible for supervising and operating the company's programming, home video, pay television, and syndication operations. He oversaw the network and syndicated launch of *Cagney and Lacey* as well as the introduction of a new version of *Hollywood Squares.*

As a result of the profit participation earnings from Filmways and Orion shows, Kellner was financially secure by the mid-1980s. This enabled him to make the leap into the risky venture being undertaken by News Corp. chairman Rupert Murdoch and FOX, Inc. chair-

Jamie Kellner.
Photo courtesy of WB

man Barry Diller in 1986: the development of a fourth network, the FOX Broadcasting Company.

Kellner was the first executive hired by Diller. At FOX, he built and then maintained the new network's affiliate base, sold programming to advertisers, and established relationships with program producers. He also formed alliances with cable operators—necessary because of FOX's inability to secure broadcast affiliates in some markets.

In his position as the head of the first new network to be created in over 30 years—a network emerging at a time of dramatic technological and industrial transformation—Kellner was on uncertain terrain. Yet he made a number of moves that appear prescient in retrospect. Among the most significant was the attempt to carve out a clear "brand identity" for FOX by targeting 18-to-49-year-olds with more explicit, graphic, and cutting-edge material than could be found on ABC, CBS, or NBC. Shows such as *Cops, Married...With Children, Beverly Hills, 90210, The Simpsons,* and *America's Most Wanted* were developed under his supervision.

Kellner recognized that a younger audience was important not only to FOX's growth in prime time, but also crucial to the network's expansion in daytime programming. Operating under the assumption that if children know about a channel, then the rest of the audience would follow, Kellner encouraged the development of the FOX Kids Network, which targeted children ages 2 to 11 with programming such as *X-Men, Beetlejuice,* and *Batman: The Animated Series.* The FOX Kids Network, which began airing shows on weekdays and Saturday mornings in the fall of 1990, operated as a joint effort between FOX and its affiliates, with profits split between the two entities.

Although the FOX Kids Network would be Kellner's first large-scale venture into children's programming and distribution, it would not be his last. He applied the lessons learned from his experiences with FOX to the strategies he employed in developing children's programming at America's fifth network, the WB. After departing from FOX in early 1993 and taking a brief break, Kellner returned to television in August of the same year to become the WB's CEO. In his move to the WB, Kellner brought with him many of the same executives who helped him develop FOX, including Garth Ancier and Susanne Daniels.

While at the WB, Kellner continued to be involved in both the business and the creative aspects of running a network, precisely as he had done at FOX. From a business perspective, he sought to make the WB even more youth-oriented than FOX by pursuing a 12-to-34 demographic in prime time. Teenagers, especially girls and young women, were particularly important to the nascent network and were targeted with such shows as *Buffy the Vampire Slayer, Charmed,* and *Dawson's Creek.*

Kellner's performance with the WB was viewed as such a success by parent company AOL Time Warner that the company elevated him to chairman and CEO of the Turner Broadcasting System in March 2001. While he continued to oversee the WB, he now supervised all of the Turner properties both domestically and internationally. These included CNN, TNT, TBS, The Cartoon Network, Turner Classic Movies, the Atlanta Braves, and the Atlanta Hawks. Among his most pressing tasks were revitalizing the sagging CNN divisions (e.g., Headline News, CNNfn) and reviving the TBS and TNT brands by making them appeal to more affluent audiences.

In February 2003, however, Kellner opted for a change of pace, leaving Atlanta and his position at Turner to return to Los Angeles and his former role as chairman and chief executive officer of the WB. With this move, he intended to direct the leadership transition for the network—a transition culminating with Kellner's retirement in summer 2004.

ALISA PERREN

See also **Ancier, Garth; AOL Time Warner; Demographics; Diller, Barry; FOX Broadcasting Company; Murdoch, Rupert; Narrowcasting; Sassa, Scott; Turner Broadcasting Systems; WB Television Network**

Jamie Kellner. Born in Brooklyn, New York. Married: Julie. Children: Melissa and Christopher. Education: degree in marketing, C.W. Post Campus of Long Island University, graduated 1969. Participant in CBS Executive Training Program, 1969; vice president for first-run programming, development and sales at Viacom; executive, Filmways, 1978; president of Orion Entertainment Group, overseeing network programming, pay television, home video, and domestic syndication operations, 1982; founding president and chief operating officer, FOX Broadcasting Company, 1986; resigned as president and appointed a member of the FOX board of directors, 1993; chief executive officer and partner of the WB, 1993; founder, chief executive officer, and chairman of the board, ACME Communications, 1997; chairman and chief executive officer of reorganized Turner TV Networks, 2001; chairman and chief executive officer, the WB, 2003. Awards: Broadcast Cable Financial Management Association Founders Award; Humanitarian Award of the National Conference for Community and Justice.

Further Reading

Block, Alex Ben, *Outfoxed: Marvin Davis, Barry Diller, Rupert Murdoch, Joan Rivers, and the Inside Story of America's Fourth Television Network,* New York: St. Martin's Press, 1991

Gunther, Marc, "This Frog Won't Be Squished," *Fortune* (September 7, 1998)

"Issues in Syndication: Jamie Kellner," *Mediaweek: NATPE '95* (January 23, 1995)

"Kellner on Out-Foxing the Competition," *Broadcasting and Cable* (January 2, 1995)

Kempner, Matt, "Hollywood Hit Maker: New Turner Broadcasting CEO Jamie Kellner Brings a Heavy Dose of Showbiz to Company," *Atlanta Journal and Constitution* (May 6, 2001)

Rice, Lynette, and Steve McClellan, "Kellner's Latest Surprise: The WB Gets New Legs," *Broadcasting and Cable* (August 11, 1997)

Rutenberg, Jim, "AOL Combines TV Networks Under a Chief," *New York Times* (March 7, 2001)

Rutenberg, Jim, "Mix, Patch, Promote and Lift: A Showman Speeds the Makeover of Ted Turner's Empire," *New York Times* (July 15, 2001)

Schmuckler, Eric, "The New Face in Toontown," *Mediaweek* (April 17, 1995)

Schneider, Michael, "Frog Prince Turns to Cable," *Variety* (March 12, 2001)

Umstead, R. Thomas, "Kellner Folds Two-Year Turner Show," *Multichannel News* (February 24, 2003)

Kendal, Felicity (1946–)

British Actor

Felicity Kendal first emerged as a favorite actor in British situation comedy in the 1970s and went on to vary her repertoire with television dramas, films, and stage plays with considerable success. She spent her childhood in India and had an early introduction to the theater on tour with the Shakespearean company run by her parents, both established theatrical performers. She made her debut on the London stage in 1967 and subsequently confirmed her reputation as a popular stage star with appearances in such plays as Alan Ayckbourn's *The Norman Conquests* (1974), Michael Frayn's *Clouds* (1978), Peter Shaffer's *Amadeus* (1979), Tom Stoppard's *Hapgood* (1988), and Chekhov's *Ivanov* (1989), for which she won the London *Evening Standard* Best Actress Award.

Kendal's theatrical links secured for her a first television role in *The Mayfly and the Frog,* which starred John Gielgud, and she made a good impression in supporting roles in such subsequent productions as *Man in a Suitcase, The Woodlanders, The Persuaders, Edward VII,* and *Home and Beauty,* among others. Producers liked her girlish good looks and bubbly confidence and audiences also quickly warmed to her.

Kendal's whimsical, puckish charm and endearingly good-humored outlook made her ideal for the role that was destined to establish her as a television star—that of Barbara Good in the BBC's *The Good Life,* in which she partnered with Richard Briers as a suburban couple determined to lead a life of independent self-sufficiency. Loyal to the point of lunacy, and ever-fetching even in mud-stained jeans and knotted headscarf, she won universal praise as the pert and long-suffering young wife of Briers, striving to understand the frustrations of her wayward cereal designer-turned-smallholder husband as he painfully sought to put some meaning back into his life by turning their

Surbiton house and garden into a small-scale farm. The accessibility of the central characters, perfectly played by Briers and Kendal, with Paul Eddington and Penelope Keith as their neighbors the Leadbeatters, ensured stardom for all four of them and a lasting place in public affections. As a direct result of the program's success, the number of smallholdings in Britain shot up to a record 51,000 by 1980.

After four seasons of *The Good Life*, the way was open for the four performers to develop their own solo careers. Kendal herself was showcased in two further sitcoms that centered around her alone. In Carla Lane's *Solo*, she returned to the theme of self-sufficiency, playing Gemma Palmer, a vulnerable but resolutely independent 30-year-old woman who throws out her faithless boyfriend and gives up her job in an attempt to reassert control of her life. In *The Mistress*, a rather more controversial sitcom also written by Lane, she was florist Maxine, trying to cope with the guilt and confusions involved in carrying on an affair with the married Luke Mansel (played by Jack Galloway). Some viewers disliked this last series, objecting to the girlish and rather innocent Felicity Kendal they remembered from *The Good Life* wrestling with such a dubious issue as adultery as she awaited her lover in her cozy pink flat, in the company of her pet rabbits, and pondered how to keep the affair secret from Luke's suspicious wife (played by Jane Asher).

Always an intelligent and sensitive actor, Kendal has been by no means confined to sitcoms, however. By way of contrast, in 1978 she played Dorothy Wordsworth in Ken Russell's biopic *Clouds of Glory* and later on she appeared with success in the miniseries *The Camomile Lawn*. In *Honey for Tea*, she was back in more familiar sitcom territory, playing American widow Nancy Belasco. In recent years she has concentrated on theater work.

DAVID PICKERING

Felicity Kendal. Born in Olton, Warwickshire, England, September 25, 1946. Education: six convents in India. Married: one son from first marriage; 2) Michael Rudman, 1983; one son. On stage, from 1947 (at age of 9 months); grew up touring with parents' theatre company in India and the Far East; in film, from 1965; London stage debut in *Minor Murder*, 1967; in television, from 1968. Recipient: Variety Club Awards, 1974, 1979, 1984; Clarence Derwent Award, 1980; Evening Standard Best Actor Award, 1989; Commander of the British Empire, 1995.

Television Series
| 1975–77 | *The Good Life* |
| 1980–82 | *Solo* |

1985–86	*The Mistress*
1994	*Honey for Tea*
2003	*Rosemary and Thyme*

Television Miniseries
| 1975 | *Edward the King* |
| 1992 | *The Camomile Lawn* |

Television Plays (selected)
1968	*The Mayfly and the Frog*
1971	*Crime of Passion*
1973	*The Woodlanders*
1973	*Love Story*
1978	*Home and Beauty*
1978	*Wings of a Song*
1978	*Clouds of Glory*
1979	*Twelfth Night*
1986	*On the Razzle* (for *Great Performances*)

Films
Shakespeare Wallah, 1965; *The Seven Percent Solution*, 1976; *Valentino*, 1977; *The Rime of the Ancient Mariner*, 1977; *Twelfth Night*, 1980; *We're Back! A Dinosaur's Story* (voice only), 1998; *Parting Shots*, 1999.

Stage
A Midsummer Night's Dream, 1947; *Minor Murder*, 1967; *Henry V*, 1968; *The Promise*, 1968; *Back to Methuselah*, 1970; *A Midsummer Night's Dream*, 1970; *Kean*, 1970; *Much Ado About Nothing*, 1971; *Romeo and Juliet*, 1972; *'Tis Pity She's a Whore*, 1972; *The Three Arrows*, 1972; *The Norman Conquests*, 1974; *Once upon a Time*, 1976; *Arms and the Man*, 1978; *Clouds*, 1978; *Amadeus*, 1979; *Othello*, 1980; *On the Razzle*, 1981; *The Second Mrs. Tanqueray*, 1982; *The Real Thing*, 1982; *Jumpers*, 1985; *Made in Bangkok*, 1986; *Hapgood*, 1988; *Much Ado About Nothing*, 1989; *Ivanov*, 1989; *Hidden Laughter*, 1990; *Tartuffe*, 1991; *Heartbreak House*, 1992; *Arcadia*, 1993; *An Absolute Turkey*, 1994; *India Ink*, 1995; *Mind Millie for Me*, 1996; *Waste*, 1997; *The Seagull*, 1997; *Alarms and Excursions*, 1998.

Publication
White Cargo (memoirs), 1998

Kennedy, Graham (1934–)

Australian Comedian, Host

In 1956, just in time for the Melbourne Olympics, Australian television began on Network Nine, destined to be the nation's most successful popular network. A year later, also on Network Nine, the long-running variety show *In Melbourne Tonight* also began and soon became immensely popular. So too did the host of the show, Graham Kennedy, who became that classic icon, a household word. He was the king of comedy, the recognized successor to Australia's previous comic king and lord of misrule, Roy Rene (Mo), whose stage had been vaudeville and radio from the 1920s to the late 1940s. With *In Melbourne Tonight,* Kennedy adapted for television Australia's rich history of very risqué music hall, vaudeville, and variety. *In Melbourne Tonight* included musical acts, game segments, burlesques of ads, and sketches, including "The Wilsons." In this segment, perhaps reminiscent of *The Honeymooners* skits on early 1950s American television, Graham played a dirty old man, married to his Joyce, carnivalizing marriage as comic disaster.

After some 15 years of *In Melbourne Tonight,* Kennedy's TV shows and appearances became more occasional. In the mid-1970s, he was host of *Blankety Blanks,* a variety quiz show that parodied other quiz shows. On *Blankety Blanks,* contestants would be asked to provide a reply that matched the responses offered by a panel of celebrities; there was no "true" answer, only answers that matched, as Kennedy would occasionally remind viewers amid the mayhem and clowning. The program tended to go sideways into nonsense and fooling, rather than go straight ahead as in a quiz "race." In the late 1980s, Kennedy was host of *Graham Kennedy Coast to Coast,* an innovative late-night program (10:30 to 11:30 P.M.) that mixed news, accompanied by its conventions of seriousness and frequent urgency, with comic traditions drawn from centuries of carnival and vaudeville, a hybridizing of genres usually considered incompatible.

Kennedy's humor was saturated with self-reflexivity. On *Blankety Blanks* he insulted the producer, chided the crew, complained about the format of the show, and chaffed with the audience. He made jokes about the props he had to use, or the young lad called Peter behind the set whose task was to pull something. The youth was addressed by Kennedy as Peter the Phantom Puller, and was frequently instructed to, "Pull it, Peter." On *Graham Kennedy Coast to Coast,* Kennedy continued to make comedy out of self-reflexivity. At various times, he showed how he could beep out words with a device on the desk in front of him. He demonstrated the cue system and revealed the cue words themselves. He discussed his smoking problem, announcing that he was a chain smoker, and, although he was not supposed to puff on it in front of viewers, he held a lit cigarette just below his desk. He presented ads, making fun of the product, revealing how much the station received for them. He showed a tiny new camera, and what it could do, and invited the audience to ring in with suggestions for how he should use it. Every night he read out telephone calls resulting from the previous night's show, some registering their disgust with his extremely "crude" jokes.

Everything served as grist for Kennedy's comedy mill: the studio, the situation of sitting in front of cameras and dealing with a producer, the off-screen personalities of his straight men (Ken Sutcliffe, a sports compere, and John Mangos, back from the United States where he had been an overseas reporter for Network Nine).

As with professional clowns from early modern Europe through pantomime, music hall, vaudeville, to Hollywood, Kennedy presented his face and body as grotesque, highlighting his protruding eyes, open gaping mouth, and long wandering tongue. His comedy was indeed risqué, calling on every aspect of the body to bring down solemnity or pomposity or pretension; his references to any and every orifice and protuberance were often such that one laughed and cried out at home, "that's disgusting." His relationship with his audience was—again as with clowns of old—competitive and interactive, particularly in the segments in which he read out and responded to phone calls. To one viewer, who must have been demanding them, Kennedy commented, "There are no limits, love, there are no limits." It is the credo of the clown through the ages, the uttering of what others only think, the saying of what cannot be said.

When Queen Elizabeth was shown in a news item visiting Hong Kong in 1989, Kennedy remarked that for a woman her age she did not have bad breasts—a purposely outrageously sexist comment, directed at a figure traditionally revered by Anglo-Australians. The night following the San Francisco earthquake, Kennedy and John Mangos staged a mock earthquake in the studio, with the ceiling apparently falling in on them. This piece of comic by-play was discussed in the press for some days. "Quality" papers such as the *Sydney Morning Herald* debated how distasteful it was. Kennedy was calling on an aspect of carnivalesque, uncrowning death with laughter. Such comedy usually remains verbal and underground, but Kennedy brought it to television.

Coast to Coast always highlighted and played with gender identity and confusion. Kennedy created his TV persona as bisexual. He might make jokes of heterosexual provenance, as in expressing his desire to make love to Jana Wendt, Australian TV's highest-rating current-affairs and news-magazine host. Alternatively, he would play up being gay. One night Sutcliffe suddenly said to Graham, "Would you like to take your hand off my knee?" Jokes flowed, and Kennedy later included the performance in his final retrospective 1989 *Coast to Coast* program. Graham and Mangos were also very affectionate to each other. In his last appearance on the show, Graham kissed Mangos's hand, and said of Ken and John that "he loved them both."

Kennedy also highlighted ethnicity on *Coast to Coast*, particularly with Greek-Australian Mangos. With George Donikian, an Armenian Australian reading out headlines every half hour, and with an American Australian listing stock exchange reports, Graham set about exploring contemporary cultural and ethnic identities in Australia. His ethnic jokes probed, provoked, teased, challenged. The jokes were uncertain, revealing his own uncertainty.

The popularity of Graham Kennedy from 1957 onward, a popularity almost coterminous with Australian television itself, was extremely important and influential for contemporary entertainment. This comedy king gave license to many princes and lesser courts. He enabled them to explore comic self-reflexivity and direct address, the grotesque body, parody, and self-parody. For if Kennedy mocked others, he just as continuously mocked himself, creating for Australian television a feature of long carnivalesque signature, comedy that destabilizes every settled category and claim to truth, including its own. Such self-parody also drew on what has been remarked as a feature of (white) Australian cultural history in the last two centuries, perhaps directly influenced by aboriginal traditions of mocking mimicry: a laconic self-ironic humor, unsettling pom-

posity, pretension, and authority. Kennedy does not belong only to cultural history in Australia; his quickness of wit in verbal play, double-entendre, sexual suggestion, inverted meanings, and festive abuse join him to a long line of great comedians across the world. What he adds to stage traditions of comedy is a mastery of the television medium itself.

JOHN DOCKER

Graham Kennedy. Born in Melbourne, Australia, February 15, 1934. Educated at Caulfield Central School and Melbourne High School. News runner for ABC Radio Australia; worked at radio station 3UZ, in the recorded music library, and as panel operator for radio personality Nicky (Cliff Nicholls), 1951–57; moved to television, working for GTV Nine Network, 1957–69, and 1972–74; popular host, GTV9's *In Melbourne Tonight;* briefly returned to radio, 1961; briefly hosted GTV9's *The Tonight Show,* 1973; film career as a character actor; worked for Ten Network, 1977–79; host of the Australian version of *Blankety Blanks,* 1977–81; occasional TV appearances, from 1981; host, *Funniest Home Videos,* from 1990. Recipient: several Logie Awards, two Penguin Awards.

Television Series

1957–69	*In Melbourne Tonight*
1973	*The Tonight Show*
1977–81	*Blankety Blanks*
1988–89	*Graham Kennedy Coast to Coast*
1990	*Graham Kennedy's Funniest Home Videos*

Films

They're a Weird Mob, 1968; *The Odd, Angry Shot,* 1978; *The Club,* 1980; *The Return of Captain Invincible,* 1982; *The Killing Fields,* 1983; *Stanley,* 1983; *Travelling North,* 1987.

Publication

"Foreword," *A Man Called Mo* (edited by Fred Parsons), 1973

Further Reading

Bakhtin, Mikhail, *The Dialogic Imagination,* Austin: University of Texas Press, 1981
Bakhtin, Mikhail, *Rabelais and His World,* Bloomington: Indiana University Press, 1984
Docker, John, *Postmodernism and Popular Culture: A Cultural History,* Melbourne: Cambridge University Press, 1994
Klages, Mary, "What to Do with Helen Keller Jokes: A Feminist Act," in *New Perspectives on Women and Comedy,* edited by

Regina Barreca, Philadelphia, Pennsylvania: Gordon and Breach, 1992

Turner, Graeme, "Transgressive TV: From *In Melbourne Tonight* to *Perfect Match*," in *Australian Television: Programs, Pleasures, and Politics,* edited by John

Tulloch and Graeme Turner, Sydney: Allen and Unwin, 1989

Welsford, Enid, *The Fool: His Social and Literary History,* London: Faber and Faber, 1935

Kennedy, John F.: Assassination and Funeral

The network coverage of the assassination and funeral of President John F. Kennedy warrants its reputation as the most moving and historic passage in broadcasting history. On Friday November 22, 1963, news bulletins reporting rifle shots during the president's motorcade in Dallas, Texas, broke into normal programming. Soon the three networks preempted their regular schedules and all commercial advertising for a wrenching marathon that would conclude only after the president's burial at Arlington National Cemetery on Monday, November 25. As a purely technical challenge, the continuous live coverage over four days of a single, unbidden event remains the signature achievement of broadcast journalism in the era of three-network hegemony. But perhaps the true measure of the television coverage of the events surrounding the death of President Kennedy is that it marked how intimately the medium and the nation are interwoven in times of crisis.

The first word came over the television airwaves at 1:40 P.M. Eastern Standard Time, when CBS News anchorman Walter Cronkite broke into *As the World Turns* with an audio announcement over a bulletin slide: "In Dallas, Texas, three shots were fired at President Kennedy's motorcade in downtown Dallas. The first reports say that President Kennedy has been seriously wounded by this shooting." Minutes later, Cronkite appeared on screen from CBS's New York newsroom to field live reports from Dallas and read news bulletins from Associated Press and CBS Radio. Eddie Barker, news director for CBS's Dallas affiliate KRLD-TV, reported live from the Trade Mart, where the president was to have attended a luncheon. As a stationary camera panned the ballroom, closing in on a black waiter who wiped tears from his face, Barker related rumors "that the president is dead." Back in New York, a voice off-camera told Cronkite the same news, which, the anchorman stressed, was "totally unconfirmed." Switching back to Dallas, Barker again reported "the word we have is that the president is dead." Though he cautioned "this we do not know for a fact,"

the visual image at the Trade Mart was ominous: workman could be seen removing the presidential seal from a podium on the dais.

Behind the scenes, at KRLD's newsroom, CBS's Dallas bureau chief Dan Rather scrambled for information. He learned from two sources at Parkland Hospital that the president had died, a report that went out prematurely over CBS Radio. Citing Rather, Cronkite reported the president's death but noted the lack of any official conformation. At 2:37 P.M. CBS news editor Ed Bliss Jr., handed Cronkite an Associated Press wire report. Cronkite took a long second to read it to himself before intoning: "From Dallas, Texas, the flash, apparently official. President Kennedy died at 1:00 P.M. Central Standard Time, two o'clock Eastern Standard Time." He paused and looked at the studio clock. "Some 38 minutes ago." Momentarily losing his composure, Cronkite winced, removed his eyeglasses, and cleared his throat before resuming with the observation that Vice President Lyndon Johnson would presumably take the oath of office to become the 36th president of the United States.

To appreciate the enormity of the task faced by the networks over the next four days, it is necessary to recall that in 1963, before the days of high-tech, globally linked, and sleekly mobile news-gathering units, the technical limitations of broadcast journalism militated against the coverage of live and fast-breaking events in multiple locations. TV cameras required two hours of equipment warm-up to become "hot" enough for operation. Video signals were transmitted cross-country via "hard wire" coaxial cable or microwave relay. "Spot coverage" of unfolding news in the field demanded speed and mobility, and since television cameras had to be tethered to enormous wires and electrical systems, 16mm film crews still dominated location coverage, with the consequent delay in transportation, processing, and editing of footage. The challenges of juggling live broadcasts from across the nation with overseas audio transmissions, of compiling instant documentaries and special reports, and of acquiring

The funeral of John F. Kennedy
Photo courtesy of the John F. Kennedy Library

and putting out raw film footage over the air was an off-the-cuff experiment in what NBC correspondent Bill Ryan called "controlled panic."

The resultant technical glitches served to heighten a national atmosphere of crisis and imbalance. NBC's coverage during that first hour showed correspondents Frank McGee, Chet Huntley, and Bill Ryan fumbling for a simple telephone link to Dallas, where reporter Robert McNeil was on the scene at Parkland Hospital. Manning the telephone and bobbling a malfunctioning speaker attachment, McGee had to repeat McNeil's words for the home audience because NBC technicians could not establish a direct audio feed. As McNeil reported White House aide Mac Kilduff's official announcement of the president's death, the phone link suddenly kicked in. Creating an eerie echo of the death notice, McGee, unaware, continued to repeat McNeil's now audible words. "After being shot at," said McNeil. "After being shot," repeated McGee needlessly. "By an unknown assailant..." "By an unknown assailant..."

Throughout Friday afternoon, information rushed in about the condition of Texas governor John Connolly, also wounded in the assassination; about the whereabouts and security of Vice President Lyndon Johnson, whom broadcasters made a determined effort to call "President Johnson"; and, in the later afternoon, about the capture of a suspected assassin, identified as Lee Harvey Oswald, a former Marine associated with left-wing causes.

So urgent was the craving for news and imagery that unedited film footage, still blotched and wet from fresh development, was put out over the air: of shocked pedestrians along the motorcade route and tearful Dallas residents outside Parkland Hospital, of the president and first lady, vital and smiling, from earlier in the day. The simultaneity of live video reports of a dead president intercut with recently developed film footage of a lively president delivering a good-humored breakfast speech that morning in Fort Worth, Texas, made for a jarring by-play of mixed visual messages. Correspondents on all three networks were apt reflections of spectator reaction: disbelief, shock, confusion, and grief. Grasping for points of comparison, many recalled the death of Franklin Delano Roosevelt on April 12, 1945. NBC's Frank McGee rightly predicted, "that this afternoon, wherever you were and whatever you might have been doing when you received the word of the death of President Kennedy, that *is* a moment that will be emblazoned in your memory and you will never forget it...as long as you live."

At 5:59 P.M. on Friday, the president's body was returned to Andrews Air Force Base, where television caught an obscure, dark, and ghostly vessel taxiing in on the runaway. When the casket was lowered from the plane, glimpses of Jacqueline Kennedy appeared on screen, her dress and stockings still visibly blood-stained. With the new first lady, Lady Bird Johnson, by his side, President Johnson made a brief statement before the cameras. "We have suffered a loss that cannot be weighed," he intoned flatly. "I will do my best. That is all I can do. I ask for your help—and God's." Speculations about the funeral arrangements and updates on the accused assassin in Dallas rounded out the evening's coverage. NBC concluded its broadcasting day with a symphonic tribute from the NBC Studio Orchestra.

On Saturday the trauma was eased somewhat by religious ritual and constitutional tradition. Close friends, members of the president's family, government officials, and the diplomatic community arrived to pay their respects at the White House, where the president's body was lying in state. Former presidents Harry Truman and Dwight Eisenhower spoke for the cameras, offering condolences to the Kennedy family and expressions of faith in democratic institutions. Instant documentary tributes to the late president appeared on all three networks: quick, makeshift compilations of home movies of Hyannisport frolics, press conference witticisms, and formal addresses to the nation. Meanwhile, more information dribbled in about Oswald, the accused assassin, whom the Dallas police paraded through the halls of the city jail. That evening CBS presented a memorial concert by the Philadelphia Orchestra with Eugene Normandy conducting.

On Sunday an unprecedented televised event blasted the story of the assassination of John F. Kennedy out of the realm of tragedy and into surrealism: the on-camera murder of Lee Harvey Oswald, telecast live. At 12:21 P.M. Eastern Standard Time, as preparations were being made for the solemn procession of the caisson bearing the president's casket from the White House to the Capitol rotunda, the accused assassin was about to be transferred from the Dallas City Jail to the Dallas County Jail. Alone of the three networks, NBC elected to switch over from coverage of the preparations in Washington, D.C., to the transfer of the prisoner in Dallas. CBS was also receiving a live feed from Dallas in its New York control room but opted to stay with the D.C. feed. Thus, only NBC carried the murder of Lee Harvey Oswald live. "He's been shot! He's been shot! Lee Oswald has been shot!" shouted NBC correspondent Tom Petit. "There is absolute panic. Pandemonium has broken out." Within minutes, CBS broadcast its own live feed from Dallas. For the rest of the day, all three networks deployed their Ampex videotape technology to rewind and replay the scene again and again. Almost every American in proximity to a television watched transfixed.

Amid the scuffle after the shooting, a journalist's voice could be heard gasping, "This is unbelievable." The next day *New York Times* television critic Jack Gould called the on-air shooting of Oswald "easily the most extraordinary moments of TV that a set-owner ever watched." In truth, as much as the Kennedy assassination itself, the on-air murder of the president's alleged assassin created an almost vertiginous imbalance in television viewers, a sense of American life out of control and let loose from traditional moorings.

Later that same afternoon, in stark counterpoint to the ongoing chaos in Dallas, thousands of mourners lined up to file past the president's flag-draped coffin in the Capitol rotunda. Senator Mike Mansfield intoned a mournful, poetic eulogy. Holding daughter Caroline's hand, the president's widow knelt by the casket and kissed the flag, the little girl looking up to her mother for guidance. "For many," recalled broadcasting historian Erik Barnouw, "it was the most unbearable moment in four days, the most unforgettable."

Throughout Sunday, tributes to the late president and scenes of mourners at the Capitol intertwined with news of the assassin and the assassin of the assassin, a Dallas strip-club owner named Jack Ruby. Remote coverage of church services around the nation and solemn musical interludes were intercut and dissolved into the endless stream of mourners in Washington. That evening, at 8:00 P.M. Eastern Standard Time, ABC telecast *A Tribute to John F. Kennedy from the Arts,* a somber variety show featuring classical music and dramatic readings from the Bible and Shakespeare. Host Fredric March recited the Gettysburg Address, Charlton Heston read from the *Psalms* and the poetry of Robert Frost, and Marian Anderson sang Negro spirituals.

The next day—Monday, November 25, a national day of mourning—bore witness to an extraordinary political-religious spectacle: the ceremonial transfer of the president's coffin by caisson from the Capitol rotunda to St. Matthew's Cathedral, where the funeral mass was to be celebrated by Richard Cardinal Cushing, and on across the Potomac River for burial at Arlington National Cemetery. Television coverage began at 7:00 A.M. Eastern Standard Time, with scenes from Washington, where all evening mourners had been filing past the coffin in the Capitol rotunda. At 10:38 A.M., the coffin was placed on the caisson for the procession to St. Matthew's Cathedral. Television imprinted a series of memorable snapshot images. During the mass, as the phrase from the president's first inaugural address came through loudspeakers ("Ask not what your country can do for you. Ask what you can

do for your country"), cameras dissolved to a shot of the flag-draped coffin. No sooner did commentators remind viewers that this day marked the president's son's third birthday, than outside the church, as the caisson passed by, little John F. Kennedy Jr. saluted. The spirited stallion Black Jack, a riderless steed with boots pointed backward in the stirrup, kicked up defiantly. Awed by the regal solemnity, network commentators were quiet and restrained, allowing the medium of the moving image to record a series of eloquent sounds: drums and bagpipes, hoofbeats, the cadenced steps of the honor guard, and, at the burial at Arlington, the final sour note of a bugle playing "Taps."

The quiet power of the spectacle was a masterpiece of televisual choreography. Besides maintaining their own cameras and crews, each of the networks contributed cameras for pool coverage. CBS's Arthur Kane was assigned the task of directing the coverage of the procession and funeral, coordinating more than 60 cameras stationed strategically along the route. NBC took charge of feeding the signal via relay communications satellite to 23 countries around the globe. Even the Soviet Union, in a broadcasting first, used a five-minute news report sent via Telestar. CBS estimated 50 engineers worked on the project and NBC 60, while ABC put its total staff at 138. Unlike the fast-breaking news from Dallas on Friday and Sunday, the coverage of a stationary, scheduled event built on the acquired expertise of network journalism.

The colossal achievement came with a hefty price tag. Trade figures estimated the total cost to the networks at $40 million, with some $22 million lost in programming and commercial revenue over the four days. Ironically, on one of the few occasions when none of the networks cared about ratings, the television audience was massive. Though multicity Nielsen ratings for prime-time hours during the Black Weekend were calculated modestly (NBC at 24, CBS at 16, and ABC at 10), during intervals of peak viewership—as when the news of Oswald's murder struck—Nielsen estimated that fully 93 percent of televisions in the nation were tuned to the coverage. As if hypnotized, many Americans watched for hours at a stretch, in an unprecedented immersion in deep-involvement spectatorship.

Not incidentally, the Zapruder film, the famous super 8mm record of the assassination shot by Abraham Zapruder, was not a part of the original televisual experience. Despite the best efforts of CBS's Dan Rather, exclusive rights to the most historically significant piece of amateur filmmaking in the 20th century were obtained by *Life* magazine. The Zapruder film was not shown on television until March 1975, when it aired on ABC's *Goodnight America.* Almost certainly, however, in 1963 it would have been deemed too gruesome and disrespectful of the feelings of the Kennedy family to have been broadcast on network television.

The saturation coverage of the assassination and burial of John F. Kennedy, and the startling murder of his alleged assassin Lee Harvey Oswald on live television, yielded a shared media experience of astonishing unanimity and unmatched impact, an imbedded cultural memory that as years passed seemed to comprise a collective consciousness for a generation. In time, it would seem appropriate that the telegenic president was memorialized by the medium that helped make him. For its part, television—so long sneered at as a "boob tube" presided over by avaricious lords of kitsch—emerged from its four days in November as the only American institution accorded unconditional praise. *Variety*'s George Rosen spoke the consensus: "In a totally unforeseen and awesome crisis, TV immediately, almost automatically, was transformed into a participating organ of American life whose value, whose indispensability, no Nielsen audimeters could

measure or statistics reveal." The medium Kennedy's Federal Communications Commission commissioner Newton Minow condemned as a "vast wasteland" had served, in extremis, as a national lifeline.

THOMAS DOHERTY

See also **Media Events**

Further Reading

Baker, Dean C., *The Assassination of President Kennedy; A Study of the Press Coverage,* Ann Arbor: University of Michigan Department of Journalism, 1965

Berry, Joseph P., *John F. Kennedy and the Media: The First Television President,* Lanham, Maryland: University Press of America, 1987

Dayan, Daniel, and Elihu Katz, *Media Events: The Live Broadcasting of History,* Cambridge, Massachusetts: Harvard University Press, 1992

McCartney, James, "Rallying Around the Flag," *American Journalism Review* (September 1994)

Watson, Mary Ann, "How Kennedy Invented Political Television," *Television Quarterly* (Spring 1991)

Kennedy, Robert F.: Assassination

Shortly after midnight on June 5, 1968, Senator Robert F. Kennedy (D-New York) was assassinated by Sirhan B. Sirhan in the ballroom of the Ambassador Hotel in Los Angeles, California. All three television networks (ABC, CBS, and NBC) began coverage at the scene just minutes after the shooting. The first broadcast included footage of a large crowd of supporters gathered in the ballroom, awaiting Kennedy's address following his California presidential primary victory. Muffled sounds emerged from the direction of the podium, the crowd became disorderly, and although the reason for the disruption was still unclear, Steven Smith, Kennedy's brother-in-law, asked everyone to clear the room. A still photograph of Kennedy sprawled on the floor was televised as reporters noted in voice-over that he had been shot by an unknown assailant. About two hours after the shooting, supplemental footage was shown of Kennedy from behind as he stepped up to the podium, with a crowd around him. Shots were heard, camera angles were jolted in the confusion, but one camera managed to focus on the senator lying injured on the floor.

Intermittent reports provided updates of Kennedy's medical condition. Reporters at the scene first noted

his condition by sight only, stating that he had been shot repeatedly but was conscious and had "good color." A physician at the scene remarked that the extent of his injuries was unknown. Later reports were provided by Kennedy's press secretary, Frank Mankiewicz, who stood on a car outside Good Samaritan Hospital to relay more technical information supplied by surgeons. At last he announced Kennedy's death some 26 hours after the shooting.

The whereabouts, identity, and motives of the assassin were vague in early accounts. Two hours after the shooting, reporters noted that a "young man had been caught" but were uncertain whether he was still in the hotel or had been taken into police custody. Described as "dark-skinned" and "curly-haired," and variously as Filipino, Mexican, Jamaican, or Cuban, Palestinian Sirhan B. Sirhan was identified nearly ten hours later by his brother Adel after a still photograph of him was shown on television. Although he made no statements to police, eyewitnesses claimed that at the time of the shooting Sirhan said, "I did it for my country." In response to the crowd's angry chant of "kill him, lynch him," anchorman Walter Cronkite reiterated that Sirhan was "presumed innocent until proven guilty."

CBS Reports Inquiry: "The American Assassins, Robert F. Kennedy," 1975.
Courtesy of the Everett Collection

Questions concerning Sirhan's motives and whether he was part of a conspiracy are mired in controversy to this day.

A description of the weapon was similarly indeterminate. In the earliest reports, a policeman stated that celebrity Roosevelt "Rosie" Grier had first grabbed the weapon but that he currently had no idea where or what type the weapon was. Within one hour of the shooting, controversy had begun to emerge in terms of conspiracy: some eyewitnesses reported that the assassin had used a six-shot revolver; others said that more than six shots had been fired. One reporter suggested that there might have been more than one gun, and more than one gunman. Two hours later, however, the weapon was identified as an Iver Johnson .22-caliber pistol, a weapon capable of eight shots. Los Angeles Police Chief Thomas Reddin stated several hours after this that the pistol had been traced to a missing gun report, though the gunman himself had not yet been identified. He was uncertain at this point whether the man in custody was actually the assailant. Special reports on the pistol's history of ownership began to air nine hours after the shooting; 18 hours after the shooting, detailed special reports related the histories of the pistol and the assassin, who by this time had been identified as Sirhan.

The issue of violence played a crucial role in many of the shooting reports. One reporter noted that the United States would, with its rash of assassinations in the 1960s, appear to outsiders to be "some sort of violent society." The Reverend Ralph Abernathy, speaker for the Southern Christian Leadership Conference, aimed his criticism more pointedly in the direction of President Lyndon Johnson and the Vietnam War by saying that Kennedy had worked against "the violence, the hatred, and the war mentality" that had been "poisoning" the United States. Kennedy's opponent in the Democratic primary, Senator Eugene McCarthy, echoed this sentiment in his condemnation of violence at home and abroad. Some 12 hours after the shooting, Johnson responded to criticism in a special address in which he denounced violence "in the hearts of men everywhere" and suggested the establishment of a commission to investigate the causes of violence in society. The commission would be jointly directed by the president and Congress and would be composed of academic, political, and religious leaders.

More immediate measures were also proposed to deal with the security of political candidates. Following an early report that police had planned no special security for Kennedy, President Johnson declared that full Secret Service protection would be provided for all leading announced candidates for national positions, rather than for the position-holders alone. In the meantime, reporters announced that Senator McCarthy, New York Governor Nelson Rockefeller, and Republican candidate Richard Nixon had called off all appearances.

Others at the Ambassador Hotel rally were also injured. Shortly after the shooting, it was reported that Jesse Unruh, Kennedy's campaign manager, had been hit, along with Paul Shrade, head of the United Automobile Workers union. Four hours later, added to the list were William Weisel, an ABC unit manager; Ira Goldstein, a California news service reporter; Elizabeth Evans, a political supporter; and Irwin Stroll, a teenage bystander.

Coverage of the shooting and its aftermath continued to be broadcast until the early evening of June 5, when networks began switching back to programs "already in progress." ABC opted not to broadcast a professional baseball game and instead had a special report on "The Shooting of RFK." Other networks informed viewers that regular programming would be interrupted occasionally to provide updated reports of Kennedy's condition. Early on the morning of June 6, a news conference was held to announce Kennedy's death. His funeral was televised on June 7, and highlights were televised on June 8.

KEVIN A. CLARK

Further Reading

Jansen, Godfrey, *Why Robert Kennedy Was Killed: The Story of Two Victims,* New York: Third Press, 1970

Melanson, Philip H., *Who Killed Robert Kennedy?* Berkeley, California: Odonian, 1993

Turner, William V., and John G. Christian, *The Assassination of Robert F. Kennedy: A Searching Look at the Conspiracy and Cover-up 1968–1978,* New York: Random House, 1978

Kennedy Martin, Troy (1932–)

British Writer

Troy Kennedy Martin began his career as a television screenwriter in 1958 and quickly emerged as a leading member of a group of writers, directors, and producers at the BBC who were pushing the limits of British television drama. In addition to writing episodes of crime series, literary adaptations, and original miniseries, Kennedy Martin became an outspoken proponent of a new approach to television drama that would exploit what he saw as the properties of the medium.

He first received widespread acclaim for his approach with the BBC police series *Z Cars,* which proved enormously popular and ran from 1962 to 1978. The series was acclaimed for the fast pace and gritty realism with which it depicted a Lancashire police force coping with the problems of a modern housing estate. Its view of the police offered a sharp contrast to the homespun philosophy of PC Dixon in the BBC's *Dixon of Dock Green,* which had been extremely popular with family audiences since its debut in 1955. Kennedy Martin wrote the first eight episodes of the first season of *Z Cars,* plus the final episode in 1978.

In 1964 he published an article in the theater magazine *Encore* in which he argued forcefully for a "new television drama." Through its attack on "naturalism," this article set the terms for a lively, if sometimes confusing, debate on realism in television drama that persists into the present. Kennedy Martin advocated using the camera to do more than just show talking heads, by freeing the dramatic structure from the limits of real time and creating more complex relations between sound and image. In particular, he wanted to exploit what he called "the total objectivity of the television camera," which gave the medium a built-in Brechtian critical dimension that worked against subjective identification with characters.

From Kennedy Martin's point of view, the value of *Z Cars* lay in its respect for reality: its refusal to idealize the police and its attempt to reveal the underlying social causes that led to crime. Yet, because the style remained "naturalistic," Kennedy Martin felt that it was soon compromised by the generic and institutional constraints that encourage identification with the police and the demonization of the criminal.

Despite his disappointment with *Z Cars,* Kennedy Martin continued to write within popular crime and ac-

tion genres, notably for Thames Television's police series *The Sweeney* (1975–78), for which he wrote six episodes. He also wrote screenplays for several action films, with the same sense of frustration that his critical intentions were subverted in the production process. *The Italian Job* (1969), directed by Peter Collinson, was Kennedy Martin's most successful film screenplay.

Some of the formal innovations that Kennedy Martin called for in his manifesto were incorporated into *Diary of a Young Man,* a six-part serial broadcast by the BBC in 1964, written by Kennedy Martin and John McGrath and directed by Ken Loach. Other writers, notably David Mercer and Dennis Potter, also explored the possibilities of a non-naturalistic television drama. Yet it was not until the 1980s that Kennedy Martin was able to produce work that fulfilled both his critical and formalist goals. First came a fairly free adaptation of Angus Wilson's *The Old Men at the Zoo* as a five-part serial, broadcast by the BBC in 1983, a powerful and disturbing science fiction parable about a political order whose logic leads to the destruction of Britain in a nuclear war.

Fears of nuclear power and government bureaucracy also drove Kennedy Martin's major achievement, *Edge of Darkness,* a political thriller broadcast in six parts on BBC 2 in late 1985 and promptly repeated in three parts on consecutive nights on BBC 1. This serial combined the "naturalistic" tradition of British television drama on social issues with a popular thriller format and elements of fantasy and myth. A police inspector, investigating the murder of his daughter, discovers that she belonged to an anti-nuclear organization that had uncovered an illegal nuclear experiment backed by the government. The break with naturalism occurs when the murdered woman simply appears beside her father and starts a conversation with him, linking his investigation to the fusion of myth and science in the ecological movement to which she had belonged.

The popularity of political thrillers on British television after 1985 confirmed the significance of *Edge of Darkness* as a key work of the decade. Although Kennedy Martin advocated the development of short dramatic forms, not unlike the music videos that emerged in the 1980s, he has made a major contribution to British television drama in the developments of the long forms of series and serials.

JIM LEACH

Troy Kennedy Martin. Born 1932. Creator of long-running TV police series *Z Cars,* though only remained with it for three months, and of *The Sweeney,* among other series; has also worked in Hollywood. British Academy of Film and Television Arts Award, 1983.

Television Series

1962–65	*Z Cars*
1964	*Diary of a Young Man* (with John McGrath)
1975–78	*The Sweeney*
1983	*Reilly—Ace of Spies*
1983	*The Old Men at the Zoo*
1985	*Edge of Darkness*

Made-for-Television Movie

1997	*Hostile Waters*

Films

The Italian Job, 1969; *Kelly's Heroes,* 1970; *The Jerusalem File,* 1972; *Sweeney II,* 1978; *Red Heat,* 1988; *Bravo Two Zero,* 1999; *The Italian Job,* 2003 (remake); *Red Dust,* 2004.

Publications

"Nats Go Home: First Statement of a New Television Drama," *Encore* (March–April 1964)
Edge of Darkness, 1990

Further Reading

Caughie, John, "Before the Golden Age: Early Television Drama," in *Popular Television in Britain: Studies in Cultural History,* edited by John Corner, London: British Film Institute, 1991
Cooke, Lez, "Edge of Darkness," *Movie* (winter 1989)
Cooke, Lez, "An Interview with Troy Kennedy Martin," *Movie* (winter 1989)
Laing, Stuart, "Banging in Some Reality: The Original *Z Cars*," in *Popular Television in Britain: Studies in Cultural History,* edited by John Corner, London: British Film Institute, 1991
Lavender, Andrew, "Edge of Darkness," in *British Television Drama in the 1980s,* edited by George W. Brandt, Cambridge: Cambridge University Press, 1993
McGrath, John, "Better a Bad Night in Bootle," *Theatre Quarterly* (1975)
McGrath, John, "TV Drama: The Case Against Naturalism," *Sight and Sound* (Spring 1977)
Petley, Julian, "A Very British Coup," *Sight and Sound* (spring 1988)
Tulloch, John, *Television Drama: Agency, Audience, Myth,* London: Routledge, 1990

Kennedy-Nixon Presidential Debates, 1960

On September 26, 1960, 70 million U.S. viewers tuned in to watch Senator John Kennedy of New York and Vice President Richard Nixon in the first-ever televised presidential debate. It was the first of four televised "Great Debates" between Kennedy and Nixon. The first debate centered on domestic issues. The high point of the second debate, on October 7, was disagreement over U.S. involvement in two small islands off the coast of China, and on October 13, Nixon and Kennedy continued this dispute. On October 21, the final debate, the candidates focused on U.S. relations with Cuba.

The Great Debates marked television's grand entrance into presidential politics. They afforded the first real opportunity for voters to see their candidates in competition, and the visual contrast between Kennedy and Nixon was dramatic. In August, Nixon had seriously injured his knee and spent two weeks in the hospital. By the time of the first debate, he was still 20 pounds underweight, his complexion still pale. He arrived at the debate in an ill-fitting shirt and refused makeup to improve his color and lighten his perpetual "five o'clock shadow." Kennedy, by contrast, had spent early September campaigning in California. He was tan and confident and well rested. "I had never seen him looking so fit," Nixon later wrote.

In substance, the candidates were much more evenly matched. Indeed, those who heard the first debate on the radio pronounced Nixon the winner. But the 70 million who watched television saw a candidate still sickly and obviously discomforted by Kennedy's smooth delivery and charisma. Those television viewers focused on what they saw, not what they heard. Studies of the audience indicated that, among television viewers, Kennedy was perceived the winner of the first debate by a very large margin.

The televised Great Debates had a notable impact on voters in 1960, on national elections since, and, indeed, on our concerns for democracy itself. The debates' effect on the election of 1960 was significant, albeit subtle. Commentators broadly agree that the first debate accelerated Democratic support for Kennedy. In hindsight, however, it seems the debates were not, as once thought, the turning point in the election. Rather than encouraging viewers to change their vote, the debates appear to have simply solidified prior allegiances. In short, many would argue that Kennedy would have won the election with or without the Great Debates.

Yet voters in 1960 did vote with the Great Debates in mind. At election time, over half of all voters reported that the Great Debates had influenced their opinion; 6 percent reported that their vote was the result of the debates alone. Thus, regardless of whether the debates changed the election result, voters pointed to the debates as a significant reason for electing Kennedy.

The Great Debates had consequences beyond the election of 1960, as well. They served as precedent around the world: Soon after the debates, Germany, Sweden, Finland, Italy, and Japan established debates between contenders for national office. Moreover, the Great Debates created a precedent in U.S. presidential politics. Federal laws requiring that all candidates receive equal air time stymied debates for the next three elections, as did Nixon's refusal to debate in 1968 and 1972. Yet by 1976, the law and the candidates had both changed, and ever since, presidential debates, in one form or another, have been a fixture of U.S. presidential races.

Perhaps most important, the Great Debates forced citizens to rethink how democracy would work in a television era. To what extent does television change debate, indeed, change campaigning altogether? What is the difference between a debate that "just happens" to be broadcast and one specifically crafted for television? What is lost in the latter? Do televised debates really help us to evaluate the relative competencies of the candidates, to assess policy options, to increase voter participation and intellectual engagement, to strengthen national unity? For some observers, such events lead to worries that television emphasizes the visual, when visual attributes seem neither the best nor most reliable indicators of a great leader. However, other analysts express confidence that televised presidential debates remain one of the most effective means to operate a direct democracy. The issue then becomes one of improved form rather than changed forum. The Nixon-Kennedy debates of 1960 brought these questions to the floor, forcing us to ponder the role of television in democratic life.

ERIKA TYNER ALLEN

See also **Political Processes and Television; U.S. Presidency and Television**

Further Reading

Hellweg, Susan A., Michael Pfau, and Steven R. Brydon, *Televised Presidential Debates: Advocacy in Contemporary America,* New York: Praeger, 1992

Jamieson, Kathleen Hall, and David S. Birdsell, *Presidential Debates: The Challenge of Creating an Informed Electorate,* New York: Oxford University Press, 1988

Kraus, Sidney, *The Great Debates: Background, Perspective, Effects,* Bloomington: Indiana University Press, 1962

Kraus, Sidney, *Televised Presidential Debates and Public Policy,* Hillsdale, New Jersey: Erlbaum, 1988; 2nd edition, Mahwah, N.J.: Lawrence Erlbaum Associates, 2000

Minow, Newton N., and Clifford M. Sloan, *For Great Debates: A New Plan for Future Presidential Debates,* New York: Priority Press, 1987

Kenya

Kenyan television is a classic example of an industry whose good chances for development have been consistently frustrated by government sensitivity and political interference. The medium's history in Kenya is marked by stunted growth due to excessive government regulation and extensive abuse by the dominant political forces.

In 1959 the Kenya Broadcasting Corporation (KBC) was established by the British colonial administration, with the objective of providing radio and television broadcasting. The proposal for the formation of a public corporation had been submitted by a commission appointed earlier in the year to report on the advantages and disadvantages of a television service for

Kenya, and the impact of such a service on radio broadcasting. The 1959 Proud Commission rejected earlier findings by another commission in 1954 that television was "economically impracticable in Kenya" and concluded that the new medium was likely to be financially self-reliant if it were set up as a full-fledged commercial outfit.

Between 1959 and 1961, and in keeping with the Proud Commission's recommendations, the colonial administration contracted a consortium of eight companies to build and operate a television service. The eight firms, seven of which were from Europe and North America, formed Television Network Ltd., which was charged with the responsibility of setting up the national television broadcasting system. The consortium, cognizant of the irreversible developments toward Kenya's political independence, created the Kenya Broadcasting Corporation as an autonomous public organization. The idea was to have the corporation wield as much independence as the British Broadcasting Corporation (BBC). By the end of 1962, a transmission station and recording studio had been set up in Kenya, and television was officially launched the following year.

The corporation created by the consortium bore a striking resemblance to the BBC. It drew its revenue from advertising, annual license fees on receiver sets, and government subventions. The vision of financially self-sustaining television service was, however, misplaced, especially since the new medium failed to attract as much advertising as the older and more popular radio broadcasting service. Within the first full financial year of television broadcasting (July 1963 to June 1964), the corporation posted a loss of nearly $1 million and had to resort to government loans and supplementary appropriations to remain afloat. Coincidentally, Kenya had gained independence, and the new government, worried about the threat to national sovereignty posed by the foreign ownership of the broadcasting apparatus, decided to nationalize the corporation in June 1964. After the takeover, the corporation was renamed Voice of Kenya (VoK) and was converted to a department under the Ministry of Information, Broadcasting, and Tourism (later renamed Ministry of Information and Broadcasting). VoK's new role, as the government mouthpiece, was to provide information, education, and entertainment. While the government adopted a capitalist approach to economic development, which embraced private-sector participation in all areas of the economy and even welcomed participation in a number of electronic broadcasting activities, private ownership of broadcasting concerns was disallowed.

Between 1964 and 1990, television and radio were owned and controlled by the state, and the two media exercised great caution in reporting politically sensitive news. During this period, several attempts were made to move away from the established broadcasting system. The Ministry of Information and Broadcasting replaced annual license fees with a one-time permit fee, and the drive for commercial self-sustenance was replaced by a politically inspired initiative for increased local content and a sharper nationalistic outlook. The objective was elusive, however, as the VoK television was only able to achieve a 40 percent local-programming content by the mid-1980s, well below the target of 70 percent local content. Television also failed to become an authoritative national medium: studies in 1985 showed that only 17 percent of the electronic media audience regarded television as the best source of information, compared to 86 percent who rated radio as their prime news source.

Several reasons have been advanced for poor performance of television in Kenya. Besides being a preserve of the educated minority in the country, the spread of ownership of television sets has been severely curtailed by the poor penetration of the national electrical power grid. Even worse is the poor transmission the country received from the 55 small transmission and booster stations, whose weak signals generally cover small areas or are constrained by the country's rugged topography. As such, household audiences have been growing mainly within the major urban areas, or near large rural centers served by electricity and near a booster station.

In 1989 the VoK was renamed Kenya Broadcasting Corporation and accorded semi-autonomous status founded on the premise that it would adopt a more commercially oriented stance. Although the corporation unveiled grandiose plans to expand news coverage and improve local programming content, it was unable to chart out an independent editorial position, and it is still widely seen as a part of the government propaganda machinery. However, some progress has been made in increased weekly on-air periods, and enhancement of color transmission. Until the early 1990s, the corporation relied on cheap but time-consuming air-mail services for the supply of foreign news footage, even though the country was serviced by Intelsat. Since 1994, the corporation has been retransmitting large chunks of the BBC World Service Television several nights per week. A second KBC channel launched in 1995 is a joint venture between the KBC and MultiChoice South Africa; this channel mainly transmits movies and international sports.

Liberalization has been slow and inconsistent. In March 1990, a second television station, the Kenya Television Network (KTN), commenced operations, offering a mixture of relayed retransmission of CNN programming and light entertainment. KTN was initiated as a joint venture between Kenya's ruling party, Kanu, and the London-based Maxwell Communications, but the British media group withdrew after the death of its founder, Robert Maxwell. Baraza Ltd.—owners of the *East African Standard* and Capital FM radio station—acquired KTN in the late 1990s. Even though it is privately owned, KTN has been unable to provide independent news coverage because of excessive political interference with its editorial direction, a problem that forced its management to scrap the transmission of local news for more than a year, between 1993 and 1994. About 95 percent of the station's programs are foreign, mainly because most of its 24-hour service is a retransmission of the CNN signal.

A second private station, Cable Television Network (CTN), launched in March 1994, has also failed to inspire major changes in Kenya's television industry. CTN unsuccessfully tried to build a subscriber base in Nairobi via overhead cables passed along existing electrical power pylons. Its intermittent transmissions have so far comprised Indian drama and films. A third private station, Stellavision TV, was licensed in the early 1990s and went on air in 1999 with primarily foreign films and entertainment.

The enactment of the Kenya Communications Act in 1998 signaled the beginning of deregulation of the airwaves in earnest. The law created the Communications Commission of Kenya (CCK) as an independent regulatory authority for broadcasting, telecommunications, and postal services. CCK is responsible for licensing, broadcast-frequency allocations, ownership and control regulation, and enforcement of fair practices. The act also provides for the transformation of KBC into a national public service broadcaster in both radio and television.

The latest entrants into the television market are Citizen TV and Nation TV. Citizen TV, owned by Royal Media, was licensed in 1997 and began transmission in 1999. Problems with government saw its license temporarily withdrawn in 2001. African Broadcasting Ltd., a subsidiary of the Nation Media Group, owns Nation TV. The station was licensed in 1998 and went on air in December 1999. Five other TV licenses have been given out since 1999, two of which are for religious broadcasting. As of 2002, these channels had not yet gone on air. The licensing of private stations, however, says little about Kenya's commitment to liberalizing the airwaves. The government has previously refused to license operators on the grounds that broadcasting frequencies are inadequate, and for fear of losing control over the information-dissemination process.

Owing to the centralized nature of Kenyan television, only a handful of small production houses have been set up in the country. Most local productions are from the KBC teams and the government camera crew located in provincial headquarters. Virtually all programs are in either English or Swahili; English is the programming language used during two-thirds of all airtime. Most of the small production houses concentrate on commercials and documentary filming. Lately, however, a few production houses have been formed that target programming opportunities as the region liberalizes its airwaves.

NIXON KARIITHI

Further Reading

Bourgault, Louise Mahon, *Mass Media in Sub-Saharan Africa,* Bloomington: Indiana University Press, 1995

Lukalo, Rose, and Lynne Wanyeki, *Up in the Air: The State of Broadcasting in Eastern Africa,* Kampala, Uganda: Panos Eastern Africa, 1997

Mwaura, Peter, *Communication Policies in Kenya,* Paris: UNESCO, 1980

Mytton, Graham, *Mass Communication in Africa,* London: Edward Arnold, 1983

Wilcox, Dennis L., *Mass Media in Black Africa: Philosophy and Control,* New York: Praeger, 1975

Kids in the Hall

Canadian Sketch Comedy Program

Kids in the Hall (KITH) was a sketch comedy program produced by Lorne Michaels's Broadway Video and cofinanced by the Canadian Broadcasting Corporation (CBC) and the U.S. cable network, Home Box Office (HBO). KITH aired in Canada on the CBC and in the United States on HBO, CBS, and another cable network, Comedy Central. The members of the KITH performance group are Dave Foley, Bruce McCulloch, Kevin McDonald, Mark McKinney, and Scott Thompson. The name derives from U.S. comedian Jack Benny's habit of attributing some of his material to aspiring comedians whom he called "the kids in the hall."

KITH was formed in 1984 when McCulloch and McKinney, who had worked together in Calgary as part of a group named the Audience, teamed up with Foley and McDonald's Toronto-based group, KITH. Thompson officially joined in January 1985. That same year, McCulloch and McKinney were hired as writers for NBC's *Saturday Night Live* (SNL) after a talent scout saw KITH in performance. Significantly, SNL had also been created by Michaels, himself an expatriate Canadian living and producing in New York. Also in 1985, Foley appeared in the film *High Stakes,* and Thompson and McDonald toured with Second City. In 1986 KITH were reunited in Toronto and Michaels finally saw them perform. He immediately envisaged a television project around them. In 1987, he moved KITH to New York and, paying each member $150 per week, had them perform in comedy clubs, write new material, and rehearse sketches. In 1988, Michaels produced their HBO special. The regular series followed.

KITH immediately attracted a cult following and broke new ground by combining shock humor with a finely developed sense of performance and a generosity of spirit, which invited audiences to question their presuppositions rather than simply to mock the targets of the humor. Characteristic of KITH's style are well-rounded personifications of both men and women, homosexuals, business executives, prostitutes, and drug users, and such creations as the half-human/half-fowl Chicken Lady, gay barfly Buddy Cole, the angry "head crusher," the annoying child Gavin, and the teenager drawn to older women. These personifications consis-

tently draw upon the inner resources of the characters themselves, showing their encounters with society rather than society's judgment upon them.

KITH also occupies an interesting place within Canadian television. First, although a Canadian show filmed in Toronto, it was produced by a New York–based company best known for turning comedians such as Steve Martin and John Belushi into major stars. KITH could therefore serve as Canadian content while gaining access to the much larger and more lucrative U.S. market. Second, although a CBC program, KITH attracted a youthful cult audience unfamiliar to the CBC and inconsistent with its core demographic. Third, KITH cracked the U.S. market by targeting an audience understood not in terms of its membership in a Canadian national cultural community but a North American audience understood in terms of its relative youth and sophistication with comedy. Fourth, the success of KITH coincided with the moment when the

Kids in the Hall.
Photo courtesy of CBC Television

Kids in the Hall

CBC attempted to change its corporate culture by adopting some of the practices of other North American networks and embracing urbanity unreservedly.

However, KITH also extended certain existing aspects of Canadian television. KITH adopted the sketch rather than the situation comedy format. Canadian broadcasting has attempted situation comedy only sparingly and unevenly, whereas its sketch comedy record reaches back at least to the 1940s with radio's *The Happy Gang.* On television, sketch comedy appeared in the early 1950s with Wayne and Shuster and has come to include *Nightcap, SCTV, The Frantics, S and M Comic Book, Codco, The Vacant Lot, Three Dead Trolls in a Baggie, This Hour Has 22 Minutes,* and others.

Within the North American context, KITH also exemplified the relative openness of Canadian broadcasting. For example, many of KITH's themes and situations were initially deemed inappropriate for U.S. network TV and it therefore debuted on HBO. When CBS did pick it up, KITH underwent certain deletions. Canadian television, however, because of the traditional preponderance of public broadcasting, is more experimental and less censorious, and has long been open to a much broader range of social, political, and cultural attitudes than would be possible on U.S. television. This created a space for KITH's shock humor and extended the CBC's commitment to more challenging material.

KITH repeated the tradition of exporting Canadian comedy to U.S. television through such notables as Lorne Michaels himself, Dan Aykroyd, Dave Thomas, Martin Short, Jim Carrey, John Candy, Catherine O'Hara, Rick Moranis, Mike Meyers, and others.

KITH was terminated by the principals themselves, who have pursued careers in the entertainment industry that highlight their skills as actors and writers, mainly in situation comedies and films. In 1996, KITH starred in the film *Brain Candy,* a comedy about a pharmaceutical company's attempt to market a new drug. In 2000, KITH undertook a North American reunion tour. In 2001, the live tour documentary *Kids in the Hall: Same Guys, New Dresses* was released. KITH enjoys a devoted fan following and has spawned websites, merchandise, and fanzines.

PAUL ATTALLAH

Performers
David Foley
Scott Thompson
Kevin McDonald
Bruce McCulloch
Mark McKinney

Producer
Lorne Michaels

Programming History
CBC
1989–95   Thursday 9:30
HBO, CBS, Comedy Central,
  Sky Channel (Europe)   various times

Further Reading

Barol, Bill, "Oh, Those Darn Kids—Black Humor from the Great White North," *Newsweek* (October 2, 1989)

Barrett, Tom, "5 Angry Kids: Scott Thompson Decries Hypocrisy of CBS Ban on Troupe's AIDS Humor," *Vancouver Sun* (February 1, 1993)

Berton, Pierre, and Sid Adilman, "A Serious Look at Canadian Comedy," *Toronto Star* (January 15, 1994)

Haslett Cuff, John, "Farewell to Those Versatile and Fearless Kids," *Globe and Mail* (January 16, 1995)

Haslett Cuff, John, "Has Too Much Freedom Spoiled the Kids?" *Globe and Mail* (October 31, 1991)

Kids of Degrassi Street, The. *See* Degrassi

Kinescope

The first and most primitive method of recording a television program, production, or news story, a kinescope is a film made of a live television broadcast. Kinescopes are usually created by placing a motion picture camera in front of a television monitor and recording the image off the monitor's screen while the program is being aired. This recording method came into wide use around 1947. Before videotape, this process was the standard industry method of creating a permanent document, for rebroadcast and for archival purposes. The term "kinescope" comes from the combination of two words: the Greek "kinetic," meaning of or related to motion, and "scope," as in an observational instrument such as a microscope.

Actually, kinescope is the name for the cathode-ray tube in a television receiver that translates electrical signals into a picture on a lighted screen. The use of the word "kinescope" to describe a filmed recording of a television broadcast was derived from this piece of equipment. Originally, such recordings were called "kinescope recordings," but, due to repeated usage in spoken language, the term was usually shortened to just "kinescope," and then often shortened again to just "kine" or "kinnie." The picture quality created by kinescopes was admittedly and understandably poor—they appeared grainy, fuzzy, even distorted—yet they were the only method for documentation available to stations and producers at that time. Although the poor picture quality of kinescopes generally prohibited any extensive reuse, many programs were rebroadcast from kinescope in order to save money, to allow broadcast at a different time or, more frequently, to expose the programs to a wider audience. Cities and locales outside of an antenna's reach and without wire or cable connection had no way of seeing programming produced in and broadcast from New York City, programming that constituted the majority of television at the time. In order for a program to be seen in outlying areas (either beyond the city limits or elsewhere across the country), kinescope films were shipped from station to station in a practice known as "bicycling."

For many stations, the airing of kinescopes (despite the very poor picture quality) was a necessary way to fill the programming day. This was especially true in the early days of educational television, which had high goals but little money with which to achieve them. Although kinescope programs could never be very timely, they could be educational and, in this case, they were the best way to fill a void. The National Educational Television and Radio Center (later NET) in Ann Arbor, Michigan, was the country's largest clearinghouse for kinescope distribution until the late 1950s.

Because kinescopes were considered so unsatisfactory, many companies attempted to find more efficient, less costly, and more aesthetically pleasing methods of recording programs. Seeking a more convenient way of producing his television specials without having to perform them live, singer Bing Crosby had his company, Bing Crosby Enterprises, create and demonstrate the first magnetic videotape recordings in 1951. The RCA and Ampex companies would also display electronic videotape recording methods before the end of the decade, with the Ampex standard eventually adopted by the television industry.

However, the true demise of the kinescope (at least as far as entertainment programming is concerned), like most things in television, was ultimately driven by economic concerns and can be attributed to *I Love Lucy* and its stars and producers, Desi Arnaz and Lucille Ball. When beginning their landmark show, the couple insisted on producing in California, their home of many years. Philip Morris, the cigar and cigarette manufacturer, already signed on as the show's sponsor, wanted the program produced in New York because more potential smokers lived east of the Mississippi, but Philip Morris would not settle for inferior kinescopes playing on the east coast. In response, Arnaz and cinematographer Karl Freund devised a method of recording performances on film. Their system used three cameras to record the live action while a director switched among them to obtain the best shot or angle. The show was later edited into the best performance in a manner much like a feature film. The result not only was a superior recording good for repeated airing throughout the country, it also presaged the move of the TV industry from New York to the west coast, where fully equipped film studios eagerly entered television production and recouped some of the losses they had encountered with the rise of the newer medium. Moreover, the new filmed product created, almost accidentally, TV's most profitable byproduct, the rerun.

The kinescope, the one and perhaps only method of television recording technology to be completely obsolete in the industry today, is now of use only in archives and museums, where the fuzzy, grainy texture often adds to the recordings' charm as artifacts and antiquities. For those who would understand and present the history of television programming, that charm is fortunately matched by the historical value of even this partial record of an era all but lost.

CARY O'DELL

Further Reading

Gross, Lynne Schafer, *Telecommunications: An Introduction to Radio, Television, and the Developing Media,* Dubuque, Iowa: Brown, 1983; 7th edition as *Telecommunications: An Introduction to Electronic Media,* Boston: McGraw-Hill, 2000

King, Larry (1933–)

U.S. Talk Show Host

Larry King, television and radio talk show host, claims to have interviewed more than 30,000 people during his career. In 1989 *The Guinness Book of World Records* credited him as having logged more hours on national radio than any other talk show personality in history.

His nationwide popularity began with his first national radio talk show, premiering over the Mutual Network in 1978. In 1985 the Cable News Network (CNN) scheduled a nightly, one-hour cable-television version of King's radio program. *Larry King Live* has become one of CNN's highest-rated shows and positioned King as the first American talk-show host to have a worldwide audience. Currently, the program reaches more than 200 countries, with a potential audience of 150 million.

Called cable television's preeminent pop-journalist, King is characterized as an interviewer, not a journalist. He is an ad-lib interviewer, who claims not to overprepare for his guest. "My lack of preparation really forces me to learn, and to listen," he says. His guests are given a wide range of latitude while responding to questions that any person on the street might ask. Rather than acting as an investigative reporter, King prides himself in asking "human questions," not "press-conference questions." He sees himself as nonthreatening, nonjudgmental, and concerned with feelings.

King's radio broadcast career began with a 1957 move to Miami, Florida, where he worked for station WAHR as a disc jockey and sports talk show host. He changed his name from the less euphonious Larry Zeiger when the general manager noted that his name was "too German, too Jewish. It's not show-business enough."

After a year, he joined WKAT, a station that gave DJs a great deal of freedom to develop their personalities. King took advantage of the opportunity by inventing a character called "Captain Wainright of the Miami State Police." Sounding like Broderick Crawford, Wainright interrupted traffic reports with crazy suggestions, such as telling listeners to save a trip to the racetrack by flagging down police officers and placing their bets with them. The Wainright character became so popular that bumper stickers appeared bearing the slogan "Don't Stop Me. I Know Capt. Wainright."

In 1958 King's celebrity status led to his first major break as host of an on-location interview program from Miami's Pumpernik Restaurant. He interviewed whoever happened to be there at the time. Never knowing who his guest would be and unable to plan in advance, he began to perfect his interviewing style, listening carefully to what his guest said and then formulating questions as the conversation progressed.

Impressed with King's Pumpernik show, WIOD employed him in 1962 to do a similar radio program originating from a houseboat formerly used for the ABC television series *Surfside Six*. Because of the show's on-the-beach location and because of the publicity it offered the television series, *Surfside Six* became an enormous success. WIOD gave King further exposure as the color commentator for broadcasts of Miami Dolphin football games. While riding a tide of popularity during 1963, he did double duty as a Sunday late-night talk show host over WLBW-TV. In 1964 he left WLBW-TV for a weekend talk show on WTVJ-TV. He added newspaper writing to his agenda with columns for *The Miami Herald, The Miami News,* and *The Miami Beach Sun-Reporter.*

Larry King, circa 2000.
Courtesy of the Everett Collection

Of this period, King said he was "flying high." Unfortunately, his life flew out of control. He ran up outrageous bills and fell $352,000 into debt. Still worse, he was charged with grand larceny and accused of stealing $5,000 from a business partner. On March 10, 1972, the charges were dropped, but the scandal nearly destroyed his career. It would take four years before he worked regularly in broadcasting again. King candidly presented this period of his life to the public in his book, *Larry King.*

From 1972 to 1975, King struggled to get back on his feet. In the spring of 1974, he took a public relations job with a horse racing track in Shreveport, Louisiana. In the fall, he became the color commentator for the short-lived Shreveport Steamers of the World Football League.

In 1975, after returning to Miami, he was rehired by a new general manager at WIOD for an evening interview show similar to his previous program. Over the next several years, he gradually recovered as a TV interviewer, a columnist for *The Miami News,* and a ra-

dio commentator for the Dolphins. Still deep in debt, he claimed bankruptcy in 1978.

In the same year, the Mutual Broadcasting Network persuaded him to do a late-night radio talk show, which debuted on January 30, 1978, in 28 cities as the *Larry King Show.* It was first aired from WIOD, but beginning in April 1978, it originated from Mutual's Arlington, Virginia, studios, which overlook the capital. Originally, the show's time slot was from midnight to 5:30 A.M. and divided into three distinct segments, a guest interview, guest responses to callers, and "Open Phone America." King greeted callers by identifying their location: "Memphis, hello."

In February 1993, King's radio talk show on Mutual (now Westwood One) moved from late night to an afternoon drive time reaching 410 affiliates. By June 1994, Westwood also began simulcasting King's CNN live show, the first ever daily "TV/radio talk show." As part of the agreement, King dropped his syndicated radio show, a move that ended his regular radio broadcasting activities.

Larry King's CNN program received a huge boost in 1992 by attracting the presidential candidates. On February 20, his interview with H. Ross Perot facilitated Perot's nomination. Viewers of *Larry King Live* learned of Perot's candidacy even before his wife did. Because of King's call-in format, Perot was approachable as he responded to questions from viewers. The interview initiated a new trend in campaigning as other candidates followed suit by sidestepping traditional news conferences with trained reporters in favor of live, call-in talk shows. The new boom in "talk show democracy" invited voters back into the political arena formerly reserved for politicians and journalists, and marked a new stage in television's influence on the U.S. political process.

In addition to his work in radio and television as a talk show host, King has made appearances (usually playing himself) in many movies, including *Ghostbusters* (1984), *Primary Colors* (1998), and *America's Sweethearts* (2001), and he has guest-starred (again playing himself) on a number of sitcoms such as *Murphy Brown, The Simpsons, The Larry Sanders Show, Frasier,* and *Spin City.* From the 1980s until November 2001, he published a weekly column for the national newspaper *USA Today.* In 2002 King signed a four-year contract with CNN.

FRANK J. CHORBA

See also **Cable News Network**

Larry King. Born Lawrence Zeiger in Brooklyn, New York, November 19, 1933. Educated at Lafayette High School. Married: 1) Freda Miller, 1952 (annulled); 2) Alene Atkins, 1961 (divorced, 1963); 3) Mickey Sutphin, 1963 (divorced, 1963); 4) Alene Atkins, 1967 (divorced, 1971); child: Chaia; 5) Sharon Lepore, 1976 (divorced, 1982); 6) Julia Alexander, 1989 (divorced, 1992); child: Andy; 7) Shawn Southwick, 1997; children: Chance Southworth and Cannon Edward. Disc jockey and host, radio interview show at various stations, Miami, Florida, 1957–71; columnist, various Miami newspapers, 1965–71; freelance writer and broadcaster, 1972–75; radio talk show host, WIOD, Miami, 1975–78; host, Mutual Broadcasting System's *Larry King Show,* from 1978; host, CNN's *Larry King Live,* since 1985; host, the Goodwill Games, 1990; columnist, *USA Today* and *The Sporting News.* Member: the Friars Club and the Washington Center for Politics and Journalism. Recipient: George Foster Peabody Award, 1982; National Association of Broadcasters' Radio Award, 1985; Jack Anderson Investigative Reporting Award, 1985; International Radio and TV Society's Broadcaster of the Year, 1989; American Heart Association's Man of the Year, 1992; named to Broadcaster's Hall of Fame, 1992.

Television Series (selected)

1985–   *Larry King Live*

Films

Ghostbusters, 1984; *Lost in America,* 1985; *Eddie and the Cruisers II: Eddie Lives!,* 1989; *Crazy People,* 1990; *The Exorcist III,* 1990; *Dave,* 1993; *Open Season,* 1996; *Courage Under Fire,* 1996; *The Long Kiss Goodnight,* 1996; *Contact,* 1997; *Mad City,* 1997; *The Jackal,* 1997; *Primary Colors,* 1998; *Bulworth,* 1998; *Enemy of the State,* 1998; *The Kid,* 1998; *The Contender,* 2000; *America's Sweethearts,* 2001; *John Q,* 2002.

Radio (selected)

Larry King Show, 1978–94; *Larry King Live,* 1994– .

Publications (selected)

Larry King (with Emily Yoffe), 1982
Tell It to the King (with Peter Occhiogrosso), 1988
Tell Me More (with Peter Occhiogrosso), 1990
When You're from Brooklyn, Everywhere Else Is Tokyo (with Marty Appel), 1992
On the Line: The New Road to the White House (with Mark Stencel), 1993
The Best of Larry King Live: The Greatest Interviews, 1995
Anything Goes! What I've Learned from Pundits, Politicians, and Presidents (with Pat Piper), 2000

Further Reading

"King of Radio: 10 Years and Counting," *Broadcasting* (January 25, 1988)
"Live with Larry King" (interview), *Broadcasting and Cable* (December 13, 1993)
Meyer, Thomas J., "The Maestro of Chin Music: With a Face Made for Radio, Larry King Has Become America's Premier Yakker on the Airwaves," *New York Times Magazine* (May 26, 1991)
Rosellini, Lynn, "All Alone, Late at Night," *U.S. News and World Report* (January 15, 1990)
Unger, Arthur, "Larry King: 'Everyman with a Mike'" (interview), *Television Quarterly* (Winter 1993)
Viles, Peter, "Larry King Faces the Day Shift with Mixed Emotions," *Broadcasting* (January 18, 1993)
Wilkinson, Alec, "The Mouthpiece and Handsomo," *The New Yorker* (March 28, 1994)

King, Dr. Martin Luther, Jr.: Assassination

Dr. Martin Luther King Jr., leader of the American civil rights movement, was assassinated on April 4, 1968, in Memphis, Tennessee, while lending support to a sanitation workers' strike. He was shot by James Earl Ray at approximately 7:05 P.M. Ray's bullet struck King as he was standing on his balcony at the Lorraine Motel; King died approximately one hour later. Although no television cameras were in the vicinity at the time of the assassination, television coverage of the event quickly followed.

News reports of King's wounding appeared first, but reporters remained consistent with the traditional news format, making early reports of the shooting seem both impersonal and inaccurate. The assassination occurred at the same time as the evening news, and several anchormen received the information during their live

The funeral of Martin Luther King, Jr.
Courtesy of AP/Wide World Photos

broadcasts; because details of the shooting were not yet clear, inaccurate information was offered in several cases. Julian Barber of WTTG in Washington, D.C., for example, mistakenly reported that King had been shot while in his car. Following this presentation of incorrect details, Barber then proceeded to introduce the station's weatherman. The rest of the newscast followed a standard format, with only minor interruptions providing information about King's condition.

Similarly, Stanislav Kondrashov recalls that Walter Cronkite had almost finished delivering his report on the *CBS Evening News* when he received word of King's wounding. Visibly shaken, he announced the shooting. Moments after the announcement, however, the news program faded into commercial advertising.

With little information available, the networks continued with their regularly scheduled programming and only later interrupted the programs with their station logos. At that point, an anonymous voice announced that King was dead.

Having received word of King's death, all three U.S. networks interrupted programming with news coverage. Awaiting President Lyndon Johnson's statement, all three featured anchormen discussing King's life and his contributions to the civil rights movement. The networks then broadcast Johnson's statement, in which he called for Americans to "reject the blind violence" that had killed the "apostle of nonviolence." In addition, the networks also covered Senator Hubert Humphrey's response and presented footage of King's prophetic speech from April 3, in which he acknowledged the precarious state of his life. Although the networks had reporters positioned in Memphis, there were no television reporters on the scene because an official curfew had been imposed on the city in an attempt to prevent violence.

According to G.D. McKnight, the immediacy of the television coverage prompted riots in more than 60 U.S. cities, including Chicago, Denver, and Baltimore. Television coverage of King's death and the riots it sparked continued for the next five days. King's life was featured on morning shows (e.g., NBC's *Today Show*), evening news programs, and special programs. The riots themselves commanded extensive television coverage (e.g., CBS's *News Nite* special on the riots). G.L. Carter suggests that the riots following King's assassination represent a significant shift from previous riotous activities, from responses dealing primarily with local issues to the national focus emerging in the wake of the King riots. National television coverage of the circumstances surrounding the King assassination may have contributed to this shift.

The King assassination is a significant moment in the history of the civil rights movement as well as in the history of the United States more generally. In death, as in life, King influenced millions of Americans. From the first reports of his shooting to the coverage of his funeral services on April 9 at the Ebenezer Church on the Morehouse College campus, television closely followed. News coverage of King's legacy continued when, on April 11, President Johnson signed the Civil Rights Bill.

VIDULA V. BAL

Further Reading

Carter, G.L., "In the Narrows of the 1960s U.S. Black Rioting," *Journal of Conflict Resolution* (1986)

Kondrashov, S., *The Life and Death of Martin Luther King,* translated by Keith Hammond, Moscow: Progress Publishers, 1981

Lewis, D.L., *King: A Biography,* Urbana: University of Illinois Press, 1970; 2nd edition, 1978

McKnight, G.D., "The 1968 Memphis Sanitation Strike and the FBI: A Case Study in Urban Surveillance," *South Atlantic Quarterly* (1984).

King of Kensington

Canadian Domestic Comedy

The five seasons of *King of Kensington* provided some of the most popular television in the more than 50-year history of television in Canada. Veteran actor Al Waxman was remembered as the "King" for the rest of his life, as was the catchy tune that opened every episode under the credits. The lyrics define King as the "people's champion," a "king without a buck...his wife says helping people brings him luck/His mother tells a slightly different story" over shots of King going down the crowded sidewalks greeting everyone with a broad smile. The song ends with a little send-up: a deep male voice drawling, "What a guy!" The series is set in the multi-ethnic open market of Kensington Street in downtown Toronto. Taped in front of a live audience, originally the series emphasized topical humor based on recent events, but given a twist by the ethnicity of the various characters. King is Jewish, Cathy his wife is a WASP, Tony the cabbie is Italian, and Nestor the postman is from the Caribbean. A Ukrainian alderman and a Francophone gambler also appeared in early episodes of this domestic comedy.

King of Kensington also focuses on the clash of cultures between Cathy and Gladys, King's rather stereotypical Jewish mother, and between Cathy's needs and Larry's willingness to help anybody. The topical references provided the show with some edginess, as the did the working-class realism of the sets, costumes, and dialogue. Larry came from a well-known Toronto high school, yet was willing to try foods like curry just then coming into popularity in the city. The fact that King was easygoing, a little overweight, and an average guy made him a very appealing protagonist.

In the second season, the topical political references disappeared, largely as a result of CBC audience research that signaled that they were not very popular. That meant, among other things, that the next four seasons would be more easily syndicated. On the other hand, the ethnic stereotypes were gradually taking on more rounded characteristics. However, despite the fact that Nestor was one of the few visible minorities in Canadian television drama and Tony was one of the few Italians, they were written out in the third season.

A bigger problem for the writers was that Fiona Reid (who played Cathy) wanted to return to the theater. She told interviewers she was reproached even years later by people she passed on the street for leaving *King*. The third season episode "Cathy's Last Stand," in which she left, is one of the best in the series—touching, a little funny, and a reprise of her history on the show, as she talks about her various unsuccessful efforts to define herself separately from King's huge persona. In a nice twist, it is established that she is leaving him, not because she does not love him any more, but because he gives so much of himself to everyone else he leaves little time for her. That characteristic is, of course, the basis for many of the show's comic situations, an intrinsic part of Larry King.

In the fourth season, Gladys marries her friend Jack who takes over the store, and King becomes the athletic director of the Kensington Community Centre. King finds a girlfriend in Tina, and life goes on. There are mediocre episodes (the Christmas episode in which everyone is snowbound in a restaurant and a pregnant woman gives birth) and better, more innovate ones (the episode in which King finds out that the tough school teacher he dreaded is both fair and a good teacher). Episodes center on topics and individuals such as night classes for immigrants, the pride of an old man struggling with impotence, a nude model in a life drawing class, a controversy about a dance for gay people, and an alderman who, in a 1979 episode, thinks the center is controlled by "a deviant ethnic conspiracy." In the decade of *M*A*S*H* and *All in the Family,* and in the context of the CBC's own tradition of topical dramas, the series did not abandon its sense of Toronto as a rapidly changing cultural, racial, ethnic, and sexually diverse mix nor its wry means of addressing relevant social issues.

The series ended with a poor young couple, the Cortinas, wanting to buy the store, but denied credit. Gladys leaves, at King's urging, to a retirement haven in Florida with Jack. King's father, a self-made success, is referred to when King obtains a second mortgage for the Cortinas and decides to continue to live in the apartment, paying them much-needed rent and not really leaving Kensington at all. Viewers who loved the series found this an appropriate conclusion with a hint of an open ending. No more episodes, no spin-offs, no movies of the week or reunions ever revived *King of Kensington.* But it remains one of the most fondly remembered series in Canadian television history.

MARY JANE MILLER

Cast

Larry King	Al Waxman
Cathy	Fiona Reid
Gladys	Helen Winston
Tony	Bob Vinci
Nestor	Ardon Bess
Tina	Rosemary Radcliffe
Jack	Peter Boretski
Gwen	Jayne Eastwood, Ron Bacon
Dorothy	Linda Rennhofer

Producers

Perry Rosemond, Jack Humphrey, Joe Partington. Some episodes coproduced and written by Louis Del Grande with David Barlow associate producer

Programming History

CBC
1975–80

Further Reading

Kentner, Peter, *TV North: Everything You Wanted To Know About Canadian Television,* Vancouver and Toronto: Whitecap, 2001

Miller, Mary Jane, "Sitcoms and Domestic Comedy," in *Turn up the Contrast 1952: CBC Television Drama Since 1952,* Vancouver: University of British Columbia Press, CBC Enterprises, 1987

Miller, Mary Jane, *Rewind and Search: Conversations with Makers and Decision Makers of CBC Television Drama,* Montreal and Kingston: McGill-Queen's University Press, 1996 *passim.*

Pevere, Geoff, and Greig Dymond, "The People's Champion: King of Kensington," in *Mondo Canuck: A Canadian Pop Culture Odyssey,* Scarborough, Ontario: Prentice Hall Canada, 1996.

Kinnear, Roy (1934–1988)

British Actor

A portly and popular comic character actor, Roy Kinnear proved to be a reliable guest star on many television programs and a dependable lead in his own right. He was born in Wigan, Lancashire, and educated in Edinburgh. When he was 17, he enrolled in the Royal Academy of Dramatic Arts, but his studies there were interrupted when National Service conscription took him to war. He later returned to the theatrical world and appeared on stage in repertory theater in the 1950s. In 1959 he joined Joan Littlewood's famous Theatre Workshop in the East End of London and appeared in some of their biggest successes.

Television made Roy Kinnear a household name; his big break was the controversial and highly popular satire series *That Was the Week That Was.* The team consisted of a group of irreverent, bright young things hell-bent on attacking the hypocrisies of the establishment. One criticism often made of the show was that the protagonists came across as smug, but Kinnear was spared from that accusation because his role in the group was that of the common man. In sketches he would usually be cast as a normal, working-class chap baffled by the complexities and machinations of the government and the media. Viewers could identify with the character and were endeared to him. Indeed, Kinnear's very ordinariness and likeability assured him a long career in the medium.

He was a regular guest star on long-running series such as *The Avengers,* often costarred in TV plays and was a semi-regular on *Minder* (as Whaley), and *George and Mildred* (as Jerry). He was not averse to appearing as a straight man (albeit a very funny one) to comedian Dick Emery in various Dick Emery shows, and his familiar face was put to use in various TV commercials. Kinnear starred in his own sitcoms, shaped around his persona: as daydreamer Stanley Blake in *A World of His Own* (BBC, 1965); as compulsive worrier George Webley in *Inside George Webley* (Yorkshire Television, 1968 and 1970); as greengrocer and ladies' hairdresser Alf Butler in *No Appointment Necessary* (BBC, 1977); as building-firm manager Joe Jones in *Cowboys* (Thames Television, 1980–81); as Sidney Pratt, manager of struggling escapologist Ernest Tanner (Brian Murphy) in *The Incredible Mr. Tanner* (London Weekend Television, 1981); as Arnold Bristow, used-car dealer and psychic in *The Clairvoyant*

(BBC, 1986); and in his last sitcom, as the tipsy headmaster, R.G. Wickham, in the short-lived *Hardwicke House* (Central, 1987), which was pulled off air halfway through its run following accusations of bad taste.

Kinnear worked regularly for more than 25 years on television. Much of his success was due to the warmth that the public felt toward him and the esteem in which he was held by his fellow professionals. Throughout this period, Kinnear still made appearances in the theater and acted in support roles in more than 50 movies. While on location for *The Return of the Musketeers* (1989), he suffered a fatal fall from his horse.

DICK FIDDY

See also **That Was the Week That Was**

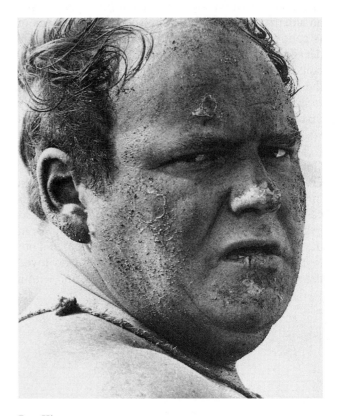

Roy Kinnear.
Courtesy of the Everett Collection

Roy Kinnear. Born in Wigan, Lancashire, England, January 8, 1934. Attended George Herriot School, Edinburgh; Royal Academy of Dramatic Arts. Married: Carmel Cryan; children: Karina, Kirsty, and Rory. Made debut as stage actor in repertory, Newquay, 1955; appeared in repertory at Nottingham, Glasgow, Edinburgh, and Perth; joined Joan Littlewood's Theatre Workshop, London, 1959, and later appeared in pantomime and with the Royal Shakespeare Company and National Theatre Company, among others; established reputation as television comedian in *That Was the Week That Was* and starred in several situation comedies; also appeared as character actor in many films. Died in Spain, September 20, 1988.

Television Series

1962	*That Was the Week That Was*
1964	*A World of His Own*
1970	*Inside George Webley*
1980	*Cowboys*
1986	*The Clairvoyant*
1987	*Hardwick House*

Made-for-Television Movies

1981	*Dick Turpin*
1984	*The Zany Adventures of Robin Hood*

Films

Sparrows Can't Sing, 1962; *Tiara Tahita,* 1962; *The Boys,* 1962; *Heavens Above!,* 1963; *The Small World of Sammy Lee,* 1963; *A Place to Go,* 1963; *The Informers,* 1963; *French Dressing,* 1964; *The Hill,* 1965; *Help!,* 1965; *The Deadly Affair,* 1966; *A Funny Thing Happened on the Way to the Forum,* 1966; *Albert Carter QOSO,* 1967; *How I Won the War,* 1967; *The Mini-Affair,* 1968; *Till Death Us Do Part,* 1968; *The Bed Sitting Room,* 1969; *Lock Up Your Daughters,* 1969; *On a Clear Day You Can See Forever,* 1970; *Scrooge,* 1970; *Taste the Blood of Dracula,* 1970; *The Firechasers,* 1970; *Egghead's Robot,* 1970; *Willie Wonka and the Chocolate Factory,* 1971; *Melody,* 1971; *Raising the Roof,* 1971; *The Alf Garnett Saga,* 1972; *Madame Sin,* 1972; *Alice's Adventures in Wonderland,* 1972; *The Pied Piper,* 1972; *That's Your Funeral,* 1973; *The Cobblers of Umbridge,* 1973; *The Three Musketeers,* 1974; *Barry McKenzie Holds His Own,* 1974; *Juggernaut,* 1974; *The Amorous Milkman,* 1974; *The Four Musketeers,* 1975; *Three for All,* 1975; *One of Our Dinosaurs Is Missing,* 1975; *Royal Flash,* 1975; *The Adventures of Sherlock Holmes' Smarter Brother,* 1975; *Not Now, Comrade,* 1976; *Chimpmates,* 1977; *Herbie Goes to Monte Carlo,* 1977; *The Last Remake of Beau Geste,* 1977; *Eskimo Nell,* 1977; *Watership Down* (voice only), 1978; *Hound of the Baskervilles,* 1978; *The London Connection/The Omega Connection,* 1979; *The Princess and the Pea,* 1979; *Mad Dogs and Cricketers,* 1979; *A Fair Way to Play,* 1980; *High Rise Donkey,* 1980; *Hawk—The Slayer,* 1980; *Hammett,* 1981; *The Girl in the Train,* 1982; *The Boys in Blue,* 1983; *1984,* 1984; *Squaring the Circle,* 1984; *Vote: June European Parliament Election,* 1984; *Pavlova,* 1984; *Pirates,* 1985; *Neat and Tidy,* 1986; *Casanova,* 1987; *Falcon's Maltester,* 1987; *The Return of the Musketeers,* 1988.

Stage (selected)

Make Me an Offer; Sparrers Can't Sing; The Clandestine Marriage; The Travails of Sancho Panza; The Cherry Orchard.

Kinoy, Ernest (1925–)

U.S. Writer

Ernest Kinoy is one of U.S. television's most prolific and acclaimed writers. His career spans five decades, from the live anthology dramas of the 1950s to the made-for-television movies of the 1990s. His best-known works, such as scripts for *The Defenders* and *Roots,* have dramatized social and historical issues. Outside of television, Kinoy is less well known than some of his contemporaries from the "Golden Age" of television, such as Mel Brooks and Paddy Chayefsky. Within the industry, however, Kinoy has always been recognized for his well-crafted television dramas. He has also written successfully for radio, film, and the stage.

Ernest Kinoy.
Photo courtesy of Broadcasting & Cable

Kinoy wrote for many shows in the 1950s, including *The Imogene Coca Show* and *The Marriage,* a series featuring Hume Cronyn and Jessica Tandy. He was best known for contributing to such live anthology dramas as *The DuPont Show of the Week, Studio One,* and *Playhouse 90.* When the Federal Communications Commission held an inquiry into the decline of the live dramas, Kinoy and other writers offered damaging testimony about network unwillingness to broadcast "serious" drama. CBS, under scrutiny, resurrected a weighty dramatic series that would soon showcase Kinoy's talents—*The Defenders.* Kinoy won two Emmy Awards writing for the series, which was created by his colleague Reginald Rose. The show followed two idealistic lawyers, a father and son, who confronted controversial issues and moral paradoxes on a weekly basis. In "Blacklist," one of Kinoy's most celebrated episodes, Jack Klugman played a blacklisted actor who finally received a serious part after ten years, only to be harassed by vehement anticommunists. In another well-known Kinoy episode, "The Non-Violent," James Earl Jones played a black minister thrown in jail with a wealthy, white civil rights activist. Like *Dr. Kildare,* another series that Kinoy wrote for, *The Defenders* was sometimes described as a New Frontier character drama for its exploration of social ethics. During this same period, Kinoy also wrote for the series *The Nurses* and *Route 66.*

In the 1970s, Kinoy shifted to made-for-television movies and feature films. He often had two or more scripts produced in a year. Notable accomplishments included *Crawlspace* (1972), a CBS movie about a family adopting a homeless man, and *Buck and the Preacher* (1972), an action-packed black western directed by Sidney Poitier for the big screen. Kinoy's television career took a new turn in 1976 when he wrote two docudramas for producer David L. Wolper: *Victory at Entebbe,* about the Israeli rescue operation in Uganda, and *Collision Course,* based on Harry Truman's struggles with Douglas MacArthur. Kinoy subsequently worked on Wolper's blockbuster docudrama *Roots* (1977), winning an Emmy for an episode he cowrote with William Blinn. Kinoy served as Wolper's head writer on *Roots: The Next Generations* (1979). In 1981 he received an Emmy nomination and Writers Guild of America Award for another of his television docudramas, *Skokie,* about street demonstrations attempted by neo-Nazis in the Jewish neighborhoods of Skokie, Illinois.

In the 1980s and 1990s, Kinoy's made-for-television movies continued to receive praise. His scripts included *Murrow* (1985), about the famous broadcaster, and TNT's *Chernobyl: The Final Warning* (1990). Kinoy is a rare presence in contemporary television. A writer known for quality drama, he has enjoyed success during each of television's five decades.

J.B. BIRD

See also **Anthology Drama;** *Defenders, The;* **"Golden Age" of Television Drama;** *Playhouse 90; Roots; Route 66*

Ernest Kinoy. Born April 1, 1925. Educated at Columbia University, New York City. Began writing career in radio; staff writer for NBC Radio, 1948–60; writer for numerous television shows, since 1950s; president, Writers Guild of America, East, 1969–71; writer of several made-for-television movies and motion pictures. Recipient: Emmy Awards, 1963, 1964, 1977.

Television Series (selected)

1948–58	*Studio One*
1954–55	*The Imogene Coca Show*
1954	*The Marriage*
1956–61	*Playhouse 90*
1960–64	*Route 66*
1961–64	*The DuPont Show of the Week*
1961–65	*The Defenders*
1961–66	*Dr. Kildare*
1962–65	*The Nurses*

Made-for-Television Movies

1972	*Crawlspace*
1973	*The President's Plane Is Missing*

1974	*The Story of Jacob and Joseph*
1976	*Victory at Entebbe*
1976	*The Story of David*
1976	*Collision Course*
1977	*The Deadliest Season*
1977	*Roots*
1979	*Roots: The Next Generations*
1980	*The Henderson Monster*
1981	*Skokie*
1985	*Murrow*
1990	*Chernobyl: The Final Warning*
1995	*Tad*
1997	*Rescuers: Stories of Courage: Two Women* (segment "The Woman on the Bicycle")

Films

Brother John, 1972; *Buck and the Preacher,* 1972

Publication

Something About a Soldier: A Comedy-Drama in Three Acts, 1962

Further Reading

Bogle, Donald, "*Roots* and *Roots: The Next Generations,*" in *Blacks in American Film and Television: An Encyclopedia,* New York: Garland, 1988

Harris, Jay S., editor, *TV Guide: The First 25 Years,* New York: Simon and Schuster, 1978

Sheuer, Steven H., *Who's Who in Television and Cable,* New York: Facts on File, 1983

Stempel, Tom, *Storytellers to the Nation: A History of American Television Writing,* New York: Continuum, 1992

Sturcken, Frank, *Live Television: The Golden Age of 1946–1958 in New York,* Jefferson, North Carolina: McFarland, 1990

Watson, Mary Ann, *The Expanding Vista: American Television in the Kennedy Years,* New York: Oxford University Press, 1990

Wilk, Max, *The Golden Age of Television: Notes from the Survivors,* New York: Delacorte Press, 1976

Kintner, Robert E. (1909–1980)

U.S. Media Executive

Robert E. Kintner was a television executive who, as network president, influenced the development of two major networks (ABC and NBC) during the tumultuous decade of the 1950s. This former journalist fused his passion for journalistic excellence and his zeal for high entertainment ratings into a successful formula that shaped network programming trends for several decades. Kintner was lauded within the industry and the press for applying the "doctrine of common sense to many a ticklish problem" and for his refreshing "cold realism." He defended the embattled television industry during the quiz show scandals of the late 1950s, and he spearheaded the move to make television a respectable journalistic medium by dedicating unprecedented network resources and air time to news and documentary programming.

Beginning his career as a reporter, Kintner established a national reputation in the late 1930s with a syndicated political column co-written with Joseph Wright Alsop, with whom he also collaborated on a number of best-selling books on U.S. politics. Kintner's entry into broadcasting came when he was hired by ABC owner and chair Edward J. Noble in 1944 as a vice president of public relations and radio news. Six years later, Kintner was named president of the ABC network, which was just beginning to provide television service and was the clear underdog in competition with NBC and CBS.

With a keen understanding of television's potential as a journalistic medium, Kintner's major coup at ABC was the network's full coverage of the Army-McCarthy hearings, which brought Senator Joseph McCarthy's tactics to public light and established ABC as a major source for public affairs coverage. On the entertainment front, under Kintner's leadership the production-weak ABC struck ground-breaking deals with Walt Disney and Warner Brothers studios for the production of weekly television series. The success of such filmed television programming as *Disneyland* (and its offshoots) and the hit western *Cheyenne* influenced the programming trends at all three networks; by the late 1950s, Hollywood studio-produced westerns dominated the Nielsen ratings.

Kintner left the ABC presidency in 1956, in a period of great network growth, and joined NBC in early 1957, where he was named president in July 1958. As

Robert E. Kintner.
Courtesy of the Everett Collection

the first journalist to head a network, Kintner took pride in the informational potential of broadcasting, and he believed that TV could fulfill its mission to society through news programming. Known affectionately as the "managing editor" of the NBC news division because of his hands-on approach, Kintner was directly responsible for the development of a strong news component at NBC. By increasing budget allocations and air time for the news division and hiring top news executives and journalists (often from CBS, with whom NBC was in ferocious competition), Kintner had by the end of the decade built a high-prestige, unequaled news division at NBC that reigned throughout the early 1960s.

The major components of Kintner's three-pronged public affairs initiative were the nightly network newscasts, the development of strong prime-time documentary series, and the preemption of regular programs to provide live coverage of breaking news events. The anchor team of Chet Huntley and David Brinkley dominated news programming during this period, and in late 1963 both NBC and CBS lengthened their evening newscasts from 15 to 30 minutes, a move that many critics credited as making television a serious information medium comparable to newspapers.

Kintner's vision of the medium as a way to educate and inform citizens about social issues was enabled by public and government pressures—especially in the wake of the quiz show scandals—to increase the prestige of the industry by increasing prime-time public affairs programming by the networks. Kintner revitalized NBC's network documentary units, which had focused mainly on cultural programming, to begin to take on serious social and political issues in series such as *NBC White Paper.* By 1962 Kintner claimed that the networks were "proving what's right with television," bringing space flights, civil rights activism, election coverage, and swiftly breaking events into U.S. living rooms. Although often gently criticized for micromanaging the NBC news division, Kintner hosted the transformation of news and informational programming from a peripheral aspect of television programming to the position of prestige in broadcasting.

This "golden age" of television journalism was directly related to the historical moment, especially the years of President John F. Kennedy's "New Frontier" initiative, marked by the charismatic charm of a made-for-media president, the dramatic struggles of the civil rights movement, the patriotic cold war-era fervor of the United States' race into space, and the coming of age of American news broadcasting with the live coverage of the aftermath of the Kennedy assassination. Kennedy's image-oriented New Frontier forged an alliance with television, an alliance described by Mary Ann Watson in *The Expanding Vista* as a "symbiotic bond" between Kennedy and the television medium, which would forever alter the relationship between the public and the president. Similarly, the centrality of television in the political process increased dramatically under Kintner's reign at NBC, with the coverage of the 1960 campaigns, the "Great Debates" between Kennedy and Nixon, paid political advertisements, and especially the election coverage (Watson reports that over 90 percent of American homes were tuned in).

Kintner was an active player in the public controversies surrounding the quiz show scandals of 1959, and he used this opportunity to redefine the mission and the structure of commercial television. Testifying before the House Subcommittee on Legislative Oversight in 1959, Kintner claimed that the networks, as well as the public, were victims of deception by those who rigged quiz shows. Although the networks were criticized by the subcommittee for "lack of diligence" in taking action, Kintner strongly defended his network, claiming that NBC was taking active steps to "investigate and safeguard the integrity of the shows" and had taken direct production control over the quiz shows away from the sponsors.

Under intense public criticism about the entertainment programming standards, as well as mounting pressure from the Federal Communications Commission and from civic and religious groups in the wake of the quiz show scandals, Kintner recognized this period as a crossroads for the TV industry, and he advocated that the industry take actions to recover public confidence. In the face of concerns about sex and violence in television shows, Kintner also defended the network in 1961 before the Senate Subcommittee on Juvenile Delinquency (the Dodd Committee), which charged the TV industry with violating moral codes, lacking imagination, and shirking its responsibilities in the drive for higher ratings.

Believed to watch more television than any of his contemporaries in the industry, Kintner's addiction to "the box" was frequently noted. He was perceived as a paradox by some critics, such as Jack Gould of the *New York Times,* who wrote about Kintner in 1965: "He can rationalize the pap of the medium with a relaxed opportunism that stands in strange contrast to his initiative in news and public affairs.... He embodies [both] the promise and problem of mass communication—how to keep up the quarterly dividend while offering both folk rock and the oratorio."

In early 1966, Kintner left NBC and was appointed as a special assistant and cabinet secretary to President Lyndon B. Johnson. In a parting interview upon leaving NBC, Kintner advocated greater experimentation in TV programming, calling for programs dealing with more controversial social, economic, and political subjects in both news and entertainment programming.

PAMELA WILSON

See also **American Broadcasting Company; Army-McCarthy Hearings; National Broadcasting Company;** *NBC White Paper; Warner Brothers Presents*

Robert Edmonds Kinter. Born in Stroudsburg, Pennsylvania, September 12, 1909. Swarthmore College, B.A. 1931. Married: Jean Rodney, 1940; children: Susan and Michael. Served in the U.S. Army during World War II. Financial news reporter, *Herald Tribune,* 1933–37; columnist, *Herald Tribune* and North American Newspaper Alliance, 1937–41; vice president of public relations, ABC, 1944–50; president, ABC, 1950–56; president, NBC, 1956–66; cabinet liaison for Lyndon B. Johnson administration, 1966–67. Recipient: Legion of Merit, World War II. Died in Washington, D.C., December 3, 1980.

Publications

Men Around the President (with Joseph Alsop), 1939
American White Paper: The Story of American Diplomacy and the Second World War (with Joseph Alsop), 1940
Broadcasting and the News, 1965

Further Reading

Barnouw, Erik, *Tube of Plenty: The Evolution of American Television,* New York: Oxford University Press, 1975; 2nd revised edition, 1990

Baughman, James L., *The Republic of Mass Culture: Journalism, Filmmaking, and Broadcasting in America Since 1941,* Baltimore: Johns Hopkins University Press, 1992; 2nd edition, 1997

Bednarski, J., "Recalling Four Days in November," *Electronic Media,* 18 (July 26, 1999)

Blair, William, "Kintner Testifies," *New York Times* (November 6, 1959)

Boddy, William, *Fifties Television: The Industry and Its Critics,* Urbana: University of Illinois Press, 1990

Curtin, Michael, *Redeeming the Wasteland: Television Documentary and Cold War Politics,* New Brunswick, New Jersey: Rutgers University Press, 1995

"Excerpts from the Testimony by President of NBC at Quiz-Show Hearing," *New York Times* (November 6, 1959)

Frank, Reuven, "The Great Coronation War," *American Heritage,* 44 (December 1993)

Frank, Reuven, "News Powered NBC's Early Days," *Electronic Media,* 20 (November 12, 2001)

Gould, Jack, "Robert Edmonds Kintner: The Man from NBC," *New York Times* (October 24, 1965)

Thomas, Cal, "Broadcast Journalism Is Dead," *Human Events,* 55 (August 13, 1999)

Watson, Mary Ann, *The Expanding Vista: American Television in the Kennedy Years,* New York: Oxford University Press, 1990

Kirck, Harvey (1928–2002)

Canadian News Anchor

Harvey Kirck, news anchor for the privately owned Canadian Television Network (CTV) from 1963 to 1984, has been called Canada's version of Walter Cronkite. In his autobiography he even noted how his retirement after 20 years was planned to ensure that he broke Cronkite's record. In fact, Kirck never exercised a similar power over the news or over the public mind, but he did become a celebrity, a recognized "Face and Voice of the News" in English-speaking Canada.

Beginning in 1948, Kirck served a long apprenticeship in private radio as an announcer who hosted programs; narrated commercials; and wrote, delivered, and occasionally reported the news. In 1960 he became a news anchor for a television station where, he claimed later, he learned the importance of being a performer: "You have to develop a bullet-proof persona, and send him out to face the damnable, merciless camera." Three years later, he joined the CTV news service, then stationed in Ottawa, as one of four men (another was Peter Jennings) who served in two pairs of co-anchors on the model of NBC's *The Huntley-Brinkley Report.* The fledgling network, only two years old, was determined to challenge the dominance of the established *The National* on the Canadian Broadcasting Corporation (CBC) (then *CBC Television News*). The peculiar arrangement of alternating pairs of co-anchors soon devolved into a more normal structure, and Kirck took over the responsibility as chief anchor as well as news editor.

After a change in the ownership structure of the network, *CTV News* was moved in 1966 to Toronto, the media hub of English Canada. It was a mixed blessing for Kirck: he lost his position as news editor while concentrating on the task of presenting the news (although he also continued to participate in the writing of the newscast). Even though CTV's resources were slight—much of the material came from U.S. sources or the private affiliates—it hoped to produce a bright and lively newscast at 11:00 P.M., with a distinctly American flavor that would contrast with the supposedly stodgy, and British, approach of the CBC. From 1971 to 1972, *CTV News* drew roughly even with CBC's *The National,* with 950,000 viewers a night in the common area covered by both networks (CTV did not then cover the country). A 1972 CBC survey discovered that *CTV News* scored higher as "more com-

plete, lively, aggressive, fresh, friendly, interesting and in-touch."

That success owed something to Kirck's persona. He was a tall, eventually heavy-set man with a craggy and weathered face that signaled experience. His voice was deep and resonant, authoritative rather than casual. He might seem a bit gruff, but he was eminently believable: a survey carried out in 1977 found that people had confidence that he fully understood what he presented.

That persona, however, was not enough to overcome the deficiencies in the quality of *CTV News.* Dur-

Harvey Kirck.
Photo courtesy of Harvey Kirck

ing the next few years, *The National* secured an apparently unshakable lead over its rival, except in the metropolitan centers, where *CTV News* moved ahead. In 1976 CTV management scored a coup by hiring away from the CBC its news anchor, Lloyd Robertson, as well as a top news producer, Tim Kotcheff. Robertson and Kirck became co-anchors, which allowed each more freedom to go on special assignment. The relationship between the two men, by all published accounts, remained good, perhaps because Kirck's salary was also increased (at Robertson's request) to the new level paid Robertson. The result established the fact that Canadian news anchors, as in the United States, were now celebrities who could command hefty salaries.

In fact, the duo made an odd couple: Robertson was smaller, younger, and handsome, with a perfect diction, whereas Kirck was taller and bulkier, older, increasingly rugged, boasting what Peter Trueman has referred to as a "tough, truck-driver delivery." There appeared to be no obvious reason for the pairing. The CTV coup did little to improve the fortunes of its flagship newscast, perhaps bringing another 100,000 viewers. In his autobiography, Kirck himself wondered what might have been the result if the network had invested funds in the newsroom and its facilities rather than big-name salaries. In 1982 the competitive situation changed dramatically when CBC moved *The National* back to 10:00 P.M. as part of a new hour of news and public affairs. Shortly afterward, Kirck retired from the nightly newscast, though he continued to appear on CTV for occasional broadcasts. He was inducted into the Broadcast Hall of Fame of the Canadian Association of Broadcasters in 2000.

PAUL RUTHERFORD

Harvey Kirck. Born in Uno Park, Ontario, October 14, 1928. Married: 1) Maggie, 1947 (divorced); 2) Renate, 1962 (divorced); 3) Brenda, 1983. Began career as radio announcer, program host, news reader, 1948–60; television announcer and news reader, 1960–63; news anchor, Canadian Television Network, 1963–84. Inducted into the Canadian Association of Broadcasters Broadcast Hall of Fame, 2000. Died of a heart attack, February 18, 2002.

Television
1963–84   *CTV News*

Publication

Nobody Calls Me Mr. Kirck (with Wade Rowland), 1985

Further Reading

Kiefl, Barry, and Stan Staple, "An Annotated Bibliography of CBC Research Reports Dealing with Radio and Television News, 1956–1988," in *Beyond the Printed Word: The Evolution of Canada's Broadcast News Heritage*, edited by Richard Lochead, Kingston, Ontario: Quarry, 1991

Nash, Knowlton, *Prime Time at Ten: Behind-the-Camera Battles of Canadian TV Journalism*, Toronto: McClelland and Stewart, 1987

Trueman, Peter, *Smoke and Mirrors: The Inside Story of Television News in Canada*, Toronto: McClelland and Stewart, 1980

Klein, Paul L. (1929–1998)

U.S. Television Executive

In the 1960s, as the head of research at NBC, Paul Klein developed a theory of Least Objectionable Programming (or L.O.P., as it was generally known) to explain the behavior of audiences in the days when three behemoth networks ruled the television landscape. In a world of limited choice, viewers do not watch particular programs, he insisted; they simply watch television. Every day at the same time the number of television sets turned on is remarkably constant—regardless of what is on the air. Viewers do not select favorite programs, but settle for those they dislike the least in order to sustain the general experience of television. Under these conditions, network programmers worry less about creating exceptional programs to attract viewers than about supplying the least objectionable program on the air at any given moment. As a unifying theory of television in the age of program scarcity, Klein's became the most widely quoted statement to emerge from within the television industry when the networks were at the height of their influence. A remarkable number of books and articles written about American television in the 1970s and 1980s felt it necessary to contend with Klein's theory—seeing it as either refreshingly honest or profoundly cynical.

Contrary to what some of Klein's critics believed, his theory of Least Objectionable Programming was not a call for more programs aimed at the lowest common denominator of mass taste, but an attempt to convince advertisers and his own supervisors at NBC that the time was ripe to overturn the old viewing patterns. The Nielsen ratings system, with its emphasis on bulk ratings—the sheer number of viewers watching a program—ignored demographic distinctions in the viewing audience, and this was a mistake. Nielsen based its ratings on the number of households viewing a given program, but it is individuals, not households, who buy products. As the industry's most vocal advocate of demographic ratings, Klein conducted a nonstop campaign in the 1960s and 1970s, and eventually saw his ideas adopted throughout the television industry.

That so much is known about Klein's opinions in the 1960s, when he was but a mid-level executive in charge of research at NBC, says much about his character. Seldom does an executive of Klein's rank achieve such wide recognition, particularly outside the industry. In the button-down world of the 1960s television business, he cultivated an unconventional image, spurning suits and ties for baggy sweaters, tempering the can-do spirit of the junior executive class with his own perpetually melancholy demeanor. Klein was arrogant and dismissive of those with whom he disagreed, willing to criticize colleagues and competitors at other networks or to send taunting letters when he had won a particular victory. In spite of such intemperate behavior, uncharacteristic of a network executive, he possessed what one reporter at the time described as "the best brain in broadcasting," and for this reason his superiors at NBC valued his advice on crucial programming decisions during the 1960s—including the network's decision to shift its entire schedule to color and, later, to present the ground-breaking situation comedy *Julia,* with its African-American star, Diahann Carroll.

Klein graduated from Brooklyn College in 1953 with a degree in mathematics and philosophy and immediately joined a Madison Avenue advertising agency, where he was responsible for research on the Philip Morris cigarette account when Morris was the chief advertiser on television's highest-rated program,

I Love Lucy. He experienced his first epiphany about the failure of bulk ratings when his research revealed that the program, despite its enormous ratings, appealed primarily to children and older women—not the target market for cigarettes. Klein sharpened his convictions about audience demographics in his next job, as the head of research at the Doyle Dane Bernbach advertising agency for six years, before finding a platform for his ideas when he took charge of the research department at NBC in 1960. When media theorist and critic Marshall McLuhan came to prominence in the 1960s, Klein not only read his books, but openly declared himself a "McLuhan thinker." From McLuhan, Klein absorbed the idea that a communications medium has a social meaning of its own, independent of any particular content—an idea that found expression in Klein's theory of Least Objectionable Programming.

By 1970 Klein was growing restless at NBC, where he had held the same job for a decade, and his career had essentially stalled. He left NBC in 1970 to pursue his own independent interests. He volunteered his audience research skills for the newly created Children's Television Workshop and, for NBC's Saturday morning children's schedule, produced a series of one-minute educational spots, called Pop-Ups, designed to teach reading to preschoolers. His larger interest was in event programming, selectively targeted viewers, and new technologies—the future of television, as he envisioned it. He founded Computer Cinema, Inc., a visionary company that foresaw the convergence of television and the computer long before anyone had even heard of the Internet. The company pioneered the development of pay-per-view programming in hotels, initially called "Hotelevision," by offering commercial-free, uncut feature films before they had appeared on the broadcast networks, distributed to hotels via satellite master antennas.

In 1976 Klein was invited to return to NBC and take charge of programming. Regular weekly series had been the staple of network broadcasting since the days of radio, but Klein believed that audiences had grown bored with series, that humdrum programming was eroding the value of the network franchise, driving away discriminating viewers. Klein was an evangelist of special-event programming, which he saw as a way to lure the economically desirable young adult viewers to NBC. Brought in at the last minute to plug holes in NBC's fall 1976 season, Klein created the "Big Event"—a 90-minute block on Sunday nights—in which he placed movies, variety shows, and miniseries. For the 1977 season, he blocked out four entire evenings of the network's schedule for special events, movies, and miniseries. Klein's critics complained that he was not paying enough attention to series development, but he believed that event programming would bond the younger, economically desirable viewers to NBC. He avidly committed NBC to the miniseries format, often scheduling installments on consecutive nights. Under his leadership, NBC developed dozens of these expensive, limited-run series. Many were banal and excessive: bloated melodramas and historical pageants like *Captains and Kings, Wheels, 79 Park Avenue,* and *Centennial,* but others were among the most ambitious television productions of the decade: *Studs Lonigan, King, Shogun,* and *Holocaust* (which set a record as NBC's highest-rated entertainment program of all time, with 120 million viewers).

However, Klein's strategy was an utter failure. NBC's ratings plunged steadily downward, reaching a ten-year low in the 1978–79 season. Meanwhile, ABC surged to first place on the strength of exactly the sort of programming that Klein eschewed: familiar, comfortable weekly series. Klein publicly criticized ABC programming chief Fred Silverman. This made for especially cruel irony when in June 1978 NBC named Fred Silverman as its new network president. Although Klein remained in charge of programming, his days at NBC were numbered from the moment Silverman signed the contract. It is an even more unfortunate irony that Klein is remembered not only for leading NBC to its ratings nadir, but also for developing the series, *Supertrain,* an expensive, ill-conceived answer to ABC's *The Love Boat* that became virtually synonymous with network folly when it was canceled due to disastrous ratings after just four episodes. In January 1979—less than three years after returning to NBC and only six months after Silverman's arrival—Klein resigned from NBC for the second time.

After leaving NBC, Klein returned to cable and satellite television. He spent the next decade developing adult-oriented and X-rated program services. He was a founder of the Playboy Channel in 1982 and served as president until 1984, when he left to create Hi-Life, a programming service designed to go beyond Playboy by offering sexually explicit X-rated films. When cable operators refused to carry the service, he criticized them and shifted his attention to an alternative form of distribution: satellites. In 1987 he founded Home Dish Only Satellite Networks, which supplied "sophisticated adult programming" aimed at hotels and the owners of backyard satellite dishes via such channels as the American Exxxtasy Channel and the Tuxxxedo Network.

One might ask how a man once considered the "best brain in broadcasting" would find himself a purveyor of pornography, but this was not really such an odd departure for Klein. Unlike most television executives who came of age in the 1950s and 1960s, he disagreed that television was solely a mass medium, obliged to provide something for everyone. He imagined a different model in which particular viewers would be drawn to programs that appealed to their tastes. In this he clearly anticipated the changes that would restructure the television landscape in the 1990s—including the vast (and largely unnoticed) profits earned by adult-oriented premium and pay-per-view channels in hotels and on direct broadcast satellite and digital cable services.

From his position outside the networks, Klein was an astute observer of the broadcast networks' declining ratings in the 1980s and 1990s. Along with his entrepreneurial ventures in cable and satellite, Klein developed movies for the networks during the 1980s and 1990s, including *The People vs. Jean Harris* (1981). In the years prior to his death in 1998, he had turned his attention to the globalization of television, lending his knowledge and experience as a consultant to emerging television markets in Eastern Europe and the countries of the former Soviet Union.

CHRISTOPHER ANDERSON

Paul L. Klein. Born in 1929. Married: Janet. Children: Molly, Adam. Education: Brooklyn College, B.A. in philosophy and mathematics, 1953. Began career as researcher at Biow advertising agency, 1953–54; research department at Doyle Dane Bernbach advertising agency, 1954–60; research department at NBC, 1960–70; independent producer, consultant, president of Computer Cinema, 1970–75; vice president in charge of programming at NBC, 1976–79; independent producer (PKO Television) and consultant, 1980–98; president of the Playboy Channel, 1982–84; president of Hi Life Network and Home Dish Only Satellite Networks, 1984–90. Died in New York City, July 4, 1998.

Further Reading

Bedell, Sally, *Up the Tube: Prime Time in the Silverman Years,* New York: Viking Press, 1981

Brown, Les, *Television: The Business Behind the Box,* New York: Harcourt Brace Jovanovich, 1971

Gitlin, Todd, *Inside Prime Time,* New York: Pantheon, 1983

Kluge, John (1914–)

U.S. Media Mogul

John Kluge ranks as one of the least-known but most powerful moguls in the history of the modern television industry in the United States. The major television networks and their affiliates deservedly draw the most attention, but Kluge proved that a group of independent TV stations could make millions of dollars. His Metromedia, Inc., pioneered independent stations operations through the 1960s and 1970s. In the mid-1980s, Rupert Murdoch offered Kluge nearly $2 billion for the Metromedia stations, which then served as the basis for Murdoch's FOX television network. This deal made Kluge one of the richest people in the United States.

It was the food business that led Kluge to television. In 1951 he invested in a Baltimore, Maryland, food brokerage enterprise, increased sales dramatically, sold his majority stake in the mid-1950s, and began to look for another industry that was growing. He found television. In 1956 Kluge was too late to enter network television, but he saw possibilities with independent TV stations. He assembled an investment group and purchased the former DuMont stations. He ran Metromedia on a tight budget, saving rent, for example, by headquartering the company across the Hudson River from New York City, in Secaucus, New Jersey. He seized upon the programming strategy of simply re-running old network situation comedies and low-budget movies. And Metromedia made millions with relatively small audiences, because costs of operation were so low.

Under his stewardship, Metromedia grew into the largest independent television business in the United States. Afterward, Kluge purchased assorted businesses to add to his Metromedia empire. Over the years he acquired the Ice Capades, the Harlem Globetrotters, music publishing companies holding such titles as *Fiddler on the Roof, Zorba the Greek,* and *Cabaret,* television production and syndication units, *Playbill* magazine, and a highly profitable direct-mail advertising division. But he did make mistakes. One disastrous misstep was Kluge's 1960s purchase of the niche magazine *Diplomat;* another came with his proposal for a fourth TV network. Neither project succeeded, and the failures cost Metromedia millions of dollars.

Kluge reached his greatest successes in television by buying the syndication rights to *M*A*S*H.* With this asset, he finally gave rival network affiliates a contest for ratings in the early fringe time period. Not one to sit still, during the early 1980s Kluge cooked up a deal to take Metromedia private. In 1984, by structuring a $1.3 billion leveraged buyout on unusually favorable terms, Kluge ended up owning three-quarters of the new company and pocketing $115 million in cash in the process. With Metromedia now private and under his full control, Kluge did not hesitate when Rupert Murdoch approached him with $2 billion to buy Metromedia's television stations.

Out of TV, Kluge attended to his other businesses. Under the Metromedia name, he began to manufacture paging devices and mobile telephones. In managing these telecommunication ventures, Kluge retraced the steps he took in his television career: buy a license in a major market at an affordable price, then wait as the market evolves, and finally cash in.

In 1995 the Actava Group, Inc., Orion Pictures Corp., MCEG Sterling, Inc., and Metromedia Interna-

John Kluge.
Photo courtesy of Broadcasting & Cable

tional Telecommunications, Inc., signed an agreement to form a global communications entity to be named Metromedia International Group, Inc. Kluge already owned a major stake in Hollywood's Orion Pictures. The new four-part alliance merged wireless cable and Hollywood production skills to sell all forms of mass communication to citizens in Eastern Europe and the former Soviet Republics.

Investing and selling has benefited Kluge enormously. His wealth, which *Forbes* estimated at $5 billion as of the mid-1990s, vaulted him onto the list of the richest people in the United States. By the beginning of the 21st century, Metromedia International was mired in the same economic downturn that pulled down numerous telecommunications enterprises. Following an unprofitable cycle and the bankruptcy of Metromedia Fiber in May 2002, several top mangers left the company in the wake of shareholder criticism. In July 2002, Kluge, at 87, resigned as chairman of the board, though he retained control of Metromedia Fiber.

In 2003 Metromedia Fiber Network Inc. was eased of some of its bankruptcy burden when the telecommunications executive Craig McCaw bought some of its debt in exchange for an agreement that he would own a significant stake in the company when it comes out of bankruptcy. Kluge agreed to back the $25 million that remains after McCaw bought suppliers' claims against the company and agreed to back half of a $50 million stock offering. In 2003 Metromedia Fiber planned to change its name to AboveNet Inc.

DOUGLAS GOMERY

John (Werner) Kluge. Born in Chemnitz, Germany, September 21, 1914. Attended Wayne State University, Detroit, Michigan; Columbia University, B.A. in economics 1937. Married: 1) Theodora Thomson, 1946 (divorced); 2) Yolanda Zucco, 1969 (divorced); children: Samantha and Joseph; 3) Patricia Rose Gay, 1981 (divorced, 1990); child: John W. Kluge II. Served in U.S. Army intelligence, 1941–45. Immigrated to United States, 1922; worked assembly line, Ford Motor Company; vice president and sales manager, Otten Brothers, 1937–41; bought radio station WGAY, Silver Springs, Maryland, 1946; president and director, WGAY, 1946–59; president, New England Fritos, 1947–55; president, Mid-Florida Radio Corporation, Orlando, 1952–59; president and director, St. Louis Broadcasting Corporation, 1953–58; president, New York Institute of Dietetics, 1953–60; president and director, Pittsburgh Broadcasting Company, 1954–59; president, treasurer, and director, Capitol Broadcasting Company, Nashville, Tennessee, 1954–59; partner, Nashton Properties, Nashville, 1954–60; owner, Kluge

Investment Company, Washington, D.C., 1956–60; president and director, Washington Planagraph Company, 1956–60; founder, with David Finkelstein, wholesale food operation Kluge, Finkelstein and Company, Baltimore, Maryland, 1956; partner in Texworth Investment Company, Fort Worth, Texas, 1957–60; president, treasurer, and director, Associated Broadcasters, Inc., Fort Worth-Dallas, 1957–59; chair of the board, Seaboard Service Systems, Inc., 1957–58; treasurer and director of television operation, Mid-Florida Radio Corporation, 1957–60; partner in Western New York Broadcasting Company, Buffalo, New York, 1957–60; president, Washington Food Brokers Association, 1958; president, Metropolitan Broadcasting Company (became Metromedia, Inc., 1961; then Metromedia Company, 1980s), 1959; bought World Wide Broadcasting (WWB), 1960, sold WWB, 1962; vice president, later president and chairman of the executive committee, United Cerebral Palsy Research and Educational Foundation, from 1972; purchased Texas-based LDS, 1983; bought Florida-based Network 1, 1984; purchased all outstanding shares (72 percent) of Metromedia Company, becoming sole owner, 1984; sold off most Metromedia assets, 1984–92; became 69 percent owner, Orion Pictures, 1988; merged Metromedia Long Distance with long-distance divisions of International Telephone and Telegraph (ITT), forming Metromedia-ITT, 1989; merged Metromedia-ITT with Resurgens Communications Group and LDDS Communications to form LDDS Metromedia Communications, 1993. Chair of the board, treasurer, director, Kluge, Finkelstein and Company, from 1993; chair of the board and treasurer, Tri-Suburban Broadcasting Corporation and Washington, Kluge and Company; chair of the board, president, and treasurer, Washington, Silver City Sales Company; director, Marriott-Hot Shoppes, Inc., Chock Full O' Nuts Corporation, National Bank of Maryland, Waldorf Astoria Corporation, Just One Break, Inc., Belding Heminway Company, Inc.; board of directors, Bear Stearns Companies, Inc., Schubert Foundation, Occidental Petroleum Corporation, LDDS Metromedia, and national advisory board, Chemical Banking Corporation; trustee, Strang Cancer Prevention Center; chair, James Madison National Council of the Library of Congress. Member: advisory council, Manufacturers Hanover Trust Company; board of governors, New York College of Osteopathic Medicine; National Association of Radio and Television Broadcasters.

Publication

The Metromedia Story, 1974

Further Reading

Fabrikant, Geraldine, "Top Shareholder Offers Deal To End Bankruptcy at Orion," *New York Times* (May 23, 1992)

Flanagan, William G., "Share and Share Unlike," *Forbes* (June 10, 1991)

Grover, Ronald, "Will Flipper Play in Estonia: Why John Kluge Is on a Buying Binge in Hollywood," *Business Week* (January 8, 1996)

"It's Redstone vs. Kluge for Orion," *Broadcasting* (February 1, 1988)

"Kluge to Sell Metromedia's Stake in Worldwide," *New York Times* (August 15, 1995)

Marcial, Gene G., "The Action May Not Be Over at Metromedia," *Business Week* (September 27, 1993)

Martin, Justin, "College Boosters," *Fortune* (May 17, 1993)

Nicklin, Julie L., "Metromedia's Kluge Gives Columbia $60 Million for Minority Scholarships," *Chronicle of Higher Education* (April 28, 1993)

Peers, Martin, "Metromedia Signs Off on Goldwyn Buy," *Variety* (February 5, 1996)

Petrozzello, Donna, "Orion the Nucleus of New Kluge Venture: Metromedia International Group Will Use Film Library to Become Global Media Concern," *Broadcasting and Cable* (September 5, 1994)

Weber, Joseph, "The Millstones at Metromedia: What's Holding Back the Building of a New Long Distance Empire," *Business Week* (March 1, 1993)

Knowledge Network

Canadian (British Columbia) Public Educational Broadcaster

The Knowledge Network is the public educational television broadcaster of the Canadian province of British Columbia, a part of the province's larger effort to extend education to all parts of the province using various delivery systems. In 1978, the province established the Open Learning Institute (OLI), to develop and deliver educational programming using distance-education methods. These methods have included correspondence courses, audio, film, teleconferencing, videodiscs, and, increasingly, digital media products for reaching outside the conventional classroom. In 1980, in order to further the goals of distance education, the province created the Knowledge Network as part of OLI. The network went to air on January 12, 1981. The Knowledge Network today reaches 100 percent of all households in British Columbia. Its mandate, however, has led it to pursue two different types of audience. On the one hand, the Knowledge Network was mandated to provide general public education programs, which might interest casual viewers. These typically involve nature documentaries, British series, international drama, and children's programming. On the other hand, the Knowledge Network was also directed to collaborate with the province's educational institutions to deliver formal instruction, which would only interest registered students. This double focus has led to a progressive diversification in the types of programs offered.

In 1988, however, OLI was substantially reorganized. Renamed the Open Learning Agency (OLA), it was reshaped into three constituents: (1) the Open School, aimed at K–12 (kindergarten through 12th grade) students and teachers and administrators; (2) the Open College, responsible for adult basic education; and (3) the Open University offering accredited university-level degree courses.

The Knowledge Network's pursuit of two different types of audience (general and specialized) is typical of virtually all educational networks in Canada. As organizations concerned with education, educational networks naturally attempt to extend and give shape to the larger projects of their respective ministries of education. Consequently, they are involved in the delivery of course material, collaborate with educational institutions, and reflect various curricula in their scheduling. As television networks, however, they also find themselves confronted with a much broader constituency (in terms of age, background, ability, education, etc.) than would be likely in any classroom. Furthermore, they reach this constituency under conditions not conducive to learning. Hence, like all other educational networks, the Knowledge Network has construed education in a broad sense. It means not only formal education, or the content of lectures and courses, but also the attempt to create a generally literate, lively, and well-educated citizenry.

The result is clear in the Knowledge Network's schedule. The Knowledge Network devotes roughly half of its 6,000 annual broadcast hours to traditional educational material (credit and noncredit courses, college and university lectures, K–12 content, etc.). Televised courses constitute a minority of its schedule, and much instructional content has migrated to its interactive website. It devotes most of its broadcasting time to content of a more general and entertaining nature, such as programs devoted to film (international, Hollywood, Canadian), general documentaries, teleplays, how-to programs, music programs, children's shows, and so on.

The very effort to construe education as both formal and informal has led to the criticism that educational networks are no longer fulfilling their mandates. For some, they are increasingly perceived as publicly funded entertainment undertakings that compete unfairly with the private sector. This perception has, in turn, led to calls to cut public funding of the educational networks, or for them to be reorganized, abolished, or sold to private interests.

PAUL ATTALLAH

Further Reading

Mugridge, Ian, and David Kaufman, editors, *Distance Education in Canada,* London and Dover, New Hampshire: Croom Helm, 1986

Open Learning and Distance Education in Canada, Ottawa: Department of the Secretary of State of Canada, 1989

Sweet, Robert, editor, *Post-secondary Distance Education in Canada: Policies, Practices, and Priorities,* Athabasca, Alberta: Athabasca University, Canadian Society for Studies in Education, 1989

Koppel, Ted (1940–)

U.S. Broadcast Journalist

When Ted Koppel addressed Catholic University's graduating class in 1994, he proclaimed, "We have reconstructed the Tower of Babel, and it is a television antenna." In Koppel's words, "We now communicate with everyone and say absolutely nothing." This may be Koppel's opinion of television in general, but few observers would accept it as a description of Koppel or his late-night ABC news and public affairs program, *Nightline* (1980–), for which he has served many functions, including managing editor, anchor, interviewer, and principal on-air reporter. Koppel and *Nightline* have repeatedly won awards and consistently attracted large audiences, even battling against such successful network stars as Johnny Carson, Jay Leno, and David Letterman. In the eyes of many TV viewers, Koppel is a celebrity, a respected, gutsy commentator, one of the best interviewers on TV, and a superb reporter. *Newsweek* once called him the "smartest man in television." Clearly, Koppel does not "say absolutely nothing."

After first working in radio news at WMCA in New York, Koppel joined ABC News in 1963 as one of the youngest news reporters to ever work for a network, and he quickly rose through the ranks of the organization. He covered Vietnam and became the bureau chief for Miami, Florida, and then Hong Kong, before being named chief diplomatic correspondent in 1971. In this capacity, he established himself as one of television's best reporters. Then on November 4, 1979, Iranians seized the U.S. embassy in Iran, taking Americans hostage, and television news took another step toward becoming the most reliable source of news. Four days later, ABC News aired at 11:30 P.M. (Eastern Standard Time) a program called *The Iran Crisis: America Held Hostage,* anchored by Frank Reynolds. Roone Arledge, ABC News president, decided this program would continue till the hostage crisis was over; the show would eventually become a regular late-night newscast. After about five months, *The Iran Crisis* became *Nightline,* and Koppel, who had anchored *The Iran Crisis* several times, became the permanent anchor for the new program. Since 1980, it has been difficult to separate Koppel from *Nightline.*

Koppel has won nine Overseas Press Club Awards, six George Foster Peabodys, ten duPont-Columbia Awards, two George Polk Awards, two Sigma Delta Chi Awards, and 37 Emmys, as well as countless other honors. In 1994 the Republic of France named him a Chevalier de l'Ordre des Arts et des Lettres. He went to South Africa for a week-long series in 1985 to analyze apartheid and subsequently won a Gold Baton duPont-Columbia prize for the series. Koppel also interviewed the scandal-plagued televangelists Jim and Tammy Faye Baker on *Nightline,* attracting 42 percent

Ted Koppel.
Courtesy of the Everett Collection

of network viewers. He brought George H.W. Bush and Michael Dukakis to TV in the last days of the 1988 presidential election when neither was giving interviews. Also, in 1988, Koppel went to the Middle East to report on Arab-Israeli problems and held a town meeting attended by hundreds of Israeli and Arab citizens. He has probably brought Henry Kissinger (who once tried to hire Koppel as his press spokesman at the U.S. State Department) to TV more than any other interviewer. Among many other accomplishments, Koppel achieved a journalistic coup by being the first Western journalist to reach Baghdad after Iraq's Sadam Hussein invaded Kuwait in 1990. Koppel eventually began his own production company so he could produce his own programs, such as *The Koppel Reports.*

Koppel's success has been earned under the scrutiny of millions of viewers, and he has had his share of critics. While dealing with enormous programming, technological, and economic changes in the business of electronic journalism (not to mention enormous egos), Koppel has persisted and has usually come out on top. However, the style of *Nightline* was established early as one of "us-versus-them" during the Iran hostage crisis. Critics such as Michael Massing have said Koppel

and *Nightline* are not impartial; some contend that, especially with Kissinger's influence, the show (and therefore Koppel) serves as a "transmission belt for official U.S. views." Fairness and Accuracy in Reporting (a watchdog organization also known by its acronym, FAIR) has charged Koppel's *Nightline* as being overly influenced by white, male, corporate guests. In other words, the audience frequently only gets one side of an issue.

However, Koppel wants to be seen as impartial, and he wants *Nightline* to be a program where "people of varying stripes and political persuasions can feel comfortable." Koppel recognizes the possibility, raised by critics, that his work can actually influence news events, but he says that all the journalist can hope for is to "bring events to the attention of people in government," and of course to the public. In his book on ABC News, Marc Gunther describes Koppel's *Nightline* as the most significant addition to television news since *60 Minutes* was created in the 1960s. If this is so, then Ted Koppel may be one of the most significant journalists working in the medium.

In 2002 Koppel and *Nightline* became the center of a controversy that grabbed a great deal of media attention. The show's parent companies, Disney and ABC, insulted Koppel and his team by considering replacing *Nightline* with other programming, such as a comedy/talk program (for a time, ABC sought to lure David Letterman to bring his program to the time period in which *Nightline* aired, but Letterman eventually re-signed with CBS). The network hoped to attract a younger audience (and the higher ad revenues that programs pitched to that demographic could earn). On the other hand, many other TV news operations (e.g., CNN, PBS) began courting Koppel to join their news lineups, while many television critics as well as on-air journalists warned that ABC's treatment of Koppel epitomized the misguided priorities of networks at the beginning of the 21st century. However, Koppel and *Nightline* remained on the air with ABC.

CLAYLAND H. WAITE

See also **American Broadcasting Company**

Ted Koppel. Born in Lancashire, England, February 8, 1940. Educated at Syracuse University, New York, B.A. in speech, 1960; Stanford University, M.A. in mass communications research and political science, 1962. Married: Grace Anne Dorney, 1963, children: Andrea, Deirdre, Andrew, and Tara. Reporter, radio station WABC, 1963–67; television reporter, Saigon Bureau of ABC News, Vietnam, 1967–68; Miami bureau chief, ABC News, 1968; Hong Kong bureau chief, 1969–71; chief diplomatic correspondent, ABC News, 1971–80, correspondent, *ABC News Closeup,*

1973–74, anchor, ABC News programs, since 1975, including *Nightline,* since 1980; anchor of *The Koppel Reports,* since 1988. Recipient: nine Overseas Press Club Awards, six George Foster Peabody Awards, ten duPont-Columbia Awards, two George Polk Awards, two Sigma Delta Chi Awards, 37 Emmy Awards. Chevalier de l'Ordre des Arts et des Lettres, 1994.

Television Series

1967–80	*ABC News* (correspondent and bureau chief)
1973–74	*ABC News Closeup* (correspondent)
1975–76	*ABC Saturday Night News* (anchor)
1980–	*Nightline* (anchor)

Television Specials

1973	*The People of People's China*
1974	*Kissinger: Action Biography*

1975	*Second to None*
1988–90	*The Koppel Reports*

Publications

The Wit and Wisdom of Adlai Stevenson, 1965
In the National Interest (with Marvin Kalb), 1977
Nightline: History in the Making and the Making of Television (with Kyle Gibson), 1996
Off Camera: Private Thoughts Made Public, 2000

Further Reading

Corcoran, John, *A Few Marbles Left: A Close-Up Look at TV News in All Its Agonizing, Maddening Idiocy (Plus Its Occasional Moments of Glory),* Chicago: Bonus Books, 2001
Gunther, Marc, *The House That Roone Built: The Inside Story of ABC News,* Boston: Little, Brown, 1994
Massing, Michael, "Ted Koppel's Neutrality Act," *Columbia Journalism Review* (March–April 1989)

Kovacs, Ernie (1919–1962)

U.S. Comedian

Ernie Kovacs, a creative and iconoclastic comedian, pioneered the use of special effects photography in television comedy. On the 50th anniversary of the beginning of television in 1989, *People Weekly* recognized him as one of television's top-25 stars of all time. During the 1950s, Kovacs's brilliant use of video comedy demonstrated the unique possibilities of television, decades before similar techniques became popular on *Rowan and Martin's Laugh-In* and the various David Letterman shows. His live shows were characterized by ad-libbed routines, enormous flexibility with the TV camera, experimentation with video effects, complete informality while on camera, and a permissiveness that expanded studio boundaries by allowing viewers to see activity beyond the set.

His routines frequently parodied other programs and introduced imaginative Kovacsian characters such as the magician Natzoh Hepplewhite, Professor Bernie Cosnowski, and Mr. Question Man, whose traits would later be echoed in Johnny Carson's Carnac the Magnificent. The best-known of his creations was the Nairobi Trio, three ape instrumentalists playing "Solfeggio" in a deadpan manner like mechanical monkeys. The high point came when the percussionist turned jerkily to the conductor and bopped him on the head with a xylophone hammer.

Following a career in radio, Kovacs's transition to television came in 1950, when he simultaneously hosted several programs on NBC's WPTZ in Philadelphia, Pennsylvania. His first show, *Deadline for Dinner,* consisted of cooking tips from guest chefs. When a guest did not show, Kovacs did his own recipe for "Eggs Scavok" ("Scavok" being his name spelled backward). In August 1950, he hosted a quiz and fashion program titled *Pick Your Ideal,* basically a 15-minute promotional for the Ideal Manufacturing Company. In November of that year, he pioneered one of TV's first morning wake-up programs. The unstructured format required improvisational abilities Kovacs had mastered on radio. The daily 90-minute slot was titled *3 To Get Ready.* (The number 3 referred to channel 3, or WPTZ).

Kovacs's off-the-wall style was extremely unorthodox in early television. He approached the medium as something totally new. While his contemporaries were treating TV as an extension of vaudeville stages, Kovacs was expanding the visible confines of the studio. His skits incorporated areas previously considered

Ernie Kovacs.
Photo courtesy of Edie Adams Archive

taboo, including dialogue with the camera crew, the audience, and forays into the studio corridor.

Impressed with his abilities, NBC network executives scheduled his first network show, *It's Time for Ernie,* in May 1951. The daily 15-minute broadcast aired from WPTZ, featuring Kovacs and music from a local combo known as the Tony deSimone Trio. In July he received his first prime-time slot as a summer replacement for *Kukla, Fran, and Ollie. Ernie in Kovacsland* opened with the music "Oriental Blues" and title cards with cartoon drawings of Ernie. A voice-over announced: "Ernie in Kovacsland! A short program—it just seems long."

Early in 1952, Kovacs reappeared on daytime TV as host for *Kovacs on the Corner,* the last of his shows to originate from Philadelphia. Similar to radio's *Allen's Alley,* Kovacs strolled along a cartoon-like set and talked to such neighborhood characters as Luigi the Barber, Pete the Cop, Al the Dog, and Little Johnny Merkin, a midget. One program segment allowed a selected audience member to say hello to folks back home. A closed window filled the screen. On the window shade was printed the phrase "Yoo-Hoo Time." When the shade was raised, the excited audience member waved, saying "Yoo-hoo!"

In April 1952, Kovacs moved to WCBS in New York as host of a local daytime comedy-variety show named *Kovacs Unlimited.* Known for its parodies of other programs, *Kovacs Unlimited* can be compared to *Saturday Night Live,* which resembles it. It was Kovacs's longest-running series out of New York, lasting 21 months.

In December, CBS aired a new, national *Ernie Kovacs Show* opposite NBC's *Texaco Star Theater* with Milton Berle. Kovacs produced and wrote the show himself, and, as with his earlier broadcasts, much of the program was improvised. Unlike other TV comedies, there was no studio audience, nor was canned laughter used. In Kovacs's view, the usefulness of an audience was diminished because they could not see the special effects. Described as his "hallucinatory world," the program featured many ingenious video effects, as though illusion and reality were confused. In his skits, paintings came to life, flames from candles remained suspended in midair, and library books spoke.

Kovacs reappeared periodically in shows over various networks. In April 1954, the DuMont network's flagship station, WABD in New York, scheduled him as a late-night rival to Steve Allen. NBC aired his show as a daytime comedy premiering in December 1955 and in prime time a year later. Kovacs's final appearances were in a monthly series over ABC during 1961 and 1962. He received an Emmy for the 1961 series sponsored by Dutch-Masters Cigars. Regulars on many of Kovacs's early shows were Edie Adams, who became his second wife; straight-men Trigger Lund and Andy McKay; and the Eddie Hatrak Orchestra.

The most extraordinary episode in Kovacs's career was the half-hour NBC broadcast, without dialogue, known as the "Silent Show." Seen on January 19, 1957, it was the first prime-time program done entirely in pantomime. Accompanied by only sound effects and music, Kovacs starred as the mute, Chaplinesque "Eugene," a character he earlier developed during the fall of 1956 when hosting *The Tonight Show.* In 1961 Kovacs and codirector Joe Behar received the Directors Guild of America Award for a second version of the program aired over ABC.

Kovacs was an avant-garde experimenter in a television era governed by norms from earlier entertainment media. In his routines, he pioneered the use of blackouts, teaser openings, improvisations with everyday objects, matting techniques, synchronization of music and sound with images, and various camera effects including superimpositions, reverse polarity (a switch making positive seem negative), and reverse scanning (flipping images upside down). Several TV documentaries have celebrated his work. These include WNJT's *Cards and Cigars: The Trenton in Ernie Kovacs*

(1980), Showtime Cable's *Ernie Kovacs: Television's Original Genius* (1982), and ABC's *Ernie Kovacs: Between the Laughter* (1984). In 1987 he was inducted into the Academy of Television Arts and Sciences Hall of Fame.

FRANK J. CHORBA

See also **Ernie Kovacs Show, The**

Ernie Kovacs. Born in Trenton, New Jersey, January 23, 1919. Attended New York School of Theatre and American Academy of Dramatic Art in Manhattan. Married: 1) Bette Wilcox, 1945 (divorced, 1954); children: Betty Lee Andrea (Elizabeth) and Kip Raleigh (Kippie); 2) Edie Adams, 1954; one daughter. As teenager, performed in stock companies, 1936–39; hospitalized, for 19 months, 1939–40; formed own stock company, 1941–43; columnist for hometown newspaper, *The Trentonian,* 1945–50; announcer, director of special events, and assistant of programming, radio station WTTM, 1942–50; first worked in television, 1950, on cooking show for WPTZ-TV; morning show, WPTZ-TV, 1950; *It's Time for Ernie,* NBC-TV, 1951; host, various shows, 1950s; first film, *Operation Mad Ball,* 1957; *Bell, Book and Candle,* 1958; first starring vehicle in British film *Five Golden Hours,* 1961. Recipient: Emmy Awards, 1957 and 1961; Directors Guild of America Award, 1961; named to Academy of Television Arts and Sciences Hall of Fame, 1987. Died in Los Angeles, California, January 13, 1962.

Television Series (selected)

1951	*It's Time for Ernie*
1951	*Ernie in Kovacsland*
1952–53, 1956	*The Ernie Kovacs Show* (originally titled *Kovacs Unlimited*)
1960–61	*Silents Please* (host)

Television Specials

1957	*Festival of Magic* (host)
1961	*Private Eye, Private Eye* (host)
1961–62	*The Ernie Kovacs Special*

Films

Operation Mad Ball, 1957; *Bell, Book and Candle,* 1958; *It Happened to Jane,* 1958; *Our Man in Havana,* 1959; *Wake Me When It's Over,* 1960; *Strangers When We Meet,* 1960; *Pepe,* 1960; *North to Alaska,* 1960; *Five Golden Hours,* 1961; *Sail a Crooked Ship,* 1961; *Cry for Happy,* 1961.

Further Reading

"Ernie Kovacs, 1919–1962, Television Performer," *People Weekly* (Summer 1989)

Lochte, Dick, "The Best of Ernie Kovacs," *Los Angeles Magazine* (October 1991)

Rico, Diana, *Kovacsland: A Biography of Ernie Kovacs,* New York: Harcourt Brace Jovanovich, 1990

Whalley, David, *The Ernie Kovacs Phile,* New York: Simon and Schuster, 1987

Zoglin, Richard, "Celebrating a Comedy Composer," *Time* (July 14, 1986)

Kraft Television Theatre

U.S. Anthology Series

Kraft Television Theatre proved to be one of the most durable and honored programs of what is sometimes referred to as the "Golden Age" of American dramatic television, airing on NBC from 1947 to 1958. Produced by the J. Walter Thompson advertising agency, this live anthology drama was designed to mesh with Kraft's overall marketing strategy, which stressed the concept of "gracious living," an appeal to middle-class, suburban, family values. *Kraft Television Theatre* featured quietly paced, intimate dramas; as one Kraft representative put it, the show was a "respectful guest in America's living rooms."

Although *Kraft Television Theatre* quickly established itself as a critical favorite after its premiere in May 1947, in Kraft's estimation the show was only as useful as its ability to move product. In this it succeeded beyond fondest expectations. The first indication of the magnitude of the program's sales prowess came from Thompson's sales department, which reported in June that McLaren's Imperial Cheese, a new Kraft product advertised only on television, was flying off grocers' shelves.

The decision to feature food preparation over hard-sell personality or price appeals was not made lightly.

Kraft Television Theatre: "Burlesque."
Photo courtesy of Kraft Foods, Inc.

Kraft's advertising personnel were concerned that using a model or a recognized spokesman would detract from the product, so Thompson designed live commercials that used a single-focus technique. Each program had, on average, a pair of two-minute breaks, at which time cameras focused on a pair of feminine hands as they demonstrated the preparation of various dishes while announcer Ed Herlihy relayed the recipe to the viewer. This careful approach paid off for Kraft; sales of advertised products rose dramatically in television cities, and, even more importantly, a poll conducted by *Television* magazine in November 1947 showed that *Kraft Television Theatre* had the highest sponsor-identification of any show on television.

Kraft and Thompson prided themselves on keeping costs at a minimum in the early years. The dramatic emphasis was on warm and engaging family fare ("realism with a modest moral," as one executive said) solicited from young playwrights in New York; all performers were selected by Thompson's casting department. Although the show was almost entirely an agency product, NBC took a great interest in the program's operation—too much, at times, for the agency's liking.

Still, *Kraft Television Theatre* remained Thompson's defining program, and through its long run (the show never went on hiatus during its 11 years on the air), it featured such outstanding plays as Rod Serling's "Patterns"; "A Night to Remember," in which the Titanic disaster was memorably reproduced; and a version of Senator John F. Kennedy's book *Profiles in Courage.* Several noted directors, including George Roy Hill, Fielder Cook, and Sidney Lumet, served their apprenticeships on the program.

In October 1954, a second *Kraft Television Theatre* debuted, this time on ABC. The addition of another series surprised many industry observers, who expected Kraft, if anything, to pare its television activities. The original *Kraft Television Theatre* was never a ratings success, but Kraft apparently never expected it to be, consistently claiming that they measured the show's popularity by the number of recipe requests it drew, not by its Nielsen ratings. The ABC version was conceived with the intent of creating another advertising vehicle for Kraft's burgeoning product line, such as the new Cheez Whiz. However, sales figures from products advertised on the ABC program did not justify the additional $2 million in costs, so Kraft pulled the show in January 1955.

By 1958 the anthology drama had yielded to serial narratives with their recurring characters and situations, and in April 1958, after a sustained period of ratings lassitude, Kraft decided to sell the rights to the program to Talent Associates, a production company headed by David Susskind. The movement from agency to package production relieved much of Kraft's financial obligation to the show, as the company could now split production costs with Susskind. *Kraft Television Theatre* remained on the air only a few more months before it was completely reconfigured by Talent Associates as *Kraft Mystery Theatre,* which lasted until September 1958.

MICHAEL MASHON

See also **Advertising, Company Voice; Advertising Agency; Anthology Drama; "Golden Age" of Television;** *Hour Glass*

Announcers
Ed Herlihy (1947–55)
Charles Stark (1955)

Programming History
NBC

May 1947–December 1947	Wednesday 7:30–8:30	
January 1948–October 1958	Wednesday 9:00–10:00	

ABC
October 1953–January 1955   Thursday
                                9:30–10:30

Further Reading

Hawes, William, *The American Television Drama: The Experimental Years,* University: University of Alabama Press, 1986

Kindem, Gorham, editor, *The Live Television Generation of Hollywood Film Directors: Interviews with Seven Directors,* Jefferson, North Carolina: McFarland, 1994

MacDonald, J. Fred, *One Nation Under Television: The Rise and Decline of Network TV,* New York: Pantheon, 1990

Skutch, Ira, *Ira Skutch: I Remember Television: A Memoir,* Metuchen, New Jersey: Scarecrow Press, 1989

Stempel, Tom, *Storytellers to the Nation: A History of American Television Writing,* New York: Continuum, 1992

Sturcken, Frank, *Live Television: The Golden Age of 1946–1958 in New York,* Jefferson, North Carolina: McFarland, 1990

Wicking, Christopher, and Tise Vahimagi, *The American Vein: Directors and Directions in Television,* New York: Dutton, 1979

Wilk, Max, *The Golden Age of Television: Notes from the Survivors,* New York: Delacorte Press, 1976

Kukla, Fran and Ollie

Children's Puppet/Variety Program

Kukla, Fran and Ollie was the first children's show to be equally popular with children and adults. The show's immense popularity stemmed from its simplicity, gentle fun and frolic, and adult wit. Burr Tillstrom's Kuklapolitan Players differed from typical puppets in that the humor derived from satire and sophisticated wit rather than slapstick comedy. At the height of the show's popularity, the cast received 15,000 letters a day and the program's ratings were comparable to shows featuring Milton Berle and Ed Sullivan.

The basic format of the show was simple: Fran Allison stood in front of a small stage and interacted with the characters. The format was derived from the puppet act Tillstrom performed for the RCA Victor exhibit at the 1939 New York World's Fair. Acting as an entr'acte for the RCA Victor Puppet Opera at the fair, Kukla and Ollie would comment on the activities, sometimes heckle the announcer, and coax the actresses and models acting as exhibit spokespersons to come up onto the stage and talk with them. Never working from a written script, Tillstrom improvised more than 2,000 performances at the World's Fair, each one different because of his personal dislike of routine. During World War II, Tillstrom and his Kuklapolitan Players performed in United Service Organization (USO) shows, at army hospitals, and for bond drives, where he met radio personality Fran Allison.

In 1947 the majority of television sets were located in taverns and saloons. Network executives were looking for a television show that could be watched at home and decided the Kuklapolitans would be the perfect "family fare." The group was contracted for 13 weeks on daytime TV and stayed for the next ten years.

The first episodes were aired daily from 4:00 to 5:00 P.M. on local Chicago television station WBKB, which was later acquired by NBC. When the network completed its New York-Chicago transmission lines in 1948, *Kukla, Fran and Ollie* began to air nationwide. By its second season, the growing adult audience prompted the network to move the show to a 7:00 P.M. half-hour time slot. By its third season, the show had 6 million viewers. In 1951 NBC cut the half-hour format to 15 minutes, which, ironically, caused the ratings to soar even higher because audiences craved more of their favorite characters, and NBC was deluged with letters of outrage from fans. After several seasons, the daily program was shifted to a weekly program on Sunday afternoons. When the series switched from NBC to ABC in 1954, it returned to a daily broadcast. Before being canceled in 1957, the series had been one of the longest-running programs on television, second only to *Kraft Television Theatre.*

With few exceptions (e.g., elaborately staged versions of *The Mikado* and an original operetta of *St. George and the Dragon,* which aired in 1953), all of the shows were improvised. Pre-show preparation consisted of a meeting of Tillstrom, Allison, director Lewis Gomavitz, musical director Jack Fascinato, costume designer Joe Lockwood, and producer Beulah Zachary to discuss the basic premise for that day's program.

The immense popularity of the show stemmed from

how it created its own unique world of make-believe. The characters were not caricatures, but rather fully developed, three-dimensional individuals with distinct histories, personalities, eccentricities, and foibles. In the show's initial episodes, the Kuklapolitans were strong characters, but not individuals. Through the simple banter between Allison and one of the "kids" (as Tillstrom, Allison, and others referred to the puppets), audiences learned more of each characters' individual history: where they went to school; their relatives; how an ancestor of Ollie's once swam the Hellespont (Dardonelle Strait) and took in too much water, thereby drowning the family's fire-breathing ability; and the time Buelah Witch was arrested by Interpol for flying too low over the United Nations building.

The leader of the troupe was Kukla, a sweet-natured and gentle clown who was something of a worrywart. Oliver J. Dragon (Ollie), atypical of traditional puppet show dragons, was a mischievous, one-toothed dragon with a penchant for getting into trouble. Other members of the Kuklapolitans included grand dame Madame Ophelia Oglepuss, Stage Manager Cecil Bill (who spoke a language comprehensible only to the other Kuklapolitans), debonair Southern gentleman Colonel R.H. Crackie, floppy-eared Fletcher Rabbit, Buelah Witch (named for producer Beulah Zachary—with the intentional misspelling), Ollie's mother Olivia Dragon, his niece Dolores (whom audiences saw grow from a noisy infant into a typical teenage dragonette), and many others. The human qualities of these characters endeared them to their audience.

It could be said that Allison acted as "straight man" to this cast of characters, but her role was much greater. A quick wit in her own right who could maintain the pace set by Tillstrom, Allison served simultaneously, according to Tillstrom, as "big sister, favorite teacher, babysitter, girlfriend, and mother." Allison was equally responsible for adding to the characters' histories. She was the first to mention Ollie's mother, inspiring Tillstrom to create the character for a future show.

The Kuklapolitans returned briefly for one season in 1961 for a daily five-minute show without Fran Allison. *Kukla, Fran and Ollie* was revived for two seasons (1969–71) for PBS, and from 1971 to 1979, the Kuklapolitans with Allison served as hosts for the Saturday afternoon *CBS Children's Film Festival*. The characters continued to appear in syndicated specials throughout the early 1980s. In all of these series and formats, the essential elements of the original series remained the same.

During its run on television, *Kukla, Fran and Ollie* received a total of nine Emmy nominations for Best Children's Program but won only once, in 1954. It was awarded a George Foster Peabody Award as the Outstanding Children's Program of 1949. In a tribute to creator Burr Tillstrom, co-worker Donald Corren stated in 1986, "The acceptance of television puppetry as a form of entertainment and communication exists because *Kukla, Fran and Ollie* was as much a part of the original television vocabulary as were 'station identification,' 'the six-o'clock news,' or the chimes that identified NBC." Because the Kuklapolitans were such vibrant characters, Tillstrom requested in his will that they never be put on display inertly unless they are moving and speaking as he intended them to be seen.

SUSAN R. GIBBERMAN

See also **Allison, Fran; Chicago School of Television; Children and Television; Tillstrom, Burr**

Host
Fran Allison

Announcer
Hugh Downs

Puppeteer
Burr Tillstrom

Musical Director
Jack Fascinato

Puppets
Kukla
Ollie (Oliver J. Dragon)
Fletcher Rabbit
Mme. Ophelia Oglepuss
Buelah Witch
Cecil Bill
Col. R.H. Crackie
Mercedes
Dolores Dragon (1950–57)
Olivia Dragon (1952–57)

Producers
Burr Tillstrom, Beulah Zachary

Programming History
NBC

November 1948–November 1951	Monday–Friday 7:00–7:30
November 1951–June 1952	Monday–Friday 7:00–7:15
ABC	
September 1954–August 1957	Monday–Friday 7:00–7:15

Further Reading

Adams, Rosemary K., "Here We Are Again: *Kukla, Fran and Ollie*," *Chicago History* (Fall 1997)

Corren, Donald, "Kukla, Me, and Ollie: Remembering Chicago's Legendary Puppeteer, Burr Tillstrom," *Chicago* (July 1986)

"End of the Affair," *Time* (September 9, 1957)

Gehman, Richard B., "Mr. Oliver J. Dragon…and Friends," *Theatre Arts* (October 1950)

Haynes, George Gleve, "Kukla, Fran, and Fletcher," *New York Times* (June 30, 1989)

"Kukla, Fran and Ollie," in *The Golden Age of Television: Notes from the Survivors,* edited by Max Wilk, Mount Kisco, New York: Moyer Bell, 1989

Mitchard, Jacquelyn, "Kukla, Fran, Ollie, and Me," *TV Guide* (November 16, 1996)

"Shed a Tear for Them," *Newsweek* (September 9, 1957)

Stover, Carol, "*Kukla, Fran and Ollie:* A Show for All Time," *Antiques and Collecting Magazine* (May 1997)

Terkel, Studs, "Burr Tillstrom, 1966 and 1978," in *The Spectator: Talk About Movies and Plays with the People Who Make Them,* by Terkel, New York: New Press, 1999

Kuralt, Charles (1934–1997)

U.S. News Correspondent

Charles Kuralt is best known for his critically acclaimed series "On the Road," television "essays" on the United States, and for his 15-year tenure as host of the equally acclaimed *CBS Sunday Morning* series. Through a CBS network career spanning four decades, this award-winning journalist and author brought the life and vitality of back-roads America to an eager audience while providing a television home for the arts, the environment, and the offbeat.

Kuralt began his career as a reporter-columnist in 1955 for the *Charlotte News*. His penchant for unusual human interest stories found a home in the *News*' daily "People" column, which in turn earned him the 1956 Ernie Pyle Memorial Award. A year later he was recruited by CBS. His first network job was to rewrite wires and cables from overseas correspondents for radio newscasts, but he quickly advanced to the position of writer for *CBS Evening News.* In 1958 he moved to the CBS television news assignment desk, where he also covered fast-breaking stories. A year later, he became a full-fledged correspondent—the youngest person ever to win that position. In 1960 his star continued to rise, as he was chosen over Walter Cronkite to host a new CBS public affairs series, *Eyewitness to History.* However, within four months he was replaced by Cronkite and was moved back to general assignment reporting. He was named chief of CBS's newly established Latin American bureau during the Kennedy administration, then chief West Coast correspondent in 1963. He also reported from various global hot spots in Africa, Europe, and Southeast Asia, including four tours of duty in Vietnam.

Contributing special reports to the documentary series *CBS Reports* and anchoring several public affairs specials in addition to his regular reporting duties, Kuralt began to tire of the grind and rivalry inherent in daily reporting. To remedy this, he devised his plan for "On the Road." After an initial negative reaction, he managed to win minimal support from network executives who granted him a three-month trial.

Kuralt's three-month trial began in October 1967, and turned into a 25-year odyssey. With cameraman Izzy Bleckman and soundman Larry Gianneschi, he logged more than 1 million miles in six motor homes while producing approximately 500 "On the Road" segments. Staying off the interstates and with no set itinerary, he drew upon viewer letters, a state-by-state clipping file, and occasional references from public relations firms and local chambers of commerce to find unusual stories and unsung heroes. He had total freedom to discover the United States.

In the early 1970s, CBS considered reassigning Kuralt, but he was ever reluctant to leave the road. He did serve as cohost with Sylvia Chase on the short-lived *CBS News Adventure* in 1970, and in May 1974, on *Magazine,* an afternoon news and features program. He also contributed pieces to another short-lived prime-time magazine show, *Who's Who* (1977). With Dan Rather and Barbara Howar concentrating on more famous, high-profile newsmakers, he brought, in typical Kuralt fashion, the *Who's Who* viewing audience such unlikely characters as the inventor of the shopping cart, champion boomerang throwers, and an 89-year-old kite flyer.

With network assurance that he could continue "On the Road," on January 28, 1979, Kuralt assumed the anchor position on the new *CBS News Sunday Morning.* Leisurely paced and low-key, in keeping with its

Charles Kuralt.
Photo courtesy of Wisonsin Center for Film and Theater Research

early Sunday morning time slot, the 90-minute show examined major headlines and provided a weekly in-depth cover story and a series of special reports on law, science, the environment, music, the arts, education, and world affairs. In essence, with its eclectic view of the United States, *Sunday Morning* became a natural extension of "On the Road," providing an outlet for topics not regularly covered on other newscasts. Commented Milton Rhodes, president of the American Council for the Arts, in the June 1987 issue of *Horizon:* "Nowhere else on television does a journalist of Kuralt's reputation discuss the arts as regularly, as fully, and as intelligently as he."

For 18 months, Kuralt combined his *Sunday Morning* activities with his ongoing "On the Road" reports, but in October 1980 he left the road to become anchor for the daily morning network news offering. *Morning with Charles Kuralt* would be criticized for being too slow-paced for the time period, and, in mid-March 1982 Kuralt was replaced as anchor and sent back out on the road. Within two years, his new "On the Road" reports became the centerpiece of yet another short-lived prime-time series, *The American Parade.*

Openly opposed to the fast-paced, minimal information format of many news broadcasts, through the years Kuralt chastised television executives for "hiring hair instead of brains." Quoted in *TV Guide* on April 2, 1994, Kuralt said, "I am ashamed that so many [anchorpersons] haven't any basis on which to make a news judgment, can't edit, can't write, and can't cover a story." As *TV Guide's* Neil Hickey reported, these are all things Kuralt could do and for which he was honored with 11 Emmy Awards and three Peabody Awards.

Into the 1990s, Kuralt continued his *Sunday Morning* efforts and for an approximate five-month period beginning in October 1990, cohosted the nightly news summary, *America Tonight,* four nights a week, with Lesley Stahl. Then on April 3, 1994, at the age of 59, he retired from CBS with a poetic good-bye to his audience at the conclusion of his *Sunday Morning* broadcast. In 1997 he came out of his short-lived retirement to host two new television offerings, *An American Moment,* a syndicated series of 90-second vignettes on American life, and *I Remember,* a weekly one-hour broadcast examining major news stories from the past 30 years. However, his health deteriorated, and in June 1997 he was diagnosed with lupus. Kuralt died of heart failure and complications from lupus on July 4, 1997, and he was buried on the campus of his alma mater, the University of North Carolina.

Described by *Newsweek* on July 4, 1983, as "our beloved visiting uncle" and a "de Tocqueville in a motor home," Kuralt worked to awaken the United States to the beauty of its landscape, the depth, and character of its people, and the qualities of excellence possible in television journalism. On the occasion of his death, Kuralt's long-time CBS associate Dan Rather echoed those sentiments in the *New York Times:* "Charles's essays were miniature movies, carefully scripted, filmed, and edited," said Rather. "They told of our life and times. They had breadth, depth, and sweep to engage the eye, ear and mind."

JOEL STERNBERG

Charles Bishop Kuralt. Born in Wilmington, North Carolina, September 10, 1934. Educated at University of North Carolina, B.A. 1955. Married: Suzanna Folsom Baird, 1962; children from previous marriage: Lisa Bowers White and Susan Guthery Bowers. Columnist and reporter, *Charlotte News* (North Carolina), 1955–57; writer, CBS News, 1957–59; correspondent, CBS News, from 1959; first host of *Eyewitness,* 1960; named CBS News chief Latin America correspondent, 1961; chief West Coast correspondent, 1963; CBS News, New York, 1964; "On the Road" correspondent and host, from 1967; *CBS Sunday Morning* correspondent, from 1979, host, from

1980. Recipient: Ernie Pyle Memorial Award, 1956; George Foster Peabody Broadcasting Awards, 1969, 1976, 1980; 11 Emmy Awards; International Radio-TV Society's Broadcaster of the Year, 1985; DuPont-Columbia Award; George Polk Award; National Association of Broadcasters Distinguished Service Award, 1996. Died in New York City, July 4, 1997.

Television Series (writer, correspondent, host)

1957–59	*CBS Evening News* (writer)
1959–1994	*CBS News* (correspondent)
1960–61	*Eyewitness to History* (host)
1970	*CBS News Adventure*
1977	*Who's Who?*
1979–94	*CBS News Sunday Morning* (correspondent, host)
1980–82	*Morning with Charles Kuralt*
1983	*On the Road with Charles Kuralt*
1984	*The American Parade*
1990	*America Tonight*
1997	*I Remember* (host)
1997	*An American Moment* (host)

Publications

To the Top of the World: The First Plaisted Polar Expedition, 1968

Dateline America, 1979

"Point of View: This New News Isn't Good News," *Chicago Tribune,* May 2, 1982

"On the Road with Charles Kuralt," *Reader's Digest,* December 1983

On the Road with Charles Kuralt, 1985

Southerners: Portrait of a People, 1986

North Carolina Is My Home, 1986

"Backroads: Journeys Through the South to Places 'Like Nowhere Else,'" *Chicago Tribune,* January 4, 1987

A Life on the Road, 1990

"The Rocky Road to Popularity," *Saturday Evening Post,* March 1991

Growing Up in North Carolina, 1993

Charles Kuralt's America, 1995

Further Reading

Baker, Russell, "Gone with America," *New York Times* (April 5, 1994)

Carman, John, "CBS Sunday Morning: Free To Be Smart," *Channels* (October 1986)

Carter, Bill, "A Charles Kuralt Visit Turns into 15 Years," *New York Times* (February 5, 1994)

"Charles Kuralt," *Variety* (July 14, 1997)

Daley, Steve, "Keillor and Kuralt on the Prairie Beat," *Chicago Tribune* (June 18, 1987)

Ferretti, Fred, "A Gourmet at Large: Charles Kuralt, Television's Man on the Road" *Gourmet* (April 1996)

Goodman, Walter, "Long Time on Less-Traveled Roads," *New York Times* (May 4, 1994)

Johnson, Steve, "Kuralt Could Never Be Replaced, Even if Networks Wanted To," *Chicago Tribune* (July 11, 1997)

Rathbun, Elizabeth, "Kuralt Returns to 'Road' Stop; Buys Minnesota Condo," *Broadcasting and Cable* (September 4, 1995)

Rather, Dan, "A Poet with a Camera in Tow," *New York Times* (July 13, 1997)

Reibstein, Larry, "The End of the Road: Charles Kuralt, Teller of Stories, 1934–1997," *Newsweek* (July 14, 1997)

Kureishi, Hanif (1954–)

British Writer, Director

Hanif Kureishi, an Anglo-Pakistani writer, is best known to international audiences as the screenwriter of *My Beautiful Launderette,* one of the greatest international successes of British television's Channel 4.

Born in London of an English mother and a Pakistani father, Kureishi documents the population of London's margins: an underclass of disenfranchised youth, immigrants from former British colonies, leftist intellectuals, sexual outlaws (gays, lesbians, and heterosexuals refusing serial monogamy), and those individuals who cross class, ethnic, and sexual boundaries. His stories are often set in the Notting Hill district, a neighborhood once at the center of the country's most violent racial unrest.

Notting Hill is also the home of film and television director, Stephen Frears, with whom Kureishi collaborated on two projects for Channel 4's Film on Four, *My Beautiful Launderette* and *Sammy and Rosie Get Laid.* Frears is one of many British directors who have worked both on films produced exclusively for televi-

Hanif Kureishi.
Photo courtesy of Hanif Kureishi

sion and on films that are theatrically released but have been funded all or in part by television (the two Frears-Kureishi films are examples of the latter). Frears has repeatedly claimed that television—not the cinema—is the best site for communicating the quality of daily life in Britain. When he encountered Kureishi's script for *My Beautiful Launderette,* he was excited by the prospect of bringing the story of the everyday lives of a group of entrepreneurial Pakistanis and disenfranchised white youth to a British television audience of up to 12 million people, 74 percent of whom never attend the cinema.

The film centers on Omar, a Pakistani caught, like so many of Kureishi's characters, between two worlds—those of his leftist intellectual father, now a bitter alcoholic, and of his Uncle Nasser, a wealthy slumlord who lets his nephew revamp one of his laundromats. Omar first employs and then becomes lovers and partners with a former school chum, Johnny, one of the hundreds of unemployed white youths in London in the 1980s. The racist attacks on Omar by the other white youth are graphically depicted, but Kureishi does not demonize the perpetrators. In the universe of his stories, the once-colonized are sometimes the new exploiters, and left versus right, us versus them dichotomies do not apply. Omar respects his father but imitates his economically successful uncle, keeping his homosexual love affair with Johnny from both.

In *Sammy and Rosie Get Laid,* Rafi, a Pakistani official and wealthy factory owner, returns to London to rekindle relationships with his son Sammy; his leftist English daughter-in-law, Rosie; and his former mistress Alice. The film condemns Rafi's association with a government that used torture on its citizens, but Kureishi endows the character with lively hedonistic impulses that underscore his affinity with his non-monogamous son and daughter-in-law, whose leftist beliefs are more in sync with the writer's.

Critics usually point to Kureishi's masterful use of irony in these two films whose characters embody Margaret Thatcher's meritocrats and entrepreneurs, but who still find their identity in some of the sensual excesses of the 1960s—most notably sexual experimentation and/or drugs—that were decried by the Thatcher regime. In 1993 the writer adapted his own novel, *Buddha of Suburbia,* as a four-hour miniseries for BBC 2. This program explores the social climate of 1970s Britain leading to the rise of the conservative government of the 1980s and 1990s. Avowedly auto-biographical, the narrative follows Karim, a young Anglo-Pakistani, through the experiments of the 1960s that mutated into a "series of scary, delirious little moments of cocksure revolt" in the 1970s. Because of its heavy use of obscene language and explicit sexual situations, the BBC moved the time for airing the series a half-hour later than originally scheduled, and it was never picked up for U.S. television distribution (although it was screened in its entirety at the 1994 San Francisco Film Festival). Kureishi has written in his "Film Diary," that "openness and choice in sexual behavior is liberating," while "ambition and competitiveness are stifling narrowers of personality." By that prescription, his major characters—ambitious, competitive, but risk-takers in sensuality—are complex studies in the contradictions of Britain from the 1970s through the 1990s.

MARY DESJARDINS

Hanif Kureishi. Born in London, December 5, 1954. Attended King's College, University of London, B.A. in philosophy. Began career as playwright with *Soaking in Hell,* produced in London, 1976; has also directed his own work.

Television Series

1993   *The Buddha of Suburbia*

Made-for-Television Movies

1984   *My Beautiful Laundrette*
1987   *Sammy and Rosie Get Laid*
1991   *London Kills Me* (also director)

Film

My Beautiful Laundrette, 1985; *Sammy and Rosie Get Laid,* 1987; *My Son the Fanatic,* 1997; *Mauvais Passe* (also known as *The Escort,* also known as *The Wrong Blonde*), 1999; *Intimacy,* 2001; *The Mother,* 2003.

Radio

You Can't Go Home, 1980; *The Trial,* 1982.

Stage

Soaking in Hell, 1976; *The Mother Country,* 1980; *The King and Me,* 1980; *Outskirts,* 1980; *Tomorrow-Today!,* 1981; *Cinders,* 1981; *Borderline,* 1981; *Artists and Admirers,* with David Leveaux, 1982; *Birds of Passage,* 1983; *Mother Courage,* 1984; *My Beautiful Laundrette,* 1986; *Sleep with Me,* 1999.

Publications

Borderline, 1981
Birds of Passage, 1983

"Introduction," *My Beautiful Laundrette,* 1986
"Film Diary," *Granta,* Autumn 1987
Sammy and Rosie Get Laid: The Script and the Diary, 1988
The Buddha of Suburbia, 1991
London Kills Me, 1991
Outskirts and Other Plays, 1992
The Black Album, 1995
The Faber Book of Pop (editor with Jon Savage), 1995
Love in a Blue Time, 1997
Intimacy, 1998
Midnight All Day, 1999
Gabriel's Gift, 2001

Further Reading

Dixon, Wheeler Winston, editor, *Re-Viewing British Cinema, 1900–1992,* Albany: State University of New York Press, 1994
"Interview with Hanif Kureishi," *Interview* (April 1990)
Wolf, Matt, "Hanif Kureishi Trades Pen for the Director's Lens," *New York Times* (July 14, 1991)

L

L.A. Law

U.S. Drama

L.A. Law, created by Steven Bochco and Terry Louise Fisher, premiered September 15, 1986, on NBC. During that television season, Bochco's groundbreaking *Hill Street Blues* wound to a close and *L.A. Law* inherited the key Thursday night anchor spot. NBC affiliates complained about *Hill Street Blues'* declining audience, and Bochco's new show delivered larger Nielsen ratings for the network's prime-time lineup and larger numbers to NBC affiliates' late-night local news.

The program ran for eight seasons, from 1986 until 1994, was nominated for more than 90 Emmy awards, and won 15 honors from the Academy of Television Arts and Sciences. These accolades included four years as best drama series, five acting awards, three writing honors, and one prize each for direction, art direction, and single camera editing. Frequently, *L.A. Law*'s creative staff dominated a category. In 1989 three categories had three nominees from the program. In 1988 *L.A. Law* produced four of the six nominees for outstanding directing in a drama series: Kim H. Friedman, Gregory Hoblit, Sam Weisman, and Win Phelps. In the program's first season, *L.A. Law* received the George Foster Peabody Award for excellence, richness, and diversity of television content.

The fictional law firm of McKenzie, Brackman, Chaney & Kuzak brought a romantic ambience to the legal, moral, and ethical battles fought inside the courtroom, in the court hallways, and behind the closed doors of attorneys' offices. The action combined several social classes: the firm's partners, associates who were employed soon after graduation, clerical workers, clients, and county employees. Critics felt the law partners' lifestyles epitomized the financial and social excesses of 1980s wealthy yuppies, characterized by the show's signature license plate affixed to a Jaguar sports car.

The characters ranged from steadfast and cautious senior partner Leland MacKenzie (played by Richard Dysart, who won the outstanding supporting actor Emmy in 1992), to arrogant Arnie Becker (Corbin Bernsen). Becker's antithesis was Benny Stulwicz (Larry Drake, who won two Emmy awards as outstanding supporting actor in 1988 and 1989), a mentally retarded office assistant who wanted to successfully maintain life's simplest essentials: a job, an apartment, a commute to work, and a marriage. In the show, Stulwicz was hired by the firm after his dying mother, a long-time client, expressed concern over her son's future. Melman and Becker subsequently watched over Stulwicz, much like surrogate parents.

Many of *L.A. Law*'s ensemble cast members can best be described in pairs, as most characters had steady romantic partnerships with other characters portrayed in the series. Alan Rachins played Douglas Brackman Jr., as a frustrated, balding managing partner. His attempts to lead the firm were frequently thwarted by his partners. Rachins played opposite his real life spouse, Joanna Frank (Steven Bochco's sister) as his wife and then ex-wife, Sheila Brackman.

L.A. Law, Rosenberg, Bernsen, Eikenberry, Rachins, Eckholdt, Dysart, Tucker, Powers, Drake, Mazar, Underwood, 1986–94.
©20th Century Fox/Courtesy of the Everett Collection

Michael Kuzak (Harry Hamlin) often served as the focal point of the program. Kuzak was sensitive, intelligent, passionate, and sexual; his dynamic courtroom maneuvers often combined logic with pleas for compassion. Opposite Kuzak was Grace Van Owen (Susan Dey), the district attorney with an icy exterior, an empathetic side, and a libido that matched Kuzak's.

The best-remembered couple linked tall, waspy Ann Kelsey (Jill Eikenberry) and short, Jewish, tax attorney Stuart Markowitz (Bochco's college friend Michael Tucker). Those two, married in real life before their characters wed on *L.A. Law,* had onscreen romantic interludes that were discussed beside office water coolers nationwide.

The strangest romantic pairing may have been that between senior partner McKenzie and Rosalind Shays (played by Diana Muldaur during the fourth and fifth season). Shays's introduction as a vicious attorney hired to boost revenues by bringing her large client list to McKenzie Brackman came in the 1989 season episode, "One Rat; One Ranger." During her short stay, Shays and the recently widowed McKenzie began dating, much to the surprise of the other characters. A

power struggle arose. Shays lost the battle and was removed from the law firm, then sued her former partners for sexual discrimination. The character dramatically exited the program when she stepped into a carriage-less elevator shaft and plummeted to her death in the March 21, 1991, episode, "Good to the Last Drop."

Taking the lead from Bochco's previous NBC hit *Hill Street Blues, L.A. Law* cast ethnic actors in roles as attorneys. These characterizations included Alfre Woodard, who guest-starred and won an acting Emmy award for the pilot episode, Blair Underwood as Jonathan Rollins, and Jimmy Smits as the fiery but self-involved Victor Sifuentes (Smits won the 1990 supporting actor Emmy, competing against colleagues Drake and Dysart). After Smits left the show, A. Martinez joined the cast as Daniel Morales.

Other notable characters included Michele Greene as recent law school graduate and single mother Abby Perkins, Vincent Gardenia as Roxanne Melman's father Murray, Sheila Kelly as clerical worker and law student Gwen Taylor, Conchata Ferrell as entertainment attorney Susan Bloom, and Kathleen Wilhoite as

Benny's childlike and slow-learning love interest Rosalie.

For *L.A. Law,* Bochco brought many storytelling devices that worked well for *Hill Street Blues.* Instead of *Hill Street*'s daily roll call that introduced each episode's plot lines and framed each potential conflict, *L.A. Law* used the weekly partner's meeting for the same narrative functions. However, the shows differed greatly in one respect. *Hill Street Blues* had strong female characters, but men outnumbered them as the central focus of the series. With *L.A. Law,* women partners, associates, and secretaries often took the forefront.

The storylines ranged from outrageous humor to thoughtful debate of social issues. Trials portrayed a gay man prosecuted for killing his lover by infecting him with AIDS, dental malpractice, a female news anchor terminated by a TV station, date rape, polluted water poisoning a trailer park's residents, age discrimination, athletes on steroids, drive-by killings, and racial profiling. On the humorous side, topics included a man prosecuted for clubbing a swan to death on a golf course, ownership of a pig eaten by a python at a music video filming, male senior citizens who wreak havoc at a home when they become test subjects for a testosterone patch, and a man who communicates solely through a rude ventriloquist's dummy.

The creative successes of the program's writers and producers engendered frequent behind-the-scene changes, and that instability contributed to real-life drama. When Bochco contemplated leaving the series to begin a long-term development deal at ABC, he replaced Fisher with writer David E. Kelley as the program's supervising producer. In 1989 a disappointed Fisher left the show as Bochco banned her from the set. The next year, Bochco left *L.A. Law* and Kelley became executive producer. Kelley revitalized the fading program by adding fresh, quirky characters to his intriguing and clever dialogue and plot lines, sometimes teaming with writer/director William Finkelstein. The show remained strong until Kelley left in 1992.

During the final season, the program's creative edge disappeared, as did the large audiences of its best years. For season five, Amanda Donohoe as C.J. Lamb, John Spencer as Tommy Mullaney, and Cecil Hoffman as Mullaney's ex-wife Zoey Clemons added color to the program.

For network "sweeps" on May 12, 2002, and as part of NBC's 75th anniversary celebration, NBC brought the cast of *L.A. Law* together for a reunion movie and an episode of the network's quiz show, *The Weakest Link.* Finkelstein wrote the reunion, *L.A. Law: The Movie,* which fared poorly with both audiences and critics.

JOAN STULLER GIGLIONE

See also **Bochco, Steven; Fisher, Terry Louise; Kelley, David E.**

Cast

Arnie Becker (1986–94)	Corbin Bernsen
Frank Kittredge (1991–92)	Michael Cumpsty
Grace Van Owen (1986–92)	Susan Dey
C.J. Lamb (1990–92)	Amanda Donohoe
Benny Stulwicz (1987–94)	Larry Drake
Leland McKenzie (1986–94)	Richard A. Dysart
Ann Kelsey (1986–94)	Jill Eikenberry
Susan Bloom (1991–92)	Conchata Ferrell
Abby Perkins (1986–91)	Michele Greene
Michael Kuzak (1986–91)	Harry Hamlin
Zoey Clemmons (1991–92)	Cecil Hoffman
Gwen Taylor (1990–93)	Sheila Kelley
Daniel Morales (1992–94)	A Martinez
Denise Ianello (1993–94)	Debi Mazar
Jane Halliday (1993–94)	Alexandra Powers
Douglas Brackman Jr. (1986–94)	Alan Rachins
Eli Levinson (1993–94)	Alan Rosenberg
Roxanne Melman (1986–93)	Susan Ruttan
Victor Sifuentes (1986–91)	Jimmy Smits
Tommy Mullaney (1990–94)	John Spencer
Stuart Markowitz (1986–94)	Michael Tucker
Jonathan Rollins (1987–94)	Blair Underwood

Creator

Steven Bochco

Executive Producers

David E. Kelley
Steven Bochco

Supervising Producers

David E. Kelley
Terry Louise Fisher
William M. Finkelstein

Producers

Ellen S. Pressman
Elodie Keene
Gregory Hoblit
James C. Hart
Michael M. Robin
Michele Gallery
Rick Wallace
Scott Goldstein
Steven Bochco

Programming History
NBC

October 1986–November 1986	Friday 10:00–11:00
December 1986–August 1990	Thursday 10:00–11:00
October 1990–February 1993	Thursday 10:00–11:00
April 1993–December 1993	Thursday 10:00–11:00
February 1994–May 1994	Thursday 10:00–11:00

Further Reading

Mason, M.S., "'L.A. Law' Raises the Bar Again: The TV Movie Picks Up 10 Years Later with the Original Cast," *Christian Science Monitor,* May 10, 2002

La Femme Nikita

U.S. Drama

La Femme Nikita (also known as *Nikita*) was one of the earliest and best programs in the cycle of "strong woman" or "tough girl" TV series that came to prominence beginning in the mid 1990s. This group also included *Xena: Warrior Princess, Buffy the Vampire Slayer, Dark Angel, Witchblade,* and *Alias,* among others. The TV version of the Nikita story was an adaptation of Luc Besson's film *Nikita* (France/Italy, 1990, also known as *La Femme Nikita*), which had already spawned two film adaptations, *Black Cat* (Hong Kong, 1991) and *Point of No Return* (United States, 1993, also known as *The Assassin*). In turn, the underlying Nikita formula is an updated and somewhat perverse retelling of the Pygmalion story (see Grindstaff and Hayward).

In the film version of Nikita, a young, drug-addicted street criminal named Nikita commits murder and is spared from a life sentence by being recruited, upon threat of death, into a clandestine crime-fighting organization. She is taught to be a polished and proper lady, as in Shaw's *Pygmalion,* but also a professional assassin and spy. Her employer requires complete commitment, and she is unable to have a normal personal life outside of her work.

The TV series follows this plot, but with a crucial difference. The TV series does begin with Nikita's arrest for murder, but in this case she is not guilty (and not a drug addict). As we learn in a much later episode, she has been framed by her soon-to-be employer, a top-secret espionage agency called Section One. This device provides the TV program with a moral problematic not present in the film, but exploited with great skill by the producers through the entire run of the series.

Nikita (Australian actress Peta Wilson) begins the TV series as a troubled young adult, but she is not a murderer. Section One forces her to become one. Her colleagues in the organization are antiheroes fighting an endless supply of terrorist villains, ostensibly the true forces of evil in the world. However, Section One itself operates entirely outside the conventional limits imposed by law. One of the cruxes of the series is that the heroes often commit worse atrocities than the villains. Nikita's struggle to retain a sense of right and wrong inside the amoral octopus that is Section One provides the basis for powerful and thought-provoking episodes.

Section One is headed by a character known as Operations (American actor Eugene Robert Glazer), who serves as a surrogate, unforgiving father of sorts for Nikita. (In a much later episode, we learn that his real name is Paul.) The "mother" in this scenario is Madeline (Canadian actress Alberta Watson), an expert at prisoner interrogation and mind games. The heir apparent to Operations is Michael, the most deadly Section One field agent, played with minimalist intensity by French Canadian Roy Dupuis. All are damaged people with traumatized personal histories revealed in particular episodes. Together they constitute a dysfunctional pseudo-family, stuck with each other's treacheries in a world largely of their own making.

Nikita and Michael (her recruiter and principal trainer) fall in and out of love throughout the series. Sometimes he corrupts her; other times she redeems him (and potentially Section One as a whole). At the end of the series, in a development long foreshadowed, Nikita ascends to the command of Section One, but it is unclear whether she has by now become totally corrupt herself or has enough residual goodness to save Section One from its depravity.

Thus *Nikita* is a story of heroic but perhaps futile individual resistance within a totalitarian collective. In this respect, the show is reminiscent of *The Prisoner,* and indeed Nikita spends much of the series plotting her escape, turning the tables on her captor-bosses, and trying to discover the true identity and purpose of Section One. Nikita updates *The Prisoner*'s comment on East-West moral equivalence in the cold war era to a similar meditation on the ethics of antiterrorism vis-à-vis terrorism itself.

Like *The Prisoner*'s Number Six, Nikita is, in effect, kidnapped. Unlike Number Six, she is an innocent, civilian female. The series takes double advantage of Peta Wilson as spectacle, drawing upon both her sexual allure and her displays of violence. At the same time, she maintains a stereotypically female vulnerability. In the midst of a stunningly warped realpolitik, Nikita never entirely loses her innocence, even though she must often keep it hidden. She is a complex character in a complicated situation, as well as a female in the traditionally male genre realm of the spy and action hero. Similarly, her liaison with Michael combines the pleasures of a steamy romance and frequent rescue scenarios with the ever-present possibility of a double-cross by either party (although, curiously, it is Michael who is most often in the "femme fatale" position).

Physically, Section One headquarters is labyrinthine and apparently underground, a sort of high-tech dungeon and panopticon for the mostly dronelike apparatchiks who work there. It is antiseptically black, brown, and gray, yet somehow dazzling to the viewer's eye: a self-contained, menacing fantasy backdrop for startling intrigue. In the occasionally glimpsed bowels of the place lie torture chambers, supercomputers, combat training areas, and laboratories for genetic engineering and other horrors. Nikita's struggle to learn the truth about Section One seems all the more challenging because of the program's claustrophobic workplace setting, in which evil becomes banal in a way not usually encountered in television drama.

The show attracted a cult following, especially among female viewers. It also served as a high-profile example of quality programming for the often-marginal USA Network. When the series was prematurely canceled in 2000, the audience rallied and persuaded USA to bring the show back for an abbreviated fifth season in 2001 to wrap up loose ends.

GARY BURNS

See also **Buffy the Vampire Slayer;** **Gender and Television;** *Xena: Warrior Princess*

Cast

Nikita	Peta Wilson
Michael	Roy Dupuis
Operations	Eugene Robert Glazer
Madeline	Alberta Watson
Walter	Don Francks
Birkoff (1997–2000)	Matthew Ferguson
Jason (2000–01)	Matthew Ferguson
Quinn (2000–01)	Cindy Dolenc
Mick Schtoppel (1999–2001)	Carlo Rota
George (1999–2001)	David Hemblen
Mr. Jones (2001)	Edward Woodward

Producers

Executive Consultant	Joel Surnow
Executive Consultant	Lawrence Hertzog
Executive Producer	Jay Firestone
Producer	Jamie Paul Rock

Programming History

1997–2001	96 episodes
USA	
January 1997–June 1997	Monday 10:00–11:00
June 1997–March 2001	Sunday 10:00–11:00

Further Reading

Brown, Jeffrey A., "Gender and the Action Heroine: Hardbodies and the Point of No Return," *Cinema Journal,* 35 (1996)

Connolly, Dawn, *La Femme Peta,* Toronto: ECW Press, 2000

Durham, Carolyn A., *Double Takes: Culture and Gender in French Films and Their American Remakes,* Hanover, New Hampshire: University Press of New England, 1998

Grindstaff, Laura, "A Pygmalion Tale Retold: Remaking La Femme Nikita," *Camera Obscura,* 47 (2001)

Hayward, Susan, "Recycled Woman and the Postmodern Aesthetic: Luc Besson's Nikita (1990)," in *French Film: Texts and Contexts,* edited by Susan Hayward and Ginette Vincendeau, 2nd edition, London: Routledge, 2000

Inness, Sherrie A., *Tough Girls: Women Warriors and Wonder Women in Popular Culture,* Philadelphia: University of Pennsylvania Press, 1999

Tasker, Yvonne, *Spectacular Bodies: Gender, Genre and the Action Cinema,* London: Routledge, 1993

Wiles, Mary M., "Mapping the Contours of Cyborg Space in the Conspiracy Film: The Feminine Ecology of Luc Besson's La Femme Nikita," *Post Identity,* 1 (1997)

La Frenais, Ian (1937–)

British Writer

Ian La Frenais ranks among British television's most accomplished comedy writers. Most of his greatest successes were collaborations with BBC writer-producer Dick Clement; with Clement he contributed several of the most enduringly popular comedy series of the late 20th century.

La Frenais's early experience as an insurance salesman in his native Newcastle-upon-Tyne was to prove invaluable when he came to write the first of the classic comedy series that he created in partnership with Clement. He happened to meet Clement while on holiday, and they devised a sketch about two cocky northern lads for Clement's director's exams. The BBC was much impressed by the scenario, and their sketch was developed into the massive hit *The Likely Lads,* which was one of the fledgling BBC 2's first big successes. The series revolved around the squabbles and contrasting aspirations of two friends, Bob Ferris (Rodney Bewes) and Terry Collier (James Bolam). La Frenais's writing showed facility with characterization and an easy grasp of northern traits and humor, as well as a certain acuteness in exposing the absurdities of the British class system in a rapidly changing world. Sequels all too often turn out to lack the flair and uniqueness of originals. In this case, however, when the series was revived some years later as *Whatever Happened to the Likely Lads?,* with Bob now engaged to be married and an even more vituperative Terry newly released from the army, the critics were unanimous in finding the humor even sharper and more effective. There was no critical dissent when the program was voted Best Situation Comedy of the Year in 1973.

Clement and La Frenais returned to the humor of northeast England at regular intervals over the years, notably in the extraordinarily successful series *Auf Wiedersehen, Pet,* about a gang of Geordie building laborers obliged to pursue their trade in Germany, and in *Spender,* which starred former *Auf Wiedersehen* bricklayer Jimmy Nail. However, the pair proved that they were by no means restricted to purely regional comedy drama, and in the mid-1970s they scored another huge hit with the classic prison comedy *Porridge,* starring the multifaceted comedian Ronnie Barker.

Barker's cockney Norman Stanley Fletcher, a habitual criminal obliged by his innate good nature to guide his young cellmate Godber (Richard Beckinsale) through the vicissitudes and dangers of life behind bars, was hailed as a masterpiece of comic invention, and the program became a favorite of prison audiences throughout the country. A sequel, *Going Straight,* which followed Fletcher's life after his release was less successful, lacking the dramatic tension that came with the confines of the original setting. In some respects, Clement and La Frenais had already had a dry run for *Porridge* in their series *Thick As Thieves,* in which two crooks (Bob Hoskins and John Thaw) competed for the love of the same woman. This series ended after just eight episodes, when Thaw began work on *The Sweeney* police series. The original plan had been to return the two central characters to prison, where their relationship would have to adjust to new circumstances.

Collaborative efforts on situation comedies in the 1990s—including the disappointing *Full Stretch,* about a luxury car-hire business—have proved less notable. With Clement, however, La Frenais enjoyed significant success as a screenwriter with his script for the cult film *The Commitments* (a triumph that prompted the pair to attempt a television version under the title *Over the Rainbow*). In the 1990s, La Frenais's solo contributions as writer were more successful, with the popular *Lovejoy* series, adaptations for television of the Jonathan Gash novels about an antiques dealer with an eye for the main chance (and for the ladies). As before, La Frenais's easy humor and skillful characterization were deemed essential to the show's success.

DAVID PICKERING

See also **Auf Wiedersehen, Pet; Likely Lads, The; Porridge**

Ian La Frenais. Born in Newcastle-upon-Tyne, England, January 7, 1937. Attended Dame Allan's School, Northumberland. Married: Doris Vartan, 1984; one stepson. Worked as insurance salesman before establishing reputation as a screenwriter and producer; formed comedy writing partnership with BBC producer Dick Clement; partner, with Clement and Allan McKeown, in Witzend Productions. Recipient: British Academy of Film and Television Arts Awards; Broadcasting Guild Awards; *Evening News* Award; Pye Television Award; Screen Writers Guild Award; Society of Television Critics Award; Writers Guild of America

Award; London Film Critics Circle Award; *Evening Standard* Peter Sellers Award, 1991.

Television Series

1964–66	*The Likely Lads* (with Dick Clement)
1968	*The Adventures of Lucky Jim* (with Dick Clement)
1972	*The Train Now Standing*
1973–74	*Whatever Happened to the Likely Lads?* (with Dick Clement)
1973	*Seven of One* (with Dick Clement)
1974	*Thick As Thieves* (with Dick Clement)
1974–77	*Porridge* (with Dick Clement)
1975	*Comedy Playhouse* (with Dick Clement)
1976–77	*On the Rocks*
1978	*Going Straight* (with Dick Clement)
1979	*Billy*
1983	*Further Adventures of Lucky Jim* (with Dick Clement)
1983–84	*Auf Wiedersehen, Pet* (with Dick Clement)
1985	*Mog* (with Dick Clement)
1986	*Lovejoy*
1990	*Spender* (with Jimmy Nail)
1990	*Freddie and Max* (with Dick Clement)
1991	*Old Boy Network* (with Dick Clement)
1993	*Tracey Ullman: A Class Act* (with others)
1993	*Full Stretch* (with Dick Clement)
1993	*Over the Rainbow* (with Dick Clement)
1995–99	*Tracy Takes On* (with Dick Clement)

Made-for-Television Movie

1983	*Sunset Limousine* (with Wayne Kline)

Television Specials (with Dick Clement)

1980	*My Wife Next Door*
1981	*Mr. and Mrs. Dracula*
1982	*There Goes the Neighbourhood*
1993	*Tracey Ullman Special*

Films (writer)

The Jokers (with Dick Clement), 1967; *The Touchables* (with Dick Clement), 1968; *Hannibal Brooks* (with Dick Clement and Tom Wright), 1969; *Otley* (with Dick Clement), 1969; *The Virgin Soldiers* (with John Hopkins and John McGrath), 1970; *Villain* (with Dick Clement and Al Lettieri), 1971; *Catch Me a Spy* (with Dick Clement), 1971; *The Likely Lads* (with Dick Clement), 1976; *It's Not the Size That Counts* (with Dick Clement and Sid Collin), 1979; *To Russia... with Elton*, 1979; *Doing Time* (with Dick Clement), 1979; *The Prisoner of Zenda* (with Dick Clement), 1979; *Water* (with Dick Clement and Bill Persky), 1985; *Vice Versa* (with Dick Clement), 1988; *Wilt* (with Dick Clement), 1989; *The Commitments* (with Dick Clement and Roddy Doyle), 1991; *Honest*, 2000.

Films (producer)

Porridge (with Dick Clement), 1979; *Doing Time* (with Allan McKeown), 1979; *To Russia... with Elton* (also director), 1979; *Bullshot*, 1983; *Water* (with Dick Clement), 1985; *Vice Versa* (with Dick Clement), 1988; *Wilt* (with Dick Clement), 1989; *The Commitments* (with Dick Clement and Marc Abraham), 1991; *Excess Baggage*, 1997; *Still Crazy*, 1998; *Honest*, 2000.

Stage (writer)

Billy, 1974; *Anyone for Denis?* (coproducer), 1982.

Publications

The Likely Lads (with Dick Clement)
Whatever Happened to the Likely Lads? (with Dick Clement)
Porridge (with Dick Clement)
Auf Wiedersehen, Pet (with Dick Clement)

La Plante, Lynda (1946–)

British Writer, Producer

Considered one of the most important contemporary British television dramatists, Lynda La Plante is energetic and prolific and has achieved success in several diverse media fields. Originally an actor, La Plante is also a best-selling novelist and currently runs her own production company, La Plante Productions, as well as having gained both popular and critical recognition for her serious and intelligent television dramas. Apart from her series *Lifeboat* (1994), which was centered on the intrigues of a coastal community (almost in the fashion of a soap opera), La Plante's dramas have been generally constructed round the imperatives of crime, punishment, and underworld intrigue.

As an actor, La Plante appeared on British television in several well-known crime series of the late 1970s and early 1980s, including *The Sweeney* and *The Gentle Touch.* Usually typecast as either a prostitute or a gangster's moll, La Plante's experience as a television actor ensured that she was grounded in the narrative dynamics of the British crime series, while also making her only too aware of the subordinate role generally assigned to female characters in the genre. Having written for her own pleasure since her childhood, La Plante began to write and submit scripts for various current police series, scripts that attempted to create roles for women that were much more intelligible, independent, and less subordinate to men. As fate would have it, one of her scripts, titled "The Women," ended up on the desk of producer Verity Lambert at Euston Films at a time when Lambert and her colleague Linda Agran were consciously looking for television dramas that would feature women at the center of both the events and the action. "The Women" became the series *Widows,* which was broadcast to great public acclaim in 1983 and which was to transform La Plante's career from actor to television dramatist.

Despite the centrality of women in her writing career—whether as characters such as Dolly Rawlins (*Widows* and *She's Out*) and Jane Tennison (*Prime Suspect*), or as producers such as Lambert—La Plante has eschewed any identification with feminism or feminist agendas. Although undeniably aware of the questions raised and changes brought about by "second-wave" feminism, she has included women's issues (such as Tennison's abortion in the *Prime Suspect* series) in incidental rather than pivotal positions in her dramas.

La Plante's female protagonists are neither saintly nor unproblematic. Dolly Rawlins murdered her husband, and Jane Tennison finds it necessary to repress her own emotional needs to the extent that she not only obscures much of her own femininity (qualities traditionally accepted as feminine such as care and compassion) but, at times, also seemingly manages to lose sight of her humanity.

Despite the problematic nature of her protagonists, some critics accuse La Plante of producing works that actively espouse ideas of the "politically correct," and which succeed in portraying all men as bastards and oppressors of women. To the contrary, La Plante has, in fact, provided some of the most disturbingly frank yet sympathetic male characters to appear on British television in recent times. In programs such as *Civvies* (but also in *Comics* and *Prime Suspect*), La Plante has uniquely explored the bonds of love between heterosexual men. Although poorly received by the public and critics (because of its brutality and lack of sentiment), *Civvies* undoubtedly portrays extraordinary love between men.

Male violence is often at the heart of La Plante's work. She does not excuse it, nor does she shy away from its reality and implications. In many ways, she is eager to get to the heart of this violence and depict it in a matter-of-fact manner. This ambition can be seen in a formalized way in *Seconds Out, Prime Suspect,* and, to a lesser extent, in *Framed,* where La Plante explores some of the dynamics of boxing. She displays obvious fascination with the ways in which dimensions of male physicality and brutality are enacted and performed in boxing competitions, training sessions, and sparring bouts.

La Plante's dramas, on the whole, do not champion either gender but try to discuss both inequalities and power relations as they exist within society. For the most part, her protagonists (both male and female) stand for reason, the ability to think intelligently, and expertise. In her dramas, La Plante is not interested in small-scale petty crime; she is preoccupied by both exceptional crimes and feats of exceptional detection. La Plante's crime dramas often focus on the minutiae of planning (*Widows, Prime Suspect, Framed, She's Out*) and the exhibition of particular skills and expertise, such as Gloria's demonstration of weapons in *She's Out.*

A concern for realism and accuracy of procedure (whether in a police station, a pathology lab, or a prison) has become one of the hallmarks of La Plante's work. Her dramas are based on her own detailed and painstaking research, and her elaborate and detailed scripts demand absolute accuracy of mise-en-scene, performance, and procedure.

The formation of her own production company, La Plante Productions, in 1994 can be interpreted as an attempt to integrate her own creative input at each stage of production. Her subsequent output has been prolific but has also taken two distinct directions. In the United Kingdom, with dramas such as *Supply and Demand, Trial and Retribution,* and *Killer Net,* La Plante has synthesized many of her earlier narrative traits and preoccupations but also has strived for a vivid engagement with televisuality by straying into the seedier aspects of cyberspace and employing graphic imagery such as the use of parallel narratives on split screens to produce an overall look of flashy finesse. In the United States, her recent productions (*The Warden, Framed,* and *Widows*) have been less innovative but have involved an American reworking of some of her greatest British hits (*The Governor, Framed,* and *Widows*).

ROS JENNINGS

See also **Mirren, Helen;** *Prime Suspects*

Lynda La Plante. Born in Liverpool, Merseyside, England, 1946. Began career as an actor, later scriptwriter and producer; founder, La Plante Productions, 1995, Cougar Films (with Sophie Ballhetechet), 2001. Recipient: Dennis Potter Writer's Award, British Academy of Film and Television Arts, 2001.

Television Series (writer)

1983, 1985	*Widows*
1991–	*Prime Suspect*
1992	*Civvies*
1992	*Framed*
1993	*Seekers*
1993	*Comics*
1994	*Lifeboat* (also producer)
1994	*In the Firing Line* (presenter)
1994	*She's Out* (also coproducer)
1995–96	*The Governor* (also producer)
1997–2000	*Trial and Retribution* (also producer)
1997	*Bella Mafia*
1998	*Supply and Demand* (also producer)
1998	*Killer Net* (also producer)
2002	*Widows* (U.S. version; also producer)

Made-for-Television Movies (writer)

1986	*Hidden Talents*
1992	*Seconds Out*
1996	*The Prosecutors* (also executive producer)
1997	*Supply and Demand* (pilot)

2001	*The Warden* (also producer)
2001	*Mind Games*
2001	*Framed* (U.S. version)

Publications

Widows, 1983
Widows II, 1985
The Legacy, 1988
The Talisman, 1988
Bella Mafia, 1990
Prime Suspect, 1991
Prime Suspect II, 1992
Framed, 1992
Civvies, 1992
Entwined, 1992
Prime Suspect III, 1993
Seekers, 1993
Cold Shoulder, 1994
The Lifeboat, 1994
She's Out, 1995
The Governor, 1995
The Governor II, 1996
Cold Blood, 1996
Trial and Retribution, 1997
Trial and Retribution II, 1998
Cold Heart, 1998
Trial and Retribution III, 1999
Trial and Retribution IV, 2000
Sleeping Cruelty, 2000
Trial and Retribution V, 2001

Further Reading

Rennert, Amy, editor, *Helen Mirren: Prime Suspect: A Celebration,* San Francisco: KQED, 1995

Lamb, Brian (1941–)

U.S. Media Executive, Founder of C-SPAN

To most causal observers, Brian Lamb *is* the Cable Satellite Public Affairs Network (C-SPAN). In his mind, however, nothing could be farther from the truth. Lamb always attributes the existence of the network and its continued success to others. The others are the cable industry, leaders within it, members of the House of Representatives and the Senate who

made it possible for the network to carry the signal they controlled, C-SPAN staffers at all levels, and the public itself. Despite his protestations, Lamb made C-SPAN happen. Now chairman and CEO of the network, he was the matchmaker who brought Congress and the cable industry together.

A native of Lafayette Indiana, Lamb attended Pur-

Brian Lamb.
Photo courtesy of C-SPAN

due University in his hometown. There he majored in speech because the school did not offer a degree in broadcasting. After completing his degree Lamb spent three days in law school by his account and then entered the navy. During the Johnson presidency he was assigned to duty in the nation's capital where he reported to the Assistant Secretary of Defense for Public Affairs. There he witnessed both network broadcasters and Pentagon officials at work shaping the news. His duty in Washington also took him to the White House as social aide.

After leaving the service he worked briefly as a freelancer for UPI Audio. He later served as a press secretary for Senator Peter Dominick (R-Colorado). An appointment as a staffer in the office of the Director of Telecommunications Policy during the Nixon administration followed. Lamb's Washington experiences taught him to be wary of what constituted news on the three broadcast networks. To him they made the nation seem like a three-newspaper town.

In the mid-1970s, Lamb moved from the world of pragmatic politics to trade journalism. While serving as Washington bureau chief for *Cablevision* magazine,

opportunity met an idea. In 1977 he took a 50 percent salary cut going half time with *Cablevision* in order to start "Cable Video." It brought 15-minute interviews with members of Congress to over a dozen cable outlets. Lamb wanted to broaden access to the political process. The cable industry needed to enhance its reputation and had a delivery system suited to his goals. The House of Representatives had been exploring the possibility of telecasting floor sessions but was wary of sound bite journalism. Lamb's willingness to carry the signal of House-directed television cameras full time, the industry's access to the satellite, and his drive made C-SPAN happen.

C-SPAN took to the air in 1979. From the outset key industry leaders made funding possible. Especially during the pivotal developmental years they kept cable system owners from abandoning a non-money making enterprise in favor of profit-producing channels. In 1986 C-SPAN 2 came on line, providing viewers with access to Senate proceedings. A third channel devoted to public affairs was launched on a 24-hour basis in 2001. It brought C-SPAN into the digital world. Some argue that what C-SPAN does is not journalism, claiming it only supplies raw material for journalists, despite the fact that the National Press Club honored Lamb for his lifelong contributions to American journalism in 2002. Whether it is called journalism or not does not matter. Public access to governmental affairs does. Legislation like the must-carry rules, the rapid changes in technology, and the vagaries of the political world matter to Lamb too.

Traces of Brian Lamb's influence can be found in all of C-SPAN's on-air formats. Gavel-to-gavel coverage came first, but it was quickly followed by programming designed to give citizens direct access to elected officials, other decision makers and journalists. Within a year of the start of the network, Lamb introduced viewers to call-in programming C-SPAN style. He hosted most of the early shows in this format. There the model of what became the network's approach to audience interaction programs developed. There Lamb perfected his interviewing style. As he saw it, the task involved promoting informed discussion between the guest and viewers and then staying out of the way of the ensuing dialogue. His would be a different kind of journalism. The style would be conversational not confrontational. No "gotcha" questions would be heard on C-SPAN. Lamb can still be seen at least once a week on *The Washington Journal,* C-SPAN's daily call-in program, where his demeanor on air led one viewer to address him as "O Great Poker Face." Committed to the style Lamb developed, the network regularly conducts in-house meetings to make sure that hosts stay out of the way of the conversations and that camera operators support that approach.

No other programming format reveals Lamb's persona better than *Booknotes*. The network experimented with the idea of book-related programs in fall of 1988, when Lamb interviewed Neil Sheehan, the author of *Bright Shining Lie*. Within a year, *Booknotes* became part of C-SPAN's regular programming. Lamb set the ground rules for the program. He would choose serious nonfiction books that might help viewers better understand U.S. history or contemporary politics. Not afraid to ask the most simple or most esoteric question, every interview makes it clear that Lamb has read the book. In the book world, the program has had a great effect. At C-SPAN it led to the development of "a network within a network," *Book TV*. As a result of the series, Lamb edited a number of books based on the interviews.

Modest about his accomplishments, Lamb has brought together a loyal group of executives, most of whom joined C-SPAN early in their careers. Like Lamb they stay out of the public eye and several appear on air. He constantly gives them credit for the network's success. Brian Lamb believes that C-SPAN is more than one person. For many observers, however, he *is* C-SPAN.

JOHN SULLIVAN

See also **C-SPAN**

Brian Lamb. Born in Lafayette, Indiana, October 9, 1941. Education, public schools, B.A. Purdue University. Served in the U.S. Navy 1963–67, during the latter part of his tour assigned to the office of the Assistant Secretary of Defense for Public Affairs and as a White House aide; after his tour he freelanced for UPI Audio and served as a Senate press secretary and as a staff member in the Office of Telecommunications Policy. Became Washington Bureau Chief for *Cablevision* magazine in the early 1970s, helped

found C-SPAN, incorporated in 1977, later became chairman and CEO; network began cablecasting, 1979; started C-SPAN 2 in 1989; a third network came on line in 2001. WCSP, C-SPAN's Washington D.C. FM radio station, began broadcasting in 1997; also carried on satellite radio. Honors: National Court Reporters Association's Charles Dickens Award, 2001; National Press Club's Fourth Estate Award for a lifetime of contributions to American journalism, 2002; DePauw University's Bernard C. Kilgore Medal for distinguished lifetime achievement in journalism (2003); National Humanities Medal, 2003.

Publications

C-SPAN: America's Town Hall (with C-SPAN staff), 1988

Booknotes: America's Finest Authors on Reading, Writing and the Power of Ideas, 1997

Booknotes: Life Stories, Notable Biographers on the People Who Shaped America, 1999

Who's Buried in Grant's Tomb? A Tour of Presidential Grave Sites (with C-SPAN staff), 1999

Booknotes: Stories from American History, 2001

Further Reading

Cole, Bruce, "Changing the Channel, A Conversation with Brian Lamb," *Humanities* (March-April 2003)

Conway, Terry, "Mixed Media," *Biblio* (February, 1998)

Ebner, Michael H., "Bringing Democracy to Television," *OAH Newsletter* (August 1999)

Frantich, Stephen, and John Sullivan, *The C-SPAN Revolution,* Norman and London: University of Oklahoma Press, 1996

Hazlett, Thomas W., "Changing Channels," *Reason* (March 1996)

West, Don, and Sara Brown, "America's Town Crier," *Broadcasting and Cable* (July 21, 1997)

Lambert, Verity (1935–)

British Producer

By the early 1980s, Verity Lambert's influence as a television producer and executive had made her not only one of Britain's leading businesswomen, but possibly the most powerful member of the nation's entertainment industry. With a résumé that lists many of the most noteworthy successes from the past 30 years,

Lambert has served as a symbol of women's advancement in the media. By the early 1990s, however, Lambert's name had also become associated with one of the more spectacular disasters in the history of the British Broadcasting Corporation (BBC).

Lambert's career did not quite suggest such dra-

Verity Lambert.
Photo courtesy of Verity Lambert

matic highs or lows when the BBC first hired her in the early 1960s. She had already worked on British ABC's *Armchair Theatre,* a prestigious commercial television series, and she had worked in American television with David Susskind. After 18 months, however, she returned to ABC, only to quit over its refusal to hire women directors. But when the BBC hired Sydney Newman away from ABC in 1963, the BBC's new head of drama in turn brought along Lambert, who, at age 27, became the corporation's youngest producer.

Lambert's BBC assignment, producing a new children's program, may be her most internationally known achievement; for its first three seasons (1963–65), Lambert guided the development and production of *Doctor Who.* Although those three seasons might easily be overlooked in the 25-plus-year history of the series, *Doctor Who* fans have repeatedly stressed Lambert's importance. During her tenure she both oversaw the creation of the original Doctor as a willful, often irresponsible pacifist, and presided over the phenomenal explosion of popular interest in writer Terry Nation's cyborg villains, the ever-hardy Daleks.

As Tulloch and Alvarado argue in *Doctor Who: The*

Unfolding Text (1983), Lambert herself represents the convergence of discourses that helped to make *Doctor Who* so original and enduring. Over the course of the 1970s, the BBC had sought to meet the challenge of ITV by broadening its own definition of high culture beyond the realm of classical literature and its adaptation. Coming from the upstart world of commercial television, Lambert's association with the production of original dramas, heavy in social realism, became part of the BBC's continuing efforts to maintain its audiences. Moreover, Lambert and *Doctor Who* were not based in the children's department, and Lambert's inexperience with and even indifference to the established conventions of children's programming helped to lay the ground for the cross-generational audiences that made the series a groundbreaking success. Perhaps it was simply assumed that, "as a woman," Lambert was somehow automatically qualified for the job. Indeed, interviewers have often emphasized Lambert's decision not to have children of her own. Lambert has just as often refused to supply the sometimes expected displays of remorse: in the early 1980s, she cheerfully claimed, "But I can't stand babies—no, I love babies as long as their parents take them away."

Lambert's career subsequent to *Doctor Who* continued to display similar mixtures of social awareness and slick commercial savvy. After producing an award-winning series of Somerset Maugham's short stories and other projects, Lambert left the BBC in 1970 for London Weekend Television. She returned to cocreate *Shoulder to Shoulder* (1974), a multipart history of the suffragette movement. The next year Lambert joined Thames Television as controller of the drama department, becoming the company's director from 1982 to 1985. During that time Lambert was responsible for a number of highly successful productions with high exposure abroad, including *Rumpole of the Bailey,* the American Emmy-winning *Edward and Mrs. Simpson,* and Quentin Crisp's landmark biography, *The Naked Civil Servant.*

In 1976 Lambert had also joined the Thames subsidiary Euston Films, and from 1979 to 1982 she served as its chief executive. At Euston Films she developed *Danger UXB,* as well as the gangster drama, *Out.* She was also responsible for the 1979 *Quatermass* sequel, *The Flame Trees of Thika,* and *Reilly: Ace of Spies,* as well as *Minder* (1979–82), the popular working-class crime series, with which she is most often associated in Britain. Series such as *Out, Reilly,* and *Minder* helped to solidify her reputation as a woman who could produce tough, male-oriented programming, a reputation she has both acknowledged and decried as sexist.

Lambert's move into feature films came when she was named head of production for Thorn-EMI, replacing the man responsible for the disastrous, big budget flops *Can't Stop the Music* and *Honky Tonk Freeway*. During what she calls this "terrible, horrible time" (1982–85), Lambert did persuade the company to join with Rank Film Distribution and Channel 4 in backing a new British Screen Finance Consortium, a step that helped further blur the distinctions in Britain between film and television production.

After leaving Thorn-EMI, her production company, Cinema Verity, produced the Meryl Streep film *A Cry in the Dark* (1988). Lambert's most public project, however, has been an elaborate, high-budget soap opera, *Eldorado* (1992–93). Like *Doctor Who*, *Eldorado* was an attempt by the BBC to prove itself competitive in a rapidly evolving market. This time, however, Lambert was not so lucky. A disaster of fully publicized dimensions, *Eldorado* was only Lambert's second experience with the genre (the first was in the 1960s, *The Newcomers*). Critics quickly turned on Lambert's "tough" *Minder* reputation and blamed her for *Eldorado*'s departures from the familiar British conventions for soap opera. The "greatest of all British television drama producers" had dared to set a soap opera in Spain, and filled it with a multilingual array of British expatriates and foreigners far removed from the milieus of either *Coronation Street* or the BBC's own "quality" soap, *EastEnders*.

Lambert defended *Eldorado* to the end and continued to produce a range of programming, from sitcoms to the gritty thriller *Comics* (1993), written by *Prime Suspect*'s Lynda La Plante.

ROBERT DICKINSON

See also **Doctor Who; Minder; Quatermass; Rumpole of the Bailey**

Verity Lambert. Born in London, England, November 27, 1935. Attended Roedean School; La Sorbonne, Paris. Began career in television, 1961; drama producer, BBC Television, 1963; drama producer, London Weekend Television, 1970; rejoined BBC, 1973; controller of drama department, Thames Television, 1974; chief executive, Euston Films, 1979–82; director of drama, Thames Television, 1981–82; director, Thames Television, 1982–85; director of production, Thorn EMI Screen Entertainment, 1982–85; independent producer for film and television from 1985; founder, Cinema Verity, 1985; MacTaggart Lecturor, Edinburgh Television Festival, 1990; governor: British Film Institute, 1981–86 (chair, production board, 1981–82); National Film and Television School, since 1984. LL.D., University of Strathclyde, 1988. Recipient: Veuve-Clicquot Businesswoman of the Year, 1982; *Woman's Own* Woman of Achievement, 1983. Order of the British Empire, 2002.

Television Series (selected)

1963–65	*Doctor Who*
1965	*The Newcomers*
1966–67	*Adam Adamant Lives*
1968	*Detective*
1969	*Somerset Maugham Short Stories*
1971–72	*Budgie*
1973–74	*Shoulder to Shoulder*
1976–77	*Rock Follies*
1978–92	*Rumpole of the Bailey*
1978–80	*Hazell*
1978	*Edward and Mrs. Simpson*
1978	*Out*
1979	*Danger UXB*
1979–93	*Minder*
1979	*Quatermass*
1980	*Fox*
1983	*Reilly: Ace of Spies*
1987	*American Roulette*
1989	*May to December*
1990	*Coasting*
1991	*GBH*
1991, 1992	*The Boys from the Bush*
1992	*Sleepers*
1992–93	*Eldorado*
1992–94	*So Haunt Me*
1993	*Comics*
1994	*Class Act*
1995	*Class Act II*
1995	*She's Out*
1997–	*Jonathan Creek*

Films

The Sailor's Return, 1978; *Charlie Muffin,* 1979; *The Knowledge,* 1979; *Not For Publication,* 1984; *Morons from Outer Space,* 1985; *Dreamchild,* 1985; *Restless Natives,* 1985; *Link,* 1986; *Clockwise,* 1986; *A Cry in the Dark,* 1988; *Heavy Weather,* 1995 (TV); *The Cazalets,* 2000 (TV).

Further Reading

Dunn, Elisabeth, "One Woman's Rise to EMInence," *Sunday Times* (London) (January 16, 1983)

Frean, Alexander, "Back to Reality After *Eldorado*," *Times* (London) (May 26, 1993)

Haining, Peter, editor, *The Doctor Who File,* London: W.H. Allen, 1986

Haining, Peter, editor, *Doctor Who: The Key to Time: A Year-by-Year Record,* London: W.H. Allen, 1984

Tulloch, John, and Manuel Alvarado, *Doctor Who: The Unfolding Text,* New York: St. Martin's Press, 1983

White, Lesley, "TV Troubleshooter Sets Her Sights on the *Eldorado* Gang," *Sunday Times* (London) (August 9, 1992)

Landon, Michael (1936–1991)

U.S. Actor, Writer, Director, Producer

Michael Landon disregarded Hollywood's traditional ways of doing business. He abhorred TV violence, preferring positive, hopeful family-oriented messages, wrote numerous scripts for physically and emotionally handicapped performers, and refused to be beholden to Hollywood or the press. He worked fast and under budget, split the savings with his crew, allowed them more family time, and earned their loyalties in the process. He also possessed a quick wit and enjoyed being sarcastic.

Landon was born Eugene Maurice "Ugey" Orowitz on October 31, 1936, in Forest Hills, New York. He was the second child of Jewish father Eli Orowitz, an RKO Radio Pictures publicist, and Catholic mother Peggy O'Neill, a Broadway showgirl. When older sister Evelyn and Eugene were children, the family moved to Collingswood, New Jersey, where he felt ostracized for being Jewish and his home life suffered due to his parents' tumultuous marriage.

Eugene's prowess throwing the javelin earned him a University of Southern California scholarship in 1954. When Eugene began college his parents also moved to Los Angeles, where his father sought publicity work. Regrettably, Hollywood shunned Eli and he resorted to movie house management. He never recovered from Hollywood's rejection, and his devastation led to divorce. As an actor, Eugene said he could cry easily by remembering how his father was treated.

After an arm injury cost him his scholarship, Eugene accompanied a friend to a Warner Brothers audition. Both were unsuccessful, but Eugene, hoping to be discovered, took a gas station job near Warner Brothers and soon was invited to the studio's acting program. He chose "Michael Landon" from a phone book and with the new name appeared in B movies, dozens of TV series, and TV dramas such as *Playhouse 90* and *Studio One*. He dabbled in music, recording *Gimme a Little Kiss, Will Ya, Huh?* in 1957 and touring with Jerry Lee Lewis, but B movies launched him into TV stardom. Landon landed the lead in 1957's *I Was a Teenage Werewolf,* an instant hit and cult classic. During the shooting of 1958's *The Legend of Tom Dooley,* he was injured using a knife and he learned his father died, but *Tom Dooley* was his big break. The film was panned, but his performance was lauded, and producer

David Dortort was sufficiently impressed to create the Little Joe Cartwright character for Landon in his NBC western series *Bonanza* (1959–73).

As the youngest of three Cartwright brothers, Little Joe was funny, caring, hotheaded, and handsome. Lorne Greene was father Ben Cartwright. Pernell Roberts (Adam) and Dan Blocker (Hoss) played his elder brothers. In appearance the brothers seemed totally unrelated, and in the series narrative it was explained that each had a different deceased mother. Off camera, as well, Greene became Landon's father figure, and Blocker was like a real brother. Roberts, however, rarely spoke to Landon. Believing *Bonanza* beneath his dignity, Roberts quit after six years.

Although *Bonanza* gave Landon the opportunity to write and direct, his star status took a personal toll. In 1956, against his mother's wishes, he married Dodie Levy, a widow several years older. Endless weekend commitments following *Bonanza*'s rigorous weeklong shooting schedule led Landon to alcohol and substance abuse, physical and mental collapse, and ultimately divorce. Landon adopted Dodie's son and two other boys, but returned the youngest to the adoption agency. The decision attracted little notice at the time, but when Landon lay dying 30 years later, tabloids exploited the story.

Landon met divorcée model Lynn Noe, 26, an extra on *Bonanza,* whom he married in 1962. He adopted her daughter Cheryl and together they had four children. Landon modified his drinking and overcame his drug addiction. A 1973 automobile accident killed three friends and left Cheryl in a three-day coma and hospitalized for months. During his bedside vigil, Landon promised God he would make the world better if she lived, and his subsequent work became filled with themes of hope, courage, forgiveness, friendship, and love.

After *Bonanza,* Landon coproduced, wrote, directed, and starred on NBC's *Little House on the Prairie* (1974–82), a series designed to compete with CBS's *The Waltons.* Coproducer Ed Friendly acquired the rights to and based the program on Laura Ingalls Wilder's *Little House* books. The pilot movie was telecast on March 30, 1974. *Little House on the Prairie* debuted in September 1974 and was instantly successful.

NBC gave Landon total control of the series, which bore little resemblance to Ingalls's stories. As farmer Charles "Pa" Ingalls, Landon played a pioneer father in 1880s Walnut Grove, Minnesota. His family included wife Caroline (Karen Grassle) and daughters Laura (Melissa Gilbert), Mary (Melissa Sue Anderson), Carrie (twins Lindsay and Sidney Greenbush—alternating), and Grace (Wendi and Brenda Turnbeaugh—alternating), who was added in 1977. The Ingalls later adopted other children. The stories were told through the narrative voice of daughter Laura.

Landon's friend Victor French played neighbor Isaiah Edwards until leaving for ABC's *Carter Country*. Landon considered the departure a breach in their friendship, but after *Carter Country's* cancellation, the two reconciled and French returned to *Little House*. Landon ceased regular appearances in the ninth season, when the series became *Little House: A New Beginning* (1982–83). In the narrative, Charles and Caroline moved to Iowa, leaving Walnut Grove to other family members.

Landon's spousal relations starkly contrasted with his TV views on family. In 1981 his affair with Cindy Clerico, a *Little House* extra, led to a nasty divorce from Lynn, made worse by the tabloids. Landon and Clerico married in 1983 and had two children. He then created, produced, wrote, directed, starred in, and owned entirely NBC's *Highway to Heaven* (1984–89), in which he played angel Jonathan Smith sent to help people in trouble. Victor French costarred as Mark Gordon, a down-on-his-luck ex-cop whose life was turned around by Jonathan. They traveled in Mark's old car, becoming tremendous friends while helping others. *Highway to Heaven* aired weekly until 1988–89, when it appeared sporadically. French died of lung cancer in 1989.

Landon starred in and/or produced several TV movies, including *The Loneliest Runner* (1976), *Little House Years* (1979), *Little House on the Prairie: Look Back to Yesterday* (1983), *Love Is Forever* (1983), *Sam's Son* (1984), and *Where Pigeons Go to Die* (1990). He was executive producer of NBC's *Father Murphy* (1981–82).

Early in 1991, Landon completed a pilot for *Us*, playing a recently released convict regaining his life. Before the series was initiated, he was diagnosed with pancreatic cancer on April 3, 1991. On May 9, he made his last public appearance on *The Tonight Show* in the second-most watched installment during friend Johnny Carson's tenure. He died July 1, 1991, at 54, but remains an enduring figure in television history with a legacy of work reflecting his dedication to making a positive difference.

W.A. KELLY HUFF

See also **Bonanza, Highway to Heaven, Little House on the Prairie**

Michael Landon. Born Eugene Maurice (Ugey) Orowitz in Forest Hills, New York, October 31, 1936. Married: 1) Dodie Levy, 1956 (divorced, 1962); children: Mark (adopted by Landon) and Josh (adopted by both); 2) Marjorie Lynn Noe, 1962 (divorced 1981); children: Cheryl (Lynn's daughter adopted by Landon), Leslie, Michael, Christopher, and Shawna; 3) Cindy Clerico, 1983; children: Jennifer and Sean. Ex-athlete who became an actor by chance. Started career in B movies and TV guest appearances before achieving stardom as Little Joe Cartwright in NBC's *Bonanza* TV series (1959–73). Moved on to produce, write, direct, and star as Charles "Pa" Ingalls in NBC's *Little House on the Prairie* (1974–82), his second longest running TV series, and NBC's *Highway to Heaven* (1984–89) that he owned entirely and on which he played Jonathan Smith, an angel. Executive producer of NBC's *Father Murphy* (1981–82) and *Little House: A New Beginning* (1982–83). Had completed *Us*, a pilot for a proposed series on CBS, at the time of his death from cancer on July 1, 1991.

Television Series

1959–73	*Bonanza*
1974–82	*Little House on the Prairie*
1981–82	*Father Murphy*
1982–83	*Little House: A New Beginning*
1984–89	*Highway to Heaven*

Films

These Wilder Years, 1956; *I Was a Teenage Werewolf*, 1957; *Maracaibo*, 1958; *High School Confidential*, 1958; *God's Little Acre*, 1958; *The Legend of Tom Dooley*, 1958; *The Errand Boy*, 1961.

Made-for-Television Movies

1973	*Love Story: Love Came Laughing* (writer, producer, director)
1974	*Little House on the Prairie* (series pilot—performer, producer, director)
1976	*The Loneliest Runner* (performer, producer, director)
1983	*Love Is Forever* (performer, producer, director)
1983	*Little House on the Prairie: Look Back to Yesterday* (performer, producer, director)
1984	*Sam's Son* (performer, producer, director)

| 1990 | *Where Pigeons Go to Die* (performer, producer, director) |
| 1991 | *Us* (series pilot—performer, producer, director) |

Recordings

Gimme a Little Kiss, Will Ya, Huh?, 1957

Further Reading

Brooks, Tim, and Marsh, Earle, *TV's Greatest Hits: The 150 Most Popular TV Shows of All Time,* New York: Ballantine Books, 1985

Brown, Les, *Les Brown's Encyclopedia of Television,* New York: Zoetrope, 1982

Carlson, Timothy, "Michael Made a Difference in Our Lives," *TV Guide* (July 13, 1991)

Carlson, Timothy, "Intimates Report Landon Knew End Was Nearing," *TV Guide* (July 13, 1991)

Carlson, Timothy, "Michael Landon's Final Days," *TV Guide* (July 20, 1991)

Daly, Marsha, *Michael Landon: A Biography,* New York: St. Martin's Press, 1987

Flynn, Harry, Pamela Flynn, and Gene Trindl, *Michael Landon: Life, Love & Laughter,* Universal City, California: Pomegranate Press, 1991

Galloway, Stephen, "Landon and *Us:* The Series that Might Have Been," *TV Guide* (July 20, 1991)

Ito, Tom, *Conversations with Michael Landon,* Chicago: Contemporary Books, 1992

Joyce, Aileen, *Michael Landon: His Triumph and Tragedy,* New York: Zebra Books, 1991

Landon, Cheryl, *Michael Landon's Legacy: 7 Keys to Supercharging Your Life,* Charlottesville, Virginia: Hampton Roads, 2001

Libman, Gary, *Little House on the Prairie,* Mankato, Minnesota: Creative Education, 1983

McNeil, Alex, *Total Television: A Comprehensive Guide to Programming from 1948 to the Present,* third edition, New York: Penguin Books, 1991

Murphy, Mary, "What Michael Landon Left Behind," *TV Guide* (June 27, 1992)

Sackett, Susan, *Prime-Time Hits: Television's Most Popular Network Programs 1950 to the Present,* New York: Billboard Books, 1993

Wheeler, Jill C., *Michael Landon,* Edina, Minnesota: Abdo and Daughters, 1992

Wilson, Cheryl Landon, and Jane Scovell, *I Promised My Dad: An Intimate Portrait of Michael Landon by His Eldest Daughter,* Thorndike, Maine: Thorndike Press, 1992

Lane, Carla

British Writer

Carla Lane is one of the most successful British sitcom writers—she has conceived of and written numerous shows that have proved tremendously popular, and she has contributed to many others. Lane carries particular significance within British television, as she is one of few British counterparts to the women writers, directors, and producers of American prime-time sitcoms.

Lane broke into television when she and Myra Taylor created *The Liver Birds,* a BBC sitcom based on two young women sharing a Liverpool bedsit and their mainly amorous adventures. Having moved to London from her native Liverpool at a time when, Lane reports, being from Liverpool was not something people were interested in, she succeeded in demonstrating her writing skills precisely by flaunting Liverpool culture. Over the following ten years and 100 episodes, a highly recognizable style developed in Lane's writing of *The Liver Birds.* The characteristics of her work include themes on sexual and personal relationships, contemporary characters, and narratives more realistic than British television comedy had hitherto allowed. Lane's comedy has always been distinctive for its lack of jokes and can be best defined as comedy-drama. She describes herself as writing dialogue not jokes, with humor emerging through characters and speech rather than action.

Butterflies (1978–82), Lane's next popular success, marked an increasing seriousness and melancholic tone in her sitcoms. This long-running BBC show presented an intimate and studied portrait of a middle-aged, suburban housewife, Ria (Wendy Craig), as she became attuned to the shortcomings of her life. Initially, the BBC argued with Lane that comedy was not ready for a married woman to be attracted to another man, but Lane persevered and Ria embarked on an adulterous affair. Although not championing women's issues, Lane writes from a woman's experience and point of view, which is clearly evident in the relationships defined in *Butterflies.* Her shows are, consequently, favorites with women viewers.

Lane furthered many of her earlier themes in ensuing sitcoms for the BBC, including *Solo* and *The Mistress* (both starring Felicity Kendal), *Leaving,* and *I Woke Up One Morning.* In addition to creating portraits of life up and down the social scale, these and other shows written by Lane took social issues as a backdrop for character development, focusing on such topics as adultery, divorce, and alcoholism. Focusing on the theme of unemployment, Lane's next major show, *Bread* (BBC, 1986–91), was once again informed and inspired by Liverpool; this program revolved around the Boswells, a working-class family consisting of a matriarch and her unemployed children. *Bread* was in no sense an instant success—it took a while for viewers to warm to the indulgent, staunchly Catholic mother and her family of unashamed scroungers—but within two years the sitcom had gained almost soap status and came close to overtaking top soap *EastEnders* in the ratings.

Lane has received official recognition for her contributions to British television in the form of an O.B.E., but her work has not always received critical approval. Some have expressed aversion to her subtle, anecdotal, and often poignant approach to programs that have been labeled as comedy. However, ratings confirm the popular appeal of her work for the BBC. Lane's success has stemmed from her insight into character construction and her skill at allowing humor to flourish in situations that are not conventionally considered for such potential, yet which exist as everyday realities.

NICOLA FOSTER

Carla Lane. Born in Liverpool, Merseyside, England. Writer for television in collaboration with Myra Taylor, notably with *The Liver Birds;* subsequently embarked on long series of successful solo series. Prominent animal rights activist. Recipient: O.B.E., 1989.

Television Series

1969–79, 1996	*The Liver Birds* (with Myra Taylor)
1971–76	*Bless This House* (with Myra Taylor)
1975	*No Strings*
1977	*Three Piece Suite*
1978–82	*Butterflies*
1981–82	*Solo*
1981, 1983	*The Last Song*
1984–85	*Leaving*
1985–87	*The Mistress*
1985–86	*I Woke Up One Morning*
1986–91	*Bread*
1992	*Screaming*
1993–94	*Luv*
1995	*Searching*

Television Specials

1975	*Going, Going, Gone...Free?*
1989	*A Night of Comic Relief*
2000	*Butterflies Reunion Special*

Language and Television

Despite the centrality of the visual image in television, this medium combines visuality with both oral and written varieties of language. Television is thus distinguished from print media by its predominantly aural-oral mode of language use, while visuality separates it from the exclusively aural medium of radio.

Orality is generally viewed as the "normal" or "natural" mode of communication through language. Being face-to-face, interactive, immediate, and non-mediated (e.g., through writing, print, or electronic media), oral communication and the oral tradition are considered by some theorists, such as Harold Innis, to be indispensable to a free and democratic life. Unlike oral communication, which is usually dialogic and participatory, written language separates the writer and the reader in space and time and relies on other senses. According to this perspective, audiovisual media, especially television, restore the preprint condition of harmony of senses by using the ear and the eye and calling into play the remaining senses of touch, smell, and taste. This view is rejected by those who argue that the "mechanized" orality of radio and television provides a one-way communication flow from the broadcaster to the hearer or viewer, thus eliminating a fundamental feature of the spoken language: its dialogue and interactivity. Television, like writing, then, overcomes the barriers of space, reaches millions of viewers, and may contribute to the centralization of power and knowledge.

Many viewers see television as an oral medium, a perception constantly reinforced by announcers, anchors, and reporters who try to engage in an informal, conversational style of speaking. Among their techniques are the use of direct forms of address, (e.g., "Good evening," "Thank you for watching," or "Please stay with us"), the maintenance of eye contact with viewers while reading the script from TelePrompTers or printed copy, and the attempt to be, or at least appear, spontaneous.

This on-the-air conversationality is, however, different from everyday talk in significant ways. For instance, television talk aims at avoiding what is natural in face-to-face conversation—errors such as false starts or pauses, and repetitions, hesitations, and silence. A manual of script writing advises the beginner: "Structure your scripts like a conversation, but avoid the elements of conversations that make them verbose, redundant, imprecise, rambling, and incomplete" (Mayeux, 1994). Furthermore, the broadcaster is required to have a good or "polished" voice and is advised "to articulate, enunciate, breathe from the diaphragm, sound authoritative, stay calm under fire, and, all the while, be conversational!" (see Freedman).

Viewers, by contrast, engage in an aural or auditory communication with the medium. Even on call-in shows, the majority of viewers are not able to speak. The few who go on the air via telephone are selected through a gatekeeping process, and are often instructed to be brief and to the point. Language, then, much like studio setup and camera position, is used to create a sense of intimate involvement, a sharing of time and space. Phil Donahue, for example, uses words such as "we," "us," "you," and "here" in order to create a sense of communion between the host and the studio and home audiences—stating, for example, "You'll forgive us, Mr. X, if we are just a little skeptical of your claim that all we need to do...." Similarly, another linguistic code, the frequent use of the present tense, is used to create a sense of audience involvement and apparently allows the host, the guest, and the home audience to share the same moment of broadcast time, even though most shows in the United States were, by the early 1990s, either pre-recorded or packaged as syndication reruns.

Despite the presence of seeming spontaneity in talk genres, they are usually semiscripted, and involve a preparation process including research, writing, editing, and presentation. As Bernard Timberg points out, over 100 professionals can be involved in producing and airing a "spontaneous" talk show like *The Tonight Show* each evening, for example, and as much as 80 percent of the interview with guests on David Letterman's talk show may be worked out in advance. Nonscripted, ad-lib, and unprepared talk shows do, however, appear both on mainstream networks (e.g., *Larry King Live*), and on low-budget or semiprofessional programs of local, community, or alternative television.

While some theorists, such as Walter Ong, admit the written bases of television's spoken language and conceptualize that language as "secondary orality," there is a tendency to explain the popularity of television by, among other things, equating its orality with that of the face-to-face speech. Some researchers see in popular talk shows (such as *The Oprah Winfrey Show* or *Kilroy*) a forum or a public sphere where audiences, in the studio and in front of the screen, engage in oppositional dialogue. Others find the talk shows essentially conformist, contributing to the maintenance of the status quo.

Romanticizing the orality of television is as problematic as denouncing it as an impoverished form of speech. Language changes continually, and television, as a social institution and powerful technology, creates new discourses, new modes of language use, new forms of translation, and new forms of communication between communities with different linguistic abilities. "Natural" and TV languages coexist in constant interaction, influencing each other and contributing to the dynamism of verbal communication. Language consists of numerous varieties rooted in socioeconomic differentiation (e.g., working-class language, legal language), gender (male and female languages), age (e.g., children's language), race (e.g., black English), geography (e.g., Texan English), ethnicity, and other formations. Each variety may include diverse styles with distinct phonological, lexical, semantic, and even syntactic features. Television genres provide a panorama of these language varieties and styles, a presentation of amazing language diversity that the viewer will rarely if ever encounter in daily face-to-face communication.

Television fosters an appreciation of the way writing and speaking merge, not only in the production of speech (the oral text), but also on the screen (in print), in genres ranging from weather and stock-market reports to commercials and game shows. Even live interviews carry captions identifying the interviewees, their status, location, or affiliation. Moreover, "writing for television" has emerged as a new art, which aims not at a literate readership but rather an aural-visual audience. It has developed, for instance, "aural writing styles" or "writing for the ear," allowing the incorporation of music and sound; "visual writing styles" for envisioning images; and "broadcast punctuation" codes for indicating the nuances of on-the-air speech. Training in this new realm of writing is provided in courses offered by academic and professional institutions and in dozens of textbooks and manuals with titles such as Max Wylie's *Writing for Television* and Richard Blum's *Television Writing*. On a different level, some popular programs in the United States have generated extensive fan writing, published and exchanged through the Internet. The fandom of the science fiction series *Star Trek*, for example, has produced no less than 120 fanzines (fan magazines), and some novels written by fans are commercially published.

Unlike radio and print media, then, which create meaning primarily through language, television engages in signification through the unity and conflict of verbal, visual, and sound codes. The dynamics of this type of signification has not been studied adequately. Viewers and media professionals often claim that the visuality of television is a sufficient form of communication, as evidenced in the popular belief that "seeing is believing" and "the camera never lies." Much like verbal language, however, the visual and sound components of the television program are polysemic (that is, they convey multiple meanings) and lend themselves to different, sometimes conflicting, interpretations. Moreover, the verbal text, far from being a mere appendage to the visual, has the power, as Masterman suggests, to "turn images on their heads." Marshal McLuhan's well-known aphorism "the medium is the message" implies that all these meanings are, to a large extent, determined by the technology of television, its audiovisuality. However, this view has been rejected by, among others, producers and script writers who are rather self-conscious about their independence and claim freedom from the dictates of the medium.

Despite this multiplicity of meanings, language in television, as in all its other manifestations, written or spoken, does not serve everyone equitably or effectively. Far from being neutral, language is always intertwined with the distribution and exercise of power in society. Dichotomies such as standard/dialect or language/vernacular point to some aspects of the unequal distribution of linguistic power. In its phonetic, morphological, and semantic systems, language is marked by differences of class, gender, ethnicity, age, race, and so on; similarly, the speakers/hearers are also divided by their idiosyncratic knowledge of language, and often communicate in "idiolects" (personal dialects).

Television attempts to control these differences and overcome the cleavages in order to reach sizable audiences. Thus, for example, the program standards department of CBS requires broadcast language to "be appropriate to a public medium and generally considered to be acceptable by a mass audience." This implies, among other things, that "potentially offensive language" must be generally avoided and "blasphemy and obscenity" are not acceptable. In conforming to standards such as these, many television genres, especially news and other information programs, have developed a language style characterized by simple, clear, and short sentences, read or spoken in an appropriate voice.

Born into this unequal linguistic environment, television followed radio in adopting the standard, national, or official language, which is the main communication medium of the nation-state. While the schools and the print media established the written standard long before the advent of broadcasting, radio and television assumed, more authoritatively than the "pronouncing" dictionaries, the role of codifying and promoting the spoken standard. In Britain, for example, broadcasters were required until the 1960s to be fluent in the British standard known as Received Pronunciation. Despite increasing tolerance for dialectalisms in many Western countries, news and other information programming on the public and private national networks continue to act as custodians of the standard language.

Thus, much like the language academy and the dictionary, television actively intervenes in the language environment and creates its own discourses, styles, and varieties. In the deregulated television market of the United States, genres known as "tabloid" or "trash" TV usually feel free to engage in potentially offensive language. Also, citing an economic imperative to compete with less-restrictive programming on cable television, dramas such as Steven Bochco's *NYPD Blue*, use language once prohibited on network television.

Television and radio have also actively participated in the exercise of gender power through language. In the United States, female voice, especially its higher pitch, was once marginalized for "lacking in the authority needed for a convincing newscast," whereas male lower-pitched voices were treated as "overly polished, ultrasophisticated." Thus, in the 1950s, Lyle Barnhart points out, about 90 percent of commercial copy in the United States was "specifically written for the male voice and personality." According to a British announcer's handbook, women were not usually "considered suitable for the sterner duties of newscasting, commentary work, or, say, political interviewing" because of their "voice, appearance, and temperament." By the 1970s, however, television responded to the social movements of the previous decade and gradually adopted a more egalitarian policy. Women now appear as newscasters, although male anchors still dominate North American network news. The 1979 edition of an

American announcer's manual added a chapter on "the new language," which recommended the use of an inclusive language that respects racial, ethnic, and gender differences.

Despite this kind of professional awareness, television's role in the much larger configuration of worldwide language use remains far more constricting. The languages of the world, estimated to number between 5,000 and 6,000, have evolved as a "global language order," a system characterized by increasing contact and a hierarchy of power relations. About 20 percent of the 5,000 existing languages are used by at least 10,000 speakers each; languages with only a few thousand speakers are too small to survive. Only about 200 languages are spoken by more than 1 million individuals. About 60 are spoken by 10 million or more individuals, comprising 90 percent of the world's population. Twelve languages are spoken by 100 million or more, accounting for 60 percent of the world's population. Although Chinese is spoken by 1 billion people, it is dwarfed by English (which has 500 million speakers) in terms of cultural power. Most of the world's languages remain unwritten, while half of them are, according to linguists, in danger of extinction. If state policy was once responsible for language death, the electronic media, including satellite television, are now seen as the main destructive force.

Before the age of broadcasting, contact between languages was primarily through either face-to-face or written communication. Overcoming spatial barriers and the limitations of literacy, radio and television have brought on-the-air languages within the reach of those who can afford the receiving equipment. However, contrary to a common belief that access to broadcasting is easier than to print media, small and minority languages have often been excluded by both radio and television. Being multilingual and multiethnic, the great majority of contemporary states seek national unity in part through a national or official language. As a result, the states and their public television systems either ignore linguistic diversity or actively eliminate it. Private television is equally exclusionist when minority audiences are not large enough to be profitably delivered to advertisers, or if state policy proscribes multilingual minority broadcasting (as is the case in Turkey). Even in Western Europe, indigenous minority languages such as Welsh in the United Kingdom had to go through a difficult struggle in order to access television. Both the centralizing states and minorities realize that television confers credibility and legitimacy on language. The use of a threatened language at home, even at school, no longer ensures its survival; language vitality depends increasingly on broadcasting.

Although broadcasting in the native tongue is increasingly viewed as a communication right of every citizen, the majority of languages, especially in developing countries, have not yet been televised. In Turkey, where Turkish is the only official language, some 12 million Kurds are constitutionally deprived of the right to broadcast in their native tongue, Kurdish. Even listening to or watching transborder programs in this language is considered an action against the territorial integrity of the state. In countries where linguistic and communication rights are respected, economic obstacles often prevent multilingual broadcasting. In Ghana, for example, there are over 60 languages or dialects, but in 1992 only six out of 55 hours of weekly television air-time were devoted to "local" languages; the rest was in English, the official language. Television production could not satisfy local tastes and demands. While the rural population could not afford the cost of a TV set, the urban elite tuned to CNN.

New technologies such as satellites, computers, cable, and video and digital recording have radically changed the process of televisual production, transmission, delivery, and reception. One major change is the globalization of the medium, which for the first time in history has created audiences of 1 billion viewers for certain programs. Satellite television easily violates international borders, but it is less successful in crossing linguistic boundaries. This has led to the flourishing of translation or "language transfer" in the forms of dubbing, subtitling, and voice-over. Although the linguistic fragmentation of the global audience is phenomenal, English-language programs, mostly produced in the United States and England, are popular throughout the world. Television has accelerated the spread of English as a global lingua franca. For instance, in Sweden, where subtitling allows viewers to listen to the original language, television has helped the further spread of English. Also, since the United States is the most powerful producer of entertainment and information, American English is spreading at the expense of other standards of the language such as Australian, British, Canadian, or Indian.

While some observers see in the new technologies the demise of minority languages and cultures, others believe these technologies empower minorities to resist and survive. Cable television, for instance, has offered opportunities for access to small and scattered minorities. In 1995, satellites empowered the refugee and immigrant Kurdish community in Europe to launch a daily program in their native tongue (Med-TV, later renamed Medya TV). Thus, unable to enjoy self-rule in their homeland, the Kurds gained linguistic and cultural sovereignty in the sky, beaming their programs to Kurdistan where the language suffers from

Turkey's harsh policy of linguicide. While this is a dramatic achievement, other experiences, such as the broadcasting of aboriginal languages in Western countries, have had mixed success.

Truly empowering is television's potential to open a new door on the prelingually deaf community. The World Federation of the Deaf in Helsinki demands the official recognition of the sign language(s) used by the deaf as one of each country's indigenous language. Television is the main medium for promoting these languages and providing translated information from print and broadcast media.

While it is possible to launch channels in sign language, it is important to note that television technology can also be used by the more powerful states to promote their linguistic and political presence among the less powerful. Thus, the Islamic Republic of Iran's state-run television was made available via satellite to the sizeable Iranian refugee and immigrant populations in Europe and North America in the early 2000s.

It is a remarkable achievement of the small screen to allow a home audience of diverse linguistic abilities to watch the same program communally. This is made possible in some instances by simultaneous broadcasting in spoken language, closed captioning, and sign language through an interpreter in an insert on the screen. In another strategy, many programs broadcast in the United States allow viewers to choose between English and Spanish versions. Television has even popularized an artificial tongue, Klingonese, the "spoken and written language" of the fictional Klingons, a powerful "humanoid warrior race" who built an empire in *Star Trek*'s universe. Fans are speaking and studying the language, which is taught in a Klingon Language Institute, with learning materials such as *The Klingon Dictionary;* an audiotape, *Conversational Klingon;* and a quarterly linguistics journal.

Television itself, then, is not a monolithic medium. Moreover, there is no great divide separating the language of television from that of other media. Throughout the world, television airs old and new films and theatrical performances, while in North America some popular TV programs such as *Roseanne* and *Star Trek* are simulcast (broadcast simultaneously) on radio. Linguistic variation is found even within a single genre in mainstream, alternative, local, or ethnic televisions. Whereas a cross-media study of each genre, such as the news, would reveal medium-specific features of language use, the diversity of genres does not allow us to identify a single, homogeneous language of television. Despite this rich variety of voices, however, it remains to be seen whether a combination of official policies and market forces reduces the overall range and heterogeneity of languages and their uses throughout the world.

AMIR HASSANPOUR

See also **Closed Captioning; Dubbing; Subtitling; Talk Show; Voice-Over**

Further Reading

Allen, Robert, "Reader-Oriented Criticism and Television," in *Channels of Discourse,* edited by Allen, Chapel Hill: University of North Carolina Press, 1987

Anepe, Titi, "Ghana," *Intermedia* (September 20, 1992)

Barnhart, Lyle, *Radio and Television Announcing,* Englewood Cliffs, New Jersey: Prentice-Hall, 1961

Blum, Richard, *Television Writing: From Concept to Contract,* New York: Hastings House, 1980

Carpignano, P., R. Andersen, S. Aronowitz, and W. DiFazio, "Chatter in the Age of Electronic Reproduction: Talk Television and the 'Public Mind,'" *Social Text* (1990)

Cormack, Mike, "Problems of Minority Language Broadcasting: Gaelic in Scotland," *European Journal of Communication* (1993)

De Swaan, Abram, "Notes on the Emerging Global Language System: Regional, National and Supranational," *Media, Culture, and Society* (1991)

Findahl, Olle, "Language in the Age of Satellite Television," *European Journal of Communication* (1989)

Fiske, John, *Television Culture,* London: Routledge, 1989

Freedman, Michael, "Foreword," in *Broadcast Voice Handbook,* by Ann S. Utterback, Chicago: Bonus Books, 1990

Gorman, James, "Klingon: The Final Frontier," *Time* (April 5, 1993)

Haney, Daniel, "Half of World's 6,000 Languages in Danger of Extinction," *Philadelphia Inquirer* (February 19, 1995)

Hassanpour, Amir, "The Med-TV Story," *InteRadio* (December 1998)

Henneke, Ben G., and Edward Dumit, *The Announcer's Handbook,* New York: Holt, Rinehart and Winston, 1959

Hourigan, Niamh, "New Social Movement Theory and Minority Language Television Campaigns," *European Journal of Communication* (2001)

Howell, W.J., Jr., *World Broadcasting in the Age of the Satellite,* Norwood, New Jersey: Ablex, 1986

Innis, Harold, *The Bias of Communication,* Toronto: University of Toronto Press, 1971

Jenkins, Henry, III, "*Star Trek* Rerun, Reread, Rewritten: Fan Writing As Textual Poaching," in *Television: The Critical View,* edited by Horace Newcomb, New York: Oxford University Press, 1976; 5th edition, 1994

Lewis, Bruce, *The Technique of Television Announcing,* New York: Hastings House, 1966

Lindahl, Rutger, *Broadcasting Across Borders: A Study on the Role of Propaganda in External Broadcasts,* Lund, Sweden: LiberLäromedel/Gleerup, 1978

Masterman, Len, *Teaching the Media,* London: Comedia, 1985

Mayeux, Peter L., *Writing for Electronic Media,* revised edition, Madison, Wisconsin: Brown and Benchmark Publishers, 1994

McLaughlin, Lisa, "Chastity Criminals in the Age of Electronic Reproduction: Reviewing Talk Television and the Public Sphere," *Journal of Communication Inquiry* (Winter 1993)

McLuhan, Marshal, *Understanding Media: Extensions of Man,* New York: McGraw-Hill, 1964

Okuda, M., and D. Mirek, *The Star Trek Encyclopedia: A Reference Guide to the Future,* New York: Pocket Books, 1994

Ong, Walter, *Interfaces of the Word: Studies in the Evolution of Consciousness and Culture,* Ithaca, New York: Cornell University Press, 1977

Orlik, Peter, *Broadcast/Cable Copywriting,* Boston: Allyn and Bacon, 1978; 4th edition, 1990

Riggins, Stephen H., editor, *Ethnic Minority Media: An International Perspective,* Newbury Park, California: Sage, 1992

Skutnabb-Kangas, T., and R. Phillipson, editors, *Linguistic Human Rights: Overcoming Linguistic Discrimination,* Berlin: Mouton de Gruyter, 1994

Timberg, Bernard, "The Unspoken Rules of Talk Television," in *Television: The Critical View,* edited by Horace Newcomb, New York: Oxford University Press, 1976; 5th edition, 1994

Tomos, Angharad, "Realizing a Dream," in *What's This Channel Four? An Alternative Report,* edited by S. Blanchard and D. Morely, London: Comedia, 1982

Walters, Roger, *Broadcast Writing: Principles and Practice,* New York: Random House, 1988

Wylie, Max, *Writing for Television.* New York: Cowles, 1970

Lansbury, Angela (1925–)

U.S. Actor

After years of winning awards and critical praise for her work on Broadway and in Hollywood, Angela Lansbury finally became a household name in a television role. Lansbury portrayed Jessica Fletcher in CBS's *Murder, She Wrote* for 12 years beginning in 1984, serving as the program's executive producer for its last four. The program, television's longest-running detective show, was canceled in 1996 amid vocal protests from its loyal fans. Since then, Jessica Fletcher has lived on in syndication and in occasional made-for-television *Murder, She Wrote* movies that Lansbury and her husband Peter Shaw have produced, and her son Anthony has directed. Other members of her family have been involved in her career, as well: her brother Bruce served as supervising producer on *Murder, She Wrote,* her son Anthony and her stepson David have served as executive producers, and her husband, to whom she credits much of her success, helped to run their production company, Corymore Productions. For her work in television, Lansbury has received 16 Emmy nominations (12 for *Murder, She Wrote*). She received her first Academy Award nomination at age 17 for her performance in *Gaslight,* and went on to receive two more Academy nominations and four Tony awards.

As a mystery writer who relied on her extraordinary powers of intuition, Lansbury's Jessica Fletcher entered prime time as a sincere if somewhat dowdy widow who, over time, transformed into a sophisticated, appealing, and successful older businesswoman. Jessica's balance of smart professional action and strong commitments to traditionally feminine practices and beliefs, along with the program's strong slate of guest performers, allowed the series to appeal to women across a range of backgrounds. By its second season, the program ranked among the top ten according to Nielsen audience ratings, and would remain in this position for most of its years on the air, attracting such big-name advertisers as the Ford Motor Company.

Murder, She Wrote has spawned three made-for-television film successors: *Murder, She Wrote: South by Southwest* (1997), *Murder, She Wrote: A Story to Die For* (2000), and *Murder, She Wrote: The Last Free Man* (2001). Lansbury has starred in a number of other made-for-television movies as well, including *The Unexpected Mrs. Pollifax* and *Mrs. Santa Claus.* Most recently, she has hosted ABC television's reintroduction of *The Wonderful World of Disney* and the Disney Channel's airing of its family programming. Today, thanks to syndication and numerous airings of quality feature films on cable film channels, hardly a week goes by when viewers cannot find the much-loved Angela Lansbury somewhere on television.

LYNN SCHOFIELD CLARK

See also **Murder, She Wrote**

Angela (Brigid) Lansbury. Born in London, England, October 16, 1925; came to United States, 1940; became U.S. citizen, 1951. Studied at Webber-Douglas School of Singing and Dramatic Art, London; Feagin School of Drama and Radio, New York. Married 1) Richard Cromwell, 1945 (divorced, 1946); 2) Peter Shaw, 1949; children: Anthony and Deirdre. Began film career as contract player with MGM, 1943; Broadway debut in *Hotel Paradiso,* 1957; stage roles

Angela Lansbury.
Courtesy of the Everett Collection

include *A Taste of Honey,* 1960, *Mame,* 1966, *Dear World,* 1969, and *Sweeney Todd,* 1979; appeared as Jessica Fletcher in the television series, *Murder, She Wrote,* 1984–96. Three Oscar nominations and 16 Emmy nominations (12 for *Murder, She Wrote*). Recipient: four Tony Awards; two Sara Siddons Awards; Woman of the Year, Harvard Hasty Pudding Theatricals, 1977; Theatre Hall of Fame, 1982; British Academy Award, 1991; Screen Actors Guild Lifetime Achievement Award, 1997; New Dramatists' Lifetime Achievement Award, 2000; Algur H. Meadows Award for Excellence in the Arts, 2000; Kennedy Center Honors, 2000; Inductee, Academy of Television Arts and Sciences Hall of Fame.

Television Series

1984–96	*Murder, She Wrote* (star)
1992–96	*Murder, She Wrote* (star and executive producer)

Television Miniseries

1984	*The First Olympics–Athens 1896*

Made-for-Television Movies

1975	*The Snow* (voice)
1982	*Sweeney Todd*
1982	*Little Gloria…Happy at Last*
1983	*The Gift of Love: A Christmas Story*
1984	*The Murder of Sherlock Holmes*
1984	*Lace*
1986	*A Talent for Murder*
1986	*Rage of Angels: The Story Continues*
1988	*Shootdown*
1989	*The Shell Seekers*
1990	*The Love She Sought*
1992	*Mrs. 'Arris Goes to Paris*
1996	*Mrs. Santa Claus*
1997	*Murder, She Wrote: South by Southwest*
1999	*The Unexpected Mrs. Pollifax*
2000	*Murder, She Wrote: A Story To Die For*
2001	*Murder, She Wrote: The Last Free Man*
2003	*Murder, She Wrote: The Celtic Riddle*
2004	*Blackwater Lightship*

Television Specials

1989	*The First Christmas Snow* (voice)
1993	*The Best of Disney* (cohost)
2000	*The Kennedy Center: A Celebration of the Performing Arts* (honoree)

Films

National Velvet, 1944; *Gaslight,* 1944; *The Picture of Dorian Gray,* 1945; *The Hoodlum Saint,* 1946; *The Harvey Girls,* 1946; *The Private Affairs of Bel Ami,* 1947; *If Winter Comes,* 1947; *The Three Musketeers,* 1948; *State of the Union,* 1948; *Tenth Avenue Angel,* 1948; *Samson and Delilah,* 1949; *The Red Danube,* 1949; *Kind Lady,* 1951; *Mutiny,* 1952; *Remains To Be Seen,* 1953; *The Purple Mask,* 1955; *A Lawless Street,* 1955; *Enjeu de la Vie,* 1955; *Please Murder Me,* 1956; *The Court Jester,* 1956; *The Reluctant Debutante,* 1958; *The Long, Hot Summer,* 1958; *Season of Passion,* 1959; *The Dark at the Top of the Stairs,* 1960; *A Breath of Scandal,* 1960; *Blue Hawaii,* 1961; *The Manchurian Candidate,* 1962; *All Fall Down,* 1962; *In the Cool of the Day,* 1963; *The World of Henry Orient,* 1964; *Mister Buddwing,* 1965; *Harlow,* 1965; *The Greatest Story Ever Told,* 1965; *The Amorous Adventures of Moll Flanders,* 1965; *Something for Everyone,* 1970; *Bedknobs and Broomsticks,* 1971; *Story of the First Christmas,* 1978; *Death on the Nile,* 1978; *The Lady Vanishes,* 1979; *The Mirror Crack'd,* 1980; *The Last Unicorn* (voice), 1982; *The Pirates of Penzance,* 1983; *The Company of Wolves,* 1985; *Beauty and the Beast* (voice), 1991; *Anastasia* (voice), 1997; *Fantasia 2000* (hostess), 2000; *The Last Unicorn* (live action remake), 2004.

Stage

1957	*Hotel Paradiso*
1960	*A Taste of Honey*
1966	*Mame*
1969	*Dear World*
1979	*Sweeney Todd*

Publications

Angela Lansbury's Positive Moves: My Personal Plan for Fitness and Well-Being, 1990

See Britain At Work, 1977
See Scotland At Work, 1979
See the South At Work, 1977
Unforgettable British Weekends: A Guide to Unusual and Celebration Holidays, 1988
Wedding Speeches and Toasts (Family Matters), 1994
The Murder, She Wrote Cookbook (contributor), 1997

Further Reading

Bonanno, Margaret Wander, *Angela Lansbury: A Biography,* New York: St. Martin's Press, 1997
Edelman, Rob, and Audrey Kupferber, *Angela Lansbury: A Life on Stage and Screen,* Citadel Press, 1999
Gottfried, Martin, *Balancing Act: The Authorized Biography of Angela Lansbury,* Boston: Little, Brown, 1999

Larry Sanders Show, The.

*See **It's Garry Shandling's Show/Larry Sanders Show, The***

Lassie

U.S. Family Drama

Lassie was a popular long-running U.S. television series about a collie dog and her various owners. Over her more than 50-year history, Lassie stories have moved across books, film, television, comic books, and other forms of popular culture. The American Dog Museum credits her with increasing the popularity of collies.

British writer Eric Knight created Lassie for a *Saturday Evening Post* short story in 1938, a story released in book form as *Lassie Come Home* in 1940. Knight set the story in his native Yorkshire and focused it around the concerns of a family struggling to survive as a unit during the depression. Lassie's original owner Joe Carraclough is forced to sell his dog so that his family can cope with its desperate economic situation, and the story becomes a lesson about the importance of interdependence during hard times. The story met with

immediate popularity in the United States and in Great Britain and was made into an MGM feature film in 1943, spanning six sequels between 1945 and 1953. Most of the feature films were still set in the British Isles, and several of them dealt directly with the English experience of World War II. Lassie increasingly became a mythic embodiment of ideals such as courage, faithfulness, and determination in front of hardship, themes that found resonance in wartime with both the British and their American counterparts. Along the way, Lassie's mythic function moved from being the force uniting a family toward a force uniting a nation. The ever-maternal dog became a social facilitator, bringing together romantic couples or helping the lot of widows and orphans.

In 1954 *Lassie* made its television debut in a series that removed the dog from Britain and placed her on

Lassie, Lassie, June Lockhart, Jon Provost, Hugh Reilly, 1954–74; 1963 episode.
Courtesy of the Everett Collection

the American family farm, where once again she was asked to help hold a struggling family together. For the next decade, the *Lassie* series became primarily the story of a boy and his dog, helping to shape our understanding of American boyhood during that period. The series' rural setting offered a nostalgic conception of national culture at a time when most Americans had left the farm for the city or suburbia. Lassie's ownership shifted from the original Jeff Miller to the orphaned Timmy Martin, but the central themes of the intense relationship between boys and their pets continued. *Lassie* became a staple of Sunday night television, associated with "wholesome family values," though, periodically, she was also the subject of controversy with parents' groups monitoring television content. *Lassie*'s characteristic dependence on cliff-hanger plots in which children were placed in jeopardy was seen as too intense for many smaller children; at the same time, Timmy's actions were said to encourage children to disobey their parents and to wander off on their own. Despite such worries, *Lassie* helped to demonstrate the potential development of ancillary products associated with television programs, appear-

ing in everything from comic books and Big Little Books to Viewmaster slides, watches, and Halloween costumes.

By the mid-1960s, actor Jon Provost proved too old to continue to play Timmy and so Lassie shifted into the hands of a series of park rangers, the focus of the programming coming to fall almost exclusively upon Lassie and her broader civic service as a rescue dog in wilderness areas. Here, the show played an important role in increasing awareness of environmental issues, but the popularity of the series started to decline. Amid increasing questions about the relevance of such a traditional program in the midst of dramatic social change, the series left network television in the early 1970s, though it would continue three more years in syndication and would be transformed into a Saturday morning cartoon series. Following the limited success of the 1979 feature film *The Magic of Lassie,* yet another attempt was made in the 1980s, without much impact on the marketplace, to revive the Lassie story as a syndicated television series. The 1994 feature film *Lassie* suggests, however, the continued association of the series with "family entertainment."

Many animal series, such as *Flipper,* saw their non-human protagonists as playful, mischievous, and childlike, leading their owners into scrapes, then helping them get out again. Lassie, however, was consistently portrayed as highly responsible, caring, and nurturing. Insofar as she created problems for her owners, they were problems caused by her eagerness to help others, a commitment to a community larger than the family, and her role was more often to rescue those in peril and to set right wrongs that had been committed. She was the perfect "mother" as defined within 1950s and 1960s American ideology. Ironically, the dogs who have played Lassie through the years have all been male.

HENRY JENKINS

See also **Children and Television**

Cast

Jeff Miller (1954–57)	Tommy Rettig
Ellen Miller (1954–57)	Jan Clayton
"Gramps" Miller (1954–57)	George Cleveland
Sylvester "Porky" Brockway 1954–57)	Donald Keeler
Matt Brockway (1954–57)	Paul Maxey
Timmy Martin (1957–64)	Jon Provost
Doc Weaver (1954–64)	Arthur Space
Ruth Martin (1957–58)	Cloris Leachman
Paul Martin (1957–58)	Jon Shepodd
Uncle Petrie Martin (1958–59)	George Chandler
Ruth Martin (1958–64)	June Lockhart

Paul Martin (1958–64)
Boomer Bates (1958–59)
Cully Wilson (1958–64)
Corey Stuart (1964–69)
Scott Turner (1968–70)
Bob Erikson (1968–70)
Garth Holden (1972–73)
Mike Holden (1972–74)
Dale Mitchell (1972–74)
Keith Holden (1973–74)
Lucy Baker (1973–74)
Sue Lambert (1973–74)

Hugh Reilly
Todd Ferrell
Andy Clyde
Robert Bray
Jed Allan
Jack De Mave
Ron Hayes
Joshua Albee
Larry Wilcox
Larry Pennell
Pamelyn Ferdin
Sherry Boucher

Dog Trainer
Rudd Weatherwax

Producers
Jack Wrather, Bonita Granville Wrather, Sheldon Leonard, Robert Golden, William Beaudine, Jr.

Programming History
451 episodes
CBS
September 1954–June 1955   Sunday 7:00–7:30
September 1955–September
 1971   Sunday 7:00–7:30

First-Run Syndication
Fall 1971–Fall 1974

Further Reading

Barcus, Francis Earle, *Children's Television: An Analysis of Programming and Advertising,* New York: Praeger, 1977

David, Jeffrey, *Children's Television, 1947–1990: Over 200 Series, Game and Variety Shows, Cartoons, Educational Programs, and Specials,* Jefferson, North Carolina: McFarland, 1995

Fischer, Stuart, *Kids' TV: The First 25 Years,* New York: Facts On File, 1983

Shayon, Robert Lewis, "Softening up Lassie," *Saturday Review* (March 3, 1956)

Late Show with David Letterman
(Late Night with David Letterman)

U.S. Talk/Comedy/Variety Show

Fans of late night television have delighted in the antics of host David Letterman in one form or another since the beginnings of his show on NBC in 1981. For 11 years, *Late Night with David Letterman* enjoyed the weeknight time slot following *The Tonight Show with Johnny Carson* (later *Tonight Show with Jay Leno*). But after being passed over as the replacement for the retiring Johnny Carson on *Tonight,* Letterman accepted CBS's multimillion-dollar offer to hop networks. The move brought Letterman and his band leader/sidekick Paul Shaffer to CBS, moved them up an hour in the schedule to run opposite *Tonight Show with Jay Leno,* and prompted renovation of the historic Ed Sullivan Theatre in New York to be the exclusive location for Letterman's new show. *The Late Show with David Letterman,* featuring Paul Shaffer and the CBS Orchestra, premiered on August 30, 1993, and within weeks had overtaken the Leno show in the ratings race.

It would be too simplistic to classify David Letterman as a talk show host, or his programs as fitting neatly into the talk show genre. Still, the format for both *Late Night* and *Late Show* resembles the familiar late night scenario. An opening monologue by the host usually plays off the day's news or current events. The monologue is followed by two or three guests who appear individually and chat with the host for five to ten minutes. Before and between the guest appearances, the host might indulge in some comedic skit or specialty bit. Despite their similarity to this basic format, however, Letterman's shows differ from others in the areas of program content, delivery, and rapport with guests.

The content of both *Late Night* and *Late Show* has remained remarkably steady over the years. Standard installments included "Viewer Mail," which became "The CBS Mailbag" after the move. During this segment, Letterman reads actual viewer letters and often responds to requests or inquiries with humorous, scripted video segments featuring Shaffer and himself. Another long-time Letterman bit is "Stupid Pet Tricks," in which ordinary people travel to the program and showcase pets with unusual talent. In one sequence Letterman hosted a dog that would lap milk out of its owner's mouth, and from that bit sprang "Stupid Human Tricks." In this segment people present unusual talents such as tongue distortion and spinning basketballs; one man vertically balanced a canoe on his chin. One of the most popular elements in Letterman's repertoire is the "Top Ten List." Announced nightly by Letterman, this list—"express from the home office in Sioux City Iowa"—features an absurdly comic perspective on current events and public controversies.

Other specialty bits have included sketches such as "Small Town News," during which Letterman reads goofy or ironic headlines from actual small town newspapers, and "Would You Like To Use the Phone?" in which Letterman invites a member of the studio audience to his desk and offers to place a phone call to someone he or she knows. Letterman sent his mother, known to fans as "Letterman's Mom," to the 1994 Winter Olympics in Lillehammer, Norway, where she interviewed First Lady Hillary Clinton and skater Nancy Kerrigan for the *Late Show*. Letterman frequently visits local businesses near his Broadway theatre: the copy shop, a local café, and a gift shop run by "Mujibar and Sirijul," two brothers who have become quite famous because of their visits to the show and their performances in skits on the program.

Letterman's style melds with the content of his program, both often unpredictable and out of control. His delivery is highly informal, and like the content, the personal performance is extremely changeable, given to sudden outbursts and frequent buffoonery. This style builds on the carefully constructed persona of "a regular guy," and Letterman often "wonders" with the audience just how a guy like him managed to become the host of one of the most popular late night shows in America. He has referred to himself as "the gap-toothed monkey boy" and frequently calls himself a "dweeb" (which his band leader Shaffer usually acknowledges as true). This "regular guy" excels at impromptu delivery and the ability to work with his audience. He often hands out "gifts and prizes" such as light bulbs, motor oil, and most notably, his trademark brand "Big Ass Ham." He has been known to send his stand-by audience to Broadway shows when they were not admitted to his taping. Letterman's relationship with his studio and viewing audiences does not always translate to his treatment of his guests, however.

Over the years of *Late Night* and *Late Show*, Letter-

Late Show with David Letterman, 1993–present. David Letterman.
Courtesy of the Everett Collection

man has hosted first ladies, vice presidents, film and television stars, national heroes, sports figures, zoo keepers, wood choppers, six-year-old champion spellers, and the girl next door. His relaxed attitude can make guests feel at home, and he can be a very gracious host if he so chooses. But there have been times when he has offended guests (Shirley MacLaine nearly hit him) and been offended by guests (Madonna offended the nation with her obscene language and demeanor on one of her visits with Letterman).

Perhaps the most significant moment in Letterman's career to date occurred in the aftermath of the September 11 attacks on the World Trade Center and the Pentagon. In what was viewed by some as an attempt to return to "normalcy," Letterman returned to his late night spot on Monday following the attacks. Somber, at times apparently stalled with emotion, he cited Mayor Rudolph Giuliani's admonition for New Yorkers to return to work and hosted guests Dan Rather and Regis Philbin. Rather twice broke into tears during their conversation, and Philbin revealed that his son had been at work in the Pentagon, though on the opposite side of the plane crash, on the 11th. *Late Night with David Letterman* was, on this occasion, something of a significant cultural marker for many viewers, an indication that late night television comedy could be the locus for powerfully shared moments of cultural significance.

Early in 2002, as Letterman's contract with CBS was set to expire, rumors circulated that the show would move to ABC, as a replacement for the news program *Nightline,* hosted by Ted Koppel. Letterman was reportedly unhappy with CBS, particularly with the local-news lead-ins it used. However, in March of 2002, Letterman did indeed renew his contract with CBS.

DAWN MICHELLE NILL

See also **Carson, Johnny; Leno, Jay; Letterman, David; Talk Shows;** *Tonight Show*

Late Night with David Letterman

Host
David Letterman

Band Leader
Paul Shaffer
with
Calvert DeForest as Larry "Bud" Melman

Programming History
NBC

February 1982–May 1987	Monday–Thursday 12:30–1:30 A.M.
June 1987–August 1991	Monday–Friday 12:30–1:30 A.M.
September 1991–September 1993	Monday–Friday 12:35–1:35 A.M.

Late Show with David Letterman
CBS

August 1993–	Monday–Friday 11:30 P.M.–12:30 A.M.

Further Reading

Adler, Bill, *The Letterman Wit: His Life and Humor,* New York: Carroll and Graf, 1994

Carter, Bill, *The Late Shift: Letterman, Leno, and the Network Battle for the Night,* New York: Hyperion, 1994

Kaplan, Peter W., "David Letterman: Vice-President of Comedy," *Esquire* (December 1981)

Latham, Caroline, *The David Letterman Story,* New York: F. Watts, 1987

Letterman, David, "The *Playboy* Interview," *Playboy* (October 1984)

Markoe, Merrill, editor, *Late Night with David Letterman: The Book,* New York: Villard, 1985

Shales, Tom, "David Letterman and the Power of Babble," *Esquire* (November 1986)

Sullivan, Robert E., Jr., "Letterman: The First 100 Nights," *Vogue* (January 1994)

Wolcott, James, "The Swivel Throne," *The New Yorker* (October 18, 1993)

Wolcott, James, "Sleepless Nights: Letterman vs. Leno Has Become a War of Attrition," *The New Yorker* (June 12, 1995)

Laverne and Shirley

U.S. Situation Comedy

Originally introduced as characters on *Happy Days,* Laverne De Fazio (Penny Marshall) and Shirley Feeney (Cindy Williams) "schlemiel-schlamazeled" their way into the Tuesday night ABC prime-time lineup and into the hearts of television viewers in 1976. The show, set in the late 1950s, centered on the two title characters and was rated the number-one program in its second year of airing. In the earliest years of the long-running sitcom, the two 20-something women shared an apartment in Milwaukee, Wisconsin, and worked at Shotz Brewery, the local beer-bottling plant. Many of the episodes focused on the humorous complications involving the women or their friends. From ditching blind dates to goofing up on the conveyor belt at the bottling plant, Laverne and Shirley "did it their way" in Milwaukee until 1980, when ABC decided to change the setting of *Laverne and Shirley* to Burbank, California, for a new twist. Aside from a change of climate and employment, now in Bradburn's Department Store, the central characters and structure of the program remained the same until Williams left the program in 1982. Following her departure, the program continued for one year under the original title, but with Laverne alone as the central character.

"There is nothing we won't try / Never heard the word impossible / This time, there's no stopping us /

We're gonna do it!" These lines from the theme song of the sitcom describe the state of mind of the program's two main characters. With the advantage of two decades of hindsight, *Laverne and Shirley* painted a picture of the 1950s from the single, independent woman's point of view. The plots of the episodes reflect concerns about holding a factory job, making it as an independent woman, and dealing with friends and relatives in the process of developing a life of one's own. Many plots revolve around the girls dating this man or that, or pondering the ideal men they would like to meet: sensitive, handsome doctors. If on the surface the characters appear to be longing to fulfill the stereotypical 1950s role of woman, their true actions and attitudes cast them as two of television's first liberated women. They think for themselves and make things happen in their social circles. Together they fight for causes, from workers' rights at the bottling plant to animal rights at the pound. They help each other and they help their friends, who add much texture and comic effect to the program.

Laverne and Shirley's two male neighbors, Lenny and Squiggy, provide much of the humor in the program with their greasy-1950s appearance and their ironic knack of entering at just the wrong time. If someone said, "Can you imagine anything more slimy and filthy than that?" in would charge Lenny and Squiggy with their famous, distorted "Hello!" Despite the fun poked at the two men, they are still portrayed as friends and thus are often caught up in the "Lucy-esque" escapades of Laverne and Shirley. Another prominent character, Carmine Ragusa or "The Big Ragu," is an energetic Italian singer. Friend to both women, Carmine is after Shirley's heart.

Laverne and Shirley gave its lead characters room to explore boundaries and break some stereotypes common in television portrayals of women prior to the 1970s. Shirley is portrayed as interested in marriage, yet she is not sure that Carmine is "the one"; instead of settling, she keeps her independence *and* her friendship with Carmine.

Among the loudest characters on the program is Frank De Fazio, Laverne's widowed father who owns the local Pizza-Bowl where everyone congregates. In his eyes Laverne is still a little girl, and he frequently checks up on her, evaluates her dates, and attempts to invalidate her decisions. Edna, Frank's girlfriend, acts as a buffer between father and daughter and becomes an even more motherly figure to Laverne after she marries Frank midway through the series' run. Although Frank expresses his overly protective and chauvinistic views, Edna's buffering reason and Laverne's stubbornness always win out. *Laverne and*

Laverne and Shirley, Cindy Williams, Penny Marshall, 1976–83.
Courtesy of the Everett Collection

Shirley was an early prime-time proponent of women's rights and placed much value in the viewpoints and experiences of 1950's women, suggesting that even in that decade women could be independent.

Since *Laverne and Shirley* was a spin-off of *Happy Days,* and because the programs aired back to back, it was easy to cross over characters from one show to another. Laverne and Shirley are often visited by Arthur Fonzarelli (better known as The Fonz), or run into Richie Cunningham or Ralph Malph (all from *Happy Days*) camping in the woods. Viewers were able to carry knowledge from one show (*Happy Days*) to the next (*Laverne and Shirley*) as characters shared experiences with each other outside the context of their own programs. The programs were thus able to layer meanings or overlap realities between previously mutually exclusive television families.

While visits to or from *Happy Days* characters were always extra fun, *Laverne and Shirley* provided seasons of hilarious antics and left behind many memorable images uniquely their own: Laverne's clothing, always decorated with a large, cursive "L"; the milk and Pepsi concoction that is her favorite beverage; the giant posters of Fabian; and Shirley's Boo-Boo Kitty, a two-foot stuffed cat that is the true ruler of her heart. Laverne and Shirley may be a female "odd couple," Shirley fanatically neat and Laverne hopelessly sloppy, but they balance each other and provide a system of mutual support, demonstrating that women can compete in the world of work as well as in the world of ideas. From a 1950s perspective, for two young women that indeed was "making our dreams come true."

DAWN MICHELLE NILL

See also **Happy Days; Marshall, Garry**

Cast

Laverne De Fazio	Penny Marshall
Shirley Feeney (1976–82)	Cindy Williams
Carmine Ragusa	Eddie Mekka
Frank De Fazio	Phil Foster
Andrew "Squiggy" Squigman	David L. Lander
Lenny Kosnowski	Michael McKean
Edna Babish De Fazio (1976–81)	Betty Garrett
Rosie Greenbaum (1976–77)	Carole Ita White
Sonny St. Jaques (1980–81)	Ed Marinaro
Rhonda Lee (1980–83)	Leslie Easterbrook

Producers

Garry Marshall, Thomas L. Miller, Edward K. Milkis, Milt Josefberg, Marc Sotkin

Programming History

112 episodes
ABC

January 1976–July 1979	Tuesday 8:30–9:00
August 1979–December 1979	Thursday 8:00–8:30
December 1979–February 1980	Monday 8:00–8:30
February 1980–May 1983	Tuesday 8:30–9:00

Further Reading

Gates, Anita, "Through Thick and Thin," *New York Times* (April 30, 1995)

Hamamoto, Darrell Y., *Nervous Laughter: Television Situation Comedy and Liberal Democratic Ideology,* New York: Praeger, 1989

Jones, Gerard, *Honey, I'm Home: Sitcoms, Selling the American Dream,* New York: Grove Weidenfeld, 1992

Marc, David, and Robert J. Thompson, *Prime Time, Prime Movers: From I Love Lucy to L.A. Law—America's Greatest TV Shows and the People Who Created Them,* Boston: Little Brown, 1992

Marshall, Garry, with Lori Marshall, *Wake Me When It's Funny: How To Break into Show Business and Stay There,* Holbrook, Massachusetts: Adams, 1995

Mitz, Rick, *The Great TV Sitcom Book,* New York: R. Marek, 1988

Newcomb, Horace, and Robert S. Alley, *The Producer's Medium: Conversations with Creators of American TV,* New York: Oxford University Press, 1983

Law & Order

U.S. Crime Drama

"In the criminal justice system, the people are represented by two separate yet equally important groups: the police who investigate crime, and the district attorneys who prosecute the offenders. These are their stories." This narrative voice-over begins each episode of *Law & Order,* currently network television's longest running drama series, comprising over 275 episodes by the end of its 12th season in 2002. Created by ex-*Miami Vice* executive producer Dick Wolf as a never-aired pilot for CBS in 1988, the series was launched at a time when law and crime hourly dramas were far less popular than half-hour sitcoms in the prime-time net-

work schedule. NBC had canceled its critically acclaimed *Hill Street Blues* in 1987, and the limited success of its replacement in the Thursday night schedule, *L.A. Law,* was already waning by 1990. With its plots often based upon contemporary headline stories, *Law & Order* has helped to revitalize the crime drama not only by hybridizing police investigation and legal prosecution, but also by reworking the narrative strategies of its genre predecessors.

The elegant and distinctive format has changed little since the show's inception. Unlike the multi-arc structure of Steven Bochco dramas such as *Hill Street*

Blues, L.A. Law, and *NYPD Blue,* each episode of *Law & Order* focuses upon the criminal and legal processes of a single homicide case, beginning as bystanders accidentally discover a murder victim, and ending after the disclosure of the jury's trial decision. Episodes are devised as discrete units, with closure and without season cliff-hangers. Although *Law & Order* shares with the Bochco crime dramas an extensive use of the hand-held camera, the series emphasizes stability and direction over distraction: signposts guide the viewer through the intricacies of the investigation, including the intertitles that punctuate the narrative to identify location changes on the Manhattan streets comprising the show's setting (several early episodes also included closing taglines documenting the fate of the criminals). The scales of justice featured in the opening credit sequence resonate as a metaphor of the tightly balanced episodic structure. Half of each episode's segments comprise a criminal investigation conducted by two police detectives guided by their lieutenant. Upon identification of a suspect and the gathering of sufficient evidence, the case is handed over to two assistant district attorneys who regularly enlist the assistance of their DA boss. After the case is prepared, the final segments of the episode feature highlights of the trial. So plot-focused is the narrative that the police and attorneys exist as a rule only in their professional capacities; the viewer's knowledge is structured to maximize identification with the point-of-view of the police and attorneys, at least one of whom remains present in every scene after the murder discovery.

The stability of narrative structure has overridden the numerous cast changes among the six principal roles, none of which are currently played by original cast members. George Dzundza left the series after the first season due to conflicts over the quality of the writing. His replacement Paul Sorvino departed after the start of the third season, complaining that the outdoor street shooting was compromising the vocal chords he wanted to preserve for opera singing. Michael Moriarity resigned in 1994 after heated network conflicts concerning his publicized disagreement with Attorney General Janet Reno on television censorship issues. In NBC's effort to introduce female characters, S. Epatha Merkerson and Jill Hennessy were hired to replace Dann Florek and Richard Brooks after the end of the third season. Three female assistant district attorneys have succeeded Hennessy since her departure in 1996. The involuntary contract termination of Chris Noth in 1995 remains a mystery to viewers (as well as the actor).

In the tightly structured, case-focused narrative of the series, intimacies between principals emerge through a number of strategies. Backstory is occasionally introduced to motivate the departure of a major character, as with the increasingly frequent references to Detective Reynaldo Curtis's wife's multiple sclerosis in the ninth season, and ADA Jamie Ross's custody battles in season eight. As the police officers and attorneys debate suspects' guilt and innocence, intimacies arise when case issues strike personal chords. On religious grounds, Sgt. Max Greevey asks to be removed from a case involving sadomasochism; past trauma inflects the perspectives of Detective Mike Logan and ADA Abby Carmichael in cases of child abuse and rape (respectively); the liberal-minded Detective Lennie Briscoe and Lieutenant Anita Van Buren clash with the conservative Curtis on child discipline and abortion cases; Briscoe's alcoholism renders him empathetic with suspects and criminals who share the affliction. Less frequently, reactions to a difficult case elicit vulnerabilities that demonstrate the tenuous "order" of these professionals' personal lives. Such crises are taken to an extreme in the sixth season finale episode "Aftershock," unique in its reworking of the established episodic structure as it begins with a murderer's execution and develops by tracing its effects upon the police and lawyers, who are driven to infidelity, drunken stupor, and tragic, accidental death. The fact that such instances occur only rarely in the series makes the intrusion of character backstory all the more resonant.

Law & Order has experienced a steady gain in popularity since the mid-1990s, surpassing *NYPD Blue* in the Nielsen ratings since the 1999–2000 season, and ranked in the top ten since 2000. It received the Emmy Award for Outstanding Drama Series in 1997 and has been nominated ten times in this category. The series is in syndication on the Arts & Entertainment Channel and the TNT network. Dick Wolf also produced the made-for-TV *Exiled: A Law & Order Movie* in 1998 and two series spinoffs, *Law & Order: Special Victims Unit* (1999–) and *Law & Order: Criminal Intent* (2001–), both of which focus more intently upon criminal investigation than prosecution. In its opening segments, the latter of these spin-offs alters the format of the original series by revealing information to which the investigators are not privy. *Special Victims Unit,* which treats the most "heinous" of criminal homicides, reintroduces Dann Florek in his role of Captain Donald Cragen. NBC has renewed *Law & Order* through May of 2005.

MICHAEL DeAngelis

See also **Police Programs; Wolf, Dick**

Cast

Sgt. Max Greevey (1990–91)	George Dzundza
Det. Mike Logan (1990–95)	Chris Noth

Captain Donald Cragen (1990–93)	Dann Florek
Exec. Asst. Dist. Attorney Ben Stone (1990–94)	Michael Moriarty
Asst. Dist. Attorney Paul Robinette (1990–93)	Richard Brooks
Dist. Attorney Adam Schiff (1990–2000)	Steven Hill
Sgt. Phil Cerreta (1991–92)	Paul Sorvino
Det. Lennie Briscoe (1992–2004)	Jerry Orbach
Lieutenant Anita Van Buren (1993–)	S. Epatha Merkerson
Asst. Dist. Attorney Claire Kincaid (1993–96)	Jill Hennessy
Exec. Asst. Dist. Attorney Jack McCoy (1994–)	Sam Waterston
Det. Reynaldo Curtis (1995–99)	Benjamin Bratt
Asst. Dist. Attorney Jamie Ross (1996–98)	Carey Lowell
Asst. Dist. Attorney Abigail Carmichael (1998–2001)	Angie Harmon
Det. Ed Green (1999–)	Jesse L. Martin
Dist. Attorney Nora Lewin (2000–)	Dianne Wiest
Asst. Dist. Attorney Serena Southerlyn (2001–)	Elisabeth Röhm

Creator/Executive Producer
Dick Wolf

Executive Producers
Jeffrey Hayes
Barry Schindel

Co-Executive Producers
Lewis J. Gould
Arthur Forney
Richard Sweren

Programming History
277 episodes (by the end of 2001–2002 season)
NBC
September 1990–present Wednesday 10:00–11:00

Further Reading

Courrier, Kevin, and Susan Green, *Law & Order: The Unofficial Companion,* New York: Renaissance Books, 1999
Delamater, Jerome H., and Ruth Prigozy, editors, *The Detective in American Fiction, Film, and Television,* Westport, Connecticut: Greenwood Publishing Group, 1998
McConnell, Frank, "Twice-told Tales: *Law & Order,*" *Commonweal* (November 1994)
Thompson, Robert J., *Television's Second Golden Age: From Hill Street Blues to ER,* Syracuse, New York: Syracuse University Press, 1997
Wood, William P., and Elizabeth Massie, *Law & Order,* New York: Ibooks, 2002

Lawrence Welk Show, The

U.S. Musical Show

One of television's most enduring musical series, *The Lawrence Welk Show,* was first seen on network TV as a summer replacement program in 1955. Although the critics were not impressed, Welk's show went on to last an astonishing 27 years. His format was simple: easy-listening music (what he referred to as "champagne music") and a "family" of wholesome musicians, singers, and dancers.

The show first ran on ABC for 16 years and was known in the early years as *The Dodge Dancing Party.* ABC canceled the show in 1971, not because of lack of popularity, but because it was "too old" to please advertisers. ABC's cancellation did little to stop Welk, who lined up more than 200 independent stations for a successful syndicated network of his own.

Part of Welk's success can be attributed to his relationship with viewers. He meticulously compiled a "fever chart," which tallied positive and negative comments from viewers' letters. Performers with favorable comments became more visible on the show. In this way, viewers also played an important role in Welk's "family" of regulars.

The Lawrence Welk Show, Lawrence Welk, 1955–82.
Courtesy of the Everett Collection

There were many show favorites throughout the years, including the Lennon Sisters, who were brought to Welk's attention by his son Lawrence Jr., who was dating Dianne Lennon in 1955. Other favorites included the Champagne Ladies (Alice Lon and Norma Zimmer); accordionist Myron Floren, who was also the assistant conductor; singer-pianist Larry Hooper; singers Joe Feeney and Guy Hovis; violinist Aladdin; dancers Bobby Burgess and Barbara Boylan; and Welk's daughter-in-law, Tanya Falan Welk.

Most of the regulars stayed with the show for years, but a few moved on—or were told to leave by Welk. In 1959, for example, Welk fired Champagne Lady Alice Lon for "showing too much knee" on camera. After receiving thousands of protest letters for his actions, he attempted to get Lon to return, but she refused.

Welk himself was the target of endless jokes. Born on a North Dakota farm in 1903 of Alsatian immigrant parents, he dropped out of school in the fourth grade. He was 21 years old before he spoke English. His thick accent and stiff stage presence were often parodied. But viewers were delighted when he played the accordion or danced with one of the women in the audience. Fans also bought millions of his albums, which contributed to the personal fortune he amassed, a fortune including a music-recording and publishing empire and the Lawrence Welk Country Club Village.

The final episode of *The Lawrence Welk Show* was produced in February 1982. After that time, however, followers of his show were still able to enjoy the programs, which were repackaged with new introductions by Welk under the title of *Memories with Lawrence Welk.* Loyal fans thirsty for more champagne music were pleased. The programs continue to be aired in syndication on many channels throughout the United States, including many public broadcasting channels.

DEBRA A. LEMIEUX

See also **Music on Television**

Regular Performers

Lawrence Welk, host
Alice Lon, vocals
Norma Zimmer, vocals
Aladdin, violin
Jerry Burke, piano-organ
Dick Dale, saxophone
Myron Floren, accordion
Bob Lido, violin
Tiny Little Jr., piano
Buddy Merrill, guitar
Jim Roberts, vocals
Rocky Rockwell, trumpet, vocals
The Sparklers Quartet, vocals
The Lennon Sisters (Dianne, Peggy, Kathy, Janet), vocals
Larry Dean, vocals
Frank Scott, piano, arranger
Joe Feeney, tenor
Maurice Pearson, vocals
Jack Imel, tap dancer
Alvan Ashby, hymns
Pete Fountain, clarinet
Jo Ann Castle, piano
Jimmy Getzoff, violin
Bobby Burgess and Barbara Boylan, dancers

Joe Livoti, violin
Bob Ralston, piano-organ
Art Duncan, dancer
Steve Smith, vocals
Natalie Nevins, vocals
The Blenders Quartet
Lynn Anderson, vocals
Andra Willis, vocals
Tanya Falan Welk, vocals
Sandi Jensen, vocals
Salli Flynn, vocals
The Hotsy Totsy Boys
Ralna English Hovis
Mary Lou Metzger
Guy Hovis
Peanuts Hucko
Anacani
Tom Netherton
Ava Barber
Kathy Sullivan
Sheila and Sherry Aldridge
David and Roger Otwell
Jim Turner

Producers

Sam Lutz, James Hobson, Edward Sobel

Programming History

ABC

July 1955–September 1963	Saturday 9:00–10:00
September 1963–January 1971	Saturday 8:30–9:30
January 1971–September 1971	Saturday 7:30–8:30
Syndicated	
1971–82	

Further Reading

Coakley, Mary Lewis, *Mister Music Maker, Lawrence Welk,* Garden City, New York: Doubleday, 1958
Schwienher, William K., *Lawrence Welk, an American Institution,* Chicago: Nelson-Hall, 1980
Welk, Lawrence, and Bernice McGeehan, *Lawrence Welk's Musical Family Album,* Englewood Cliffs, New Jersey: Prentice-Hall, 1977

Laybourne, Geraldine (1947–)

U.S. Media Executive

Geraldine Laybourne is chairwoman and chief executive officer of Oxygen Media, a cable television/online network launched on February 2, 2000. She developed Oxygen after a two-year tenure in which she was in charge of Disney/ABC Television's cable operations. However, Laybourne gained her greatest renown for her work at Nickelodeon, a cable network targeted to children, where she was president until 1996. Laybourne was largely responsible for the overwhelming success the network achieved in the 1980s and 1990s, a time when Nickelodeon garnered a larger audience of child viewers than ABC, CBS, NBC, and FOX, combined.

Laybourne began her tenure at Nickelodeon in 1980. Her prior background featured stints in both education and children's television programming, experiences that would serve her well at Nickelodeon. She then joined her husband, Kit (a professional animator), as an independent producer of children's television programming. From this position she began, in 1979, to work with the new cable network Nickelodeon in the production of pilot programs. A year later she was named the company's program manager.

During Nickelodeon's early years, Laybourne was instrumental in several key decisions that ultimately led to the network's long-term success. Nickelodeon came into being as a noncommercial program source created largely to serve as a goodwill tool through which cable system operators could win both franchise rights and subscribers. The company began to accept corporate underwriting in 1983 and became advertiser-supported a year later. Although it continued to devote fewer minutes per hour to advertising than most cable or broadcast commercial program sources, the initial decision to accept advertising was extremely controversial. The end result of the decision, however, was that Nickelodeon became an extremely profitable operation.

In 1985 Laybourne initiated the launch of the complementary evening service Nick at Nite, which breathed new life into old television series such as *The Dick Van Dyke Show, The Mary Tyler Moore Show, Get Smart,* and *Dragnet.* Nick at Nite took series that had been syndicated for years and presented them in an original, tongue-in-cheek environment designed to create a unique program flow and to appeal to an affluent "baby boomer" audience. Nick thus expanded Nickelodeon's programming hours, widened the network's appeal to new audience segments, and ultimately led to the launch of another 24-hour program service from Nickelodeon called TV Land.

With a number of accomplishments under her belt, Laybourne was named president of Nickelodeon in 1989, and in 1992 she became vice chair of corporate parent MTV Networks (owned by Viacom). In these positions, Laybourne continued her efforts to build the brand equity of the Nickelodeon name. To this end, Nickelodeon opened its own production studio at Universal's Orlando, Florida, theme park; it licensed con-

Geraldine Laybourne.
Photo courtesy of Nickelodeon/M. Malabrigo

sumer products to companies such as toy manufacturers Mattel and Hasbro; and it produced a magazine aimed at children, which regularly included a question-and-answer section with "The Boss Lady," as Laybourne came to be known by Nickelodeon's young viewers.

Nickelodeon has also produced programs aired on outlets other than the cable network itself. For instance, its youth-oriented game show *Double Dare* was syndicated to broadcast stations, and its 1991 sitcom *Hi Honey, I'm Home* represented a cable landmark in that its episodes aired within the same week on both the cable network Nickelodeon and the broadcast network ABC. Such synergistic strategies became even more prevalent after Paramount Communication's takeover of Viacom in 1994. For example, Nickelodeon played a central role in the cross-media promotional strategies Paramount employed leading up to the successful 1995 theatrical release of *The Brady Bunch Movie,* and Nickelodeon's popular *Rugrats* series became a Paramount feature film in 1998, with a sequel released in 2000.

Under Laybourne's leadership, Nickelodeon grew from a fledgling, noncommercial programmer that existed largely to serve the cable industry's public image purposes, to a profitable and acclaimed program source that has become a core service in the channel lineups of virtually every U.S. cable system. In so doing, Laybourne became one of the foremost figures among cable television programmers, as well as one of the most influential women in the television industry. Her launch of Oxygen—with partners that include Oprah Winfrey, Microsoft cofounder and cable television magnate Paul Allen, and the Hollywood production team of Marcy Carsey, Tom Werner, and Caryn Mandabach—represented an ambitious step to create a multimedia content provider targeted to women. Although Oxygen initially struggled, it nevertheless promised to present Laybourne with many opportunities to exercise her unique and prescient vision of television's role in contemporary society.

DAVID GUNZERATH

Geraldine Laybourne. Born Geraldine Bond, May 19, 1947. Educated at Vassar College, New York, B.A. in art history, 1969; University of Pennsylvania, M.S. in elementary education, 1971. Married: Kit Laybourne, 1970; children: Emily and Sam. Started career as administrator, architectural firm of Wallace, McHarg, Roberts and Todd, Philadelphia, 1969–70; teacher, Concord Academy, Concord, Massachusetts, 1972–73; festival coordinator, American Film Festival, New York, 1974–76; cofounder, Media Center for Children, New York, 1974–77; partner, Early Bird Specials Company, New York, 1978–80; program manager, Nickelodeon, 1980; various acquisition, scheduling, and programming positions, Nickelodeon, 1981–86; senior vice president and general manager, Nick at Nite, 1986–87, executive vice president and general manager, 1987–89, president, from 1989; vice chair of MTV Networks, from 1992; vice president for cable operation, Disney/ABC, 1996–98; chairwoman and chief executive officer, Oxygen Media, since 1998.

Further Reading

Brooker, Katrina, "Oxygen Is Can't-See TV; That's a Good Thing," *Fortune* (January 8, 2001)
Burgi, Michael, "Disney/ABC Eyes Cable Nets," *MediaWeek* (January 1, 1996)
Dempsey, John, "Mighty Mouse Nips at Nick," *Variety* (December 18, 1995)
Mifflin, Lawrie, "Nickelodeon Executive To Head Disney/ABC Cable Unit," *New York Times* (December 16, 1995)

Le Mesurier, John (1912–1983)

British Actor

As the gentle, genteel, and serenely gallant Sergeant Frank Wilson in *Dad's Army,* John Le Mesurier remains one of the best-loved actors in the history of the British situation comedy. With its provocative use of wartime sing-a-long tunes, perfectly and piously pitched scripts, and an ensemble acting team who instinctively fed off each other's momentum, the series ran from 1968 until 1977. During that time, a stage version, a radio series, and a feature film spin-off opened new doors for the home guard homage. The show is still repeated to huge audience figures.

Like the majority of the cast, Le Mesurier's major television fame came late and after a lengthy, enjoyable "apprenticeship" on the stage and in film. A jobbing actor for 20 years before finally being recognized as a supporting comic face to be reckoned with, he had made his television debut as early as 1938 and his first film appearance some ten years later. Typically, he was inauspicious and incognito, miles down the cast list and turning in a competent, albeit workmanlike, performance. However, in 1949 he embraced big-screen comedy, when he turned in a majestic contribution as a frustrated and flustered headwaiter in *Old Mother Riley's New Venture*. With an unsmiling, bottled-up tension, furtive eyes, a worried look of impending disaster, and "head-in-hands" dismay at the mayhem all around him, the "type" would hold the actor in good stead for the next 30 years or more. Importantly, much more than the theater, Le Mesurier saw television and film as his natural medium, where every subtle nuance could be captured by the camera and magnified tenfold. His early, major television assignment also allowed him to exercise his great versatility. He played the doctor in the Dorothea Brooking–produced BBC production of *The Railway Children*, and featured as the ill-fated and foppish Eduardo Lucas in *Sherlock Holmes: The Second Stain*, with Alan Wheatley as the great detective (both 1951). He was cast in *The Granville Melodramas*, a 1955 epic for Rediffusion for director/producer Cyril Butcher. More importantly, that same year, he found his perfect niche in British cinema. Under the wing of the Boulting Brothers, Le Mesurier scored a success in the army satire *Private's Progress* opposite Terry-Thomas, and kick-started a glittering run of uneasy, tense, bombastic, and petulant character studies. He clocked up an amazing score of appearances well into the 1970s, effortlessly complementing the world's funniest comedians, from Norman Wisdom to Peter Sellers.

Displaying a clear skill for comedy acting and reacting, television didn't take long to grab Le Mesurier for a never-ending supply of judges, doctors, military men, and crusty colonels opposite the cream of British comedy talent. Writers Ray Galton and Alan Simpson, having ushered their hit radio series *Hancock's Half Hour* onto television, turned to an array of "proper" actors to fully complement the hapless flights of fancy of star comedian Tony Hancock. Le Mesurier proved both a long-standing member of the *Hancock* repertory company and one of the star's closest friends in the business, appearing in all of his subsequent ill-fated attempts to make it big in feature films. Le Mesurier's

contributions to *Hancock* stand alone: the plastic surgeon in *The New Nose*, the officious RAF officer in *The Lift*, the National Trust trustee in *Lord Byron Lived Here*, the hypochondriac doctor in *The Cold*. All were basically the same figure of stern, befuddled authority, but played with real dramatic conviction. Not surprisingly, Le Mesurier would stooge for television comedians for much of the rest of his television career, working alongside Dick Emery, Harry Worth, Morecambe and Wise, and, in the 1960s, on the Galton and Simpson scripted series, Frankie Howerd. It was like *Hancock* with added innuendo. The actor also found himself featured in celebrity-based American television drama (*Douglas Fairbanks Presents* and *Errol Flynn Theatre*) and ATV action serials (*Dangerman: Affair of State*, in November 1960) and a starring role in *Armchair Theatre: Three on the Old Tar Fiddle* with Norman Rossington and Raymond Huntley. Produced by Charles Jarrot, it was broadcast on January 17, 1961. An ever-reliable general-purpose actor was how Le Mesurier liked to see himself, chalking up appearances in *The Avengers* (Mandrake, January 1964) and *Play of the Week* (Bachelors, November 1964). His film roles, while almost entirely swamped by comedy fare, throw up excellent opportunity for compelling character studies, notably as the bereaved father in Val Guest's superior crime thriller *Jigsaw* in 1962. Television, sporadically, employed him in equally dramatic presentations, including *Sunday Night Theatre: The Trial of Mary Lefarge*, with Yvonne Mitchell, and Harold Pinter's *Tea Party*, the second specially commissioned play for the European Broadcasting Union broadcast on March 25, 1965, and produced by Sydney Newman.

Le Mesurier himself was less than happy with moving away from his fast-growing reputation for comedy. He was content to "stay in his own backyard" and feverishly work away at developing his standard, scene-stealing persona of officious bureaucracy. His first major television series, the ITV situation comedy *George and the Dragon*, came at the end of 1966. Although most certainly playing "third fiddle" to the central comic pairing of Sid James and Peggy Mount, Le Mesurier grabbed his featured role of the kindly, tolerant, and deceptively bemused Colonel for whom the leading characters work.

The scripts, by Vince Powell and Harry Driver, were never really taxing, but the series, thanks in no small part to the inspired casting, proved extremely popular, running to four series. However, the show's untimely demise was rather timely for Le Mesurier. That same year, 1968, saw the launch of the program that would make him one of Britain's best-loved actors, *Dad's*

Army. His effete, charming, and magnetic style gave him a touch of the Jack Buchanans and proved the perfect contrast with Arthur Lowe's bluff, bombastic Captain Mainwaring. Le Mesurier's Wilson was the lesser man in rank only. Eventually the character became the man and the man became the character. A gentle, trusting, and endearingly vague soul in real life, Le Mesurier seemingly liked to indulge in alcohol, certain substances, traditional jazz, and dreamy days in blissful ignorance. However, his acting career continued to be diverse and diverting during the run of his most popular television series. Although his film output was slightly less prolific than before, the small screen delighted in offering him guest roles in everything from *Jason King* (1971) to *Orson Welles' Great Mysteries* (1975). He featured in the Richard Burton and Sophia Loren NBC's Hallmark of Fame remake of *Brief Encounter* for director Alan Bridges and enhanced a Crown Court case, *Murder Most Foul.* Dabbling with anarchic comedy, Le Mesurier played a mild-mannered but mildly-mad scientific farmer in a one-off guest appearance in *The Goodies,* played a health farm obsessive in a John Cleese–scripted *Doctor At Large episode* ("Mr. Moon") and even joined forces with his ex-wife, comedy actress Hattie Jacques, in a 1972 episode of *Sykes.* Stricken with ill health while rehearsing a play, *The Miser,* in Perth, Australia, he was rushed to hospital and enforced to adopt an alcohol-free lifestyle, which led to his haggard appearance in the last series of *Dad's Army.* After a year, Le Mesurier returned to moderate drinking and to his old dashing self. A high-profile appearance in *Brideshead Revisited,* a role in Val Guest's Ealing community styled TV movie *The Shillingbury Blowers* and a brilliantly emblematic appearance in the final *Ripping Yarns:* "Roger of the Raj," with Michael Palin, followed. Le Mesurier made appearances alongside Jon Pertwee in *Worzel Gummidge,* narrated the children's favorite *Bod,* and provided voice-overs for a long-running advertising campaign for Homepride Baking Flour. He also accepted another assignment for David Croft and Jimmy Perry with a single appearance in their "latest" BBC comedy success, *Hi-De-Hi,* as well as recreating his *Dad's Army* creation for radio. It was a fitting closure to a career that simply tried and succeeded in spreading as much happiness as possible. He died in 1983 at the age of 71. His dying words, just before slipping into a final coma, were "it's all been rather lovely."

ROBERT ROSS

See also **Dad's Army**

John Le Mesurier. Born April 5, 1912, Bury St. Edmunds, Suffolk, England. Married: 1) June Melville, 1939 (divorced 1947); 2) Hattie Jacques, 1949 (divorced 1965); two sons Robin and Kim; 3) Joan Malin, 1965. Died November 15, 1983, Ramsgate, Kent, England.

Television Series
George and the Dragon (1966–68)
Dad's Army (1968–77)

Films (selected)
Death in the Hand (1948); *Blind Man's Bluff* (1951); *Mother Riley Meets the Vampire* (1952); *Dangerous Cargo* (1954); *Josephine and Men; A Time To Kill* (1955); *The Battle of the River Plate; The Baby and the Battleship; Brothers in Law* (1956); *Happy Is the Bride; The Admirable Crichton* (1957); *Law and Disorder; I Was Monty's Double; The Captain's Table; Blood of the Vampire; Too Many Crooks; Carlton-Brown of the F.O.* (1958); *Ben-Hur; I'm All Right Jack; The Wreck of the Mary Deare; The Hound of the Baskervilles; Follow A Star; School for Scoundrels* (1959); *Jack the Ripper; Doctor in Love; The Pure Hell of St. Trinian's; The Bulldog Breed* (1960); *The Rebel; Very Important Person; On the Fiddle* (1961); *Go to Blazes; The Waltz of the Toreadors; Only Two Can Play; The Wrong Arm of the Law* (1962); *The Pink Panther; Hot Enough for June; The Mouse on the Moon* (1963); *The Moon-Spinners* (1964); *The Early Bird; Those Magnificent Men in Their Flying Machines* (1965); *The Sandwich Man; The Wrong Box* (1966); *Casino Royale* (1967); *The Italian Job; The Magic Christian* (1969); *Doctor in Trouble* (1970); *Confessions of a Window Cleaner* (1974); *The Adventures of Sherlock Holmes' Smarter Brother* (1975); *Jabberwocky* (1977); *The Spaceman and King Arthur* (1979); *The Fiendish Plot of Dr. Fu Manchu* (1980).

Stage (selected)
Dangerous Corner, French Without Tears, Gaslight, Hamlet, An Inspector Calls, The Three Sisters, Twelfth Night, The Winslow Boy.

Lear, Norman (1922–)

U.S. Writer, Producer

Norman Lear had one of the most powerful and influential careers in the history of U.S. television. He first teamed with Ed Simmons to write comedy (Lear tells numerous stories relating how he persisted in seeking the attention of comedians like Danny Thomas, trying to convince them he could write their kind of material). After a time it worked, and Thomas bought a routine from Lear and Simmons. David Susskind, too, noticed their work and signed them to write for *Ford Star Revue,* a musical comedy-variety series that lasted only one season, 1950–51, on NBC. Lear and Simmons then moved to *The Colgate Comedy Hour,* a high-budget NBC challenge to Ed Sullivan on Sunday evenings. It was a success, lasting five years. The partners wrote all the Jerry Lewis and Dean Martin material for the famous comedy team's rotating regular appearances on the show.

After the *Colgate* years, Lear began writing on his own, and in 1959 he teamed with Bud Yorkin to create Tandem Productions. Tandem produced several feature films, and Lear selectively took on the tasks of executive producer, writer, and, on the film *Cold Turkey,* director.

In 1970 Lear and Yorkin moved into television. While in England Lear had seen a comedy, *Till Death Us Do Part,* which became an inspiration for *All in the Family.* ABC was interested in the idea and commissioned a pilot, but after it was produced the network rejected it, leaving Lear with a paid-for, free-standing pilot. He took it to CBS, which had recently brought in a new president of the network, Robert Wood. The timing was fortuitous. Anxious to change the bucolic image cast by shows like *The Beverly Hillbillies,* Wood reacted positively to Lear's approach and gave Tandem a green light.

All in the Family first aired on January 12, 1971. Wood commented in a 1979 interview that CBS had added several extra phone operators to handle an expected flood of reactions to the contentious nature of the program and especially the bigoted lead character Archie Bunker. The calls never came.

The series did, however, attract its share of protests and strong reactions. Over its early life, there was a continuous flow of letters that objected to language and themes and challenged Lear for his "liberal" views. Later, in 1979, Lear remarked that he responded to such criticism by stating, "I'm not trying to say anything. I am entertaining the viewers. Is it funny? That was the question." Later, when attacks on the show asked how he dared to express his views, he altered his response: "Why wouldn't I have ideas and thoughts and why wouldn't my work reflect those ideas?" And, of course, his programs did.

Lear's pioneering television work brought an even more controversial series, *Maude,* to CBS in 1972. Lear once described the acerbic and openly liberal Maude as the flip side of Archie Bunker. Perhaps that was true in the beginning, but, unlike Archie, Maude's positions on issues were not presumed to be ridiculous

Norman Lear.
Photo courtesy of Norman Lear

and her approaches to social issues were almost always presented sympathetically. The most famous episodes of *Maude* dealt with her decision to have an abortion. Reflecting the U.S. Supreme Court's 1973 decision legalizing abortion, Maude and husband Walter worked out their response to her midlife pregnancy with dignity and compassion. That show sparked a storm of protest from Roman Catholics. If some viewers accepted Archie as the bigot he was, some of the religious community took Maude equally seriously.

Lear and Yorkin also moved black families to network prime time with *Good Times* and *The Jeffersons.* Lear's satiric bent was also evident in *Mary Hartman, Mary Hartman,* a pioneering show he wanted to air in the daytime as part of the soap-opera scene. When that attempt failed, he syndicated the series and found it frequently relegated to late-night fringe time schedules. Still, Lear saw the show as depicting "the worst of what was going on in society." At the other end of the spectrum, Lear collaborated with Alex Haley and brought a classy drama, *Palmerstown, U.S.A.,* to the air in 1980.

Always present at story conferences of every series, even when he had as many as six on the air at one time, Lear's influence could be seen in every show. During most of the 1970s, he even performed as the "warm up" entertainer for the audiences assembled to watch weekly tapings of his shows, a production schedule that ran from late summer to early spring. He was fond of describing various episodes as sensitive, requiring his constant attention for just the right touch. He and executive assistant Virginia Carter spent several hours one Sunday evening discussing a single dramatic development—how to treat Walter Findley's alcoholism and Maude's response.

When Lear left active involvement in television production in 1978, he left a company without a creative rudder. Few projects reached the small screen and those that did were poorly received. Much of Lear's own attention turned to the development of various media-related industries, cable television, motion picture theaters, and film production companies.

By 1980 Lear was alarmed by the radical religious fanaticism of Christian fundamentalists. At first he thought he would use a television series to respond. He developed a series concept, "Good Evening, He Lied," in which the costar of the show would be a woman newswriter in her 30s, very professional, trying to do her job as a writer for an egotistical, airhead male news anchor. A moralist at heart, Lear also proposed to have the woman be a devout, mainstream Protestant Christian, openly practicing her faith. It was a fine idea and demonstrated anew Lear's genuine respect for sincere religious convictions. NBC approved the idea, but

Lear did not pursue the production. He became convinced that another approach would be more effective for him, and he founded People for the American Way to speak out for Bill of Rights guarantees and monitor violations of constitutional freedoms. By the mid-1990s, the organization had become one of the most influential and effective voices for freedom.

In the 1990s, Lear returned to television with several efforts. Neither *Sunday Dinner,* addressing what Lear calls "spirituality," nor *704 Hauser,* involving a black family moving into Archie Bunker's old house, found an audience. Lear's voice is still heard through public appearances. He has not abandoned television, but he is less frequently involved directly with the medium. It is possible, however, no single individual has had more influence through the medium of television than Norman Lear.

ROBERT S. ALLEY

*See also **All in the Family;** **Comedy, Domestic Settings; Family Viewing Time;** Good Times; **Hemsley, Sherman;** Jeffersons, The; Maude; **O'Connor, Carroll***

Norman Lear. Born in New Haven, Connecticut, July 27, 1922. Attended Emerson College, 1940–42. Married: 1) Charlotte Rosen (divorced); child: Ellen; 2) Frances Loeb (divorced); children: Kate and Maggie; 3) Lyn Davis; children: Benjamin, Brianna, and Madeline. U.S. Air Force, 1942–45, Air Medal with four Oak Leaf Clusters. Career in public relations, 1945–49; comedy writer, various television programs, 1950s; writer-producer, television specials, 1960s; creator, producer, and writer, television series, 1970s, including *All in the Family, Sanford and Son, Maude,* and *Mary Hartman, Mary Hartman;* founded Act III Communications, comprised of television station and motion picture theater ownership, motion picture and television production, 1987. President, American Civil Liberties Association of Southern California, 1973; trustee, Museum of Television and Radio; founder, People for the American Way, 1980; founder, Business Enterprise Trust, 1988; member, Writers Guild of America; Directors Guild of America; American Federation of Television and Radio Artists; Caucus of Producers, Writers, and Directors. Recipient: four Emmy Awards; George Foster Peabody Award; Broadcaster of the Year, International Radio and Television Society, 1973; Mark Twain Award, International Platform Association, 1977; Valentine Davies Award, Writers Guild of America, 1977; William O. Douglas Award, Public Counsel, 1981; Gold Medal of the International Radio and Television Society, 1981; Distinguished American Award, 1984; Mass Media Award, American

Jewish Committee of Institutional Executives, 1987; National Medal of the Arts, 1999. Among the first inductees to the Academy of Television Arts and Sciences Hall of Fame, 1984.

Television Series

1950–51	*Ford Star Revue* (co-writer)
1950–55	*The Colgate Comedy Hour* (writer)
1955–56	*The Martha Raye Show* (writer)
1955	*The George Gobel Show* (producer, director)
1971–83	*All in the Family* (producer, writer)
1972–77	*Sanford and Son* (producer)
1972–78	*Maude* (producer, writer)
1975	*Hot L Baltimore* (producer)
1975–84	*One Day at a Time* (producer)
1975–78	*Mary Hartman, Mary Hartman* (producer)
1976	*The Nancy Walker Show* (producer)
1976–77	*All's Fair* (producer)
1977	*All That Glitters* (producer)
1978	*Apple Pie* (producer)
1979–81	*The Baxters* (producer)
1980–81	*Palmerstown, U.S.A* (producer, with Alex Haley)
1984	*A.k.a. Pablo* (producer)
1991	*Sunday Dinner* (producer)
1992–93	*The Powers That Be* (producer)
1994	*704 Hauser* (producer)

Television Specials

1961	*The Danny Kaye Special*
1963	*Henry Fonda and the Family*
1965	*Andy Williams Special and Series*
1970	*Robert Young and the Family*
1982	*I Love Liberty*
1991	*All in the Family 20th Anniversary Special*

Films

Scared Stiff, 1953; *Come Blow Your Horn* (coproducer, with Bud Yorkin), 1963; *Never Too Late,* 1965; *Divorce American Style,* 1967; *The Night They Raided Minsky's,* 1968; *Start the Revolution Without Me,* 1970; *Cold Turkey* (also director), 1971; *Stand by Me* (executive producer), 1986; *Princess Bride* (executive producer), 1987; *Fried Green Tomatoes,* 1991.

Further Reading

Adler, Richard, *All in the Family: A Critical Appraisal,* New York: Praeger, 1979

Arlen, Michael, "The Media Dramas of Norman Lear," *The New Yorker* (May 10, 1975)

Cowan, Geoffrey, *See No Evil: The Backstage Battle over Sex and Violence on Television,* New York: Simon and Schuster, 1979

Landy, Thomas M., "What's Missing from This Picture?" (interview), *Commonweal* (October 9, 1992)

Newcomb, Horace, "The Television Artistry of Norman Lear," *Prospects: An American Studies Annual* (1975)

Leave It to Beaver

U.S. Situation Comedy

Leave It to Beaver, a series both praised for its family-bolstering innocence and panned for its homogenized sappiness, served as a bridge between the waning radio comedy and the blossoming of the television "sitcom." The show was created by Joe Connelly and Bob Mosher, two writers who first worked together at the J. Walter Thompson advertising agency in New York. Leaving the agency in 1942 to devote their talents to radio comedy writing, the duo worked on shows starring Edgar Bergen, Frank Morgan, and Phil Harris before securing jobs on the wildly popular *Amos 'n' Andy* program. Over a period of 12 years, they earned writers' credits on more than 1,500 radio and television scripts for that series; continuing to create material for the show's radio version right up to *Beaver's* third year. Although *Amos 'n' Andy* now is viewed as a distorted repository of racial stereotyping and segregated casting, Connelly and Mosher's experience on that program helped them refine a flair for extracting humor from uncomplicated yet likable characters immersed in unremarkable situations with which the audience could easily identify.

Connelly and Mosher's first solo television effort was a short-lived anthology series for actor Ray Milland. This uncharacteristic failure, they revealed in a *New York Times* interview with Oscar Golbout, taught

Leave It to Beaver, (top) Tony Dow, Barbara Billingsley, Hugh Beaumont, Jerry Mathers, 1957–63.
Courtesy of the Everett Collection

them to restrict themselves to writing "things we know about." They followed up on this resolution by taking a situation Connelly had observed while driving his son to parochial school and crafting it into *The Private War of Major Benson,* a theatrical feature starring Charlton Heston that won the pair an Academy Award nomination in 1956. It was from such real-life simplicity that *Leave It to Beaver* was born. In 1957 Connelly and Mosher developed a concept for an adult-appealing show about children. Unlike such predecessors (and competitors) as *The Life of Riley, The Adventures of Ozzie and Harriet,* and *Father Knows Best,* it would not be the parents who served as *Beaver*'s focal point but rather, their offspring. The stories would be told from the kids' point of view as Connelly and Mosher recalled it and observed it in their own children. Mosher was the father of two children and Connelly the parent of six. While all of these offspring served as sources for the show's dialogue and plot lines, Connelly's eight-year-old son Ricky was the inspiration for Beaver, his 14-year-old son Jay the model for Beaver's older brother Wally.

Remington Rand picked up the project that became a co-owned vehicle in which Connelly and Mosher had 50 percent and comedian George Goebel's Gomalco Production controlled the other half. The creative and casting aspects of the show were put together by dominant talent agency MCA (then known as the Music Corporation of America).

From its inception, *Beaver* was fashioned as a traditional family unit with two sons. Beaver Cleaver was near eight when the show began, and his brother Wally was 12. Although Beaver's real name was Theodore, the nickname was emphasized to suggest a toothy, perky youngster who was "all boy." Early in the series, Beaver explains that he acquired the moniker as a baby when toddler Wally could only pronounce Theodore as "Tweeter." Parents Ward and June modified the sound to the slightly more dignified "Beaver," which would be the show's namesake. The pilot script was, in fact, titled *Wally and Beaver* to emphasize the project's child's-eye viewpoint. Sponsor Remington Rand felt this might suggest a nature program, however, so the series became *Leave It to Beaver.*

Beaver ran on network television from October 1957 to September 1963, the first season on CBS and the following five on ABC. Paralleling the network shift, the show's production relocated from Republic Studio to Universal Studios after the second year—and the on-screen Cleavers moved from a modest, picket-fenced house at 485 Maple Drive to a larger abode at 211 Pine Street—both in the small and vaguely Midwestern town of Mayfield. A library of 234 episodes was produced, in which the characters were allowed to

naturally age with their actors. Beaver went from a dirt-loving little boy to a gawky teen about to enter high school. Wally matured from a preteen just beginning to take an interest in girls to a poised young man ready to leave for college. In the show's first seasons, when actor Jerry Mathers was at his cutest, his Beaver character was the program's centerpiece. As he became a more gangling preadolescent, more plot attention was directed toward Wally, whose portrayer Tony Dow was developing into a handsome teenager. Through it all, father Ward (played by Hugh Beaumont, a Methodist lay preacher and religious film actor) and mother June (grade-B film and TV drama veteran Barbara Billingsley) observed and nurtured their children with quiet selflessness and obvious love.

Despite its six-year-run as a prime-time network offering, *Beaver* never made the coveted top-25 list. Nevertheless, its down-to-earth writing, low-key acting, and uncontrived storylines served as a memorable and well-crafted icon for the positive if unremarkable joys of middle-class family life in general and suburban kid-dom in particular. If *Beaver*'s ignoring of significant social issues was a common flaw of the programs of its time, its unpretentious advocacy of personal responsibility and self-respect was an uncommon virtue. Admittedly, as critic Robert Lewis Shayon observed, Ward and June Cleaver were "Mr. and Mrs. Average-American living in their typical *Good Housekeeping* home." But what happened in and around that home was a consistent and continuous celebration of all those minor but precious family victories that could be won even when the children themselves were required to be the decision makers.

Less than three months after *Beaver* left the air, the assassination of President John F. Kennedy changed the nation's view of itself and its times. Connelly and Mosher went off to write *The Munsters,* and a country preoccupied with civil rights strife, Vietnam, Woodstock, and Watergate would find little relevance in *Beaver*'s radio-derived simplicity. But by the late 1970s, the show's uncomplicated and nonabrasive observations reacquired appeal. On superstation WTBS and scores of other outlets, *Beaver* reruns enjoyed significant ratings success. Beaver and Wally appeared on packages of Kellogg's Corn Flakes in 1983, and the show's cast members have since been featured in a variety of retrospective projects. A striking example of the wistful admiration for all the series still represents was uncovered in a 1994 *Parenting* magazine poll. Predictably, 40 percent of respondents said the contemporary super-hit *Roseanne* reflected their family life—but a full 28 percent picked *Beaver* instead. What Wally once observed about his brother may be true of the program as a whole: "He's got that little kid expression on his face all the time, but he's not really as goofy as he looks." After almost half a century, *Beaver* continues its on-air exposure with frequent airings on such nostalgia-oriented cable networks as TV Land.

PETER B. ORLIK

See also **Mosher, Bob and Joe Connelly**

Cast

June Cleaver	Barbara Billingsley
Ward Cleaver	Hugh Beaumont
Beaver (Theodore) Cleaver	Jerry Mathers
Wally Cleaver	Tony Dow
Eddie Haskell	Ken Osmond
Miss Canfield (1957–58)	Diane Brewster
Miss Landers (1958–62)	Sue Randall
Larry Mondelo (l958–60)	Rusty Stevens
Whitey Whitney	Stanley Fafara
Clarence "Lumpy"	
Rutherford (1958–63)	Frank Bank
Fred Rutherford	Richard Deacon
Gilbert Bates (1959–63)	Stephen Talbot
Richard (1960–63)	Richard Correll

Producers

Harry Ackerman, Joe Connelly, Bob Mosher

Programming History

234 episodes
CBS

October 1957–March 1958	Friday 7:30–8:00
March 1958–September 1958	Wednesday 8:00–8:30
ABC	
October 1958–June 1959	Thursday 7:30–8:00
July l959–September 1959	Thursday 9:00–9:30
October 1959–	
September 1962	Saturday 8:30–9:00
September 1962–	
September 1963	Thursday 8:30–9:00

Further Reading

Applebaum, Irwyn, *The World According to Beaver,* New York: Bantam, 1984

Golbout, Oscar, "A Gift from the Children," *New York Times* (December 8, 1957)

Leibman, Nina C., *Living Room Lectures: The Fifties Family in Film and Television,* Austin: University of Texas Press, 1995

Shayon, Robert Lewis, "Beaver's Booboo," *Saturday Review* (February 1, 1958)

Shepard, Richard, "Busy 'Beaver' and His Brother," *New York Times* (October 30, 1960)

Spigel, Lynn, *Make Room for TV: Television and the Family Ideal in Postwar America,* Chicago: University of Chicago Press, 1992

"TV's Eager Beaver," *Look* (May 27, 1958)

Leno, Jay (1950–)

U.S. Talk Show Host, Comedian

With his sanitized comedy appealing to middle-class sensibility and ordinary, nice-guy demeanor, Jay Leno rose from comedy hall fame to win the coveted host seat of NBC's *Tonight Show* in 1992. In so doing, Leno followed in the footsteps of the great past hosts, Johnny Carson, Jack Paar, and Steve Allen.

Leno began his stand-up career in Boston and New York comedy clubs and strip bars. During the 1970s, he became a popular warm-up act for such divergent performers as crooner Johnny Mathis and country singer John Denver, and he wrote scripts for the sitcom *Good Times,* starring Jimmy Walker. He obtained similar work for David Letterman, who, after he began hosting *Late Night with David Letterman,* granted Leno more than 40 appearances on that program. Leno

became a popular guest on the Merv Griffin and Mike Douglas shows and on *The Tonight Show,* and by 1986 he was named one of several guest hosts for the latter program. An untiring success-seeker, Leno still spent 300 days a year on the road.

As a popular stage and television stand-up comic, Leno strives not to offend, offering nonracist, nonsexist, anti-drug humor. Like forerunners George Carlin and Robert Klein and contemporary Jerry Seinfeld, Leno is not capricious. His focus is on ridiculing the mundane, the idiocies of social life. His feel-good approach avoids cynicism and promotes patriotism. In 1991, for example, he performed for U.S. military personnel stationed in the Middle East. Despite his penchant for politically liberal jokes, Leno insists that his

Jay Leno.
©*CJ Contino/Everett Collection*

humor is nonideological and thus apolitical. Hence, he appeals to a conventional and politically diverse—that is, broad—American public.

Although he was the exclusive guest host for *The Tonight Show* since 1987, Leno's selection as Carson's successor caused surprise and controversy in the industry. Letterman—whose popular late, late show had followed *Tonight* for years and created expensive advertising slots—had been slated for the job. However, NBC was attracted to the more cooperative Leno, matching his wit to the older *Tonight Show* audience. Moreover, an aggressive Leno promoted himself, working the affiliate-station personnel, who in turn boosted his popularity ratings. Ultimately, Leno was simply more affordable than Letterman, allowing *The Tonight Show* to maintain its $75 million to $100 million profit base.

Seeking Letterman's fans, Leno's *Tonight Show* featured a renovated stage; young, popular guests; and the music of popular jazz musician Branford Marsalis. Controversy came to the set early on, when NBC fired Leno's long-time, tumultuous manager Helen Kush-

nick, and later when Marsalis, in a wrangle over artistic control, quit and was replaced by Kevin Eubanks. Thereafter, Leno faired decently in the ratings, but he failed to impress reviewers as had Carson and Paar. Accustomed to practicing his routines many times before a show, Leno suffered agitation with his new, full-week schedule. Moreover, a year into the show, Leno was faced with a rating war against CBS's new *Late Show*, hosted by highly paid competitor Letterman.

During the *Late Show*'s first three years, it regularly bested the *Tonight Show* in the ratings, particularly with the younger audiences. This was particularly damaging as *Tonight* had the advantage of airing a full hour earlier than *Late Show* across 30 percent of the nation. Leno, in comparison to Letterman, was an unseasoned monologist, and a sometimes distracted interviewer, lacking ad-libbing skills. To boost ratings, Leno agreed to hire new *Tonight* writers and hawk advertiser's goods—Hondas and Doritos—on air. In early 1995, *Tonight* revamped the show from a talk to a variety format, creating a comfortable, comedy club-type studio for Leno. A more responsive and fluid Leno raised *Tonight*'s ratings to competitive levels, and by 1996 the program had intermittently regained its status, held since 1954, as the most popular late night show in the United States. By 2002 *The Tonight Show with Jay Leno* was consistently winning over its competitors, *The Late Show with David Letterman* and ABC's news program *Nightline*.

Leno was frustrated by his make-or-break *Tonight Show* role, but he was not broken by it. Rather, he responded predictably to this midcareer trauma with more strenuous effort on the set and increased appearances at Las Vegas clubs and college campuses. A popular comic, Leno has been named Best Political Humorist by *Washingtonian Magazine* and one of the Best-Loved Stars in Hollywood by *TV Guide*.

PAULA GARDNER

*See also **Carson, Johnny; Late Show with David Letterman; Letterman, David; Talk Shows; Tonight Show***

Jay Leno (James Douglas Muir Leno). Born in New Rochelle, New York, April 28, 1950. Educated at Emerson College, B.A. in speech therapy, 1973. Married: Mavis Nicholson. Performed as stand-up comedian at such venues as Carnegie Hall and Caesar's Palace; in television, from 1977; in movies, from 1978; numerous appearances on *Late Night with David Letterman*, 1970s and 1980s; exclusive guest host on *The Tonight Show Starring Johnny Carson*, 1987–92; host, *The Tonight Show with Jay Leno*, since 1992.

Television Series

1977	*The Marilyn McCoo and Billy Davis Jr. Show*
1986	*Saturday Night Live* (one-time host)
1987–92	*The Tonight Show Starring Johnny Carson* (exclusive guest host)
1992–	*The Tonight Show with Jay Leno* (host)

Television Specials (selected)

| 1986 | *Showtime Special* (host) |
| 1987 | *Jay Leno's Family Comedy Hour* |

Films

The Silver Bears, 1978; *American Hot Wax,* 1978; *Collision Course,* 1988.

Publication

Leading with My Chin, 1998

Further Reading

Carter, Bill, *The Late Shift: Letterman, Leno and the Network Battle for the Night,* New York: Hyperion, 1994

Freeman, Michael, "Look Who's Laughing Now," *Mediaweek* (May 1, 1995)

Kaufman, Joan, "Profile (Whew!) of a Funny Man," *People* (November 30, 1987)

Stengel, Richard, "Midnight's Mayor," *Time* (March 16, 1992)

Tauber, Peter, "Jay Leno: Not Just Another Funny Face," *New York Times Magazine* (February 26, 1989)

Leonard, Herbert B. (1922–)

U.S. Producer

Herbert B. Leonard was one of many Hollywood veterans to try his hand as a telefilm producer in the early 1950s, but few were as successful, and none made the transition with such outstanding results. Like other alumni of the studio system, Leonard started his television career by turning out formulaic fare in the B-movie vein, but by 1960 he was producing two of the most literate and visually arresting series of the sixties, or any decade: *Naked City* and *Route 66*.

Leonard started in the movie business as a production manager for producer Sam Katzman at Columbia in 1946. During this apprenticeship, overseeing the logistics of low-budget potboilers, westerns, and swashbucklers—and the *Jungle Jim* series for which Katzman is perhaps most famous—Leonard developed a knack for efficient production, and an affinity for location shooting that would mark his later television work.

After nearly eight years with Katzman, Leonard struck out on his own as an independent television producer. For his first effort Leonard secured the rights to the old Rin-Tin-Rin feature film property and turned the concept into a juvenile-oriented western series, *The Adventures of Rin Tin Tin,* which joined the heroic German shepherd with a young orphan boy at a frontier cavalry fort in the 1880s. This project launched Leonard as an "in-house" independent with Screen Gems, Columbia's television subsidiary, whereby the studio provided pilot financing and production facilities in return for distribution rights and a cut of the profits. With *Rin Tin Tin* a hit on ABC, Leonard mounted two more half-hour series, *Tales of the 77th Bengal Lancers* and *Circus Boy. Circus Boy* was a variation on *Rin Tin Tin,* centering on the adventures of an orphan and an elephant with a traveling circus in the 1890s, and *77th Bengal Lancers* followed the exploits of a British cavalry troop in 19th-century colonial India—all the elements of a TV western in a more exotic setting. Both series were sold to NBC for fall 1956, and by early 1958 Leonard was in pre-production on two more half-hour entries, *Rescue 8* and *Naked City.* The former was a syndicated adventure series about the Los Angeles Fire Department Rescue Squad, notable for its unprecedented location shooting in and around L.A., with spectacular rescues staged in real locations.

For *Naked City,* Leonard not only left the studio, but the state. The producer became intrigued by *Naked City*'s potential as a series after seeing the 1948 feature *The Naked City* when Columbia acquired it for television release in 1957. Although Screen Gems sales execs were lukewarm to the idea, Leonard purchased the rights to the film property, and hired Stirling Silliphant to write the pilot. Leonard described the show to *Vari-*

ety as "a human interest series about New York," a vehicle for anthology-type stories as seen through the eyes of two detectives. He also announced that he would be shooting the ABC series entirely on location in New York, on both counts ("entirely on location" and "in New York") a major departure from the standard telefilm practice of the time. *Naked City* made an impact on critics with its gritty style and authentic look, but its stories were constrained by the 30-minute format, and its downbeat dramatics could not dent the ratings of the established *Red Skelton Show;* it was not renewed for autumn 1959.

By then Leonard was already planning his next series. Brainstorming for a vehicle for a young actor named George Maharis (who had caught Leonard's eye in a couple of supporting roles on *Naked City*), Leonard and Silliphant came up with the idea for *Route 66:* two restless young men roaming the highways of the United States in a Corvette, searching for meaning. Screen Gems was even less enthusiastic about this concept than it had been about *Naked City,* and flatly refused to finance the pilot, so Leonard put up his own money and assembled a crew in Kentucky to shoot the pilot in February 1960. A few weeks later, with a rough cut in hand, the studio sales force changed its tune and sold the show to CBS.

Meanwhile, *Naked City* had not been forgotten. In the autumn of 1959, an advertising executive approached Leonard with the idea of mounting *Naked City* for the following season, again on ABC, this time a 60-minute program. The network also agreed to finance the pilot. After some initial hesitation due to his *Route 66* demands, Leonard agreed, turning to Silliphant for the pilot script, and by February of 1960 pilot shooting had been completed. With Silliphant heavily involved in *Route 66,* Leonard hired Howard Rodman as story editor and frequent scripter on the revised *Naked City.* Yet another hour-long Leonard-Silliphant project, *Three-Man Sub* (a peripatetic adventure whose premise is explained by the title), made it to the pilot stage in late 1959—shot on location around the Mediterranean—but did not sell. In March 1960, *Variety* trumpeted Leonard as the "Man of the Hours," the only independent producer to have two one-hour series in production that season.

Although supervising two successful network series, Leonard found the time to launch yet another project far from Hollywood in 1961, *Tallahassee 7000.* The syndicated half-hour entry featured Walter Matthau (with a southern accent) as an investigator for the Florida Sheriff's Bureau, and was shot on location all over Florida. The series was cast in the hard-boiled mold, with Matthau providing first-person voice-over narration à la Mike Hammer.

Route 66 marked the end of Leonard's relationship with Screen Gems. He went on to produce a handful of feature films and made-for-TV movies in the 1960s and 1970s and set up a production equipment rental house as a sideline, using all the gear he had accumulated in his years on the road. In the late 1980s, Leonard revived his first TV project in a Canadian-produced series, *Rin Tin Tin K-9 Cop,* with the modern "Rinty" now in the public service as a police dog.

Route 66 and *Naked City* remain high watermarks of American television drama, and set Herbert B. Leonard apart as one of the industry's most innovative producers of any era.

MARK ALVEY

See also **Naked City; Route 66; Silliphant, Stirling**

Herbert B. Leonard. Born in New York City, October 8, 1922.

Television Series

1954–59	*The Adventures of Rin Tin Tin* (executive producer)
1956–58	*Circus Boy* (executive producer)
1956–57	*Tales of the 77th Bengal Lancers*
1958–59 (syndicated)	*Rescue 8* (executive producer)
1960 (syndicated)	*Tallahassee 7000* (executive producer)
1958–59	*Naked City* (30-minute version; executive producer)
1960–63	*Naked City* (60-minute version; executive producer)
1960–64	*Route 66* (executive producer)
1988–89	*Rin Tin Tin K-9 Cop* (also known as *Katts and Dog;* executive producer)

Made-for-Television Movies

1972	*The Catcher* (executive producer)
1975	*Friendly Persuasion* (executive producer)
1975	*Except for Me and Thee*

Films

Conquest of Cochise, 1953 (associate producer); *The Perils of Pauline,* 1967 (producer, director); *Popi,* 1969 (producer); *Going Home,* 1971 (producer, director).

Further Reading

Alvey, Mark, "Wanderlust and Wire Wheels: The Existential Search of *Route 66,*" in *The Road Movie Book,* edited by

Steven Cohan and Ina Rae Hark, New York: Routledge, 1997

"Case History of a TV Producer," *Variety* (October 14, 1959)

Gomery, Douglas, "Sam Katzman," in *The International Dictionary of Films and Filmmakers,* Vol. 4, edited by James Vinson, Chicago: St. James Press, 1987

"Herb Leonard as Man of the Hours," *Variety* (March 30, 1960)

Jenkins, Dan, "Talk About Putting a Show on the Road!" *TV Guide* (July 22, 1961)

"Leonard's 60-Min. 'Route 66' Pilot," *Variety* (December 9, 1959)

"On Location," *Broadcasting* (January 27, 1958)

"Pact Martin Milner for 'Route 66' Series," *Variety* (February 3, 1960)

Thompson, Richard, "Sam Katzman," in *Kings of the Bs,* edited by Todd McCarthy and Charles Flynn, New York: E.P. Dutton, 1975

"We Can Make 'Em Just as Cheap or Cheaper in N.Y.: Herb Leonard," *Variety* (February 26, 1958)

Leonard, Sheldon (1907–1997)

U.S. Actor, Director, Producer

For nearly two decades, from the early 1950s through the late 1960s, Sheldon Leonard was one of Hollywood's most successful hyphenates, producing—and often directing and writing—a distinctive array of situation comedies, of which three justly can be considered classics (*The Danny Thomas Show, The Andy Griffith Show,* and *The Dick Van Dyke Show*). Although he assayed the hour-long espionage form with conspicuous success as well, the sitcoms remain the Leonard hallmark. Long before *Taxi, Cheers,* and MTM Productions, Leonard was overseeing the creation of literate, character-driven ensemble comedies that blended the domestic arena with the extended families of the modern workplace.

Like many independent producers in television's formative years (Bing Crosby, Desi Arnaz, Jack Webb, Dick Powell), Leonard began his show business career in front of the cameras. After six years acting on Broadway (during which time he also took his first stab at directing, for road companies and summer theater), in 1939 Leonard made the move to Hollywood, where he would go on to appear in 57 features over the next 14 years. It was not long before the actor was equally busy in radio, with regular roles on several programs (*The Jack Benny Show, The Lineup,* and *Duffy's Tavern,* to name only a few), and guest parts on dozens of others. Although Leonard played a variety of characters in both media, the Brooklyn-toned actor—described as "Runyonesque" in most biographical sketches—is best remembered for his incarnations of quietly menacing gangsters.

As the 1940s wore on, Leonard decided to take up writing for radio, selling scripts to such anthology shows as *Broadway Is My Beat.* Already demonstrat-

ing the business savvy befitting a future producer, Leonard retained the ownership of his radio scripts after production, thus building a library of salable properties. It was not long before Leonard turned his writing talents to the new medium of television, writing teleplays (some adapted from his radio scripts) for the filmed anthologies. Next Leonard tried his hand at directing some installments, an experience that signaled a new chapter in his show business career.

His apprenticeship behind him, Leonard signed on as director of the Danny Thomas series *Make Room for Daddy* in 1953. He was promoted to producer in the show's third year, remaining its resident producer-director for six more seasons. Between 1954 and 1957 the energetic director also found time to produce and direct the pilot and early episodes of *Lassie* and *The Real McCoys* (which was produced by Thomas's company), write and direct installments of (fittingly enough) *Damon Runyon Theatre,* as well as act in a 1954 summer replacement series, *The Duke.* In 1961 Leonard became executive producer of the Thomas series (renamed *The Danny Thomas Show*), at which time he and the comedian teamed up to form their own production firm.

T and L Productions would go on to make a lasting mark on television comedy. At its peak in 1963, T and L had four situation comedies in prime time, with Leonard serving as executive producer on all four: *The Danny Thomas Show, The Dick Van Dyke Show, The Andy Griffith Show,* and *The Bill Dana Show.* Through their own separate companies, Leonard and Thomas also owned an interest in a fifth sitcom, *The Joey Bishop Show,* although Leonard had no creative role in the series after directing the pilot. To complete the T

Sheldon Leonard, 1966.
Courtesy of the Everett Collection

and L comedy empire, the partners each owned an interest in *My Favorite Martian* by virtue of Thomas's financing and Leonard's direction of the pilot, and also owned *The Real McCoys'* syndication package. Although the Bishop and Dana programs were short-lived, Thomas's, Van Dyke's, and Griffith's series were all certifiable top-ten Nielsen hits.

As the titles of the hit programs suggest, the foundation of the T and L formula was the comic performer, around whom a premise was formed and an extended "family" of kin and coworkers built. There were certain clear resemblances among the series, notably the reflexive Dick Van Dyke and Joey Bishop shows, which followed the *Danny Thomas* model by focusing on the professional and private lives of people in show business (a TV writer in *The Dick Van Dyke Show,* nightclub performers in the others). *The Andy Griffith Show* is in some ways antithetical to the noisy, urban sensibility of show-biz shows, although the slow-paced rural realism of *The Real McCoys* could not have been far from Leonard's mind when he created the premise. Yet all the programs had something more in common, something *Television* magazine called the "T and L trademark": "It's good clean comedy with a small moral," in the words of one 1963 observer—or, as a *Television* reporter put it, "a combination of comedy and sentiment." While this mix was certainly not

unique to the T and L sitcoms during the 1960s, it underlines their emphasis on characters, relationships, and emotion over situation and slapstick. One need look no further for proof of this than *The Andy Griffith Show* character Deputy Barney Fife, who, in even his most outrageously broad moments, is underlined with a humanity that keeps him believable.

Leonard's influence on television comedy is bound up in the T and L hits, but it also transcends them. He can be credited with spotting the potential of bucolic raconteur Andy Griffith and (with writer Artie Stander) transforming him into wise and gentle Andy Taylor, sheriff of a fictional town called Mayberry. It was Leonard who recognized the story and character quality in a failed pilot written by and starring Carl Reiner and resurrected it by casting Dick Van Dyke in the lead role—retaining Reiner's writing talents. The excellence of the T and L programs is surely due in no small part to Leonard's commitment to the quality of the scripts, exemplified by his cultivation of writing talent, his promotion of writers to producers, and the extremely collaborative nature of the writing process on all the shows. Indeed, Leonard had an equally profound impact on the medium through the writers he mentored, notably Danny Arnold (*Barney Miller*), and the teams of Garry Marshall and Jerry Belson (*The Odd Couple, Happy Days*), and Bill Persky and Sam Denoff (*That Girl, Kate and Allie*).

Leonard's impact on television is attested to by the long-standing popularity of the *Griffith* and *Van Dyke* programs in syndication. Just as significant in terms of industry practice, Leonard pioneered the strategy of launching new series via spin-offs, thereby avoiding the expense of pilots. Both the Andy Griffith and Joey Bishop shows began with "backdoor pilots" (directed by Leonard) aired as episodes of *The Danny Thomas Show;* similarly, Bill Dana's José Jimenez character began as a recurring character on the Thomas show before setting out on his own series. While the Dana and Bishop vehicles were flops, Leonard scored a long-running success with another spin-off in 1964, when he and *The Andy Griffith Show* producer Aaron Ruben sent a popular resident of Mayberry off into six years of military misadventures on *Gomer Pyle, U.S.M.C.*

Leonard and Thomas parted company in 1965, and Leonard shifted generic gears, mounting the globe-trotting espionage series *I Spy.* Among a spate of spy shows popular in the mid-1960s, *I Spy* distinguished itself for its mix of humor and suspense, and its exotic locales (Leonard and company spent several months each season shooting exteriors around the world in such faraway places as Hong Kong, England, France, Morocco, and Greece). But the most significant aspect of the series was Leonard's decision to cast African-

American comedian Bill Cosby opposite Robert Culp as the series' two leads. If the move seems less than startling in retrospect, one need only look back at the *Variety* headline announcing the Cosby hire, dubbing the actor "Television's Jackie Robinson." Thanks to sharp writing and the chemistry of its leads, *I Spy* was hip without being campy, as witty as it was exciting. The series was nominated for the Outstanding Dramatic Series Emmy every year of its three-year run and earned Leonard an Emmy nomination for directing in 1965.

Leonard returned to the sitcom form in 1967 with the short-lived *Good Morning, World* (written and produced by Persky and Denoff), another reflexive, quasi-show-biz format in *The Dick Van Dyke Show* vein, concerning a team of radio deejays, which also anticipated the ensemble comedy style of the MTM shows of the 1970s. The producer shifted genres again in the spring of 1969 with the lighthearted mystery *My Friend Tony,* but the program was not renewed after its trial run. Leonard's most innovative comedy project came along in the fall of that year, *My World and Welcome to It,* a whimsical comedy based on the stories of James Thurber and interspersed with animated versions of Thurber's cartoons. Despite critical acclaim and an Emmy for Outstanding Comedy Series for 1969, the series was not a ratings success and was canceled after one season. Leonard's final forays into situation comedy were less prestigious: *Shirley's World,* a Shirley MacLaine vehicle in *The Mary Tyler Moore Show* mold, and *The Don Rickles Show,* an ill-fated attempt to package the master of insult comedy in a domestic sitcom.

Throughout the 1950s and 1960s, Leonard had continued to take on the occasional acting job, re-creating his radio role as the racetrack tout on *The Jack Benny Show,* appearing as Danny Williams's agent on *The Danny Thomas Show,* and doing a gangster turn in an episode of *The Dick Van Dyke Show.* Still typecast after almost 40 years, Leonard acted the tough guy yet again in 1975 as the star of the short-lived series *Big Eddie* (as a gambler-turned-sports promoter), and once more in 1978 in the made-for-TV movie *The Islander* (as a mobster). That same year Leonard discharged executive producer duties and acted in the TV movie *Top Secret,* a tale of international espionage starring and coproduced by Bill Cosby. Later, Cosby recruited Leonard to fill the executive producer slot on *I Spy Returns,* a 1993 TV-movie sequel that reunited Culp and Cosby as the swinging (and now seasoned) secret agents.

Few individuals have had the longevity in the television business that Sheldon Leonard had, and even fewer have had long-run success comparable to his string of hits spanning nearly two decades. Fewer still have had the remarkable impact on the medium, both creatively and institutionally. It might be an exaggeration to say that without Sheldon Leonard there would have been no spin-offs, and no Cosby, but it is certain that both phenomena hit the screens of the United States when they did through Leonard's efforts. Certainly, without him neither Rob and Laura Petrie nor Mayberry would exist as we know them. At the end of his 1995 autobiography, Leonard vowed a return to do battle with the networks on the field of television creativity. Although that engagement was cut short by Leonard's death in 1997, his contribution to the literature that is American television comedy continues to play out in syndication, and may well do so forever.

MARK ALVEY

See also **Andy Griffith Show; Danny Thomas Show; I Spy**

Sheldon Leonard. Born Sheldon Leonard Bershad in New York City, February 22, 1907. Syracuse University, B.A. 1929. Married: Frances Bober, 1931; one child: Andrea. Began career as actor in Broadway plays, 1930–39; numerous radio roles, 1930s and 1940s; acted in films, 1939–61; radio scriptwriter, 1940s; screenwriter, 1948–57; director of television, from 1953; producer of television, from 1955; guest appearances as actor on television, 1960s and 1970s; president of T and L Productions; partner and officer, Mayberry Productions, Calvada Productions, Sheldon Leonard Enterprises. Member: vice president and trustee, Academy of TV Arts and Sciences; national trustee, board of governors, vice president, Directors Guild of America; Academy of Motion Picture Arts and Sciences. Recipient: Christopher Award, 1955; Emmy Awards, 1957, 1961, 1969; Best Comedy Producer Awards, 1970 and 1974; Golden Globe Award, 1972; Sylvania Award, 1973; Cinematographers Governors Award; Directors Guild of America Aldrich Award; Man of the Year Awards from National Association of Radio Announcers, Professional Managers Guild, B'nai B'rith; Arents Medal, Syracuse University; Special Achievement Award, NAACP; Special Tribute Award, NCAA; TV Hall of Fame, 1992. Died in Beverly Hills, California, January 10, 1997.

Television Series

1953–56	*Make Room for Daddy* (director; producer, 1955–61; actor, 1959–61)	
1953–62	*General Electric Theater* (director)	
1953–64	*The Danny Thomas Show* (also producer, 1961–64)	
1954–71	*Lassie* (director)	
1954–57	*The Jimmy Durante Show* (director)	

1954	*The Duke* (summer replacement series; actor)
1955–56	*Damon Runyon Theatre* (director)
1957–63	*The Real McCoys* (director)
1960–68	*The Andy Griffith Show* (executive producer, director, and writer)
1961–66	*The Dick Van Dyke Show* (executive producer and director)
1963–65	*The Bill Dana Show* (executive producer and director)
1963	*My Favorite Martian* (director of pilot only)
1964–69	*Linus the Lionhearted* (voice for animated series)
1964–70	*Gomer Pyle, U.S.M.C* (executive producer and director)
1965–68	*I Spy* (executive producer and director)
1967–68	*Good Morning, World* (producer)
1969	*My Friend Tony* (executive producer)
1969–70	*My World and Welcome to It* (producer)
1971	*From a Bird's Eye View* (U.K. series; executive producer)
1971–72	*Shirley's World* (producer)
1972	*The Don Rickles Show* (executive producer)
1975	*Big Eddie* (actor)

Made-for-Television Movies

1978	*Top Secret* (actor and executive producer)
1978	*The Islander* (actor)
1993	*I Spy Returns* (executive producer)

Films (actor)

Another Thin Man, 1939; *Buy Me That Town,* 1941; *Tall, Dark and Handsome,* 1941; *Rise and Shine,* 1941; *Tortilla Flat,* 1942; *Street of Chance,* 1942; *Lucky Jordan,* 1942; *To Have and Have Not,* 1944; *Her Kind of Man,* 1946; *It's a Wonderful Life,* 1946; *Zombies on Broadway,* 1945; *Somewhere in the Night,* 1946; *The Gangster,* 1947; *Violence,* 1947; *Sinbad the Sailor,* 1947; *If You Knew Susie,* 1948; *My Dream Is Yours,* 1949; *Take One False Step,* 1949; *Iroquois Trail,* 1950; *Behave Yourself,* 1951; *Here Come the Nelsons,* 1952; *Young Man with Ideas,* 1952; *Stop You're Killing Me,* 1952; *Diamond Queen,* 1953; *Money from Home,* 1954; *Guys and Dolls,* 1955; *Pocketful of Miracles,* 1961.

Radio (actor; selected)

The Jack Benny Show; The Lineup; Duffy's Tavern.

Publications

"The World Is His Back-Lot," as told to Morris J. Gelman, *Television* (April 1966)
And the Show Goes On: Broadway and Hollywood Adventures, 1995

Further Reading

Haber, Deborah, "Kings Among the Jesters," *Television* (September 1963)
Kelly, Richard, *The Andy Griffith Show,* Winston-Salem, North Carolina: John F. Blair, 1981
Smith, Ronald L., *Cosby,* New York: St. Martin's Press, 1986
"Television's Jackie Robinson," *Variety* (December 23, 1964)
Waldron, Vince, *The Official Dick Van Dyke Show Book,* New York: Hyperion, 1994
Weismann, Ginny, and Coyne Steven Sanders, *The Dick Van Dyke Show: Anatomy of a Classic,* New York: St. Martin's Press, 1983

Leslie Uggams Show, The

U.S. Music/Variety Show

The Leslie Uggams Show, which premiered in September 1969, was the first network variety show to feature an African-American host since the mid-1950s *Nat "King" Cole Show.* Uggams's show took over the CBS Sunday night slot vacated by *The Smothers Brothers Comedy Hour,* the controversial variety show CBS had censored and then forcibly removed from the airwaves the previous April. Produced by Ilson and Chambers, the same team who put together the beleaguered Smothers program, Uggams's show was given very little opportunity to prove itself and find an audience against the popular *Bonanza* on NBC. CBS pulled the plug in midseason, replacing the show with Glen Campbell's *Goodtime Hour* in December 1969.

Leslie Uggams had achieved a modest amount of success both on Broadway and in television. As a teenager she was a regular player on the *Sing Along with Mitch* musical variety show broadcast on NBC in the early 1960s. However, many critics argued that she was too much of a novice to deal successfully with the performance rigors of a variety show. Questions were raised about why Uggams was chosen to replace the politically contentious Smothers program. Industry observers noted that CBS, suffering from a public relations problem due to its censorious activity, needed to rehabilitate its reactionary image. A black-hosted variety show that included a certain amount of social commentary on race issues might repair some of the damage.

The Leslie Uggams Show was noteworthy for the number of African Americans who participated in the show's production, including technical personnel. Regular cast members included actors Johnny Brown and Lillian Hayman. Resident dancers, singers, and orchestra were racially integrated, and the show boasted a black choreographer, conductor, and writer.

A major feature of the show was a continuing segment called "Sugar Hill" about a working-class black family. Uggams played the wife of a construction worker in the sketch. They lived together with Uggams's mother (Lillian Hayman), unemployed brother (Johnny Brown), and a "hippie" sister, in an unintegrated apartment that resembled *The Honeymooners*' home far more than the lavish and much commented upon integrated apartment building of television's other African-American family, the Bakers of *Julia*.

The show's quick demise generated protest and concern among black organizations from the Harlem Cultural Council, the Southern Christian Leadership Conference, the National Association for the Advancement of Colored People, and the Urban League. Whitney Young Jr., head of the Urban League, publicly expressed his concern over what he considered an overhasty cancellation. He argued the show was not given any time to prove itself or institute necessary changes. He also pointed out that CBS's action diminished opportunities for black performers and technicians. Twenty-eight African Americans were put out of work by the cancellation, according to Young. CBS countered that the show's demise had not generated much protest from viewers. While the canning of the Smothers Brothers had resulted in thousands of letters of complaint, the Uggams decision led to about 600 letters of disapproval.

While Leslie Uggams did not prove successful in a variety format, she did manage more notable achievements in dramatic acting. She went on to play major roles in the 1970s black-oriented miniseries, *Roots* and *Backstairs at the White House*. The first African American to really succeed in a variety show would be Flip Wilson in the season following the demise of the Uggams show.

ANIKO BODROGHKOZY

Regular Performers
Leslie Uggams
Dennis Allen
Lillian Hayman
Lincoln Kilpatrick
Allison Mills
Johnny Brown

Music
Nelson Riddle and His Orchestra
The Howard Roberts Singers

Dancers
The Donald McKayle Dancers

Programming History
CBS
September 1969–December 1969 Sunday 9:00–10:00

Further Reading

MacDonald, J. Fred, *Blacks and White TV: Afro-Americans in Television Since 1948,* Chicago: Nelson-Hall Publishers, 1983; 2nd edition, 1992

Letterman, David (1947–)

U.S. Talk Show Host, Comedian

David Letterman has cultivated a national following of ardent fans with his offbeat humor and sophisticated smart-aleck comic style. That style was honed on his nighttime talk show on NBC, *Late Night with David Letterman,* which debuted in 1982 in the hour following *The Tonight Show Starring Johnny Carson.* Roughly a decade later, in 1993, Letterman changed time periods and networks, as *The Late Show with David Letterman* began broadcasting on CBS at 11:30 P.M., a more accessible and lucrative time slot.

Letterman rose to fame as talk show host and celebrity during a period in television history when late-night talk, a unique TV genre, began to stretch beyond the confines of the solid, long-standing appeal of NBC's *Tonight Show.* His influence and appeal increased steadily until, by 1995, he was the most-watched and highest-paid late-night television talk show host in the United States. In 1996, however, NBC's *The Tonight Show with Jay Leno* began occasionally overtaking Letterman's programs in the ratings, and by the early 21st century, Leno's show was regularly attracting a larger audience than Letterman's. Although he has slipped a bit in the ratings, Letterman's audience remains considerable (and represents a demographic that advertisers greatly desire), and he remains a favorite of critics, many of whom prefer his more pointed and acerbic style of comedy to the milder, "nice guy" humor of his *Tonight Show* rival.

Letterman began his career in broadcasting in his native Indianapolis, Indiana, where he worked in both television (as an announcer and weekend weatherman) and radio (as a talk show host). In 1975 he moved to Los Angeles, where he wrote comedy, submitted scripts for television sitcoms, and even appeared on various sitcoms and game shows. He performed stand-up routines at the Comedy Store, where he met Leno, by then a seasoned comedian, and Merrill Markoe, with whom he would later have a long-time professional and personal relationship. In 1978 Letterman made his first appearance as a stand-up comic on *The Tonight Show Starring Johnny Carson.* Shortly thereafter he was hired by NBC to host a morning television talk show, which was broadcast from New York. Although the program lasted only a short time, it was the comic forerunner to his late-night NBC hit.

Late Night with David Letterman, programmed to follow the familiar Carson formula, was a different kind of talk show, a format in which the comedy usually outshone the interviews. Letterman's fascination with humor of the mundane, his quirky antics (Stupid Pet Tricks, Elevator Races, the Top Ten List), and his overall irreverence came on the heels of a new, hip style of comedy exemplified by NBC's late-night comedy sketch program, *Saturday Night Live* (*SNL*). His style was attractive to a younger television audience that had been loyal supporters of *SNL* since the mid-1970s. However, Letterman retained *The Tonight Show* comedy/interview format. Letterman was neither as emotionally nor as politically involved in his interviews as Paar had been. More like Carson, he exhibited a cool detachment from, and more middle-American stance toward, the political and social events of the day.

During his tenure at NBC, Letterman occasionally served as guest host on *The Tonight Show* in Carson's absence. He shared that job with several others, most notably Joan Rivers and Leno. Letterman's interview style on both *The Tonight Show* and *Late Night* was sometimes easygoing, sometimes mocking. Indeed, a number of guests found him to be a mean-spirited interviewer, and some celebrities claimed he was adolescent at best, highly offensive at worst. Nevertheless, he had a loyal following of late-night watchers, and he inspired a large number of discussions, references, and imitations among fans, in the media, and throughout popular culture.

By the early 1990s, speculation centered on which of the two most successful young comedians, Leno or Letterman, would be Carson's successor upon his retirement. After intense network negotiations with both potential *Tonight Show* hosts—and considerable public attention—Leno succeeded Carson. At that point, Letterman accepted a generous offer from CBS to host his own show, and the two men became direct competitors at 11:30 P.M. on weeknights. On CBS, Letterman's popularity grew. He maintained much the same approach to comedy he had at NBC, but he softened some of his angry edge and irreverence. Some commentators attributed the changes to a desire, on both his part and the network's, to broaden his audience in the earlier time slot.

In the late 1990s and early 2000s, *The Late Show* was regularly visited by political figures eager to reach Letterman's large and diverse audience, including viewers who might not watch more traditional news programming. During his tenure as New York City mayor, Rudolph Giuliani made a number of appearances, not just for interviews but also as a reader of Top Ten lists and participant in comedy sketches. Other notable politicians to appear with Letterman have included President Bill Clinton, presidential candidates Al Gore and George W. Bush, Hillary Clinton (when she was running to become senator for New York), and U.S Attorney General John Ashcroft (who played piano with *The Late Show* band). The ability of such political leaders to stand up to the jibes of Letterman and to make the audiences laugh has increasingly been seen as a kind of test of their suitability for office. Similarly, news anchors such as Tom Brokaw, Dan Rather, and even Ted Koppel (whose *Nightline* program directly competed with *The Late Show*) have frequently sat for interviews with Letterman, who gives them exposure to viewers outside of the aging demographic group most likely to watch network news.

In 2000 Letterman underwent heart bypass surgery after doctors discovered he had potentially life-threatening arterial blockages. When he returned to his program several weeks after his surgery, the *Late Show* host allowed himself a rare display of emotion, bringing his doctors and nurses onstage to thank them publicly for their care. More generally, this health scare helped focus popular and critical attention on Letterman's maturation and his evolving status as a late-night fixture of considerable influence.

Over the next couple of years, two other notable events would throw even more light on the power wielded by *The Late Show* and its host in the television medium and American popular culture more broadly construed. On September 17, 2001, Letterman was the first comedic talk show host to return to the airwaves after the terrorist attacks on the United States of September 11. When the show opened, he appeared at his desk (foregoing the usual fanfare, music, and introductory humorous monologue) and spoke without a script for several minutes about his own sorrow, anger, and horror at the losses that had occurred. Admitting to the audience that he was unsure if he should be on the air, he told them, "We're going to try and feel our way through this, and we'll just see how it goes." Letterman then followed his commentary with two interviews: a serious discussion with CBS anchorman Dan Rather about the event that had occurred and a conversation with favorite *Late Show* guest Regis Philbin (who had also been on the last program before Letter-

man had surgery and the first after he returned to health). The approach taken by Letterman that night (including his tentative return to humor in a moment or two of gently mocking Philbin) was widely praised in the press, and other late-night comedians clearly took their cue from him as they too opened their first post-attack shows with personal, joke-free reflections on the event.

In April 2002, several months after *The Late Show* had settled back into its familiar comedy-talk format, Letterman again grabbed headlines, this time when it was revealed that ABC was making a bid to lure him away from CBS. If Letterman were to sign with ABC, it was announced, his show would replace *Nightline,* the venerable late-night news program that aired opposite *The Late Show* and *The Tonight Show.* To many observers, ABC's willingness to sacrifice news analysis for Letterman's more advertiser-friendly—and therefore potentially more lucrative—comedic fare signaled the degree to which U.S. networks had come to privilege profits over the public interest. Ultimately, Letterman decided to re-sign with CBS for several more years.

Prior to weekday taping sessions, sidewalks outside the Ed Sullivan Theater in New York City, venue for *The Late Show,* are typically the site of long stand-by lines of those hoping for seats inside the already packed house. Letterman clearly remains a celebrity whose voice resonates in contemporary American culture.

KATHERINE FRY

See also *Late Show with David Letterman (Late Night with David Letterman);* Leno, Jay; Talk Show

David Letterman. Born in Indianapolis, Indiana, April 12, 1947. Graduated from Ball State University, 1969. Married: Michelle Cook (divorced). Began career as radio announcer, TV weatherman and talk show host, Indianapolis; performer, Comedy Store, Los Angeles, from 1975; writer for television, Hollywood, from 1970s; frequent guest host on *The Tonight Show,* 1978–82; performed and wrote songs for the Starland Vocal Band; host, *Late Night with David Letterman,* 1982–93; host, *The Late Show with David Letterman,* since 1993. Recipient: numerous Emmy Awards.

Television Series

1974	*Good Times* (writer)
1977	*The Starland Vocal Band Show*
1978–82	*The Tonight Show Starring Johnny Carson* (guest host)
1978	*Mary* (performer and writer)
1980	*The David Letterman Show*

| 1982–93 | *Late Night with David Letterman* |
| 1993– | *The Late Show with David Letterman* |

Television Specials

1977	*Paul Lynde Comedy Hour* (writer)
1978	*Peeping Times* (actor)
1995	*The Academy Awards* (host)

Further Reading

Adler, Bill, *The Letterman Wit: His Life and Humor,* New York: Carroll and Graf, 1994

Carter, Bill, *The Late Shift: Letterman, Leno, and the Network Battle for the Night,* New York: Hyperion, 1994

Levin, Gerald

Former CEO, Time Warner

Gerald M. Levin was chairman and chief executive officer of AOL Time Warner/Time Warner for almost a decade (1993–2002) and retired in May 2002. He served in this role during an era of significant change for one of the largest media companies in the world and presided over the sale in 2000 of Time Warner to Internet service provider AOL.

He joined Time Inc. in 1972 after a brief career as an attorney and international investment banker. At Time Inc. he worked in the fledgling Home Box Office (HBO) pay-cable television subsidiary, starting out as a programming executive and eventually becoming chairman of the division. In 1975, during his tenure at HBO, Levin pioneered the use of telecommunications satellites for pay-cable television program distribution. At the time, HBO was using microwave technology to distribute programming to cable systems in Pennsylvania and New Jersey. Levin proposed that all national program distribution be accomplished by satellite transmission, a concept that transformed the U.S. premium-cable industry and led to a dramatic increase in the number of satellite-delivered cable networks. HBO experienced rapid growth after it became available via satellite and became a standard pay-cable offering during the late 1970s and 1980s. By 1979 Levin was a group vice president supervising all cable television operations, and eventually moved into the vice chairman's position in 1988. His ascension within the Time corporate hierarchy marked a transition from print-oriented managers to others, such as Levin, who were involved with electronic media.

Time Inc. merged with Warner Communications in 1990, and, as Time's chief strategist, Levin had an influential role in negotiating the complicated merger between two dissimilar corporate cultures. At the time,

Time Warner published books and magazines, distributed recorded music, made motion pictures, and operated cable television production and distribution companies. From 1992 to 1995, Levin and Time

Gerald Levin, 2001.
©CJ Contino/Everett Collection

Warner were the focus of a public furor over recorded music lyrics that some critics claimed were anti-social. Levin defended the constitutional First Amendment rights of the recording artists and film directors who created works for the company, but Time Warner finally dodged the controversy by divesting the music division that produced the most controversial recordings.

Levin also played a central role in the 1996 acquisition of Turner Broadcasting. The Turner purchase brought all of that company's cable programming assets to Time Warner, including the worldwide operations of CNN. The grand strategy was to create a vertically integrated media behemoth that would control not only the means of production in entertainment, news, and publishing, but also multiple channels of distribution for this content.

Levin was an ardent champion of Time Warner's Full Service Network (FSN), a 100-plus-channel cable television system that was first introduced in Orlando, Florida. The Full Service Network used large computer servers to provide digitized programming, such as feature films, on viewer demand. The FSN project was canceled after several years of operation, but the company learned a great deal about digital interactive services in the process.

The desire to have a major media presence on the Internet led to the purchase of Time Warner by America Online (AOL) in 2000. The deal was initiated by AOL CEO Steve Case in a series of meetings with Gerald Levin. The strategy was that the sale would facilitate the distribution of Time Warner programming by using the Internet to reach the large installed base of AOL subscribers. While Levin again worked hard to merge two dissimilar corporate cultures, the sale was initially not a good one for AOL Time Warner shareholders. Internal struggles at the company led to Ted Turner's "demotion" to board member and later to Levin's departure. Though announced as a voluntary retirement, some accounts indicated the exit was forced by influential members of the board, including Turner. AOL struggled to maintain its base of subscribers after the merger, and its poor performance provided a somber note for Gerald Levin's retirement.

Levin's ascension within Time Inc. (and later in Time Warner) reflects the increasing centrality of electronic communication in mass media companies. He was a champion of electronic media services, and his early ability to foresee the role of technology in media distribution was an important element of his tenure as the chief executive of one of the world's largest media organizations.

Since his retirement Gerald Levin has dedicated his time and energy to several charitable programs, in particular the creation of the Holistic Mental Health Institute in Los Angeles, California.

PETER B. SEEL

See also **Case, Steve; HBO; Time Warner**

Further Reading

Klein, Alec, *Stealing Time: Steve Case, Jerry Levin, and the Collapse of AOL Time Warner,* New York: Simon and Schuster, 2003

Levinson, Richard (1934–1987)

U.S. Writer

Richard Levinson teamed with William Link to write and produce some of the most memorable hours of U.S. network television in the history of the medium. Moving easily from series to made-for-television movies, the partners created, wrote, and produced at a level that led many of their peers to describe them as the Rolls and Royce of the industry. They received two Emmys, two Golden Globe Awards, three Edgar Allan Poe Awards from the Mystery Writers of America, the Writers Guild of America Award, and the Peabody Award.

As high school classmates, Levinson and Link made early use of wire recordings as an aid to developing their dramatic writing skills, then continued their collaboration through university studies at the University of Pennsylvania. Following graduation and military service, the two moved to New York to pursue a career in television, only to discover that the production end of the business had largely moved west. In 1959, their drama about army life, "Chain of Command," was produced as an installment of *Desilu Playhouse,* then chosen by *TV Guide* as one of the best programs of the

Richard Levinson.
Courtesy of the Everett Collection/CSU Archives

season. With that success, the team, known fondly by many of their associates as "the boys," moved to Los Angeles, where in 1960 they were the first writers placed under contract by Four Star Productions.

For the first ten years of their work in Hollywood, Levinson and Link wrote episodes for various television series. In 1967 they created one of their own: *Mannix.* However, that series was taken in a direction opposite to their original intention by head writer Bruce Geller. In 1969 the partners first grappled with contemporary problems in a pilot for the lawyers segment of *The Bold Ones.* Their work on this series presaged their use of television to explore serious social and cultural themes in the made-for-television-movie format. They wrote and produced nine "social issue" films as well as launched one of the most popular of all television detectives, Lt. Columbo.

Frustrated by Hollywood production routines, Levinson and Link had returned briefly to New York earlier in the decade to write a stage play titled *Prescription: Murder.* That play introduced the Columbo character and became the foundation for the *Columbo* series, starring Peter Falk, which began on television

in 1971 as part of *The NBC Mystery Movie.* As Levinson noted in an interview, "Columbo was a conscious reaction against the impetuous force of Joe Mannix." *Columbo* was, at one point, the most popular television show in the world. Translated into numerous languages, the show still retains enormous popularity.

In November 1983, Link and Levinson went to Toronto to film an HBO movie, *The Guardian,* examining urban violence, fear, and responses to those realities. After a long and frustrating effort to cast the film on a very tight budget, Link and Levinson chose Louis Gossett Jr. to play the title character, John Mack, and Martin Sheen to play the protagonist, Mr. Hyatt. In the movie, Hyatt and his fellow tenants in a New York apartment feel so threatened by the growing violence in the neighborhood that they hire a professional "guardian," only to discover that this man quickly establishes his own authority over them, one by one. In the course of the story, Mack successfully intimidates all the tenants even as he physically subdues and ultimately kills one intruder. One after another, the tenants trade freedom for security. Hyatt resists until he is threatened by a street gang and Mack saves his life.

As always, Levinson worried about the climax of the piece, left intentionally ambiguous. The final scene in *The Guardian* is an exchange of glances between Mack and Hyatt as the latter leaves the building for work the morning following his rescue. Sheen noted in an interview on the set that he played the expression to convey a sense of "What have I done?" Levinson, however, saw in the final frame on Hyatt a "spark of hope." In either interpretation, the underlying question of the drama is made clear: does security demand denial of freedom? Sheen saw it as a parable and related the story to his own concerns regarding U.S. military-political issues and the belief that the only way to get security is to give up more and more freedom. For the writers, the television movie was "only" posing questions. But they saw the implications of what they were doing. In the end, the decent character was not a hero, and the frozen stare could signal either hope or despair.

Long and intense conversations between the writers on such issues regularly led to that same conclusion: "We don't have to have the answers, we just raise the questions." For Levinson, however, the posing of such questions set his personal direction as a dramatist. One sees this in the *Crisis at Central High* (1981), where Joanne Woodward portrayed assistant principal Elizabeth Huckaby in a drama about racial integration set in Little Rock, Arkansas, in 1958. Although evenhanded, the moral high ground in the movie belongs to Huckaby and integration. Levinson's moral questions are equally evident in the sympathetic treatment of Private Eddie Slovik in the story of the only U.S. soldier executed for desertion in World War II, *The Execution of Private Slovik* (1974), and they inform the search for responsibility and judgment in *The Storyteller* (1977), an exploration of the role of television in instigating social violence.

In the summer of 1986, just a few months prior to his premature death, Levinson explored the problems inherent in another high-profile social issue—terrorism—in his last script, "United States vs. Salaam Ajami." The television movie was finally aired in early 1988 as *Hostile Witness*. In the film, he sought to provide a valid defense for a Lebanese terrorist charged in a U.S. court for a crime committed in Spain against an American tour group. In the story, the terrorist is kidnapped and brought to justice in a federal court in Virginia. Striving to achieve an objective portrayal of the motives for the terrorist and introduce to the audience some comprehension of such an individual's rationale, Levinson was determined to raise philosophical questions, but he wanted no weaknesses in the case against the terrorist.

In 1987 Levinson died at the age of 52. When Link accepted their joint election into the Television Hall of Fame in November 1995, his words were almost all devoted to Levinson, who would, he said, be pleased with the recognition.

ROBERT S. ALLEY

See also **Columbo; Detective Programs; Johnson, Lamont; Link, William**

Richard Levinson. Born in Philadelphia, Pennsylvania, August 7, 1934. Educated at University of Pennsylvania, B.S. in economics, 1956. Served in U.S. Army, 1957–58. Married: Rosanna Huffman, 1969; one child: Christine. With partner William Link, wrote scripts for many television series, created a number of television series, and wrote and produced made-for-television movies dealing with social problems; associated with Universal Studios, 1966–77; co-president, with Link, Richard Levinson/William Link Productions, 1977–87. Recipient (all with William Link): Emmy Awards, 1970 and 1972; National Association for the Advancement of Colored People Image Award, 1970; two Golden Globe Awards; Silver Nymph Award, Monte Carlo Film Festival, 1973; Peabody Award, 1974; Edgar Awards, Mystery Writers of America, 1979, 1980, 1983; Christopher Award, 1981; Paddy Chayefsky Laurel Award, Writers Guild of America, 1986; Ellery Queen Award, Mystery Writers of America, 1989, for lifetime contribution to the art of the mystery; elected to Academy of Television Arts and Sciences Hall of Fame (posthumously), 1995. Died in Los Angeles, California, March 12, 1987.

Television Series (episodes written with William Link; selected)

1955–65	*Alfred Hitchcock Presents*
1958–60	*Desilu Playhouse*
1961–77	*Dr. Kildare*
1963–67	*The Fugitive*

Television Series (created with William Link)

1967–75	*Mannix*
1969–73	*The Bold Ones*
1970–77	*McCloud*
1971–77, 1989–90	*Columbo*
1971	*The Psychiatrist*
1973–74	*Tenafly*
1975–76	*Ellery Queen*
1980	*Stone*
1984–96	*Murder, She Wrote*
1985	*Scene of the Crime*
1986–88	*Blacke's Magic*
1987	*Hard Copy*

Made-for-Television Movies (with William Link)

1968	*Istanbul Express*
1969	*The Whole World Is Watching*
1970	*My Sweet Charlie*
1971	*Two on a Bench*
1972	*That Certain Summer*
1972	*The Judge and Jake Wyler* also with David Shaw)
1973	*Tenafly*
1973	*Partners in Crime*
1973	*Savage*
1974	*The Execution of Private Slovik*
1974	*The Gun*
1975	*Ellery Queen*
1975	*A Cry for Help*
1977	*Charlie Cobb: Nice Night for a Hanging*
1977	*The Storyteller*
1979	*Murder by Natural Causes*
1981	*Crisis at Central High*
1982	*Rehearsal for Murder*
1982	*Take Your Best Shot*
1983	*Prototype*
1984	*The Guardian*
1985	*Guilty Conscience*
1985	*Murder in Space*
1986	*Vanishing Act*
1986	*Blacke's Magic*
1988	*Hostile Witness*

Films (with William Link)

The Hindenberg, 1975; *Rollercoaster,* 1977.

Stage (with William Link; selected)

Merlin, 1982; *Killing Jessica,* 1986; *Guilty Conscience,* 1986.

Publications (with William Link)

Prescription: Murder (three-act play), 1963
Fineman (novel), 1972
Stay Tuned: An Inside Look at the Making of Prime-Time Television, 1981
The Playhouse (novel), 1984
Guilty Conscience: A Play of Suspense in Two Acts, 1985

Off Camera: Conversations with the Makers of Prime-Time Television, 1986

Further Reading

Broughton, Irv, *Producers on Producing: The Making of Film and Television,* Jefferson, North Carolina: McFarland, 1986

Burger, Richard, *The Producers: A Descriptive Directory of Film and Television Directors in the Los Angeles Area,* Venice, California: R. Burger, 1985

Newcomb, Horace, and Robert S. Alley, *The Producer's Medium: Conversations with Creators of American TV,* New York: Oxford University Press, 1983

Liberace Show, The

U.S. Musical Program

Certainly among the most popular early television celebrities and performers, both Liberace the individual and his television program were among the most persistently derided. Oddly folksy and campy at the same time, Liberace and his show defined a certain strata of showmanship in the post–World War II era.

Born Wladziu (Walter) Valentino Liberace in suburban Milwaukee, Wisconsin, Liberace was interested in music from the age of four and won a scholarship to the Wisconsin College of Music at the age of seven, studying there for 17 years. Reputedly at the advice of family friend and renowned pianist Paderewski, the youngster decided that he too would someday be known by just one name. Although he was classically trained, he began to perform pop hits in local clubs as a teen. By the early 1940s, he was establishing himself in New York night spots; ads offered a phonetic guide for his fans ("Libber-*ah*-chee"). Playing cocktail lounges and intermissions for big bands, he received a rave *Variety* notice in 1945 while appearing at the Persian Room, which led to strings of dates across the United States. He won a small role in the film *South Seas Sinner* (1950).

In 1950 Don Fedderson, the general manager of Los Angeles station KLAC-TV, saw Liberace perform before a small audience at the Hotel del Coronado in San Diego, California, and immediately offered him a chance to appear on the new medium of television. The resultant series was so popular that it drew network at-tention, and when Liberace appeared on NBC as a summer replacement for Dinah Shore in 1952 (15-minute shows twice a week in prime time), he began to create a sensation. For a subsequent series, he wisely accepted what was at the time an unorthodox format of filming programs for syndication. As a result, when Liberace became a television fixture throughout the country by the mid-1950s, he also became very rich. The program was one of several shows featuring KLAC talent produced by Fedderson and syndicated by Guild Films. (Betty White was in another KLAC production, starring in *Life with Elizabeth* from 1953 to 1955.) Fedderson would go on to produce many successful television series, often for CBS, including *My Three Sons* and *Family Affair.*

Liberace's TV shows were famous for offering a range of popular and classical standards, and featured tributes to composers, musicians, and genres of music—everything from "The Beer Barrel Polka" to "September Song" to "Clair de Lune." Visually, they showcased Liberace in direct address to the audience and in flamboyant performance, always smiling and often winking. No one in early television worked harder to create a star persona. Ever-present candelabras, piano-shaped objects large and small, and especially his outrageous and glamorous costumes defined Liberace's celebrity. Sentimental but ostentatious, the program also featured his elder brother George as violin accompanist and orchestral arranger, plus regular

Liberace.
Courtesy of the Everett Collection

and affectionate mentions of their mother, Frances. The show was immediately successful, appearing on 100 stations by October 1953 (more than any network program) and nearly 200 stations a year later. Liberace quickly sold out the Hollywood Bowl, Carnegie Hall, and other venues for live performances. A series of hit albums and a brief resumption of his movie career followed.

Liberace soon experienced the effects of overexposure: some local stations, desperate for programming, played his shows twice a day, five days a week. His career suffered a considerable slump after only a few years. In response, a short-lived daytime series in the late 1950s tried and failed to feature a scaled-down, tempered Liberace. A change of management and a return to extravagance in a series of Las Vegas venues restored his notoriety, and he made many guest appearances on TV variety and talk shows through the 1960s and 1970s. In a memorable film cameo, he played a quite earnest casket salesman in the black comedy *The Loved One* (1965). In the late 1960s, one last TV series was briefly produced in London.

Liberace's popularity was typically met in the press with equal parts disbelief and disdain. The arrangements of his classical pieces were noted as simplifications, and his mix of classical and popular styles raised hackles about an encroaching middle-brow aesthetic. His personal eccentricities were detailed at length. More tellingly, the size and devotion of his following was seen to be problematic. That his audience was largely female, and often middle-aged, wrought clichéd anxieties about insubstantial and wayward popular culture; it even was suggested that he was not providing quality performances but rather represented for his fans an object to be mothered. In response to his critics, he uttered a still-famous retort: "I cried all the way to the bank." In two instances, however, he responded with successful lawsuits—one against London *Daily Mirror* columnist "Cassandra" (William Neil Connor), and another against the infamous scandal magazine *Confidential.* Each had discussed his behavior or his appeal in terms that inferred homosexuality.

In retrospect, Liberace's career seems due for reconsideration as a kind of "queer" open secret. The concern that his audience was mostly female, the regular speculation about his love life (When would he marry?), and the criticism of his attention to his mother all can be seen as touchstones for social anxieties of the time about appropriate gender roles and definitions. Indeed, if Liberace's appeal was grounded in a decidedly unthreatening masculinity, marked by good manners and simplistic pieties, it also inspired a range of critical attention that often revealed a tendency to sexualize him. The libelous incidents were the culmination of this tendency and perhaps revealed more than they intended about "normative" attitudes about postwar male behavior. To be sure, there was nothing about Liberace that corresponded to "queer" underground culture or the avant-garde of the 1950s—no one appeared to be more mainstream. However, the contradictions within his very successful career and persona raise further questions about postwar society and culture. Liberace died of AIDS-related complications on February 4, 1987.

MARK WILLIAMS

See also **Music on Television**

Regular Performers
Liberace
George Liberace and Orchestra (1952)
Marilyn Lovell (1958–59)
Erin O'Brien (1958–59)
Dick Roman (1958–59)
Darias (1958–59)
Richard Wattis (1969)
Georgina Moon (1969)
Jack Parnell Orchestra (1969)
The Irving Davies Dancers (1969)

Producers
Joe Landis (NBC; 1952); Louis D. Sander, Robert Sandler (syndicated; 1953–55); Robert Tamplin, Bernard Rothman, Colin Cleeves (CBS; 1969)

Programming History
NBC
July 1952–August 1952   Tuesday/Thursday
                                7:30–7:45

Syndicated
1953–55
ABC

October 1958–April 1959
CBS

July 1969–September 1969

Various times

30-minute daytime

Tuesday 8:30–9:30

Further Reading

Donovan, Richard, "'Nobody Loves Me but the People,'" *Collier's* (September 3, 1954 and September 17, 1954)
Liberace, *Liberace: An Autobiography,* New York: Putnam's, 1973
Taubman, Howard, "A Square Looks at a Hotshot," *New York Times Magazine* (March 14, 1954)
"Why Women Idolize Liberace," *Look* (October 19, 1954)

License

U.S. Broadcasting Policy

Under the Communications Act of 1934, the U.S. Federal Communications Commission (FCC) is responsible for the "fair, efficient, and equitable distribution" of television broadcast airwaves for use by the American public. As a result, any person or other entity (other than the federal government) wishing to operate a television broadcast facility must apply for and receive a government-issued license in order to reserve a transmission frequency for its television signal. These broadcast licenses are subject to review and renewal by the FCC every seven years for radio and every five years for television, unless the FCC determines a shorter period to be in the public interest.

In the United States, private individuals and companies are permitted to own and operate television stations for commercial and noncommercial use. However, because of their limited availability on the broadcast spectrum, the airwaves themselves are considered a finite public resource that is "owned" and regulated by the federal government on behalf of the American people. During the first half of the 1920s, when commercial broadcasting was in its infancy, pioneers in the industry had unfettered and virtually unlimited access to what was then an abundance of electromagnetic frequencies. By 1926, when the number of broadcast stations increased from 536 to 732, Congress became concerned that the rapid proliferation of broadcasters would quickly deplete available airwaves. In addition, advances in transmission technology enabled powerful, city-based operators to boost their signal range, effectively drowning out smaller, rural facilities. The chaos and cacophony of broadcasting in the mid-1920s ultimately led Congress to pass regulatory legislation in 1927, and again in 1934, requiring all station owners to apply for a broadcast license and meet specific criteria for eligibility before a license is issued or renewed.

Until the 1990s, the essential aspects of broadcast license grants largely stayed the same. In 1991, Congress amended the Communications Act to permit the FCC to choose new licensees by lottery, in an effort to streamline what had become a costly and burdensome hearing process. Following the Supreme Court's decision in *Adarand Contractors, Inc. v .Pena* (1995), which placed all federal affirmative-action programs under strict scrutiny, the FCC introduced a gender- and race-neutral bidding system that gave preferential credit to small-business applicants.

In 1998, seeking to recognize the revenue potential of license grants, Congress enacted Section 309(j) of the act, which mandated an auction process for new licensees. Once the highest bidder is selected, opposing parties have ten days in which to file a petition to deny. If there is no objection, or if the FCC does not act on the petition to deny, the successful bidder pays the amount of the bid and is issued a construction permit. In order to assure diversity among licensees, the FCC granted a 25 percent "bidding credit" to minority-owned and women-owned applicants.

In determining who will or will not get a broadcast license, the FCC considers a wide range of factors that can vary or be waived under different circumstances. A successful applicant must be a U.S. citizen or an entity controlled by U.S. citizens, must be in good financial health, and cannot broadcast to more than 35 percent of the total national audience. While the FCC still enforces some restrictions designed to limit the dominance of a licensee in local markets, the period following the Telecommunications Act of 1996 has been marked by a movement away from licensing and ownership regulation. By the year 2001, the FCC had eased regulations that had been enforced for decades, including the duopoly rules, which had strictly prevented a licensee from owning more than one television facility in a market; the dual network prohibition, which prevented one company from owning two broadcast networks; and various rules relating to the public interest qualifications of license applicants.

MICHAEL M. EPSTEIN

See also **Allocation; Deregulation; Federal Communications Commission; "Freeze" of 1948**

Further Reading

Bittner, John R., *Law and Regulation of Electronic Media,* Englewood Cliffs, New Jersey: Prentice-Hall, 1994

Burgess, John, "FCC Proposes Lottery for Issuing Licenses: Public Interest Group, Broadcasters Criticize Plan for TV and Radio," *Washington Post* (January 31, 1991)

Carter, T. Barton, Marc A. Franklin, and Jay B. Wright, *The First Amendment and the Fifth Estate: Regulation of Electronic Mass Media,* 4th edition, Westbury, New York: Foundation Press, 1996

Cox, Kenneth A., *Broadcasting in America and the FCC's License Renewal Process: An Oklahoma Case Study,* Washington, D.C.: Federal Communications Commission, 1968

"Forty Megahertz and a Mule: Ensuring Minority Ownership of the Electromagnetic Spectrum," *Harvard Law Review* (March 1995)

Ginsburg, Douglas, H., Michael H. Botein, and Mark K. Director, *Regulation of the Electronic Mass Media: Law and Policy for Radio, Television, Cable, and the New Technologies,* St. Paul, Minnesota: West Publishing, 1979; 2nd edition, 1991

Legal Guide to Broadcast Law and Regulation, Washington, D.C.: National Association of Broadcasters, 1988

Lippman, John, "Preferences Get Static in Broadcasting," *Los Angeles Times* (February 22, 1992)

Streeter, Thomas, *Selling the Air: A Critique of the Policy of Commercial Broadcasting in the United States,* Chicago: University of Chicago Press, 1996

Wharton, Dennis, "Controversial 'Diversity' Policy Upheld in Surprise Supreme Court Decision," *Variety* (July 4, 1990)

"When Citizens Complain: *UCC v. FCC* a Decade Later," *Proceedings of the Mass Communication Law Section, Association of American Law Schools December 27, 1977,* New York: Association of American Law Schools and the Communications Media Center, New York Law School, 1978

License Fee

The term "license fee" has two meanings when applied to television. The first indicates a means of supporting an entire television industry. The second indicates support for the production of specific programs. When applied in the first sense a license fee is a form of tax used by many countries to support indigenous broadcasting industries. The fee is levied on the television receiver set and paid at regular intervals.

In the United States, a receiving-set license fee for the support of broadcasting was considered and rejected very early in radio's infancy. At this time the new medium was considered a public resource, and the idea of support from advertisers was thought inappropriate. The license fee was one of several funding proposals, including municipal or state funding and listener contributions, offered by various sources in the 1920s. The license fee idea took two distinct forms. The first was modeled on the British scheme of taxing receivers in viewers' homes. At that time, the British levy was 10 shillings per receiving set. The second approach, proposed by RCA's David Sarnoff, called for a tax (2 percent) on the sale price of receivers. The success of toll broadcasting (broadcasting paid for by ad-

vertisers) near the midpoint of that decade squelched further discussion on the issue.

In the early days of U.S. television, the idea of a receiving-set license fee was briefly raised again by those who pointed to the failures and inadequacies of radio's commercial nature. Because most early television stations were owned by broadcasters with long experience in AM radio, however, it was almost inevitable that advertising would provide the primary economic support for the new medium.

This was not the case in Great Britain. The license fee was in place from the earliest days of the British broadcasting service, having been mandated by the 1904 Wireless Telegraphy Act (and reaffirmed for radio and television in the Wireless Telegraphy Act of 1949). The level of the fee is set by Parliament through its Treasury Department. The BBC is allowed to make its recommendation, and, once set, the fee is collected by the Post Office, which is also responsible for identifying and tracking down those who attempt to avoid paying the fee (approximately 6 percent of the audience). The resulting income supports the broadcasting authority (the BBC) and its programming. As a public corporation supported by these fees (none of the income can be distributed elsewhere), the BBC is theoretically insulated from day-to-day influence by Parliament.

The 10 shillings fee remained in force until the end of World War II. The year 1946 saw a doubling of the radio fee, and when black-and-white television was first introduced, its fee was £2 (double that of radio). The license fee for radio was dropped in 1971, and today, only the color television fee remains, rising periodically, for example from £46 in 1981 to £109 20 years later.

Although the BBC has occasionally toyed with the idea of running commercials to increase revenues in difficult economic periods, the license fee is well entrenched there. Said a BBC spokesperson when testifying on the future of British broadcasting in 1977,

> The license fee system involves each member of the viewing public . . . in the feeling that he is entitled to a direct say in what he gets for his money. At the same time, the license fee system puts the broadcasters in a more direct relationship with the public than any other system of financing would. It reinforces a frame of mind in the BBC which impels us constantly to ask ourselves the question: "What ought we to be doing to serve the public better?"

Such a system for supporting a nation's broadcasting can be considered valuable in three respects. First, it assigns the costs for broadcasting directly to its consumers. Second, this tends to create a mutual and reciprocal sense of responsibility between the broadcasters and the audience members, which—third—frees the broadcasters from control and influence by governments (as might be the case where direct government support exists) or advertisers (as might be the case in commercial systems). Against these benefits is the problem of complacency. An increasing number of nations with license fees also allow limited commercial broadcasting, in part to overcome this tendency.

Many countries other than Great Britain, including Israel, Malta, France, the Netherlands, and Jordan, have some form of license fees. Some base their fee on color television only (like Great Britain) and some on color television and radio (for example, Denmark). Two-thirds of the countries in Europe, one-half in Africa and Asia, and 10 percent of those in the Americas and Caribbean rely, at least in part, on a license fee to support their television systems. Common among them is a philosophy of broadcasting that sees it as a "public good." A great many countries, however, if not all those reliant on a license-fee structure for funding

are now facing a new form of competition. Cable and satellite television have become common throughout the world, requiring subscription or payment fees in addition to the television license. These newer forms of distribution have also provided viewers with more programming options and, as audiences for state-supported systems decline in number, governments press the managers of state-supported broadcasting systems more severely to explain why the license fee should remain in place or be raised. In efforts to sustain or increase viewership, these circumstances have led to greater attention to numbers of viewers, to the creation of ratings systems to measure them, and to altered programming designed to attract larger audiences. In some views, these conditions have led to a severe erosion of the very notion of "public service broadcasting."

The second definition of license fee is applied most often in U.S. television, though its use is growing throughout television production communities elsewhere. It refers to funding that supports independent television production for broadcast networks or other television distributors such as cable companies. In this context, the license fee is the amount paid by the distributor to support production of commissioned programs and series. In exchange for the license fee, the distributor receives rights to a set number of broadcasts of commissioned programs. Following those broadcasts, the rights to the program revert to the producer. This form of production financing is central to the economic system of commercial television because the distributor's license fee rarely funds the full cost of program production. Producers or studios still must often finance part of their production costs and hope to recoup that amount when a program returns to their control and can be sold into syndication to other distribution venues. Nevertheless, the initial funds, in the form of a license fee, generally enable production to begin.

KIMBERLY B. MASSEY

See also **British Television; Public Service Television**

Further Reading

Barnouw, Erik, *A History of Broadcasting in the United States,* Vol. I: *A Tower in Babel, to 1933,* New York: Oxford University Press, 1966

Head, S.W., *World Broadcasting Systems: A Comparative Analysis,* Belmont, California: Wadsworth, 1985

Sterling, Christopher H., and John M. Kittross, *Stay Tuned: A Concise History of American Broadcasting,* Belmont, California: Wadsworth, 1978; 3rd edition, Mahwah, New Jersey: Lawrence Erlbaum Associates, 2002

Life of Riley, The

U.S. Situation Comedy

The Life of Riley, an early U.S. television sitcom filmed in Hollywood, was broadcast on NBC from 1949 to 1950 and from 1953 to 1958. Although the program had a loyal audience from its years on network radio (1943–51), its first season on television, in which Jackie Gleason was cast in the title role, failed to generate high ratings. William Bendix portrayed Riley in the second version, and the series was much more successful, among the top 25 most watched programs from 1953 to 1955. Syndicated in 1977, the series has been telecast on many cable systems.

The Life of Riley was one of several blue-collar, ethnic sitcoms popular in the 1950s. Chester A. Riley was the breadwinner of an Irish-American nuclear family living in suburban Los Angeles. Although most of the program took place within the Riley household, his job as an airplane riveter sometimes figured prominently in weekly episodes. Riley's fixed place in the socioeconomic structure also allowed for occasional barbs directed at the frustrations of factory employment and at the pretensions of the upper classes. After *The Life of Riley* was canceled, blue-collar protagonists like Riley would not reappear until *All in the Family* premiered in the 1970s.

A pilot for *The Life of Riley* starred Herb Vigran and was broadcast on NBC in 1948. Six months later, the series appeared on NBC with Riley played by Gleason; however, Riley's malapropisms and oafish behavior were poorly suited to Gleason's wisecracking nightclub style. Bendix, who had played Riley on radio and in a movie version, was originally unable to play the part on television due to film obligations. When he did assume the role, however, he became synonymous with the character.

Bendix played Riley in a manner that resembled many of his supporting roles in Hollywood films of the 1940s: as a heavy-handed, obstinate, yet ultimately sensitive lummox. Each week Riley first became flustered, then overwhelmed by seemingly minor problems concerning his job, his family, or his neighbors. These small matters escalated to the verge of disaster once Riley became involved. Riley's catch phrase—"What a revoltin' development this is!"—expressed his frustration and became part of the national idiom. His patient wife, Peg (originally played by Rosemary DeCamp, then by Marjorie Reynolds), managed to keep the family in order despite her husband's calamitous blunders.

Other central characters included Riley's studious and attractive daughter, "Babs" (Gloria Winters, Lugene Sanders), and his younger, respectful son, "Junior" (Lanny Rees, Wesley Morgan). Riley also had several neighbors, friends, and coworkers. The most significant of these was Jim Gillis (Sid Tomack, Tom D'Andrea), Riley's smart-aleck neighbor whose schemes often instigated trouble.

The narrative structure of the series was much like that of any half-hour sitcom: Each week, stasis within the Riley household would be disrupted by a misunderstanding on Riley's part or by Riley's bungled efforts to improve his or his family's status. Catastrophe was ultimately averted by a simple solution, usually the clarification of a fact by Peg or another character besides Riley. Order was thus restored by the end of the episode.

The postwar suburban lifestyle conditioned much of the program's content. Mirroring trends established during the postwar economic boom, the Riley family lived comfortably, though not lavishly, aided—and sometimes baffled—by many of the latest household consumer gadgets. Gender roles typical of the era were also represented with Chester earning the family's single paycheck while Peg maintained the household. Similarly, Babs's problems typically concerned dating, while Junior's were related to school. Most of the problems in the Riley household occurred when the private and public realms merged, usually when Riley interfered with Peg's responsibilities.

Like many sitcoms of the 1950s, *The Life of Riley* reinforced the promise of suburban gratifications open to hard-working, white Americans. Even so, Riley's incompetence set him apart from his television counterparts. More so than Ozzie of *Ozzie and Harriet,* Riley's ineptitude called into question the role of the American father and therefore of the entire family structure, thus preceding some 1960s sitcoms such as *Green Acres* and *Bewitched* that carried that theme even further.

WARREN BAREISS

See also **Gleason, Jackie**

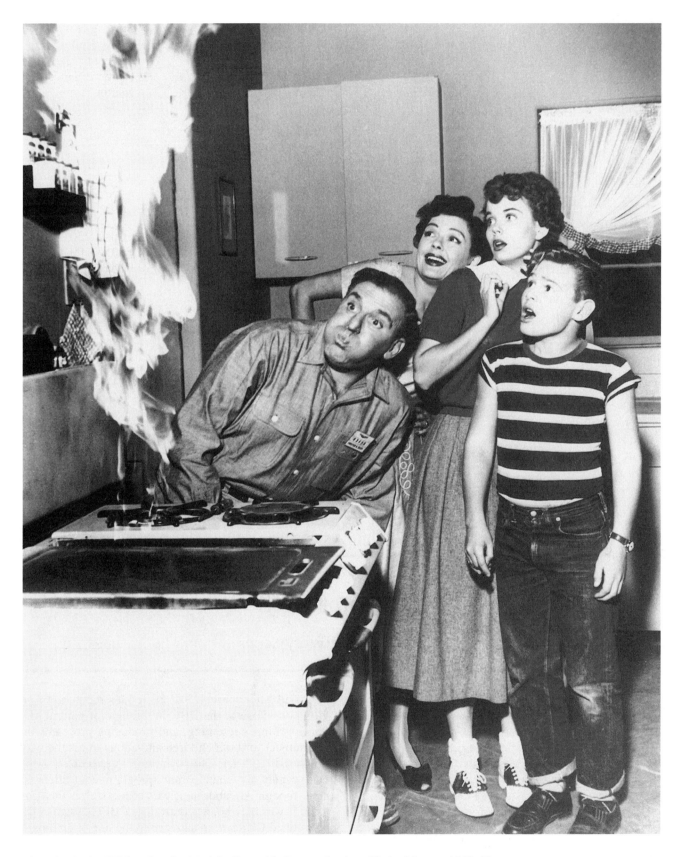

The Life of Riley, William Bendix, Marjoire Reynolds, Lugene Sanders, Wesley Morgan, 1953–58.
Courtesy of the Everett Collection

Cast (1949–50)

Chester A. Riley	Jackie Gleason
Peg Riley	Rosemary DeCamp
Junior	Lanny Rees
Babs	Gloria Winters
Jim Gillis	Sid Tomack
Digby "Digger" O'Dell	John Brown

Producer
Irving Brecher

Programming History
26 episodes
DuMont
October 1949–March 1950   Tuesday 9:30–10:00

Cast (1953–58)

Chester A. Riley	William Bendix
Peg Riley	Marjorie Reynolds
Junior	Wesley Morgan
Babs Riley Marshall	Lugene Sanders
Jim Gillis	
(1953–55, 1956–58)	Tom D'Andrea
Honeybee Gillis	
(1953–55, 1956–58)	Gloria Blondell
Egbert Gillis (1953–55)	Gregory Marshall
Cunningham	Douglas Dumbrille
Dangle	Robert Sweeney
Riley's Boss	Emory Parnell
Waldo Binney	Sterling Holloway
Otto Schmidlap	Henry Kulky
Calvin Dudley (1955–56)	George O'Hanlon
Belle Dudley (1955–56)	Florence Sundstrom
Dan Marshall (1957–58)	Martin Milne

Producer
Tom McKnight

Programming History
212 episodes
NBC

January 1953–September 1956	Friday 8:30–9:00
October 1956–December 1956	Friday 8:00–8:30
January 1957–August 1958	Friday 8:30–9:00

Further Reading

Brooks, T., and E. Marsh, *The Complete Directory to Prime Time Network TV Shows: 1946–Present,* New York: Ballantine Books, 1988

Hamamoto, Darrell Y., *Nervous Laughter: Television Situation Comedy and Liberal Democratic Ideology,* New York: Praeger, 1989

Lipsitz, George, "The Meaning of Memory: Family, Class, and Ethnicity in Early Network Television Programs," in *Time Passages: Collective Memory and American Popular Culture,* Minneapolis: University of Minnesota Press, 1990

Terrace, V., *Fifty Years of Television: A Guide to Series and Pilots, 1937–1988,* New York: Cornwall, 1991

Terrace, V., *Television: 1970–1980,* San Diego, California: Barnes, 1981

Life on Earth

British Natural History Series

The genesis of *Life on Earth* came from several sources. The BBC had, during the 1970s, gained a reputation for producing landmark 13-part documentary series in which a noted expert in a particular field presented a definitive filmed account of that subject, using spectacular photography on diverse locations. These series had included *Civilisation* (1969) on the history of Western art, *The Ascent of Man* (1973) on the history of science, and *Alistair Cooke's America* (1976) on the history of the United States. What better to continue the line than the story of life on Earth?

David Attenborough had gained his reputation as a program maker at the BBC in the field of natural history: writing, presenting, and producing programs on the subject for both children and adults. As is the way in the BBC, this led to promotion to executive status and eventually channel and program controllership and, though Attenborough was successful at this (indeed it was he who, as controller of BBC 2, had commissioned *Civilisation* and started the line of landmark documentary series), he grew dissatisfied and longed to return to his roots as a program maker.

By the late 1970s, the natural history program had evolved to the point at which constantly improving photographic techniques, allied to a seemingly inexhaustible supply of subject matter, meant that returning series like *The World About Us* (BBC) and *Survival* (Anglia), as well as the output of National Geographic, filled television screens with a constant stream of outstanding programming. Yet no overall survey of the subject had been attempted. The stage was set for *Life on Earth,* and it was to prove a turning point in the coverage of its subject.

Life on Earth took as its subject the evolution of species, which it traced through the development of all the major forms of life, from the single cell to homo sapiens. The 13 hour-long episodes were as follows:

1. "The Infinite Variety," explaining the Darwinian theories of evolution and natural selection and how they produced such an enormous variety of life forms;
2. "Building Bodies," on the origins of life and how single cells developed into primitive creatures in the seas;
3. "The First Forests," on the development of plant life on the land;
4. "The Swarming Hordes," exploring the diversity of insect life and how it depends on plant life;
5. "Conquest of the Waters," on the variety of species of fish;
6. "Invasion of the Land," considering the crucial stage of evolution when fish took to the land and developed into amphibians;
7. "Victors of the Dry Land," on reptiles, including dinosaurs;
8. "Lords of the Air," considering the theory that birds may have evolved from dinosaurs and exploring the spectacular variety of species;
9. "The Rise of the Mammals," on another crucial stage of evolution;
10. "Themes and Variations," considering how the wide variety of mammal life evolved from a common ancestor;
11. "The Hunters and the Hunted," on how the relationship between predators and their prey drives evolution and behavior patterns;
12. "Life in the Trees," on the evolution of primates;
13. "The Compulsive Communicators," on human beings.

Although it told a coherent story, much of the success of *Life on Earth* was due to the succession of spectacularly photographed sequences on particular species, such as birds of paradise or big cats hunting on the African plain, and, despite the plethora of natural history programs available, *Life on Earth* represented a step forward in the presentation of the subject on television. It took three years to make, with a number of photographic units at work all over the world. Their work was linked by Attenborough's authoritative script and narration and his pieces to camera filmed in all the relevant locations. Of these, the one that made the greatest impact, and has become a definitive moment in British television history, was his close encounter with a family of mountain gorillas in episode 11.

Life on Earth became a worldwide success and sparked an even greater demand for natural history programming, leading eventually to the emergence of a number of specialist channels devoted to the subject. For Attenborough himself, its success meant more of the same. He went on to present two very similar series, exploiting the vast array of potential subject matter, but arranging the latest spectacular wildlife sequences in different contexts. Thus *The Living Planet* (BBC, 1984) presented life on Earth from the perspective of habitat, while *The Trials of Life* (BBC, 1990) compared the approach of different species to the same problems. After that, he expanded several of the individual parts of *Life on Earth* into full-length series with *The Private Life of Plants,* (BBC, 1995), *The Life of Birds* (BBC, 1998) and *The Blue Planet* (BBC, 2001) on life in the seas.

STEVE BRYANT

See also **Attenborough, David**

Writer/Presenter/Narrator
David Attenborough

Producers
Christopher Parsons, Richard Brock, John Sparks

Programming History
13 episodes
BBC
January 16, 1979–March 10, 1979

Further Reading

Attenborough, David, *Life on Earth,* London: BBC/Collins, 1979

Lifetime

U.S. Cable Network

Lifetime Television ranks among the oldest U.S. cable networks, and made substantial gains in audience size in the early 21st century. Throughout its nearly 20 years of existence, Lifetime has focused on serving the needs of female audience members, although it has varied its emphasis and strategy in seeking audiences of both sexes. As "Television for Women" (its slogan claims), Lifetime enacted one of the earliest narrowcast experiments, and yielded noteworthy success because of the degree to which women both are and are not a niche audience.

Lifetime Television was born from the merger of two cable networks in 1984. Daytime, a joint venture of Hearst and ABC, and the Viacom-owned Cable Health Network, had both launched in 1982, but struggled in this early era of limited cable distribution as neither network reached a large enough audience to command sizable advertising revenue. The newly created Lifetime retained programming from the original networks, with a heavy reliance on advertiser-created series and specials, many which featured pharmaceuticals and other health products, such as hormone supplements and diet aids. By the late 1980s, Lifetime began establishing its identity by acquiring off-net syndication rights to *Cagney & Lacey,* and by continuing original production of a series canceled by NBC, *The Days and Nights of Molly Dodd.*

The network experimented with other original dramatic series without success but began developing "World Premier Movies" produced originally for Lifetime in 1990, the form that most defined the network's reputation. These made-for-Lifetime films have shifted narrative focus slightly but formulaically rely on a plot centered on a female character (often played by an established, but fading television actress) facing a challenging personal and/or professional situation, but surmounting the obstacles by the film's conclusion. Most of the films are fictional, but some notable successes have been based on the lives of real women or news.

Although its films and series implicitly named the network's focus for some time, Lifetime launched its signature "Television for Women" slogan in 1995, and continued to establish itself with films about female protagonists who struggle through crises to succeed in the end. Viacom sold its share of Lifetime to partners Hearst and Cap Cities/ABC in 1994, shortly before Cap Cities/ABC merged with the Walt Disney Company in 1995.

Lifetime spent nearly $8 million developing four pilots in 1998, three of which aired during the 1998–99 television season. The investment paid off when the two-hour time slot in which the network scheduled the three series (*Any Day Now, Maggie,* and *Oh Baby*) increased the number of female 18-to-49-year-old viewers by nearly 200,000 viewers per week (46 percent). Lifetime's development of comedy series has been unsuccessful, with *Maggie* failing in the first year and *Oh Baby* in the second. *Any Day Now* developed a core following and drew critical attention for its stories about ethnic difference and racism in American culture. Lifetime has since emphasized dramatic series, debuting *Strong Medicine,* a medical series featuring two female doctors working in a women's health clinic in 2000, and *The Division,* a detective procedural set in a predominately female squad in 2001. Throughout the 1990s, Lifetime attempted to appeal to a general female audience without emphasizing the fragmented and diversified nature of this group, yet provided some of the only non-white, non-upper-middle-class female characters on U.S. television.

In the midst of experimenting with original programming, Lifetime entered another transitional phase. Despite six relatively successful years, Lifetime did not renew the contract of CEO Douglas McCormick, who had held the position since 1993, and named Carole Black the new Lifetime CEO in March 1999. Thus, Lifetime employed its first female CEO, recruiting Black from KNBC in Los Angeles, where she served as the station's general manager and was

Lifetime™
Television for Women

credited with bringing more women viewers to its newscasts. Black expanded the Lifetime programming budget to $236 million, a 20 percent increase over 1998.

Positive critical reception and some audience gains by the original series that Lifetime schedules in a block on Sunday nights contributed to the rising status and viewership of the network, although its made-for-Lifetime movies continue to reach the largest audience. This success led the network to create a second network, Lifetime Movie Network (LMN), in September 1998. Programming for LMN consists of movies, miniseries, and theatrical films from the Lifetime library, as well as some purchased from second-run distributors. Although early market surveys reported a ready audience for the network, with 93 percent of women who watched Lifetime aware of its films, the network had a slow start. Stymied mainly by lack of distribution, a year after its launch LMN reached only five million households. LMN increased its reach to over 15 million by mid-2001, the same year it launched another network, Lifetime Real Women. This network features reality programming such as *Unsolved Mysteries, Intimate Portraits* (Lifetime's self-produced biography series), and films based on true stories, but receives limited distribution. Branching out with subnetworks has allowed the "mother" network to focus on narrative series.

Black inherited a solid network and expanded its gains. In 2001 Lifetime ranked 17th in projected revenue among all U.S. networks with $715 million. Lifetime also possesses a large potential audience base, reaching 83.8 million cable and satellite homes, approximately 90 percent of those available. Nielsen Media Research ranked Lifetime the second most watched cable network with an average of 992,000 viewers per day (behind Nickelodeon), and, more significantly, Lifetime drew an average of 1.58 million viewers in prime time, which earned it the distinction of the most watched cable network in 2001. Despite the current viability of the network, Black faces pressure to continue its growth and to prevent new competitors from eroding its grip on the female cable audience. Lifetime now faces direct competition in the niche women's market with Oxygen Media launching in 2000 as an integrated cable and Web media company, and the rebranding of Romance Classics Network as the Women's Entertainment Network (WE) in 2001.

AMANDA LOTZ

See also **Gender and Television; Narrowcasting**

Further Reading

Bronstein, Carolyn, "Mission Accomplished? Profits and Programming at the Network for Women," *Camera Obscura* (special volume on "Lifetime: A Cable Network for Women"), 33–34 (1994)

Byars, Jackie, and Eileen R. Meehan, "Once in a Lifetime: Constructing the 'Working Woman' Through Cable Narrowcasting," *Camera Obscura* (special volume on "Lifetime: A Cable Network for Women"), 33–34 (1994)

Hundley, Heather Lyn, "Defining Feminine Programming and Co-opting Liberal Feminism: A Discursive Analysis of Lifetime's Original Movies," Ph.D. diss., University of Utah, 1999

Johnson, Eithne, "Lifetime's Feminine Psychographic Space and the *Mystery Loves Company Series*," *Camera Obscura* (special volume on "Lifetime: A Cable Network for Women"), 33–34 (1994)

Meehan, Eileen, and Jackie Byars, "Telefeminism: How Lifetime Got Its Groove," in *Television and New Media,* Vol. 1 (2000)

Wilson, Pamela, "Upscale Feminine Angst: *Molly Dodd,* the Lifetime Cable Network and Gender Marketing," *Camera Obscura* (special volume on "Lifetime: A Cable Network for Women"), 33–34 (1994)

Likely Lads, The

British Comedy

When the BBC's second television channel began in 1964, it was generally intended to provide the sort of minority-interest, factual, and cultural programming that was being marginalized by the BBC's struggle for popularity against the commercial channel ITV. It was also intended to advance the technology of television by transmitting on the new 625-line standard, which would pave the way for the introduction of color. To receive it, viewers needed to buy a new television set—and to sell the new sets in large enough numbers, the new channel needed some popular programming.

In the field of comedy, *The Likely Lads* provided the perfect vehicle, being both innovative and within the tradition of popular entertainment. It launched the comedy career of the writing team of Dick Clement and Ian La Frenais and proved one of the infant channel's most enduring successes.

The protagonists are two young friends, Terry Collier and Bob Ferris, recently out of school and starting out in their first jobs. Their interests are predictable—girls, drinks, football, and fun. However, they are a new breed of working-class heroes. They have some money in their pockets and the Swinging Sixties are getting underway. The first scene of the first episode, "Entente Cordiale," sees them coming home from a holiday in Spain—the sort of thing that had been unavailable to their kind in earlier years but that had come to be taken for granted by their generation.

The setting, the northeast of England, was also fairly new—to television, anyway. In many ways, *The Likely Lads* was television's response to the portrayal of north country youth in such films of the early 1960s as *A Kind of Loving* and *Billy Liar*. Indeed, the two young actors chosen for the lead roles—James Bolam as Terry and Rodney Bewes as Bob—had begun their careers in minor roles in these films.

As the series progressed, the two characters emerged, and their differences were to form the basis for the comedy and the development of the show. Both the lads have a sharp intelligence but use it differently, and they reach different conclusions about what they want out of life. Terry is a cynic. He knows his class and his place in society, and his sole aim is to get what he can, when he can. Bob has ambitions. He thinks he can make a better life for himself but lacks confidence. Terry's crazy schemes scare him, but it is usually his friend who comes off worse.

There were three series of *The Likely Lads* between 1964 and 1966, a total of 20 episodes. In the final episode, "Good-bye to All That," Bob decides to join the army. Missing his friend, Terry signs up too, only to find that Bob has been discharged for having flat feet and that he, Terry, is committed for five years.

So, the likely lads went their own ways and the actors into different projects with varying success. But, with the spread of color television in the early 1970s, the BBC instituted a policy of reviving its biggest comedy successes of the 1960s. Following *Steptoe and Son* and *Till Death Us Do Part,* the decision was made to bring back *The Likely Lads*. However, unlike the other two sitcoms, *The Likely Lads* was not the same as it had been. The new title, *Whatever Happened to the Likely Lads?* reflected the fact that seven years had passed since they last appeared. The actors were older, and the characters had aged with them. Terry had seen the world (Germany and Cyprus) with the army. Bob had been successful at work, and, as the series opened in 1973, he is buying a new house and is about to marry his childhood sweetheart, Thelma (Bridgit Forsyth), and settle down to a respectable middle-class life.

Terry's return, and his withering contempt for what he sees as Bob's betrayal of his working-class roots, threatens to spoil Bob's plans and ruin his marriage, which takes place as the series progresses. At the same time, the shifting economic circumstances of the Northeast are reflected in Terry's feeble attempts to find employment or any sort of a role in a place that has changed so much in his absence.

Whatever Happened to the Likely Lads? provided, among all the laughs, a social commentary equal to anything found in the serious drama of the time. Two series were made in 1973 and 1974, a total of 26 shows. The actors, particularly James Bolam, tried subsequently to shake off their roles, but there are still many in Britain who wonder what Terry and Bob are up to now.

STEVE BRYANT

See also **La Frenais, Ian**

Cast

Terry Collier	James Bolam
Bob Ferris	Rodney Bewes

Producers
Dick Clement, James Gilbert, Bernard Thompson

Programming History

The Likely Lads
20 25-minute episodes
BBC

December 1964–January 1965	6 episodes
June 1965–July 1965	6 episodes
June 1966–July 1966	8 episodes

Whatever Happened to the Likely Lads?
26 30-minute episodes, 1 45-minute special
BBC

January 1973–April 1973	13 episodes
January 1974–April 1974	13 episodes
December 24, 1974	Christmas special

Further Reading

Grant, Linda, "The Lad Most Likely to..." *The Guardian* (August 12, 1995)

Ross, Deborah, "What Really Happened to the Likely Lad?" *Daily Mail* (July 17, 1993)

Link, William (1933–)

U.S. Writer

William Link and Richard Levinson formed one of the most notable writing and producing teams in the history of U.S. television. Working in both series and made-for-television movie forms, they moved easily from what they considered light entertainment to the exploration of serious and immensely complicated social problems. Their collaboration was of much longer standing than even their television careers suggest, for they had begun to work together in the early years of high school in Philadelphia, Pennsylvania. Even at that time the two wrote plays together, inspired by radio dramas, which they frequently wire recorded. After graduating from the University of Pennsylvania and completing service in the U.S. Army, they quickly formed an adult partnership that was to last until Levinson's death in 1987. Intent upon building a career in television, they followed the migration of talent to California in 1960 and were quickly identified for their talents.

After almost ten years of working with series television, the "boys," as they were identified by Martin Sheen, who often starred in their movies, began to explore "social issues." It may have begun with their questions regarding the violence of television shows such as *Mannix,* their own creation. As Link put it in an interview, "Dick and I did not know whether television violence had an effect or not, but we just decided we were not going to do that kind of writing anymore." *Columbo* was the natural answer. In Link's words, "It portrayed a bloodless murder followed by a cat-and-mouse game. Columbo was a meat-and-potatoes cop who brought low the rich and famous."

The partners made these social concerns explicit in the character of Ira Davidson, central figure in their made-for-television movie *The Storyteller* (1977). In that piece, Davidson, a television writer, engages his producer in a debate about TV violence. The producer questions the writer's deletion of violent scenes from his original treatment. Davidson replies that he could tell the story just as well without vehicular mayhem. The producer then accuses him of acquiring a conscience just when nonviolence was fashionable and insists he does not want the Parent Teachers Association or anyone else telling him what kind of television to make. He wants to use violence when it works for the

plot without interference from the network. Ira responds, "Agreed." Surprised, the producer says, "Agreed? But I thought . . . ." Ira ends the discussion by stating, "I was telling you what I am going to do. What you do is your business."

Discussing those social dramas, Link commented, "The best things come to you—they fall into your hand or you see a human life situation like *That Certain Summer*—and you say that would make a good drama. It's hard to begin by saying, 'Let's do a social drama.' These things just occur to you." Link's philosophy of filmmaking is summed up in remarks he made in the early 1980s:

> In the films where we have serious intentions, we tend to understate. This comes from a feeling that if you're going to deal with subjects such as homosexuality, or race relations, or gun control, you should show some aesthetic restraint and not wallow in these materials like a kid who's permitted to write dirty words on a wall. Our approach is that if you're going to use these controversial subjects—play against them. Don't be so excited by your freedom that you go for the obvious. The danger, of course, is that sometimes you get so muted that you boil out the drama. In *The Storyteller* we were so concerned with being fair and with balance that we lost energy and dramatic impact.

When Link spoke movingly about Levinson upon their induction into the Television Hall of Fame in 1995, the extremely difficult task of admitting to himself that there was no longer "Link and Levinson" was completed. Even as he oversaw the final production of the made-for-television movie *United States v. Salaam Ajami* (aired as *Hostile Witness,* 1988), that fact perhaps led to reviving a story idea Levinson had rejected.

Link wrote and produced *The Boys* (1991), dealing with a writing partnership in which one man smokes, while the other informs his colleague that he has contracted cancer from secondhand cigarette smoke. Here was a social drama on two levels. While not strictly autobiographical, the drama was surely related to individual experience. Levinson smoked heavily during most of his adult years, and the practice most probably shortened his life. *The Boys,* then, was personal, but it also dealt with a real social issue.

After Levinson's death, Link remained active as a

William Link.
Courtesy of the Everett Collection/CSU Archives

writer-producer at Universal, working on new stories for *Columbo*. By continuing to hold on to the producer credit, he held creative control over the words. As Link expressed it in an interview:

> We produce for two reasons. One is to protect the material. And the second is that we've discovered that producing is an extension of writing. The day before they're going to shoot it, you walk on a set designed for a character you've written. You say to the art director, "The man we've written would not have these paintings. He would not have that dreadful objet d'art sitting there. It's much too cluttered for a guy of his sensibilities. So clean out the set...." We created that person as a character. We're also interested in how it's extended.

In the late 1980s, Link served as supervising executive producer of *The ABC Mystery Movie*. Leaving Universal in 1991, he became executive producer and writer for *The Cosby Mysteries* on NBC. He also became an actor in the series when Bill Cosby insisted on casting him as a saxophone instructor for Cosby's character. Appearing infrequently, Link was a natural for the part.

William Link has a lively sense of humor and frequently employs it to assail what he perceives as the current decay of the industry he loves. He is an avid reader of mysteries, extremely knowledgeable concerning music and cinema, and an active collector of Latin American art. He and his wife, Margery Link, live surrounded by the collection.

ROBERT S. ALLEY

See also ***Columbo;*** **Detective Programs; Johnson, Lamont; Levinson, William**

William Link. Born in Philadelphia, Pennsylvania, December 15, 1933. Educated at University of Pennsylvania, B.S., 1956. Served in U.S. Army, 1956–58. Married: Margery Nelson, 1980. Scriptwriter with partner Richard Levinson for many television series; with Levinson created a number of television series; also with Levinson wrote and produced many made-for-television movies dealing with social problems; wrote *The Boys,* 1991, loosely based on the partnership with Levinson; writer-producer, *The Cosby Mysteries,* 1994–95; as actor, appeared as Sapolsky in *The Cosby Mysteries,* 1994; producer of television series and made-for-television movies, from 1995. Recipient (all with Richard Levinson): Emmy Awards, 1970 and 1972; Image Award, National Association for the Advancement of Colored People, 1970; Golden Globe Award, 1972; Silver Nymph Award, Monte Carlo Film Festival, 1973; Peabody Award, 1974; Edgar Awards, Mystery Writers of America, 1979, 1980, 1983; Christopher Award, 1981; Paddy Chayefsky Laurel

Award, Writers Guild of America, 1986; Ellery Queen Award, Mystery Writers of America, 1989, for lifetime contribution to the art of the mystery; Academy of Television Arts and Sciences Television Hall of Fame, 1995.

Television Series
1994–95	*The Cosby Mysteries*

Television Series (selected episodes written with Richard Levinson)
1955–65	*Alfred Hitchcock Presents*
1958–60	*Desilu Playhouse*
1961–77	*Dr. Kildare*
1963–67	*The Fugitive*

Television Series (created with Richard Levinson)
1967–75	*Mannix*
1969–73	*The Bold Ones*
1971–77, 1989–90	*Columbo*
1971	*The Psychiatrist*
1973–74	*Tenafly*
1975–76	*Ellery Queen*
1980	*Stone*
1984–96	*Murder, She Wrote*
1985	*Scene of the Crime*
1986–88	*Blacke's Magic*
1987	*Hard Copy*

Made-for-Television Movies
1989–90	*The ABC Mystery Movie*
1991	*The Boys*

Made-for-Television Movies (with Richard Levinson)
1968	*Istanbul Express*
1969	*The Whole World Is Watching*
1970	*My Sweet Charlie*
1971	*Two on a Bench*
1972	*That Certain Summer*
1972	*The Judge and Jake Wyler* (also with David Shaw)
1973	*Tenafly*
1973	*Partners in Crime*
1973	*Savage*
1974	*The Execution of Private Slovik*
1974	*The Gun*
1975	*Ellery Queen*
1975	*A Cry for Help*
1977	*Charlie Cobb: Nice Night for a Hanging*
1977	*The Storyteller*
1979	*Murder by Natural Causes*
1981	*Crisis at Central High*
1982	*Rehearsal for Murder*
1982	*Take Your Best Shot*
1983	*Prototype*
1984	*The Guardian*
1985	*Guilty Conscience*
1985	*Murder in Space*
1986	*Vanishing Act*
1986	*Blacke's Magic*
1988	*Hostile Witness*
1990	*Over My Dead Body*

Credited as creator on 18 *Columbo* made-for-television movies, 1989–1998

Films (with Richard Levinson)
The Hindenberg, 1975; *Rollercoaster*, 1977.

Stage (with Richard Levinson; selected)
Merlin, 1982; *Killing Jessica*, 1986; *Guilty Conscience*, 1986.

Publications (with Richard Levinson)

Prescription: Murder (three-act play), 1963

Fineman (novel), 1972

Stay Tuned: An Inside Look at the Making of Prime-Time Television, 1981

The Playhouse (novel), 1984

Guilty Conscience: A Play of Suspense in Two Acts, 1985

Off Camera: Conversations with the Makers of Prime-Time Television, 1986

Further Reading

Broughton, Irv, *Producers on Producing: The Making of Film and Television,* Jefferson, North Carolina: McFarland, 1986

Burger, Richard, *The Producers: A Descriptive Directory of Film and Television Directors in the Los Angeles Area,* Venice, California: R. Burger, 1985

Newcomb, Horace, and Robert S. Alley, *The Producer's Medium: Conversations with Creators of American TV,* New York: Oxford University Press, 1983

Little House on the Prairie

U.S. Drama Series

After *Bonanza* ended its successful run (1959–73) on NBC, the popular Michael Landon, who had played Little Joe Cartwright, was offered numerous TV opportunities. In addition to his acting duties, *Bonanza* had given Landon the chance to write and direct. He wanted to create a new series, yet he was unsure of what sort of project he wanted to pursue.

Ed Friendly, a former network vice president and coproducer of *Rowan & Martin's Laugh-In,* was a savvy television veteran. Like Landon, he was looking for a new television series. To that end, he had acquired the dramatic rights for Laura Ingalls Wilder's nostalgic nine-volume *Little House on the Prairie* book series from her family estate. Until Landon entered the picture, Friendly was unable to generate any interest in producing a television series based on the books. Networks were unimpressed with the no frills, values-oriented approach such a series would require. As luck would have it, Friendly proposed *Little House* to Landon at a time when his daughter, Leslie, was immersed in the *Little House* book series.

NBC had witnessed the success of CBS's *The Waltons* and commissioned *Little House on the Prairie* as direct competition for the program. That was perfect for Landon, who differed from many of his Hollywood peers. He opposed TV violence, eschewed traditional Hollywood business models, and used *Little House on the Prairie* to convey positive family values. Landon wanted a show that families could watch together and he wanted to feature themes that would be important to a modern generation. Landon wrote, directed, and starred in the series from 1974 to 1982. Initially, he coproduced *Little House on the Prairie* with Friendly, but everyone knew from the outset that Landon was in charge. Friendly wanted the series to remain true to Laura Ingalls Wilder's *Little House* book series, but Landon had other ideas.

Those viewers who tuned in to *Little House on the Prairie* expecting to see a *Bonanza* clone may have been disappointed. Both series were one-hour dramas and both were period pieces from the late 1800s, but the similarities ended there. There were no fights, shootings, or other instances of violence as there had been on *Bonanza*. Rather than the massive, sprawling Ponderosa ranch of the Cartwright clan, there was the

humble Ingalls family log cabin. Instead of the eligible bachelor named Little Joe Cartwright, Michael Landon had a new alter ego in the settled, frontier family man named Charles "Pa" Ingalls. Landon's on-screen character may have been different, but his creative work delighted audiences.

Although Landon considered the *Little House* books to be depressing, he knew the setting would work for a program that would be uplifting. From the beginning, Landon let Friendly know the direction the series would take; there was little relationship between the books and TV series. Landon blamed much of the inconsistency on the physical location for shooting the series. For example, Landon refused to have his character wear a beard as the real Charles Ingalls had done. Simi Valley, California, where the program was filmed, could reach temperatures of up to 110 degrees—something that would certainly not be commonplace in Minnesota, where the Ingalls family lived. Landon refused to let the child actors go shoeless like the children of the book. He was careful not to let them step on the thorns, glass, or snakes that were frequently discovered on the California set. And there was the fact that the main character in the book was Laura Ingalls—not her father. Since Landon was to play the father, he wanted that character to be the centerpiece of the production.

Friendly wanted the series to be like the books, but during production of the pilot commissioned by NBC, Landon's intentions became obvious to Friendly. Friendly knew the cards were stacked against him, because NBC was in Landon's corner. The two-hour *Little House on the Prairie* pilot aired on March 30, 1974, garnering a 26.2 rating and a 45 share. As a result, NBC picked up the series. It debuted on September 11, 1974, on NBC and was instantly successful with viewers. Friendly did all he could to wrestle control from Landon, but he knew there would be no series without Landon. Friendly gave up his fight before the series aired, but he may have found some solace in that numerous television critics panned the series. Many compared it unfavorably with *The Waltons*.

As farmer Charles "Pa" Ingalls, Landon played a pioneer father in the 1870s. Ingalls had built a farm near the border of Kansas and Oklahoma in the 1870s, but he was forced to move when the federal government set aside the land for a Native American reservation. Ingalls, his wife Caroline (Karen Grassle), and their three daughters moved hundreds of miles to Walnut Grove, Minnesota. In Walnut Grove, the real-life Ingalls family lived in squalor. Charles situated the house on the banks of Plum Creek, where he literally made it from sod and mud. As the family crops paid off, Ingalls built a modest wooden house that had glass windows. Although the frontier was a difficult place to make a home or living, Landon did not want the TV family of *Little House on the Prairie* to live in such a primitive home. The TV series was uplifting to many viewers, but it was equally depressing to others, with its weekly disasters ranging from swarming locusts, to blindness, illness, and prejudice.

The daughters were Mary (Melissa Sue Anderson), who was the eldest, Laura (Melissa Gilbert), who narrated the stories, Carrie (twins Lindsay and Sidney Greenbush—alternating), and Grace (Wendi and Brenda Turnbeaugh—alternating) who was added in 1977. The Ingalls characters later adopted other children.

When the series began, Landon believed the show was good for a four-year run. Its popularity kept it going for eight years, when Landon discontinued his regular appearances. He continued to produce the program for a ninth season when the show transformed into *Little House: A New Beginning* (1982–83). Charles and Caroline moved to Iowa, leaving Walnut Grove to other family members. After the series ended, Landon produced three *Little House* TV movies for NBC: *Look Back to Yesterday* (1983), *Bless All the Dear Children* (1984), and the appropriately named *The Last Farewell* (1984). During its nine-year run, *Little House on the Prairie* finished the year in the top 20 programs six times and was in the top ten two times (1977–78, 1980–81). Its highest annual rating was a tie for sixth in 1977–78. It has remained popular in syndication.

W.A. KELLY HUFF

See also **Bonanza; Landon, Michael**

Cast

Charles "Pa" Ingalls	Michael Landon
Caroline "Ma" Ingalls	Karen Grassle
Laura Ingalls Wilder	Melissa Gilbert
Mary Ingalls Kendall (1974–81)	Melissa Sue Anderson
Carrie Ingalls	Lindsay and Sidney Greenbush (twins)
Grace Ingalls (1978–82)	Wendi and Brenda Turnbeaugh (twins)
Lars Hanson (1974–78)	Karl Swenson
Nels Oleson	Richard Bull
Harriett Oleson	Katherine MacGregor
Nellie Oleson Dalton (1974–81)	Alison Arngrim
Willie Oleson	Jonathan Gilbert
Dr. Hiram Baker	Kevin Hagen
Reverend Robert Alden	Dabbs Greer
Isaiah Edwards (1974–77, 1982–83)	Victor French
Grace Snider Edwards (1974–77)	Bonnie Bartlett
Jonathan Garvey (1977–81)	Merlin Olsen
Alice Garvey (1977–80)	Hersha Parady
Andrew "Andy" Garvey (1977–81)	Patrick Laborteaux
Albert Quinn Ingalls (1978–82)	Matthew Laborteaux
Eva Beadle Sims (1974–78)	Charlotte Stewart
Adam Kendall (1978–81)	Linwood Boomer
Hester Sue Terhune (1978–83)	Ketty Lester
Almanzo Wilder (1979–83)	Dean Butler
Eliza Jane Wilder (1979–80)	Lucy Lee Flippin
James Cooper Ingalls (1981–82)	Jason Bateman
Cassandra Cooper Ingalls (1981–82)	Missy Francis
Nancy Oleson (1981–83)	Allison Balson
Alica Sanderson-Edwards (1975–77)	Kyle Richards
Percival Dalton	Steve Tracy
Jenny Wilder (1982–83)	Shannon Doherty
John Carter (1982–83)	Stan Ivar
Sarah Carter (1982–83)	Pamela Roylance
Mrs. Melinda Foster	Ruth Foster
Jeb Carter (1982–83)	Lindsay Kennedy
Jason Carter (1982–83)	David Friedman
Etta Plum (1982–83)	Leslie Landon
Rose Wilder (1982–84) (uncredited)	Brenda and Michelle Steffin (twins)

Producer
Michael Landon

Programming History

1974–1983	183 episodes
NBC	
September 1974–August 1976	Wednesday 8:00–9:00

September 1976–August 1982   Monday 8:00–9:00
September 1982–March 1983   Monday 8:00–9:00

Further Reading

Brooks, Tim, and Earle Marsh, *TV's Greatest Hits: The 150 Most Popular TV Shows of All Time,* New York: Ballantine Books, 1985

Brown, Les, *Les Brown's Encyclopedia of Television,* New York: Zoetrope, 1982

Daly, Marsha, *Michael Landon: A Biography,* New York: St. Martin's Press, 1987

Flynn, Harry, Pamela Flynn, and Gene Trindl, *Michael Landon: Life, Love & Laughter.* Universal City, California: Pomegranate Press, 1991

Ito, Tom, *Conversations with Michael Landon,* Chicago: Contemporary Books, 1992

Joyce, Aileen, *Michael Landon: His Triumph and Tragedy,* New York: Zebra Books, 1991

Libman, Gary, *Little House on the Prairie,* Mankato, Minnesota: Creative Education, 1983

McNeil, Alex, *Total Television: A Comprehensive Guide to Programming from 1948 to the Present,* 3rd edition, New York: Penguin Books, 1991

Sackett, Susan, *Prime-Time Hits: Television's Most Popular Network Programs 1950 to the Present,* New York: Billboard Books, 1993

Wheeler, Jill C., *Michael Landon,* Edina, Minnesota: Abdo and Daughters, 1992

Littlefield, Warren (1952–)

U.S. Media Executive

Warren Littlefield was an executive at NBC from 1979 to 1998, and currently produces prime-time programming for several networks through his production outfit, the Littlefield Company, which he cofounded in 1999. Littlefield served as president of the entertainment division of NBC from 1991 to 1998, during which time he was responsible for the development of prime-time, late-night, and Saturday-morning entertainment programming. Under Littlefield's guidance, NBC rose from last place in almost every Nielsen rating category to become the top-ranked network for 11 of Littlefield's last 16 years at NBC, setting a record for consecutive years at number one. Littlefield contributed to the development of many of the series that defined "quality programming" in the 1980s and 1990s. NBC's entertainment programming received 168 Emmy Awards under his leadership.

Littlefield began his career in the mid-1970s as a gofer at a small media production company in New York City. By 1977 Littlefield was a vice president at Westfall Productions, where he developed and produced prime-time specials and movies, most notably the CBS movie *The Last Giraffe,* shot exclusively on location in Kenya. After a brief stint at Warner Brothers, Littlefield was hired by NBC's Brandon Tartikoff in December 1979 as manager of comedy development. He quickly worked his way up the executive the ladder from vice president for comedy development in 1981 to senior vice president for prime time in 1987.

Throughout the 1980s, Littlefield oversaw the development of several critically acclaimed and financially successful situation comedies, including *Cheers, Family Ties, The Cosby Show,* and *The Golden Girls.* He is also credited with casting Will Smith in NBC's successful *Fresh Prince of Bel Air.*

In 1990 Littlefield was appointed president of NBC Entertainment, making him second only to Tartikoff among NBC's program executives. When Tartikoff left NBC for Paramount in 1991, Littlefield replaced him at the helm. During the 1990s, Littlefield developed the NBC dramas and situation comedies *Seinfeld, ER, Friends, Frasier, Mad About You, Just Shoot Me, 3rd Rock from the Sun, NewsRadio, Law & Order,* and *Homicide: Life on the Street.* Shortly before leaving NBC, he was also involved with the development of *Will and Grace, Providence,* and *The West Wing* (owned by NBC Studios). In addition to these comedic and dramatic series, Littlefield acquired the film classic *It's a Wonderful Life* and presented the initial network broadcast of *Schindler's List* without commercials (underwritten by Firestone) to over 60 million Americans.

Littlefield is also widely regarded as the NBC executive who hired and supported Jay Leno over David Lettterman as the host of *The Tonight Show* following Johnny Carson's retirement. Littlefield also oversaw the hiring of Conan O'Brien to replace David Letterman in NBC's 12:30 spot, when Letterman moved to CBS in 1993.

In interviews, Littlefield takes credit for branding NBC as the network that, in his words, offered "quality" programming to the "upscale" or "key" demographic of "college-educated, urban-based young adults earning over $75,000 a year." Delivering that audience to advertisers was largely responsible for NBC's renaissance, which, according to Littlefield, "distinguished [NBC from the other networks], and I made advertisers pay a tremendous premium for that." Indeed, Littlefield points out that during his last three years at NBC, upfront ad sales totaled $2 billion more than its nearest competitor.

As NBC's ratings began to fade in the late 1990s, Littlefield was replaced by Scott Sassa. Littlefield entered into a nonexclusive production venture with the network through his newly formed Littlefield Company. In 2001 Littlefield (and the Littlefield Company) entered into a multiyear agreement with the network television division of Paramount, and has since coproduced the sitcom *Do Over* for the WB network and the dramedy *Keen Eddie* for FOX. Although both programs received some critical praise and loyal followings when they debuted in 2003, including fan communities on the Web, both programs were canceled before finishing their first seasons. In 2003 the Bravo cable network, which is owned by NBC's parent company General Electric, purchased the rights to *Keen Eddie* and is scheduled to run all 13 episodes in 2004. With NBC's marketing and promotions behind it and the scheduled release of the series on DVD, *Keen Eddie* is expected to recoup its initial losses.

Littlefield's "multi-ethnic situation comedy" *Like Family,* which also premiered on the WB in 2003 finished near the bottom of the Nielsen ratings but scored well enough in the key demographic categories of women aged 12–34, teens, and female teens to merit being picked up for an additional nine episodes for the 2004 season. Although the program does not explicitly address racism in the tradition of the politically charged *All in the Family,* it is a rare example of a racially diverse family situation comedy. (In the pilot, a white single mother and her 16-year-old son move in with a middle-class African-American family.) In January 2004, Littlefield was also producing the drama *Repo Man* for NBC with *Keen Eddie* writer Joel Wyman, and developing a new dramedy for ABC entitled *Joe Green and Eugene* with *Keen Eddie* star Mark Valley.

Littlefield's career is thus illustrative of the shifting landscape of television over the past 25 years from broadcasting to narrowcasting. Indeed, while one could argue that Littlefield has experienced a relative lack of success in recent years as a producer when compared with his years as an NBC executive, in an era of increased channels and fragmented audiences— combined with increased media conglomeration and product integration—Littlefield's projects have remained consistently profitable through niche marketing and cross-promotion.

JAMES CASTONGUAY

*See also **Cheers; Cosby Show, The; Family Ties; Frasier; Friends; Golden Girls, The; Homicide: Life on the Street** ; Law & Order; **Narrowcasting; Seinfeld; Tartikoff, Brandon; Tonight Show***

Warren Littlefield. Born in Montclair, New Jersey, May 11, 1952. B.A. in psychology, Hobart and William Smith Colleges, 1974. Vice president, Westfall Productions, 1977. Hired as NBC's manager of comedy development, 1979. Named vice president for comedy development, 1981. Named senior vice president for prime time, 1987. President of the entertainment division of NBC, 1991–98. Cofounded the Littlefield Company in 1999. With the Littlefield Company, entered into a multiyear agreement with the network television division of Paramount, 2001.

Further Reading

Andreeva, Nellie, "WB Net Smiles on 4 Comedies," *Hollywood Reporter* (November 11, 2003)

Carter, Bill, "NBC To Name New President for Network Entertainment," *New York Times* (October 26, 1998)

Frutkin, Alan James, "Back on Stage," *MediaWeek* (September 9, 2002)

Goodman, Tim, "NBC Looking a Lot Like Must-Sink TV," *San Francisco Chronicle* (December 31, 2000)

"Keep Doing It Until You Get It Right," *Television Week* (October 13, 2003)

Pennington, Gail, "'Keen Eddie' May Have Been Too Smart for Network TV," *Post-Dispatch* (August 26, 2003)

Schneider, Michael, "In Dog-Eat-Dog Business, Littlefield Hung Tough," *Electronic Media* (November 2, 1998)

"Warren Littlefield: The View from the Other Side of the Desk," *Washington Post* (June 1, 2003)

Zoglin, Richard, and Jeffrey Ressner, "Still Standing in Burbank," *Time* (March 18, 1996)

Live with Regis and Kathie Lee/Live with Regis and Kelly. *See* **Philbin, Regis**

Loach, Ken (1937–)

British Director

Ken Loach is Britain's most renowned and controversial director of socially conscious television drama. He is also an internationally acclaimed director of feature films whose radical political messages consistently provoke strong responses in audiences and politicians alike. In 1965 he received the British Television Guild's TV Director of the Year Award, while the 1990s brought prizes and nominations at the Cannes Film Festival. His considerable body of work, documenting British society since the 1960s, is an acknowledged source of inspiration to his contemporaries.

Loach worked for a brief spell as a repertory actor before joining the BBC in 1963 as a trainee television director. Significantly, this was during the progressive director-generalship of Sir Hugh Greene and coincided with Sydney Newman's influential appointment as head of BBC drama. Loach's earliest directorial contribution was on episodes of the ground-breaking police series *Z Cars,* but he first attracted serious attention with *Up the Junction,* a starkly realistic portrayal of working-class life in south London, which in 1965 was one of the earliest productions in the BBC's innovative *Wednesday Play* slot. This success marked the beginning of a long and fertile creative collaboration with story editor and producer Tony Garnett, which led to the recognition of their particular mode of documentary drama as the "Loach-Garnett" style. It also positioned Loach as an exponent of television's foray into the "social realist" British New Wave, popular in film, theater, and novels.

Loach collaborated with Garnett on a number of other celebrated *Wednesday Play* productions, including David Mercer's famous play about schizophrenia, *In Two Minds* (1967), which Loach later made into a feature film, *Family Life* (1971), and two significant industrial drama-documentaries written by ex-coal miner Jim Allen: *The Big Flame* (1969) and *The Rank and File* (1971). These productions demonstrated Loach's passionate concern to ignore theatrical artificiality in favor of authentic dramas on topical, important issues—dramas that give a voice to politically marginalized sections of society. By far the most powerful work from this period of Loach's career, however, is *Cathy Come Home* (1966), a study of the effects of homelessness and bureaucracy on family life. This remains one of the most seminal program events in the history of British television.

Cathy Come Home, written by former journalist Jeremy Sandford, exploded with tremendous force upon the complacent, affluent, post-Beatles culture of the Swinging Sixties. Drawing attention to disturbing levels of social deprivation far in excess of those claimed by government, the play led to a public outcry, questions in Parliament, the establishment of the housing charity Shelter, and a relaxation of policy on the dissolution of homeless families. Reflecting years afterward on this *succés de scandale,* Loach explained that, though he may have believed at the time in the potential of television drama for effecting social change, he had subsequently come to realize it could do nothing more than provide a social critique, promoting awareness of problems capable of resolution only through political action.

It was not only the subject matter of *Cathy,* and of Loach's television work generally, that struck contemporary audiences and critics as innovative; his chosen form and style were distinctive and provocative too. Above all, he was concerned to capture a sense of the real, extending a range of practiced cinema-vérité techniques to produce a sense of immediacy and plausibility that would in turn produce recognition in the spectator and inspire collective action. Lightweight, handheld camera; grainy 16mm film stock; a black-and-white aesthetic; location shooting; natural lighting; direct, asynchronous sound; blending of experienced and nonprofessional performers; authentic regional accents and dialects; overlapping dialogue; improvised acting; expressive editing; incorporation of statistical information: all these strategies combined in varying degrees to create a compelling and original documentary effect markedly at odds with the look of traditional "acted" television drama.

In 1975 the distinctive Loach-Garnett style was employed in a notable exploration, nearly 400 minutes in length, of British labor history, which functioned as a poignant commentary on the parlous state of contemporary industrial relations. This was the four-part BBC serial *Days of Hope,* scripted by Jim Allen, which follows a northern British working-class family through the turbulent years of struggle from the end of World War I to the general strike of 1926. Loach, already subject to criticism for preferring the docudrama form (deemed reprehensible in some quarters for its potential confusion of fact and fiction), now found himself embroiled in an academic debate about the extent to which radical television drama, using the conventions of bourgeois realism, could be truly "progressive." Loach insisted that his priority was populist political discourse rather than a rarefied, aesthetic debate of interest only to a critical elite. In other words, *Days of Hope* and the other strike dramas that preceded it were intended to open the eyes of ordinary people to the emancipatory potential of free collective bargaining within any capitalist culture.

Loach made his first feature film, *Poor Cow,* at the height of his television fame in 1967. He became a major founding partner, with Tony Garnett, of the independent production company, Kestrel Films, for which he made half a dozen low-budget films between 1969 and 1986. His first project at Kestrel Films was *Kes,* a moving story of a young boy and his pet kestrel set against a bleak northern industrial landscape. Some of the Kestrel Films projects were intended for television screening as well as limited theatrical release.

The Thatcher years put Loach increasingly in conflict with those who took exception to the left-wing thrust of his work and wanted to censor it or lessen its impact. Finding it difficult to ensure transmission of the kind of television drama he considered important, he turned for a while almost exclusively to straight documentary, convinced that the nonfiction form could more speedily and directly address the key social and political questions of the day. If anything, however, this route led Loach into even greater problems with censorship, culminating in the controversial withdrawals of the four-part series *Questions of Leadership*

Ken Loach.
Photo courtesy of Ken Loach

(1983) and *Which Side Are You On?* (1984), a polemical documentary about the socially disruptive miners' strike. It was probably this unsavory experience, and the greater freedom afforded by cinema, that drove Loach away from television at the end of the 1980s.

The 1990s and beyond brought Ken Loach renewed success and established him as one of Britain's foremost film directors, albeit not of mainstream commercial films. Beginning with his political thriller about a military cover-up in Ulster, *Hidden Agenda,* which was reviled and praised in roughly equal measure on its first screening at Cannes, Loach has gone on to make roughly one feature film each year, usually with an early television showing in mind. These are, without exception, films of integrity that continue their director's lifelong principle of bringing issues of oppression, inhumanity, and hypocrisy to the public's attention. The political content is, if anything, more foregrounded than in the earlier television work; the uncompromising focus on the disadvantaged or voiceless sections of society remains the same. Though he made brief returns to the television drama-documentary genre in 1997 with *The Flickering Flame* (about a strike by Liverpool dock workers) and in 2001 with *The Navigators* (about the chaotic aftermath of rail privatization in Britain), Loach continues to reserve his creative energies chiefly for cinema. After a lifetime of eschewing filming in the United States, he relented in 2000 with *Bread and Roses,* a typical Loach vehicle about a strike by non-unionized janitors in Los Angeles.

TONY PEARSON

See also **Cathy Come Home; Docudrama; Garnett, Tony; Wednesday Play, The; Z Cars**

Ken Loach. Born in Nuneaton, Warwickshire, England, June 17, 1937. Attended King Edward School, Nuneaton; St. Peter's College, Oxford. Married: Lesley Ashton, 1962; two sons and two daughters. Began career as actor with repertory company in Birmingham; joined BBC drama department as trainee, 1961; director with producer Tony Garnett, beginning with *Up the Junction,* 1965; founder, with Garnett, of Kestrel Films production company, 1969; has worked on a freelance basis, chiefly for Central Television, since the 1970s. Fellow, St. Peter's College, Oxford, 1993. Recipient: British Television Guild Television Director of the Year Award, 1965; British Academy of Film and Television Arts Award, 1967; Cannes Festival Special Jury Prize, 1990.

Television Series

1962–78	*Z Cars*
1975	*Days of Hope*
1983	*Questions of Leadership* (not transmitted)

Television Specials

1964	*Catherine*
1964	*Profit By Their Example*
1964	*The Whole Truth*
1964	*The Diary of a Young Man*
1965	*Tap on the Shoulder*
1965	*Wear a Very Big Hat*
1965	*Three Clear Sundays*
1965	*Up the Junction*
1965	*The End of Arthur's Marriage*
1965	*The Coming Out Party*
1966	*Cathy Come Home*
1967	*In Two Minds*
1968	*The Golden Vision*
1969	*The Big Flame*
1969	*In Black and White* (not transmitted)
1970	*After a Lifetime*
1971	*The Rank and File*
1973	*A Misfortune*
1976	*The Price of Coal*
1979	*The Gamekeeper* (also co-writer)
1980	*Auditions*
1981	*A Question of Leadership*
1983	*The Red and the Blue*
1984	*Which Side Are You On?*

1985	*Diverse Reports: We Should Have Won* (editor)
1988	*The View from the Woodpile*
1989	*Split Screen: Peace in Northern Ireland*
1991	*Dispatches*
1997	*The Flickering Flame*
2001	*The Navigators*

Films (director)

Poor Cow, 1967 (also co-scriptwriter); *Kes,* 1969 (also co-scriptwriter); *The Save the Children Fund Film,* 1971; *Family Life,* 1971; *Black Jack,* 1979 (also co-scriptwriter); *Looks and Smiles,* 1981; *Fatherland,* 1986; *Hidden Agenda,* 1990; *Singing the Blues in Red,* 1990; *Riff Raff,* 1991; *Raining Stones,* 1993; *Ladybird, Ladybird,* 1994; *Land and Freedom,* 1995; *Carla's Song,* 1996; *My Name Is Joe,* 1998; *Bread and Roses,* 2000; *The Navigators,* 2001; *Sweet Sixteen,* 2002; *11/09/01-September 11* ("United Kingdom" segment), 2002; *Ae Fond Kiss,* 2004.

Further Reading

Bennett, Tony, Susan Boyd-Bowman, Colin Mercer, and Janet Woollacott, *Popular Television and Film,* London: British Film Institute, 1981

Brandt, George, editor, *British Television Drama,* Cambridge: Cambridge University Press, 1981

Hacker, Jonathan, and David Price, *Take 10: Contemporary British Film Directors,* Oxford: Oxford University Press, 1991

Keighron, Peter, and Carol Walker, "Working in Television: Five Interviews," in *Behind the Screens: The Structure of British Television in the Nineties,* edited by Stuart Hood, London: Lawrence and Wishart, 1994

Kerr, Paul, "The Complete Ken Loach," *Stills* (May/June 1986)

Levin, G. Roy, *Documentary Explorations: Fifteen Interviews with Film-makers,* Garden City, New York: Doubleday, 1971

McKnight, George, editor, *Agent of Challenge and Defiance: The Films of Ken Loach,* London: Flicks Books, 1995

Pannifer, Bill, "Agenda Bender," *Listener* (January 3, 1991)

Petley, Julian, "Questions of Censorship," *Stills* (November 1984)

Petley, Julian, "Ken Loach—Politics, Protest and the Past," *Monthly Film Bulletin* (March 1987)

Shubik, Irene, *Play for Today: The Evolution of Television Drama,* London: Davis-Poynter, 1975

Taylor, John, "The *Kes* Dossier," *Sight and Sound* (Summer 1970)

Tulloch, John, *Television Drama: Agency, Audience and Myth,* London: Routledge, 1990

Local Television

Even though television networks and syndicators have garnered the lion's share of historical and critical attention in the United States, these entities could not have existed without local television. In the early struggles surrounding the establishment of television, crucial decisions were made with regard to the structure of the new industry. Central to many of those decisions were those of the Federal Communications Commission (FCC). The commission grounded the organization, financing, and regulation of the television industry for the existing radio model of broadcasting, which had ensured nationwide service. Thus local TV stations came to serve as the infrastructure of the industry. Local stations negotiated the role TV would play in their communities, coordinating the new medium to local rhythms, interests, sentiments, and ideologies. They have contributed immeasurably to the growth, allure, and impact of television in the United States. The considerable history—or rather, series of histories—of local television are still being written.

All of the earliest television stations were necessarily local stations. Most began in an "experimental" status, noncommercial and sporadically scheduled. Applications for early broadcasting stations had come from a range of potential participants, but many of the first to become truly operational were owned by radio networks or broadcast equipment manufacturers with strong financial reserves; costs for construction and research-and-development were high, and revenues were low or nonexistent for many years. Much of the television industry was developed by those who could withstand continuing financial losses. Stations independent of corporate ties were started by newspapers, automobile dealers, and other local entrepreneurs in major cities across the country. These groups and individuals had also often owned radio stations or were otherwise experienced in radio.

The advantages of multiple station ownership were clear to some of these early investors, but they were faced with regulatory restrictions. Companies that hoped to attain a network-like reach were allowed to own only a handful of stations—up to five in the early years—each in a different market. As the technology for linking stations emerged, station affiliations grew. A few cities featured stations owned and operated by the existing national broadcasting networks, but most had stations affiliated with more than one network, and some areas had so few stations that each could feature multiple affiliations, often for many years. And some cities did maintain additional, fully independent channels.

But in every city and market, local stations worked to invent, adapt, and expand what television had to offer to their specific audiences. Each station produced a great deal of its own programming, increasingly so as the television schedule expanded to include more daytime and weekend hours. Viewers had a different relationship to the performers and personalities on local stations, a sense of accessibility and proximity that was inflected by all things regional—from speech patterns to weather systems to fashion tastes. Station personnel tended to perform in different capacities and roles throughout the programming day—news reader at one point, talk-show host at another, children's show performer in still another—all lending them a familiarity and informality that often proved welcome by the audience. Local television could even seem quasi-interactive, and many programs included responses to viewer mail or even phone calls to viewers. For most local programs, budget constraints translated to a lack of production spectacle, but the same financial restriction led to a yen for ingenuity. In some cases this could afford marvelous and bizarre performers and programming formats, often outside the boundaries of what networks—already seeking a "national" audience—would deem suitable.

Certain programming similarities existed among stations, of course, especially regarding TV's emerging relationship to the rhythms of everyday life, a relationship that presumed a family work-week and school-day, conventional gender roles, and regularized daily patterns of behavior and involvement. Kids' shows quickly became a late afternoon staple. Cooking and homemaking shows were popular around midday. Movies and sports programs could dominate evening and weekend hours. Most of the conventions of television news were also developed at the local level, typically out of necessity rather than conscious design or analysis.

Word quickly spread when a programming innovation proved successful at a local station, often ensuring imitations at other stations and in other markets. Many stations featured disc jockeys who played favorite records, cartoon show emcees in the guise of friendly authority figures, afternoon movie hosts who proffered quizzes and giveaways. In some instances, local talent went on to national success: Ernie Kovacs and Dick Clark began locally in Philadelphia; Dave Garroway, Burr Tillstrom, and Fran Allison first appeared on TV in Chicago; Liberace, Alan Young, and Betty White started their TV careers on local Los Angeles stations.

But local television was more than just a supplement to the networks. In fact, many original formats and regional distinctions emerged in local TV before being subsumed or displaced by network schedules and priorities. In Chicago, for example, pioneer telecasters like William Eddy and Jules Herbuveaux helped to develop a casual but intelligent style of programming that became known as the "Chicago School." Many of these programs, featuring the likes of Garroway; Kukla, Fran and Ollie; and even Studs Terkel; appeared on NBC affiliate WNBQ. But when Chicago became networked to the East Coast in 1949, many of the most popular shows were retooled according to standards in the New York offices or were dropped entirely, and the regional style quickly evaporated.

Los Angeles was in a slightly different situation, for the network lines did not arrive until late 1951, and only one or two national "feeds" were possible for some time thereafter. Partially due to this, Los Angeles was a strongly independent early TV market: it had a full complement of seven stations by January 1949, yet the network affiliates were the last on the air. Network stars such as Milton Berle were enormously popular, of course, even via kinescope, but for many years local programs dominated the ratings. The leading station until the mid-1950s was KTLA, owned by Paramount Pictures, Inc., and run by German émigré Klaus Landsberg, who had helped to telecast the 1936 Olympics before coming to this country later in the decade. Often utilizing "remote" coverage, programming in Los Angeles was surprisingly diverse, reflecting local tastes in a variety of musical shows and featuring any number of sporting events. The 1951 network link-up was complemented by a shift in TV production from New York to Los Angeles, especially after NBC and CBS opened elaborate new facilities there in 1952. The independent stations, which had dominated, were no longer able to compete with network practices, with the stars and spectacle that national advertising rates could afford.

The same pattern prevailed at almost every local station. Nationally syndicated shows blossomed on local stations through the 1950s, followed in turn by reruns of network programs, which began to be syndicated in the early 1960s. Of course there have been exceptions to the hierarchies of the network-dominated system, and the boom in UHF stations in the 1960s ensured a fair amount of locally produced programming. Some stations have even been able to produce work syndicated outside their own markets, sometimes via regional networks. But as more network programs became available for syndication, the demand for them generally meant fewer opportunities for programming tailored to local tastes. Nearly all of television began to reflect past or present nationally distributed fare. Even the Prime Time Access Rule, designed to promote local programming by blocking out network shows for an hour each weeknight, resulted in a boom for the syndication industry. Measured against the costs of original production and the possibility of lower return in advertising dollars, the expense of acquiring syndicated offerings still seemed a clear economic advantage. Game shows such as *Jeopardy!* and *Wheel of Fortune* and slick "infotainment" programming such as *Entertainment Tonight* became television institutions.

The new technologies of the modern television era have complicated these dynamics. Cable television systems brought a range of new national competitors to existing local broadcast stations, but they also created local access channels. Public access television has in many cases featured informative and alternative programming (often syndicated among stations), as well as a range of often peculiar and amusing fare. But hopes that these channels might produce an enhanced televisual public sphere seem all but exhausted. Many of the politically oriented and activist users of access television are likely to turn to the Internet as a site for communicating with interest groups that share concerns and extend beyond the local arena.

Satellite technology has similarly both enhanced and threatened local television. The availability of international newsfeeds enabled even local newscasts to compete with what was available from cable networks and raised opportunities for examining the local ramifications of nonlocal incidents. But satellites have also made available a ready stream of sensationalistic footage and feature stories of little consequence. Conversely, a few local stations have come to enjoy national distribution via cable and satellite: the so-called "superstations," such as TBS, WOR, WGN, and KTLA. But many other local stations have faced being eclipsed by these same delivery systems, especially since satellite programming packages typically include network affiliates from other parts of the country, but none of the local broadcast stations from the audience's "home" area.

As a result of these shifts in technology and programming strategy, the future of local television seems uncertain. Certainly the dollar value of local stations has only escalated, especially in light of the competition for affiliates, which resulted from the rise of FOX and other fledgling networks. The extent to which these stations will continue to provide truly local service—whether by audience demand or by regulatory edict—remains to be seen. But whatever the changes in technology, industrial organization, or commercial exigency, it will continue to be important to study the consumption and effects of local television—the medium's role in helping define the very concept of the local.

MARK WILLIAMS

Further Reading

Godfrey, Donald, and Michael Murray, editors, *Television in America: Pioneering Stations*. Ames: Iowa State University Press, 1996

Lone Ranger, The

U.S. Western

The Lone Ranger originated on WXYZ radio in Detroit, Michigan, in 1933. Created by George W. Trendle and written by Fran Striker, the show became so popular it was one of the reasons why several stations linked together to share programming on what became the Mutual Broadcasting System. Aimed primarily at the children's audience, *The Lone Ranger* made a successful transition to ABC television in 1949. Several characteristics were unique and central to the premise of this western, and the initial episode that explained the legend was occasionally repeated so young viewers would understand how the hero gained his name and why he wore a mask. The Lone Ranger is one of six Texas Rangers who are ambushed while chasing a gang of outlaws led by Butch Cavendish. After the battle, one "lone ranger" survives and is discovered by Tonto, a Native American who recognizes the survivor as John Reid, the man who had saved his life earlier. Tonto thereafter refers to the ranger as *kemo sabe,* which is translated as "trusty scout." After Tonto helps him regain his strength, the ranger vows to hide his identity from Cavendish and to dedicate his life to "making the West a decent place to live." He and Tonto dig an extra grave to fool Cavendish into believing all six rangers had died, and the ranger dons a mask to protect his identity as the single surviving ranger. Only Tonto knows who he is...the Lone Ranger. After he and Tonto save a silver-white stallion from being gored by a buffalo, they nurse the horse back to health and set him free. The horse follows them and the Lone Ranger decides to adopt him and give him the name Silver. Shortly thereafter, the Lone Ranger and Tonto encounter a man who, it turns out, had been set up to take the blame for murders committed by Cavendish. They establish him as caretaker in an abandoned silver mine, where he produces silver bullets for the Lone Ranger. Even after the Cavendish gang is captured, the Lone Ranger decides to keep his identity a secret. Near the end of this and many future episodes, someone asks about the identity of the masked man. The typical response: "I don't rightly know his real name, but I've heard him called...the Lone Ranger."

The Lone Ranger exemplifies upstanding character and righteous purpose. He engages in plenty of action, but his silver bullets are symbols of "justice by law," and were never used to kill. For the children's audience, he represented clean living and noble effort in the cause of fighting crime. His values and style, including his polished manners and speech, were intended to provide a positive role model. The show's standard musical theme was Rossini's "William Tell Overture," accompanied by the Lone Ranger voicing a hearty "Hi-Ho, Silver, away" as he rode off in a cloud of dust.

Clayton Moore is most closely associated with the TV role, but John Hart played the Lone Ranger for two seasons. The part of Tonto was played by Jay Silverheels. After the original run of the program from 1949 to 1957, it was regularly shown in reruns until 1961, and later in animated form. *The Lone Ranger* has also been the subject of comic books and movies. Both the original and animated versions of the program have been syndicated.

Perhaps no fictional action hero has become as established in our culture through as many media forms as the Lone Ranger. Clayton Moore made personal appearances in costume as the Lone Ranger for many years, until a corporation that had made a feature length film with another actor in the role obtained a court injunction to halt his wearing the mask in public. Moore continued his appearances wearing oversized sunglasses. He later regained the right to appear as the Lone Ranger, mask and all.

B.R. SMITH

See also **Western; Wrather, Jack**

Cast

The Lone Ranger (1949–52, 1954–57)	Clayton Moore
The Lone Ranger (1952–54)	John Hart
Tonto	Jay Silverheels

Producers

Sherman Harris, George W. Trendle, Jack Chertok, Harry H. Poppe, Paul Landers

Programming History

221 episodes
ABC

September 1949– September 1957	Thursday 7:30–8:00
June 1950–September 1950	Friday 10:00–10:30

Further Reading

Calder, Jenni, *There Must Be a Lone Ranger,* London: Hamilton, 1974

Glut, Donald F., and Jim Harmon, *The Great Television Heroes,* New York: Doubleday, 1975.

Goldstein, Richard, "Clayton Moore, Television's Lone Ranger and a Persistent Masked Man, Dies at 85," *New York Times* (December 29, 1999)

MacDonald, J. Fred, *Who Shot the Sheriff? The Rise and Fall of the Television Western,* New York: Praeger, 1987

Rothel, David, *Who Was That Masked Man? The Story of the Lone Ranger,* San Diego, California: A. Barnes, 1981

West, Richard, *Television Westerns: Major and Minor Series, 1946–1978,* Jefferson, North Carolina: McFarland, 1987

Yoggy, Gary A., *Riding the Video Range: The Rise and Fall of the Western on Television,* Jefferson, North Carolina: McFarland, 1995

Loretta Young Show, The

U.S. Drama Anthology

The Loretta Young Show, airing on NBC from 1953 to 1961, was the first and longest-running prime-time dramatic anthology series to feature a female star as host, actor, and producer. Film star Loretta Young played a variety of characters in well over half of the episodes, but her glamorous, fashion-show entrances as host became one of the most memorable features of this prime-time series.

Premiering under the title *Letter to Loretta,* the series was renamed *The Loretta Young Show* during the first season. Originally, the series was framed as the dramatization of viewers' letters. Each teleplay dramatized a different letter/story/message. Even after the letter device was dropped, Young still introduced and closed each story. At the beginning of each episode, she entered a living room set (supposedly her living room) through a door. Turning around to close the door and swirling her designer fashions as she walked up to the camera, Young was consciously putting on a mini-fashion show, and the spectacular entrance became Young's, and the series', trademark. Glamour and fashion had been important elements of her film star image, and she considered them central to her television image and appeal. (As an indication of how strongly Young felt about this aspect of the series, she later won a suit against NBC for allowing her then-dated fashion openings to be seen in syndication.)

The successful format and style of *The Loretta Young Show* spurred other similar shows. *Jane Wyman Theater* (1955–58), *The DuPont Show with June Allyson* (1959–61), and *The Barbara Stanwyck Show* (1960–61) were prime-time network series that attempted to capitalize on Young's success. Similar syndicated series included *Ethel Barrymore Theater* (1953), *Crown Theater with Gloria Swanson* (1954), and *Ida Lupino Theater* (1956).

When original sponsor Procter and Gamble snapped up the proposed *Loretta Young* series, Young and her husband, Thomas Lewis, hired Desilu (credited on-screen as DPI) to do the actual filming for the first season's episodes. At a time when television was often broadcast live from New York, the series was filmed in Hollywood, where Desilu was already a major force in telefilm production. The first five seasons of the show were produced by Lewislor Enterprises, a company created by Young and Lewis to produce the series. They were co-executive producers the first three seasons, but when Lewis and Young split personally and professionally by the end of the third season, Young became sole executive producer (though she chose not to identify herself in the credits). When Lewislor's five-year contract with NBC was up, Young formed Toreto Enterprises, which produced the series' last three seasons.

Young played a variety of characters, but stories most often centered around her as mother, daughter, wife, or single woman (often a professional) finding romance. (Another unique aspect of the series was that Young acted in every episode the first two seasons and ultimately in well over half of all the episodes.) Presenting both melodramas and light romantic comedies, the series was designed as and considered to be women's programming. (In fact, NBC reran episodes on its daytime schedule, which was targeted to women.) Young chose stories for their messages, lessons to be learned by characters and audiences. Her introductory remarks always framed the stories in specifically didactic terms, and she closed each episode with words of wisdom quoted from the Bible, Shakespeare, or another authoritative source.

Stories affirmed postwar, middle-class ideas about the home, families, and gender roles. Single working women found love and were transformed. Mothers learned how to be better mothers. Women found true happiness within the domestic/heterosexual sphere of the middle-class home. Yet characters sometimes had to stand up for their convictions, putting them at odds with the men in their lives. Women demonstrated strength, intelligence, and desire. This was a series that put women front stage and center, especially when Young portrayed the characters. Even when she did not act, themes of women's fiction, such as the play of emotions and the focus on character relationships, were present in the stories. Occasionally, the show explicitly addressed social issues of the day, such as U.S. aid to war-ravaged Korea, the plight of East European refugees, and alcoholism. It stands out as a rare prime-time network drama series where a woman tells her stories.

Unlike many of the live anthology dramas, big-name guest stars were not a regular feature of *The Loretta Young Show*. The biggest stars appeared as guest hosts during Young's illness in the fall of 1955.

The Loretta Young Show, Loretta Young, 1953–61.
Courtesy of the Everett Collection

Barbara Stanwyck, Joseph Cotten, Claudette Colbert, and several other film stars hosted the show in Young's absence. Marking the importance of her swirling entrances, none of the guest hosts came through the door to open the show. Over the years, guest actors included Hume Cronyn, Merle Oberon, Hugh O'Brian, and Teresa Wright.

The Loretta Young Show won various industry awards, including three Emmys for Young as best actress. It also was honored by numerous educational, religious, and civic groups. The series and its star were praised by these groups for promoting family- and community-based ideals in the rapidly changing postwar United States.

The Loretta Young Show represents a type of television programming that no longer exists. The various anthology dramas of the 1950s disappeared as programs with continuing characters came to exemplify series television in the 1960s. TV series that worked through the image of the glamorous Hollywood star would forever remain a phenomenon of 1950s television, the period in which the Hollywood studio system that had created larger-than-life stars came to a close. The 1950s space for strong female stars also closed because television now had a permanent place in American homes. The industry no longer felt the need to attract specifically female audiences in prime time as a strategy to secure domestic approval for the medium.

MADELYN M. RITROSKY-WINSLOW

See also **Anthology Drama; Young, Loretta**

Hostess
Loretta Young

Substitute Hostesses (1955)
Dinah Shore
Merle Oberon
Barbara Stanwyk

Producers
Loretta Young, John London, Ruth Roberts, Bert Granet, Tom Lewis

Programming History
225 episodes
NBC
September 1953–
    June 1958   Sunday 10:00–10:30
                      (as *Letter to Loretta,* September
                      1953–February 1954)
October 1958–
    September 1961   Sunday 10:00–10:30

Further Reading

Atkins, J., "Young, Loretta," in *International Dictionary of Films and Filmmakers,* Vol. 3: *Actors and Actresses,* edited by N. Thomas, Detroit, Michigan: St. James Press, 1992

Bowers, R.L., "Loretta Young: Began as a Child-Extra and Exuded Glamour for Forty Years," *Films in Review* (1969)

Morella, Joe, and Edward Z. Epstein, *Loretta Young: An Extraordinary Life,* New York: Delacorte Press, 1986

Siegel, S., and B. Siegel, *The Encyclopedia of Hollywood,* New York: Facts on File, 1990

Young, Loretta, as told to Helen Ferguson, *The Things I Had To Learn,* Indianapolis, Indiana: Bobbs-Merrill, 1961

Lou Grant

U.S. Drama

Created by executive producers Gene Reynolds with James L. Brooks and Allan Burns, *Lou Grant* drew on the comedy character of the executive producer of TV news in the long-running *Mary Tyler Moore Show.* But the new series transformed that comic persona into a serious, reflective, committed newsman at a major metropolitan newspaper.

As he developed the concept for the series, Reynolds drew on his experience researching the TV series *M*A*S*H.* He haunted Toronto newspaper offices to learn firsthand how they operate, how principals interact, procedures for processing news stories, what issues trouble professional news-gatherers, how they thrash out the daily agenda to be distributed to the mass public. From tape-recorded interviews came the seeds of storylines and snatches of dialogue to capture the flavor and cadences of newspeople in action.

The series sought weekly to explore a knotty issue facing media people in contemporary society, focusing on how investigating and reporting those issues affect the layers of personalities populating a complex newspaper publishing company. The program served as a vehicle for dramatic reflection, analyzing sometimes bold and sometimes tangential conflicts in business practices, government, media, and the professions. Topics treated dramatically included gun control, invasion of privacy, confidential sources, child abuse, Vietnamese refugees, and news reporting versus publishing economics. Mingled with each episode's issue was interplay of personalities, often lighthearted, among featured characters.

Reynolds risked undercutting issue-oriented themes by importing Lou Grant (Ed Asner) from the long-running comedy about a flaky TV newsroom to act as city editor of a daily newspaper. Asner not only effectively adapted the original comedic character to the serious role of *Lou Grant;* off-screen the actor spoke out increasingly about social and political issues, possibly causing some audience disaffection in its final years.

The series (1977–82) received critical acclaim for exploring complicated challenges involving media and

Lou Grant, Ed Asner, 1977–82.
Courtesy of the Everett Collection

society. It received a Peabody Award in 1978, Emmy Awards in 1979 and 1980 for outstanding drama series, plus other Emmys for writing and acting during its five years on the air. Yet it never ended any season among the top 20 most popular prime-time programs. First scheduled the last hour of Tuesday evenings (10:00 P.M.), in the second and following seasons it was aired on Mondays at that time. It enjoyed strong lead-in shows *M*A*S*H* and *One Day at a Time,* but competing networks scheduled Monday night football (ABC) and theatrical movies (NBC), both at midpoint when *Lou Grant* came on. Scheduling was thus probably a "wash" as a factor; audiences were perhaps deterred more by the substantive issues explored, which called for attentive involvement, unlike more passive TV entertainment.

Lou Grant is also significant in the history of MTM Productions as the "bridge" program between comedies such as *The Mary Tyler Moore Show* and later, more complex dramas such as *Hill Street Blues.* Few independent production companies have had such visible success in crossing lines among television genres. The transformation of Asner's character, then, and the focus on serious social issues pointed new directions for the company and, ultimately, for the history of American television.

JAMES A. BROWN

See also **Asner, Ed; Brooks, James L.;** *Mary Tyler Moore Show, The;* **Reynolds, Gene; Tinker, Grant**

Cast

Lou Grant	Edward Asner
Charlie Hume	Mason Adams
Joe Rossi	Robert Walden
Billie Newman McCovey	Linda Kelsey
Margaret Pynchon	Nancy Marchand
Art Donovan	Jack Bannon
Dennis "Animal" Price	Daryl Anderson
National Editor (1977–79)	Sidney Clute
National Editor (1979–82)	Emilio Delgado
Foreign Editor (1977–80)	Laurence Haddon
Financial Editor (1978–79)	Gary Pagett
Adam Wilson (1978–82)	Allen Williams
Photo Editor (1979–81)	Billy Beck
Carla Mardigian (1977)	Rebecca Balding
Ted McCovey (1981–82)	Cliff Potts
Linda (1981–82)	Barbara Jane Edelman
Lance (1981–82)	Lance Guest

Producers

Allan Burns, James L. Brooks, Gene Reynolds

Programming History

110 episodes
CBS

September 1977–January 1978	Tuesday 10:00–11:00
January 1978–September 1982	Monday 10:00–11:00

Further Reading

Feuer, Jane, Paul Kerr, and Tise Vahimagi, editors, *MTM: "Quality Television,"* London: British Film Institute, 1984

Gitlin, Todd, *Inside Prime Time,* New York: Pantheon, 1985; revised edition, 1994

Schatz, Thomas, "*St. Elsewhere* and the Evolution of the Ensemble Series," in *Television: The Critical View,* edited by Horace Newcomb, New York: Oxford University Press, 1987

Schudson, Michael, "The Politics of *Lou Grant,*" in *Television: The Critical View,* edited by Horace Newcomb, New York: Oxford University Press, 1987

Tinker, Grant, and Bud Rukeyser, *Tinker in Television: From General Sarnoff to General Electric,* New York: Simon and Schuster, 1994

Low Power Television

Television Transmission Technology

Television translators are broadcast devices that receive a distant station's signal from over the air, automatically convert the frequency, and re-transmit the signal locally on a separate channel. Until 1980, the operators of these devices were required solely to rebroadcast the program service of a licensed full-service TV station and were banned from originating all but 60 seconds per hour for fundraising inserts. In 1980 the Federal Communications Commission (FCC) announced that it would accept applications to waive the 60-second cap, so that translators could broadcast original programs—to an unlimited extent—from any suitable source. This liberalization was made permanent in 1982, with the creation of a new broadcast service, low power television, called LPTV.

The name derives from the fact that LPTV stations, like the TV translators that continue to operate, cannot employ transmitter powers in excess of 1,000 watts. This imposes a practical ceiling on the effective radiated power, using a high-gain antenna, of 20 kilowatts or so under ideal conditions. It contrasts with regular, full-service TV operations, which are permitted up to 100 kilowatts of effective power (channels 2 to 6), 316 kilowatts (channels 7 to 13), or 5,000 kilowatts in the UHF bands (channels 14 to 69). As of the end of 1995, the FCC had licensed 1,787 LPTV stations, with 1,224 operating at UHF, the remainder at VHF. The total number of LPTVs exceeds the number of licensed full-service TV stations in the United States—some 1,180 commercial and 363 noncommercial stations, or 1,543 total.

Prior to the official launch of LPTV services, the FCC had granted waivers to permit origination of programs in several instances, notably for rural educational programming in upstate New York, and for the satellite-fed bush stations in Alaska, where there was no practical alternative for delivering television programming to isolated villages. The first low power television station was constructed in 1981 by John W. Boler in Bemidji, Minnesota. Boler had been a pioneer broadcaster in Fargo, North Dakota, and built the Bemidji facility as a smaller version of a traditional independent TV station, with regular evening news, studios, a sales force, and even a mobile van.

LPTV service expanded just as the equipment manufacturers were introducing significant cost and feature improvements for all broadcast components. It became possible for a crew of one to record programs with a camcorder on inexpensive S-VHS cassette and use them to offer a watchable broadcast picture. Satellite services also expanded, giving LPTV operators a choice of program fare from new networks.

Mark J. Banks, a professor at Slippery Rock University in Pennsylvania, performed mail and telephone surveys of low power television stations in 1988, 1990, and 1994. In the most recent survey, his sample of 456 stations yielded completed interviews with only 129, but the results are somewhat informative. Seventy-one percent of the LPTV stations were commercial, 17 percent public or educational, 10 percent religious, and 2 percent operated on a scrambled, subscription basis. A plurality, 40 percent, were in rural areas, but almost as many, 37 percent, were urban, with the remainder suburban or a mixture. The largest "group owners" are Alaska Public Broadcasting and Trinity Broadcasting Network. LPTV was designed to favor minority ownership, but only 8 percent described themselves as minority controlled.

The surveys over time indicated reduced dependency on satellite-fed program services, in favor of increased local programming. Stations reporting use of satellite services dropped from 87 percent in 1988 to 55 percent in 1994. Conversely, the amount of station time devoted to local programming has grown. The 63 percent reporting local programming said their most popular categories were, in order, sports, news, talk, community events, public affairs, and children's programs. Locally originating stations derive their greatest revenue by far from the sale of local advertising, and total revenue is up, to an average of $240,000 per station per year.

Low power television has achieved a solid niche, providing new services to rural areas that cannot support full-service TV and to ethnic and religious groups in large urban areas. The full-service TV broadcasters, commercial and noncommercial, opposed LPTV from its inception, and sooner or later may succeed in eradicating it. The FCC no longer assigns any priority to assuring program delivery to underserved audiences and, as of the end of 1995, the agency had made no provision for LPTV in the future to change over to some form of advanced, digitized TV system.

MICHAEL COUZENS

See also **Microwave**

Further Reading

Banks, Mark J., "A Survey of Low Power Television," *Community Television Business* (Part 1, December 19, 1994; Part 2, January 16, 1995; Part 3, January 30, 1995; Part 4, February 13, 1995)

Biel, Jacquelyn, *Low Power Television: Development and Current Status of the LPTV Industry,* Washington, D.C.: National Association of Broadcasters, 1985
Coe, Steve, "Nielsen to Measure LPTV's," *Broadcasting and Cable* (November 13, 1995)
Federal Communications Commission, *Report and Recommendations in the Low Power Television Inquiry* (BC Docket No. 78–153), Washington, D.C., September 9, 1980
"New Low Power Lobby Formed," *Broadcasting* (August 6, 1984)

Lumet, Sidney (1924–)

U.S. Director, Producer, Writer

When Sidney Lumet brought his powerful television influence to the Hollywood cinema of the late 1950s, it was in the company of four other notable American directors who also had emerged from the Golden Age of live television: Arthur Penn, John Frankenheimer, Franklin J. Schaffner, and Robert Mulligan. Their urgent, realist approach—a sharp combination of television drama adaptations reflecting social realism and technically tight production experience—was instrumental in reshaping the face of cinema for the next decade. Like his Golden Age contemporaries, Lumet's training ground had been on-the-spot television.

Following military service during World War II, Lumet returned to New York stage work. In 1947, exasperated by the pompous practice of the newly-formed Actor's Studio, he formed his own Actor's Workshop. When the group realized that they did not have a director, Lumet found himself drifting into the role.

In 1950 he was invited to join CBS Television as an assistant director by his old friend Yul Brynner, then a staff director at the network. When Brynner left to do *The King and I* on Broadway, Lumet took over the mystery anthology series *Danger* from him and was promoted to staff director. It was the beginning of what would be some 500 television productions as director; his on-the-spot training ground where he began to develop his clarity of storytelling, his skill for handling actors, and his artistry in coordinating tightly structured drama production.

For *Danger,* a McCarthy-era series produced by Martin Ritt and with scripts often supplied by blacklisted writers (Abraham Polonsky, Walter Bernstein, and others) under "front" names, Lumet directed around 150 half-hour episodes between 1951 and 1953. During this period he also directed episodes of the family comedy *Mama* (also known as *I Remember Mama*) and the newspaper adventure *Crime Photographer* series before moving on to the drama-documentary *You Are There.* (Lumet's replacement on *Danger* was John Frankenheimer.)

With the team of Charles Russell producing and Lumet directing, *You Are There* was unique in television for its multidimensional approach to history, presenting reenactments of major events in history in a current affairs news style. From the multiple episodes he directed between 1953 and 1955, Lumet singles out as personally satisfying works "The First Salem Witch Trial" ("because we did it the same week that Ed Murrow did his McCarthy show [on *See It Now*], so we like to think we were slight contributors to the general attack on him," he explained to writer Frank R. Cunningham) and "The Death of Socrates" (which featured an astonishing line-up of on-screen talent: Paul Newman, Barry Jones, John Cassavetes, Robert Culp, Richard Kiley, E.G. Marshall, Sheppard Strudwick).

When Lumet began directing original plays for television in 1956, his first critical success came with Reginald Rose's tension-charged drama on mob violence "Tragedy in a Temporary Town" for *The Alcoa Hour.* Lumet's cameras gave the production a crisp, chilling authority and drew some fine performances from the cast, especially Lloyd Bridges' poignant portrayal as the man facing the mob and denouncing it into shamefaced dispersal.

It was at this time that the success of the feature adaptation of Paddy Chayefsky's *Marty* for United

Sidney Lumet.
©*Columbia Pictures/Courtesy of the Everett Collection*

Artists had prompted Hollywood to look to television for new talent and material. For the film version of Rose's *Twelve Angry Men,* star and coproducer Henry Fonda selected Lumet as his director (marking Lumet's feature debut). The play had been directed on television (*Studio One*) in 1954 by Franklin Schaffner. *Twelve Angry Men* won wide critical approval, opening the door to television-to-cinema traffic, and appeared to cement Lumet's career as a big-screen director.

During April and May of 1958, he directed three notable and much-praised productions for *Kraft Television Theatre:* "Three Plays by Tennessee Williams" (a color telecast from New York, incorporating "Moony's Kid Don't Cry," "The Last of My Solid Gold Watches," and "This Property is Condemned," all introduced by Williams), an adaptation of Hemingway's "Fifty Grand," and Robert Penn Warren's Pulitzer Prize novel "All the King's Men" (the latter broadcast in two parts).

After three less-than-successful feature ventures (*Stage Struck, That Kind of Woman, The Fugitive* *Kind*), Lumet returned to television in 1960 and shone again. The two-part presentation (on tape) of Reginald Rose's drama-documentary *The Sacco-Vanzetti Story* (NBC) was a gripping account of the notorious judicial transgression of 1920, when two alleged Italian anarchists were found guilty of murder and robbery, and were eventually executed following a lengthy and highly controversial trial. Once again, Lumet showed a fine, sure hand in his grasp of the lengthy production (with a cast of 175) and the sharply edged portrayals, notably by the two principals (Martin Balsam as Nicolas Sacco and Steven Hill as Bartolomeo Vanzetti).

Lumet's television triumph of 1960, however, was his four-hour rendition of Eugene O'Neill's play about assorted barflies in a 1912 saloon, "The Iceman Cometh." Produced for the PBS *Play of the Week* strand, the mammoth drama was shown in two parts and scheduled at 10:30–12:30 due to the "mature nature" of the play. The *Variety* (November 16, 1960) review was ecstatic: "Television drama soared to triumphant, poetic dimensions…[and] was a landmark for the video medium, a reference point for greatness in television drama." Leading the large cast were Jason Robards Jr. as Hickey and Myron McCormack as Larry Slade, with James Broderick, Roland Winters, and Robert Redford among this modern-day Greek chorus. Considered the high mark of that season's *Play of the Week* showcase, "the sure, talented, creative hands of director Sidney Lumet seemed everywhere in evidence."

From 1962 onward, beginning with *A View from the Bridge,* Lumet was active on the big screen, enjoying the greatest commercial success of his career in 1976 with *Network* (a forceful indictment of television as a profit machine).

In January 2001, Lumet returned to television as writer, director, and executive producer on the cops-and-courtrooms drama series *100 Centre Street* (the address of the court building in lower Manhattan). In a nod to old acquaintances, Arthur Penn was invited to direct an episode during the series' second season. Although its themes and characters are more in keeping with Lumet's NYPD (*Serpico, Prince of the City*) and legal (*The Verdict, Guilty as Sin*) films than with the live dramas of his early days, *100 Centre Street* nevertheless displayed all the hallmarks familiar to the director's favorite subject matter.

TISE VAHIMAGI

See also **Golden Age of Television Drama**

Sidney Lumet. Born in Philadelphia, Pennsylvania, June 25, 1924. Married: 1) Rita Gam (divorced); 2) Gloria Vanderbilt, 1956 (divorced, 1963); 3) Gail Jones, 1963 (divorced, 1978); 4) Mary Gimbel, 1980.

Father Yiddish actor Baruch Lumet, with whom he made stage debut, aged four. Educated at Professional Children's School, New York, and Columbia University extension school. Child actor in theater and films: Yiddish Theatre, New York, 1928; Broadway debut in *Dead End*, 1935; film actor from 1939. Military service in Signal Corps, U.S. Army, 1942–46. Resumed acting career and formed off-Broadway stage group; also stage director, 1947. Assistant director, then director for TV, from 1950.

Television Plays/Episodes (selected)

1951–53	*Danger*
1951	*Crime Photographer*
	Mama
1953–55	*You Are There*
	"The First Salem Witch Trial," *You Are There*
	"The Death of Socrates," *You Are There*
	"The Fate of Nathan Hale," *You Are There*
1954	"The Philadelphia Story," *The Best of Broadway*
1955	"The Show-Off," *The Best of Broadway*
	"Stage Door," *The Best of Broadway*
	"The Death of Stonewall Jackson," *You Are There*
	"The Liberation of Paris," *You Are There*
1956	"Tragedy in a Temporary Town," *The Alcoa Hour*
1957	"No Deadly Medicine," *Studio One*
1958	"Three Plays by Tennessee Williams," (also known as "Three By Tennessee"), *Kraft Television Theatre*
	"Fifty Grand," *Kraft Television Theatre*
	"All the King's Men" (two parts), *Kraft Television Theatre*
	The DuPont Show of the Month
1960	"The Hiding Place," *Playhouse 90*
	The Sacco-Vanzetti Story (two parts)
	John Brown's Raid (two parts)
	"The Dybbuk," *Play of the Week*
	"The Iceman Cometh" (two parts), *Play of the Week*
	"Rashomon," *Play of the Week*
2001–2002	*100 Centre Street* (also writer and executive producer)

Films (selected)

Twelve Angry Men, 1957; *Stage Struck*, 1958; *That Kind of Woman*, 1959; *The Fugitive Kind*, 1960; *A View from the Bridge*, 1962; *Fail Safe*, 1964; *The Pawnbroker, The Hill*, 1965; *The Deadly Affair*, 1967; *The Anderson Tapes*, 1971; *Serpico*, 1973; *Murder on the Orient Express*, 1974; *Dog Day Afternoon*, 1975; *Network*, 1977; *Prince of the City*, 1981; *The Verdict*, 1982; *Guilty as Sin*, 1993; *Gloria*, 1999; *The Set-Up*, 2004.

Stage (as director)

The Doctor's Dilemma, Picnic, 1955; *The Night of the Auk*, 1956; *Caligula*, 1960; *Nowhere To Go But Up*, 1962.

Publications

Making Movies, 1995

Further Reading

Cunningham, Frank R., *Sidney Lumet: Film and Literary Vision*, 2nd edition, Lexington: University Press of Kentucky, 2001

Moskowitz, Gene, "The Tight Close-Up," *Sight and Sound*, Vol. 28 (1959)

"TV to Film: A History, a Map and a Family Tree," *Monthly Film Bulletin* (January 1983)

Lumley, Joanna (1946–)

British Actor

Joanna Lumley's lengthy career in television has been marked chiefly by two components—her image as glamorous and refined, and the characters she has played in three popular series, which span three decades. Her work over the years has been varied, encompassing theater, film, and several major advertising

Joanna Lumley.
©*GM/ Courtesy of the Everett Collection*

campaigns, as well as television drama, comedy, and regular celebrity appearances. Equally, her work has been of widely varying standards, ranging from the flimsy and trite to award-winning performances.

A former model in the Swinging Sixties, Lumley landed her first major television role in *The New Avengers* (1976–77), in which she played special agent Purdey, alongside Gareth Hunt (Gambit) and Patrick Macnee (Steed). The show evidently seemed to be more concerned to promote Lumley's legs than her character's crime-fighting skills—not only did her costume consist of a skin-tight trouser suit and kinky high boots, but Purdey's prime weapon was her immobilizing karate kick. In spite of this fetishistic fixation, Lumley became most synonymous with the pudding-bowl haircut named after her character, Purdey, and widely imitated by women and girls alike.

Shortly after *The New Avengers* came *Sapphire and Steel* (1979–82), an offbeat science fiction series in which Lumley costarred with David McCallum. The two played mysterious agents who traveled through time and space, whilst the ethereal Sapphire (Lumley) costumed in a long, floaty dress communed with psychic forces. Although this and the previous show were popular with both children and adults, Lumley claimed she was becoming frustrated with the parts

she was playing, primarily as they did not mimic real women.

For the remainder of the 1980s, Lumley was involved in less memorable productions, although she remained in the public eye, as the face for several advertisements, as a regular guest on TV chat shows, and with certain notable film appearances, particularly as head girl-turned-prostitute in *Shirley Valentine* (1989). However, it was her performance with Ruby Wax (on *The Full Wax*) as a washed-up, drugged-out actress that initiated the revival of her career. This performance instantly transformed her from an idealized myth of feminine perfection to a more complex and humorous persona. Shortly after revealing her talent for comedy and self-parody, through a stroke of pertinent casting, Lumley became Patsy Stone, the aging, neurotic "Fash-Mag-Slag," conceived of by Jennifer Saunders for *Absolutely Fabulous* (1992–96). This casting was central to the success of *Absolutely Fabulous* and to the renaissance of Lumley's career. Lumley gives an immensely entertaining performance, but also, because of her on- and off-screen persona, she creates in Patsy a hilarious and hideous satire around the expectations of glamour and refinement assigned to her. As a character, Patsy has several functions that covered new ground in television culture: she overturned ageist assumptions by opening up a space in television for the representation of women of all ages as humorous; as an "unruly woman" she violated, in a highly entertaining way, the unspoken feminine sanction against making a spectacle of herself; and she confronted and redefined the values of beauty, consumerism, and decorum inferred upon women, particularly of a certain age and social class.

Since playing what must surely be her ideal role, and achieving high critical acclaim with several awards, including BAFTAs and an Emmy, Lumley's subsequent work was not nearly so demanding on her talents. She played a down-at-heel aristocrat in the mediocre *A Class Act* and in a documentary-drama, *Girl Friday,* she had to fend for herself on an inhospitable desert island, with emphasis on how she copes without couture clothes, haute cuisine, and cosmetics. Both of these shows revolve around Lumley's conventional image, but neither seeks to recognize the contradictions apparent since *Absolutely Fabulous* in Lumley's persona as the epitome of high class. While there may generally be a lack of recognition of Lumley's specific capabilities as an actor, all her major roles share a common interest in casting her as an independent woman—she is nobody's wife or side-kick. However, it seems ironic that *Absolutely Fabulous,* while giving Lumley a new lease of life and promoting her to an international audience, has remained an almost unique forum for her talent as a comedy actor.

NICOLA FOSTER

See also Absolutely Fabulous; Avengers; Coronation Street; Saunders, Jennifer

Joanna Lumley. Born in Srinagar, Kashmir, India, May 1, 1946. Married: 1) Jeremy Lloyd (divorced, 1971); 2) Stephen Barlow, 1986; child: James. Established reputation as a top model before starting career as an actor on both stage and screen; costar, in *The New Avengers* adventure series and other shows, notably in *Absolutely Fabulous*. Officer of the Order of the British Empire. Recipient: British Academy of Film and Television Arts Award, 1993; Emmy Award, 1994.

Television Series

1973	*Coronation Street*
1976–77	*The New Avengers*
1979–82	*Sapphire and Steel*
1986	*Mistral's Daughter*
1992	*Lovejoy*
1992–96	*Absolutely Fabulous*
1993	*Cluedo*
1993	*Class Act*
1998	The Tale of Sweeney Todd (TV movie)
1999	*Nancherrow* (TV movie)

Films (selected)

Some Girls Do, 1968; *On Her Majesty's Secret Service,* 1969; *Tam Lin/The Devil's Widow,* 1970; *Games That Lovers Play,* 1972; *Don't Just Lie There, Say Something,* 1973; *The Satanic Rites of Dracula/Count Dracula and His Vampire Bride,* 1973; *The Trail of the Pink Panther,* 1982; *Curse of the Pink Panther,* 1983; *The Glory Boys,* 1984; *Shirley Valentine,* 1989; *James and the Giant Peach,* 1996; *Cold Comfort Farm,* 1996; *James and the Giant Peach,* 1996; *Prince Valiant,* 1997; *Mad Cows,* 1999; *Parting Shots,* 1999; *Maybe Baby,* 2000; *The Magic Roundabout Movie,* 2004; *The Ugly Americans,* 2004.

Recordings

The Hundred and One Dalmatians, 1984; *Invitation to the Waltz,* 1985.

Stage

Don't Just Lie There, Say Something; Othello; Private Lives; Noel and Gertie; Blithe Spirit; Me Old Cigar; Hedda Gabler.

Publications

Stare Back and Smile (autobiography), 1989
Forces Sweethearts, 1993

Lupino, Ida (1918–1995)

U.S. Actor, Director

Ida Lupino's career in television plays much like a re-run of her career in the cinema. Originally charting her course in each medium primarily as an actor, she apparently fell into directing as a matter of circumstance. Making her debut on CBS television's *Four Star Playhouse* in December 1953 as a performer, it was not until three years later that Lupino was commissioned to direct an episode for *Screen Directors Playhouse,* "No. 5 Checked Out," for which she also wrote the script. Eventually, after more frequent invitations to helm episodes from a variety of series, Lupino would, over the course of the next 15 years, establish a reputation as the most active woman director working behind the cameras during this formative period in television's history.

Economic necessity, it would seem, played as much a part as creative opportunities in Lupino's decision to work almost exclusively within television for the remainder of her career as director. By the mid-1950s, Lupino had been offered fewer leading roles, and her activities as a film director had gradually diminished. Although she would continue to act in even more television episodes than she would direct (over 50), her unique position in the fledgling industry rested more upon her reputation as a filmmaker than as a leading lady, in particular upon the critical and commercial

Ida Lupino.
Courtesy of the Everett Collection

success of her most widely seen cinematic work, *The Hitch-Hiker.*

In fact, after 1960, Lupino earned the nickname "the female Hitch" (as in Hitchcock) for her specialty work in action-oriented television genres that employed her talent at creating suspense. For example, Richard Boone, the star of the popular *Have Gun—Will Travel* series, of which Lupino eventually directed four episodes, had admired her hard-boiled style and offered her a script by Harry Julian Fink, famed for his graphic descriptions of physical violence. From that point on, although she would direct many sitcoms (e.g., *The Donna Reed Show, The Ghost and Mrs. Muir*) and various dramatic programs (e.g., *Mr. Novak, Dr. Kildare*), Lupino would be commissioned primarily for westerns (*The Rifleman, The Virginian, Dundee and the Culhane, Daniel Boone, Tate, Dick Powell's Zane Grey Theater*), crime dramas (*The Untouchables, The Fugitive, 77 Sunset Strip*), and mysteries (*The Twilight Zone, Kraft Suspense Theatre, Alfred Hitchcock Presents*). Perhaps the only series that Lupino genuinely shaped as director is *Thriller,* a mystery anthology hosted by Boris Karloff, for which she directed at least ten episodes in its first two seasons. At times

lamenting publicly that she had become so typecast as an action director that she was overlooked for love stories, Lupino otherwise exploited her anomalous stature as a woman specializing in shoot-outs and car chases, at one point turning down Hitchcock's offer of a lead role in one episode of his series in order to replace him as its director.

This figure of Lupino as a "female Hitch," whose nomenclature suggests the freedom to call her own shots and her status as auteur, is rather misleading within the context of the U.S. television industry, whose creative efforts are shaped and controlled almost exclusively by producers rather than by directors. Thus, although she directed episodes of *The Untouchables* and *The Fugitive,* whose intricate weekly subplots and relatively large guest casts required her creative input, her influence on formulaic series such as *Gilligan's Island* or *Bewitched* was minimal. For this reason, in contrast to her body of cinematic works (most of which she also co-wrote or coproduced), Lupino's scattered work in television resists an auteurist approach because of the very nature of the industry. More of a freelance substitute than a series regular, Lupino never pursued long-term contracts with any particular producer or network. Such job security generally was reserved for her male colleagues.

On the other hand, Lupino's continued interest in acting may have been equally responsible for her irregular directing schedule; it undoubtedly strengthened her reputation as a director who worked well with fellow actors. Although praised for her abilities to link scenes smoothly, to cooperate with the crew, and to come in on time and under budget, Lupino's most sought-after capacities were her skill at handling players of both sexes and her sensitivity to the problems and needs of her cast, qualities derived from her own training and experience as an actress.

Although Lupino was one of the first woman directors during the early years of American television production, it is odd that she is rarely referenced as a "groundbreaker" for other women entering the industry. Unlike Lucille Ball, Loretta Young, Joan Davis, and other women who were involved as producers in early television programming, Lupino had little creative control over the programs she directed. To contextualize Lupino's role as a director in relation to other women working contemporaneously as producers is not meant to suggest, however, that a critical analysis of Lupino's work is irrelevant to television history and feminist inquiry. What remains significant about Lupino as a "woman director" was her unique ability to succeed in an occupation that was (and still is) dominantly coded as "masculine." Constructed as an outsider and an anomaly, Lupino as a TV director was more often than not represented merely as a woman, her directorial skill either de-emphasized or ignored altogether in the popular press.

After a decade of professional activity spanning all three networks, a variety of genres, and an irregular schedule, Lupino's commitment to directing, like acting, could not have been said to be total. Working at a period in her life in which her desire for a career chafed at her equally strong desire to raise and care for her family, Lupino suffered the dilemma of the average woman of the time. She was forced to negotiate a notion of "work" dictating that her choices should threaten neither the spheres over which patriarchy dominated, such as the television industry, nor her identity as a wife and mother, whose "natural" place belonged in the home rather than in the studio. It should come as no surprise, therefore, that the nickname bestowed upon Lupino by her production crews—"Mother"—worked to contain her in the dominant role for women at the time.

MARY CELESTE KEARNEY AND JAMES MORAN

Ida Lupino. Born in London, England, February 4, 1918. Educated at the Clarence House School, Sussex; Royal Academy of Dramatic Arts, London. Married: 1) Louis Hayward, 1938 (divorced, 1945); 2) Collier Young, 1948 (divorced, 1951); 3) Howard Duff, 1951 (divorced, 1972); child: Bridget Mirella. Leading film role debut, 1932; actor in numerous British films; star in American films, from 1933; under contract with Paramount, 1933–37; under contract to Warner Brothers, 1940–47; cofounded Emerald Productions, 1949; producer, director, and co-scriptwriter, *Not Wanted,* 1949; director and co-writer, *Never Fear,* 1950; co-owner, Filmmakers, 1950–80; television director, from 1953; worked exclusively in television, from 1957–66. Recipient: New York Film Critics Award, 1943. Died in Burbank, California, August 3, 1995.

Television Series (selected; guest director)

1953–62	*General Electric Theater*
1955–56	*The Screen Directors Playhouse*
1955–65	*Alfred Hitchcock Presents*
1956–59	*On Trial*
1957–58	*Mr. Adams and Eve* (also star)
1957–63	*Have Gun—Will Travel*
1958–63	*The Rifleman*
1958–64	*77 Sunset Strip*
1958–66	*The Donna Reed Show*
1959–61	*Manhunt*
1959–63	*The Untouchables*
1959–65	*The Twilight Zone*
1960	*Tate*
1960–61	*Dante's Inferno* ("Teenage Idol"; pilot)

1960–61	*Hong Kong*
1960–62	*Thriller*
1961–63	*The Dick Powell Show*
1961–66	*Dr. Kildare*
1962–63	*Sam Benedict*
1962–71	*The Virginian*
1963–64	*The Breaking Point*
1963–65	*Mr. Novak*
1963–65	*The Kraft Suspense Theatre*
1963–67	*The Fugitive*
1963–67	*Bob Hope Presents the Chrysler Theater*
1964–65	*The Rogues*
1964–67	*Gilligan's Island*
1964–70	*Daniel Boone*
1964–72	*Bewitched*
1965–67	*Please Don't Eat the Daisies*
1965–69	*The Big Valley*
1967	*Dundee and the Culhane*
1968–70	*The Ghost and Mrs. Muir*
1969–71	*The Bill Cosby Show*

Made-for-Television Movies

1971	*Women in Chains*
1972	*Strangers in 7A*
1972	*Female Artillery*
1973	*I Love a Mystery*
1973	*The Letters*

Films

Her First Affaire, 1932; *Money for Speed,* 1933; *High Finance,* 1933; *The Ghost Camera,* 1933; *I Lived With You,* 1933; *Prince of Arcadia,* 1933; *Search for Beauty,* 1934; *Come On, Marines!,* 1934; *Ready for Love,* 1934; *Paris in Spring,* 1935; *Smart Girl,* 1935; *Peter Ibbetson,* 1935; *Anything Goes,* 1936; *One Rainy Afternoon,* 1936; *Yours for the Asking,* 1936; *The Gay Desperado,* 1936; *Sea Devils,* 1937; *Let's Get Married,* 1937; *Artists and Models,* 1937; *Fight for Your Lady,* 1937; *The Lone Wolf Spy Hunt,* 1939; *The Lady and the Mob,* 1939; *The Adventures of Sherlock Holmes,* 1939; *The Light That Failed,* 1939; *They Drive By Night,* 1940; *High Sierra,* 1941; *The Sea Wolf,* 1941; *Out of the Fog,* 1941; *Ladies in Retirement,* 1941; *Moontide,* 1942; *Life Begins at 8:30,* 1942; *The Hard Way,* 1943; *Forever and a Day,* 1943; *Thank Your Lucky Stars,* 1943; *In Our Time,* 1944; *Hollywood Canteen,* 1944; *Pillow to Post,* 1945; *Devotion,* 1946; *The Man I Love,* 1946; *Deep Valley,* 1947; *Escape Me Never,* 1947; *Road House,* 1948; *Lust for Gold,* 1949; *Not Wanted* (directed, produced, co-wrote), 1949; *Woman in Hiding,* 1949; *Outrage* (director, coproducer, co-screenwriter), 1950; *On Dangerous Ground*, 1951; *Hard, Fast, and Beautiful* (director and coproducer), 1951; *Beware, My Lovely*, 1952; *Jennifer*, 1953; *Private Hell 36*, 1954; *Women's Prison*, 1955; *The Big Knife*, 1955; *While the City Sleeps*, 1956; *Strange Intruder*, 1956; *The Trouble with Angels* (director and coproducer); *Backtrack*, 1969; *Junior Bonner*, 1972; *Deadhead Miles*, 1972; *The Devil's Rain*, 1975; *The Food of the Gods*, 1976; *My Boys Are Good Boys*, 1978.

Further Reading

Donati, William, *Ida Lupino: A Biography*, Lexington: University Press of Kentucky, 1996

Gianakos, Larry James, *Television Drama Series Programming: A Comprehensive Chronicle*, Metuchen, New Jersey: Scarecrow, 1978

Heck-Rabi, Louise, *Women Filmmakers: A Critical Reception*, Metuchen, New Jersey: Scarecrow, 1984

Kearney, Mary Celeste, and James M. Moran, "Ida Lupino As Director of Television," in *Queen of the 'B's: Ida Lupino Behind the Camera*, edited by Annette Kuhn, New York: Greenwood, 1995

Nolan, Jack Edmund, "Ida Lupino," *Films in Review* (1965)

Stewart, Lucy Ann Liggett, *Ida Lupino As Film Director: 1949–1953: An Auteur Approach*, New York: Arno, 1980

Vermilye, Jerry, "Television: The Director's Chair," *Ida Lupino: A Pyramid Illustrated History of the Movies*, New York: Pyramid Publications, 1977

Weiner, Debra, "Interview with Ida Lupino," in *Women and the Cinema*, edited by Karyn Kay and Gerald Peary, New York: Dutton, 1977

Lyndhurst, Nicholas (1961–)

British Actor

Nicholas Lyndhurst emerged as a prominent star among a new generation of British situation comedy performers in the early 1980s, although he had by then already amassed a considerable number of years' television experience, having started out as a child actor.

Lyndhurst made the transition from child performer to adult star in stages, beginning as an actor in a string of children's dramas and adventures such as *The Tomorrow People, Heidi,* and *The Prince and the Pauper* (in which he played the dual leading role). He also tried his hand as a presenter for children's television, cohosting for a time the series *Our Show* on Saturday mornings (with Susan Tully and others). In 1978 his selection for the part of Ronnie Barker's son in *Going Straight,* the sequel to the classic prison comedy *Porridge,* marked the start of his emergence as an adult performer, a process that continued with his casting as Wendy Craig's teenage son Adam in the long-running situation comedy *Butterflies.*

The final stage in the transition to a mature performer came in the hugely successful comedy series *Only Fools and Horses,* in which Lyndhurst was entrusted with the role of Rodney, the hapless and much put-upon younger brother of David Jason's immortal "Del Boy" Trotter. As Rodney, a part he played for some ten years, Lyndhurst was endearingly naive, sensitive, and idealistic—the perfect foil to Jason's streetwise would-be millionaire. Frequently rendered speechless at his brother's tricks and deceptions and all too often living up to the "plonker" tag that his exasperated sibling bestowed upon him, Rodney was widely praised as a beautifully realized comic creation.

Toward the end of the long run of *Only Fools and Horses,* Rodney was allowed to get married (to the long-suffering trainee banker Cassandra), and much humor was devised from the inevitable difficulties he experienced as a new husband. Subsequent situation comedies that were constructed around Lyndhurst further developed the theme of not dissimilar Rodney-style characters, bemused and indignant though not necessarily quite as dimwitted as Rodney, trying to cope with the demands of wives or girlfriends. In *The Two of Us,* for instance, Lyndhurst's character, computer programmer Ashley, wrestled with independent girlfriend Elaine's reluctance to get married, despite his entreaties, and with her contrasting views on just about any subject he cared to raise. In *Goodnight Sweetheart,* meanwhile, his character Gary Sparrow agonized over whether he should stay true to his brash and pushy wife in their modern London flat or whether he should desert her for the barmaid with whom he had formed a relationship while exploring wartime London after finding a way to travel some 50 years back through time.

Memories of the highly successful *Only Fools and Horses* series, kept fresh through regular repeats of old episodes, have perhaps dominated perceptions of the sort of roles Lyndhurst is capable of playing. Typecast though he may have been, he remains, however, unsurpassed in his portrayal of the hen-pecked husband or lover, well-meaning but frequently nonplused by the tricks that fate plays on him. In 1999 he finally had a chance to demonstrate his skills in a different type of role when he was cast, with great success, as the unpleasant Uriah Heep in the Dickens classic *David Copperfield.*

DAVID PICKERING

Nicholas Lyndhurst. Born in Emsworth, Hampshire, England, April 20, 1961. Attended Corona Stage Academy, 1980. Began career as television performer, from a young age; comedy performer as Rodney Trotter in *Only Fools and Horses;* star, several situation comedy series.

Television Series and Miniseries

1976	*Our Show*
1978	*Going Straight*
1978–82	*Butterflies*
1981–96	*Only Fools and Horses*
1986	*To Serve Them All My Days*
1986–90	*The Two of Us*
1990–92	*The Piglet Files*
1993–99	*Goodnight Sweetheart*
1999	*David Copperfield*
2000	*Thin Ice*

Films

Endless Night, 1971; *Bequest to the Nation,* 1973; *Bullshot,* 1983; *Gun Bus,* 1986.

Stage (selected)

The Foreigner; Straight and Narrow; Harding's Luck; Trial Run; Black Comedy; The Private Ear.